UNIVERSITY CASEBOOK SERIES

CASES AND MATERIALS

ECONOMIC JUSTICE:

RACE, GENDER, IDENTITY AND ECONOMICS

by

EMMA COLEMAN JORDAN
Professor of Law
Georgetown University Law Center

ANGELA P. HARRIS
Professor of Law
Boalt Hall—School of Law, University of California, Berkeley

FOUNDATION PRESS

NEW YORK, NEW YORK

2005

© 2005 By FOUNDATION PRESS

395 Hudson Street
New York, NY 10014
Phone Toll Free 1–877–888–1330
Fax (212) 367–6799
fdpress.com

Printed in the United States of America

ISBN 1–58778–904–3

 TEXT IS PRINTED ON 10% POST CONSUMER RECYCLED PAPER

For the late E. W. Coleman and M. H. Coleman,
my daughters Kristen and Allison and my sisters Betty, Jean and Earlene

*

INTRODUCTION

We live in a society organized according to two master principles: capitalism and democracy. Although principles and their associated values, institutions, and norms are integral to American life, they often seem to exist in different worlds. Capitalism is often thought of as belonging to the "private" sphere, whereas democracy belongs in the "public" sphere. Capitalism is the business of business organizations and of economic analysis; democracy is the business of politicians, voters and political analysis. Within the academy, a similar split seems to have created two cultures, like the "two cultures" of science and the humanities of which C.P. Snow originally spoke. Economic analysis has developed a culture of scientific expertise in which developing testable hypotheses with mathematical rigor, constructing quantitative analyses, and making predictions are principal values. Although social scientists increasingly analyze democratic institutions in this way as well, discussions of democracy have more traditionally been the bailiwick of moral philosophers, and more recently critical theorists, who use the language of morality, justice, and the methodological tools associated with the humanities to pursue the "ought" rather than the "is."

The split obtains in legal scholarship as well. In the last few decades, the law and economics movement has had a tremendous impact on legal studies. Like its parent discipline: economics, law and economics focuses on questions of transactional efficiency and tends to ignore questions of distribution or justice. It seeks to accurately describe how legal rules work (or don't work), and to the extent it is normative rather than descriptive, the assumed goal is greater efficiency. Traditional legal scholarship, however, has taken the pursuit of distributional justice, fairness, and democratic process as central to its analyses. In the last few decades, critical legal scholarship has developed an even more openly moral discourse of justice, focused on the pursuit of equality. Traditional and critical scholars, however, have seldom ventured into the territory of efficiency or the systematic analysis of transactions, just as law and economics scholars have seldom ventured into the territory of fairness and equality.

Interesting exchanges between the two cultures have begun to occur in the recent years. Economics generally, and law and economics in particular, has begun to alter its once iron-clad assumption that people always act as rational maximizers; with the abandonment of perfect rationality, economic analysis is increasingly equipped to address issues, like cooperative behavior, that involve trust as well as immediate self-interest, and motivations more complicated than direct instrumentality. For their part, philosophers and traditional scholars—and even a few critical scholars—have become increasingly interested in what economic analysis can tell us about institutions and the aggregate behavior of groups in response to incentives. New sub-disciplines like "socio-economics" have emerged to explore the convergence between traditional legal scholarship and law and economics. Yet, a productive conversation between critical legal scholarship and law and economics has only tentatively begun. This casebook is offered as a means of furthering that conversation.

The phrase "economic justice" signals our aim: rather than maintaining the tacit assumption that "justice" has nothing to do with economics and economics nothing to do with social justice, we hope to engage the two cultures with one another. What can economics tell us about democracy and the law? What can theories of justice tell us about economic theory and the law? Why is there no legal language of "class" in the United States, and what might one look like? Rather than asking students to specialize in one or the other discourse, as current legal pedagogy implicitly does, this casebook openly engages students in the project of learning from both discourses, and using each as a means to gain insights on the other.

Moreover, our project here is not only to engage traditional legal scholarship with law and economics, but more specifically critical legal scholarship with law and economics. Critical legal scholarship is not only distinctive in its wholehearted embrace of a moral perspective on politics and law and in its commitment to equality as the master principle; it is also distinctive in its ambition to place issues that have long stymied American society, especially the issue of racial and gender justice, at the center of its normative agenda. Race and gender are so thorny, in part, because they introduce a third principle—community—into the debate between liberty and equality. Neither traditional legal analysis nor economic analysis has paid much attention to the question of who constitutes America, what full citizenship means to those who were originally not included in the American vision, and how a multicultural, multinational society can function within a single economic and political system. Neither traditional legal analysis nor economic analysis has adequately addressed issues like the market value of racialized culture and sexual difference, the borders of national and cultural community, and the problem of remediating long-standing inequalities in both economic and social spheres.

In this casebook, we use the problem of racial and gender injustice as a vehicle for engaging both critical theory and economic theory. Just as race, gender, and class seem inextricably intertwined, economic and critical analysis both seem crucial to unraveling the knot of racial and gender inequality. Moreover, economic analysis and critical analysis may need to influence and be influenced by one another in order for a truly incisive and transformative dialogue about race and gender to emerge in the legal academy and in American society more generally.

This casebook involves students in creating this dialogue. In Chapter 1, we identify a central tension between the culture of traditional legal analysis, with its claims of neutrality and the culture of critical race theory with its emphasis on subjective narrative. We ask whether legal analysis is (or should it be) a science? Or is legal reasoning inherently interpretive, more art than science? Is the law a neutral and objective forum for conflict resolution, or is it a tool of the powerful? As legal scholars concerned with the impact of subordination in law and in markets, we examine the role that traditional legal analysis plays in reinforcing the rational choice, efficiency, and wealth maximization assumptions of traditional economic views of the operation of markets. It is not surprising to find that claims of neutrality play as central a role in traditional legal theory, as they do in traditional economic analysis.

The challenge to the premise of legal neutrality has brought to the surface the conflict between the two cultures of law. In this first chapter we extend the anti-subordination critique to classic market economics and to law and economics. We believe that the question of method—whether there is an objective science of society, or whether knowledge is inherently perspectival—is of such central importance to understanding the structure of economic inequality that it is the indispensable starting point from which we must begin the three-way conversation between the traditionalists in economics, the traditionalists in law, and the anti-subordination-oriented legal theorists.

The central organizing question of this first chapter is what methods and normative assumptions are most useful in evaluating the complex landscape of law, markets, and culture? What tools are best suited to sort truth from ideology and myth? What would "truth" look like if we found it? We begin with these questions because we believe that unless these intensely contested, yet often invisible, first premises of analysis are explored, it will be impossible to make sense of the claims and arguments of the traditionalists in economics and in law or the contradictory positions of critical race and feminist scholars concerned with the problem of intertwined structures of subordination. Throughout this book we will use a variety of tools to pursue our interest in fostering a conversation between economics and the critical perspectives. We will use methodologies and insights from political theory, sociology, psychology, and behavioral economics, as well as the various schools of modern legal thought.

Chapter 2 introduces students to two ways of thinking about the idea of economic justice: one drawing on the Weberian notion of class stratification, and the other drawing on Marx (who drew on early economists like Adam Smith and John Stuart Mill) and the notion of political economy. It introduces students as well to the concept of the United States as a capitalist democracy in which capitalism and democracy popularly inhabit two different spheres, a "public" and a "private," and it helps students see how law is actively engaged in creating and maintaining both spheres, as well as in drawing the line between them. Chapter 2 also engages students in trying to answer the question: why there is no developed discourse of economic inequality within American constitutional law. In pursuing answers to this question, the chapter introduces themes that will reappear throughout the book, including racial injustice and the tangled relationship between racial inequality and economic inequality.

Chapter 3 introduces students to the basic principles of economic theory and the key ideological assumptions that undergird the discipline of economics and thereby law and economics. The work of this chapter operates through an engagement with "neo-classical," free-market economics. We use familiar cases from the first year curriculum in torts and property to explore actual examples of judicial reasoning that relies upon the law and economics theoretical premises.

Chapters 4 and 5 extend the exploration of the basic tenets of modern economic theory as it has been applied in legal reasoning. Chapter 4 is concerned with the critiques of classic market theory coming from those who share its basic premises. Chapter 5 introduces students to the major challenges to market economics from those who reject the basic premises of that field. In this chapter, we explore the challenges to price theory, rational choice, and wealth maximization premises that have come from those who do not share the faith in markets and private ordering. Within law, these criticisms include doctrinalists who are unconvinced by the positive claim that the common law converges on efficiency, critical legal scholars who reject the normative premise that wealth maximization is a coherent value for evaluating the legal rules that govern the distribution of material goods in a democracy, and from humanistic legal scholars who reject the materialism inherent in the efficiency and wealth maximization norms of modern law and economics.

In Chapters 6 and 7 we take up the data that confirms the picture of economic inequality. Beyond the numbers, we listen to the voices and narratives of those who are at the bottom rung of wealth and income. We see the role of class and the influence of material culture in degrading the participation of those who have the least influence in the common forums of this society. Finally, these two chapters are concerned with the barriers to economic mobility.

Chapters 8, 9, 10, 11, and 12 take up specific topics that illuminate the interactions among race, gender, and economic inequality, and the sometimes complementary, sometimes conflicting values of liberty, equality, and community. Chapter 8 concerns the family; Chapter 9 concerns culture and identity; Chapter 10 explores the questions arising from the market value of culture; Chapter 11 concerns underground and informal economies; and Chapter 12 concerns economic borders to community.

Finally, Chapter 13 addresses questions of remediation and transformation. How might familiar legal debates like the one on "affirmative action" be transformed when seen from a perspective that incorporates a sophisticated understanding of the relationship between race and class, and a vision that is enriched by both efficiency and justice concerns?

*

ACKNOWLEDGEMENTS

The idea for creating teaching materials to introduce law students to a systematic examination of the interdisciplinary dimensions of increasing economic inequality and the role of identity in the distribution of wealth first occurred to me more than ten years ago. My decision to create this casebook arose from my mounting frustration with the conceptual limitations of the consumer protection features of commercial law and banking, the two traditional areas in which I had been working over the course of my career. I deeply appreciate the contributions of Nancy Ota who came to Georgetown Law Center in 1992–93 as a graduate Fellow in the Future Law Professor Program to work with me. She invested her unique imagination and commitment to assist me in creating the first set of teaching materials for the first course on Economic Justice.

This casebook owes much to the confidence and support I enjoyed from my publisher, Steven Errick. His enthusiasm and shared vision for the innovations of this effort and his never-failing generosity in responding to and initiating additional publishing opportunities for the Economic Justice topic were important at critical points in the process. Steve's departure in the weeks before this book went to press was a real personal loss. I look forward to working with the new publisher, John Bloomquist in future editions.

I especially want to thank the many Georgetown University Law Center students who enrolled in the early courses in Economic Justice, and who became my most enthusiastic cheering section (offering rap and pop lyrics, African proverbs, Equal Access to Justice/E.A.T. Justice, a socially conscious business venture and strong counterarguments) as this project moved forward to completion. I learned so much from our intense classroom investigations of some of my then forming hypotheses about educational capital, wealth and income inequalities, intergenerational economic effects, linguistic differences, the relationship of the Constitution to economic outcomes, and the limits of conventional market theory. The richness and complexity of this project owe much to my students.

From my Georgetown law students, I chose outstanding research assistants who worked with passion and conviction on the research for this book. They found many truly important additions to the materials. They designed the critical copyright accounting system, chased elusive copyright holders with the zeal of a "repo" man/woman. They kept me laughing when I might have otherwise turned grouchy. They discussed this newly emerging field with me with intelligence and energy. My special thanks go to Angela Ahern '05, Rashida Baskerville '06, Katherine Buell '04, Cassandra Charles '05, Kenneth Leichter '06, William Morriss '05, Michael Radolinski '06, and Joshua Soszynski '07.

Shaping the boundaries of this project required many hours of conversation with colleagues. Steven Salop was exceptionally generous with his time and the contents of his library on economics. The time we spent talking about economics and shuttling from my office to his across the hall, undoubtedly accelerated my understanding of the intellectual framework of modern economics. I benefited greatly from the expertise and gentle prodding of several colleagues: Alex Aleinikoff, William Braxton, Jerry Kang (during his visit in 2004–5), Carrie Menkel-Meadow, Michael Seidman, Gerry Spann, Rebecca Tushnet, Kathy Zeiler and the colleagues who participated in the Georgetown Law Center Summer Faculty Workshop in 2004. If there are any errors in what follows, it must be because I didn't listen to their sage advice.

This project could not have been finished without the superb institutional arrangements in place at Georgetown University Law Center to support faculty manuscripts. Georgetown enjoys an organizational structure that would be the envy of most casebook writers. I received several summer research grants to allow me to devote time to developing and completing the project. In their capacities as lead manuscript editor and faculty services librarian for this book, Zinta Saulkans and Jennifer Locke and her staff were truly indispensable to achieving a high technical quality for the final manuscript. Diane McDonald, my faculty assistant, Derreck Brown, Sylvia Johnson, Toni Patterson, Ronnie Reese, and Anna Selden in the Office of Faculty Support were always optimistic in the face of frustrations and the unexpected nightmares of formatting, and other technical meltdowns. They were responsive to my many requests during the development of this book. Finally, the Office of Information Systems and Technology introduced me to new equipment and software for managing the project. My special thanks go to Dianne H. Ferro Mesarch, Dimo Michailov, Pablo Molina and Barry Wileman.

In 2001, Angela Harris visited at Georgetown from Boalt Hall at the Univ. of California at Berkeley. As we discussed her work on class and race, it became clear that I could benefit from working with her on this casebook. When she agreed to join the project, I could not know then what a terrific contributor she would be. Her intelligence and humor made the work flow effortlessly to conclusion. We truly had fun doing this work; my only regret is that I didn't think to ask her to join me sooner.

Finally, I want to thank my two daughters Kristen and Allison for their patience and understanding during the many hours I devoted to completing this project.

EMMA COLEMAN JORDAN

Washington, D.C. August, 2005

I would like to thank my students at Boalt and at Georgetown (Wealth and Class Relations, fall 2000; Wealth and Class Relations, fall 2001; and Law, Markets, and Culture, fall 2004) for their excitement, hard work, and insight as we tried to think through the complicated mutual entanglements of "fairness," "efficiency," "markets," "culture," and "law," and as we struggled toward an institutional theory of human flourishing.

I would like to thank my assistant, Ayn Lowry, for her skill and dedication at tracking down copyright holders across the globe, and for her enthusiasm for this project despite the many last-minute headaches it caused.

I owe a huge debt to my co-author, Emma Coleman Jordan, for talking me into joining and then sticking with the project, and for her wonderful combination of brilliant vision, sisterly solidarity, and can-do spirit.

Last, but not least, I would like to thank my amazing research assistants, Tucker Bolt Culbertson and Naomi Ruth Tsu, for everything: research, pep talks, proofreading, formatting, article suggestions, critical feedback, and, of course, cookies.

ANGELA HARRIS

Berkeley, California
August 2005

*

SUMMARY OF CONTENTS

xv

*

TABLE OF CONTENTS

TABLE OF CASES

Principal cases are in bold type. Non-principal cases are in roman type. References are to Pages.

CASES AND MATERIALS

ECONOMIC JUSTICE:

RACE, GENDER, IDENTITY AND ECONOMICS

*

CHAPTER 1

Race, Markets and Neutrality in Two Disciplines

Introduction and Overview

Almost fifty years ago, Charles P. Snow, the British novelist and physicist, identified an important communications gap between the literary and scientific cultures. In a now famous lecture, he used the metaphor of "two cultures" to represent the often incompatible world views of science and literature. He worried that the progress of knowledge in the western world would be compromised by the incomprehension then existing between scientists on one hand, and scholars in the humanities on the other. For Snow, science embodied a culture of objectivity, neutrality, and detached factual inquiry. Literary intellectuals, on the other hand were concerned with questions of meaning, identity, and history.

We conclude that an analogous gap exists today between two groups of legal scholars who think seriously about markets. On one hand, traditional law and economics scholars, like economists, are interested in questions of rational choice, efficiency, wealth maximization, and production and transactions costs. On the other hand, legal scholars concerned with questions of identity, including race, gender and sexual orientation have focused their scholarly investigations on issues of subordination, identity, cultural context, and legal indeterminacy. These two groups of scholars might have much to learn from each other. However, these "two cultures" of law, with few exceptions, remain in separate conversations, with separate world views and separate, even antagonistic, operating assumptions about how to evaluate market phenomena.

In this book, we investigate the problems of the market domain with respect for both cultures. We suspect that the economics perspective, with its reliance on scientific measurement and numerical representation of experience, offers much that can be useful. Our vantage point as scholars who have been active in anti-subordination theory, however, also leads us to be attentive to questions of identity, culture, context, history, and dominance.

Central to the tension between the two cultures of law is the question of method. Is legal analysis (or should it be) a science? Or is legal reasoning inherently interpretive, more art than science? Is the law a neutral and objective forum for conflict resolution, or is it a tool of the powerful? Scholars concerned with the problem of subordination—especially subordination based on race and gender identity—have challenged the claims of neutrality of traditional legal theory. This challenge has brought to the surface the conflict between the two cultures of law. In this book we extend the anti-subordination critique to classic market economics and to law and economics. We believe that the question of method—whether there is an objective science of society, or whether knowledge is inherently perspectival—is of such central importance to understanding the structure of economic inequality that it provides a promising field upon which to begin the three-way conversation between the traditionalists in economics, the traditionalists in law, and the anti-subordination-oriented legal theorists.

As legal scholars concerned with the impact of subordination in law and in markets, we want to examine the role that traditional legal analysis plays in reinforcing the rational choice, efficiency, and wealth maximization assumptions of traditional economic views of the operation of markets. It is not surprising to find that claims of neutrality play as central a role in traditional legal theory as they do in traditional economic analysis.

We turn now to the central organizing question of this first chapter: what methods and normative assumptions are most useful in evaluating the complex landscape of law, markets, and culture? What tools are best suited to sort truth from ideology and myth? What would "truth" look like if we found it? We begin with these questions because we believe that unless these intensely contested, yet often invisible, first premises of analysis are explored, it will be impossible to make sense of the claims and arguments of the traditionalists in economics and in law or the contradictory positions of critical race, feminist and other scholars concerned with the problem of intertwined structures of subordination. Throughout this book we will use a variety of tools to pursue our interest in fostering a conversation between economics and the critical perspectives. We will use methodologies and insights from sociology, psychology, and behavioral economics, as well as the various schools of modern legal thought.

To begin our discussion we have chosen a now-famous narrative account by Professor Patricia Williams. Williams is a part of the critical race theory movement, described below. Our choice to begin with a narrative reflects our view about neutrality and truth. Stories can provide a potent starting point for identifying and examining buried assumptions. As you work through this material keep in mind the structure and sources of the neutrality claims identified above. See if you can detect them on your own.

A.   CRITICAL RACE THEORY: NARRATIVE, NEUTRALITY AND THE MARKETPLACE

The Death of the Profane

THE ALCHEMY OF RACE AND RIGHTS 44–51 (1991).

■ PATRICIA J. WILLIAMS

Buzzers are big in New York City. Favored particularly by smaller stores and boutiques, merchants throughout the city have installed them as screening devices to reduce the incidence of robbery: if the face at the door looks desirable, the buzzer is pressed and the door is unlocked. If the face is that of an undesirable, the door stays locked. Predictably, the issue of undesirability has revealed itself to be a racial determination. While controversial enough at first, even civil-rights organizations backed down eventually in the face of arguments that the buzzer system is a "necessary evil," that it is a "mere inconvenience" in comparison to the risks of being murdered, that suffering discrimination is not as bad as being assaulted, and that in any event it is not all blacks who are barred, just "17-year-old black males wearing running shoes and hooded sweatshirts."

The installation of these buzzers happened swiftly in New York; stores that had always had their doors wide open suddenly became exclusive or received people by appointment only. I discovered them and their meaning one Saturday in 1986. I was shopping in Soho and saw in a store window a sweater that I wanted to buy for my mother. I pressed my round brown face to the window and my finger to the buzzer, seeking admittance. A narrow-eyed, white teenager wearing running shoes and feasting on bubble gum glared out, evaluating me for signs that would pit me against the limits of his social understanding. After about five seconds, he mouthed "We're closed," and blew pink rubber at me. It was two Saturdays before Christmas, at one o'clock in the afternoon; there were several white people in the store who appeared to be shopping for things for *their* mothers.

I was enraged. At that moment I literally wanted to break all the windows of the store and *take* lots of sweaters for my mother. In the flicker of his judgmental gray eyes, that saleschild had transformed my brightly sentimental, joy-to-the-world, pre-Christmas spree to a shambles. He snuffed my sense of humanitarian catholicity, and there was nothing I could do to snuff his, without making a spectacle of myself.

I am still struck by the structure of power that drove me into such a blizzard of rage. There was almost nothing I could do, short of physically intruding upon him, that would humiliate him the way he humiliated me. No words, no gestures, no prejudices of my own would make a bit of difference to him; his refusal to let me into the store—it was Benetton's, whose colorfully punish ad campaign is premised on wrapping every one of the world's peoples in its cottons and woolens—was an outward manifestation of his never having let someone like me into the realm of his reality. He had no compassion, no remorse, no reference to me; and no desire to acknowledge me even at the estranged level of arm's-length transactor. He saw me only as one who would take his money and therefore could not conceive that I was there to give him money.

In this weird ontological imbalance, I realized that buying something in that store was like bestowing a gift, the gift of my commerce, the lucre of my patronage. In the wake of my outrage, I wanted to take back the gift of appreciation that my peering in the window must have appeared to be. I wanted to take it back in the form of unappreciation, disrespect, defilement. I wanted to work so hard at wishing he could feel what I felt that he would never again mistake my hatred for some sort of plaintive wish to be included. I was quite willing to disenfranchise myself, in the heat of my need to revoke the flattery of my purchasing power. I was willing to boycott Benetton's, random white-owned businesses, and anyone who ever blew bubble gum in my face again.

My rage was admittedly diffuse, even self-destructive, but it was symmetrical. The perhaps loose-ended but utter propriety of that rage is no doubt lost not just to the young man who actually barred me, but to those who would appreciate my being barred only as an abstract precaution, who approve of those who would bar even as they deny that they would bar *me*.

The violence of my desire to burst into Benetton's is probably quite apparent. I often wonder if the violence, the exclusionary hatred, is equally apparent in the repeated public urgings that blacks understand the buzzer system by putting themselves in the shoes of white storeowners—that, in effect, blacks look into the mirror of frightened white faces for the reality of their undesirability; and that then blacks would "just as surely conclude that they would not let themselves in under similar circumstances." (That some blacks might agree merely shows that some of us have learned too well the lessons of privatized intimacies of self-hatred and rationalized away the fullness of our public, participatory selves.)

On the same day I was barred from Benetton's, I went home and wrote the above impassioned account in my journal. On the day after that, I found I was still brooding, so I turned to a form of catharsis I have always found healing. I typed up as much of the story as I have just told, made a big poster of it, put a nice colorful border around it, and, after Benetton's was truly closed, stuck it to their big sweater-filled window. I exercised my first amendment right to place my business with them right out in the street.

So that was the first telling of this story. The second telling came a few months later, for a symposium on Excluded Voices sponsored by a law review. I wrote an essay summing up my feelings about being excluded from Benetton's and analyzing "how the rhetoric of increased privatization, in response to racial issues, functions as the rationalizing agent of public unaccountability and, ultimately, irresponsibility." Weeks later, I received the first edit. From the first page to the last, my fury had been carefully cut out. My rushing, run-on-rage had been reduced to simple declarative sentences. The active personal had been inverted in favor of the passive impersonal. My words were different; they spoke to me upside down. I was afraid to read too much of it at a time—meanings rose up at me oddly, stolen and strange.

A week and a half later, I received the second edit. All reference to Benetton's had been deleted because, according to the editors and the faculty adviser, it was defamatory; they feared harassment and liability; they said printing it would be irresponsible. I called them and offered to supply a footnote attesting to this as my personal experience at one particular location and of a buzzer system not limited to Benetton's; the editors told me that they were not in the habit of publishing things that were unverifiable. I could not but wonder, in this refusal even to let me file an affidavit, what it would take to make my experience verifiable. The testimony of an independent white bystander? (a requirement in fact imposed in U.S. Supreme Court holdings through the first part of the century).

Two days *after* the piece was sent to press, I received copies of the final page proofs. All reference to my race had been eliminated because it was against "editorial policy" to permit descriptions of physiognomy. "I realize," wrote one editor, "that this was a very personal experience, but any reader will know what you must have looked like when standing at that window." In a telephone conversation to them, I ranted wildly about the significance of such an omission. "It's irrelevant," another editor explained in a voice gummy with soothing and patience; "It's nice and poetic" but it doesn't "advance the discussion of any principle.... This is a law review, after all." Frustrated, I accused him of censorship; calmly he assured me it was not. "This is just a matter of style," he said with firmness and finality.

Ultimately I did convince the editors that mention of my race was central to the whole sense of the subsequent text; that my story became one of extreme paranoia without the information that I am black; or that it became one in which the reader had to fill in the gap by assumption, presumption, prejudgment, or prejudice. What was most interesting to me in this experience was how the blind application of principles of neutrality, through the device of omission, acted either to make me look crazy or to make the reader participate in old habits of cultural bias.

That was the second telling of my story. The third telling came last April, when I was invited to participate in a law-school conference on Equality and Difference. I retold my sad tale of exclusion from Soho's most glitzy boutique, focusing in this version on the law-review editing process as a consequence of an ideology of style rooted in a social text of neutrality, I opined:

> Law and legal writing aspire to formalized, color-blind, liberal ideals. Neutrality is the standard for assuring these ideals; yet the adherence to it is often determined by reference to an aesthetic of uniformity, in which difference is simply omitted. For example, when segregation was eradicated from the American lexicon, its omission led many to actually believe that racism therefore no longer existed. Race-neutrality in law has become the presumed antidote for race bias in real life. With the entrenchment of the notion of race-neutrality came attacks on the concept of affirmative action and the rise of reverse discrimination suits. Blacks, for so many generations deprived of jobs based on the color of our skin, are now told that we ought to find it demeaning to be hired, based on the color of our skin. Such is the silliness of simplistic either-or inversions as remedies to complex problems.

> What is truly demeaning in this era of double-speak-no-evil is going on interviews and not getting hired because someone doesn't think we'll be comfortable. It is demeaning not to get promoted because we're

judged "too weak," then putting in a lot of energy the next time and getting fired because we're "too strong." It is demeaning to be told what we find demeaning. It is very demeaning to stand on street corners unemployed and begging. It is downright demeaning to have to explain why we haven't been employed for months and then watch the job go to someone who is "more experienced." It is outrageously demeaning that none of this can be called racism, even if it happens only to, or to large numbers of, black people; as long is it's done with a smile, a handshake and a shrug; as long as the phantom-word "race" is never used.

The image of race as a phantom-word came to me after I moved into my late godmother's home. In an attempt to make it my own, I cleared the bedroom for painting. The following morning the room asserted itself, came rushing and raging at me through the emptiness, exactly as it had been for twenty-five years. One day filled with profuse and overwhelming complexity, the next day filled with persistently recurring memories. The shape of the past came to haunt me, the shape of the emptiness confronted me each time I was about to enter the room. The force of its spirit still drifts like an odor throughout the house.

The power of that room, I have thought since, is very like the power of racism as status quo: it is deep, angry, eradicated from view, but strong enough to make everyone who enters the room walk around the bed that isn't there, avoiding the phantom as they did the substance, for fear of bodily harm. They do not even know they are avoiding; they defer to the unseen shapes of things with subtle responsiveness, guided by an impulsive awareness of nothingness, and the deep knowledge and denial of witchcraft at work.

The phantom room to me is symbolic of the emptiness of formal equal opportunity, particularly as propounded by President Reagan, the Reagan Civil Rights Commission and the Reagan Supreme Court. Blindly formalized constructions of equal opportunity are the creation of a space that is filled in by a meandering stream of unguided hopes, dreams, fantasies, fears, recollections. They are the presence of the past imaginary, imagistic form—the phantom-roomed exile of our longing.

> It is thus that I strongly believe in the efficacy of programs and paradigms like affirmative action. Blacks are the objects of constitutional omission which has been incorporated into a theory of neutrality. It is thus that omission is really a form of expression, as oxymoronic as that sounds: racial omission is a literal part of original intent; it is the fixed, reiterated prophecy of the Founding Fathers. It is thus that affirmative action is an affirmation; the affirmative act of hiring—or hearing—blacks is a recognition of individuality that replaces blacks as a social statistic that is profoundly interconnective to the fate of blacks and whites either as sub-groups or as one group. In this sense, affirmative action is as mystical and beyond-the-self as an initiation ceremony. It is an

act of verification and of vision. It is an act of social as well as professional responsibility.

The following morning I opened the local newspaper, to find that the event of my speech had commanded two columns on the front page of the Metro section. I quote only the opening lines: "Affirmative action promotes prejudice by denying the status of women and blacks, instead of affirming them as its name suggests. So said New York City attorney Patricia Williams to an audience Wednesday."

I clipped out the article and put it in my journal. In the margin there is a note to myself: eventually, it says, I should try to pull all these threads together into yet another law-review article. The problem, of course, will be that in the hierarchy of law-review citation, the article in the newspaper will have more authoritative weight about me, as a so-called "primary resource," than I will have; it will take precedence over my own citation of the unverifiable testimony of my speech.

I have used the Benetton's story a lot, in speaking engagements at various schools. I tell it whenever I am too tired to whip up an original speech from scratch. Here are some of the questions I have been asked in the wake of its telling:

Am I not privileging a racial perspective, by considering only the black point of view? Don't I have an obligation to include the "salesman's side" of the story?

Am I not putting the salesman on trial and finding him guilty of racism without giving him a chance to respond to or cross-examine me?

Am I not using the store window as a "metaphorical fence" against the potential of his explanation in order to represent my side as "authentic"?

How can I be sure I'm right?

What makes my experience the real black one anyway?

Isn't it possible that another black person would disagree with my experience? If so, doesn't that render my story too unempirical and subjective to pay any attention to?

Always a major objection is to my having put the poster on Benetton's window. As one law professor put it: "It's one thing to publish this in a law review, where no one can take it personally, but it's another thing altogether to put your own interpretation right out there, just like that, uncontested, I mean, with nothing to counter it."

———

NOTES AND QUESTIONS

1. Shared claims of neutrality: legal neutrality and economic neutrality. In their declarations of "truth," legal opinions are presented as objective, indifferent, and neutral. Similarly, the market is based on the notion that a willing buyer and a willing seller will participate in an arm's-length transaction according to their preferences. The sum total of these discrete transactions is a market expressing cumulative preferences that are neutral, in that they do not reflect central government control. It was Adam Smith, one of the founding fathers of modern economics, who asserted that the greater good for all could be best achieved through such a market of free exchanges, guided by the invisible hand. But, what happens when only one party is willing to participate in a transaction? How do individual preferences and choices affect the market? What role does legal neutrality play in weakening or reinforcing these preferences?

2. Wechslerian principles of neutrality. Lawyer and legal scholar Herbert Wechsler promoted constitutional interpretation based on neutral principles, not the immediate results of particular cases. He described the "ad hoc evaluation" based on individual outcome as "the deepest problem of our constitutionalism." Herbert Wechsler, *Toward Neutral Principles of Constitutional Law*, 73 HARV. L. REV. 1 (1959).

> A principled decision, in the sense I have in mind, is one that rests on reasons with respect to all the issues in the case, reasons that in their generality and their neutrality transcend any immediate result that is involved. When no sufficient reasons of this kind can be assigned for overturning value choices of the other branches of the Government or of a state, those choices must, of course, survive. Otherwise, as Holmes said in his first opinion for the Court, "a constitution, instead of embodying only relatively fundamental rules of right, as generally understood by all English-speaking communities, would become the partisan of a particular set of ethical or economical opinions. . . ." *Id.* at 19.

Wechsler recognizes the potential for constitutional decisions that do not reflect personal views of justice, and he points to use of the Fourteenth Amendment to remedy racial discrimination as "the hardest test." *Id.* at 26. Though he claimed to be in favor of desegregated schools, he says:

> I find it hard to think the judgment [in *Brown v. Board of Education*] really turned upon the facts. Rather, it seems to me, it must have rested on the view that racial segregation is, in principle, a denial of equality to the minority against whom it is directed; that is, the group that is not dominant politically and, therefore, does not make the choice involved. For many who support the Court's decision this assuredly is the decisive ground. But this position also presents problems. Does it not involve an inquiry into the motive of the legislature, which is generally foreclosed to the courts? Is it alternatively defensible to make the measure of validity of legislation the way it is interpreted by those who are affected by it? In the context of a charge that segregation *with equal facilities* is a denial of equality, is there not a point in *Plessy* in the statement that if "enforced separation stamps the colored race with a badge of inferiority" it is solely because its members choose "to put that construction upon it"? . . .

> For me, assuming equal facilities, the question posed by state-enforced segregation is not one of discrimination at all. Its human and its

constitutional dimensions lie entirely elsewhere, in the denial by the state of freedom to associate, a denial that impinges in the same way on any groups or races that may be involved.

* * *

But if the freedom of association is denied by segregation, integration forces an association upon those for whom it is unpleasant or repugnant.... Given a situation where the state must practically choose between denying the association to those individuals who wish it or imposing it on those who would avoid it, is there a basis in neutral principles for holding that the Constitution demands that the claims for association should prevail? (I should like to think there is, but I confess that I have not yet written the opinion. To write it is for me the challenge of the school-segregation cases.)

Id, at 33–34.

The requirement of neutrality in law, as described by Wechsler, limits the judiciary's ability to make law based on value judgments. Is it more important for the legal system to make decisions based on neutral principles or outcomes? Are "neutral" principles really neutral, or do they promote value judgments as well? Is the refusal of the courts to inquire into the motive of the legislature a neutral principle or one which upholds the power of the political majority? In what ways has this philosophy influenced the development of the common law? We return to the question of motive in *Washington v. Davis* infra at 44.

Williams challenges the "blind application of principles of neutrality," claiming, "[b]lacks are the objects of a constitutional omission which has been incorporated into a theory of neutrality." WILLIAMS, *supra*, at 50. How would Williams respond to Wechsler's question whether there is a neutral principle upon which *Brown v. Board of Education* could have, or should have, been decided?

3. Neutrality of facts in appellate opinions. Courts use the law as a screen through which certain facts emerge as relevant while other facts are sifted out as irrelevant. *See* Richard Delgado, *Storytelling for Oppositionists and Others: A Plea for Narrative*, 87 MICH. L. REV. 2411, 2428 (1989). Sometimes the facts after they pass through this screen are startlingly dissimilar to the experiences of the parties involved.

For example, the Supreme Court's opinion in *United States v. Cruikshank*, 92 U.S. 542 (1875) did not include any significant discussion of the facts, only stating the indictments at issue:

The general charge ... that of "banding," and ... that of "conspiring" together to injure, oppress, threaten, and intimidate Levi Nelson and Alexander Tillman, citizens of the United States, of African descent and persons of color, with the intent thereby to hinder and prevent them in their free exercise and enjoyment of rights and privileges "granted and secured" to them "in common with all other good citizens of the United States by the constitution and law of the United States." United States v. Cruikshank, 92 U.S. 542, 548 (1875).

The Court found that the charges were insufficiently specific under the Civil Rights Enforcement Act of 1870, and the convictions were overturned. *Id.* at 559. The Court failed to mention that the charges stemmed from the "bloodiest violence of the Reconstruction." ENCYCLOPEDIA OF AFRICAN AMERICAN CIVIL RIGHTS: FROM EMANCIPATION TO THE PRESENT 541 (Charles D. Lowery & John F. Marszalek, eds., 1992). On Easter Sunday of 1873 in Colfax, Louisiana, 280 African Americans were massacred. *Id.* at 541. In *Cruikshank*, the Court overturned the only convictions among scores of federal prosecutions for the Colfax Riot, but the significance of the opinion's blow to the post-Civil War civil rights movement is lost without a factual setting.

Rather than failing to include significant facts, Justice Cardozo seems to have invented his own version of what took place in the famous torts case *Palsgraf v. Long Island Railroad*. After reading Cardozo's impossible account of Mrs. Palsgraf being injured from across the station platform after a small package exploded, her attorney requested a rehearing because "there was an apparent error in the understanding of the facts of the case." Manz, *Palsgraf, Cardozo's Urban Legend?*, 107 DICK. L. REV. 785, at 818 (spring 2003). Manz asserts that the importance of this case, despite its questionable fact pattern, does not indicate disregard for the truth so much as academic interest in the opinion itself, not the underlying event. Manz, *supra* at 789. As Wechsler advocated, principled reasoning, not the immediate outcome, is important. *See* Wechsler, *supra* text at note 2. Perhaps the outcome of this case is relevant, however. Mrs. Palsgraf was reportedly upset by the lost case for the rest of her life. Manz, *supra* at 840. Additionally, Cardozo's version of the facts has raised questions about his attitudes toward women and the poor. *Id.* at 786. For more on the Palsgraf case factual history, see JOHN T. NOONAN, JR., PERSONS AND MASKS OF THE LAW (1976).

The law review board attempted to screen references to Williams's race as irrelevant and the role of Benetton's as unverifiable. Is Williams correct in asserting that these facts were relevant to her story?

Questioning the neutrality of law, Richard Delgado observed:

Traditional legal writing purports to be neutral and dispassionately analytical, but too often it is not. In part, this is so because legal writers rarely focus on their own mindsets, the received wisdoms that serve as their starting points, themselves no more than stories, that lie behind their quasi-scientific string of deductions. The supposedly objective point of view often mischaracterizes, minimizes, dismisses, or derides without fully understanding opposing viewpoints. Implying that objective, correct answers can be given to legal questions also obscures the moral and political value judgments that lie at the heart of any legal inquiry. Delgado, *supra* at 2440–41.

Delgado is describing the indeterminacy of the law and challenging the notion of neutral application—central themes in the critical legal studies movement. *See* RICHARD W. BAUMAN, CRITICAL LEGAL STUDIES: A GUIDE TO THE LITERATURE 3 (1996). Although "[n]o single manifesto" can summarize the diversity of critical legal thought, "[t]he critique of law, its theories, and its institutions is meant to break down hierarchies of gender, race, class, or so-called merit." *Id.* at 3–4.

4. Challenging neutrality in practice. Law students generally learn the language of law through legal writing courses, which teach the tone, culture, factual analysis, and reasoning of the practice of law. Kathryn M. Stanchi, *Resistance is Futile: How Legal Writing Pedagogy Contributes to the Law's Marginalization of the Outsider*, 103 DICK. L. REV. 1, 11 (1998).

In addition to internalizing the labels of "relevant" and "irrelevant" facts, students learn how to write objectively. The dominant perspective is described as neutral and objective, and the subjective is disregarded as personal, as opposed to professional. *Id.* at 40. "[O]bjectivity is a hallmark of legal language, of the professional voice." *Id.* at 35.

To counteract the negative effects of objectivity, instructors must incorporate critical legal theory into teaching lawyering skills, but critical writing has generally been focused on legal scholarship instead of the practice of law. Stanchi, *supra* at 56; Brook K. Baker, *Transcending Legacies of Literacy and Transforming the Traditional Repertoire: Critical Discourse Strategies for Practice*, 23 WM. MITCHELL L. REV. 491, 516 (1997).

> Developing a critical discourse is fraught with contradictions arising from lawyers' competing obligations to act and write zealously on behalf of clients on the one hand, and to resist dogma and write transformatively in furtherance of community interests and social justice on the other. Nonetheless, legal writing specialists might consider the efficacy of increased reliance on: (1) using subversive outsider-narratives; (2) confronting and avoiding appeals to bias; and (3) using a more dialogic, less adversarial, more feminist discourse. *Id.* at 517.

Narratives, when subversive instead of hegemonic, use an individual story to reveal a collective wrong. *Id.* at 528–29, 532. The adversarial nature of legal representation allows lawyers to use almost any relevant tactic and prevents only the most blatant appeals to biases. The backlash of color-blind jurisprudence restricts the means to counteract stereotypes, employing biases as well. *Id.* at 543. Using feminist ideals to counteract the male ideology of legal representation as combat, "a nonadversarial advocacy might tone down excessive rhetoric, decrease competitive posturing, and instead engage in a more serious legal, moral, and political dialogue with opponents and legal decision-makers." *Id.* at 555–56.

How might Williams have used her experience in a discrimination suit against Benetton's? Could she find a role for her narrative in the formality of legal documents, thereby avoiding appeals to biases and creating a dialogue about retailers' use of buzzers? *See* Williams at 48, in which she claims omission of her race would make the reader participate in old habits of cultural bias.

5. Narratives in legal discourse. Narratives are a powerful means of constructing moral and social realities, which are indeterminate and therefore subject to interpretation. Richard Delgado, *Storytelling for Opposition-*

ists and Others: A Plea for Narrative, 87 MICH. L. REV. 2411, 2415–16 (1989) (illustrating how the reality of a single event changes with the perspective of five different stories).

The stories of the dominant ingroup are used to construct a "shared reality in which its own superior position is seen as natural," by picking and choosing facts to justify the world as it is. But " 'neutrality' can feel [different] from the perspective of an outsider." *Id.* at 2412, 2421, 2425.

Members of outgroups use counterstories, which directly challenge the stories of the ingroup, as (1) a means of self-preservation and (2) a means of lessening their own subordination. *Id.* at 2436.

> [S]tories about oppression, about victimization, about one's own brutalization—far from deepening the despair of the oppressed, lead to healing, liberation, mental health. They also promote group solidarity. Storytelling emboldens the hearer, who may have had the same thoughts and experiences the storyteller describes, but hesitated to give them voice. Having heard another express them, he or she realizes, I am not alone.

> Yet, stories help oppressed groups in a second way—through their effect on the oppressor. Most oppression . . . does not seem like oppression to those perpetrating it. It is rationalized, causing few pangs of conscience. The dominant group justifies its privileged position by means of stories, stock explanations that construct reality in ways favorable to it. . . .

> This story is drastically at odds with the way most people of color would describe their condition. . . . Counterstories can attack that complacency.

> What is more, they can do so in ways that promise at least the possibility of success. Most civil rights strategies confront the obstacle of blacks' otherness. The dominant group, noticing that a particular effort is waged on behalf of blacks, increases its resistance. Stories at times can overcome that otherness, hold that instinctive resistance in abeyance. Stories are the oldest, most primordial meeting ground in human experience. Their allure will often provide the most effective means of overcoming otherness, of forming a new collectivity based on the shared story.

> *Id.* at 2436–38.

Listeners asked Patricia Williams why she did not feel obligated to include the salesman's side of the story and why her individual experience was worth their attention. How could Williams, had she chosen to answer the questions, have defended putting "[her] own interpretation right out there"?

6. Significance of Williams's self description. While describing her face in a manner that reinforces connections with this country's segregated history, is Williams giving short shrift to descriptive accuracy? What relationship should the accuracy of Williams's self description have with her publication of the Benetton's story in a law review? If the law review editors believe Williams's description was wholly inaccurate, should they refuse to publish her work? Would the answer change if Williams's piece were written in the traditional, "objective" law review style? For an especially heated exchange between two critical legal scholars about exactly the point raised in the notes above, and the credibility of Patricia Williams's Benetton story, see Mark Tushnet, *The Degradation of Constitutional Discourse*, 81 GEO. L.J. 251, 265–78 (1992) and Gary Peller, *The Discourse of Constitutional Degradation*, 81 GEO. L.J. 313 (1992). *See generally* Richard Posner, *The Skin Trade*, THE NEW REPUBLIC, Oct. 13, 1997, at 40; DANIEL A. FARBER AND SUZANNA SHERRY, BEYOND ALL REASON (1997).

One possible criticism that can be made of Williams's decision to describe her face as round and brown is that it paints a much more familiar picture of racism. Discrimination against Patricia Williams implies a difficult problem which can not be solved simply by assimilation or affirmative action. Law review readers who believe in marketplace neutrality will not want to believe in discrimination against Patricia Williams because it may raise issues of their own culpability for not finding ways of combating prejudice beyond assimilation.

Does Williams's article lose some of its effectiveness by perpetuating a comforting picture of racism? *See also* Devon W. Carbado & Mitu Gulati, *The Law and Economics of Critical Race Theory: Crossroads, Directions, and a New Critical Race Theory*, 112 YALE. L.J. 1757, 1817 (2003) (book review).

7.   Williams and anonymous clerk. In *Death of the Profane*, Williams describes not one, but two transactions. First, there is the actual transaction between her and the clerk: the gift of her commerce in exchange for his permission to enter Benetton's. Second, there is the hypothetical exchange which never took place: Williams's money in exchange for Benetton's sweater. When analyzing the situation in this way, doesn't it seem simply as though Williams didn't meet the clerk's asking price for admittance? Obviously, the clerk undervalued Williams's cultural capital. Since the clerk did not open the door, should Williams have pressed a twenty dollar bill against the window in order to sweeten her offer? Would it indicate that the market was functioning properly, at least in the first exchange, if the clerk who refused Williams entry was fired because of bringing bad publicity to Benetton's?

8.   Note on Williams's "marketplace." Williams's poignant personal account details her exclusion from participating in the marketplace, an environment where, theoretically, a willing buyer and a willing seller make a connection based on each of their preferences and enter into agreements to buy and sell products and services. The marketplace is fundamentally associated with freedom, functional objectivity, and deference to personal preference. DEBORAH WAIRE POST ET AL., CONTRACTING LAW 1 (1996). In making exchanges for goods and services, willing buyers and sellers usually engage in single transactions or once-only interactions. CRAIG CALHOUN ET AL.,

STRUCTURES OF POWER AND CONSTRAINT: PAPERS IN HONOR OF PETER M. BLAU 134 (1990). These transactions are not based on personal trust between these buying and selling actors; rather, individuals depend on the independent system of law, official contracts, courts, and enforcement agencies to regulate interaction and exchange in the marketplace. *Id.* In this case, Williams requesting to enter Benetton's was an offer to participate in the marketplace, a manifestation of intent to enter into an exchange of her money for a Benetton's product. POST, *supra* at 196. However, Williams's offer created the power of acceptance in the sales associate—the "narrow-eyed, white teenager"—and in denying her admittance into the store, the young clerk abruptly ended a potential exchange in the retail market. *Id.* Therefore, economists may claim that there was no acceptance on the part of the sales clerk, thereby making no obligation on the part of Benetton's to sell Williams any goods or services. The absence of an acceptance failed to complete the formation of a contract between Benetton's to sell goods and Williams to grant "the gift of her commerce."

Though the marketplace paradigm explicates exchanges between buying and selling actors in a straightforward, ostensibly neutral model, it largely ignores several ideological, cultural, and social implications of everyday human interaction. The simple paradigm assumes that actors voluntarily enter into these transactions and that these buyers and sellers do not consider salient issues, such as the other actor's race, class, gender, or ethnicity. *Id.* at 2. As societal norms, citizens' biases, and the nation's socioeconomic hierarchy play a large role in social life, economic models of exchange in the marketplace fail to consider the varied rule systems that constitute and control social transactions. CALHOUN, *supra* at 142.

Williams challenges the simple economic model by asserting that the market is not an impartial setting, but a partial milieu where market players are significantly influenced by their own prejudices and self-indulgence to exclude certain actors from participating in the process of exchange. Williams claims the white clerk's rejection of her admittance into the store was an overt "manifestation of his never having let someone like me into the realm of his reality"; this clerk was only a willing seller to certain willing buyers, not buyers like Williams. Rather than a simple economic transaction, where two players are interested in generating an efficient exchange with one another, negotiating, and creating bilateral decisions, Williams is not given a chance to enter into the bargain; she is on the receiving end of a unilateral decision. According to Williams, a critical race scholar, the marketplace is not an environment where players are on equal footing and make decisions based on individual preferences, but a place where her "round brown face" banishes her from creating stable economic relationships.

9. *Death of the Profane* as demonstrating market power. At first glance, Professor Williams's experience seems to imply a market failure. However, market economics does not say that businesses (like Benetton's) always make correct decisions; it says that when businesses make bad decisions, they are punished by lost profits which provide an incentive to make better decisions in the future. According to this model, if a business does not stop making bad decisions, its competitors will eventually drive it out of business. With this in mind, is Williams's story an example of the market in action? Benetton's has certainly suffered for its bad decision. Not only did Professor Williams not patronize Benetton's, she also posted a sign in Benetton's window and immortalized the episode in a law review article. Will the loss of business and bad publicity generated by this incident lead Benetton's to change its ways, demonstrating that there wasn't a market failure after all?

10. *Death of the Profane* **as demonstrating market impotence.** If Williams's experience was not a market failure, does that mean that the market provides no means of dealing with any particular act of injustice, and that it can only (theoretically) work to minimize possible future injustice? However, if the market can not deal with actual acts of injustice, does that argue strongly for legislative solutions?

11. Does a famous black face make any difference? In the summer of 2005, Oprah Winfrey, the billionare entertainer and entrepreneur, went shopping in Paris. Just fifteen minutes after closing, Oprah approached the very exclusive Hermes store, accompanied by a small party of friends. She noticed a group of people still milling about in the store, and she tried to enter. She was firmly turned away by a clerk. Oprah's best friend, Gayle King, who witnessed the incident reports that: " 'People were in the store and they were shopping. **Oprah** was at the door and she was not allowed into the store.' '**Oprah** describes it herself as "one of the most humillating moments of her life." ' "

King said it's unlikely that Winfrey will shop there again: *Store Sorry for Closed Door Policy* CHI. TRIB., June 24, 2005, at p. 23.

Oprah was as enraged as Patricia Williams at this shopping slight. Oprah turned her considerable publicity apparatus to respond to the store's refusal. Although she received an apology, she has promised to devote an entire show to the episode when she begins taping for the new season in the fall of 2005.

Does the Oprah incident reinforce, undercut, or complicate the racial explanation of Patricia Williams story? Like Williams, Oprah concluded that this was an example of racism. What weight should we give the store's explanation that it refused entry to Oprah because it was preparing for a special promotional event? Does it matter that the store did not fire or demote the clerk who denied entry to Oprah and friends?

12. Buzzer's role in market model. Does the buzzer fit into the conventional model of the market discussed above? Rather than a traditional negotiation between a willing buyer and a willing seller, the buzzer creates a unilateral decision made by an unwilling seller to exclude a willing buyer from the market. What factors might have influenced the clerk's decision to exclude Williams?

13. Buzzer and racism in marketplace. Williams notes that some deemed the buzzer system to be a "necessary evil" to mitigate the risk of crime in retail establishments. Another possible interpretation of the cultural and social context of the buzzer is that it symbolizes an elevated economic status or a means to establish economic segregation, utilized to prevent theft by excluding people who do not look as if they could afford the merchandise.

If the buzzer system was created to serve this purpose, why did the sales clerk choose to exclude Williams from the store? What is the basis of his belief that a black woman like Williams cannot afford clothes from Benetton's? Did the clerk exclude Williams based on the pervasive cultural representations of African Americans' socioeconomic background in the media or in the courts? Teun A. Van Dijk's study of racism and prejudice at a micro level observed interpersonal communication in everyday life. Van Dijk asserts that the media and the law are major vehicles that create ethnic prejudices in society. TEUN A. VAN DIJK, COMMUNICATING RACISM: ETHNIC PREJUDICE IN THOUGHT AND TALK 361 (1987). These representations of minorities may have a deleterious effect on interpersonal relations in the marketplace:

> Prejudices about aggression and crime of ethic groups largely derive from biased media stories that mention the ethnic backgrounds of suspects, which are again based on police reports or court trials, as well as on media articles about crime statistics or crime "waves" that are also partly derived from information supplied by the authorities. This is one of the most socially destructive ethnic prejudices, and there is much empirical evidence that the law and the media together help construct public attitudes about crime, deviance, or similar negative properties attributed to ethnic minority groups. *Id.* at 364.

Do you share Van Dijk's view? Do court trials aid in creating derogatory beliefs about the socioeconomic status of minorities and thus reinforce the legitimacy of the buzzer system?

An article in the *Washington Post Magazine* created heated debate concerning the buzzer system when it ran a column that supported the use of locks and buzzers as a security measure to discriminatorily screen young black male customers entering retail shops.

> As for me, I'm with the store owners, although I was not at first.... Young black males commit an inordinate amount of urban crime.... [R]ace is only one factor in their admissions policy. Age and sex count, too. And while race is clearly the most compelling factor, ask yourself what their policies would be if young white males were responsible for most urban crime.

> A nation with our history is entitled to be sensitive to race and racism—and we are all wary of behavior that would bring a charge of racism. But the mere recognition of race as a factor—especially if those of the same race recognize the same factor—is not in itself racism. This may apply as much to some opponents of busing or public housing in their own neighborhood as it does to who gets admitted to jewelry stores. Let he who would open the door throw the first stone.

Richard Cohen, *Closing the Door on Crime*, WASH. POST, Sept. 7, 1986 (magazine), at W13; *see also* Jane Gross, *When "By Appointment" Means Keep Out*, N.Y. TIMES, Dec. 17, 1986, at B1.

Was race "only one factor" in the exclusion of Williams, a successful female law professor? How does race as a factor in exclusion affect the model of the market described above? Is using race as a factor in excluding a willing buyer from the market racist? If not, what would meet the commentator's definition of racism?

14.   More screening based on race. Discriminatory screening practices are not an isolated occurrence. In New York, small shops on the Upper Eastside have used, in addition to locks and buzzers, signs that read, "Men by appointment only." *Fear of Blacks, Fear of Crime*, N.Y. TIMES, Dec. 28, 1986, at § 4, 10. In addition, an African American man in Philadelphia filed a complaint with the Human Rights Commission after he was denied entrance to Mums & Pops Confectionary, which employs a lock and buzzer system. *See* Tamar Charry, *Bitter Sweets Battle*, PHILADELPHIA CITY PAPER, Dec. 7–14, 1995.

The retailers employing such security measures seem to equate blackness with criminality, and the *New York Times* editorial board warned, "discrimination, cumulatively, can be as poisonous as mugging or burglary." *Fear of Blacks, supra.* "Fearful whites need to put themselves in the shoes of innocent blacks. Doing so will not dissipate fear, but it can steadily inspire the understanding and reason that keep fear in its place." *Id.* A letter to the editor disagreed "that a society in which prejudice is rampant is as bad as one in which violent crime is rampant." Michael Levin and Margarita Levin, *Howard Beach Turns a Beam on Racial Tension*, N.Y. TIMES, Jan. 11, 1987, at § 4, 30. The letter concluded that an innocent black person would not let himself into the shop if standing in the owner's shoes. After reading Williams's description of the humiliation and rage she felt, do you think she would agree with the letter's conclusion? For an array of responses to a hypothetical involving decisions to screen customers based on race, see *The Jeweler's Dilemma* in THE NEW REPUBLIC, November 10, 1986, at 18.

15.   Law and economics criticisms of critical race narrative methodology. Judge Richard Posner, a leading law and economics scholar, faults the critical race narrative methodology as non scientific, selective, and unreliable when compared to economic methodology. Posner, Overcoming Law, 368–384, "Nuance, Narrative and Empathy in Critical Race Theory." This argument is discussed in the next section of this chapter.

B.   A LAW AND ECONOMICS CHALLENGE TO THE NEUTRALITY OF THE CRITICAL RACE NARRATIVE METHODOLOGY

Nuance, Narrative, and Empathy in Critical Race Theory

OVERCOMING LAW 368–84 (1995).

■ RICHARD POSNER

The Alchemy of Race and Rights describes its author, Patricia Williams, as a young black female law professor of contracts and commercial law whose abiding interest is the plight of the American black. Or plights, for she is particularly concerned with the lack of fit that her condition of being a black professional woman makes with the attitudes and expectations of the predominantly white community in which, as a professor in an academic field that has relatively few women, very few blacks, and therefore almost no black women, she mainly circulates. The lack of fit induces in her at times a sense of disorientation that is almost vertiginous. So it is a book about both "privileged" blacks like herself and her underprivileged coracialists at the bottom of the social totem pole.

The book offers a black feminist perspective on a variety of practices and institutions: law's pretense to objectivity and impersonality, surrogate motherhood, consumerism, constitutional protection of hate speech and condemnation of governmental efforts at affirmative action, the inept and insensitive behavior of well-meaning white liberal academics, and above all white racism in what she considers its hydra-headed manifestations. There is little that is new in the paraphrasable content of her criticisms. The novelty is the form, which can aptly be described as literary, in which Williams has cast her discussion of these legal and social issues. She is not unique in employing literary methods in legal scholarship; earlier and essentially isolated examples of this genre to one side, it is the methodological signature of critical race theory. But she is one of the most skillful practitioners of the genre.

The subtitle of the book—"Diary of a Law Professor"—is a clue to her technique. The book is not literally a diary, although it contains some excerpts from the author's diary. But it is like a diary in presenting the author's analyses of legal and social issues in the form of reactions to her daily experiences, whether as consumer, law professor, television viewer, or daughter. The reader comes to understand that Williams's way of coping with the many stresses of her life is to write down her reactions to stressful or arresting events as soon after they occur as she can. Writing in a diary-like format is thus a form of therapy. But it also gives scope for her powerful gift for narration. * * *

The rhetorical highlight of the book, however, is the description of an episode at a Benetton clothing store. "Buzzers are big in New York City. Favored particularly by smaller stores and boutiques, merchants throughout the city have installed them as screening devices to reduce the incidence of robbery: if the face at the door looks desirable, the buzzer is pressed and the door is unlocked. If the face is that of an undesirable, the door stays locked. Predictably, the issue of undesirability has revealed itself to be a racial determination," as Williams discovers one Saturday afternoon when she

> was shopping in Soho and saw in a store window a sweater that I wanted to buy for my mother. * * *

The power of this sketch lies in its compression, its vivid contrasting of the round brown face with the sales clerk's narrow eyes and pink bubble gum, its use of physical exclusion as a metaphor for social exclusion, its suggestion that the least significant of whites (this gum-chewing bubble-blowing teenage sales clerk) is utterly comfortable with exercising power over an older and more accomplished black, and its elegant summation of the clerk's reaction to her ("evaluating me for signs that would pit me against the limits of his social understanding"). Yet here at the very pinnacle of Williams's art the careful reader will begin to feel a sense of disquiet. Did Williams really press her face against the window—that is, did her face actually touch the glass? Or is she embroidering the facts for dramatic effect—making the insult to her seem even graver than it was because it shattered a childlike eagerness and innocence? Also, how does she know that the sales clerk refused to let her in the store because she's black? The only evidence she cites is that, since Christmas was approaching, it was unlikely that the store had closed, and that there were other shoppers in the store. The second point has no force. Stores normally stop admitting customers before all the customers already in the store have left—otherwise the store might never be able to close. The first point has greater force. Although many stores close early on Saturday, the likelihood that a Benetton store in New York City during the Christmas shopping season would be one of them is slight. Yet Williams does not suggest that she has tried to find out whether the store was open. She does not suggest that she saw any customers admitted after she was turned away. The absence of a sign indicating that the store was closed would be some evidence that it was not, but she doesn't say anything about the presence or absence of a sign. Many stores list their hours on the front door. She makes no mention of this either. In all likelihood the store was open, but I am surprised that she—a lawyer—did not attempt to verify the point.

But of course the attempt might have been futile. And it is even possible, though I find no clues to this in the text, that her anger at the episode reflects in part a pervasive, debilitating uncertainty that confronts blacks in their encounters with whites. Not every disappointment that a black person encounters is a result of discrimination, and yet it may be impossible to determine which is and which is not. We like to know where we stand with other people, and this may be difficult for blacks in their dealings with whites.

Yet she had told us at the outset, in defense of doing legal scholarship in the form of story telling, "that one of the most important results of reconceptualizing from 'objective truth' to rhetorical event will be a more nuanced sense of legal and social responsibility" (p. 11). Unless "nuanced" is a euphemism for fictive, Williams has promised to get the particulars of an event or situation right, rather than submerging them in a generality, such as that whites hate blacks. That promise implies an effort to find out what *really* was going on in that white teenager's mind when he told her the store was closed. Maybe, as I said, it was closed; or maybe it wasn't but the clerk had his hands full with the customers inside. Maybe he was a disloyal employee who wanted to get his employer in trouble; maybe he was lazy, mischievous, rude, irresponsible, or just plain dumb.

The Alchemy of Race and Rights suppresses every perspective other than that of the suffering, oppressed black. * * *

This is a pattern. In discussing the case of Bernhard Goetz, who shot four black youths in a subway car and was acquitted of all but an illegal weapons charge even though he could not have been acting in *reasonable* self-defense, Williams disparages white fear of black crime by characterizing the criminal records of Goetz's victims as mere "allegations" by asking rhetorically how the community would have reacted to Goetz's action if he had been black and his victims white *and the crime had occurred in a department store rather than in the subway*—an added fictive touch that magnifies the malignant irrationality of Goetz's action—and by reciting irrelevant statistics showing that whites commit more crimes than blacks. What is omitted is that the prison population is almost half black, although blacks are only 12 percent of the population, and that urban street (and subway) crime is committed mostly by blacks. Black criminality is a serious social problem. To pretend otherwise is an evasion. AIDS, drug addiction, homophobia, neglect of children, anti-Semitism, and poor political leadership are other problems of the black community that Williams ignores. * * *

Mention of black anti-Semitism brings me back to the question of Beethoven's color. That Beethoven was black is a typical and recurrent claim of the Afrocentrist movement, members of which have also asserted that melanin is positively correlated with intelligence, that the ancient Greeks stole philosophy from black Egyptians and, specifically, that Alexander the Great pillaged the library at Alexandria to steal Egyptian philosophical ideas for his old tutor, Aristotle (never mind that Alexander *founded* Alexandria and that the library was built long after his death), that Napoleon shot off the sphinx's nose so that no one would know that the sphinx had Negroid features, that not only Beethoven but also Haydn, Cleopatra, and Lincoln were black, that Beethoven's blackness is shown by (among other things) his confidence in his abilities, a confidence similar to that of Mohammed Ali, that Dwight Eisenhower's mother was black, that America was first discovered by Africans, that AIDS was invented by whites to exterminate the black race, that the telephone and carbon steel were invented in Africa along with science, medicine, and mathematics, that "the [African] Blacks' conception of God was on a scale too grand to be acceptable to Western minds"—and that Jews controlled the African slave trade and today are plotting with the Mafia the financial destruction of the black race. *Not all Afrocentrists are anti-Semitic; but irresponsible claims appear to be the hallmark of the movement* [emphasis added], and I should have thought that Williams, as a lawyer and an academic, would have wanted to place as much distance as possible between herself and it rather than to embrace uncritically one of its representative wild claims.

Could it be—despite Martha Nussbaum's argument that imaginative literature in general and the novel in particular renders social reality with a degree of balance, nuance, and concreteness that provides a needed antidote to the partial visions furnished by abstract, generalizing social-scientific approaches, such as that of economics—that one-sidedness is an endemic risk of the literary depiction of reality, rather than a particular characteristic of Patricia Williams? * * *

We accept one-sidedness in literature, moreover, because we make allowance for *autres temps, autres moeurs* and because factual accuracy and scholarly detachment are not rules of the literature game. But they are rules of the scholarly game, and Williams is writing as a scholar. If my criticisms of her in this chapter should turn out to be one-sided, misleading, and tendentious, she would not be impressed by my rejoining that mine is only one voice in an ongoing conversation and I can leave it to others to rectify any omissions or imbalance in my contribution.

If one-sidedness is the other side of literature's empathetic concreteness, empathetic awareness of strangers' pains and pleasures is the unexpected other side of the economist's Gradgrindian detachment. Consider rent control. The beneficiaries are plain to see: they are the tenants when the rent-control law is adopted. The victims are invisible: they are the future would-be tenants, who will face a restricted supply of rental housing because landowners will have a diminished incentive to build rental housing and owners of existing apartment buildings will prefer to sell rather than to rent the apartments in them. Economics brings these victims before the analyst's eye; literature, and the type of legal scholarship that imitates literature, does not.

Maybe economic scholarship is not *really* empathetic. The economist does not enter imaginatively into the distress of the disappointed quester for rental housing; all he does is tote up some additional costs. But that may be a sounder way of doing policy than by cultivating empathy. A jurisprudence of empathy can foster short-sighted substantive justice because the power to enter imaginatively into another person's outlook, emotions, and experiences diminishes with physical, social, and temporal distance.[30] Compare the maxims *tout comprendre c'est tout pardoner* and no man is a villain in his own eyes (an actor's adage). The second maxim should remind us that when we succeed in looking at the world through another's eyes, we lose the perspective necessary for judgment. We find ourselves in a stew of rationalization, warped perception, and overmastering emotion. (Any lawyer knows the risk of overidentification with his client.) The *tout comprendre* maxim expresses a different point: To understand another person completely is to understand the causality of his behavior, to see that behavior as the end of a chain of causes and thus as determined rather than responsible. It is to understand the person as completely as a scientist understands an animal, which is to say as a phenomenon of nature rather than as a free agent. If we understand a criminal's behavior as well as we understand a rattlesnake's behavior, we are unlikely to accord him much dignity and respect.

---

30. A more basic point is that the internal perspective—the putting oneself in the other person's shoes—that is achieved by the exercise of empathetic imagination lacks normative significance [Emphasis added].

The project of empathetic jurisprudence invites us to choose between achieving a warped internal perspective and an inhumanly clinical detachment: between becoming too hot and too cold. The affective dimension of empathy leads to identification with the person whose fate or welfare is at stake; the intellectual dimension leads to embedding the person in a web of causes that transforms him from a free human being into (in Nietzsche's phrase) an irresponsible piece of fate. I take back nothing I said in discussing the German judges about the importance of remembering that other human beings are—human. That does not require us to be able to crawl into their minds. Indeed, a lively awareness that other people are in an important sense closed to us—that they have their own plans and perspectives, into which we can enter imperfectly if at all—is one of the planks of the liberal platform. It is a presupposition of individuality.

Another problem with Williams's method is a lack of clarity. Here is the ending of the chapter in which Williams stands up for rights against the critical legal studies movement: "Give [rights] to trees. Give them to cows. Give them to history. Give them to rivers and rocks. Give to all of society's objects and untouchables the rights of privacy, integrity, and self-assertion; give them distance and respect" (p. 165). "What does it *mean* to give rights to history, or to entitle cows to privacy, integrity, and self-assertion? Is the reference to cows meant to put us in mind of Hindu doctrine regarding the sacredness of animals? Is Williams an animist, a 'Green'? Is she the second coming of Walt Whitman? (likely Carl Sandburg.) How can all this be squared with her being a fashion-conscious shopper. * * *

Narrative has two aspects, Narrative in the sense of the telling of a story is the way we make sense of a sequence of events unfolding in history.31 Black scholars like it because they believe that the current condition of the American black population cannot be understood without reference to the history of Negro slavery. But despite Williams's references to her great-great-grandmother, a slave, her book does not employ historical narration.

Narration is also a literary technique. To present an issue, such as the clash between critical legal studies and critical race theory, in the form of a story, * * * is to reinforce or replace abstract argument with a portrait. Portraits, including the verbal portraits that we call literature—works that depict rather than overtly argue—can change minds. This role of verbal portraiture, as also of photographs, is especially valuable in situations in which we have difficulty *seeing* important aspects of a problem because it involves people whose experiences are remote from ours. In education and occupation Patricia Williams is like other establishment legal figures, but in race and all that that connotes in this country (at least when the race is black) she is not, and maybe one has to learn to see the world through her eyes as well as one's own before one can fully evaluate the arguments pro and con various racial policies. On this view the very one-sidedness of her presentation, however questionable by the conventional standards of scholarship and even by the professed standards of critical race theory (which promised us, remember, nuance), has value in providing insight into the psychology and rhetoric of many blacks. But if whites must acquire a stereoscopic biracial perspective in order to cope effectively with our society's racial problems, blacks must too.

―――――

NOTES AND QUESTIONS

1. Standards of proof and burden of persuasion in narrative. What standards of proof and persuasion does Judge Posner rely upon to assess the Williams narrative? *See* Richard H. Gaskins; BURDENS OF PROOF IN MODERN DISCOURSE, (1993) (New Haven: Yale University Press).

2. Throwing rhetorical stones from glass houses? Does Posner's essay exhibit any of the problems that he sees in Williams work? Lack of clarity, exaggeration for rhetorical effect, manipulation of empathy, one-sidedness?

3. Difference between legal and economic standards of proof. Is the Posner essay structured by the standards of economic proof, or legal proof?

4. Finding "truth" in law or economics. What would persuade Judge Posner that a report of racism or microaggression is "true"?

5. Valuing collective experience. What place does group experience with subordination have in the Posnerian schema? *But see* Charles R. Lawrence, III, *The Id, the Ego, and Equal Protection: Reckoning with Unconscious Racism*, 39 STAN. L. REV. 317 (1987) (arguing for "cultural meaning test" based on a community's collective experience as the targets of racism).

6. Statistics as a scientific form of collective experience. In economics, collective experience is represented in statistical forms of aggregate data, including the mode, mean, average, and regression analysis. *Mode* is the value or item occurring most frequently in a series of observations or statistical data. *Mean* is the sum of all the members of the set divided by the number of items in the set. *Average* is something, as a type, number, quantity, or degree, that represents a midpoint between points on a scale of valuation. In statistics, *regression analysis* is a mathematical method of modeling the relationships among three or more variables. It is used to predict the value of one variable given the values of the others.

―――――――――――――――――

C. THE NARRATIVE OF POST-MODERN RACISM: THE "MICROAGRESSIONS"

Popular Legal Culture: Law as Microaggression

98 YALE L.J. 1559 (1989).

■ PEGGY C. DAVIS

[*The scene is a courthouse in Bronx, New York. A white assistant city attorney "takes the court elevator up to the ninth floor. At the fifth floor, the doors open. A black woman asks: 'Going down?' 'Up,' says [the city attorney]. And then, as the doors close: 'You see? They can't even tell up from down. I'm sorry, but it's true.' "]*

The black woman's words are subject to a variety of interpretations. She may have thought it efficient, appropriate, or congenial to ask the direction of the elevator rather than to search for the indicator. The indicator may have been broken. Or, the woman may have been incapable of competent elevator travel. The city attorney is led, by cognitive habit and by personal and cultural history, to seize upon the pejorative interpretation.

The city attorney lives in a society in which blacks are commonly regarded as incompetent. The traditional stereotype of blacks includes inferior mentality, primitive morality, emotional instability, laziness, boisterousness, closeness to anthropoid ancestors, occupational instability, superstition, care-free attitude, and ignorance. Common culture reinforces the belief in black incompetence in that the black is "less often depicted as a thinking being." If, for example, the city attorney watches television, she has observed that whites, but not blacks, are likely to exert authority or display superior knowledge; that whites, but not blacks, dispense goods and favors; and that blacks are disproportionately likely to be dependent and subservient. Cognitive psychologists tell us that the city attorney shares with all human beings a need to "categorize in order to make sense of experience. Too many events occur daily for us to deal successfully with each one on an individual basis; we must categorize in order to cope." In a world in which sidewalk grates routinely collapsed under the weight of an average person, we would walk around sidewalk grates. We would not stop to inspect them and distinguish secure ones from loose ones: It is more efficient to act on the basis of a stereotyping heuristic. In a world in which blacks are commonly thought to be incompetent (or dangerous, or musical, or highly sexed), it is more efficient for the city attorney to rely on the generalization than to make individuating judgments.

It is likely that the city attorney assimilated negative stereotypes about blacks before she reached the age of judgment. She will, therefore, have accepted them as truth rather than opinion. Having assimilated the stereotypes, the city attorney will have developed a pattern of interpreting and remembering ambiguous events in ways that confirm, rather than unsettle, her stereotyped beliefs. If she sees or hears of two people on a subway, one white, one black, and one holding a knife, she is predisposed to form an impression that the black person held the knife, regardless of the truth of the matter. She will remember examples of black incompetence and may fail to remember examples of black competence.

Psychoanalysts tell us that the stereotype serves the city attorney as a mental repository for traits and impulses that she senses within herself and dislikes or fears. According to this view, people manage normal developmental conflicts involving impulse control by projecting forbidden impulses onto an outgroup. This defense mechanism allows the city attorney to distance herself psychologically from threatening traits and thoughts. In this respect, the pejorative outgroup stereotype serves to reduce her level of stress and anxiety.

Historians tell us of the rootedness of the city attorney's views. During the early seventeenth century, the circumstances of blacks living in what was to become the United States were consistent with principles of open, although not equal, opportunity. African–Americans lived both as indentured servants and as free people. This early potential for egalitarianism was destroyed by the creation of a color-caste system. Colonial legislatures enacted slavery laws that transformed black servitude from a temporary status, under which both blacks and whites labored, to a lifelong status that was hereditary and racially defined. Slavery required a system of beliefs that would rationalize white domination, and laws and customs that would assure control of the slave population.

The beliefs that served to rationalize white domination are documented in an 1858 treatise. In many respects, they echo the beliefs identified one hundred years later as constitutive of the twentieth century black stereotype:

> [T]he negro, . . . whether in a state of bondage or in his native wilds, exhibits such a weakness of intellect that . . . 'when he has the fortune to live in subjection to a wise director, he is, without doubt, fixed in such a state of life as is most agreeable to his genius and capacity.' . . .
>
> . . . So debased is their [moral] condition generally, that their humanity has been even doubted. . . . [T]he negro race is habitually indolent and indisposed to exertion. . . . * * *
>
> The negro is naturally mendacious, and as a concomitant, thievish. . . .
>
> . . . Lust is his strongest passion; and hence, rape is an offence of too frequent occurrence.

The laws and customs that assured control of the slave population reinforced the image of blacks as incompetent and in need of white governance. The master was afforded ownership, the right to command labor, and the virtually absolute right of discipline. Social controls extending beyond the master-slave relationship served to exclude the slave—and in some respects to exclude free blacks—from independent, self-defining activity. * * * Social relationships between whites and blacks were regulated on the basis of caste hierarchy: Breaches of the social order, such as "insolence" of a slave towards a white person, were criminally punishable.

This history is part of the cultural heritage of the city attorney. The system of legal segregation, which maintained caste distinctions after abolition, is part of her life experience. This "new system continued to place all Negroes in inferior positions and all whites in superior positions." The city attorney is among the

> two-thirds of the current population [that] lived during a time when it was legal and customary in some parts of this country to require that

blacks sit in the back of a bus, give up their seats to whites, use different rest rooms and drinking fountains, and eat at different restaurants.

The civil rights movement and post–1954 desegregation efforts are also part of the city attorney's cultural heritage. As an educated woman in the 1980s, she understands racial prejudice to be socially and morally unacceptable. Psychological research that targets her contemporaries reveals an expressed commitment to egalitarian ideals along with lingering negative beliefs and aversive feelings about blacks. "Prejudiced thinking and discrimination still exist, but the contemporary forms are more subtle, more indirect, and less overtly negative than are more traditional forms."

Recent research also suggests that the city attorney can be expected to conceal her anti-black feelings except in private, homoracial settings. Many of her white contemporaries will suppress such feelings from their conscious thoughts. White Americans of the city attorney's generation do not wish to appear prejudiced. "[T]he contemporary form[ ] of prejudice is expressed [at least in testing situations] in ways that protect and perpetuate a nonprejudiced, nondiscriminating self-image." Americans of the city attorney's generation live under the combined influence of egalitarian ideology and "cultural forces and cognitive processes that ... promote prejudice and racism." Anti-black attitudes persist in a climate of denial.

The denial and the persistence are related. It is difficult to change an attitude that is unacknowledged. Thus, "like a virus that mutates into new forms, old-fashioned prejudice seems to have evolved into a new type that is, at least temporarily, resistant to traditional ... remedies."

II.   THE VIEW FROM THE OTHER SIDE OF THE LENS: MICROAGGRESSION

Return to the fifth floor and to the moment at which the elevator door opened. The black woman sees two white passengers. She inquires and perceives the response to her inquiry. She sees and hears, or thinks she sees and hears, condescension. It is in the tone and body language that surround the word, "Up." Perhaps the tone is flat, the head turns slowly in the direction of the second passenger and the eyes roll upward in apparent exasperation. Perhaps the head remains lowered, and the word is uttered as the eyes are raised to a stare that suggests mock disbelief. The woman does not hear the words spoken behind the closed elevator doors. Yet she feels that she has been branded incompetent, even for elevator travel. This feeling produces anger, frustration, and a need to be hypervigilant against subsequent, similar brandings.

The elevator encounter is a microaggression. "These are subtle, stunning, often automatic, and non-verbal exchanges which are 'put downs' of blacks by offenders." Psychiatrists who have studied black populations view them as "incessant and cumulative" assaults on black self-esteem.

Microaggressions simultaneously sustain defensive-deferential

thinking and erode self confidence in Blacks.... [B]y monopolizing ... perception and action through regularly irregular disruptions, they contribute to relative paralysis of action, planning and self-esteem. They seem to be the principal foundation for the verification of Black inferiority for both whites and Blacks.

The management of these assaults is a preoccupying activity, simultaneously necessary to and disruptive of black adaptation.

[The black person's] self-esteem suffers ... because he is constantly receiving an unpleasant image of himself from the behavior of others to him. This is the subjective impact of social discrimination. ... It seems to be an ever-present and unrelieved irritant. Its influence is not alone due to the fact that it is painful in its intensity, but also because the individual, in order to maintain internal balance and to protect himself from being overwhelmed by it, must initiate restitutive maneuvers ... —all quite automatic and unconscious. In addition to maintaining an internal balance, the individual must continue to maintain a social facade and some kind of adaptation to the offending stimuli so that he can preserve some social effectiveness. All of this requires a constant preoccupation, notwithstanding ... that these adaptational processes ... take place on a low order of awareness.

Vigilance and psychic energy are required not only to marshall adaptational techniques, but also to distinguish microaggressions from differently motivated actions and to determine "which of many daily microaggressions one must undercut."

The microaggressive acts that characterize interracial encounters are carried out in "automatic, preconscious, or unconscious fashion" and "stem from the mental attitude of presumed superiority." They are the product of the factors described in Part I. The elevator incident represents their least insidious form. This is so for three reasons. First, the black woman at the elevator initiated an interaction, thereby providing social cues that would predictably result in an expressed judgment. The microaggression she suffered was avoidable. The black woman can in the future decline to initiate an exchange with a white stranger. To the extent that she minimizes such exchanges, she can protect against further insult. Moreover, the microaggression was arguably content-based. The reaction of the city attorney can be interpreted as a response to the woman's question—to the data gathered in the interaction—rather than a response to the person. Susceptibility to content-based microaggression can be minimized or controlled, not only by avoiding interactions, but also by avoiding ambiguity when interactions occur: The black woman might have said, "The indicator is broken. Is this elevator going up or down?" The more frequent and more insidious microaggressions, however, are unavoidable in that they are neither initiated by blacks nor based in any apparent way on the behavior of blacks. Finally, the elevator incident is benign among microaggressions because the white woman's implicit assertion of superiority did not culminate in an achievement of subordination. A fictitious continuation of the elevator incident illustrates microaggressions that are not only unprovoked in the sense described above but also complete in their achievement of subordination:

[The city attorney decides to leave the elevator. She is standing at the right side of the car—directly opposite, but several feet away from, the black woman. Although she might easily exit by walking a path angled toward the center of the car, she takes a step directly forward. After a moment's hesitation, the black woman steps aside.]

This is microaggression in its most potent form. It is the direct descendent of an aspect of color-caste behavior described fifty years ago as "deference":

> The most striking form of ... "caste behavior" is deference, the respectful yielding exhibited by the Negroes in their contacts with whites. According to the dogma and to a large extent actually, the behavior of both Negroes and white people must be such as to indicate that the two are socially distinct and that the Negro is subordinate. Thus ... [i]n places of business the Negro should stand back and wait until the white has been served before receiving any attention, and in entering or leaving he should not precede a white but should stand back and hold the door for him. On the streets and sidewalks the Negro should "give way" to the white person.

The wordless interchange was not initiated by the black woman. It was not based upon any action taken by her. It was a natural manifestation of an imbedded interactive pattern in which "skin color determines whether or not one is expected to operate from an inferior or superior vantage point. Both races have come to expect and accept as unremarkable that the blacks' time, energy, space, and mobility will be at the service of the white." The inferiority of the black is more than an implicit assertion; it is a background assumption that supports the seizure of a prerogative.

* * *

———

NOTES AND QUESTIONS

1. Neutrality in law: its sources. In the public law debates over constitutional principle, the once well-accepted idea that legal rules are neutral, formal, and even scientific has been a vigorously contested terrain. In the 1980s, critical legal scholars mounted a broad challenge to the neutrality of legal rules. They argued that legal rules are indeterminate, lacking in objective neutrality, controlled instead by context, politics, and discretionary incorporation of the decision maker's perspective. However, when we turn to the debates about the rules that control outcomes in the market, skepticism about neutrality and rationality has emerged among legal scholars more recently.

In what follows we offer a preliminary map, tracing the role of the neutrality claim in legal theory. We start with the formalism of Christopher C. Langdell, a late 19th century dean of Harvard Law School, who introduced the study of appellate cases and the classification of legal subjects into categories that he defined as based upon a scientifically rigorous organization of legal thought, derived from provable "principles" of law. Langdell's formalism thus served to introduce the early framework of the neutrality claim through its assertion that legal reasoning was based upon "scientifically provable premises."

In the practice of law, legal neutrality is featured in several professional norms. First, we have the expectation of professional detachment in which the lawyer serves as a vigorous advocate on behalf of the client, without becoming so identified with the client as to lose perspective on sound professional assessments of what best serves the client's interest. Second, in litigation, neutrality expectations are on display in the rules that govern judicial conduct. Judges are expected to maintain an even temperament. Our chosen garb for judges, black robes, strips them of their ordinary clothing and the signifiers of class status that are a part of ordinary "street" clothing. Thus, the black robe is chosen to signal to participants in the legal process that judges have left behind personal identity in the service of their professional obligation of fair treatment and neutrality for every litigant.

In the dynamics of the courtroom, we can see the contest model of truth-seeking neutrality at work. In the contest model opposing lawyers may introduce palpably false testimony, misleading evidence, and they may use harsh tactics to destroy the credibility of witnesses who speak the objective truth. However, in the contest model, neutrality does not depend upon the truth or unbiased participation of litigants, but depends instead upon the dynamics of contested assertions. Neutrality emerges from the competing vectors of truth introduced by the interested parties. The contest model is also carried over into our expectations for jury deliberation. Juries are expected to rely upon their diverse identities, experience, and preferences to arrive at a verdict in both the criminal and civil cases. The verdict is the product of a contest of competing points of view, ultimately produces a compromise that represents a fair and neutral adjudication of the disputed claims.

In constitutional frameworks, the ideal of neutrality finds its home in the Equal Protection Clause. The equality norm has, at least since Wechsler (see note 2, supra at page 8), merged with legal formalism to insist on the application of "neutral principles." The concept of legal neutrality therefore can be traced to many complex and mutually reinforcing structures in legal theory, legal practice, and doctrine.

2. Neutrality in economics: its sources. In the market domain, belief in the insights of the first modern economist, Adam Smith, is still very firmly entrenched. Smith's central argument, in the 1759 classic the *Theory of Moral Sentiments*, was that private markets operate on the self-interested decisions of each individual participant. He argued that society achieved its maximum productivity when individuals were left alone to figure out from whom they wanted to buy and to whom they wanted to sell. Smith's famous metaphor for the social good that would arise from the cumulative impact of these buyer-seller decisions is the "invisible hand." In the centuries since Smith wrote, the argument that individuals are "led by an invisible hand to promote'' what was good for society by choosing what was good for themselves has been enormously influential across all social-science disciplines, such as law, sociology, psychology, and economics.

Traditional economic analysis does not incorporate variables for either culture or identity. The language of economic analysis is built upon the implicit assumption that economic activity is natural and pre-political, and that economic actors possess abstract, identity-free preferences, devoid of the influences of culture or the dynamics of social groups. We adopt an opposing view that economic institutions are suffused with cultural power. We know that identity matters, and that economic subordination is not an abstract preference to those excluded from participation in the material comforts of our wealthy economic system.

As in traditional models of legal practice, traditional economic methodologies are framed with the claim of neutrality in seeking truth. Truth seeking in the hard sciences, like mathematics, physics, and chemistry depends upon the use of the scientific method, in which researchers do not have a normative stake in the outcome of the investigations. So, empiricism, and experimental procedures that can be duplicated by any trained scientist, insure that the ''truth'' is not subject to manipulation. Economics associates itself with the scientific culture. This association plays a role in advancing the neutrality premises, as well. In this culture, professional detachment is a prerequisite. There is a preference for laboratory experiments over *in vivo* (life), in which variables can be controlled, unlike the messy multivariate environments of real human interaction.

Despite the association of economics with the physical sciences and mathematics, we notice that contemporary economics imposes crucial limitations upon its fields of inquiry. For example, questions of distribution—who has how much wealth—have been defined as outside the scope of research for the discipline. The problems of economic inequality and the structures of identity-based subordination have no place in the equations featuring wealth maximization, zero transactions costs, rational choice, and perfect competition.

3. Critical race theory objections to neutrality frameworks: sources and central themes. Critical race theory rejects the neutrality and objectivity of law, elevating a personal, subjective, outsider experience to the center of jurisprudence, and demanding non-neutral laws to eradicate the ramifications of oppression. In addition to its anti-neutrality position, critical race theory explores other themes, including the following characteristic viewpoints:

   a.   **Race as a social construction.** Critical race theorists deem the notion of race developed as a function of communal needs, economics, and politics. This belief aids in explaining the simplicity and prevalence of race as a social category (the mere existence of race) and the derogatory and positive connotations related to particular racial identities.

Because race is a social construct, it does not exist a priori; rather, it is created by discourses in politics, law, and science. In addition, the constructs that support race formation are mutable and volatile. The meaning of race, the number of racial groupings, and the cultural definition of particular racial personalities have all changed over time.

b. **Narrative.** Critical race scholars write narratives to liberate themselves from the constraining effects of conformity. With narratives, scholars can choose from a range of techniques—autobiographies, parables, and self-portraits—to communicate race and equality issues. Narrative provides a framework about the character of discrimination from the view of those who experience it and also challenges the "truth" (the objective reasoning) of American jurisprudence. Carbado & Gulati, *supra*, at 1784–86. Though there is some "storytelling" in the legal world—in the courtroom and in legal documents—stories told through a detached lens fail to capture central experiences.

c. **Color-blind society.** Critical race theorists reject the notion of colorblindness and embrace race consciousness. According to these scholars, colorblindness promotes nonwhites to assimilate and to deny their racial background because association with that group would cause these nonwhites to appear to be different. Critical race theory scholars argue that one simply cannot be "blind" to race because it is impossible not to notice an individual's attributes without having first thought about such traits at least once before. Neil Gotanda elaborates on this notion as he discusses the difference between medical colorblindness and liberal theorists' "nonrecognition" of race:

> A medically color-blind person is someone who cannot see what others can. It is a partial nonperception of what is "really" there. To be racially color-blind, on the other hand, is to ignore what one has already noticed. The medically color-blind individual never perceives color in the first place; the racially color-blind individual perceives race and then ignores it.... The characteristics of race that are noticed ... are situated within an already existing understanding of race.... This preexisting race consciousness makes it impossible for an individual to be truly nonconscious of race.

Neil Gotanda, *A Critique of "Our Constitution is Color–Blind,"* 44 Stan. L. Rev. 1, 18–19 (1991).

d. **Race as performative identity.** Legal scholars Devon Carbado and Mitu Gulati argue that the social definition of an individual's racial identity is a function of the way that person "performs" his or her race—for example, how an Asian person presents her "Asianness." In everyday encounters, people create or project specific images of race. This implies that the simplicity of an African American's racial identity partly originates from (1) the image of blackness he presents, and (2) how that racial projection is interpreted. Carbado and Gulati argue that they often have to suppress their racial or ethnic attributes in speech, clothing, and hair in order to dispel derogatory stereotypes about their demographic groups. This implies that racial minorities have some power to configure the parameters upon which they are experienced.

The racial "performance" an individual exhibits can span a wide range, and that individual's susceptibility to racism largely depends on where he falls on the racial spectrum:

> On one side of the spectrum are "conventional" black people. They are black prototypes—that is, people who are perceived to be stereotypically black. Their performance of blackness is consistent with society's understanding of who black people really are. On the other side are "unconventional" black people—people who are not stereotypically black. Their performance of blackness is outside of what society perceives to be conventional black behavior. A black person's vulnerability to discrimination is shaped in part by her racial position on this spectrum. The less stereotypically black she is, the more palatable her identity is. The more palatable her identity is, the less vulnerable she is to discrimination. The relationship among black unconventionality, racial palatability, and vulnerability to discrimination creates an incentive for black people to signal—through identity performances—that they are unconventionally black. These signals convey the idea that the sender is black in a phenotypic but not a social sense. Put another way, the signals function as a marketing device. They brand the black person so as to make clear that she is not a black prototype.

Devon W. Carbado & Mitu Gulati, *The Law and Economics of Critical Race Theory*, 112 YALE L.J. 1757, 1769 (2003) (book review).

e. **Essentialism.** To "essentialize" about race is to assume that a specific racial or gender personality has a singular and particular essence, isolated from other parts of identity. Some critical race scholars choose not to follow this essentialized methodology and are instead committed to intersectionality, a theory that insinuates that people's identities are intersectional—that is raced, gendered, sexually oriented, etc.—and that people's susceptibility to racism is a function of their specific intersectional identities. *Id. See* Kimberlé W. Crenshaw, *Mapping the Margins: Intersectionality, Identity Politics, and Violence Against Women of Color*, 43 STAN. L. REV. 1241 (1991); Angela P. Harris, *Race and Essentialism in Feminist Legal Theory*, 42 STAN. L. REV. 581 (1990).

f. **Identity privilege.** Critical race theorists argue that because racial discrimination is an enduring social predicament, there will be victims and recipients of this discrimination.

g. **Multiracialism.** A primary premise of critical race theory is a multiracial concept. This implies that the effects of racism are larger than any particular racial group. Certain critical race scholars condemn the black/white paradigm, asserting that most legal and political discussions concerning race focus on black and white experiences, failing to consider or marginalizing the experiences of nonblack minorities.

D. Economics and Law: Two Cultures in Tension

Economics and Law: Two Cultures in Tension

54 TENN. L. REV. 161 (1986).

■ James Boyd White

* * *

Many people think of economics solely as a scientific, conceptual, and cognitive system, apparently unaware that there are any other dimensions of meaning in economic talk. But all expression is loaded with values, ethical and otherwise; all expression defines a self and another and proposes a relation between them; all expression remakes its language; in these senses all expression proposes the creation of a community and a culture. All expression, in short, is ethical, cultural, and political, and it can be analyzed and judged as such. To claim that economics is a science is perhaps to claim that it cannot be judged in such terms. But "sciences" are cultures too, with their own created worlds and values. One way to describe my aim in this talk, then, is to say that it reverses the usual flow: we are used to economic analyses of this or that aspect of our common life—voting, the family, war, etc. I propose here to begin what I would call a rhetorical or cultural analysis of a certain kind of economics.

* * *

III. Economics as a Language of Theory

Neoclassical microeconomics proceeds upon certain assumptions that can be summarized this way. The universe is populated by a number of discrete human actors, each of whom is competent, rational, and motivated solely by self-interest. External to the human actors is a natural universe that affords what are called "resources," which are acted upon by human actors to create something called "wealth." Partly for reasons of practicality, this kind of economics defines economic activity, and hence wealth, in terms of the process of exchange by which one actor exchanges some item within his dominion for an item within the dominion of another, or, far more commonly, for money which is the medium of exchange. To look at everything from the point of view of exchange is, naturally enough, to regard the universe as a collection of items for potential exchange, and in this sense to itemize it. When an exchange takes place these items enter the economic system and become part of what we mean by productivity. Where no exchange actually takes place—as where wealth is created and consumed by the same person, or where leisure is chosen over work—the economic effect of the actor's decision is not disregarded by professional economics, as it often is in popular economic thought, but it is still measured by the value of an imagined exchange, the one the actor has forgone. The central principle of the system is that everything is at least hypothetically interchangeable and thus of necessity quantifiable in ways that permit meaningful commensuration, at any rate by the actors who are faced with the choices to which economics speaks.

As the natural universe is itemized by these real or imagined exchanges, the social world is atomized, conceived of as a set of actors of equal competence, without race, gender, age, or culture. Each actor is assumed to be motivated by an unlimited desire to acquire or consume. Since each is interested only in its own welfare, each is in structural competition with all the others. This in turn creates a severe scarcity with respect to the resources. Where there is no scarcity, as there once was not with respect to clean air or water, there can be no economics of this kind. The final ingredient is money, a medium in which surplus can be accumulated with convenience and, in principle, without limit. So far as possible, all human interaction is reduced to the single model of exchange. Economics is the study of what life would be like on such assumptions.

Exchange is a method of determining value, which, tautologically, is said to be the price for which items are sold. This is the value that is put upon them by the economic system, and the only kind of value that economics can express. Obviously individuals may put different values on different items—indeed, this is ordinarily necessary for the exchange to occur in the first place—but although these private values drive the economic system, they are not directly expressible in its terms.

In the world of economics individual actors function according to what economists call "rationality." This is a reasoning process that consists of identifying items of potential consumption or dominion in the world, calculating their value in dollar or other common terms, and then estimating various kinds of positive and negative risks. Reason is thus reducible to calculation and risk assessment. * * *

> * * *

IV.   ECONOMICS AS A SYSTEM OF VALUES

We can start with the question of value. In its purest form economics claims to be a value-free social science. But as I suggested earlier I think it in fact enacts a set of values, including political ones, values to which the speaker of the language cannot avoid finding himself at least in part committed.

A.   *In the World*

Think, for example, of the way in which economics defines the economic actor and the processes by which he functions. He is for the most part

...we ought to lead
...nce of "tastes" or
...a language can
... in oneself or
...ich not. To the
...may be worse
...a discourse.
...in the only
...and on the
...e model of

...desires
...ould be
...e. This
...most
...ation
...e i...

...ge, sex, race and cultural
...ulating economic rela-
...f his own wishes and
...term is used, to mean
...as an individual, not as
...establishes contractual or
...ed to be motivated by self-
...f competition, acquisition, and
...es and other actors, for in the
...those desires.

...may have other values—indeed the
...ling them "tastes" or "preferences"—
...altruism, for peace and quiet, for heavy
...nature unspoiled, for beautiful or ugly art,
...es will drive his participation in the exchange
...to withdraw from it. But in either case they are
...the method of exchange: either by an actual exchange
...by a hypothetical or imagined exchange that is forgone
...mplicated case by a combination of exchanges made and
...th cases these external values are converted by the discourse
...acquisitive or instrumental values—the desire to extend the
...on of the will—that all economic actors are assumed to have, for this
...ly kind of value about which economics can directly talk.
...ly "value the external values in their original form, the system is
...the system itself. That is, it regards individual values as simply
...t it demeans them. Economics of cou... recognizes that these
...imply that n... ...ling them "tastes" or "prefer-
...ich they are reflected in the activity of exchange.
...cannot, in principle, talk about any value other
...mental one that it universalizes. (Indeed it
...er, but merely assumes and acts upon it.)
...s apologists claim, but to make self-
...value, for it is the only one
...t it the other way, it is to
...r some purposes, as if

...soni...
...onomist...
...roof appro...
...ed by logic a...
...ke certain other
...ers to submit to
...o they necessarily
...d valuable way to
...n.

...ience is thus false in at
...ience, for no science
...alue-free, for no science
...premises from which it

...ested values it
...reedom," that
...lue that are
...n the exchange
...es" among which
...nt on all the great
...dness in art and music,
...and folly in conduct and

judgment, and the greatest of all questions, which is ho
our lives. Economic analysis assumes as a given the exist
"preferences" which drive the system, but economics as
provide no way of talking about these values, whethe
another, no way of thinking about which to prefer and wh
extent that economics does reach out for these questions it
than silent, for silence after all can be a mode of controllin
When economics tries to speak about these matters it does s
way it knows how to speak, in purely quantitative terms
assumption that all human transactions can be reduced to th
exchange.

* * *

For the purposes of economic analysis all human wishes and
are thus reduced to the same level, as though no principled choices
made among them, as though it didn't matter what choices one mad
in turn means that it is impossible to talk in these terms about our
important choices as individuals and communities, or about the educ
of mind or heart, for any impulse that we or others may happen to ha
as good, valid, and entitled to respect as any other.

* * * We must and do have preferences, as the economist knows; a
these necessarily commit those who have them to the inquiry of better ar
worse, as well as to that of greater and less. To refuse to engage in thi
inquiry—to privatize it—as economics in its neutral phase neces reduce all
is to deny an essential and necessary aspect of time, is intellect ally and
value to self-interest. it does the rest of the economist one's children or onese to live
ethically intolerable. How could educate one's children or onese to live
in a world that was neutral on all the great questions of life, exept that it
reduced them to acquisition, competition, and calculation?

B.   Among Economists

There is another dimension to economics, as a discourse am
mists. Here too, in the discourse, values are of necessity e
example, economics necessarily values the reduction of life to
I describe, for this is what it achieves. It values linear re
competition for dominance. This last is especially so among e
it is ostensibly a premise of economic discourse, as a rule of
ate to a science, that we will believe only what we are for
fact to believe. This means that economic conversations—
academic discussions—are often attempts to compel ot
one's views, or to resist such submission. In doing
perform a claim that this is the most appropriate a
converse on these subjects, itself a most dubious positi

* * *

The claim that microeconomics is a value-free s
least two ways. First, even as a science it is not
can be. It values the positivist and behavioris

assumed to be an individual of indeterminate age, sex, race and cultural background, but of adequate competence at manipulating economic relations. He acts as one who is both perfectly aware of his own wishes and wholly rational—in the special sense in which that term is used, to mean "calculating"—in his pursuit of them. He exists as an individual, not as part of a community, except insofar as he establishes contractual or exchange relations with others. He is assumed to be motivated by self-interest, which in turn is defined in terms of competition, acquisition, and dominion, at least in relation to resources and other actors, for in the process of exchange the self is reduced to those desires.

Of course a particular individual may have other values—indeed the economist insists that he must, calling them "tastes" or "preferences"—perhaps including a "taste" for altruism, for peace and quiet, for heavy metal music, for appreciating nature unspoiled, for beautiful or ugly art, and so forth. These values will drive his participation in the exchange process, or his decision to withdraw from it. But in either case they are themselves valued by the method of exchange: either by an actual exchange that takes place or by a hypothetical or imagined exchange that is forgone (or in a more complicated case by a combination of exchanges made and forgone). In both cases these external values are converted by the discourse into the acquisitive or instrumental values—the desire to extend the dominion of the will—that all economic actors are assumed to have, for this is the only kind of value about which economics can directly talk.

With respect to the external values in their original form, the system is purportedly "value neutral." That is, it regards individual values as simply exogenous to the system itself. Economics of course recognizes that these values exist, but it demeans them by calling them "tastes" or "preferences," names that imply that no serious conversation can proceed on such subjects. And economics itself is by definition not about those values, but about the process by which they are reflected in the activity of exchange. This means that economics cannot, in principle, talk about any value other than the acquisitive or instrumental one that it universalizes. (Indeed it does not talk about this value either, but merely assumes and acts upon it.) This is not to be "value free," as its apologists claim, but to make self-interest the central, indeed almost the only, value, for it is the only one that can be talked about in these terms. To come at it the other way, it is to claim that all values can be talked about, at least for some purposes, as if they were selfish, quantifiable, and interchangeable.

  * * *

Yet economics is troubling not only for the self-interested values it directly asserts, but also for the very neutrality, the "value freedom," that it claims. It is in principle neutral on all questions of value that are external to the acquisitive and competitive ones enacted in the exchange game, which it lumps together as "tastes" or "preferences" among which no distinctions can be drawn. But this is to be silent on all the great questions of human life: questions of beauty and ugliness in art and music, sincerity and falsity in human relations, wisdom and folly in conduct and judgment, and the greatest of all questions, which is how we ought to lead our lives. Economic analysis assumes as a given the existence of "tastes" or "preferences" which drive the system, but economics as a language can provide no way of talking about these values, whether in oneself or another, no way of thinking about which to prefer and which not. To the extent that economics does reach out for these questions it may be worse than silent, for silence after all can be a mode of controlling a discourse. When economics tries to speak about these matters it does so in the only way it knows how to speak, in purely quantitative terms and on the assumption that all human transactions can be reduced to the model of exchange.

* * *

For the purposes of economic analysis all human wishes and desires are thus reduced to the same level, as though no principled choices could be made among them, as though it didn't matter what choices one made. This in turn means that it is impossible to talk in these terms about our most important choices as individuals and communities, or about the education of mind or heart, for any impulse that we or others may happen to have is as good, valid, and entitled to respect as any other.

* * * We must and do have preferences, as the economist knows; and these necessarily commit those who have them to the inquiry of better and worse, as well as to that of greater and less. To refuse to engage in this inquiry—to privatize it—as economics in its neutral phase necessarily does, is to deny an essential and necessary aspect of human life. To reduce all value to self-interest, as it does the rest of the time, is intellectually and ethically intolerable. How could one educate one's children or oneself to live in a world that was neutral on all the great questions of life, except that it reduced them to acquisition, competition, and calculation?

B. Among Economists

There is another dimension to economics, as a discourse among economists. Here too, in the discourse, values are of necessity enacted. For example, economics necessarily values the reduction of life to terms such as I describe, for this is what it achieves. It values linear reasoning and competition for dominance. This last is especially so among economists, for it is ostensibly a premise of economic discourse, as a rule of proof appropriate to a science, that we will believe only what we are forced by logic and fact to believe. This means that economic conversations—like certain other academic discussions—are often attempts to compel others to submit to one's views, or to resist such submission. In doing so they necessarily perform a claim that this is the most appropriate and valuable way to converse on these subjects, itself a most dubious position.

* * *

The claim that microeconomics is a value-free science is thus false in at least two ways. First, even as a science it is not value-free, for no science can be. It values the positivist and behaviorist premises from which it functions, the reduction of reason to calculation, the performed conversion of the world into quantifiable units, and so on. Second, economics attributes motives and values to its actors, those of acquisitiveness and self-interest, and invests itself in these attributions, which it assumes to be universal. This assumption is qualified by the recognition that one actor may choose to act for others, but in the end economics always reduces motive to self-interest, the only kind of motive it can conceive of and speak about. The reduction of all human interaction to the model of exchange, actual or imagined, simply erases whole fields of life and thought, from art to morals, for economics recognizes no ground, other than competitive survivability, upon which one can choose one form of life or one work of art over another, or even upon which one can choose to favor the market and its methods of analysis over others.

In saying that "value-free" economics is actually committed to certain values, both in the assumptions it makes about the world and in the conventions by which its own discourse operates, I do not mean to suggest that the field is in this respect peculiar. Quite the contrary. As I say above I think that all systems of discourse commit their users to values and do so in both domains, that is in one's account of the "other world" one talks about and in the here-and-now world one creates by talking. Science does this, and so do law and literary criticism too. Economics is not to be blamed, then, for having values. But no one should be allowed to claim value-neutrality where it does not exist, and economics, like other disciplines, can be praised or blamed for the values it has. All of us, economists and lawyers and lecturers among the rest, should be held responsible for the values we enact in our talking.

All this is not to say that economics is wrong to do what it does, namely, to isolate the practices of exchange for study, especially when its results are applied to spheres of life that are in fact characterized by exchanges that take place on conditions roughly matching the assumptions of the discourse. This is, after all, a good deal of the economic life of the investor or entrepreneur in a capitalist economy. But it is to say that this study would lead to insanity unless it were premised on a recognition that these activities, and the culture they and their study together create, require subordination to other activities and cultures, both at the level of the individual and of the polity.

V. Economics as a Political System

An economist might agree with most of this and say that the language and practices in which he engages as an economist must somehow be put together with the languages and practices that make up the rest of his life, both public and private. This would raise the wonderfully interesting and important question, how this might be done, and with what effect on economics itself, a question to which I shall return below.

But another line of justification is possible as well, one that neither denies the political character of this discourse nor seeks to subordinate it to other languages and practices, but affirmatively celebrates the politics and ethics that this kind of economics entails, mainly on the ground that the market is affirmatively desirable both as a model of life and as a political and social institution. The premises of the analytic method, in other words, can be regarded as the proper premises upon which to build our collective life. In talking this way the economist moves off the ground of purportedly pure science. He begins to use his language not as a "filing system" but as a way of expressing overt social and political attitudes, largely in support of the institution of the market. I should stress that not all economists would take this step. But some would. They are of course perfectly entitled to do so, but only to the extent that their politics and ethics, not their economics, persuade us of the rightness of their vision.

A.   *Justifying the Market as a Model of Life*

The institution of the market is celebrated by its proponents because in their view it is democratic—each person brings to the market his own values and can "maximize" them his own way—and because it is creative and open, leaving the widest room for individual choice and action. The market establishes a community based upon a competitive process that allows each person freedom to choose what to do with what is his. These merits mean, for some economists at least, that all social institutions ought to be modified to approximate the market—to conform to the analytic model of life as exchange—or at least to be analyzed and judged on that presumption.

The market is further justified, when such justification is thought necessary, in either of two rather conflicting ways. The first is to say that the market is good because it promotes efficiency, that is to say it maximizes the "welfare" of all participants in the process. It does this by definition, because each person participates in the process only because he thinks he gets more that way than he would any other way, and who are we to tell him differently? In maximizing the welfare of all participants it does the same for society as a whole, which is nothing more or less than the sum of all the participants in the market. The obvious trouble with this is that it takes for granted not only the existing values (or "tastes") of the actors, but also the existing distributions among them of wealth, capacity, and entitlement, which it has no way of criticizing. Yet these may of course be eminently criticizable.

The "welfare" defense of the market would justify all transactions— including the sale of oneself into slavery or prostitution—that are not in an obvious sense "coerced" by another because they are marginal improvements for the actors involved. But an economy might provide a different set of starting points for its actors, so that such degrading activities would no longer be "improvements" for anyone. We would all benefit from living in such a world. But the economist has no way of saying this. On the premises I have described he cannot deny the desirability of redistribution, but he cannot affirm it either. Even to discuss the question requires a shift of discourse, to ways of talking that economics of the sort I have been discussing excludes.

The second ground upon which the market is justified is that not of its gross effects but of its fairness. In one version this justification rests upon the ethical standing of voluntary action and holds that the results of the market process are justified with respect to every actor because the choices by which the market works are voluntary. In another version, it becomes the affirmative celebration of autonomy or liberty: whether or not it is efficient, the market is good because it gives the widest possible range to freedom of choice and action. Here the claim moves beyond justifying market results by the voluntary character of the choices upon which they rest to the point of asserting autonomy as the central social and political value. The obvious trouble with this line of defense, in both of its forms, is that it assumes that all exchanges are for all actors equally voluntary and equally expressive of autonomy, a position that common sense denies.

* * *

The market purports to rest upon an assumption of the equality of all the actors in the system. In fact, it rests upon a different assumption, namely, the equality of every dollar in the system. Since some players have many more dollars, and through this fact are at a competitive advantage, it is a system that actively supports inequality among its actors.

It is not too much to say, I think, that the modern celebration of the market as the central social institution—the most fair, the most respecting of autonomy, and the most efficient—threatens to destroy the single greatest achievement of Western political culture: the discovery that a community can govern itself through a rule of law that attempts to create a fundamental moral and political equality among human beings. The great phrase in the Declaration of Independence—"all men are created equal"— is partly a theological statement about the conditions under which we are created and partly a political statement about the obligation of the government to acknowledge, indeed to create or recreate, that equality. This value is the heart of what is meant both by equality under law and by our democratic institutions more generally, resting as they do on the premise that each person's vote is worth exactly what everyone else's is. The ideology of the market, if it prevailed in its desire to convert all institutions into markets, would destroy this set of political relations and would create another in its stead, based upon the dollar.

* * *

The market ideology claims to be radically democratic and egalitarian because it leaves every person free to do with her own what she will. But this freedom of choice is not equally distributed among all people. The market is democratic not on the principle of one person one vote, but on the far different principle of one dollar, one vote. One could hardly make a greater mistake than to equate, as so much modern public talk carelessly does, the "free market" with democracy.

There are two distinct points here. First, the exchange transactions that the market celebrates are not entitled to the special respect claimed for them as free and voluntary, and hence fair, unless each person has roughly the same amount of money and the same competence and freedom in its use, which is demonstrably not the case. The accumulations of wealth it permits thus cannot be justified by the fairness of the transactions by which the accumulation occurs. Second, if the advocates of the market succeeded in converting other institutions into markets, the result would be to transfer to those who have wealth not only the economic power that inescapably follows it but also the political power that in our democratic tradition the people have claimed for themselves and have exercised through the institutions of self-government. This would validate and institutionalize private economic power held by one person over another, of the rich over the poor. If we were to yield entirely to its claims, we would gradually find our traditional government, which operates by collective deliberation on a premise of fundamental equality of citizens, replaced by a private-sector government of the few over the many, wholly unregulated by collective judgment.

VI. ECONOMICS AS A SYSTEM OF ECONOMIC ANALYSIS

But it is not only as a system of value and politics that this kind of economics, and the ways of thought it encourages, are troubling. I think that it is distorted and unrealistic as a way of imagining, thinking about, and shaping the processes of production and exchange that we think of as the economy itself.

A. *The Social and Natural Matrix*

The first distortion I wish to consider has to do with the relationship between the exchange system and the cultural and natural world that it necessarily presupposes. What I mean is this. The economic activity of exchange takes place under natural and cultural conditions that are absolutely essential to it, but about which economics has no way of talking except by itemization, quantification, and conversion into the material of actual or hypothetical exchange. All talk about exchanges, that is, necessarily presupposes that the exchangers live in the natural world of sun, air, and water, subject to the powers of growth and health and disease, a world the organization of which is complex far beyond our understanding. Each of the exchangers is part of that world in another sense as well, for each is himself an organism, and one that incompletely understands both himself and his relation to the natural world upon which he absolutely depends for his existence. The language of economics similarly assumes the existence of a society and culture, a set of human understandings and expectations upon which each exchanger can rely: that promises will normally be kept, that one can get one's money home without being robbed, that it is worth thinking about the future, for oneself or for one's children, and so on. What is more, the actor's motives or values (what the economists call his "preferences") are themselves formed by interactions both with his culture and with nature. This is how we are made as individuals, how we cohere as a community, and how we connect ourselves to the past and to the future.

But on all this economics is silent, for it begins to speak only when an actor has, at least in his mind, identified some item in the world and begun to think of exchanging it for something else. It is his judgment of its worth, in exchanging it or in declining to do so, that is for the economist its value. But what confidence can we have in such judgments of worth, by actors necessarily imperfectly aware both of themselves and of the cultural and natural worlds they inhabit? To put it in epistemological terms, the economist assumes that there is nothing to be known about the natural or cultural world that cannot be known through the process of exchange itself. But in order to judge the value of an item now, or to predict one for the future (which is very much the same thing), one must make estimates about possible changes in the social, cultural, and natural matrix in which all exchange takes place, and about the effect of this and similar exchanges upon that matrix. There is no reason to be especially confident in anyone's capacity to make such estimates.

* * *

This is to talk about it in terms of knowledge, the knowledge that the economist assumes we have. But it can be cast in terms of value as well, for the language of economics assumes that the relation between humanity and nature should be one of dominion, that the expanded assertion of control by individual actors over nature—called "natural resources"—is inherently a good thing. But why should one grant such an assumption? As Wendell Berry repeatedly points out in his works on agricultural economics, modern agriculture can be considered a great technological success only if one uses the measure of present-day output per man-hour, disregarding both the destructive effects of modern farming on soil and water and the costs, natural and economic, of the fossil fuels used for both fertilizer and power. If productivity over decades or per acre is the test, as in a world of five billion perhaps it should be, our agriculture falls well below that of many more "primitive" peoples. If one includes the meaning of the work the farmer does, its rhythms and its harmonies or disharmonies with nature, the picture is complicated further; still further if one asks how important it is in a nuclear age for a particular polity, or for humanity, that the capacity for fruitful and stable survival on a small scale be maintained. Economic language assumes, with what a theologian like James Gustafson might call a foolish pride, that man's wants and wishes are the ultimate measure of value; it then claims that these wishes are constrained only in ways that traders can see and account for. These are assumptions of fact and value that one might generously regard as dubious.

The only kind of meaning economics can reflect is one that can be expressed in the medium of exchange, that is, quantifiable and comparative. This is in turn to give the world itself a meaning of a new kind, reflected in the Japanese phrase for the blue sky that can rarely be seen over Tokyo these days: it is called a "recession sky."

* * *

D. *Erasing Community*

For similar reasons this kind of economics has the greatest difficulty in reflecting the reality of human community and the value of communal institutions. Its necessary tendency seems to be to destroy the idea of public action, indeed the idea of community itself. This is partly because this methodology tends to resolve all communities and organizations into the individual human actors who constitute them, partly because commitment to the market system leads one to think that everything that can be made the subject of the market should be. The idea is that every economic actor should pay for what he wants, and should not have to pay for what he doesn't want. But this tends to destroy our public institutions, all of which extend benefits far beyond those who would pay (if they were reduced to markets) or who do pay (when they are supported by taxes). Such institutions reflect a communal judgment that we need to educate ourselves and each other, that our "tastes" are not all of equal value but need to be formed, and formed well rather than badly. Public universities, libraries, orchestras, museums, parks—all these would fall before the ideology that denies the existence and reality of community and reduces all institutions, all human production, to the language of the market.

Think here of the way economists explain why people who will probably never visit, say, the Everglades or an art museum are happy to have their taxes used to maintain them. The economist says it is because the actor wants to maintain the option of visiting them some day, and calls this an "option demand." But may it not be that the voter simply takes pleasure in what other people have and in what other people can do, in belonging to a community that is good for all its members? Or that he respects their desires and wants a community based on that kind of mutual respect? This possibility is systematically denied by the assumption of economic talk, that individuals and communities are in principle incapable of generosity, or more precisely, that "altruism" can adequately be talked about as a species of selfishness.

The language of self and self-interest not only fails to reflect the reality of community and of shared interests, it draws attention away from those aspects of life and devalues them. To continue to talk on these assumptions, even hypothetically, is to encourage "self-interest" in an ethical sense and to erode the commitments we have to each other that underlie such essential practices of citizenship as the willingness to pay taxes, to work for the local school, or to serve in the army, upon which everything depends. To adopt the economic view would in fact threaten the very existence of community, for on these premises no one would conceivably die or seriously risk his life for his community: at the point of danger one's self-interest in survival would outweigh all other self-interests. And to speak of all "tastes" as if they were equivalent is to invite oneself and others to think that they are, and to confirm the premises of our culture, already drummed into the mind by the consumer economy, that the consumer is king, that whatever you happen to want is a good that you should seek to satisfy, that no distinction can be drawn between the beautiful and ugly, the wise and foolish, and so on. It is to confirm a vulgar view of democracy that makes the preference or will supreme, as if we functioned by instant referendum. It erases the sense that a democracy is a mode of communal self-constitution and self-education that may have higher ends than the satisfaction of wants, namely the creation of a community of a certain sort, at once based upon a set of responsibilities and offering us a set of opportunities for civic and social action.

———

NOTES AND QUESTIONS

1. **Effect of terminology on White's critique.** White states that "all systems of discourse commit their users to values ... [and that] economics is [not] wrong to do what it does." James Boyd White, *Economics and Law: Two Cultures in Tension*, 54 TENN. L. REV. 161, 176 (1986). If all White wishes is for economics to acknowledge that it is no different from other systems of discourse, does his critique of law and economics have any value? Would the problems White identifies with law and economics be solved by acknowledging that law and economics has values without making any substantive changes to the discipline? Would White be satisfied with this solution?

2. **Pernicious nature of law and economics.** At the close of his article, White states that "to continue to talk on ... [law and economics'] assumptions, even hypothetically, is to encourage 'self interest' in an ethical sense and to erode the commitments we have to each other that underlie such essential practices of citizenship as the willingness to pay taxes, to work for the local school, or to serve in the army, upon which everything depends. To adopt the economic view would in fact threaten the very existence of community...." *Id.* at 192. If White is correct about the dire consequences of even hypothesizing in an economic framework, how can he assert that economics is not wrong to "do what it does"? *Id.* at 176.

———

E.   JUDGING RACE: THE DOCTRINE OF DISCRIMINATORY INTENT

Note About Neutrality in Form, Discriminatory Impact and the Paradox of Statistical Correlation vs. Motivation

The debate about race, neutrality, and markets has not been limited to economic theories of rationality contesting the subjective narratives of critical race scholars. Conflicting perspectives about neutrality also extend to disputes about what evidence can trigger a constitutional violation of the Equal Protection Clause. In this debate, the liberal and conservative positions have been reversed. Civil rights advocates sought to rely upon scientific measures of statistical racial disparity to show that the impact of a facially neutral policy violated the Equal Protection standard. The Court rejected statistical measures of the disparate impact of the employment screening test on black applicants.

For "facially neutral" policies, such as this employment screening test, the Court introduced a motive-focused standard that required evidence of intentional racial discrimination to establish a violation of the Fourteenth Amendment. The demise of disparate impact theory to prove an Equal Protection violation was a major setback for the use of civil rights legal theory seeking to challenge government policies and practices, even though such policies did not contain a race-specific classification.

Consider how this case contributes to our understanding of the uses of the concept of neutrality. Does the fact that scientific tools, such as statistical proof of disproportionate harm to racial minority groups, were rejected in this case turn the conservative (scientific) vs. liberal (empathetic, seeking to enter the subjective experience of another) on its head? As you read the case that follows, recall that it was Judge Posner who said:

> Maybe economic scholarship is not *really* empathetic. The economist does not enter imaginatively into the distress of the disappointed quester for rental housing; all he does is tote up some additional costs. But that may be a sounder way of doing policy than by cultivating empathy. A jurisprudence of empathy can foster short-sighted substantive justice . . . [1]

Posner, OVERCOMING LAW, *supra* at 381.

On the basis of the observations above, had he been a Justice, do you think Judge Posner would have dissented in the following case?

Washington v. Davis

426 U.S. 229 (1976).

■ MR. JUSTICE WHITE DELIVERED THE OPINION OF THE COURT.

This case involves the validity of a qualifying test administered to applicants for positions as police officers in the District of Columbia Metropolitan Police Department. The test was sustained by the District Court, but invalidated by the Court of Appeals. We are in agreement with the District Court and hence reverse the judgment of the Court of Appeals.

[The action was filed by black applicants to become police officers in the District of Columbia. The claimants were unsuccessful in passing a test that was designed to measure verbal skills, vocabulary and reading. They introduced evidence in the District Court showing that a greater percentage of blacks failed, than did whites. In addition, the claimants alleged that the

----

1. A more basic point is that the internal perspective—putting oneself in the other person's shoes—that is achieved by the exercise of empathic imagination lacks normative significance.

test had not been validated, by accepted test measurement methodology, to provide reliable test results for predicting future job performance.]

The central purpose of the Equal Protection Clause of the Fourteenth Amendment is the prevention of official conduct discriminating on the basis of race. It is also true that the Due Process Clause of the Fifth Amendment contains an equal protection component prohibiting the United States from invidiously discriminating between individuals or groups. *Bolling* v. *Sharpe*, 347 U.S. 497 (1954). But our cases have not embraced the proposition that a law or other official act, without regard to whether it reflects a racially discriminatory purpose, is unconstitutional *solely* because it has a racially disproportionate impact.

Almost 100 years ago, *Strauder* v. *West Virginia*, 100 U.S. 303 (1880), established that the exclusion of Negroes from grand and petit juries in criminal proceedings violated the Equal Protection Clause, but the fact that a particular jury or a series of juries does not statistically reflect the racial composition of the community does not in itself make out an invidious discrimination forbidden by the Clause. "A purpose to discriminate must be present which may be proven by systematic exclusion of eligible jurymen of the proscribed race or by unequal application of the law to such an extent as to show intentional discrimination." A defendant in a criminal case is entitled "to require that the State not deliberately and systematically deny to members of his race the right to participate as jurors in the administration of justice."

The rule is the same in other contexts [a 1964 case] upheld a New York congressional apportionment statute against claims that district lines had been racially gerrymandered. The challenged districts were made up predominantly of whites or of minority races and their boundaries were irregularly drawn. The challengers did not prevail because they failed to prove that the New York Legislature "was either motivated by racial considerations or in fact drew the districts on racial lines"; the plaintiffs had not shown that the statute "was the product of a state contrivance to segregate on the basis of race or place of origin." * * *

The school desegregation cases have also adhered to the basic equal protection principle that the invidious quality of a law claimed to be racially discriminatory must ultimately be traced to a racially discriminatory purpose. That there are both predominantly black and predominantly white schools in a community is not alone violative of the Equal Protection Clause. The essential element of *de jure* segregation is "a current condition of segregation resulting from intentional state action." *Keyes* v. *School Dist. No. 1,* 413 U.S. 189, 205 (1973). "The differentiating factor between *de jure* segregation and so-called *de facto* segregation ... is *purpose* or *intent* to *segregate*." *Id.,* at 208. See also *id.,* at 199, 211, and 213. The Court has also recently rejected allegations of racial discrimination based solely on the statistically disproportionate racial impact of various provisions of the Social Security Act because "[t]he acceptance of appellants' constitutional theory would render suspect each difference in treatment among the grant classes, however lacking in racial motivation and however otherwise rational the treatment might be."

This is not to say that the necessary discriminatory racial purpose must be express or appear on the face of the statute, or that a law's disproportionate impact is irrelevant in cases involving Constitution-based claims of racial discrimination. A statute, otherwise neutral on its face, must not be applied so as invidiously to discriminate on the basis of race. *Yick Wo v. Hopkins,* 118 U.S. 356 (1886). It is also clear from the cases dealing with racial discrimination in the selection of juries that the systematic exclusion of Negroes is itself such an "unequal application of the law . . . as to show intentional discrimination." A prima facie case of discriminatory purpose may be proved as well by the absence of Negroes on a particular jury combined with the failure of the jury commissioners to be informed of eligible Negro jurors in a community, or with racially nonneutral selection procedures. With a prima facie case made out, "the burden of proof shifts to the State to rebut the presumption of unconstitutional action by showing that permissible racially neutral selection criteria and procedures have produced the monochromatic result."

Necessarily, an invidious discriminatory purpose may often be inferred from the totality of the relevant facts, including the fact, if it is true, that the law bears more heavily on one race than another. It is also not infrequently true that the discriminatory impact—in the jury cases for example, the total or seriously disproportionate exclusion of Negroes from jury venires—may for all practical purposes demonstrate unconstitutionality because in various circumstances the discrimination is very difficult to explain on nonracial grounds. Nevertheless, we have not held that a law, neutral on its face and serving ends otherwise within the power of government to pursue, is invalid under the Equal Protection Clause simply because it may affect a greater proportion of one race than of another. Disproportionate impact is not irrelevant, but it is not the sole touchstone of an invidious racial discrimination forbidden by the Constitution. Standing alone, it does not trigger the rule, that racial classifications are to be subjected to the strictest scrutiny and are justifiable only by the weightiest of considerations. * * *

As an initial matter, we have difficulty understanding how a law establishing a racially neutral qualification for employment is nevertheless racially discriminatory and denies "any person . . . equal protection of the laws" simply because a greater proportion of Negroes fail to qualify than members of other racial or ethnic groups. Had respondents, along with all others who had failed Test 21, whether white or black, brought an action claiming that the test denied each of them equal protection of the laws as compared with those who had passed with high enough scores to qualify them as police recruits, it is most unlikely that their challenge would have been sustained. Test 21, which is administered generally to prospective Government employees, concededly seeks to ascertain whether those who take it have acquired a particular level of verbal skill; and it is untenable that the Constitution prevents the Government from seeking modestly to upgrade the communicative abilities of its employees rather than to be satisfied with some lower level of competence, particularly where the job requires special ability to communicate orally and in writing. Respondents, as Negroes, could no more successfully claim that the test denied them equal protection than could white applicants who also failed. The conclusion would not be different in the face of proof that more Negroes than whites had been disqualified by Test 21. That other Negroes also failed to score well would, alone, not demonstrate that respondents individually were being denied equal protection of the laws by the application of an otherwise valid qualifying test being administered to prospective police recruits.

Nor on the facts of the case before us would the disproportionate impact of Test 21 warrant the conclusion that it is a purposeful device to discriminate against Negroes and hence an infringement of the constitutional rights of respondents as well as other black applicants. As we have said, the test is neutral on its face and rationally may be said to serve a purpose the Government is constitutionally empowered to pursue. Even agreeing with the District Court that the differential racial effect of Test 21 called for further inquiry, we think the District Court correctly held that the affirmative efforts of the Metropolitan Police Department to recruit black officers, the changing racial composition of the recruit classes and of the force in general, and the relationship of the test to the training program negated any inference that the Department discriminated on the basis of race or that "a police officer qualifies on the color of his skin rather than ability."[13] * * *

A rule that a statute designed to serve neutral ends is nevertheless invalid, absent compelling justification, if in practice it benefits or burdens one race more than another would be far reaching and would raise serious questions about, and perhaps invalidate, a whole range of tax, welfare, public service, regulatory, and licensing statutes that may be more burdensome to the poor and to the average black than to the more affluent white....

We also hold that the Court of Appeals should have affirmed the judgment of the District Court granting the motions for summary judgment

---

13. It appears beyond doubt by now that there is no single method for appropriately validating employment tests for their relationship to job performance. Professional standards developed by the American Psychological Association in its Standards for Educational and Psychological Tests and Manuals (1966), accept three basic methods of validation: "empirical" or "criterion" validity (demonstrated by identifying criteria that indicate successful job performance and then correlating test scores and the criteria so identified); "construct" validity (demonstrated by examinations structured to measure the degree to which job applicants have identifiable characteristics that have been determined to be important in successful job performance); and "content" validity (demonstrated by tests whose content closely approximates tasks to be performed on the job by the applicant). These standards have been relied upon by the Equal Employment Opportunity Commission in fashioning its Guidelines on Employee Selection Procedures, 29 CFR pt. 1607 (1975), and have been judicially noted in cases where validation of employment tests has been in issue.

filed by petitioners and the federal parties. Respondents were entitled to relief on neither constitutional nor statutory grounds. * * *

■ MR. JUSTICE STEVENS concurring. . . .

While I agree with the Court's disposition of this case, I add these comments on the constitutional issue discussed. . . .

The requirement of purposeful discrimination is a common thread running through the cases summarized in Part II. These cases include criminal convictions which were set aside because blacks were excluded from the grand jury, a reapportionment case in which political boundaries were obviously influenced to some extent by racial considerations, a school desegregation case, and a case involving the unequal administration of an ordinance purporting to prohibit the operation of laundries in frame buildings. Although it may be proper to use the same language to describe the constitutional claim in each of these contexts, the burden of proving a prima facie case may well involve differing evidentiary considerations. The extent of deference that one pays to the trial court's determination of the factual issue, and indeed, the extent to which one characterizes the intent issue as a question of fact or a question of law, will vary in different contexts.

Frequently the most probative evidence of intent will be objective evidence of what actually happened rather than evidence describing the subjective state of mind of the actor. For normally the actor is presumed to have intended the natural consequences of his deeds. This is particularly true in the case of governmental action which is frequently the product of compromise, of collective decision-making, and of mixed motivation. It is unrealistic, on the one hand, to require the victim of alleged discrimination to uncover the actual subjective intent of the decision-maker or, conversely, to invalidate otherwise legitimate action simply because an improper motive affected the deliberation of a participant in the decisional process. A law conscripting clerics should not be invalidated because an atheist voted for it.

My point in making this observation is to suggest that the line between discriminatory purpose and discriminatory impact is not nearly as bright, and perhaps not quite as critical, as the reader of the Court's opinion might assume. I agree, of course, that a constitutional issue does not arise every time some disproportionate impact is shown. On the other hand, when the disproportion is as dramatic as in *Gomillion* v. *Lightfoot,* 364 U.S. 339, or *Yick Wo* v. *Hopkins,* 118 U.S. 356, it really does not matter whether the standard is phrased in terms of purpose or effect. Therefore, although I accept the statement of the general rule in the Court's opinion, I am not yet prepared to indicate how that standard should be applied in the many cases which have formulated the governing standard in different language. * * *

My agreement . . . rests on a ground narrower than the Court describes. I do not rely at all on the evidence of good-faith efforts to recruit black police officers. In my judgment, neither those efforts nor the subjective good faith of the District administration, would save Test 21 if it were otherwise invalid.

There are two reasons why I am convinced that the challenge to Test 21 is insufficient. First, the test serves the neutral and legitimate purpose of requiring all applicants to meet a uniform minimum standard of literacy. Reading ability is manifestly relevant to the police function, there is no evidence that the required passing grade was set at an arbitrarily high level, and there is sufficient disparity among high schools and high school graduates to justify the use of a separate uniform test. Second, the same test is used throughout the federal service. The applicants for employment in the District Columbia Police Department represent such a small fraction of the total number of persons who have taken the test that their experience is of minimal probative value in assessing the neutrality of the test itself. That evidence, without more, is not sufficient to overcome the presumption that a test which is this widely used by the Federal Government is in fact neutral in its effect as well as its "purpose" as that term is used in constitutional adjudication. * * *

■ Mr. Justice Brennan and Mr. Justice Marshall dissent

[I]t should be observed that every federal court, except the District Court in this case, presented with proof identical to that offered to validate Test 21 has reached a conclusion directly opposite to that of the Court today. * * *

––––––––

Empirical Evidence

Pervasive Prejudice, Unconventional Evidence of Race and Gender Discrimination 3–8 (2001).

■ Ian Ayres

Indeed, there seems to be a widespread, implicit belief (at least among white males) that race and gender discrimination is not a serious problem in retail markets. The civil rights laws of the 1960s focused on only a handful of non-retail markets-chiefly concerning employment, housing, and public accommodation services. Indeed, the most gaping hole in our civil rights law concerns retail gender discrimination. No federal law prohibits gender discrimination in the sale of goods or services. A seller could flatly refuse to deal with a potential buyer of a car or a paperclip because of her gender. And while the civil rights laws of the 1860s prohibited race discrimination in contracting, the civil rights laws a century later only prohibited sex discrimination in a narrow range of "titled" markets. The thousands of other markets that make up our economy are completely unregulated with regard to gender (as well as to religion and national origin) discrimination and only somewhat more regulated with regard to race. And only a handful of cities and states (chief among them California) make up for this failing by prohibiting gender discrimination in contracting generally.

The non-regulation of retail discrimination seems to be premised on a vague coterie of assumptions: (1) retail discrimination does not exist because retailers have no motive to discriminate; (2) retail discrimination does not exist because competition forces retailers not to discriminate; and (3) any retail discrimination that does occur does not have serious consequences because of effective counterstrategies by potential victims. It is also argued that any discrimination in the sale of goods or services is less important than the potential effects of discrimination in the markets for employment and housing. But without denying the primacy of employment, the current regulatory regime leaves approximately 66 percent of the dollars we spend-and 35 percent of the dollars we earn-unregulated (with respect to gender discrimination) or less regulated (with respect to race discrimination).

In this book, I contest the idea that race and gender discrimination in the retail sale of goods is nonexistent or unimportant. My thesis is that race and gender discrimination is neither a thing of the past nor is it limited to the narrow set of "titled" markets regulated by the civil rights legislation of the 1960s (Title VII, Title II, and so on). The book's primary contribution is empirical, but let me begin with a few theoretical reasons why we should take the possibility of retail discrimination seriously.

RETAILERS MAY HAVE A MOTIVE TO DISCRIMINATE

The argument that discrimination in the sale of goods and services does not exist because retailers lack any disparate treatment motive is itself premised on the twin ideas that discriminating against economically marginal groups would not be profitable and that racial animus would not manifest itself in discrete retail transactions.

The latter idea is that while animus might cause race discrimination in the more relational settings employment, apartment rental, and restaurants-which civil rights laws regulate, regulated retail transactions are sufficiently discrete that seller and/or customer prejudice would not induce disparate treatment. There are, however, several problems with this theory. First, as pointed out by Ian MacNeil, contractual arrangements are not as discrete as initially appear. Barbers may have much more tactile and repeated contact with their customers than one-time sellers of a house, but the law much more vigorously regulates the latter transaction. Second, the thought that prejudice is less likely to be acted upon in discrete transactions is premised on a narrow theory of what might be called "associational" animus-that is, that bigots don't like associating with particular groups. But, * * * there are other types of animus that might persist even in discrete markets. For example, if sellers enjoy extracting an extra dollar of profit from people of color more than from whites, we might expect to see disparate racial treatment in pricing or quality of service. Finally, appreciating the pervasive discretion given to employees as agents open up the possibility that even profit-maximizing principals will by necessity countenance some disparate treatment by their subordinates.

Discriminating retailers may also be actuated by profit. Sellers may have a profit-maximizing incentive to price discriminate against minorities and women-even if sellers believe that members of these groups are on average poorer. It has long been known that "statistical discrimination" might cause rational, profit-maximizing sellers to charge more to groups that on average cause sellers to incur higher costs. Thus, as a theoretical matter, the drivers of taxis might discriminate against African American men if the drivers perceive a higher chance of being robbed by such passengers. But, more provocatively, focusing on the example of new car sales, I argue that profit-maximizing sellers may engage in "revenue-based" race and gender disparate treatment. Dealerships may discriminate not because they expect higher costs but because they expect to be able to extract higher revenues. This is a surprising possibility because, as an empirical matter, people of color have a substantially lower ability to pay for new cars. But profit-maximizing sellers care far more about the variability in willingness to pay than in the mean willingness. The presence of a few minority members who are willing to pay a large markup can make it rational for the dealership to offer higher prices to all members of the group-even if group members are on average poorer.

It is correct and useful to ask whether sellers would plausibly be motivated to engage in a particular type of discrimination. But treating this issue seriously opens up a variety of dimensions where discrimination in the retail sale of goods and services could be a plausible seller strategy for either profit or non-profit-based reasons.

COMPETITION MAY NOT DRIVE OUT RETAIL DISCRIMINATION

Nobel-prize winning economist Gary Becker emphasized how competition could provide a much-needed antidote for the disease of discrimination. Non-discriminating sellers could earn higher profits by picking up the sales of those minorities and/or women excluded from equal access to the discriminating sellers. One problem with this theory is that it focuses on the ability of competition to drive out discriminating sellers, but competition may not be as effective at driving out the preferences of discriminating customers. If fixed costs of production limit the number of firms selling and if a substantial number of, say, white customers prefer dealing with a firm that discriminates against (by excluding or offering inferior service to) people of color, then firms may decide that it is more profitable to exclude minorities than to lose the patronage of whites.

As an empirical matter, however, my guess is that most firms would not find overt race or gender discrimination to be a profit-maximizing strategy. While Lester Maddox may have increased his sales by excluding African Americans, in most markets a "whites only" or "males only" policy or overtly charging higher prices to particular demographic groups would lead to a general negative consumer reaction-by both minorities and progressive white consumers.

A more important limitation on competition is consumer information. In order for discrimination to cause the competitive shift of consumers toward nondiscriminatory sellers, consumers must know which sellers are discriminating and which are not. There is thus an important informational prerequisite for competition to have the predicted Beckerian effect. But as described above, there are many aspects of treatment where consumers may not be able to compare how sellers treat similarly situated counterparts. Retail discrimination is most likely to persist where consumers do not learn the benchmark treatment of fellow consumers. Thus, while there is little opportunity for a single fast food franchise to charge different prices for hamburgers, it is possible for a dealership to charge different prices to potential buyers of cars. Since bargained prices diverge from the list price, it is very difficult for a consumer to know whether she has received a nondiscriminatory price. And it will be more difficult for a nondiscriminatory seller to credibly market itself on the basis that the race or gender of customers do not influence its bargaining strategy.

Markets in which price or other terms of trade are individually bargained for provide much greater opportunities for race or gender discrimination than markets with homogeneous product attributes and posted prices. However, even retailers that sell standardized products at posted prices might discriminate on the basis of race or gender with regard to discretionary aspects of service. Anyone watching the *Prime Time* segment could vividly see that record and department stores could substantially increase the "transaction costs" of minority customers. This is not just an issue of whether the retailer provides "service with a smile" but, as in the *Prime Time Live* testing, whether the retailers make minority customers wait substantially longer before being served (or whether the minority customers are conspicuously shadowed to scrutinize whether they are shoplifting).

Retailers may also discriminate in their willingness to accommodate private and somewhat idiosyncratic consumer requests. For example, Jane Connor is currently testing retailers in Binghamton, New York, to see whether there are racial differences in their willingness to accede to a request to use a restroom or a request to return a sweater without a receipt. Economists (and others) tend to ignore or downplay the harms of such discrimination. But nontrivial injury may be visited on people of color in terms of both higher transactions costs and taking more precaution to comply strictly with retailer policies. One audit study showed that African Americans in Washington, D.C., had to wait 27 percent longer to hail a cab If this seems a minor inconvenience, white readers should try to imagine what their life would be like if *every* (or even just many) transactions took 27 percent longer. Even a single incident can impose real psychological costs. Consider, for example, Patricia Williams's story of being denied entrance to an open Benneton store by a gum-chewing, buzzerwielding store clerk.

———————

NOTES AND QUESTIONS

1. Statistical discrimination. Statistical discrimination exists when a seller or provider of services or property owner treats two equally suitable persons differently, solely on the basis of the average characteristics of members of a race, gender, or other subordinated group.

2. References for statistical discrimination. For more extensive discussion of statistical discrimination, see D.J. Aigner & G.C. Cain, *"Statistical Theories of Discrimination in the Labor Market,"* 30 Indus. & Lab. Rel. Rev. 175 (1977); K.J. Arrow, *"The Theory of Discrimination;" in* Discrimination in Labor Markets, (Ashenfelter and Rees eds.) (1973); A. Moro & P. Norman, *"A General Equilibrium Model of Statistical Discrimination."* 114 J. of Econ. Theory. (2004); S. Schwab, *"Is Statistical Discrimination Efficient?"*, 76 Amer. Econ. Rev. 228 (1986); P. Norman, *"Statistical Discrimination and Efficiency"*, 70 Rev. of Econ. Studies, 615 (2003).

3. Does statistical discrimination account for the proliferation of stereotypes and the presence of negative cognitive associations for subordinated groups whose average characteristics are the product of a societal history of exclusion from opportunity?

———

F. Neutrality Challenges From Other Social Science Methodologies:

1. Cognitive Psychology—Scientific Evidence of Cognitive Bias?

Racism lost its explicit social endorsement in the aftermath of the civil rights revolution that followed in the more than half-century since the 1954 Supreme Court decision in *Brown v. Board of Education*. Hostile racial attitudes and prejudicial belief systems gradually went underground, flourishing in the subterranean world of personal cognition, family norms, and private conversations in racially homogeneous settings. Until recently, this bias was undetectable by scientifically reliable assessment tools. Moreover, both economic theory and legal theory operated on heuristics that assumed that significant racial bias no longer existed.

As Ian Ayres has shown, with a series of empirical research studies of racial discrimination in retail markets, this assumption is probably false. *See* Ayres, Pervasive Prejudice? Unconventional Evidence of Race and Gender Discrimination, *infra* at 777. However, notwithstanding Ayres pathbreaking empirical research, the difficulty for those seeking to challenge the neutrality heuristics of economics and law has been to find ways to identify individual biases, and more importantly to link those biases to racially harmful behavior.

Note on the Implicit Association Test (I.A.T.)

The development of the Implicit Association Test has provided a method to penetrate the web of latent individual bias. The test, in its most widely used version, is administered to individuals who choose to take it on the internet. Test takers are asked to sort a randomly shown series of faces into two categories: black American or white American. The test instructions encourage speedy responses using two keys on the computer keyboard that require the use of either the left or right hand. In the second stage of the test, a sequence of value-laden words, such as "joy" and "failure" appear on the screen. The test taker is asked to associate these words with a random distribution of the same set of faces representing the two racial groups. In the final step, the words and faces are reversed, and the test taker is asked again to associate the words with the, now racialized faces. The existence of bias is measured by the time difference between the length of time it takes to match the faces to words that are consistent with the racial stereotype, and the length of time required to match the faces with words associated with the other group, so that matching blacks with joy takes longer than matching blacks with "failure." The test is built on the psychological phenomenon of cognitive dissonance, in which there is discrepancy between beliefs, and new facts require more mental effort to process. The test results, from tens of thousands of self-selected test takers who described themselves as liberal, identified 88 percent of white test takers as having an anti-black bias. Perhaps even more interesting than the bias of whites against blacks, were the results of black bias against other blacks, revealing an internalization of the cultural tilt against all blacks. A startling 48 percent of blacks showed an anti-black bias.

The test is not without its critics who charge that even if it accurately measures interior states of mind, it should not be the basis for policymaking, or legal intervention by government, because it only reveals "thoughts". Psychologist, Hal Arkes, argues that the problem with the test is "where we are going to set our threshold of proof for saying something represents prejudice. My view is the implicit prejudice program sets the threshold at a historical low." Quoted in, Shankar Vedantam, "See No Bias", *The Washington Post Magazine*, 12, at 40, January 23, 2005.

Taking the I.A.T. We encourage you to take a moment to take the test for yourself. The website is https://implicit.harvard.edu. A full explanation of the research design can be found at https://implicit.harvard.edu/implicit/demo/faqs.html.

Pro–Black Bias. Courtland Milloy, a black columnist for the *Washington Post*, took the Implict Association Test. He reports that his results told him that: "your data suggest a strong automatic preference for Black relative to White." White notes:

> For some readers, no doubt, this is confirmation that I am a reverse racist ... The last thing I wanted [was] to end up in that group of African Americans who showed a pro-white or anti-black bias [48 percent]. ... A conscious effort is what it has taken for me not to absorb the worst of white society's stereotypes about blacks.

Courtland Milloy, "Out From Under the Thumb of White Bias", *Washington Post*, B1, January 26, 2005.

———

Civil Rights Perestroika: Intergroup Relations After Affirmative Action

86 CAL. L. REV. 1251 (1998).

■ LINDA HAMILTON KRIEGER

Here at the University of California at Berkeley, there was a surreal quality to November 6, 1996, the day after voters, in enacting Proposition 209, elected to end affirmative action in California state hiring, contracting, and education. The few protests that had been organized ended quickly and quietly. At the law school, students seemed uncharacteristically subdued: quietly resigned—or quietly pleased. In the newspapers that morning and on the mornings that followed, articles about Texaco executives referring to their African–American employees as "niggers" and "black jelly beans" were oddly juxtaposed against others in which Proposition 209's triumphant sponsors heralded a glorious new era of truly equal opportunity and the long-awaited dawning of a colorblind society.

Now, many months later and well into the first of Berkeley's "post-affirmative action" years, the atmosphere here is no less strange. On the first day of classes in 1997, the halls and courtyards swarmed with television cameras and reporters, attempting, I noted with a sense of irony, to identify the lone African–American member of Boalt Hall's first "colorblind" class. We were no longer supposed to consider race, but race was everywhere in these halls on that first morning of the new school year. * * *

If history is any guide, the trend started in California will spread to other states and to the national stage in the months ahead. The 105th Congress witnessed the introduction of three separate bills that would have "nationalized" Proposition 209, and, events in Houston notwithstanding, many States are contemplating similar legislation.

But before proceeding further down this road, it might be wise to pause and ask some hard questions. * * * What can we expect to occur with respect to intergroup relations, and with race relations in particular, in a post-affirmative action environment? If affirmative action is eliminated, will remaining policy tools prove adequate to effectuate racial and gender equity and to prevent the resegregation of American society? Will the idea of "colorblindness" suffice as a theoretical model for understanding what it means not to discriminate? Or will we find instead that affirmative action actually served to mask a "multiplicity of sins"—critical failings in our approach to intergroup relations and serious defects in the tools available to make the equal opportunity society a reality instead of a hazy, unattainable dream?* * *

[This article] inquires whether, absent preferential forms of affirmative action, remaining policy tools would prove adequate to control discrimination and prevent the further segregation of American society. It concludes that these remaining tools, which include a colorblindness model of nondiscrimination, an objective concept of merit, and individualized adjudication as a primary policy enforcement tool, are unequal to the task. In short, we still lack adequate tools for coping successfully with the problems of intergroup competition and cooperation in a pluralistic society.

This failure, which I will argue has been masked to a certain extent by preferential forms of affirmative action, derives from a misunderstanding of the nature and sources of intergroup bias, from a failure to recognize its tendency to persist over time, and from over-reliance on limited adjudicatory and regulatory approaches to address what is fundamentally a complex cultural problem. Accordingly, I argue that unless we develop a broadened understanding of intergroup bias and new approaches to reducing it, the problems of discrimination and inequality of opportunity will worsen in a post-affirmative action environment.

[D]iscrimination does not solely derive from stable, dispositional traits internal to actors we call "discriminators." Rather, intergroup bias increases or decreases in response to contextual, environmental factors which shape how social actors perceive, judge, and make decisions about members of their own and other social reference groups. Accordingly, an anti-discrimination policy grounded in an individualized search for discriminatory intent cannot be expected to succeed either in identifying and preventing intergroup bias or in managing social tendencies toward intergroup conflict. If we are to solve the problem of intergroup discrimination, we must attend more closely to the ecology of intergroup relations. Eliminating affirmative action before we have developed an effective alternative theoretical and doctrinal approach to managing intergroup bias is a strategy more risky than many might assume. * * *

II

AFTER AFFIRMATIVE ACTION: RECOGNIZING DISCRIMINATION IN THE LAND OF THE COLORBLIND

What might we expect if every institution in the nation—every college and university, every corporation, every state and local public agency, and every arm and organ of the federal government—suddenly prohibited its employees from considering the race, sex, or national origin of applicants or employees in hiring, contracting, promotion, or admission to educational programs? What would happen if every employment and admissions decision maker was told simply to "be colorblind," to base his or her decisions only on "considerations of merit"? Would they do it? Could they do it? Could we identify those who did not do it, whose decisions were tainted by intergroup bias?

The answers to these questions are, quite simply, "no," "no," and "no." Perhaps constitutions can be colorblind. Perhaps official government or corporate policies can be colorblind. But human beings living in a society in which history, ideology, law, and patterns of social, economic, and political distribution have made race, sex, and ethnicity salient, cannot be colorblind. The "colorblindness" approach to nondiscrimination will prove ineffective because it provides neither a framework for enabling people to recognize the effects of race, gender, or national origin on their perceptions and judgments, nor the tools required to help them counteract those effects. Indeed, a color blindness-centered interpretation of the nondiscrimination principle, coupled with well-meaning people's awareness that they do categorize along racial and ethnic lines, may exacerbate the very intergroup anxiety and ambivalence that lead to what social psychologists refer to as aversive racism.

Furthermore, decision makers cannot base selection decisions only on colorblind considerations of merit for the simple reason that merit has a color. Conceptions of merit are socially and politically constructed and are shaped by the same ingroup preferences that give rise to other subtle forms of intergroup bias. Affirmative action preferences have, in many ways, diverted our attention from the biases inherent in the construction of merit. But if preferences are eliminated, this problem and the inequities it generates will soon rise into sharp relief.

Finally, there is substantial reason to doubt that remaining law enforcement tools, particularly the adjudication of individual disparate treatment cases, will prove effective in identifying and remedying subtle but pervasive forms of intergroup bias. For a variety of reasons, reliance on individual disparate treatment adjudication can be expected to result in the serious underidentification of discrimination by judicial decision makers, victims, and private fact finders.

A. The Inefficacy of Colorblindness as a Normative Construct

[E]xisting antidiscrimination law constructs intergroup bias as something that occurs when a "discriminatory purpose" motivates a decision. In other words, in order for a decision to be considered "discriminatory" under a statute such as Title VII, the disparate treatment plaintiff must show that the employer chose to take the negative action against him because of his membership in a particular protected class. Thus, to say that discrimination is intentional means that the decision stands in a particular sort of close relation to the target person's group status. Specifically, in the decision maker's mental process, there must be some syllogistic connection between the two.

So, for example, existing antidiscrimination law understands cognitive stereotypes as causing discrimination through the operation of a conscious, syllogistic reasoning process, through which the decision maker uses a person's group status in the following sort of way:

Major Premise: Women with young children are preoccupied with family responsibilities and do not put their jobs first;

Minor Premise: This applicant is a woman with young children;

Conclusion: This applicant cannot be expected to put the job first.

Current antidiscrimination law further conceives gender role expectations, or normative stereotypes, as causing discrimination through the operation of a similar sort of syllogistic reasoning:

Major Premise: Women with young children should be preoccupied with family responsibilities and should not hold jobs that will compete with the responsibilities associated with raising children;

Minor Premise (1) The rigors of this job can be expected to conflict with family responsibilities associated with raising young children;

Minor Premise (2) This applicant is a mother with young children;

Conclusion: This applicant should not hold this job.

According to the existing jurisprudential model of discrimination, personal animosity may also lead to discrimination through the operation of implicit syllogistic reasoning:

Major Premise: Working with black coworkers makes me feel uncomfortable;

Minor Premise: This applicant is black;

Conclusion: Working with him would make me feel uncomfortable.

In each of these contexts, the decision maker's thinking moves directly through the target person's group status. So long as we understand discrimination as operating in this way, we can rely on a color-blindness model of nondiscrimination to function as an effective normative principle. A social decision maker can refrain from discriminating simply by refraining from any syllogistic use of the target person's group status, in other words, by being "colorblind."

But as I have also attempted to demonstrate, not all discrimination is of this sort. Much discrimination has little connection with discriminatory motive or intent. This sort of discrimination occurs when an individual's group status subtly, even unconsciously, affects a decision makers' subjective perception of relevant traits, on which ostensibly non-discriminatory decision are subsequently based. This form of discrimination results from a variety of categorization-related cognitive biases, and can result in disparate treatment based on race, sex, national origin, or other factors, even among the well-intentioned.

I do not wish to rehash the evidence supporting this proposition described at length elsewhere. Rather, using related but more recent research, I wish to demonstrate that only "color-consciousness" can control these cognitive forms of intergroup bias. This research strongly suggests that cognitive biases in social judgment operate automatically, without intention or awareness, and can be controlled only through subsequent, deliberate "mental correction" that takes group status squarely into account.

1. Automatic Processes in Intergroup Judgment

In his early work on perceptual readiness, Jerome Bruner observed that when a person receives information with the goal of forming an impression, his or her first cognitive task is to fit that information into some existing knowledge structure. As Bruner described, only when behavioral information is encoded in this way does it becomes useful, or even meaningful.

Of course, in many situations incoming information is ambiguous in that it is susceptible to varied interpretations. A student's volunteered but halting response to a question can be interpreted as reflecting dull-wittedness—or courageous engagement with a difficult subject. An employee's hesitancy in the face of an important decision may evince timidity—or prudence. As Bruner suggested, "All perception is generic," meaning that observed actions, like objects, take on meaning only when they are assigned to a particular trait construct—a preexisting knowledge structure residing in the observer's mind.

In their attempts to understand this process more fully, cognitive psychologists originally assumed that assigning an action to a particular trait construct depended primarily on the extent of the "match" between the features of the action and those of the construct. Then in the late 1970s through the early 1980s, encouraged no doubt by Amos Tversky and Daniel Kahneman's seminal work on the availability heuristic, various researchers began investigating the role of trait construct accessibility in social perception. Their work showed that the readiness with which a person will characterize a particular behavior in terms of any given trait construct is a function of that construct's availability in memory at the time the behavior is perceived. Any activity, conscious or unconscious, that "primes" a particular trait construct will tend to increase its accessibility and the corresponding likelihood that ambiguous information will be assimilated or encoded in a manner consistent with that trait.

Social stereotypes bias perception in this general manner. As numerous researchers have demonstrated, one learns at an early age stereotypes of the major social groups in the United States. These stereotypes have a long history of activation, and are likely to be highly accessible, regardless of whether they are believed. They are invoked automatically when people encounter members of a stereotyped outgroup. Once activated, stereotypes serve to "prime" the trait constructs with which they are associated. Incoming behavioral information, especially if capable of various interpretations, is accordingly assimilated into those traits associated with the stereotype.

This tendency to assimilate ambiguous information into stereotypic trait constructs might not be so serious if people were aware that they were doing it. To understand the significance of this process and its implications for the debate over affirmative action, it is useful to understand a phenomenon which attribution theorists refer to as spontaneous trait inference.

People are highly concerned with understanding why things happen in their social environments. Rightly or wrongly, we assume that understanding why something has happened will improve our power to predict or even control what will happen in the future. To the extent that personality traits play an important role in understanding people's actions, one might expect the process of translating observed behaviors into trait-related meanings to occur with great frequency. Given that social perception and judgment processes become increasingly efficient with repeated execution, one might further hypothesize that trait inference processes could become so overlearned as to operate without intention or awareness, much like the processes involved in recognizing a word or a face.

This hypothesis appears to be correct. In a number of studies replicated in a variety of contexts by other researchers, New York University psychologist James S. Uleman and his colleagues demonstrated that European-American subjects spontaneously encode behaviors into stable trait constructs without intention or awareness. Thus, there is a strong tendency, at least among European Americans, to attribute stable dispositional qualities spontaneously, as part of the process of perceiving and encoding information about another person's behavior. To say that trait inference is "spontaneous" however is not quite the same as saying it is "automatic," and the difference is critical to equal opportunity policy.

Through the early-1980s, it was generally believed that a particular mental process was either entirely automatic or entirely deliberate. Over time, however, cognitive processes came to be understood as falling along a continuum. On one side of that continuum lie "controlled processes," which require substantial processing capacity and occur with greater levels of focus and awareness. On the other side lie fully automatic processes, which occur without intention or awareness, are difficult if not impossible to control once triggered, and interfere little with other ongoing mental activity. Eventually, it became apparent that complex mental processes such as causal attribution and other forms of social inference were neither exclusively automatic nor exclusively controlled, but rather combined aspects of both. Specifically, social inference came to be understood as comprising a chain of three sequential subprocesses: "categorization," in which the person perceived is identified and placed within an existing categorical structure; "characterization," in which spontaneous dispositional inferences are drawn from the observed behavior; and "correction," in which those dispositional inferences are adjusted to account for situational factors. While categorization and characterization are automatic, correction is controlled. It requires deliberate, effortful mental processing and will compete for cognitive resources with other information processing demands. * * *

The significance of these processes and their implications for the colorblindness approach to nondiscrimination can hardly be overemphasized. Very little information shapes a social perceiver's impression of a target person. Rather, it is the perceiver's interpretation of the raw information that influences social judgment. If the target's social group membership influences these interpretations, and if one is unaware of the effect of such status on those interpretations, how can we expect a colorblindness approach to nondiscrimination to function successfully as a normative principle? Given the realities of social perception, we can anticipate that similarly situated people will be treated differently based on their group membership, because decision makers, influenced by these subtle forms of intergroup bias, will not perceive them as similarly situated at all. Nothing in the colorblindness approach to nondiscrimination provides social decision makers with the tools required to recognize or to correct for biases of this sort.

According to spontaneous trait inference theory, only the application of deliberate, controlled, corrective processes can prevent stereotypes and subtle ingroup priming valences from biasing interpersonal judgment. As social cognition researchers Patricia Devine and Susan Fiske observe, it is neither that nonprejudiced individuals "do not notice" such traits as gender or ethnicity nor that the presence of a member of another group does not "prime" the stereotypes associated with those groups. Rather, insofar as cognitive sources of bias are concerned, the difference between people who discriminate and those who do not is that members of the latter group notice the influences of stereotypes on their thinking and counteract those influences by consciously adjusting responses in a nonprejudiced direction. This process, however, is effortful: it requires both strong motivation and a great deal of capacity, attention, and practice. In short, controlling the biases stemming from such processes as spontaneous trait inference is substantially more complicated than it might at first seem.

2. Controlled Processes and Nondiscrimination: Taming the Beast of Automaticity

The major sources of error in human judgment divide into two broad types. Errors of the first type stem from a failure to know or apply normative rules of inference. Errors of the second type result from a phenomenon which Timothy Wilson and Nancy Brekke refer to as "mental contamination." Mental contamination occurs when a person's judgment or behavior is corrupted by unconscious or uncontrollable mental processes which she would rather not have influence her behavior or decisions. Judgment errors deriving from rule ignorance or incorrect rule application are easier to remedy than those resulting from mental contamination. Normative rules of inference, like the rule of regression to the mean, supply specific procedures for solving the problems to which they pertain and can be consciously learned and deliberately applied.

Correcting judgmental errors resulting from mental contamination is more difficult, in large part because simply teaching people a particular decision rule is unlikely to control biases of which they are unaware. This will be particularly true if the biases in question are difficult to recognize, or easily mistaken for valid, decision-relevant considerations. A supervisor evaluating employees for promotion, or a professor considering which student to hire as a research assistant, may know the rule, "don't discriminate against the black guy." But that kind of rule, in this case the colorblindness rule, cannot be applied in the same way as cost-benefit analysis or the rule of regression to the mean. It can be applied to eliminate facial discrimination—that is, a conscious, explicit policy of excluding a certain group of persons from consideration. It might even be applied to eliminate the conscious, deliberate use of group status as a proxy for decision-relevant traits like initiative or writing ability. But it cannot be applied to prevent or correct biases caused by emotional discomfort, the subconscious effects of stereotypes, causal attribution, or spontaneous trait inference, because it fails to provide a specific set of procedures or techniques which can be applied to the evaluation or decision task at hand. A normative decision rule, such as one prohibiting discrimination on the basis of race, cannot be applied to eliminate a source of bias if the decision maker is unaware that her judgment might be biased or is unable to control the effects of such bias for lack of applicable remedial tools.

As Wilson and Brekke explain, four discrete conditions must be satisfied if people are to control the effects of nonconscious biases. First, one must become aware of the nature of the particular mental process which threatens to bias one's judgment. Second, one must be motivated to correct its unwanted influence once it has been recognized. Third, one must be able to discern the direction and magnitude of the bias, lest it be "overcorrected" and judgment skewed in the opposite direction. And finally, one must have sufficient control over his or her mental processes to correct the effect of the unwanted influences. While it is beyond the scope of this Article to review all of the problems encountered at each of these four stages, those with the most serious implications for the colorblindness model of nondiscrimination warrant attention here.

a. Unawareness of Mental Process

During the fall of 1996, while the campaign on Proposition 209 swirled around the University, I was teaching a class on employment discrimination law. Every day, I called on a different student to respond to questions about the cases prepared for that day's class. Most of my students were Caucasian; only three of sixty-five were African American. Let us assume for purposes of illustration, that one day I had called on one of these three African–American students, and that he experienced a certain amount of difficulty answering various questions. He was not unprepared, but many of his answers were halting and somewhat confused, leaving me with the initial impression that he was not particularly capable.

I flatly reject the belief that African–American law students are less intelligent than others. If asked at the beginning of the semester to predict how any one of my three African–American students would perform relative to their classmates, I would have vigorously objected to making a prediction in the absence of individuating information. Given that I am familiar with certain normative rules of inference such as the principle of regression to the mean, I would probably, if pushed, have predicted that his or her performance would be about average.

But it is also true that, although I reject them as untrue, I am aware of the stereotypes associated with intelligence, academic achievement, and African–American males. I too was exposed to those stereotypes at a very early age, before I developed my own powers of critical and moral intelligence and made a conscious decision to reject these stereotypes as inaccurate and unfair. But my nonprejudiced beliefs did not displace the stereotypes, which exist alongside and function independently of these beliefs. The stereotypes are triggered whether I believe in them or not. And, once triggered, those stereotypes prime the trait constructs associated with them, constructs like "not too bright" or "underachieving," rather than "grappling courageously with a difficult subject."

So, what should one conclude if I had taken from this hypothetical encounter the initial impression that the student in question was "not particularly capable?" His performance had not been very good. Why then, should I even question whether the student's race had anything to do with my judgment?

If such a situation were to arise, I would likely question my initial impression only if: (1) I was aware of the possibility that negative stereotypes of African–American males, or some other aspects of the situation had subtly influenced my judgment; and (2) I was motivated to do something about it.

Of course, other subtle cognitive sources of bias besides racial stereotypes could have "contaminated" my judgment as well. If I approached the issue mindfully, I would probably have noticed that over the course of the semester, a number of students I had called on had performed relatively poorly, some just as poorly as the student in question. But try as I might, if I had not made contemporaneous notes, I probably could not now remember just who those students were. I would remember the African–American student, but I would most likely have forgotten the others.

This scenario illustrates a common unconscious source of bias—the polarized evaluation of distinctive members of an otherwise largely homogeneous group. It is well-established that people pay particularly close attention to distinctive stimulus objects, such as a "token" woman or minority group member. And the more attention we pay to something, the more about it we perceive, encode, and store in memory. Indeed, under conditions of high attention, we are more likely to encode an event visually, which makes it more readily available in memory and more influential in the formation of subsequent judgments. Accordingly, the poor performance of a distinctive minority student is more likely to be remembered, and will tend to be charged with a more powerful negative valence, than the poor performance of a majority white student.

If I were unschooled in these sorts of salience or expectancy-related biases, I would likely remain unaware that the student's race had played any role in the formation of my initial impression that he was "not particularly capable." But could I fairly deny that he had been negatively judged, at least in part, because of his race?

The colorblindness approach to nondiscrimination is dangerous because it leads a decision maker to believe that, so long as she is not consciously thinking about race, she is not discriminating. But social cognition theory teaches that, in a culture pervaded by racial stereotypes, or where persons of one race constitute a small minority in an otherwise homogeneous group, one must think about race in order not to discriminate. In short, the colorblindness principle discourages the first step prerequisite to controlling cognitive sources of intergroup bias.

b.   The Role of Motivation

All "dual process" models of social inference posit that in order to correct errors caused by an automatic mental process, people must not only be aware of the process, but must also be motivated to control its biasing effects. Of course, the development of awareness itself requires motivation. Despite early controversy on particular issues, it is now relatively well-accepted that people lack awareness of a large proportion of mental processing, including the processes comprising impression formation.

Developing self-awareness of such processes and correcting for the various biases inherent in them is in any context objectively difficult. Even after they are activated, the controlled processes required for mental correction require a great deal of capacity and attention and will compete for cognitive resources with other mental demands. But in the context of intergroup discrimination, the order is taller still. Increasing awareness of and sustained attention to the biasing effects of racial, ethnic, or gender stereotypes on one's social judgments is apt to engender fear of moral opprobrium and substantial psychological discomfort. Thus, especially in the context of reducing intergroup bias, there is little reason to assume that people will expend the effort or bear the psychological discomfort associated with mental correction unless they have strong motivations for so doing. Thus, the colorblindness approach not only fails to provide incentives for developing an awareness of mental contamination, but the model itself and the rhetoric that often accompanies it actually establish disincentives for so doing. * * *

c.   The Limits of Mental Correction

As Timothy Wilson and Nancy Brekke observe, even if a person becomes aware that some unwanted mental process has tainted her judgment, she may not be able to determine the magnitude of the resulting bias. For example, in my hypothetical interaction with my African–American student, I might have become aware that stereotype or salience-related biases had influenced my assessment of his performance. But assuming that I were eventually required to formulate an evaluation, how far, if at all, should I adjust it? There is really no way for me to assess how much of my impression is fairly attributable to bias and how much to the student's flawed performance.

Even more troubling is the question whether "correction" is feasible at all. Once the initial impression that the student was "not particularly capable" had been formed, would I be able to erase it from my mind, or prevent it from influencing my impressions of him in connection with future interactions?

There is ample reason to fear that I would not. In a series of now classic studies, Stanford psychologist Lee Ross and his colleagues demonstrated that, even after a belief is discredited, the causal explanations generated to support it persist, giving the discredited belief a kind of cognitive life after death. More recently, University of Texas psychologists Daniel Gilbert and Randall Osborne extended these observations to the process of spontaneous trait inference. Their work demonstrates that once a trait inference is made, subsequent efforts to adjust it may prove ineffective. As they observed, misperceptions are "metastatic." Controlled processing may correct the original misperception, but it often fails to eliminate subsidiary changes that the original misperception engendered. These endure and influence subsequent judgments of the person perceived. It is easier to forbear from action based on a biased impression than to eliminate the impression itself.

Assuming I realized that my impression formation process was potentially biased, I might have decided to reject the view that the student was not particularly capable. I might even have decided not to take action based on my initial impression of his in-class performance, for example, deciding not to use it in calculating his grade. But I would probably not be able to erase the impression from my mind. Given its enduring presence, I would likely experience any adjustments in my subsequent behavior toward or expressed beliefs about the student as a form of racial preferencing. "After all," I might tell myself, "if the student weren't African–American, I wouldn't be bending over backwards like this." What the colorblindness perspective would allow me to forget, or never teach me in the first place, is that if the student were not African–American, I probably would not have remembered his performance at all. * * *

[Krieger's discussion of how conceptions of "merit" are "defined and assessed through the same complex, largely unconscious cognitive processes which subtly bias social judgment in other contexts and give rise to more easily recognizable forms of discrimination" is omitted.]

b.   Schematic Expectancies and the Problem of Ingroup Favoritism * * *

    iii.   Ingroup Helping Discrimination and the Leniency Effect

Patterns of modern discrimination turn in large measure on the answer to one simple question: Who gets cut slack, and who does not? What happens when an employee violates a rule? Is she subjected to discipline under established policies, or are her transgressions overlooked, or attributed to factors beyond her control? When an ambiguous aspect of a person's background can be interpreted in various ways, one negative, one neutral, which attribution is made? And when a person simply needs help, does she receive it?

Type II bias in large measure shapes people's tendencies to assist or ignore, to excuse others' transgressions or hold them accountable under objective standards of conduct. The earliest, and perhaps still the most vivid of the studies illustrating this effect, was conducted in the early 1970s, in front of a Kansas supermarket. In this study, one black woman and one white woman, whom researchers matched for age and social class-related appearance, dropped a bag of groceries while leaving a supermarket, right in the path of oncoming shoppers. Researchers investigated whether white shoppers would help a white "bag dropper" more frequently than a black bag dropper.

The results were complex and intriguing. Overall, the experimenters found no significant effect of race on the provision of help per se: approximately the same percentage of incoming white shoppers in either condition stopped to help. Subsequent analysis of the data however, revealed an important, if more subtle, phenomenon. When the bag dropper was white, sixty three percent of those who stopped continued to provide assistance until the job was done. When the bag dropper was black, helpers tended to pick up one or two items and then leave, providing complete assistance only thirty percent of the time.

Additional studies provide further evidence of an ingroup helping bias. In 1977, Samuel Gaertner and John Dovidio conducted an experiment in which white subjects were led to believe that they were participating in an investigation of extrasensory perception (ESP). Researchers assigned subjects to serve as either a "sender" or a "receiver," and paired each with a partner/confederate, who was either white or black. Senders and receivers sat in different rooms. Researchers told some subjects that a second person was sitting with their partner in the other room, and told other subjects that the partner was alone.

During the course of the "ESP" experiment, researchers staged an emergency. Subjects heard the sound of falling chairs and the screams of the partner in the other room, followed by prolonged silence. Researchers investigated whether the partner's race would effect the rates at which subjects would go to the aid of their partner.

When subjects believed that their partner was alone in the other room, the partner's race had no significant effect on responses. However, when subjects believed that there was another person in the room with the partner, race made a dramatic difference. Where the apparently imperiled partner was white, seventy-five percent of subjects offered aid, but where the partner was black, the rate dropped to thirty-seven percent. Perhaps even more significantly, subjects showed greater physiological arousal, measured by change in heart rate, when the partner/confederate was white than when he was black.

Gaertner and Dovidio interpreted these results as indicating that whites do not deliberately avoid providing assistance to blacks. However, when features of the situation are ambiguous, when it is unclear whether help is called for, they tend to resolve uncertainty in favor of helping whites and against helping blacks. * * *

As the tendency to assist is biased, so is the tendency to overlook or excuse transgression. For example, in a 1974 field study of whites' reactions to apparent shoplifting, Max Dertke and his colleagues demonstrated that when the shoplifter/confederate was black, white shoppers spontaneously reported and followed up on an observed shoplifting incident at a much higher rate than when the shoplifter/confederate was white. * * *

One can easily see how over time, these subtle forms of ingroup favoritism would result in markedly different outcomes for ingroup and outgroup members. If decision makers react to members of their own social reference groups with more positive associations, a quicker willingness to help, and a stronger inclination to ignore or excuse shortcomings, it is easy to predict who will be systematically advantaged in hiring and promotion decisions. Disparities will develop even absent hostile animus or negative actions directed towards the outgroup. * * *

[Krieger's discussion of how current anti-discrimination law is poorly equipped to control Type II discrimination is omitted.]

D. Individualized Adjudication, Hypothesis Testing, and Causal Attribution: The Effects of Intergroup Bias

Consider for a moment the judgment task involved in adjudicating an individual employment discrimination suit. Determining in any given case whether discrimination has occurred is fundamentally an exercise in causal attribution. The employer has taken some negative action, most frequently a termination of employment, against the plaintiff. The jury's role is to determine why that negative action was taken. Was it, as the plaintiff alleges, because the decision maker discriminated against her because of her membership in a protected group? Or was it, as the defendant argues, because of some legitimate, nondiscriminatory reason, usually some malfeasance or deficiency on the plaintiff's part? In a hiring case, did the plaintiff fail to get the job because the decision maker took her group status into account in making the challenged decision? Or did the decision maker believe that some other candidate would do a better job? The trial of such a case will essentially entail a battle between two competing causal theories. Seeking to convince the jury that discrimination is to blame, the plaintiff will portray the decision makers as discriminators. Seeking to convince the jury that the plaintiff is to blame, the defendant will do everything possible to make his or her deficiencies salient.

Why should we expect a jury to approach this social decision task free from the various forms of intergroup bias that distort intergroup perception and judgment in other contexts? As we have seen, unconscious stereotypes about members of different social groups create implicit expectancies in the minds of social perceivers. These expectancies in turn distort the perception, interpretation, and recall of information about members of the targeted groups, pulling subsequent social judgments in a stereotype-consistent direction. Stereotypic expectancies and other forms of intergroup bias also affect causal attribution, causing unconscious distortions in the interpretation and perceived predictiveness of past behavior.

Attributing the causes of employment decisions implicates the very processes of social perception and judgment bound up in the challenged employment decisions themselves. Unless the demographic characteristics of fact finders vary in some dramatic way from those of the decision makers, we cannot reasonably expect that the level of intergroup discrimination reflected in employment decisions will vary in any meaningful way from the level reflected in discrimination verdicts. Indeed, the analytical structure and content of disparate treatment adjudications, focusing as it does on the plausibility of defendant's proffered legitimate nondiscriminatory reasons for a challenged employment decision, can be expected to potentiate those forms of intergroup bias caused by stereotypic expectancies. Discrimination adjudications therefore may be even more vulnerable to cognitive forms of intergroup bias than the decision tasks which give rise to them.

An employer's determination, for example, whether a particular employee should be terminated is not much different from a court's determination whether an employer believed in good faith that a particular employee deserved to be terminated. Similarly, an employer judging whether a particular candidate is best qualified for a position is not particularly different from a court judging whether a particular candidate would reasonably have been viewed by a well-intentioned employer as the best qualified person for a position. Expectancy confirmation effects, such as those illustrated in Darley's and Gross's study discussed above, will distort both types of judgments. Thus, there is no reason to believe that the incidence of stereotype-induced judgment error in discrimination adjudications will differ in any significant way from its incidence in employment or educational decision making. Indeed, if as Darley and Gross suggest, exposure to ambiguous but ostensibly diagnostic collections of information potentiates expectancy confirmation bias, we can expect disparate treatment adjudications, with their "information rich texture," to suffer even more from such biases than hiring or educational admissions decisions, where relatively little diagnostic information is available and decision makers may be more on guard against making stereotypic judgments.

In short, from a cognitive process standpoint we cannot expect disparate treatment adjudications to be any less subject to subtle forms of intergroup bias than the decisions which give rise to them. Correspondingly, we cannot expect individualized adjudication of disparate treatment claims to be particularly effective in identifying or redressing cognitive discrimination. For this reason as for others, disparate treatment adjudication, like the colorblindness model of nondiscrimination and reliance on an objective concept of merit, is an extremely weak tool for combating cognitive forms of intergroup bias. We cannot expect these policies to do the work once accomplished by disparate impact theory, numerical standards, and the systematic, self-critical analysis of selection procedures. Unfortunately, when a person is color-blind, there is simply much he will not see. * * *

———

What is the explanation for the stubborn persistence of pervasive discrimination today? In what follows, R.A. Lenhardt draws on sociological research to argue that the focus should be on the racial harm, including citizenship harms arising from exclusion, instead of either disparate impact, or intent.

2. Sociology and Law: Stigma Theory

Understanding the Mark: Race, Stigma, and Equality in Context

79 N.Y.U. L. Rev. 803 (2005).

■ R.A. Lenhardt

* * *

* * * In fact, we are approaching a state in which many minority youths arguably stand a greater chance of being incarcerated than of obtaining a college degree and entering the economic mainstream. According to a recent study, of the approximately two million people in adult correctional facilities in the United States, an astounding 1.2 million, or 63%, are African–American or Latino, even though these groups together comprise only 25% of the total population.

These statistics paint a devastating picture of increasing racial separation and inequality along several fundamental life axes and demonstrate how far away we actually are from remedying the problem of racial disadvantage. The truth is that, in many ways, we are as racially divided a society today as we were before the Supreme Court's landmark decision in *Brown v. Board of Education* and the enactment of the Civil Rights Act of 1964. Where we live, go to school, and work are all still greatly determined by race. The question we must ask is: Why? What accounts for the stubborn persistence of the color line DuBois identified so many years ago? Why do racial disparities still exist?

For some time, the only legal framework available for understanding questions of racial inequity and disadvantage, reflected in cases such as *Washington v. Davis*, was that of intentional discrimination. Then, more than fifteen years ago, Professor Charles Lawrence revolutionized legal scholarship by arguing that the source of racial harm lay principally in unconsciously racist acts. Drawing on psychoanalytic theory and cognitive psychology, Lawrence's article, *The Id, The Ego, and Equal Protection: Reckoning with Unconscious Racism*, challenged the view that only intentionally discriminatory conduct ran the risk of imposing racial harm. Because of the cognitive processes and meanings associated with race in this country, Lawrence argued, racial motive was most often reflected in unconscious conduct bearing a disparate racial impact. He maintained that the messages communicated by facially neutral governmental actions were the best indicator of racist motive, and he therefore advocated greater judicial attention to the cultural or racial meaning of policy choices and initiatives.

This Article seeks to advance the conversation about the nature and contours of racial harm by asserting that we should be concerned, not with the meanings associated with conduct, but rather with the meanings associated with race itself. My argument is that racial stigma, not intentional discrimination or unconscious racism, is the true source of racial injury in the United States. This theory accounts for the persistence of racial disparities that mark the color line, as well as the incidence of intentionally discriminatory or racialized behavior. It conceives of these problems as a function of racial stigma, not vice versa. In this respect, it is perhaps the most comprehensive theory of racial harm advanced thus far.

[Lenhardt defines racial stigma as consisting of the following 4 characteristics:]

I.   WHAT IS RACIAL STIGMA?

* * * Brands were used as a way of identifying African slaves as human property up until the latter part of the eighteenth century and as a method of punishment well into the nineteenth century. When we talk about racial stigma today, however, we are almost never referring directly to the brands and cuts that were used to demarcate slave or outsider status. We plainly mean something different, something less physical and perhaps more cognitive in nature. The question is: What?

Even as the term racial stigma has become part of common parlance, it has escaped clear definition. An informal survey of individuals on the street likely would generate as many definitions as people interviewed. For some, it refers to demeaning racial insults or stereotypes. For others, it is synonymous with the concept of racial inferiority. Still others see it principally as a by-product of discriminatory treatment that excludes or denies a benefit on the basis of race. The connotation given the term seems to vary by individual and even by context.

Significantly, this holds true even among courts and legal scholars, who ordinarily might be expected to have a more uniform understanding of a concept that has been embraced as a key constitutional principle in the race context. The legal approach to racial stigma, for the most part, has mirrored the strategy that former Justice Potter Stewart infamously adopted in obscenity cases: "I know it when I see it." By contrast, with only a few refinements, social scientists seem to have employed the same basic understanding of stigma for some time. In this Section, I thus look principally outside the legal arena to social science for direction in defining what racial stigma is and how it functions.

1.   DEHUMANIZATION AND THE IMPOSITION OF VIRTUAL IDENTITY

Most lawyers are probably familiar with the social research on racial stigma that Dr. Kenneth Clark completed nearly fifty years ago as an expert in the litigation surrounding *Brown v. Board of Education*. In the social science world, however, the work of another social scientist—Erving Goffman—is most often cited in connection with questions surrounding the problem of racial stigma. Nearly forty years after it was first published, Goffman's book, STIGMA: NOTES ON THE MANAGEMENT OF SPOILED IDENTITY, continues to be regarded as one of the definitive texts in this area.

In Stigma, Goffman concerned himself with a single purpose: defining the problem of stigma. Looking to a variety of psychological, sociological, and historical studies and texts, he explored a range of stigma-inducing conditions and situations, including the so-called "tribal" or group-based stigmas such as "race, nation, and religion." Although Goffman also studied the etiology and function of stigmas relating to physical deformities and character "blemishes" attributed to a variety of conditions, the many insights he garnered through his research are extremely relevant to the race-focused inquiry that I take up here. Even today, virtually all social scientists accept the broad definition of stigma developed through his work, namely that "stigmatized persons possess an attribute that is deeply discrediting and that they are viewed as less than fully human because of it." * * *

2. Shared Negative Meanings about the Racially Stigmatized

* * * Racial stigma, at bottom, concerns the relationship between a group of individuals perceived as essentially similar and shared community beliefs about that group and the attributes they possess. While racist attitudes are held at an individual level as well, the group-level responses to racial difference are most important here. Part of the strength of the "societal devaluations" associated with race in this country is that "they cannot be dismissed as the ravings of some idiosyncratic bigot." They are shared and consensual, which means that they cannot easily be ignored. This, perhaps even more than the precise character of the messages conveyed about race, is what makes racial stigma such a powerful social force. The meanings ascribed to an attribute—i.e., that dark skin or an accent provide meaningful evidence of intellectual or moral inferiority—begin to form what constitutes "a socially shared sense of 'reality.'" * * *

3. The Automatic Nature of Responses to the Racially Stigmatized

The next stigma factor that contributes to broad-scale racial inequality relates to the automatic or unconscious nature of the responses the no stigmatized—and sometimes even minorities themselves—have to the racially stigmatized. The prevailing constitutional paradigm in the race context is, of course, the discrimination model discussed earlier. Under that model, embodied in cases such as Washington v. Davis, only conduct and policies that reflect discriminatory intent or motive can be actionable. No remedies exist for racialized, unconsciously committed behavior or policies that have merely a discriminatory impact.* * *

4. The Reinforcing Nature of Racial Stigma and Stereotypes

As previously noted, when asked to define racial stigma, people often confuse it with the problem of racial stereotypes, which have historically been defined as inaccurate or overbroad generalizations, but have more recently come to be understood as "cognitive categories" employed in processing information. Most "profoundly stigmatized social identities" have a myriad of well-accepted stereotypes associated with them: "Blacks are dumb"; "Latinos are lazy"; "Asians are smart, but conniving." The terms racial stigma and racial stereotype are, however, two analytically distinct concepts. Whereas racial stigma provides the negative meanings associated with race and accounts for the initial affective reactions individuals often have toward racial minorities, racial stereotypes help to explain the persistence of certain attitudes about and responses toward race and the racially stigmatized. In this way, they also are directly related not just to discrimination but to the broader problem of racial inequality.

Racial stigma and stereotypes, in some sense, play mutually reinforcing roles in the dehumanization and marginalization—social, as well as economic and political—of minority groups. On the one hand, racial stigma contributes to the development of negative racial stereotypes about stigmatized groups. It is thought that the social meanings conveyed by racial stigma actually influence the cognitive processes that lead to stereotype formation. As Glenn Loury notes, "The 'social meaning of race'—that is, the tacit understanding associated with 'blackness' [or dark skin] in the public's imagination, especially the negative connotations—biases the social cognitions and distorts the specifications of observing agents, inducing them to make causal misattributions [or categorizations] detrimental to" racial minorities.

CHAPTER 2

STATES, MARKETS AND THE PROBLEM OF GOVERNANCE

Introduction

Many decades ago, economist Arthur Okun observed:

American society proclaims the worth of every human being. All citizens are guaranteed equal justice and equal political rights. Everyone has a pledge of speedy response from the fire department and access to national monuments. As American citizens, we are all members of the same club.

Yet at the same time, our institutions say "find a job or go hungry," "succeed or suffer." They prod us to get ahead of our neighbors economically after telling us to stay in line socially. They award prizes that allow the big winners to feed their pets better than the losers can feed their children.[a]

Okun's point was that the United States is a capitalist democracy, with a "split-level institutional structure." Thus, many of the social institutions in which Americans live their daily lives are organized around capitalist "market" principles, according to which inequality of many kinds is a fact of life. At the same time, other social institutions in which Americans live their daily lives—particularly those institutions connected to government—are organized around egalitarian, "democratic" principles. In addition, democracy and equality are touchstones for how Americans talk about their group identities outside the state. When people speak of their racial and gender identities, for example, they often speak of the importance of social, cultural, and legal equality.

Legal rules create, regulate, and maintain both our "capitalist" institutions and our "democratic" ones. This book is designed to introduce readers to descriptive and normative issues concerning the operation of law in a capitalist democracy. Thinking about what might constitute "economic justice" requires us to think about markets, about culture, and about the state, and to think about their interrelationship. It requires us, as well, to think about how law operates in both capitalist and democratic realms, and about the shadow of the law in social worlds not governed directly either by state or market.

a. ARTHUR M. OKUN, EQUALITY AND EFFICIENCY: THE BIG TRADEOFF 1 (1975).

This chapter introduces a number of questions. In what ways does the law shape our market culture and our political culture? How does our society negotiate the tensions between the inequalities our market culture produces and exploits and the equality idealized by our political culture? What role does the law play in these negotiations? Which aspects of our social life should be governed by market principles and which by non-market principles? How should our society negotiate the resulting tensions? What role should the law play in negotiating these tensions? In light of all these considerations, what does economic justice mean?

It may be useful to begin with some terminology. The broadest way to think about economic justice is through the idea of political economy. Our capitalist democracy is made up of different kinds of institutions, some labeled political and some economic, and different sorts of institutions are organized according to different rules and norms. What is the relationship between the political and the economic realms? How do the norms of each differ? How does the law constitute and regulate each of these realms, and how does it conceptualize the relationship between them? Finally, how might the conventional distinctions between the political and the economic be criticized?

A.   LAW AND POLITICAL ECONOMY

Before economics existed as a discipline, there was political economy. As we will see in greater detail in chapter 3, the foundational thinkers in economics—including Adam Smith, Thomas Malthus, David Ricardo, and Karl Marx—considered their subject to include not only economic activity in the modern sense, but also the connection between economic activity and human flourishing. Adam Smith's great works, for example, include the *Wealth of Nations* and *The Theory of Moral Sentiments*: books that travel far beyond the contemporary purview of the discipline of economics.

In contemporary times, however—perhaps partly as a consequence of the nineteenth-century ideology of domesticity described in the excerpt from Frances Olsen below—we tend to think about the social world as being divided into separate spheres. The most common division—between the state, the market, and the family—places the political in the sphere of the state and the economic in the sphere of the market. This division, which we can call structural liberalism, suggests that the realms of the state, the market, and the family are inherently very different.

The assumption that the state, the market, and the family are separate and very different spheres of life has led to a number of consequences. One consequence is the way these spheres are described. As the excerpt from Olsen below explains in more detail, the state is usually conceptualized as public, whereas the family is usually described as private. The market is sometimes described as public and sometimes as private. The public/private distinction, moreover, is imagined as a relationship of opposites.

A second consequence of structural liberalism is the emergence of different kinds of methods to describe and analyze different spheres. Thus, in contemporary life, people often use the language of economics and efficiency to talk about market institutions, whereas they use the moral language of fairness or equity to talk about state institutions. Efficiency and equity, like the public and the private, are popularly believed to be opposites, inherently in tension with one another. The language of economics, moreover, employs rhetoric of objectivity and neutrality, eschewing questions of values, meaning, and justice. The language of fairness and equity, in contrast, has recently attracted postmodern and critical thinkers who are skeptical of concepts of objectivity and neutrality.

Structural liberalism affects how students are trained and what experts see as the proper domain of their expertise. A third consequence of structural liberalism, then, is a specialization of expertise between those who study the world of facts and those who study the world of meaning—a dichotomy deplored by C.P. Snow in a famous article on what he called the two cultures of the sciences and the humanities. Students in economics departments learn very little about moral philosophy or other disciplines that take fairness seriously. Conversely, philosophy students and humanities scholars typically know very little about economics. The split continues in professional life. Economic experts and policymakers tend not to use the language of fairness or investigate questions of distribution, while experts and policymakers interested in questions of justice and fairness tend not to have much to say about economic efficiency. The essay by Anthony Taibi excerpted below deplores this consequence of structural liberalism from the perspective of people who care about racial justice.

A fourth consequence of structural liberalism is the tendency to speak of the division between state, family, and market not only as a descriptive truth but as a prescription for action. For instance, it is commonly debated whether and when government should or should not intervene in the market, or whether and when government should or should not interfere with the family. This kind of debate can be very misleading, however, for at some level the state is always involved in creating and maintaining both market and family institutions. Governments, for example, formulate and enforce contract and property rights, without which markets could not function; and markets are regulated by domestic and international trade rules, including antitrust laws and tariff regulation. Similarly, marriage is a recognized legal institution with rights and responsibilities that are formulated by legislatures and enforced by courts, as well as being a private relationship of love and intimacy. It is important, therefore, not to confuse description with prescription, and to understand that arguments for or against government interference in the market or the family are really arguments about the costs and benefits of specific kinds of government action.

As you read the materials below, consider the various ways in which state, market, and family are defined as being separate and distinct. Consider also the ways in which they are interrelated with one another, and the ways in which they are all regulated by law. How is the split between public and private reflected in constitutional law? How is the distinction between political and civil rights, on the one hand, and social and economic rights, on the other, reflected in international and in U.S. law? How might things be different?

1.   STRUCTURAL LIBERALISM AND ITS CRITIQUES

The Family and the Market: A Study of Ideology and Legal Reform

96 HARV. L. REV. 1497 (1983).

■ FRANCES OLSEN

* * * In the early nineteenth century, as men's work was largely removed to the factory while women's work remained primarily in the home, there came to be a sharp dichotomy between "the home" and "the [workaday] world." This dichotomy took on many of the moral overtones developed in the theological dichotomy between heaven and earth. Often the home was referred to as "sacred," and home life was the reward for which men should be willing to suffer in the earthly world of work. The family and home were seen as safe repositories for the virtues and emotions that people believed were being banished from the world of commerce and industry. The home was said to provide a haven from the anxieties of modern life—"a shelter for those moral and spiritual values which the commercial spirit and the critical spirit were threatening to destroy."

At the same time that the home was being glorified, it was being devalued. The woman's sphere was for men "the object of yearning, and yet of scorn." Ann Douglas has pointed out that, while men sentimentalized the family and exalted domesticity, they continued to behave in the marketplace as if they believed that "profane," worldly goals represented the greatest good. * * *

Further, while the world of the marketplace was decried for being selfish, debasing, and exploitative, it was also admired and esteemed. Self-reliance, progress, modernization—each had positive connotations that were associated with the world of commerce and industry. Rationality, discipline, and a focus on objective reality were considered desirable aspects of the "male" sphere of the market. Moreover, although the values of domesticity were used to criticize the destructiveness of marketplace values and the pursuit of wealth, they nevertheless served to "undercut opposition to exploitative pecuniary standards in the work world, by upholding a 'separate sphere' of comfort and compensation, instilling a morality that would encourage self control, and fostering the idea that preservation of home and family sentiment was an ultimate goal."

Given this simultaneous glorification and denigration of both the home and the marketplace, it should be no surprise that the sharp split between the two spheres had complex effects upon women. The market/family dichotomy tended to exclude women from the world of the marketplace while promising them a central role in the supposedly equally important domestic sphere. The dichotomy encouraged women to be generous and nurturant but discouraged them from being strong and self reliant; it insulated women from the world's corruption but denied them the world's stimulation. While the dichotomy tended to mask the inferior, degraded position of women, it also provided a degree of autonomy and a base from which women could and did elevate their status. * * *

A.   The Free Market and the Private Family: The Principle of Nonintervention

Although the woman's sphere has been described as "private" and contrasted with the "public sphere of the marketplace and government," such a characterization can be misleading. There are two different dichotomies involved in this contrast: on one hand, a dichotomy between the market, considered public, and the family, considered private; on the other hand, a dichotomy between the state, considered public, and civil society, considered private. Both the market and the family are thought of as part of "private" civil society in opposition to the "public" state. Calling both the marketplace and the state "public" can thus confuse our thinking about the two dichotomies.

It is important to recognize the distinction between the state/civil society dichotomy and the market/family dichotomy, because the former dichotomy plays itself out in an analogous manner on both sides of the latter. In discourse on the market, the state/civil society dichotomy appears as the issue of state regulation of the economy; in discourse on the family, it appears as the issue of state interference in the family. The classic laissez-faire arguments against state regulation of the free market find a striking parallel in the arguments against state interference with the private family. The two sets of arguments, and the ideals that underlie them, share a great deal more than just hostility to government. Both are constructed of similar elements and subject to similar attacks; our understanding of each is enriched by our understanding of the other.

1. The Free Market.—It is possible briefly to summarize the basic themes of laissez-faire theory without denying the richness or complexity of the theory. Laissez-faire theory depends upon the notion of a free and autonomous market. Although the free market does not have to be considered an object or a thing, "the market" must at least be considered a coherent and sensible way of talking and thinking about economic relations among people. Further, laissez-faire theory posits that the market is "natural" in that it reflects actual supply and demand, and "autonomous" in that it was not created by the state and can function independently of the state. Laissez faire theory both assumes and asserts that it makes sense to advocate state neutrality with respect to the market. Economic and social inequalities that persist after the institution of the liberal state (that is, the institution of "political equality") are deemed to be natural and beyond the proper scope of state activity. Thus, although laissez-faire theorists believe that people should be considered equal in their relations with the state, these theorists characterize the domination and subordination that accompany economic and social inequality in civil society as private matters that do not implicate the political state. A departure from laissez-faire policies is asserted to constitute an effort by the state to alter an inequality that otherwise exists quite independently of the state. Enforcement of contract, tort, and property law is compatible with laissez-faire doctrine only as long as the courts merely facilitate free market transactions without jeopardizing or compromising state neutrality.

Some critics of laissez faire accept the claim that laissez-faire policies would actually represent state neutrality with respect to an autonomous free market, but nevertheless reject these policies and urge that the state should regulate the economy to lessen some of the damaging effects of free market inequality. Thus, proponents of laissez-faire policy have had to assert not only that nonintervention is possible, but also that it is preferable to any form of state intervention.

Two classic arguments have been advanced to support nonintervention. The first is based on the theory that, although the natural market functions effectively, it is fragile. Just as introducing rabbits into Australia disrupted the continent's natural ecology, so, too, the attempt to mitigate human suffering by tinkering with one aspect of the market may cause quite unexpected and severe suffering with regard to other aspects of the market.

The second classic argument emphasizes the extreme strength and durability of the market. The claim here is that the free market is characterized by strong natural forces that will overcome and nullify any but the most radical efforts to impose state control on the economy, and that nothing less than socialism or total state abolition of the free market will have any lasting effect. Such theorists consider a court's refusal to enforce "harsh" or "oppressive" contract terms or a legislature's attempt to abolish cognovit notes to be reforms doomed to failure. The very same "unequal bargaining position" that is appealed to in support of such reforms can be used to demonstrate their futility. One contract term may be forbidden, but it will be replaced by another or by an adjustment in price; thus, assuming that the basic conditions of supply and demand remain unchanged, bargaining power will stay about the same, and parties will continue to form contracts that reflect this bargaining power.

2.   *The Private Family.*—* * *

The basic assumptions that underlie arguments in favor of the private family are similar to those underlying the arguments in favor of the free market. The first assumption is that "the family" is a coherent way of talking about certain relations among people. Another assumption is that the family is capable of existing in some sense apart from state activity, as a natural formation rather than only as a creation of the state.

The issue of state neutrality with respect to the family is more complicated than that of neutrality with respect to the market. Neutrality toward the market means treating the participants in economic life as juridical equals. The state is said to take a neutral stance toward the family, however, when it ratifies the preexisting social roles within the family.

In contrast to the market, in which universal selfish behavior is supposed to result in the betterment of society, the family has generally been expected to be based on less individualistic principles. The good of all is to be achieved not by each family member's pursuit of individual goals, but rather by sharing and sacrifice among family members. At one time the social good was thought to require the husband to control his wife; and children were, and to an extent still are, expected to obey their parents for the sake of a better society. Parents have often been expected to sacrifice their immediate individual interests for the sake of their children. The morality of altruism has been supposed to animate the family to the same extent that the morality of individualism has been supposed to pervade the marketplace.

The state has traditionally been expected to facilitate sacrifice and sharing within the family by ratifying the social roles assigned to family members; thus, it would be considered intervention for the state to treat the members of a family as juridical equals. At one time, for example, the father's social role entitled him to control the children. If the mother were to leave him and take the children with her, the courts would ordinarily be expected to force her to return them to him; for courts to refuse to do so would be considered state interference with the family.

Today, courts are still ordinarily expected to ratify the social role of parents as disciplinarians. For example, if a court were to allow a child to recover tort damages from her parents for confining her to her room as punishment, most people would consider this a serious state intrusion into the family, even though the parents' act would have been false imprisonment had it been committed by a third party.

The notion of noninterference in the family depends upon some shared conception of proper family roles, and "neutrality" can be understood only with reference to such roles. For example, one of the bases upon which statutes limiting access to contraceptives have been struck down is that such statutes intrude upon the marital relation. Governmental programs providing minors with access to contraceptives, however, are also condemned as state interference in the family. Thus, "interference" is not a simple description of state action or inaction, but rather a way of condemning particular state policies, usually those aimed at changing the status quo. The status quo itself is treated as something natural and not as the responsibility of the state. Actual inequality and domination in the family— as in the free market—are represented as private matters that the state did not bring about, although it could undertake to change them.

* * *

B. *Standard Critiques of the Free Market and the Private Family*

1. The Market.—The attack upon the accuracy and coherence of the laissez-faire image of the free market had two major components. First, the notion that the market is private and capable of existing separately from the state was challenged. Commentators argued that "systems advocated by professed upholders of laissez faire" were "in reality permeated with coercive restrictions of individual freedom." Furthermore, these coercive restrictions did not conform to "any formula of 'equal opportunity' or of 'preserving the equal rights of others.'" State interference, it was claimed, was unavoidable and would inevitably "affect the distribution of income and the direction of economic activities." Because government neutrality was an impossibility, a laissez-faire economy was a false ideal.

The second component of this attack was a demonstration that the government was not in fact neutral, but instead benefited certain entrepreneurs at the expense of working people. In making this argument, some commentators assumed that it would be theoretically possible to fashion workable laissez-faire policies, but pointed out that in practice these were "never . . . carried out consistently." The extreme version of this argument would suggest that laissez faire is a smokescreen used by representatives of large industries to limit popular control of business. The same industries, it could be argued, would not really want an across-the-board laissez-faire policy, because they actually depend upon probusiness regulation.

An argument that draws on both components of the attack on laissez faire treats so called "private law as a state grant of partial sovereignty to one of the economic actors." Thus, contract law does not simply put into effect the agreement of the parties; rather, the mechanisms for enforcing contract put "the sovereign power of the state at the disposal of one party to be exercised over the other party." Similarly, private property is seen to confer on its owner the "sovereign power [of] compelling service and obedience" from those who need access to the property. This vision of property and contract law undermines the notion that the state can be a noncoercive, neutral arbiter in the market.

2. The Family.—Arguments similar to those developed in the attack on laissez faire have been used to undermine the basis for state refusal to "intervene" in the private family. One such argument attempts to demonstrate that the state cannot be neutral because it cannot help imposing coercive restrictions upon the freedom of family members. For example, although noninterventionists argue that the state should not interfere to prevent wife abuse, courts will have to deal somehow with cases in which battered wives kill their husbands. The simple principle of nonintervention in the family gives no clear direction for deciding such cases; it will not dictate whether criminal charges should be brought against these women or whether wife battering should mitigate or provide a defense to homicide. Yet the determination of such questions will inevitably affect the distribution of power within violent marriages and thus the social relations of families.

The second component of the attack on the private nature of the family is the claim that, even if the state could be neutral vis-à-vis the family, it in fact is not. The theory of the private family, it is argued, is not consistently carried out. Instead, the assertion that family affairs should be private has been made by men to prevent women and children from using state power to improve the conditions of their lives. By insisting that the family should not be subject to state regulation, men have been able to retain their excessive power. Furthermore, men in fact use the coercive power of the state to reinforce and consolidate their authority over wives and children.

The argument that nonintervention serves to empower husbands to dominate their wives and children has been particularly useful in the attack upon the claimed neutrality of the state with respect to the family. During the first half of the nineteenth century, state neutrality meant the ratification and reinforcement of social roles within the family that were openly hierarchical. Husbands were expected to control their wives, and wives were expected to obey their husbands. Nineteenth century feminists attacked the state for granting husbands sovereignty within the family, and asserted that the state itself was creating inequality when it endorsed separate social roles and realms of activities for the different members of the family. According to Lucretia Mott, the subjugation of wives by husbands was not apostolic but was "done by law and public opinion." Lucy Stone and Henry Blackwell protested that the marriage laws "confer[red] upon the husband an injurious and unnatural superiority, investing him with legal powers which no honorable man would exercize, and which no man should possess."

* * *

One response to feminist attacks on the claimed neutrality of the state was the gradual enactment of laws that seemed more neutral. During the late nineteenth century and the twentieth century, much of the law providing for juridical superiority of the male was replaced by statutes and court decisions providing for juridical equality. The effect of this legal change upon the actual subordination of women has been debated, but what is of interest here is the extent to which the assertion of state neutrality between juridically equal husbands and wives is open to the same attacks as is the asserted state neutrality between juridically equal entrepreneurs and workers. The move toward legal equality does represent a change in the mode of explaining or denying the inferior status of women. It can be seen as a shift from a direct to an indirect mode of legitimating the subordination of women. Just as the notion of different, essentially incomparable spheres had replaced the claim that God created women inferior to men, so the notion of separate spheres was supplanted by the claim that men and women were actually equal.

* * *

I do not advocate replacing the present dichotomies with an all powerful state and an all embracing market any more than I would advocate making women just like men. The state as it now exists must be ended at the same time that civil society as it now exists is ended; and when we transform the contemporary family, we must simultaneously transform the market. * * *

Contract Law, the Free Market, and State Intervention: A Jurisprudential Perspective

STATE, SOCIETY AND CORPORATE POWER 17, 17–23 (Marc R. Tool & Warren J. Samuels eds., 2d ed. 1989).

■ ROBERT B. SEIDMAN

It frequently is argued that the more the state plans, the more power is placed in the hands of the planners. Social engineering begets power, and Lord Acton long ago warned us that power tends to corrupt.

The classical response has been the celebration of the free market economy. Social engineering and planning are perceived as the very opposites of the free market; intervention is the opposite of nonintervention. The legal expression of social engineering is perceived as a set of commands directed by the state to various citizens. The legal expression of the free market is perceived as facilitative law, of which the law of contract is the archetype. As social engineering is the opposite of a free market, so command law is the opposite of facilitative law.

* * *

Many sorts of law on their face are rules expressing how the lawmaker expects the targets of the law to behave, on pain of sanction. Criminal law and tort law fit this model nicely. A rule is promulgated; if a person violates the rule he is punished, either directly as in criminal law, or through the imposition of a judgment for damages.

Many other sorts of rules, however, seem to be cut from a different bolt of cloth. Contract law does not require people to do anything. It merely prescribes that if certain agreements are entered upon, and broken, the courts may be required to levy a sanction. General corporation laws do not require anyone to enter upon a corporation. They provide a facilitative form. If parties wish to enter into a corporate relationship, the law prescribes some of the consequences. Because role occupants are not required to enter upon particular contracts, or to enter into particular organizations, the facilitative form seems to free the role occupant of coercion and to release him from the shadow of overarching power.

Is it true that facilitative law frees the role occupant from coercion? We shall denote the two contrary answers to this question as the classical and the anticlassical views.

THE CLASSICAL PERSPECTIVE

The classical paradigm asserts that facilitative law does free the citizen from state coercion. Long ago Sir Henry Maine said that the movement of all progressive societies heretofore has been from status to contract. By this

Sir Henry meant that "the Individual is substituted for the Family, as the unit of which civil laws take account. . . . Starting, as from one terminus of history, from a condition of society in which all the relations of Persons are summed up in the relations of Family, we seem to have steadily moved towards a phase of social order in which all these relations arise from the free agreement of individuals."

Jurisprudential theories were developed which gave ideological support for the theme of contract. Thomas Hobbes said that the definition of injustice "is no other than the nonperformance of Covenant." Nietzsche, perhaps sarcastically, was even more extravagant: "To breed an animal that is able to make promises—is that not precisely the . . . task which Nature set for herself as regards man"?

Contract is a device for social cooperation. In a highly complex society, people must do many different things. Manufacturers must buy from suppliers, employ labor, sell to customers; landlords must rent to tenants; submanufacturers must contract with manufacturers; wholesalers and retailers and customers must interact with each other to keep the vast engine of the economy moving.

Without planned organization of the interchanges necessitated by the division of labor, it seems preferable for every man to seize his own opportunity. Through contract, the parties to an exchange define the norms of conduct for the occasion. The market becomes a giant communication system, by its "Invisible Hand" advising individuals the sort of norms to demand and accept in order to maximize their personal benefit.

From the point of view of the parties to the contract, they merely exercise a personal freedom to conduct their affairs in accordance with their emergent needs and desires. They exercise freedom by themselves determining the norms to which they will be bound.

The notion that contract law embodies "freedom" is closely intertwined with the ideal type of the market economy. If perfect competition prevails, then, by definition, no individual has the power to affect market price. The availability of other potential bargaining partners, who offer their services or goods on terms and conditions defined not by themselves, but by the Invisible Hand of the market, protect the parties each from arbitrary power in the other.

What ideal type of legal order is apt for this ideal conceptualization of the economic order? Unless one can exclude others from interfering with his possession of things, he will not purchase them. The law of property and of torts purports to guarantee rights of peaceable possession. Unless there are guarantees that the law of marginal utility will not continue to operate after a bargain is struck, promises for future performance become mere pious intentions. The law of contract purports to ensure that promises, once made, will be kept.

The classical view implies a model of the state as a value neutral framework whose task it is to ensure only that in case of dispute these bodies of law are enforced. It presupposes a sharp discontinuity between the private sphere, between state action and state non-action. The former consists of intervention and social engineering; the latter consists of adjudicating disputes arising in the private sector. In this view, the laissez-faire ideal of the state is the very opposite of social engineering. State inaction is markedly different from state action.

We can summarize the classical perspective in a series of propositions. (1) Facilitative law permits the parties to an interaction to determine their own norms of conduct. (2) The perfect competitive market ensure that neither party has power over the other. (3) The state is a neutral, impartial framework within which bargaining can take place peaceably and conflict can be resolved peaceably. (4) The state, by limiting its function to conflict resolution, does not engage in ordering the society; there is, therefore, a sharp discontinuity between state inaction and state action. (5) Facilitative law therefore ensures "voluntariness."

THE ANTICLASSICAL PERSPECTIVE

The anticlassical paradigm is at issue with the classical on all but the first of these propositions. Facilitative law does permit the parties to the transaction to determine between themselves the norms defining their interchange. Through it, the state delegates to the contracting parties a portion of its sovereign power. The two parties legislate for themselves in the act of bargaining; they lay down rules; the state proceeds to enforce them. "From this point of view the law of contract may be viewed as a subsidiary branch of public law, as a body of rules according to which the sovereign power of the state will be exercised in accordance to the rules agreed upon between the parties to a more or less voluntary transaction."

Parties to bargains are seldom of equal bargaining strength. To the extent that they are not, contract, however it may appear to the parties, is not a matter of freedom of choice, but of command. Is it significantly different to say to a man, "I will pay you a wage if you will work for me?" rather than, "You will get no wage unless you work for me"? Two hundred years ago Lord Chancellor Northington expressed it succinctly: "Necessitous men are not, truly speaking, free men."

At law, to treat unequals notionally as equals is in fact to elevate the stronger to a position of domination. In a bargaining situation, the stronger imposes upon the weaker the norms of conduct which he desires. * * *

The power to create norms of conduct, that is, to legislate, plus the use of state power to enforce them are two of the three familiar attributes of government. The net result of contract law is to transfer to the economically superior classes in the community the most significant powers of the state, all under the fictional disguise of equality and freedom. Facilitative law and "voluntariness" begin with notions of "freedom." They end by subjecting the weaker party to the power of the stronger. Facilitative law manipulates the weaker party, as does planning law or social engineering. The principal difference lies in who does the manipulating.

* * *

The anticlassical understanding of facilitative law, therefore, focuses upon the framework of institutions within which bargains are struck and upon the power relationships of the parties. A bargain implies "freedom" only in that, *given the available alternatives*, both parties prefer the bargain struck. It is the framework which structures the alternatives available to each party which determines the extent of their volitional freedom.

It is further argued that the model of the value neutral state providing an impartial framework within which conflict can be resolved peaceably is not only empirically but also theoretically impossible. A decision-making structure—and the state is, par excellence, a decision-making structure—cannot be value neutral. The rules that define any decision-making process necessarily limit the range of potential inputs, conversion processes, and feedback functions. These rules, to that degree, predetermine the outputs, that is, the decisions. The state, perceived as a framework for the resolution of conflict, is a decision-making structure. No more than can any other decision-making structure can it be value neutral. * * *

The state must, willy-nilly, favor some and disadvantage others. For the state to stand by and permit the private activity of citizens to determine the configurations of the economy is as much state action as overt intervention. *Cui bono*? is not simply a possible query; it is the most significant question of all.

We can summarize the anticlassical model in a set of propositions. (1) Facilitative law permits the parties to an interaction to determine their own norms of conduct. (2) Facilitative law ensures that the more powerful party to an interchange will impose his desires upon the weaker. Further, the perfectly free market does not and cannot exist as a protection against the imposition of private power. (3) The state, by enforcing private agreements, lends its reserve monopoly of violence to enforce the norms agreed upon by the parties to the interchange. (4) Since every decision-making function is necessarily value laden, the state is not and cannot be a value neutral arbiter. (5) The enforcement of private bargains made under the guise of facilitative law is therefore as much a form of state intervention as more direct commands from the state to citizens. (6) Facilitative law therefore ensures that the state will delegate its power to the more powerful party to the exchange.

    * * *

NOTES AND QUESTIONS

1. Structural liberalism across political spectrum. Structural liberalism, as Olsen and Seidman describe it, governs the thinking of political conservatives and libertarians as well as traditional liberals. As chapter 3 explores in more detail, those on the political right typically argue that political freedom and individual happiness require a relatively small public sphere and a large private sphere; those on the political left typically argue the opposite. Political conservatives and liberals also argue over whether there should be some kind of minimum "social safety net" for people at the very bottom of the economy and, if so, the size and composition of this net. Both sides of the debate, however, treat the public sphere and the private sphere as being inherently different; their arguments are over the relative size and priority of these spheres.

2. Jurisprudential critiques of public/private distinction. As Olsen's and Seidman's excerpts indicate, one criticism of the so-called "public/private distinction" is that it conceals normative assumptions about the role of law. Several generations of legal theorists have made this point. For example, in the 1920s, scholars identifying themselves with the Legal Realist movement sharply criticized the view that rules that abridge common law rights, especially property rights, constitute state "intervention" in the market. For the Legal Realists, property rights are already a creation of the state, so changing their distribution is not a special "intervention" in anything. The idea of "laissez-faire" economics—that one should allow the market to "naturally" allocate goods without state intervention—is therefore an illusion; markets themselves are a creation of the state. *See, e.g.*, Robert L. Hale, *Coercion and Distribution in a Supposedly Non–Coercive State*, 38 POL. SCI. Q. 470 (1923); Morris R. Cohen, *Property and Sovereignty*, 13 CORNELL L.Q. 8 (1927); Robert L. Hale, *Rate Making and the Revision of the Property Concept*, 22 COLUM. L. REV. 209 (1922); Note, *Peppercorn Theory of Consideration and the Doctrine of Fair Exchange*, 35 COLUM. L. REV. 1090 (1935).

The critique was picked up in the 1980s by the Critical Legal Studies movement and by the feminist legal theory movement, movements with which Olsen herself was affiliated. CLS scholars attacked dichotomies of all sorts in legal rhetoric, including the public/private distinction, arguing that they inhibited clear thinking about justice and social change. *See, e.g.*, MARK KELMAN, A GUIDE TO CRITICAL LEGAL STUDIES 103 (1987) (observing that CLS scholars have both reiterated the Realist point that "the state is inextricably involved in the supposedly private realm," and "noted the extent to which coercion and choicelessness can readily exist in the realms traditionally denominated private"). Feminist scholars, like Olsen, criticized the public/private distinction for its tendency to ignore the politics of the family. For more recent versions of the feminist argument, see, Susan Moller Okin, *Justice and Gender: An Unfinished Debate*, 72 FORDHAM L. REV. 1537 (2004); Tracy E. Higgins, *Why Feminists Can't (or Shouldn't) Be Liberals*, 72 FORDHAM L. REV. 1629 (2004).

A version of this argument applied to contemporary United States constitutional law has been made by Cass Sunstein. Sunstein argues that the justices of the Supreme Court tend to treat common law distributions of wealth labeled "private"—for example, distributions in the form of property and contract rights—as the "baseline" from which to perceive state action. As a result, state-initiated social welfare programs look like "intervention," or "takings." *See also* Gary Peller & Mark Tushnet, *Charles L. Black, Jr.: State Action and a New Birth of Freedom*, 92 GEO.

L.J. 779 (2004) (tracing a form of the argument to an essay by Charles Black published in 1967).

----

2. STRUCTURAL LIBERALISM AND CONSTITUTIONAL LAW

It is often observed that the United States constitutional structure protects some kinds of rights—political and civil rights—but not others, namely social and economic rights. Sometimes this is explained as stemming from the distinction between positive and negative rights: the U.S. Constitution attempts to protect citizens from the abuse of government power, but does not require the government to provide its citizens with anything. Other times, the lack of economic and social rights in the U.S. Constitution is explained as an outgrowth of structural liberalism: the kind of governance appropriate to the market does not include rights. In any case, political liberals who favor a strong welfare state have frequently found themselves stymied by the lack of constitutional support. Consider the opinion in DeShaney, below, and its relationship to structural liberalism.

DeShaney v. Winnebago County Dep't of Soc. Servs.

489 U.S. 189 (1989).

■ CHIEF JUSTICE REHNQUIST delivered the opinion of the Court.

Petitioner is a boy who was beaten and permanently injured by his father, with whom he lived. Respondents are social workers and other local officials who received complaints that petitioner was being abused by his father and had reason to believe that this was the case, but nonetheless did not act to remove petitioner from his father's custody. Petitioner sued respondents claiming that their failure to act deprived him of his liberty in violation of the Due Process Clause of the Fourteenth Amendment to the United States Constitution. We hold that it did not.

I

The facts of this case are undeniably tragic. Petitioner Joshua DeShaney was born in 1979. In 1980, a Wyoming court granted his parents a divorce and awarded custody of Joshua to his father, Randy DeShaney. The father shortly thereafter moved to Neenah, a city located in Winnebago County, Wisconsin, taking the infant Joshua with him. There he entered into a second marriage, which also ended in divorce.

The Winnebago County authorities first learned that Joshua DeShaney might be a victim of child abuse in January 1982, when his father's second wife complained to the police, at the time of their divorce, that he had previously "hit the boy causing marks and [was] a prime case for child abuse." The Winnebago County Department of Social Services (DSS) interviewed the father, but he denied the accusations, and DSS did not pursue them further. In January 1983, Joshua was admitted to a local hospital with multiple bruises and abrasions. The examining physician suspected child abuse and notified DSS, which immediately obtained an order from a Wisconsin juvenile court placing Joshua in the temporary custody of the hospital. Three days later, the county convened an ad hoc "Child Protection Team" consisting of a pediatrician, a psychologist, a police detective, the county's lawyer, several DSS caseworkers, and various hospital personnel to consider Joshua's situation. At this meeting, the Team decided that there was insufficient evidence of child abuse to retain Joshua in the custody of the court. The Team did, however, decide to recommend several measures to protect Joshua, including enrolling him in a preschool program, providing his father with certain counselling services, and encouraging his father's girlfriend to move out of the home. Randy DeShaney entered into a voluntary agreement with DSS in which he promised to cooperate with them in accomplishing these goals.

Based on the recommendation of the Child Protection Team, the juvenile court dismissed the child protection case and returned Joshua to the custody of his father. A month later, emergency room personnel called the DSS caseworker handling Joshua's case to report that he had once again been treated for suspicious injuries. The caseworker concluded that there was no basis for action.

For the next six months, the caseworker made monthly visits to the DeShaney home, during which she observed a number of suspicious injuries on Joshua's head; she also noticed that he had not been enrolled in school, and that the girlfriend had not moved out. The caseworker dutifully recorded these incidents in her files, along with her continuing suspicions that someone in the DeShaney household was physically abusing Joshua, but she did nothing more. In November 1983, the emergency room notified DSS that Joshua had been treated once again for injuries that they believed to be caused by child abuse. On the caseworker's next two visits to the DeShaney home, she was told that Joshua was too ill to see her. Still DSS took no action.

In March 1984, Randy DeShaney beat 4-year-old Joshua so severely that he fell into a life-threatening coma. Emergency brain surgery revealed a series of hemorrhages caused by traumatic injuries to the head inflicted over a long period of time. Joshua did not die, but he suffered brain damage so severe that he is expected to spend the rest of his life confined to an institution for the profoundly retarded. Randy DeShaney was subsequently tried and convicted of child abuse.

Joshua and his mother brought this action under 42 U.S.C. § 1983 in the United States District Court for the Eastern District of Wisconsin against respondents Winnebago County, DSS, and various individual employees of DSS. The complaint alleged that respondents had deprived Joshua of his liberty without due process of law, in violation of his rights under the Fourteenth Amendment, by failing to intervene to protect him against a risk of violence at his father's hands of which they knew or should have known. The District Court granted summary judgment for respondents.

The Court of Appeals for the Seventh Circuit affirmed.[1] * * *

The Due Process Clause of the Fourteenth Amendment provides that "[n]o State shall . . . deprive any person of life, liberty, or property, without due process of law." Petitioners contend that the State deprived Joshua of his liberty interest in "free[dom] from . . . unjustified intrusions on personal security," by failing to provide him with adequate protection against his father's violence. The claim is one invoking the substantive rather than the procedural component of the Due Process Clause; petitioners do not claim that the State denied Joshua protection without according him appropriate procedural safeguards, but that it was categorically obligated to protect him in these circumstances.

But nothing in the language of the Due Process Clause itself requires the State to protect the life, liberty, and property of its citizens against invasion by private actors. The Clause is phrased as a limitation on the State's power to act, not as a guarantee of certain minimal levels of safety and security. It forbids the State itself to deprive individuals of life, liberty, or property without "due process of law," but its language cannot fairly be extended to impose an affirmative obligation on the State to ensure that those interests do not come to harm through other means. Nor does history support such an expansive reading of the constitutional text. Like its counterpart in the Fifth Amendment, the Due Process Clause of the Fourteenth Amendment was intended to prevent government "from abusing [its] power, or employing it as an instrument of oppression." * * * Its purpose was to protect the people from the State, not to ensure that the State protected them from each other. The Framers were content to leave the extent of governmental obligation in the latter area to the democratic political processes.

Consistent with these principles, our cases have recognized that the Due Process Clauses generally confer no affirmative right to governmental aid, even where such aid may be necessary to secure life, liberty, or property interests of which the government itself may not deprive the individual.[2] * * * As we said in *Harris v. McRae*: "Although the liberty protected by the Due Process Clause affords protection against unwarranted *government* interference . . ., it does not confer an entitlement to such [governmental aid] as may be necessary to realize all the advantages of that freedom."[3] If the Due Process Clause does not require the State to provide

---

1. 812 F.2d 298 (1987).

2. See, *e.g., Harris v. McRae*, 448 U.S. 297, 317–318 (1980) (no obligation to fund abortions or other medical services) (discussing Due Process Clause of Fifth Amendment); *Lindsey v. Normet*, 405 U.S. 56, 74 (1972) (no obligation to provide adequate housing) (discussing Due Process Clause of

Fourteenth Amendment); see also *Youngberg v. Romeo*, [457 U.S. 307,] 317 ("As a general matter, a State is under no constitutional duty to provide substantive services for those within its border").

3. 448 U.S., at 317–318 (emphasis added).

its citizens with particular protective services, it follows that the State cannot be held liable under the Clause for injuries that could have been averted had it chosen to provide them. As a general matter, then, we conclude that a State's failure to protect an individual against private violence simply does not constitute a violation of the Due Process Clause.

* * *

■ JUSTICE BLACKMUN, dissenting.

Today, the Court purports to be the dispassionate oracle of the law, unmoved by "natural sympathy." * * * But, in this pretense, the Court itself retreats into a sterile formalism which prevents it from recognizing either the facts of the case before it or the legal norms that should apply to those facts. As JUSTICE BRENNAN demonstrates, the facts here involve not mere passivity, but active state intervention in the life of Joshua DeShaney—intervention that triggered a fundamental duty to aid the boy once the State learned of the severe danger to which he was exposed.

The Court fails to recognize this duty because it attempts to draw a sharp and rigid line between action and inaction. But such formalistic reasoning has no place in the interpretation of the broad and stirring Clauses of the Fourteenth Amendment. Indeed, I submit that these Clauses were designed, at least in part, to undo the formalistic legal reasoning that infected antebellum jurisprudence, which the late Professor Robert Cover analyzed so effectively in his significant work entitled Justice Accused (1975).

Like the antebellum judges who denied relief to fugitive slaves, see *id.*, at 119–121, the Court today claims that its decision, however harsh, is compelled by existing legal doctrine. On the contrary, the question presented by this case is an open one, and our Fourteenth Amendment precedents may be read more broadly or narrowly depending upon how one chooses to read them. Faced with the choice, I would adopt a "sympathetic" reading, one which comports with dictates of fundamental justice and recognizes that compassion need not be exiled from the province of judging. Cf. A. Stone, Law, Psychiatry, and Morality 262 (1984) ("We will make mistakes if we go forward, but doing nothing can be the worst mistake. What is required of us is moral ambition. Until our composite sketch becomes a true portrait of humanity we must live with our uncertainty; we will grope, we will struggle, and our compassion may be our only guide and comfort").

Poor Joshua! Victim of repeated attacks by an irresponsible, bullying, cowardly, and intemperate father, and abandoned by respondents who placed him in a dangerous predicament and who knew or learned what was going on, and yet did essentially nothing except, as the Court revealingly observes, *ante*, at 193, "dutifully recorded these incidents in [their] files." It is a sad commentary upon American life, and constitutional principles— so full of late of patriotic fervor and proud proclamations about "liberty and justice for all"—that this child, Joshua DeShaney, now is assigned to live out the remainder of his life profoundly retarded. Joshua and his mother, as petitioners here, deserve—but now are denied by this Court—

the opportunity to have the facts of their case considered in the light of the constitutional protection that 42 U.S.C. § 1983 is meant to provide.

————

State Action Is Always Present

3 Chi. J. Int'l L. 465 (2002).

■ Cass R. Sunstein

What is the place of social and economic guarantees in a democratic constitutional order? Do such guarantees place a special strain on the judiciary? Do they help poor people? What is the relationship between such guarantees and doctrines involving state action and the horizontal application of constitutional norms?

[In his article *State Action, Social Welfare Rights, and the Judicial Role*, [4]Mark Tushnet] casts new light on [these questions] by analyzing a number of cases in which courts have, or have not, taken their constitutions to alter background rules of property, contract, and tort. Tushnet contends that the rise of the activist state, understood as some form of social democracy, unsettles preexisting understandings of the relationship between constitutional norms and the private sector. In the classical liberal state, the constitution does not apply horizontally; there are no economic guarantees; and what counts as state action is relatively clear. But once the state assumes "affirmative obligations," constitutional norms might well be triggered, and the state's failure to alter the background rules of property and contract law might well raise serious constitutional problems. To borrow from Tushnet's summary of his complex account: In a "thin social democratic nation," such as Canada, courts are placed in a new and extremely difficult position, being forced either to "enforce obviously arbitrary lines between what they treat as state action and what they do not," or to work out "the set of entitlements people should have in a thicker social democracy."

Much of what Tushnet says is highly illuminating, but I think that there are several gaps in his discussion. I emphasize two points here. First, the classical liberal state assumes affirmative obligations, and does so no less than the social democratic state. The obligations are different, but they are not less affirmative. The widespread neglect of this point, within the legal and political culture, has led to serious failures in analysis, and the failures are not innocuous. Second, state action is always present. The constitutional question, in any system that has a state action requirement, is not whether there is state action, but whether the relevant state action is unconstitutional. That is a hard question on the merits, but it is not a hard state action question. A thin social democracy may struggle with constitutional issues, but by virtue of its status as a thin social democracy, it ought not to have any special struggle with questions involving state action or

---

4. 3 Chi. J. Int'l L. 435 (2002).

horizontal effect. A nation that currently embraces social democracy might create, at the constitutional level, social and economic rights, or it might not. A nation that currently rejects social democracy might offer, at the constitutional level, social and economic rights, or it might not. The legal questions involve the merits.

I now offer some details about these two points.

1. The so called activist state is no more activist than what preceded it. Tushnet speaks of the "rise of the activist state," which he contrasts with the "classical liberal state." In his view, the "activist state . . . is defined by the fact that it has affirmative obligations." This is the conventional understanding. But the conventional understanding is an unfortunate way of seeing the relevant categories. Most of the so-called negative rights require governmental assistance, not governmental abstention. Those rights cannot exist without public assistance. Consider, for example, the right to private property. As Bentham wrote, "Property and law are born together, and die together. Before laws were made there was no property; take away laws, and property ceases." In the state of nature, private property cannot exist, at least not in the way that it exists in a free society. In the state of nature, any property "rights" must be protected either through self-help—useful to the strong, not to the weak—or through social norms. This form of protection is far too fragile to support a market economy or indeed the basic independence of citizens. As we know it, private property is both created and protected by law; it requires extensive governmental assistance.

The same point holds for the other foundation of a market economy, the close sibling of private property: freedom of contract. For that form of freedom to exist, it is extremely important to have reliable enforcement mechanisms in the form of civil courts. The creation of such mechanisms requires action, not abstention. Nor is the point—the dependence of rights on public assistance—limited to the foundations of a market economy. Take, for example, the right to be free from torture and abuse, perhaps the defining "negative" freedom. Of course it is possible to say this right is a "negative" safeguard against public intrusion into the private domain. But as a practical matter, this right requires a state apparatus willing to ferret out and to punish the relevant rights violations. If the right includes protection against private depredations, it cannot exist simply with governmental abstention. If the right is limited to protection against public abuse of power, it can be satisfied by abstention; but in practice, abstention from torture and abuse must be guaranteed by a public apparatus that will deter and punish misconduct. Some rights require the government to protect against its own rights violations. If we go down the list of conventional private rights, we will see this same point at every turn.

There is a larger implication, with direct relevance to the question of social and economic rights. All constitutional rights have budgetary implications; all constitutional rights cost money. If the government plans to protect private property, it will have to expend resources to ensure against both private and public intrusions. If the government wants to protect people against unreasonable searches and seizures, it will have to expend resources to train, monitor, and discipline the police. If the government wants to protect freedom of speech, it must, at a minimum, take steps to constrain its own agents; and these steps will be costly. It follows that insofar as they are costly, social and economic rights are not unique.

Now it is possible that such rights are unusually costly. To ensure, for example, that everyone has housing, it will be necessary to spend more than must be spent to ensure that everyone is free from unreasonable searches and seizures. But any such comparisons are empirical and contingent; they cannot be made on an a priori basis. We could imagine a society in which it costs a great deal to protect private property, but not so much to ensure basic subsistence.

2. *State action is always present, and the real question involves the merits—the meaning of the relevant constitutional guarantees.* Much discussion of the state action question, and the "horizontal" application of constitutional norms, seems to me confused, because it disregards the extent to which the state is present in the arrangements under challenge.
* * *

————

NOTES AND QUESTIONS

1. Constitutional law and "status quo neutrality." Sunstein argues that the assumptions of structural liberalism wrongly influence constitutional decision making. Elsewhere he has criticized what he calls "status quo neutrality":

> [T]he understanding that I mean to challenge defines neutrality by taking, as a given and as the baseline for decision, the status quo, or what various people and groups now have: existing distributions of property, income, legal entitlements, wealth, so-called natural assets, and preferences. A departure from the status quo signals partisanship; respect for the status quo signals neutrality. When government does not interfere with existing distributions, it is adhering to the neutrality requirement, and it rarely needs to justify its decision at all. When it disrupts existing arrangements, it is behaving partially, and is thus subject to constitutional doubt. Current rights of ownership are not seen as a product of law.
>
> Even more than this, the very categories of government "action" and "inaction" are given their content by the status quo. Courts answer the question whether government has acted by reference to existing practices and existing distributions. Decisions that upset those practices and distributions are treated as "action." Decisions that do not are perceived to stay close to nature and thus to amount to no action at all.

Cass R. Sunstein, The Partial Constitution 3 (1993).

Is *DeShaney* a reflection of status quo neutrality? If Sunstein is correct that constitutional law should give no special protection to existing distributions, how should courts decide which acts of redistribution are legitimate?

2. Structural liberalism in United States constitutional jurisprudence. Structural liberalism is reflected in United States constitutional jurisprudence in several ways. First, U.S. constitutional law guarantees rights to poor people but, with a few exceptions, not the financial ability to exercise those rights. *See, e.g.,* Harris v. McRae, 448 U.S. 297, 317–18 (1980) (no constitutional obligation to fund abortions even though the right to abortion is constitutionally protected); Lindsey v. Normet, 405 U.S. 56, 74 (1972) (no constitutional obligation to provide adequate housing); *see also Youngberg*, 457 U.S. at 317 ("As a general matter, a State is under no constitutional duty to provide substantive services for those within its border"). A partial exception is the Supreme Court jurisprudence requiring state funding for the constitutional right to legal representation for indigent defendants. *But see* David Cole, "A Muted Trumpet," in No EQUAL JUSTICE: RACE AND CLASS IN THE AMERICAN CRIMINAL JUSTICE SYSTEM 63–95 (1999) (arguing that inadequate funding of this right leaves indigent defendants without effective protection from the power of the state).

Second, U.S. constitutional law treats legislative decisions with respect to social welfare as entitled to the greatest judicial deference: thus, although government decisions made on the basis of race and gender receive heightened constitutional scrutiny, government decisions made affecting poverty will be upheld as long as the Court can discern a real or imaginary "rational basis" for them. *See, e.g.,* Dandridge v. Williams, 397 U.S. 471 (1970); San Antonio Indep. Sch. Dist. v. Rodriguez, 411 U.S. 1, 28–29 (1973) (wealth is not a "suspect classification").

Third, U.S. constitutional law subjects legislative actions that alter or threaten to alter common law property rights to heightened scrutiny. *See, e.g.,* Pa. Coal Co. v. Mahon, 260 U.S. 393 (1922) (establishing that government regulations can effect a "taking" of private property, triggering the right to compensation under the Fifth Amendment); RICHARD A. EPSTEIN, TAKINGS: PRIVATE PROPERTY AND THE POWER OF EMINENT DOMAIN (1985) (arguing for broad constitutional protection of existing private property rights). The law of "takings" is complex, however, reflecting the desire to defend state police power to redefine property rights as well as the desire to limit this power. *See* Frank I. Michelman, *Property, Utility, and Fairness: Comments on the Ethical Foundations of "Just Compensation" Law*, 80 HARV. L. REV. 1165 (1967); Stewart Sterk, *The Federalist Dimension of Regulatory Takings Jurisprudence*, 114 YALE L.J. 203 (2004).

In the New Deal period, the Supreme Court famously (or infamously) sought to give constitutional protection to contract rights, striking down labor legislation, price regulation, and restrictions on entry into business in the name of freedom of contract. *See, e.g.,* Lochner v. New York, 198 U.S. 45 (1905) (striking down state regulation of hours in the baking industry). The "*Lochner* era" came to an end with the Court's decision in *West Coast Hotel Co. v. Parrish*, 300 U.S. 379 (1937) (upholding a state law establishing a minimum wage for women). *Lochner* has been criticized by scholars as an attempt to entrench a libertarian or laissez-faire conception of markets and the role of government into the Constitution. *See* Cass R. Sunstein, Lochner's *Legacy*, 87 COLUM. L. REV. 873, 874–75 (1987); CASS R. SUNSTEIN, THE PARTIAL CONSTITUTION (1993). While the Supreme Court in *Lochner* sought to limit government power over markets in the name of economic liberty, the President and some national legislators sought to establish broad economic rights as foundations of the New Deal. See the excerpt from William Forbath, below.

Fourth, U.S. constitutional law limits the protection of constitutional rights to the "public" sphere. As *DeShaney* indicates, actions that occur in the "private" sphere of the family are not perceived as involving state action, even when the state has taken on the task of monitoring and regulating families. *See also* United States v. Morrison, 529 U.S. 598 (2000).

3. Explaining public/private distinction in United States constitutional law. Why does the United States Constitution protect private property rights but not public social welfare rights? There are many responses to this question.

One response is doctrinal. As one casebook on constitutional law observes:

> The Constitution contains several provisions that expressly restrict government's power to interfere with market ordering and the private economic interests of individuals. The fifth and fourteenth amendments, for example, provide that "[n]o person shall [be] deprived of [property] without due process of law." Article I, section 10 provides that "[n]o State shall [pass] any [Law] impairing the Obligation of Contracts." And the fifth amendment provides that "private property" shall not "be taken for public use, without just compensation."

GEOFFREY R. STONE ET AL., CONSTITUTIONAL LAW 813 (3d ed. 1996).

In contrast, the Constitution does not contain any explicit social welfare rights.

A second response points to the structure of the Constitution, which creates procedural obstacles to the significant redistribution of wealth and power. Examining the *Federalist Papers* and James Madison's fear of the propertyless mob, Jennifer Nedelsky argues that "[t]he Framers' preoccupation with property generated a shallow conception of democracy and a system of institutions that allocates political power unequally and fails to foster political participation." JENNIFER NEDELSKY, PRIVATE PROPERTY AND THE LIMITS OF AMERICAN CONSTITUTIONALISM: THE MADISONIAN FRAMEWORK AND ITS LEGACY 1 (1990). The concern is that people without wealth and property are kept at arms' length from political power. Thus, Nedelsky writes, "When we try to understand why Americans, and particularly poor Americans, don't vote, we should remember that the basic structure of our institutions was not designed to encourage their participation." *Id.* at 215.

In a more tendentious vein, Charles Beard has argued that the U.S. Constitution was the product of "special interest" groups concerned to

protect their economic privilege. CHARLES A. BEARD, AN ECONOMIC INTERPRETA-
TION OF THE CONSTITUTION OF THE UNITED STATES (Transaction Publishers
1998) (1913). Beard notes that four groups were completely disfranchised
from participation in the Constitutional Convention: slaves, indentured
servants, men who could not qualify for voting under the property tests
imposed by the state constitutions and laws, and women. BEARD, AN
ECONOMIC INTERPRETATION OF THE CONSTITUTION OF THE UNITED STATES at 24. He
then offers some further observations:

> The movement for the Constitution of the United States was originat-
> ed and carried through principally by four groups of personalty inter-
> ests which had been adversely affected under the Articles of Confedera-
> tion: money, public securities, manufactures, and trade and shipping.
>
> The first firm steps toward the formation of the Constitution were
> taken by a small and active group of men immediately interested
> through their personal possessions in the outcome of their labors.
>
> No popular vote was taken directly or indirectly on the proposition to
> call the Convention which drafted the Constitution.
>
> A large propertyless mass was, under the prevailing suffrage qualifica-
> tions, excluded at the outset from participation (through representa-
> tives) in the work of framing the Constitution.
>
> The members of the Philadelphia Convention which drafted the Con-
> stitution were, with a few exceptions, immediately, directly, and per-
> sonally interested in, and derived economic advantages from, the
> establishment of the new system.
>
> The Constitution was essentially an economic document based upon
> the concept that the fundamental private rights of property are anteri-
> or to government and morally beyond the reach of popular majorities.
>
> The major portion of the members of the Convention are on record as
> recognizing the claim of property to a special and defensive position in
> the Constitution.
>
> In the ratification of the Constitution, about three-fourths of the adult
> males failed to vote on the question, having abstained from the
> elections at which delegates to the state conventions were chosen,
> either on account of their indifference or their disfranchisement by
> property qualifications.
>
> The Constitution was ratified by a vote of probably not more than one-
> sixth of the adult males.

BEARD, AN ECONOMIC INTERPRETATION OF THE CONSTITUTION, supra at 324–25.

Most efforts at making the political process less beholden to economic
interests have focused on strengthening campaign finance restrictions. The
Supreme Court's decision in *Buckley v. Valeo*, 424 U.S. 1 (1976), striking
down limits on the amount a candidate may spend from personal or family
funds as violative of the First Amendment, has been a significant obstacle
to these reform efforts. Critics of the decision in *Buckley* argue that the
majority wrongly took the existing distribution of wealth as "natural."
Thus, Cass Sunstein argues:

We should view [*Buckley*] as the modern-day analogue of [*Lochner*]: a decision [that takes] the market status quo as just and prepolitical, and [uses it] to invalidate democratic efforts at reform. Reliance on [existing distributions] is [treated as] government neutrality.... [But] it should be clear that elections based on those distributions are ... subject to a regulatory system, made possible and constituted through law. That law consists, first, in legal rules protecting the present distribution of wealth, and more fundamentally, in legal rules allowing candidates to buy speech rights through markets.

Cass R. Sunstein, *Free Speech Now*, 59 U. CHI. L. REV. 255, 291–92 (1992).

For an argument that the Supreme Court's decision in *Austin v. Mich. Chamber of Commerce*, 494 U.S. 652 (1990) "implicitly recognizes that poor people, although formally enfranchised, suffer severe marginalization from the processes of self-government because of their economic incapacity" and that "wealth-based distribution of political power is a democratically illegitimate phenomenon of considerable constitutional import," *see* Stephen Loffredo, *Poverty, Democracy, and Constitutional Law*, 141 U. PA. L. REV. 1277, 1286 (1993).

A third answer to the puzzle focuses on the contingencies of United States history. For example, Akhil Amar argues below that the constitutional revolution represented by Reconstruction should be understood as having fundamentally altered the allocation of social and economic rights. William Forbath suggests that the promise of economic reconstruction symbolized by the slogan "forty acres and a mule" was never fulfilled, however, because of repeated failures to completely dismantle racial subordination. *See* William E. Forbath, *Caste, Class, and Equal Citizenship*, 98 Mich. L. Rev. 1 (1999).

A fourth answer to the question why the U.S. Constitution protects common law property rights but not social welfare rights points to the centrality of ideology. American political ideology contains a strong libertarian strand, which stresses skepticism toward, if not fear of, "big government" and perceives a strong connection between freedom, property rights, and a weak national government. Consider the excerpt by Mary Ann Glendon, below, in this light. For an ideological analysis that examines the American focus on property rights as the key to individual liberty, *see* David Abraham, *Liberty Without Equality: The Property–Rights Connection in a "Negative Citizenship" Regime*, 21 LAW & SOC. INQUIRY 1 (1996).

---

3. STRUCTURAL LIBERALISM IN "PRIVATE" LAW

Un-Making Law: The Classical Revival in the Common Law

28 SEATTLE U. L. REV. 1 (2004).

■ JAY M. FEINMAN

The common law—the law of contracts, torts, and property—is in the throes of a potentially remarkable transformation. The transformation is pervasive; many changes already have been adopted, more are in process, and still more have been proposed. If they all come to pass, the law will have experienced a once–in-a-century remaking. More precisely, we may be observing the "un-making" of law, to use Stephen Sugarman's phrase, as the principal common-law developments of the twentieth century are rolled back. In this sense, the changes are both radical and regressive, representing a classical revival, instituting in the twenty-first century common law a barely updated version of the classical law that reigned in the Gilded Age at the end of the nineteenth century. Even more broadly, the changes in the law and the vision that animates them are part of a more general transformation of American government and society.

This article describes the possibility of a classical revival in the common law and situates the revival in its historical context. * * *

* * * This remarkable fact is best understood in this context: The un-making of the common law is part of the effort by conservatives and business interests to elevate the market and diminish the government.

I. ORIGINS: CLASSICAL LEGAL THOUGHT AND CRITIQUE

Contracts, torts, and property have ancient origins, but most of their history is barely relevant to understanding modern law. The story really begins with classical legal thought, the body of law usually seen as dominant from 1870 to 1920. * * * Classical legal thought is the thesis, and the combination of sociological jurisprudence, legal realism, and related Progressive ideas comprise a critique that is the antithesis of classicism. Thesis and antithesis are resolved to a considerable extent in the synthesis of modern law, the law that begins to take shape after World War II and achieves its mature form in the 1970s. Because in this resolution the critique supplemented and modified classical law but did not supplant it altogether, this modern body of law is often called "neoclassical law."

A. *Classical Law*

Classical legal thought once was seen as the age of *Lochner*, in which a conservative bench and bar reformulated the law to serve the interests of the new corporate oligarchs. More recent scholarship has shown that picture to be incomplete or misleading; although the effects of classical jurisprudence may have served big business, the motivations of its authors were more complex, including the important development of an autonomous legal science and the preservation of traditional values against emerging monopoly capitalism. In any case, the inquiry here is less about causes and consequences and more about the body of classical law as a coherent whole against which later critics would react, the essential elements of which are being revived in our time. This section briefly summarizes the content, structure, and method of classical law.

[Thomas] Grey defines the three essential characteristics of classical legal thought:

First, it must be *determinate*, its judgments following from the application of norms to facts, without the exercise of discretion or contestable judgment. Second, it must be *systematic*, forming a coherent structure of relatively abstract concepts and principles. Finally, it must be *autonomous*, deriving its norms from distinctively legal sources, rather than from the contestable claims of religion, philosophy, or political economy.

The substantive vision of classical legal thought is a world of independent individuals, each of whom acts within a broad sphere of legal autonomy to pursue his own self-interest. The role of government is precisely defined and narrowly circumscribed. The legislature has limited authority to regulate narrowly and traditionally defined harmful activities. The courts, applying a complete, coherent, and formal body of law, police the boundaries of legislative authority and define the ground rules for interaction among private individuals, namely, the rules of contract, tort, and property.

Classical contract law described a broad realm in which individuals could exercise their autonomy by consenting to agreements with other autonomous individuals. Individuals could accept the liability of an enforceable contract by exercising consent and could be free from liability unless consent had been exercised. The entire body of contract doctrine flowed from this single principle. * * *

While contract law defined a broad scope of individual autonomy, tort law encompassed a much narrower realm in which the law recognized liability for harm wrongfully committed. Tort liability, unlike contract liability, was not created by the consent of the parties, but neither was it imposed by the courts. Instead, tort law was corrective justice through which the law provided recompense when one person caused injury by invading the preexisting right to bodily security held by another person. For liability to be imposed, corrective justice required that the defendant must have been at fault and must have caused the injury. In classical tort law, each of these elements had a fixed meaning. * * *

The law of property was more of an agglomeration, because of its antique categories and doctrinal variety. Nevertheless, a core concept of classical property law developed. Blackstone's concept of property as "sole and despotic dominion" was dephysicalized and commodified. Where once property had largely been associated with land, the generalization of the market in classical law led to an understanding of property as "everything which has exchangeable value," as Justice Swayne wrote in dissent in the *Slaughterhouse Cases*. Property was defined by the ability to be exchanged, and the purpose of property was to be exchanged. An individual's right to own property included the creation, exchange, and accumulation of wealth of all kinds, from dynastic trusts to corporate wealth. The state could control property rights only in limited ways, under traditional doctrines and consistent with the ability of an owner to realize the value of property; classical property law "sanctioned capitalist accumulation, the starkest sort of property-as-wealth ... and it created a large private domain of unregulated and unregulatable market activity."

The classical ideal was realized through a rigid structure that drew sharp distinctions between realms of authority and areas of law. First, public law was distinguished from private law. Public law encompassed the area in which the legislature could legitimately exercise its regulatory and coercive authority—the police power. Private law, by contrast, was defined and governed by individual rights to own property, to contract, and to take any other action that did not invade the rights of other persons. Because its content flowed from legal rights, private law did not require the kinds of policy choices that the legislature made in public law. Second, within private law, clear lines were drawn between contracts, torts, and property. Each subject had a proper sphere of authority, defined by the subjects' respective organizing principles of consent, fault, and ownership.

In exercising the police power, the legislature could consider political and distributive concerns, so that legislative choice was, in a technical sense, unprincipled. Courts, by contrast, were nonpolitical institutions that did not exercise discretion or make political judgments. They could maintain this posture by applying the distinctive decisional method of formal legal reasoning. A court engaged in legal reasoning began with the few basic propositions that lay at the heart of the common law, such as "an exercise of consent creates a contract;" sometimes these principles were obvious, while in other instances they were defined by induction from an examination of cases. Judges then used inexorable, deductive logic to generate narrower doctrinal rules and decisions in individual cases, all of which were merely specific instances of the basic propositions. Any preexisting rules or decided cases that did not conform to the derived logic were discarded. The task was made simpler by devices such as the prevalence of binary categories. A statement was either a manifestation of willingness to enter into a bargain sufficient to constitute an offer or it was not; there was no intermediate category of, say, a promise which could be relied on even though it was not an offer.

For some, of whom Langdell was the most notable, the primary attraction of classical legal reasoning was its claim to be a scientific method, an application of the rigorous, logical process of induction and deduction that simultaneously developed in the natural and social sciences. For others, the primary attraction of the classical method was political, in the sense that it guaranteed that rights would be defined and protected without the exercise of potentially redistributive choice by the courts.

B.   The Critique of Classical Law

The critique of classical legal thought began almost at the moment of classical thought's creation. In *The Common Law* in 1881, Holmes was the theorist and objectivist who outlined much of the structure and content of classical law even as he rejected its conceptualist method. By the late 1890s, in "Privilege, Malice, and Intent" and "The Path of the Law," as pragmatist, skeptic, and empiricist Holmes had begun the process of undermining classical law's integrity.

Holmes was followed by successive waves of pragmatists, Progressives, sociological jurisprudents, and legal realists through the 1930s who revealed in detail the weaknesses of classical law. The divergence in intellectual approach and political orientation among the critics was great. The dispute between Roscoe Pound and Karl Llewellyn is the most famous, but any movement, or even succession of movements, that includes Cardozo, Frank, Corbin, Moore, Sturges, and Fuller will be very diverse. What each of these critics minimally shared was distaste for at least some elements of classical thought, commonly the grand classical claims to abstraction, autonomy, and rigor.

From the perspective of the subsequent developments, a useful entry point in seeing how classical law collapsed is by examining the most arcane, scholastic effort at critique of the twentieth century. Wesley Newcomb Hohfeld attempted to construct a new taxonomy of legal relationships in his exquisite tables of "Jural Correlatives" and "Jural Opposites," but the destructive effect of his work was more important than the reconstruction. Hohfeld explained that general concepts such as ownership were descriptive rather than normative, that they were in fact composed of many different legal relations, and that the concepts were two-sided, so that obligation rather than entitlement could be described as the basis of legal relationships. To say that one owns property, for example, simply summarizes a set of legal relationships between the owner and non-owners. The relationships can be specified more precisely, as in the right to exclude and the privilege to enter, or the relationships can be reversed, focusing on the obligations they impose on the non-owner rather than the benefits they bestow on the owner; a duty to not trespass is the consequence of a right to exclude. The lawyer economist Robert Hale applied and contextualized the analysis, dissecting "liberty," "property," "freedom," and "coercion" to show that these concepts represented the exercise of legal power, not the absence of it, and so lacked the axiomatic content ascribed to them by classical law. Property, for example, consisted of a set of Hohfeldian interests that enabled an owner to exercise the power of the state in withholding access to the property from others unless they bargained on his terms. "The law has delegated to him a discretionary power over the rights and duties of others." Similarly, bargains are not free contracts but rather mutual coercions set against a background of market inequality established by legal entitlements. By the time the critique had crested in 1930, Felix Cohen would summarize much of the classical method as "transcendental nonsense," or the use of such empty concepts to reach circular results.

Under this view, courts in common-law cases were engaged in the allocation of rights, not the application of rights, and in that respect they were as much public law entities engaged in distributional judgments as the legislature. Contract, property, and tort law all necessarily involve discretion in imposing legal liability. Nor could the discretion be vitiated by a formal, rule-based body of doctrine, because the traditional concepts were incapable of providing that degree of formality. The inadequacy of language and the complexity of facts made the ideal unrealizable; rules could not be both precise and comprehensive, so judges, not rules, decided the cases. Therefore the public-private distinction in general and the organizing principles of the common law subjects in particular were incapable of carrying the weight the classicists attributed to them.

If the common law involved policy choices, its individualist, market-oriented principles were at least incomplete if not invalid. The critics offered to supplement or replace those principles from two directions. The first direction, grounded in their scientific and functionalist bent, was empirical. Law ought to attend to the realities of the world, complex as they might be. The principles of individualism and the market were found wanting when tested against the circumstances of lack of personal choice in an imperfect world, concentrations of economic power, and networks of social relations. The second direction, grounded as much in the critics' Progressive politics as in their academic approach, focused on the collectivist concern of social welfare as an antidote to excessive individualism. Here, too, concern for instrumental policymaking to achieve Progressive social objectives required departure from the classical ideal. In each of the subjects, the critique demonstrated that the classical method and substance needed to be discarded in favor of a more complex, functional analysis.

* * *

C.   The Critique Consolidated

The critique of classical legal thought flourished in the 1920s and early 1930s, undermining the classical claims to abstraction, coherence, and autonomy. The critique initially had its greatest impact in the legal academy, but it also made its way into the mainstream of the law. * * *

* * *

The core concept of classical law was individual autonomy, derived from abstract principle and embodied in the right to own property, the right to contract, and the right to act without being subject to unwarranted tort liability. The critique demonstrated that the concept of autonomy was at best incomplete and at worst illusory. Neoclassical law began by balancing individual autonomy and non-individualist considerations of social welfare. Neoclassical tort law, for example, merged corrective justice principles in an individual case with social interests in compensation and accident prevention.

A particularly important area for this balancing is the market. Market transactions in the real world are often not characterized by the exercise of autonomy, but are plagued by inequality and market failures. For example, the market may not provide low-income workers and consumers with meaningful choices to realize basic human needs. Moreover, the market is not the measure of all things. Non-market values such as community, collective responsibility, and protection of the disadvantaged also are important. Accordingly, the law regulates and intervenes in market transactions. Contract law, for example, balances assent with fairness norms derived from commercial practice and from the broader society. Under neoclassical law, this approach was unavoidable. Law constructs social relations, including market relations, through its doctrines, by prescribing terms of ownership and exchange. Therefore, law is necessarily constitutive and regulatory.

Neoclassical courts had to immerse themselves in the world they regulated. In the decision of individual cases, courts need to construct detailed accounts of the events and context to reach proper conclusions. Each case is also representative of a larger area of social process, and courts, now engaged overtly in regulating that social process, need a broad understanding of it. Once engaged in that kind of detailed contextual inquiry, potentially in every case and actually in many cases, courts are faced with choices about social policy. Courts as much as legislatures necessarily and appropriately engage in policymaking when they formulate and apply doctrine, typically in the form of vague standards that leave play for contextual and policy inquiries in future cases. For example, where the original Restatements were typically cast as syllogistic rules, the second Restatements are replete with standards made up of "factors to be considered."

Therefore, by the 1970s, the full effects of the critique, in revised form, were finally felt in the law. The generalization of negligence and the rise of products liability in torts, consumerism and the adoption of flexible rules in contracts, and a regulatory property law best exemplified by the revolution in landlord-tenant law, created in a mature form the kind of law for which the critics of classicism, in their reformist mode, had been striving. The second round of Restatements solidified many of the developments. By 1980, neoclassical law had arrived.

II. The Transformation of Contract, Tort, and Property Law

The contemporary changes adopted, underway, and proposed in the common law subjects are diverse and broad-ranging, but they share a common core. Despite a century of critique and neoclassical development, the changes attempt to revive elements of the classical common law. This part highlights some of the most significant developments in each of the subjects.

A. Contract Law

Two major developments in neoclassical contract law were the contextualization of previously abstract doctrine and the recognition of the necessity of regulating market transactions. In the 1960s and 1970s, these developments culminated in a wave of progressive legislation and well-known judicial decisions. Statutes such as the Uniform Commercial Code and the Truth in Lending Act mandated more disclosure of contract terms. The U.C.C. also expanded formation doctrines. A contract could be found based on the bargain in fact, even though the moment of its formation was undetermined and previously essential terms such as price and quantity were missing. Courts also expanded on the process of contract interpretation; insurance contracts in particular were interpreted according to the reasonable expectations of the subordinate party, and a relaxed parol evidence rule undermined the primacy of written agreements. Courts also recognized the full complexity of contractual settings; promissory estoppel expanded to provide a remedy for reliance (and, arguably, even reasonable expectations without reliance) created by promises that failed the traditional standards of assent and consideration. And courts felt free to review the fairness of contracts, especially between parties of unequal bargaining power; unconscionability enabled courts to strike down oppressive contract terms, from the cross-collateral clause in a consumer installment sale in *Williams v. Walker–Thomas Furniture Co.* to the arbitration provision signed by an experienced concert promoter in *Graham v. Scissor Tail, Inc.*

The classical revival challenges these developments, arguing that the law has departed from the core principle governing contract law: Courts should simply enforce the contracts people make. In this view, neoclassical contract law makes two mistakes.

First, it diminishes personal freedom, of which freedom of contract is an essential element in a market economy. As Judge Kozinski of the Ninth Circuit writes,

> Perhaps most troubling, the willingness of courts to subordinate voluntary contractual arrangements to their own sense of public policy and proper business decorum deprives individuals of an important measure of freedom. The right to enter into contracts—to adjust one's legal relationships by mutual agreement with other free individuals—was unknown through much of history and is unknown even today in many parts of the world. Like other aspects of personal autonomy, it is too easily smothered by government officials eager to tell us what's best for us.

Second, because parties are the best judges of their own interest, and because the market, left to its own devices, will produce the best results for society, detrimental results are likely to happen when courts interfere with contracts. Richard Epstein explains the superiority of the enforcement of contracts over legal intervention:

> [Contract] law can facilitate (not compel, but facilitate) sizable productive interactions which will continue to expand over time and transactions until they embrace all individuals who possess the minimum capacity to engage in contracting at all. The system goes forward in a benevolent fashion because the exchanges are mutually beneficial. . . . The background knowledge of the uniform incentives moving self interested parties is a more reliable guide to their interests than any public vetting of their deal.

The solution to these problems is to revert to a simple model of contract based on an ideal market, strictly enforcing the bargains that parties make, not reading beyond the four corners of a document in enforcing a contract, and certainly not evaluating the bargains for fairness.

The model is so simple that it can ignore the complexities of the modern world. * * *

As a result, law under the classical revival emphasizes abstraction over contextualization. In general, this means less attention to the factual details of a particular case or of the class of cases of which it is representative and more attention to the complexities of real-world contracting as a means of better understanding and regulating the parties' contract. Contract law also becomes more abstract in a particular way. The process of abstraction moves the principles of contract to more closely resemble those of an ideal market, and the market model achieves primacy as the source of contract doctrine.

Under the classical revival, formality reigns at two levels. First, the contract doctrine itself becomes more formal; ostensibly clear, rigid rules are favored over flexible standards. Second, the substance of the rules favors formality in contracting practices. Written contracts (including standard form contracts) are favored over oral contracts; the interpretation of contracts looks primarily to their plain meaning; and parties are given great freedom to define the terms of their relationships without examination or intervention by the law. The practical consequence of the implementation of this vision is that businesses can use contract law more effectively to control relationships with their customers and employees because they can more easily dictate the terms of dealing, avoid being legally bound except on their own terms, avoid review by the courts of the fairness of those terms, and control how disputes are resolved under their contracts. The sections that follow illustrate the principles and their consequences by discussing formation doctrines, including approaches to form contracts and rolling contracts; the decline of reliance; the parol evidence rule; and the enforcement of mandatory arbitration clauses.

* * *

A useful summary of the structure of the classical revival is provided by an article by William Powers, Jr., *Border Wars*, 72 TEX. L. REV. 1209, 1210–11 (1994), in which Powers discusses the bad faith tort in the context of the larger "border wars" between contract law and tort law. Powers defines the "basic paradigms" of private law, each of which has a "prime directive" or central organizing principle:

· The tort or negligence paradigm reflects the basic norm that people should act reasonably under the circumstances. If people do not act reasonably, this norm demands that they should then compensate those whom they foreseeably injure....

· [T]he property paradigm gives individuals entitlements to do as they please with their own property....

· The contract paradigm expresses the basic norm that individuals should be able to agree between and among themselves how to allocate resources. Contract law does not itself give entitlements or independently evaluate the reasonableness of each party's conduct;

instead, it establishes a structure within which individuals can voluntarily bargain and reach their own agreements.

Each paradigm assigns authority for development of the content of the law to a different institution. The contract and property paradigms assign responsibility to individuals through actions in the private market. Tort, on the other hand, assigns power to courts and juries.

When the paradigms potentially overlap, conflicts between them can be resolved by a resort to their purposes, which are reflected in the structure of the common law under the classical revival. * * *

* * *

2.   Method

The challenges to neoclassical private law include a new orientation to legal method as well as to substance and structure. The method is more formal than neoclassical law, and there has been much academic discussion of this "new formalism" in both public and private law. But formalism is too broad a term to capture what is going on in the new approach to legal method.

Classical legal thought defined the problem of legal method as keeping legal reasoning (the decision from legal doctrine, as done in courts) distinct from policy oriented legislative reasoning. Classical law resolved this problem through a legal method that was autonomous and determinate: courts could deductively apply legal rules and principles without regard for their social consequences to produce certain results in particular cases. The critique of classical legal thought undermined the claims of autonomy and determinacy. Critics demonstrated that the classical structure, principles, and method were inadequate to the task of producing a formal legal system. Courts necessarily engaged in the allocation of rights, not just the application of rights, and so were engaged in the making of public policy.

Some of the most policy-oriented of the critics were unconcerned by this similarity and urged the courts to embrace a legislative role. But that path was too extreme for most legal scholars, ordinary judges and lawyers and, ultimately, the social and political environment in which they operated. Accordingly, as neoclassical law matured it developed a distinctive legal method that preserved a role for doctrine and a relatively autonomous legal method. Under neoclassical law, ordinary cases are handled by a deductive method in which doctrinal principles are applied straightforwardly to sets of facts. The principles are adequate for ordinary cases, but not for unusual cases, and it is recognized that even in the ordinary cases their application is always provisional. The principles are based on policy, they are typically cast as standards rather than rules, and they require detailed factual determinations, all of which leaves considerable but not unlimited room for judicial discretion.

The classical revival rejects the neoclassical resolution of the problem of legal method. It attempts to solve the problem by reinstating elements of the classical approach in a revised form—an "anti-antiformalism"—it being not so much classical formalism as a formalist reaction to the critique and its neoclassical progeny.

This method has its roots in the substance of the classical revival. The core of the substance is an idealized market in which autonomous individuals contract to maximize their wealth. This resembles the classical ideal of the market, but it gives more room for state intervention to maintain the conditions under which the market can operate by enforcing legal rules that support the market and, to a very limited extent, to correct market failures and provide remedies in non market transactions.

This substance has methodological consequences. First, there is a preference for determinate rules over standards. Rules clarify the rights and obligations of market participants; this facilitates market transactions by enabling parties to plan more effectively and by reducing the opportunities for judicial interference. Second, the rules are such that they require less extensive factual inquiry. In particular cases, courts may engage in considerable discussion of the facts, but the purpose of doing so is to provide, as it were, the middle term of a syllogism; if certain facts are present, then a result follows from the rule. This contrasts with neoclassical law, in which fact finding serves as part of the balancing process in the application of a standard and as a basis for policy making in the formulation of rules, subrules, and exceptions to rules.

These forms of rule preference permit a relatively effective deductive process to operate at several levels. Rules are derived from market principles, sub rules are derived from more general rules, and individual results are derived from the sub rules. As a result, courts have less discretion in defining rules of law and juries have less discretion in applying them.

So far this description resembles the method of classical legal thought, with a shift in emphasis from rights derived from abstract, quasi-natural principle to rights derived from the ideal market. But there is an important difference. Policy was largely absent in classical law, but after decades of critique and neoclassical law, it is hard for the challenge to neoclassical law to forsake that development entirely. Policy is part of the challenge, but in particular ways.

First, the policy arguments are constrained by the market-oriented substance. Neoclassical law embodied a conflict of policies, which can be captured as market versus non-market or individualist versus collectivist; that is what made it neoclassical. Not so in the current challenges; the policies argued are substantially weighted in support of the ideal market. If neoclassical policy argument reflects a form of pluralist, interest group politics, the policy argument of its challengers reflects a kind of universalism or social absolutism, in which only market concerns deserve substantial weight because they benefit everyone.

Second, policy tends to be applied wholesale rather than retail. In neoclassical law, policy arguments were applied quite particularly, on individual issues of doctrine. In the recent challenges, the tendency is more to make policy arguments in support of market solutions generally, and the arguments simply resonate at the level of particular doctrinal issues. This is formalist reasoning in the sense that the market norms are presumed to generate sub-rules in a relatively direct fashion and with particular results. Grey nicely sums up this element of the new formalism as "treating doctrinal elaboration as a search for coherent structures of general concepts and principles, rather than as a process of gap-filling sublegislation ancillary to particularized dispute resolution."

III.   CONCLUSION: THE CLASSICAL REVIVAL IN CONTEXT

Grant Gilmore famously remarked that there are alternating tides in law, just as in art, architecture, music, and fashion—classicism to romanticism, formality to flexibility, and back again. One might consider the changes in the common law to be little more than a reflection of political fashion in the current, more conservative era that follows the liberalism of the 1960s and 1970s. In context, however, the classical revival is remarkable.

In historical context, the revival represents a conceptual regress. Despite alternating styles, law has generally been assumed to progress over time. Rules and decisions will always be inadequate and mistakes will always be made, but at least they will be new mistakes, not repetitions of past errors. The appropriate metaphor for legal development is a spiral, back and forth but continually upward. The classical revival, in its reinstatement of an ostensible formality and reliance on principles assumed to be fundamental, simply updates positions that the critique of classical legal thought demonstrated to be flawed almost a century ago. The movement is radical, not conservative, in rejecting that demonstration. Justice Scalia asserts that there are categorical rules of property; Hohfeld knew better in 1917. Tort reformers argue for a simple principle of fault as the basis of personal injury law; Leon Green showed in 1928 that no simple principle existed. Judge Alex Kozinski claims that we need to restore the "sanctity of contract;" Robert Hale explained why that was a bankrupt concept in 1943. Professor Epstein states there are simple rules that can govern a complex world; Hohfeld, Green, Hale, and other scholars, and Benjamin Cardozo, Roger Traynor, and scores of other judges have known better for generations.

This error is puzzling as an intellectual matter, but its origins are very clear if the classical revival is seen in its contemporary context. The unmaking of the common law is consistent with the contemporary campaign by political conservatives and business interests to reshape American government, law, and society.

Ronald Reagan proclaimed the principal item on the agenda of this campaign most baldly in his first inaugural address: "Government is not the solution to our problems; government is the problem." If government is the problem, then the solution is to reduce the reach of government. Anti-tax activist Grover Norquist declared the movement's ambition to be cutting the size of federal, state, and local government in half, to "get it down to the size where we can drown it in the bathtub." Many government programs can be reduced or eliminated altogether; others will be cut by shifting responsibility from the federal government to the states and from government to the market. Publicly supported retirement and health care will be replaced by private investment accounts instead of Social Security and HMOs and private prescription insurance instead of Medicare. Public support of education will be replaced by voucher-funded school choice. Public welfare, already reformed "as we know it" under centrist Democrat Bill Clinton, will be supplanted by voluntary, faith-based initiatives. Tax cuts will starve government across the board.

In this vision, government is the problem because it interferes with individual freedom, particularly the individual freedom to pursue self-interest through the market. Conservatives idealize and worship the market as the single social institution that produces efficient, just, and democratic results: "One market under God," as Thomas Frank has styled it.

The master narrative of the vision of market centrality is Reagan-esque: Once upon a time there was a golden age when a man (always a man) could stand on his own two feet, his rights inviolate. Individual liberty, personal responsibility, and economic opportunity were the foundations of American life. Society was organized and controlled by two institutions: the market and the state. The market was primary; through it, people could maximize their potential, realize their dreams, and rise or fall on their own merits. The state was subordinate; beyond its minimal functions of guaranteeing physical security, providing public goods, and protecting individual rights, government offered only the possibility of unwise and pernicious interference in the social order created by the market.

The narrative is hardly new or unique. Judge Posner traces the ideology's roots to the classical liberalism of John Stuart Mill:

> [T]he government's role is to provide an unobtrusive framework for private activities. Government provides certain goods, such as national defense and (in some versions) education, that private markets will not provide in sufficient quantities. But beyond that it merely protects a handful of entitlements (property rights and some personal liberties) that are necessary to prevent markets from not working at all or from running off the rails.

But the breadth of the market fervor in the modern conservative era is striking. "More than anything else," said Reagan, "I want to see the United States remain a country where someone can get rich." In this narrative, the ideal state of affairs was corrupted by liberal politicians and judges who expanded the role of government and thereby disrupted the natural and just order of things. When government spread beyond its proper role of protecting individual rights and preserving market competition through fixed rules known in advance, it began down "The Road to Serfdom," as Austrian economist Friedrich Hayek entitled his 1944 book which became an instant best seller in the United States.

The mainstream discourse of conservatism seldom makes explicit the place of the common law in this picture, but a vision of the common law is central to the conservative ideology, and the conservative ideology is central to contemporary changes in the common law. The ideal of individual freedom and limited government and the classical revival conceptions of property, contract, and tort law are mutually reinforcing. The protection of absolute private property is "the foundation from which America's prosperity was launched." The "sanctity of contract" also is a condition of freedom, according to Judge Kozinski. The role of courts, therefore, is simply to enforce the contracts the parties appear to have made, not to assess their reasonableness or fairness: "Like other aspects of personal autonomy, [freedom of contract] is too easily smothered by government officials eager to tell us what's best for us." Tort law supplements property and contract law in the relatively few cases of wrongful acts that cause injury. The Reagan Administration's Tort Policy Working Group called fault "the only vehicle in tort law capable of distinguishing wrongful (or undesirable) from beneficial (or desirable) conduct," but the fault principle has been corrupted by activist judges and grasping lawyers.

The radical conservative, business-oriented agenda in property, contract, and tort law fits well with the broader ideology of individualism and the free market. This ideology also promotes an understanding of the common law as nonpolitical. The common law is portrayed exclusively as a realm of corrective justice, righting wrongs between individuals according to objective principles of law, as contrasted with the political choices made in electoral politics and in legislation. In this understanding, the choice of common-law rules that favor the conservative conception of private property, freedom of contract, and limited tort law is not a political choice; indeed, it is hardly a choice at all. Instead, the substance of the common law and the process of judicial decision-making reside as a neutral background against which "real" political conflicts are played out. The common law, like the interstate highway system, is simply part of the natural, nonpolitical infrastructure of society. In this way, conservatives attempt to withdraw from the realm of politics the allocation of economic, political, and social values by the common law.

But like the interstate highway system, the conservative vision of the common law is neither natural nor nonpolitical. Instead, it furthers the economic interests of big business and the political interests of conservative politicians, and it promotes an ideology in support of those interests. Contemporary conservatives are "rolling back the twentieth century," returning America to the Gilded Age, with George W. Bush playing the part of William McKinley. Classical legal thought reigned in the Gilded Age, and the classical revival in the common law presents the same challenge to what throughout the twentieth century became the mainstream of American law as conservatism generally presents to the mainstream of American government.

B.   RESTRUCTURING STRUCTURAL LIBERALISM

As Sunstein and others argue, the U.S. Constitution's allocation of rights is not the only possible allocation. The United Nations International

Covenant on Economic, Social, and Cultural Rights represents a different approach. As the Glendon excerpt below suggests, the United States Constitution predates the Covenant, but more recently written constitutions, such as the Constitution of South Africa, show the influence of the Covenant. Compare the South African Constitution, excerpted below, to the United States Constitution and to the Covenant.

The United States also has a "social citizenship" tradition. Consider the speech by President Franklin D. Roosevelt below, along with the commentary by William Forbath.

———

International Covenant on Economic, Social and Cultural Rights

UNITED NATIONS

ARTICLE 6

1.   The States Parties to the present Covenant recognize the right to work, which includes the right of everyone to the opportunity to gain his living by work which he freely chooses or accepts, and will take appropriate steps to safeguard this right.

2.   The steps to be taken by a State Party to the present Covenant to achieve the full realization of this right shall include technical and vocational guidance and training programmes, policies and techniques to achieve steady economic, social and cultural development and full and productive employment under conditions safeguarding fundamental political and economic freedoms to the individual.

ARTICLE 7

The States Parties to the present Covenant recognize the right of everyone to the enjoyment of just and favourable conditions of work which ensure, in particular:

(a) Remuneration which provides all workers, as a minimum, with:

(i) Fair wages and equal remuneration for work of equal value without distinction of any kind, in particular women being guaranteed conditions of work not inferior to those enjoyed by men, with equal pay for equal work;

(ii) A decent living for themselves and their families in accordance with the provisions of the present Covenant;

(b) Safe and healthy working conditions;

(c) Equal opportunity for everyone to be promoted in his employment to an appropriate higher level, subject to no considerations other than those of seniority and competence;

(d) Rest, leisure and reasonable limitation of working hours and periodic holidays with pay, as well as remuneration for public holidays. * * *

ARTICLE 8

1.   The States Parties to the present Covenant undertake to ensure:

(a) The right of everyone to form trade unions and join the trade union of his choice. * * *

ARTICLE 9

The States Parties to the present Covenant recognize the right of everyone to social security, including social insurance. * * *

ARTICLE 11

1.   The States Parties to the present Covenant recognize the right of everyone to an adequate standard of living for himself and his family, including adequate food, clothing and housing, and to the continuous improvement of living conditions. * * *

2.   The States Parties to the present Covenant, recognizing the fundamental right of everyone to be free from hunger, shall take, individually and through international co operation, the measures, including specific programmes, which are needed:

(a) To improve methods of production, conservation and distribution of food by making full use of technical and scientific knowledge, by disseminating knowledge of the principles of nutrition and by developing or reforming agrarian systems in such a way as to achieve the most efficient development and utilization of natural resources;

(b) Taking into account the problems of both food-importing and food-exporting countries, to ensure an equitable distribution of world food supplies in relation to need. * * *

ARTICLE 13

1.   The States Parties to the present Covenant recognize the right of everyone to education. They agree that education shall be directed to the full development of the human personality and the sense of its dignity, and shall strengthen the respect for human rights and fundamental freedoms. They further agree that education shall enable all persons to participate effectively in a free society, promote understanding, tolerance and friendship among all nations and all racial, ethnic or religious groups, and further the activities of the United Nations for the maintenance of peace.

2.   The States Parties to the present Covenant recognize that, with a view to achieving the full realization of this right:

(a) Primary education shall be compulsory and available free to all;

(b) Secondary education in its different forms, including technical and vocational secondary education, shall be made generally available and accessible to all by every appropriate means, and in particular by the progressive introduction of free education;

(c) Higher education shall be made equally accessible to all, on the basis of capacity, by every appropriate means, and in particular by the progressive introduction of free education;

(d) Fundamental education shall be encouraged or intensified as far as possible for those persons who have not received or completed the whole period of their primary education;

(e) The development of a system of schools at all levels shall be actively pursued, an adequate fellowship system shall be established, and the material conditions of teaching staff shall be continuously improved.

* * *

———

Rights in Twentieth–Century Constitutions

59 U. CHI. L. REV. 519, 523–26, 535–36 (1992).

■ MARY ANN GLENDON

A renowned European legal historian recently compiled a list he described as representing the "basic inventory" of rights that have been accepted by "most western countries" at the present time. The list includes, first and foremost; human dignity; then personal freedom; fair procedures to protect against arbitrary governmental action; active political rights (especially the right to vote); equality before the law; and society's responsibility for the social and economic conditions of its members. An American reader of this list is apt to be struck both by the omission of property rights, and by the inclusion of affirmative welfare obligations. Yet the list cannot be faulted as description of the law on the books of "most western countries." Welfare rights (or responsibilities) have become a staple feature of post-war international declarations and have been accorded a place beside traditional political and civil liberties in the national constitutions of most liberal democracies. It is the eighteenth-century American Constitution that, with the passage of time, has become anomalous in this respect.

As Gerhard Casper has pointed out, these differences regarding the rights that are accorded constitutional status in various countries are not merely a function of the age of the documents establishing those rights. To a great extent, the differences are legal manifestations of divergent, and deeply rooted, cultural attitudes toward the state and its functions. Historically, even eighteenth- and nineteenth-century continental European constitutions and codes acknowledged state obligations to provide food, work, and financial aid to persons in need. And continental Europeans today, whether of the right or the left, are much more likely than Americans to assume that governments have affirmative duties actively to promote the well-being of their citizens. The leading European conservative parties, for example, accept the subsidization of child-raising families, and the funding of health, employment, and old age insurance at levels most Americans find scarcely credible. By contrast, it is almost obligatory for American politicians of both the right and the left to profess mistrust of government.

These divergent attitudes toward the state have found constitutional expression in what are sometimes called "negative" and "positive" rights. The American Bill of Rights is frequently described as a charter of "negative" liberties, protecting certain areas of individual freedom from state interference. Judge Posner has succinctly stated the position: "The men who wrote the Bill of Rights were not concerned that the federal government might do too little for the people, but that it might do too much to them." The Supreme Court, while willing to accord procedural due process protection to statutory welfare entitlements, has consistently declined to recognize constitutional welfare rights. * * *

These statements contrast markedly with the attitudes of the post World War II European constitution makers who supplemented traditional negative liberties with certain affirmative social and economic rights or obligations. The idea of government underlying the "positive rights" in European constitutions has a complex history. In part, it represents a transposition to the modern state of the feudal notion that an overlord owed certain protection to his dependents in exchange for their service and loyalty. More proximately, it reflects the programs of the major European political parties—one large group animated by Christian social thought, and another by socialist or social democratic principles. As Casper has observed, it was only natural that peoples accustomed to the notion of a state with affirmative responsibilities would carry that idea forward when they added bills of rights to their constitutions.

* * *

In view of the long-standing American rights tradition, and the recent history of expansive judicial protection of a broad spectrum of individual and minority rights, [a] third aspect of American distinctiveness may at first glance seem puzzling. I refer to the dubious distinction of the United States as the only liberal democracy that has not ratified a number of important human rights instruments, notably the two United Nations Covenants on Civil and Political Rights, and on Economic, Social and Cultural Rights. This reticence, no doubt, is due in large part to our prudent unwillingness to submit to the jurisdiction of international organizations dominated by critics of the United States. But, particularly where economic and social rights are concerned, our reluctance is also attributable to our prevailing ideas about which sorts of needs, goods, interests, and values should be characterized as fundamental rights. Another likely reason is that the American civil litigation system is not well equipped to handle the potential consequences of characterizing a new set of interests as fundamental rights.

* * *

[E]very country in the democratic world is experiencing a tension between the two ideals that are linked together in the deceptively bland title of this symposium—a regime of rights and a welfare state. Every country is grappling with a set of problems that are in a general way similar: how to provide needed social aid without undermining personal responsibility; how to achieve the optimal mix of markets and central planning in a mixed economy; and how to preserve a just balance among individual freedom, equality, and social solidarity under constantly changing circumstances. The problem of "the Bill of Rights in the Welfare State" is nothing less than the great dilemma of how to hold together the two halves of the divided soul of liberalism—our love of individual liberty and our sense of a community for which we accept a common responsibility.

Below the surface of that dilemma lies a more serious one. Neither a strong commitment to individual and minority rights, nor even a modest welfare commitment like the American one, can long be sustained without the active support of a citizenry that is willing to respect the rights of others; that is prepared to accept some responsibility for the poorest and most vulnerable members of society; and that is prepared to accept responsibility, so far as possible, for themselves and for their dependents.

* * *

Constitution of the Republic of South Africa

CHAPTER 2—BILL OF RIGHTS

Rights

7. (1) This Bill of Rights is a cornerstone of democracy in South Africa. It enshrines the rights of all people in our country and affirms the democratic values of human dignity, equality and freedom.

    (2) The state must respect, protect, promote and fulfil the rights in the Bill of Rights.

    (3) The rights in the Bill of Rights are subject to the limitations contained or referred to in section 36, or elsewhere in the Bill.

Application

8. (1) The Bill of Rights applies to all law, and binds the legislature, the executive, the judiciary and all organs of state.

(2) A provision of the Bill of Rights binds a natural or a juristic person if, and to the extent that, it is applicable, taking into account the nature of the right and the nature of any duty imposed by the right.

(3) When applying a provision of the Bill of Rights to a natural or juristic person in terms of subsection (2), a court

    a. in order to give effect to a right in the Bill, must apply, or if necessary develop, the common law to the extent that legislation does not give effect to that right; and

    b. may develop rules of the common law to limit the right, provided that the limitation is in accordance with section 36(1).

(4) A juristic person is entitled to the rights in the Bill of Rights to the extent required by the nature of the rights and the nature of that juristic person.

Equality

9. (1) Everyone is equal before the law and has the right to equal protection and benefit of the law.

(2) Equality includes the full and equal enjoyment of all rights and freedoms. To promote the achievement of equality, legislative and other measures designed to protect or advance persons, or categories of persons, disadvantaged by unfair discrimination may be taken.

(3) The state may not unfairly discriminate directly or indirectly against anyone on one or more grounds, including race, gender, sex, pregnancy, marital status, ethnic or social origin, colour, sexual orientation, age, disability, religion, conscience, belief, culture, language and birth.

(4) No person may unfairly discriminate directly or indirectly against anyone on one or more grounds in terms of subsection (3). National legislation must be enacted to prevent or prohibit unfair discrimination.

(5) Discrimination on one or more of the grounds listed in subsection (3) is unfair unless it is established that the discrimination is fair.

* * *

Environment

24. Everyone has the right—

a. to an environment that is not harmful to their health or well being; and

b. to have the environment protected, for the benefit of present and future generations, through reasonable legislative and other measures that

    i. prevent pollution and ecological degradation;

    ii. promote conservation; and

iii. secure ecologically sustainable development and use of natural resources while promoting justifiable economic and social development.

Property

25. (1) No one may be deprived of property except in terms of law of general application, and no law may permit arbitrary deprivation of property.

(2) Property may be expropriated only in terms of law of general application

a. for a public purpose or in the public interest; and

b. subject to compensation, the amount of which and the time and manner of payment of which have either been agreed to by those affected or decided or approved by a court.

(3) The amount of the compensation and the time and manner of payment must be just and equitable, reflecting an equitable balance between the public interest and the interests of those affected, having regard to all relevant circumstances, including

a. the current use of the property;

b. the history of the acquisition and use of the property;

c. the market value of the property;

d. the extent of direct state investment and subsidy in the acquisition and beneficial capital improvement of the property; and

e. the purpose of the expropriation.

(4) For the purposes of this section

a. the public interest includes the nation's commitment to land reform, and to reforms to bring about equitable access to all South Africa's natural resources; and

b. property is not limited to land.

(5) The state must take reasonable legislative and other measures, within its available resources, to foster conditions which enable citizens to gain access to land on an equitable basis.

(6) A person or community whose tenure of land is legally insecure as a result of past racially discriminatory laws or practices is entitled, to the extent provided by an Act of Parliament, either to tenure which is legally secure or to comparable redress.

(7) A person or community dispossessed of property after 19 June 1913 as a result of past racially discriminatory laws or practices is entitled, to the extent provided by an Act of Parliament, either to restitution of that property or to equitable redress.

(8) No provision of this section may impede the state from taking legislative and other measures to achieve land, water and related

reform, in order to redress the results of past racial discrimination, provided that any departure from the provisions of this section is in accordance with the provisions of section 36(1).

(9) Parliament must enact the legislation referred to in subsection (6).

Housing

26.   (1) Everyone has the right to have access to adequate housing.

(2) The state must take reasonable legislative and other measures, within its available resources, to achieve the progressive realisation of this right.

(3) No one may be evicted from their home, or have their home demolished, without an order of court made after considering all the relevant circumstances. No legislation may permit arbitrary evictions.

Health care, food, water and social security

27.   (1) Everyone has the right to have access to

    a.   health care services, including reproductive health care;

    b.   sufficient food and water; and

    c.   social security, including, if they are unable to support themselves and their dependants, appropriate social assistance.

(2) The state must take reasonable legislative and other measures, within its available resources, to achieve the progressive realisation of each of these rights.

(3) No one may be refused emergency medical treatment.

* * *

Education

29.   (1) Everyone has the right

    a.   to a basic education, including adult basic education; and

    b.   to further education, which the state, through reasonable measures, must make progressively available and accessible.

(2) Everyone has the right to receive education in the official language or languages of their choice in public educational institutions where that education is reasonably practicable. In order to ensure the effective access to, and implementation of, this right, the state must consider all reasonable educational alternatives, including single medium institutions, taking into account

    a.   equity;

    b.   practicability; and

    c.   the need to redress the results of past racially discriminatory laws and practices.

(3) Everyone has the right to establish and maintain, at their own expense, independent educational institutions that

    a.   do not discriminate on the basis of race;

    b.   are registered with the state; and

    c.   maintain standards that are not inferior to standards at comparable public educational institutions.

(4) Subsection (3) does not preclude state subsidies for independent educational institutions.

* * *

Limitation of rights

36. (1) The rights in the Bill of Rights may be limited only in terms of law of general application to the extent that the limitation is reasonable and justifiable in an open and democratic society based on human dignity, equality and freedom, taking into account all relevant factors, including

    a.   the nature of the right;

    b.   the importance of the purpose of the limitation;

    c.   the nature and extent of the limitation;

    d.   the relation between the limitation and its purpose; and

    e.   less restrictive means to achieve the purpose.

(2) Except as provided in subsection (1) or in any other provision of the Constitution, no law may limit any right entrenched in the Bill of Rights.

* * *

Enforcement of rights

38. Anyone listed in this section has the right to approach a competent court, alleging that a right in the Bill of Rights has been infringed or threatened, and the court may grant appropriate relief, including a declaration of rights. The persons who may approach a court are-

    a.   anyone acting in their own interest;

    b.   anyone acting on behalf of another person who cannot act in their own name;

    c.   anyone acting as a member of, or in the interest of, a group or class of persons;

    d.   anyone acting in the public interest; and

    e.   an association acting in the interest of its members.

INTERPRETATION OF BILL OF RIGHTS

39. (1) When interpreting the Bill of Rights, a court, tribunal or forum

    a.   must promote the values that underlie an open and democratic society based on human dignity, equality and freedom;

    b.   must consider international law; and

  c. may consider foreign law.

(2) When interpreting any legislation, and when developing the common law or customary law, every court, tribunal or forum must promote the spirit, purport and objects of the Bill of Rights.

(3) The Bill of Rights does not deny the existence of any other rights or freedoms that are recognised or conferred by common law, customary law or legislation, to the extent that they are consistent with the Bill.

———

Justiciable Social Rights as a Critique of the Liberal Paradigm

38 TEX. INT'L L.J. 763, 779–93 (2003).

■ JEANNE M. WOODS

  * * *

V. SOUTH AFRICAN SOCIAL RIGHTS JURISPRUDENCE

A. Soobramoney: *The Utilitarian Calculus*

The 1996 South African Constitution contains an extensive panoply of socio-economic rights and duties. In contrast to previous efforts to constitutionalize social rights, the Constitution contains a unique bill of rights that integrates social rights with the more traditional fundamental freedoms. The absence of a structural hierarchy of rights effectively merges the public and private spheres, engaging the state in the formerly private endeavor of securing the social and economic pre conditions to the full realization of human freedom. The state is obligated to "take reasonable legislative and other measures, within its available resources, to achieve the progressive realization of each of these rights." This constitutional formulation of the state's duty reflects the collective character of social rights, whose realization requires the resources and effort of the whole society.

The Constitutional Court was presented with its first opportunity to interpret this language barely a year after the 1996 Constitution took effect, posing an unenviable challenge to a new judiciary with precious little precedent to guide it. *Soobramoney v. Minister of Health* involved a forty-one year old unemployed diabetic who suffered from chronic renal failure, necessitating regular kidney dialysis. Because Mr. Soobramoney suffered from a combination of serious ailments rendering his condition irreversible, the treatment was calculated to prolong his life but would not cure him. He had exhausted his personal funds and sought treatment at the state hospital in Durban. Due to an insufficient number of dialysis machines in the public health sector, however, the hospital rationed their use, limiting them to patients who were eligible for a kidney transplant. Under the guidelines developed by the hospital, Mr. Soobramoney was ineligible for a transplant because of his complicated medical history. The plaintiff invoked several provisions of the South African Constitution, claiming violations of his rights to life, health, and emergency medical treatment.

In the Court's first pronouncement on social rights, it affirmed their integral connection to human dignity, freedom, and equality, without which the aspirations of the new constitutional dispensation would "have a hollow ring." Noting, however, that in Section 27(2) the state's duty with regard to health care was circumscribed by the "available resources" the Court read additional limiting language into the provision, restating the obligation of the state as "dependent upon the resources available *for such purposes.*" Thus, the Court indicated that it would not consider the state's resources as a whole, but in effect limited the state's duty to whatever resources it had already allocated to health care in general, and dialysis treatment in particular.

The Court also declined to give serious consideration to the plaintiff's right to life claim, reasoning that resort to the right to life in Section 11 was obviated by Section 27's specific protection of health care. Cautioning that its "purposive" approach to constitutional interpretation may not always require a "generous" construction of the rights afforded by the Constitution, the Court narrowly construed the right to emergency medical treatment in Section 27(3), holding it to be a negative right that does not confer affirmative obligations on the state, and declining to impute any positive obligations from the right to life in Section 11. The Court defined an "emergency" as an urgent, sudden occurrence for which advance preparation was not possible and a constitutional violation as state denial of available treatment, implying that there must be some misconduct or improper motive for the denial, such as racial discrimination. In the Court's view, such a narrow construction was necessary in order to conserve the resources needed to effectuate the state's overall health care obligations.

The Court's analysis under Sections 27(1) and (2) was similarly circumspect. It rejected the claim that the positive right to health required the state to make additional resources available for dialysis treatment, emphasizing that the regional health budget was already overspent, and that a dramatic increase of the health budget would be required to accommodate all similarly situated patients in South Africa, which would imperil other state social obligations. Applying a reasonableness test to the guidelines imposed by the hospital administration, the Court announced what appeared to be an overly deferential standard of review with regard to social rights, cautioning that it would "be slow to interfere with rational decisions taken in good faith by the political organs and medical authorities whose responsibility it is to deal with such matters."

Expressing sympathy for the appellant (who died three days after the decision), the Court acknowledged "[t]he hard and unpalatable fact ... that if the appellant were a wealthy man he would be able to procure [dialysis] treatment from private sources...." The Court nonetheless reasoned that the state has to manage its limited resources, and that "[t]here will be times when this requires it to adopt a holistic approach to the larger needs of society rather than to focus on the specific needs of particular individuals within society."

Thus, the Court adopted a utilitarian perspective advancing the health of the population as a whole versus "doing everything for each individual patient until you run out of funds and everybody else gets nothing." Such reasoning is extremely problematic in a rights context. The point of giving policy choices the priority status of fundamental rights is to avoid the utilitarianism inherent in majority decision making. Utilitarianism in this context is premised on a presumption of fixed and limited resources. While such a presumption is contained in the language of the constitutional provision itself, it is troubling that the Court arbitrarily embellished this language with the additional qualification that the resources be available "for such purposes."

In a concurring opinion, Justice Sachs asserted that "the rationing of access to life prolonging resources is ... integral to ... a human rights approach to health care." He proposed a "new analytical framework" for collective rights, which substituted interdependence for autonomy as its bedrock principle:

> Traditional rights analyses ... have to be adapted so as to take account of the special problems created by the need to provide a broad framework of constitutional principles governing the right of access to scarce resources and to adjudicate between competing rights bearers. When rights by their very nature are shared and inter-dependent, striking appropriate balances between the equally valid entitlements or expectations of a multitude of claimants should not be seen as imposing limits on those rights ... but as defining the circumstances in which the rights may most fairly and effectively be enjoyed.

Soobramoney may be understood especially in light of the Court's subsequent jurisprudence, discussed below as a first step in defining the minimum normative core of the social rights guaranteed by the South African Constitution. Under this analysis, the relief sought by Mr. Soobramoney required access to a level of health care that exceeded the minimum core of the right to health. Similarly, although the majority opinion did not reach this issue, the case suggests that the minimum core of the right to life does not require the state to provide extraordinary life support measures that would not lead to a cure of the patient's illness.

Nevertheless, both the majority and concurring opinions beg the question whether the collective right to health actually conflicted with the individual's right to health and life in this context, that is, whether the state should be allowed to treat dialysis as an extraordinary resource that must be rationed for the poor in a country whose white citizens enjoy one of the highest standards of living in the world. The majority opinion made no mention of the resources available in the private sector, nor did it suggest that the state should do anything further to respond to the epidemic of kidney disease. In acknowledging that a person's wealth determined whether he would live or die, yet failing to interpret the constitutional rights to health and life to avoid this outcome, the Court missed an important opportunity to give meaning to the new social contract, suggesting a retreat from the challenge of justiciable social rights.

B.   Grootboom: *Collective Remedies for Legislative Commands*

The Constitutional Court's decision in *Government of the Republic of South Africa v. Grootboom* reassured social rights advocates that it was indeed willing to adjudicate positive rights claims. Contrary to the complaint that justiciable social rights remove policy choices from the legislative prerogative, the South African Constitutional Court demonstrated that violations of these rights can be remedied by a court without intruding unduly on legislative discretion.

The case arose under Section 26 of the South African Constitution which provides, in pertinent part:

(1) Everyone has the right to have access to adequate housing.

(2) The state must take reasonable legislative and other measures, within its available resources, to achieve the progressive realization of this right.

As part of the legacy of apartheid, millions of Black South Africans live in intolerable conditions. To alleviate the acute shortage of adequate housing in the country, the South African government developed an ambitious long term plan to build quality housing. However, a desperate need for emergency housing existed, which was not addressed in the plan. The Court found that this omission was a fatal constitutional flaw and ordered the Constituent Assembly to develop a program to accommodate those in desperate need with temporary shelter short of the sophisticated dwellings contemplated by the government plan.

The case was brought by a group of families who lived in Wallacedene, a squatter camp in the Western Cape, in what the Court described as "appalling conditions." When their situation became intolerable, they were forced to move out and settled on private land that had been earmarked for public housing. They were evicted by the government in a brutal manner reminiscent of the forced removals of the apartheid era: their shacks and belongings were destroyed, and the families were left homeless.

The Court found that the plaintiffs' housing situation was exacerbated by extreme poverty, noting that "a quarter of the households in Wallacedene had no income at all.... In some cases, their shacks are permanently flooded during the winter rains, others are severely overcrowded and some are perilously close to busy roads." The case was appealed by the government to the Constitutional Court after a lower court ordered the state to accommodate the families in basic shelter until permanent housing could be provided.

While commending the "major achievement" represented by the government's comprehensive housing program, the Court determined that the plan was not a reasonable effort to promote the constitutional right of access to adequate housing, because it excluded a significant segment of the population—those in desperate need. Noting that the United Nations

Committee on Economic, Social and Cultural Rights has formulated the concept of a state's "minimum core obligation," the Court stated that it was possible to ascertain the meaning of this standard in international law and apply it to the rights enumerated in the South African Constitution: "Minimum core obligation is determined generally by having regard to the needs of the most vulnerable group that is entitled to the protection of the right in question." A reasonable measure must therefore address the needs of this group.

In developing this concept the Court gave more teeth to the reasonableness standard than it appeared willing to do in *Soobramoney*. While giving assurances that it would not substitute its judgment on the wisdom of legislative measures for that of the political branches, the Court outlined the parameters of reasonableness in terms of the minimum core obligation: A reasonable legislative program "must be balanced and flexible and make appropriate provision for attention to housing crises and to short, medium and long term needs." It must take into account "[t]hose whose needs are the most urgent and whose ability to enjoy all rights therefore is most in peril...." Mere statistical success is not enough.

Similarly, the Court found added normative weight in the criterion in Section 26(2) of "progressive realization," a phrase that was not part of the analysis in *Soobramoney*, although it is also contained in the health care provision. Under this standard, consistent with the meaning that term is given in international law, the measures promulgated by the state must be calculated to realize the rights in question for everyone incrementally. Again, the Court cited the analysis of the Committee on Economic, Social and Cultural Rights, which declared that the requirement of progressive realization of the right to housing "imposes an obligation to move as expeditiously and effectively as possible towards that goal."

Accordingly, the Court found that the government's program lacked the requisite momentum:

> The absence of this component [emergency shelter] may have been acceptable if the nationwide housing programme would result in affordable houses for most people within a reasonably short time. However the scale of the problem is such that this simply cannot happen. Each individual housing project could be expected to take years.... The result is that people in desperate need are left without any form of assistance with no end in sight.

Emphasizing that the state has "the obligation to devise, fund, implement and supervise measures to provide relief to those in desperate need," the Court ordered the government to create a program that includes "reasonable measures ... to provide relief for people who have no access to land, no roof over their heads, and who are living in intolerable conditions or crisis situations." The opinion observed that the right to housing protects not only the most vulnerable in society, but people at all economic levels of society. However, the Court ruled that there was no positive individual right to housing on demand.

Grootboom represents a major milestone in the vindication of justiciable social rights. The decision has enriched the jurisprudence on the meaning of two fundamental concepts in international human rights law: that of minimum core obligation and progressive realization. Significantly, the case illustrates that because of the collective character of social rights these standards do not necessarily impose limitations on rights, but can be stringent criteria by which a court can measure states' compliance.

At the same time, the decision evidences the possibilities of judicial restraint. While undertaking the novel task of discovering the normative content of a constitutional right that is subject to the unusual condition of resource availability, the Court utilized textbook judicial methods to determine the reasonableness of a legislative measure. If its intervention could be labeled redistributive, it merely redistributed resources within the government program; the Court did not disturb the legislative determination of what resources were available. Thus, while the protection of fundamental rights required the judiciary to exercise a policy choice, the Court left to the legislature the ultimate policy decision of how much of the state's resources to commit to the right to housing.

The Court's ruling does, however, represent a victory for the organized efforts of housing rights advocacy groups, which could prompt the legislature to reconsider the adequacy of its housing budget. By highlighting the priority status of the right to housing and the plight of those deprived of that right, judicial review serves as a catalyst for social change.

C. Treatment Action Campaign: *Negative Rights and Positive Remedies*

In *Minister of Health v. Treatment Action Campaign*, the South African Constitutional Court revisited the issue of the scope of the right to health in the context of the tragic AIDS epidemic—a public health crisis of enormous proportions. The government appealed a High Court ruling finding it in breach of its constitutional obligation with respect to the right to health. In the decision, the High Court cited estimates that 10% of the South African population is HIV-positive, including 24% of pregnant women. Approximately 70,000 infants are infected annually through mother-to-child transmission. Clinical trials showed that the anti-retroviral drug Nevirapine could significantly reduce this risk if administered during labor. The manufacturer of the drug had offered to supply it to South African health authorities free of charge for five years. However, the Health Ministry instituted a limited pilot program administering the drug to pregnant women at a few selected public health clinics throughout the country.

The petitioners, apparently learning the lessons of *Soobramoney* and *Grootboom*, did not argue that every pregnant woman had a right to be provided Nevirapine on demand, but they challenged the government's failure to design a comprehensive nationwide program. They further argued that the state should not prohibit the administration of the drug by doctors and other health care professionals in the public health sector so long as patients have given informed consent to treatment. The High

Court's opinion, authored by Justice Botha, focused on Section 27(2) of the Constitution, framing the issue as whether the limited treatment program constituted a reasonable governmental measure to ensure the progressive realization of the right to health.

Citing *Grootboom*, the Court identified the factors to be considered in making a determination of reasonableness: (1) provision of appropriate financial and human resources; (2) reasonable implementation of the plan; and (3) the inclusion of all relevant segments of society. While acknowledging that the standard of progressive realization contemplates that the right to health care would not be achievable immediately, the Court pointed out that the program lacked an "unqualified commitment to reach the rest of the population in any given time or at any given rate." In view of the enormity of the threat to human life and health, the Court ruled that the phased implementation of the Nevirapine program was discriminatory. It reasoned that the state violated the negative obligation to desist from impairing the right to health care implicit in Section 27(1) by prohibiting the use of Nevirapine outside the pilot sites, and that the government had no justification for not making the drug widely available to the public. Moreover, the Court determined that the state had also violated the positive obligation in Section 27(2) to achieve the progressive realization of the right, concluding that "[t]he programme of the respondents lacks the impetus that is required for a programme that must move progressively. If there is no time-scale, there must be some other built-in impetus to maintain the momentum of progression.... That does no justice to the exigency of the case."

On appeal the Constitutional Court affirmed the essential elements of the High Court's ruling. Declaring that economic and social rights are "[c]learly" justiciable, the Court added that "when it is appropriate to do so, courts ... must ... use their wide powers to make orders that affect policy as well as legislation." In citing its earlier decision in *Soobramoney* in support of justiciability, the Court implicitly distinguished that case on its facts, opining that the plaintiff had simply failed to make out a violation of the right to health.

In preliminary comments, the Court sought to clarify its elaboration of the concept of "minimum core" in *Grootboom*, rejecting an argument by amici that this principle vests everyone with an individual right to the satisfaction of basic needs. Rather, the Court explained, the concept of minimum core provides a standard by which to assess the reasonableness of a governmental measure. Under this standard, the government program must address the needs of the most vulnerable in society, "[t]hose whose needs are the most urgent and whose ability to enjoy all rights therefore is most in peril...."

The case before it required the Court to consider the claim of a uniquely vulnerable group—infants threatened with the transmission of HIV/AIDS from their mothers at birth—that the government violated the negative dimension of their right to health by confining the use of Nevirapine to the pilot sites. It found that the allegedly prohibitive costs cited by the government as justification for its policy were associated with the development of a comprehensive long-term program, not with the provision of a single dose of the drug to mothers and their babies at birth. Dismissing concerns raised by the government regarding the efficacy and safety of the drug as unsupported by the evidence, the Court ruled that the government had breached its obligation under Sections 27(1) and (2) by its insistence that Nevirapine be administered only under the most optimal conditions. Thus, the government's program would not achieve the progressive realization of the right to health care mandated in Section 27(2) of the constitution, because it entailed "waiting for a protracted period before taking a decision on the use of Nevirapine beyond the research and training sites...."

After concluding that restricting access to Nevirapine in public health centers was unreasonable, the Court considered the implications of this determination for the government's AIDS policy, emphasizing the need for "a concerted national effort to combat the HIV/AIDS pandemic." It ruled that the government's policy "fails to meet constitutional standards because it excludes those who could reasonably be included where such treatment is medically indicated to combat mother to child transmission of HIV." While reiterating that this ruling does not grant everyone the right to individual treatment on demand, the court stressed that "[e]very effort must ... be made to [achieve this goal] as soon as reasonably possible." In the meantime, "[t]he policy will have to be that Nevirapine must be provided where it is medically indicated at those hospitals and clinics within the public sector where facilities exist for testing and counselling."

The Court acknowledged that since the case was first brought, the government had made significant adjustments in its AIDS policy, relaxing its rigid restrictions on the availability of Nevirapine, making substantial additional funds available for HIV treatment, and establishing comprehensive programs to combat mother-to-child transmission in three of the nine provinces in the country. Nevertheless, the Court found that additional relief was necessary, and ordered the government to "devise and implement within its available resources a comprehensive and co-ordinated programme to realise progressively the rights of pregnant women and their newborn children to have access to health services to combat mother–to-child transmission of HIV" which must include counseling, testing, and treatment.

The government was further ordered "without delay" to (a) remove the restrictions on Nevirapine; (b) make it available at public hospitals and clinics when medically indicated; (c) provide counselors at these sites; and (d) expand the availability of testing and counseling facilities throughout the public health sector to "facilitate and expedite the use of Nevirapine for the purpose of reducing the risk of mother-to-child transmission of HIV." Thus, while taking pains to insist that it was not creating a private right of action, the Court's ruling nonetheless requires the government to provide specific medical treatment to a specific population.

This ruling highlights the speciousness of Erica De Wet's distinction between traditional individual rights and social rights framed as constitutional commands addressed to state, which she calls "objective legal norms." Because in her view only individual entitlements are rights, De Wet does not regard legislative commands as generating correlative enforceable rights, since they do not, in terms, entitle individuals to relief on demand. Nevertheless, as this case illustrates, a court order enforcing a constitutional legislative command ultimately will benefit specific individuals. The perceived dilemma she posits is resolved if social rights are understood as collective rights, for which individual remedies are not necessarily the most efficacious response.

D. *Reconciling the Results*

The South African case law has evolved from the rejection of individual rights claims for life-preserving dialysis treatment, to recognition of collective rights to comprehensive government programs to address urgent social needs for housing and health care. Permeating these decisions is the influence of the two often-countervailing components of the social construction of rights: ideology and practice. On the one hand, pervasive individualist norms, such as the public/private dichotomy and the principle of free choice, inhibit the expansion of rights analysis beyond traditional first generation liberties. On the other, popular movements stimulate legal developments that can lead to more encompassing definitions of rights.

Both kidney disease and AIDS are serious, life-threatening harms. However, the AIDS epidemic has all of the characteristics of a classic "public" health crisis: a communicable disease that threatens the entire population. As such, AIDS more readily falls within the traditional scope of liberal state responsibility. In contrast, kidney disease, no matter how widespread, is seen as a "private" misfortune; its victims, while generating sympathy, may even be deemed "undeserving" of an urgent public response by having made bad lifestyle choices. Notably, in *Treatment Action Campaign*, the beneficiaries of constitutional relief were not the infected mothers, but the innocent—hence "deserving"—infants to whom the disease was transmitted *in utero*. Hopefully, these mothers will survive long enough to care for their children.

The fact that public housing has long been imbued with assumptions of government responsibility may also explain the *Grootboom* Court's willingness to intercede. Mass homelessness evokes the specter of rampant crime, disease, and public unrest. Interestingly, the court in this case identified individuals and other agents, as well as the state, as duty-holders of the right to housing. In contrast, in *Soobramoney* the Constitutional Court was markedly unwilling to recognize any duty in the private sector for the provision of dialysis treatment, despite the fact that the identical language on which it relied to eliminate the public/private distinction is contained in the section on the right to health.

Finally, the Court more readily acknowledged rights and correlative state duties where there was a history of political struggle demanding their recognition. Both the housing and AIDS cases took place against the backdrop of tenacious local and international movements on those issues.

In light of the huge domestic and international outcry over the South African government's handling of the AIDS crisis, the Court was apparently unwilling to presume the good faith of the authorities, as it had in *Soobramoney*. With each case, the Court has been more willing to question the adequacy of the government's allocation of resources to pressing social needs.

VI. TOWARD A GLOBAL SENSE OF COMMUNITY

The new South African jurisprudence demonstrates that there are no institutional obstacles to the realization of collective rights where the political will exists to enforce them. The cases also show that the full protection of social rights cannot be achieved without a reevaluation and reconstruction of liberal rights discourse.

According to economist Michel Chossudovsky, the world's poor countries, with 85.2% of the population, share only 21.5% of its income, while rich nations—14.8% of the population—account for 78.5%. As the chasm widens between the planet's privileged minority and its impoverished masses, the need for international recognition of collective rights has never been more apparent. Such a development is needed to fulfill the promise of universality proclaimed by human rights discourse. As Felice points out, in many cultures "the concept of collective human rights ... has an historical basis that runs far deeper ... than does the Western concept of individual rights." Moreover, individual rights are inadequate to protect disempowered groups when collective rights have not been realized.

The argument that a scarcity of resources renders social rights unattainable is unpersuasive. It is well documented that the world's abundant resources are sufficient to meet minimum core needs. World poverty is a function not of scarcity, but of distribution. [Michael] Walzer defines the available resources of the community as "the past and present product, the accumulated wealth of its members—not some 'surplus' of that wealth.... Socially recognized needs are the first charge against the social product; there is no real surplus until they have been met." He criticizes the inherently undemocratic nature of the right to unlimited accumulation in the face of dire need: "Men and women who appropriate vast sums of money for themselves while needs are still unmet act like tyrants, dominating and distorting the distribution of security and welfare."

To Walzer's definition I would add that the available resources include not just the wealth produced within a given state but that of the global community as a whole. This conception flows not only from the recognition of humanity's interdependence in the age of globalization but from elementary principles of justice: the international slave trade, colonialism, apartheid, physical and cultural genocide of indigenous peoples and continued inequities in North–South relations provide ample grounds to support an inclusive definition of available resources. Moreover, these historical experiences are constitutive of the human person in the twenty-first century. They are part of our collective identity. They are who we are. The rapid globalization of the economy and communications, as well as objective threats to global human welfare—such as nuclear war, environmental degradation, and the AIDS epidemic—lend urgency to the need for a collective conceptualization of the self that transcends geographical boundaries.

Thus, the available resources of South Africa include not only the monies directly at the disposal of the state; they include the immense wealth in the hands of the white minority—riches wrung from the suffering of the African people. It is possible that when the total resources of the country are taken into account, kidney dialysis could be considered a component of the minimum core right to health. Moreover, many rich nations are heavily indebted to the Black majority of South Africa for their government's economic, political, diplomatic, and military support of the apartheid regime. Similarly, the available resources of the "Third World" include those of the industrialized nations whose development was made possible by colonial exploitation.

Despite its theoretical weaknesses, the collective right of peoples to development offers a potential conceptual framework within which the issue of scarcity of resources can be addressed. Originally formulated by Senegalese jurist Keba M'Baye, the United Nations General Assembly adopted the Declaration on the Right to Development in 1986. The Declaration defines the right to development in both individual and collective terms. It is "an inalienable human right by virtue of which every human person and all peoples are entitled to participate in, contribute to, and enjoy economic, social, cultural and political development, in which all human rights and fundamental freedoms can be fully realized."

Critics correctly point out that the Declaration is vague as to the juridical basis and normative content of the right to development, including the identity of the rights-holders and duty-holders. Tanzanian scholar Issa Shivji criticizes the concept as essentially a demand for charity "based on an illusory model of co-operation and solidarity." When seen as part of the global demand for economic, social, and cultural rights, however, the right to development has the potential to surmount welfarist constraints. As William Felice argues, the right to development establishes an emerging principle in international law that "there is a collective international responsibility for the human condition."

VII.   CONCLUSION

In order for human rights discourse to evolve in the twenty-first century, the eighteenth-century fiction of natural, self-evident rights must give way to the realization that all rights are social constructs. They are the product of collective struggles: particular demands made on organized society in particular historical times and places. They represent values that, as a result of these struggles, society has agreed to prioritize. Critical scholars have deconstructed, denounced, and defended rights discourse, and have vigorously debated the efficacy of reifying fundamental values in legal form. Nevertheless, rights ideology is a powerful transformative force and a potent weapon in the hands of the dispossessed. Just as individual rights-talk served as a catalyst in the democratic revolutions of Europe and the United States, so too will the demand for second-and third-generation rights play a galvanizing role in the ongoing struggle of the world's impoverished millions to realize fully the dream of human dignity.

The Economic Bill of Rights

Excerpt from January 11, 1944 message to Congress on the State of the Union.

■ FRANKLIN D. ROOSEVELT

It is our duty now to begin to lay the plans and determine the strategy for the winning of a lasting peace and the establishment of an American standard of living higher than ever before known. We cannot be content, no matter how high that general standard of living may be, if some fraction of our people–whether it be one-third or one-fifth or one-tenth–is ill-fed, ill-clothed, ill-housed, and insecure.

This Republic had its beginning, and grew to its present strength, under the protection of certain inalienable political rights—among them the right of free speech, free press, free worship, trial by jury, freedom from unreasonable searches and seizures. They were our rights to life and liberty.

As our nation has grown in size and stature, however—as our industrial economy expanded—these political rights proved inadequate to assure us equality in the pursuit of happiness.

We have come to a clear realization of the fact that true individual freedom cannot exist without economic security and independence. "Necessitous men are not free men." People who are hungry and out of a job are the stuff of which dictatorships are made.

In our day these economic truths have become accepted as self evident. We have accepted, so to speak, a second Bill of Rights under which a new basis of security and prosperity can be established for all—regardless of station, race, or creed.

Among these are:

The right to a useful and remunerative job in the industries or shops or farms or mines of the nation;

The right to earn enough to provide adequate food and clothing and recreation;

The right of every farmer to raise and sell his products at a return which will give him and his family a decent living;

The right of every businessman, large and small, to trade in an atmosphere of freedom from unfair competition and domination by monopolies at home or abroad;

The right of every family to a decent home;

The right to adequate medical care and the opportunity to achieve and enjoy good health;

The right to adequate protection from the economic fears of old age, sickness, accident, and unemployment;

The right to a good education.

All of these rights spell security. And after this war is won we must be prepared to move forward, in the implementation of these rights, to new goals of human happiness and well being.

America's own rightful place in the world depends in large part upon how fully these and similar rights have been carried into practice for our citizens.

The New Deal Constitution in Exile

51 DUKE L.J. 165, 176–222 (2001).

■ WILLIAM E. FORBATH

* * * On the hustings, in radio addresses, and in more sustained debates, speeches, and writings, the lawmakers and [President Franklin D. Roosevelt] argued not simply that Congress had the *power* under the Constitution, rightly understood or amended, to regulate agriculture, industry, and labor. They argued that citizens had fundamental economic and social rights under the Constitution, rightly understood or amended; and Congress, therefore, had the *duty* to exercise its power to govern economic and social life in a way that sought to secure those rights. Making these arguments, New Dealers drew on a half-century-old tradition of constitutional discourse that I have dubbed the "social citizenship" tradition. It provided them not only a rights rhetoric, but also a constitutional narrative, modes of interpretation, and conceptions of the allocation of interpretive authority.

The narrative, of course, was about a "changing," "living" Constitution; more specifically, it was about constitutional change and continuity in an industrialized America. * * *

In Congress, after [*Schechter Poultry Corp. v. United States*, 295 U.S. 495 (1935) (, invalidating a provision of the National Industrial Recovery Act of 1933 as beyond the power of Congress)] in May 1935, and, with growing intensity, after [*Carter v. Carter Coal Co.*, 298 U.S. 238 (1936) (, invalidating a provision of the Bituminous Coal Conservation Act of 1935 as beyond the power of Congress)] in May 1936, proposals for constitutional amendments multiplied. "[H]aving in mind the Supreme Court's [decision in *Schechter*]," scores of New Deal congressmen would declare that "the time has come to extend the Bill of Rights to embrace such guarantees as 'the right to honest work,' an industry wide 'minimum standard of hours, wages, and fair competition,' and the like."

* * *

Accompanying these substantive ideas was a set of views about the allocation of interpretive and enforcement authority. It was clear that "[s]omebody should determine whether an act of Congress is repugnant to the Constitution." Only on rare occasions, however, and only in respect of certain constitutional provisions was the Court the proper somebody. The Constitution was a "statesman's document," whose general "abstract phrases" were best "interpreted in the legislative laboratory where and when the statute [was] being made." Until the late nineteenth century, New Dealers pointed out, the houses of Congress, the president, and the people at the polls were (almost) the sole wielders of a constitutional veto over congressional statutes.

Now that Congress had affirmative obligations as well as duties of self-restraint in respect of rights protection, this allocation of interpretive authority to Congress was all the more imperative. The right to work, "the equal right ... to a share of the Nation's employment asset"—these were modern rights that the Constitution, rightly understood, both authorized and obliged Congress to protect, and advocates insisted on the right of Congress "to determine for itself the meaning of [the Constitution's general rights protecting] provisions" in recognizing a modern social right to work. To those who insisted on "the traditional legal habit of looking upon rights as negative," these advocates first objected that seventeenth-and eighteenth-century ideas had imparted a rigidity that ill-served "legislators who must implement" the Constitution. * * * To be sure, social rights did not lend themselves to judicial enforcement, but judicial enforcement was not always the proper test of a right.

     * * *

From the first New Deal onward, the president set himself a task of constitutional narration and interpretation, to elaborate and win the nation's support for a "re definition of [inherited constitutional] rights in terms of a changing and growing social order." Thus, Roosevelt situated those rights in terms of their eighteenth century meaning. Quoting Jefferson, he evoked an agrarian past when America had "no paupers. The great mass of our population [was] of laborers ... [and m]ost of the laboring class possess[ed] property...." For these smallholder-citizens, the rights "involved in acquiring and possessing property," together with the ballot and the freedom to live by one's "own lights," ensured liberty and equality.

Well into the nineteenth century, Roosevelt's grand rights-interpreting narrative continued, roughly comparable conditions endured. If industrial concentration and industrial depressions tore away from many Americans the kind of economic independence and decent work that underwrote republican citizenship, still the frontier remained open, land remained cheap, and the scale of commerce and production in much of the nation remained small and local. So, for almost a century, in pre-industrial and industrializing America, the "old and sacred possessive [common law] rights" of property and labor, enshrined in the Court's Constitution, retained much of their social meaning for the "welfare and happiness" of ordinary Americans.

By the end of the nineteenth century, however, the frontier had closed, free land was "no more," and "our industrial combinations had become great uncontrolled and irresponsible units of power within the State." These new conditions robbed the old rights of their original meaning. All Americans understood this social historical sea change, Roosevelt suggested, and all had access to the insight that new contexts demanded new meanings lest old texts be distorted and old values lost.

* * * A mature industrial society could not be governed by a laissez-faire Constitution, insulating industry and finance from the modern claims of liberty and equality. America needed an "economic constitutional order." The terms of our basic rights "are as old as the Republic," but new conditions demand new readings. * * * A right "to make a living—a living decent according to the standard of the time" was at the heart of the new interpretation of the constitutional promise of liberty that Roosevelt had expounded throughout the 1936 election campaign.

* * *

[T]he social citizenship tradition held that lawmakers, and not the courts, were the appropriate interpreters and guardians of an important subset of fundamental rights, including the rights to social provision, decent labor standards, and decent work. It was patent to generations of populists and progressives that the courts not only would not, but also could not and should not translate the general rights-declaring provisions of the Reconstruction Amendments into specific guarantees of social and economic rights in industrial America. That required redistributive legislation and administrative machinery and a broad national political will to support them. The only important contribution the courts could make to this essentially political and legislative task was to allow the process to go forward. * * *

II. THE COUNTERREVOLUTION AND THE DEFEAT OF SOCIAL CITIZENSHIP

* * * To understand the present exile of the "right to live" and to make a living, we must examine the fate of the New Deal mandate.

A. *The Solid South, the Counterrevolution, and the Fracturing of Social Citizenship*

That fate was decided by the sway of Jim Crow over the politics of New Deal lawmaking. The nation's betrayal of Reconstruction prevented the legislative enactment of the New Deal vision of national citizenship. Measures instituting rights to decent work and social provision for all Americans enjoyed broad support, yet they expired in Congress. Thanks to their numbers, their seniority, and their control over key committees, southern Democrats had a hammerlock on Congress. The Solid South's national representatives generally supported the New Deal until the late 1930s. They demanded, however, that New Deal social provision and labor standards respect states' rights, by resting on state, and not national, administration and standard setting. Also, they insisted that key bills exclude the main categories of southern labor, else Congress would fall guilty of doing what it had done so often in the past, using legislation to "overcome the splendid gifts of God to the South." 'If southern agricultural labor were covered, how "were they going to get blacks to pick and chop cotton when Negroes [on federal work programs] were receiving . . . more than twice as much as they had ever been paid." The outrage to "our region" also "outrage[d] the Constitution," by threatening to "set up a dangerous and all powerful board . . . in Washington" in "utter violation of States' rights, local self-government, [and] local self-determination of our own sociological and economic problems."

At stake was the South's labor market, with its unique fusion of class and caste relations and its low wages. Social Security is a prime illustration of the Solid South's sway over reforms affecting that market. Roosevelt's Committee on Economic Security fashioned the administration's proposals to appease the Southern Bourbons. The Committee's blueprints adopted state-level autonomy—though with national minimum standards—in both unemployment insurance and assistance for the needy aged, dependent children, and blind. Only the old age benefits program would be purely federal. Nonetheless, when the blueprints arrived in Congress, the Dixiecrats demanded more from the sponsors of the administration bill. National standards for unemployment and old age insurance also vanished and the core principle of a national commitment to include all employed persons in the unemployment and old-age insurance schemes was abandoned. Finally, the Dixiecrats expelled agricultural and domestic workers from the nation's core social insurance programs, thereby expelling the majority of black Americans, who worked in these two sectors.

So it went across the array of core reforms. Whether the arena was agricultural or industrial recovery, industrial relations or labor standards, broad, inclusive bills—bills with national rather than local standards and administration—enjoyed solid support from the northern Democrats (and from disenfranchised southern blacks and poor whites). But the bills failed. For his first term, Roosevelt seemed entirely willing to oblige his party's powerful southern bloc and the "racial civilization" they prized. Then, however, as the 1936 election approached and business opposition to the New Deal intensified, Roosevelt grew more attentive to two crucial constituencies: the insurgent new industrial unions of the CIO and the black voters of the large cities of the North. As these groups began to bulk large in his 1936 reelection bid, Roosevelt's social and economic rights talk grew more universal and robust—and the southern attacks began. Governor Talmadge of Georgia called a "Grass Roots" convention to uphold the Constitution against "Negroes, the New Deal and . . . Karl Marx." For his part, Senator Carter Glass of Virginia challenged the white South to show "spirit and courage enough to face the new Reconstruction era that northern so called Democrats are menacing us with."

In the fall of 1937, after the Court had handed down *West Coast Hotel Co. v. Parrish* and *Jones & Laughlin*, and its steadfastness in upholding the old Constitution seemed to be crumbling, the New Deal's foes in Congress were galvanized. The old Constitution found a new redoubt, and

the counterrevolution authored a manifesto. A group of conservative southern Democrats in the Senate met with like-minded Republican senators to
consider a more formal alliance against the New Deal. If the judicial
safeguards for state sovereignty and individual liberty were eroding, they
agreed, they must invest renewed vigor in the century-old Constitution of
congressional constitutional precedent and practice. They drafted a "statement of principles"—it became known as the "Conservative Manifesto"
that reaffirmed their devotion to the Constitution of states' rights ("the
vigorous maintenance of States' rights, home rule, and local self-government"), liberty of contract (and the "common law principles of free men"),
and the property rights of the owners of capital ("the constitutional
guaranties of the rights . . . of property"). The attempt at forming a new
conservative party foundered, but the coalition and its role as bulwark for
the old Constitution held firm and prevailed.

The conservative coalition managed to cripple or undo administration
measures in the areas of labor reform and social insurance. World War II,
in turn, brought labor shortages and a burgeoning of national governmental controls on local and state economies. With this, southern congressmen
openly joined ranks with the minority-party Republicans to thwart
Roosevelt's executive reorganization plan, to gut the administration's 1945
Full Employment Bill, and to abolish the National Resources Planning
Board (NRPB).

The conservative coalition's accomplishments in destroying these agencies and thwarting these measures meant that Roosevelt's famous "second,
economic Bill of Rights" would find no enduring legislative and institutional embodiments, and the maturation of the idea of legislated fundamental
rights would cease. * * *

The constitutional bad faith—the willful blindness toward the Reconstruction Amendments' condemnation of racial caste—that for half a century enabled both parties and all three branches of the federal government to
condone or support Jim Crow and disenfranchisement produced the anomaly of a reactionary core, the Solid South, at the heart of Roosevelt's New
Deal liberal coalition. In the face of the Fifteenth Amendment's bar on
race-based disenfranchisement, the southern state governments disenfranchised black citizens through such racially "neutral" measures as the poll
tax and literacy tests. From the Southern oligarchs' perspective, these had
the additional benefit of also disenfranchising a majority of the region's
poor and working class whites, which enabled the Dixiecrat oligarchy to
choose the bulk of the South's congressional delegation. The upshot was
the derailing of the New Deal "revolution" by a Dixiecrat-led counterrevolution.

Put simply, the absence of *political* citizenship led to the defeat of
social citizenship in America. Not only were most black Americans excluded
from the benefits of the main New Deal programs, but this constitutional
bad faith at black America's expense also deprived all Americans of the
institutional foundations and political constitutional legacy of social citizenship. Broad social and economics rights talk fell into disuse after the

decisive defeats that the New Deal agenda suffered in the 1940s. Blocked by the Dixiecrats at every legislative crossroad, the CIO, social citizenship's only powerful, organized constituency, gradually abandoned its efforts to "complete the New Deal."

* * *

White America and the federal government's abandonment of Reconstruction did more than deprive black Americans of civil and political rights for almost another century. By allowing the emergence and consolidation of the Solid South, this constitutional bad faith prevented all Americans from securing the boon of social citizenship. From the perspective of this history, the New Deal constitutional legacy that is under attack today by restorationist scholars and judges is a marred one. The vast expansion of national governmental power has been constitutionally enshrined, but the reason for its expansion has not.

Nevertheless, this history may yield a constitutional imperative that binds citizens and lawmakers, the true authors and interpreters of the political Constitution. If this history proves persuasive, then perhaps the New Deal constitutional revolution was left unfinished. Its expansion of national authority rested on an unkept promise, and the fate of this promise of social citizenship was decided by the nation and government's complicity with Jim Crow. If I am right about these historical matters, then the question of social citizenship was concluded illegitimately and must be reopened. Even further, those who defend the main contours of congressional power under the New Deal Constitution may be obliged to make good faith efforts to enact the social citizenship rights it promised. The Court will not do anything to mend the broken constitutional links between racial and economic justice, but we can.

* * *

Forty Acres and a Mule: A Republican Theory of Minimal Entitlements

13 HARV. J.L. & PUB. POL'Y 37 (1990).

■ AKHIL REED AMAR

Let me begin by mapping out what, for this Federalist Society audience, I take to be common ground. Pure socialism is bad. A system of private property, at least up to a point, is good. A regime in which the state controlled all resources would threaten both individual liberty and true democracy. * * *

I will now move from this common ground to stake out a position that for this group may seem far less obvious. Private property is such a good thing that every citizen should have some. Indeed, a minimal entitlement to property is so important, so constitutive, and so essential for both individual and collective self-governance that to provide each citizen with that minimal amount of property, the government may legitimately redistribute property from other citizens who have far more than their minimal share. But wait—there's more. The notion of minimal entitlements is not simply constitutive, it is constitutional—not just constitutionally permissible, meaning that the government *may* distribute or redistribute to insure every citizen a minimal stake in society, but constitutionally obligatory. The government *must* do so. * * *

Now that I have your attention, let me explain. There is a tradition deep in American constitutional law that I shall refer to as the "R/republican tradition," with both a lowercase and a capital "R." This tradition was a driving force behind a number of significant political movements that helped shape the American political experience. These include Abraham Lincoln's Republican party in the 1860s (and before it the Free Soil party), Thomas Jefferson's Democratic Republicans at the turn of the Nineteenth Century, and before that, the ideological platform of a group of commonwealth writers, most prominently James Harrington, in England in the Seventeenth and Eighteenth Centuries.

In this R/republican tradition, there is a recognition that for one truly to be a citizen in a democracy and to participate in the democratic process, one needs a minimum amount of independence. Economic independence is necessary if the citizen is to be able to deliberate on the common good, the *res publica*, the thing public. (Hence the word republicanism.) According to this tradition, the problem of poor people is that, in a real way, they have no wills of their own. You may give them the right to vote, but they will alienate that right. They will sell it either to rich people or to foreign tyrants. They lack some minimal stake in society sufficient to connect their own personal interests with that of the larger public interest. * * *

I suggest that there are two basic ways of dealing with the R/republican notion that in order for a democracy to work, people must have a stake in society. The first way is the dark side–the exclusionary side–of the R/republican vision. It is the Athenian solution, and I would suggest the original American solution. That solution is to enslave people, to ruthlessly disfranchise people who do not have property, to adopt poll taxes and property qualifications. * * *

This original R/republican solution was radically modified by the Civil War and the Thirteenth Amendment. The solution to the problem is no longer the Athenian solution of enslavement. It is now an inclusionary solution, a solution that says We the People of the United States will not allow a degraded caste of people to exist in our society. It is a solution that provides people with inalienable property rights in their own persons. Moreover, I suggest, it is a vision that, especially under section two of the Thirteenth Amendment, * * * provides for forty acres and a mule. It is a vision that provides a right to sustenance and shelter: minimum sustenance, minimum shelter.

* * *

When the Reconstruction Amendments are viewed as a whole, a radically different vision of society emerges. Precisely because the Fifteenth Amendment gave former slaves the right to vote, and the Fourteenth Amendment made them citizens by dint of their birth, we should interpret the Thirteenth Amendment to guarantee each American a certain minimum stake in society. Otherwise, We the People of the United States really failed to set the slaves free—free from economic dependence. Without guaranteeing independence, it would have been both futile and dangerous under R/republican principles to have extended the rights of equal citizenship and equal votes to freedmen. * * *

* * * I have not, at least here, argued that this Thirteenth Amendment vision of forty acres and a mule is judicially enforceable under section one of the Thirteenth Amendment. There may very well be a variety of institutional limitations on courts that make them unsuitable for the tak. Rather, I would like to stress the obligation—not only a moral obligation, but a legal, a *constitutional* obligation—of Congress, under section two of the Thirteenth Amendment. Congress has both a constitutional right and a constitutional duty to implement this vision.

NOTES AND QUESTIONS

1. Social citizenship and economic and social rights. The term social citizenship was discussed in a famous essay by T.H. Marshall written in the 1940s. T.H. MARSHALL, *Citizenship and Social Class, in* SOCIOLOGY AT THE CROSSROADS 67 (1963). Marshall argued that the concept of citizenship was steadily broadening in order to ensure a fully participatory democracy, and that as part of this evolution the liberal state would expand its recognition of rights claims. Marshall envisioned a progression from civil rights (the classical eighteenth-century rights limiting the exercise of state power against citizens, such as freedom of speech and association) to political rights (rights, like the right to vote and to run for public office, that guarantee the citizen's technical ability to participate in a democratic government) to, finally, social rights, which would include "the whole range from the right to a modicum of economic welfare and security to the right to share to the full in the social heritage and to live the life of a civilized being according to the standards prevailing in the society." *Id.* at 74.

C.B. Macpherson makes a similar distinction between civil rights, which are rights against the state, and social rights, which are "claims for benefits to be guaranteed by the state." C.B. MACPHERSON, *Problems of Human Rights in the Late Twentieth Century, in* THE RISE AND FALL OF ECONOMIC JUSTICE AND OTHER ESSAYS 25 (1985).

Compare Roosevelt's *Economic Bill of Rights* to the United Nations' *International Covenant on Economic, Social and Cultural Rights,* and to the South African Constitution. What are the similarities and differences? Which rights identified in these texts are civil rights, which are political rights, and which are social rights?

2. Judicial role in enforcing economic and social rights. As both the Woods excerpt and the Forbath excerpt suggest, the implementation of social rights, including economic rights, may look very different than the implementation of political and civil rights. What is the role of the courts in enforcing social rights? Would an economic bill of rights in the United States necessarily change the relationship between the branches of government? Would it change what we mean by a right in the first place? Would a gradualist approach to fundamental rights, represented by South African constitutional law, be alien to United States legal culture? Would it be helpful or hurtful to political and legal movements for social change?

3. Race, class, and political economy. What is the relationship between race and class? Much ink has been spilled on this question. For example, some Marxists have insisted that racial exploitation is merely a cover for capitalist exploitation, while others have insisted that racial exploitation has a psychological and social dynamic that is independent of economic relations. *See* Martha R. Mahoney, *Class and Status in American Law: Race, Interest, and the Anti–Transformation Cases*, 76 S. CAL. L. REV. 799 (2003); Frances Lee Ansley, *Stirring the Ashes: Race, Class and the Future of Civil Rights Scholarship*, 74 CORNELL L. REV. 993 (1989). It seems generally agreed, however, that whether or not race and class exploitation are autonomous or one a subset of the other, they are certainly intertwined in United States history. Both Amar and Forbath suggest, for instance, that African American subordination and resistance are tied to political economy. Is this true of other racialized groups?

4. Racial liberation movements and economic development movements: some convergences. Scott Cummings traces the history of community economic development back to the famous dialogues between W.E.B. DuBois and Booker T. Washington. Although DuBois emphasized political action and Washington emphasized private investments in human capital and business development, both men saw economic development as key to black empowerment in the post-slavery era, and both championed the development of black businesses. Scott L. Cummings, *Community Economic Development as Progressive Politics: Toward a Grassroots Movement for Economic Justice*, 54 STAN. L. REV. 399, 410–11 (2001).

Many years later, another grassroots movement for black economic justice was spearheaded by women rather than men. The National Welfare Rights Organization (NWRO) was led by African American women, such as Johnnie Tillmon, who implemented local organizing campaigns designed to educate women receiving Assistance to Dependent Children (ADC), a program that was later renamed Aid to Families with Dependent Children (AFDC), about their rights to grants for food, rent, clothing, and furniture, and to force welfare offices to pay them. *See* GUIDA WEST, THE NATIONAL WELFARE RIGHTS MOVEMENT: THE SOCIAL PROTEST OF POOR WOMEN (1981). The hope was that "a mass welfare drive would expand benefits to millions of eligible persons and ultimately force the federal government to drastically reorganize the welfare—possibly through the imposition of a national guaranteed minimum income." Cummings, *supra* at 418.

Legal scholars as well as organizers looked forward to a constitutional right to welfare, *see, e.g.,* Frank I. Michelman, *The Supreme Court 1968 Term—Foreword: On Protecting the Poor Through the Fourteenth Amendment*, 83 Harv. L. Rev. 7 (1969), and at its peak, the NWRO claimed 22,000 dues paying members nationwide. Cummings, *supra*, at 419. The NWRO eventually collapsed, however, and in the 1980s President Ronald Reagan would use the image of black "welfare queens" as a central rallying point for the destruction of AFDC and other means-tested entitlement programs. *Id.* at 422. AFDC was ultimately abolished by President Clinton, who replaced the program with Temporary Assistance for Needy Families (TANF).

Analyzing the failure of the NRWO, some scholars argue that the effort of African American women to demand political inclusion based on a right to welfare conflicted with a long-standing ideology that identified female economic prosperity with marriage and dependency on a man earning a "family wage," not the state. *See* Rickie Solinger, Beggars and Choosers: How the Politics of Choice Shapes Adoption, Abortion, and Welfare in the United States (2001); Linda Gordon, Pitied But Not Entitled: Single Mothers and the History of Welfare, 1890–1935 (1994). Others argue that the welfare rights movement was politically vulnerable and ultimately failed because it was not tied to the principle of the inherent dignity and value of wage work, a principle deeply embedded in United States conceptions of citizenship. *See* William E. Forbath, *Constitutional Welfare Rights: A History, Critique and Reconstruction*, 69 Fordham L. Rev. 1821 (2001).

Another debate among historians concerning the convergence of the struggle for black liberation and the struggle for economic justice involves the Civil Rights Movement of the 1960s. Forbath argues that Civil Rights Movement leaders such as Martin Luther King, Jr. had a well-developed agenda for economic justice, but that it foundered, like the New Deal era agenda, on the rock of racial subordination. *See* William E. Forbath, *Caste, Class, and Equal Citizenship*, 98 Mich. L. Rev. 1 (1999). Risa Goluboff argues that the National Association for the Advancement of Colored People Legal Defense and Education Fund (commonly called the "NAACP Inc. Fund" or "Inc. Fund") must bear a share of the blame for the contemporary understanding of rights against racial discrimination as not comprehending economic rights. Goluboff argues that the Inc. Fund subordinated the complaints of black tenant farmers and sharecroppers, whose problems involving involuntary servitude, peonage, and wage ceilings were profoundly linked to the political economy of the South, to cases in which workers, "because they were black, were denied privileges extended to white workers in the same unions, the same jobs, the same companies, the same industries." Risa L. Goluboff, *"We Live's in a Free House Such As It Is": Class and the Creation of Modern Civil Rights*, 151 U. Pa. L. Rev. 1977, 2012 (2003). According to Goluboff, "As NAACP lawyers contemplated their attack on racial inequality in the 1940s, labor-related inequality as experienced by African Americans working in southern agriculture stood outside their framework." *Id.* at 2010.

Scholars also have questioned whether African Americans have been well served by their historic alliance with the political left. David Bernstein suggests that the traditional "liberal," pro-union, pro-civil rights position has disserved Chinese American and African American agricultural, service, and industrial workers, who would have been benefitted more from adherence to laissez-faire ideology and anti-union political movement. *See* David Bernstein, Lochner, *Parity, and the Chinese Laundry Cases*, 41 WM. & MARY L. REV. 211 (1999); David E. Bernstein, *The Law and Economics of Post–Civil War Restrictions on Interstate Migration by African–Americans*, 76 TEX. L. REV. 781 (1998); David Bernstein, *The Davis–Bacon Act: Vestige of Jim Crow*, 13 NAT'L BLACK L.J. 276 (1994). *But see* Kendall Thomas, *Rouge et Noir Reread: A Popular Constitutional History of the Angelo Herndon Case, in* CRITICAL RACE THEORY: THE KEY WRITINGS THAT FORMED THE MOVEMENT 465 (Kimberlé Crenshaw et al. eds., 1995) (describing the solidarity between African American radicals and the Communist Party).

5. Basing economic rights in Reconstruction Constitution. Do the Reconstruction Amendments provide, as Akhil Amar suggests, an imaginative resource for rethinking economic rights? For another attempt to use antislavery constitutionalism as a foundation for economic justice and anti-subordination vision generally, see Peggy Cooper Davis, *Neglected Stories and Progressive Constitutionalism*, 4 WIDENER L. SYMP. J. 101 (1999).

CHAPTER 3

CLASSIC MARKET THEORY AND LAW AND ECONOMICS

A. CLASSIC MARKET THEORY

Economics is the study of how scarce resources—land, capital, and labor—can best be allocated to satisfy human wants. Although it would be impossible to cover the whole of economic theory in a single chapter, this section describes some basic assumptions about human nature, the organization of society, and the role of government that have influenced the development of our modern economic and legal systems.

Economic analyses can be divided into two types: *positive* and *normative*. Positive economics attempts to describe in a rigorous way how markets operate, without judging whether the outcomes are good or bad. Normative economics takes the pursuit of greater efficiency as the primary good in governance, and frequently argues that governance through markets is superior to governance by direct state regulation. As you read the excerpts below, ask yourself which arguments are positive and which are normative, and why it makes a difference. Ask yourself, also, in what ways contemporary economic analysis has diverged from the work of Adam Smith.

Both strands of economic analysis—positive and normative—owe a central debt to the work of Adam Smith (1723–1790). Smith was a popular, absent-minded professor of moral philosophy—a field that at the time incorporated theology, ethics, justice, and political economy—at Scotland's University of Glasgow. Smith is called the "father of modern economics" because "[he] was the first to explain in detail the role of human beings in the development of markets and how these markets function to solve the basic economic problems that confront any society: what goods to produce, how to produce them, and to whom they should be distributed."

From the sixteenth through the nineteenth centuries, European nations generally solved these problems through mercantilism, an economic system in which the government regulated and dictated economic activity. Mercantilism used tools such as monopolies, subsidies, tariffs, and restrictive labor policies to build up a nation's gold and silver reserves, the theoretical source of economic power. Despite the restrictive regulations mercantilism involved, the English economy was expanding, in part through illegal market activities.

Smith's emphasis on the role of people in economic development was pioneering. His work defined the classical school of economics, which explains the economy in the context of human behavior. *The Theory of Moral Sentiments* (1759) explored the ethics and principles motivating human behavior and argued that people are mainly driven by self-interest, tempered by an "impartial spectator," or conscience. In the *Wealth of Nations* (1776), his most famous work, Smith used his theory of human nature to show how individuals acting in their own self-interest, unregulated by the state, could nevertheless collectively maximize the wealth of all. Smith argued that "[s]elf interest leads to market exchange, which fosters the division of labor, which leads in turn to specialization, expertise, dexterity, and improved machinery and ultimately creates greater wealth." Most famously, Smith described the results of this system of undirected market exchange as "the invisible hand": even purely self-interested behavior can result in a better life for all, as if an invisible hand had ordered the result.

Smith's assumption, shared by most contemporary economists, that people are chiefly motivated by self-interest is a controversial one. The following excerpt examines in more detail Smith's beliefs about human nature.

Adam Smith's View of Man

19 J.L. & ECON. 529 (1976).

■ R. H. COASE

* * * It is sometimes said that Adam Smith assumes that human beings are motivated solely by self-interest. Self-interest is certainly, in Adam Smith's view, a powerful motive in human behaviour, but it is by no means the only motive. I think it is important to recognise this since the inclusion of other motives in his analysis does not weaken but rather strengthens Adam Smith's argument for the use of the market and the limitation of government action in economic affairs.

* * * In *The Theory of Moral Sentiments*, man's actions are influenced by benevolence. In the *Wealth of Nations*, this motive is apparently absent. This view is supported by a much-quoted passage: "It is not from the benevolence of the butcher, the brewer, or the baker, that we expect our dinner, but from their regard to their own interest. We address ourselves, not to their humanity but to their self-love, and never talk to them of our own necessities but of their advantages." What is not quoted is something which Adam Smith says earlier in the same paragraph: "In civilized society [man] stands at all times in need of the co-operation and assistance of great multitudes, while his whole life is scarce sufficient to gain the friendship of a few persons." This puts a completely different complexion on the matter. For that extensive division of labour required to maintain a civilized standard of living, we need to have the co-operation of great multitudes, scattered all over the world. There is no way in which this co-operation could be secured through the exercise of benevolence. Benevolence, or love, may be the dominant or, at any rate, an important factor within the family or in our relations with colleagues or friends, but as Adam Smith indicates,

it operates weakly or not at all when we deal with strangers. Benevolence is highly personal and most of those who benefit from the economic activities in which we engage are unknown to us. * * *

Looked at in this way, Adam Smith's argument for the use of the market for the organisation of economic activity is much stronger than it is usually thought to be. The market is not simply an ingenious mechanism, fueled by self-interest, for securing the co-operation of individuals in the production of goods and services. In most circumstances it is the only way in which this could be done. Nor does government regulation or operation represent a satisfactory way out. A politician, when motivated by benevolence, will tend to favour his family, his friends, members of his party, inhabitants of his region or country (and this whether or not he is democratically elected). Such benevolence will not necessarily redound to the general good. And when politicians are motivated by self-interest unalloyed by benevolence, it is easy to see that the results may be even less satisfactory.

The great advantage of the market is that it is able to use the strength of self-interest to offset the weakness and partiality of benevolence, so that those who are unknown, unattractive, or unimportant, will have their wants served. But this should not lead us to ignore the part which benevolence and moral sentiments do play in making possible a market system. Consider, for example, the care and training of the young, largely carried out within the family and sustained by parental devotion. If love were absent and the task of training the young was therefore placed on other institutions, run presumably by people following their own self-interest, it seems likely that this task, on which the successful working of human societies depends, would be worse performed. At least, that was Adam Smith's opinion: "Domestic education is the institution of nature— public education the contrivance of man. It is surely unnecessary to say which is likely to be the wisest." Again, the observance of moral codes must very greatly reduce the costs of doing business with others and must therefore facilitate market transactions. As Adam Smith observes, "Society ... cannot subsist among those who are at all times ready to hurt and injure one another...."

Adam Smith allows for a good deal of folly in human behaviour. But this does not lead him to advocate an extensive role for government. Politicians and government officials are also men. Private individuals are constrained in their folly because they personally suffer its consequences: "Bankruptcy is perhaps the greatest and most humiliating calamity which can befall an innocent man. The greater part of men, therefore, are sufficiently careful to avoid it." But, of course, men who bankrupt a city or a nation are not necessarily themselves made bankrupt. Adam Smith, therefore, continues: "Great nations are never impoverished by private, though they sometimes are by public prodigality and misconduct." As he later observes: "[Kings are and ministers] are themselves, always, and without any exception, the greatest spend thrifts in the society. Let them look well after their own expence, and they may safely trust private people with theirs. If their own extravagance does not ruin the state, that of their subjects never will."

* * *

It is wrong to believe, as is commonly done, that Adam Smith had as his view of man an abstraction, an "economic man," rationally pursuing his self-interest in a single-minded way. Adam Smith would not have thought it sensible to treat man as a rational utility-maximiser. He thinks of man as he actually is—dominated, it is true, by self-love but not without some concern for others, able to reason but not necessarily in such a way as to reach the right conclusion, seeing the outcomes of his actions but through a veil of self-delusion. No doubt modern psychologists have added a great deal, some of it correct, to this eighteenth-century view of human nature. But if one is willing to accept Adam Smith's view of man as containing, if not the whole truth, at least a large part of it, realisation that his thought has a much broader foundation than is commonly assumed makes his argument for economic freedom more powerful and his conclusions more persuasive.

As the Coase excerpt above suggests, Smith's theory was influential in part because it sought to provide a better policy solution than mercantilism to the problem of production and exchange in a mass society. Smith showed how a system of competition, under which producers competed to offer the highest quality goods at the lowest possible prices, could encourage the efficient allocation of resources without the need to resort to government coercion. The excerpt that follows updates Smith's basic insight.

The Advantages of a Free–Enterprise Price System

INVISIBLE HAND 64–68 (Adrian Klaasen ed., 1965).

■ W. ALLEN WALLIS

* * *

Suppose you were asked how to organize [the population of the United States] to utilize the resources available to them for their material satisfactions. You can imagine you have a fairly detailed inventory of the natural resources of the country, of the people and their knowledge, energies and abilities and of their wants. Imagine that all these resources are as unorganized as a set of chessmen just poured out of their box and awaiting organization on the chessboard. [The next issue concerns deciding how to organize the supply to meet the demand.]

[O]ne of the first things you are going to need is some way of establishing goals and measuring achievement. Which of the many things wanted are going to be produced, in what quantities, and with what priorities?

After you establish these goals and priorities, you will need a method of assigning the various pieces of capital, the various natural resources and the various people to particular activities. Each will have several alternative uses; you will need a method of deciding which use to assign it or him to, and of coordinating the resources assigned to cooperate in each task.

Then, third, you will have to have some system for dividing the product among the people: who gets how much of what, and when?

Fourth, you will probably realize that for one reason or another your system [will create mismatches between supply and demand]. You will need some system of adjustment to [account for these mismatches], until your method of measuring achievement and your method of allocating resources can get the basic situation corrected.

A fifth kind of problem you may worry about is that of providing for the expansion and improvement of your capital, equipment and technological knowledge.

These five functions have to be provided for when you establish any organization, even a small and relatively simple one. When we consider the large and complex organization of an entire economy, what are some of the alternative ways of arranging for them?

The most obvious way to arrange things is the way an army does. You set up a commander or a general staff. They decide on goals, they decide who shall do what to attain them, they decide how to apportion the product; and they issue orders accordingly. Another method is that used in beehives and ant colonies, in which caste and custom determine who does what. Things go on in the same way, generation after generation.

A third way is to introduce money and let each person decide what activities that others will pay for he will engage in, and what things that others offer for money he will buy. This is a method that no one really invented. It requires careful and sometimes complicated analysis to discover how it will really work. Indeed, it was only with the recognition that this is in fact a method of organizing society that the scientific study of economics began, back in 1776.

Under this system, goals are set by the money offers of individuals for goods and services. Resources are allocated to one activity or another by the desires of their owners for money income. Goods are distributed to individuals according to their willingness and ability to pay the prices. Thus prices become the crucial organizing element in such an economy. Indeed, this system is often called the "price system."

The price system has two outstanding features. First, it is by all odds the most efficient system of social organization ever conceived. It makes it possible for huge multitudes to cooperate effectively, multitudes who may hardly know of each other's existence, or whose personal attitudes toward one another may be indifference or hostility. Second, it affords a maximum of individual freedom and a minimum of coercion. And since people can cooperate effectively in production even when their attitudes on other issues are hostile, there is no need for unity and conformity in religion, politics, recreation and language—or even in patriotism and goodwill, except in the very broadest senses.

> * * *

NOTES AND QUESTIONS

1. **Markets, price theory, and the invisible hand.** Are there times when price theory fails to adequately serve the communication function Wallis identifies? Are there technical obstacles in some situations to using the price system for the allocation of goods? Theories of "market failure," discussed in the next chapter, take up these questions.

2. **Smith and professional economists.** For many modern economists, Smith was a great economist, perhaps the greatest ever. Adam Smith was not truly an economist as we understand that discipline today. Smith laid many of the foundations of modern economics with the *Wealth of Nations*, "but not for another century did economics truly become established as . . . a separate discipline." Skousen, *supra* at 195. As an academic, Smith was appointed professor of Logic at the University of Glasgow in 1751, and transferred to the chair of moral philosophy in 1752. ROBIN PAUL MALLOY & JERRY EVENSKY, ADAM SMITH AND THE PHILOSOPHY OF LAW AND ECONOMICS 34 (1994). As a moral philosopher, Smith drew on the work of contemporary thinkers such as Hume, Franklin, and Montesquieu when writing both *The Theory of Moral Sentiments* and the *Wealth of Nations*. SKOUSEN, *supra* at 38, 41–42.

3. **Economic analysis and the rational actor.** Although Adam Smith's understanding of "economic man" incorporated benevolence, altruism, and sympathy, the tradition of "neoclassical" economics that followed in his footsteps focused on modeling self-interested behavior rather than other-directed behavior. In contemporary terms, economic analysis adopts some version of "rational choice" theory: individuals enter a market with specific preferences, and they act so as to satisfy those preferences to the greatest extent possible at the lowest possible cost. Rational actor theory has been much criticized; these critiques will be taken up in the next chapter.

4. **Modern evolution of classic market theory: victory of neoclassical theory.** Historian Michael Bernstein notes that an important debate within the discipline of economics took place around the turn of the twentieth century. On the one hand were:

> those determined to preserve for economics a pride of place, grounded in rigorous theory, among the social sciences. For these scholars it was clear that, in the words of the eminent Alfred Marshall, "the raison d'être of economics as a separate science [wa]s that it deal[t] chiefly with the part of [people's] action which [wa]s most under the control of

measurable motives." It was necessarily the case, therefore, that economists had to employ "selective principles" in order to understand human behavior. Utilizing "a series of deductions from the fundamental concept of scarcity," the discipline's practitioners were thus in a position to engage in truly "analytical" studies that were, given a "correspondence [between] original assumptions and the facts," realistic approximations of social conduct. While history, institutions, law, and ideology could provide more detailed and nuanced explanations of actual economic events, the core analytical principles of economic explanation remained distinct.

MICHAEL A. BERNSTEIN, A PERILOUS PROGRESS: ECONOMISTS AND PUBLIC PURPOSE IN TWENTIETH-CENTURY AMERICA 45–46 (2001).

For these scholars, the discipline of economics could provide an "objective science of society." *Id.* at 45. These "neoclassical" economists were drawn to rigorous mathematical models of economic behavior.

On the other side of the debate were the "institutionalists," a group of economists, many of them involved in public policy work for the federal government, who sought a broader scope for economics. Institutionalist economics was rooted in the work of Thorstein Veblen, who in the late 1890s and early 1900s attacked neoclassical theory for its excessive abstraction from the real world of economic behavior and posited that the search for social "status"—not just the desire for financial profit—motivated much of economic production, by spurring the desire for conspicuous consumption. According to Bernstein:

> [T]he institutionalists conceived of economics as a far more catholic field in which any claims to realism rested perforce on broadly construed disciplinary boundaries. Indeed, both [Wesley] Mitchell and Veblen themselves had aggressively attacked the manner in which neoclassical investigators ignored human activity that could not be understood simply as the "rational" and calculating response of individuals to the constraints of the market. To their minds "such institutions as the market, trade, contract, property, and competition" were themselves the product of political, cultural, and historical circumstances all of which were worthy of the economist's attention.

Id. at 46.

Accordingly, the institutionalists were empiricist rather than theoretical and mathematical in their bent. Ultimately, however, it was the neoclassicists who won the battle and ascended to power over the institutionalists.

5. Cold War and discipline of economics. Michael Bernstein argues that "[i]n its theoretical and methodological trajectory, the American economics profession was decisively affected by the pressures, constraints, and opportunities afforded by the Cold War preoccupations of the federal government, colleges and universities, and private foundations and 'think tanks.'" *Id.* at 94. During World War II, mathematically-driven developments in economics such as "activity analysis" and "linear programming" made it possible for economists to help the War Department plan resource allocation and distribution plans (for example, to calculate the most efficient supply shipments). During the Cold War, the federal government, both directly and through organizations such as the RAND Corporation (originally Project RAND under the supervision of the Air Force) and the National Science Foundation, generously supported research into "game theory" and other mathematical approaches to the problem of modeling competitive behavior. Game theory, for example, demonstrated how strategic behavior could be modeled mathematically, and these models could be applied to problems such as nuclear deterrence. Macroeconomic theory was also appealing to government funders, because of the promise that it could be directly applied to the project of sustaining the American economy and preserving and protecting the nation's security. For example, in 1954, the staff of the Council of Economic Advisers initiated "a series of wide-ranging discussions on the matter of 'emergency economic stabilization' in the event of a nuclear exchange." *Id*. at 104. The idea was that "in the event of a nuclear attack civil defense authorities should be given the power to set wages, prices, and rents—as well as to ration goods and services. To be effective, plans for such a contingency would need to be set up in advance." *Id*.

The issues of national security and national prosperity were intertwined, and both of them seemed uniquely suited to economists' strengths. Bernstein observes:

> High rates of growth, robust levels of employment, and stable prices were the standards by which a capitalist society could demonstrate its advantages over command economies premised upon socialist or communist designs. As the emblematic "Kitchen Debate" between Soviet premier Nikita Khrushchev and Vice President Richard Nixon had suggested in 1959, winning the Cold War involved more than husbanding a credible nuclear deterrent, deploying fleets, garrisons, and air wings around the world, and utilizing special forces in counterinsurgency campaigns. It also required that an economic system deliver the goods to the people. Prosperity was an essential weapon in the struggle for the hearts and minds of any society.

Id. at 107.

By the 1950s, argues Bernstein, "No longer the study of 'the nature and causes of the wealth of nations' (as Adam Smith had claimed), or 'a critical analysis of capitalist production' (as Karl Marx suggested), economics had become the formal study of 'the adaptation of scarce means to given ends.'" *Id*. at 95. The means to this study should be apolitical and objective. Thus, "[g]one from a rising number of nationally ranked graduate programs in economics, by the late 1950s, were agendas that acquainted the student with the work of a Thorstein Veblen, a Joseph Schumpeter, or a Karl Polanyi—not to mention a Karl Marx. In their place were 'core' course sequences that emphasized neoclassical theory, most often in its mathematical representations." *Id*. at 123. Although the 1960s and 1970s saw a challenge by a "New Left" within the economics profession—which formed organizations such as the Union for Radical Political Economics (URPE), and identified and attacked logical inconsistencies at the heart of neoclassical economics—neoclassical economics continued to define the discipline up to the end of the twentieth century.

6. Economic theory and the rise and fall of Keynesian macroeconomics. As we have seen, Adam Smith wrote primarily against the "mercantilism" of his time, a system in which the state heavily controlled economic behavior, often by granting monopolies in crucial trading industries to particular organizations and individuals. Smith's metaphor of the invisible hand suggested that a market free of such government intervention would provide more prosperity for everyone, and that such a market would be self-regulating. In 1936, however, an Englander named John Maynard Keynes [1883–1946], published a book called *The General Theory of Employment, Interest, and Money* [hereafter the *General Theory*] that paved the way for a new discipline of "macroeconomics." Keynes was many things during his illustrious career: "a brilliant student at England's most famous prep school; an equally brilliant student and then professor at Kings College in Cambridge; a financier who made a fortune for himself, and, later for Kings College by overseeing its endowment fund; president of a life-insurance company; patron of the arts; husband of a famous Russian ballerina; member of the influential 'Bloomsbury set' of intellectuals; esteemed official of the British Treasury; board member of the Bank of England; and the principal designer of the international financial system after World War II." CHARLES SACKREY & GEOFFREY SCHNEIDER, INTRODUCTION TO POLITICAL ECONOMY 80–81 (3d ed. 2002).

Keynes's innovation begins with the "business cycle": over time, national economies tend to experience periods of growth, followed by periods of seeming economic collapse, involving sudden drops in wages, mass unemployment, and drastically reduced spending power (known as recessions). The most famous of these in the United States was, of course, the Great Depression, which followed the stock crash of 1929. Classical economists argued that during these depressions, falling wages would lower costs and prices and invite a greater demand for goods and services. Thus, downturns in the business cycle are always self-correcting. Keynes argued, however, that "a *general* fall in wages . . . would likely cause an eventual *decline* in the demand for goods and services that workers buy, rather than an increase encouraged by the lower prices." *Id.* at 92. Moreover, falling wages could reduce the optimism of capitalists and encourage them to reduce investment in new equipment. The result would be a downward spiral for the economy rather than a self-correcting equilibrium. As a policy matter, then, Keynes argued that an active rather than passive government response to recessions and depressions was required:

> "[A]s investment and consumption spending fell, the government should take up the slack in demand by borrowing money to increase its own expenditures * * * And it didn't matter for what those expenditures were made. As this spending worked its way through the economy, it would ultimately produce a better outlook for businesses, which

meant more investment on capital goods. * * * [T]his would start the whole process moving back upward to recovery and economic growth.

Id. at 97.

Keynesian theory and policy quickly became mainstream. The massive government spending involved in the United States' participation in World War II appeared to prove Keynes right about the ability of governments to take action against economic recessions, and the Cold War period saw the adoption of Keynesian macroeconomic policy on a broad scale. Sackrey and Schneider observe:

> A symbolic highpoint of the influence of Keynes occurred in 1963, when in a speech at Yale University John Kennedy used the idea of the Keynesian multiplier to justify the cut in personal income taxes he was urging on the Congress as a way to cause a sluggish economy to grow faster. The essentially Keynesian basis of domestic U.S. economic policy remained in place for about 25 years, and, in 1971, an economic conservative, Richard Nixon, argued that "we are all Keynesians now."

Id. at 98.

Nevertheless, the rise of Keynesian macroeconomics was followed by a fall. Beginning in the late 1960s, the American national economy began to experience persistent and growing inflation. In the early 1970s, the Organization of Petroleum Exporting Countries (OPEC) announced a plan to dramatically cut petroleum production, setting off a series of global economic shocks. Soon the American economy was experiencing high inflation and high unemployment at the same time—a situation, nicknamed "stagflation," thought to be impossible by professional economists. Real incomes fell dramatically and capital investments stagnated, and Keynesian theorists seemed helpless to address the problem. Into the breach stepped new macroeconomic theories. The "new classical" economists argued that government interventions in the market were futile because economic actors would always be able to anticipate and adjust their behavior to such interventions. "Supply-side" economists argued that the country's economic woes were caused by

> high levels of government spending, high taxation of income, and extensive governmental regulation of economic affairs. Excessive income taxation, it was argued, stifled productive effort, for example, by discouraging overtime work. It robbed individuals of the fruits of enterprise and risk-bearing. Finally, it distorted economic decision making so as to slow growth and create the very fiscal pressure that contributed to the problems of "stagflation" in the first instance. The solution would involve a radical reduction in taxes, a systematic shrinking of government spending programs and, thus, federal agency budgets, and the elimination of costly regulatory measures.

MICHAEL A. BERNSTEIN, A PERILOUS PROGRESS, *supra* at 164.

These scholarly arguments were supported by a new turn in electoral politics against "big government." Ronald Reagan's decisive 1980 victory over Jimmy Carter for the presidency symbolized a new consensus in the electorate that government did not work, that private businesses should be as free of regulation as possible, and that taxes should be cut in order to reward individual initiative and let the "invisible hand" do its work. Although few professional economists agreed with the excesses of "Reaganomics," a general mood in favor of laissez-faire economics, deregulation, and "privatization" now characterized the electorate and dominated thought in the Beltway.

B.   LIBERTARIANISM

Created Equal

FREE TO CHOOSE: A PERSONAL STATEMENT 128–49 (1980).

■ MILTON FRIEDMAN & ROSE FRIEDMAN

"Equality," "liberty"—what precisely do these words from the Declaration of Independence mean? Can the ideals they express be realized in practice? Are equality and liberty consistent one with the other, or are they in conflict?

Since well before the Declaration of Independence, these questions have played a central role in the history of the United States. The attempt to answer them has shaped the intellectual climate of opinion, led to bloody war, and produced major changes in economic and political institutions. This attempt continues to dominate our political debate. It will shape our future as it has our past.

In the early decades of the Republic, equality meant equality before God; liberty meant the liberty to shape one's own life. The obvious conflict between the Declaration of Independence and the institution of slavery occupied the center of the stage. That conflict was finally resolved by the Civil War. The debate then moved to a different level. Equality came more and more to be interpreted as "equality of opportunity" in the sense that no one should be prevented by arbitrary obstacles from using his capacities to pursue his own objectives. That is still its dominant meaning to most citizens of the United States.

Neither equality before God nor equality of opportunity presented any conflict with liberty to shape one's own life. Quite the opposite. Equality and liberty were two faces of the same basic value—that every individual should be regarded as an end in himself.

A very different meaning of equality has emerged in the United States in recent decades—equality of outcome. Everyone should have the same level of living or of income, should finish the race at the same time. Equality of outcome is in clear conflict with liberty. The attempt to promote it has been a major source of bigger and bigger government, and of government-imposed restrictions on our liberty.

EQUALITY BEFORE GOD

When Thomas Jefferson, at the age of thirty-three, wrote "all men are created equal," he and his contemporaries did not take these words literally. They did not regard "men"—or as we would say today, "persons"—as equal in physical characteristics, emotional reactions, mechanical and intellectual abilities. * * *

The clue to what Thomas Jefferson and his contemporaries meant by equal is in the next phrase of the Declaration—"endowed by their Creator with certain unalienable rights; that among these are Life, Liberty, and the pursuit of Happiness." Men were equal before God. Each person is precious in and of himself. He has unalienable rights, rights that no one else is entitled to invade. He is entitled to serve his own purposes and not to be treated simply as an instrument to promote someone else's purposes. "Liberty" is part of the definition of equality, not in conflict with it.

Equality before God—personal equality—is important precisely because people are not identical. Their different values, their different tastes, their different capacities will lead them to want to lead very different lives. Personal equality requires respect for their right to do so, not the imposition on them of someone else's values or judgment. Jefferson had no doubt that some men were superior to others, that there was an elite. But that did not give them the right to rule others.

If an elite did not have the right to impose its will on others, neither did any other group, even a majority. Every person was to be his own ruler—provided that he did not interfere with the similar right of others. Government was established to protect that right—from fellow citizens and from external threat—not to give a majority unbridled rule. * * *

Similarly, Alexis de Tocqueville, the famous French political philosopher and sociologist, in his classic *Democracy in America*, written after a lengthy visit in the 1830s, saw equality, not majority rule, as the outstanding characteristic of America. "In America," he wrote,

> the aristocratic element has always been feeble from its birth; and if at the present day it is not actually destroyed, it is at any rate so completely disabled, that we can scarcely assign to it any degree of influence on the course of affairs. The democratic principle, on the contrary, has gained so much strength by time, by events, and by legislation, as to have become not only predominant but all-powerful. There is no family or corporate authority....

> America, then, exhibits in her social state a most extraordinary phenomenon. Men are there seen on a greater equality in point of fortune and intellect, or, in other words, more equal in their strength, than in any other country of the world, or in any age of which history has preserved the remembrance.

> * * *

It is striking testimony to the changing meaning of words that in recent decades the Democratic party of the United States has been the chief instrument for strengthening that government power which Jefferson and many of his contemporaries viewed as the greatest threat to democracy. And it has striven to increase government power in the name of a concept of "equality" that is almost the opposite of the concept of equality Jefferson identified with liberty and Tocqueville with democracy.

* * *

EQUALITY OF OPPORTUNITY

Once the Civil War abolished slavery and the concept of personal equality—equality before God and the law—came closer to realization, emphasis shifted, in intellectual discussion and in government and private policy, to a different concept—equality of opportunity.

Literal equality of opportunity—in the sense of "identity"—is impossible. One child is born blind, another with sight. One child has parents deeply concerned about his welfare who provide a background of culture and understanding; another has dissolute, improvident parents. One child is born in the United States, another in India, or China, or Russia. They clearly do not have identical opportunities open to them at birth, and there is no way that their opportunities can be made identical.

Like personal equality, equality of opportunity is not to be interpreted literally. Its real meaning is perhaps best expressed by the French expression dating from the French Revolution: *Une carriere ouverte aux les talents*—a career open to the talents. No arbitrary obstacles should prevent people from achieving those positions for which their talents fit them and which their values lead them to seek. Not birth, nationality, color, religion, sex, nor any other irrelevant characteristic should determine the opportunities that are open to a person—only his abilities.

On this interpretation, equality of opportunity simply spells out in more detail the meaning of personal equality, of equality before the law. And like personal equality, it has meaning and importance precisely because people are different in their genetic and cultural characteristics, and hence both want to and can pursue different careers.

Equality of opportunity, like personal equality, is not inconsistent with liberty; on the contrary, it is an essential component of liberty. If some people are denied access to particular positions in life for which they are qualified simply because of their ethnic background, color, or religion, that is an interference with their right to "Life, Liberty, and the pursuit of Happiness." It denies equality of opportunity and, by the same token, sacrifices the freedom of some for the advantage of others.

Like every ideal, equality of opportunity is incapable of being fully realized. The most serious departure was undoubtedly with respect to the blacks, particularly in the South but in the North as well. Yet there was also tremendous progress—for blacks and for other groups. The very concept of a "melting pot" reflected the goal of equality of opportunity. So also did the expansion of "free" education at elementary, secondary, and higher levels—though, as we shall see in the next chapter, this development has not been an unmixed blessing.

The priority given to equality of opportunity in the hierarchy of values generally accepted by the public after the Civil War is manifested particularly in economic policy. The catchwords were free enterprise, competition, laissez-faire. Everyone was to be free to go into any business, follow any occupation, buy any property, subject only to the agreement of the other parties to the transaction. Each was to have the opportunity to reap the benefits if he succeeded, to suffer the costs if he failed. There were to be no arbitrary obstacles. Performance, not birth, religion, or nationality, was the touchstone.

One corollary was the development of what many who regarded themselves as the cultural elite sneered at as vulgar materialism—an emphasis on the almighty dollar, on wealth as both the symbol and the seal of success.

* * *

Another corollary, of course, was an enormous release of human energy that made America an increasingly productive and dynamic society in which social mobility was an everyday reality. Still another, perhaps surprisingly, was an explosion in charitable activity. This explosion was made possible by the rapid growth in wealth. It took the form it did—of nonprofit hospitals, privately endowed colleges and universities, a plethora of charitable organizations directed to helping the poor—because of the dominant values of the society, including, especially, promotion of equality of opportunity.

Of course, in the economic sphere as elsewhere, practice did not always conform to the ideal. Government *was* kept to a minor role; no major obstacles to enterprise were erected, and by the end of the nineteenth century, positive government measures, especially the Sherman Anti–Trust Law, were adopted to eliminate private barriers to competition. But extralegal arrangements continued to interfere with the freedom of individuals to enter various businesses or professions, and social practices unquestionably gave special advantages to persons born in the "right" families, of the "right" color, and practicing the "right" religion. However, the rapid rise in the economic and social position of various less privileged groups demonstrates that these obstacles were by no means insurmountable.

In respect of government measures, one major deviation from free markets was in foreign trade, where Alexander Hamilton's *Report on Manufactures* had enshrined tariff protection for domestic industries as part of the American way. Tariff protection was inconsistent with thoroughgoing equality of opportunity * * * and, indeed, with the free immigration of persons, which was the rule until World War I, except only for Orientals. Yet it could be rationalized both by the needs of national defense and on the very different ground that equality stops at the water's edge—an illogical rationalization that is adopted also by most of today's proponents of a very different concept of equality.

Equality of Outcome

That different concept, equality of outcome, has been gaining ground in this century. It first affected government policy in Great Britain and on the European continent. Over the past half-century it has increasingly affected government policy in the United States as well. In some intellectual circles the desirability of equality of outcome has become an article of religious faith: everyone should finish the race at the same time. As the Dodo said in *Alice in Wonderland*, "*Everybody* has won, and *all* must have prizes."

For this concept, as for the other two, "equal" is not to be interpreted literally as "identical." No one really maintains that everyone, regardless of age or sex or other physical qualities should have identical rations of each separate item of food, clothing, and so on. The goal is rather "fairness," a much vaguer notion—indeed, one that it is difficult, if not impossible, to define precisely. "Fair shares for all" is the modern slogan that has replaced Karl Marx's, "To each according to his needs, from each according to his ability."

This concept of equality differs radically from the other two. Government measures that promote personal equality or equality of opportunity enhanced liberty; government measures to achieve "fair shares for all" reduce liberty. If what people get is to be determined by "fairness," who is to decide what is "fair"? As a chorus of voices asked the Dodo, "But who is to give the prizes?" "Fairness" is not an objectively determined concept once it departs from identity. "Fairness," like "needs," is in the eye of the beholder. If all are to have "fair shares," someone or some group of people must decide what shares are fair—and they must be able to impose their decisions on others, taking from those who have more than their "fair" share and giving to those who have less. Are those who make and impose such decisions equal to those for whom they decide? Are we not in George Orwell's *Animal Farm*, where "all animals are equal, but some animals are more equal than others"?

In addition, if what people get is determined by "fairness" and not by what they produce, where are the "prizes" to come from? What incentive is there to work and produce? How is it to be decided who is to be the doctor, who the lawyer, who the garbage collector, who the street sweeper? What assures that people will accept the roles assigned to them and perform those roles in accordance with their abilities? Clearly, only force or the threat of force will do.

The key point is not merely that practice will depart from the ideal. Of course it will, as it does with respect to the other two concepts of equality as well. The point is rather that there is a fundamental conflict between the *ideal* of "fair shares" or of its precursor, "to each according to his needs," and the *ideal* of personal liberty. This conflict has plagued every attempt to make equality of outcome the overriding principle of social organization. The end result has invariably been a state of terror: Russia, China, and, more recently, Cambodia offer clear and convincing evidence.

* * *

The far less extreme measures taken in Western countries in the name of equality of outcome have shared the same fate to a lesser extent. They, too, have restricted individual liberty. They, too, have failed to achieve their objective. It has proved impossible to define "fair shares" in a way that is generally acceptable, or to satisfy the members of the community that they are being treated "fairly." On the contrary, dissatisfaction has mounted with every additional attempt to implement equality of outcome.

Much of the moral fervor behind the drive for equality of outcome comes from the widespread belief that it is not fair that some children should have a great advantage over others simply because they happen to have wealthy parents. Of course it is not fair. However, unfairness can take many forms. It can take the form of the inheritance of property—bonds and stocks, houses, factories; it can also take the form of the inheritance of talent—musical ability, strength, mathematical genius. The inheritance of property can be interfered with more readily than the inheritance of talent. But from an ethical point of view, is there any difference between the two? Yet many people resent the inheritance of property but not the inheritance of talent.

Look at the same issue from the point of view of the parent. If you want to assure your child a higher income in life, you can do so in various ways. You can buy him (or her) an education that will equip him to pursue an occupation yielding a high income; or you can set him up in a business that will yield a higher income than he could earn as a salaried employee; or you can leave him property, the income from which will enable him to live better. Is there any ethical difference among these three ways of using your property? Or again, if the state leaves you any money to spend over and above taxes, should the state permit you to spend it on riotous living but not to leave it to your children?

The ethical issues involved are subtle and complex. They are not to be resolved by such simplistic formulas as "fair shares for all." Indeed, if we took that seriously, youngsters with less musical skill should be given the greatest amount of musical training in order to compensate for their inherited disadvantage, and those with greater musical aptitude should be prevented from having access to good musical training; and similarly with all other categories of inherited personal qualities. That might be "fair" to the youngsters lacking in talent, but would it be "fair" to the talented, let alone to those who had to work to pay for training the youngsters lacking talent, or to the persons deprived of the benefits that might have come from the cultivation of the talents of the gifted?

* * *

Still another facet of this complex issue of fairness can be illustrated by considering a game of chance, for example, an evening at baccarat. The people who choose to play may start the evening with equal piles of chips, but as the play progresses, those piles will become unequal. By the end of the evening, some will be big winners, others big losers. In the name of the ideal of equality, should the winners be required to repay the losers? That would take all the fun out of the game. Not even the losers would like that.

They might like it for the one evening, but would they come back again to play if they knew that whatever happened, they'd end up exactly where they started?

This example has a great deal more to do with the real world than one might at first suppose. Every day each of us makes decisions that involve taking a chance. Occasionally it's a big chance as when we decide what occupation to pursue, whom to marry, whether to buy a house or make a major investment. More often it's a small chance, as when we decide what movie to go to, whether to cross the street against the traffic, whether to buy one security rather than another. Each time the question is, who is to decide what chances we take? That in turn depends on who bears the consequences of the decision. If we bear the consequences, we can make the decision. But if someone else bears the consequences, should we or will we be permitted to make the decision? * * *

The system under which people make their own choices—and bear most of the consequences of their decisions—is the system that has prevailed for most of our history. It is the system that gave the Henry Fords, the Thomas Alva Edisons, the George Eastmans, the John D. Rockefellers, the James Cash Penneys the incentive to transform our society over the past two centuries. It is the system that gave other people an incentive to furnish venture capital to finance the risky enterprises that these ambitious inventors and captains of industry undertook. Of course, there were many losers along the way—probably more losers than winners. We don't remember their names. But for the most part they went in with their eyes open. They knew they were taking chances. And win or lose, society as a whole benefited from their willingness to take a chance.

The fortunes that this system produced came overwhelmingly from developing new products or services, or new ways of producing products or services, or of distributing them widely. The resulting addition to the wealth of the community as a whole, to the well-being of the masses of the people, amounted to many times the wealth accumulated by the innovators. Henry Ford acquired a great fortune. The country acquired a cheap and reliable means of transportation and the techniques of mass production. Moreover, in many cases the private fortunes were largely devoted in the end to the benefit of society. The Rockefeller, Ford, and Carnegie foundations are only the most prominent of the numerous private benefactions which are so outstanding a consequence of the operation of a system that corresponded to "equality of opportunity" and "liberty" as these terms were understood until recently.

    * * *

There is no inconsistency between a free market system and the pursuit of broad social and cultural goals, or between a free market system and compassion for the less fortunate, whether that compassion takes the form, as it did in the nineteenth century, of private charitable activity, or, as it has done increasingly in the twentieth, of assistance through government—provided that in both cases it is an expression of a desire to help others. There is all the difference in the world, however, between two kinds of assistance through government that seem superficially similar: first, 90 percent of us agreeing to impose taxes on ourselves in order to help the bottom 10 percent, and second, 80 percent voting to impose taxes on the top 10 percent to help the bottom 10 percent—William Graham Sumner's famous example of B and C deciding what D shall do for A. The first may be wise or unwise, an effective or an ineffective way to help the disadvantaged—but it is consistent with belief in both equality of opportunity and liberty. The second seeks equality of outcome and is entirely antithetical to liberty.

WHO FAVORS EQUALITY OF OUTCOME?

There is little support for the goal of equality of outcome despite the extent to which it has become almost an article of religious faith among intellectuals and despite its prominence in the speeches of politicians and the preambles of legislation. The talk is belied alike by the behavior of government, of the intellectuals who most ardently espouse egalitarian sentiments, and of the public at large.

* * *

For intellectuals, the clearest evidence is their failure to practice what so many of them preach. Equality of outcome can be promoted on a do-it-yourself basis. First, decide exactly what you mean by equality. Do you want to achieve equality within the United States? In a selected group of countries as a whole? In the world as a whole? Is equality to be judged in terms of income per person? Per family? Per year? Per decade? Per lifetime? Income in the form of money alone? Or including such nonmonetary items as the rental value of an owned home; food grown for one's own use; services rendered by members of the family not employed for money, notably the housewife? How are physical and mental handicaps or advantages to be allowed for?

However you decide these issues, you can, if you are an egalitarian, estimate what money income would correspond to your concept of equality. If your actual income is higher than that, you can keep that amount and distribute the rest to people who are below that level. If your criterion were to encompass the world—as most egalitarian rhetoric suggests it should—something less than, say, $200 a year (in 1979 dollars) per person would be an amount that would correspond to the conception of equality that seems implicit in most egalitarian rhetoric. That is about the average income per person worldwide.

What Irving Kristol has called the "new class"—government bureaucrats, academics whose research is supported by government funds or who are employed in government financed "think tanks," staffs of the many so-called "general interest" or "public policy" groups, journalists and others in the communications industry—are among the most ardent preachers of the doctrine of equality. Yet they remind us very much of the old, if unfair, saw about the Quakers: "They came to the New World to do good, and ended up doing well." The members of the new class are in general among the highest paid persons in the community. And for many among them, preaching equality and promoting or administering the resulting legislation has proved an effective means of achieving such high incomes. All of us find it easy to identify our own welfare with the welfare of the community.

Of course, an egalitarian may protest that he is but a drop in the ocean, that he would be willing to redistribute the excess of his income over his concept of an equal income if everyone else were compelled to do the same. On one level this contention that compulsion would change matters is wrong—even if everyone else did the same, his specific contribution to the income of others would still be a drop in the ocean. His individual contribution would be just as large if he were the only contributor as if he were one of many. Indeed, it would be more valuable because he could target his contribution to go to the very worst off among those he regards as appropriate recipients. On another level compulsion would change matters drastically: the kind of society that would emerge if such acts of redistribution were voluntary is altogether different—and, by our standards, infinitely preferable—to the kind that would emerge if redistribution were compulsory.

Persons who believe that a society of enforced equality is preferable can also practice what they preach. They can join one of the many communes in this country and elsewhere, or establish new ones. And, of course, it is entirely consistent with a belief in personal equality or equality of opportunity and liberty that any group of individuals who wish to live in that way should be free to do so. Our thesis that support for equality of outcome is word-deep receives strong support from the small number of persons who have wished to join such communes and from the fragility of the communes that have been established.

　　　* * *

CONSEQUENCES OF EGALITARIAN POLICIES

In shaping our own policy, we can learn from the experience of Western countries with which we share a common intellectual and cultural background, and from which we derive many of our values. Perhaps the most instructive example is Great Britain, which led the way in the nineteenth century toward implementing equality of opportunity and in the twentieth toward implementing equality of outcome.

Since the end of World War II, British domestic policy has been dominated by the search for greater equality of outcome. Measure after measure has been adopted designed to take from the rich and give to the poor. Taxes were raised on income until they reached a top rate of 98 percent on property income and 83 percent on "earned" income, and were supplemented by ever heavier taxes on inheritances. State-provided medical, housing, and other welfare services were greatly expanded, along with payments to the unemployed and the aged. Unfortunately, the results have been very different from those that were intended by the people who were quite properly offended by the class structure that dominated Britain for centuries. There has been a vast redistribution of wealth, but the end result is not an equitable distribution.

Instead, new classes of privileged have been created to replace or supplement the old: the bureaucrats, secure in their jobs, protected against inflation both when they work and when they retire; the trade unions that profess to represent the most downtrodden workers but in fact consist of the highest paid laborers in the land—the aristocrats of the labor movement; and the new millionaires—people who have been cleverest at finding ways around the laws, the rules, the regulations that have poured from Parliament and the bureaucracy, who have found ways to avoid paying taxes on their income and to get their wealth overseas beyond the grasp of the tax collectors. A vast reshuffling of income and wealth, yes; greater equity, hardly.

The drive for equality in Britain failed, not because the wrong measures were adopted—though some no doubt were; not because they were badly administered—though some no doubt were; not because the wrong people administered them—though no doubt some did. The drive for equality failed for a much more fundamental reason. It went against one of the most basic instincts of all human beings. In the words of Adam Smith, "The uniform, constant, and uninterrupted effort of every man to better his condition"—and, one may add, the condition of his children and his children's children. Smith, of course, meant by "condition" not merely material well-being, though certainly that was one component. He had a much broader concept in mind, one that included all of the values by which men judge their success—in particular the kind of social values that gave rise to the outpouring of philanthropic activities in the nineteenth century.

When the law interferes with people's pursuit of their own values, they will try to find a way around. They will evade the law, they will break the law, or they will leave the country. Few of us believe in a moral code that justifies forcing people to give up much of what they produce to finance payments to persons they do not know for purposes they may not approve of. When the law contradicts what most people regard as moral and proper, they will break the law—whether the law is enacted in the name of a noble ideal such as equality or in the naked interest of one group at the expense of another. Only fear of punishment, not a sense of justice and morality, will lead people to obey the law.

When people start to break one set of laws, the lack of respect for the law inevitably spreads to all laws, even those that everyone regards as moral and proper—laws against violence, theft, and vandalism. Hard as it may be to believe, the growth of crude criminality in Britain in recent decades may well be one consequence of the drive for equality.

* * *

We in the United States have not gone as far as Britain in promoting the goal of equality of outcome. Yet many of the same consequences are already evident—from a failure of egalitarian measures to achieve their objectives, to a reshuffling of wealth that by no standards can be regarded as equitable; to a rise in criminality, to a depressing effect on productivity and efficiency.

CAPITALISM AND EQUALITY

Everywhere in the world there are gross inequities of income and wealth. They offend most of us. Few can fail to be moved by the contrast between the luxury enjoyed by some and the grinding poverty suffered by others.

In the past century a myth has grown up that free market capitalism—equality of opportunity as we have interpreted that term—increases such inequalities, that it is a system under which the rich exploit the poor.

Nothing could be further from the truth. Wherever the free market has been permitted to operate, wherever anything approaching equality of opportunity has existed, the ordinary man has been able to attain levels of living never dreamed of before. Nowhere is the gap between rich and poor wider, nowhere are the rich richer and the poor poorer, than in those societies that do not permit the free market to operate. That is true of feudal societies like medieval Europe, India before independence, and much of modern South America, where inherited status determines position. It is equally true of centrally planned societies, like Russia or China or India since independence, where access to government determines position. It is true even where central planning was introduced, as in all three of these countries, in the name of equality.

* * *

In 1848 John Stuart Mill wrote: "Hitherto it is questionable if all the mechanical inventions yet made have lightened the day's toil of any human being. They have enabled a greater population to live the same life of drudgery and imprisonment, and an increased number of manufacturers and others to make fortunes. They have increased the comforts of the middle classes. But they have not yet begun to effect those great changes in human destiny, which it is in their nature and in their futurity to accomplish."

No one could say that today. You can travel from one end of the industrialized world to the other and almost the only people you will find engaging in backbreaking toil are people who are doing it for sport. To find people whose day's toil has not been lightened by mechanical invention, you must go to the non-capitalist world: to Russia, China, India or Bangladesh, parts of Yugoslavia; or to the more backward capitalist countries—in Africa, the Mideast, South America; and until recently, Spain or Italy.

CONCLUSION

A society that puts equality—in the sense of equality of outcome—ahead of freedom will end up with neither equality nor freedom. The use of force to achieve equality will destroy freedom, and the force, introduced for good purposes, will end up in the hands of people who use it to promote their own interests.

On the other hand, a society that puts freedom first will, as a happy by-product, end up with both greater freedom and greater equality. Though a by-product of freedom, greater equality is not an accident. A free society releases the energies and abilities of people to pursue their own objectives. It prevents some people from arbitrarily suppressing others. It does not prevent some people from achieving positions of privilege, but so long as freedom is maintained, it prevents those positions of privilege from becoming institutionalized; they are subject to continued attack by other able, ambitious people. Freedom means diversity but also mobility. It preserves the opportunity for today's disadvantaged to become tomorrow's privileged and, in the process, enables almost everyone, from top to bottom, to enjoy a fuller and richer life.

NOTES AND QUESTIONS

1. Operation of government and market in Wealth of Nations. In his second book, the *Wealth of Nations*, Adam Smith advocated a limited role for government in economic life. Nevertheless, Smith advocated government authority to ensure the provision of four basic necessities:

1. The need for a well-financed militia for national defense
2. A legal system to protect liberty, property rights, and to enforce contracts and payment of debts
3. Public works—roads, canals, bridges, harbors, and other infrastructure projects
4. Universal public education to counter the alienating and mentally degrading effects of specialization (division of labor) under capitalism

MARK SKOUSEN, THE MAKING OF MODERN ECONOMICS 33 (2001).

Additionally, Smith identifies three characteristics necessary for a self-regulating economics system:

1. Freedom: the right to produce and exchange products, labor, and capital
2. Self-interest: the right to pursue one's own business and to appeal to the self interest of others
3. Competition: the right to compete in the production and exchange of goods and services

Id. at 22.

2. Friedman's political philosophy. Milton Friedman is associated with the libertarian school of political philosophy. According to this school, the best government is the smallest, least intrusive government possible, "consistent with the maximum freedom for each individual to follow his own ways, his own values, as long as he doesn't interfere with anybody else who's doing the same." *Uncommon Knowledge, Take it to the Limits: Milton Friedman on Libertarianism* (American Public Television broadcast, Feb. 10, 1999), *available at* http://www.uncommonknowledge.org/99winter/324.html

Friedman does not justify his advocacy of a free market society by some external referent like wealth maximization. Instead he says that:

> A free society, I believe, is a more productive society than any other. . . . But that is not why I am in favor of a free society. I believe and

hope that I would favor a free society even if it were less productive than some alternative.... I favor a free society because my basic value is freedom itself.

RUBIN PAUL MALLOY & JERRY EVENSKY, ADAM SMITH AND THE PHILOSOPHY OF LAW AND ECONOMICS 160 (1994).

3. Libertarianism and law and economics. Friedman's libertarian political philosophy is often associated with the law and economics movement discussed *infra* at 153. As one commentator put it "law and economics scholars will—with only rare exceptions—take positions comparable with libertarian conservatives." Michael McConnell, *The Counter–Revolution in Legal Thought,* 41 POL'Y REV. 18, 24 (1987). For more on libertarianism, especially as it relates to law and economics see this text, *infra* at 154, note 7 & 8 at 192, 294.

4. Friedman's equality.

    a.   Friedman's negative definitions of equality. Friedman, when introducing what he asserts are distinct stages in the progression of equality, defines what each stage was not. For example, Friedman states that Thomas Jefferson "did not regard men ... as equal in physical characteristics, emotional reactions, mechanical and intellectual abilities." FRIEDMAN, *supra,* at 154. Why does Friedman do this? Does he mean to imply that the only alternative interpretation of equality to the one he ascribes to the founding fathers is literal physical equality? If there are other possible interpretations of the Declaration of Independence, why should we choose Friedman's? For example, Charles Black asserts that the Declaration of Independence can be read as guaranteeing every person a right to a livelihood. Charles Black, *Further Reflections on the Constitutional Justice of Livelihood,* 86 COLUM. L. REV. 1103 (1986) (arguing that the right to pursuit of happiness and the elimination of poverty are not simply matters of compassion. Black argues that these rights can be derived from the preamble to, and Ninth Amendment of, the Constitution and the Declaration of Independence). Given that there are alternative readings of the Declaration of Independence that are vastly more persuasive than the literal equality Friedman addresses, should his refusal to address those alternatives make us skeptical about his main claims?

    b.   Friedman's use of straw-men when discussing equality of outcome. When discussing personal equality and equality of opportunity, Friedman cites admired historical and cultural figures such as Jefferson, de Tocqueville, and Lincoln. When discussing equality of outcome, Friedman cites the Dodo from *Alice in Wonderland* and Karl Marx. If, as Friedman claims is the case, "equality of outcome ... has become almost an article of religious faith among intellectuals," why did Friedman not cite a supporter of equality of outcome who is both nonfictional and non-discredited? FRIEDMAN, *supra* at 157. A possible example of an individual who believed in equality of outcome would be Martin Luther King, Jr. who stated that a political alliance between organized labor and African Americans could bring about the American dream which King interpreted as "a dream of equality of opportunity, of privilege and property widely distributed, a dream of a nation where all our gifts and resources are held not for ourselves but as instruments of service for the rest of humanity. . . ." STEPHEN B. OATES, LET THE TRUMPET SOUND: A LIFE OF MARTIN LUTHER KING, JR. 187 (1994). Does the fact that Friedman chose to attribute equality of outcome to a fictional dodo rather than the infinitely more persuasive Dr. King detract from the persuasiveness of his conclusions?

c. Effect of Dr. King on Friedman's piece. Including the views of Dr. King would have had three effects on Friedman's piece. First, because Dr. King believed that his dream was the realization of the American dream, including his views would have demonstrated that Friedman's assertion that equality of outcome is a radical departure from traditions of liberty is highly questionable. Second, including the voice of Dr. King, or any minority leader, would have drawn attention to the fact that, to minorities, formal equality is inadequate because it ignores the handicaps placed upon them by private discrimination, both past and present. *See* MARTIN LUTHER KING, JR., WHY WE CAN'T WAIT 134 (1964); T. Alexander Aleinikoff, *A Case for Race–Consciousness*, 91 COLUM. L. REV. 1060 (1991). This insufficiency of formal equality would have led to the third effect of including Dr. King, tying wealth redistribution to Friedman's second duty of government, "establishing an exact administration of justice." MILTON FRIEDMAN & ROSE FRIEDMAN, *The Role of Government, in* FREE TO CHOOSE: A PERSONAL STATEMENT 27, 29 (1980). Dr. King stated that American society had done "something special *against* the Negro for hundreds of years [and] must . . . do something special *for* him, in order to equip him to compete on a just and equal basis." WHERE DO WE GO FROM HERE (quoted in OATES, *supra* note 2b, at 426). Linking wealth redistribution to justice would have been anathema to a libertarian like Friedman. For a history of the development of affirmative action, including its origins as a compensatory measure, *see* Erin E. Byrnes, *Unmasking White Privilege to Expose the Fallacy of White Innocence: Using a Theory of Moral Correlativity to Make the Case for Affirmative Action Programs in Education*, 41 ARIZ. L. REV. 535 (1999).

5. Equality and liberty. Friedman sees equality of outcome as antithetical to liberty, but he claims equality of opportunity to be a companion to liberty. How do barriers to equality interfere with liberty? What can be done to remove those barriers?

a. Private barriers. In *Capitalism and Freedom*, Friedman said, "[T]he

> preserves of discrimination in any society are the areas that are most monopolistic in character, whereas discrimination against groups of particular color or religion is least in those areas where there is the greatest freedom of competition." MILTON FRIEDMAN (WITH THE ASSISTANCE OF ROSE D. FRIEDMAN), CAPITALISM AND FREEDOM

109 (1962). The invisible hand of the market ideally promotes society's welfare through competition and self-interest, and equality of opportunity ideally allows such competition by rendering characteristics such as birth, race, and sex irrelevant. Friedman resigns himself to the fact that equality of opportunity is an ideal which cannot be fully realized while he applauds government efforts to legally reinforce the ideal of competition. If supposedly irrelevant characteristics in reality impede equality of income, and therefore its partner liberty, what justifies government intervention to remove some private barriers to competition but not others? What similarities and differences exist between the concentration of wealth and monopolistic trade practices?

> The Sherman Anti–Trust Act is a "positive government measure . . . adopted to eliminate private barriers to competition." The Act outlaws monopolies and contracts, combinations, or conspiracies to restrain trade. Sherman Antitrust Act, 15 U.S.C. §§ 1–7 (2000). At common law, contracts in restraint of trade were void and unenforceable, but in 1890 Congress deemed such contracts illegal and created a civil action for damages. Denison Mattress Factory v. Spring-Air Co., 308 F.2d 403, 407 (5th Cir. 1962). In 1910, the Supreme Court affirmed the dissolution of the Rockefellers' Standard Oil Company, which controlled approximately ninety percent of the petroleum trade, and stock was transferred back to the many subsidiary companies. Standard Oil Co. v. United States, 221 U.S. 1 (1911). By controlling the petroleum trade, Standard Oil had been able to fix prices and restrain trade, violating the principles of the price system. Antitrust law gave the Court the tools to promote a competitive oil market. *Id.* at 33. If the triumphs of antitrust law over obstacles to competition are favorable in this situation, can we ignore other private obstacles to competition, such as race and gender inequality, because they are "not insurmountable"? If measures such as the Fourteenth Amendment and the Civil Rights Acts have not completely eliminated such barriers, what else can be done to improve competition?

b. Equality of access. Friedman compares the unfairness of inherited property to inherited talent, and he uses access to musical training for an untalented child instead of a musically gifted child to illustrate the impossibility of fairness. But suppose that the talented child was too poor to afford private music lessons and lived in an impoverished school district that had cut the music program for financial reasons, as so many schools have been forced to do, and his musical talent was never developed. And suppose the untalented child, whose family was wealthy, had unlimited access to music lessons, which did little to improve her skill. While we cannot, and probably would not want to, evenly distribute talents and interests throughout the population, it is at least possible that resources could be distributed in such a manner that makes them available to all. Perhaps equality of outcome is not possible or desirable, but meaningful freedom to choose demands true equality of access.

C. LAW AND ECONOMICS

The Uses of History in Law and Economics

4 THEORETICAL INQUIRIES L. 659 (2003).

Ron Harris

* * *

The debate over the intellectual origins of the law and economics field is still at a very preliminary stage. Some outside observers suggest a peculiar connection between the law and economics movement and either institutional economics or else legal realism, or a combination of the two in the form of the "first great law & economics movement." Insiders disdainfully repudiate such intellectual origins. They point to Chicago (not Yale, Columbia, or Wisconsin), to economics (not law), and to the neo-classical (not institutional or historical) school of economics as the bedrock of the field. Thus, the official, internal history of the field begins in Chicago. The questions that then arise are, When and who? * * * But most stress as the immediate origins, both in terms of time and substance, the contributions of two economists: Ronald Coase and Gary Becker, circa 1960. Coase, in his seminal 1960 article [*The Problem of Social Cost*, 3 J.L. & ECON. 1 (1960)], reintroduced transaction costs (after doing so for the first, relatively unnoticed, time twenty-three years earlier in the context of his *The Nature of the Firm*), but this time with direct reference to the relevance of legal liability rules in a world with transaction costs. Becker, after completing his doctoral dissertation in 1955 (published in 1957), extended the realm of neo-classical theory by employing it in the analysis of non-market behavior. His starting point was racial discrimination; he then proceeded to the family (until then a black box for economists), and, by the late 1960s, arrived at crime and punishment. Thus the work of Coase and Becker planted the roots of the modern incarnation of law and economics in Chicago and in the neo-classical tradition.

* * *

Both Coase and Becker, the intellectual founders of law and economics, were economists by training and much more interested in the study of economics than law. Ironically, the new field of law and economics that their work launched focused mainly on the law. Both noted this a few years ago at a [University of] Chicago Law School round table on the future of law and economics. Becker noted, "I am certainly not an expert in law and economics.... [A] relatively small fraction of my time over the years has been spent on this subject." Coase confessed, "[N]ow an economist isn't really interested in this part of Law and Economics—the use of economics to analyze the law—at least this economist isn't." Despite the fact that

Coase and Becker laid the theoretical foundations of law and economics and occupy a mythical position in its official history, they were not awarded the Nobel Prize for their contribution to this field, but, rather, for their work in economics in general. Nor did they operate in the field of law and economics as later defined by Posner, and they failed to shift the field's research agenda to studying the effects of the law on the economy or the economy on the law.

It was Richard Posner who, in fact, set and shaped the boundaries of the Chicago School of Law and Economics, limiting them to the economic analysis of the law. This school of thought marginalized and may even have prevented other potential connections between law and economics. The boundaries set by Posner and his colleagues held strong for at least three decades. A discussion of the reasons for this is beyond the scope of this article. I believe that it is related to Posner's personal interest and eminent position in the field. Limiting the boundaries of law and economics made sense for a newly formed field, as it enabled concentrating on research resources and rapidly advancing learning on a narrow front. Moreover, law and economics was institutionalized as a discipline in law schools rather than in economics departments. By analyzing legal rules and providing prescriptions for legal reforms, law and economics scholars could participate in the major areas of discourse within legal academia. They could even demonstrate the power of their coherent and rigorous theory over the confused intuitions of other legal scholars. This further expanded their sphere of activity within the law schools. Only in the last decade has research transgressing these boundaries begun to appear.

In sum, on the assumption that law has no methodology of its own to contribute to the study of economics, three potential outcomes of the interaction between the disciplines of economics and law appeared around 1960: 1) the study of the effects of law on the economy; 2) the study of the effects of the economy on legal change; and 3) the application of economic methodology to the analysis of law. Until recently, only the third of these possible research agendas was considerably advanced within the field of law and economics. The narrow scope of the newly created field partly explains its a-historical nature and its lack of interaction with economic and legal history.

In addition to developing a normatively-based policy analysis, Posner and colleagues developed a positive branch of law and economics. The two were unified in the framework of the theory of the common law's tendency toward efficiency. This theory deals with the effects of law on economic growth or the effects of economic growth on the law. It also can be understood as encompassing both the positive and normative research agendas by creating identification between them, at least insofar as the common law is concerned. * * * [R]efining and defending this general theory of the common law's tendency toward efficiency consumed a great deal of the time and energy of law and economics scholars and impinged on their interest in positive theories. Instead, they were occupied with proposing and examining theoretical mechanisms that might explain the tendency toward efficiency in the common law. * * * This weak start at positive research further removed law and economics scholars from engaging in the first two research agendas, which seemed important to both Coase and Becker. The interest in these two agendas was developed outside law and economics in fields such as New Institutional Economics, Historical New Institutional Economics, and the Wisconsin School of Legal History. Only recently has law and economics expanded its agenda to include these two issues.

More specifically, Chicago law and economics scholars claimed to be interested not only in legal rules but also in how legal incentives affect individuals' behavior. However, their research did not focus on studying the behavior of individuals, and the behavior of societies and basic social structures and trends was entirely beyond the scope of their research agenda. The behavior of individuals was assumed to be affected by changes in legal rules that affected individual incentives. Law and economics aimed at changing behavior but, in fact, studied rules and their change. As its other name, economic analysis of the law, implies, law and economics mainly aspired to normatively evaluate legal rules and prescribe their modification. Only rarely, when legal rules functioned within a market setting, as in the case of anti-trust and securities regulation, did Chicago law and economics scholars inquire into the behavior of individual agents more closely. It was more often the case that the legal rules were analyzed in non-market settings and the behavior of individuals was assumed rather than studied. * * *

From its inception, Chicago law and economics involved the application of neo-classical tools, which reached a powerful phase in the 1950s and 1960s in the Chicago School of Economics. Neo-classical economics at [the University of Chicago] was remarkably a-historical. The detachment of economics from change over real time, and thus from history, began with the marginalist revolution and [Alfred Marshall], continued with Keynes, and culminated in Chicago in the 1950s.

For economics, the 1950s was a decade of high theory. It was one of markets, allocation, and equilibrium; of abstraction and deduction; of marginalism and incremental change; of optimization and mathematization. It was one in which the basic assumptions of neo-classical theory still held strong. This decade was a low point in economic theory in terms of interest in history and change over real time. Theory was mainly static, not dynamic. Insofar as dynamic elements played a role in economic theory, they were reflected in shifts of curves, moves from point to point along curves, or leaps from one equilibrium to the next, over a single time period. Time was not discussed in terms of months or years or decades; the flow of time was not treated differently for different historical eras. Not only was change over time neglected, but there was also a perception that the past of any given system had no bearing on its present and certainly not on its future. Since any given current regime of functions, allocations, and equilibria is not burdened by its past, it can serve as a good starting point for future predictions. An economic theoretician thus did not have to reconstruct the passage of time, as did historians—and some sociologists, anthropologists, political scientists, lawyers, literary critics, and philosophers. Imagining change was confined to the two-dimensional classroom world of blackboard curves and to figures in books. This static state of economic theory thus hindered the development of a history-conscious law and economics.

This was the economic theory applied in the late 1960s and early 1970s by Richard Posner and his colleagues at the University of Chicago Law School. By that point, law and economics had acquired all its familiar characteristics: reliance on the neo-classical assumption that individuals are rational maximizers; equating change in legal rules with change in relative prices; and adoption of Kaldor–Hicks efficiency ("potential Pareto efficiency," in more obscure terms) in the sense of wealth maximization as a standard of evaluation.

The a-historical neoclassical characteristics of law and economics dominated the field. Well into the 1980s and beyond, law and economics was still engaged in adapting price theory to non-market legal behavior as part of a wider project of the expansion of economics. It focused on the application of price theory to the specific contours of the law: judge-made law and legislation; property, contracts, and torts; liability rules; and remedies. Law and economics scholars were engaged in intense normative and policy debates with critics from rival jurisprudential and doctrinal schools. These debates revolved around the imperialistic tendencies of economics, its unrealistic assumptions (e.g., of rationality), and its ideological bias in favor of efficiency considerations at the expense of distributive considerations. As long as the debates at the normative and policy level were intense, law and economics scholars were not likely to find much time or motivation to turn to the study of history.

* * *

In the first edition of *Economic Analysis of Law* (1972), what Posner termed "the economic logic of the common law" was the first theoretical argument in law and economics to draw the attention of scholars in the emerging field of the history of law. * * * Posner based his thesis that common law exhibits a tendency toward efficiency on a few historical examples from nineteenth-century America, including: enterprise liability for faulty products; industrial accidents; railroad-crossing accidents; damage caused by train engine sparks; and the impossibility doctrine in contracts. He claimed that these examples, when viewed in the framework of his positive theory of common law, confirm his thesis. These examples also serve to counter arguments that common law is either irrelevant to economic growth or encourages economic growth by subsidizing big business and increasing social inequality.

Posner did not base his claims on thorough historical research, but he most decidedly challenged historians. His positive theory of the law was historical in nature. It purported to explain how law changes over time. This explanation was too deterministic for most legal historians. It subjected their micro-historical interpretations to his macro theory and, in a sense, made them secondary to it. Furthermore, he used concrete examples rooted in time and place that are central to the work of many American legal historians. In doing so, he called into dispute concrete historical studies. It is not surprising that several legal historians, in response to this challenge, criticized Posner for misunderstanding the history of legal doctrines and their social and economic effects. In each of the editions of *Economic Analysis of Law*, Posner's discussion of the positive theory of common law's tendency toward efficiency grew in length, increasing from the four-and-a-half pages in the first edition to six-and-a-half pages in the 1977 second edition to nine-and-a-half pages in the 1986 third edition. * * * These increases in length were not the result of more historical studies conducted to test or confirm the theory. Rather, greater space was devoted to criticizing legal historians for not understanding economic theory, including the theory of the common law's tendency toward efficiency and the concept of efficiency. Legal historians became more critical of Posner, and Posner became more critical of legal historians, particularly those who viewed the law as subsidizing business, redistributing wealth, and oppressing the weak.

Posner had to answer not only to legal historians, but also to other legal scholars, even some with an economic orientation. These legal scholars questioned his thesis on a theoretical rather than empirical-historical level. What in the common law, they asked, could lead it to produce efficient rules? Some law and economics scholars tried to support Posner's claim and counter the growing criticism against it, by explaining its theoretical logic. Some suggested that judges are the agents who steer the common law toward efficiency; even if they are not aware that they maximize efficiency, they behave as if they are doing so. Justice and common sense considerations lead to efficient judgments. Other scholars saw litigants in general (losing litigants or repeat litigants) as the agents of the drive toward efficiency: inefficient rules will be rooted out by ongoing litigation. By the mid–1980s, the debate over the tendency of the common law toward efficiency, both on the historical and theoretical levels, had exhausted itself.

　　　* * *

Though not one of the first fields within economics to apply theoretical novelties, over time, law and economics adopted extensions and modifications of the basic models of price theory to account for, among other things, transaction costs, risk sensitivity, and information a-symmetry. A main new feature of research in the 1980s and early 1990s was the addition of game theory tools to the law and economics analysis. Another was the gradual opening up of law and economics to public choice analysis. * * * Law and economics has become more empirical and more comparative in recent years. * * *

Contrary to these trends in economic theory and the research agenda of law and economics, some Chicago law and economics scholars still view price theory as the sole economic tool for analyzing the law. They believe that despite its imperfections, it cannot be successfully replaced by any other theoretical framework. Moreover, they argue that the use of multiple theoretical frameworks will cause incoherence and complications, which would result in less rigorous tools, more limited applicability, and less insightful conclusions. They view the future of their field as developing along three main trajectories: first, sophistication within the neo-classical price theory paradigm, by employing heavier mathematical, game theoretic, and micro tools; second, expansion into the relatively neglected areas of public law; and third, the filling in of the remaining gaps in the analysis of private law. * * *

The Economic Approach to Law

THE PROBLEMS OF JURISPRUDENCE 353–92 (1990).

■ RICHARD A. POSNER

    * * *

THE APPROACH

The basic assumption of economics that guides the version of economic analysis of law that I shall be presenting is that people are rational maximizers of their satisfactions—*all* people (with the exception of small children and the profoundly retarded) in all of their activities (except when under the influence of psychosis or similarly deranged through drug or alcohol abuse) that involve choice. Because this definition embraces the criminal deciding whether to commit another crime, the litigant deciding whether to settle or litigate a case, the legislator deciding whether to vote for or against a bill, the judge deciding how to cast his vote in a case, the party to a contract deciding whether to break it, the driver deciding how fast to drive, and the pedestrian deciding how boldly to cross the street, as well as the usual economic actors, such as businessmen and consumers, it is apparent that most activities either regulated by or occurring within the legal system are grist for the economic analyst's mill. It should go without saying that nonmonetary as well as monetary satisfactions enter into the individual's calculus of maximizing (indeed, money for most people is a means rather than an end) and that decisions, to be rational, need not be well thought out at the conscious level—indeed, need not be conscious at all. Recall that "rational" denotes suiting means to ends, rather than mulling things over, and that much of our knowledge is tacit.

Since my interest is in legal doctrines and institutions, it will be best to begin at the legislative (including the constitutional) level. I assume that legislators are rational maximizers of their satisfactions just like everyone else. Thus nothing they do is motivated by the public interest as such. But they want to be elected and reelected, and they need money to wage an effective campaign. This money is more likely to be forthcoming from well-organized groups than from unorganized individuals. The rational individual knows that his contribution is unlikely to make a difference; for this reason and also because voters in most elections are voting for candidates rather than policies, which further weakens the link between casting one's vote and obtaining one's preferred policy. The rational individual will have little incentive to invest time and effort in deciding whom to vote for. Only an organized group of individuals (or firms or other organizations—but these are just conduits for individuals) will be able to overcome the informational and free-rider problems that plague collective action. But such a group will not organize and act effectively unless its members have much to gain or much to lose from specific policies, as tobacco farmers, for example, have much to gain from federal subsidies for growing tobacco and much to lose from the withdrawal of those subsidies. The basic tactic of an interest group is to trade the votes of its members and its financial support to candidates in exchange for an implied promise of favorable legislation. Such legislation will normally take the form of a statute transferring wealth from unorganized taxpayers (for example, consumers) to the interest group. If the target were another interest group, the legislative transfer might be effectively opposed. The unorganized are unlikely to mount effective opposition, and it is their wealth, therefore, that typically is transferred to interest groups.

* * * [B]ecause of the costs of transactions within a multi-headed legislative body, and the costs of effective communication through time, legislation does not spring full-grown from the head of the legislature; it needs interpretation and application, and this is the role of the courts. They are agents of the legislature. But to impart credibility and durability to the deals the legislature strikes with interest groups, courts must be able to resist the wishes of current legislators who want to undo their predecessors' deals yet cannot do so through repeal because the costs of passing legislation (whether original or amended) are so high, and who might therefore look to the courts for a repealing "interpretation." The impediments to legislation actually facilitate rather than retard the striking of deals, by giving interest groups some assurance that a deal struck with the legislature will not promptly be undone by repeal. An independent judiciary is one of the impediments.

Judicial independence makes the judges imperfect agents of the legislature. This is tolerable not only for the reason just mentioned but also because an independent judiciary is necessary for the resolution of ordinary disputes in a way that will encourage trade, travel, freedom of action, and other highly valued activities or conditions and will minimize the expenditure of resources on influencing governmental action. Legislators might appear to have little to gain from these widely diffused rule-of-law virtues. But if the aggregate benefits from a particular social policy are very large and no interest group's ox is gored, legislators may find it in their own interest to support the policy. Voters understand in a rough way the benefits to them of national defense, crime control, dispute settlement, and the other elements of the night watchman state, and they will not vote for legislators who refuse to provide these basic public services. It is only when those services are in place, and when (usually later) effective means of taxation and redistribution develop, that the formation of narrow interest groups and the extraction by them of transfers from unorganized groups become feasible.

The judges thus have a dual role: to interpret the interest-group deals embodied in legislation and to provide the basic public service of authoritative dispute resolution. They perform the latter function not only by deciding cases in accordance with preexisting norms, but also—especially in the Anglo–American legal system—by elaborating those norms. They fashioned the common law out of customary practices, out of ideas borrowed from statutes and from other legal systems (for example, Roman law), and out of their own conceptions of public policy. The law they created exhibits, according to the economic theory that I am expounding, a remarkable (although not total—remember the extension of the rule of capture to oil and gas) substantive consistency. It is as if the judges wanted to adopt the rules, procedures, and case outcomes that would maximize society's wealth.

I must pause to define "wealth maximization," a term often misunderstood. The "wealth" in "wealth maximization" refers to the sum of all tangible and intangible goods and services, weighted by prices of two sorts: offer prices (what people are willing to pay for goods they do not already own); and asking prices (what people demand to sell what they do own). If A would be willing to pay up to $100 for B's stamp collection, it is worth $100 to A. If B would be willing to sell the stamp collection for any price above $90, it is worth $90 to B. So if B sells the stamp collection to A (say for $100, but the analysis is qualitatively unaffected at any price between $90 and $100—and it is only in that range that a transaction will occur), the wealth of society will rise by $10. Before the transaction A had $100 in cash and B had a stamp collection worth $90 (a total of $190); after the transaction A has a stamp collection worth $100 and B has $100 in cash (a total of $200). The transaction will not raise measured wealth—gross national product, national income, or whatever—by $10; it will not raise it at all unless the transaction is recorded, and if it is recorded it is likely to raise measured wealth by the full $100 purchase price. But the real addition to social wealth consists of the $10 increment in *nonpecuniary* satisfaction that A derives from the purchase, compared with that of B. This shows that "wealth" in the economist's sense is not a simple monetary measure, and explains why it is a fallacy (the Earl of Lauderdale's fallacy) to think that wealth would be maximized by encouraging the charging of monopoly prices. The wealth of producers would increase but that of consumers would diminish—and actually by a greater amount, since monopoly pricing will induce some consumers to switch to goods that cost society more to produce but, being priced at a competitive rather than a monopoly price, appear to the consumer to be cheaper. The fallacy thus lies in equating business income to social wealth.

Similarly, if I am given a choice between remaining in a job in which I work forty hours a week for $1,000 and switching to a job in which I would work thirty hours for $500, and I decide to make the switch, the extra ten hours of leisure must be worth at least $500 to me, yet GNP will fall when I reduce my hours of work. Suppose the extra hours of leisure are worth $600 to me, so that my full income rises from $1,000 to $1,100 when I reduce my hours. My former employer presumably is made worse off by my leaving (else why did he employ me?), but not more than $100 worse off, for if he were, he would offer to pay me a shade over $1,100 a week to stay—and I would stay. (The example abstracts from income tax.)

Wealth is *related* to money, in that a desire not backed by ability to pay has no standing—such a desire is neither an offer price nor an asking price. I may desperately desire a BMW, but if I am unwilling or unable to pay its purchase price, society's wealth would not be increased by transferring the BMW from its present owner to me. Abandon this essential constraint (an important distinction, also, between wealth maximization and utilitarianism—for I might derive greater utility from the BMW than its present owner or anyone else to whom he might sell the car), and the way is open to tolerating the crimes committed by the passionate and the avaricious against the cold and the frugal.

The common law facilitates wealth-maximizing transactions in a variety of ways. It recognizes property rights, and these facilitate exchange. It also protects property rights, through tort and criminal law. (Although today criminal law is almost entirely statutory, the basic criminal protections—for example, those against murder, assault, rape, and theft—have, as one might expect, common law origins.) Through contract law it protects the process of exchange. And it establishes procedural rules for resolving disputes in these various fields as efficiently as possible.

The illustrations given thus far of wealth-maximizing transactions have been of transactions that are voluntary in the strict sense of making everyone affected by them better off, or at least no worse off. Every transaction has been assumed to affect just two parties, each of whom has been made better off by it. Such a transaction is said to be Pareto superior, but Pareto superiority is not a necessary condition for a transaction to be wealth maximizing. Consider an accident that inflicts a cost of $100 with a probability of .01 and that would have cost $3 to avoid. The accident is a wealth-maximizing "transaction" (recall Aristotle's distinction between voluntary and involuntary transactions) because the expected accident cost ($1) is less than the cost of avoidance. (I am assuming risk neutrality. Risk aversion would complicate the analysis but not change it fundamentally.) It is wealth maximizing even if the victim is not compensated. The result is consistent with Learned Hand's formula, which defines negligence as the failure to take cost-justified precautions. If the only precaution that would have averted the accident is not cost-justified, the failure to take it is not negligent and the injurer will not have to compensate the victim for the costs of the accident.

* * *

The wealth-maximizing properties of common law rules have been elucidated at considerable length in the literature of the economic analysis of law. Such doctrines as conspiracy, general average (admiralty), contributory negligence, equitable servitudes, employment at will, the standard for granting preliminary injunctions, entrapment, the contract defense of impossibility, the collateral-benefits rule, the expectation measure of damages, assumption of risk, attempt, invasion of privacy, wrongful interference with contract rights, the availability of punitive damages in some cases but not others, privilege in the law of evidence, official immunity, and the doctrine of moral consideration have been found—at least by some contributors to this literature—to conform to the dictates of wealth maximization. * * * It has even been argued that the system of precedent itself has an economic equilibrium. Precedents are created as a by-product of litigation. The greater the number of recent precedents in an area, the lower the rate of litigation will be. In particular, cases involving disputes over legal as distinct from purely factual issues will be settled. The existence of abundant, highly informative (in part because recent) precedents will enable the parties to legal disputes to form more convergent estimates of the likely outcome of a trial, and as noted in previous chapters, if both parties agree on the outcome of trial they will settle beforehand because a trial is more costly than a settlement. But with less litigation, fewer new precedents will be produced, and the existing precedents will obsolesce as changing circumstances render them less apt and informative. So the rate of litigation will rise, producing more precedents and thereby causing the rate of litigation again to fall.

This analysis does not explain what drives judges to decide common law cases in accordance with the dictates of wealth maximization. Prosperity, however, which wealth maximization measures more sensitively than purely monetary measures such as GNP, is a relatively uncontroversial policy, and most judges try to steer clear of controversy: their age, method of compensation, and relative weakness vis-a-vis the other branches of government make the avoidance of controversy attractive. It probably is no accident, therefore, that many common law doctrines assumed their modern form in the nineteenth century, when laissez-faire ideology, which resembles wealth maximization, had a strong hold on the Anglo–American judicial imagination * * *.

It may be objected that in assigning ideology as a cause of judicial behavior, the economist strays outside the boundaries of his discipline; but he need not rest on ideology. The economic analysis of legislation implies that fields of law left to the judges to elaborate, such as the common law fields, must be the ones in which interest-group pressures are too weak to deflect the legislature from pursuing goals that are in the general interest. Prosperity is one of these goals, and one that judges are especially well equipped to promote. The rules of the common law that they promulgate attach prices to socially undesirable conduct, whether free riding or imposing social costs without corresponding benefits. By doing this the rules create incentives to avoid such conduct, and these incentives foster prosperity. In contrast, judges can, despite appearances, do little to redistribute wealth. A rule that makes it easy for poor tenants to break leases with rich landlords, for example, will induce landlords to raise rents in order to offset the costs that such a rule imposes, and tenants will bear the brunt of these higher costs. Indeed, the principal redistribution accomplished by such a rule may be from the prudent, responsible tenant, who may derive little or no benefit from having additional legal rights to use against landlords— rights that enable a tenant to avoid or postpone eviction for nonpayment of rental—to the feckless tenant. That is a capricious redistribution. Legislatures, however, have by virtue of their taxing and spending powers powerful tools for redistributing wealth. So an efficient division of labor between the legislative and judicial branches has the legislative branch concentrate on catering to interest-group demands for wealth distribution and the judicial branch on meeting the broad-based social demand for efficient rules governing safety, property, and transactions. Although there are other possible goals of judicial action besides efficiency and redistribution, many of these (various conceptions of "fairness" and "justice") are labels for wealth maximization,[1] or for redistribution in favor of powerful interest groups; or else they are too controversial in a heterogeneous society, too ad hoc, or insufficiently developed to provide judges who desire a reputation for objectivity and disinterest with adequate grounds for their decisions.

Finally, even if judges have little commitment to efficiency, their inefficient decisions will, by definition, impose greater social costs than their efficient ones will. As a result, losers of cases decided mistakenly from an economic standpoint will have a greater incentive, on average, to press for correction through appeal, new litigation, or legislative action than losers of cases decided soundly from an economic standpoint—so there will be a steady pressure for efficient results. Moreover, cases litigated under inefficient rules tend to involve larger stakes than cases litigated under efficient rules (for the inefficient rules, by definition, generate social waste), and the larger the stakes in a dispute the likelier it is to be litigated rather than settled; so judges will have a chance to reconsider the inefficient rule.

Thus we should not be surprised to see the common law tending to become efficient, although since the incentives to judges to perform well along any dimension are weak (this is a by-product of judicial independence), we cannot expect the law ever to achieve perfect efficiency. Since wealth maximization is not only a guide in fact to common law judging but also a genuine social value and the only one judges are in a good position to promote, it provides not only the key to an accurate description of what the judges are up to but also the right benchmark for criticism and reform. If judges are failing to maximize wealth, the economic analyst of law will urge them to alter practice or doctrine accordingly. In addition, the analyst will urge—on any legislator sufficiently free of interest-group pressures to be able to legislate in the public interest—a program of enacting only legislation that conforms to the dictates of wealth maximization.

Besides generating both predictions and prescriptions, the economic approach enables the common law to be reconceived in simple, coherent terms and to be applied more objectively than traditional lawyers would think possible. From the premise that the common law does and should seek to maximize society's wealth, the economic analyst can deduce in logical—if you will, formalist—fashion (economic theory is formulated nowadays largely in mathematical terms) the set of legal doctrines that will

1. EDWARD W. RYAN, IN THE WORDS OF ADAM SMITH: THE FIRST CONSUMER ADVOCATE 1 (1990). For example, it is unclear whether Weinrib's Kantian theory of tort law (see Chapter 11) has different substantive implications from the economic theory; the differences may be in vocabulary only.

n law doctrine, judges
nsistent with efficien-
ry of the common law

ous in its own right.
t is a bad theory, and
eral cannot be, and it

ntly incomplete as a
ut the distribution of
distribution of rights
rive the policies that
not go far enough,
d be just to start off
he others. If wealth
of rights, it is a

this point may have
completely silent on
se identical nascent
rs and in the other
mparison a century
iety was wealthier
ther illustrate the
distribution). Al-
ler modern condi-
rganizing produc-
ing World War II
lfare of the slave

ion tell us some-
ts is incomplete.
t some people in
ives than as free
t to punish by
not psychotic or
ganized, undisci-
es in a way that
t is not market
other sources of
uld be maxim-
vision were not
gh is built into
es than as free
o one thinks it
no evidentiary
trusted to be

and can compare
. After translating
e analyst will find
oximations to the
tically valid. * * *

its many separate
ds of thousands of
formulas may seem
s for doubting this
non law is seen to be
the common law is
alysis, the prevention
on, and the promotion
octrines and decisions.
y re-characterizing the
tract that the parties
rohibitive, and contract
at remedy if any would
undertaking considered
it a crime is no different
her to prosecute; a plea
by insolvent defendants
costs of their crimes, the
e left to tort law. Such
he common law really is
d be simplified by exposing
cture beneath the garb of

it differs fundamentally in
st of a rule derived from
ity of the derivation but the
the rule of capture to oil and
was replaced (albeit through
ient rules. The other rules of
ewise.

TIVE THEORY

ation *should* guide legal policy,
elds (plus those statutory fields
efficiency—antitrust law being a
as separate from the question
nsofar as the positive theory may
e normative theory. Actually the
s, illustrating again the lack of a
" propositions. One of the things
t, although not inflexibly; so if

efficiency is the animating principle of much commo
have some obligation to make decisions that will be c
cy. This is one reason why the positive economic the
is so contentious.

The normative theory has been highly contenti
Most contributors to the debate over it conclude that
although many of the criticisms can be answered, sev
is those I shall focus on.

The first is that wealth maximization is inhere
guide to social action because it has nothing to say abo
rights—or at least nothing we want to hear. Given the
(whatever it is), wealth maximization can be used to de
will maximize the value of those rights. But this doe
because naturally we are curious about whether it wou
with a society in which, say, one member owned all t
maximization is indifferent to the initial distributio
truncated concept of justice.

Since the initial distribution may dissipate rapidly,
little practical significance. Nor is wealth maximization
the initial distribution. If we could compare two otherwi
societies, in one of which one person owned all the othe
of which slavery was forbidden, and could repeat the co
later, almost certainly we would find that the second so
and the first had abolished slavery (if so, this would fu
limited effect of the initial distribution on the current
though it has not always and everywhere been true, un
tions of production slavery is an inefficient method of
tion. The extensive use of slave labor by the Nazis dur
may seem an exception—but only if we disregard the w
laborers.

This response to the demand that wealth maximizat
thing about the justice of the initial distribution of righ
Suppose it were the case—it almost surely *is* the case—th
modern American society would be more productive as sl
persons. These are not antisocial people whom we wa
imprisoning (a form of slavery that is tolerated); they are
profoundly retarded; they just are lazy, feckless, poorly or
plined people—people incompetent to manage their own liv
will maximize their output, even though the relevant outp
output alone but also leisure, family associations, and any
satisfaction to these people as well as to others. Wealth w
ized by enslaving these people, provided the costs of super
too high—but the assumption that they would not be too h
the proposition that their output would be greater as slav
persons, for it is net output that we are interested in. Yet
would be right to enslave such people, even if there were
problems in identifying them, the slave masters could be

benign, and so on; and these conditions, too, may be implicit in the proposition that the net social output of some people would be greater if they were slaves.

It is no answer that it would be inefficient to enslave such people unless they consented to be enslaved, that is, unless the would-be slave-master met the asking price for their freedom. The term *"their* freedom" assumes they have the property right in their persons, and the assumption is arbitrary. We can imagine assigning the property rights in persons (perhaps only persons who appeared likely to be unproductive) to the state to auction them to the highest bidder. The putative slave could bid against the putative master, but would lose. His expected earnings, net of consumption, would be smaller than the expected profits to the master, otherwise enslavement would not be efficient. Therefore he could not borrow enough—even if capital markets worked without any friction (in the present setting, even if the lender could enslave the borrower if the latter defaulted!)—to outbid his master-to-be.

This example points to a deeper criticism of wealth maximization as a norm or value: like utilitarianism, which it closely resembles, or nationalism, or Social Darwinism, or racialism, or organic theories of the state, it treats people as if they were the cells of a single organism; the welfare of the cell is important only insofar as it promotes the welfare of the organism. Wealth maximization implies that if the prosperity of the society can be promoted by enslaving its least productive citizens, the sacrifice of their freedom is worthwhile. But this implication is contrary to the unshakable moral intuitions of Americans, and . . . conformity to intuition is the ultimate test of a moral (indeed of any) theory.

* * *

[S]uppose it were the case—it may be the case—that some religious faiths are particularly effective in producing law-abiding, productive, healthy citizens. Mormonism is a plausible example. Would it not make sense on purely secular grounds, indeed on purely wealth-maximizing grounds, for government to subsidize these faiths? Practitioners of other religious faiths would be greatly offended, but from the standpoint of wealth maximization the only question would be whether the cost to them was greater than the benefits to the country as a whole.

Consider now a faith that both has few adherents in the United States and is feared or despised by the rest of the population. (The Rastafarian faith is a plausible example.) Such a faith will by assumption be imposing costs on the rest of the community, and given the fewness of its adherents, the benefits conferred by the faith may, even when aggregated across all its adherents, be smaller than the costs. It could then be argued that wealth maximization warranted or even required the suppression of the faith. This example suggests another objection to wealth maximization, one alluded to in the discussion of slavery: its results are sensitive to assumptions about the initial distribution of rights—a distribution that is distinct from the initial distribution of wealth (which is unlikely to remain stable over time), but about which wealth maximization may again have relatively little to say. If Rastafarians are conceived to have a property right in their religion, so that the state or anyone else who wants to acquire that right and suppress the religion must meet their asking price, probably the right will not be sold. Asking prices can be very high—in principle, infinite: how much would the average person sell his life for, if the sale had to be completed immediately? But if rights over religious practices are given to the part of the populace that is not Rastafarian, the Rastafarians may find it impossible to buy the right back; their offer price will be limited to their net wealth, which may be slight.

No doubt in this country, in this day and age, religious liberty is the cost-justified policy. The broader point is that a system of rights—perhaps the system we have—may well be required by a *realistic* conception of utilitarianism, that is, one that understands that given the realities of human nature a society dedicated to utilitarianism requires rules and institutions that place checks on utility-maximizing behavior in particular cases. For example, although one can imagine specific cases in which deliberately punishing an innocent person as a criminal would increase aggregate utility, one has trouble imagining a system in which government officials could be trusted to make such decisions. "Wealth maximizing" can be substituted for "utilitarian" without affecting the analysis. Religious liberty may well be both utility maximizing and wealth maximizing, and this may even be why we have it. And if it became *too* costly, probably it would be abandoned; and so with the prohibition of torture, and the other civilized political amenities of a wealthy society. If our crime rate were much lower than it is, we probably would not have capital punishment—and if it gets much higher, we surely will have fewer civil liberties.

But at least in the present relatively comfortable conditions of our society, the regard for individual freedom appears to transcend instrumental considerations; freedom appears to be valued for itself rather than just for its contribution to prosperity—or at least to be valued for reasons that escape the economic calculus. Is society really better off in a utilitarian or wealth-maximizing sense as a result of the extraordinarily elaborate procedural safeguards that the Bill of Rights gives criminal defendants? This is by no means clear. Are minority rights welfare maximizing—when the minority in question is a small one? That is not clear either, as the Rastafarian example showed. The main reasons these institutions are valued seem not to be utilitarian or even instrumental in character. *What* those reasons are is far from clear; indeed, "noninstrumental reason" is almost an oxymoron. And as I have suggested, we surely are not willing to pay an infinite price, perhaps not even a very high price, for freedom. * * *

Still, hypocritical and incoherent as our political ethics may frequently be, we do not permit degrading invasions of individual autonomy merely on a judgment that, on balance, the invasion would make a net addition to the social wealth. And whatever the philosophical grounding of this sentiment, it is too deeply entrenched in our society at present for wealth maximization to be given a free rein. The same may be true of the residue of corrective-justice sentiment.

I have said nothing about the conflict between wealth maximization and equality of wealth, because I am less sure of the extent of egalitarian sentiment in our society than that of individualistic sentiment (by "individualism" I mean simply the rivals to aggregative philosophies, such as utilitarianism and wealth maximization). Conflict there is, however, and it points to another important criticism of wealth maximization even if the critic is not an egalitarian. Imagine that a limited supply of growth hormone, privately manufactured and sold, must be allocated. A wealthy parent wants the hormone so that his child of average height will grow tall; a poor parent wants the hormone so that his child of dwarfish height can grow to normal height. In a system of wealth maximization the wealthy parent might outbid the poor parent and get the hormone. This is not certain. Amount of wealth is only one factor in willingness to pay. The poor parent might offer his entire wealth for the hormone, and that wealth, although meager, might exceed the amount of money the wealthy parent was willing to pay, given alternative uses to which he could put his money. Also, altruists might help the poor parent bid more than he could with only his own resources. The poor might actually be better off in a system in which the distribution of the hormone were left to the private market, even if there were no altruism. Such a system would create incentives to produce and sell the hormone sooner, and perhaps at a lower price, than if the government controlled its distribution; for the costs of production would probably be lower under private rather than public production, and even a monopolist will charge less when his costs fall.

But what seems impossible to maintain convincingly in the present ethical climate is that the wealthy parent has the *right* to the hormone by virtue of being willing to pay the supplier more than the poor parent can; more broadly, that consumers have a right to purchase in free markets. These propositions cannot be derived from wealth maximization. Indeed, they look like propositions about transactional freedom rather than about distribution only because I have assumed that the growth hormone is produced and distributed exclusively through the free market. An alternative possibility would be for the state to own the property right in the hormone and to allocate it on the basis of need rather than willingness to pay. To argue against this alternative (socialist medicine writ small) would require an appeal either to the deeply controversial idea of a natural right to private property, or to purely instrumental considerations, such as the possibility that in the long run the poor will be better off with a free market in growth hormone—but to put the question *this* way is to assume that the poor have some sort of social claim by virtue of being poor, and thus to admit the relevance of egalitarian considerations and thereby break out of the limits of wealth maximization.

A stronger-seeming argument for the free-enterprise solution is that the inventor of the hormone should have a right to use it as he wishes, which includes the right to sell it to the highest bidder. But this argument seems stronger only because we are inclined to suppose that what has happened is that *after* the inventor invented it the government decided to rob him of the reward for which he had labored. If instead we assume that

Congress passes a law in 1989 which provides that after the year 2000 the right to patent new drugs will be conditioned on the patentee's agreeing to limit the price he charges, we shall have difficulty objecting to the law on ethical, as distinct from practical, grounds. It would be just one more restriction on free markets.

* * * Although the advocate of wealth maximization can argue that to the productive should belong the fruits of their labor, the argument can be countered along the lines [that] production is really a social rather than individual effort[] to which it can be added that wealth may often be due more to luck (and not the luck of the genetic lottery, either) than to skill or effort. Furthermore, if altruism is so greatly admired, as it is by conservatives as well as by liberals, why should not its spirit inform legislation? Why should government protect only our selfish instincts? To this it can be replied that the spirit of altruism is voluntary giving. But the reply is weak. The biggest reason we value altruism is that we *desire* some redistribution—we may admire the altruist for his self-sacrifice but we would not admire him as much if he destroyed his wealth rather than giving it to others—and we think that voluntary redistribution is less costly than involuntary. If redistribution is desirable, some involuntary redistribution may be justifiable, depending on the costs, of course, but not on the principle of the thing.

There is a still deeper problem with founding wealth maximization on a notion of natural rights. The economic perspective is thoroughly (and fruitfully) behaviorist. "Economic man" is not, as vulgarly supposed, a person driven by purely pecuniary incentives, but he is a person whose behavior is completely determined by incentives; his rationality is no different from that of a pigeon or a rat. The economic task from the perspective of wealth maximization is to influence his incentives so as to maximize his output. How a person so conceived could be thought to have a *moral* entitlement to a particular distribution of the world's goods—an entitlement, say, to the share proportional to his contribution to the world's wealth—is unclear. Have marmots moral entitlements? Two levels of discourse are being mixed.

* * *

The strongest argument for wealth maximization is not moral, but pragmatic. Such classic defenses of the free market as chapter 4 of Mill's *On Liberty* can easily be given a pragmatic reading. We look around the world and see that in general people who live in societies in which markets are allowed to function more or less freely not only are wealthier than people in other societies but have more political rights, more liberty and dignity, are more content (as evidenced, for example, by their being less prone to emigrate)—so that wealth maximization may be the most direct route to a variety of moral ends. The recent history of England, France, and Turkey, of Japan and Southeast Asia, of East versus West Germany and North versus South Korea, of China and Taiwan, of Chile, of the Soviet Union, Poland, and Hungary, and of Cuba and Argentina provides striking support for this thesis.

Writing in the early 1970s, the English political philosopher Brian Barry doubted the importance of incentives. "My own guess," he said, "is that enough people with professional and managerial jobs really like them (and enough others who would enjoy them and have sufficient ability to do them are waiting to replace those who do not) to enable the pay of these jobs to be brought down considerably ... I would suggest that the pay levels in Britain of schoolteachers and social workers seem to offer net rewards which recruit and maintain just enough people, and that this provides a guideline to the pay levels that could be sustained generally among professionals and managers." He rejected the "assumption that a sufficient supply of highly educated people will be forthcoming only if lured by the anticipation of a higher income afterwards as a result," adding that "it would also be rash to assume that it would be an economic loss if fewer sought higher education." He discussed with approval the Swedish experiment at redistributing income and wealth but thought it hampered by the fact that "Sweden still has a privately owned economy." He worried about "brain drain" but concluded that it was a serious problem only with regard to airline pilots and physicians; and a nation can do without airlines and may be able to replace general practitioners "with people having a lower (and less marketable) qualification." (Yet Barry himself was soon to join the brain drain, and he is neither a physician nor an airline pilot.) He proposed "to spread the nastiest jobs around by requiring everyone, before entering higher education or entering a profession, to do, say, three years of work wherever he or she was directed. (This would also have educational advantages.) To supplement this there could be a call-up of say a month every year, as with the Swiss and Israeli armed forces but directed towards peaceful occupations."

At least with the benefit of hindsight we can see that Barry wrote a prescription for economic disaster. It may be impossible to lay solid philosophical foundations under wealth maximization, just as it may be impossible to lay solid philosophical foundations under the natural sciences, but this would be a poor reason for abandoning wealth maximization, just as the existence of intractable problems in the philosophy of science would be a poor reason for abandoning science. We have reason to believe that markets work—that capitalism delivers the goods, if not the Good—and it would be a mistake to allow philosophy to deflect us from the implications, just as it would be a mistake to allow philosophy to alter our views of infanticide.

A sensible pragmatism does not ignore theory. The mounting evidence that capitalism is more efficient than socialism gives us an additional reason for believing economic theory (not every application of it, to be sure). The theory in turn gives us greater confidence in the evidence. Theory and evidence are mutually supporting. From the perspective of economic theory, brain drain is not the mysterious disease that Barry supposes it to be; it is the rational response to leveling policies by those whose incomes are being leveled downward.

    * * *

My pragmatic judgment is, moreover, a qualified one. All societies depart from the precepts of wealth maximization. The unanswered question is how the conditions in these societies would change if the public sector could somehow be cut all the way down to the modest dimensions of the night watchman state that the precepts of wealth maximization seem to imply. That is a difficult counterfactual question (it seems that no society's leadership has both the will and the power to play the guinea pig in an experiment with full-fledged wealth maximization) * * * . Until it is answered, we should be cautious in pushing wealth maximization; incrementalism should be our watchword.

The fact that wealth maximization, pragmatically construed, is instrumental rather than foundational is not an objection to its use in guiding law and public policy. It may be the right principle for that purpose even though it is right only in virtue of ends that are not solely economic. At least it may be the right default principle, placing on the proponent of departures from wealth maximization the burden of demonstrating their desirability.

Even if my observations on comparative economic performance in the Third World and elsewhere are correct, do such matters belong in a book on jurisprudence? They do. The object of pragmatic analysis is to lead discussion away from issues semantic and metaphysical and toward issues factual and empirical. Jurisprudence is greatly in need of such a shift in direction. Jurisprudence needs to become more pragmatic.

COMMON LAW REVISITED

The case for using wealth maximization as a guiding principle in common law adjudication is particularly strong. The common law judge operates within a framework established by the Constitution, which, by virtue of a number of the amendments, not only rules out of bounds the ethically most questionable applications of wealth maximization but largely eliminates the problems of incompleteness and indeterminacy that result from the uncertain relationship between wealth maximization and the initial distribution of rights. That initial distribution is more or less a given for the common law judge. A related point is that such a judge operates in a domain where distributive or egalitarian considerations can play at best only a small role. The judge whose business is enforcing tort, contract, and property law lacks effective tools for bringing about an equitable distribution of wealth, even if he thinks he knows what such a distribution would be. He would be further handicapped in such an endeavor by the absence of consensus in our society on the nature of a just distribution, an absence that undermines the social acceptability of attempts to use the judicial office to achieve distributive goals. A sensible division of labor has the judge making rules and deciding cases in the areas regulated by the common law in such a way as to maximize the size of the social pie, and the legislature attending to the sizes of the slices.

The case is strongest in those common law areas where the relevant policies are admitted to be economic. Suppose the idea of an implied warranty of habitability—which entitles a tenant to sue his landlord if the premises fall below the standards of safety and comfort specified in the local housing code—is defended, as normally it is defended, on the ground that it is needed to protect tenants from deception and over reaching by landlords and will not lead to a reduction in the stock of housing available to poor people or to higher rentals than the poor are willing and able to pay. If research demonstrates that these assumptions are incorrect, the proponent, if fair-minded, will have to withdraw the proposal. In this example, in principle (for the necessary research is difficult to conduct), legal questions can be made determinate by the translation of a legal question into a social-scientific one in a setting of common ends, and therefore the valid Benthamite project of placing law on a more scientific basis can be advanced without injury to competing values.

If it could be shown or if it is conceded that common law decision making is indeed not an apt field for efforts to redistribute wealth, then it may be possible to ground wealth maximization (as used to guide such decision making) in a more powerful normative principle of economics, the Pareto principle. A transaction is Pareto superior when it makes at least one person better off and no one worse off. A simple contract approximates a Pareto-superior transaction. Neither party would sign the contract unless he thought he would be better off as a result. So, assuming adequate information (which does not mean assuming omniscience) and no adverse effects on third parties, the contract will be Pareto superior. At least this will be so on an ex ante basis, for as things turn out one of the parties (perhaps both) may be made worse off by the contract. This possibility is inevitable if there is uncertainty, and uncertainty is inevitable.

The ethical appeal of the Pareto principle is similar to that of unanimity. If everyone affected by a transaction is better off, how can the transaction be socially or ethically bad? There are answers to this question, yet a Pareto-superior transaction makes a powerful claim for ethical respect because it draws on intuitions that are fundamental to both utilitarianism and Kantian individualism-respect for preferences, and for persons, respectively. It may seem paradoxical to derive a norm of wealth maximization from the principle of Pareto superiority, when the hallmark of the latter is compensation of all potential losers (for remember that no one must be made worse off by the transaction if it is to be Pareto superior), while wealth maximization requires only that the winners' gains exceed the losers' losses. But if, as in the contract example, compensation is permitted to be ex ante, the paradox disappears.

The difference between the ex ante and ex post perspectives is fundamental, and failure to attend to it underlies much confused thinking about markets and transactional competence. Because many choices are made, unavoidably, under conditions of uncertainty, a fair number must turn out badly. Ex post, they are regarded as mistaken and engender regret, yet ex ante they may have been perfectly sensible. Suppose I have a choice between two jobs. One would pay me $50,000 every year with certainty the other either $500,000 a year (with a 90 percent probability) or nothing (with a 10 percent probability). The expected income in the first job is $50,000 and in the second $450,000. (Notice the use of Bayesian probability, mentioned in Chapter 6.) The second, however, involves uncertainty. If I am risk averse—and let us assume I am—I will value an uncertain expectation at less than its actual equivalent. Hence the second job will not really be worth $450,000 to me, and let us suppose it will be worth only one-third as much—$150,000. Still, that is more than $50,000, so I will take the second job. But I am unlucky, the 10 percent chance materializes, and my income is zero. I would be less (or more) than human if I did not regret my choice, rail against my fate, berate myself for having chosen stupidly. But in fact I made the right choice—and would make it again, given the same uncertainty as before.

Consider now the case where negligence is the more efficient principle, in a wealth-maximizing sense, than strict liability because when all the costs and benefits are toted up the negligence regime turns out to produce the greater excess of benefits over costs. If so, the sum of liability and accident insurance premiums will be lower in the negligence regime and all drivers will be better off ex ante, although ex post, of course, some may do better in a regime of strict liability. Actually, not all will be better off even ex ante. Some people who are more prone to be injured than to injure will be worse off, since negligence favors injurers relative to strict liability, and some who are more prone to injure than to be injured will be better off. The "losers" will lose little, though—a matter of slightly higher insurance premiums. And both the "winners" and the vast majority of drivers who are neither disproportionately likely to injure than to be injured nor vice versa will be better off. Complete unanimity will be unattainable, but near unanimity can be presumed and the few losers will hardly be degraded, their autonomy wrecked, or their rights destroyed by having to pay a few dollars a month more in automobile insurance premiums.

I am painting with slightly too rosy a palette. Some people will lack the knowledge, intelligence, and foresight to buy insurance (I am putting to one side the deliberate risk takers); some may not be able to afford adequate insurance; and insurance that pays off as generously as common law damages may not be available in the market. When a person becomes a victim of a serious accident in which the injurer is not at fault, it may spell a financial disaster not attributable to the choices or the deserts of the victim—a disaster that strict liability could have avoided. An alternative, of course, is social insurance—the famous safety net. If cases of catastrophic uninsured nonnegligent accidental injury are rare, social insurance may be a better solution than a strict liability system that would require compensation through the tort system in all accident cases.

The essential point is that the availability of insurance, private or social, is necessary to back wealth maximization with the ethical weight of the Pareto principle. Once it is so backed, however, wealth maximization provides an ethically adequate guide to common law decision making—indeed a superior guide to any other that has been suggested. And the adequacy of private and public insurance markets, on which this conclusion depends, is an empirical, a studiable, issue.

No doubt most judges (and lawyers) think that the guiding light for common law decision making should be either an intuitive sense of justice or reasonableness, or a casual utilitarianism. But these may all be the same thing, and if pressed such a judge would probably have to admit that what he called utilitarianism was what I am calling wealth maximization. Consider whether a thief should be permitted to defend himself at trial on the ground that he derived greater pleasure from the stolen item than the pain suffered by the owner. The answer obviously is no, but it is offered more confidently by the wealth maximizer than by the pure utilitarian. The former can point out that the thief is bypassing the market system of exchange and that the pleasure he derives from the good he has stolen has no social standing because his desire for the good is not backed by willingness to pay. These are separate points. The thief might be willing to pay if he had to—that is, he might value the good more than its owner—yet prefer theft because it is a cheaper way for him to acquire the good. So theft might be utility maximizing, although this is unlikely because a practice of theft would result in enormous, utility-reducing expenditures on protection of property.

Since utility is more difficult to estimate than wealth, a system of wealth maximization may seem a proxy for a utilitarian system, but it is more; its spirit is different. Wealth maximization is an ethic of productivity and social cooperation—to have a claim on society's goods and services you must be able to offer something that other people value—while utilitarianism is a hedonistic, unsocial ethic, as the last example showed. And an ethic of productivity and cooperation is more congruent with the values of the dominant groups in our society than the pure utilitarian ethic would be. Unfortunately, wealth maximization is not a pure ethic of productivity and cooperation, not only because even lawful efforts at maximizing wealth often make some other people worse off, but more fundamentally because luck plays a big role in the returns to market activities. What is worse, it is always possible to argue that the distribution of productivity among a population is itself the luck of the genetic draw, or of upbringing, or of where one happens to have been born, and that these forms of luck have no ethical charge. There are counterarguments, of course, but they are not decisive. So, once again, the foundations of an overarching principle for resolving legal disputes are rotten, and one is driven back to the pragmatic ramparts.

* * *

NOTES AND QUESTIONS

1. Increase of wealth through theft. Posner claims that society's wealth will not be increased by transferring a BMW to an individual who can not pay for it, even if that individual would enjoy the BMW more than anyone who could pay for it. However, is this why this is true? If, for example, the BMW is worth $50,000 to A and $60,000 to B, then transferring the BMW from A to B will increase society's wealth by $10,000, regardless of whether B pays for the BMW or not. If B pays nothing, then A will be $50,000 worse off from having his car stolen, but B will be $60,000 better off for having stolen the car, a net gain to society of $10,000. This transfer, in which society's wealth is maximized even though one party to the transfer is left worse off, is based on the idea of Kaldor–Hicks efficiency which states that a transaction is efficient if "the winners win more than the losers lose." Guido Calabresi, *The Pointlessness of Pareto: Carrying Coase Further*, 100 YALE L.J. 1211, 1221 (1991).

2. **Place of poor in law and economics.** In Posner's view, society's wealth is generated not through money but through individual preferences. *See* the stamp collection example discussed *supra* at note 2. However, Posner distinguishes law and economics from utilitarianism by stating that only those preferences backed by money should "count." Does this reliance on money, which admittedly does not increase society's wealth not have the effect of simply shutting the poor out of the law and economics equation? Is Posner explicitly calling on the law to treat the rich (who have the money to back up their preferences in the market) differently from the poor (who, under Posner's framework, can only have preferences for the necessities of life, and sometimes not even those)? Additionally, Posner states that slavery is inefficient and that Nazi use of slave labor only looks efficient when the welfare of the slaves is ignored. POSNER, *supra* at 375–76. But, since slave laborers in Nazi Germany had no money, do we not have to ignore their preferences? How can Posner's statement about paying attention to the welfare of slaves be squared with his assertion that "a desire not backed by ability to pay has no standing?"

3. **Relationship between price and wealth.** Under Posner's analysis, the price of a commodity actually has no relationship to the wealth generated by its exchange. To use his stamp collection example from page 175, if B paid $1,000,000 for A's stamp collection, then society would be better off because A would have gained $1,000,000 and lost $90.00, while B would have lost $1,000,000 and gained $100. In all cases, because B values the stamp collection more highly than A and money is fungible, society's wealth is maximized by the exchange, even if it is blatantly unfair to either A or B. This is a direct result of the wealth maximizing properties of Kaldor–Hicks efficiency, discussed in Calabresi, *supra*.

4. **Inefficiency of tort.** Posner claims that the common law "establishes procedural rules for resolving disputes ... as efficiently as possible." THE PROBLEMS OF JURISPRUDENCE, *supra* at 357. However, tort law is notoriously inefficient at resolving disputes and several alternative statutory systems such as no-fault insurance and worker's compensation might provide better methods of adjudication. In particular, no-fault auto insurance might return over 90 percent of premium dollars in the form of benefits, compared with only 50 percent for liability insurance. DAN B. DOBBS & PAUL T. HAYDEN, TORTS AND COMPENSATION: PERSONAL ACCOUNTABILITY AND SOCIAL RE-

sponsibility for Injury 898 (4th ed. 2001). How can such inefficiency in the tort system be squared with Posner's claims about the procedural benefits of the common law?

5. **Effect of family privilege.**

    a. **Intergenerational persistence of wealth**. Posner's claim that the initial distribution of wealth will dissipate within three generations is almost certainly incorrect. The study by Becker and Tomes on which he based his statements on has since been criticized for, among other things, estimating an individual's lifetime income from one year's income. Gary Solon, *Intergenerational Income Mobility in the United States*, 82 Am. Econ. Rev. 393, 395 (1992); *see also* Bhashkar Mazumder, Federal Reserve Bank of Chicago, The Mis-Measurement of Permanent Earnings: New Evidence from Social Security Earnings Data (2001), *available at* http://www.chicagofed.org/publications/workingpapers/papers/Wp2001–24.pdf (critiquing the use of short-term averages of earnings as a proxy for permanent earnings). Newer research indicates that the actual requirement for regression to the mean is between four and six generations. Alan B. Krueger, *The Apple Falls Close to the Tree, Even in the Land of Opportunity*, N.Y. Times, Nov. 14, 2002, at C2.

    b. **Effect of legacy on meritocracy**. In 1998, nine students from Groton boarding school in Massachusetts applied for admission to Stanford University; only one was admitted. Her SAT score was lower than seven of the eight other Groton grads who applied to Stanford and both her SAT scores and class rank were significantly lower than the class ranks and test scores of the vast majority of students admitted to Stanford. However, she had something other students' didn't have: a father who was chairman of Stanford's board and who had given $25,000,000 to Stanford in 1992. Does the policy of preferential admission of the children of alumnae and donors cast doubt on Posner's arguments about the rapid dissipation of the initial distribution of wealth? Even if a free market would lead to dissipation of the initial wealth distribution, do policies like legacy admissions serve to maintain the initial distribution of wealth, perhaps indefinitely? For more, see Daniel Golden, *College Ties*: *For Groton Grads, Academics Aren't Only Keys to Ivy Schools*, Wall St. J., Apr. 25, 2003, at A1.

6. **Morality in law and economics.** Is law and economics amoral? Judge Posner notes that "it would be possible in a system unflinchingly dedicated to wealth maximization to come up with results that would be deeply, perhaps universally, offensive." Richard Posner, *Law and Economics is Moral*, *in* Adam Smith and the Philosophy of Law and Economics 174 (Rubin Paul Malloy & Jerry Evensky eds., 1994). One such specific proposal is child trafficking which Posner believes

> is a form of transaction that would be wealth maximizing and would repair a serious imbalance in the supply and demand for babies for adoption. We have in this country an enormous production of illegiti-

mate births and, on the other hand, a terrible shortage of babies for adoption. This is clearly a disequilibrium, and it results in part from refusing to allow an explicit trade in babies.

Id. at 173.

Should the fact that law and economics can justify such schemes which even Posner admits are "deeply, perhaps universally, offensive" undermine the persuasive authority of law and economics?

7. Libertarianism and persuasive power of law and economics. In its statement of principles, the Libertarian party of the United States declares that:

> People should not be forced to sacrifice their lives and property for the benefit of others. They should be left free by government to deal with one another as free traders; and the resultant economic system, the only one compatible with the protection of individual rights, is the free market.

LIBERTARIAN PARTY, STATEMENT OF PRINCIPALS, *available at* http://www.lp.org/issues/platform_all.shtml#sop.

This economic position seems to mirror the law and economics of Judge Posner which recommends that the legal system act as much like the free market as possible when resolving disputes. Indeed, many of the thinkers most closely associated with law and economics, including Judge Posner himself, identify as libertarians. Given the conservative nature of libertarianism, does this association undermine claims of Law and Economics as a value-neutral method of jurisprudence?

8. Contradictions between libertarianism and utilitarianism. Ayn Rand, an influential libertarian thinker, stated:

> Parasites, moochers, looters, brutes and thugs can be of no value to a human being—nor can he gain any benefit from living in a society geared to their needs, demands and protection, a society that treats him as a sacrificial animal and penalizes him for his virtues in order to reward them for their vices, which means: a society based on the ethics of altruism.

AYN RAND, THE VIRTUE OF SELFISHNESS 32 (1964).

Such sentiments are very similar to the consequence of the money requirement in law and economics which results in the preferences of the destitute having zero weight. Thus, it seems that libertarianism and law and economics are a perfect match for one another. However, on closer examination, is there not a contradiction between libertarianism, which focuses on the primacy of the individual, and law and economics, which bases its normative appeal on the good of the community? Some libertarians, like Posner, support economic individualism only to the extent that it is the most effective way of providing for the well-being of everyone. Others, like Rand, seem to favor a devil take the hindmost approach to the marketplace. For more on this tension, see Gary Lawson, *Efficiency and Individualism*, 42 DUKE L.J. 53 (1992) (explaining difficulties relating to interpersonal comparisons of utility and addresses the tension between individualism and social wealth); Larry Alexander & Maimon Schwarzschild, *The Uncertain Relationship Between Libertarianism and Utilitarianism*, 19 Quinnipiac L. Rev. 657 (2000) (tracing the development of the jurisprudence of Epstein and noting the contradiction between his early libertarian philosophy and his later utilitarian bent.); Heidi Li Feldman, *Law and Economics: Libertarianism with a Twist*, 94 Mich. L. Rev. 1883 (1996) (questioning Epstein's attempt to justify a libertarian state through rule utilitarianism).

1. Law and Economics in Judicial Reasoning

A. An Early Precursor

Learned Hand's opinion in *U.S. v Carroll Towing Co.* is a classic of tort law. It is recognized for introducing an algebraic representation (negligence =PL > B) of the economic cost benefit test to replace the more vague and general common law standard of "reasonable care." In the arguments of the law and economics movement, the Hand formulation is taken as an expression of the goal of economic efficiency. The Hand formulation fits neatly into both the positive and normative claims of law and economics. The positive argument is that the common law has been constructed so as to pursue efficiency as its goal. This argument has been vigorously contested by torts scholars who have argued that many nineteenth-century tort cases are quite inconsistent with the efficiency interpretation. *See* Gary T. Schwartz, The *Character of Early American Tort Law*, 36 UCLA L. Rev. 641 (1989); Gary T. Schwartz, *Tort Law and the Economy in Nineteenth–Century America: A Reinterpretation*, 90 Yale L.J. 1717 (1981).

Other scholars have disputed the normative claim, that tort law *should* pursue efficiency and wealth maximization as primary goals. *Carroll Towing Company*, is often used to support the normative position as well. The cost benefit approach to personal injury rules is designed to allow the party whose activities will inflict injury to continue to do so, as long as the burden of taking precaution exceeds the combined probability of injury multiplied by the gravity of injury should it occur. Legal philosopher Jules Coleman argued that corrective justice, rather than economic efficiency, explains the arc of tort common law developments. Jules Coleman, Risk and Wrongs, 374–382 (1992).

Now, read this familiar case and decide whether it supports either the Posnerian positive or normative efficiency claims.

———

United States v. Carroll Towing Co.
159 F.2d 169 (2d Cir.1947).

■ L. Hand, Circuit Judge.

* * *

On June 20, 1943, the Conners Company chartered the barge, "Anna C." to the Pennsylvania Railroad Company at a stated hire per diem, by a charter of the kind usual in the Harbor, which included the services of a bargee, apparently limited to the hours 8 A.M. to 4 P.M. On January 2, 1944, the barge, which had lifted the cargo of flour, was made fast off the end of Pier 58 on the Manhattan side of the North River, whence she was later shifted to Pier 52. At some time not disclosed, five other barges were moored outside her, extending into the river; her lines to the pier were not then strengthened. At the end of the next pier north (called the Public Pier), lay four barges; and a line had been made fast from the outermost of these to the fourth barge of the tier hanging to Pier 52. The purpose of this line is not entirely apparent, and in any event it obstructed entrance into the slip between the two piers of barges. The Grace Line, which had chartered the tug, "Carroll," sent her down to the locus in quo to "drill" out one of the barges which lay at the end of the Public Pier; and in order to do so it was necessary to throw off the line between the two tiers. On board the "Carroll" at the time were not only her master, but a "harbor-master" employed by the Grace Line. Before throwing off the line between the two tiers, the "Carroll" nosed up against the outer barge of the tier lying off Pier 52, ran a line from her own stem to the middle bit of that barge, and kept working her engines "slow ahead" against the ebb tide which was making at that time. The captain of the "Carroll" put a deckhand and the "harbormaster" on the barges, told them to throw off the line which barred the entrance to the slip; but, before doing so, to make sure that the tier on Pier 52 was safely moored, as there was a strong northerly wind blowing down the river. The "harbormaster" and the deckhand went aboard the barges and readjusted all the fasts to their satisfaction, including those from the "Anna C." to the pier.

After doing so, they threw off the line between the two tiers and again boarded the "Carroll," which backed away from the outside barge, prepara-tory to "drilling" out the barge she was after in the tier off the Public Pier. She had only got about seventy-five feet away when the tier off Pier 52 broke adrift because the fasts from the "Anna C," either rendered, or carried away. The tide and wind carried down the six barges, still holding together, until the "Anna C" fetched up against a tanker, lying on the north side of the pier below—Pier 51—whose propeller broke a hole in her at or near her bottom. Shortly thereafter: i.e., at about 2:15 P.M., she careened, dumped her cargo of flour and sank. The tug, "Grace," owned by the Grace Line, and the "Carroll," came to the help of the flotilla after it broke loose; and, as both had syphon pumps on board, they could have kept the "Anna C" afloat, had they learned of her condition; but the bargee had left her on the evening before, and nobody was on board to observe that she was leaking. The Grace Line wishes to exonerate itself from all liability because the "harbormaster" was not authorized to pass on the sufficiency of the fasts of the "Anna C" which held the tier to Pier 52; the Carroll Company wishes to charge the Grace Line with the entire liability because the "harbormaster" was given an over-all authority. Both wish to charge the "Anna C" with a share of all her damages, or at least with so much as resulted from her sinking. The Pennsylvania Railroad Company also wishes to hold the barge liable. The Conners Company wishes the decrees to be affirmed.

The first question is whether the Grace Line should be held liable at all for any part of the damages. The answer depends first upon how far the "harbormaster's" authority went, for concededly he was an employee of some sort. Although the judge made no other finding of fact than that he was an "employee," in his second conclusion of law he held that the Grace Line was "responsible for his negligence." Since the facts on which he based this liability do not appear, we cannot give that weight to the conclusion which we should to a finding of fact; but it so happens that on cross-examination the "harbormaster" showed that he was authorized to pass on the sufficiency of the facts of the "Anna C." He said that it was part of his job to tie up barges; that when he came "to tie up a barge" he had "to go in and look at the barges that are inside the barge" he was "handling"; that in such cases "most of the time" he went in "to see that the lines to the inside barges are strong enough to hold these barges"; and that "if they are not" he "put out sufficient other lines as are necessary." That does not, however, determine the other question: i.e., whether, when the master of the "Carroll" told him and the deckhand to go aboard the tier and look at the fasts, preparatory to casting off the line between the tiers, the tug master meant the "harbormaster" to exercise a joint authority with the deckhand. As to this the judge in his tenth finding said: "The captain of the Carroll then put the deckhand of the tug and the harbor master aboard the boats at the end of Pier 52 to throw off the line between the two tiers of boats after first ascertaining if it would be safe to do so." Whatever doubts the testimony of the "harbormaster" might raise, this finding settles it for us that the master of the "Carroll" deputed the deckhand and the "harbormaster," jointly to pass upon the sufficiency of the "Anna C's" fasts to the pier. The case is stronger against the Grace Line than Rice v. The Marion A. C. Meseck, was against the tug there held liable, because the tug had only acted under the express orders of the "harbormaster." Here, although the relations were reversed, that makes no difference in principle; and the "harbormaster" was not instructed what he should do about the fast, but was allowed to use his own judgment. The fact that the deckhand shared in this decision, did not exonerate him, and there is no reason why both should not be held equally liable, as the judge held them.

We cannot, however, excuse the Conners Company for the bargee's failure to care for the barge, and we think that this prevents full recovery. * * * As we have said, the deckhand and the "harbormaster" jointly undertook to pass upon the "Anna C's" fasts to the pier; and even though we assume that the bargee was responsible for his fasts after the other barges were added outside, there is not the slightest ground for saying that the deckhand and the "harbormaster" would have paid any attention to any protest which he might have made, had he been there. We do not therefore attribute it as in any degree a fault of the "Anna C" that the flotilla broke adrift. Hence she may recover in full against the Carroll

Company and the Grace Line for any injury she suffered from the contact with the tanker's propeller, which we shall speak of as the "collision damages." On the other hand, if the bargee had been on board, and had done his duty to his employer, he would have gone below at once, examined the injury, and called for help from the "Carroll" and the Grace Line tug. Moreover, it is clear that these tugs could have kept the barge afloat, until they had safely beached her, and saved her cargo. This would have avoided what we shall call the "sinking damages." Thus, if it was a failure in the Conner Company's proper care of its own barge, for the bargee to be absent, the company can recover only one third of the "sinking" damages from the Carroll Company and one third from the Grace Line. For this reason the question arises whether a barge owner is slack in the care of his barge if the bargee is absent.

* * *

It appears from the foregoing review that there is no general rule to determine when the absence of a bargee or other attendant will make the owner of the barge liable for injuries to other vessels if she breaks away from her moorings. However, in any cases where he would be so liable for injuries to others obviously he must reduce his damages proportionately, if the injury is to his own barge. It becomes apparent why there can be no such general rule, when we consider the grounds for such a liability. Since there are occasions when every vessel will break from her moorings, and since, if she does, she becomes a menace to those about her; the owner's duty, as in other similar situations, to provide against resulting injuries is a function of three variables: (1) The probability that she will break away; (2) the gravity of the resulting injury, if she does; (3) the burden of adequate precautions. Possibly it serves to bring this notion into relief to state it in algebraic terms: if the probability be called P; the injury, L; and the burden, B; liability depends upon whether B is less than L multiplied by P: i.e., whether $B < PL$. Applied to the situation at bar, the likelihood that a barge will break from her fasts and the damage she will do, vary with the place and time; for example, if a storm threatens, the danger is greater; so it is, if she is in a crowded harbor where moored barges are constantly being shifted about. On the other hand, the barge must not be the bargee's prison, even though he lives aboard; he must go ashore at times. We need not say whether, even in such crowded waters as New York Harbor a bargee must be aboard at night at all; it may be that the custom is otherwise, as Ward, J., supposed in "The Kathryn B. Guinan," supra; and that, if so, the situation is one where custom should control. We leave that question open; but we hold that it is not in all cases a sufficient answer to a bargee's absence without excuse, during working hours, that he has properly made fast his barge to a pier, when he leaves her. In the case at bar the bargee left at five o'clock in the afternoon of January 3rd, and the flotilla broke away at about two o'clock in the afternoon of the following day, twenty-one hours afterwards. The bargee had been away all the time, and we hold that his fabricated story was affirmative evidence that he had no excuse for his absence. At the locus in quo-especially during the short January days and in the full tide of war activity-barges were being constantly "drilled" in and out. Certainly it was not beyond reasonable expectation that, with the inevitable haste and bustle, the work might not be done with adequate care. In such circumstances we hold—and it is all that we do hold—that it was a fair requirement that the Conners Company should have a bargee aboard (unless he had some excuse for his absence), during the working hours of daylight.

* * *

B. Modern Cases

It is easy to forget that Professor Posner is also a judge whose views on law and economics extend beyond the realm of theory into the judicial arena. In this Seventh Circuit opinion, we see two University of Chicago law and economics scholars, Judges Easterbrook and Posner, carve out a separate rationale in a concurrence in a case in which they agree with the holding. Can you identify the tenets of law and economics legal theory upon which their opinion is based? What is the difference between the views of Judges Cudahy and Posner and Easterbrook? Do you agree with the Posner/Easterbrook analysis of the disparate impact of the rent control ordinance on the "poor" and the "middle class"?

In the second case in this section, Judge Posner is using law and economics reasoning to define the standard applicable under the common law as restated in the American Law Institute Restatement of the Law of Torts section 520 on strict liability for ultrahazardous activity liability. Like *Chicago Board of Realtors, Indiana Harbor* is strictly a question of law for the judge to decide what legal standard is applicable to resolve the dispute. In *Indiana Harbor*, Posner explores the relationship between two tort liability regimes: negligence, as we have discussed in *U.S. v. Carroll Towing Company* above, and strict liability. He decides that strict liability is inappropriate for the shipper/manufacturer of a highly flammable chemical that leaked while in a Chicago railyard near occupied homes. One component of the Restatement test for whether an activity is abnormally dangerous or ultrahazardous is whether the activity is unusual or inappropriate in the area in which the accident occurred. Consider Posner's opinion, that:

> ... It is no more realistic to propose to reroute the shipment of all hazardous materials around Chicago than it is to propose the relocation of homes adjacent to the Blue Island switching yard to more distant suburbs. It may be less realistic. Brutal though it may seem to say it, *the inappropriate use* to which land *is* being put in the Blue Island yard and neighborhood may be, not the transportation of hazardous chemicals, but *residential living*. The analogy is to building your home between the runways at O'Hare.

Indiana Harbor Belt R.R. Co. v. American Cyanamid Co., 916 F.2d 1174, 1181 (7th Cir. 1990) (emphasis added).

———

Chicago Board of Realtors, Inc. v. City of Chicago

United States Court of Appeals, Seventh Circuit, 819 F.2d 732 (1987).

■ POSNER, CIRCUIT JUDGE, concurring.

[In 1986, the Chicago City Council passed a Residential Landlord and Tenant ordinance. It codified the "implied warrant of habitability," which is a doctrine of property law that requires landlords to provide a baseline of quality in the housing they let, a duty which is independent of the tenant's obligation to pay rent. The ordinance was upheld against a challenge by property owners who questioned its constitutionality. In his opinion for the court, Judge Cudahy ruled that the ordinance was sufficiently specific and reasonable under the government's police power.

In the concurrence that follows, Judge Posner, joined by Judge Easterbrook, laid out a policy analysis of the ordinance.]

We agree with Judge Cudahy's opinion as far as it goes, and we therefore join it. But in our view it does not go far enough. It makes the rejection of the appeal seem easier than it is, by refusing to acknowledge the strong case that can be made for the unreasonableness of the ordinance. It does not explain how the district judge's denial of a preliminary injunction against such an interference with contract rights and economic freedom can be affirmed without violating the contract clause and the due process clause of the Constitution. So we are led to write separately, and since this separate opinion commands the support of two members of this panel, it is also a majority opinion.

The new ordinance rewrites present and future leases of apartments in Chicago to give tenants more legal rights than they would have without the ordinance. It requires the payment of interest on security deposits; requires that those deposits be held in Illinois banks; allows (with some limitations) a tenant to withhold rent in an amount reflecting the cost to him of the landlord's violating a term in the lease; allows a tenant to make minor repairs and subtract the reasonable cost of the repair from his rent; forbids a landlord to charge a tenant more than $10 a month for late payment of rent (regardless of how much is owing); and creates a presumption (albeit rebuttable) that a landlord who seeks to evict a tenant after the tenant has exercised rights conferred by the ordinance is retaliating against the tenant for the exercise of those rights.

The stated purpose of the ordinance is to promote public health, safety, and welfare and the quality of housing in Chicago. It is unlikely that this is the real purpose, and it is not the likely effect. Forbidding landlords to charge interest at market rates on late payment of rent could hardly be thought calculated to improve the health, safety, and welfare of Chicagoans or to improve the quality of the housing stock. But it may have the opposite effect. The initial consequence of the rule will be to reduce the resources that landlords devote to improving the quality of housing, by making the provision of rental housing more costly. Landlords will try to offset the higher cost (in time value of money, less predictable cash flow, and, probably, higher rate of default) by raising rents. To the extent they succeed, tenants will be worse off, or at least no better off. Landlords will also screen applicants more carefully, because the cost of renting to a deadbeat will now be higher; so marginal tenants will find it harder to persuade landlords to rent to them.

Those who do find apartments but then are slow to pay will be subsidized by responsible tenants (some of them marginal too), who will be paying higher rents, assuming the landlord cannot determine in advance who is likely to pay rent on time. Insofar as these efforts to offset the ordinance fail, the cost of rental housing will be higher to landlords and therefore less will be supplied—more of the existing stock than would otherwise be the case will be converted to condominia and cooperatives and less rental housing will be built.

The provisions of the ordinance requiring that interest on security deposits be paid and that those deposits be kept in Illinois banks are as remote as the provision on late payment from any concern with the health or safety of Chicagoans, the quality of housing in Chicago, or the welfare of Chicago as a whole. Their only apparent rationale is to transfer wealth from landlords and out-of-state banks to tenants and local banks—making this an unedifying example of class legislation and economic protectionism rolled into one. However, to the extent the ordinance seeks to transfer wealth from landlords to tenants it could readily be undone by a rent increase; the ordinance puts no cap on rents. Cf. Coase, *The Problem of Social Cost*, 3 J. Law & Econ. 1 (1960).

The provisions that authorize rent withholding, whether directly or by subtracting repair costs, may seem more closely related to the stated objectives of the ordinance; but the relation is tenuous. The right to withhold rent is not limited to cases of hazardous or unhealthy conditions. And any benefits in safer or healthier housing from exercise of the right are likely to be offset by the higher costs to landlords, resulting in higher rents and less rental housing.

The ordinance is not in the interest of poor people. As is frequently the case with legislation ostensibly designed to promote the welfare of the poor, the principal beneficiaries will be middle-class people. They will be people who buy rather than rent housing (the conversion of rental to owner housing will reduce the price of the latter by increasing its supply); people willing to pay a higher rental for better-quality housing; and (a largely overlapping group) more affluent tenants, who will become more attractive to landlords because such tenants are less likely to be late with the rent or to abuse the right of withholding rent—a right that is more attractive, the poorer the tenant. The losers from the ordinance will be some landlords, some out-of-state banks, the poorest class of tenants, and future tenants.* * *

A growing body of empirical literature deals with the effects of governmental regulation of the market for rental housing. The regulations that have been studied, such as rent control in New York City and Los Angeles, are not identical to the new Chicago ordinance, though some—regulations which require that rental housing be "habitable"—are close. The significance of this literature is not in proving that the Chicago ordinance is unsound, but in showing that the market for rental housing behaves as economic theory predicts: if price is artificially depressed, or the costs of landlords artificially increased, supply falls and many tenants, usually the poorer and the newer tenants, are hurt. * * * The single proposition in economics from which there is the least dissent among American economists is that "a ceiling on rents reduces the quantity and quality of housing available." * * *

Indiana Harbor Belt R.R. Co. v. American Cyanamid Co.

916 F.2d 1174 (7th Cir. 1990).

■ POSNER, CIRCUIT JUDGE.

American Cyanamid Company * * * is a major manufacturer of chemicals, including acrylonitrile, a chemical used in large quantities in making acrylic fibers, plastics, dyes, pharmaceutical chemicals, and other intermediate and final goods. On January 2, 1979, at its manufacturing plant in Louisiana, Cyanamid loaded 20,000 gallons of liquid acrylonitrile into a railroad tank car that it had leased from the North American Car Corporation. * * * [The car was brought to] the Blue Island railroad yard * * * in the Village of Riverdale, which is just south of Chicago and part of the Chicago metropolitan area.

* * * Several hours after it arrived, employees of the switching line noticed fluid gushing from the bottom outlet of the car. The lid on the outlet was broken. After two hours, the line's supervisor of equipment was able to stop the leak by closing a shut-off valve controlled from the top of the car. No one was sure at the time just how much of the contents of the car had leaked, but it was feared that all 20,000 gallons had, and since acrylonitrile is flammable at a temperature of 30° Fahrenheit or above, highly toxic, and possibly carcinogenic (*Acrylonitrile*, 9 International Toxicity Update, no. 3, May–June 1989, at 2, 4), the local authorities ordered the homes near the yard evacuated.* * *

[The plaintiff] asserts that the transportation of acrylonitrile in bulk through the Chicago metropolitan area is an abnormally dangerous activity, for the consequences of which the shipper (Cyanamid) is strictly liable to the switching line, which bore the financial brunt of those consequences because of the decontamination measures that it was forced to take.* * *

The question whether the shipper of a hazardous chemical by rail should be strictly liable for the consequences of a spill or other accident to the shipment en route is a novel one in Illinois, despite the switching line's contention that the question has been answered in its favor by two decisions of the Illinois Appellate Court that the district judge cited in granting summary judgment.* * *

The parties agree that the question whether placing acrylonitrile in a rail shipment that will pass through a metropolitan area subjects the shipper to strict liability is, as recommended in Restatement (Second) of Torts § 520, comment *l* (1977), a question of law, so that we owe no particular deference to the conclusion of the district court. They also agree * * * that the Supreme Court of Illinois would treat as authoritative the provisions of the Restatement governing abnormally dangerous activities. The key provision is section 520, which sets forth six factors to be considered in deciding whether an activity is abnormally dangerous and the actor therefore strictly liable.

The roots of section 520 are in nineteenth-century cases. [In *Guille v. Swan*, 19 Johns. (N.Y.) 381 (1822) a] man took off in a hot-air balloon and landed, without intending to, in a vegetable garden in New York City. A crowd that had been anxiously watching his involuntary descent trampled the vegetables in their endeavor to rescue him when he landed. The owner of the garden sued the balloonist for the resulting damage, and won. Yet the balloonist had not been careless. In the then state of ballooning it was impossible to make a pinpoint landing.

Guille is a paradigmatic case for strict liability. (a) The risk (probability) of harm was great, and (b) the harm that would ensue if the risk materialized could be, although luckily was not, great (the balloonist could have crashed into the crowd rather than into the vegetables). The confluence of these two factors established the urgency of seeking to prevent such accidents. (c) Yet such accidents could not be prevented by the exercise of due care; the technology of care in ballooning was insufficiently developed. (d) The activity was not a matter of common usage, so there was no presumption that it was a highly valuable activity despite its unavoidable riskiness. (e) The activity was inappropriate to the place in which it took place—densely populated New York City. The risk of serious harm to others (other than the balloonist himself, that is) could have been reduced by shifting the activity to the sparsely inhabited areas that surrounded the city in those days. (f) Reinforcing (d), the value to the community of the activity of recreational ballooning did not appear to be great enough to offset its unavoidable risks.

* * * The baseline common law regime of tort liability is negligence. When it is a workable regime, because the hazards of an activity can be avoided by being careful (which is to say, nonnegligent), there is no need to switch to strict liability. Sometimes, however, a particular type of accident cannot be prevented by taking care but can be avoided, or its consequences minimized, by shifting the activity in which the accident occurs to another locale, where the risk or harm of an accident will be less ((e)), or by reducing the scale of the activity in order to minimize the number of accidents caused by it ((f)). * * * By making the actor strictly liable—by denying him in other words an excuse based on his inability to avoid accidents by being more careful—we give him an incentive, missing in a negligence regime, to experiment with methods of preventing accidents that involve not greater exertions of care, assumed to be futile, but instead relocating, changing, or reducing (perhaps to the vanishing point) the activity giving rise to the accident. * * * The greater the risk of an accident

((a)) and the costs of an accident if one occurs ((b)), the more we want the actor to consider the possibility of making accident-reducing activity changes; the stronger, therefore, is the case for strict liability. Finally, if an activity is extremely common ((d)), like driving an automobile, it is unlikely either that its hazards are perceived as great or that there is no technology of care available to minimize them; so the case for strict liability is weakened.

The largest class of cases in which strict liability has been imposed under the standard codified in the Second Restatement of Torts involves the use of dynamite and other explosives for demolition in residential or urban areas.* * *

Against this background we turn to the particulars of acrylonitrile. Acrylonitrile is one of a large number of chemicals that are hazardous in the sense of being flammable, toxic, or both; acrylonitrile is both, as are many others.* * *

[W]e can get little help from precedent, and might as well apply section 520 to the acrylonitrile problem from the ground up. To begin with, we have been given no reason * * * for believing that a negligence regime is not perfectly adequate to remedy and deter, at reasonable cost, the accidental spillage of acrylonitrile from rail cars * * * More important, although acrylonitrile is flammable even at relatively low temperatures, and toxic, it is not so corrosive or otherwise destructive that it will eat through or otherwise damage or weaken a tank car's valves although they are maintained with due (which essentially means, with average) care. No one suggests, therefore, that the leak in this case was caused by the *inherent* properties of acrylonitrile. It was caused by carelessness—whether that of the North American Car Corporation in failing to maintain or inspect the car properly, or that of Cyanamid in failing to maintain or inspect it, or that of the Missouri Pacific when it had custody of the car, or that of the switching line itself in failing to notice the ruptured lid, or some combination of these possible failures of care. Accidents that are due to a lack of care can be prevented by taking care; and when a lack of care can * * * be shown in court, such accidents are adequately deterred by the threat of liability for negligence.

It is true that the district court purported to find as a fact that there is an inevitable risk of derailment or other calamity in transporting "large quantities of anything." 662 F.Supp. at 642. This is not a finding of fact, but a truism: anything can happen. The question is, how likely is this type of accident if the actor uses due care? For all that appears from the record of the case or any other sources of information that we have found, if a tank car is carefully maintained the danger of a spill of acrylonitrile is negligible. If this is right, there is no compelling reason to move to a regime of strict liability, especially one that might embrace all other hazardous materials shipped by rail as well. This also means, however, that the amici curiae who have filed briefs in support of Cyanamid cry wolf in predicting "devastating" effects on the chemical industry if the district court's decision is affirmed. If the vast majority of chemical spills by railroads are preventable by due care, the imposition of strict liability should cause only a slight, not as they argue a substantial, rise in liability insurance rates, because the incremental liability should be slight. The amici have momentarily lost sight of the fact that the feasibility of avoiding accidents simply by being careful is an argument against strict liability.

* * *

The district judge and the plaintiff's lawyer make much of the fact that the spill occurred in a densely inhabited metropolitan area. Only 4,000 gallons spilled; what if all 20,000 had done so? Isn't the risk that this might happen even if everybody were careful sufficient to warrant giving the shipper an incentive to explore alternative routes? Strict liability would supply that incentive. But this argument overlooks the fact that, like other transportation networks, the railroad network is a hub-and-spoke system. And the hubs are in metropolitan areas. Chicago is one of the nation's largest railroad hubs. In 1983, the latest year for which we have figures, Chicago's railroad yards handled the third highest volume of hazardous-material shipments in the nation. East St. Louis, which is also in Illinois, handled the second highest volume. * * * With most hazardous chemicals (by volume of shipments) being at least as hazardous as acrylonitrile, it is unlikely—and certainly not demonstrated by the plaintiff—that they can be rerouted around all the metropolitan areas in the country, except at prohibitive cost. Even if it were feasible to reroute them one would hardly expect shippers, as distinct from carriers, to be the firms best situated to do the rerouting.* * *

The difference between shipper and carrier points to a deep flaw in the plaintiff's case. * * * [H]ere it is not the actors—that is, the transporters of acrylonitrile and other chemicals—but the manufacturers, who are sought to be held strictly liable. * * * A shipper can in the bill of lading designate the route of his shipment if he likes, 49 U.S.C. § 11710(a)(1), but is it realistic to suppose that shippers will become students of railroading in order to lay out the safest route by which to ship their goods? Anyway, rerouting is no panacea. Often it will increase the length of the journey, or compel the use of poorer track, or both. When this happens, the probability of an accident is increased, even if the consequences of an accident if one occurs are reduced; so the expected accident cost, being the product of the probability of an accident and the harm if the accident occurs, may rise. * * * It is easy to see how the accident in this case might have been prevented at reasonable cost by greater care on the part of those who handled the tank car of acrylonitrile. It is difficult to see how it might have been prevented at reasonable cost by a change in the activity of transporting the chemical. This is therefore not an apt case for strict liability.

We said earlier that Cyanamid, because of the role it played in the transportation of the acrylonitrile—leasing, and especially loading, and also it appears undertaking by contract with North American Car Corporation to maintain, the tank car in which the railroad carried Cyanamid's acrylonitrile to Riverdale—might be viewed as a special type of shipper (call it a "shipper-transporter"), rather than as a passive shipper. But neither the district judge nor the plaintiff's counsel has attempted to distinguish Cyanamid from an ordinary manufacturer of chemicals on this ground, and we consider it waived. Which is not to say that had it not been waived it would have changed the outcome of the case. The very fact that Cyanamid participated actively in the transportation of the acrylonitrile imposed upon it a duty of due care and by doing so brought into play a threat of negligence liability that, for all we know, may provide an adequate regime of accident control in the transportation of this particular chemical.

In emphasizing the flammability and toxicity of acrylonitrile rather than the hazards of transporting it, as in failing to distinguish between the active and the passive shipper, the plaintiff overlooks the fact that ultra-hazardousness or abnormal dangerousness is, in the contemplation of the law at least, a property not of substances, but of activities: not of acrylonitrile, but of the transportation of acrylonitrile by rail through populated areas. * * * Natural gas is both flammable and poisonous, but the operation of a natural gas well is not an ultrahazardous activity. * * * Whatever the situation under products liability law (section 402A of the Restatement), the manufacturer of a product is not considered to be engaged in an abnormally dangerous activity merely because the product becomes dangerous when it is handled or used in some way after it leaves his premises, even if the danger is foreseeable. * * * The plaintiff does not suggest that Cyanamid should switch to making some less hazardous chemical that would substitute for acrylonitrile in the textiles and other goods in which acrylonitrile is used. Were this a feasible method of accident avoidance, there would be an argument for making manufacturers strictly liable for accidents that occur during the shipment of their products (how strong an argument we need not decide). Apparently it is not a feasible method.

The relevant activity is transportation, not manufacturing and shipping. This essential distinction the plaintiff ignores. But even if the [defendant] is treated as a transporter and not merely a shipper, [the plaintiff] has not shown that the transportation of acrylonitrile in bulk by rail through populated areas is so hazardous an activity, even when due care is exercised, that the law should seek to create—perhaps quixotically—incentives to relocate the activity to nonpopulated areas, or to reduce the scale of the activity, or to switch to transporting acrylonitrile by road rather than by rail. * * * It is no more realistic to propose to reroute the shipment of all hazardous materials around Chicago than it is to propose the relocation of homes adjacent to the Blue Island switching yard to more distant suburbs. It may be less realistic. Brutal though it may seem to say it, the inappropriate use to which land is being put in the Blue Island yard and neighborhood may be, not the transportation of hazardous chemicals, but residential living. The analogy is to building your home between the runways at O'Hare.

* * *

The case for strict liability has not been made. Not in this suit in any event. We need not speculate on the possibility of imposing strict liability on shippers of more hazardous materials, such as [bombs], any more than we need differentiate (given how the plaintiff has shaped its case) between active and passive shippers. We noted earlier that acrylonitrile is far from being the most hazardous among hazardous materials shipped by rail in highest volume. Or among materials shipped, period.* * *

The judgment is reversed (with no award of costs in this court) and the case remanded for further proceedings, consistent with this opinion, on the plaintiff's claim for negligence.

————

90–Day Hazmat Ban Is Passed; Measure Will Bar Shipments in D.C.

Washington Post, Feb. 2, 2005, at B01.

■ Eric M. Weiss and Spencer S. Hsu

The D.C. Council yesterday approved a temporary ban on shipments of hazardous materials through the nation's capital, becoming the first jurisdiction in the nation to halt such cargo in response to the threat of terrorism. Council members, who approved the 90–day emergency legislation 10 to 1, said reassurances from federal officials were not enough to safeguard residents. Mayor Anthony A. Williams (D) said through a spokesman that he will sign the bill as soon as possible.

Although the legislation does not require congressional review, the council is also considering a bill for a permanent ban, which would be subject to review by Congress.

The D.C. action sets up a potential legal battle with rail giant CSX Corp., which owns and operates the major freight line that runs through the city, passing within four blocks of the U.S. Capitol. Senior federal officials opposed the action, noting that they have pushed CSX to voluntarily reroute dangerous materials. But the officials have declined to make public exactly what safeguards are being taken.

"This is the nation's capital, and we need the toxics out," said council member Kathy Patterson (D–Ward 3), the measure's chief sponsor.

A CSX rail line in the District moves 8,500 chemical cars a year through the city, though only a fraction of those chemicals are toxic when inhaled. The legislation bans the most dangerous types of material, including certain classes of explosives, flammable gases and poisonous gases and materials. It also requires all rail and truck firms carrying other hazardous materials to obtain permits from the city's Transportation Department. Ban advocates say they expect about 5 to 10 percent of rail shipments to fall under the prohibition.

A chief U.S. Naval Research Laboratory scientist projected that in a worst-case scenario, a release of chlorine from a 90–ton tanker car during a Fourth of July celebration on the Mall could kill 100 people a second and 100,000 in 30 minutes.

Council member Carol Schwartz (R–At Large) cast the only vote against the measure. Marion Barry (D–Ward 8) was at a funeral and did not vote.

Schwartz, who is chairman of the council's public works committee, said CSX officials privately assured her that the company has been rerouting the most dangerous cargo since the Madrid train bombing in March. Therefore, she said, the legislation is unnecessary and would trigger a legal battle.

"We are better served by cooperating with the feds rather than by confronting them," Schwartz said.

The U.S. Department of Homeland Security and the U.S. Department of Transportation issued separate statements suggesting that federal and industry officials have taken safety measures that go beyond the D.C. ban but declined to say what material is being rerouted.

"We will also continue to explore other options that might be available with regards to routes for transporting hazardous materials through the national Capital region," the Department of Transportation said.

The Transportation Security Administration last year conducted a security study and hazardous material response plan for 42 miles of rail corridor in the Washington area. It is implementing a $7 million long-term plan for low-tech measures such as fencing and added patrols as well as more sophisticated safeguards, including intrusion detection systems and video surveillance.

The rail industry and transportation lawyers have closely watched the D.C. legislation. Although the consensus of legal analysts is that the law would not pass a federal court challenge, it feeds a national debate about the power of communities to control the flow of toxic shipments, spurred by the Sept. 11, 2001, terrorist attacks and by recent rail accidents.

Spokesman Robert T. Sullivan said CSX had grave reservations about the bill but stopped short of promising a legal challenge.

"We will review it again and make a determination about exactly what to do," Sullivan said. "But when you get into cities dictating how commodities can move, it frustrates interstate commerce."

Industry groups reiterated that shipping hazardous materials by rail is generally safer than using trucks. They noted that chemicals such as chlorine are used to purify half of the nation's water systems and predicted that a D.C. ban would set off a series of prohibitions that would cripple the U.S. rail system.

A coalition of environmental, labor and civic groups, mobilized to pass the ban, called it a landmark.

"This is probably the most important vote D.C. Council members will ever take," said Rick Hind, legislative director of the Greenpeace Toxics Campaign, which mounted a two-year lobbying effort to pass the ban with Friends of the Earth and the local Sierra Club.

Ultimately, whether the city will be allowed to implement a permanent ban may be decided by Congress, which has been reluctant to impose new restrictions on the rail industry since 2001, analysts said.

"Congress may feel compelled to say there are certain circumstances where we shouldn't let materials like this go close to particular sites," said James B. Reed, transportation program director for the National Council of State Legislatures. "But under existing law, it would probably be preempted under a court challenge." On May 3, 2005, the District of Columbia Court of Appeals ruled in favor of the railway, granting an injunction enforcing the HazMat ban. The court found that although under the Federal Rail Safety Act a city could adopt a more protective standard than the Federal Rule, the action must however be limited to eliminating "an essentially local safety or security hazard." In addition the local provision must not "burden interstate commerce." The court found that protecting the Capitol building was not an "essentially local hazard" and that the city ordinance burdened interstate commerce. The injunction sought by the CSX Railway Co. was therefore granted. CSX Transportation, Inc. v. Anthony Williams, 406 F.3d 667 (D.C.Cir.2005).

NOTES AND QUESTIONS

1. **Role for judges in deciding economic common law cases.** In *The Economic Approach to Law*, The Problems of Jurisprudence 353–92 (1990), Posner argues that:

> The judge whose business is enforcing tort, contract, and property law lacks effective tools for bringing about an equitable distribution of wealth, even if he thinks he knows what such a distribution would be. He would be further handicapped in such an endeavor by the absence of consensus in our society on the nature of a just distribution, an absence that undermines the social acceptability of attempts to use the judicial office to achieve distributive goals. *A sensible division of labor has the judge making rules and deciding cases in the areas regulated by the common law in such a way as to maximize the size of the social pie*, and the legislature attending to the sizes of the slices.

Richard A. Posner, *The Economic Approach to Law*, in The Problems of Jurisprudence 353, 388 (1990)(emphasis added).

Does this decision upholding the landlord tenant ordinance "increase the size of the social pie?"

2. **Importance of empirical support for economic assumptions.** In the following excerpt *Posner* next takes up a hypothetical, not unlike the *Chicago Board of Realtors* case above, in which a common law judge is asked to rule on the validity of a landlord-tenant ordinance:

> The case is strongest in those common law areas where the relevant policies are admitted to be economic. Suppose the idea of an implied warranty of habitability—which entitles a tenant to sue his landlord if the premises fall below the standards of safety and comfort specified in

> the local housing code—is defended, as normally it is defended, on the
> ground that it is needed to protect tenants from deception and over
> reaching by landlords and will not lead to a reduction in the stock of
> housing available to poor people or to higher rentals than the poor are
> willing and able to pay. If research demonstrates that these assump-
> tions are incorrect, the proponent, if fair-minded, will have to with-
> draw the proposal.

Posner, *supra* at 388.

Posner argues that "[a] growing body of empirical literature deals with
the effects of governmental regulation of the market for rental housing."
Chicago Bd. of Realtors, 819 F.2d at 742. However, does Posner base his
majority opinion in *Chicago Board of Realtors* on the existence of empirical
research showing the characteristics of the rental housing market in
Chicago in response to a housing ordinance with the features of the
Chicago ordinance? Does comparing Chicago with New York and Los
Angeles, where studies were done but the ordinances are different, meet a
judge's burden of persuasion to develop the empirical basis for economic
reasoning in an action seeking an injunction?

3.   Is economic reasoning precedent? What is the basis for Posner's
agreement with the holding of the Cudahy opinion, if he disagrees with
Cudahy's conclusion that the ordinance is Constitutional? Consider this
passage from the Posner/Easterbrook concurrence:

> It does not explain how the district judge's denial of a preliminary
> injunction against such an interference with contract rights and eco-
> nomic freedom can be affirmed without violating the contract clause
> and the due process clause of the Constitution. So we are led to write
> separately.

Id. at 741.

Since the ordinance was ultimately upheld, is the economic reasoning
just a rhetorical flourish in the case—an "advisory opinion"—not a common law precedent based upon economic reasoning, even though it is a
"majority opinion?"

Is the key piece of economic reasoning that might qualify as precedent
found in this passage of the Posner opinion?:

> Their only apparent rationale is to transfer wealth from landlords and
> out-of-state banks to tenants and local banks—making this an unedify-
> ing example of class legislation and economic protectionism rolled into
> one. However, to the extent the ordinance seeks to transfer wealth
> from landlords to tenants it could readily be undone by a rent increase;
> the ordinance puts no cap on rents. Cf. Coase, *The Problem of Social
> Cost*, 3 J. LAW & ECON. 1 (1960).

Id. at 742.

Thus, Posner can support the legislation despite his misgivings about
its constitutionality or efficiency because landlords retain wealth-maximiz-

ing options to control the price of rental housing in response to any of the intrusive features of the ordinance.

———

2. The Problem of Incompatible Property Uses: The Roles for Private Bargaining and Judicial Injunctions

A central tenet of the law and economics approach to legal reasoning has been the Coase Theorem. The theorem asserts that when there are no barriers to transactions between parties, the affected parties will bargain so as to obtain an efficient allocation of resources regardless of how the legal rule or decision would assign the rights initially. The major assumption of this theorem is that there are no transactions costs. What happens when transactions costs are substantial—does that change the assessment of whether the bargaining has produced an efficient outcome?

We now examine the problem of how to structure the remedies for property owners whose uses are incompatible. Where one owner's use presents continuing invasions of the rights of others, either because of pollution, noise, particulate discharge, or because the adjoining structure blocks the light or view of the other property owner. The question in law and economic terms is: for the efficient distribution of property value, does it ultimately matter whether the court grants the injunction or not? Will the parties seek to bargain in the shadow of the court decision, so that the party who values the right the most will buy the right to engage in the incompatible use from the party who values it less?

Boomer v. Atlantic Cement Co.

257 N.E.2d 870 (N.Y. 1970).

■ Bergan, Judge.

Defendant operates a large cement plant near Albany. These are actions for injunction and damages by neighboring land owners alleging injury to property from dirt, smoke and vibration emanating from the plant. A nuisance has been found after trial, temporary damages have been allowed; but an injunction has been denied.

The public concern with air pollution arising from many sources in industry and in transportation is currently accorded ever wider recognition accompanied by a growing sense of responsibility in State and Federal Governments to control it. Cement plants are obvious sources of air pollution in the neighborhoods where they operate.

But there is now before the court private litigation in which individual property owners have sought specific relief from a single plant operation. The threshold question raised by the division of view on this appeal is whether the court should resolve the litigation between the parties now before it as equitably as seems possible; or whether, seeking promotion of the general public welfare, it should channel private litigation into broad public objectives.

* * *

It seems apparent that the amelioration of air pollution will depend on technical research in great depth; on a carefully balanced consideration of the economic impact of close regulation; and of the actual effect on public health. It is likely to require massive public expenditure and to demand more than any local community can accomplish and to depend on regional and interstate controls.

A court should not try to do this on its own as a by-product of private litigation and it seems manifest that the judicial establishment is neither equipped in the limited nature of any judgment it can pronounce nor prepared to lay down and implement an effective policy for the elimination of air pollution. This is an area beyond the circumference of one private lawsuit. It is a direct responsibility for government and should not thus be undertaken as an incident to solving a dispute between property owners and a single cement plant—one of many—in the Hudson River valley.

The cement making operations of defendant have been found by the court at Special Term to have damaged the nearby properties of plaintiffs in these two actions. That court, as it has been noted, accordingly found defendant maintained a nuisance and this has been affirmed at the Appellate Division. The total damage to plaintiffs' properties is, however, relatively small in comparison with the value of defendant's operation and with the consequences of the injunction which plaintiffs seek.

The ground for the denial of injunction, notwithstanding the finding both that there is a nuisance and that plaintiffs have been damaged substantially, is the large disparity in economic consequences of the nuisance and of the injunction. This theory cannot, however, be sustained without overruling a doctrine which has been consistently reaffirmed in several leading cases in this court and which has never been disavowed here, namely that where a nuisance has been found and where there has been any substantial damage shown by the party complaining an injunction will be granted.

The rule in New York has been that such a nuisance will be enjoined although marked disparity be shown in economic consequence between the effect of the injunction and the effect of the nuisance.

* * *

Although the court at Special Term and the Appellate Division held that injunction should be denied, it was found that plaintiffs had been damaged in various specific amounts up to the time of the trial and damages to the respective plaintiffs were awarded for those amounts. The effect of this was, injunction having been denied, plaintiffs could maintain successive actions at law for damages thereafter as further damage was incurred.

The court at Special Term also found the amount of permanent damage attributable to each plaintiff, for the guidance of the parties in the event both sides stipulated to the payment and acceptance of such permanent damage as a settlement of all the controversies among the parties. The total of permanent damages to all plaintiffs thus found was $185,000. This basis of adjustment has not resulted in any stipulation by the parties.

This result at Special Term and at the Appellate Division is a departure from a rule that has become settled; but to follow the rule literally in these cases would be to close down the plant at once. This court is fully agreed to avoid that immediately drastic remedy; the difference in view is how best to avoid it.

One alternative is to grant the injunction but postpone its effect to a specified future date to give opportunity for technical advances to permit defendant to eliminate the nuisance; another is to grant the injunction conditioned on the payment of permanent damages to plaintiffs which would compensate them for the total economic loss to their property present and future caused by defendant's operations. For reasons which will be developed the court chooses the latter alternative.

If the injunction were to be granted unless within a short period—e.g., 18 months—the nuisance be abated by improved methods, there would be no assurance that any significant technical improvement would occur.

The parties could settle this private litigation at any time if defendant paid enough money and the imminent threat of closing the plant would build up the pressure on defendant. If there were no improved techniques found, there would inevitably be applications to the court at Special Term for extensions of time to perform on showing of good faith efforts to find such techniques.

Moreover, techniques to eliminate dust and other annoying by-products of cement making are unlikely to be developed by any research the defendant can undertake within any short period, but will depend on the total resources of the cement industry Nationwide and throughout the world. The problem is universal wherever cement is made.

* * *

On the other hand, to grant the injunction unless defendant pays plaintiffs such permanent damages as may be fixed by the court seems to do justice between the contending parties. All of the attributions of economic loss to the properties on which plaintiffs' complaints are based will have been redressed.

The nuisance complained of by these plaintiffs may have other public or private consequences, but these particular parties are the only ones who have sought remedies and the judgment proposed will fully redress them. The limitation of relief granted is a limitation only within the four corners of these actions and does not foreclose public health or other public agencies from seeking proper relief in a proper court.

It seems reasonable to think that the risk of being required to pay permanent damages to injured property owners by cement plant owners would itself be a reasonable effective spur to research for improved techniques to minimize nuisance.

* * *

JASEN, JUDGE (dissenting).

I agree with the majority that a reversal is required here, but I do not subscribe to the newly enunciated doctrine of assessment of permanent damages, in lieu of an injunction, where substantial property rights have been impaired by the creation of a nuisance.

It has long been the rule in this State, as the majority acknowledges, that a nuisance which results in substantial continuing damage to neighbors must be enjoined. * * * To now change the rule to permit the cement company to continue polluting the air indefinitely upon the payment of permanent damages is, in my opinion, compounding the magnitude of a very serious problem in our State and Nation today.

* * *

The harmful nature and widespread occurrence of air pollution have been extensively documented. Congressional hearings have revealed that air pollution causes substantial property damage, as well as being a contributing factor to a rising incidence of lung cancer, emphysema, bronchitis and asthma.

* * *

I see grave dangers in overruling our long-established rule of granting an injunction where a nuisance results in substantial continuing damage. In permitting the injunction to become inoperative upon the payment of permanent damages, the majority is, in effect, licensing a continuing wrong. It is the same as saying to the cement company, you may continue to do harm to your neighbors so long as you pay a fee for it. Furthermore, once such permanent damages are assessed and paid, the incentive to alleviate the wrong would be eliminated, thereby continuing air pollution of an area without abatement.

* * *

It is not my intention to cause the removal of the cement plant from the Albany area, but to recognize the urgency of the problem stemming from this stationary source of air pollution, and to allow the company a specified period of time to develop a means to alleviate this nuisance.

* * *

———

Fontainebleau Hotel Corp. v. Forty–Five Twenty–Five, Inc.

114 So.2d 357 (Fla. Dist. Ct. App. 1959).

PER CURIAM

This is an interlocutory appeal from an order temporarily enjoining the appellants from continuing with the construction of a fourteen-story addition to the Fontainebleau Hotel, owned and operated by the appellants. Appellee, plaintiff below, owns the Eden Roc Hotel, which was constructed in 1955, about a year after the Fontainebleau, and adjoins the Fontainebleau on the north. Both are luxury hotels, facing the Atlantic Ocean. The proposed addition to Fontainebleau is being constructed twenty feet from its north property line, 130 feet from the mean high water mark of the Atlantic Ocean, and 76 feet 8 inches from the ocean bulkhead line. The 14–story tower will extend 160 feet above grade in height and is 416 feet long from east to west. During the winter months, from around two o'clock in the afternoon for the remainder of the day, the shadow of the addition will extend over the cabana, swimming pool, and sunbathing areas of the Eden Roc, which are located in the southern portion of its property.

In this action, plaintiff-appellee sought to enjoin the defendants-appellants from proceeding with the construction of the addition to the Fontainebleau (it appears to have been roughly eight stories high at the time suit was filed), alleging that the construction would interfere with the light and air on the beach in front of the Eden Roc and cast a shadow of such size as to render the beach wholly unfitted for the use and enjoyment of its guests, to the irreparable injury of the plaintiff; further, that the construction of such addition on the north side of defendants' property, rather than the south side, was actuated by malice and ill will on the part of the defendants' president toward the plaintiff's president; and that the construction was in violation of a building ordinance requiring a 100–foot setback from the ocean. * * *

The defendants' answer denied the material allegations of the complaint, pleaded laches and estoppel by judgment.

The chancellor heard considerable testimony on the issues made by the complaint and the answer and, as noted, entered a temporary injunction restraining the defendants from continuing with the construction of the addition. His reason for so doing was stated by him, in a memorandum opinion, as follows:

> "In granting the temporary injunction in this case the Court wishes to make several things very clear. The ruling is not based on any alleged presumptive title nor prescriptive right of the plaintiff to light and air nor is it based on any deed restrictions nor recorded plats in the title of the plaintiff nor of the defendant nor of any plat of record. It is not based on any zoning ordinance nor on any provision of the building code of the City of Miami Beach nor on the decision of any court, nisi prius or appellate. It is based solely on the proposition that no one has a right to use his property to the injury of another. In this case it is clear from the evidence that the proposed use by the Fontainebleau will materially damage the Eden Roc. There is evidence indicating that the construction of the proposed annex by the Fontainebleau is malicious or deliberate for the purpose of injuring the Eden Roc, but it is

scarcely sufficient, standing alone, to afford a basis for equitable relief.''

This is indeed a novel application of the maxim *sic utere tuo ut alienum non laedas*. This maxim does not mean that one must never use his own property in such a way as to do any injury to his neighbor. * * * In Reaver v. Martin Theatres, 52 So.2d 682, under this maxim, it was stated that 'it is well settled that a property owner may put his own property to any reasonable and lawful use, so long as he does not thereby deprive the adjoining landowner of any right of enjoyment of his property *which* is *recognized and protected by law, and so long as his use is not such a one as the law will pronounce a nuisance.*' [Emphasis supplied.]

No American decision has been cited, and independent research has revealed none, in which it has been held that—in the absence of some contractual or statutory obligation—a landowner has a legal right to the free flow of light and air across the adjoining land of his neighbor. Even at common law, the landowner had no legal right, in the absence of an easement or uninterrupted use and enjoyment for a period of 20 years, to unobstructed light and air from the adjoining land.* * *

There being, then, no legal right to the free flow of light and air from the adjoining land, it is universally held that where a structure serves a useful and beneficial purpose, it does not give rise to a cause of action, either for damages or for an injunction under the maxim *sic utere tuo ut alienum non laedas*, even though it causes injury to another by cutting off the light and air and interfering with the view that would otherwise be available over adjoining land in its natural state, regardless of the fact that the structure may have been erected partly for spite.* * *

We see no reason for departing from this universal rule. If, as contended on behalf of plaintiff, public policy demands that a landowner in the Miami Beach area refrain from constructing buildings on his premises that will cast a shadow on the adjoining premises, an amendment of its comprehensive planning and zoning ordinance, applicable to the public as a whole, is the means by which such purpose should be achieved. (No opinion is expressed here as to the validity of such an ordinance, if one should be enacted pursuant to the requirements of law. Cf. City of Miami Beach v. State ex rel. Fontainebleau Hotel Corp., Fla.App.1959, 108 So.2d 614, 619; certiorari denied, Fla.1959, 111 So.2d 437.) But to change the universal rule—and the custom followed in this state since its inception—that adjoining landowners have an equal right under the law to build to the line of their respective tracts and to such a height as is desired by them (in the absence, of course, of building restrictions or regulations) amounts, in our opinion, to judicial legislation.* * *

* * *

The record affirmatively shows that no statutory basis for the right sought to be enforced by plaintiff exists. The so-called Shadow Ordinance enacted by the City of Miami Beach at plaintiff's behest was held invalid in City of Miami Beach v. State ex rel. Fontainebleau Hotel Corp., supra. It also affirmatively appears that there is no possible basis for holding that plaintiff has an easement for light and air, either express or implied, across defendants' property, nor any prescriptive right thereto—even if it be assumed, arguendo, that the common-law right of prescription as to 'ancient lights' is in effect in this state. And from what we have said heretofore in this opinion, it is perhaps superfluous to add that we have no desire to dissent from the unanimous holding in this country repudiating the English doctrine of ancient lights.

* * *

While the chancellor did not decide the question of whether the setback ordinance had been violated, it is our view that, even if there was such a violation, the plaintiff would have no cause of action against the defendants based on such violation. The application of simple mathematics to the sun studies filed in evidence by plaintiff in support of its claim demonstrates conclusively that to move the existing structure back some 23 feet from the ocean would make no appreciable difference in the problem which is the subject of this controversy. * * * The construction of the 14–story addition is proceeding under a permit issued by the city pursuant to the mandate of this court in City of Miami Beach v. State ex rel. Fontainebleau Hotel Corp., supra, which permit authorizes completion of the 14–story addition according to a plan showing a 76–foot setback from the ocean bulkhead line. Moreover, the plaintiff's objection to the distance of the structure from the ocean appears to have been made for the first time in the instant suit, which was filed almost a year after the beginning of the construction of the addition, at a time when it was roughly eight stories in height, representing the expenditure by defendants of several million dollars. In these circumstances, it is our view that the plaintiff has stated no cause of action for equitable relief based on the violation of the ordinance—assuming, arguendo, that there has been a violation.

Since it affirmatively appears that the plaintiff has not established a cause of action against the defendants by reason of the structure here in question, the order granting a temporary injunction should be and it is hereby reversed with directions to dismiss the complaint.

Reversed with directions.

NOTES AND QUESTIONS

1. Courts or markets. One of the key insights of the Coase Theorem is that the market solution to conflicts such as those present in *Boomer* and *Fontainebleu* will ultimately prevail over any judicial determination of the respective rights. This can be understood as a normative commentary on the respective benefits of these two mechanisms for resolving disputes. Is this preference for markets consistent with the libertarian commitments of the law and economics school in which government actors are given a marginal role in allocating economic resources?

2.   The deal. Did the court impose a deal on the parties by granting an injunction against the cement plant, conditioned on the plant paying its neighbors the amount of permanent damages determined by the court? If the court imposed a deal, is this inconsistent with the Coase Theorem? Once the court granted the conditional injunction, what would you expect the bargaining between the parties to include?

3.   No transactions costs. The Coase Theorem assumes that there are no transactions costs. Imagine a scenario in which there *are* transactions costs. What might the costs include if the court had granted the permanent injunction in *Boomer*, and the plant had chosen to initiate a series of Coasian bargains with the plaintiffs, seeking to buy the right to pollute?

Might the costs include legal expenses such as the cost of retaining lawyers and drafting documents to support the agreements allowing the plant to pollute? If these costs ever exceed the value to the defendant of the right to pollute, would you expect the Coasian bargain to take place?

What if one or more of the plaintiffs has a strong moral opposition to environmental and personal injury damage caused by pollution? This plaintiff becomes a "hold out" who flatly refuses to compromise. The hold out says, "I will not sell my lungs to you for any price." What might the impact of a hold out be on the hypothetical exchange? Does the principled hold out have monopoly power in this situation? Can the hold out demand that the plant be shut down? Does it matter what motivation the hold out has to oppose the bargain? Is a mercenary who simply wants to exact an exorbitant settlement in the same position as the environmentally conscious hold out? What if the hold out demands that the defendants set up a fund for free private education and health care for as long as it operates in that community? What would expect the limit of the defendants willingness to respond to these third party directed demands?

3.   THE PROBLEM OF REDISTRIBUTION

An especially thorny and controversial issue for law and economics theory has been the problem of economic inequality and what its response should be, if any, to the social and economic effects of the vast wealth disparities among market participants. One answer, given by the neoclassical modern economists such as Friedman, Becker, and Coase has been to regard the distribution of wealth in society as the product of market competition, and therefore not a suitable target for government intervention. In this view, as forcefully argued by Milton Friedman in the essay "Created Equal," above, central government-controlled economic equality in the distribution of wealth is antithetical to liberty. Friedman observes:

> In some intellectual circles the desirability of equality of outcome has become an article of religious faith: everyone should finish the race at the same time. As the Dodo said in *Alice in Wonderland*, 'Everybody has won, and *all* must have prizes."

* * *

Everywhere in the world there are gross inequities of income and wealth. They offend most of us. Few can fail to be moved by the contrast between the luxury enjoyed by some and the grinding poverty suffered by others.

In the past century a myth has grown up that free market capitalism— equality of opportunity as we have interpreted that term—increases such inequalities, that it is a system under which the rich exploit the poor.

Nothing could be further from the truth.

MILTON FRIEDMAN & ROSE FRIEDMAN, *Created Equal, in* FREE TO CHOOSE 134, 146 (1980).

Libertarian aims include expanding the zone of individual autonomy and reducing the zone of governmental control. For libertarians, economic inequality, though regrettable, is unavoidable—even natural.

More recently, modern law and economics scholars have tried to grapple directly with the problem of fairness, defined as some form of redistribution, and the conflict between fairness and efficiency, defined as maximizing market forces without government intervention. Law and economics scholars Kaplow and Shavell have framed these arguments in complex detail in *Fairness Versus Welfare*, 114 HARV. L. REV. 961 (2001) in which they argue that legal policy should be concerned with the effect of such policies on the well-being of individuals, and not with notions of fairness that extend beyond the welfare of the individual to "notions of fairness, such as corrective justice and retributive justice. . . ." *Id.* at 1381.

In what follows, law and economics scholar Mitchell Polinsky, offers a more accessible account of the tension between efficiency and equity. What solution does Polinsky ultimately identify as the acceptable avenue for attending to questions of fairness, however defined? Does this position differ markedly from the libertarian position articulated by Friedman?

————

Efficiency and Equity

AN INTRODUCTION TO LAW AND ECONOMICS 7–10 (3d ed. 2003).

■ A. MITCHELL POLINSKY

For the purposes of this book, the term *efficiency* will refer to the relationship between the aggregate benefits of a situation and the aggregate costs of the situation; the term *equity* will refer to the distribution of income among individuals. In other words, efficiency corresponds to "the size of the pie," while equity has to do with how it is sliced. Economists traditionally concentrate on how to maximize the size of the pie, leaving to others—such as legislators—the decision how to divide it. The attractiveness of efficiency as a goal is that, under some circumstances described below, everyone can be made better off if society is organized in an efficient manner.

IS THERE A CONFLICT?

An important question is whether there is a conflict between the pursuit of efficiency and the pursuit of equity. If the pie can be sliced in any way desired, then clearly there is no conflict—with a bigger pie, everyone can get a bigger piece. If, however, in order to create a bigger pie, its division must be quite unequal, then, depending on what constitutes an equitable division of the pie, there may well be a conflict between efficiency and equity. It may be preferable to accept a smaller pie (less efficiency) in return for a fairer division (more equity).

The potential conflict between efficiency and equity can be illustrated by a simple example. Suppose that the government must decide whether to build a dam and that the Dean of Stanford Law School and I are the only two individuals affected by it. Currently, without the dam, the Dean has $65 and I have $35, so total income is $100. The dam would cost $30 to build, consisting of $30 worth of my labor but none of the Dean's. The dam would create benefits worth $40, all of which would go to the Dean because the only feasible location for building the dam happens to be on her property. Should the dam be built?

On efficiency grounds, the dam clearly should be built because it creates benefits of $40 and costs only $30, thereby creating net benefits of $10. But the equity effects need to be considered as well. Before the dam is built, the Dean has $65 and I have $35. After the dam is built, the Dean will have $105 (including the $40 benefit) and I will have $5 (after subtracting my $30 cost). Whether these distributional consequences are desirable depends on what constitutes a fair distribution of income. Suppose that the most equitable distribution of income involves the Dean receiving 60 percent of income and my receiving 40 percent. If the dam is not built, then the Dean should have $60 and I should have $40. If the dam is built and total income rises by $10, the Dean should have $66 and I should have $44.

But suppose, regardless of whether the dam is built, it is impossible to redistribute income between the two of us. Therefore, the choice is between the Dean's having $65 and my having $35 if the dam is not built, and the Dean's having $105 and my having $5 if the dam is built. Building the dam is more efficient but less equitable. How this conflict between efficiency and equity should be resolved depends on how important efficiency is relative to equity. If promoting equity is very important, it might be more desirable to sacrifice some efficiency for more equity by not building the dam (in other words, "damn" the Dean).

Alternatively, suppose it is possible to costlessly redistribute income between the Dean and me. Then, given the preferred distribution of income, if the dam is not built, $5 would be transferred from the Dean to me, so that she would end up with $60 and I would have $40. If the dam is built, $39 would be transferred from the Dean to me, so that she would end up with $66 and I would have $44. Clearly, since total income is distributed according to the percentages desired and we both are better off with the dam, the dam should be built. There is no conflict between efficiency and equity.

Note that, if it is possible to redistribute income at no cost, the dam should be built regardless of what constitutes an equitable distribution of income. If, for example, an egalitarian income distribution is desired, then without the dam the Dean and I each have $50 and with the dam we each could have $55. If, alternatively, equity required that everything should go to the Dean, the dam should be built because she then could have $110 rather than $100.

The dam example illustrates two important general observations. If income cannot be costlessly redistributed, there may be a conflict between efficiency and equity. Whether there is in fact a conflict depends on the specific distributional consequences of pursuing efficiency and on what constitutes an equitable distribution of income. However, if income can be costlessly redistributed, there is no conflict between efficiency and equity. This is true regardless of the specific distributional consequences of pursuing efficiency and regardless of what constitutes an equitable distribution of income. In other words, if income can be costlessly redistributed, it is always preferable to maximize the size of the pie because the pie can be sliced in any way desired.

Whether income can be costlessly distributed is discussed [below]. Although the conclusion there is that income redistribution is generally costly, it is argued nonetheless that efficiency should be the principal criterion for evaluating the legal system. This argument rests on the observations, explained at length [below], that it is often impossible to redistribute income through the choice of legal rules and that, even when it is possible, redistribution through the government's tax and transfer system may be cheaper and is likely to be more precise. In other words, the potential conflict between efficiency and equity when income redistribution is costly should be considered in the design of the government's tax and transfer system, but not generally in the choice of legal rules. Thus, *for purposes of discussing the legal system*, a reasonable simplifying assumption is that income can be costlessly redistributed.

* * *

Before proceeding, it is worth mentioning several other standard assumptions of economic analysis that will be made in analyzing the efficiency of legal rules. First, all benefits and costs can be measured in terms of a common denominator—dollars. It is important to emphasize that this assumption is made for expositional simplicity. It is not essential to economic analysis and does not exclude considerations that might be thought of as noneconomic—such as the protection of life and limb. Second, individuals themselves determine the dollar values to place on their benefits and costs. This is known as the assumption of *consumer sovereignty*. It is an acceptable assumption if one believes that individuals generally know what is best for themselves. Third, the values that individuals place on their benefits and costs are "stable" in the sense that these values are not affected by changes in public policy. For example, an individual's evaluation of the desirability of cleaner air is assumed not to depend on whether the legal system establishes a right to clean air. This is known as the assumption of *exogenous preferences*. Finally, individuals (and, when relevant, firms) maximize their benefits less their costs. This is known as the assumption of *utility maximization* (or, when firms are involved, profit maximization).

———

Efficiency and Equity Reconsidered

INTRODUCTION TO LAW AND ECONOMICS 147–156 (3d ed. 2003).

■ A. MITCHELL POLINSKY

The discussion of efficiency and equity [above] showed that there is no conflict between these goals if income can be redistributed costlessly. In essence, this is because any inequity in the distribution of income caused by the pursuit of efficiency could be corrected at no cost. The assumption that redistribution was costless was made at the end of that chapter. We now consider this assumption, first with respect to the redistribution of income by means of government's tax and transfer system and then with respect to redistribution by the choice of legal rules.

REDISTRIBUTION BY TAXES AND TRANSFERS

In general, the redistribution of income by taxes and transfers is costly in the following sense. * * * If the price of a good equals its cost of production, only those individuals who value the good more than its cost will purchase it. This was seen to be efficient. The good used to illustrate this point * * * was a lawnmower that cost $100 to produce. Suppose that rich people are more likely to purchase lawnmowers than poor people because they are more likely to live in houses than in apartment buildings. Then, by imposing an excise tax on purchases of lawnmowers, the government would raise more tax revenue from the rich than from the poor. Assuming that the revenue is spent in a way that does not disproportionately favor the rich—say it benefits everyone equally—then the net effect of the tax would be to redistribute income from the rich to the poor. However, an inevitable byproduct of this redistribution is that the price of lawnmowers will be "distorted"—that is, the effective price of lawnmowers, including the tax, will exceed their cost of production. As a consequence, too few lawnmowers will be bought. For example, if the excise tax is $10 per lawnmower, then everyone who values a lawnmower more than the production cost of $100 but less than $110 will not purchase one, an inefficient outcome given that they value the good more than its cost of production. In general, to redistribute income by excise tax it is necessary to sacrifice some efficiency with respect to consumption decisions. This loss of efficiency is a cost of redistributing income.

The same kind of problem applies to income taxes, although not in as obvious a way. To see the distortion from income taxes, first note that leisure is commodity desired by consumers just like any other commodity. The "price" of an hour of leisure is the income forgone by not working that hour. For example, suppose that the wage rate in the widget industry is $25 per hour. * * * If widget workers did not have to pay income taxes, then they would give up $25 to consume an hour of leisure. Thus, those individuals who valued another hour of leisure more than $25 would "buy" more leisure by working an hour less. But suppose widget workers faced a 20 percent income tax. Then for every hour worked, they would pay $5 to the government and retain $20. The "price" of leisure therefore would fall to $20 per hour. Now individuals who value leisure more than $20 per hour will work less. Assuming that the $25 per hour wage reflects a worker's contribution to the value of the widgets produced, the income tax will cause an inefficient consumption decision regarding leisure. For example, a worker who values leisure at $21 per hour will work less even though the value of the worker's time in terms of widget production is $25 per hour. As in the case of the excise tax, the income tax distorts the price of some commodity—in this case leisure—and causes inefficient consumption decisions. Thus, it too imposes a cost in order to redistribute income.

Redistributing income by transfers rather than by taxes does not avoid the problem of distorting consumption decisions. For instance, suppose the government subsidizes the price of electricity for low-income individuals. Then the individuals who receive the subsidy will face an effective price of electricity that is below the cost of producing electricity and they therefore will buy too much of it relative to what is efficient. In general, any kind of tax or transfer used to redistribute income will distort the price of some commodity and will have this kind of efficiency cost.

Can Legal Rules Redistribute Income?

Given the cost of redistributing income by taxes and transfers, the question naturally arises whether the legal system should be used to redistribute income. That legal rules *can* be used to redistribute income was suggested by the discussion * * * of the distributional aspects of the Coase Theorem. In the example in that chapter—of the factory polluting the residents—recall, for example, that when there were no transaction costs, the choice between the right to pollute and the right to clean air redistributed income by the $150 cost of the smokescreen (the least-cost solution to the conflict). It does not follow from that discussion, however, that legal rules always affect the distribution of income. To understand why, it will be useful to distinguish between legal disputes in which the parties are in some kind of contractual relationship, including a market relationship, and disputes in which the parties are, in effect, "strangers" prior to the dispute. The breach of contract and products liability examples would be characterized as *contractual disputes*, while the nuisance law, automobile accident, and pollution control examples would be described as *disputes between strangers*. (The products liability example is one of the first type because the victim is a consumer; it would be of the second type if the victim were a third party). It will be shown below that legal rules often cannot redistribute income in contractual disputes, whereas legal rules always can redistribute income in disputes between strangers.

To see why it is frequently difficult, if not impossible, to use legal rules to redistribute income in contractual disputes, consider * * * breach of contract. * * * [T]he seller of widgets might want to breach the contract with the initial buyer if an offer from a third party materialized. Suppose it is desirable for equity reasons to redistribute income from the seller to the buyer. Giving the buyer the remedy of expectation damages makes the buyer as well off if the contract is breached as he would have been had it been performed. Giving the buyer the remedy of reliance damages or restitution damages makes the buyer worse off if the contract is breached. However, because the contract price the buyer and seller negotiate depends on what the remedy is, it does not follow that the buyer is better off with the expectation remedy. Clearly, the seller will demand a higher price and the buyer will be willing to pay more if the buyer receives a larger payment in the event of a breach, the buyer may not be any better off with the expectation remedy. In general, the parties will take any distributional effects of breach of contract remedies into account when they negotiate the contract price; thus, how the joint benefits of entering into the contract are shared between the parties depends primarily, if not exclusively, on their relative bargaining strengths, not on the remedies available to them.

An analogous observation can be made about the products liability application when the victim of the product accident is a consumer of the good. Suppose, for example, that it is desirable for equity reasons to redistribute income from producers to consumers. * * * [U]nder the rule of negligence, producers will meet the standard of care, and, therefore, consumers will bear their own losses. But under the rule of strict liability, consumers will be fully compensated for their losses (assuming, if there is a defense of contributory negligence, they meet the standard of care applicable to them). Consumers will not, however, be better off as a class under strict liability because, in a competitive long-run equilibrium, the price of the good will rise by an amount equal to the producers' expected liability. In general, then, whenever the parties to a dispute are in some kind of contractual or market relationship, it may be difficult, if not impossible, to use the legal system to redistribute income.

To see why legal rules can be used to redistribute income in disputes between strangers, reconsider the discussion of automobile accidents * * *. In the simplest version of the example employed there, the pedestrian's expected accident losses depended solely on whether the driver chose to drive slowly, moderately, or rapidly. Under a negligence rule, the pedestrian will bear her own losses because the driver will choose to meet the standard of care—to drive moderately—whereas under a strict liability rule the driver will have to compensate the pedestrian for her losses. Because there is no contractual or market relationship between the parties, there is no contract price or market price that can be adjusted when legal rules change. Thus, shifting from one liability rule to the other will redistribute income by the amount of the expected losses.

Analogous observations can be made with respect to the nuisance law and pollution control applications. In the nuisance example * * *—of a polluting factory next to a single resident—the choices of the entitlement and the remedy for protecting the entitlement have distributional consequences. Given the entitlement, a party generally is better off if it is protected by an injunctive remedy rather than by a damage remedy (with liability equal to actual damages); although the damage remedy guarantees that the protected party will be fully compensated for damages, the injunctive remedy gives that party the right to hold out for more. And under either remedy, a party obviously is better off if the entitlement is more favorable to the party.

In the pollution control example * * * in which the pollution victims are third parties, the distributional effects of choosing between strict liability and negligence to control the polluting industry are similar to those discussed in the automobile accident context. Under negligence, the victims bear their own losses, whereas under strict liability, the producers—and ultimately consumers of the product—bear these losses. In general then, whenever the parties to a dispute are "strangers"—that is, not in a contractual or market relationship—the choice of legal rules will have distributional consequences.

SHOULD LEGAL RULES BE USED TO REDISTRIBUTE INCOME?

Having now identified the types of situations in which the legal system is most likely to have distributional effects, we can return to the question of whether legal rules *should* be used in these situations to promote distributional equity. The answer to this question depends in part on the "cost" of using legal rules to redistribute income relative to the cost of using taxes or transfers.

There are two senses in which redistribution through the legal system may be costly. The first relates to the administration costs of using the legal system. Suppose, for example, that the consumers of the goods produced by some polluting industry are high-income individuals, while the victims living near the polluting factories are low-income individuals. By making the firms strictly liable for the pollution damages, income will be transferred from rich people to poor people. A similar transfer could be accomplished by taxing high-income individuals and transferring the proceeds to low-income persons. The tax and transfer system is a *much* less expensive way to redistribute income than is the legal system. Roughly speaking, to transfer a dollar through a private lawsuit from a defendant to a plaintiff costs on average about a dollar in administrative costs of both parties and costs of the court system. To transfer a dollar through the tax and transfer system costs only a fraction of this amount.

Legal redistribution also may be costly in a second sense: Inefficient rules may have to be chosen in order to achieve the desired result. For example, * * * of driver-pedestrian accidents in which both parties are risk averse and the pedestrian cannot affect expected losses. It was seen that negligence is efficient because the driver will meet the standard of care and the pedestrian will be able to buy a first-party accident insurance policy with full coverage; strict liability may not be efficient because of the moral hazard problem (which could result in the driver not being able to buy a liability insurance policy with full coverage and/or in the driver not taking appropriate care). But if drivers are wealthier than pedestrians, strict liability may be preferable to negligence on equity grounds. The loss of efficiency from using strict liability rather than negligence is a "cost" of redistributing income from drivers as a class to pedestrians as a class.

There may be instances in which redistribution through the legal system is not costly in this sense. For example, suppose that in some types of nuisance disputes the parties can be expected to bargain in a cooperative way. Then, * * * any entitlement will lead to the efficient outcome, whether protected by an injunctive remedy or a damage remedy. Thus, the choices of the entitlement and the remedy can be used to redistribute income without causing an inefficient resolution of the nuisance dispute. In general, however, not all legal rules will be efficient, so it often may be necessary to choose an inefficient legal rule in order to promote equity.

An additional consideration in deciding whether to use the legal system to promote distributional equity is the "precision" of legal redistribution. Legal rules will not be able to redistribute income systematically unless the status of the parties in a certain type of dispute corresponds closely to the groups between which redistribution is desired. For example, in automobile accidents involving drivers and pedestrians, there probably is not a close correspondence between the income of a party and whether that party is a driver or a pedestrian. It may be that higher income persons are more likely to be drivers than pedestrians, but certainly there are many low-income drivers and high-income pedestrians. Thus, liability rules regarding driver-pedestrian accidents are not very precise instruments for accomplishing income redistribution. In nuisance and pollution control disputes, there may be a closer correspondence between the income of a party and whether that party is victim or an injurer. The purchasers of the goods produced by some polluting industry may be mainly higher-income people, while the victims of the pollution may be primarily lower-income persons. Thus, in some kinds of disputes, the choice of a legal rule might contribute towards the implementation of distributional goals.

Even where there is a close correspondence between the status of the parties in a certain kind of dispute and the groups between which redistribution is desired, legal rules still might not be able to achieve redistribution as systematically as an income tax system. This is because redistribution through the legal system only may occur when a dispute arises, and not all members of a given income class will be involved in a dispute. For instance, even if the goods produced by a polluting industry were consumed exclusively by rich persons and the pollution victims were all poor people, not every rich person necessarily purchases this commodity and not every poor person lives near a factory in this industry. Thus, the legal rule used to control the pollution dispute will, as best, redistribute income from a subset of one income class to a subset of another. In sum, the legal system is not nearly as precise as the tax system in redistributing income.

The initial discussion of efficiency and equity * * * showed that, if it is costly to redistribute income, there may be a tradeoff between efficiency and equity. In other words, it may be desirable to choose an inefficient policy in order to promote the desired distribution of income. [This discussion] has shown that income redistribution generally *is* costly, whether it is accomplished by the tax and transfer system or by the legal system. Nonetheless, several reasons have been suggested * * * why the choice of legal rules should be based primarily on efficiency considerations. In some circumstances—contractual dispute—legal rule often will have little or no effect on the distribution of income. In situations in which the legal system does have distributional consequences—disputes between strangers—legal rules still should be based primarily on efficiency considerations because legal rules generally are more costly than taxes and transfers as means of redistributing income and less precise. Thus, the justification for the assumption made * * * that income could be redistributed without cost * * * is not only that this simplified the subsequent exposition by allowing us to focus on the efficiency analysis of legal rules. As this chapter has shown, the justification also is that, even when the cost of redistributing income is taken into account, there are reasons why the efficiency analysis should be of principal importance.

4. Politics

Public Choice and the Future of Public-Choice-Influenced Legal Scholarship

50 Vand. L. Rev. 647 (1997) (reviewing Maxwell L. Stearns, Public Choice and Public Law: Readings and Commentary (1997)).

David A. Skeel, Jr.

* * *

At a general level, the distinctive characteristic of public choice is its "use of economic tools to deal with the traditional problems of political science." Perhaps the most basic of these tools is the assumption of individual rationality. In contrast to much traditional political analysis, public choice assumes that all of the relevant players tend to act in their own self-interest, and explores the implications of self-interest for the legislative and other institutional decisionmaking processes.

The public choice literature thus can, and in my view should, be seen as including any analysis that incorporates or explicitly challenges the self-interestedness premise in addressing institutional decisionmaking processes. The literature that fits within this definition consists of two principal branches. The first can be described as interest group analysis, and the second is social choice.

The central insight of interest group analysis is that concentrated interest groups often benefit at the expense of more widely scattered groups, even if the diffuse group has much more at stake overall. Although this insight is now so familiar that it seems obvious to many, it was far from obvious when it emerged in the public choice literature. Whereas many theorists assumed that interest group competition tends to produce public-regarding legislation, public choice suggested that self-interested behavior by each of the relevant actors could lead to strikingly different outcomes.

The reasoning is as follows. For a self-interested voter, taking the time to inform herself and to vote intelligently is an unattractive proposition, since the likelihood that her vote will affect the outcome of an election is minuscule. Although voters as a group would benefit if each took the time to vote intelligently, ordinary voters simply do not have an incentive to do so. By contrast, because the members of a concentrated interest group have more at stake with respect to the issues that concern them, they tend both to inform themselves and to participate actively in the political process.

The interest group branch of public choice suggests that the distinction between ordinary voters and concentrated interest groups is not lost on legislators. Self-interested legislators are likely to focus principally on getting reelected, since legislators who fail to do so quickly become ex-legislators. Because interest groups are better informed than ordinary voters, and serve as an important source of political funding, legislators have a tremendous incentive to be responsive to interest group perspectives.

Like the interest group literature itself, I have focused principally on the advantages interest groups have in the legislative process. But this analysis, and in particular its self-interest assumption, also has generated important insights into related areas such as the incentives of agency bureaucrats and * * * the nature of the judicial process.

The second branch of public choice is social choice. At the heart of much of the recent social choice literature is Kenneth Arrow's famous impossibility theorem. Arrow's Theorem demonstrates that it is impossible to design a system that will always both aggregate the preferences of a group of decisionmakers in a rational fashion, and satisfy a short list of fairness requirements. If there is a particular kind of inconsistency, referred to as multipeakedness, across the preferences of a group of decisionmakers (each of whose individual preferences is wholly consistent), the voting procedure will cycle endlessly among the possible outcomes unless one or more of the fairness requirements is relaxed.

To see this, assume that Voter 1 prefers outcome A to B, and B to C; Voter 2's preferences are B, C, A; and Voter 3's ranking is C, A, B. In a pairwise vote between A and B, outcome A would prevail (with Voter 1 and Voter 3 voting for A). Outcome C would prevail over A in a similar vote (on the strength of votes from Voter 2 and Voter 3). But, in a third vote between C and B, B would prevail, despite the fact that it loses to outcome A, which C defeats. On closer consideration, it quickly becomes clear that

...t the other two in pairwise voting, and
...unstable. This cycling occurs because the
...Preferences are multipeaked only if the
...ree about which choice is best (or second best
...e about the relationship among the choices. If
...ayed from smallest to largest, or conservative to
...uld disappear. Cycling would not occur even if the
...ose a different first choice.

...ent literature has focused on the trade-off posed by the
...ipeaked preferences. A voting institution that adheres to
...s criteria will cycle endlessly in these circumstances, but
...r more of the requirements introduces the possibility of path
...and path manipulation. To give a familiar example, Congress's
...against reconsidering an outcome that has been defeated in an
...te counteracts the risk of cycling. In the illustration above, for
...outcome C would prevail under this rule, since outcome B could
...introduced after it lost to outcome A. Yet the cost of eliminating
...that the order of voting determines the outcome-the result is path
...t. The rule, therefore, vests significant power in anyone who has
...y to manipulate the order of the voting.

...discussion thus far suggests a rough rule of thumb for distinguish-
...en the interest group and social choice branches of public choice.
...the important contributions of interest group theory stem from
...ght that not all voters are equal due to the organizational advan-
...enjoyed by members of a concentrated group. Social choice, on the
...hand, explores the dynamics of voting under conditions where voters
...at least initially assumed to have an equal voice. In fact, the literature
...cycling shows that voting pathologies can emerge even if each voter
participates fully.

Despite this distinction, it is important to emphasize that the line
between interest group theory and social choice is a rough one, and it
quickly blurs in both directions. The two branches of public choice analysis
share a common history, and commentators often employ both in their
efforts to understand a particular voting institution. Consider the extensive
literature on logrolling. From a social choice perspective, logrolling may act
as a solution to cycling concerns, since legislators avoid cycling by trading
votes on matters they are relatively indifferent about for votes on matters
about which they care deeply. Interest group theory raises questions as to
whether the "solution" is an attractive one, however, given that logrolling
could enhance interest groups' ability to obtain private benefits from the
legislative process.

An additional source of confusion is that the term public choice is used
in two ways. I have characterized public choice as a general term comprising both interest group theory and social choice, and many commentators
do likewise. But other commentators use public choice more narrowly, as a
synonym for interest group analysis. When a commentator indicates that

she will tell a "public choice story" about a given issue, it is o[...]
narrower definition that she has in mind.

B.   Related Concepts

Having explored in some detail what we mean when we tal[...]
public choice, we still must consider how several related modes of ana[...]
interact with public choice. Two of the most important are game theory a[...]
collective action theory. I will focus on these, then conclude with[...] bri[...]
description of the emerging literature employing "positive politic[...] [...]ry."

Game theory refers to the economic analysis of strategic[...]
action—the choices that individuals make when they recognize the o[...]
depends in part on the decisions made by others. The "game" in[...]
theory, then, is the interaction between two or more independent dec[...]
makers, each of whom attempts to account for the actions of the ot[...]
Game theoretic analysis formalizes this interaction by precisely specif[...]
the players involved, the information available to each at any given po[...]
and the different outcomes that would result from each set of "moves" [...]
players might make.

The most familiar game theory insight is the prisoners' dilemma. I[...]
the prisoners' dilemma, two prisoners who have committed a crime and[...]
cannot communicate with one another must each decide whether to confess. Although the prisoners would be better off if neither confessed than if
both confessed, the best outcome results from confessing when the other
prisoner refuses to do so. As a result, both have an incentive to confess and
the game often results in the least desireable outcome—two confessions.

The irony of the prisoners' dilemma—that the actions of individuals
behaving in their own best interests can produce outcomes that are
undesirable for all of them—has led to valuable insights in a wide range of
areas. One of the most important is in public choice. Recall the interest
group insight that diffuse groups tend to fare poorly in the legislative
process. The principal reason for this is that while the members of a diffuse
group might be better off if each participated in an informed fashion, each
member has little incentive to do so. In other words, diffuse groups tend to
face a debilitating prisoners' dilemma problem. Interest group analysis thus
depends in important respects on a concept taken straight from game
theory.

In contrast, the central insight in social choice theory, Arrow's Theorem, does not involve game theory in its initial formulation. The principled
voting requirement precludes voters from considering the preferences and
likely actions of other voters, thus ruling game theoretic interactions out of
bounds. Yet once we move beyond the initial formulation—as we must,
given that *no* institution can both satisfy the fairness requirements and
guarantee rational outcomes—strategic interaction quickly reenters the
picture. The agenda control and strategic voting concerns that have animated much of the social choice literature are classic examples of strategic
interaction, and are particularly amenable to game theoretic analysis.

As should be clear by now, game theory is a useful tool in any context where we wish to consider the nature of strategic interaction between two or more decisionmakers. Because strategic interaction is integral to much of public choice, it is not surprising that we find so much game theoretic analysis in the public choice literature. The second term we need to fit into our picture is collective action—not to be confused with the misleadingly similar term "collective choice." As with game theory, we can see the relevance of collective action theory most easily by focusing on the interest group branch of public choice. Recall that the prisoners' dilemma from game theory is a useful tool for explaining the barriers that often prevent large groups from acting in concert. The collective action literature starts from precisely the same insight, that free riding prevents many groups from acting collectively.

Collective action theorists take the obstacles to collective action as their starting point, and ask how it is that some groups do succeed in acting collectively. These theorists have identified two factors that seem particularly important to successful group action. First, smaller groups have a significant advantage as compared to large ones, both because members may have a larger individual stake in successful action and because members can more easily police one another against free riding. Second, groups that have access to "selective incentives"—that is, mechanisms for rewarding or punishing members for contributing or failing to contribute to the collective action—are more likely to prove effective.

A moment's reflection will make clear that collective action analysis is central to the distinction between concentrated and diffuse groups in interest group analysis, and to any effort to predict which groups will prove successful in legislative and other decisionmaking processes. The collective action literature is less immediately relevant to social choice, since social choice tends to focus on the voting decisions made by isolated individuals within a decisionmaking process. Yet as soon as we move beyond stylized assumptions about the voting process, and integrate interest group questions such as why some voters vote and others don't into our social choice analysis, collective action concerns come back into play.

In attempting to relate game theory and collective action to public choice, it is tempting to suggest that the former apply broadly to aspects of legislative, market, and judicial behavior, whereas public choice is uniquely concerned with the legislative process. Yet this would be a mistake. Although public choice has focused primarily on legislative behavior, it increasingly has been employed to explore courts and markets as well * * *.

Before we turn to the applications of public choice, however, we should briefly consider one final term: positive political theory. Positive political theory uses game theory to explore relationships among decisionmaking institutions such as Congress, administrative agencies, and the courts. It differs from public choice in that it focuses on the strategic interactions among political decisionmaking institutions, and on institutional structures, rather than on the individuals who comprise the institutions. Positive political theory does take account of the problems of multi-individual decisionmaking that preoccupy collective action theory and the two branches of public choice. But it does so indirectly. Positive political theory incorporates these considerations into its characterization of an institution. It then takes intra-institution concerns as a given, in a sense, in order to emphasizes strategic interactions between and among institutions.

In short, this new perspective makes direct use of game theoretic analysis; though it has a different focus than either branch of public choice, it is closely connected to both.

III.   PUBLIC CHOICE AND THE LEGAL LITERATURE

As is usually the case when legal academics draw on nonlegal insights, public choice did not enter legal discourse until well after it had captured the attention of economists and political scientists. It was not until the mid–1970s that legal scholars first explored the implications of public choice, even though many of the seminal insights of both interest group theory and social choice had been in place for over a decade. Since then, public choice has taken the legal literature by storm. In this Part, I will briefly describe the diffusion of public choice into the legal literature. I then will speculate as to the future of public-choice-influenced legal scholarship.

A.   *Law and Public Choice: The First Wave*

The first wave of public choice inquiry in the legal literature can be seen as a classic illustration of legal academics sticking to their area of comparative advantage. Whereas much of the extant economic and political science public choice literature focused on the legislative process, legal academics asked what the implications of public choice are for the legal system.

The first wave took as its starting point the social choice and interest group insights that the legislative process cannot guaranty outcomes that are both fair and rational, and that concentrated interest groups will exert disproportionate influence over the process. The obvious issue raised by the prospect of legislative dysfunction was the proper role for judges to play. How should public choice affect our view of the nature of statutory interpretation and, more generally, of judicial review?

Three commentators prompted a vigorous debate on this question by offering distinct visions of statutory interpretation in a post-public choice world. The starkest proposal was that of Judge Frank Easterbrook. Judge Easterbrook suggested that courts not only should recognize the role of interest groups in the political process, but that they also should enforce any interest group bargains reflected in the legislative product. Rather than trying to "correct" the process in some way, judges should interpret statutes in accordance with the realities of how they were enacted. Judge Richard Posner initially staked out a position similar to Judge Easterbrook's, though he subsequently shifted his focus to a perspective less obviously tied to the insights of public choice.

Professor Jonathan Macey responded to Judge Easterbrook and to Judge Posner's initial position by proposing a more independent, and more aggressive, role for courts. While agreeing that courts should enforce clear interest group bargains, Professor Macey contended that courts should refuse to enforce "implicit" bargains-that is, interest group deals that legislators disguise by defending the provision in question in public-regarding terms. Professor Macey contended that by refusing to enforce implicit bargains, courts could raise the costs to interest groups of obtaining private interest legislation, and in doing so moderate the influence of interest groups.

In addition to their political conservatism, each of the commentators shared a view that the pessimistic insights of public choice do, in fact, accurately describe the legislative process. Not surprisingly, this perspective prompted a backlash of sorts. Most prominently, Daniel Farber and Philip Frickey acknowledged that the public choice account of legislation is accurate in important respects, but contended that many of the dire conclusions of public choice are overstated. In their view, judges should simply police the political process for obvious defects, and should otherwise let the political process run its course.

Although generally sympathetic to public choice, William Eskridge shared some of Professors Farber and Frickey's concerns as to its limitations. Professor Eskridge's model of statutory interpretation called for judges to show solicitude for underrepresented minorities when they exercise judicial review. Cass Sunstein has used public choice insights in somewhat similar fashion, and has argued that courts should interpret statutes and the Constitution so as to curb interest group excesses.

Despite the sophistication of the debate, nearly all of the proposals suffered from a single, obvious weakness: in striking contrast to their sober portrayal of legislators, the proposals tended to assume that judges are somehow above the fray and can be wholly objective in interpreting the statutes that come before them. Yet there is no reason to believe that the judicial process is immune from interest group activity and the other kinds of distortions that characterize legislation. Once we subject judges to the same public choice scrutiny previously reserved for legislators, it becomes much more difficult to blithely assume that statutory interpretation can counteract the problems of legislative decisionmaking.

Interestingly, the literature on the evolution of the common law has proceeded on a somewhat analogous track, with overly optimistic early accounts giving way to more realistic assessments of the judicial process. Starting in the early 1970s, Judge Posner contended that common law rules tend to become efficient over time, due in large part to judges' unarticulated preference for efficient, rather than inefficient, rules. Other commentators argued for the efficiency of the common law on other grounds. Yet the differential interests of different kinds of litigants, and other biases in the cases that go to trial, suggest that any tendency toward common law efficiency is likely to be, at most, a weak one.

The first wave of public choice scholarship has thus complicated, rather than simply clarified, our understanding of the roles of legislators and judges. The extent to which interest group influence and the distortions identified by social choice undermine the legislative process remains unclear. In addition, the ability of the judiciary to counteract these influences on legislative decisions is open to question. The obvious next step is to engage in a more nuanced comparison of decisionmaking institutions. As we shall see, this raises intriguing questions as to the future of public-choice-influenced legal scholarship.

B.   Catching the Next Wave

It seems safe to say, as I have just noted, that the next wave of public choice scholarship will reflect an increasing interest in comparative institutional analysis. Rather than simply identifying the flaws of a particular institution, public-choice-influenced legal scholars will consider the comparative attributes of each of the relevant institutions.

Evidence of just such a trend already exists. A recent book by Neil Komesar contends that there is an urgent need for comparative institutional analysis in order to counteract the distortions of single institution analysis in law-and-economics scholarship. Professor Komesar's transaction costs model emphasizes the interests that affected individuals or groups have, their costs of participation, and how these factors change as we shift our focus among markets, the legislative process, and the judicial system.

With the enhanced sensitivity to comparative institutional analysis, we can expect to see increasingly sophisticated applications of public choice insights in the legal literature. Ironically, however, existing comparative analysis has tended to fall into precisely the same trap that its advocates criticize: the assumption that there exists an objective, unbiased context where institutional distortions can be corrected. Thus, comparative analysis often begins with a nuanced assessment of the respective institutions, then shifts to a prescriptive mode whose proposals depend on implementation by an unbiased decisionmaker. Most frequently, the analysis awards this status to courts, whose limitations are ignored when it comes time to act on the insights of the comparative analysis.

It is easy enough to see the reason for this oversight. Because legal scholarship is at its heart prescriptive, comparative analysts feel a natural urge to progress from descriptive analysis to proposals for change. In doing so, however, they face a strong temptation to forget the real world limitations of the institutions with which they are concerned.

The obvious antidote to this problem is to pursue the analysis all the way down—that is, to resist the temptation to address correctives to a hypothetically unbiased decisionmaker. Yet this poses an intriguing dilemma for future public choice scholarship. Given the typically prescriptive nature of legal scholarship, what role can the next wave of public choice literature, with its enhanced sensitivity to institutional limitations, play? What can so relentlessly descriptive an analysis aspire to?

CHAPTER 4

BEYOND CLASSIC MARKET THEORY– INTERNAL CRITIQUES

In recent years, developments in the field of law and economics have proliferated rapidly. Many of these developments call into question various aspects of the classic market theory introduced in the previous chapter. This chapter presents examples of three kinds of challenges to classic market theory that have been raised by scholars working within the tradition of economic analysis.

First, price theory has been subject to increasing critique as scholars recognize the differences between the functioning of markets in the imaginary world of perfect competition assumed by neoclassical economics and the functioning of markets in the real world. One direction the literature on the economic analysis of law has taken concerns the question of when markets "fail" and the role that law and government should play in responding to "market failure." The fields of antitrust law, consumer protection law, and environmental law (among others) are built on the assumption of such market failures, and the concomitant necessity of government intervention to address them. The concept of "market failure" itself, however, has been challenged by economists. Price theory has also been challenged by "transaction cost economics," which relaxes traditional neoclassical economics' assumption that economic interaction is costless, and by "institutional economics," which recognizes that markets function differently depending on the organizational context in which bargaining takes place.

Second, the "rational choice" theory of human behavior on which neoclassical economics relies has been challenged from a number of different directions. "Social norms" scholars argue that people respond not only to prices and their own idiosyncratic preferences, but to the preferences of their reference group—preferences that are malleable. In the other direction, behavioral economists and evolutionary economists argue, respectively, that biologically-driven cognitive limitations of human beings and biologically-influenced preferences of human beings shape market behavior.

Finally, traditional neoclassical economics assumes that natural resources are costless and infinite, and that capitalist economies are capable of growing forever. The field of environmental economics, or ecological economics, attempts in various ways to account for finite resources, the "services" that the biosphere produces for human endeavor, and the value of present resources and goods for future generations.

A.   BEYOND PRICE THEORY

Consumer Sovereignty: A Unified Theory of Antitrust and Consumer Protection Law

65 ANTITRUST L.J. 713, 723–28 (1997).

■ NEIL W. AVERITT & ROBERT H. LANDE

It is axiomatic that perfect competition, the perfect functioning of a competitive market, will maximize the welfare of consumers. Markets that diverge significantly from perfect competition may not do so. If a market's characteristics differ dramatically from those required for perfect competition, a condition termed "market failure" can exist. The overall level of consumer welfare may then be far below what it otherwise would be, and wealth that Congress assigned to consumers may be "unfairly" acquired by firms with market power.

Although economists generally agree on the fundamental concept of perfect competition, there is no universally agreed upon list of factors that define perfect competition or whose absence may lead to market failure. But the disagreements generally arise only over taxonomic matters—views of which concepts are implicit in others, which are assumed as necessary predicates or subsets of one another and are caused by other factors that themselves prevent markets from functioning optimally.

A leading scholar of the subject, Edwin Mansfield, believes that perfect competition requires four conditions: product homogeneity,[42] relatively small buyers and sellers,[43] mobile resources,[44] and perfect information.[45]

---

42. Mansfield describes product homogeneity as follows:

[P]erfect competition requires that the product of any one seller be the same as the product of any other seller. This is an important condition because it makes sure that buyers do not care whether they purchase the product from one seller or another, as long as the price is the same. Note that the product may be defined by a great deal more than the physical characteristics of the good.

EDWIN MANSFIELD, MICROECONOMICS: THEORY & APPLICATIONS 232 (5th ed. 1985).

43. According to Mansfield:

[P]erfect competition requires each participant in the market, whether buyer or seller, to be so small, in relation to the entire market, that he or she cannot affect the product's price.... Of course, if all producers act together, changes in

output will certainly affect price, but any producer acting alone cannot do so.

Id.

44. In this regard, Mansfield states:

[P]erfect competition requires that all resources be completely mobile. In other words, each resource must be able to enter or leave the market, and switch from one use to another, very readily. More specifically, it means that labor must be able to move from region to region and from job to job; it means that raw materials must not be monopolized; and it means that new firms can enter and leave an industry.

Id. at 233 (footnote omitted). "Sunk costs," a key feature of barriers to entry, are best included within this category.

45. Mansfield describes perfect information as follows:

Jack Hirshleifer has considered the converse situation and provided a list of three possible imperfections that can prevent a market from functioning perfectly: imperfect information, time lags,[47] and transaction [costs].[48] Significant problems in any of these areas can cause competition to be suboptimal.

Additional market failures are added to some other lists. These further potential problems include coerced decisionmaking, barriers to the entry of new firms, circumstances of natural monopoly, positive or negative externalities,[49] and situations involving "public goods,"[50] "free riders,"[51] "pris-

[P]erfect competition requires that consumers, firms, and resource owners have perfect knowledge of the relevant economic and technological data. Consumers must be aware of all prices. Laborers and owners of capital must be aware of how much their resources will bring in all possible uses. Firms must know the prices of all inputs and the characteristics of all relevant technologies. Moreover, in its purest sense, perfect competition requires that all of these economic decision-making units have an accurate knowledge of the future together with the past and present.

Id.

47. According to Hirshleifer:

A perfect market would instantaneously digest the inputs and proclaim the correct market-clearing price. But no such magic machine exists in the real world. So a farmer bringing vegetables to a city produce market may by cleverness or chance realize a sale at a price higher than the (unknown) true equilibrium. Or, unluckily, the farmer may accept a price lower than might have been obtained.

Id. at 418–19.

48. On the subject of transaction costs, Hirshleifer states:

Markets that are perfect would also be costless. In the real world, market "middlemen" such as wholesalers and retailers, brokers, dealers, and jobbers exist, and obviously must be paid for their services. While these middlemen improve the perfection of the market in other respects, the fees and payments they receive constitute a burden on the process of exchange. Transaction taxes, in which *government* collects "middleman" payments (possibly reflecting actual services

to taxpayers, but possibly not), are another important factor.

Id. at 419.

49. Robert Cooter and Thomas Ulen have defined the problem of externalities as follows:

Exchange inside a market is voluntary and mutually beneficial; in contrast, an economic effect external to a market exchange may be involuntary and harmful. So, a harmful externality is defined as a cost or benefit that the voluntary actions of one or more people imposes or confers on a third party or parties without their consent. An example of an external cost is pollution.... The reason the market fails in the presence of external costs is that the generator of the externality does not have to pay for harming others, and so exercises too little self-restraint.... We would like the firm to take into account all the costs of production, including the costs imposed on others, in choosing its profit-maximizing output.... When this is accomplished, the externality is said to have been "internalized" in the sense that the private firm now takes it into consideration.

ROBERT COOTER & THOMAS ULEN, LAW AND ECONOMICS 45–46 (1988) (emphasis added).

50. According to Cooter and Ulen:

A public good is a commodity with two very closely related characteristics: first, consumption of the good by one person does not leave less for any other consumer ... and second, the costs of excluding non-paying beneficiaries who consume the good are so high that no private profit-maximizing firm is willing to supply the good. Consider the conventional example of a public good: national defense. The fact that one citizen is secure from the threat of invasion by a foreign oner's dilemmas,"[52] "lemons,"[53] and adverse selection.[a] Despite disputes

army does not leave any less security for other citizens. Furthermore, it is difficult to exclude any citizen from enjoying the security provided to others. Because of these two characteristics, public goods are not likely to be provided at all by the market, or if they are privately provided, provided in less than socially optimal amounts.

Id. at 46.

51. Cooter and Ulen provide a classic example of the free-rider problem:

[T]here is a strong inducement for consumers of the privately-provided public good to try to be "free riders": they hope to benefit at no cost to themselves from the payment of others. The related problem for the private supplier of a public good like national defense is that it is very costly to exclude nonpaying beneficiaries of the service. The attempt to distinguish those who have from those who have not subscribed to the private defense company is almost certain to fail.... As a result ..., it is not likely that the private company will be able to induce many people to purchase defense services. If private profit-maximizing firms are the only providers of national defense, too little of that good will be provided.

Id. at 47–48. For a different type of "free rider" problem, see Jerry Green & Jean–Jacques Laffont, *Characterization of Satisfactory Mechanisms for the Revelation of Preferences for Public Goods*, 45 ECONOMETRICA 427 (1977). These authors are concerned with "free riders" who are willing to pay something, but less than others. This situation might arise, for example, if many people would wish to use a bridge, but would be willing to pay significantly different prices for this service. If those deciding whether to construct the bridge could not price discriminate among potential users, they might not be able to collect enough revenue to make the project profitable. Thus, it is possible that the relevant decision makers will decide not to build the bridge, even though it would be socially desirable to do so.

52. Cooter and Ulen explain how a prisoner's dilemma situation, in which the two participants seek to coordinate their actions, while at the same time being uncertain and

to some degree distrustful of the other's course of action, can result in a suboptimal outcome for each affected party.

In this two person, non-cooperative game two suspects in a crime are taken into custody, put in separate cells, and not allowed to communicate. The authorities offer each prisoner the opportunity to confess to the crime. Suppose that if either prisoner confesses and his partner does not, the confessor will receive half a year in prison and the non-confessor will receive 10 years. If they both confess, they will each receive 5 years in prison. And if neither confesses, they will each receive 1 year in prison. The prisoners will be best off if neither of them confesses. But if either prisoner adopts the strategy of not confessing, he might be left open to a long prison sentence if his partner confesses. In these circumstances, the best strategy is for each prisoner to confess. Thus, each will spend 5 years in prison. Note how different the solution to this game would have been if the participants could have communicated. Presumably, they would have coordinated their strategies so that each would have refused to confess, with the result that each would have spent only 1 year in prison.

COOTER & ULEN, *supra* note 52, at 93 n. 3.

53. George Akerlof identified an interesting market failure that might be caused by imperfect consumer information. In certain markets, consumers might not be able to easily obtain sufficient information regarding the quality of specific goods and might confuse the quality of particular goods with the quality of most goods on the market. Over time, competition from inferior goods (which can sell at a lower price due to their lower cost) could drive goods of higher quality (which have higher costs and, therefore, higher prices) from the market. Eventually, only low quality "lemons" might be left on the market. *See* George A. Akerlof, *The Market for "Lemons": Quality Uncertainty and the Market Mechanism*, 84 Q.J.ECON. 488 (1970).

a. Robert Cooter and Thomas Ulen describe adverse selection in this way:

[Adverse selection] arises because of the high cost to [insurance companies] of over taxonomy, this basic list of factors that can plausibly cause competition to become suboptimal is relatively noncontroversial.

Far more controversial is the question of just how often market failures occur and, therefore, how often remedial action under the antitrust or consumer protection statutes might be appropriate. This controversy may be illustrated by the role of imperfect information, perhaps the most important single market failure. Even Chicago School adherents concede that information often is imperfect. Much of what separates "post-Chicago" antitrust from Chicago School antitrust, however, are differing beliefs concerning the frequency and degree to which information is imperfect, the implications this has for competition, and whether government intervention is likely to correct the situation more optimally or more rapidly than the market.

Proponents of post-Chicago views are perhaps more inclined than the Chicago School to believe that important informational and other market failures may exist because they have come to believe that there are a number of ways in which such failures, perhaps small in themselves, can interact with and reinforce each other. In the final analysis, there is no substitute for close study of the facts of individual cases.

Everything for Sale

Everything for Sale 16–19, 24–28 (1996).

■ Robert Kuttner

* * * The theory of markets posits several interrelated assumptions.

Three have to do with competition. In a stylized free market, consumers are said to possess "perfect information." This is almost never literally true, but is often close enough to be a reasonable approximation. Second, there is said to be "perfect competition"—many suppliers and freedom to

accurately distinguishing between high- and low-risk insurees. Although the law of large numbers helps the company in assessing probabilities, what it calculates from the large sample are average probabilities. The insurance premium must be set using this average probability of a particular loss. For example, insurance companies have determined that unmarried males between the ages of 16 and, say, 25, have a much higher likelihood of being in an automobile accident than do other identifiable groups of drivers. As a result, the insurance premium charged to members of this group is higher than that charged to other groups whose likelihood of accident is much lower.

But even though unmarried males between the ages of 16 and 25 are, on average, much more likely to be involved in an accident, there are some young men within the group who are even more reckless than average and some who are much less reckless than the group's average. If it is difficult for the insurer to distinguish these groups from the larger group of unmarried males aged 16 to 25, then the premium that is set equal to the average likelihood of harm within the group will seem like a bargain to those who know they are reckless and too high to those who know that they are safer from their peers.

Robert Cooter & Thomas Ulen, Law and Economics 50 (2d ed. 1997).

shop around. Barriers to entry are necessarily low—anybody must be free to open a supermarket. This, in turn, means that producers are not monopolists, and don't have the market power to dictate prices. (Supermarkets do engage in opportunistic price hikes, but prices that are wildly out of line with competitors do not stick for very long, because word spreads and shoppers are driven away.) Prices are thus set by the interplay of supply and demand. Though there may be other forms of regulation, such as food inspection and labeling, there is little direct price regulation from third parties such as government. Third, free markets must have "mobility of factors": capital and labor, as well as consumers, are free to go elsewhere if they don't like their compensation.

A second set of assumptions is behavioral. Firms, by definition, have the single-minded goal of maximizing profits; consumers pursue the goal of rationally maximizing their well-being ("utility") by pursuing the most satisfying products at the best available price. Preferences are said to be set "exogenously"—they reflect the consumer's own tastes. * * * A perfect market also presumes the absence of significant "externalities"—social costs or benefits, such as pollution or public health, not fully captured in the price of the immediate market transaction. * * *

What describes supermarkets pretty well describes the production and sale of most consumer goods. It describes the setting of prices for many, but not all, raw materials used by producers. A relatively free market also characterizes many, if not most, services bought by consumers and producers alike. If you don't like your barber, there is likely to be another one down the block. There is no shortage of restaurants, hotels, tax preparers, photocopiers, dry cleaners from which to choose. Likewise, if your business is dissatisfied with the computer-repair service, management consultant, ad agency, office-cleaning company, office space itself, there are many more to choose from, all competing on the basis of quality and price, all—remarkably—earning a roughly normal profit. In all of these realms, the market mechanism mostly works.

This brief description of how the marketplace operates * * * allows us to appreciate why most economists are so enraptured with markets. Students of economics often hear their teachers compare markets to self-regulating systems in nature. Listening to an economist rhapsodize on how marvelously markets continuously adjust, how they deliver a humble cornflake from stalk to table through several chains of production and distribution without help from a commissar, is a bit like hearing a physicist marveling at the equipoise of the physical universe, or a doctor explaining the wonder of the self-regulating systems of the human body.

When a particular market does not work like a supermarket or a textbook one, the question is what to do about it. Free-market economists, almost intuitively, think market failure is limited to a fairly narrow set of special cases, and that the solution to market failure is more market. But is it? And when is it? And by what criteria do we know? * * *

Consider a market profoundly different from the market for retail groceries—the market for health care. This is no small, special case, since it consumes 15 percent of the entire economy, roughly as much as food does. * * * Health care is anything but a textbook free market, yet market forces and profit motives in the health industry are rife.

On the supply side, the health industry violates several conditions of a free market. Unlike the supermarket business, there is not "free entry." You cannot simply open a hospital, or hang out your shingle as a doctor. This gives health-care providers a degree of market power that compromises the competitive model—and raises prices. On the demand side, consumers lack the special knowledge to shop for a doctor the way they buy a car, and lack a perfectly free choice of health-insurer. Since society has decided that nobody shall perish for lack of medical care, we partly de-link effective demand from private purchasing power, which is also inflationary.

Health care also offers substantial "positive externalities"—diffused benefits not calculated in the instant transaction. The value to society of mass vaccinations far exceeds the profits that can be captured by the doctor or drug company. If vaccinations and other public-health measures were left to private supply-and-demand, society would seriously underinvest. The health system also depends heavily on extra-market norms. Physicians and nurses are guided by ethical constraints and professional values that limit the opportunism that their specialized knowledge and power might otherwise invite.

The fact that health care is a far cry from a perfect market sets up a chain of perverse incentives. In ordinary markets, sellers maximize profits by minimizing costs. But in health care, the profit maximizer's object is to maximize insurance reimbursement. The more complex the procedure and the more inflated the cost base, the more money can be billed to the insurance company. In recent years, private and government insurers have tried to crack down—by intensively reviewing what doctors and hospitals do, publishing book-length schedules or permissible procedures and reimbursements. Providers have fought back, by further complicating their own billing. All this inflates the cost of the whole system.

Worse, the insurance industry's efforts to reduce inflation (in a highly imperfect market) have created a second-order set of inefficiencies. Increasingly, consumers lack the ability to shop around for doctors or insurance plans. Often, they are locked in either because they get health insurance through their jobs, or because a "pre-existing condition" makes them unattractive to other insurers. They then become easy prey for insurance plans that seek to save costs by denying them care that they need, and to which they are ostensibly entitled.

Increasingly, too, insurance companies seek to minimize costs simply by refusing to insure people likely to become sick. This process of risk selection and segmentation, known as medical underwriting, is itself very expensive. So is the endless point-counterpoint of complex preapprovals and reviews of treatments. And so is the proliferation of paperwork. The providers and the insurers are each behaving "rationally" as profit maximizers, but their behavior does not yield a general good; the result is irrational for the system as a whole.

Thus, health care violates all the premises of an efficient free market—perfect competition, perfect information, mobility of factors, and so on. Yet, unless we want people dying from preventable diseases for lack of private purchasing power, the cure does not lie in liberation of the health "market." * * *

Here is the nub of the issue. Are most markets like supermarkets—or like health markets? And when a market exhibits resistance to market forms of discipline, what is the remedy? The conundrum of the market for health care is a signal example of a concept that will recur throughout this book: The General Theory of the Second Best. The theory, propounded by the economists Richard Lipsey and Kelvin Lancaster in 1956, and largely ignored today, holds that, when a particular market departs significantly from a pure market and yields an outcome that is not "optimal" in market terms, attempts to make it more marketlike in some, but not all, respects will have indeterminate results for economic efficiency—and sometimes perverse ones.

The Second Best theorem suggests that when there are multiple "distortions" in the price and supply disciplines of a given market, the removal of one distortion in the attempt to create a purer market will not necessarily improve the overall outcome. A second-best market typically has second-best forms of accountability—professional norms, government supervision, regulation, and subsidy—to which market forces have adapted. For example, if the health-care system is already a far cry from a free market on both the demand side and the supply side, removing one regulation, and thereby making the health system more superficially marketlike, may simply increase opportunism and inefficiency. In many economic realms, the "second-best" outcome of some price distortion offset by regulation and extra-market norms may be the best outcome practically available. The hapless attempt to get incrementally closer to the "first-best" state of a pure free market—in an arena like health care, where price signals are necessarily distorted—may lead to third-best outcomes. * * *

THE THREE EFFICIENCIES

* * * A review of both economic history and economic theory suggests that there are three very different concepts of efficiency in economic life. We might call them Smithian, Keynesian, and Schumpeterian. For the most part, the study of markets is dominated by issues of allocation—the efficiency of Adam Smith. Keynesian efficiency, by contrast, addresses the potential output that is lost when the economy is stuck in recession, performing well below its full-employment potential. Increasing allocative efficiency in such circumstances doesn't help. It may even hurt—to the extent that intensified competition in a depressed economy may throw more people out of work, reduce overall purchasing power, and deepen the shortfall of aggregate demand. The economy of the 1990s has offered the paradox of escalating gains to productivity via Smithian efficiency, coexisting with declining purchasing power and declining job security for most ordinary people. Resources are allocated in a more marketlike manner, but

overall performance is nonetheless mediocre and living standards are mostly stagnant.

By contrast, World War II is history's great example of an event that grossly violated allocative efficiency yet stimulated broad improvements in living standards. During the war, the United States had wage and price controls, rationing, coerced savings, monopolistic military contracts, and a variety of other affronts to free-market pricing. There was massive state intervention throughout the economy. During the peak of the war effort, nearly 50 percent of production was in response to government procurement contracts, most of which entailed monopoly pricing.

All of this violated ordinary supply and demand; it was profoundly inefficient in an allocative sense. Yet in a Keynesian sense the war was stunningly efficient. In 1941, the economy had still not fully recovered from the Great Depression. Unemployment remained at over 11 percent, and growth from June 1940 to June 1941 was less than 2 percent. But by June 1942, the economy was at full employment. Industry, which had resisted making investments because demand was slack, suddenly poured billions of dollars into war-production plants. Industry was recapitalized, at state-of-the-art technology. A generation of skilled workers was trained to operate it. Although nearly half of what was produced during the war was literally manufactured only to be blown up, the stimulus of war production rekindled economic growth. GNP increased by about 50 percent in just four years, a rate that has never been equaled before or since. By war's end, civilian purchasing power was one-third higher than it had been before Pearl Harbor. Although private-savings rates rose, much of the money that paid for the war was borrowed, through war bonds. But despite a record debt/GDP ratio of 119.8 percent at the war's end—more than double the "dangerous" ratio of the mid-1990s—this high debt was perfectly compatible with the two decades of record growth that followed.

Standard free-market economics simply does not know how to treat these two very different kinds of efficiency in the same analytical frame. * * * If a Keynesian intervention reduces allocative efficiency by distorting market prices, but appropriately stimulates demand, standard market economics is literally unable to calculate *a priori* whether the trade-off is worth the candle.

The postwar boom was also built on what I am terming "Schumpeterian" efficiencies. Joseph Schumpeter was the great prophet of technical progress as the engine of growth, and the defender of imperfect competition as the necessary agent of technical progress. Large, oligopolistic firms often turn out to have the deepest pockets. They keep on innovating, to defend their privileged market position and to fend off encroachment. Innovation within a structure of stable oligopoly may be more reliable than innovation in a context of fierce and mutually ruinous price competition. Casual readers (or nonreaders) of Schumpeter may remember him as the prophet of "creative destruction," a phrase that he indeed coined to describe the onrushing turbulence of capitalism. But the usual cartoon of Schumpeter gets his meaning backward. Schumpeter's concern was how a market system could endure *despite* its many propensities toward ruinous competition. He was no advocate of creative destruction.

The modern economy offers many examples of Schumpeterian efficiency. The old regulated Bell telephone monopoly generated excess profits, many of which were plowed back into Bell Labs. A regulated rate structure also created pricing incentives for investing in ever more advanced switching technology, since profits grew with the rate base, and the rate base grew with the base of installed capital. * * *

James Kurth, a political economist at Swarthmore, has coined the useful phrase "Military Schumpeterianism." This is an ingenious twist on the oft-repeated observation that the postwar boom was built on "Military Keynesianism," by which commentators meant the reliable stimulus of defense spending; this substituted for a more explicit and aggressive Keynesianism of large deficit spending for civilian purposes, socialized savings, public-works investment, and so on. Kurth's point is that, though large and persistent military outlays may have indeed had macroeconomic benefits, defense contracts also had immense benefits for technical innovation, industrial stabilization, and market leadership—the efficiency of Schumpeter.

A series of long-term military contracts to a prime vendor produced assaults against allocative efficiency—the hundred-dollar hammers, thousand-dollar toilet seats, cost-plus windfalls regularly exposed in congressional investigations—yet also produced stunning technical advances and market leadership. Who thinks that Boeing would be the world's leader in aircraft sales absent World War II and the Cold War? * * *

As a matter of technical economics, there is a Schumpeter/Smith disjuncture that parallels the Keynes/Smith disjuncture. An economy that is performing according to the precepts of allocative efficiency is likely to have both avoidable unemployment and collective underinvestment in technological advance. A perfectly competitive market will spend too little on innovation both because profits will be too low, and because of well-known "externality" dilemmas.

An externality, please recall, is a cost or benefit to the economy as a whole that is not captured by a party to an immediate transaction. A negative externality is a cost, such as pollution, that is imposed on others. A positive externality, such as the broad gain from a new invention or from training an employee, is a benefit to society whose economic return is not fully realized by the innovator. Because investments in innovation are risky and because they often benefit competitors, market forces tend to underinvest in innovation. Indeed, the more "perfect" the competition, the less money is left over to invest in innovations that have broadly diffused benefits but that may not pay off to the investor for decades, if ever. The greater the rate of creative destruction, the less available are the monopoly "rents" that are the innovator's reward and necessary shelter. (In economic terminology, a "rent" is a super-normal profit that would be competed away in a perfect market.)

The more the economy relies on casino-like capital markets, the less the availability of patient capital. But when is oligopoly relatively "efficient," and when is competition mutually ruinous? From a purely Smithian perspective, the question is nonsensical *ex hypothesis*. Oligopoly is never efficient, because more competition is always better. However, as Douglass North, the first economic historian to win the Nobel Prize in economics, observed in his 1993 Nobel Lecture, "It is adaptive rather than allocative efficiency which is the key to long run growth." This is, of course, the efficiency of technical progress—of Schumpeter. * * *

Another problem with allocative efficiency: the market's allocation of resources is only "efficient" based on a given distribution of income—one that reflects not only the verdicts of prior efficient markets, but also historical accidents. "Property is not theft," wrote R.H. Tawney, rebutting the anarchist Proudhon, "but a good deal of theft becomes property." Remarkably, the set of goods purchased by the existing income distribution is deemed simultaneously "efficient"—and substantially arbitrary.

In principle, we could have a wide range of possible income distributions and start the economic game again, and the usual supply-and-demand discipline would efficiently resume. Though this happens occasionally (as in the case of land reforms, or social revolutions), for the most part the allocative efficiency of the market presumes the actual income distribution bequeathed to us by recent history. By market criteria, therefore, it is allocatively efficient for a millionaire to spend an extra fifty dollars on a fine after-dinner cigar, and for a pauper to starve in the streets for lack of money to eat. The price system doesn't care about that: its job is simply to match willing buyers with available sellers, and to be a buyer you need money.

Conventional economics usually replies that it is still more efficient to let market-determined supply and demand determine prices and prizes; if we don't like the social consequences, we can always redistribute income after the fact. Fine—but who are "we"? This rather airy conclusion innocently overlooks how wealth buys, among other things, power—and how power resists income redistribution.

The usual construct of purely allocative efficiency also begs the question of "Efficiency for what?" Market pricing is an arguably efficient means, not an end. The goals, values, habits, and institutions of a good society may include an essentially market economy, but must be set by extra-market processes and forces. In their enthusiasm for the market mechanism, many theorists insist market values are an end, not a means, and that whatever society results from market forces is by definition the best available, as well as one that has delivered just rewards.

Milton Friedman and his disciples have made valiant but ultimately unconvincing efforts to infer extra-market values from the functioning of the market mechanism. If markets thrive on well-informed consumers, then a market society requires free expression. If markets express voluntary exchange and free choice, then they are the natural handmaiden of liberal democracy. This sounds plausible in the abstract, until we remember that Nazism, fascism, Latin American military dictatorships, East Asian autocracies, and a wide range of other authoritarian regimes coexisted all too well with a basically capitalist form of production and exchange. Liberal democratic values, not to mention social ones, must be found elsewhere. Taken to an extreme, markets tend to destroy them.

NOTES AND QUESTIONS

1. Price theory, imperfect markets, and "rents." While the concept of supply and demand is widely known and frequently discussed, non-economists may not understand the precise meaning of the terms. JEFFERY L. HARRISON, LAW AND ECONOMICS IN A NUTSHELL 7 (2d ed. 2000). Demand is the range of prices and the amount of a good or service consumers are willing and able to purchase in a given market at a given time, not including those potential consumers who cannot or will not pay for the good or service. *Id.* Supply is the range of prices and the amount of the good or service available for sale at each price in a given market at a given time. *Id.* at 11. The equilibrium price combines supply and demand to establish the price and quantity toward which the market tends to gravitate. *Id.* at 14.

This model assumes perfect market competition in which the sellers are price takers, passively reacting to the market-determined price. A perfect market depends on such factors as multiple suppliers with homogenous products, availability of information about prices and other relevant considerations, easiness for suppliers to enter the industry, and no single supplier large enough to affect prices by increasing or decreasing its output. An imperfect market exists if such a factor is absent and therefore a seller is able to raise prices above those of a competitive market. *Id.* at 20–22. Under perfect conditions, competitors will make a normal profit, or the minimum profit necessary to stay in business. If competition is imperfect, however, the seller may be able to make an economic profit (or "rent"), which is profit in excess of a normal profit. Competition is therefore important in determining prices. *Id.* at 24–26.

2. Market failures and "government intervention." The concept of market failure is popularly used by scholars and policymakers to explain when government mechanisms, rather than market mechanisms, should allocate a resource. As the excerpts above indicate, there may be many situations in which markets can be said to fail. In the legal literature, market failures are popularly pointed to as a reason for antitrust law, consumer protection law, and environmental law. Antitrust law responds to the market failures represented by oligopoly and monopoly power; consumer protection law responds to the market failures traceable to asymmetrical information between consumers and firms; and environmental law responds to the market failures caused by the negative externalities of pollution and the positive externalities of clean air and water.

But, assuming that government action is necessary, what should the government do? Debates have raged in the legal and economic literature for some time about whether market failures are better addressed by "command and control" government regulation, or whether government should seek to create more "marketlike" structures for bargaining. For example, rather than telling factory owners how much of which toxic substances they may emit into the environment, governments could create a system of tradeable emission permits, allowing firms to bargain with one another for the right to pollute. For a discussion of the more fundamental problems environmental pollution poses to traditional economic analysis, see section C below.

3. New theories of market failure: informational economics. Market failures have long been assumed to exist with respect to certain "public goods" such as environmental cleanliness and police and fire protection. More recently, economists such as Joseph Stiglitz and George Akerlof have argued that "market failure" is not limited to these kinds of goods, but is pervasive throughout all kinds of markets. These economists identify asymmetric information as a source of market failure. Consider the excerpt by Joseph Stiglitz (who won a Nobel Prize for his work) below.

Keynesian Economics and Critique of First Fundamental Theorem of Welfare Economics

Market Failure or Success: The New Debate 41, 48–57, 58 (Tyler Cowen & Eric Crampton eds.).

■ Joseph E. Stiglitz

[Stiglitz begins by arguing that traditional neoclassical economics assumes that there is perfect information and that there is a complete set of markets for everything that can be exchanged.]

The assumption that there is a complete set of markets, including a complete set of risk and futures markets is important in the standard competitive paradigm but unrealistic. * * *

The incompleteness of markets can itself be explained by transaction costs, an important component of which is information costs. There are costs associated with establishing a market. If there were markets for each of the millions of commodities, each of the billions of contingencies, each of the infinity of future dates, then so much of societies' resources would be absorbed in organizing these transactions that there would be little left over to be bought and sold on each of these markets!

Once we recognize the myriad events that affect us, we recognize the impossibility of having even a complete set of risk markets (insurance against all contingencies). Each firm is affected not only by the events that affect the industry but by idiosyncratic events—the illness of its president, a breakdown in one of its machines, the departure of a key salesperson. The firm itself can buy insurance for many of the risks it faces, such as that its trucks get into accidents or that its factories burn down, but most of the risks it faces cannot be insured against. The notion that there be markets for each of these risks is mind-boggling. * * *

Consider * * * the market for labor. Each individual is different, in myriad ways. A complete set of markets would entail there being a different market for each type of labor—a market for Joe Stiglitz's labor, which is different from the market for Paul Samuelson's labor, which in turn is different from the market for plumbers, which in turn is different from the market for unskilled labor, and so on. If we are careful in defining markets for homogenous commodities (Joe Stiglitz's labor delivered at a particular date, in a particular state, at a particular location), then there is only one trader on one side of the market (Joe Stiglitz). If we expand the markets to embrace all theoretical economists, then it is obviously more competitive. But we have had to drop the assumptions that commodities are homogenous and that the set of markets is incomplete; there is not a separate market for each homogenous commodity. * * *

[B]eyond that, asymmetries of information greatly limit the opportunities to trade, a notion captured in the familiar maxim: I wouldn't want to buy something from someone who is willing to sell it to me. Of course the old principles concerning differences in preferences and comparative advantage providing motives for trade still remain valid, but there is another motive for trading, which can be put baldly as "cheating." While in traditional exchanges both parties are winners, I can get you to pay more for something than it is worth—to buy a used car that is a lemon—I win and you lose. Farmers have a strong incentive to sell their crops on futures markets, but most do not avail themselves much of this opportunity, and for good reason. Those markets are dominated by five large trading companies, who have every incentive to be more informed by the small farmer. The differential information means the farmer is at a disadvantage; the trading companies can make a profit off the farmer's relative ignorance. Knowing this, a choice is made to bear the risk rather than pay the price.

Asymmetries of information give rise to market imperfections in many markets, other than the insurance market, futures markets, and the market for used cars. Consider, for instance, the market for "used labor," workers who already have a job. Their present employer normally has more information concerning their abilities than do prospective employers. A prospective employer knows that if it makes an offer to attract an employee from another firm, the other firm will match it, if the worker is worth it, and will not if the worker is not. Thus, again, the prospective employer is in a heads you win, tails I lose situation: it is only successful in hiring the new employee if it has offered higher wages than the current (well-informed) employer thinks the worker is worth. To be sure, there are instances when the prospective employee's productivity at the new firm will be higher than at the old job—the employee is better matched for the job—or where there are other (nonpecuniary) reasons why the individual may wish to move (to be near relatives, or get away from them). As a result there is *some* trade in the used labor market, but apart from younger workers who are trying to get well matched with a firm, these markets tend to be thin. * * *

Asymmetries of information give rise to two problems, referred to as the (adverse) selection and the incentive or moral hazard problems. Both are seen most clearly in the context of insurance markets, but they arise in a variety of other contexts as well. The first problem results in firms being unable to obtain insurance on their profits: clearly the firm is more informed about its prospects than any insurance firm could be, and the insurance firm worries that if the firm is willing to pay the premium, it is getting too good of a deal. That is, there is a high probability that the insurance firm will have to pay off on the policy.

Moral hazard also leads to limited insurance. The more complete the insurance coverage, the less incentive individuals or firms have to take actions that ensure that the insured-against event does not occur. Because the actions that would be required to reduce the likelihood of the insured-against event occurring are often not observable (and/or it cannot be verified that the insured took the requisite actions), the payment of the insurance cannot be made contingent on the individual or firm taking those actions. Thus health insurance firms would like those they insure not to smoke or to be in places where they suffer the consequences of "second-hand smoke," that is, smoking by others. But insurance firms cannot observe these actions, and hence cannot require those they insure not to smoke.

The provision of *complete* insurance would greatly attenuate incentives, so much so in many cases that for the insurance firm to break even would require charging such a high premium that the policy would be unattractive. Thus, in general, whenever there is moral hazard, there will be incomplete insurance. * * *

It should be clear of course that for traders to have incentives to gather information required that information not be perfectly disseminated in the market. If, simply by looking at market prices, those who do not spend money to acquire information can glean all the information that the informed traders who have spent money to acquire information have, then the informed traders will not have any informational advantage; they will not be able to obtain any return to their expenditures on information acquisition. Accordingly, *if there were a complete set of markets, information would be so well conveyed that investors would have no incentives to gather information.* (Of course with all participants having the same [zero] information, incentives to trade would be greatly reduced.) To put the matter differently, the assumptions of "informed" markets and "a complete set of markets" may be mutually exclusive. * * *

The problems with the assumption of a complete set of markets run deeper. [Elsewhere] I emphasize the importance of innovations, but it is hard to conceive of there being markets for contingencies (states) that have not yet been conceived of: surely an event such as the discovery of the principles underlying atomic energy and the subsequent development of commercial atomic power is an event of immense economic importance, in particular for owners of other energy resources. Yet how could markets in these risks—or in the risks associated with lasers or transistors—have existed before the underlying concepts had been developed? This is a fundamental incoherence between the ideas of a complete set of markets and notions of innovation. * * *

Another critique of the fundamental theorem of welfare economics is that it *assumes* that there is perfect competition, that every firm is a price taker. Most markets are in fact not perfectly competitive. One reason is that when information is imperfect and costly, markets will normally not be perfectly competitive. Imperfect information confers on firms a degree of market power. Though there is competition, it is not the perfect competition of textbook economics, * * * it is *more* akin to monopolistic competition. * * * Because of imperfect information, if a firm raises its price, not all the firm's customers will immediately be able to find a firm that charges a lower price for the same commodity: indeed customers may well infer that other firms have raised their prices as well. By the same token, if it lowers its price, it does not instantly garner for itself all the customers from the higher-priced stores. Search is costly, and so those in the market rarely know the prices being charged by all the firms selling every good in which they are interested.

The imperfections of competition arise not only, however, from imperfect information but also from fixed costs, many of which are information-related costs. There are fixed costs that arise directly in production—the overhead costs of running a firm—and fixed costs associated with acquiring information about how to produce. This means that there is unlikely to be a very large number of firms producing every quality of every good at every location at every date in every state of nature. As we have noted before, with even small fixed costs, many of these "markets" will have relatively few suppliers. * * *

Finally, we think of one of the great virtues of market economies is its ability to "solve" information problems efficiently. Yet when information is costly, firms act to take advantage of that. In doing so, they may *create* noise—they create, some times deliberately, information problems for consumers.

Temporary price reductions ("sales"), though we normally do not view them from this perspective, create price dispersion. Costly search gives firms good reason to charge different prices, or to temporarily reduce prices. Low-priced firms can gather themselves a larger customer base, but the high-priced firms can still survive, serving only those who have high search costs and who have not had the good fortune to find a low-priced firm. The high-priced firms compensate for the smaller scale of their sales with a higher profit (price) per sale. * * *

Thus, while price dispersion gives rise to search and other activities directed at reducing the "noise" of the market, and search limits the extent to which prices may differ in the market, the fact of the matter is that the existence of imperfect information—costly search—is what creates the price dispersion in the first place. The price dispersion itself arises, in part, not in response to exogenous changes in economic circumstances, or the differences in economic circumstances facing different firms, but endogenously, as part of the market equilibrium where each firm recognizes the consequences of the fact that search is costly. * * *

These results * * * reduce the confidence we have in the presumption that markets are efficient. There are two important differences between the new market failures, based on imperfect and costly information and incomplete markets, and the older market failures associated with, for instance, public goods and pollution externalities: the older market failure were, for the most part, easily identified and limited in scope, requiring well-defined government interventions. Because virtually all markets are incomplete and information is always imperfect—moral hazard and adverse selection problems are endemic to all market situations—the market failures are pervasive in the economy. * * *

The new information paradigm has revealed that "market failures" are indeed pervasive in the economy. They appear in virtually every transaction among private parties in the economy, and while they may be small in each case, cumulatively they are important. Moreover the market failures are not like those concerning air pollution, for which a well-defined and effective government policy can often easily be designed. This pervasiveness of failures, while it reduces our confidence in the efficiency of market solutions, also reduces our confidence in the ability of the government to correct them. Most important from our perspective, neither the theory nor the practice of socialism paid any attention to these problems.

The Failure of Market Failure

18 J. Pol'y Anal. & Mgt. 558–64, 571, 572 (1999).

■ Richard O. Zerbe Jr. & Howard E. McCurdy

The question of the proper role of government in the marketplace is an old and fundamental one. Public officials throughout the world grapple with this issue, deciding which public services to provide or how to regulate the activities of individuals and firms, a task made more urgent by recent efforts to privatize public responsibilities and "reinvent" government. In the search for objective standards by which such decisions can be made, public officials have increasingly turned to the concept of market failure. Use of the market failure concept is widespread, both in teaching curricula and in practicing government circles.

* * *

The concept of market failure initially appeared as a means of explaining in economic terms why the need for government expenditures should arise. It constituted, according to its presenters, "a normative judgment about the role of government and the ability of markets to establish mutually beneficial exchanges.''

* * *

* * * In one leading textbook on the new science of policy analysis, David Weimer and Aidan Vining reach a conclusion that appears frequently in the literature: "When is it legitimate for government to intervene in private affairs? In the United States, the normative answer to this question has usually been based on the concept of *market failure*—a circumstance where the pursuit of private interest does not lead to an efficient use of society's resources or a fair distribution of society's goods." Textbooks on microeconomics and public finance commonly present the concept of market failure as a general justification for government intervention.

As it matured, the market failure concept took on an additional characteristic—that of a diagnostic tool by which policymakers learned how to objectively determine the exact scope and type of intervention. Expansion of this normative concept into a diagnostic tool appeared in conjunction with the growth of policy analysis as a field of study and university training. One scholar argues: "The welfare theorem lets [us] classify inefficiencies as due to monopoly externalities, and so on. This helps us to understand and perhaps to solve such inefficiencies just as a doctor's diagnosis . . . is part of treatment."

* * *

What began as a simple attempt to provide a normative explanation for the existence of government expenditures has developed into a quasi-scientific full-scale diagnostic test with the prescription of cures. Some textbooks even present tables that allow students to identify appropriate interventions for different types of market and government failures. This appears to be a powerful and attractive model. It looks scientific. It seems to provide an objective test for governmental intervention. It appears to be something that can be usefully taught in schools.

Inevitably, such concepts and teachings find their way into public policy. Recently the U.S. government issued Executive Order 12866 [1993], which requires federal officials to conduct an economic analysis as a means of determining the need for proposed regulations. Guidelines for carrying out this order require officials to make a finding of "whether the problem constitutes a significant market failure" as a prerequisite for recommending government intervention. The guidelines further provide instructions for identifying types of failures, comparing potential interventions, and guarding against "unintentional harmful effects on the efficiency of market outcomes." The resulting regulatory impact analyses make reference to a variety of market failure concepts. * * *

An extensive flowering of the market failure concept has occurred in the field of law. The number of law review articles and court decisions using the concept run into the thousands, with 239 references turned up by a search of law reviews for the 12 months between June 1995 and June 1996 alone. These references occur not just in monopoly, antitrust, and environmental issues, but appear to span virtually the entire corpus of law. References are found, for example, in family law articles, in connection with setting product standards, in references to the plight of refugees, in connection with health care, and with regard to problems of creating markets in less developed countries, as well as in securities law, the creation of financial derivatives, moral legal theory, contracts, occupational injuries, controls on credit card interest rates, intellectual property, discrimination in insurance markets, the information superhighway, and zoning. Similarly, court decisions that refer to market failure and to externalities are made with great frequency.

Long before social scientists applied diagnostic skills to public affairs, doctors of medicine guessed that diseases of the body could be traced to imbalances in bodily "humors." By the 18th century, this fit of deductive reasoning had been elevated to the level of a diagnostic procedure. The approach led doctors to prescribe a variety of ineffective and often dangerous remedies, such as bleeding or purging. It eventually was replaced by more scientifically valid approaches, such as the discovery of antibiotics and the theory of germs. The theory of market failures, this paper will show, is little better grounded than the outdated belief in bodily humors.

A fundamental problem with the concept of market failure, as economists occasionally recognize, is that it describes a situation that exists everywhere. While the ubiquity of market failures seems well accepted, the consequences of this observation are not. * * *

Market failures are thought to occur when the market fails to produce public goods, or inadvertently produces externalities, or gives rise to natural monopolies, or disenfranchises parties through information asymmetries, or creates undesirable income distributions. All of these forms are types of externalities, since each consists of nonmonetary effects not taken into account in the decisionmaking process, which is the classic definition of externalities. Hence, when we charge that the market failure concept has certain shortcomings, we mean to apply this statement to all forms of externalities including nonmarket failures by government institutions.

The core argument against market failure analysis is derived from the study of transactions. Externalities arise when parties engage in transactions. The effect of transactions on market behavior was first analyzed in the 1930s, beginning with an examination of brokerage charges and other costs of exchange. This quickly expanded into an analysis of the relationship between property rights and the cost of transactions. The property rights approach began with an article by R.H. Coase, now well known in the discipline of economics. Coase argued that individuals form firms because use of the price system is not costless. In other words, entrepreneurs create firms in an effort to reduce the transaction costs associated with using the price system. This approach developed mainly after Coase's 1960 article on "The Problem of Social Cost" * * *.

The property rights approach is important because it defines the condition under which externalities entirely disappear. Transaction costs in this respect are defined as *the resources necessary to transfer, establish, and maintain property rights*. As property rights become more extensive and complete, transaction costs approach zero. In a similar fashion, as transaction costs decline, property rights become more complete as it is cheaper to defend them or transfer property.

Only when property rights are perfect do transaction costs vanish. In a zero transaction cost world, with well-specified rights, there would be markets for everything and all markets would clear, producing efficient outcomes for any collective problem that parties chose to resolve. This condition is expressed by the so-called "weak form" of the Coase Theorem.[3] * * *

No such world, of course, can ever exist. This realization is critical to understanding why the market failure model fails. * * *

    * * *

Market failures may be defined as departures from the optimum with respect to an operating price system that is costless. The existence of unpriced but nonzero transaction costs means that some trades are not created—trades that would be undertaken if the cost of the unpriced transactions were zero (or less than the net monetary impact to be gained). Failure to undertake these trades creates a market failure.

Market failures disappear only when the cost of operating the price system is zero. In the real world, however, this never occurs. People incur costs resolving, transferring, and maintaining property rights. This occurs wherever transactions take place. Unpriced transaction costs, as a consequence, appear everywhere. Since unpriced transaction costs are ubiquitous, this gives rise to a situation in which externalities and hence market failures can be found wherever transactions occur.

How then does an analyst distinguish between externalities that require government attention and those that do not? The market failure approach owes much of its success to the fact that sophisticated users have focused on the provision of goods with large net benefits where government has an advantage with respect to transaction costs. For example, market failure analysts have focused on goods with high exclusion costs, such as clean air. These are goods for which the government can better exploit its advantage in coercion to effect substantial per unit reductions in transaction costs and in which the potential markets—clean air and water, police and fire services, and the like—are large. The choice of these markets, however, is essentially ad hoc (aside from their transaction cost features).

---

3. The first formal statement of the Coase Theorem did not appear until 1966, when George Stigler offered that "the Coase Theorem . . . asserts that under perfect competition private and social costs will be equal." Since this original formulation, the theorem has been stated in numerous ways, including: "if one assumes rationality, no transaction costs, and no legal impediments to bargaining, *all* misallocations of resources would be fully cured in the market by bargains" and "if transaction costs are zero the structure of the law does not matter because efficiency will result in any case." Paradoxically, the Coase Theorem has spawned a huge literature dealing with the artificial world of zero transaction costs, but Coase meant to emphasize real world analysis.

Going beyond these obvious cases, the market failure concept can also be applied to situations that most analysts would consider trivial and not worthy of government attention, which analysts recognize and tend to avoid. When a neighbor fails to plant more flowers even though this would increase property values in the neighborhood by more than the cost of planning, an externality and a market failure exist. The highway driver who drives too slowly fails to consider the time costs he or she imposes on other drivers, thereby creating an externality. (Since the government owns the highway we should probably say that a nonmarket failure exists.) Wherever moral hazard or adverse selection may be found, externalities arise. Companies providing fire insurance worry that policyholders will ignore efficient fire prevention measures; flood insurance may induce people to build in flood plains; government insurance for savings and loan companies may induce investments that are too risky; and * * * colleges granting tenure to professors may find they work too little thereafter.

Externalities exist anytime there is inefficiency in the law affecting markets. A law that encourages inefficient breach of contract produces an externality, as does a tort law that sets the penalty for reckless driving so low that too much reckless driving occurs. A person who inadvertently issues a fraudulent check may not take into account the burden he or she imposes on other users of checks. Suppose that buying a car involves title transfer fees imposed by the state. If these fees are set too high, some trades will not be made. The car manufacturer will produce too few cars, just as a monopolist would.

As these situations suggest, analysts in search of externalities and market failures can find them anywhere they look, providing a universal justification for any sort of government intervention that one might want to undertake. Supporters of the market failure concept avoid this problem by focusing on failures that are "big." In its worst form, this amounts to little more than the substitution of the ideological biases of the analyst. * * *

    * * *

The issue of government intervention is largely an empirical and not a theoretical one. As Nelson says, "there is no satisfactory normative theory regarding the appropriate roles of government in a mixed economy." No theory captures the variety of institutional arrangements that people have developed to resolve collective problems. The market failure concept is not inherently empirical and as such cannot provide answers to empirical questions.

The most important empirical question is this: What are the net benefits (if any) of any particular institutional arrangement? The only general statement that can be made about government intervention on Kaldor–Hicks efficiency grounds is that government should intervene where the costs of intervention are less than the benefits. No simple diagnostic scheme can indicate whether the costs of intervention will be less than the benefits for any general class of cases. Empirical analysis invites the analyst to consider the particular costs that govern each case.

* * *

For thinking about intervention decisions, the transaction cost concept provides analysts with insights into the relationship between government and the marketplace not otherwise apparent. It provides insights into the accumulation of institutional arrangements that exist in practice and it avoids the endless quest for "failures" either in the private or public sector that provide a basis for government intervention. The transaction cost concept is correct in principle, we believe, although not all of its facets have been worked out.

The transaction cost concept invites the analysis to answer a key question: What are the transaction costs that affect the search for collective solutions, and in each case how are those costs affected by government laws and actions?

The transaction cost approach does tend to restore law to a more central role in the study of government. The strengthening of private property rights often lowers transaction costs and thereby permits private parties to achieve collective solutions in situations where the costs of litigation and bargaining would otherwise be prohibitive. In such cases, government intervention through the strengthening of private property rights may improve the market. Such markets are inefficient not because of any inherent "failures," but because the government has neglected to provide the appropriate institutional framework.

* * *

Transaction cost analysis calls attention to the characteristics of government that give it an advantage relative to other institutions in its ability to lower transaction costs. There is one such advantage: the power of coercion. A classic definition of government is that of an institution that monopolizes the use of force or coercive powers over a given territory. The government may change laws and use force to compel compliance with them; it may force payment for goods through taxation and it may use police powers to forbid or compel actions. The most general statement about government intervention is that it should perform those functions for which its powers of coercion give it an absolute advantage. This is also a positive prediction about what government will do, since in failing to perform these functions government sacrifices both wealth and power. What are the important market failures to which its advocates refer? They are simply instances in which government action can lower transaction costs sufficiently to produce significant welfare gains.

* * *

Better empirical analysis, more attention to net benefits, and a deeper understanding of transaction costs would all help to improve the process of policy analysis. Continued reliance on the market failure concept will not.

* * *

———

NOTES AND QUESTIONS

1. Transaction cost economics, the theory of the firm, and the economic analysis of law. Recently, legal scholars have begun to abandon traditional price theory and take up transaction cost economics, or TCE, as a way of thinking about the economic analysis of law. One use to which TCE has been put, as the preceding excerpt suggests, is to provide a different way of thinking about the question of what mix of facilitative ("market") mechanisms and coercive ("government") mechanisms for the allocation of resources and production of goods will best further social welfare. Another use to which TCE has been put is in thinking about why corporate actors, or "firms," exist in markets, and what the possibilities and limitations of firms are vis-à-vis economic production and distribution. *See, e.g.*, Alan J. Meese, *Intrabrand Restraints and the Theory of the Firm*, 83 N.C. L. REV. 5 (2004) (using TCE to justify antitrust law); Reuven S. Avi–Yonah, *Corporations, Society, and the State: A Defense of the Corporate Tax*, 90 VA. L. REV. 1193 (2004) (using TCE to justify corporate taxation).

2. Beyond the market and the firm. Are there ways to organize economically productive activity outside markets and firms? What prospects does the "information economy" and technology such as the Internet offer to projects of democracy and economic justice? In the excerpt below, Yochai Benkler offers one perspective.

———

Freedom in the Commons: Towards a Political Economy of Information

52 DUKE L.J. 1245, 1250–58, 1259–61, 1262, 1265–66, 1267–69, 1272, 1273–74, 1276 (2003).

■ YOCHAI BENKLER

A. HOW WE GOT HERE

For over 150 years, new communications technologies have tended to concentrate and commercialize the production and exchange of information, while extending the geographic and social reach of information distribution networks. When large-volume mechanical presses and the telegraph were introduced, newspapers changed from small-circulation, local efforts, into mass media—intended to reach ever larger and more dispersed audiences. Of practical necessity, as the size of the audience and its geographic and social dispersion increased, public discourse adapted to an increasingly one-way model. Information and opinion flowed from ever more capital-intensive commercial and professional producers to consumers who, over time, became passive and undifferentiated. This model was easily adopted and amplified by radio, television, and later, cable and satellite communications.

The Internet presents the possibility of a radical reversal of this long trend. It is the first modern communications medium that expands its reach by decentralizing the distribution function. Much of the physical capital that embeds the intelligence in the network is diffused and owned by end users. Network routers and servers are not qualitatively different from the computers that end users use, unlike broadcast stations or cable systems that are vastly different from the televisions to which they transmit. What I hope to persuade you of today is that this basic change in the material conditions of information and cultural production and distribution can have quite substantial effects on how we perceive and pursue core values in modern liberal societies.

In the wake of the hype-economy of the late 1990s, it is all too easy to treat any such claim about an Internet "revolution" as a figment of an overstimulated imagination. The dazed economy makes it seem as though the major leap—if there ever was one—has already happened, and that "normal"—gradual, predictable, nondisruptive—technological progression has set in. But to think so would be a mistake. It would be a mistake not, primarily, in the domain of technological prognostication. It would be a mistake of paying too much attention to e-commerce and stock values, which are reflections of the utility of the new medium to old modes of production and exchange. What we need instead is a focus on the basic characteristics of the medium around which information and cultural production can now be organized, and on how this medium interacts with an economy that has advanced to the stage where information and cultural production form its core.

For the moment, I will suggest that we call the combination of these two trends—the radical decentralization of intelligence in our communications network and the centrality of information, knowledge, culture, and ideas to advanced economic activity—the *networked information economy*. By "networked information economy," I mean to describe an emerging *stage* of what in the past has been called more generally "the information economy" or "the information society." I would use the term in contradistinction to the earlier stage of the information economy, which one could call the "*industrial* information economy."

The "information economy," conjuring up the Big Five (accounting firms or recording companies, your choice), began as a response to the dramatic increase in the importance of usable information as a means of controlling our economy. James Beniger's study of what he called *The Control Revolution* showed how the dramatic increase in physical production and distribution capabilities in the nineteenth century created a series of crises of control over the material world—crises resolved through the introduction of more efficient modes of producing and using information to control physical processes and the human behavior that relates to them. Ranging from the introduction of telegraph to control the rolling stock of railroads, which, as Chandler has shown, made Western Union the first nationwide prototype for modern corporate organization, to the invention of double-entry bookkeeping, scientific management, and brand advertising, that economy was largely driven by a concern with control of material flows into, through, and out of the new, unmanageably productive factories. The "cultural" offshoots of that moment—Hollywood, the broadcast networks, and the recording industry—were also built around maintaining control over the use and transmission paths of their products. For the first time, music or performance could be captured in a thing, a thing that could be replicated millions of times, and which therefore had to be made to capture the attention and imagination of millions. This first stage might best be thought of as the "industrial information economy."

"The networked information economy" denotes a new stage of the information economy, to succeed this older industrial stage. It is a stage in which we can harness many more of the richly diverse paths and mechanisms for cultural transmission that were muted by the capital structure of communications, a capital structure that had led to the rise of the concentrated, controlled form, whether commercial or state-run. The most important aspect of this new stage is the possibility it opens for reversing the control focus of the information economy. In particular, it permits the reversal of two trends in cultural production, trends central to the project of control: concentration and commercialization. Although the claim that the Internet leads to some form or another of "decentralization" is not new, the fundamental role played in this transformation by the emergence of nonmarket, nonproprietary production and distribution is often overlooked, if not willfully ignored.

I imagine you sitting there, managing a bemused nod at my utopianism as you contemplate AOL Time Warner, or Microsoft's share in Comcast's purchase of AT&T Broadband. Decentralization and nonmarket production indeed! But bear with me. That the dinosaurs are growing bigger in response to ecological changes does not mean that, in the end, it will not be these warm-blooded furry things that will emerge as winners.

What, then, would make one think that sustaining productivity and growth are consistent with a shift towards decentralized and nonmarket-based modes of production? And how would these organizational characteristics affect the economic parameters within which practical political imagination and fulfillment must operate in the digitally networked environment?

Certain characteristics of information and culture lead us to understand them as "public goods" in the technical economic meaning of the term, rather than as pure "private goods" or standard "economic goods." Economists usually describe "information" as "nonrival." The analytic content of the term applies to all cultural forms, and it means that the marginal cost of producing information, knowledge, or culture is zero. Once a scientist has established a fact, or once Tolstoy has written *War and Peace*, neither the scientist nor Tolstoy need spend a single second on producing additional *War and Peace* manuscripts or studies for the one-hundredth, one-thousandth, or one-millionth user. Economists call such goods "public," because a market will never produce them if priced at their marginal cost—zero. Given that welfare economics claims that a market is producing a good efficiently only when it is pricing the good at its marginal cost, a good that can *never* be sold both at a positive price and at its marginal cost is fundamentally a candidate for substantial nonmarket production.

Information has another quirky characteristic in the framework of mainstream welfare economics—it is both the input and the output of its own production process. This has important implications that make property rights and market-based production even less appealing as the exclusive mechanisms for information and cultural production than they would have been if the sole quirky characteristic of information were the public goods problem. These characteristics form the standard economic justification for the substantial role of government funding, nonprofit research, and other nonproprietary production in our information production system, and have been understood as such at least since Nobel Laureate Kenneth Arrow identified them in this context four decades ago.

The standard problems that economics reveals with purely market-based production of information and culture have now been coupled with a drastic decline in the physical capital costs associated with production and distribution of this public good. As I mentioned, one primary input into information or cultural production is pre-existing information, which is itself a public good. The other inputs are human creativity and the physical capital necessary to generate, fix, and communicate transmissible units of information and culture—like a recording studio or a television network. Ubiquitously available cheap processors have radically reduced the necessary capital input costs. What can be done now with a desktop computer would once have required a professional studio. This leaves individual human beings closer to the economic center of our information production system than they have been for over a century and a half. And what places human beings at the center is not something that is homogeneous and largely fungible among people—like their physical capacity to work or the number of hours they can stay awake. Those fungible attributes of labor were at the center of the industrial model that Fredrick Taylor's scientific management and Henry Ford's assembly line typified. Their centrality to industrial production in the physical economy was an important basis for concentration and the organization of production in managed firms. In contrast, human beings are central in the networked information economy because of attributes in which they differ widely—creativity, wisdom, taste, social experience—as well as their effort and attention. And human beings use these personal attributes not only in markets, but also in nonmarket relations. From our homes to our communities, from our friendships to our play, we live life and exchange knowledge and ideas in many more diverse relations than those mediated by the market. In the physical economy, these relationships were largely relegated to spaces outside of our production system. The promise of the networked information economy and the digitally networked environment is to bring this rich diversity of living smack into the middle of our economy and our productive lives.

In the physical economy, we settled more or less on two modes of making production decisions. The first was the market. The second was corporate hierarchy. Markets best coordinated some economic activities, while managers were better at organizing others. The result was that most individuals lived their productive life as part of corporate organizations, with relatively limited control over how, what, or when they produced; and these organizations, in turn, interacted with each other largely through markets. We came to live much of the rest of our lives selecting from menus of goods, heavily advertised to us to try to fit our consumption habits to the decisions that managers had made about investment in product lines.

B. EXAMPLES OF CHANGE

What is emerging in the networked information economy is a wider scope for two very different phenomena. The first is a much-expanded role for nonmarket enterprises familiar to us from the real world—both professional, like National Public Radio, nonprofit academic research, philharmonic orchestras, or public libraries, and nonprofessional, like reading groups or fan clubs. The second phenomenon is radical decentralization, which can be seen at the simplest level in the information available on the World Wide Web from an amazing variety of individuals and networks of individuals. The most radically new and unfamiliar element in this category is *commons-based peer production* of information, knowledge, and culture, whose most visible instance has been free software. Here, digital networks seem to be permitting the emergence of radically new relationships between individuals and their information environment, and, more dramatically, radically new roles that individuals play in the production process.

The role of nonmarket enterprises in information and cultural production has always been great, though appreciation for its centrality has waned over the past two decades. Think, most obviously, of science and news. In science, perhaps more than in any other cultural form, the nonprofit academic enterprise, funded by government grants, philanthropy, and teaching, has been the center of basic science, while market-based research was at the periphery. In most fields, the best scientists make the most fundamental advances in academic settings. Firms then take this science, refine it, and then apply it. They do very valuable and important work, but the core of the scientific enterprise has been people who forgo monetary rewards and work instead for glory, immortality, or the pure pleasure of learning something new. If you think of news, the story is more mixed, with commercial providers like the *New York Times* or CNN playing a tremendously important role. Still, public professional producers—like NPR or PBS in the United States, or the BBC in the United Kingdom—play a crucial role, far beyond what we usually see in, for example, automobile or wheat production.

The difference that the digitally networked environment makes is its capacity to increase the efficacy, and therefore the importance, of many more, and more diverse, nonmarket producers. A Google search for "presidential debates," for example, shows CNN as the first commercial site to show up, but it is tenth on the list, while C-SPAN, a nonprofit funded by commercial cable providers shows up fifth. Both are preceded and surrounded by nonmarket organizations, like the Commission on Presidential Debates, a museum, an academic site, and a few political action sites. If you search for "democracy" in Google, PBS is the first media organization to show up, at ninth place, and no commercial entity shows up until a story in *The Atlantic* magazine some ninety-five links into the search. A number of the most highly ranked sites are nonprofit sites devoted to disseminating information about candidates. Consider for example what DemocracyNet, the League of Women Voters website, created for the city-council elections in Raleigh, North Carolina in 2001. What one sees as compared to, say, the local television news broadcasts—is a facility that allows individuals to post questions in writing to the candidates and that allows the candidates to respond directly. For example, we see each candidate's response to the question of whether or not there should be a living-wage ordinance. The site does not provide pages on pages of analysis—one might see a line or two, although some candidates may have written more in response to questions that are more central to their agenda. But you actually see the difference between the candidates on this particular question. It is worth going to the site and looking around. The point here is that because of the low capital costs, a nonprofit organization is capable of providing information down to the level of city council elections that is richer than anything we have gotten from the commercial broadcast media. There is, then, both an increase in the number of nonmarket producers and an increase in their effectiveness.

The networked information economy departs more dramatically from the industrial information economy in the possibilities it opens for radically decentralized collaborative production, a phenomenon I call "peer production." Peer production describes a process by which many individuals, whose actions are coordinated neither by managers nor by price signals in the market, contribute to a joint effort that effectively produces a unit of information or culture. Now this is not completely new. Science is built by many people contributing incrementally—not operating on market signals, not being handed their research marching orders by their dean—but independently deciding what to research, bringing their collaboration together, and creating science. The *Oxford English Dictionary* was created in roughly the same way in the nineteenth century—laboriously and over many years. But what we see in the networked information economy is a dramatic increase in the importance and the centrality of information produced in this way.

Free software has become the quintessential instance of peer production in the past few years. Over 85 percent of emails are routed using the sendmail software that was produced and updated in this way. Over the past six years the Apache web server software has risen from being nonexistent to capturing over 60 percent of the market in server software. Choosing the server software that runs one's site is not a situation in which a few hundred or a few thousand dollars will cause a company to adopt a particular application, but superior performance will, and it is in such a market that we see tremendous adoption of software produced by peer production. Similarly, Windows NT and Sun's Solaris are steadily losing ground to the GNU/Linux operating system, which is produced in this way and already runs on some 30 percent of servers connected to the Web.

While free software is the most visible instance of peer production, in fact, peer production is ubiquitous in the digitally networked environment. We see it happening all around. Think of the web itself. Go to Google, and plug in any search request. The particular collection of information you see did not exist before you actually ran the search, and now it exists on your search page. How was it produced? One nonprofit, another person who is a hobbyist, a third company that has as part of its business model to provide certain information for free—all sorts of individuals and groups, small and large, combine on your Google results page to provide you the information you wanted.

But we also see this phenomenon occur less diffusely as well. The Mars "clickworkers" project was an experiment run by NASA that allowed 85,000 people to collaborate on mapping Mars craters. People looked at images of Mars's surface online and mapped craters, and after six months, when NASA did an analysis comparing the results from the Internet to the mapping done by the trained Ph.D.s they had used previously, they described the outcomes as "practically indistinguishable." Massive multi-player online games, like EverQuest or Ultima Online, are another example. There, thousands or tens of thousands of people play a game whose effect is to tell a story together, instead of going to the movies and receiving the story as a finished good.

Or compare "Wikipedia" (www.wikipedia.com), an online encyclopedia produced by distributed contributors, to encyclopedia.com, produced by Columbia Encyclopedia. Look up the term "copyright" on encyclopedia.com and you see "right granted by statute to the author," etc., and there is a bit of analysis, and some discussion of the Berne Convention, for example, and so on. Now we go to Wikipedia, enter the same search term, and we see a similar copyright discussion. One might agree or disagree with it, as one might, as a professional, agree or disagree with any short encyclopedia definition. But it is there, it is plausible, it may even be better than the definition offered in encyclopedia.com, and it is collaboratively produced by about 2000 volunteers.

But how are we supposed to know whether any of this is any good? What creates relevance and accreditation? The Internet also provides instances of relevance and accreditation happening through distributed peer production. * * *

How do * * * decentralized relevance-and accreditation-production enterprises compare to market mechanisms for ascertaining relevance? Perhaps most interesting in this regard is the competition between Google and Overture. Google ranks search results based on counting "votes," as it were, that is, based on how many other websites point to a given site. The more people who think your site is sufficiently valuable to link to it, the higher you are ranked by Google's algorithm. Again, accreditation occurs on a widely distributed model, in this case produced as a byproduct of people building their own websites and linking to others. Overture is a website that has exactly the opposite approach. It ranks sites based on how much the site pays the search engine. So we have a little experiment, the market vs. distributed voting. How do these compare?

Here is what Google produces when we search for "Barbie": We see barbie.com, with "Activities and Games for Girls Online!", and we see barbiebazaar.com, with "Barbie, Barbie dolls, Barbie doll magazine, etc.," but then very quickly we start seeing sites like adiosbarbie.com, "A Body Image Site for Every Body." We see more Barbie collectibles, but then we see "Armed and Dangerous, Extra Abrasive: Hacking Barbie with the Barbie Liberation Organization." Further down we see "The Distorted Barbie," and all sorts of other sites trying to play with Barbie.

What happens when we run the same search on Overture, the search engine used by Go.com, which is the Internet portal produced by Disney? We get "Barbies, New and Preowned" at Internetdoll.com, BarbieTaker wholesale Barbie store, "Toys for All Ages" at Amazon.com, and so on. The Barbie Liberation Organization is nowhere to be found. Whether Overture is better than Google's list depends on whether you are shopping for Barbie dolls or interested in understanding Barbie as a cultural phenomenon, but it certainly is not normatively neutral, and it certainly offers a narrower range of information sources. Unsurprisingly, different things emerge when the market determines relevance than when people vote on what is most important to them. For those who find the choices of market actors a persuasive source of insight, it is at least interesting to note that AOL replaced Overture with Google as its search engine in 2002, and uses the Open Directory Project database for its directory.

C. THE IMPACT OF THE CHANGE

In all these communities of production, individuals band together, contributing small or large increments of their time and effort to produce things they care about. They do so for a wide range of reasons—from pleasure, through socially and psychologically rewarding experiences, to economic calculation aimed at receiving consulting contracts or similar monetary rewards. At this point, what is important to see is that these efforts mark the emergence of a new mode of production, one that was mostly unavailable to people in either the physical economy (barring barn raising and similar traditional collective efforts in tightly knit communities) or in the industrial information economy. In the physical world, capital costs and physical distance—with its attendant costs of communication and transportation—mean that most people cannot exercise much control over their productive capacities, at least to the extent that to be effective they must collaborate with others. The digitally networked environment enables more people to exercise a greater degree of control over their work and productive relationships. In doing so, they increase the productivity of our information and cultural production system beyond what an information production system based solely on the proprietary industrial model could produce.

* * *

So let me speak about the relationship between democracy, autonomy, and social justice and the choice between a more concentrated and commercial information and cultural production system and one that is more decentralized and includes more nonmarket production.

A.   Democracy

The industrial model of mass media communications that dominated the twentieth century suffers from two types of democratic deficits that could be alleviated by a greater role for commons-based production. The first deficit concerns effective political participation, the second deficit concerns cultural politics, or the question of who gets to decide the cultural meaning of social choices and conditions. Both deficits, and the potential role of emerging trends in information production in redressing them, are already present in the examples I gave of the emergence of nonmarket and radically decentralized production. DemocracyNet and Adios Barbie are the most obvious.

The primary thrust of the first deficit is the observation that in the mass-mediated environment only a tiny minority of players gets to participate in political public discourse and to affect decisionmaking directly. As Howard Jonas, chairman of a growing telecommunications company, incautiously described his ambitions, "Sure I want to be the biggest telecom company in the world, but it's just a commodity.... I want to be able to form opinion. By controlling the pipe, you can eventually get control of the content." The high cost of mass media communications translates into a high cost of a seat at the table of public political debate, a cost that renders individual participation all but impossible. The digitally networked environment makes it possible for many individuals and groups of similar beliefs to band together, express their views, organize, and gain much wider recognition than they could at a time when gaining recognition required acceptance by the editors of the mass media.

* * *

What radical decentralization of information production promises is the correction of some of the main maladies of the electronic mass media—the centralization of power to make meaning, the increased power of corporate interest in influencing the agenda, and the inescapable sound-bite character of the discussion.

The second democratic deficit of the mass-mediated communications environment concerns what some, like Niva Elkin Koren and William Fisher, have called "semiotic democracy," a term originally developed by John Fiske to describe the extent to which a medium permits its users to participate in structuring its message. In the mass media model, a small group of actors, focused on maintaining and shaping consumer demand, has tremendous sway over the definition of meaning in society—what symbols are used and what they signify. The democracy implicated by this aspect is not political participation in formal governance, but rather the extent to which a society's constituents participate in making sense of their society and their lives. In the mass media environment, meaning is made centrally.

Commercial mass media owners, and other professional makers of meaning who can buy time from them, largely define the terms with which we think about life and develop our values. Television sitcoms, Barbie dolls, and movies define the basic set of symbols with which most of us can work to understand our lives and our society. In the pervasively networked environment, to the contrary, meaning can be produced collaboratively, by anyone, for anyone. Again, as with public political discourse, this will result in a more complicated and variegated, perhaps less coherent, story about how we should live together as constituents of society. But it will be a picture that we made, not one largely made for us and given to us finished, prepackaged, and massively advertised as "way cool."

B.   AUTONOMY

Autonomy, or individual freedom, is the second value that I suggest can be substantially served by increasing the portion of our information environment that is a commons and by facilitating nonmarket production. Autonomy means many things to many people, and some of these conceptions are quite significantly opposed to others. Nonetheless, from an autonomy perspective the role of the individual in commons-based production is superior to property-based production almost regardless of the conception one has of that value.

First, the mass media model, and its core of an owned and controlled communications infrastructure, provides substantial opportunities for individuals to be manipulated by the owners of the media. That is, for any number of business reasons, media owners can decide to disclose or reveal information to their consumers, or change the efficacy with which certain information is available to certain users. When they do so, they can, if they choose to, shape the options that individuals know about.

* * *

Second, decentralization of information production and distribution has the capacity qualitatively to increase both the range and diversity of information individuals can access. In particular, the commercial mass media model has generally presented a relatively narrow range of options about how to live, and these options have been mostly variations on the mainstream. This is so largely because the economies of that model require large audiences to pay attention to anything distributed, constraining the content to that which would fit and attract large audiences. Decentralization of information production, and in particular expansion of the role of nonmarket production, makes information available from sources not similarly constrained by the necessity of capturing economies of scale. This will not necessarily increase the number of different ways people will actually live, but it will increase the number of different ways of living that each one knows about, and thereby enhance their capacity to choose knowledgeably.

A different type of effect of commons-based nonmarket production, in particular peer production, on autonomy is relevant only within a narrower set of conceptions of autonomy—those usually called "substantive." These are conceptions of autonomy that recognize that individuals are always significantly constrained—by genes, environment, and social and economic constraints—and consider the institutions of a society in terms of their effect on the relative role that individuals can play in planning and pursuing their own life plan. The networked information economy promises the possibility of an expansion of elements of autonomous choice into domains previously more regimented by the decisions of firm managers in the market. In particular, the shift can alter two central organizational constraints on how our lives are shaped—the organization of production and the organization of consumption. Much of our day-to-day time is occupied with, and much of our well being shaped by, production and consumption, work and play. In the twentieth century, the economics of mass production led to a fairly regimented workday for most people, at the end of which most people went into a fairly regimented pattern of consumption and play at the mall or in front of the television set. Autonomy in these domains was largely limited to consumer sovereignty—that is, the ability to select finished goods from a range of products available in usefully reachable distribution channels.

Peer production and otherwise decentralized nonmarket production can fundamentally alter the producer/consumer relationship with regard to culture, entertainment, and information. We are seeing the emergence of a new category of relationship to information production and exchange—that of "users." Users are individuals who are sometimes consumers, sometimes producers, and who are substantially more engaged participants, both in defining the terms of their productive activity and in defining what they consume and how they consume it. To the extent that people spend more of their production and consumption time in this ambiguous category of "user," they can have a greater autonomy in self-defining their productive activity, and in making their own consumption goods. The substantive capacity of individuals to control how their life goes—day to day, week to week—would increase to cover aspects of life previously unavailable for self-governance by individuals seeking to put together an autonomously conceived and lived life.

C.   Justice

Finally, as we think about the relationship between the structure of information and cultural production and liberal society, there is the question of how the transition to more commons-based production will affect social justice, or equality. Here in particular it is important to retain a cautious perspective as to how much can be changed by reorganizing our information production system. Raw poverty and social or racial stratification will not be substantially affected by these changes. Education will do much more than a laptop and a high speed Internet connection in every home, though these might contribute in some measure to avoiding increasing inequality in the advanced economies, where opportunities for both production and consumption may increasingly be known only to those connected.

For some individuals and societies, where access to capital, not education, is a primary barrier to development, however, there is some promise that a substantial commons in the information economy will provide valuable opportunities.

* * *

Building * * * a commons would * * * add a more competitive layer of goods and services from market-based sources, as well as nonmarket sources, thereby providing a wider range of information and cultural goods at lower cost. On the consumption side this has an unusual flavor as an argument within a social-democratic framework. Proposing a mechanism that will increase competition and decrease the role of government-granted and regulated monopolies is not exactly the traditional social-democratic way. But lower prices are a mechanism for increasing the welfare of those at the bottom of the economic ladder, and in particular, competition in the provision of a zero-marginal-cost good, to the extent it eventually drives the direct price of access and use to zero, will have this effect. More importantly, access to such resources, free of the usual capital constraints, will permit easier access to production opportunities for some in populations traditionally outside the core of the global economy—particularly in developing nations. Such access could provide, over the long term, somewhat greater equity in the distribution of wealth globally, as producers in peripheral economies take these opportunities to compete through a globally connected distribution medium, access to which is relatively unaided by wealth endowments.

D. THE BATTLE OVER THE INSTITUTIONAL ECOLOGY

* * *

What decentralized and nonmarket information production generally, and peer production in particular, need, is a space free of the laws developed to support market-and hierarchy-based production. In the late eighteenth and early nineteenth centuries, market-based production was replacing artisan and guild-based production, and law developed the framework that that transition needed—modern property and contract law. In the late nineteenth and early twentieth centuries, larger-scale production in corporate hierarchies was necessary to coordinate the complex production decisions that technology had made possible. Law developed to accommodate these properties by developing corporate law, antitrust law, labor law, securities laws, and later, consumer protection law. Some of the newer laws had to conflict with, and partly displace, contract and property law. One example is the power that corporate law gives managers to make decisions independent of the wishes of those traditionally seen as "the owners" of the corporation, its shareholders. Similarly, labor law and consumer protection law partially displaced contract law. National policy too was harnessed to advance railroad construction, electrification, and eventually the highway system that this new, larger-scale system of production and distribution of material goods required.

As we enter the twenty-first century, law and policy must once again develop to accommodate newly emerging modes of production. The primary need is to develop a *core common infrastructure*—a set of resources necessary to the production and exchange of information, which will be available as commons—unowned and free for all to use in pursuit of their productive enterprises, whether or not market-based. Building the core common infrastructure will require a combination of both legal and policy moves to develop a series of sustainable commons in the information environment, stretching from the very physical layer upon which it rests—the radio frequency spectrum—to its logical and content layers. The idea is not to replace the owned infrastructure, but rather to build alongside it an open alternative. Just as roads do not replace railroads or airport landing slots, the core common infrastructure will be open to be used by all, and biased in favor of none.

At the physical layer, we should focus on two primary policy objectives. The first is to permit the free utilization of radio frequencies, so as to develop a market in end-user-owned equipment that will create an ownerless network. The dramatic emergence of WiFi over the past year or so points in the general direction, but metaphorically, think of this option as one that replaces railroads—owned and managed infrastructure—with sidewalks, roads, and highways—infrastructure that is open for all who have the necessary equipment—a car, bike, or legs. The main difference is that the infrastructure in spectrum will be built by individual and private equipment owners, more like the Internet than like the public highway system, and will have an even more decentralized capital investment structure than the Internet because physical connectivity itself will be provided cooperatively, by individuals.

The second policy in the physical-layer objective is to begin to move towards public investment in open infrastructure, alongside the private infrastructure. A variety of municipalities, frustrated with the slow rate of broadband deployment, in particular in the last mile, have begun to work on deploying fiber to the home networks. Chicago CityNet is probably the most ambitious effort, in terms of scope, hoping to use the city's own purchasing power to drive investment in fiber, which would then be available on a nondiscriminatory basis for all to use.

    * * *

Conclusion

We are at a moment in our history at which the terms of freedom and justice are up for grabs. We have an opportunity to improve the way we govern ourselves—both as members of communities and as autonomous individuals. We have an opportunity to be more just at the very core of our economic system. The practical steps we must take to reshape the boundaries of the possible in political morality and to improve the pattern of liberal society will likely improve productivity and growth through greater innovation and creativity. Instead of seizing these opportunities, however, we are sleepwalking. We shuffle along, taking small steps in the wrong direction, guided by large political contributions, lobbyists, and well-financed legal arguments stretching laws written for a different time, policy arguments fashioned for a different economy. The stakes are too high, however, for us to take our cues from those who are well adapted to be winners in the economic system of the previous century. The patterns of press culture became settled for five hundred years within fifty years of Gutenberg's invention; radio had settled on the broadcast model within twenty-five years of Marconi's invention. Most of the major decisions that put the twentieth century broadcast culture in place were made in the span of six years between 1920 and 1926. The time to wake up and shape the pattern of freedom and justice in the new century is now.

———

NOTES AND QUESTIONS

1. **Institutional economics.** Another offshoot of Coase's work, related to transaction cost economics, has been the development of "institutional economics," also referred to as "new institutional economics" or NIE to distinguish it from the turn of the century movement inspired by Thorstein Veblen. The distinctive feature of institutional economics is its interest in the "rules of the game" that structure market behavior. As Alan Meese explains:

> [A]ll economic cooperation takes place against a backdrop of numerous "rules of the game" produced and enforced by the State. The law of contract empowers individuals and firms to make enforceable promises to each other, and such promises are the basis of cooperation. The law of property, including that of intellectual property, vests exclusive control of most resources in particular persons or entities and thus facilitates cooperative bargaining between potential users. Property law also facilitates the enforcement of bargains, by making self-help possible. (A franchisor can "terminate" a franchisee because trademark law allows the franchisor to exclude others from use of its trademark.) Finally, the law of tort facilitates bargains by, for instance, deterring fraudulent statements and thus ensuring that parties need not take wasteful precautions to verify a trading partner's representations.
>
> These "rules of the game" include more than just generally-applicable common law rules of contract, property, and tort. They also include statutory provisions and common law rules that facilitate the creation and operation of various types of business organizations such as partnerships, limited liability companies, and corporations. Each such business code, backed up by common law rules of agency and fiduciary duties, creates a distinctive series of presumptive or "default" rules that enable individuals to select and tailor that form of organization that best suits the particular enterprise they have chosen. Thus, when a firm acts, either alone or in concert, it does so because the State has recognized its authority to do so. When combined with other back-

ground "rules of the game," such rules (hopefully) minimize the cost of creating and running a business organization.

Taken together, these various rules—contract, property, tort, and the law of business entities—all create what economists call the "institutional framework." When they construct such frameworks, states recognize and facilitate the innumerable forms of cooperation that characterize the modern economy. As noted at the outset, some such cooperation takes place between firms, other cooperation occurs within them. By changing this framework, states can in turn alter the cost of entering and preserving relationships, thus affecting the allocation of resources and the nature and amount of social output. Indeed, what economists and others call a "private" market is in fact a social institution, constructed by innumerable background rules, created or enforced by the State.

Of course, cooperation between economic actors is not always a good thing. Society in general and consumers in particular should not rejoice if Ford and General Motors cooperate when setting prices or if Microsoft and Dell cooperate to exclude Netscape from its most efficient channel of distribution. As a result, an institutional framework that simply enforces all commercial contracts will not suffice to maximize social welfare. A society that wishes to reap the most possible gains from economic activity must therefore construct an institutional framework that minimizes the cost of beneficial cooperation while deterring that cooperation which injures society.

Alan J. Meese, *Intrabrand Restraints and the Theory of the Firm*, 83 N.C. L.Rev. 5, 11–14 (2004).

2. Peer production, freedom, and democracy. Benkler argues that the "networked information economy" makes possible important transformations in the American (and perhaps the global) political economy, including advances for democracy, autonomy, and social justice. Is his argument persuasive? What kinds of changes would be necessary to get there? Are those changes likely?

B. Beyond the "Rational Actor"

In addition to identifying the limits of price theory, contemporary economists and scholars of the economic analysis of law have begun to question another fundamental assumption of neoclassical market theory: the "rational actor." The literature on "social norms" evolved to explain the puzzle that people often engage in behavior that is from a neoclassical perspective "irrational": for example, people vote even though the likelihood of their vote making a difference is very small, and drivers stop at stoplights in the middle of the night even when their chances of being caught by the police are very low. Legal scholars became interested in social norms as an alternative to legal rules: Are legal rules really necessary in some situations? Can, and should, the state change "norms" to prevent unwanted behavior ex ante rather than simply punishing that behavior ex post? The social norms literature does not directly dispute the notion that people act rationally, but it makes accounts of the "inputs" spurring market behavior—"preferences"—more complex.

More recently, a literature in "behavioral economics" has emerged, drawing on cognitive psychology to suggest that economic behavior is influenced not only by social norms, but also by inherent quirks of human cognition. Legal scholars have put behavioral economics to use in a number of fields to explain why rules intended to cause certain kinds of behavior may fail to work properly, or may have unintended consequences.

Social Norms and Social Roles

96 COLUM. L. REV. 903, 904–14, 959–61, 967–68 (1996).

■ CASS R. SUNSTEIN

I. TALES OF RATIONALITY AND CHOICE

A. *Ultimatums and Fairness*

Economists have invented a game: the ultimatum game. The people who run the game give some money, on a provisional basis, to the first of two players. The first player is told to offer some part of the money to the second player. If the second player accepts that amount, he can keep what is offered, and the first player gets to keep the rest. But if the second player rejects the offer, neither player gets anything. Both players are informed that these are the rules. No bargaining is allowed. Using standard assumptions about rationality, self-interest, and choice, economists predict that the first player should offer a penny and the second player should accept.

This is not what happens. Offers usually average between 30% and 40% of the total. Offers of less than 20% are often rejected. Often there is a 50-50 division. These results cut across the level of the stakes and across diverse cultures.

B. *Littering*

Why do people litter? Why don't they throw things out instead? Social psychologist Robert Cialdini tried to find out. He placed flyers under the windshield wipers of cars and waited to see what drivers would do with them. Cialdini made arrangements so that before reaching their cars, some people would see someone (a Cialdini associate) walk past them, pick up from the street a bag from a fast-food restaurant, and throw it in the trash can. Of the group who both saw the responsible behavior and noticed the flyers, almost none threw them on the street. In the control experiment, with no one showing responsible behavior, over 1/3 of the drivers threw the flyers on the street.

C. Smoking, Rationality, and Race

About 400,000 Americans die each year from smoking-related causes. Government has tried to reduce smoking through educational campaigns designed to inform people of the risks. Indeed the government has now initiated a large-scale program to reduce smoking, especially among teenagers. Despite this fact, about one million Americans begin smoking each year, many of them teenagers, and people worry that educational campaigns will succeed, if at all, only with well-educated people.

But consider this. Nationally, 22.9% of white teenagers smoked in 1993, a number that basically has been unchanged in the last decade. But in the same year, only about 4.4% of African-American teenagers smoked, a number that is four times smaller than the number a decade before. What accounts for this difference? Part of the explanation appears to lie in differing understandings of what is fashionable. And part of that difference may lie in a private antismoking campaign in the African-American community, symbolized most dramatically by posters in Harlem subways showing a skeleton resembling the Marlboro man and lighting a cigarette for a black child. The caption reads: "They used to make us pick it. Now they want us to smoke it."

D. Recycling in the Hamptons

In East Hampton, New York—part of the famous and wealthy "Hamptons"—what used to be called the East Hampton Dump is now the East Hampton Recycling and Disposal Center. At the East Hampton Recycling and Disposal Center, there are separate bins for green glass, clear glass, newspapers, tin cans, paper other than newspaper, and more.

Almost every day in August (the most popular period in the Hamptons), residents can be found patiently separating their garbage for placement in the relevant bins. Sometimes this takes a long time. The people at the Center tend to own expensive cars—Mercedes Benzes, BMWs—that are parked near the bins. As they separate their garbage, they look happy.

E. John Jones

John Jones lives in California. Here is a description of some aspects of his behavior.

1. He buys smoke alarms and installs them in three rooms in his house.

2. He loves chocolate and ice cream, and eats a lot of both. He also eats a fair amount of frozen foods; he makes sure that they are "lean" whenever he has a choice. According to his doctor, he is slightly over his ideal weight.

3. On warm days, he likes to ride his bicycle to and from work, and he enjoys riding his bicycle on busy city streets, even though he has heard about a number of collisions there.

4.   He is happily married. He tries to share the work around the house, but he doesn't much like domestic labor. He does less than his share. He acknowledges that this is both true and unfair, and he supports many policies that are conventionally described as "feminist."

5.   He buckles his seat belt whenever he is in a car. His own car is a Volvo, and he bought it partly because it is said to be an especially safe car.

6.   He is not worried about the risk of an earthquake in California. On some days, he says that he doesn't think that an earthquake is very likely; on other days, he claims to be "fatalistic about earthquakes."

7.   He does not recycle. He considers recycling a personal "irritation." He is mildly embarrassed about this, but he has not changed his behavior.

8.   He considers himself an environmentalist; his votes reflect his enthusiasm for environmentalism. He supports aggressive regulation designed to encourage conservation and to protect people from risks to their life and health. In fact he is in favor of mandatory recycling, notwithstanding his own failure to recycle.

9.   In his own mind, his resources fall in various mental "compartments." Some money is reserved for retirement. Some money is saved for charitable donations. Some money is kept for vacation. Some money is for monthly bills. His forms of mental accounting are very diverse. He is fully aware of this.

Is Jones inconsistent or irrational? Is Jones risk-averse or risk-inclined? What is Jones's dollar valuation of a human life, or of his own life?

F.   The Point of this Article

My goal in this article is to challenge some widely held understandings of rationality, choice, and freedom, and to use that challenge to develop some conclusions about human behavior and the appropriate uses and domain of law. I particularly seek to understand and defend the place of law in "norm management."

I urge that behavior is pervasively a function of norms; that norms account for many apparent oddities or anomalies in human behavior; that changes in norms might be the best way to improve social well-being; and that government deserves to have, and in any case inevitably does have, a large role in norm management. As I will suggest, norm management is an important strategy for accomplishing the objectives of law, whatever those objectives may be. One of my goals is to show how this is so.

Part of my motivation is therefore practical. Consider the following table:

Deaths from Preventable Risks in the United States

Risk	Percent of Total Deaths	(Range)	Total Deaths /yr
Tobacco	19	14–19	400,000
Diet/activity	14	14–27	300,000
Alcohol	5	3–10	100,000
Microbial	4	—	90,000
Toxic agents	3	3–6	60,000
Firearms	2	—	35,000
Sexual behavior	1	—	30,000
Motor vehicles	1	—	25,000
Illicit drugs	<1	—	20,000

Existing social norms encourage much risk-taking behavior; and almost all of these risks of death could be much reduced with different norms. Consider smoking, diet/activity, alcohol, firearms, sexual behavior, motor vehicles, and illicit drugs as causes of death. In all these cases, new norms could save lives. A regulatory policy that targets social norms may well be the cheapest and most effective strategy available to a government seeking to discourage risky behavior. It may complement or work more efficiently than existing regulatory approaches.

Social norms are also part and parcel of systems of race and sex equality. If norms changed, existing inequalities would be greatly reduced. It is thus transparently important to see whether shifts in social norms, brought about through law, might operate to save lives and otherwise improve human well-being.

But part of my motivation is theoretical. It involves a conceptual puzzle. In the last decade there has been an intense debate about whether and to what extent law should try to change people's "preferences." But the term "preferences" is highly ambiguous, and it is not clear what the participants in this debate are actually disputing when they say that "preferences" should or should not be respected by law. I attempt to clarify possible meanings of the term. I also suggest that when the idea of a "preference" is unpacked, it becomes plain that the term is often too abstract and coarse-grained to be a reliable foundation for either normative or positive work. We will thus find reason to doubt the elaborate edifice of social science based on the notion of "preference." The ultimate task is to separate positive, descriptive, and normative inquiries more sharply and, in the process, to try to untangle different motivational states and their influences on choices.

More particularly, I aim to make a set of conceptual or descriptive points:

1. Existing social conditions are often more fragile than might be supposed, because they depend on social norms to which—and this is the key point—people may not have much allegiance. What I will call norm entrepreneurs—people interested in changing social norms—can exploit this fact. If successful, they produce what I will call norm bandwagons and

norm cascades. Norm bandwagons occur when small shifts lead to large ones, as people join the "bandwagon"; norm cascades occur when there are rapid shifts in norms. Successful law and policy try to take advantage of learning about norms and norm change.

2.   Sometimes people do not behave as economists predict. Many important and well-known anomalies in human behavior are best explained by reference to social norms and to the fact that people feel shame when they violate those norms. Thus when people deviate from economic predictions—when they appear not to maximize their "expected utility"—it is often because of norms.

3.   There is no simple contrast between "rationality" or "rational self-interest" and social norms. Individual rationality is a function of social norms. The costs and benefits of action, from the standpoint of individual agents, include the consequences of acting inconsistently with social norms. Many efforts to drive a wedge between rationality and social norms rest on obscure "state of nature" thinking, that is, on efforts to discern what people would like or prefer if social norms did not exist. Those efforts are doomed to failure.

4.   For many purposes, it would be best to dispense with the idea of "preferences," despite the pervasiveness of that idea in positive social science and in arguments about the appropriate domains of law and the state. In normative work, the idea of "preferences" elides morally important distinctions among the motivations and mental states of human agents. In positive work, the idea is too coarse-grained, in the sense that it disregards contextual factors that produce diverse choices in diverse settings. People's choices are a function of norms, which operate as "taxes" or "subsidies"; and the content of norms depends on the context. Instead of speaking of "preferences," we might assess choice in terms of (1) intrinsic value, (2) reputational effects, and (3) effects on self-conception.

I also aim to make two normative claims involving the appropriate domain of law. These claims have a great deal to do with law's expressive function, by which I mean the function of law in expressing social values with the particular goal of shifting social norms.

1.   There can be a serious obstacle to freedom in the fact that individual choices are a function of social norms, social meanings, and social roles, which individual agents may deplore, and over which individual agents have little or no control. Norms can tax or subsidize choice. Collective action—in the form of information campaigns, persuasion, economic incentives, or legal coercion—may be necessary to enable people to change norms that they do not like.

2.   Some norms are obstacles to human well-being and autonomy. It is appropriate for law to alter norms if they diminish well-being by, for example, encouraging people to shorten their lives by driving very fast, using firearms, or taking dangerous drugs. It is appropriate for law to alter norms if they diminish autonomy by, for example, discouraging people from becoming educated or exposed to diverse conceptions of the good.

G. An Insufficiently Charted Domain

Libertarians, some economic analysts of law, and many liberals give inadequate attention to the pervasive functions of social norms, social meanings, and social roles. Often it is said that in a free society, governments should respect both choices and preferences. But the case for respecting these things depends partly on their consequences and genesis, and as I have indicated, the determinants of choices (indeed the very meaning of the term "preference") remain obscure. We should agree that social norms play a part in determining choices; that people's choices are a function of their particular social role; and that the social or expressive meaning of acts is an ingredient in choice. Of course norms vary a great deal across cultures, and sometimes even within cultures. We should try to see when social norms, social roles, and social meanings are obstacles to human well-being, and whether something might be done to change them, even if people are making "choices," even if there is neither force nor fraud, and whether or not there is "harm to others."

One of my central points here is that individual agents have little control over social norms, social meanings, and social roles, even when they wish these to be very different from what they are. This is not an argument against norms, meanings, and roles. Human beings can live, and human liberty can exist, only within a system of norms, meanings, and roles; but in any particular form, these things can impose severe restrictions on well-being and autonomy.

As I have suggested, agents who seek to make changes in norms face a collective action problem. For example, it is impossible for an individual to alter norms determining whether the act of smoking seems daring, or the act of recycling seems exotic, or the act of opposing sexual harassment seems humorless. This is so even though the relevant norms greatly influence behavior. If, for example, smokers seem like pitiful dupes rather than exciting daredevils, the incidence of smoking will go down. If people who fail to recycle are seen as oddballs, more people will recycle. If the role of secretary is not associated with susceptibility to unwanted sexual attention, there will be less unwanted sexual attention. The point bears very much on current public disputes. If single parenthood is stigmatized, social practices will change accordingly; if homosexual marriages are consistent with social norms, social practices will be much altered. In all of these cases, individual actors need to act together in order to produce the relevant shifts.

More particularly, I hope to draw attention to the fact that people's conception of appropriate action and even of their "interest" is very much a function of the particular social role in which they find themselves. This is true of (for example) judges, lawyers, doctors, parents, children, waiters, wives, husbands, colleagues, friends, and law school deans. Attention to the place of social role shows that for many purposes, the contrast between "rationality" and social norms is unhelpful. What is rational for an agent is a function of, and mediated by, social roles and associated norms. And when social norms appear not to be present, it is only because they are so taken for granted that they seem invisible.

At the same time, norms and roles—operating as taxes on or subsidies to action—can create a division between the judgments and desires that are displayed publicly and the judgments and desires that would be displayed without current norms and roles. People's private judgments and desires diverge greatly from public appearances. For this reason current social states can be far more fragile than is generally thought—small shocks to publicly endorsed norms and roles decrease the cost of displaying deviant norms and rapidly bring about large-scale changes in publicly displayed judgments and desires. Hence societies experience norm bandwagons and norm cascades. Norm bandwagons occur when the lowered cost of expressing new norms encourages an ever-increasing number of people to reject previously popular norms, to a "tipping point" where it is adherence to the old norms that produces social disapproval. Norm cascades occur when societies experience rapid shifts toward new norms. Something of this kind happened with the attack on apartheid in South Africa, the fall of Communism, the election of Ronald Reagan, the use of the term "liberal" as one of opprobrium, the rise of the feminist movement, and the current assault on affirmative action.

To spell out the most general point emerging from the discussion: The notion of a "preference" can be deeply confusing, and in many of its uses, it impairs both positive and normative analysis of law. In its standard form, a preference is supposed to be something that lies behind choices and that is more abstract and general than choices are. But what lies behind choices is not a thing but an unruly amalgam of things—aspirations, tastes, physical states, responses to existing roles and norms, values, judgments, emotions, drives, beliefs, whims. The interaction of these forces will produce outcomes of a particular sort in accordance with the particular context. Hence we might say that preferences are constructed, rather than elicited, by social situations, in the sense that they are very much a function of the setting and the prevailing norms.

This point bears on the role of government, which cannot avoid affecting social norms. A market economy will, for example, have predictable effects on norms, and historically it has been justified on just this ground, as a way of softening social divisions by allowing people to interact with one another on a mutually beneficial basis. A good deal of governmental action is self-consciously designed to change norms, meanings, or roles, and in that way to increase the individual benefits or decrease the individual costs associated with certain acts. Thus government might try to inculcate or to remove shame, fear of which can be a powerful deterrent to behavior. The inculcation of shame operates as a kind of tax; the removal of shame might be seen as the elimination of a tax or even as a kind of subsidy.

There is a thin line between education and provision of information on the one hand and attempted norm-change on the other. In fact we will see that in the process of norm management, government has a number of tools. In a democratic society, it ought to be willing to use them.

* * *

John Jones, the protagonist of the fifth tale, is in one way quite usual: There is an evident and pervasive difference between people's choices as consumers and their choices as citizens. This is because people are choosing quite different things. In their private capacity, people may watch silly situation comedies; but they may also support, as citizens, the use of government resources to assist public broadcasting. Some people seek stringent laws protecting the environment or endangered species even though they do not use the public parks or derive material benefits from protection of endangered species—and even though in their private behavior, they are unwilling to do much to protect environmental amenities. The mere existence of certain environmental goods seems to be highly valued by political participants, even if they are not willing to back up the valuation with dollars in private markets. Of course many people give to organizations that support environmental protection. But what people favor as political participants can be different from what they favor as consumers. It is in part for this reason that democratic outcomes are distinct from those that emerge from markets.

In fact a good deal of empirical work shows that people's judgments about politics are not a product of their self-interest, narrowly understood. People without health care are not more likely to support laws creating a right to health care; people recently victimized by crime are not more likely to support aggressive policies against crime. Norms and values are instead the principal determinant of political judgment.

The disjunction between political and consumption choices presents a puzzle. Would it make sense to say that consumer behavior is a better or more realistic reflection of "actual" preferences than is political behavior? In light of the fact that choices depend on context, and do not exist in the abstract, the very notion of a "better reflection" of "actual" preferences is a confusing one; there is no such thing as an "actual" (in the sense of unitary or acontextual) preference in these settings. The difference might be explained by the fact that political behavior reflects judgments made for a collectivity. For this reason it reflects a variety of social norms that are distinctive to the context of politics.

Because of the governing norms, citizens may seek to implement individual and collective aspirations in political behavior but not in private consumption. As citizens, people may seek the aid of the law to bring about a social state that they consider to be higher than what emerges from market ordering. People may, in their capacity as political actors, attempt to promote altruistic or other-regarding goals, which diverge from the self-interested preferences sometimes characteristic of markets. Political decisions might also vindicate metapreferences or second-order preferences. People have wishes about their wishes, and sometimes they try to vindicate those second-order wishes, including considered judgments about what is best, through law. And norms with respect to public discussion may impose "taxes" on public statements of various sorts—perhaps requiring them to be "laundered," perhaps inducing conformity by punishing certain dissident views that might be reflected in other spheres.

In all of these ways, the norms at work in democratic arenas can produce different choices from those produced by markets. It would be wrong to say that the market choices are more "real" or "true." The question of which choices should govern for purposes of law and policy depends on a range of contextual issues that cannot be resolved by reference to notions of "choice" and "preference" alone. * * *

* * *

Many claims about the appropriate limits of law are insufficiently appreciative of the pervasive effects of social norms, social meanings, and social roles. In fact these effects have yet to receive much attention. But—to say the least—the impact of law on human behavior is an important matter for lawmakers to understand, and that impact has everything to do with social norms. An understanding of norms will therefore help illuminate effective regulatory policy. Many of the most dramatic gains in health and safety policy are a product of changes in norms, meanings, and roles. Many of the most severe problems in current societies are a product of unfortunate norms, meanings, and roles.

Norms relate to some broader issues as well. Often it is said that the common law, and a liberal regime dedicated to freedom, take "preferences" as they are and do not seek to change them. But the term "preferences" is highly ambiguous. If the term is meant to refer to "choices," it should be understood that choices are very much a function of context, including governing norms, meanings, and roles. Certainly the particular choices made by people in markets—in their capacity as consumers or laborers—do not suggest global or acontextual valuations of relevant goods. If the term "preferences" is meant to refer not to choices but to the motivational and mental states behind choices, it is important to recognize that those mental states include assessments of social norms, the expressive meaning of acts, and the expectations associated with a dazzling variety of social roles. Norms and roles affect both public action and public talk, in ways that can much disguise how people think privately. This point has large implications. In many settings, it would be best to dispense with the idea of "preferences," and to shift instead to more concrete ideas, including intrinsic value, reputational effects, and effects on self-conception.

We have also seen that norms can be far more fragile than they appear. Hence "norm entrepreneurs" can help solve collective action problems, and hence "norm bandwagons" and cascades are common. Sometimes law interacts with the efforts of norm entrepreneurs, facilitating or blunting their efforts, and sometimes law ratifies or accelerates—or halts—norm bandwagons and cascades.

While social life would be impossible without norms, meanings, and roles, individual people have little control over these things. The result can be severe limits on human well-being and autonomy. Certainly there is a problem with existing norms when all or almost all people would seek a change. There may well be a problem when reputational incentives lead people to do what they would otherwise refuse to do, at least if the relevant norms deny people the preconditions for autonomy or otherwise undermine well-being. In fact lives are shortened and unjustified inequalities are perpetuated by the existence of many current norms.

People need collective help if they want to change norms, meanings, or roles. Collective help may be futile or counterproductive; it may be illegitimately motivated. But these matters require an inquiry into the particular context. The issue should not be foreclosed by resort to confusing claims about the need to respect private choice.

Law and Behavioral Science: Removing the Rationality Assumption From Law and Economics

88 CAL. L. REV. 1051, 1053–56, 1057–58, 1060–75 (2000).

■ RUSSELL B. KOROBKIN & THOMAS S. ULEN

INTRODUCTION

The law-and-economics movement has suffered from the truthfulness of one of its most important postulates: the law of diminishing marginal returns. Although law and economics was once viewed as a revolutionary approach to legal scholarship that applied the principles of microeconomics price theory to the analysis of legal rules, the value of its new insights is gradually diminishing. The movement's vast initial successes were so sweeping that the current pliers of the trade have been forced to search for more narrow niches to fill. As a result, the discipline often seems to be devolving into a subdiscipline of applied economics that happens to focus substantively on legal matters. What began as a form of legal analysis that employed economics as a tool is now too often economic analysis that uses law as a target. Mathematical elegance often becomes the primary goal, with usefulness in the realm of law, that combines logic with human experience, a mere afterthought.

The seminal insight that economics provides to the analysis of law is that people respond to incentives—a generalized statement of price theory. From this insight, two important corollaries follow. First, the law can serve as a powerful tool to encourage socially desirable conduct and discourage undesirable conduct. In the hands of skillful policymakers, the law can be used to subsidize some behaviors and to tax others. Second, the law has efficiency consequences as well as distributive consequences. Intentionally or unintentionally, legal rules can encourage or discourage the production of social resources and the efficient allocation of those resources. Although efficiency need not be the sole or primary goal of legal policy, economic analysis of law teaches that policymakers ignore the efficiency implications of their actions at society's peril. Legal rights that are unobjectionable in the abstract are not free but rather must be measured against their opportunity costs.

Law and economics is, at root, a behavioral theory, and therein lies its true power. The concern of law and economics with how actors in and subject to the legal system respond to legal directives (and would respond to hypothesized changes in those directives) now permeates the mainstream of legal academic thought, far beyond the boundaries of scholarship that is self-consciously part of the law-and-economics tradition. This concern was by no means "invented" by the law-and-economics movement but certainly universalized by it. Indeed, it is so widely acknowledged and accepted that it hardly bears mentioning in the modern legal academy that law does not exist in a vacuum; rather, it has real effects on private behavior, and those effects should be considered and accounted for when examining alternative legal regimes.

To speak coherently of the legal implications of viewing law as a series of incentives, analysts have to make assumptions about the consequences of those incentives to the people subject to the legal system. To satisfy this need, early law-and-economics scholars imported from economics a series of assumptions about how people respond to incentives, known generally as "rational choice theory." There is considerable debate within both the economics and law-and-economics communities about precisely what rational choice theory is and is not. As it is applied implicitly or explicitly in the law-and-economics literature, however, it is understood alternatively as a relatively weak, or "thin," presumption that individuals act to maximize their expected utility, however they define this, or as a relatively strong, or "thick," presumption that individuals act to maximize their self-interest.

Rational choice theory provided what was, no doubt, the best series of assumptions upon which to begin to develop the application of price theory to legal rules. The use of rational choice theory enabled the law-and-economics movement, in its early days, to achieve significant advances in understanding the interaction between legal rules and society. But now that the movement has reached intellectual maturity, the rationality assumption severely limits its continued scholarly development. There is simply too much credible experimental evidence that individuals frequently act in ways that are incompatible with the assumptions of rational choice theory. It follows that the analysis of the incentive effects of legal rules based on such implausible behavioral assumptions cannot possibly result in efficacious legal policy, at least not in all circumstances.

* * *

In response to these trends, a new movement is emerging in the legal academy that builds on the core insights of law-and-economics scholarship but takes seriously the shortcomings of rational choice theory. This movement, which we call "law and behavioral science," lacks a single, coherent theory of behavior. Although such a general theory may someday develop and would be welcome, the movement's current lack of concern about this shortcoming identifies law and behavioral science as a species of legal pragmatism. As we argue in this Article, one can analyze the appropriate legal command in any given circumstance without a grand, overarching theory of behavior so long as one has a due regard for the relevant decision-making capabilities of the actors in that specific setting. By borrowing from psychological and sociocultural theories in addition to economics, the law-and-behavioral-science approach consciously chooses to emphasize its external usefulness in analyzing legal problems rather than either its internal elegance or universal applicability. Its ultimate goal, quite simply, is to understand the incentive effects of law better than modern law and economics is able to do by enlisting more sophisticated understandings of both the ends of those governed by law and the means by which they attempt to achieve their ends.

* * *

I. The Uses and Shortcomings of Rational Choice Theory

Rational choice theory is the heart of modern microeconomic theory. It is such a powerful, straightforward, compelling, and useful construct that scholars in a wide range of disciplines contiguous to economics, such as political science, history, international relations, sociology, finance and accountancy, and, of course, law, have adopted rational choice theory as their central account of human decision making. Unfortunately for the purposes of precise analysis, there is no single, widely accepted definition of rational choice theory. Although the use of the assumption that actors behave rationally is pervasive among law-and-economics scholars, the assumption is most often implicit. As a result, there is rarely a discussion in the legal literature about what, exactly, constitutes rational behavior. In actuality, there are probably nearly as many different conceptions of rational choice theory as there are scholars who implicitly employ it in their work.

The variety of conceptions of rational choice theory makes critiquing the theory something akin to shooting at a moving target. We will simplify the task somewhat by positing that versions of the theory can be aligned along a spectrum and then addressing four specific points along the spectrum representing the most common conceptions of the theory, as it is employed in legal scholarship.

A. Conceptions of Rational Choice Theory

The different conceptions of rational choice theory can be understood as points along a continuum of how specific and precise the predictions of the theory are. On the left side of the spectrum are "thin" conceptions of rational choice theory—that is, conceptions in which the theory is relatively undemanding and in which it is relatively easy for the behavior of actors to be consistent with the theory. On the right side of the spectrum are "thick" conceptions of the theory—that is, conceptions with more robust behavioral predictions that are more easily falsifiable by empirical evidence. Figure 1 illustrates the construct, with the dominant conceptions of the theory in bold:

RATIONAL CHOICE THEORY SPECTRUM

"Thin" Conceptions --------------------------------------- "Thick" Conceptions

| Definitional Version | Expected Utility Version | Self–Interest Version | Wealth Maximizing Version |

1. The Definitional Version

In its thinnest version, rational choice theory is definitional in nature. This conception postulates only that, as Richard Posner has written, "man is a rational maximizer of his ends," without providing any predictions regarding what ends an individual might attempt to maximize or what means he might employ in such an effort. On this account, rationality is understood as suiting means to ends, but no normative theory of either means or ends is assumed.

One can conceive of a situation in which the prediction of this thin theory (that economic decision makers choose means well suited to achieving their ends) would not hold—namely, when an individual chooses an action contrary to his goals. But in practice the definitional version of rational choice theory is nonfalsifiable, because both the means and the ends of behavior are defined by observing the behavior itself. Put another way, rational behavior is understood as "the way people act." Because we assume a priori that people "rationally maximize their ends" (or their "utility"), we characterize as rational any behavior that we see and any behavior that can be justified as "rational" merely by noting its existence. Even behavior that seems anomalous, such as clucking like a chicken whenever a bell sounds, is presumed to be well suited to achieving the ends of the clucker.

On this thin understanding, everything confirms the rationality of behavior, and nothing refutes it. As Arthur Leff noted in an early critique of the law-and-economics movement, this use of rational choice theory substitutes a definition for a normative or empirical proposition.

2. The Expected Utility Version

The next conception of rational choice theory, and the one most dominant in modern microeconomics, is often termed "expected utility theory." This conception, like the definitional version, is "thin" in the sense that it does not specify what preferences or goals decision makers will pursue. As before, the particular preferences or tastes contained in the actors' utility functions are exogenous, that is, given from outside the maximization problem. The expected utility version is, however, "thicker" than the definitional version because it does specify the means (or at least some of the means) by which actors will seek to satisfy their goals and preferences.

The assumption that economic decision making can be shown to be the result of the maximization of expected utility, subject to constraints, is a thicker model of human behavior in that it posits a more formal model of individual decision making than does the version of rational choice theory considered in the previous Section. Consider expected utility theory's account of decision making under uncertainty. Suppose that an individual must choose between a certain and an uncertain course of action—for example, between a certain return on an investment and an uncertain return on a more speculative investment. Suppose, further, that outcome O^1 occurs with certainty but that outcomes $O^2, \ldots, O^n$ are probabilistic: only one of them will eventuate, but they are all possible. How would the rational choice theorist predict that the actor will decide which investment to choose? The actor will presumably attach a utility to each possible outcome—$U(O^1)$, $U(O^2)$, and so forth, along with a probability of each outcome's occurring—p^1, p^2, and so on. Calculating the value of the certain course of action is straightforward. Because O^1 is certain to occur, $p^1 = 1$, so that the expected utility to the actor of O^1 equals $U(O^1)$. The uncertain investment presents more of a challenge to evaluate because the uncertain outcomes are mutually exclusive, $p^2 \ldots p^n = 1$. The decision maker can reduce the multiple possibilities to a single expected utility by solving:

$$EU(uncertain\ action) = p^2 U(O^2) \ldots p^n U(O^n).$$

The rational consumer then compares the expected utility of the certain course of action with the expected utility of the uncertain course of action, and selects the one with the higher value.

Stripped of its mathematical adornments, the basic requirement of expected utility theory is that decision makers conduct an explicit or implicit cost-benefit analysis of competing options and select the optimal method of achieving their goals (that is, the method that maximizes expected benefits and minimizes expected costs, or maximizes net expected benefits), subject to external constraints.

If an actor makes a decision that does not maximize net expected benefits to him, then he violates the behavioral predictions of the expected utility version of rational choice theory. But because it is impossible to know what choices are optimal for a particular decision maker without knowing the contours of his utility function, and because utility functions are difficult to elicit, the behavioral predictions of expected utility theory often are not directly verifiable or falsifiable. Fortunately, there are some necessary (but not sufficient) conditions of rational behavior under the expected utility model that analysts can observe. These are usually understood to include the following:

(1) *Commensurability*: actors should be able to compare the utility consequences of all alternatives to each other;

(2) *Transitivity*: if an actor prefers choice A to choice B and choice B to choice C, he should then prefer choice A to choice C;

(3) *Invariance*: the preference between two or more choices should not depend on how the choice is presented or structured, so long as the outcome possibilities are constant;

(4) *Cancellation*: a choice between options should not depend on features of the options that are identical; and

(5) *Dominance*: an actor should never choose an option in which every feature is only as good as the features of a competing option, and at least one feature is not as good.

If an actor fails to follow one or more of these principles, he cannot be making decisions consistent with the expected utility model. Consequently, the predictions of the model are testable, at least at some minimum level.

3. The Self–Interest Version

Still thicker versions of rational choice theory start from expected utility theory's predictions about the manner in which actors will attempt to achieve their utility, and add predictions about the actors' goals and preferences—that is, about the content of the actor's utility function. Perhaps the most common assumption about ends, that actors will seek to maximize what is in their self-interest, can be traced to Adam Smith's famous statement:

> It is not from the benevolence of the butcher, the brewer, or the baker that we expect our dinner, but from their regard to their own interest. We address ourselves, not to their humanity but to their self-love, and never talk to them of our necessities but of their advantages.

The implication is that if we can figure out what course of action will most profit the decision maker, we will be able to predict his course of action. This is an advance over the thin conceptions of rational choice in that it suggests falsifiable predictions about substantive behaviors, not just predictions about decision-making procedures.

Such thick versions of rational choice theory dominate the law-and-economics literature, although the assumption is almost always implicit rather than explicit. Consider, for example, the simple prediction that if there is no punishment for littering, people will litter (the cost to an individual of disposing of his litter in a lawful manner exceeds the cost to him of observing his individual litter on the ground). This prediction implicitly relies on the assumption that individuals are concerned with punishments they might receive, the disutility that they will suffer from looking at their own litter, and the time and energy it takes to dispose of litter, but not with the disutility others will suffer from looking at their litter. Or consider the prediction that if punitive damages were to be abolished or capped, more defective products would be produced. This prediction relies on the assumption that product manufacturers are concerned with their own bottom line, and are concerned with the health and safety of their customers only to the extent that those issues demonstrably affect that bottom line. Unlike the thin versions of rational choice theory, the self-interested version can lead to the creation of directly falsifiable behavioral predictions.

Suspecting an ambush, defenders of rational choice theory might at this point observe that it is plausible to hypothesize that a decision maker's "self-interest" might be served by taking account of the well-being of others, not just his or her own wants and desires. Unfortunately, expanding the conception of "self-interest" to include other-regarding preferences in addition to selfish ones would rob the notion of "self-interest" of all of its predictive value. We would no longer be able to predict that people would litter if doing so risks no punishment, or that products would be more dangerous without products liability law, because people walking in the park may or may not gain utility from keeping the park tidy for their neighbors, and manufacturers may or may not gain utility from preventing harm to their customers. Adam Smith's prediction would have to be rewritten to read:

> It is from *either* the benevolence of the butcher, the brewer, or the baker that we expect our dinner, *or* from their regard to their own interest. We address ourselves, to their humanity *and/or* their self-love, and talk to them of our necessities *and/or* of their advantages.

The point is not that we believe actors seek to fulfill only selfish preferences—in fact, we argue quite the opposite below. But if "self-interest" is defined to include anything that produces satisfaction for the decision maker, then the self-interest version of rational choice theory is no different from the thin expected utility version.

4.   The Wealth Maximization Version

The thickest conceptions of rational choice theory provide even more specific predictions about the ends of decision makers than does the self-interest version. The most common of these very thick conceptions is "wealth maximization": the prediction that actors will attempt to maximize their financial well-being or monetary situation. Nearly all law-and-economics literature on business organizations, following the neoclassical economic theory of firms, is built on the explicit or implicit assumption that firms seek to maximize profits. And much law-and-economics literature on individual behavior makes an analogous assumption (usually implicitly), at least in circumstances in which money is at stake.

B.   *Limitations of Rational Choice Theory in Legal Analysis*

None of the conceptions of rational choice theory discussed above is optimal for the purpose of understanding how actors will respond to the incentives that the law creates. The deficiencies of the different conceptions arise from one or both of two shortcomings: their inadequacy in predicting future behavior and the implausibility of their predictions. * * *

1.   The Inadequacy of Thin Versions of Rational Choice Theory

Thin conceptions of rational choice theory can serve as a useful tool for social scientists attempting to explain, classify, or label human behavior from an ex post perspective. By positing that actors will seek to maximize their utility, scholars can observe behavior and then reason backwards to an understanding of preferences (ends) and strategies (means). Thin versions of rational choice theory thus can be viewed as useful for recognizing that people usually act the way they do for a reason and, consequently, that observable actions provide clues for understanding these unobservable "reasons." However, these advantages are of little use to the makers of legal policy, who need to choose among competing legal rules. Policymakers need to predict future behavior under various legal scenarios, not merely understand past actions in hindsight.

The inadequacy of rational choice theory is most obvious in its thinnest, definitional version, which offers no behavioral predictions at all. Consider, as an example, the parable of Buridan's ass, who faced a choice between two equidistant haystacks as a source of nourishment. The definitional version of rational choice theory could offer no prediction as to which haystack the ass would choose, or whether he would choose neither. Because this version of the theory interprets all acts as rational, it would conclude, *ex post*, that it was rational for the ass to stand still and die of starvation. Because he believed this version of rational choice theory to be the behavioral premise underlying the law-and-economics movement, Leff disparagingly referred to law and economics as "American legal nominalism."

The expected utility version of rational choice theory, although it rises above mere tautology, is scarcely more adequate for generating behavioral predictions *ex ante*. In virtually any imaginable situation of importance to legal policy, expected utility theory alone yields indeterminate predictions; not only does the theory fail to yield a single, unique behavioral prediction (the result that would be of most use to a policymaker), but it also fails to eliminate many conceivable possible actions. This version of rational choice theory, like the definitional version, is helpless in predicting the action of Buridan's ass, because it provides no theory or account of the content of the ass's utility function. If we knew, for example, that survival was the ass's sole preference, then expected utility theory would lead to the prediction that the ass would choose one of the two haystacks. On the other hand, if we knew that the ass placed a higher value on avoiding difficult decisions than on remaining alive, expected utility theory would predict that the ass would stand still and perish. But without some theory about the content of the ass's preferences, either standing still or choosing a haystack could be rational. Expected utility theory can yield only the prediction that the ass will not violate one of the observable necessary conditions of expected utility theory. For example, it would lead to a prediction that the ass will not announce that he cannot compare the value of choosing a haystack with the value of standing still and dying, because to do so would violate the principle of commensurability.

To use an example of direct relevance to legal policy, consider the following question: if society wishes to reduce crime, assuming all other policy decisions are held constant, should it increase or decrease the length of prison sentences? Note that, although the former appears to be the obvious answer, it is only correct if we assume that most people prefer to live outside of prison than to be incarcerated. But recall that thin versions of rational choice theory cannot aid us in creating this assumption. Virtually no predictions can be made about decisions or behaviors without thickening the conception of rational choice theory to include some predictions about the content of preferences.

2. The Implausibility of Thin and Thick Versions

Thin conceptions of rational choice theory, such as expected utility theory, are not only inadequately specified to be valuable to policymakers concerned with the incentive effects of law, but the behavioral predictions that they do make are also implausible as predictions of general applicability: that is, they have been demonstrated, as an empirical matter, to be substantially incorrect, at least under some conditions.

Thick conceptions of rational choice theory substantially avoid the inadequacy problem. They can be used to generate predictions about how actors will respond to alternative legal regimes and, thus, can serve as a useful tool for policymakers. A thick conception of rational choice theory, for example, could enable us to predict that Buridan's ass would value life sufficiently that it would be utility-maximizing to choose one of the haystacks, even if that meant suffering the pain of making a difficult choice. Thick conceptions, however, trade the inadequacy problem of thin conceptions for even more pronounced implausibility problems than those that plague thin conceptions. The predictions that they make about the preferences of actors (in addition to predictions about the means actors will use to satisfy their preferences) are demonstrably incorrect, at least in many circumstances. Buridan's ass, of course, did not choose either of the haystacks, thus falsifying the prediction that would be produced by any thick conception of rational choice theory.

Thin and thick conceptions of rational choice theory share two types of implausibility problems. First, actors often fail to maximize their expected utility, but instead make suboptimal choices among competing options given a set of preferences and use a range of heuristics—rules of thumb rather than complex cost-benefit analysis. This "bounded rationality" results from the high cost of processing information, the cognitive limitations of human beings, or a combination of the two. * * *

Second, while all but the thinnest versions of rational choice theory assume that decision makers conduct a cost-benefit analysis that is invariant to factors external to their choice, context is quite important to behavior. How individuals will respond to legal rules depends on what reference points individuals recognize when making decisions. Decisions and behaviors are often affected by such factors as how an actor perceives choices relative to the status quo, whether choices are consistent or inconsistent with an actor's habits or traditions, and the temporal distance of the rule's effects. * * *

Thick versions of rational choice theory face yet an additional implausibility problem. There is substantial evidence that decision makers often behave in ways that are inconsistent with their direct self-interest. Individuals form preferences not merely according to their subjective conceptions of well-being, but also in accordance with norms that are often socially constructed and sometimes evolutionarily adaptive. Some preferences well established in the behavioral sciences, such as a commitment to notions of fairness or social justice even at a cost to the self, might be ingrained by social or genetic forces, or by both. * * *

C. The Responses of Rational Choice Theory to Criticisms

Defenders of rational choice theory, when confronted with the sorts of criticisms that we have voiced, generally respond in one of three ways, none of which is satisfying.

The first defense is an evolutionary account of decision making, which asserts that actors who fail to make rational decisions cannot survive in a competitive world. In the competition for resources, utility maximizing behavior will drive out nonmaximizing behavior. The argument is most compelling in the context of business enterprises. Organizations will seek to maximize profits, and those that fail to do so will be put out of business by a lack of customers, capital, or both. Even when complexity or ambiguity would appear to make optimization impossible or unduly costly, those that manage to optimize, even by chance, will survive, and their strategies will be emulated by competitors.

We find this account unconvincing as it pertains to individuals. With rare exception, individuals who fail to maximize their utility are not "driven out of the market." They might (although not necessarily) enjoy less happiness than their more rational counterparts, but they will live to make decisions another day.

Even with regard to business enterprises, for which the evolutionary force of economic rationality might be most forceful, the account is unlikely to be true in most circumstances. Certainly, firms that make clearly suboptimal decisions routinely or in extremely important circumstances may be driven out of business, but competition in product or capital markets is rarely so perfect that a firm that occasionally makes decisions that fail to maximize profits will face bankruptcy or be taken over by firms that do maximize. In any event, if it were true that competition drives imperfectly rational behavior out of business markets, such results would not occur instantaneously, and at any given moment in time a substantial number of participants in markets would likely be imperfectly rational actors who have not yet learned their lessons.

A weaker version of this defense concedes that many individual and even some firm mistakes are not fatal, but stresses that actors learn from experience and correct failures of rationality. This argument doubtlessly has validity, in the sense that there are circumstances in which correctives are possible within the rational choice theory. But we do not think that this point merits the weight that defenders place on it. First, many * * * behaviors * * * are persistent, even when experimenters bring them to the attention of their subjects. Second, learning from experience is a long-term strategy, and there will always be a substantial number of imperfectly rational actors who have not yet learned their lessons.

The second argument offered by defenders of rational choice theory when confronted with criticism is that rational choice theory, while not perfect, is the best single available behavioral theory. The theory's defenders contend that, even if the criticisms are accurate, they do not amount to a coherent theory of decision making that does a better job of predicting a wide range of human behavior than does rational choice theory. As we shall see, imperfectly rational actors undoubtedly utilize many different decision-making strategies, no single one of which provides a general behavioral description more realistic than rational choice theory. In a commonly heard phrase around the academy, "It takes a theory to beat a theory," and these criticisms, even if correct, do not amount to a theory.

This rejoinder to the criticisms is sound, as far as it goes, but not particularly relevant to the project of developing a more nuanced understanding of behavior for use by legal policymakers. Rational choice theory is descriptively and prescriptively accurate more often than any other single theory of behavior, or so even its critics generally believe. But the elegance and parsimony that a single, universal theory of behavior such as rational choice can provide is of far less importance, if it is of any importance at all, to legal policymakers than to economists. The reason is that most laws are geared toward specific portions of the populations or to people who play specific roles.

To be useful for legal policy, behavioral theories need to predict (with reasonable success) the likely responses to legal rules of the particular classes of actors to whom the rules are geared, whether or not the responses of other classes of actors would likely be identical. For instance, if policymakers are considering revising products liability law, they need a prediction of how product manufacturers, on one hand, and product consumers, on the other, will likely respond to competing proposals. The predicted responses of these two groups need not be identical, nor need they be the same as they would be for other groups operating in different contexts. Of course, it is possible that the predicted responses of the consumers of heavy machinery to a given phenomenon would be different from the predicted responses of consumers of toasters to that same phenomenon. If this is in fact the case, rather than default to a reliance on rational choice theory, policymakers should consider whether it would be efficacious for the law to approach products liability for industrial goods, which have a more limited, sophisticated market, differently than for mass consumer goods.

There is no doubt that a single, universally applicable theory of behavior is convenient and highly desirable. But if universality is inconsistent with sophistication and realism, legal policymakers are better off foregoing universality and, instead, creating a collection of situation-specific minitheories useful in the analysis of discrete legal problems. Moreover, there is a great deal to be said for an incremental approach to theorybuilding—that is, grafting on just enough theory to deal with the matter at hand rather than attempting to construct a universal theory. * * *

The third defense is to respond to evidence of a purported failing of rational choice theory by explaining how the anomaly in question could possibly be consistent with the theory if viewed from a different angle. This strategy avoids the problem of directly refuting or proving rational choice theory wrong, but in doing so the defender implicitly retreats to a conception of rational choice theory that is so thin that it can have no predictive value.

Consider, as an example, the contention that rational individuals will not pay attention to sunk costs when choosing between options because such costs cannot affect the marginal utility to be derived from future activities. This leads to the prediction that an individual who has bought an expensive ticket to the symphony will be no more likely to attend than an individual who has been given a free ticket, assuming the two have an equal appreciation for classical music and that all other things are also equal. There is ample evidence that many people would in fact be more likely to attend the performance if they have paid for the ticket, reasoning that "the money would be wasted if I don't go."

A clever proponent of rational choice theory might respond to this apparent violation of the theory by asserting that rational people are fully aware of the fact that they may be reluctant later to attend a particular concert, and, knowing that they will both enjoy the concert if they attend and that they will feel guilty if they allow an expensive ticket to go unused, they purchase a ticket in advance as a precommitment strategy to ensure their attendance. In other words, pre-purchase is used as a means to control one's tendency not to do things that may appear to be painful but are really desirable in the long run.

Responses like this provide a useful way to understand behavior ex post (although the ex post account might well be inaccurate), but they also demonstrate the problem with relying on rational choice theory to inform future-oriented policymaking. The response makes it impossible to use rational choice theory to predict whether a person will be more likely to attend the symphony if he has purchased a ticket in advance (and has, therefore, "sunk" money into a symphony ticket) than if he were given the ticket for free. This defense of rational choice theory, in fact, demonstrates our basic contention that the theory can provide a plausible description of behavior only when the theory is adopted in such a thin form that it has little prescriptive value.

D. Modifying the Behavioral Predictions of Rational Choice Theory

To claim that rational choice theory is an insufficient behavioral model on which to base legal policy is not to argue that individuals behave irrationally (although they certainly do in some circumstances). Rather, it is to assert that legal scholars seeking to understand the incentive effects of law in order to propose efficacious legal policy should not be limited to rational choice theory. The goal of the law-and-behavioral-science movement is not, at least at this stage, to replace rational choice theory with an inconsistent paradigm but to modify the implausible elements of rational choice theory and supplement the inadequate elements in order to create a tool with more predictive power in specific situations.

* * *

———

NOTES AND QUESTIONS

1.   Bounded rationality: data. Theorists of bounded rationality have identified a host of cognitive quirks of human beings that, Korobkin and Ulen argue, undermine the concept of the neoclassical "rational actor." These include the following:

(1) Complex decisions and "satisficing." Traditional economic theory would suggest that the more information that should be provided to people, the better they will be able to satisfy their preferences. But in fact people have limited abilities to process information and limited time in which to do so. Thus, when faced with very complex consumer decisions (Which cell phone plan should I adopt? Which health care insurance plan should I adopt?), people adopt decision-making shortcuts, and they look for a "good enough" outcome, rather than the "optimal" outcome.

(2) People tend systematically to make mistakes about probabilities relating to representativeness and risk. People assume that memorable events are more common than they are. For example, most people believe that homicides and car accidents kill more Americans than diabetes and stomach cancer, presumably because of the greater media coverage provided to the former two, although the two diseases kill far more people.

(3) People tend to interpret the world in self-serving ways. That is, even if they intellectually recognize the probabilities of certain events, they predict that good things will disproportionately happen to them and bad things will disproportionately happen to other people. For example, newlyweds are likely to represent the odds of their divorce as zero or close to zero, even though it is common knowledge that half of all marriages end in divorce.

(4) People employ "hindsight bias" to interpret events in the past as having been inevitable.

(5) People exhibit the "endowment effect": they place a higher monetary value on items they own than on those that they do not own. Thus, people tend to demand more money to have an item taken away from them than they would pay to acquire the same item.

2.   Bounded rationality: reliability of the theory. The theory of bounded rationality rests on experimental findings, usually involving students and other test subjects paid to participate in a research study. Should these findings be extrapolated to the real world?

Are these findings culture-specific, or might they vary cross-culturally? Consider, for example, Robin Paul Malloy's attempt to demonstrate the famous "prisoner's dilemma" to a group of Chinese legal scholars, lawyers, and officials:

> Using the classic scenario, I informed all players that they had just committed a serious criminal offense, such as a robbery. I told them they and their partner had both been arrested and that the police would deal with each of them individually. Then I separated the teams and isolated each player from the other member of his or her team. * * *
>
> In this classic arrangement, self-interest is supposed to lead each player to snitch on the other so that we end up with a less than optimal strategy being selected. Clearly both players are best off when they each remain silent, but the incentive structure of the game motivates the rational self-interested player to cooperate with the police. This is because neither player wants to be left "holding the bag," so to speak, in the event that the other player uses a cooperation strategy in order to pin the crime on his or her accomplice.
>
> In all six teams, each composed of players who did not know each other prior to attending this training program, every single player opted to remain silent. Thus, not one of the twelve players was convicted and no one acted in the way that traditional law and economic approaches would predict. When we took class time to discuss the outcome I explained how the pay-off matrix was supposed to encourage them to snitch on each other. Participants in the exercise responded that they understood the costs and the incentives presented by the matrix. They said that they understood that the incentive structure encouraged them to cooperate with the police but none of them gave credence to the incentives. They interpreted the incentive structure from within a community understanding in which no one in China trusts the police. Any incentive structure offered by the police would, therefore, not be expected to be honored. The best course of action when dealing with the police, I was told, was to say nothing.

ROBIN PAUL MALLOY, LAW AND MARKET ECONOMY: REINTERPRETING THE VALUES OF LAW AND ECONOMICS 12–13 (2000).

3. Bounded rationality: implications. Does the idea of bounded rationality destroy the foundations of neoclassical economics, as Korobkin and Ulen claim? Or might neoclassical economics find a way to mathematically model bounded rationality in a way that preserves the basic theory?

4. Bounded rationality and public policy. How should law and public policy respond to the fluidity of people's preferences, and the theory of bounded rationality? In the excerpt that follows, updating his earlier work on social norms, Cass Sunstein (writing with Richard Thaler) concludes that some form of government paternalism is both inevitable and desirable.

Libertarian Paternalism Is Not an Oxymoron

70 U. Chi. L. Rev. 1159, 1159–66, 1184–86, 1188–90, 1199–1201, 1202 (2003).

■ Cass R. Sunstein & Richard H. Thaler

* * *

Consider two studies of savings behavior:

- Hoping to increase savings by workers, several employers have adopted a simple strategy. Instead of asking workers to elect to participate in a 401(k) plan, workers will be assumed to want to participate in such a plan, and hence they will be enrolled automatically unless they specifically choose otherwise. This simple change in the default rule has produced dramatic increases in enrollment.

- Rather than changing the default rule, some employers have provided their employees with a novel option: *Allocate a portion of future wage increases to savings*. Employees who choose this plan are free to opt out at any time. A large number of employees have agreed to try the plan, and only a few have opted out. The result has been significant increases in savings rates.

Libertarians embrace freedom of choice, and so they deplore paternalism. Paternalists are thought to be skeptical of unfettered freedom of choice and to deplore libertarianism. According to the conventional wisdom, libertarians cannot possibly embrace paternalism, and paternalists abhor libertarianism. The idea of libertarian paternalism seems to be a contradiction in terms.

Generalizing from the two studies just described, we intend to unsettle the conventional wisdom here. We propose a form of paternalism, libertarian in spirit, that should be acceptable to those who are firmly committed to freedom of choice on grounds of either autonomy or welfare. Indeed, we urge that libertarian paternalism provides a basis for both understanding and rethinking a number of areas of contemporary law, including those aspects that deal with worker welfare, consumer protection, and the family. In the process of defending these claims, we intend to make some objections to widely held beliefs about both freedom of choice and paternalism. Our emphasis is on the fact that in many domains, people lack clear, stable, or well-ordered preferences. What they choose is strongly influenced by details of the context in which they make their choice, for example default rules, framing effects (that is, the wording of possible options), and starting points. These contextual influences render the very meaning of the term "preferences" unclear.

Consider the question whether to undergo a risky medical procedure. When people are told, "Of those who undergo this procedure, 90 percent are still alive after five years," they are far more likely to agree to the procedure than when they are told, "Of those who undergo this procedure, 10 percent are dead after five years." What, then, are the patient's "preferences" with respect to this procedure? Repeated experiences with such problems might be expected to eliminate this framing effect, but doctors too are vulnerable to it. Or return to the question of savings for retirement. It is now clear that if an employer requires employees to make an affirmative election in favor of savings, with the default rule devoting 100 percent of wages to current income, the level of savings will be far lower than if the employer adopts an automatic enrollment program from which employees are freely permitted to opt out. Can workers then be said to have well-defined preferences about how much to save? This simple example can be extended to many situations involving the behavior of workers and consumers.

As the savings problem illustrates, the design features of both legal and organizational rules have surprisingly powerful influences on people's choices. We urge that such rules should be chosen with the explicit goal of improving the welfare of the people affected by them. The libertarian aspect of our strategies lies in the straightforward insistence that, in general, people should be free to opt out of specified arrangements if they choose to do so. To borrow a phrase, libertarian paternalists urge that people should be "free to choose." Hence we do not aim to defend any approach that blocks individual choices.

The paternalistic aspect consists in the claim that it is legitimate for private and public institutions to attempt to influence people's behavior even when third-party effects are absent. In other words, we argue for self-conscious efforts, by private and public institutions, to steer people's choices in directions that will improve the choosers' own welfare. In our understanding, a policy therefore counts as "paternalistic" if it attempts to influence the choices of affected parties in a way that will make choosers better off. Drawing on some well-established findings in behavioral economics and cognitive psychology, we emphasize the possibility that in some cases individuals make inferior decisions in terms of their own welfare— decisions that they would change if they had complete information, unlimited cognitive abilities, and no lack of self-control. In addition, the notion of libertarian paternalism can be complemented by that of *libertarian benevolence*, by which plan design features such as default rules, framing effects, and starting points are enlisted in the interest of vulnerable third parties. We shall devote some discussion to this possibility.

Libertarian paternalism is a relatively weak and nonintrusive type of paternalism, because choices are not blocked or fenced off. In its most cautious forms, libertarian paternalism imposes trivial costs on those who seek to depart from the planner's preferred option. But the approach we recommend nonetheless counts as paternalistic, because private and public planners are not trying to track people's anticipated choices, but are self-consciously attempting to move people in welfare-promoting directions. Some libertarians are likely to have little or no trouble with our endorsement of paternalism for private institutions; their chief objection is to paternalistic law and government. But as we shall show, the same points that support welfare-promoting private paternalism apply to government as well. It follows that one of our principal targets is the dogmatic anti-paternalism of numerous analysts of law, including many economists and economically oriented lawyers. We believe that this dogmatism is based on a combination of a false assumption and two misconceptions.

The false assumption is that almost all people, almost all of the time, make choices that are in their best interest or at the very least are better, by their own lights, than the choices that would be made by third parties. This claim is either tautological, and therefore uninteresting, or testable. We claim that it is testable and false, indeed obviously false. In fact, we do not think that anyone believes it on reflection. Suppose that a chess novice were to play against an experienced player. Predictably the novice would lose precisely because he made inferior choices—choices that could easily be improved by some helpful hints. More generally, how well people choose is an empirical question, one whose answer is likely to vary across domains. As a first approximation, it seems reasonable to say that people make better choices in contexts in which they have experience and good information (say, choosing ice cream flavors) than in contexts in which they are inexperienced and poorly informed (say, choosing among medical treatments or investment options). So long as people are not choosing perfectly, it is at least possible that some policy could make them better off by improving their decisions.

The first misconception is that there are viable alternatives to paternalism. In many situations, some organization or agent must make a choice that will affect the behavior of some other people. There is, in those situations, no alternative to a kind of paternalism—at least in the form of an intervention that affects what people choose. We are emphasizing, then, the possibility that people's preferences, in certain domains and across a certain range, are influenced by the choices made by planners. The point applies to both private and public actors, and hence to those who design legal rules as well as to those who serve consumers. As a simple example, consider the cafeteria at some organization. The cafeteria must make a multitude of decisions, including which foods to serve, which ingredients to use, and in what order to arrange the choices. Suppose that the director of the cafeteria notices that customers have a tendency to choose more of the items that are presented earlier in the line. How should the director decide in what order to present the items? To simplify, consider some alternative strategies that the director might adopt in deciding which items to place early in the line:

1.   She could make choices that she thinks would make the customers best off, all things considered.

2.   She could make choices at random.

3.   She could choose those items that she thinks would make the customers as obese as possible.

4.   She could give customers what she thinks they would choose on their own.

Option 1 appears to be paternalistic, but would anyone advocate options 2 or 3? Option 4 is what many anti-paternalists would favor, but it is much harder to implement than it might seem. Across a certain domain of possibilities, consumers will often lack well-formed preferences, in the sense of preferences that are firmly held and preexist the director's own choices about how to order the relevant items. If the arrangement of the alternatives has a significant effect on the selections the customers make, then their true "preferences" do not formally exist.

Of course, market pressures will impose a discipline on the self-interested choices of those cafeteria directors who face competition. To that extent, those directors must indeed provide people with options they are willing to buy. A cafeteria that faces competition and offers healthy but terrible-tasting food is unlikely to do well. Market-oriented libertarians might urge that the cafeteria should attempt to maximize profits, selecting menus in a way that will increase net revenues. But profit maximization is not the appropriate goal for cafeterias granted a degree of monopoly power—for example, those in schools, dormitories, or some companies. Furthermore, even those cafeterias that face competition will find that some of the time, market success will come not from tracking people's ex ante preferences, but from providing goods and services that turn out, in practice, to promote their welfare, all things considered. Consumers might be surprised by what they end up liking; indeed, their preferences might change as a result of consumption. And in some cases, the discipline imposed by market pressures will nonetheless allow the director a great deal of room to maneuver, because people's preferences are not well-formed across the relevant domains.

While some libertarians will happily accept this point for private institutions, they will object to government efforts to influence choice in the name of welfare. Skepticism about government might be based on the fact that governments are disciplined less or perhaps not at all by market pressures. Or such skepticism might be based on the fear that parochial interests will drive government planners in their own preferred directions (the public choice problem). We agree that for government, the risks of mistake and overreaching are real and sometimes serious. But governments, no less than cafeterias (which governments frequently run), have to provide starting points of one or another kind; this is not avoidable. As we shall emphasize, they do so every day through the rules of contract and tort, in a way that inevitably affects some preferences and choices. In this respect, the anti-paternalist position is unhelpful—a literal nonstarter.

The second misconception is that paternalism always involves coercion. As the cafeteria example illustrates, the choice of the order in which to present food items does not coerce anyone to do anything, yet one might prefer some orders to others on grounds that are paternalistic in the sense that we use the term. Would anyone object to putting the fruit and salad before the desserts at an elementary school cafeteria if the result were to increase the consumption ratio of apples to Twinkies? Is this question fundamentally different if the customers are adults? Since no coercion is involved, we think that some types of paternalism should be acceptable to even the most ardent libertarian. In the important domain of savings behavior, we shall offer a number of illustrations. To those anti-libertarians who are suspicious of freedom of choice and would prefer to embrace welfare instead, we urge that it is often possible for paternalistic planners to make common cause with their libertarian adversaries by adopting policies that promise to promote welfare but that also make room for freedom of choice. To confident planners, we suggest that the risks of confused or ill-motivated plans are reduced if people are given the opportunity to reject the planner's preferred solutions.

The thrust of our argument is that the term "paternalistic" should not be considered pejorative, just descriptive. Once it is understood that some organizational decisions are inevitable, that a form of paternalism cannot be avoided, and that the alternatives to paternalism (such as choosing options to make people worse off) are unattractive, we can abandon the less interesting question of whether to be paternalistic or not, and turn to the more constructive question of how to choose among the possible choice-influencing options. To this end we make two general suggestions. First, programs should be designed using a type of welfare analysis, one in which a serious attempt is made to measure the costs and benefits of outcomes (rather than relying on estimates of willingness to pay). Choosers should be given more choices if the welfare benefits exceed the welfare costs. Second, some results from the psychology of decisionmaking should be used to provide ex ante guidelines to support reasonable judgments about when consumers and workers will gain most by increasing options. We argue that those who are generally inclined to oppose paternalism should consider these suggestions uncontroversial.

* * *

The inevitability of paternalism is most clear when the planner has to choose starting points or default rules. But if the focus is on welfare, it is reasonable to ask whether the planner should go beyond the inevitable, and whether such a planner can also claim to be libertarian. To illustrate the problem, return to the simple cafeteria example discussed above. Putting the fruit before the desserts is a fairly mild intervention. A more intrusive step would be to place the desserts in another location altogether, so that diners have to get up and get a dessert after they have finished the rest of their meal. This step raises the transaction costs of eating dessert, and according to a standard economic analysis the proposal is quite unattractive—it seems to make dessert eaters worse off and no one better off. But many people face problems of self-control, and the results include illness and disease, small and large. Once the costs of self-control are incorporated into the analysis, we can see that some diners would prefer this arrangement, namely those who would eat a dessert if it were put in front of them but would resist temptation if given a little help. To fit with libertarian principles, the planner could arrange two lines in the cafeteria: the tempting line and the non-tempting line. The tempting line would include everything, whereas the non-tempting line would make unhealthy foods less available. Since people could choose either line, this passes the libertarian test. (As a solution to the self-control problem, it might not be entirely adequate, because people would be tempted to join the tempting line.)

Hence it is possible to preserve freedom of choice, and to allow opt-outs, but also to favor self-conscious efforts to promote welfare by helping people to solve problems of bounded rationality and bounded self-control. Efforts of this kind need not attempt to give people what they would choose ex ante, even in cases in which preferences exist; but such efforts would nonetheless allow people to move in their preferred directions.

In the domain of employee behavior, there are many imaginable illustrations. Employees might be automatically enrolled in a 401(k) plan, with a right to opt out, but employers might require a waiting period, and perhaps a consultation with an adviser, before the opt-out could be effective. Thaler and Benartzi have proposed a method of increasing contributions to 401(k) plans that also meets the libertarian test. Under the Save More Tomorrow plan, * * * employees are invited to sign up for a program in which their contributions to the savings plan are increased annually whenever they get a raise. Once employees join the plan, they stay in until they opt out or reach the maximum savings rate. In the first company to use this plan, the employees who joined increased their savings rates from 3.5 percent to 11.6 percent in a little over two years (three raises). Very few of the employees who join the plan drop out. We believe that this is successful libertarian paternalism in action. In fact, the ideas of automatic enrollment and Save More Tomorrow provide quite promising models for increasing saving; they might well be more effective than imaginable economic incentives, as for example through decreased taxes on savings.

The same sort of strategy might be used in many domains. Moving from paternalism to protection of third parties, employers (or the state) might seek to increase charitable giving from workers. Is it possible to produce a form of libertarian benevolence, and if so, how might this be done? Moral suasion may or may not succeed, but compare a system of Give More Tomorrow. Because workers appear quite willing to part with a fraction of their future raises, such a system, like Save More Tomorrow, would be highly appealing to many people. In fact the ideas explored here might well be used to produce significant increases in charitable donations (of course, there are obvious complexities about institutional design and appropriate default beneficiaries).

It should now be clear that the difference between libertarian and non-libertarian paternalism is not simple and rigid. The libertarian paternalist insists on preserving choice, whereas the non-libertarian paternalist is willing to foreclose choice. But in all cases, a real question is the cost of exercising choice, and here there is a continuum rather than a sharp dichotomy. A libertarian paternalist who is especially enthusiastic about free choice would be inclined to make it relatively costless for people to obtain their preferred outcomes. (Call this a *libertarian* paternalist.) By contrast, a libertarian paternalist who is especially confident of his welfare judgments would be willing to impose real costs on workers and consumers who seek to do what, in the paternalist's view, would not be in their best interests. (Call this a libertarian *paternalist*.)

Rejecting both routes, a non-libertarian paternalist would attempt to block certain choices. But notice that almost any such attempt will amount, in practice, to an effort to impose high costs on those who try to make those choices. Consider a law requiring drivers to wear seat belts. If the law is enforced, and a large fine is imposed, the law is non-libertarian even though determined violators can exercise their freedom of choice—at the expense of the fine. But as the expected fine approaches zero, the law approaches libertarianism. The libertarian paternalism that we are describing and defending here attempts to ensure, as a general rule, that people can easily avoid the paternalist's suggested option.

* * *

We are now in a position to categorize a diverse set of paternalistic interventions: minimal paternalism, required active choices, procedural constraints, and substantive constraints.

a) Minimal paternalism. Minimal paternalism is the form of paternalism that occurs whenever a planner (private or public) constructs a default rule or starting point with the goal of influencing behavior. So long as it is costless or nearly costless to depart from the default plan, minimal paternalism is maximally libertarian. This is the form of paternalism that we have described as inevitable.

b) Required active choices. Unsure of what choices will promote welfare, a planner might reject default plans or starting points entirely and force people to choose explicitly (what we have described as the strategy of required active choices). This approach finds an analogue in information-eliciting default rules in contract law, designed to give contracting parties a strong incentive to say what they want. To the extent that planners force people to choose whether or not people would like to choose, there is a paternalistic dimension to their actions. ("Choosing is good for both freedom and welfare," some appear to think, whether or not people agree with them!) We think that the argument for requiring choices stands or falls largely on the welfare consequences.

c) Procedural constraints. A slightly more aggressive form of paternalism occurs when the default plan is accompanied by procedural constraints designed to ensure that any departure is fully voluntary and entirely rational. When procedural constraints are in place, it is not costless to depart from the default plan. The extent of the cost, and the aggressiveness of the paternalism, will of course vary with the extent of the constraints. The justification for the constraints will depend on whether there are serious problems of bounded rationality and bounded self-control; if so, the constraints are justified not on the ground that the planner disagrees with people's choices, but because identifiable features of the situation make it likely that choices will be defective. Such features may include an unfamiliar setting, a lack of experience, and a risk of impulsiveness. The Age Discrimination in Employment Act is our principal example here.

d) Substantive constraints. Alternatively, a planner might impose substantive constraints, allowing people to reject the default arrangement, but not on whatever terms they choose. On this approach, the planner selects the terms along which the parties will be permitted to move in their preferred directions. The Model Termination Act and the Fair Labor Standards Act are illustrations. The extent of the departure from libertarianism will be a function of the gap between the legally specified terms and the terms that parties would otherwise reach. Here too the justification for the constraint depends on bounded rationality and bounded self-control.

e) A thin line. A planner might reject freedom of choice on the ground that those who reject the default plan will err all or almost all of the time. Such a planner will impose significant costs on those who depart from the plan. As we have said, there is a thin line between non-libertarian paternalists and libertarian paternalists who impose high costs, procedural or substantive, on those who reject the plan. Almost all of the time, even the non-libertarian paternalist will allow choosers, at some cost, to reject the proposed course of action. Those who are required to wear motorcycle helmets can decide to risk the relevant penalty, and to pay it if need be. Employers and employees might agree to sub-minimum wage work and risk the penalties if they are caught. In this particular sense, penalties are always prices.

III.   How to Choose: The Toolbox of the Libertarian Paternalist

How should sensible planners choose among possible systems, given that some choice is necessary? We suggest two approaches to this problem. If feasible, a comparison of possible rules should be done using a form of cost-benefit analysis, one that pays serious attention to welfare effects. In many cases, however, such analyses will be both difficult and expensive. As an alternative, we offer some rules of thumb that might be adopted to choose among various options. In general, it makes sense to experiment with possible approaches to identify their results for both choices and outcomes. We have emphasized automatic enrollment plans and Save More Tomorrow because studies have suggested that both of these have a great deal of potential. In other domains, plans are likely to be proposed in the face of highly imperfect information; more data will reveal a great deal. Large-scale programs are most justified if repeated experiments have shown that they actually work.

* * *

The argument for libertarian paternalism seems compelling to us, even obvious, but we suspect that hard-line anti-paternalists, and possibly others, will have objections. We respond to three possible objections here.

The first objection is that by advocating libertarian paternalism, we are starting down a very slippery slope. Once one grants the possibility that default rules for savings or cafeteria lines should be designed paternalistically, it might seem impossible to resist highly non-libertarian interventions. Critics might envisage an onslaught of what seem, to them, to be unacceptably intrusive forms of paternalism, from requiring motorcycle riders to wear helmets, to mandatory waiting periods before consumer purchases, to bans on cigarette smoking, to intrusive health care reforms of many imaginable kinds. In the face of the risk of overreaching, might it not be better to avoid starting down the slope at all?

There are three responses. First, in many cases there is simply no viable alternative to paternalism in the weak sense, and hence planners are forced to take at least a few tiny steps down that slope. Recall that paternalism, in the form of effects on behavior, is frequently inevitable. In such cases, the slope cannot be avoided. Second, the libertarian condition, requiring opt-out rights, sharply limits the steepness of the slope. So long as paternalistic interventions can be easily avoided by those who seek to adopt a course of their own, the risks emphasized by anti-paternalists are minimal. Third, those who make the slippery slope argument are acknowledging the existence of a self-control problem, at least for planners. But if planners, including bureaucrats and human resource managers, suffer from self-control problems, then it is highly likely that other people do too.

A second and different sort of objection is based on a deep mistrust of the ability of the planner (especially the planner working for the government) to make sensible choices. Even those who normally believe that everyone chooses rationally treat with deep skepticism any proposal that seems to hinge on rational choices by bureaucrats. Part of the skepticism is based on a belief that bureaucrats lack the discipline imposed by market pressures; part of it is rooted in the fact that individuals have the welfare-promoting incentives that are thought to come from self-interest; part of it is rooted in the fear that well-organized private groups will move bureaucrats in their preferred directions. We happily grant that planners are human, and thus are both boundedly rational and subject to the influence of objectionable pressures. Nevertheless, as we have stressed, these human planners are sometimes forced to make choices, and it is surely better to have them trying to improve people's welfare rather than the opposite. In emphasizing the important effect of plan design on choice (a point under-appreciated by economists, lawyers, and planners), we hope to encourage plan designers to become more informed. And by arguing for a libertarian check on bad plans, we hope to create a strong safeguard against ill-considered or ill-motivated plans. To the extent that individual self-interest is a healthy check on planners, freedom of choice is an important corrective.

A third objection would come from the opposite direction. Enthusiastic paternalists, emboldened by evidence of bounded rationality and self-control problems, might urge that in many domains, the instruction to engage in only libertarian paternalism is too limiting. At least if the focus is entirely or mostly on welfare, it might seem clear that in certain circumstances, people should not be given freedom of choice for the simple reason that they will choose poorly. In those circumstances, why should anyone insist on libertarian paternalism, as opposed to unqualified or non-libertarian paternalism?

This objection raises complex issues of both value and fact, and we do not intend to venture into difficult philosophical territory here. Our basic response is threefold. First, we reiterate our understanding that planners are human, and so the real comparison is between boundedly rational choosers with self-control problems and boundedly rational planners facing self-control problems of their own. It is doubtful that the comparison can sensibly be made in the abstract. Second, an opt-out right operates as a safeguard against confused or improperly motivated planners, and in many contexts, that safeguard is crucial even if it potentially creates harm as well. Third, nothing we have said denies the possibility that in some circumstances it can be advisable to impose significant costs on those who reject the proposed course of action, or even to deny freedom of choice altogether. * * * Our only qualification is that when third-party effects are not present, the general presumption should be in favor of freedom of choice, and that presumption should be rebutted only when individual choice is demonstrably inconsistent with individual welfare.

* * *

In our view, libertarian paternalism is not only a conceptual possibility; it also provides a foundation for rethinking many areas of private and public law. We believe that policies rooted in libertarian paternalism will often be a big improvement on the most likely alternative: inept neglect.

C.   Beyond Traditional Macroeconomics: "Ecological Economics"

The problem of pollution has long been recognized to pose a problem of market failure, because clean air and water is not a good that can be restricted to those who can pay for it. Proposals to address this market failure have often focused on creating markets for pollution, through, for example, tradable emissions permits. A deeper criticism of neoclassical economics is that such economic analysis treats the earth's resources as infinite, when in fact the depletion of nonrenewable resources should be counted as a cost. As Douglas Kysar explains:

> Conventional economists often state that growth of human economic production is not checked by restrictions imposed by nature. In other words, they treat the human economic process as an open system that draws resources and emits wastes through a relatively undefined and unexamined relationship with nature. In contrast, ecological economists view the means of production and nature as components of the same closed system. On this account, the human economic process faces hard constraints imposed by the absolute or temporal scarcity of nonrenewable resources and renewable resources, as well as by the limited capacity of ecological mechanisms to absorb the pollution produced by exploitation of those resources. As a consequence of such constraints, society must remain cognizant of the extent and quality of existing resource stocks, as well as the capacity for natural systems to absorb waste outputs created during the transformation of those stocks into human goods.

Douglas Kysar, *Law, Environment, and Vision*, 97 Nw. U. L. Rev. 675, 680 (2003).

One effect of taking the finite resources of the planet seriously is the effort to catalog and quantify the "services" provided by the natural world in order to internalize their costs. Another effect has been the recognition that questions of sustainability and scale should play a role in macroeconomic analysis. Drawing on the pioneering work of Herman Daly, Kysar argues:

> Markets, through their twin devices of price information and economic incentives, are unparalleled in their effectiveness at allocating resources efficiently. They do not, however, resolve the altogether separate problems of achieving distributive justice and ecological sustainability. Put differently, economists recognize that a Pareto-optimal allocation of resources can be achieved with respect to any given distribution of income, including ones that might be described as unjust. Similarly, a Pareto-optimal allocation of resources can be achieved with respect to any given scale of the human economy, including ones that might lead to ecological peril. "Ecological criteria of sustainability, like ethical criteria of justice, are not served by markets." Thus, Daly argues that "[o]ptimal scale, like distributive justice, full employment, or price level stability, is a macroeconomic goal," requiring unique macroeconomic policy instruments.

Id. at 683–84.

In the following excerpt, Kysar introduces to a legal audience the emerging field of ecological economics. In what ways does ecological economics echo the internal critiques of microeconomics? In what ways does it undermine the neoclassical vision altogether?

Sustainability, Distribution, and the Macroeconomic Analysis of Law

43 B.C. L. Rev. 1, 4–7, 17–18, 19, 20–26, 28–34, 35–38, 39–44, 63–71 (2001).

■ Douglas A. Kysar

Since its inception, law and economics has attracted criticism from scholars who find its assumptions unrealistic. For a long time, this response was purely critical in form, exposing as flawed the behavioral assumptions of law and economics without proposing corresponding changes to increase its veracity. In recent years, however, a group of scholars has devoted considerable insight and energy to the project of behavioral law and economics. This emerging subdiscipline fuses traditional neoclassical economic analysis with lessons drawn from cognitive psychology and decision theory research. The result is a law and economics grounded in assumptions that comport better with observed real-world behavior than the stylized rational actor model featured in conventional law and economics. The fruits of this effort are now dominating new research in law journals, such that it is no overstatement to conclude, "The future of economic analysis of law lies in new and better understandings of decision and choice."

With a few notable exceptions, this project to improve the veracity of law and economics assumptions has focused exclusively on the foundational principles of microeconomics. A group of dedicated scholars within economics, biology, and ecology departments have undertaken a parallel project to reform the assumptions of *macro*economics. These scholars—who have banded together under the moniker, *ecological economists*—adopt the same methodology as legal behavioral economists. They examine the most robust findings from disciplines outside of economics and utilize those findings to steer economic analysis toward what they believe is greater real-world relevance. As behavioralists instill microeconomic analysis with the teachings of cognitive psychology and decision theory, ecological economists bring the findings of ecology, biology, and environmental science to macroeconomics.

This Article introduces the field of ecological economics and analyzes its potential use as a macroeconomics for legal analysis. * * *

Ecological economics * * * is built around a more complex understanding of human economic goals than traditional economic analysis. Economists recognize two primary functions served by the market: the allocation of resources among competing uses (allocation) and the distribution of wealth among market participants (distribution). In grossly simplified terms, economists believe that the first function suggests market policies designed to maximize allocative efficiency, while the second function requires a social decision best left to the political process. Ecological economists argue that a third function served by the market has been overlooked by conventional analysis: moderation of the scale of human economic activity vis-à-vis the ecological superstructure upon which all life and activity depends (scale). While allocation determines the purposes for which resources are used, scale determines the rate and amounts of resources that are used.

Like their orthodox counterparts, ecological economists offer a norm to accompany this concept. Just as economists almost instinctively believe that allocative efficiency should be maximized, ecological economists tend to believe that the scale of the economy should be sustainable, that is, capable of reproduction in perpetuity (or its practical equivalent). Readers who are uncomfortable with some of the more dramatic implications of sustainability should bear in mind that the fundamental insight of ecological economics is a recognition of the concept of scale, not necessarily the norm of sustainability. Whether or not one accepts all of the implications of sustainability as a norm, ecological economists seek acknowledgment that human economic activity impacts the environment and that the size and rate of that impact is a legitimate subject of social and legal influence.

* * *

B. Some Fundamentals

Although the field is still relatively new and ill-formed, several fundamental concepts have gained sufficient acceptance to be called "standard" ecological economics. This Section examines those concepts in detail.

1. The Relationship Between Ecological and Economic Systems

"The vision of modern economics in general, and especially of macroeconomics, is the familiar circular flow diagram." The economy is viewed as a self-contained system within which exchange value circulates between producers and consumers. The macroeconomic loop makes no accounting of the actual resource materials from which goods are produced, or the waste matter into which goods are transformed during consumption. Physical dimensions of economic activity simply do not exist in the textbook circular flow diagram. Thus, resource depletion, environmental pollution, impairment of necessary environmental services such as water filtration or carbon absorption, or indeed any other relationship between economic activity and factors outside of the narrow universe of value exchange are ignored by standard macroeconomics. As [pioneering ecological economist Herman] Daly put it, "It is exactly as if a biology textbook proposed to study an animal only in terms of its circulatory system, without ever mentioning its digestive tract...."

Ecological economists believe that this conception is misguided. Human economic activity impacts the ecological sphere in all phases of production and consumption, in ways both patently obvious, such as the clear-cutting that has occurred in the majority of the forested areas of the globe, and deceptively subtle, such as the rise of greenhouse gases in the atmosphere from 277 ppmv (parts per million by volume) to 367 ppmv since pre-Industrial times. * * *

* * *

Humans are setting in motion complex feedback loops whose little-understood mechanisms could become self-perpetuating. Melting of polar ice caps through global warming could cause the release of billions of tons of methane gas trapped beneath crystal structures on the edges of continental shelves. One cubic meter of this methane gas has the same ultraviolet radiation trapping effect as twenty cubic meters of carbon dioxide, the most voluminous greenhouse gas produced by human activity.

* * *

Nevertheless, even international institutions such as the World Bank continue to rely on the rarefied macroeconomic conception of exchange found at the beginning of standard texts. As Daly notes, "Things are no better when [one] turn[s] to the advanced chapters at the end of most macroeconomic texts, where the topic is growth theory." For years the theory was stated as a simple function involving K and L, capital and labor. Resource flows and waste output flows were not even a factor in the equation. Thus, the only constraints on economic growth appeared to be the availability of man-made capital and human labor. * * *

* * *

As an example of the orthodox view, many economic forecasters view China, with its 1.2 billion people, as an untapped market for goods associated with the affluent Western lifestyle. In other words, forecasters see the glimmer of economic growth in the development of China. Other commentators, however, argue that if the entire Chinese population were to adopt the lifestyle of consumers in a nation like the United States, the consequent ecological footprint would be catastrophic. Indeed, it does not appear that the Chinese could even eat like Americans, let alone buy, build, drive, and discard like Americans: "If the current world grain harvest, averaging 1.75 billion tons thus far during the 1990s, were boosted by roughly 15 percent to 2 billion tons, that harvest—if equitably distributed—could support [only] 2.5 billion people at the American level of consumption." To be sure, growth in consumption levels in China will be accompanied by growth in the nation's own productive capacity. It is far from clear, however, that arable land and agricultural productivity can be multiplied in the way that factories can.

2.   The Laws of Thermodynamics

Assuming that environmental frontiers are not limitless, economics as the science of scarcity therefore must confront the scarcity of natural as well as man-made resources. While mainstream economists believe that they have found a theoretical avenue around this challenge, ecological economists confront it directly, incorporating the laws of thermodynamics into their analysis in order to better understand the quality of physical exchanges that occur between the ecological system and the economic subsystem. As [Vanderbilt economist Nicholas] Georgescu–Roegen demonstrated, such application reveals a disturbing truth about human economic activity (and indeed, about all activity within the material universe). The fixed quantum of matter-energy with which the universe is endowed must necessarily move from a state of high-availability to low-availability, of low-entropy to high-entropy, and of order to chaos. Thus, physical throughput in the human economy must always be conceived of as at least a partial liquidation of capital, rather than a mere expenditure of income.

For ecological economists, such cold fatalism is not cause for despair; it is cause for reform. Humanity is somewhat in control of the rate with which it advances entropic activity. A solar heated house only utilizes an infinitesimal fraction of the sun's several billion years of activity. A house heated by coal-fired electricity, on the other hand, transforms millions of years of condensed solar energy into greenhouse gases that persist in the atmosphere for decades. The economic argument for refusing to adopt the use of renewable energy sources immediately, on a widespread basis, is no longer as strong as it once was. The cost of solar cells has declined from more than $70 per watt in the 1970s to $4 per watt today (in 1994 dollars), while the world market has grown from 34 megawatts in 1988 to an estimated 125 megawatts in 1997. The fastest growing energy market in the past decade has not been oil, coal, or natural gas, but wind power, growing from 2000 megawatts in 1990 to 7600 megawatts in 1997, and remarkably achieving cost-competitiveness with its heavily subsidized, arguably unsustainable counterparts. But most of this development is occurring outside of the United States. Nations such as China, Mexico, Kenya, and Vietnam all currently use solar electrification to provide power to remote rural villages. In the view of ecological economists, nothing prevents industrialized nations such as the United States from doing the same besides entrenched political power and a failure to perceive the true costs of current practices. In light of this situation, * * * [i]t is not that Cadillacs prevent future spades and plows; it is that sport-utility vehicles prevent future wind turbines and solar cells.

3. Optimal Scale and Sustainability

The foregoing discussion establishes another of the foundational principles of ecological economics: "The macroeconomy is an open subsystem of the ecosystem and is totally dependent upon it, both as a source for inputs of low-entropy matter-energy and as a sink for outputs of high-entropy matter-energy." Given such a conception, an inescapable question arises regarding how much the economic subsystem can grow before it places an unsustainable burden on the natural ecosystem. Conventional economists fail to address this issue because the macroeconomy is conceived of as the superstructure—conceptually, nothing exists "around" the macroeconomy. Thus, there is no reason to suspect that it cannot grow ad infinitum.

As Daly has noted, this failing is surprising given that every other economic concept involves a limit or point at which marginal benefits do not exceed marginal costs. More than one commentator has speculated that the disappearance of limits in macroeconomics serves as a theoretical expedient to avoid difficult questions of distribution. Instead of adopting such an approach, Daly argues that the logic of marginal analysis must apply with equal force to macroeconomics—that is, there must be a point at which the benefits from an increase in the scale of the economy are outweighed by the environmental and social costs entailed by such an increase. Economists and other thinkers interested in the welfare of humanity must therefore confront the issue of determining the optimal scale of the economy.

The most widely cited attempt to articulate a principle for limiting the scale of economic activity comes from the 1987 report of the United Nations World Commission on Environment and Development, popularly known as the *Brundtland Report*. This report urged nations to undergo only *sustainable development*, which it defined as development that "meets the needs of the present without compromising the ability of future generations to meet their own needs." As Susan Smith has explained, two principles underlie this notion of sustainable development: "[T]he Earth's finite capacity to accommodate people and industrial development, and a moral imperative not to deprive future generations of natural resources essential to well-being and quality of environment." Following the release of the *Brundtland Report*, several international agreements and statements of principles have further developed this goal of keeping human activity within the carrying capacity of the earth, including the Framework Convention on Climate Change, the Convention on Biological Diversity, the Rio Declaration, Agenda 21, and the Statement of Forest Principles.

While these developments were initially viewed as an important step toward reaching a consensus to restrict the scale of the global economy, they have come under fire more recently for lacking the conceptual clarity needed to avoid unsustainable growth. Among ecological economists, Daly has been especially critical of the *Brundtland Report*'s ambiguity: "Sustainable development is a term that everyone likes, but nobody is sure of what it means." Although the international community has agreed that it should not compromise the "needs" of future generations, it has not attempted to define what those "needs" will be. Should future generations be afforded only the natural resources necessary to maintain a basic level of subsistence? Should the "aesthetic" needs of the unborn be considered within the sustainable development rubric? What assumptions should be made about the ability of technological advancements to alleviate resource scarcities in the future? What type of allowance should be made for the limit of science's ability to recognize and assess the impact of economic activity on ecosystem viability?

* * *

* * * Daly has advocated the necessity of a "steady-state economy" in which the scale of human economic activity—that is, "the physical scale or size of the human presence in the ecosystem as measured by population times per capita resource use"—does not exceed the point at which marginal macroeconomic benefits equal macroeconomic costs. Economists have typically ignored this type of marginal analysis at the macroeconomic level, opting to believe that micro-level consumption choices generally reflect Pareto improvements, and that therefore the aggregate of such choices must also reflect enhancements in social welfare. In Daly's view, however, prices only measure the scarcity of resources relative to each other. Micro-level choices may result in an efficient allocation of resources in relation to everything else, but they cannot determine an efficient *absolute* level of resource use. Therefore, just as full employment and fair distribution are macroeconomic goals that are not fully resolved by unfettered microeconomic activity, Daly believes that optimal scale is an issue that must be addressed by policy instruments operating on a macroeconomic level.

"A necessary requirement for this optimal scale is that the economy's *throughput*—the flow beginning with raw material inputs, followed by their conversion into commodities, and finally into waste outputs—be within the regenerative and absorptive capacities of the ecosystem." In other words, in order to be truly sustainable, the material scale of the economy must be within the carrying capacity of the earth. Giving flesh to the concept of "carrying capacity" is a challenging task that needs to be addressed before Daly's sustainable development can become a fully operable concept. Daly provides two fundamental principles toward that end: "Renewable resources should be exploited in a manner such that: (1) harvesting rates do not exceed regeneration rates; and (2) waste emissions do not exceed the renewable assimilative capacity of the local environment." Non-renewable resources should be depleted at a rate equal to the rate of creation of renewable substitutes.

These principles of resource use, however, are only the first step in what is an essentially scientific exercise. Determining whether a given level of population and per capita resource use is sustainable requires the expertise of ecologists, biologists, and environmental scientists, as well as economists. In Daly's view, the practitioners of economics should continue to practice their bread and butter of maximizing the market's allocative efficiency, but only after the optimal scale of that market has been determined by social consensus with input from both economic and noneconomic experts.

A second task that is not exclusively economic involves determining the desirable mix of population size and resource intensity that will be used to consume society's annual quota of natural capital and services. As noted above, the scale or level of physical throughput in the economy can be thought of as the product of population times per capita resource use. This definition implies that a smaller population could lead a more resource-intensive lifestyle than a larger one, while staying within ecologically-imposed constraints of sustainability. Conversely, a larger population must reduce its per capita resource use in order to maintain the ecological footprint of a smaller one. Because the level of throughput must not be allowed to exceed the point at which ecosystem losses exceed economic gains, society must make a conscious tradeoff between these two determinant factors of the scale of its economy. Obviously, such a tradeoff entails a moral, not merely an economic, choice. * * *

* * *

4. Measuring the Human Economy

Economics is fundamentally a quantitative discipline. As Samuelson puts it in his renowned textbook, "economics focuses on concepts that can actually be measured." Following the lead of John Maynard Keynes and Simon Kuznets, macroeconomists have focused exclusively on quantifying the productive capacity of the human economy. However, as seen in the last Section, a second constraint on economic growth exists—the carrying capacity of the ecosystem. Moreover, even ignoring ecological limits to growth, there is little reason to suppose that increases in the sheer magnitude of the human economy are always desirable from the perspective of social welfare. Recognizing the practical worth of quantification (and the need to confront conventional economists in their own language), ecological economists have begun to focus attention on the task of measuring the intersection of economic and ecological spheres. This Section addresses the response of ecological economists to traditional indexes of social welfare such as the gross national product (GNP), while the next Section outlines efforts to quantify the value of the ecological sphere.

Current national accounting measures produce a variety of results that would strike noneconomists as odd. For instance, when the Exxon Valdez oil spill necessitated $2.1 billion in clean-up costs, the U.S. GNP rose by that same amount, despite the fact that ten years later only two of the twenty-three most damaged wildlife species have recovered and 40% of area fishermen suffer depression over their destroyed livelihoods. Similarly, as Superfund contributors muster the $31 billion needed to clean the 1355 worst locations on the EPA's list of nearly 40,000 hazardous waste sites, GNP views the expenditure as an increase in economic welfare, rather than just a restoration. GNP also ignores basic accounting principles by treating the unsustainable exploitation of natural capital as pure income. Centuries of logging and construction have resulted in the loss of all but 1% to 5% of the original forest cover of the United States, yet GNP has made no allowance along the way for the depreciation of scarce natural capital.

Social as well as ecological costs frequently appear as gains under GNP accounting. When the estimated one third of American adults who are obese spent $39 billion in one year on health care costs for obesity-related diseases, the macroeconomic indicators recorded an unmitigated credit. When the position of the United States as home to 1.7 million prisoners and the largest incarceration system in the world necessitated a doubling of state spending on prisons in the last decade, GNP rose to reflect the social "progress" of unprecedented prison construction. And when the American divorce rate doubled between 1970 and the present, GNP recorded an increase from the real estate transactions, attorney bills, and other expenditures necessitated by the higher number of family fractures.

Such arguably counterintuitive results are an outgrowth of the "cowboy economy" in which more of anything is simply better, regardless of what it is. Standard national accounting measures such as GNP, and more recently gross domestic product (GDP), seek only to quantify the value of monetary transactions that occur in a given economy, with no distinction among purposes and no recognition of adverse consequences that result from such transactions. No allowance is made for the irreversible depletion of natural resource inputs, or the externalized costs of waste outputs. Indeed, such environmental costs are frequently treated as economic gains, leading to a perverse national incentive structure: A policy of maximizing GNP is "practically equivalent to a policy of maximizing depletion and pollution."

Nor is any accounting attempted of other "noneconomic" spheres such as the livelihood of communities, the stability of families, or the safety of schools. Unexamined pursuit of increases in GNP can lead to parasitic growth. Commercialization of social functions traditionally performed outside the economic sphere—such as the replacement of stay-at-home parenting by child care, prepared meals by convenience food, social networks by self-help tapes, and community activities by commercial entertainment—is a consequence encouraged by any national agenda that seeks to maximize GNP.

Nobel Prize-winning economist Simon Kuznets, one of the chief architects of the concept of GNP, warned that the measurement of GNP should never be mistaken for true national progress: "Distinctions must be kept in mind between quantity and quality of growth, between its costs and return, and between the short and the long run. Goals for 'more' growth should specify more growth of what and for what." Many policymakers, however, have largely ignored this advice, seeking continual, indiscriminate growth in GNP as the ready salve for all manner of national problems. Ecological economists, on the other hand, have criticized GNP as a concept that fosters unsustainable economic practices while failing to achieve its aim of approximating human welfare. In its stead, Daly and theologian John Cobb, Jr., have offered a substitute national wealth accounting measure that corrects for many of the GNP's failings.

Called the Index of Sustainable Economic Welfare (ISEW), Daly and Cobb's measure begins with total consumption expenditure data gathered by the U.S. Bureau of Economic Analysis and then proceeds to make a series of adjustments to arrive at a best estimate of sustainable economic welfare. The first adjustment, for income inequality, attempts to account for the fact that "an additional thousand dollars in income adds more to the welfare of a poor family than it does to a rich family." This notion, which many accept as a consequence of the principle of diminishing marginal utility of income, has important implications for the calculation of economic welfare. If income distribution becomes more uneven over a period of time, unadjusted dollar flows for that period will overstate welfare. To correct for this distortion, Daly and Cobb alter consumption expenditure data to reflect the degree of income inequality in the economy.

Next, Daly and Cobb add factors representing positive income streams from four sources that are currently absent from official consumption data—household labor, existing consumer durables, public streets and highways, and public spending on health and education. Conversely, deductions are made for expenditures that arguably do not contribute to improvement in economic welfare. For example, a portion of private spending on education is deducted to represent the "competitive" nature of such spending. Similarly, the authors disallow some private expenditures on health care because they view them as attributable to "growing health risks due to urbanization and industrialization." Other costs deducted from total expenditures because of their "defensive" nature include the costs of commuting, purchases of personal pollution control equipment such as air and water filters, and damages due to vehicular accidents.

Having attempted to refine the calculation of economic welfare in accord with certain social realities, Daly and Cobb then turn to the realities of the environment in relation to the economic subsystem. They first deduct amounts relating to the current environmental damage imposed by economic activity, including the annual cost of water pollution, air pollution, noise pollution, loss of wetlands, and loss of farmland. These costs are the least controversial of Daly and Cobb's estimates of environmental damage, as they represent tangible, present costs with little scientific dispute as to their existence. Moreover, the authors adopt a purposefully conservative approach to valuation of these costs. For instance, they do not include the costs of water pollution from nonpoint sources or the health-related costs of air pollution.

The authors also attempt to account for the long-term environmental costs associated with economic activity. First, Daly and Cobb recognize that the consumption of nonrenewable resources constitutes in part "a cost borne by future generations that should be subtracted from (debited to) the capital account of the current generation." To price this cost, the authors rely on the marginal cost of producing a renewable substitute: "For each unit of nonrenewable resource depleted, we have estimated the amount of money that would have to be invested in a process to create a perpetual stream of output of a renewable substitute for it." Second, Daly and Cobb undertake the daunting task of estimating the economic impact of long-term build-up of thermal waste in the environment. Such accounting is of course destined to be inexact, but Daly and Cobb's rough approximation seems at least preferable to the alternative of measuring the costs of global warming and ozone depletion at precisely zero. In a final set of adjustments, Daly and Cobb alter ISEW to account for changes in the domestic and international capital position of the national economy. These adjustments reflect the fact that current economic welfare can be maintained only if growth in the domestic capital stock keeps pace with population growth.

　　　＊　＊　＊

＊ ＊ ＊ [W]hile the first subtotal of ISEW showed a consumer gain of $1737 billion for 1990, the end result revealed only $818 billion in net economic welfare created during the year. One can think of the $919 billion differential as a very rough estimate of the total cost of environmental and social externalities created by economic activity in 1990. Given that this amount is actually greater than the net value created that year, it is arguably an analytical strain to continue to refer to environmental and social costs as mere "externalities," a term suggesting only minor effects of limited interest. To the contrary, under Daly and Cobb's calculations, externalities appear to be a dominant effect of market transactions, suggesting that "it is time to restructure basic concepts and start with a different set of abstractions that can embrace what was previously external."

Contrasting the ISEW with GNP over a time series is also revealing. According to Daly and Cobb, GNP and ISEW both rose from 1951 until the 1970s (although the rate of growth in ISEW decreased from 1.57% to 0.21% between the 1960s and 1970s). In the 1980s, however, GNP continued to rise while ISEW actually declined by 0.43% per year. This decline suggests that continued increases in the scale of the human economy (as approximately signaled by increases in GNP) are anti-economic; that is, they impose more welfare costs than benefits (as signaled by decreases in

ISEW). Thus, beginning in the late 1970s and early 1980s, the United States may well have shifted from the cowboy to the spaceman economy, with all its attendant problems.

Of course, Daly and Cobb's figures are easily contestable, as would be any attempt to track and price the total social and environmental costs of human economic activity. Nevertheless, even without deducting for resource depletion and long-term environmental costs—the two most controversial and difficult to quantify aspects of ISEW—the pattern of change in ISEW remains largely the same. This suggests, at an absolute minimum, that undifferentiated growth in GNP is not necessarily consonant with economic welfare and that reliance on GNP as a measure of national success should be reevaluated.

5. Valuing Ecosystem Services

In addition to reforming the measurement of national accounts, ecological economists have also devoted significant attention to quantifying the worth of ecosystem services. The attempt to place a monetary value on the elements of nature has long been controversial. Many view such attempts as an almost heretical failure to appreciate that nature is "priceless." Rutgers University biologist David Ehrenfeld provides a representative, if charged, example of this view: "I am afraid that I don't see much hope for a civilization so stupid that it demands a quantitative estimate of the value of its own umbilical cord." Others attack the practice from the opposite extreme, believing that the survey methods frequently used to price natural resources are fraught with complexities that render valuations wildly overstated. Nevertheless, economists, policymakers, and courts continue to place economic values on natural resources through the use of such techniques as restoration or replacement cost valuations, travel cost valuations, hedonic pricing, and contingent or willingness-to-pay valuations.

Commonly, the practice of commodifying nature occurs in the context of calculating after-the-fact damages awards for contamination of natural resources. Ecological economists have recently adopted a different approach, seeking to quantify the value of services provided by ecosystems *before* irreversible human disruption. The significance of focusing on ecosystem services, rather than natural resources, is that they are seen by researchers as largely irreplaceable and therefore more fundamental to human survival. Moreover, while the economy may be able to signal and adjust to specific resource scarcities, the services provided by the earth are generally not subject to economic signaling. Thus, in order to ensure the long-term sustainability of human economic activity, ecological economists believe that natural services which lack practical man-made substitutes should be given a quantified presence within economic decisionmaking. By generating even approximate figures for the value of these services, ecological economists hope to impress upon private and public decisionmakers the environmental costs of contemplated development schemes.

A celebrated example of such thinking can be seen in the City of New York's decision to reclaim watershed areas in the Catskills mountains rather than build a capital-intensive water treatment facility. The Catskills have long been the primary source of purified water for New York City, but in recent years the water failed EPA standards for drinking water due to development in the mountains as well as increased sewage, pesticide, and fertilizer contamination. The city estimated that a purification plant would cost $4 billion to build plus annual operating costs, while restoring the natural integrity of the Catskills through land acquisition and restoration would cost only around $660 million. Thus, the City decided to invest in "natural capital" as a more efficient and aesthetically desirable alternative to the traditional industrial solution.

The City of New York's choice was easy to make because the treatment plant option provided a clear and reliable measure of the worth of the Catskills watershed services. As James Salzman has noted, "Replacement cost provides an effective method for valuing services because one can compare dollar investments in natural capital and physical capital to determine payback periods and overall costs." Ecological economists believe that if valuations of ecosystem services are available to policymakers at crucial decision times in that manner, economic development will become much more consonant with sustainable use patterns. For instance, researchers studying alternative management strategies for mangrove forests in Indonesia have found that when nontimber uses, including fish, locally used products, and erosion control, are included in cost-benefit calculations, sustainable timber practices are significantly more economic than traditional ones, yielding $4,800 per hectare rather than merely $3,600.

* * *

Of course, in their totality, ecosystem services consist of the very ability to support human life, rendering their aggregate value equivalent to the very value one places on human existence. Economic tools are simply not designed to measure such concepts. By attempting to price the various subcomponents of ecosystems, however, ecological economists have begun to speak in a language that economists and policymakers can fathom and operationalize. As the Catskills watershed and Indonesian mangrove examples point out, the resulting dialogue can yield surprising agreement between environmental and economic interests. *The Economists' Statement on Climate Change*, signed by over 2500 economists, including eight Nobel Laureates, offers an unqualified endorsement of such collaborative exercises in the context of reducing greenhouse emissions: "[S]ound economic analysis shows that there are policy options that would slow climate change without harming American living standards, and these measures may in fact improve U.S. productivity in the longer run." Ecological economists believe that such "sound economic analysis" can become commonplace in the debate over competing business and environmental concerns.

6.   Discount Rates and Intergenerational Equity

A final issue of concern to ecological economists is the use of discount rates in regulatory and investment decisionmaking. When evaluating a particular investment decision, economists typically reduce expected costs and benefits to present value using a discount rate, or a percentage factor that adjusts the amount of a value over time. For instance, using a discount rate of 10%, an investment yielding $110 in year two is worth only $100 in year one. If the investment costs $105 to make in year one, it is not an economic choice. Such reasoning holds well in the context of paper investment decisions. However, when the expected yield consists of saved lives, preserved ecosystem services, and other nontangible benefits to present and future generations, it is not altogether obvious that the same analysis should apply. Nevertheless, economists have long taken discounting to be the appropriate response to questions of environmental importance. As early as 1913, economists noted that "[t]he primary problem of conservation, . . . expressed in economic language, is the determination of the proper rate of discount on the future with respect to the utilization of our natural resources."

Frequently, discount rates are determined based on the prevailing real rate of interest charged in capital markets. However, positive interest rates, which can be said to represent the growth potential of man-made capital, are a poor indicator of the growth potential of natural capital. The fact that capital may grow in a bank at 10% per year does not necessarily imply that an old growth forest will regenerate at an equal rate. A timber company adopting a 10% discount rate to determine harvesting schedules will "rationally" clear forests faster than they can regrow, essentially liquidating the natural capital of the forest rather than consuming only its annual income. In this manner, use of positive discount rates in development strategy can lead to an "optimal" choice that is unsustainable—"the impoverishment of future generations as a result of the profligacy of present generations in such cases is not just an incidental, but a desirable outcome of the decision making process."

Besides encouraging unsustainable investment strategies, discounting can also discourage ecologically desirable government regulations. Because society must often pay the costs of environmental regulation long before the benefits accrue, discounting of future costs and benefits frequently counsels against the adoption of environmentally-protective measures. Daniel Farber and Paul Hemmersbaugh provide an extreme illustration by positing the case of two alternative designs for a nuclear waste repository. The designs will cost the same amount and will both be paid for entirely in the first year. If the first design is adopted, no workers will be killed during construction but one billion people will be killed in five hundred years due to a radiation leak from the repository. If the second design is adopted, between one and two workers will likely be killed during construction but no leaks and therefore no deaths will occur in five hundred years. Using a discount rate of 5%, the regulator selecting between designs "will choose the first option because one billion lives 500 years hence have a lower present value than one life today." Similar reasoning applies in less extreme, more common settings. Preventing greenhouse gas emissions, water contamination, species extinction, resource depletion, and many other environmental harms imposes current costs while offering mainly future benefits. As such, the measures routinely fail cost-benefit analyses that use a high positive discount rate.

Still, though, the impact of discounting on the environment is difficult to generalize. As Daly has pointed out, high positive discount rates can have two competing effects on natural resource exploitation. Although a high rate will shift the allocation of capital and labor to projects that exploit resources more quickly, the rate will also limit the total number of projects that are undertaken given that expected project benefits must overcome a higher opportunity cost value. Conversely, a low discount rate may slow the rate of resource extraction, but it may also increase the total number of extractive projects undertaken by making the projects appear more economic. Thus, the total effect of discounting on the environment is ambiguous, leading to what Richard Norgaard and Richard Howarth have called "the conservationist's dilemma."

Norgaard and Howarth have attempted to solve this dilemma by separating the questions of intragenerational resource allocation, for which discounting is an appropriate policy tool, and intergenerational resource distribution, for which discounting is not. Economists frequently recognize that unfettered market outcomes will not necessarily result in a just distribution of resources between generations, just as they do not necessarily result in distributive justice within generations. Stiglitz, for instance, noted that "[t]here is ... no presumption that the intertemporal distribution of income which emerges from the market solution will be 'socially optimal....' " Most economists, however, believe that the use of a discount rate is sufficient to solve the problem of intergenerational equity. As Stiglitz put it, "if the government correctly controls the rate of interest ... then there would be no objection to the competitive determination of the rate of utilization of our natural resources."

However, as Norgaard and Howarth point out, the discount rate cannot simultaneously serve the purpose of intragenerational allocative efficiency and intergenerational distributive equity. As noted above, governments often look to market rates of interest in setting discount rates for policy proposals, yet interest rates, like prices, quantities, and other market outcomes, are dependent upon the initial distribution of resources, including intergenerational distributions. "Since all of the variables that go into the calculation of net present value of a project or policy proposal depend on the intergenerational distribution of income, what might appear to be a good social investment under one income distribution may be marginal or worse under another." In other words, relying upon market rates of interest to guide social policies affecting intergenerational resource distribution presupposes the very judgment to be made.

Because he recognizes that discounting acts as a subtle proxy for important decisions of intergenerational equity in this manner, famed economist Robert Solow has suggested that the discount rate should be determined directly by society rather than by reference to market interest rates. Selection of a social discount rate, however, must be determined in large part by society's view of the initial intergenerational distribution of resources. Following selection of the rate, a new equilibrium will emerge in which resources are distributed differently among generations. That new equilibrium will cause the current generation to reconsider its choice of the appropriate discount rate, which will result in still another equilibrium, and so on.

Thus, relying upon use of a discount rate to automatically "correct" the problem of intergenerational distribution is problematic, no matter how the rate is determined. Intergenerational distributive questions are rate-determining, not rate-determined. In other words, the decision whether to curtail greenhouse emissions should depend directly on whether society wishes to risk depriving future generations of climate stability, not on whether the discount rate will permit it to happen. As Norgaard and Howarth put it, "Questions which are fundamentally matters of equity should be treated as such."

Returning to Farber and Hemmersbaugh's example helps to illustrate these considerations. On the standard approach, if a proposed regulation would save the lives of one billion people five hundred years from now, the value of those lives is discounted to a present value. In essence, economists attempt to measure what it is worth to society *now* to save the lives of a billion people in the future. As Farber and Hemmersbaugh demonstrate, it turns out not to be worth very much. However, the use of the present generation's valuation of the worth of a future generation's lives is a normative judgment that should not be obscured by arithmetic. As Lisa Heinzerling powerfully put it, "Generating numbers that are ultimately irrelevant to the questions to be resolved does more than waste precious regulatory resources. It changes the apparent nature of the decision itself, and permits politics and ideology to hide behind a mask of technical expertise."

* * *

III. Law and Ecological Economics

Although few in number, there have been significant efforts to incorporate macroeconomic concepts into legal economic analysis. Moreover, certain specific subject areas have benefited greatly from scholarly application of macroeconomic insights, including international trade regulation, foreign and domestic monetary policy, as well as immigration, administrative, employment, taxation, environmental, and criminal law. Despite these efforts, however, the law and economics movement remains primarily restricted to the application of microeconomic concepts to legal theory. This traditional exclusion of macroeconomic subject matter from law and economics raises an obvious question: Do we really need a macroeconomics for legal analysis?

The answer to this question requires a clear exposition of the subjects with which economics is concerned. As Daly has pointed out, there are three general dimensions to the economic problem: optimal allocation of inputs among uses, equitable distribution of wealth, and maintenance of economic scale within sustainable limits. The first dimension is the domain of microeconomics, while the latter two belong to macroeconomics. In both economic and legal economic analyses, attention has focused almost exclusively on the first of these dimensions. Traditionally, economists have argued that the best way to solve the distribution problem is to provide an effective answer to the allocation problem. By ensuring that resources are allocated to their most efficient uses, one maximizes the amount of wealth created, and hence, the amount of wealth available for distribution throughout society. Increases in economic productivity, therefore, can result, at least theoretically, in higher absolute levels of income for everyone and the possibility of significant upward mobility for some. In addition to providing an explicit laissez-faire response to the question of distribution, this growth-oriented policy also provides an implicit laissez-faire answer to the scale problem: by relying on economic growth as a response to the problem of inequitable distribution, economists necessarily believe that the optimal scale of the economy is always "bigger."

Law and economics scholars have adopted a similar, albeit far more refined, position. Most law and economics thinkers accept Steven Shavell and Louis Kaplow's forceful argument that legal rules should be constructed to achieve optimal allocation of resources among competing uses, without concern for the distributional effects of such rules. As they argue, for every inefficient but desirably redistributive legal rule, one can imagine an alternate legal rule coupled with a redistributive tax scheme that would achieve the same desired wealth transfer without the efficiency loss. For that reason (along with its comparative administrative advantage at transferring wealth), the tax and transfer system should be the exclusive means for the government to address distributional concerns. Of course, because redistribution of income through the tax and transfer system is simply a matter of setting politically-determined levels of redistribution, its interest to legal economists has been somewhat negligible. Despite a recent provocative attempt to reconsider Shavell and Kaplow's argument on empirical and theoretical grounds, its hold over the discipline remains. Consequently, the question of equitable distribution, and with it the field of macroeconomics, has been largely removed from the domain of law and economics.

Thus, both economists and legal economists have found theoretical grounds for ignoring the problem of wealth distribution and the lesser-recognized problem of sustainable scale. Meanwhile, wealth disparities have risen to record levels, a fact that might reflect contemporary America's lack of political resolve to use the tax and transfer system in the manner hypothesized by Shavell and Kaplow. This failure cannot be considered a direct or intended consequence of Shavell and Kaplow's reasoning, of course. Their argument contemplates removing distributional issues from analysis of legal rules; it does not advise ignoring such issues in all aspects of political discussion.

Yet the *effect* of their analysis might be to do just that—economics, and in particular growth economics, has become the dominant language of political speech, to the point of largely drowning out other dialects. As one scholar put it, "the increasing domination of homo economicus is evidenced by the fact that public discourse has become hostage to economics and has begun to dance to, instead of call, the economic tune: it is thoroughly infiltrated by the economic mindset and attuned to its interests." Before such economics occupied the bulk of the political landscape, it may have been appropriate to ignore distributional concerns on the assumption that they would be dealt with by the moral and political will of the people. Now it has become arguably tantamount to assigning a zero value to the goal of equitable distribution. In other words, when economists and legal economists exclude certain issues from their discussion on the assumption that some other discipline or some *other* mechanism will address the excluded concern, they may in effect be relegating that concern to the dustbin of politics.

In the terms of Shavell and Kaplow's argument, while it may be true that "any regime with an inefficient [but redistributive] legal rule [can be replaced with an] efficient legal rule and a modified income tax system in which all individuals are better off," the modified income tax system necessary to ensure that such a Pareto improvement actually eventuates may not be possible within a given political climate, including perhaps the current one. As a practical matter, therefore, Shavell and Kaplow's argument may demonstrate only that *potential* Pareto improvements may be gained by excluding distributive effects from the selection of legal rules. Whether legal decisionmakers should continue to ignore distributional effects when it is confidently known that the necessary "modified income tax system" will not be adopted—that is, when it is known that the redistribution necessary to achieve the Pareto improvement will not occur—is a question not directly addressed by Shavell and Kaplow's argument, as they themselves acknowledge.

Precisely the same analysis applies to the goal of sustainable scale. Although it has not appeared within the legal economic literature, one could make an argument against the consideration of scale effects of legal rules that tracks Shavell and Kaplow's reasoning. The same response, however, would apply: whether ignorance of scale effects is justified in the face of legislative recalcitrance is a separate, and more difficult, question. Indeed, with respect to scale, the problem is worse because no mechanism analogous to the tax and transfer system exists to regulate the scale of the economy, even if economic discourse does not crowd the issue out of political attention. The problem of achieving a sustainable scale of the human economy is left as a macroeconomic goal better addressed through unique, macro-economic policy instruments—yet no such instruments are in place. And to compound the problem, the current accepted wisdom regarding the distribution problem—that growth in the scale of the economy will raise absolute wealth levels for all market participants—directly conflicts with the goal of maintaining society's ecological footprint within sustainable parameters.

In short, current economic wisdom attempts to "solve" two of society's most urgent problems by trading them off against each other, and current legal economic wisdom appears to have found reasons for ignoring both.

The inconsistency is not recognized because mainstream macroeconomics does not acknowledge the problem of regulating scale. Perpetual growth is considered a viable response to the distribution problem because no adverse consequences to such growth are recognized. In effect, economists believe that they have found the global free lunch. Critics of this economic policy are at a decided disadvantage in popular and scholarly debates because they cannot point to any harmful effects of growth. Instead, they can only argue that economic growth has not achieved the goal of reducing wealth inequality. But that failure is not enough to overcome the compelling force of Pareto improvement: if a few people are better off because of economic growth, and no one is worse off, how can growth be opposed?

Ecological economists reveal the fallacy of this position by making the problem of sustainable scale an issue of explicit concern. Through the lens of ecological economics, growth economics becomes assailable not only because wealth increases might not "trickle down" in the predicted fashion, but also because the biophysical demands entailed by economic growth may have pushed the human economy toward unsustainable levels. Once one accepts the foundational principle of ecological economics—that the level of material throughout in the economy is subject to ecological constraints—the macroeconomic concerns of distribution and scale can no longer be pushed to the side in the ever-intensifying pursuit of allocative efficiency. Indeed, as noted above, there is some reason to believe that economic growth in America in the latter decades of the twentieth century has become harmful to society on net, once one considers the environmental and social externalities that are not ordinarily accounted for by macroeconomic indicators. Under such conditions, scale and distribution can no longer remain the neglected stepsiblings of allocation within the family of economic aspirations.

For at least two reasons, then, law and economics may be incomplete without some form of macroeconomics to inform its analysis. First, because no political mechanism analogous to the tax and transfer system exists to regulate the scale of the macroeconomy, legal economic scholars cannot safely ignore the scale effects of alternative legal rules in the way that they have ignored distributive effects. Second, because the traditional response of economists to the distribution problem is in direct conflict with the goal of sustainable scale, law and economics' continued ignorance of both problems may result in the discipline's long-term marginalization. In other words, if natural limits turn out to constrain the scale of the human economy in the manner hypothesized by ecological economists, then the economist's practice of postponing the problem of distribution by punting on the problem of scale will not be viable in the long run. In light of this possibility, legal economic scholars may be wise to address both problems now by allowing ecological economic insights to inform their analysis.

This methodological approach would have two obvious but important effects. First, it would force legal scholars to confront the problem of maintaining a sustainable economy in their relevant analyses. By incorporating ecological economic insights into legal policy discussion, legal scholars could essentially leapfrog mainstream economic thought to provide both the theoretical impetus for and the practical construction of policy tools that ensure long-term sustainability. The practical benefit of confronting the problem of scale is potentially enormous. Recently, 1586 scientists from 63 countries, including 104 of the 178 living Nobel Prize winners in the sciences, signed the World Scientists' Call for Action at the Kyoto Climate Summit which stated that "the scientific community ha[s] reached a consensus that grave threats imperil the future of humanity and the global environment." The United States' failure to heed this call to action from many of the world's most learned scientific experts demonstrates the stranglehold that mainstream economic ideology has on the political mindscape. By incorporating ecological economic insights into their policy analysis, however, legal economic scholars could take an important step toward harmonizing economic and scientific concerns.

A secondary effect of such an effort likely would be to revitalize the debate over distributional equity. If it is accepted that sustainability requires limits to the physical strain placed by humans on the ecosphere, absolute growth in the scale of the human economy would no longer be available as an answer to the problem of inequitable distribution. Instead, society would have to address the problem directly as a necessary subissue to the problem of determining a permissible level of resource throughout that does not jeopardize the viability of future generations. Of course, Shavell and Kaplow's argument that distributional concerns are more efficiently addressed through the tax and transfer system than through legal rulemaking would still apply under such a worldview. However, legal scholars and legal decisionmakers would have renewed interest in making certain that the goal of equitable distribution is actually being served, or at least examined, by other political mechanisms. The difficult question of political philosophy not addressed by Shavell and Kaplow's argument might then become an issue of some urgency.

　　* * *

CONCLUSION

At the time Adam Smith developed the image of rational market behavior, science in general was captivated by Enlightenment notions of limitless human intellectual ability. That microeconomists have clung to these notions longer than practitioners of any other discipline reflects what Alfred North Whitehead called the fallacy of misplaced concreteness—a failure to recognize that one's abstract theories continually must be informed by the reality from which they were abstracted. Indeed, it has only been in recent years that scholars of behavioral law and economics have made progress in upsetting the presumption of rationality in legal economic analysis by incorporating the decidedly nonrational findings of cognitive psychologists.

A similar historical analysis applies to macroeconomics. *When the core concepts of macroeconomics developed, the world contained four billion less people than it does today.* The preanalytic vision which informed the development of neoclassical thought was that of a world in which human activity was but a tiny fraction of global activity. Human use of resources and production of wastes was considered costless because the regenerative and absorptive capacities of the earth appeared to have no limits. Today, evidence to the contrary arrives with regularity, to the point that the Royal Society of London and the United States National Academy of Sciences issued an unprecedented joint action statement, warning: "The future of our planet is in the balance. Sustainable development can be achieved, but only if irreversible degradation of the environment can be halted in time. The next 30 years may be crucial." The continued dominance within economics of a view of nature as limitless demonstrates that macroeconomic theorists also may have committed Whitehead's anti-rationalist fallacy: "an arbitrary halt at a particular set of abstractions."

Yet surprisingly little recognition has been given to the fact that macroeconomics rests on what is arguably now a discredited world-view. Among economists, increasing divergence between theory and reality is accounted for by increasing recognition of "externalities," much like the Ptolemaic astronomers who attempted to save their model of circular planetary motion through desperate addition of epicycles. However, lest society is to risk growing beyond the biophysical limits of the earth (not to mention the point at which marginal costs of macroeconomic growth exceed marginal benefits), it seems appropriate to develop an alternative economics, one grounded in scientifically plausible visions of the relationship between economic and ecological spheres. What seems needed is a body of market principles built on the assumptions that natural resources are limited, that ecosystem services have value, and that the size of the human economy is a legitimate subject for social control. Because ecological economists have provided just that, their teachings may be of great use to legal scholars in the years to come.

––––––

NOTES AND QUESTIONS

1. Bounded rationality, self-interest, and ecological economics. Does economic theory explain why ecological economics remains at present a marginal rather than a central stream within the discipline of economics? That is, are politicians and policymakers concerned with their own short-term self-interest over an altruistic concern for the earth or for future generations? Are politicians and policymakers afflicted with problems relating to bounded rationality when it comes to environmental issues?

2. The fall of neoclassical theory? Based on the critiques outlined in this chapter, what useful insights, if any, remain from classical market theory? Do the critiques outlined in this chapter challenge Adam Smith's original insights, or only the reduction of his work in neoclassical economics?

CHAPTER 5

BEYOND CLASSIC MARKET THEORY: EXTERNAL CRITIQUES

As the influence of law and economics scholarship grew in the legal academy, so did the depth and breadth of criticism directed to its organizing concepts. In this chapter, we explore the challenges to price theory, rational choice, and wealth maximization premises that have come from those who do not share the law and economics faith in markets and private ordering. Within law, the criticisms spanned a broad range of perspectives. There were doctrinalists who were unconvinced by the positive claim that the common law converges on efficiency, to critical legal scholars who rejected the normative premise that wealth maximization is a coherent value for evaluating the legal rules that govern the distribution of material goods in a democracy. The dialogue has, at times, been heated and deeply engaged. As Anita Bernstein's review of the thirty-five-year period of development of the law and economics school shows, the outside challengers have often used colorful language to report their findings that: the central tenets of law and economics were "incoherent," "dubious in the extreme," "garbage in and garbage out," and a "cult."

Ironically, critical race theorists, one group of scholars with perhaps the most incompatible world view, have largely ignored law and economics, even as their narrative methodology became the target of direct criticism from leaders of law and economics. For scholars who believe that the problem of racial subordination is a central conundrum of modern and post-modern legal thought, the law and economics model of rational choice must surely be an unpersuasively thin account of how racial identity and cultural difference works in the markets. This casebook is our contribution to engaging law and economic reasoning and identifying alternative constructions of identity, law, culture, and markets.

In this chapter we explore several of the most powerful challenges to law and economics. First, we take up the most important and central claim of law and economics, that people make economic choices on the basis of a rational assessment of their own self-interest. Second, we examine the commodification challenge to markets. In this view of markets, price theory and the wealth maximization premises impose prices on aspects of human interaction that cannot and should not be reduced to a pecuniary value. This argument insists that some "aspects of social life are inappropriate for the market." Arguing for recognition of the personal aspects of some monetary transactions, Margaret Radin urges acceptance of commodification in some spheres, while refusing to try to completely separate the two value systems. She urges us to accept her view that "[i]ncomplete commodification" allows the human impulses of altruism, social justice, community, and individuality to thrive alongside markets in which commodities with pecuniary values are exchanged. We extend this discussion to include the modifying arguments of some legal feminists who have worried that the commodification idea undercuts women's economic autonomy when they work overtime in the unpaid roles of caregivers at home.

The idea that market participants assert their preferences based upon a reasoned appraisal of their own self-interest is a major point of criticism for both internal and external critics. Much of the external criticism has been concerned with the failure of rational choice theory to account for differences in identity and cultural context. Unlike the internal critics, who rely primarily upon the insights of psychology, external critics turn to several of the other social sciences such as sociology, anthropology, and linguistics to construct a view of the economic actor that reveals the race, gender, and other identity variables that contribute to market decisions. More importantly, some scholars have based their objections on the so far underdeveloped, but promising, exploration of the role of systematic subordination in markets.

Law and economics scholarship, like neoclassical economics, is actively hostile to the idea of using government intervention to equalize the vast disparities in wealth that form the predicate to market participation. Ironically, this hostility to government intervention disappears when government policy increases the wealth of the already wealthy. In the policy realm, this contradictory approach to redistribution can be seen in the enthusiasm for tax cuts that increase the amount of wealth the upper income brackets retain, while reducing the size of government expenditures to provide subsistence for those left behind by market competition. Kevin Phillips, a popular writer on economic history and policy, writes: "Laissez-faire is a pretense. Government power and preferment have been used by the rich, not shunned." WEALTH AND DEMOCRACY xiv (2002).

In this chapter, we will explore the major arguments that legal scholars who do not share the economic premises of neoclassical economics have made to highlight the shortcomings of that perspective.

A.   An Overview

Whatever Happened to Law and Economics?

64 Md. L. Rev. 101 (2005).

■ Anita Bernstein

* * * "Every fresh contribution to the economic analysis of tort law," wrote Ernest Weinrib in 1989, "adds a new storey to an edifice whose bottom has long since disappeared into the sand."

* * * Then came Leonard Jaffee * * *: "So, I have two big gripes against Law and Economics. One is that it's sick and spreads sickness. The other's that it doesn't work in ways it claims, or do what it pretends." * * * According to David Gray Carlson, "[t]here are two types of law-and-economics: one that is dubious and another that is dubious in the extreme." In her 2004 book, *The Triumph of Venus*, Jeanne Schroeder, who'd majored in economics in college, declared that "most law-and-economic proposals are classic cases of GIGO (garbage in—garbage out): nonfalsified theories are applied to untested assumptions in order to produce nonverifiable conclusions. Law-and-economics has all the characteristics of a cult."

These attacks arrayed in the background, I make here a somewhat different claim: that law and economics is no longer amenable to critique. This movement, in my view, is not an edifice whose bottom has disappeared into the sand. Instead it is not an edifice at all. In past decades, it did take shape as a unique structure; the Chicago school bore distinctive characteristics. A scholar generating new work in law and economics during this "edifice" era would borrow precepts from neoclassical economics and apply them to the law, in an effort either to describe, in material terms, how law affects and responds to aggregations of human beings ("positive" law and economics) or to propose measures designed to improve these consequences ("normative" or "prescriptive" law and economics). Many practitioners, Richard Posner foremost among them, dealt in both description and prescription. The combination brought to law the most philosophical strand in microeconomic theory, welfare economics.

Today the Chicago edifice shares attention with other types of law and economics. Anyone reading this far has undoubtedly heard that law and economics contains multitudes—an array of literatures, sub-movements, and schools of thought. Perhaps it does. Certainly a scholar trained in both economics and law has the vocabulary to combine the two disciplines in ways that would not hew to the descriptions of Chicago-style welfare economics, or to any other fraction of the genre. But observers with no stake in the cliché about diversity can see how well it serves insiders, who get from it a basis to say that their movement is big *and* a ready retort to semi-disavow anything in it that provokes criticism: "Well, that's one of the other schools." Law and economics can claim pluralism when pluralism suits, monolithic unity when pluralism threatens to splinter its power.

This inclination within the movement to have it both ways impels me to take a second look at its premise that law and economics is distinct from all other disciplines yet eclectic and pluralistic, the academy's big tent. The two postures are not only in tension with each other but perhaps also, I start to suspect, questionable in isolation. For law and economics to be valid, two conditions must obtain: law and economics needs a foundation of meaningful concepts and a boundary to fence out what it rejects or does not believe. If these two elements are missing, then its distinctive aspects may be unsound and its variations, offshoots, and alliances may be incoherent. In this Article I explore this question of foundations under, and boundaries around, the movement.

* * * [M]y rhetorical question, *Whatever happened...?* broaches an argument that although a generation ago law and economics stood—as an edifice, if you like—it no longer endures. The movement was done in by a blend of some claims that were wrong with other claims that came across in legal circles as too right—and also too trivial to reject. Law and economics combined too little accuracy with too much: While ill founded, dubious, or tautological premises were eroding its credibility, other notions from the movement, consistent with what diverse thinkers and audiences believed, blurred the line between law and economics on one hand and everything else in jurisprudence on the other. Withdraw the mistakes and exaggerations from law and economics and what you get is either positive scholarship declaring 5 to be the sum of 3 and 2, or some indistinguishable share of the centrist, forward-looking quasi-utilitarian mélange of advice to policy-minded lawyers that now dominates the legal academy, unconfined to any sector.

During the last decade, members of the movement labored to stop the fall. Unable to do much about errors, they worked on the second front, the crisis of too much acceptance, mainly by trying to claim successful outsider movements as their own, rather than reacting to them as threats or challenges. When psychology dealt blows to the ideal of a rational actor, for instance, economic analysts invoked the label of "behavioral economics" to describe claims that were directly contrary to neoclassical dogma. Led by Robert Ellickson, they used the word "norms" to summarize phenomena inconvenient to the edifice. This capacious label not only could obscure what did not fit the neoclassical model, but also aid a contention that human behaviors deviating from the paradigm—behaviors that reveal altruism, expenditures that appear to waste rather than accrete money, refusals to cheat or defect in games, and the like are consistent with law and economics, rather than refutations of its core premises. This cooptation strategy reached a height in 2002 with the publication of *Fairness Versus Welfare*, a book from two scholars identified with the law and economics movement who declared victory by asserting that Welfare accounted for everything that jurisprudence pursues, except for a handful of silly vestigial claims which the authors disparaged as Fairness. This putative victory, however, would be better described as submergence into a larger whole. Part of the law and economics edifice has disappeared into the sand; part has joined the sand itself.

So much for Weinrib's edifice; Jeanne Schroeder had a different one-word critique. Schroeder called law and economics a "cult" in order to rebuke it for falling short of scientific standards. Yet cults are characterized by more than just clinging to a dogma that gets reality wrong. They are social groups. They contain members who disdain nonmembers, and who have been known to enjoy thinking that outsiders feel hostility towards them. I quote Schroeder's insult with approval even though one might debate her charges of falsity—as a concise description of a movement done in by the twin stabbings of excessive inaccuracy and trivial accuracy. Stripped of its distinctive intellectual features, no longer able to give descriptions or policy recommendations that could not have come from sources outside the movement, law and economics now functions mainly as a faculty club with opaque, arbitrary criteria for membership.

Where do *The Costs of Accidents* and Guido Calabresi fit in this picture? Away from the missteps. Calabresi's book, in contrast to the one by Kaplow and Shavell, focuses on Welfare without perceiving it as a prizefighter that has beaten or should beat a straw man, hapless Fairness. It draws readers in with its clarity and reason, never trying to exclude or intimidate anyone. It is a model, indeed, of what law and economics scholarship can contribute in the eras following refutation of its core tenets: a wide social science that invites participants to consider the common good.

I.   ERRORS: WHAT HAS CRUMBLED, WHAT HAS NEVER BEEN

Consider how the tenets and distinguishing features of law and economics are faring at the thirty-fifth anniversary of *The Costs of Accidents*.

A.   *Three Precepts*

1.   Rational Choice.—On the first page of *Economic Analysis of Law,* Richard Posner declared a first axiom: "man is a rational maximizer of his ends in life." This individual knows what he wants and chooses means to reach his goals. The world through economists' eyes begins here, at the point where an individual makes a choice among alternatives. Rational choice is the "first and most basic" of "the critical early moves" in law and economics. Only if individuals can know what they want and act instrumentally on their desires can the other central precepts of the discipline— among them preferences, opportunities, and a consciousness of scarcity— make sense.

Moreover, Posner continues,

> the concept of rationality used by the economist is objective rather than subjective, so that it would not be a solecism to speak of a rational frog. Rationality means little more to an economist than a disposition to choose, consciously or unconsciously, an apt means to whatever ends the chooser happens to have.

According to this construction of rationality, the chooser will not lose the designation of "rational" just because her choices are self-destructive, perverse, opaque, inconsistent, unstable over time, resistant to Arrovian ordinal ranking, or dependent on the unpredictable choices that others make. Her choices can even defy the downward-sloping demand curve. As Arthur Leff noted decades ago, when

> a society dentist raises his prices and thereby increases his gross volume of business, it is no violation of the principle of the inverse relation between price and quantity. It only proves that buyers now perceive that they are buying something else which they now value more highly, "society dentistry" say, rather than "mere" dentistry.

Because "whatever ends the chooser happens to have" emerge from her behavior rather than from her own testimony or other expression, any means in this "objective" sense can be "apt."

One critique of Chicago-style law and economics argues that rational choice according to this school remains vulnerable to challenges that philosophy has long been expressing, perhaps "since the fourth century B.C." For openers, explains philosopher and classics scholar Martha Nussbaum, law and economics regards preferences as "exogenous, i.e., not significantly shaped by laws and institutions," whereas "the endogeneity of preferences has been recognized by almost all the major writers on emotion and desire in the history of Western philosophy." To speak of choice as if it originated entirely inside the actor is simply wrong. Furthermore, individuals do not simply make choices: they value their power to do so. People "do not typically view as equivalent two states of the world, one produced by their own agency and the other not." Ends, which law and economics sees as fixed, actually vary over time and through discourse; human beings deliberate about them. The concept of "preferences" sloppily throws together what philosophers have kept separated as five distinct phenomena: "belief, desire, perception, appetite, and emotion."

Along with old writings that cast the economists' version of rational choice into question, newer ones have refuted this concept through experimentation and revision. The neoclassical conception of rationality had fancied that human beings make choices within a preference ordering that is complete and transitive, subject to perfect and costlessly acquired information. Reality began to sully the premise. In the mid-twentieth century Herbert Simon established a beachhead for empiricism in economics with his identification of "bounded rationality," whereby a subject makes the best choices she can, given her limited "knowledge and computational capacities and skills." Simon's work brought about behavioral economics, the branch of microeconomics that focuses on the choices individuals make rather than the processes of their decisionmaking. "Choice," manifested in behaviors rather than the trail of conscious strategy that precedes them, came to subsume "rational": if some actor did it, then we'll say she made a choice in pursuit of her own ends.

* * * [T]his outcome cannot sit well in law and economics because of how much it gives away. * * * Posner "assumes that adding an account of 'nonrationality' in market relations would be tantamount to abandoning theory entirely in favor of a mere all-inclusive description of empirical behavior lacking any explanatory or predictive power." He concludes that "behavioral economics merely describes human actions [and does a poor job of doing so] but has no theory of action." * * *

* * * [T]he dilemma for law and economics is clear. Neoclassical assertions of rationality—abstract, laboratory-crystalline, severed from ordinary experience—stray too far from empirical fact to explain or predict much. Posner's "rational frog" expresses this limitation succinctly: we believe the frog pursues her own ends, but we have nothing but her behavior to look at when we seek support for that belief. To the extent that economic analysts accept variety in human behavior, especially behavior that defies well-ordered pursuit of transparent ends, they became less able to explain and predict because they have conceded that human behavior is either random or, alternatively, obedient to some logic alien to the rational actor model, and thus beyond their ken.

Economic analysts regret this defeat and hope they can undo it. "Deviations from the rational-actor assumption can and should be incorporated into economic analysis," declares the Harvard law and economics website. The cooptation strategy cannot, however, readily accommodate material so contrary to a first principle of economic analysis.

2. Efficiency vs. Wealth Maximization vs. Welfare.—What do, or should, individuals or societies or legal systems choose to pursue? Economic analysts have shuttled between terms to describe the goal. Two leading contenders have been "efficiency" (or sometimes allocative "efficiency") and "wealth maximization." A third term, "welfare," has arisen more recently. None is stable. * * *

If "efficiency" stands in for utilitarianism, Posner argued, then efficiency is inferior to wealth maximization as a description of what individuals and societies pursue, or should be understood as pursuing. Utilitarianism, in Posner's rendering, seeks a "surplus of pleasure over pain," but gives its followers no guidance as to whose pleasure counts (are animals included?), no distinction between average and total happiness, and no metric to evaluate success and failure. Wealth maximization as an alternative ideal avoids these difficulties by insisting on "value in dollars or dollar equivalents." In Posner's summation: The only kind of preference that counts in a system of wealth maximization is thus one that is backed up by money—in other words, that is registered in a market. * * *

The reliance on prices adds other complications to the wealth maximization criterion. * * * Price is a function of demand, and demand will vary in response to preexisting distributions of wealth. It is thus idle—or instead politically significant, . . . —to contemplate wealth maximization without attention to how much wealth each maximizer already has. With a dollar the only metric and with the marginal utility of money a sure fact, wealth maximization "has the result of weighting the preferences of wealthy persons more heavily than the preferences of poorer persons"—that is, the rich get extra ballots in the form of dollars they don't need to save. *Tant pis* for wealth maximization.

Following this critique of the wealth-maximization criterion, "welfare" has arisen as a kind of successor to the old precursor of wealth maximization, "efficiency." Louis Kaplow and Steven Shavell have led the charge among economic analysts to promote this word as summation of what societies and individuals pursue. To many, welfare seems more capacious, perhaps more humanistic, than "efficiency" or any other word standing in for utilitarianism. Yet because it does not repair what "wealth maximization" once purported to fix—that is, vagueness, indeterminacy, disagreements about measurement—"welfare" carries economic analysts back to their old condition of not being able to describe what they seek.

We see here a dilemma similar to that which haunts the economist's view of rational choice. The movement can cling to "efficiency" and remain vulnerable to criticisms about tautology, circularity, vagueness, and evasion of pertinent political questions. Alternatively, it can focus on "wealth maximization," a path that adds misdescription to the mix and cannot escape similar perils of tautology. Or try "welfare," which in application cannot be distinguished from efficiency and its perils.

3.   *Faith in Markets.*—Following *The Problem of Social Cost*, both descriptive and normative strands of law and economics evinced some enthusiasm for what they called "the market." Coase had recharacterized costs. Whereas earlier thinking, following Pigou, had seen costs as detriments that one entity imposes on another, to Coase costs were instead phenomena that obstructed market functions. The market, always central in all of microeconomics, took on after Coase even more fundamental importance to its cousin law and economics. Efficiency, for instance, could be defined as the outcome that a free market would produce. In this normative sense, the existence of a market makes efficiency (or wealth maximization) possible.

The normative truism about markets making wealth has not much occupied law and economics. In an alternative, descriptive sense, however, law and economics has seen markets wherever human beings deal with one another, including venues far from commercial transactions. Marriage and family formation take place in markets, according to Gary Becker and others. Individuals negotiate their sexual relations as trades. Scarce body parts like kidneys, say economists, could profitably become the objects of regulated exchange. The adoption of infants takes place within a market whether we like it or not, said Posner in the famously career-thwarting paper he wrote with Elisabeth Landes. Gestational surrogacy for pay is a service that American law has long been condoning. * * * In a recent essay, Claire Hill defends the faith-in-markets perspective within law and economics, and urges "skeptics" who don't want to see markets applied to "the personal sphere" to reconsider their position.

Yet even if "the market" can shed light on "the personal sphere," the law and economics project of identifying unseen markets—in human bodies and intimate associations and the like—seems to have run its course. At the risk of signing a death certificate before the patient has died, and thus compelling myself to lie next to Morton Horwitz and Owen Fiss, I will venture to say that today "the market" does not account for much novelty or centrality in this field, neither its normative nor its more recent descriptive versions. Coase's masterpiece, always amenable to divergent readings, now sounds like a warning that markets always fail, rather than a promise that exchange will work perfectly after the friction of transaction costs has been removed.

Accompanying this decline of the market in law and economics scholarship, a generation of writings skeptical of this institution has taken critical hold. The most important external criticism of the market appears in literature on "incommensurability" and "commodification." Work in this genre rejects the market insofar as this artifact assigns a cash value to anything capable of being transferred from one possessor to another. The leading scholar in this field identifies her thesis, first expressed in her title *Market-Inalienability*, as directly hostile to law and economics, whose "methodological archetype" she calls "universal commodification."

* * *

* * * "[M]arket failure" has become almost as familiar a phrase in law and economics as "the market" itself. Same recipe as the one that cooked up "behavioral economics": When truisms fail, or get refuted, reassert ownership of all material under question by adding a layer of counter-jargon. * * *

II. What Little Remains of Law and Economics

Now that rational choice, utilitarianism, efficiency, wealth maximization, markets, predictive power, and coherence have been questioned, abandoned, or smudged beyond recognition, the list of essential features defining law and economics gets shorter. I offer here all I could come up with: only three items, and even that small total contains some redundancy.

A. The Policymaker Ascendant

The insightful critic Jeanne Schroeder has noticed something central to law and economics that seems to have escaped members of the movement and other observers: "Law and economics is a policy science," whereas some other sectors of jurisprudence have no desire to form policy or, as Schroder puts it, "give advice to the government." Not everyone writing scholarship about the law takes the perspective of the legislator or a judge. One important contributor, the "speculative theorist or critical legal scholar," instead focuses on "the position of the governed—those who are subjected to the law." * * *

* * *

Here, then, we see a piece of what remains in law and economics: an inclination to address governing entities more than governed individuals as ends of inquiry in themselves. Desires or resistances of human beings enter policymaking only in the aggregate. While the critical legal scholar works to "free the legal subject from manipulation by the law," the policymaker works to articulate the best manipulation.

* * *

* * * [A]s soon as law and economics lost its distinctive character (thanks to too much refutation and too much acceptance), its adherents lost their basis for dividing the legal academy into members and nonmembers. Nevertheless their inclination to sort people into two piles without transparent criteria for division—the kind of dichotomous sorting that a Jeanne Schroder-style "cult" would do—remains. Unconstrained by genuine criteria for membership, decisionmakers in the academy and beyond—to the extent that law and economics extends beyond law schools—are now free to substitute prejudices for standards.

The most widely suspected prejudice is of political conservatism. Consider the possibility that

> facile assumptions have been carefully chosen to push forward a politically conservative agenda. Viewed in this light, the choreography is unsurpassed. First, equate utility with ability to pay, but assume away the issue of initial wealth distribution and bargaining inequalities. Next, combine with the inevitability of common-law efficiency. The result is a bias away from government regulation toward a nineteenth-century, almost Lochneresque, laissez-faire conception of the primacy of private law. The ability of good rhetoric to make this all appear natural is remarkable.

* * *

IV.   CONCLUSION: WHERE NOW?

* * * Writers frequently depict law and economics as an aging giant. Their metaphors of decline and old age perhaps rush too fast to judgment: In addition to premature proclamations of death, and wishful thinking that the movement had "peaked," the literature on law and economics includes a 1991 claim about a "mid-life crisis." I have already fretted about hurrying to entomb law and economics. That said, this birthday of a great book, marking indeed "a generation of influence," does invite thought about the state of the movement it helped inaugurate.

Conceding that dichotomous thinkers within the law and economics movement might be inclined to classify the reflections in this Article as hostile to their cause, I maintain that the Article has depicted law and economics as evolving, rather than entirely refuted or spent. This Article has indeed argued that the core tenets of the movement are refuted and spent. It has also contended that law and economics has failed to rescue itself by its tactic of trying to claim for itself various refutations of these tenets. But my reflections find a paradox in law and economics: the movement while deteriorating has been thriving. It reached heights scaled by no other jurisprudential school. Its success has consisted mainly of telling lawyers, lawmakers, and legal scholars how and why they must keep their eye on the welfare ball when making policy—but it has also fostered other triumphs: the importation of interdisciplinary findings into law and across campuses; the insistence on (if not quite the achievement of) empirical research as integral to legal policy; and the touch of science—whose perils and pretensions I have noted but that also can spur lawyers to reach for more rigorous work.

* * *

NOTES AND QUESTIONS

1.   Rational choice. Rational choice is the central claim of law and economics. As Bernstein notes, only if rational choice obtains can the "central precepts of the discipline—among them preferences, opportunities, and a consciousness of scarcity—make sense." Bernstein, *supra*, at 106. As we have explored in the previous chapter, chapter 4 at 269, behavioral economics, while sharing law and economics' faith in the market mechanism, has seriously eroded the viability of this central claim of rigid rationality. Daniel Kahneman, an experimental psychologist and a Nobel prize winner in economics, is a celebrated founder of behavioral economics and a leader in challenging the rationality assumptions of neoclassical economics. His website summarizes his influence as follows:

> Although he never took an economics course, Princeton psychologist Daniel Kahneman received the Nobel Prize in economic sciences in 2002. The award recognized Kahneman's life-long work in integrating psychological research and economic science. His work showed economists how people don't always make reasoned choices, over-turning long held views and opening up a new field of research.
>
> Kahneman has studied the importance of context in decision-making and the shortcuts people take ever since the 1970s, when he began publishing his groundbreaking work with the late Amos Tversky. His findings on the psychological motives that determine decisions have implications for economists, especially in areas such as individual savings behavior or participation in the stock market.
>
> Kahneman and Tversky's landmark paper on decision-making under circumstances where there is uncertainty was published in *Econometrica* in 1979. Prior to this publication, economists assumed humans made rational decisions. Economics was also a non-experimental science that relied on real-world observations. Today, largely because of Kahneman's work, experimental economics is burgeoning.
>
> Kahneman notes that his research has had a wide impact because his paper was published in an economics rather than a psychology journal. "It legitimized a certain approach to thinking about decision-making, which eventually, through the work of other economists, became influential in economics itself," he says.

Daniel Kahneman, *Case Study: Can I Trust My Intuitions, available at* http://webscript.princeton.edu/~psych/psychology/research/kahneman/case.php. Daniel Kahneman & Amostversky, *Prospect Theory: An Analysis of Decision Under Risk*, 47 Econometrica 263 (1979).

2.   What are the sources of preferences? Bernstein endorses Nussbaum's argument that "law and economics regards preferences as 'exogenous, i.e., not significantly shaped by laws and institutions,' whereas 'the endogeneity of preferences has been recognized by almost all the major writers on emotion and desire in the history of Western philosophy.' To speak of choice as if it originated entirely inside the actor is simply wrong."

Bernstein, *supra* at 328 (quoting Martha C. Nussbaum, *Flawed Foundations: The Philosophical Critique of (a Particular Type of) Economics*, 64 U. Chi. L. Rev. 1197, 1197–98 (1997)).

Can you identify the primary "laws and institutions" that shape preferences for race and gender discrimination?

3. Blurring the line between law and economics and everything else.

> Law and economics combined too little accuracy with too much: While ill founded, dubious, or tautological premises were eroding its credibility, other notions from the movement, consistent with what diverse thinkers and audiences believed, blurred the line between law and economics on one hand and everything else in jurisprudence on the other.

Bernestein, *supra*, at 104.

How persuasive is Bernstein's observation that law and economics is a "faculty club" of like-minded scholars who are seeking to preserve their influence in the academy by infinite adaptability and inclusiveness? Is the problem of porous conceptual borders a weakness or a strength in intellectual discourse? *See* Richard H. Gaskins, Burdens of Proof in Modern Discourse (1993).

4. Scientific discipline or cult? Bernstein makes two distinct, but related arguments: First, that law and economics cannot sustain its claim to scientific rigor. Second, that its adherents maintain their influence through policing membership in the genre according to prospective members' willingness to advance a politically conservative agenda. This, she concludes, is a cult—a secular belief system rooted in libertarianism.

> **a. Scientific Discipline?** As we discussed in chapter 1 at pp. 1–2, 17–23, 33–43, law and economics distinguishes itself from other genres of legal thought by claiming to be objective and scientific. Posner asserts that: "the concept of rationality used by the economist is objective rather than subjective ..." If, as Bernstein argues, the scientific foundations of law and economics have "disappeared into the sand," what is left of its contribution to modern legal thought?

> **b. Cult.** Is Bernstein's argument on this point internally contradictory? On one hand, she argues that law and economics has preserved itself by inclusion: "Unable to do much about errors, [law and economics scholars] worked on the second front, the crisis of too much acceptance, mainly by trying to claim successful outsider movements as their own, rather than reacting to them as threats or challenges. When psychology dealt blows to the ideal of a rational actor, for instance, economic analysts invoked the label of 'behavioral economics' to describe claims that were directly contrary to neoclassical dogma." Bernstein, *supra*, at 104. On the other hand, she claims that they have preserved their intellectual identity by exclusion.

"Yet cults ... are social groups. They contain members who disdain nonmembers, and who have been known to enjoy thinking that outsiders feel hostility towards them.... [L]aw and economics now functions mainly as a faculty club with opaque, arbitrary criteria for membership....

Unconstrained by genuine criteria for membership, decisionmakers in the academy ... are now free to substitute prejudices for standards.

The most widely suspected prejudice is of political conservatism."

Id at 105, 129.

Can both criticisms be true?

5. Policy science? Legal scholar Jeanne Schroder suggests that "law and economics is policy science ... [that] seeks to give advice to the government." Jeanne L. Schroder, *Rationality in Law and Economics Scholarship*, 79 OR. L. REV. 147, 151 (2000). If this observation is convincing, would this make law and economics an oxymoron, a movement to reduce the sphere of government power, whose primary function now is giving advice to the government?

B. NORMATIVE CRITIQUES OF ECONOMIC ANALYSIS

The normative challenges to law and economics span a broad range of contentions. The views collected in what follows include some of the most powerful claims of scholars who are unconvinced that law and economics provides a persuasive framework through which to evaluate individual and collective decision making about allocation of the basic material goods and services required for modern life.

The challenges include skepticism about the reliability of virtually all of the central premises of modern law and economics. Among the criticized premises are: rational choice, efficiency, cost benefit analysis, wealth maximization, and the relationship between preferences expressed as monetary units and democratic participation in markets and governance. Some have challenged the gendered impacts of separating household tasks from the market economy. Finally, justice is a major theme of external criticism of law and economics. This chord has focused on law and economics' aggressive refusal to consider preexisting economic distributions. The justice critics question whether law and economics' valorization of markets over fairness for those left out, or pushed out of opportunities for work and wealth accumulation is just in a society, such as ours, with a large material surplus.

We turn to two outside scholars, Rachel Moran and James Boyd White, who each in turn survey the landscape of the major normative criticisms of law and economics. Moran presents a direct comparison between law and economics and critical race theory. White argues that economics is not a science, but is rather an alternative system of values posing as a scientific enterprise. White's alternative is a humanistic value system.

1.   BEYOND: RATIONAL CHOICE

THE ELUSIVE NATURE OF DISCRIMINATION: BY VALDES, CULP, AND HARRIS

55 STAN. L. REV. 2365, 2367, 2375, 2377, 2378, 2379, 2380, 2382–83, 2385–88, 2390, 2395, 2396–97, 2401–03, 2412–14, 2416, 2417–18 (2003) (reviewing IAN AYRES, PERVASIVE PREJUDICE? UNCONVENTIONAL EVIDENCE OF RACE AND GENDER DISCRIMINATION (2001) and CROSSROADS, DIRECTIONS AND A NEW CRITICAL RACE THEORY (Francisco Valdes et al. eds., 2002)).

■ RACHEL F. MORAN

* * *

In contrast to law and economics, critical race theory has concerned itself with how race is constructed through unconscious bias and institutional structures. Race scholars do not presume that rational choice is the sine qua non of human behavior. Instead, they try to unpack the reflexive habits and hidden assumptions that guide racial judgments. Rather than worry about whether statistical discrimination is rational, critical race theorists question whether it is just. In analyzing how privilege is perpetuated, race scholars see social networks as only one example of the patterns and practices that entrench inequality. As a result, race theory has moved well beyond the marketplace to explore how everything from public bureaucracies to family life can make racial difference seem both natural and inevitable.

* * *

II.   CRITICAL RACE THEORY: AN UNRULY DISCIPLINE AT THE CROSSROADS

* * *

* * * [Kevin] Johnson, for instance, argues that "during its first full decade, Critical Race Theory has failed to explore fully the relationship between race and immigration law" in part because of "the longstanding assumption that race relations in the United States exclusively concern African Americans and whites." * * *

* * *

* * * This is a crucial crossroad because the ideal "postsubordination" world, to use Valdes's term, remains a contested and uncertain destination.

* * *

Another crossroad for critical race theory is determining whether it shares a unifying methodology. * * *

* * *

Still another crossroad for critical race theorists is determining the appropriate relationship between theory and praxis. At the outset of the volume, Charles R. Lawrence comments that "we cannot teach about liberation without actively engaging in its politics." * * *

Even so, the relationship between theory and praxis remains among the least developed areas in race scholarship. Undoubtedly, this inattention can be explained in part by the relatively small number of critical race theorists working in the academy. * * *

* * *

* * * As a quantitative researcher, Ayres devotes himself to examining the aggregate consequences of discrimination. He measures price differentials in the retail car market, disparate delays in obtaining a kidney, and unequal levels of bail. Because Ayres is measuring tangible effects of discrimination, he focuses on average differences and their statistical significance. Never does he attempt to explore what it might feel like to be the victim of discrimination. In marked contrast, critical race theorists are strongly committed to exploring the victim's perspective. Compare, for example, Ayres's treatment of retail car sales with Devon Carbado's discussion of what might be termed "shopping while black." * * *

* * *

As *Pervasive Prejudice?* and the *Crossroads* reader make clear, there are divergent schools of thought about the nature and incidence of discrimination and inequality. Ayres draws heavily on rational choice theory, and his studies are situated in particular markets like car sales or bail bonds. The challenge for theorists like Ayres is to understand why discrimination persists under competitive conditions. By contrast, the anthology by Valdes, Culp, and Harris rejects the characterization of the world as presumptively rational, and it refuses to focus primarily on market transactions as the relevant site for studying racism. Critical race theorists are working to redefine the relevance of rationality in analyzing discrimination and to reconceptualize the role of institutions, both private and public, in perpetuating inequality.

A. Rational Choice and Irrational Animus

Kenneth J. Arrow has pointed out that "rational choice theory" is broader than "economic theory." As he explains:

> Rational choice theory means that the individual actors act rationally (that is, by maximizing according to a complete ordering) within the constraints imposed by preferences, technology, and beliefs, and by the institutions which determine how individual actions interact to determine outcomes. Further, the beliefs are themselves formed by some kind of rational process. By economic theory, we mean that in some sense, markets are the central institution in which individual actions interact and that other institutions are of negligible importance.

Ayres's work falls squarely within both traditions and assesses whether discrimination persists today. When he finds that it does, its resilience becomes a puzzle. After all, the ideal market is one of competitive, impersonal exchange. If discrimination is a costly, inefficient practice, it should disappear as those who irrationally engage in prejudiced behavior go out of business.

To address the robustness of discrimination, Gary Becker early on posited a taste for discrimination, a special disutility that whites attach to interaction with nonwhites. Becker's analysis treated rational behavior as the norm, and discrimination reflected an individual preference that endured even after being labeled antisocial. So long as the taste remained widespread, discrimination could persist in a competitive market. Becker's work continues to be highly influential among market theorists today. It is no accident, for example, that in his study of retail car sales, Ayres juxtaposes rational behavior with an irrational preference, or animus.

There are several problems with Becker's approach. It salvages the image of individuals as profit-maximizers by simply creating a new trait, the taste for discrimination. As Arrow notes, "introducing new variables easily risks turning the 'explanation' into a tautology" in much the same way that concepts like phlogiston have been used to save scientific theories once their explanatory value is lost. The taste for discrimination is unique in Becker's theory of market behavior. Why is it, after all, that this trait so singularly overrides a pure commitment to the pursuit of profit? The salience of a taste for discrimination seems especially surprising if market transactions are impersonal. The arm's-length quality of bargaining ought to reduce the significance of individual traits like race. Assuming that Becker's approach was a useful snapshot of market behavior when he wrote in the mid-1950s, most scholars would agree that racial animus has since declined, though not disappeared, as a result of civil rights reforms. So, why does widespread discrimination persist? Market theorists have proposed two key responses, each of which complicates the notion of discrimination.

1. Statistical discrimination.

Some scholars have focused on statistical discrimination, the practice of using race as a proxy for other traits, such as productivity, skills, and training, when individualized information is limited and expensive to obtain. The scarcity of information leads markets to work imperfectly, even when racial animus is not a factor. Race can function as a statistical proxy when rational actors believe that the performance of one racial group is on average different from that of another, based on previous statistical experience or prevailing social beliefs. For example, in Ayres's study of the retail car market, salespeople rationally seek to maximize revenues by using race and gender as proxies for the ability to bargain effectively for a lower price. Somewhat more subtly, race and gender can be statistical proxies when the variability of performance within a group varies by race. George Akerlof has described how uncertainty about quality can drive down prices for used cars, so that even those in good condition must be priced like "lemons." Akerlof argues that the "Lemons Principle" can explain an employer's refusal to hire members of racially disadvantaged groups based on concerns about the consistency and reliability of their skills, particularly if credentials are not trustworthy signals of merit.

The line between statistical discrimination and racial animus, while theoretically clear, can be hard to draw in practice. In one recent study, participants were asked to evaluate a taxi driver's decision not to pick up a black passenger. In the scenario, the cabdriver slows down to pick a person up one night in Chicago, but when he discovers that the fare is a young black man, he speeds by without stopping. As the scenario explains: "Even though [the driver] knows that he can be fined for not stopping, he fears that he might have to drive to a dangerous neighborhood and thinks: 'I'd rather be fined than have my wife a widow.'" Based on the scenario, participants must determine whether the cab driver's decision is rational or whether he is prejudiced against blacks. This assessment turns heavily on the observer's own commitment to rationality and racial attitudes. In particular, those who emphasize cognitive solutions and have negative views of blacks are most apt to describe the driver's behavior as motivated by statistical estimates rather than animus.

Although described as rational behavior unrelated to prejudice, statistical discrimination can reflect and reinforce patterns of racial exclusion and inequality. When employers use race as a proxy for productivity or reliability, their actuarial guesses may depend on incomplete information tainted by patterns of segregation. By refraining from hiring nonwhites, employers never encounter evidence that disconfirms their predictions. Perhaps most disturbingly, rational nonwhites who are aware of patterns of statistical discrimination should reduce investment in their human capital, knowing that their efforts will be neither recognized nor rewarded by the market. A statistical estimate sadly becomes a self-fulfilling prophecy.

If discrimination persists as a rational strategy for dealing with imperfect information, economists face some awkward dilemmas. In contrast to socially undesirable animus, statistical discrimination appears to be precisely the kind of rational, interest-maximizing behavior that is normatively appropriate under market theory. For those who nonetheless wish to eliminate racial disparities, it becomes necessary to step outside the economic model. As Edmund S. Phelps writes:

> A sensitive person, I have been warned, might read this paper [on statistical discrimination] as expressing an impression on the part of the author that most or all discrimination is the result of beliefs that blacks and women deliver on the average an inferior performance. Actually, I do not know (nor claim to know) whether in fact most discrimination is of the statistical kind studied here. But what if it were? Discrimination is no less damaging to its victims for being statistical. And it is no less important for social policy to counter.

By shifting to the victim's perspective and demanding that government officials address the problem, a classic economist like Phelps begins to sound a bit like a critical race theorist. Indeed, Patricia J. Williams has written eloquently about the individual pain of being rendered nothing but a second-class statistical estimate:

> I am one, I am many.

I am amiable, orderly, extremely honest, and a very good neighbor indeed. I am suspect profile, market cluster, actuarial monster, statistical being.

My particulars battle the generals.

'Typecasting!' I protest.

'Predictive indicator,' assert the keepers of the gate.

'Prejudice!' I say.

'Precaution,' they reply.

Hundreds, even thousands, of me hover in the breach.

* * *

B.   Critical Race Theory: Beyond Rationality and Animus

Critical race theory rejects the centrality of individual animus in the market and insists on a richer picture of personal psychology, social relations, and institutional life than economic models can provide. Like economists, critical race theorists worry about the role of individual psychology in discrimination. Unlike economists, however, race scholars do not presume that conscious rational choice governs everyday judgments. Largely rejecting accounts of statistical discrimination as efficient behavior, critical race theory treats stereotypes as harmful and misleading vestiges of past discrimination. Because the social construction of race is a pervasive feature of American life, race scholars must struggle with the problem of institutional racism in a range of settings that transcend social networks and the marketplace.

* * *

Market theories of racial animus and statistical discrimination largely ignore the victim's perspective. Occasionally, economists point out that pervasive discrimination may undermine incentives for people of color to develop their human capital, so that the perception that nonwhites are less capable than whites becomes a self-fulfilling prophecy. Critical race theorists go much further in exploring the impact of being sorted, stigmatized, and stereotyped on the basis of race. Indeed, one of critical race theory's central missions has been an exploration of the victim's perspective. Stereotyping not only limits the capacity to perceive others as individuals because of their race, but it also limits the capacity of the stigmatized to imagine and develop their fullest potential. Patricia J. Williams goes so far as to label racism "spirit murder," the death of possibility that comes with "disregard for others whose lives qualitatively depend on our regard" through "a system of formalized distortions of thought" and "social structures centered on fear and hate, a tumorous outlet for feelings elsewhere unexpressed."

* * *

In focusing on the victim's perspective, critical race theory sets itself the task of listening to the disadvantaged, not just to document their harm but to "persuade, outrage, and stir to action." Race scholars use a variety of techniques to "look to the bottom," but storytelling has occupied an especially prominent place. In contrast to psychological studies that keep victims at a safe and objective distance, narrative has the power to make unique human connections. Stories can transport white readers across the color line momentarily, so that they begin to appreciate the individual experiences of nonwhites. As Angela Harris explains, "The shock of being addressed suddenly not as disembodied rational consciousness, but as a particular person caught in complex and idiosyncratic webs of emotion and intuition, is itself discomfiting and sometimes disarming." At the same time, narrative creates a sense of inclusion among those who share a common racial identity, and when artfully deployed, it can enable whites and nonwhites alike to reimagine the boundaries of human possibility. With this power comes new perils. Unlike conventional psychological studies, narrative must struggle to avoid essentializing racial experience by creating the impression that one person's account is emblematic of an entire group's experience. Paradoxically, the very stories that are designed to be individuating and idiosyncratic can, when imbued with larger symbolic significance, become a new source of stereotypes.

* * *

For economic theorists, the key puzzle has been why discrimination persists in competitive markets. So far, two important answers have emerged: statistical discrimination and social networks. Each of these approaches has important implications for law and policy. Those who focus on statistical discrimination must grapple with how to police the use of racial proxies. Should policymakers continue to punish only intentional misconduct? Should inaccurate racial generalizations also be penalized? Is the rational use of race as a proxy ever a basis for legal intervention? Economists exploring the role of social networks must consider the extent to which the law can counteract what are often largely private, informal associations. Should affirmative action programs be used to break down barriers imposed by exclusionary networks? If so, can the programs generate or redistribute social capital by setting the stage for interracial contact?

* * *

Because statistical discrimination supplements rather than supplants Becker's theory of racial distaste, the law should continue to recognize claims for disparate treatment, that is, conscious discrimination born of racial animus. In addition, statistical discrimination should be eradicated when it reflects inaccurate generalizations about race, regardless of whether the motive is benign. An economic theorist might expect distorted racial thinking to disappear naturally through competition, but if markets fail to correct these inefficiencies, state intervention could be appropriate. The real dilemma for the economic theorist is whether the government should ever ban the rational use of race as a proxy for other traits because it entrenches inequality.

* * *

In other cases, courts have been reluctant to disrupt the market's rational pricing mechanisms to redress allegedly inequitable results. So, litigators have had little success in pressing comparable worth claims, which argue that women receive less pay than men for the same type of work. Judges have found that employees are free to bargain for wages, and if women get bad deals, they should use market remedies, such as searching for better jobs, organizing for better pay, and seeking raises and promotions. Here, market theorists would likely applaud the courts' reticence to monitor wages on a broad scale in pursuit of gender equity. Pervasive wage regulation could make it hard to distinguish between remedies for sexism and penalties for otherwise rational pricing decisions.

* * *

Richard McAdams has made an important contribution to bridging the gap between critical race theory and law and economics by analyzing racial discrimination as a form of status production. Although he embraces rational choice theory, McAdams rejects Becker's reliance on animus as an explanation for racial discrimination. Instead, McAdams turns to critical race theory to identify status as a factor of critical relevance to racial subordination. McAdams posits that self-esteem is a basic interest that individuals pursue as a form of pleasure. Because an individual's regard is affected by group membership, people have a stake in whether their group's status is enhanced or diminished. Group members can pursue an indirect strategy of raising their standing by lowering the status of other group traits, a practice that McAdams defines as "discrimination." * * * McAdams believes that "affirmative action is an investment in which we bear certain costs today for the hope of a greater return tomorrow," a return that has so far proven uncertain.

* * * Status-based theories that emphasize symbolic politics must be supplemented by analyses of material inequality. Only by examining the practices of particular institutions can scholars avoid reifying status in ways that obscure the contingencies of racial discrimination. Haney Lopez also refuses to link status to rational choice theory, for he believes that unconscious racism is a significant source of status production. Indeed, Haney Lopez defines institutional racism as "racial status-enforcement influenced in an unrecognized manner by racial institutions." Though he criticizes some elements of status theory, Haney Lopez rightly infers that critical race theorists can fruitfully draw on rich and sometimes conflicting theories of status and power to explore race and racism.

2. *The limits of law reform: beyond the market.*

Efforts to explain group subordination through theories of status and power are closely linked to another important development in critical race theory. Race scholars increasingly are shifting their attention from individual psychology to organizational structures that reflect and replicate racial inequality. Here, the key challenge is to move from the phrase "institutional racism" to comprehensive accounts of the patterns and practices that generate racial disadvantage in public institutions, market settings, and private life. Here, I will describe some promising examples in each area.

Public institutions. As previously mentioned, Haney Lopez's historical account of the grand jury selection process in Los Angeles demonstrates how high-level officials with substantial formal discretion actually made decisions tightly bound by informal institutional norms. In truth, these informal constraints proved more powerful than explicit formal mandates. For example, even when the judges received official memoranda advising them to diversify the jury pool, they persisted in selection practices that largely excluded Mexican Americans. Based on these findings, Haney Lopez argues that focusing on animus fundamentally misconceives the nature of racism. The intent requirement under equal protection law has become a constitutional straightjacket, one that paralyzes efforts to reach policies and practices that, though not consciously biased, entrench racial inequality. Haney Lopez concludes:

> Courts and commentators must answer why the Equal Protection Clause curtails some racism—for example, that resulting from the conscious desire to harm minorities—while other forms remain lawful—for instance, institutional racism in taxation, welfare, public services, and so on. They should not presume to resolve this issue, however, by supposing the racial neutrality of government actions that disproportionately harm minorities but do not evince a racial purpose. Institutional analysis cautions that racial status-enforcing government action is likely to reflect institutional racism.

Haney Lopez's work is an intriguing start, but critical race theorists have much work left to do in evaluating other public institutions. Courts, agencies, and legislatures differ dramatically in the ways that they allocate discretion and hold officials accountable. Judges have considerable leeway to make decisions, but this deference reflects their professional training and socialization, personal integrity and accomplishment, and collegial consultation and cooperation. Outside the courts, bureaucracies often constrain official power through centralized rules and hierarchical oversight. Differences in organizational structure undoubtedly have important implications for defining institutional racism and evaluating racial remedies. As a result, Haney Lopez's conclusions are not necessarily generalizable, and only further research will reveal the robustness of his analysis in other public settings.

* * *

Private life. Outside the marketplace, critical race theorists increasingly have turned their attention to the role of sex, marriage, and family in the reproduction of inequality. Building on the insights of feminist legal theorists, race scholars acknowledge that there is no bright-line boundary between public and private life. Even in the realm of feeling, seemingly the most interior aspect of personal life, people are trapped within a sociopolitical economy of emotion, one that replicates boundaries of race and gender.

* * *

Although critical race theorists have devoted considerable energy to imagining a world free of subordination, perhaps some of their greatest contributions will come in documenting the day-to-day policies and practices that make inequality a seemingly inevitable feature of everyday life. This work promises to be deeply interdisciplinary, drawing on such fields as anthropology, history, political science, psychology, and sociology. Race scholars will apply a range of methods in doing these case studies, but the results can unify the field by offering a coherent and compelling portrait of how racism transcends individual animus and invades the innermost reaches of our lives.

* * * [T]he concept of discrimination has grown diffuse and fragmented. To counter images of discrimination as conscious animus, critical race theorists have described unconscious racism. In response to a framework of individual transgressions, race scholars have insisted that institutional racism is at least equally if not more significant in perpetuating inequality. Although individual discrimination might be corrected through consciousness-raising or incremental legislation, subordination is so deeply entrenched that it can be eliminated only through profound transformations of the body politic. The simple truth is that once Bull Connor and Lester Maddox are gone, once angry parents are not screaming, "Two, four, six, eight, we don't want to integrate," and once spittle isn't running down the faces of civil rights protesters, it is hard to say precisely what discrimination means. * * *

NOTES AND QUESTIONS

1. Can law and economics and critical race theory be combined? In the mid 1990s, legal scholar, Edward L. Rubin urged the combination of critical race theory and law and economics. Rubin perceived enough common ground between these two, often antagonistic, schools of legal reasoning to suggest that they could be combined:

> [C]ontemporary law and economics and outsider scholarship share a common ground—the effort to locate law, social policy, and social change in a closely analyzed institutional context. What is particularly promising about the effort is that institutional analysis has also become a major theme in the academic fields that gave rise to both these schools. To develop a new synthesis of discourse for legal scholarship, ideas from all these fields must be incorporated, for most scholars agree that law can no longer sustain itself as an autonomous discipline. Whether these complex and disparate elements can actually be integrated is an open question—there is nothing inevitable about the process—but synthesis seems like an appealing alternative to the currently fragmented state of legal scholarship.

Edward L. Rubin, *The New Legal Process, the Synthesis of Discourse, and the Microanalysis of Institutions*, 109 HARV. L. REV. 1393, 1394 (1996).

Two critical race theorists, Devon Carbado and Mitu Gulati, endorse Rubin's proposal for collaboration and synthesis between the two schools, noting that:

> The argument for a collaboration between economics and [critical race theory ('CRT')] (and feminist theory and gay and lesbian legal studies) was made with force in a 1996 essay by Ed Rubin. Rubin argued that the common critical approach to institutional analysis shared by law and economics ('L&E') and CRT—both fields reject claims about the neutrality and objectivity of legal rules, albeit for different reasons would, if combined, produce not only an exciting new methodology for legal inquiry, but one with potential to succeed the Legal Process school as a unifying discourse in legal academia. In the six years since the piece was published, however, there has been little collaborative work between CRT and L&E. If anything there has been increased antagonism.

> This makes little sense. Like Rubin, we believe that L&E and CRT should engage each other and that the results of this engagement would be fruitful.

Devon W. Carbado *The Law and Economics of Critical Race Theory* 112 Yale L.J. 1757, 1761 (2003) (book review).

2. Is statistical discrimination rational but unjust? Statistical discrimination occurs when unequal treatment is the result of cognitive short cuts that rely on the decision maker's experience with the average member of the disfavored group, or decisions based upon statistical portraits of the behavior of members of the group that may be accurate for the aggregate, but that are not accurate for any one individual in the group.

In the excerpt above, Moran has identified a central problem of rationality analysis:

> Although described as rational behavior unrelated to prejudice, statistical discrimination can reflect and reinforce patterns of racial exclusion and inequality. When employers use race as a proxy for productivity or reliability, their actuarial guesses may depend on incomplete information tainted by patterns of segregation.

Moran, *supra*, at 2387.

Moran agrees with Cass Sunstein, infra at 384, 391, 393, that:

> [S]ometimes discrimination is caused by employer practices that result precisely from economic self-interest, rather than from the employer's noneconomic goals.

> * * *

> If race or sex can be a good signaling device, an employer might discriminate not because he hates or devalues blacks or women, or has a general desire not to associate with them, or is "prejudiced" in the ordinary sense, but because he believes (on the basis either of plausible assumptions or actual experience) that the relevant stereotypes have sufficient truth to be a basis for employment decisions.

CASS R. SUNSTEIN, FREE MARKETS AND SOCIAL JUSTICE 153, 156 (1997).

The Moran and Sunstein passages raise the following issues:

1. Since statistical discrimination relies on mental shortcuts, they reduce the cost of individual evaluation. Therefore, does this form of decision making provide a competitive advantage?

2. Are the portraits of average behavior of the disfavored group themselves the product of past discrimination? Statistical discrimination therefore locks in the disadvantages of the past. In this way, invidious discrimination can morph into "benign" statistical discrimination, if it is not sanctioned.

3. Is the very accuracy of statistical discrimination-based exclusions a symptom of the persistence of societal disadvantages placed upon the subordinated group?

4. The greater wealth and market power advantage of the majority will be further multiplied by reliance on statistical discrimination. In this instance, rational choices are morally offensive because they are a link in the chain of extending historic subordination.

---

2.   BEYOND: WEALTH MAXIMIZATION AND PRICE THEORY

a.   Humanism vs. Materialism

Economics and Law: Two Cultures in Tension

54 TENN. L. REV. 161, 166–67, 172–73, 174–75, 178, 182–83, 184–85, 191–93 (1986).

■ JAMES BOYD WHITE

* * *

Many people think of economics solely as a scientific, conceptual, and cognitive system, apparently unaware that there are any other dimensions of meaning in economic talk. But all expression is loaded with values, ethical and otherwise; all expression defines a self and another and proposes a relation between them; all expression remakes its language; in these senses all expression proposes the creation of a community and a culture. All expression, in short, is ethical, cultural, and political, and it can be analyzed and judged as such. To claim that economics is a science is perhaps to claim that it cannot be judged in such terms. But "sciences" are cultures too, with their own created worlds and values. One way to describe my aim * * *, then, is to say that it reverses the usual flow: we are used to economic analyses of this or that aspect of our common life—voting, the family, war, etc. I propose here to begin what I would call a rhetorical or cultural analysis of a certain kind of economics.

* * *

IV. Economics as a System of Values

We can start with the question of value. In its purest form economics claims to be a value-free social science. But as I suggested earlier I think it in fact enacts a set of values, including political ones, values to which the speaker of the language cannot avoid finding himself at least in part committed.

A. In the World

Think, for example, of the way in which economics defines the economic actor and the processes by which he functions. He is for the most part assumed to be an individual of indeterminate age, sex, race and cultural background, but of adequate competence at manipulating economic relations. He acts as one who is both perfectly aware of his own wishes and wholly rational—in the special sense in which that term is used, to mean "calculating"—in his pursuit of them. He exists as an individual, not as part of a community, except insofar as he establishes contractual or exchange relations with others. He is assumed to be motivated by self-interest, which in turn is defined in terms of competition, acquisition, and dominion, at least in relation to resources and other actors, for in the process of exchange the self is reduced to those desires.

Of course a particular individual may have other values—indeed the economist insists that he must, calling them "tastes" or "preferences"—perhaps including a "taste" for altruism, for peace and quiet, for heavy metal music, for appreciating nature unspoiled, for beautiful or ugly art, and so forth. These values will drive his participation in the exchange process, or his decision to withdraw from it. But in either case they are themselves valued by the method of exchange: either by an actual exchange that takes place or by a hypothetical or imagined exchange that is forgone (or in a more complicated case by a combination of exchanges made and forgone). In both cases these external values are converted by the discourse into the acquisitive or instrumental values—the desire to extend the dominion of the will—that all economic actors are assumed to have, for this is the only kind of value about which economics can directly talk.

With respect to the external values in their original form, the system is purportedly "value neutral." That is, it regards individual values as simply exogenous to the system itself. Economics of course recognizes that these values exist, but it demeans them by calling them "tastes" or "preferences," names that imply that no serious conversation can proceed on such subjects and economics itself is by definition not about those values, but about the process by which they are reflected in the activity of exchange. This means that economics cannot, in principle, talk about any value other than the acquisitive or instrumental one that it universalizes. (Indeed it does not talk about this value either, but merely assumes and acts upon it.) This is not to be "value free," as its apologists claim, but to make self-interest the central, indeed almost the only, value, for it is the only one that can be talked about in these terms. To come at it the other way, it is to claim that all values can be talked about, at least for some purposes, as if they were selfish, quantifiable, and interchangeable.

* * *

Yet economics is troubling not only for the self-interested values it directly asserts, but also for the very neutrality, the "value freedom," that it claims. It is in principle neutral on all questions of value that are external to the acquisitive and competitive ones enacted in the exchange game, which it lumps together as "tastes" or "preferences" among which no distinctions can be drawn. But this is to be silent on all the great questions of human life: questions of beauty and ugliness in art and music, sincerity and falsity in human relations, wisdom and folly in conduct and judgment, and the greatest of all questions, which is how we ought to lead our lives. Economic analysis assumes as a given the existence of "tastes" or "preferences" which drive the system, but economics as a language can provide no way of talking about these values, whether in oneself or another, no way of thinking about which to prefer and which not. To the extent that economics does reach out for these questions it may be worse than silent, for silence after all can be a mode of controlling a discourse. When economics tries to speak about these matters it does so in the only way it knows how to speak, in purely quantitative terms and on the assumption that all human transactions can be reduced to the model of exchange.

* * *

For the purposes of economic analysis all human wishes and desires are thus reduced to the same level, as though no principled choices could be made among them, as though it didn't matter what choices one made. This in turn means that it is impossible to talk in these terms about our most important choices as individuals and communities, or about the education of mind or heart, for any impulse that we or others may happen to have is as good, valid, and entitled to respect as any other.

* * * We must and do have preferences, as the economist knows; and these necessarily commit those who have them to the inquiry of better and worse, as well as to that of greater and less. To refuse to engage in this inquiry—to privatize it—as economics in its neutral phase necessarily does, is to deny an essential and necessary aspect of human life. To reduce all value to self-interest, as it does the rest of the time, is intellectually and ethically intolerable. How could one educate one's children or oneself to live in a world that was neutral on all the great questions of life, except that it reduced them to acquisition, competition, and calculation?

* * *

The second ground upon which the market is justified is that not of its gross effects but of its fairness. In one version this justification rests upon the ethical standing of voluntary action and holds that the results of the market process are justified with respect to every actor because the choices by which the market works are voluntary. In another version, it becomes the affirmative celebration of autonomy or liberty: whether or not it is efficient, the market is good because it gives the widest possible range to freedom of choice and action. Here the claim moves beyond justifying market results by the voluntary character of the choices upon which they rest to the point of asserting autonomy as the central social and political value. The obvious trouble with this line of defense, in both of its forms, is that it assumes that all exchanges are for all actors equally voluntary and equally expressive of autonomy, a position that common sense denies.

* * *

The market purports to rest upon an assumption of the equality of all the actors in the system. In fact, it rests upon a different assumption, namely, the equality of every dollar in the system. Since some players have many more dollars, and through this fact are at a competitive advantage, it is a system that actively supports inequality among its actors.

It is not too much to say, I think, that the modern celebration of the market as the central social institution—the most fair, the most respecting of autonomy, and the most efficient—threatens to destroy the single greatest achievement of Western political culture: the discovery that a community can govern itself through a rule of law that attempts to create a fundamental moral and political equality among human beings. The great phrase in the Declaration of Independence—"all men are created equal"— is partly a theological statement about the conditions under which we are created and partly a political statement about the obligation of the government to acknowledge, indeed to create or recreate, that equality. This value is the heart of what is meant both by equality under law and by our democratic institutions more generally, resting as they do on the premise that each person's vote is worth exactly what everyone else's is. The ideology of the market, if it prevailed in its desire to convert all institutions into markets, would destroy this set of political relations and would create another in its stead, based upon the dollar.

* * *

The market ideology claims to be radically democratic and egalitarian because it leaves every person free to do with her own what she will. But this freedom of choice is not equally distributed among all people. The market is democratic not on the principle of one person one vote, but on the far different principle of one dollar, one vote. One could hardly make a greater mistake than to equate, as so much modern public talk carelessly does, the "free market" with democracy.

There are two distinct points here. First, the exchange transactions that the market celebrates are not entitled to the special respect claimed for them as free and voluntary, and hence fair, unless each person has roughly the same amount of money and the same competence and freedom in its use, which is demonstrably not the case. The accumulations of wealth it permits thus cannot be justified by the fairness of the transactions by which the accumulation occurs. Second, if the advocates of the market succeeded in converting other institutions into markets, the result would be to transfer to those who have wealth not only the economic power that inescapably follows it but also the political power that in our democratic tradition the people have claimed for themselves and have exercised through the institutions of self-government. This would validate and institutionalize private economic power held by one person over another, of the rich over the poor. If we were to yield entirely to its claims, we would gradually find our traditional government, which operates by collective deliberation on a premise of fundamental equality of citizens, replaced by a private-sector government of the few over the many, wholly unregulated by collective judgment.

* * *

VI.   ECONOMICS AS A SYSTEM OF ECONOMIC ANALYSIS
D.   *Erasing Community*

For similar reasons this kind of economics has the greatest difficulty in reflecting the reality of human community and the value of communal institutions. Its necessary tendency seems to be to destroy the idea of public action, indeed the idea of community itself. This is partly because this methodology tends to resolve all communities and organizations into the individual human actors who constitute them, partly because commitment to the market system leads one to think that everything that can be made the subject of the market should be. The idea is that every economic actor should pay for what he wants, and should not have to pay for what he doesn't want. But this tends to destroy our public institutions, all of which extend benefits far beyond those who would pay (if they were reduced to markets) or who do pay (when they are supported by taxes). Such institutions reflect a communal judgment that we need to educate ourselves and each other, that our "tastes" are not all of equal value but need to be formed, and formed well rather than badly. Public universities, libraries, orchestras, museums, parks—all these would fall before the ideology that denies the existence and reality of community and reduces all institutions, all human production, to the language of the market.

Think here of the way economists explain why people who will probably never visit, say, the Everglades or an art museum are happy to have their taxes used to maintain them. The economist says it is because the actor wants to maintain the option of visiting them some day, and calls this an "option demand." But may it not be that the voter simply takes pleasure in what other people have and in what other people can do, in belonging to a community that is good for all its members? Or that he respects their desires and wants a community based on that kind of mutual respect? This possibility is systematically denied by the assumption of economic talk, that individuals and communities are in principle incapable of generosity, or more precisely, that "altruism" can adequately be talked about as a species of selfishness.

The language of self and self-interest not only fails to reflect the reality of community and of shared interests, it draws attention away from those aspects of life and devalues them. To continue to talk on these assumptions, even hypothetically, is to encourage "self-interest" in an ethical sense and to erode the commitments we have to each other that underlie such essential practices of citizenship as the willingness to pay taxes, to work for the local school, or to serve in the army, upon which everything depends. To adopt the economic view would in fact threaten the very existence of community, for on these premises no one would conceivably die or seriously risk his life for his community: at the point of danger one's self-interest in survival would outweigh all other self-interests. And to speak of all "tastes" as if they were equivalent is to invite oneself and others to think that they are, and to confirm the premises of our culture, already drummed into the mind by the consumer economy, that the consumer is king, that whatever you happen to want is a good that you should seek to satisfy, that no distinction can be drawn between the beautiful and ugly, the wise and foolish, and so on. It is to confirm a vulgar view of democracy that makes the preference or will supreme, as if we functioned by instant referendum. It erases the sense that a democracy is a mode of communal self-constitution and self-education that may have higher ends than the satisfaction of wants, namely the creation of a community of a certain sort, at once based upon a set of responsibilities and offering us a set of opportunities for civic and social action.

* * *

NOTES AND QUESTIONS

1. When rational is wrong. White argues that the central defect of law and economics is that it is a scholarly discipline that masks its commitment to materialism with scientific precepts that do not withstand close scrutiny of their value-laden premises that elevate materialism over fairness.

The challenge for scholars working with both economics and the injuries of subordination is to create an alternative to the economic vocabulary for understanding how humans accumulate the resources to fulfill their basic needs. Since Adam Smith, the vocabulary of rationality has been dominant. In the following, Charles Pouncy argues for a "robust expression" of the "concept of economic justice" as an alternative to the neoclassical lexicon:

> The concept of economic justice finds no robust expression in the law of the United States.
>
> Economic justice is not a concern of neoclassical theory. Neoclassical theory is not designed to achieve economic justice, and in fact intervenes to prevent it.

Id. at 23.

> Neoclassical theory intervenes in consensus reality to support the notion of colorblind economics, an economic system in which markets negate the impact of irrational criteria, such as race, in economic decision-making.

Id. at 28.

Neoclassical theory works in concert with the preservative nature of law to prevent the development of a jurisprudence of economic justice. *Id.*

Racism and classism are insulated from approbation by . . . economic rationality.

Id. at 17.

When we combine the belief that the individual is the proper unit of economic analysis and that individuals base their decisions on their perception of their own best interests, then discrimination and racism are transformed from indicia of hatred or irrational hatred to good business decisions.

Id. at 20.

Charles R.P. Pouncy, *Economic Justice and Economic Theory: Limiting the Reach of Neoclassical Ideology*, 14 U. FLA. J. L. & PUB. POL'Y 11, 11 (2002).

2. Effect of terminology on White's critique. White states that "all systems of discourse commit their users to values . . . [and that] economics is [not] wrong to do what it does." James Boyd White, *Economics and Law: Two Cultures in Tension*, 54 TENN. L. REV. 161, 176 (1986). If all White wishes is for economics to acknowledge that it is no different from other systems of discourse, does his critique of law and economics have any value? Would the problems White identifies with law and economics be solved by acknowledging that law and economics has values without making any substantive changes to the discipline? Would White be satisfied with such a solution?

3. The pernicious nature of law and economics. At the close of his article, White states that "to continue to talk on . . . [law and economics'] assumptions, even hypothetically, is to encourage 'self interest' in an ethical sense and to erode the commitments we have to each other that underlie such essential practices of citizenship as the willingness to pay taxes, to work for the local school, or to serve in the army, upon which everything depends. To adopt the economic view would in fact threaten the very existence of community . . ." *Id.* at 192. If White is correct about the dire consequences of even hypothesizing in an economic framework, how can he assert that economics is not wrong to "do what it does?" *Id.* at 176.

b. The Commodification Critique

Justice and the Market Domain

MARKETS AND JUSTICE 165–89 (John W. Chapman & J. Roland Pennock eds., 1989).

■ MARGARET JANE RADIN

I. INTRODUCTION: THE METAPHOR OF THE WALL

It has been traditional to view some aspects of social life as inappropriate for the market. We speak of a metaphorical wall between the market and other realms of social life, much as we speak of a wall between church and state. There is a traditional understanding that important political activities, like voting, are on the nonmarket side of the wall. There is also an understanding that certain special kinds of interactions between persons are on the nonmarket side of the wall—that is, are morally required to be kept there—even if some people desire to "marketize" them. It is this latter understanding that I wish to explore and question here. Does justice require that we delineate and protect a nonmarket domain? In general, how might a theory of social justice take into account the question of the domain of the market?

A traditional liberal view is that the market appropriately encompasses most desired transactions between people, with a few special exceptions. Those few exceptions—for example, the way we acquire a spouse or a child—are morally and legally protected from the market. I want to suggest that the traditional view is wrong in granting too much ground to the market. The metaphor of a wall between a market and nonmarket realm is inapposite because it wrongly suggests a large realm of pure free-market transactions to which special kinds of personal interactions form a special exception. It wrongly suggests that a laissez-faire market regime is prima facie just.

* * *

In order to frame this discussion it is necessary to notice that there is another way to deny the appositeness of the wall metaphor, and that is to say that in principle there is no limit to the market. Someone who holds this view thinks of the market as encompassing the social world. She thinks not only that social justice does not require us to protect a nonmarket domain, but also that social justice requires a universal market structure. This is the approach taken by some of the contemporary theorists who bring economics to bear on political and legal theory. Hence, it is possible to see an imaginary battle being waged. The traditional liberal view, asserting that there must be a realm of personal interactions walled off from the market, is striving to hold some territory against the oncoming forces of economics and the notion that everything is grist for the market mill.

In my view, both sides are wrong, and so is the battle. Instead of trying to defend the small piece of ground representing the list of special non-market personal interactions, it would be better to try to reclaim for peaceful co-existence some of the territory the traditional liberal view concedes to the market. The traditional liberal view is wrong because it assumes that not much is on the nonmarket side of the wall, and the battle lines prevent us from appreciating the nonmarket aspects of many of our market relations. They prevent us from seeing fragments of a nonmarket social order embedded or latent in the market society. They prevent us from thinking about social justice in terms of fostering this latent co-existent nonmarket order.

II. UNIVERSAL COMMODIFICATION VS. THE WALL

A. *The Market as Methodological Archetype*

Let us first consider a sketch of an archetype representing the economic view, and then consider the reasons given by its opponents for walling off a few special things from the market. Some law-and-economics theorists can be understood to endorse a methodological archetype that is sometimes referred to as market-imperialism, but which I prefer to call universal commodification. Under universal commodification, all things desired or valued—from personal attributes to good government—are goods or commodities. Commodities are usually pictured as objects separate from the self and social relations. Hence, universal commodification is a form of objectification. It assimilates personal attributes, relations, and desired states of affairs to the realm of objects. Universal commodification implies that all things can and should be separable from persons and exchanged through the free market, whenever some people are willing to sell and others are willing to buy. All human attributes are conceived of as possessions bearing a value characterizable in money terms, and all human interactions are conceived as exchanges understandable in terms of gains from trade.

The language in which this conceptual scheme is couched is the rhetoric of the market. Under universal commodification, the human universe of social interaction—from government to love and sexuality—is conceived and described in the rhetoric of trading objects for money. Hobbes conceived of the value of a person in market rhetoric: "the *Value* or WORTH of a man, is as of all other things, his Price; that is to say, so much as would be given for the use of his Power." In Hobbes's conception, everything about a person that others need, desire, or value is a possession that is priced. The Hobbesian person fits into the archetype of universal commodification. The Hobbesian conception of the political order likewise conceives of politics in market rhetoric. Modern Hobbesians view political activity as fully describable in terms of "rent seeking" by those who can achieve monetary gain from the capture of portions of Leviathan's power.

* * *

For one who is willing to conceive of everything (corneas for transplant, sexuality, babies for adoption) in market rhetoric, the only explanation for why some things might be held out of the market is market failure: free riders and holdouts, administrative costs, information costs, and so on. Judge Richard Posner, for example, apparently views a ban on selling oneself into slavery as justified by information costs. Finding no apparent market failures that would suggest noncommodification of children, he suggests that a free market in babies would be a good idea.

B.   *Three Attempts to Maintain the Wall*

Those who advocate the traditional wall to claim a few things for a domain that is in principle off limits to the market rely on reasons other than market failure. Three prevalent kinds of arguments are deployed in trying to keep something—babies, blood, kidneys—on the nonmarket side of a metaphorical wall. The first is an argument based upon the degradation and invasion of personhood occasioned by allowing sales. The second is an argument based upon creating or preserving opportunities for altruism. The third is a slippery slope argument that I call a domino theory, claiming that to allow sales for some people who choose them will foreclose non-market sharing for those who don't choose the market regime. As we shall see, the second and third arguments are related, because the argument based upon opportunities for altruism assumes the domino theory is true. But the two arguments are not coextensive, for, as we shall see, the domino theory is also applied to cases that do not fit the argument about altruism.

I shall argue that these arguments are too general for the task they have been put to, that is, to show that universal commodification is wrong because there must remain certain specific pockets of nonmarket social interactions. Instead, they seem to point toward a more generalized non-market perspective. That is, these arguments have been aimed at shoring up a wall between the market and nonmarket domains, but in fact they undermine the wall metaphor. These arguments fail to capture what is wrong about universal commodification.

Personhood prophylaxis. The first strand of argument is often thought of in connection with organ transplants, especially from living people. The argument holds that we must prevent poor people from being forced to sell their kidneys and corneas. The general idea is that it is somehow degrading to be selling off one's body parts, and that this is an injury to personhood that society should prevent. Thus I characterize the argument as aimed at personhood prophylaxis. In this strand of argument it is also thought that in some sense such sales are the result of coercion and do not represent a voluntary act on the seller's part.

Of course, it is problematic whether this kind of action that results from poverty should count as coerced. Does poverty "coerce" someone into selling a kidney, or does someone, because she is poor, choose to sell a kidney? A hard choice is not a non-choice. But the main problem with the personhood prophylaxis form of argument is that it seems cruelly smug. Under what circumstances do people need money badly enough to sell a kidney? Perhaps to feed, clothe, and house their children, or to support elderly or handicapped relatives. It may appear to observers that selling a kidney is degrading, but if these are the circumstances, it seems more degrading instead to have to endure the state of affairs that the sale was supposed to ameliorate.

      * * *

Preserving opportunities for altruism. According to the second strand of argument, something should be held off the market when permitting sales would foreclose, or fail to create, opportunities for altruism that ought to be open. With regard to human blood, for example, Richard Titmuss claimed that altruism is encouraged if society permits only donation, and discouraged if society permits both gifts and sales. In the Titmuss style of argument, altruism is encouraged by donation rather than sale because giving is thought to be communitarian and to emphasize interdependence, whereas market transactions are thought to be individualistic and to emphasize isolation. A donor's experience in being responsible for saving a stranger's life is said to bring us closer together, cement our community, in a way that buying and selling cannot. Interdependence is also emphasized by the possibility of reciprocity. A donor's sense of obligation today could be partially founded on the recognition that she might well need to become a recipient tomorrow. A recipient's sense of gratitude and acknowledgment of dependence upon others' altruism rather than upon her own wealth creates solidarity and interdependence.

According to this argument, altruism is foreclosed if both donations and sales are permitted. If sales are not allowed, donations have no market value and remain unmonetized. If sales are allowed, then even gifts have a market equivalent. My giving a pint of blood is like giving $50 of my money. According to this argument, such monetization discourages giving. We are more willing to give health, perhaps life itself, to strangers than we are to give them $50 of our money.

* * *

Even accepting a need to find gift objects that must remain completely unmonetized, it still seems that the argument about opportunities for altruism is more general than its proponents have thought. Many kinds of gift objects or volunteer services that can be given on a one-shot basis and do not require much special training might still fit the argument: gifts of old clothes or books; services like reading to blind people, being a subject for experimentation, driving voters to the polls, census-taking, and so on. Why do we not think of keeping these things completely unmonetized? Maybe those who make the argument about opportunities for altruism would further try to cabin it by suggesting that, in addition to being things that can be given on a one-shot basis, the things that must be kept unmonetized are extremely important, perhaps meaning the difference between life or death, to the recipient. But such an attempt to cabin the argument must fail, because it is unclear why the level of importance should matter in this way. There seems to be no reason why we must make altruism dramatic in order to preserve it.

The domino theory. The third strand of argument, the domino theory, holds that there is a slippery-slope leading from toleration of any sales (of something) to an exclusive market regime (for that thing). Although it is a necessary supposition of the argument about opportunities for altruism, the domino theory is more often brought up in connection with prostitution and sale of babies. The domino theory implicitly makes two claims: first, as a background normative premise, that it is important for a nonmarket regime to exist; and second, as an empirical premise, that a nonmarket regime cannot co-exist with a market regime. The market drives out the nonmarket version, hence the market regime must be banned.

The domino theory covers more than just the territory supposedly conducive to altruism, since those who argue that sexuality must remain nonmonetized do not argue that the reason is so that it may be altruistically given. Indeed, as I suggested earlier, it seems that the concept of altruism already presupposes more distance, remoteness, or impersonality between people than we wish to countenance in our ideals of sexuality. Those who are against monetized sex are probably against altruistic sex also.

Preserving opportunities for altruism does not, then, seem to be the main reason for asserting that noncommercial sex must remain possible. Nor does it seem to be the main reason at work in the inclination to ban baby selling, although it can play a part, as my earlier discussion indicated. Rather, it appears that the uncommodified version must remain possible because commodification somehow destroys or deeply disfigures the possible value of sex itself or the value of the baby itself.

With babies this does not seem difficult to understand. Superficially, at least, it seems to fail to treat children as persons to make them all realize that they have a definite commercial value, and that this is all their value amounts to, even if their parents did not choose to sell them or did not obtain them by purchase; the domino theory asserts that this will be the result of permitting sales for those who choose them. Is it similarly an injury to personhood to commercialize sex? If noncommercial sex becomes impossible, as we are here assuming, the argument that the answer is yes asserts that we shall all be deprived of a significant form of human bonding and interrelation. If disrespect for personhood has an individualistic flavor, perhaps this would be better put as disrespect for humanity or human relations. Under this analysis, noncommercial sex is a component of human flourishing, like the need for opportunities to express altruism. Commercial friendship is a contradiction in terms, as is commercial love. If opportunities for noncommercial friendship and love were not available, we would not be human. The argument we are reviewing asks us to see sexuality analogously.

But let us finally focus on the domino part of the theory. Is it the case that if some people are allowed to sell babies or sexual services, those things will be thereby commercialized for everyone? The argument that the answer is yes assumes that once the fact of market value enters our discourse, it must be present in, and dominate, every transaction. The fact of pricing brings with it the conceptual scheme of commodification. We cannot know the price of something and know at the same time that it is priceless. Once something has a price, money must be a part of the interaction, and the reason or explanation for the interaction, when that something changes hands. A sale cannot simultaneously be a gift. If our children know that the going rate of babies is $10,000, they will know that they are worth $10,000. They will know that they are worth as much as an economy car, but not as much as a house. Worse, if they know that the market price of "good" babies is $10,000, whereas the price of "medium-grade" babies is only $8,000, they will be anxiously comparing themselves with the "good" grade of child in hopes that they measure up. One can fill in the analogous argument regarding sexuality.

III. Incomplete Commodification:

The Metaphor of Coexistence

A. *Coexistence of Market and Nonmarket Interaction*

The domino theory assumes that we cannot both know the price of something and know that it is priceless. We cannot have a sale that is also, and "really," a gift. Is this assumption correct? Or does it grant too much to universal commodification at the outset, by assuming that thinking in money terms is what comes most "naturally" to us? Perhaps it is not true that an interaction cannot be both a sale and a gift at the same time; that we cannot both know the price of something, and know that it is unmonetizable or priceless. This kind of critique of the domino theory would see a nonmarket aspect to much of the market. I shall elaborate it somewhat by considering work and our ideals about work.

Because this is a market society, most people must be paid for their work if they are to live, yet the kind of work we all hope to have—I think— is that which we would do anyway, without money, if somehow by other means our necessities of life were taken care of. Our ideals about work—at least for many of us—do not turn on capitalist rationality. What we hope to get out of working is not all money, nor understandable in money terms (unless the archetype of universal commodification describes our conceptual scheme).

Inspired by Hannah Arendt, I think it is helpful here to introduce a distinction between work and labor, though it is not the same one she had in mind. It is possible to think of work as always containing a noncommodified human element; and to think of the fully commodified version as labor. I think we can understand the difference between working and laboring the way we understand the difference between playing notes and playing music. Laborers play notes, workers play the music. * * *

Many people have the sense, however, that these ideals about work are declining. As market rationality takes over, there is less and less room for working with care. Many kinds of work are becoming impersonal, some say. (Health care is a primary example.) What does it mean to say they are becoming impersonal? That seems to be simply to say that market rhetoric fully characterizes the process of interaction between seller and buyer. This is to say that to the participants in the interaction the services or things are completely commodified. The relation between health-care provider and patient, for example, is no different from that between the proverbial seller and buyer of widgets.

Putting it this way suggests that complete noncommodification—complete removal from the market—is not the only alternative to complete commodification. Incomplete commodification is also possible. Incomplete commodification describes a situation in which things are sold but the interaction between the participants in the transaction cannot be fully or perspicuously described as the sale of things. If many kinds of sales retain a personal aspect even though money changes hands, those interactions are not fully described as sales of commodities. There is an irreducibly nonmarket or nonmonetized aspect of human interaction going on between seller and recipient; to them the things sold are incompletely commodified. That there should be the opportunity for work to be personal in this sense does seem to be part of our conception of human flourishing—which is why those who see increasing depersonalization deplore it. Complete commodification of work—pure labor—does violence to our notion of what it is to be a well-developed person.

B. *Incomplete Commodification and the Ideals of Personhood and Community*

Now it may be clear why I think it gives up the ball game to argue that certain specific items (for example, blood) must remain completely noncommodified so as to keep open opportunities for altruism, especially if those who argue this way hope that these sporadic opportunities may lead the way to a less commodified society. The way to a less commodified society is to see and foster the nonmarket aspect of much of what we buy and sell, rather than to erect a wall to keep a certain few things completely off the market and abandon everything else to market rationality.

If social justice would be improved by a less commodified society, then, rather than walling off a few transactions from the pure free market, we should seek to deepen and consolidate the nonmarket countercurrents that cut across the market. One way that we already do this to some extent is, of course, with regulation. At least, that is one way of interpreting what regulation means. Such an interpretation would be consistent with prevalent critiques of liberal notions of the individual and society.

Liberal conceptions of personhood and community (individuality and sociality) have been criticized for expressing and creating an alienated, crassly commercial form of life. Liberal personhood has seemed to postulate an abstract, isolated subject radically separate from a world of objects (and other subjects). * * *

Incomplete commodification as an expression of a nonmarket order co-existent with a market order can be related to this shift in conception of the ideals of personhood and community. The kinds of goods that deviate most from laissez-faire are those related to human beings' homes, work, food, environment, education, communication, health, bodily integrity, sexuality, family life, and political life. For these goods it is easiest to see that preservation and fostering of the nonmarket aspect of their provision and use is related to human flourishing and social justice—to personhood and community as reconceived to meet the critique of liberalism. Once we accept that pervasive incomplete commodification is related to appropriate ideals of personhood and community, it is clear why the arguments for piecemeal noncommodification of specific items are unsatisfactory. It seems that the values of personhood and community require not that certain specific exceptional things be insulated by a wall while everything else is governed by market forces; rather, it seems that the values of personhood and community pervasively interact with the market and alter many goods from their pure free-market form.

　　　* * *

IV. Some Ramifications for a Theory of S.C. Justice

　　* * *

B.   Incomplete Commodification and the Form of a Theory of Justice

Now I wish to explore whether we can think more satisfactorily about social justice and the market if we abandon the metaphor of walls (and spheres). Before proceeding, it will be useful to take note of prevalent forms of theorizing about social justice. In one kind of theorizing, we concentrate on justice for the community as a whole. This is often conceptualized in terms of distribution of goods or wealth. A theory of justice in this form can (though of course it need not) cohere with a universal commodifying view of the social order. For example, Robert Nozick's unpatterned entitlement theory replicates the market in its global reliance on entitlement (private property) and just transfer (free contract). Hobbesian theories likewise conceive distributive justice to be the outcomes of unfettered market trades, with adjustments for market failures that mimic what a free market would have achieved.

In another kind of theorizing, we concentrate on social justice as just deserts for individuals, or respect for personhood. This kind of theory too can be captured by universal commodification; for example, when the person's deserts are conceived of as negative freedom to buy and sell all things in markets. Although it would oversimplify matters to attribute such a conception to Rawls, it is possible to see Rawls's theory as tending in this direction. For Rawls, a version of negative liberty is the primary requirement of social justice. All the bases of self-respect necessary to respect persons are conceived of as primary "goods," which at least perpetuates the rhetoric of fungible possessions and objectification.

Whether we are theorizing about justice for the community or for individuals, the still-prevalent liberal metaphor of social contract seems itself to perpetuate market rhetoric. Modern contractualists do not always mean the language of contract to imply monetary exchange or implicit monetizability of all individual and social value. Yet contract is a linchpin of universal commodification, and in the liberal tradition the contract metaphor must draw its power from the normative power of promises to exchange commodities. It is hence possible to see theories of justice that are couched in contract rhetoric as tending toward universal commodification—reduction to monetary terms of the broader normative ideas of social commitment, agreement, and consensus.

Positing the propriety of pervasive coexistence of market and non-market aspects to human interactions is an alternative both to theories that imply or can be understood to countenance universal commodification and to "wall" theories of social justice like Walzer's. Incomplete commodification would be reflected both in a theory of overall distributive fairness and a theory of proper treatment of individuals. Key principles for both these aspects of justice in such an alternative theory are that who should get what things of value depends upon the appropriate relation between persons and things, and between persons and other people.

For example, if we accept as appropriate a close connection between persons and their housing, then housing should be socially provided in such a way not only that everyone may have the shelter necessary for physical survival, but also that everyone may have the continuity of residence (often) necessary for proper self-development. Housing, both rented and owned, is appropriately incompletely commodified: it has special nonmarket significance to participants in market interactions regarding it, and it is appropriately socially regulated in recognition of the propriety of this self-investment. This is not because, as Walzer might have it, housing belongs to the "sphere" of security and welfare, in which distribution should be according to the principle of need, rather than to the "sphere" of money and commodities, in which distribution is appropriately according to the principle of free exchange. Rather it is because, although we value the efficiency of the market, at the same time housing must be incompletely commodified in recognition of its connection with personhood.

Who gets what depends upon appropriate relations between persons and other people, and not just between persons and things. People engaged in market interactions are not just acquiring things, they are relating to each other. A theory of social justice should recognize that these interactions often are (and ought to be able to be) valued for themselves and specifically, and not merely instrumentally and fungibly. As critics of Rawls (for example) have often noted, many kinds of solidarity and interrelations between people are central to our conception of human flourishing and hence must not be excluded from a theory of social justice.

* * *

D. Further Implication for Justice as Respect for Personhood

Pursuing a bit further the idea that both the overall distribution pattern and individual desert depend upon appropriate connections between persons and their contexts of things and other people, I shall comment on three kinds of connections between what I have said about the considerations counseling rejection of the wall metaphor, and the notion of justice as respect for personhood. Here I mean to discuss, first, the significance for social justice of the dilemma created when it seems we cannot respect personhood by choosing either the market or the nonmarket solution to a problem. Second, I want to note the significance of incomplete commodification, based on respect for personhood and the fostering of community, for the justification of regulation. Finally, I want to bring up the ultimate question of market rhetoric: Is it possible that it is unjust to think and talk about some things in the discourse of commodification?

The dilemma of commodification. First, there is the observation that the prophylactic personhood argument—that people should not be allowed to sell their organs, etc., because that is degrading to personhood—calls attention to a more pervasive problem of social justice. If people are so desperate for money that they are trying to sell things we think cannot be separated from them without significant injury to personhood, we do not cure the desperation by banning sales. Nor do we avoid the injury to personhood. Perhaps the desperation is the social problem we should be looking at, rather than the market ban. Perhaps worse injury to personhood is suffered from the desperation that caused the attempt to sell a kidney or cornea than would be suffered from actually selling it. The would-be sellers apparently think so. Then justice is not served by a ban on "desperate exchanges."

These considerations change the arena of argument from considerations of appropriateness to the market to explicit considerations of social justice. If neither commodification nor non-commodification can put to rest our disquiet about harm to personhood in conjunction with certain specific kinds of transactions—if neither commodification nor non-commodification can satisfy our aspirations for a society exhibiting equal respect for persons—then we must rethink the larger social context in which this dilemma is embedded. We must think about wealth and power redistribution.

* * *

One's body is bound up with one's personhood, which is why when organs are donated it is a significant expression of human interrelation. But to preserve organ donation as an opportunity for altruism is also one way of keeping from our view the desperation of poor people. Hence, one who thinks social progress can be brought about by forcing unjust conditions upon our attention might agree with the universal commodifier that sales should be permitted. The progressive thinks, in other words, that fellow feeling is better served by permitting sales so that the spectacle will awaken fellow feeling in the rest of us, to eliminate poverty. The universal commodifier, on the other hand, thinks that even altruism is monetizable, and, in cases where there are willing buyers and willing sellers, it must be worth less than sales. This type of alliance between the far right and the far left is a sure sign that something is incoherent about the middle way.

If it appears that we cannot respect personhood either with commodification or non-commodification, given the surrounding social circumstances, for example with organ-selling, and if we agree that this means we ought to change the surrounding circumstances, we are still faced with the question of whether or not we should permit commodification while we try to do that. If we opt to permit sales for those who choose, as the libertarian and radical might both recommend, we risk complete commodification—if the domino theory correctly predicts the resulting social consciousness, given the level of commodification already present. Complete commodification makes the supposed goal of greater respect for persons in a less commodified future even less imaginable. But perhaps this risk is not as bad as the degradation of personhood and reinforcement of powerlessness brought about by the regime of enforced non-commodification. Obviously, I have no handy algorithm for making this decision.

Regulation and community. A second connection between justice and my discussion of the arguments surrounding the wall metaphor is the question of nonefficiency justification for regulation—that is, socially mandated deviations from the laissez-faire market regime for many things that are bought and sold. If everything is appropriately fully commodified unless efficiency dictates otherwise, then exceptions from the laissez-faire regime are justified only where the market for some reason cannot achieve efficient outcomes. This in fact is the position of many economists on regulation. It makes many types of regulation (for example, residential rent control) difficult to justify; when these types of regulation are frequently imposed anyway by the political order, they are seen as obvious examples of selfish rent-seeking by powerful interest groups. But as I have argued above, there is another way to view regulation of many things that are important to human personhood and community, and that is as incomplete commodification. If we stubbornly intuit that these things that are very important to human life, health, and self and community development ought not to be completely monetized, then regulation that does not (theoretically) meet an efficiency test is in principle justified. Then the response of the political order in imposing the constraints on commodification may be seen as a good-faith working out of community values, so that persons and the community may properly flourish, rather than interest-group rent-seeking.

Can market rhetoric be unjust? The third question that I would like to raise here has to do with whether social justice (as respect for persons) and the rhetoric of universal commodification are connected. I think that conceiving of politics as mere rent-seeking, and essential human attributes as mere scarce commodities, expresses and fosters a conception of human flourishing inferior to that expressed and fostered by a discourse that recognizes personhood and community as essentially unmonetized and not fungible. But is it unjust to think of these aspects of human life in terms of commodities? Does Richard Posner act unjustly in trying to convince us that the right way to think of children is as commodities, and that the right way to think of much that legislatures do is in terms of rent-seeking?

NOTE ON MARKET COMMODIFICATION

Stanford Law Professor Margaret Jane Radin has written extensively on topics covering the limits of private property and freedom of contract. Her work on justice and the market domain has been highly influential in shaping debates about theories of economic justice. A discussion of her work follows:

In her piece on universal commodification in the marketplace, Radin rejects two premises: (1) the traditional economic view that universal commodification is the best vehicle to ensure social justice, and (2) the traditional liberal view that some "nonmarket" goods and services, such as sex and reproduction, should be excluded from the market. Opposing complete commodification in the market, Radin endorses incomplete commodification: rather than building a barrier to exclude certain items from the market and reserving everything else to "market rationality," individuals must recognize and promote the nonmarket aspect of the goods and services they purchase. In order to achieve social justice, Radin encourages advancing the individuality of personhood against the mass forces of commercial interest, elevating individual preference (as opposed to majority preference), and reducing the zones of commodification.

In order to translate Radin's rhetoric into practice, individuals could embark on several tasks. First, rather than abuse certain services, individuals should humanize services. People must realize that their personal behavior may have damaging implications on individuals who provide them with services, such as restaurant servers and blue-collar workers. Accordingly, when associating with workers in the service sector, customers should respect service providers with just compensation and reverence. Second, individuals need to abandon the notion of "human hierarchy" and respect all life, regardless of a person's background. The commodification of human beings lends to the notion that an American life is worth more than another life. This idea is prevalent in news broadcasts; when reporting major disasters, the media often stresses the loss of or injury to an American life, rather than covering the tragedies of peoples of other nationalities. Rather than placing one life before another, all lives should be treated with a similar amount of deference. A third way to instill nonmarket values to promote justice is to scrutinize work conditions. Rather than examining the labor environment from a macro perspective, if market actors examine conditions at the margin, individuals may have a more accurate view of how labor policies affect workers. With this knowledge, individuals can work to change the workplace to ameliorate conditions and improve labor life.

NOTES AND QUESTIONS

1. Market inalienability. Proponents of universal commodification say that as long as there are willing buyers and sellers and an item is separable from a human being, actors should be able to exchange that item in the market. Radin opposes this premise and argues that some items are inalienable, making them exempt from market transactions. Unless some items are excluded from the market domain, people may begin to think of themselves as commodities and life will no longer have the same value. In a law journal note, Khiara M. Bridges distinguishes those scholars who endorse market alienability from those who oppose it:

> Those in this school of thought believe that if the body were made alienable in the market, people would begin to conceptualize themselves in market terms. A liver, the potential to produce and carry another life within the womb, or the remains of a terminated pregnancy (and all the emotions associated with it) is then a commodity or good whose price is determined by the intersection of supply and demand. Once this conceptualization has occurred, the theory continues, the damage is done: The individuals in society no longer think of themselves as incorporeal persons housed within physical temples. Thus, humanity is irreparably damaged. In contrast, these theorists believe that those activities that do not cause individuals to "price" their incorporeal persons or the physical manifestation of such do not need to be shielded from market rhetoric.

Khiara M. Bridges, Note, *On the Commodification of the Black Female Body: The Critical Implications of the Alienability of Fetal Tissue*, 102 Colum. L. Rev. 123, 130 (2002).

Though some products may serve as contributions for altruistic purposes, certain goods cannot be sold. The items that are essential to "personhood" should be inalienable. Paul Littlepage, who holds a master of sciences in microbiology from the University of California, Davis, and undergraduate degrees in both microbiology and physiology from Southern Illinois University, elaborates on Radin's theory of market inalienability:

> Radin defines items that are market-inalienable as those which should not be sold or traded in the market. According to Radin, an item that is market inalienable is not necessarily inseparable from a person. Instead, Radin's theory posits that market trading should not be used as the social mechanism for separating that item from the person. In other words, Radin allows that people may give certain resources away, but they cannot sell them.

> Radin's theory of market-inalienability is designed to promote the concept of "human flourishing." Thus she maintains that the resources that qualify as non-alienable are those that are important to personhood. Under her theory, in an ideal world, markets would not necessarily be abolished, but all things important to personhood would be protected by market-inalienability.

Paul Littlepage, *Compensated Siting Proposals and Environmental Justice: Should Communities Be Allowed to Sell Their Health Rights?*, 21–JUN Environs Envtl. L. & Pol'y J. 3, 10 (1998). Radin differentiates market inalienability from other forms of alienability:

> Market-inalienability negates a central element of traditional property rights, which are conceived of as fully alienable. But market-inalienability differs from the nontransferability that characterizes many nontraditional property rights—entitlements of the regulatory and welfare state—that are both nongiveable and nonsalable. Market-inalienability also differs from the inalienability of other things, like voting rights, that seem to be moral or political duties related to a community's normative life; they are subject to broader inalienabilities that preclude loss as well as transfer. Unlike the inalienabilities attaching to welfare entitlements or political duties, market-inalienability does not render something inseparable from the person, but rather specifies that market trading may not be used as a social mechanism of separation. Finally, market-inalienability differs from the inalienability of things, like heroin, that are made nontransferable in order to implement a prohibition, because it does not signify that something is social anathema. Indeed, preclusion of sales often coexists with encouragement of gifts. For example, the market-inalienability of human organs does not preclude—and, indeed, may seek to foster—transfer from one individual to another by gift.

Margaret Jane Radin, *Market-Inalienability*, 100 HARV. L. REV. 1849, 1854–55 (1987).

The means by which to make certain goods inalienable is to change legal rules governing property and its transfer. Is it possible to change laws to make certain products inalienable? What problems may ensue if certain rules are changed to disallow the commodification of some products?

> While commodification has something to do with market transfers, it is a mistake to *equate* commodification with the legality of such transfers. First, a focus on legal rules is unlikely to devote adequate attention to the many ways in which people are commodified independently of the direct power of the law. Second, equating commodification with the legal rules governing market transfers wrongly ignores the possibility of resistance to power, undermining from the outset any effort to look beyond particular issues to broader social change.

Stephen J. Schnably, *Property and Pragmatism: A Critique of Radin's Theory of Property and Personhood*, 45 STAN. L. REV. 347, 385 (1993).

If Radin's goal—the aim of making some products inalienable—becomes a reality, people may lose the legal right to make a market transfer of an item or a body part. Does making certain products market-inalienable strip an individual of a valuable legal right? University of Miami professor of law Stephen J. Schnably argues that differentiating products in an alienable/inalienable dichotomy assumes that people are passive and do not want to engage in certain market transactions:

> In Radin's conception, commodification utterly disempowers people; the only solution is for the state to counter commodification by imposing rules of market-inalienability. This conception of commodification ignores the potential for resistance. For all Radin's concern for personhood, her theory views individuals as the passive beneficiaries of a personhood-respecting state.

> The problem with such an account is that it depicts an essentially static society—a society in which the sources of change remain hidden and obscure. Radin's failure to examine consensus critically or to address the effects of power in the shaping of consensus gives her theory an implicit conservative bias.

> The problem can be restated in Radin's terminology. Treating people as passive objects renders the double bind pervasive and unresolvable. If commodification leaves people as utterly disempowered as Radin's treatment implies, then the only way to promote decommodification is for the state to disable people by stripping them of the right to sell some relevant attribute. Alternatively, the state could partially decommodify them by partially disabling them—that is, by limiting the terms under which they may sell that attribute. Any measure that advances partial or complete decommodification will be vulnerable to the charge that it disrespects the very objects of its protection by prohibiting them from entering into a market transaction to which they would otherwise agree.

Schnably, *supra,* at 379–80.

2.   Personhood. Radin argues that some items, which are "personal," should not be bought or sold because the exchange of such items can damage the personhood of individuals. Because some items are instinctively tied to our humanity, they should be excluded from the market. Timothy S. Hall, *Bargaining with Hippocrates: Managed Care and the Doctor–Patient Relationship*, 54 S.C. L. Rev. 689, 727–28 (2003). Radin deems that certain aspects of life are integral to human beings, and to attach a dollar value to these life aspects would dehumanize them:

> I believe that a better view of personhood should understand many kinds of particulars—one's politics, work, religion, family, love, sexuality, friendships, altruism, experiences, wisdom, moral commitments, character, and personal attributes—as integral to the self. To understand any of these as monetizable or completely detached from the person * * * is to do violence to our deepest understanding of what it is to be human.

Margaret Jane Radin, Contested Commodities 56 (1996).

What items would Radin consider to be essential to "human flourishing" or "personhood"? Is human body tissue an item too personal to be part of the market? In *Moore v. Regents of the University of California*, 793 P.2d 479 (Cal. 1990), the California Supreme Court encountered this issue. There, the court rejected a patient's claim that his property rights had been violated when his physician and other medical employees made commercial use of the patient's surgically removed spleen without first requesting his permission or sharing the profits. At first thought, it is probable that Radin would disagree with the decision because such a case may provide an incentive for destitute people to sell their organs, thereby injuring their personhood. However, Radin asserts that banning sales of organs fails to cure individuals' desperation for resources; instead, legislators should look at the poverty problem itself rather than the market for organs in determining whether some items are essential to personhood.

Based on the *Moore* decision, should the sale of human organs be regulated on the free market? An alternative to the complete commodification of items essential to one's "personhood" is allowing the government to regulate such transactions. Such a plan would not completely dehumanize products pertinent for "human flourishing," would make certain products market-inalienable, and would aid in increasing the supply of needed human organs:

> First, the removal of tissue should be both consensual and limited to circumstances that are consistent with the contributor?s dignity and bodily integrity. Second, the use of such excised tissue for research and commercial purposes should be consensual. Third, the proceeds from such use should be shared with tissue sources in a manner likely to best accommodate the host of ethical and practical considerations that have surfaced in debates between the regimes of inalienability and private property.

Requirements of informed consent and other rules of inalienability could address the first two objectives. For example, tissue could be deemed inalienable if its possessor did not give informed consent and if its removal were not medically necessary or would substantially impair the contributor's essential bodily functions. The third objective, the focus here, would be handled as described below, by a combination of market inalienability rules and a liability rule pertaining to tissues of exceptional value.

* * *

Private sales of tissue from its original source would be banned. If people chose to contribute their tissue, researchers could use it without up-front cost, but commercial users would be required to compensate the sample source after the fact if the commercial utility of the tissue met statutory eligibility criteria. A statutorily-established compensation tribunal would interpret and apply these criteria. The tribunal would also use statutory standards to calculate the measure of compensation to be paid.

* * *

Guidelines and precedents developed by the tribunal would enhance the fairness and predictability of the process. Prices would be determined according to the characteristics and uses of the tissue, not the personal circumstances of the contributors.

* * *

Although tissue itself could not be sold, there could still be a role, and remuneration, for patient groups, physician networks or other organizations that might assemble large pools of tissue samples pertaining to a particular disease or condition. These parties could charge researchers or companies for their collection services, even though any compensation for the materials themselves would be governed by the tribunal and owed to the original source. Sources could designate the collecting organization as the beneficiary of any compensation, although this would have to be handled carefully in the clinical context so as not to raise the specter of conflict of interest or undue influence. Collecting organizations might also negotiate for non- financial terms, such as commitments regarding the use of their samples to address problems of special interest to their group.

Charlotte H. Harrison, *Neither* Moore *nor the Market: Alternative Models for Compensating Contributors of Human Tissue*, 28 AM. J.L. & MED. 77, 96–98 (2002). (Arguing for banning private sales and imposing government regulation on the transfer of needed human tissue).

For more on notions of personhood, please see Sarah E. Waldeck, *Encouraging a Market in Human Milk*, 11 COLUM. J. GENDER & L. 361 (2002); Zachary M. Garsek, *Napster Through the Scope of Property and Personhood: Leaving Artists Incomplete People*, 19–SPG ENT. & SPORTS LAW. 1 (2002); Radhika Rao, *Property, Privacy and the Human Body*, 80 B.U. L. REV. 359 (2000).

3. Altruism. Some scholars suggest that making all products market alienable discourages individuals from making donations, for example, the market for blood samples. Price incentives offered by markets would decrease opportunities for philanthropy and cause the supply of blood donations to diminish. Could a market for blood and a blood donation be mutually exclusive? Would the existence of a market take away individuals' "right to give?" *See* Richard M. Titmuss, The Gift Relationship: From Human Blood to Social Policy 198, 237 (1971).

4. Incomplete commofidication. Rather than monetizing all goods and services, Radin advances partial commodification, where items are exchanged but the relations between the buyer and seller remain personal and nonmonetized. By retaining personal interactions with others, individuals advance the ideals of personhood and human flourishing and change many items from their standard market form. Examples of partial commodification include labor and housing. In these two domains, money is exchanged, but "[t]here is an irreducibly nonmarket or nonmonetized aspect of human interaction going on between seller and recipient."

Why is commodification so unappealing? How could monetizing all goods have a damaging impact on personhood? One consequence of attaching a dollar value to personal health rights is that it might exploit the poor.

Radin has explored commodification in the markets in babies or in sexual services. Any buying and selling in these markets is "commodified," meaning such sales dehumanize women and drain women's private power. Therefore, when sexual and reproductive activities are "commodified," there is a "threat to the personhood of women, who are the 'owners of these commodities.'" However, noncommofidication of reproductive and sexual services can also hurt women's personhood. Radin calls this dilemma faced by women the "double bind":

> The threat to personhood from commodification arises because essential attributes are treated as severable fungible objects, and this denies the integrity and uniqueness of the self. But if the social regime prohibits this kind of commodification, it denies women the choice to market their sexual or reproductive services, and given the current feminization of poverty and lack of avenues for free choice for women, this also poses a threat to the personhood of women. The threat from enforced noncommodification arises because narrowing women's choices is a threat to liberation, and because their choices to market sexual or reproductive services, even if nonideal, may represent the best alternatives available to those who would choose them.

> Thus the double bind: both commodification and noncommodification may be harmful.

Margaret Jane Radin, *The Pragmatist and the Feminist*, 63 S. Cal. L. Rev. 1699, 1699–1700 (1990). Incomplete commodification can serve as a remedy for the damage caused to women's personhood. Government regulatory restriction of particular exchanges in these markets can serve to mitigate the damage to women's personhood without impairing women's financial stability. *See* Margaret Jane Radin, *Market-Inalienability*, 100 HARV. L. REV. 1849 (1987).

What are some possible policies that would put incomplete commofidication into practice?

For more on commodification, please see Margaret J. Radin, *Rent Control and Incomplete Commodification: A Rejoinder*, 17 PHIL. & PUB. AFF. 80 (1988); Michelle B. Bray, Note, *Personalizing Personality: Toward a Property Right in Human Bodies*, 69 TEX. L. REV. 209, 241 (1990); Barbara Rothman, *Reproductive Technology and the Commofidication of Life, in* EMBRYOS, ETHICS AND WOMEN'S RIGHTS 95 (Elaine Baruch et al. eds., 1988); Elizabeth Anderson, *Is Women's Labor a Commodity?*, 19 PHIL. & PUB. AFF. 71 (1990).

c. A Feminist Critique of Both Commodification Theory and Law and Economics

Commodification and Women's Household Labor

9 YALE J.L. & FEMINISM 81(1997).

■ KATHARINE SILBAUGH

I. INTRODUCTION

A woman washes a kitchen floor. She puts the mop away and drives to the corner market. She consults a shopping list, and purchases groceries from it, carefully choosing the least expensive options. A four-year-old child is tugging at her leg while she does this, and she tries to entertain him, talking to him about the mopped floor, the grocery items. When she returns from the store, she prepares lunch from what she has brought home with her. She and the child both eat lunch. After lunch, she and the child collect laundry and she runs a load. She takes the garbage out to the curb. Then she reads him a story. They play a game where she comes up with a word, and he tries to name its opposite. Sometimes there is no opposite, and that is particularly funny to both of them. She has done housework.

There is no way to tell from this description whether these activities were market or non-market, whether her work is a commodity or not. Would it help to categorize her work if you knew the location? Is this her home? Suppose that she is a paid domestic worker, and this housework is a commodity. She leaves her employer's home. She goes home and does exactly the same thing there, but this time she is preparing dinner. The second child is her own. Whether these activities are viewed as a commodity is contextual, not activity-based.

Should we think and talk about unpaid domestic labor—housework—using market, or economic, language? What follows is a defense of economic discourse on the subject of law and housework. It is written in response to the common criticism aimed at scholars who have examined domestic labor through an economic lens. It is a response to what is commonly called a "commodification critique," and particularly as that critique is formulated within feminist discourse.

In *Turning Labor into Love: Housework and the Law*, I examined the treatment of household labor in tax law, torts, family law, social security, welfare, contracts and labor law. I argued that characterizations of domestic labor by legal actors almost never include an emphasis on its economic productivity, instead focusing on housework as an expression of the affectionate emotions associated with the family setting where housework occurs. By setting up a dichotomy between the language of economic productivity and the language of emotions, I argued that legal actors have used the language of emotions to deny material security to those who perform domestic labor. From this I concluded that a more clearly articulated understanding of the economically productive aspects of home labor would, on balance, benefit those who perform the labor, who are still primarily women. I did not, however, address commodification problems with that conclusion. The most explicit writing on commodification in legal discourse has addressed the commodification of other aspects of women's experience: sexuality and reproduction. This critique has been raised in response to some recent work on domestic labor, including my own.

I want to reject current categorical thinking about women's home activity. I argue that economic understandings are very useful, and that they do not and need not supply a complete understanding of human activities. I will make the case that economic understandings are representations of a given activity, as are sentimental or emotional understandings, and that they can and should co-exist. Margaret Jane Radin, the foremost legal scholar who has addressed commodification concerns, has also argued that multiple understandings can co-exist. Her goal, however, is to bring non-market understandings to market activities, in search of a less commodified society.

This Article questions that goal. My central argument is that the entirely emotional understanding of home labor is itself an impoverished one. If one conceded that the use of economic rhetoric could habituate people to thinking about a topic differently, as critics of economic language assert, that would not necessarily make the case *against* the use of such rhetoric in all contexts. I make the uncommon case here for the value of bringing market understandings to non-market activities where they can co-exist with non-economic conceptions. The broader implication of the thesis is that we should not assume that analyses that can remake relations are always doing a disservice, especially where those relations are already fraught with problematic analyses. In certain contexts it may be a very conservative claim that economic analysis is bad *because* it has the power to change the way we view something.

My claim is that gender equality requires us to take the economics of home labor seriously. This argument turns on a comparison between wage labor and home labor, which are similar both in content and in many of the motivations that drive workers. I argue that the difference in the treatment between them may be difference based on gender. I discuss the tendency to raise commodification concerns when women's interests are at stake, and question whether resistance to market reasoning in these contexts is a form of resistance to women's economic power. I then examine some legal doctrines touching on home labor that could benefit from economic analysis. If importing economic reasoning into these areas transforms our understanding of them, I posit that women would *benefit* from that transformation. I conclude that as long as so many of women's activities remain non-market and as long as women's economic welfare is a concern of feminists, economic analysis of non-market activities is affirmatively desirable. My objective is to show what can be gained by allowing economics to inform, without dominating, the discourse on policy and doctrine surrounding home labor. Concern over women's lives becoming entirely commodified seems by comparison an abstract worry.

II.   THE COMMODIFICATION OBJECTION: SETTING OUT THE CASE AGAINST ECONOMICS

A.   *The Basic Problem with Commodification*

The standard argument against commodification, often referred to as the "commodification critique," is that certain human attributes or certain resources should lie wholly or partially beyond exchange, because to allow exchange would be inconsistent with a vision of personhood or human flourishing. Prohibiting exchange may not be enough; it may be necessary to discourage economic analysis and discourse about these attributes. "[M]any kinds of particulars—one's politics, work, religion, family, love, sexuality, friendships, altruism, experiences, wisdom, moral commitments, character, and personal attributes [are] . . . integral to the self. To understand any of these as monetizable . . . is to do violence to our deepest understanding of what it is to be human."

Elizabeth Anderson has reviewed commodification concerns and applied them to women's reproductive labor in a piece interestingly titled, "Is Women's Labor a Commodity?" She defines a commodity as something to which "the norms of the market are appropriate for regulating its production, exchange and enjoyment." The application of market norms is inappropriate where they "fail to value *the thing* in an appropriate way." If it is appropriate to apply "use" as the proper mode of valuation, then market norms are acceptable and we may treat something as a commodity. If instead, a mode of valuation such as respect, "love, admiration, honor and appreciation," are more appropriate, then we should not treat something as a commodity. To value something differently than as a commodity is, according to Anderson, to recognize a "special intrinsic worth" to that item. This essentialist notion that things have an intrinsic worth turns out to be important to anti-commodification arguments. Anderson argues, "When women's labor is treated as a commodity, the women who perform it are degraded." Degradation means that "something is treated in accordance with a lower mode of valuation than is proper to it." Finally Anderson believes that commodifying women's labor leads to exploitation of women. This is so because women's noncommercial motivations are taken advantage of without offering anything but commercial responses.

Anderson's work draws on a notion of incommensurability of value that is seen in the work of Martha Nussbaum. As applied to the domestic labor context, the problem of incommensurability would arise with the need to give the labor a market value when it is not commensurable to market goods or services. They may not be commensurable where, for example, one is measured on a valuation scale that can translate into dollars, where another is measured on one that cannot, such as love, admiration, wonder, or respect. While these scholars have not applied their critiques directly to housework, it can be argued that there is no perfectly accurate market replacement for unpaid work, for example child-care, that a family member performs.

The commodification critique applies to an *analysis* of the economy of the home and the family labor that occurs there, as well as to the actual purchase and sale of that labor. To Anderson, market norms have an "expressive significance" as well as a practical one, and can thus infect non-market conceptions of women's labor. The argument posits that talk matters: you can pervert the personalness of something by talking about it as if it were fungible. Identifying an "economy," meaning a set of implicit valuations and exchanges, is possible even where "real markets" are either prohibited or practically impossible to imagine: organs for transplantation, sexual contacts, candidates for marriage partnerships, religious convictions, love, or a person's politics. Although in many cases this is just talk, to a commodification skeptic, that talk itself does damage to the integrity of the attribute in question: sexuality, love, marriage, health.

James Boyd White has made this case most powerfully, arguing that expression is never transparent, but instead constitutes and transforms the reality it describes. Says White: "the languages we speak, and the cultural practices they at once reflect and make possible, form our minds by habituating them to certain modes of attention, certain ways of seeing and conceiving of oneself and of the world." White concludes that economic language should be "vigorously resist[ed]" because "[t]he conventions of this discourse necessarily habituate its user[s] to thinking in terms of self-interest as a central principle." In passing, he applies this critique to an economic understanding of home labor, noting that:

> The segmentation of the exchange model tends to misvalue the work we do for ourselves, which is most of the traditional work of women.... This is especially true of people who raise their own children. Such work cannot be segmented into functions and then made the material of the market process, actual or hypothetical, for what the child requires is the sustained presence of, and interaction with, a loving and respectful person, something no alternative can supply. Similarly, housework has a different meaning when one is maintaining one's own home rather than acting as a servant for others.

To those who see a difference between real and rhetorical markets, the difference tends to be treated as one of degree. Under this view, it might not hurt personhood as much to talk about markets in certain attributes as it does to create such markets, but talk certainly doesn't *help*. By condemning talk as well as trades, skeptics take away the opportunity to make the affirmative case for the benefits of an economic perspective. For legal analysts, this conflation of actual buying and selling and market analysis proves problematic * * *.

* * *

C.   *Feminism and Economic Skepticism*

Feminists rank high among those who are skeptical of economists. This skepticism proceeds on two fronts in the domestic labor context. The two parts are a negative reaction to economics as a way to describe home activities, and an affirmatively positive response to love and affections as a descriptively accurate way of understanding and explaining productivity in the home.

1.   *Offense at Economics*

Some feminists have a visceral dislike for economic analysis. While there are many reasons for this, I believe two are most strongly at play. The first is situational: Many feminists don't trust the current practitioners of economic analysis. The second is more substantive: Many feminists do not accept the implicit notion of fungibility at play in economic analysis.

The problem of distrust may come from two characteristics of economic discourse. The first is a driving, relentless essentialism among economists. Much economic literature reads like much more than a useful tool with which to explain certain phenomenon. It instead reads like the *raison d'être* of that phenomenon, its beginning and end. Everyone has her favorite example of a social phenomenon being mercilessly pushed into an economic model producing logically clean but absurd explanations: adoption, marriage, heroic rescues, voting, altruism, religion, childbirth, sexuality. This kind of relentless essentialism among economists leaves reasonable people with what appears to be a decision to either embrace the whole absurd end of the spectrum or jump ship entirely. I will argue that it is fully possible and desirable to use economics to assist in understanding a social phenomenon without turning away from other possible explanations or understandings. But this does not describe much of the dominant economic analysis practiced in the *legal* academic community. The idea of extending this sort of essentialism into the social relations surrounding family labor seems to carry the risk of damaging the complex context of dependencies and moral and emotional commitments made there.

The second reason many feminists distrust practitioners of economic analysis is that they often employ assumptions with suspect origins. Moreover, although these are almost always identified at the outset as assumptions, by the end of the equation they seem to have assumed the status of fact. In legal discourse, when an assumption is used in an economic model, we usually see the burden of proof implicitly shifted to critics of the model to disprove the factual assumption despite the frequent lack of evidence in favor of the assumption from the outset. There is the well-known joke about the economists on a desert island with a case of food in tin cans.

They begin their plan for opening the cans by saying, "First, let's assume a can opener." It's funny when it's a can opener. It is not so funny, or at least it shouldn't be, when the empirically unsupported assumption is that women want children more than men do, that women have higher inherent value when they are young and men are worth more when they are older, that husbands and wives in most cases have the perfect trust and agency necessary to treat them as a single economic unit (individuals are selfish and self-interested but family heads are altruistic), or that rapists would pay for sex somehow if they had the necessary wealth of money, power, or looks themselves. Having those assumptions implicitly raised to the level of facts over the course of an economic analysis is particularly problematic.

I think of the implicit elevation of assumption to fact as "assumption slippage." It must be noted that this slippage is a dynamic process: Readers of economic texts, particularly in the legal community, are participants in its occurrence as much if not sometimes more than economic authors. Much of the most prominent economic analysis of family and gender relations, particularly that associated with Gary Becker, relies on very questionable assumptions that appear to come right out of the pages of *The Total Woman* and from there they help to build economic rationalizations for very conventional mid-twentieth century middle class suburban gender relations. In the words of Barbara Bergmann, "to say that New Home Economists [Becker et al.] are not feminists in their orientation would be as much of an understatement as to say that Bengal tigers are not vegetarians." Isabel Y. Sawhill has offered a critique of the lack of empirical basis for some of the basic assumptions of the New Home Economists who are prominent in the field. As economists know from their training but their legal readers quickly forget, an economic model is only as good as its assumptions. Hence, the implicit standard in economic scholarship is that unproved assumptions must be plausible before a model based on them is acceptable, even with caveats. In the context of home labor, those assumptions are very important. Assuming altruistic heads of households reduces the need to worry about disparate human capital investments made within the family. The assumption that women desire children more than men do provides an explanation for what otherwise might be tricky distributional results that occur within families. If these are to be the assumptions on which an economic analysis of home labor is to proceed, many people do not want any part of it.

I cannot join the routine conclusion that the problems with Gary Becker's work are so far-reaching as to make his work as a whole of limited use. We are indebted to Becker for raising extraordinarily important economic questions about the functioning of the family. Becker has brought us many ideas that are extremely helpful in thinking about family relations, including the very notion that in economic terms the home is a place of production and not just a place of consumption. If he has proceeded from unsupportable or incomplete assumptions, those can be corrected and the analysis and its outcomes adjusted accordingly. Indeed, examining and critiquing these assumptions has been a large implicit part of the feminist response to law and economics already, and should continue to be so.

However, critiquing assumptions does not inflict a fatal blow to methodology. It would be a mistake to hold these questionable assumptions out as an indictment of an entire mode of analysis. This is a standard to which most scholars would not wish to be held, and feminists are no exception.

There is, however, an extremely important lesson about the scope of the usefulness of economic analysis to be learned from assumption slippage and the response to it: empiricism counts. Empirical research and data need to drive any real search for policy solutions to basic problems, or even to clear understandings of the problems themselves. Law professors are not in a great position at this time to do empirical research and must rely on fields outside of law or economics, such as sociology, to inform economic understandings. Doing so is not without its own difficulties for lawyers untrained in understanding and sorting sociological research. The most that economic understandings can do is to highlight some empirical questions that need to be answered. Even answers to empirical questions do not close debates over facts. If we are confident that a resource is scarce as a matter of empirical fact, we can either treat that as a given or instead ask *why* it is scarce. That which has an empirical basis is not thereby natural or inevitable, and so even provable assumptions should be open for well-framed criticisms. But once again, economics can assist in the framing task itself.

I do not wish to be understood as overstating the ease of remembering that we are dealing with hypothetical models when we use economic analysis. I think the risk of forgetting is more serious when we *cannot* verify the empirical assumption. We move quickly on from it, sensing that the unavailability of data threatens to make an *otherwise* elegant model useless. Perversely, the less supportable an assumption, the less contestable it is, and the more it acquires the status of fact. It may be that James Boyd White's concern with the culture of economic discourse is played out most seriously when data is least available.

The next level of concern over economic analysis does not center solely on the supposed "priors" of its practitioners. It is a more substantive criticism: A rejection of the suggestion that many attributes of family life and work are fungible, and thus that the study of value can proceed by observing choices people make. Fungibility is the idea that goods, services, or attributes can be placed on a single metric of value and then traded off against one another on that metric. Fungible things can be replaced by something else that falls in the same place on the metric, such as similar services by a different person, or simply money measured in the right amount, without regret. On this account, economics is entirely concerned with theoretically measurable maximized choice among alternatives, rather than being concerned with the personal experience of choice, methods of provisioning in general (whether by voluntary exchange, gift-giving, or coercion), or with the process of developing what economists call preferences. Radin concedes that whether we think the fact of choice between alternatives proves fungibility, as many economists believe, or instead prove nothing about fungibility, is largely a matter of intuition. Joseph Raz argues that the meaning we give to a choice is its conventional understanding, and if that does not include a trade along a single metric, then no such fungibility can be inferred. Raz taps into many people's response to the talk of fungibility when thinking about marriage, romantic partners, and family work choices that are implicit in an economic analysis of home labor.

There is a similar negative response to the notion of bargaining within marriage or within family relations, which is an important element of an economic understanding of home labor. Though a bargaining model is often thought of as an improvement on Becker's notion of an altruistic head of household which can justify a failure to examine interspousal conflict, the bargaining model itself draws a negative response from many. While many would acknowledge much day-to-day bargaining within the family, it is also thought that a bargaining analysis fails to capture the altruistic behavior layered alongside self-interested behavior in family relations. It is difficult to predict much about behavior if one can rely neither on complete self-interest nor on complete altruism, and a bargaining analysis of family labor puts forward assumptions about family behavior to which many respond negatively.

2. *The Aptness of the Emotional Understanding*

The former critique, that family labor is not fungible and not always strategic, is also frequently stated in the affirmative: Family labor is uniquely emotional. In *Turning Labor into Love*, I bring an operative mode of analysis to the surface—home labor is viewed as an expression of familial emotions. In discussing this argument with others, I would routinely hear that this is the mode of analysis at play in law because it is an accurate characterization of family behavior. What is wrong with the affections characterization? Family care *is* all about affections. Should courts ignore the emotional motivations behind caring for a child or preparing a meal for a partner or spouse? While I will argue below that this idea can co-exist with an economic understanding of home labor, many feel that an economic understanding demotes or denigrates the emotional significance of home labor: this is the essence of the domino theory at play. These criticisms of the commodification of home labor through the use of economic rhetoric and analysis, in many general respects, represent a subset of criticisms of all commodification and economic rhetoric. The family context, however, raises the concerns discussed above in a particularly bright light.

I believe that feminist skepticism of economics is understandable but should be avoided. * * * [K]eeping economic understandings away from women's activities represents a particularly gendered understanding of those activities that is itself costly. * * *

2. *Women as Non-commodifiable: Questioning the Origins of an Idea*

Does concern about the comparison between wage labor and home labor commodification grow out of an implicit assumption that there is something intrinsically different about home labor? We might want to ask whether it is coincidental, or instead highly relevant, that that intrinsic difference at play in analysis also cuts along gender lines: women's work, hereby, would be essentially non-marketable. Consider the problems with assuming that women are inclined to make gifts of attributes of their personalities. Women serve, men sell. It is a familiar notion about which many feminists have been skeptical.

a. The Gender Line: Cashless Women

At a practical level, women should at least be wary of anti-commodification arguments, because these arguments arise when women receive money for something, not when women are paying money for something. The argument is used most frequently in legal discourse when talking about women receiving money for surrogate parenting and sexual contact, and herein for household labor. While Radin extends the argument into gender neutral territories, such as housing, most of the commodification red flags are raised by her and by others when discussing *women's* commodification.

One might respond that the emphasis of the anticommodification argument is that some aspect of women's personhood is going to be sold, not that women are about to receive money. It is the sale that is objectionable, not that women may end up with cash. Consider, though, that it is not uncommon to find people who approve of altruistic transfer in these same areas, for example, human egg donation and surrogacy. In fact, the current fee caps in both of these fields reflect that ideal in practice: donors are not supposed to be *too* motivated by money, so fees are held down to ensure that there is a partially altruistic motivation for donating. In these cases, it seems arguable that the difference that a woman *experiences* may simply be whether money comes to her, and how much, as compared to other wage labor that she might similarly perform from partially altruistic motivation. This difference occurs in the name of non-commodification. It is worth asking whether Anderson's concern about exploitation due to the commodification of women's reproductive capacity might just as easily turn into exploitation from non-commodification, not just in a "nonideal" world. Here the mixed motivations of women are exploited by highlighting the altruistic aspects of those motives in a discriminatory fashion. Only *women's* mixed motives relating to feminine activities are highlighted and offered as justification for leaving women without cash. Mixed motivations in the labor force at large do not require regulatory practices aimed at keeping wages down.

Social practices also exist where the characterization of the problem as "withholding money from women" seems even more apt at the practical level than "preventing the sale of women," given the particular form that current decommodification takes. Prostitutes and pimps have a relationship that results where prohibition on sale ensures that although a female attribute is being sold, a woman is not getting most of the money. The "transitional balancing" questions raised by commodification and prostitution have been widely debated elsewhere. I raise it to illustrate that protecting women from sale does not necessarily go hand in hand with preventing women from receiving cash. Women can be sold and remain relatively cashless. Few would argue that the current form of the criminalization of prostitution is intended or designed for the protection of prostitutes, and so the lack of connection between non-commodification (and its female cashlessness) and sale is hardly remarkable. But in the reproductive areas of surrogacy and egg donation, non-commodification ideals drive the policy of leaving women relatively cashless despite their (partial?) sale.

We do not usually see the anticommodification argument raised as forcefully when things typically associated with male personhood are being sold. While it may be that women's personhood is more at risk for being inappropriately objectified and commercialized, we should at least consider an alternative understanding of why commodification concerns focus on women's issues. It may have as much to do with notions of femininity and a desire to elevate a romantic essentialism about femininity as it does with a desire to protect women's integrity. Consider Anderson's argument that women's reproductive labor is inappropriately alienated by surrogacy because a surrogate mother must "divert [her labor] from the end which the social practices of pregnancy rightly promote—an emotional bond with her child." It is not clear why the end which Anderson prefers for women's labor must be extinguished by money, but it is clear that her argument leaves women without money for their labor. If a reinscription of the public-private spheres ideology on which market rhetoric thrives occurs around women's home labor, it may depend on a particular notion of femininity that has as one of its characteristics cashless women. Perhaps Anderson recognizes this, but sees it as a necessary trade-off for the preservation of familial bonds. She does not explain though, why it is a trade-off; why markets and monetary exchange cannot coexist with expressions of affection in a realistic reflection of women's mixed motivations. We have the example of wage labor as an area where monetary exchange and mixed motivations coexist.

3. BEYOND: COST-BENEFIT ANALYSIS

Myths and Markets

PRICELESS: ON KNOWING THE PRICE OF EVERYTHING AND THE VALUE OF NOTHING 35–40 (2004).

■ FRANK ACKERMAN & LISA HEINZERLING

COSTS, BENEFITS, AND BIASES

Despite its inegalitarian premises, cost-benefit analysis presents itself as the soul of rationality, an impartial, objective standard for making good decisions. Of course some environmental programs and regulations make sense, the analysts say; it's just that we have to figure out which ones are sensible, and which are not. Who could object to a careful comparison of the pros and cons of public policies?

Yet cost-benefit analysis has become a powerful weapon in the hands of vocal opponents of regulation. This is no coincidence. There are, in fact, built-in biases in cost-benefit methods. The problem is not only that those who start from an antienvironmental perspective have often used cost-benefit analysis to support their preconceptions. Even when the methods are applied in good faith by neutral or environmentally inclined investigators, we will see that the results tilt strongly toward endorsement of business as usual, and rejection of health and environmental protection. This is not obvious from the description of the methods and objectives of cost-benefit analysis, which sounds noble and nonpartisan.

Cost-benefit analysis tries to set an economic standard for measuring the success of government projects and programs. In other words, cost-benefit analysis seeks to perform, for public policy, a calculation that happens routinely in the private sector. In evaluating a proposed new initiative, how do we know if it is worth doing or not? The answer is much simpler in business than in government.

Private businesses, striving only to make money, will produce something only if they believe that someone is willing to buy it. That is, the profit motive reliably steers firms toward producing things for which the expected benefits to consumers, measured by consumer willingness to pay for them, are greater than the costs of production. It is technologically possible to produce men's business suits in brightly colored polka dots. Successful producers suspect that few people are willing to pay for such products, and usually stick to minor variations on suits in somber, traditional hues. If some firm *did* happen to produce a polka-dot business suit, no one would be forced to buy it; the producer would bear the entire loss resulting from the unsold suits.

Government, in the view of many critics, is in constant danger of requiring the production of polka-dot suits—and making people pay for them. Policies, regulations, and public spending do not face the test of the marketplace; there are no consumers who can withhold their dollars from the government until it produces regulations dressed in navy blue and charcoal gray. There is no single quantitative objective for the public sector comparable to profit maximization for businesses. Even with the best of intentions, critics suggest, government regulations and programs can easily go astray for lack of an objective standard by which to judge whether they are meeting citizens' needs.

Cost-benefit analysis sets out to do for government what the market does for business: add up the benefits of a public policy and compare them to the costs. But there is no ledger that presents the costs and benefits of public undertakings to every member of society. Cost-benefit analyses have to create that ledger, a task that often turns into a multiyear, multimillion-dollar research effort. Calculations of costs and benefits involve challenging questions of very different varieties. We begin with the costs.

Many public policies impose measurable economic costs. For example, the government may require a certain kind of pollution-control equipment, which businesses must pay for. Even if a regulation only sets a ceiling on emissions, it results in costs that can be at least roughly estimated through research into available technologies and business strategies for compliance.

Although the calculation should be straightforward, in practice there is a tendency to overestimate the costs of regulations in advance of their implementation. Massachusetts Institute of Technology researcher Nicholas Ashford argues that compliance costs typically drop after a regulation is implemented, for three reasons: pollution-control technology gets cheaper as industry produces more of it; over time, managers learn how to comply with regulations more cost-effectively; and regulations encourage innovation, which can dramatically reduce the cost of compliance. Confirming this perspective, a study by the Office of Technology Assessment of occupational safety and health regulations found many cases in which actual compliance costs were lower than anyone had expected. For example, the Occupational Safety and Health Administration (OSHA) 1974 standard for vinyl chloride, a known human carcinogen, lowered the permissible workplace exposure from 500 parts per million (ppm) to 1 ppm. Industry predicted total economic catastrophe, and OSHA's own consultants predicted compliance costs would reach $1 billion. The actual costs were about a quarter of a billion dollars, as industry quickly developed a new control technology that improved the production process as well as lowered worker exposures.

Similar patterns show up in other regulations. One study found that costs estimated in advance of regulation were more than twice actual compliance costs in eleven out of twelve cases. Another study found that advance cost estimates were more than 25 percent higher than actual costs for fourteen out of twenty-eight regulations; advance estimates were more than 25 percent too low in only three of the twenty-eight cases. Before the 1990 Clean Air Act Amendments took effect, industry had anticipated that the cost of sulfur reduction under the amendments would be $1,500 per ton. In 2000, the actual cost was under $150 per ton.

In a related vein, many companies have begun to discover that environmental protection can actually be good for business. Increased energy efficiency, profitable products made from waste, and decreased use of raw materials are just a few of the cost-saving and profit-making results of turning more corporate attention to environmentally protective business practices. Harvard Business School analyst Michael Porter maintains that carefully crafted, moderately demanding regulations can inspire business to create profitable, environmentally friendly innovations. Cost-benefit analyses typically do not take such money-saving possibilities into account in evaluating the costs of regulation. Indeed, prominent conservative policy analysts, such as Robert Hahn of the American Enterprise Institute, have expressed great skepticism that the government could discover cost savings where the market had not—much like the old joke about the economist who refuses to pick up the twenty-dollar bill in the street on the theory that if it were real, someone else would have picked it up already.

Despite these problems, the cost side is the easy part of cost-benefit analysis. In principle, one could correct for the potential sources of bias in estimating the costs of regulations and other public policies. No such correction is possible in assessing the benefits of regulation, because the benefits are, literally, priceless. Herein lies the fatal flaw of cost-benefit analysis: to compare costs and benefits in its rigid framework, they must be expressed in common units. Cancer deaths avoided, wilderness and whales saved, illnesses and anxieties prevented—all these and many other benefits must be reduced to dollar values to ensure that we are spending just enough on them, but not too much. * * * [M]ost of what we think is important about human life, health, arid the environment is lost in this translation. By monetizing the things we hold most dear, economic analysis ends up cheapening and belittling them.

In comparing monetized benefits to monetized costs, and making this comparison the criterion for judging public policies protecting people and the environment, the analysis also stacks the deck against such policies. In practice, most cost-benefit analyses could more accurately be described as "complete cost-incomplete benefit" studies. Most or all of the costs are readily determined market prices, but many important benefits cannot be meaningfully quantified or priced, and are therefore implicitly given a value of zero. Thus, despite the common claims that cost-benefit analysis is philosophically and politically impartial, its very methodology systematically disfavors protections of goods that, like health and environmental protection, are priceless.

Perhaps recognizing the likely political unpopularity of a method that requires translation of lives, health, and nature into dollars, many policy analysts have started to take a different tack in arguing for cost-benefit analysis. They do not just say that they want to create economic efficiency—after all, few people go to the polls or pull the voting lever in pursuit of efficiency. They say, instead, that what they're after is the same as what environmentalists are after: saving more lives, protecting more health, preserving more natural resources. The government, they say, often issues rules that are insanely expensive, all out of proportion to their benefits—a problem that could be solved by the use of cost-benefit analysis to screen proposed regulations and shifting money to more efficient uses. * * *

NOTES AND QUESTIONS

1. Cost-benefit analysis and Kaldor–Hicks and Pareto optimality premises. Two leading scholars of the critical legal theory movement have also criticized three central ideas of law and economics: cost-benefit analysis and the Kaldor–Hicks and Pareto optimality premises. *See* MARK KELMAN, *Is the Kaldor–Hicks Position Coherent?*, *in* A GUIDE TO CRITICAL LEGAL STUDIES 141–50 (1987); Duncan Kennedy, *Cost-Benefit Analysis of Entitlement Problems: A Critique*, 33 STAN. L. REV. 387, 422–45 (1981).

2. Effect of case or controversy on entitlement background. Critical legal scholars like Kennedy would argue that accepting a pre-existing entitlement background is a political choice because it is inattentive to the possibility of redistribution. (Arguments about the validity of background entitlements are made by both Kennedy and Kelman.) However, would a doctrinalist or a formalist not argue that judges are only supposed to decide the case before them? Does a judge not have to take the world outside of his particular case or controversy as given in order to do his/her job and decide that particular case or controversy? On the other hand, how can a judge understand the dynamics of any particular case or controversy without examining the context out of which that case arises?

3. Effect of real-world politics on critical legal studies (CLS). Kelman argues that, in many cases, wealth effects stemming from the existing entitlement scheme will be great enough to determine the outcome of costless bargaining. He uses the existence of such situations, and the fact that law and economics doesn't have much to say about them, as a criticism. However, could any other theory of jurisprudence do better? Indeed, in a case involving a dispute with Native American land ownership, the Supreme Court did try to invoke the force of law in *Worcester v. Georgia*, 31 U.S. 515 (1832). The decision was ignored and the Cherokee were dispossessed of their land. Can law and economics be criticized for remaining silent in a situation where the operative premise is "might makes right?"

4. Further problems with Coase. Aside from the general indeterminacy problem noted by critical legal scholars, there is a deeper problem with analyzing legal claims based on the Coase theorem and Pareto efficiency. Specifically, if the Coase theorem is correct and the result of a transaction is the same regardless of a court's decision, why would parties go to the extra trouble and expense of going to court? Additionally, if a change is Pareto efficient, that is, if it makes no one worse off and at least one person better off, why has it not already happened?

5. Asymmetry of no-transaction-cost modeling. Some participants in the judicial system would benefit greatly from an elimination of transaction costs, while other would benefit hardly at all. For example, a large business would benefit greatly from no transaction cost bargaining because it could avoid spending money on advertising, would not need to employ focus groups, and could generally avoid all the costs which attend selling their product to the outside world. By contrast, a neighborhood would gain very little from costless bargaining. While a lack of transaction costs would allow neighbors to resolve disputes equitably, it would not significantly improve the neighborhood's relationship with the outside world because, for the most part, that relationship is an ad-hoc one between individuals which involves very low transaction costs anyway. Why then does Kennedy argue that there is no reason to expect that trying to replicate the result of costless bargaining will not necessarily benefit any one class of factors over any other?

6. CLS's endorsement of law and economics? When litigants go to court, their primary purpose is to generate substantial wealth effects such that they will be richer and, perhaps, the person or organization they sue will be poorer. For example, punitive damage awards are made to change the behavior of tortfeasors. Pain and suffering awards are made to allow victims of torts to change their consumption patterns in order to offset their losses. With this in mind, why is the observation that changing the entitlement background generates wealth effects a critique? If I sue Ford for manufacturing automobiles that explode when rear-ended, I am trying to make it too costly for Ford to continue producing such cars. I want to change the outcome of efficient bargaining. Does the CLS analysis of wealth effects not simply demonstrate the power of cost-benefit decision making concerning entitlements?

7. Additional reading. Guido Calabresi, *The Pointlessness of Pareto: Carrying Coase Further*, 100 YALE L.J. 1211 (1991); Jeffrey L. Harrison, *Piercing Pareto Superiority: Real People and the Obligations of Legal Theory*, 39 ARIZ. L. REV. 1 (1997); Jeffrey L. Harrison, *Egoism, Altruism, and Market Illusions: The Limits of Law and Economics*, 33 UCLA L. REV. 1309 (1986); Eleanor M. Fox, *The Politics of Law and Economics in Judicial Decision Making: Antitrust as a Window*, 61 N.Y.U. L. REV. 554 (1986); Louis B. Schwartz, *With Gun and Camera Through Darkest CLS-Land*, 36 STAN. L. REV. 413 (1984);. GEORGE C. CHRISTIE & PATRICK H. MARTIN, JURISPRUDENCE (2d ed. 1995).

---

4. BEYOND: MARKET THEORY

Why Markets Don't Stop Discrimination

FREE MARKETS AND SOCIAL JUSTICE 3–9, 151–63 (1997).

■ CASS R. SUNSTEIN

We are in the midst of a period of mounting enthusiasm for free markets. This is of course true in many of the former Communist nations. It is true for much of the West as well, prominently including England and the United States.

Free markets are often defended as an engine of economic productivity, and properly so. But they are also said to be required for social justice, and here things become far more complex. Certainly there are connections between free markets and social justice. A system aspiring to social justice aspires to liberty, and a system of free markets seems to promise liberty, because it allows people to trade goods and services as they wish. In fact, a system of free markets seems to promise not merely liberty but equality of an important sort as well, since everyone in a free market is given an equal right to transact and participate in market arrangements. This form of equality should not be trivialized or disparaged. For example, race and sex discrimination has often consisted of exclusions of certain classes of people from the market domain. In both South America and the United States, discriminatory practices frequently took the form of incursions on free markets in employment.

An appreciation of the virtues of free markets has been an important part of the economic analysis of law, perhaps the most influential development in legal education in the last quarter-century, and a development with growing effects on public policy in the United States and abroad. As it operates in law schools, economic analysis is concerned above all with the consequences of legal rules. Often its practitioners have asked whether intrusions on free markets have desirable consequences. If the minimum wage is increased, what, exactly, will happen? What are the real-world consequences of bans on discrimination, legal rules for controlling air pollution, and rent control laws? There are limits to how much economic theory can say on such issues; empirical evidence is necessary. But by looking at the effects of law on incentives, economics can point in the right direction. Often it can show that the consequences of intrusions on markets will be unfortunate or even perverse. The economic analysis of law has produced significant advances, many of which are discussed in this book. Much remains to be learned.

This * * * is not, however, a simple celebration of free markets, and it raises a number of questions about economic analysis of law in its conventional form. Free markets can produce economic inefficiency and (worse) a great deal of injustice. Even well-functioning economic markets should not be identified with freedom itself. Freedom is a complex notion, to say the least, and free markets can sharply limit freedom as that term is usually understood. In fact, free markets depend on a range of coercive legal interventions, including the law of property, which can be a serious intrusion on the freedom of people who lack ownership rights. And it should not be necessary to emphasize that important forms of equality—including race and sex equality—can be undermined, not promoted, by free markets. Race discrimination is often fueled by market forces.

Moreover, economics—at least as it is used in the conventional economic analysis of law—often works with tools that, while illuminating, may be crude or lead to important errors. Consider, for example, descriptive or "positive" economics. The economic analysis of law has been built on a certain conception of human rationality, in which people are seen as "rational profit-maximizers." For some purposes, this is a helpful foundation. Certainly it is true that most people try, most of the time, to find ways of promoting their own ends. But it is not always clear in what sense human beings can be said to be "rational" or "profit-maximizers." The motivational foundations of human behavior have enormous complexity. Sometimes people do not seem at all rational. Sometimes they are ignorant and sometimes they seem to defeat their own goals. People rely on rules of thumb, or heuristic devices, that cause them badly to misunderstand probabilities and facts; this can lead to irrationality for individuals and societies alike. Sometimes people undervalue their own futures, or suffer from weakness of will, or choose what they know, on reflection, they ought not to choose. Sometimes people care not just about social outcomes, but also about the "meaning" of such outcomes, that is, the values expressed in and by the outcomes. This point very much bears on law, in such areas as environmental protection, race and sex equality, and occupational safety and health.

Above all, social norms are an important determinant of behavior, and they have received far too little attention from those interested in free markets, economic analysis of law, and social justice. A number of puzzles and anomalies underlie human decisions. Analysis of law, economic or otherwise, would do well to incorporate an understanding of these puzzles and anomalies. * * *

Thus far, I have been discussing descriptive or positive economics. If we turn to the evaluative side—to questions about what the law should be or do—economic analysis of law encounters equally serious problems. In its usual form, economics offers an inadequate understanding of social welfare. Often it is concerned with the satisfaction of existing preferences. This is far from an unworthy goal; the frustration of peoples' preferences can lead to misery and injustice. But in any society, existing preferences should not be taken as natural or sacrosanct. They are a function of context. Sometimes they are a product of deprivation, injustice, or excessive limits in available opportunities.

Moreover, the economists' conception of social welfare is too "flat," insofar as it evaluates diverse social goods along the same metric. People care about things not just in terms of amounts, but also in different ways. Some human goods, like cash, are simply for use. But people value things for reasons other than use. They respect other people; sometimes they love each other; they see some things, like a painting or a beach, as objects of awe and wonder. A well-functioning legal system attempts to make space for people's diverse valuation of diverse human goods. This point bears on the uses and the limits of free markets.

More particularly, this book develops seven basic themes:

1. *The myth of laissez-faire.* The notion of "laissez-faire" is a grotesque misdescription of what free markets actually require and entail. Free markets depend for their existence on law. We cannot have a system of private property without legal rules, telling people who owns what, imposing penalties for trespass, and saying who can do what to whom. Without the law of contract, freedom of contract, as we know and live it, would be impossible. (People in Eastern Europe are learning this lesson all too well.) Moreover, the law that underlies free markets is coercive in the sense that in addition to facilitating individual transactions, it stops people from doing many things that they would like to do. This point is not by any means a critique of free markets. But it suggests that markets should be understood as a legal construct, to be evaluated on the basis of whether they promote human interests, rather than as a part of nature and the natural order, or as a simple way of promoting voluntary interactions.

2. *Preference formation and social norms.* It is important not only to know what choices and preferences are, but also to know how they are formed, and whether they are really connected with human well-being. Unjust institutions can breed preferences that produce individual and collective harm. Severe deprivation—including poverty—can be an obstacle to the development of good preferences, choices, and beliefs. For example, a society in which people "prefer" to become drug addicts, or violent crimi-

nals, has a serious problem. Such preferences are likely to be an artifact of existing social norms, and those norms may disserve human freedom or well-being.

In this light a society should be concerned not simply and not entirely with satisfying the preferences that people already have, but more broadly with providing freedom in the process of preference-formation. Social practices, including law, will inevitably affect preferences. There is no way for a legal system to remain neutral with respect to preference formation. In these circumstances it is fully legitimate for government and law to try to shape preferences in the right way, not only through education, but also (for example) through laws forbidding racial discrimination, environmental degradation, and sexual harassment, and through efforts to encourage attention to public issues and to diverse points of view.

3. *The contextual character of choice.* Choices are a function of context. If someone takes a job that includes a certain danger, or chooses not to recycle on a Tuesday in March, or discriminates against a certain female job candidate, we cannot infer a great deal about what he "prefers" or "values." All of these choices might be different in a different context. Our discriminator may support a law banning discrimination; people who do not recycle in March may recycle in May or June, and they may well support laws that mandate recycling. Economists and economically oriented analysts of law sometimes think that they can derive, from particular choices, large-scale or acontextual accounts of how much people value various goods. This is a mistake, involving extravagant inferences from modest findings.

4. *The importance of fair distribution.* It is necessary to know not simply whether a society is rich in economic terms, but also how its resources are distributed. Thus a problem with gross domestic product, as a measure of social well-being, is its obliviousness to distributional concerns. Free markets can help fuel economic growth, and economic growth can improve people's lives. But many citizens are not benefited by growth, and at a minimum government should take steps to combat human deprivation and misery in the midst of growth. In any case, it is important to develop standards for measuring social well-being that allow people, in their capacity as citizens and voters, to focus on the issue of distribution.

5. *The diversity of human goods.* I have noted that human beings value things not just in different amounts, but also in different ways. They value a friend in one way; a park in another; a species in another; a spouse in another; an heirloom in another; a large check in another; a pet in still another. The way they value a funny movie is qualitatively different from the way they value a tragedy, a mountain, a beach, or a car. Insofar as economics uses a single metric or scale of value, it flattens qualitative differences. For some purposes the flattening is very useful, but for other purposes it is harmful. Such qualitative differences can be crucial to private life, public life, and social science.

These points help show the inadequacy, in some settings, of social ordering through markets. Some goods should not be sold on markets at all; consider the right to vote or the right to be free from discrimination on the basis of sex. Markets work best when (what we rightly treat as) consumption choices are at issue. In a liberal society, some choices should be understood not to involve consumption choices at all. For example, the choice to vote, and the decision how to vote, are not best understood as involving mere consumption. How a person votes should depend not on anyone's "willingness to pay," but on the reasons offered for and against a certain candidate. The right to vote is debased if it is understood as simply a matter of "buying" something.

This claim bears on a range of issues involving the use of markets for distributing such goods as reproductive capacity, sex, endangered species, and environmental amenities in general. Some goods are best allocated on the basis of an inquiry not into economic value, but into the reasons offered for any particular allocation.

6. *Law can shape preferences.* We have seen that no market can exist without legal rules. Legal rules must also allocate entitlements. In a system of private property, it is necessary to say who owns what, at least in the first instance. It is also necessary to create rules of tort law, saying who can do what to whom, and who must pay for injuries and harms. As a great deal of empirical work has shown, these legal rules, allocating basic entitlements, have effects on choices and preferences. Someone who has been given a legal entitlement—to chocolate bars, clean air, freedom from sexual harassment, environmental goods—may well value the relevant good more than he would if the good had been allocated to someone else in the first instance. The preference-shaping effects of the initial allocation via law raise important questions for the analysis of law and free markets. They suggest that government and law may not be able to leave preferences "as they are."

7. *Puzzles of human rationality.* Are human beings rational? What criteria should we use to answer that question? These questions have become all the more urgent in light of recent work attempting to apply economic models of rationality to race and sex discrimination, family choice, pollution problems, aging, even sexual encounters (and hence to the problem of AIDS). Such work has been highly illuminating, but it is important to know in exactly what sense people might be said to be (or not to be) "rational" when they choose spouses, recycle garbage, reject employees of certain kinds, or engage in sexual or risky activity. Any views on such matters may well depend on a controversial account of what it means to be rational.

* * *

[I] claim that the term "preference" is highly ambiguous and that people's "preferences," as they are expressed in the market domain, should not be deemed sacrosanct. On the contrary, market "preferences" are sometimes a product of background injustice or of social norms that people do not really like. Acting as citizens, people should be permitted to change those norms. I also argue that human goods are not commensurable; there is no metric by which we can assess such goods as environmental quality, employment, more leisure time, less racial discrimination, and so forth. My discussion of "measuring well-being" is designed to respond to this problem; my general treatment of incommensurability shows how the absence of a unitary metric plays a large role in both law and daily life.

[T]he basic goal is to show that markets have only a partial and instrumental role in the protection of rights. In a claim of special relevance to current disputes in the United States, I argue that free markets are not likely to stop discrimination on the basis of race and sex. On the contrary, markets often promote discrimination.

* * *

[I]t would be far too ambitious to attempt to announce a theory of justice. But debates that seem intractable at the most abstract levels may admit of solutions when the question is narrowed and sharpened, and hence an inquiry into the relation between markets and justice may be most productive when we draw close attention to the setting in which market remedies are proposed. * * * Achievement of social justice is a higher value than the protection of free markets; markets are mere instruments to be evaluated by their effects. Whether free markets promote social justice is an impossible question to answer in the abstract. Far more progress can be made by examining the contexts in which markets, adjustments of markets, and alternatives to markets are proposed as solutions.

* * *

I argue [however] that under plausible assumptions and in many settings, markets will not stop discrimination and that reliance on competitive pressures would be a grave mistake for a government intending to eliminate discriminatory practices. Indeed, markets are often the problem rather than the solution. They guarantee that discrimination will persist. Enthusiasm for markets as an anti-discrimination policy is at best wishful thinking.

I. Why Markets Produce Discrimination: Standard Accounts

As a provisional matter, let us define discrimination as a decision by a market actor to treat one person differently from another because that person is black or female. It is irrelevant for present purposes whether the differential treatment is based on hostility, fear, taste, unconscious devaluation, selective empathy and indifference, employer self-interest, unwarranted generalizations, or an accurate perception of facts about group members. This definition has a degree of vagueness, and it is certainly disputable whether government should ban all of the conduct that it identifies. But the definition has the advantage of tracking both current law and some ordinary intuitions about the problem.

On one view, the notion that competitive markets act against discrimination, so defined, might seem odd or even idiosyncratic. In the history of the United States as well as other nations, markets and discrimination have accompanied one another at numerous points and in numerous places. Surely, governmentally imposed discrimination, because of its centralized character, has especially egregious effects; but to point to the comparative strength of collective controls is not to say that decentralized markets work in the opposite direction. Indeed, there is good empirical evidence that government programs have succeeded in reducing discrimination produced by the market. The enactment of civil rights legislation appears to have led to increases in black and female employment in various sectors. At least in general, the disputed question has to do not with the direction of change but with the degree of the improvement.

Moreover, study after study has shown that the market often devalues the products and enterprises of both blacks and women. This should not be surprising. In a system with a significant amount of race and sex prejudice, covert and overt, conscious and unconscious, the "willingness to pay" criterion—as it is reflected in the purchasing and selling decisions of employers, employees, consumers, and others—will ensure that those subject to discriminatory attitudes will be at a comparative disadvantage in the market. At least this is so when the participation of disfavored groups is highly visible, as indeed it often is. In this context, the most natural initial judgment is that if discrimination is the problem, markets are hardly the solution.

But the judgment, as stated, seems too crude. Suppose a set of companies in a competitive industry—call them "D companies"—decides not to sell to or employ an identifiable segment of the community; suppose too that the D companies must compete with nondiscriminators engaged in the same line of work ("ND companies"). In the long run, the D companies should be at a significant disadvantage. They will be unable to draw on as large a pool of workers; they will be unable to sell to as large a group of purchasers. In practice, their discriminatory behavior will place a tax on their operations. To say the least, businesses that impose on themselves a tax not faced by their competitors are unlikely to fare well.

As patrons and prospective employees drift to ND companies, the D companies will be driven out. Eventually, the consequences should be nothing short of disastrous for discrimination in general. It is this understanding that accounts for the plausible claim that an effective antidiscrimination policy consists of reliance on decentralized markets.

Notwithstanding its plausibility (and even, in some settings, its accuracy), I want in this section to make three arguments against this claim. In setting out these arguments, I make no claim to special originality. All of them can be found, at least in some form, in standard economic discussions of the problem.

Third Parties

An influential approach to the problem of discrimination, captured in the account just offered, attributes the phenomenon to employers' "taste" for discrimination. On this view, employers discriminate because they do not like to associate with blacks, women, or others. The engine that drives discrimination is employer preferences—not economic self-interest, narrowly defined. Indeed, economic self-interest is in conflict with employers' taste for discrimination. This idea has a degree of truth to it; certainly, it explains many practices by employers. But sometimes discrimination is caused by employer practices that result precisely from economic self-interest, rather than from the employer's noneconomic goals. The reason is that third parties are frequently in a position to impose financial punishments on nondiscriminatory employers. Suppose, for example, that purchasers or fellow employees refuse to buy from or work for a company that does not discriminate. Third parties can pressure employers in the direction of discrimination, even if employers would, other things being equal, choose not to discriminate or have no particular view about whether to discriminate or not. Ironically, it is the failure to discriminate that operates as a tax on the employer's business, rather than vice versa. And when this is so, reliance on competitive pressures will force employers to behave in a discriminatory manner if they wish to survive.

The phenomenon is hardly unusual. Consider, for example, a shopkeeper whose customers do not like dealing with blacks or women; a commercial airline whose patrons react unfavorably to female pilots; a university whose students and alumni prefer a primarily male or white faculty; a law firm whose clients prefer not to have black lawyers; or a hospital whose patients are uncomfortable with female doctors or black nurses. The persistence of private segregation in major league baseball is a familiar example of this phenomenon.

In all of these cases, market pressures create rather than prevent discrimination. An employer who wants to act nondiscriminatorily will be punished, not rewarded. Indeed, an employer who wants not to be a discriminator will be engaging in what is, from his point of view, a form of affirmative action. From his point of view, discrimination is in fact neutral, in the sense that it is a quite ordinary form of profit-maximization through catering to consumer demand. From his point of view, a refusal to discriminate is also economically harmful to him; if he is a nondiscriminator, it is not for the sake of profits, but in order to promote the long-range goal of race and sex equality. If discrimination is to be eliminated, it may well be as a result of legal rules forbidding discrimination from continuing.

Ideas of precisely this sort played a role in the passage of the Civil Rights Act of 1964. Many restaurants and hotels sought regulation constraining their own behavior by outlawing discrimination. Their goal was to obtain the force of the law to overcome the effects of private racism (in the form of violence as well as competitive sanctions). They sought to overcome, through law, the discrimination-producing consequences of market pressures. They sought to "hide behind the law" to do what, in a sense, they wanted to do: to behave nondiscriminatorily. Without the force of law, they would encounter third-party pressures, including social norms * * *, that would push them in the direction of discrimination.

On this account, it remains necessary to explain why third parties are not themselves hurt by their "taste." At least part of the reason lies in the fact that third parties often are not market actors in the ordinary sense—that is, they will not suffer competitive injury in markets if they indulge their discriminatory preferences. Consider, for example, ordinary people who prefer not to fly in airplanes piloted by blacks or women (or having black or male stewards). At least in many cases, the harm suffered by people who indulge their prejudice—perhaps higher prices of some form or another—will not drive them out of any "market," but instead, and more simply, will make them somewhat poorer. For a customer, a racist or sexist taste operates like any other taste, such as the taste for high-sugar cereals, luxury cars, or fancy computers; the taste may increase prices, but market pressures need not make the taste disappear.

In a competitive market that contains private racism and sexism, then, the existence of third-party pressures can create significant spheres of discrimination. To be sure, sometimes the participation of blacks or women (or the handicapped) is invisible; in any case, racism and sexism are currently not so widespread as to make it costly for all employers to act in a nondiscriminatory fashion. Because of their decentralized character, markets are usually far less effective than governmental controls in perpetuating discrimination, as the experience in South Africa has (at least sometimes) showed. Moreover, third-party effects will probably produce a degree of occupational segregation instead of, or as well as, discrimination. But discriminatory practices in many areas are likely to persist over time precisely because of the market, which by its very nature registers consumer preferences, including discriminatory ones.

There is an additional problem here. Suppose that society includes a number of traders who want to interact with blacks or women as well as a number of traders who do not. Suppose, too, that it is difficult for traders who are themselves indifferent to race and sex distinctions to tell which traders are discriminators (a frequent phenomenon in competitive markets). If these conditions are met, discrimination is likely to be a rational strategy for traders. New companies will do poorly if they refuse to discriminate. All this suggests that markets will frequently have great difficulty in breaking down discrimination, if discriminatory tastes are even somewhat widespread.

Statistical or Economically Rational Discrimination

I have referred to the common-sense understanding that employers treat blacks and women differently because of hostility or prejudice on their part—an idea that often accompanies the claim that markets are an enemy of discrimination. This form of hostility or prejudice is frequently described as "irrational." But the category of irrational prejudice is an ambiguous one. Perhaps we can understand it to include (a) a belief that members of a group have certain characteristics when in fact they do not, (b) a belief that many or most members of a group have certain characteristics when in fact only a few do, and (c) reliance on fairly accurate group-based generalizations when more accurate classifying devices are relatively inexpensive and available. In all of these cases, it is possible to say that someone is acting on the basis of irrational prejudice.

Suppose instead, however, that discriminatory behavior is a response to generalizations or stereotypes that, although quite overbroad and from one point of view invidious, provide an economically rational basis for employment decisions. Such stereotypes may be economically rational in the sense that it is cheaper to use them than it is to rely on more fine-grained approaches, which can be expensive to administer. Stereotypes and generalizations, of course, are a common ingredient of day-to-day market decisions. There are information costs in making distinctions within catego-ries, and sometimes people make the category do the work of a more individualized and often far more costly examination of the merits of the particular employee.

Such categorical judgments are not only pervasive; they are entirely legitimate in most settings. We all depend on them every day. Employers rely on "proxies" of many sorts, even though those proxies are overbroad generalizations and far from entirely accurate. For example, test scores, employment records, level of education, and prestige of college attended are all part of rational employment decisions. Emphasis on these factors is a common form of stereotyping; at least in ordinary circumstances, it would be odd to say that such factors reflect hostility or prejudice of the sort that the law should ban. People may use stereotypes not because they are very accurate, but because they are less costly to use than any more individual-ized inquiry.

There can be no question that at least in some contexts, race and sex operate as similar proxies. In various ways, blacks differ from whites and women differ from men; there are "real differences" between the two groups. * * * Indeed, in light of past and present discrimination against blacks and women, it would be shocking if group-based differences were not present. Women, for example, are more likely than men to be the primary caretakers of children and more likely to leave the employment market because of that role. Along every indicator of social welfare—poverty, education, employment, vulnerability to private (or public) violence, partic-ipation in violent crime—blacks are less well-off than whites. And in light of those differences, it is fully possible that in certain settings, race- and sex-based generalizations are economically rational as proxies for relevant characteristics. Indeed, it is fully possible that race or sex is, in some contexts, every bit as accurate a signaling device as, say, test score, education, and previous employment. (Notably, the use of those proxies may itself have discriminatory consequences and indeed might be counted as a form of discrimination. But I put this point to one side for now.)

If race or sex can be a good signaling device, an employer might discriminate not because he hates or devalues blacks or women, or has a general desire not to associate with them, or is "prejudiced" in the ordinary sense, but because he believes (on the basis either of plausible assumptions or actual experience) that the relevant stereotypes have sufficient truth to be a basis for employment decisions. For example, an employer might believe that women are more likely to leave a high-pressure job than men, or that they are less suited for physically demanding employment; he might think that blacks are less likely to have the necessary training. With respect to the handicapped, the same scenario is of course readily predictable: "Real differences" call for differential treatment. As I understand it here, statistical discrimination occurs when the employer does not harbor irrational hatred or discriminatory feelings, but instead acts according to stereotypes of the sort that are typically relied on by market actors, and that are no less false than ordinary stereotypes.

It is important to be careful with this point. I do not mean to deny that ordinary, irrational prejudice accounts for a significant amount of discrimination, or even that it is hard both in practice and in principle to distinguish between ordinary prejudice and economically rational stereotyping. Sometimes employers who refuse to follow a stereotype will find employees who will move them far ahead in the marketplace. Moreover, the decision about *what kinds* of economically rational stereotypes should be adopted might itself reflect prejudice. Sometimes people refuse such stereotypes because they perceive them to be unfair. People are highly selective in their creation and selection of the very categories with which they view people—as college graduates? as children of successful parents? as nonreligious? as white males? as tall? as good-looking? People are also selective in their decisions about which categories ought to count in various sectors of social and economic life. Thus, for example, the use of sex as a proxy for flexibility with respect to overtime work may be fully rational; but other proxies may be nearly as good or better. Selectivity in the choice of the proxy may be a product of prejudice. People also tend to notice events that are consistent with previously held stereotypes and to disregard events that are inconsistent with them. This is a built-in obstacle to changes in social norms and social "knowledge," even when the governing norms increasingly fail to mirror reality.

One might agree with all this and still acknowledge what seems undoubtedly true: Discrimination sometimes persists because it is economically rational to rely on a race-or sex-based generalization. And if this is so—if discrimination of this sort is a significant part of modern practice—then markets will be the furthest thing from a corrective. If discrimination is rational, then discriminatory behavior is rewarded in the marketplace. Efforts to view people through more finely tuned (and hence more expensive) devices than stereotypes will be punished.

Moreover, if discrimination is rooted in economically rational stereotypes, it remains necessary to ask what is wrong with it. The (apparent) social consensus that prejudice is irrational tends to downplay the difficulty of finding firm moral foundations for antidiscrimination law. Contemporary American law consistently condemns discrimination even if it is fully rational—that is, if it is as accurate as other generalizations typically used in the labor market. It is no defense to a claim of race or sex discrimination that the practice under attack is reasonable stereotyping. And because contemporary law singles out one kind of rational stereotyping and bans it, the distinction between affirmative action and antidiscrimination norms is extremely thin and perhaps invisible in principle. This is because in some settings, an antidiscrimination norm itself operates to bar economically rational behavior in the interest of long-term social goals. It does so selectively; in the interest of producing a racially improved future, the law forbids rational racial stereotyping when it allows stereotyping of most other kinds. An antidiscrimination norm even requires innocent victims— for example, customers who must pay higher prices—to be sacrificed in the interest of that goal.

Indeed, the distinction between affirmative action and antidiscrimination is crisp only to those who see discrimination as always grounded in hostility and irrationality, which it clearly is not. To say this is hardly to say that there are no differences between affirmative action and an antidiscrimination principle that forbids economically rational behavior. But it is to say that a great failure of the assault on affirmative action is its failure to account for the ways in which a requirement of nondiscrimination involves very much the same considerations.

However we may think about this more adventurous claim, the central point remains. Markets will not drive out discrimination precisely to the extent that discrimination consists of economically rational stereotyping.

The Effects of Discrimination on Human Capital

Suppose that there is widespread discrimination for any number of reasons: employers have a taste for discrimination; third parties impose pressures in discriminatory directions; race or sex is used as a proxy for productivity (whether or not productivity includes the losses produced by the reactions of third parties). If any of these things is so, markets will perpetuate discrimination for yet another reason, one having to do with harmful effects on investment in human capital.

The central point here is that the productivity of blacks or whites and women or men is endogenous to, or a product of, the existence of discrimination in the labor market. Since this is so, it is a mistake to see productivity within any social group as static or independent of decisions by employers. Such decisions will have important dynamic effects on the choice of blacks and whites or women and men to invest in human capital. Decisions about education, training, drug use, trade-offs between work and leisure, and employment programs will be affected by existing patterns of discrimination. In a market that contains such discrimination, blacks and women will invest relatively less in such programs. Indeed, lower investments on their part are perfectly rational. As market actors, women should invest less than men in training to be (say) pilots, economists, politicians, or lawyers if these professions discriminate against women and thus reward their investment less than that of men.

The result can be a vicious circle or even spiral. Because of existing discrimination, the relevant groups will probably invest less in human capital; because of this lower investment, the discrimination will persist or perhaps increase because its statistical rationality itself increases; because of this effect, investments will decrease still further; and so on. Markets are the problem, not the solution.

Undoubtedly, this picture is too bleak in many settings. Proxies not rooted in sex and race have frequently evolved and employers have used them; such proxies are ordinarily far more accurate, and employers who use them sometimes prosper. More generally, the extraordinary persistence of blacks and women in attempting to enter professions dominated by whites and men is one of the most striking phenomena of the post-World War II period. Blacks and women frequently appear to invest huge amounts of human capital even in sectors that treat them inhospitably. In fact, some people respond to discrimination by increasing rather than decreasing their investments in human capital. In Western history, some racial and ethnic groups have prospered as a result of such investments, notwithstanding discriminatory tastes on the part of employers, customers, and fellow employees. But there can be little question that discrimination does have a large effect on human capital in many contexts, and that the discouraging reception, known to be accorded to blacks and women, perpetuates the exclusion of both groups from certain sectors of the economy. And when this is so, reliance on markets as an antidiscrimination policy is badly misconceived.

In General: Reinforcing Effects

The three arguments thus far—coupled with the existence of race- and sex-based hostility or devaluation on the part of employers—build on standard economic accounts of discrimination. It is notable that none of the various effects unambiguously reflects a market failure in the conventional sense. The incorporation of racist or sexist preferences is efficient, if the efficiency criterion is based on private willingness to pay; so, too, with profit-maximizing reactions to the desires of third parties and with statistical discrimination. In all of these cases, governmental interference will probably produce an efficiency loss, at least in the short term.

The only possible exception is the effect of discrimination on human capital. In that case, it is possible to conceive of discrimination as producing a serious externality, in the form of harmful effects on outsiders—prospective labor market entrants—with corresponding efficiency losses. But it is important to note that there is an optimal level of investment in human capital, and it is not entirely clear why and to what extent existing investments that are adaptive to employer behavior in the labor market should be seen as suboptimal. In fact any generalization that is used in the labor market will have a signaling effect that will shift investments in human capital, and it is not easy to develop a model revealing which signals produce suboptimal investments. In general, then, markets will perpetuate discrimination for reasons that are unrelated to the market failures that provide traditional economic grounds for legal intervention.

Moreover, and crucially, each of these effects reinforces the others in potentially powerful ways. If there is ordinary prejudice, it will interact with statistical discrimination so as to produce more of both. People tend to notice events consistent with their prejudice and disregard events that are inconsistent with them, and the result will be more in the way of both prejudice and statistical discrimination. If third parties attempt to promote discrimination, they will increase the existence of both prejudice and statistical discrimination. Employers will hire fewer blacks and women, who in turn will appear less frequently in desirable positions, with consequent reinforcing effects on both prejudice and statistical discrimination.

In addition, if there is prejudice and statistical discrimination, and if third parties promote discrimination, victims of discrimination will decrease their investments in human capital. Such decreased investments will be a perfectly reasonable response to the real world. And if there are decreased investments in human capital, then prejudice, statistical discrimination, and third-party acts will also increase. Statistical discrimination will become all the more rational; prejudice will hardly be broken down but, on the contrary, strengthened; consumers and employers will be more likely to be discriminators.

Of course, it would be necessary to compile detailed factual evidence to assess the magnitude of the relevant effects. In the abstract, it is hard to know how large they will be. But we know enough to realize that the various effects can be mutually reinforcing and might present a disaster for victims of discrimination and for society as a whole.

By this point the fact that markets often perpetuate discrimination should present no puzzle at all. Markets can be an ally of discrimination. To be sure, the precise relationship between markets and discrimination will depend on particular circumstances. The likelihood that markets will promote discrimination should increase if third-party prejudice is widespread, if stereotypes or generalizations are accurate, and if ordinary racism and sexism are pervasive. But what may be surprising is not that markets produce discrimination, but that discrimination has decreased as much as it has. And all this follows from quite conventional economic approaches to the problem.

II. Markets and Discrimination: Noneconomic Accounts

In this section, I provide two additional arguments against the view that markets will prevent discrimination. Neither of them is standard within economics, but both of them have considerable explanatory power.

Preference and Belief Formation

In economic theory, preferences and beliefs are usually taken as given—an approach that is often helpful in building models for understanding social life. But in the context of discrimination, and elsewhere as well, this approach will cause both descriptive and normative problems. The central point here is that preferences are endogenous to current laws, norms, and practices. Once those laws, norms, and practices are entrenched, there are special obstacles to bringing about change through market ordering.

In the setting at hand, the problem is that private preferences, on the part of both discriminators and their victims, tend to adapt to the status quo, and to do so in a way that makes significant change hard to achieve.

The reduction of cognitive dissonance is a powerful motivating force: People attempt to bring their beliefs and perceptions in line with existing practice. The victims of inequality may well try to reduce dissonance by adapting their preferences to the available opportunities. Consider the story of the fox who concludes that he does not want unavailable grapes because he considers them sour; the reason that he considers them sour is that they are unavailable. Or people may adapt their aspirations to the persistent and often irrationally held belief that the world is just. The beneficiaries of the status quo tend to do the same, concluding that the fate of the victims is deserved, is something for which victims are responsible, or is part of an intractable, given, or natural order. All of these claims have played an enormous role in the history of discrimination on the basis of race and sex.

There is of course extremely powerful evidence in the psychological literature for the thesis that human beings try to reduce dissonance. Some work here reveals that people who engage in cruel behavior change their attitudes toward the objects of their cruelty and thus devalue them. Observers tend to do the same. The phenomenon of blaming the victim has clear motivational foundations. The notion that the world is just, and that existing inequalities are deserved or desired, plays a large role in the formation of preferences and beliefs. The reduction of cognitive dissonance thus operates as a significant obstacle to the recognition that discrimination is a problem, or even that it exists. Adaptation of beliefs to a social status quo can also affect social norms. The social norms governing women's work may be quite hard to change; the social meaning of being female, or being black, may be nearly intractable.

This problem can be tied quite tightly to the operation of a market economy, whose participants are self-consciously involved in catering to existing tastes and in perpetuating and reinforcing them. Markets, partly because of this effect, are an engine of productivity and respect for individual autonomy in most circumstances; but in this setting, they sometimes perpetuate inequality. This is especially true in the context of sex discrimination, where advertising and consumption powerfully reinforce existing stereotypes, with consequences for the development of preferences and beliefs. Consider, for example, the multiple ways in which the beauty industry, broadly understood, attempts to define and to commodify femininity, in efforts to reach men and women alike. Women as well as men have often adapted their preferences and beliefs to a system of sex inequality.

The inevitable effect of a discriminatory status quo on preferences and beliefs is related to the phenomenon, noted previously, of decreased investment in human capital. In both cases, the response to discrimination is endogenous rather than exogenous and has the consequence of perpetuating existing inequalities. But with respect to preferences and beliefs, the effect is especially pernicious. Here the consequence is not merely to shift investments in self-development but, instead, to make people believe that the existing regime, including discrimination, presents no problem at all.

Once preferences and beliefs are affected, the likelihood of social change through markets diminishes dramatically. Here, as well, there is a mutually reinforcing effect among the various sources of market discrimination. The effect of discrimination on preferences and beliefs fortifies existing prejudice, produces a decrease in investment in human capital, leads to more in the way of statistical discrimination, and increases the unwillingness of third parties to deal with blacks and women.

Baselines and Discrimination Law

Almost by definition, markets incorporate the norms and practices of advantaged groups. Conspicuous examples include the many ways in which employment settings, requirements, and expectations are structured for the able-bodied and for traditional male career patterns. Here the market, dependent as it is on the criterion of private willingness to pay, is extremely unlikely to eliminate discrimination (understood as such by reference to widespread [sic] intuitions). To say that the refusal to provide flexible time, child care, or building access for the disabled does not count as "discrimination" is to rely on an exceptionally narrow conception of what discrimination is—a conception that is repudiated in much of current American law, that is inconsistent with an approach that is alert to discriminatory purposes or effects, and that in any case will do very little about existing inequalities.

In these circumstances, a legal system committed to an antidiscrimination principle might in some cases restructure market arrangements so as to put members of disadvantaged groups on a plane of greater equality— not by allowing them to be "like" members of advantaged groups, but by changing the criteria themselves, at least when those criteria do not have a firm independent justification. Consider the conventional test of American discrimination law: Is the member of the disadvantaged group "similarly situated" to the member of the advantaged group? That is: Have women, who are otherwise the same as men, or disabled people, who are otherwise the same as the able-bodied, been treated differently from men or the able-bodied? The problem with this test is that it itself reflects inequality, since it takes the norms and practices of the advantaged groups as the baseline against which to measure equality. And here market ordering, dependent as it is on the criterion of private willingness to pay, will inevitably present a problem.

Ideas of this sort underlie recent efforts to ban discrimination on the basis of pregnancy and disability. As in the case of statistical discrimination, these forms of discrimination are perfectly rational from the standpoint of employers and others. The argument for legal controls is that, in these settings, the criteria used in private markets are hardly prepolitical or natural, have neither good moral status nor powerful independent justification, and at the least should be overridden when their predictable consequences are exclusion or second-class citizenship for certain social groups.

In the case of disability, for example, the handicapped face a wide range of obstacles to participation in both public and private spheres. These obstacles are not a function of "handicap" itself (a most ambiguous concept; what would handicap mean in an entirely different world?) but instead are the inevitable consequence of humanly created barriers, including stairs, doors, and standards in general made by and for the able-bodied. The market in these circumstances is wholly nonresponsive. In light of the humanly created barriers, the market itself may not much value the contributions of handicapped people, which are by hypothesis relatively low if measured by normal productivity standards, understood as these are through the lens of willingness to pay. Discrimination of this sort may well require a legal remedy. And though the specification of the content of that remedy is a difficult question, markets will not respond, even in the long run.

The point, then, is that the valuation of the market will be a reflection of prevailing norms and practices, and those norms and practices sometimes are what an antidiscrimination principle is designed to eliminate or reduce. When this is so, reliance on markets will be unsuccessful. The rationale for antidiscrimination laws in these cases becomes more controversial, complex, and difficult. Certainly the cost of change is highly relevant; an effort to restructure the world would not be worthwhile if it impoverished most or many people. But my basic point remains: Private markets will not stop discrimination.

III.   What's Wrong with Discrimination

Thus far, the discussion has been entirely descriptive and explanatory. I have sought to show why markets are unlikely to eliminate discrimination on the basis of race, sex, and disability. But it will not have escaped notice that I have only provisionally defined discrimination—a highly protean concept, in light of the foregoing remarks—or said what is wrong with it. Indeed, one of the largest gaps in present civil rights theory consists of the absence of a full-fledged explanation of just what discrimination is and why we should eliminate it. In this highly tentative section, I want to say something about the appropriate characterization of the claim of discrimination and about how that claim should be treated.

Discrimination should, I suggest, be understood to include any decision that treats an otherwise similarly qualified black, woman, or handicapped person less favorably than a white, male, or able-bodied person, whether the reason for the decision lies in malice, taste, selective empathy and indifference, economic self-interest, or rational stereotyping. This understanding of discrimination picks up not merely overt unequal treatment, but also requirements that are neutral "on their face" but would not have been adopted if the burdened and benefited groups had been reversed. It does not pick up measures merely having discriminatory effects, unless those effects are, in the sense indicated, tied up with racial, sexual, or other bias.

It follows that the claim of discrimination, best understood, is not for prevention of certain irrational acts, or of "prejudice," but instead for the elimination, in places large and small, of something in the nature of a caste system. Hence the antidiscrimination principle is best conceived as an anticaste principle. The concept of caste is hard to define, and I will have to be tentative and somewhat vague about it. I do not mean at all to suggest that the caste-like features of current practices are precisely the same, in nature or extent, as those features of genuine caste societies. I do mean to say that the similarities are what make the current practices a reason for collective concern.

The motivating idea behind an anticaste principle is that without very good reason, legal and social structures should not turn differences that are irrelevant from the moral point of view into social disadvantages. They certainly should not be permitted to do so if the disadvantage is systemic. A systemic disadvantage is one that operates along standard and predictable lines in multiple important spheres of life and that applies in realms—such as education, freedom from private and public violence, wealth, political representation, and political influence—that are deeply implicated in basic participation as a citizen in a democratic society.

In the areas of race and sex discrimination, and of disability as well, the problem is precisely this sort of systemic disadvantage. A social or biological difference has the effect of systematically subordinating the relevant group and of doing so in multiple spheres and along multiple indices of social welfare: poverty, education, political power, employment, susceptibility to violence and crime, and so forth. That is the caste system to which the legal system is attempting to respond.

* * *

NOTE ON CIVIC REPUBLICANISM

Sunstein's work on markets is informed by his earlier constitutional and political theory that expands community participation in republican government known as "civic republicanism." Sunstein rejects traditional pluralist politics, where interest groups heavily influence government officials, and instead advocates a republican approach to politics. Largely relying on Lockean social contract theory, Sunstein stresses that a successful republican politic can be achieved if four goals are met: (1) deliberation, which involves communication among the citizenry, (2) equalizing political opportunity among all members of the community, (3) universalism, which emphasizes mediation and mutual agreement, and (4) citizenship, which stresses the need for citizens to participate in the political process and limit the influence of self-interested factions.

Consider the following themes underlying Sunstein's civic republicanism and accompanying questions.

NOTES AND QUESTIONS

1.   **John Locke's social contract theory.** Sunstein's analysis of participatory politics is premised on the notion that American society is governed
by a social contract, a theory where people agree to participate and support
each other through a government mechanism. Great social thinkers of the
seventeenth and eighteenth centuries, including Thomas Hobbes, John
Locke and Jean–Jacques Rousseau deemed that justice flowed from the
social contract, because every citizen in society consented to be governed by
a lawmaking body. This premise is alluring because we as citizens are
mandated to comply with the rules of justice (and the governments that
implement these rules) because we have assented to do so:

> It is as if we made a contract with the state, or more properly with
> each other, that we would live together according to certain rules,
> which are also—according to our best rational calculations—in our own
> interest as well. In return for our obedience to the rules, everyone else
> will obey them too (or be threatened and forced to do so).

ROBERT C. SOLOMON, A PASSION FOR JUSTICE: EMOTIONS AND ORIGINS OF THE
SOCIAL CONTRACT 55 (1990). As a Christian academic, Locke pondered how it
is that human behavior follows conceptions of right represented in natural
and divine law. RICHARD C. SINOPOLI, THE FOUNDATIONS OF AMERICAN CITIZEN-
SHIP: LIBERALISM, THE CONSTITUTION AND CIVIC VIRTUE 39 (1992). In writing *True
End of Civil Government*, Locke emphasized that the consent of all citizens
was necessary to obey laws executed by the government and form a
community. Within this community, the majority can act upon the remaining citizens to effectively manage one, unified body politic:

> Men being, as has been said, by nature all free, equal, and indepen-
> dent, no one can be put out of his estate and subjected to the political
> power of another without his own consent, which is done by agreeing
> with other men, to join and unite into a community for their comforta-
> ble, safe, and peaceable living, one amongst another, in a secure
> enjoyment of their properties, and a greater security against any that
> are not of it. This any number of men may do, because it injures not
> the freedom of the rest; they are left, as they were, in the liberty of the
> state of nature. When any number of men have so consented to make
> one community or government, they are thereby presently incorporat-
> ed, and make one body politic, wherein the majority have a right to act
> and conclude the rest.
>
> * * *
>
> And thus every man, by consenting with others to make one body
> politic under one government, puts himself under an obligation to
> everyone of that society to submit to the determination of the majority,
> and to be concluded by it; or else this original compact, whereby he
> with others incorporates into one society, would signify nothing, and be
> no compact if he be left free and under no other ties than he was in
> before in the state of nature.

Social Contract: Essays By Locke, Hume and Rousseau 56–57 (Greenwood Press 1980) (Sie Ernest Barker ed., 1947). Locke's basic premise is that though we are influenced by the state's coercive powers, citizens share sufficient adherence to government and obedience laws for a majority of the time.

Drawing on Locke's ideals, it is evident that the objectives of social contract theory are to establish the legitimate forms of government and to decipher the justification of any given individual's duty to obey a legitimate state. A government is legitimate only if it is the outcome of a collective agreement of "free, equal and rational individuals." Elizabeth S. Anderson, *Women and Contracts: No New Deal*, 88 Mich. L. Rev. 1792, 1793–94 (1990) (reviewing Carole Pateman, The Sexual Contract (1988)).

In his commentary on deliberation, Sunstein states that citizens and representatives should work towards a common good to promote social welfare. How does this notion relate to the Lockean social contract theory? Sunstein declares republicans should provide outlets for the exercise of citizenship. To accomplish this goal, he deems a state should be limited in size and scope. Does this idea further the notions of a social contract? Would Locke consider the size of a state significant in determining whether a social contract exists between the state and the citizens?

2. Deliberation. Sunstein argues that politics is a strength if it occurs through communication and deliberation. In this framework, political actors can advise each other to attain a degree of separation from popular preferences and subject these preferences to extensive analysis. By detaching themselves from the heavy influence of interest groups and sharing ideas with one another, government officials can reach more rational and collective decisions for the common good. Both political participation and deliberation are needed for a strong politic, but deliberation is needed to manage and mitigate the heavy pressures exerted by intermediary organizations to influence public policies. Though the two notions go hand in hand, deliberation differs from mere political participation in that it helps strengthen the political process:

> If the common good is entirely a matter of an agency's decisionmaking procedure, participation and deliberation will often, but not always, be complementary, and citizens who participate in agency decisions will be afforded all of the advantages of a deliberative process. Likewise, deliberation depends upon participation because for the common good to prevail throughout the process, members of the affected community must be allowed to participate directly in its deliberations. * * * * * *
>
> As a conceptual matter, deliberation is quite separable from participation. Participation helps to ensure that agency decisions are responsive to the will of the public, transparent, and open. Deliberation, by contrast, removes decision events from the immediate influence of the public, slowing down the political process and giving it a deeper legitimacy; it ensures that collective decisions are something more than

the consensus of "mere majorities." While participation encourages breadth in the agency decisionmaking process, deliberation is more concerned with depth.

Jim Rossi, *Participation Run Amok: The Costs of Mass Participation for Deliberative Agency Decisionmaking*, 92 Nw. U. L. Rev. 173, 211, 212 (1997).

Rossi is arguing that because deliberation lessens the pace of political procedures, government officials are less likely to be influenced by the clout of factions in making policy. Rather than pluralism, which Sunstein views as simply majoritarianism, with deliberation, politicians can make their own rational decisions, effectively working for a greater common good:

> Deliberative democracy presumes that the public interest is more than the result of a contest between competing private interests. Politics is understood to be a process in which private interests are subordinated in "an ongoing process of collective self-determination." Because the self is understood to be "socially situated," it is only partially knowable apart from knowledge of others. As a result, a political process based merely on inputting private preferences is unsatisfactory because the political process must also shape preferences in order to permit the "'intersubjective' constitution of individual selves."
>
> * * *
>
> Sunstein understands the administrative process to be deliberative. The administrator's superior technical sophistication makes it possible for agency policy to be governed by reason, not power. The expert administrator for Sunstein, though, is less Platonic guardian than informed citizen—a person whose superior knowledge facilitates deliberative democratic performance. Their technical expertise enables participants in the administrative process with "disparate views" to push past their unreflective, personal preferences and find consensus.

Note, *Civic Republican Administrative Theory: Bureaucrats as Deliberative Democrats*, 107 Harv. L. Rev. 1401, 1402–03, 1406–07 (1994). Because government officials have the requisite technical knowledge to render reasonable decisions, their choices should be viewed as legitimate. Conversely, ordinary citizens may lack the civic competence to make reasonable recommendations to officials who produce policy:

> Civic competence is a central preoccupation of people who want citizens to base political choices on a broad and accurate understanding of their consequences. Such desires, however, are dashed by evidence that citizens spend little time and effort engaging in politics. The finding that many Americans cannot answer common survey questions about a wide range of political phenomena, for example, dampens many observers' confidence in civic competence.

Arthur Lupia, *Deliberation Disconnected: What It Takes to Improve Civic Competence*, 65 Sum. Law & Contemp. Probs. 133, 133–34 (2002). It is arguable that Sunstein would aver that because proficient politicians engage in deliberation, they are more likely than lesser competent ordinary citizens to issue legitimate policies.

In light of Sunstein's thoughts on deliberation rather than participation, is it arguable that Sunstein and other civic republicans doubt that the common man can effectively make decisions for the greater good? Does Sunstein's criticism of political participation conflict with his ideas of political equality?

For more information on deliberation in decision-making, please refer to Morton J. Horwitz, *Republicanism and Liberalism in American Constitutional Thought*, 29 Wm. & Mary L. Rev. 57 (1987); Cass R. Sunstein, *Democratizing America Through Law*, 25 Suffolk U. L. Rev. 949 (1991); Cass R. Sunstein, *Well-Being and the State*, 107 Harv. L. Rev. 1303, (1994); Mark Seidenfeld, *A Civic Republican Justification for the Bureaucratic State*, 105 Harv. L. Rev. 1511 (1992); Frederick Schauer, *Deliberating about Deliberation*, 90 Mich. L. Rev. 1187 (1992); Robert C. Post, *The Constitutional Concept of Public Discourse: Outrageous Opinion, Democratic Deliberation and* Hustler Magazine v. Falwell, 103 Harv. L. Rev. 601 (1990).

3. Political equality. According to Sunstein, political equality should develop the value and ensure the legitimacy of the deliberative process. Martin H. Redish & Gary Lippman, *Freedom of Expression and the Civic Republican Revival in Constitutional Theory: The Ominous Implications*, 79 Cal. L. Rev. 267, 285 (1991). Sunstein articulates that unequal power in the polity is unfavorable because it degrades the possibility of political equality. In order to attain political equality, citizens and officials must have more access to the political process and wealth effects should be evenly distributed. Reviewing Sunstein's piece, Karan Bhatia elaborates on the civic republican position on political equality:

> Political equality ensures that all individuals and groups have equal access to the political process, and thus ensures that the attainment of the public interest is not distorted by disparities in political influence. While acknowledging that political equality and economic equality are at least conceptually distinct, Sunstein strongly implies that the latter is vital for the former, pointing out that Madison and Montesquieu both envisioned economic equality as a precondition for republicanism and suggesting that "[d]ramatic differences in wealth ... are, in this view, inconsistent with the underlying premises of a republican polity."

Karan Bhatia, *Republican Reform of Government*, 93 Colum. L. Rev. 1300, 1309 (1993) (reviewing George F. Will, Restoration: Congress, Term Limits and the Recovery of Deliberative Democracy (1992)) (quoting Cass R. Sunstein, *Republican Revival*, 97 Yale L.J. 1539, 1552–53 (1988)). Sunstein's central premise is that a more even distribution of resources would equalize political power among government actors and individual citizens. Though this is a praiseworthy objective, without the requisite time and money, several citizens are left without political power and have no voice in decisionmaking. Society's increased stress on making financial donations has several repercussions for political equality. A 1990 study found that a family in the bottom fifth income bracket was significantly less active in politics than a family in the top tenth income bracket. In comparing these two income levels, less wealthy families are less likely to vote, they are approximately half as likely to contact a government official, they are only one-third as likely to participate in informal activity in the community, and only one-tenth as likely to make a campaign contribution. Kay Lehman Schlozman, et. al. *Civic Participation and the Equality Problem, in* Civic Engagement in American Democracy, 443 (Theda Skocpol & Morris P. Fiorina, eds., 1999).

Bearing in mind Sunstein's thoughts on deliberation and the need for government actors to make rational decisions without the influence of interest groups, how can he reconcile this with the need for political equality in society? Are the two notions mutually exclusive, or can they exist in harmony?

For more on political equality, please refer to Cass R. Sunstein, *Political Equality and Unintended Consequences*, 94 Colum. L. Rev. 1390 (1994); Ronald Dworkin, Sovereign Virtue: The Theory and Practice of Equality 184–210 (2000); Howard Gillman, The Constitution Besieged: The Rise and Demise of *Lochner* Era Police Powers Jurisprudence (1993); Anne Phillips, The Politics Of Presence 27–56 (1995); Robert A. Dahl, On Democracy (1998).

4. Universalism. The third tenet of civic republicanism, universalism, puts forth that mediation and political truth are necessary to produce a common good for society:

> This commitment to universalism manifests itself in "a belief in the possibility of mediating different approaches to politics, or different conceptions of the public good, through discussion and dialogue." Two concepts are embedded in this commitment. The first is an emphasis on consensus. Mediation produces "substantively correct outcomes, understood as such through the ultimate criterion of agreement among political equals." The second is a notion of the common good or "political truth" discernible through deliberative dialogue.

Bhatia, *supra*, at 1309–10. The roots of universalism are prevalent in Aristotle's writings, in which the great philosopher articulated that a political community is a group of citizens who share common values and believe in similar norms. In this community, the virtue of justice is prevalent and partially natural, "that which everywhere has the same force and does not exist by people's thinking this or that." 2 Aristotle, Nicomachean Ethics, bk. V ch. 7, *in* The Complete Works of Aristotle 1134b18–1134b19 (W.D. Ross & J.O. Urmson trans., Jonathan Barnes ed., 1984).

With universalism, a politic can achieve justice by making decisions for the greater common good. Sunstein's universalist notions draw similarities to thoughts of liberal republicans, who deem that public policies are sound only when they protect private interests:

> Liberal republicans believe that community values emerge from a well-ordered political process, and that these values derive authority because they are supported by a consensus among political equals. * * * Liberal republicans argue that rights should be designed to protect important private interests that must be guaranteed by a legitimate

government, and that judicial review is legitimate when judges enforce community values or uphold these rights.

Kenneth Ward, *The Allure and Danger of Community Values: A Criticism of Liberal Republican Constitutional Theory*, 24 HASTINGS CONST. L.Q. 171, 186 (1996). In fact, Sunstein declares that republicanism continues to protect private autonomy—but only when such independence is justified in a public context. Though citizens share distinct views regarding public policies and may fail to reach an agreement during deliberation, Sunstein relies on his "belief in the possibility of mediating ... different conceptions of the public good, through discussion and dialogue" to reach a consensus. Is Sunstein's view a little too idealistic? Florida State University professor of law Steven G. Gey asserts that Sunstein's view of universalism portrays his "blind faith" in citizens partaking in the political process. Gey argues that if even one of the civic republicans' expressions of faith is in fact false, the government runs the risk of becoming a totalitarian system:

> These statements amount to little more than assertions of blind faith: faith that there will be a dialogue in which all members of society can participate equally; faith that this dialogue will result in an agreement about the important issues of value in society; and faith that the agreement produced by the process is not a false one—no one is coerced into agreement against his or her will.
>
> The entire structure of the civic republican system rests on these expressions of faith. If the expressions of faith are well-founded, there will be little problem. Indeed, there will be cause for celebration, for society will have proceeded to the highest level of harmony imaginable to even the most optimistic political philosopher. But if even one of the civic republicans' expressions of faith proves false, the civic republican model will produce instead a governmental system that can only be called totalitarian. It will be totalitarian because civic republicanism does not incorporate the natural limitations found in pluralist systems.

Steven G. Gey, *The Unfortunate Revival of Civic Republicanism*, 141 U. PA. L. REV. 801, 841–42 (1993).What are some "natural limitations" common to a pluralistic form of government, and why are they not present in the civic republican model?

For more on universalism and the civic republican model, please refer to Martin H. Redish & Gary Lippman, *Freedom of Expression and the Civic Republican Revival in Constitutional Theory: The Ominous Implications*, 79 CAL. L. REV. 267 (1991); Linda R. Kerber, *Making Republicanism Useful*, 97 YALE L.J. 1663 (1998).

5. Citizenship. The final principle of civic republicanism, citizenship, is intended to restrict the overarching power of interest groups by encouraging citizens to scrutinize the conduct of their representatives. Sunstein deems that in current society, individuals are unfortunately isolated from the political process and that the nation has lost a sense of community values. With political participation, citizens can reach a consensus of shared virtues and collective norms could be established. Hope M. Babcock, *De-*

mocracy's Discontent in a Complex World: Can Avalanches, Sandpiles, and Finches Optimize Michael Sandel's Civic Republican Community?, 85 GEO. L.J. 2085, 2090 (1997). Consequently, individuals should participate in making the laws that govern their lives, not only in a government contexts, but also in other circumstances:

> A civic republican conception of citizenship supposes that people must be engaged in framing the rules and administering the institutions that govern all aspects of their communal lives. These institutions include the workplace as well as governments, the fact that workers have little power over many of the decisions that immediately affect their lives is itself a serious participatory loss. Because industrial democracy can provide the foundation for active citizenship in conventionally "public" realms, its consequences reach beyond the workplace.

Paul Brest, *Further Beyond the Republican Revival: Toward Radical Republicanism*, 97 YALE L.J. 1623, 1626 (1988). Civic republicans emphasize the need for participation in order for citizens to have some control over policies that affect their lives. However, in order for individuals to participate in the political process, the size of the republic must be limited—a large republic runs the risk of decreasing the relationship between citizens and their representatives and reduces opportunities for participation. Karan Bhatia briefly describes the need for a small republic:

> Sunstein uses the terms "citizenship" and "participation" interchangeably. Participation in government serves several functions in the republican calculus. Obviously, it is instrumental to deliberation. Equally important, Sunstein argues, participation nurtures feelings of empathy, virtue, and community essential to a healthy republic. The importance of citizen participation makes representation at best a necessary evil in a republican scheme. This explains why republics are commonly thought of as small and decentralized.

Bhatia, *supra*, at 1310. With a small republic, citizens will have a better chance to deliberate and work towards a common good; sharing similar views regarding institutions and foundations, individuals can reach agreements relatively easily. Is Sunstein correct in assuming that a small republic would encourage political participation? What are some ways in which a small republic may be an impediment to an efficient government system?

Inclusion of citizenship highlights the need for deliberation and participation. Though citizenship and discussion among community members are appealing, Sunstein may be too idealistic in assuming that all individuals will participate and reach a consensus in making policy decisions:

> Once again, the civic republicans are faced with an insoluble dilemma. On the one hand, if the community is truly organic, every citizen must have a say in the community's discussions and must participate in the process in order to develop the properly virtuous attitudes and values. On the other hand, if the community forces citizens to participate against their will, a strongly motivated minority will be able to manip-

ulate the political process by obtaining support for their favored policies from unwilling participants in exchange for an agreement to support the unwilling participants in some later policy dispute. Unless the civic republicans make the unrealistic and utopian presumption that all citizens agree about important policy matters before political deliberation begins, their organic community dissolves into a system indistinguishable from the one whose problems civic republicanism is supposed to cure.

Gey, *supra* at 820. Gey's disagreement with Sunstein centers in on the fact that many citizens can be apathetic regarding political participation, making the possibility of every citizen taking part in the political process quite futile. However, if every citizen is forced to partake in deliberative decision-making, political bargaining and the struggle between interest groups may intensify, which is an unattractive pluralistic notion. Gey, *supra*, at 820. Is Gey correct that Sunstein's impractical view of complete political participation by community members runs the risk of increasing the force of influential interest groups?

Vanderbilt University Professor of Law Suzanna Sherry would probably agree with Gey's views. She asserts that most citizens are not prepared enough to participate politically, and that unless deliberation is limited to a select few elites, Sunstein's idealized system may try to change the values of ordinary citizens:

> First, the neo-republican ideal of deliberative democracy borders on the utopian. The vast majority of Americans are neither inclined nor equipped to engage in the kind of sustained, reasoned deliberation contemplated by the republicans. Moreover, republican suggestions for promoting rational deliberation may actually have the effect of "undermining public political participation, especially among poorer groups." The republican revival will not go beyond a small corps of elite law professors if it does not face up to the citizenry's lack of interest. However, neither of the two most promising ways of coming to terms with that problem is politically acceptable to most neo-republicans: either we could acknowledge that real political participation will necessarily be limited to the few because only the few are civic minded enough to participate, or we might attempt to change the values of the many so that they too are interested in participating in our rational political discussions. The first solution conflicts with the egalitarianism of modern republicans, and the second with their unwillingness to abandon the ethical relativism of modern liberalism.

Suzanna Sherry, *Responsible Republicanism: Educating for Citizenship*, 62 U. CHI. L. REV. 131, 137–38 (1995). Is Sherry correct in asserting that Sunstein's model may alter citizens' choices and values? What are some mechanisms by which the government can change citizens' views so they could partake in the deliberation process?

For more discussion on citizenship in the civic republican model, please refer to Kathryn Abrams, *Law's Republicanism*, 97 YALE L.J. 1591 (1988); Frank I. Michelman, *Law's Republic*, 97 YALE L.J. 1493 (1988); J. David

Hoeveler, Jr., *Original Intent and the Politics of Republicanism*, 75 MARQ. L. REV. 863 (1992); Daniel Rodgers, *Republicanism: The Career of a Concept*, 79 J. AM. HIST. 11, 12–13 (1992); G. Edward White, *Reflections on the "Republican Revival": Interdisciplinary Scholarship in the Legal Academy*, 6 YALE J.L. & HUM. 1, 13, 22 (1994); JOYCE ABBLEBY, LIBERALISM AND REPUBLICANISM IN THE HISTORICAL IMAGINATION (1992); Adrian Oldfield, *Citizenship and Community: Civic Republicanism and the Modern World, in* THE CITIZENSHIP DEBATES: A READER, 75–92 (Gerson Shafir ed., 1998).

Marxism and Socialism

Marxism

The fall of the Soviet Union brought with it an intellectual disintegration of Marxist theory. However, Johns Hopkins University geographer, David Harvey writes eloquently of the history of postmodernity. Harvey argues that postmodernist culture is an extension of the "basic rules of capitalistic accumulation." In the following passage, Harvey summarizes the major insights of Marx and Engels.

The Condition of Postmodernity: An Enquiry Into the Origins of Cultural Change

Blackwell (1989) at 99–106.

■ DAVID HARVEY

In *The Communist Manifesto* Marx and Engels argue that the bourgeoisie has created a new internationalism via the world market, together with "subjection of nature's forces to man, machinery, application of chemistry to agriculture and industry, steam navigation, railways, electric telegraphs, clearing of whole continents for cultivation, canalization of rivers, whole populations conjured out of the ground." It has done this at great cost: violence, destruction of traditions, oppression, reduction of the valuation of all activity to the cold calculus of money and profit. Furthermore:

Constant revolutionizing of production, uninterrupted disturbance of all social relations, everlasting uncertainty and agitation, distinguish the bourgeois epoch from all earlier times. All fixed, fast-frozen relationships, with their train of venerable ideas and opinions, are swept away, all new-formed ones become obsolete before they can ossify. All that is solid melts into air, all that is holy is profaned, and men at last are forced to face with sober sense the real conditions of their lives and their relations with their fellow men. Karl Marx, The Communist Manifesto.

But what is special about Marx is the way he dissects the origin of this general condition.

Marx begins *Capital*, for example, with an analysis of commodities, those everyday things (food, shelter, clothing, etc.) which we daily consume in the course of reproducing ourselves. Yet the commodity is, he avers, "a mysterious thing" because it simultaneously embodies both a use value (it fulfils a particular want or need) and an exchange value (I can use it as a bargaining chip to procure other commodities). This duality always renders the commodity ambiguous for us; shall we consume it or trade it away? But as exchange relations proliferate and price-fixing markets form, so one commodity typically crystallizes out as money. With money the mystery of the commodity takes on a new twist, because the use value of money is that it represents the world of social labour and of exchange value. Money lubricates exchange but above all it becomes the means by which we typically compare and assess, both before and after the fact of exchange, the value of all commodities. * * *

The advent of a money economy, Marx argues, dissolves the bonds and relations that make up "traditional" communities so that "money becomes the real community." We move from a social condition, in which we depend directly on those we know personally, to one in which we depend on impersonal and objective relations with others. As exchange relations proliferate, so money appears more and more as "a power external to and independent of the producers," so what "originally appears as a means to promote production becomes a relation alien" to them. Money concerns dominate producers. Money and market exchange draws a veil over, "masks" social relationships between things. This condition Marx calls "the fetishism of commodities." * * *

The conditions of labour and life, the sense of joy, anger, or frustration that lie behind the production of commodities, the states of mind of the producers, are all hidden to us as we exchange one object (money) for another (the commodity). We can take our daily breakfast without a thought for the myriad people who engaged in its production. All traces of exploitation are obliterated in the object (there are no finger marks of exploitation in the daily bread). We cannot tell from contemplation of any object in the supermarket what conditions of labour lay behind its production. The concept of fetishism explains how it is that under conditions of capitalist modernization we can be so objectively dependent on "others" whose lives and aspirations remain so totally opaque to us. * * *

As commodity producers seeking money, * * * we are dependent upon the needs and capacity of others to buy. Producers consequently have a permanent interest in cultivating "excess and intemperance" in others, in feeding "imaginary appetites" to the point where ideas of what constitutes social need are replaced by "fantasy, caprice, and whim." The capitalist producer increasingly "plays the pimp" between the consumers and their sense of need, excites in them "morbid appetites, lies in wait for each of [their] weaknesses—all so that he can demand the cash for this service of live." Pleasure, leisure, seduction, and erotic life are all brought within the range of money power and commodity production. Capitalism therefore "produces sophistication of needs and of their means on the one hand, and a bestial barbarization, a complete, unrefined, and abstract simplicity of need, on the other." Advertising and commercialization destroy all traces of production in their imagery, reinforcing the fetishism that arises automatically in the course of market exchange.

Furthermore, money, as the supreme representation of social power in capitalist society, itself becomes the object of lust, greed, and desire. Yet here, too, we encounter double meanings. Money confers the privilege to exercise power over others—we can buy their labour time or the services they offer, even build systematic relations of domination over exploited classes simply through control over money power. Money, in fact, fuses the political and the economic into a genuine political economy of overwhelming power relations * * *. The common material languages of money and commodities provide a universal basis within market capitalism for linking everyone into an identical system of market valuation and so procuring the reproduction of social life through an objectively grounded system of social bonding. Yet within these broad constraints, we are "free," as it were, to develop our own personalities and relationships in our own way, our own "otherness," even to forge group language games, provided, of course, that we have enough money to live on satisfactorily. Money is a "great leveler and cynic," a powerful underminer of fixed social relations, and a great "democratizer." As a social power that can be held by individual persons it forms the basis for a wide-ranging individual liberty, a liberty that can be deployed to develop ourselves as free-thinking individuals without reference to others. Money unifies precisely *through* its capacity to accommodate individualism, otherness, and extraordinary social fragmentation. * * *

Participation in market exchange presupposes a certain division of labour as well as a capacity to separate (alienate) oneself from one's own product. The result is an estrangement from the product of one's own experience, a fragmentation of social tasks and a separation of the subjective meaning of a process of production from the objective market valuation of the product. A highly organized technical and social division of labour, though by no means unique to capitalism, is one of the founding principles of capitalist modernization. This forms a powerful lever to promote economic growth and the accumulation of capital, particularly under conditions of market exchange in which individual commodity producers (protected by private property rights) can explore the possibilities of specialization within an open economic system. This explains the power of economic (free market) liberalism as a founding doctrine for capitalism. It is precisely in such a context that possessive individualism and creative entrepreneurialism, innovation, and speculation, can flourish, even though this also means a proliferating fragmentation of tasks and responsibilities, and a necessary transformation of social relations to the point where producers are forced to view others in purely instrumental terms. * * *

Capitalists when they purchase labour power necessarily treat it in instrumental terms. The labourer is viewed as a "hand" rather than as a whole person * * *, and the labour contributed is a "factor" (notice the reification) of production. The purchase of labour power with money gives the capitalist certain rights to dispose of the labour of others without necessary regard for what the others might think, need, or feel. The omni-presence of this class relation of domination, offset only to the degree that the labourers actively struggle to assert their rights and express their feelings, suggests one of the founding principles upon which the very idea of "otherness" is produced and reproduced on a continuing basis in capitalist society. The world of the working class becomes the domain of that "other," which is necessarily rendered opaque and potentially unknowable by virtue of the fetishism of market exchange. And I should also add parenthetically that if there are already those in society (women, blacks, colonized peoples, minorities of all kinds) who can readily be conceptualized as the other, then the conflation of class exploitation with gender, race, colonialism, ethnicity, etc. can proceed apace with all manner of invidious results. Capitalism did not invent "the other" but it certainly made use of and promoted it in highly structured ways. * * *

The "coercive laws" of market competition force all capitalists to seek out technological and organizational changes that will enhance their own profitability vis-à-vis the social average, thus entraining all capitalists in leap-frogging processes of innovation that reach their limit only under conditions of massive labour surpluses. The need to keep the labourer under control in the workplace, and to undercut the bargaining power of the labourer in the market (particularly under conditions of relative labour scarcity and active class resistance), also stimulates capitalists to innovate. Capitalism is necessarily technologically dynamic, not because of the mythologized capacities of the innovative entrepreneur (as Schumpeter was later to argue) but because of the coercive laws of competition and the conditions of class struggle endemic to capitalism.

The effect of continuous innovation, however, is to devalue, if not destroy, past investments and labour skills. *Creative destruction* is embedded within the circulation of capital itself. Innovation exacerbates instability, insecurity, and in the end, becomes the prime force pushing capitalism into periodic paroxysms of crisis. Not only does the life of modern industry become a series of periods of moderate activity, prosperity, over-production, crisis, and stagnation, "but the uncertainty and instability to which machinery subjects the employment, and consequently the conditions of existence, of the operatives become normal." Furthermore:

"All means for the development of production transform themselves into means of domination over, and exploitation of, the producers' they mutilate the labourer into a fragment of a man, degrade him to the level of an appendage of a machine, destroy every remnant of charm from his work and turn it into a hated toil; they estrange from him the intellectual potentialities of the labour-process in the same proportion as science is incorporate in it as an independent power; they distort the conditions under which he works, subject him during the labour-process to a despotism the more hateful for its meanness; they transform his life-time into working-time, and drag his wife and child beneath the wheels of the Juggernaut of capital." Karl Marx, Capital, vol. 1, at 604 (1955,c1952). Edited by Friedrich Engels. (Translated from the 3d German ed. by Samuel Moore and Edward Aveling. Rev., with additional translation from the 4th German ed., by Marie Sachey and Herbert Lamm) Imprint Chicago, Encyclopaedia Britannica.

Socialism
A Future for Socialism

EQUAL SHARES: MAKING MARKET SOCIALISM WORK 7–12 (Erik Olin Wright ed., 1996).

■ JOHN ROEMER

1. Introduction

The demise of the Communist system in the Soviet Union and Eastern Europe has caused many to believe that socialism cannot exist, either in the present world or as an ideal. I shall argue that it can, but that it requires some revision of standard views of what constitutes socialism. If one thought socialism were coextensive with the Soviet model, then clearly it would be dead. I shall defend the idea of market socialism.

The term "market socialism" comes to us from what has been called the socialist calculation debate of the 1930s, in which the two principal protagonists were Oscar Lange and Friederich Hayek. Lange argued that what economists now call neoclassical price theory showed the possibility of combining central planning and the market; while Hayek retorted that planning would subvert at its heart the mechanism which is the source of capitalism's vitality. Hayek's criticisms of Lange's market socialism, and more recently those of Janos Kornai, are for the most part on the mark. But the experiences of capitalism, as well as of socialism, since 1945, suggest ways of reformulating the concept of market socialism in response to the Hayekian critique of its intellectual ancestor. This reformulation is my task.

Economic theory does not yet enable us to write a complete balance sheet of the benefits and costs of the market mechanism. During the 1930s, when Lange and Hayek wrote about market socialism, the Soviet Union was undergoing rapid industrialization. There was, apparently, full employment in that country, while workers and machines were massively idle in the industrialized capitalist world. Hayek therefore wrote from a defensive position, while Lange may well have felt that his proposal was fine-tuning for a socialist system that was, inevitably, the face of the future. Today, the tables are turned. Yet both the pro-socialists of the 1930s and the pro-capitalists of today jump too quickly to conclusions, for we understand fully the effects of markets only in very special circumstances.

Economic theory can explain how, if all economic actors are small relative to the market and cannot individually affect prices, if externalities are absent, and if there is a sufficient number of insurance and financial markets, the equilibrium in a market economy will engender an allocation of resources that is Pareto efficient—that is, efficient in the sense that no other allocation of resources exists which could render everyone simultaneously better off. But this kind of static efficiency may be relatively unimportant compared to the dynamic efficiency with which markets are often credited—that they produce innovations in technology and commodities more effectively than any other economic mechanism could. Although we seem to have much evidence of market dynamism, we have no adequate economic theory of it; nor do we have a controlled experiment which would permit a skeptical scientist confidently to assert that markets are superior to planning in this dynamic sense. The real-life experiments are severely polluted, from a scientific viewpoint: the most dynamic economies of the 1960s onwards (Japan and the East Asian tigers) have used markets with a good dose of planning, and the Communist economies not only had planning and the absence of markets but also political dictatorship, a background condition an experimental designer would like to be able to alter.

The social scientist must, therefore, be more agnostic about the effects of the market than are elementary economics textbooks and the popular press. Indeed, contemporary economic theory has come to see markets as operating within the essential context of non-market institutions, most notably: firms; contract law; the interlinking institutions between economic institutions and other actors, such as between the firm and its stockholders; and the state. Large capitalist firms are centrally planned organizations (in which internal transactions are not mediated by a price system), usually run by managers hired to represent the interests of shareholders. This they do imperfectly, as their own interests do not typically coincide with the interests of shareholders. Contract law is an essential supplement to the market: long-term contracts are, indeed, instruments which render it costly for parties to them to return to the market during the life of the contract. Furthermore, in different capitalist economies different kinds of non-market institutions have evolved. We do have somewhat of a real-life experiment which can help in evaluating alternative economic mechanisms. Germany and Japan, for example, have very different institutions through which owners of firms monitor their managements from those in the United States and the United Kingdom.

In short, the market does not perform its good deeds unaided; it is supported by a myriad cast of institutional characters which have evolved painstakingly over time, and in a variety of ways, in various market economies. My central argument is that these institutional solutions to the design problems of capitalism also suggest how the design problems of socialism may be solved in a market setting.

To see why this may be so, I will first quickly, and necessarily inadequately, summarize the theory of income distribution of Hayek, more generally, of the Austrian school of economics. According to this view, the distribution of income in a market economy is, in the long run, determined by the relative scarcity of various factors of production, principally human talents, including entrepreneurial talent. Property rights should, in the long run, be viewed as themselves derivative of talent. Firms are indeed just the means through which entrepreneurs capitalize their talent; in turn, it is profits from firms which enable their owners to purchase real estate and other natural resources, so that, in the long run, natural resources, too, are owned by talented people or their descendants. Furthermore, any attempt to interfere with the operation of markets—that is, with the institution that maximizes the freedom to compete in the economic sphere—will only reduce overall welfare, as it will inevitably result in conditions which inhibit entrepreneurs from bringing their talents fully into play.

Were this 'naturalistic' view correct, egalitarians would have little remedy for inequality other than education, serving to develop the talents of as many as possible, and perhaps inheritance taxes. What I believe the institutional view of capitalism that I have outlined shows, however, is that the advanced capitalist economy is in large part the product of large, complex institutions, whose operation depends upon the combined efforts of many 'ordinary' people—ordinary in the sense that their talents are not of the rare variety that the Hayekian view envisions, but result from training and education. The wealth of society is not due primarily to rugged and rare individuals, but is reproducible, according to blueprints which are quite well understood. The market is necessary to implement competition and to economize on information, but not so much to cultivate the inspiration of rare geniuses.

A particular way in which the modern view of capitalism suggests a future for socialism is in its understanding of the firm as a nexus of principal-agent relationships. * * * Indeed the mechanisms that have evolved (or been designed) under capitalism that enable owners to control management can be transported to a socialist framework.

In contrast to the "thin" Hayekian and neoclassical views, which see markets as a minimal structure organizing competition among talented individuals, the modern 'thick' view sees markets as operating within the context of complex, man-made institutions, through which all individual contributions become pasteurized and refined. These two views of the market are, I suggest, substantially different, and the latter 'thick' view, unlike the former, is amenable to the coexistence of markets and socialism. Income distribution, in particular, is more malleable under the thick view; the door is opened to reducing inequality substantially, short of massive education, as the reallocation of profits will, if properly done, have little or no deleterious effect on economic efficiency.

In what follows, I will try to flesh out these vague claims.

2.   What Socialists Want

I believe socialists want:

1.   equality of opportunity for self-realization and welfare;

2.   equality of opportunity for political influence; and

3.   equality of social status

By self-realization, I mean the development and application of one's talents in a direction that gives meaning to one's life. This is a specifically Marxian conception of human flourishing, and is to be distinguished, for instance, from John Rawls's notion of fulfillment of a plan of life, which might consist in enjoying one's family and friends, or eating fine meals, or counting blades of grass. These activities do not count as self-realization, this being a process of self-transformation that requires struggle in a way that eating a fine meal does not. One does, however, derive welfare from enjoying one's family and eating fine meals, and so I do attribute value to these activities in the socialist's reckoning, for (1) requires equality of opportunity for self-realization and welfare.

That equality of *opportunity* for self-realization and welfare is the goal, rather than equality of self-realization and welfare, requires comment. Were equality of welfare the goal rather than equality of opportunity for welfare, then society would be mandated to provide huge resource endowments to those who adopt terribly expensive and unrealistic goals. Suppose I, a poor athlete, come to believe that my life has been worthless unless I reach the top of Mount Everest on foot. This may require a large amount of money, to hire sufficient Sherpas and other support services to make that journey possible. Equality of opportunity for welfare, on the other hand, puts some responsibility on me for choosing welfare-inducing goals that are reasonable. It is certainly tricky to decide what allocation of resources will give all people an equal opportunity for welfare or self-realization, but I hope the principle is clear from this example. What distinguishes socialists or leftists from conservatives is, in large part, the view of how deeply one must go in order to equalize opportunities. Conservatives believe in going not very deeply: if there is no discrimination in hiring and everyone has access to education through a public school system or vouchers, then the conservative standard of equality of opportunity is met. Socialists believe that those guarantees only touch the surface. Equality of opportunity requires special compensation or subsidy for children who have grown up in homes without access to privilege. Most generally, equality of opportunity requires that people be compensated for handicaps they suffer, induced by factors over which they have no control. * * *

It is, however, impossible to maximize three objectives at once. That is, the kind of social organization that maximizes the equal level of opportunity for self-realization may well induce highly unequal levels of political influence.

There are two responses to this problem. The first says: there is a form of society in which all three objectives are equalized simultaneously, when 'the free development of each becomes the condition for the free development of all,' or some such thing. I think this is an unsubstantiated and utopian claim. The second response says that one must admit the possibility of trade-offs among the three objectives. This, in fact, is what most of us do. For instance, a lively debate has taken place in the socialist movement on the question: 'Which is primary, democracy or equality?' Is equality of opportunity for political influence more important that equality of opportunity for self-realization and welfare? Socialists have different answers to this question. For example, Western socialists assign more importance to equality of opportunity for political influence than most Soviet socialists did. Some socialists did not support the Sandinistas because of the lack of press freedom and democracy in Nicaragua.

I will not offer here any particular preference order over the three equalisanda. I shall be concerned only with investigating the possibility of equalizing income without any unacceptable loss in efficiency. Indeed, I believe raising the income of the poor is the most important single step to improving their opportunities for self-realization and welfare.

––––––––

NOTE ON RADICAL THEORY

According to radical theory, which studies the socio-historic process of the political economy under capitalism, capitalism cannot meet the needs of the people collectively. Centuries of capitalism have failed to provide everyone with health care, a living wage, and a secure livelihood. Neither the conservative free market nor liberal welfare conceptions of capitalism meet the needs of society. Like Friedman, most economists identify a human capital gap, which can be overcome by increased education and technological training, as the main cause of wage and opportunity dispari- ties. Radical theorists reject this conception. They conclude that, so long as the present capitalist economic system exists, differentials in pay, income, and employment opportunities will exist for women, minorities, and the disabled. "Neither the market nor civil rights laws can undermine the structure of inequality nor prevent its reproduction." We must return to basic questions that neoclassical economists claim the price system an- swered: What purposes should our economy serve? "What is work, who controls it, and what is its purpose?"

––––––––

NOTES AND QUESTIONS

1. **Markets and socialism.** Is Roemer's argument that the decentralized economy of private markets can be reconciled with the central planning that is characteristic of socialism? What changes would be required to make such a major conversion of the political economy of the United States?

2. **Equality of opportunity.** Roemer is careful to avoid making an explicit argument for equality of outcome. Would his carefully articulated definition of equal opportunity meet with approval from Milton Friedman? Reconsider Friedman's essay, *Created Equal, in* FREE TO CHOOSE: A PERSON- AL STATEMENT, at p. 153.

3. **The "R" word: redistribution.** Progressive philosopher and activist Cornel West argues that:

> The historic role of American progressives is to promote redistributive measures that enhance the standard of living and quality of life for the have-nots and have-too-littles. Affirmative action was one such redis- tributive measure that surfaced in the heat of battle in the 1960s among those fighting for racial equality.
>
> * * *
>
> In American politics, progressives must not only cling to redistributive ideals, but must also fight for those policies that—out of compromise

and concession—imperfectly conform to those ideals. Liberals who give only lip service to these ideals, trash the policies in the name of *realpolitik,* or reject the policies as they perceive a shift in the racial bellwether give up precious ground too easily. And they do so even as the sand is disappearing under our feet on such issues as regressive taxation, layoffs or takebacks from workers, and cutbacks in health and child care.

CORNEL WEST, RACE MATTERS 63, 65 (1993).

What are the most significant differences between affirmative action and the market socialism that Roemer advocates?

4.   Does Roemer address the social, cultural, and psychological phenomena of commodification, alienation, and fetishism that Harvey conveys as the major Marxist criticisms of capitalism?

CHAPTER 6

WEALTH AND INEQUALITY

Introduction

As Deborah Malamud has observed:

Class is all but invisible in contemporary American social discourse. At most, it is a fleeting image, a rarely detected underlayer to the complex texture of race, ethnicity, and gender that captures our society's attention. For many, America stands as the model of the classless society, one in which most people think of themselves as middle class (or at least as potentially so, with hard work and a little luck) and in which middle-classness is the socioeconomic face of "American-ness." The recognized exception, the chronic poor, is seen as an aberration rather than evidence of a general system of class in the United States.

Similarly, American law does not recognize class. Constitutional equal protection doctrine and antidiscrimination statutes are the major mechanisms through which American law recognizes and redresses hierarchy in American society. Both are silent on the question of class. Welfare law advocates have utilized litigation and other mechanisms to argue that "the poor" is a legally significant group, that "poverty" is a suspect classification, and that welfare benefits are "new property" entitled to protection. Scholars have exhibited interest in addressing the question of how the law contributes both to the creation of cycles of poverty and to the social construction of poverty. But the very location of this work within poverty advocacy and theory has meant that it has drawn attention not to class as a general social phenomenon but to the aberrational nature of poverty and our social tolerance for it. Thus poverty is marked, middle-classness unmarked; poverty is figure, middle-classness ground. Poverty needs social, culture, and legal explanation. Middle-classness does not.

Deborah C. Malamud, *"Who They Are—Or Were": Middle–Class Welfare in the Early New Deal*, 151 U. PA. L. REV. 2019, 2019 (2003).

In this chapter, we will attempt to make visible the invisible category of class. Part A examines the difficulties in conceptualizing and measuring "class." Part B provides some historical perspectives on the law's role in shaping the class structure and relations we have today. Part C looks at income and wealth inequality at present and points at future trends.

A. DEFINING "CLASS"

Martha Mahoney notes that social and political theory has been dominated by two different concepts of class. One concept of class—"status-class"—draws on the work of sociologist Max Weber, and "analyzes economic participation through a focus on distribution and the market and emphasizes status as an important aspect of structural inequality."[a] In contrast, economist and theorist Karl Marx's concept of class "emphasizes class relations in a system of production and the exploitation of labor by capital."[b] A class analysis in the Weberian tradition, then, might divide American society into upper, middle, and lower classes (looking for indicia of stratification); a class analysis in the Marxist tradition might divide American society into capitalists and workers (looking for relations of power and exploitation). Another way to distinguish the two theories of class is to note that Weberian theories take a "snapshot" of existing class relations; Marxist theories attempt to explain historically how classes emerge and evolve.

To the extent that Americans are comfortable thinking about class relations at all, they usually focus on status. The excerpt that follows points out some of the difficulties in measuring and analyzing status-class.

―――――

Class–Based Affirmative Action: Lessons and Caveats

74 TEX. L. REV. 1847, 1852–93 (1996).

■ DEBORAH C. MALAMUD

Two basic models of economic inequality compete in the American ideological marketplace, each with two major versions. * * *

One view—which I will call economic individualism—depicts the American economic order as completely open to economic mobility for those individuals with the gumption to pursue it. The economic individualist view admits (as it must) that at any given moment individuals occupy a wide range of positions on a continuum of economic attainment. But this distribution is seen as a result of, rather than a constraint on, free market forces. So long as there is sufficient mobility by individuals, the inequalities in the rewards accorded to different positions are of no theoretical or political importance.

A more moderate version of economic individualism—and the only form of economic individualism that an advocate of class-based affirmative action could embrace—is what one might call pro-interventionist economic individualism. Here, it is admitted that past economic position is a con-

---

a. Martha R. Mahoney, 76 S. CAL. L. REV. 799, 817 (2003).　　**b.** *Id.*

straint on future economic position; for example, that lack of economic resources can interfere with an individual's capacity to make the investments in human capital necessary for advancement. It is thus perceived as necessary to make a modest level of economic assistance available on the basis of need at certain key junctures of personal economic development—financial aid for college, for example. Once modest assistance is given, previous experiences of economic disadvantage are deemed no longer relevant to future success.

The other major perspective on economic inequality posits the existence of class—a structured system of inequality (as opposed to a simple unequal distribution of economic outcomes among individuals) that is intrinsic to the economic realm and that is not fundamentally altered by the economic mobility of individuals. What distinguishes class perspectives from individualist perspectives on economic inequality is that class perspectives are inherently social (as opposed to individual) and diachronic (as opposed to synchronic). Class is social in the dual sense that the class system is inherent in and perpetuated by the structure of economic relations in the society and that shared class position has the potential for being mobilized as the basis for both group identity and political action. Class is diachronic in the triple sense that class position is (1) intergenerationally transmitted, (2) mediated through the strategic behavior of social actors over time, and (3) incapable of being understood without reference to patterns of change in the economic organization of the society.

Finally, there is an alternative version of a belief in class, which builds on the meaning of class just described, but goes beyond it. In this view, class is said to interact with race, gender, and ethnicity (and perhaps other elements of social identity, such as place of residence) in interlocking and mutually defining structures, and it is their interaction that is seen to shape both consciousness and life chances. * * *

II. MEASURING ECONOMIC INEQUALITY

A. *The Shape of Economic Inequality: Continua, Categories, and Conflicts*

On the broadest level, economic inequality can be represented in one of three ways. Under one view, relative economic advantage is represented as *gradational*: as a continuous sliding scale of relative economic position, rank ordered according to one or more specified criteria. The continuum may then be divided for convenience into categories (such as "lower class," "lower middle class," "upper middle class," etc.) by assigning labels to certain ranges on the continuum. But the validity of the gradational model does not turn on any notion that the theorist's groupings identify groups of people with similar patterns of consciousness and action.

Under the *categorical* approach, economic space is divided in a noncontinuous manner on the basis of the criterion that is, according to the relevant theory, the most significant indicator of economic status. The classic example of a categorical approach is the importance placed by some scholars on the distinction between blue-collar (manual) and white-collar (nonmanual) employment. It is generally contended that the theorists' categories capture "native" distinctions—in other words, that they describe patterns of affinity and difference that motivate social action. Thus, the fact that the values and behavior patterns of some skilled blue-collar workers appear to be closer to those of white-collar workers than to those of their unskilled blue-collar brethren is, for a categorical theorist (but not for a gradational theorist), a challenge to the theory or evidence of a flaw in methodology.

Finally, under what [Erik Olin] Wright calls the *relational* approach, the groups that matter for the analysis of economic inequality are identified not merely by patterns of affinity and difference, but also by their intrinsically antagonistic social relations with other economic groups. Just as the elements within such classic pairings as "parent and child" and "master and servant" take their meaning only in relationship to each other, relational perspectives see each economic grouping as existing only with reference to and in tension with the others. Different terms are used to describe the field in which economic groups operate (for example, "the market" or "relations of production") and the nature of the tension among them (for example, "domination," "hegemony," "exploitation," or "exclusion")—terminologies that often do a better job of identifying putative alliances with Weberian, neo-Marxist, or classical Marxist social theory than of describing different social realities. But what identifies an approach as relational is its emphasis on the structured nature of group relations and on the intrinsically antagonistic nature of group interests. * * *

B. Whose Economic Inequality?: Individual Versus Household or Family as the Relevant Unit of Analysis

In discussing economic inequality, one cannot go far without confronting the question of whose economic position is to be measured. Many studies use the individual worker as the unit of analysis. But in any household or family with more than one worker, each worker's economic position is potentially modified by that of the others—not only as to the availability of second (or third) incomes, but in *all* the many ways in which economic position affects life chances. Indeed, the household or family is the most appropriate unit of analysis without regard to the number of income earners in the household. This is demonstrated by the work of sociologist Greg J. Duncan, who has shown on the basis of longitudinal data that changes in household composition account for much of the intragenerational economic change in the status of families.

Family and *household* are not the same concept. Family may or may not involve blood or marital ties, as work on gay and lesbian kinship demonstrates. Divorce creates families and households of numerous shapes, and decision rules must be developed to determine the economic saliency of noncustodial parents, of custodial stepparents, of the subsequent spouses of noncustodial parents, and so forth. Even in the absence of divorce (or widowhood), families may not fit the nuclear family image: family-based households often include other relatives whose economic experiences can be quite salient to all members of the household well beyond the effects of any income-sharing that may take place. Substituting the "traditional" nuclear family for the isolated individual as the unit for measuring class position is thus only a small step in the right direction, and it creates myriad problems of its own. Furthermore, class not only is shaped by family and household composition, but at times also shapes family and household composition. Measuring class position with reference to the nuclear family mirrors middle class kinship ideology, but fails both to accord validity to other classes' conceptions of family life (a flaw on the level of cultural adequacy) and to make available for measurement the wide range of relationships upon which individuals are empowered to draw for resources under these alternative conceptions (a flaw on the level of technical adequacy).

Furthermore, household or family is important in the dimension not only of space (the sharing of the space of a common household), but also in the dimension of time. For example, it is undisputed that at least to some extent, the economic characteristics of a person's family of origin shape that person's economic prospects and attainment over the life span. There is room for debate over the extent to which this is true, the length of time for which it is true, and the mechanisms that cause it to be true. But for our present purposes, what matters is the existence of *"intergenerational* inertia," because of which the intergenerational family is the appropriate unit for understanding a family's economic status.

The complexity of "family" as a unit existing in time and space is well demonstrated by an example used by Frank Parkin. Picture two families, in each of which the father is a blue-collar worker and the mother is a high school graduate who is not employed outside the home. In one family, the mother is the child of a blue-collar worker: she has married within her own class. In the other, the mother is the child of a white-collar worker, meaning that she has "married down." According to a study cited by Parkin, the son of the within-class marriage has a forty-two percent chance of going to college, while the son of the mother who "married down" has an eighty percent chance of going to college. In the dimension of space, it is the child's interaction with his nonworking mother that is determinative of his college prospects. In the dimension of time, the key to understanding the child's life chances lies in the grandparental generation. Without considering the economic status of the high school boys in light of their families viewed in the dimensions of time and space, the boys would appear to be similarly situated. In reality, they are not.

C.   Trajectory

Sophisticated analyses of economic inequality take into consideration not merely a *snapshot* of an individual's (or household's or family's) economic circumstances, but a longer view. Jobs that require significant investments in human capital tend to have rising trajectories. In contrast, some occupations are quintessential "young man's (or woman's) games"— such as sports, dance, or physically dangerous service or industrial jobs—in which work opportunities and earnings decline over time. Furthermore,

Pierre Bourdieu correctly points out that in periods of economic change, there exists a "collective trajectory"—the mobility of an entire occupation, class fragment, or class—that does much to shape both political attitudes and the class's capacity to maintain its socioeconomic position. At the extreme, rising or falling group trajectories can destabilize basic elements of the class structure. In all of these aspects, economic position must be understood as playing out over time. There can be doubt as to whether the downwardly mobile family (intra- or inter-generational) is better or worse off than the upwardly mobile family at the point at which their trajectories cross. But it is clear that a snapshot is an oversimplification of the true position of economically mobile families.

D. Measuring Relative Economic Status: The Constituent Elements of Economic Inequality

Up to this point, I have mentioned in passing a number of factors that shape the economic situations of individuals and families: occupation, income, education, orientation toward educational attainment, and numerous extra-economic characteristics (including race and gender). When I have asked students to identify their "class," they have referred to a good number of these factors and some others. But each factor raises its own problems of definition and measurement, and their interactions are complex. I am pessimistic about the capacity of the legal system to capture enough of these complexities to achieve anything resembling a culturally adequate account; and even technical adequacy may be beyond its reach.

1. Wealth.—I mention wealth first precisely because it is so invisible in most studies of economic inequality: indeed, it is common to think of "socioeconomic status" as a product of earned income, occupation, and education, with no regard to wealth at all. Perhaps wealth is ignored because Americans are far more private about their wealth than about their incomes. As one working man said to Paul Fussell, classes "can't be [defined by] money, ... because nobody ever knows that about you for sure."

"Wealth" in the sense of ownership of productive assets is no longer at the core of theories of economic inequality. But that is no justification for ignoring wealth as an element of economic status. Wealth is "distributed far less equally than income" in American society. Wealth barriers are strongly resistant to intergenerational mobility, and inequalities in wealth have greatly increased in the United States since the mid–1970s.

Wealth has a major impact on life chances, in that it diminishes the dependency of an individual's economic well-being upon occupation, income, educational attainment, or any of the other conventionally measured elements of relative economic position. Even the expectation of future wealth is highly significant in assessing an individual's economic circumstances. For example, a recent college graduate who expects to inherit wealth in the near future can accept a "meaningful" low-paying job in social services, the humanities, or the arts and can even create the appearance that he is living on his salary. But he knows that if he ever wants to buy a house, he need not save in advance for a down payment (an obstacle that would be insurmountable for nonwealthy people of his income); he knows that he need not save money for retirement, limit himself to jobs that provide health benefits, or worry that his choices will render him unable to afford to raise children. Wealth is thus a source of personal economic freedom in a broader sense: it is the freedom to take risks, to make mistakes, to be cushioned from market forces. To fail to consider wealth is to understate the extent both of economic inequality in the United States and of its intergenerational transmission. * * *

2. *Occupation.*—Occupation is of central importance to the sociological study of class; indeed, it is common for studies that claim to be about "social mobility" to in fact be solely concerned with occupational mobility. For classical Marxist theory, class is largely determined by position in relations of production, and the locus of attention is therefore on occupation. Marxism is not alone in stressing occupation: so do numerous other neo-Weberian, neo-Marxist, and structuralist theories. Where these theories disagree is on *why* occupation is so central to class. For classical Marxists, occupation matters because the all-important exploitative relationship between capital and labor is most clearly experienced through work. For social scientists in a Weberian tradition, occupation plays an important role in shaping life chances, although it may well not be the central line of political cleavage in a society. For any number of social scientists, in contrast, there is no perceived necessity to theorize the centrality of occupation; instead, occupation is used as a convenient proxy for other important criteria (for example, income, human capital investment, or likelihood of participation in internal labor markets) or for their combined effects.

The central tool of occupation-based class analysis is some sort of scheme for grouping and ranking occupations. These scales are works of social construction on a number of different levels, in which some principled basis must be found for decisionmaking—from the level of deciding how many occupational "classes" there are, to defining and labeling them, to assigning "jobs" to them.

Occupations might be ranked according to one or more of a number of criteria, some of which are the "social prestige" or honor they command, the quantity and quality of credentials or training necessary to perform them, the degree of supervisory or managerial authority they involve, the amount of autonomy they afford, and their income-earning potential. Shortcuts might be used—such as the white-collar versus blue-collar distinction—on the theory that they capture interrelationships of a number of the important criteria. The rankings can be designed to give priority to one criterion (for example, white-collar versus blue-collar employment) and then consider other criteria for purposes of secondary fine-tuning. But unless the ranking system is to be unworkably complex, choices must be made that are bound to produce unnuanced results. Indeed, the results often seem counterintuitive or downright wrong to lay sensibilities (and perhaps to expert sensibilities as well). For example, where collar color plays a central role in the occupational hierarchy, it is considered "upward mobility" to move, via deindustrialization, from a position as a skilled machinist to one as a file clerk. * * *

The picture within categories is no more compelling. Take, for example, the category "service class"—the "top" category—in the occupational scheme of Erikson and Goldthorpe. The category is defined not in terms of the "service sector," but rather in terms of the authors' distinction between "service relationships" and relationships governed by labor contracts—with the former involving the exercise of "delegated authority or specialized knowledge and expertise" and therefore requiring the employees to be accorded a fair measure of autonomy. This means, of course, that the category is (as it should be) theory-driven, based on the view that autonomy and discretion are central to the definition of class relations. But even given the authors' theoretical approach, the category includes occupations that vary widely in respects that are theory-relevant. For example, it includes "supervisors of non-manual workers" in the same category as "large proprietors" and "higher-grade professionals"—meaning that Bill Gates of Microsoft is grouped together with the Microsoft employees who have the power to hire and fire secretaries. All professionals and high-level technicians are included in the top category as well (meaning, for example, that a high school teacher and a physician would be in the same category).

These problems of aggregation have important consequences. Frank Parkin has observed that "there is what might be called a social and cultural 'buffer zone' " between classes and that "[m]ost mobility, being of a fairly narrow social span, involves the movement into and out of th[ese] zone[s] rather than movement between the class extremes." This means that the ability to detect mobility between groups crucially depends on where the lines between the groups are drawn.

Even after "occupations" have been defined and ranked, the work of social construction continues. The "occupations" found in social scientific occupational scales are not necessarily the "jobs" that people are hired to do, which are in turn not necessarily the "jobs" that people actually do. The process of assigning a person's "job" (in either sense) to one of a restricted number of "occupational" categories is a complex process, one that produces inevitable distortions. Take the job of "secretary," routinely classified in occupational scales as "white-collar clerical." Then consider the differences between a member of a secretarial pool in a medium-sized company and a secretary for a Supreme Court Justice or for the CEO of a major corporation. Or, for another example, consider the job of "professor," likely to be classified as "professional/managerial" in most scales. Then examine the differences between a professor who strings together part-time and temporary teaching jobs and a tenured professor at a major research university. In both of these comparisons, both individuals in the pair would be classified as having the same "occupation," but there are likely to be gaps between them in prestige, autonomy, job-related social networks, job benefits, and other aspects of life and work (beyond differences in income) that would go uncaptured by their occupational classification. The latter example points, in particular, to the dangers of occupational schemes that do not reflect the important concerns of segmented labor market theory.

Finally, the problems inherent in systems of occupational classification go far deeper than mere problems of measurement. As Frank Parkin notes,

> Sociological models are almost bound to take on something of the imprint of the age in which they are put together; and the model of class recommended in a period of general affluence and economic growth is likely to look a strange and awkward thing in a period haunted by the anxieties of inflation, recession, and economic stagnation.

Many of the leading occupational frameworks have an anachronistic quality to them: they are based on theories that no longer match the realities of work. With the demise of private-sector unions, there are likely to be fewer reasons in the future to be concerned about the class placement of good blue-collar jobs. Privatization is putting pressure on the line between public and private employment. Overseas outsourcing and decreasing stability of tenure in white-collar work, including such highly trained "knowledge" work as computer programming, is increasing the commonality of job conditions across the collar color line. Cost-containment pressures are limiting the autonomy of the traditional professions. The middle classes are far from becoming an undifferentiated proletariat. But the field is wide open for social scientists to theorize the emerging economic order (or orders)—and, in particular, to theorize the elements of comparative advantage among the different segments of the middle classes. * * *

3. *Income.*—Many scholars focus on income rather than on occupation as the major force in determining relative economic advantage. So do many lay people. For a number of reasons, income-based measures are particularly compatible with the economic individualist perspective. A stress on income suggests that the "goodies" that constitute relative economic advantage (for example, knowledge, education, cultural refinement, residence in safe suburbs, etc.) are commodities that can be purchased with money. An income measure is (at least potentially) agnostic as to the source of income and therefore tacitly rejects the theoretical position that the labor process is at the center of economic relations. Finally, mobility studies that focus on income tend to show higher rates of intergenerational economic mobility in the United States than do occupation-based studies.

Income-based measures also have the practical advantage that the measurement of income is more straightforward than the construction and implementation of occupational hierarchies. But income measurement presents a number of methodological problems that are capable of generating troublesome inaccuracies, both in measuring individual cases and in depicting economic mobility.

First among the issues in income measurement is the question of whose income it is appropriate to measure. Many studies of income inequality look solely at the incomes of individual earners—in part because this information is easily obtained (from employers and from tax returns, for example). But households routinely pool income, so that the more accurate measure of economic position is "family" or "household" income—the measurement of which is complex. Even at the level of the individual, conventional measures of income tend to understate the economic position of high-income individuals and families by excluding the value of employee benefits (for example, pensions and health benefits). And high-income taxpayers have the greatest opportunities to shelter income from taxation, which means that relying on tax returns as the source of income data understates their economic advantage.

Once a measure of income is agreed upon, there remains the question of how (if at all) to determine which income levels correspond to meaningful "breaks"—whether for purposes of a gradational or a categorical scheme. The first question is whether the breaks are to be determined in absolute terms, in relative terms, or in terms of the purchasing power of the income. Another important question is the number of groupings to use. A fairly common approach is to divide individuals into quintiles according to income and then study mobility between quintiles. But mobility between two adjacent quintiles—the most common form of mobility—may not be much mobility at all: it may simply represent a trading of positions between those with income locations at the quintile boundaries. As is the case with occupations, aggregation is necessary for the sake of simplicity, but the data loss inherent in aggregation makes the data harder to interpret—and may well overstate the degree of income mobility in this country. * * *

* * * Education is most often quantified as the number of years studied or the highest degree attained. But to treat education as a commodity in this fashion is to miss differences that are palpably relevant in work and in life. On the college level, for example, educational attainment is routinely judged in real life by type of school (four-year college versus community college, accredited versus unaccredited, day versus night program, and so forth); quality of school (often measured by selectivity or by academic reputation); content of study (with superiority of attainment measured for different purposes along a number of potentially conflicting dimensions ranging from raw difficulty to likelihood of producing cultural literacy); grades and honors; outside enrichment activities (overseas studies, for example); and numerous other more subjective judgments about the student's "character" as reflected through her curricular choices. * * *

5. *Consumption.*—It was turn-of-the-century economist Thorstein Veblen who most colorfully pointed to patterns of consumption as definitive of class aspiration and class position. Just as inflation can be measured by the relative cost of a fixed "basket" of food items, middle class status is often described as the possession of a "basket" of middle class goods. When middle class status is so defined, mobility into the middle classes is made easier to the extent that the items in the basket are easy to identify (through advertising, popular culture, and so forth) and easy to afford (as the Levittowns democratized suburbanization for white urbanites).

At first glance, it would seem easy to create a quick material index to capture the key elements of middle class material consumption. The consumption choice that most defines ascent into the middle classes is home ownership—which is why federal tax policy subsidizes home ownership and why the fact that young people cannot afford homes is viewed as a breach of faith with the middle class. A conventional consumption index might include such elements as home ownership; type of home (stand-alone versus townhouse versus mobile home); location (with suburban rating highest, except for the most exclusive city homes); home size; the ownership of cars (divided by old and new); the purchase of private primary or secondary education; number and kind of home electronics (with class ascending as the ratio of computers and cellular phones to televisions increases); the eating of meals outside of the home; and perhaps the nature of preferred leisure activities. Such a list—reworked as required by location (for example, the lack of home ownership and cars for many affluent New Yorkers)—could provide broad brush strokes to draw a line between lower and middle classes.

But as anyone with a good ear for the culture knows, these elements of consumption are not so much measures of class unity as they are fields for the social process (and processing) of distinction. Houses can be large because they have many bedrooms (for many children) or because they offer grand spaces for entertaining. Their grounds can be groomed "just right," too poorly, or too well ("If there's no crabgrass at all, we can infer an owner who spends much of his time worrying about slipping down a class or two. . . ."). The living room can be furnished from antique markets or from Sears. Cars can be utilitarian objects or displays of wealth and taste; they can be old in order to demonstrate patrician nonconcern with material values or because the family cannot afford new. Food cooked at home can be traditional or gourmet. The gulfs in consumption within the "middle class" category are, in short, huge. The advertising industry knows this, and it markets goods not to some broad aggregate "middle class," but to very carefully defined segments within it, defined as much by class aspiration and cultural orientation as by income.

The literature on consumption-based markers of class identity always generates laughter because it so sharply points out the anxiety of our attempts to manipulate social status. But consumption is no laughing matter. The material world is a minefield for the class-mobile, and every dollar spent a potentially fatal misstep. Consumption choices shape opportunities for conversation and for the formation of friendships and professional networks. (If tennis is the game of choice at your office, being a top-notch bowler does you no good; and try inviting your boss to dinner if your only table is in the kitchen.) They are, at the very least, the most easily observed markers of who you are and where you fit into the social hierarchy; they may in fact be an important part of the constitution of the self.

In sum, consumption is central to our (often unarticulated) cultural understandings of class. * * *

6. *Consciousness.*—Categorical and relational models of class are built upon the claim that the "classes" they describe have the potential for some degree of consciousness of themselves as classes. Class consciousness is important to students and practitioners of politics and for Marxist theorists, for whom the capacity of groups to organize and take action on the basis of class is all-important. It is also important to culturally oriented class theorists, for whom the system of *beliefs* about economic inequality is an important component of the system of economic inequality. And understanding the consciousness of social actors is necessary if their dignity is to be respected. * * *

7. *Interactions Among the Elements of Economic Inequality.*—The various measures of economic inequality I have reviewed are not independent of one another, but cannot freely substitute for one another. The acquisition of credentials may have some value in and of itself, but its greatest value is in securing a job that utilizes those credentials (or purports to utilize them) and brings one into contact with coworkers who have attained similar or greater educational levels. Access to high culture is limited by lack of income, but high income alone does not guarantee the "right" kind of understanding and the entree into cultured circles that goes with it. Within prestigious occupations, status declines in relation to the relative status of one's clients. Impressive attainments of cultural capital are of little use without the income and occupation to put them to work and the education to announce their presence on the surface of a resume. Resources can be rendered far less meaningful in their impact by coming too early or too late in the lifespan. Yet there is *some* measure of tolerance for gaps in the personal economic armor, *some* capacity for substitution.

What this means is that the relationships among the elements of economic privilege are not simply additive or multiplicative. They are structural. The factors contributing to relative economic advantage exist in a delicate balance and interact in space and time, as is generally true of the elements of society and culture. Their effects are likely to be nonhomogenous—meaning that the analysis of important socioeconomic factors and their interrelationships must be "disaggregated," with an eye to spotting relevant discontinuities. No easily administered, quantitative, composite index of the elements of economic inequality can capture their complex interrelationships.

To the extent that social scientific studies can simultaneously recognize and order the complexities of class, theory allows them to do so. At some point, it is necessary to stress one element and de-emphasize the others—to decide, for example, whether class or economic inequality is or is not fundamentally grounded in the realm of work. That is the role of theory. But the corollary of the centrality of theory is that in shopping for a measurement method and in deciding which factors form the core of relative economic advantage, the legal system will be buying a social theory—whether it admits it or not, and whether it wants one or not. * * *

8. *Outside Interactions: Race, Gender, and the Danger of False Claims of "Holding Class Constant."*—Up until this point, we have discussed class

as though it were a hermetically sealed category, impervious to other forms of inequality. But it is not. Just as economic variables interact, there are important interactions between each of those elements (and their interactions) and "outside" elements, such as race and gender.

Gender issues in class analysis are obscured (or perhaps underscored) by the fact that studies of social mobility commonly look only at the experience of men. The reason is that one of the most vexing problems in research on class and economic inequality is how to determine the economic position of women—both their individual status and their contributions as wage-earners and domestic producers to the economic status of their households and families. It should be obvious that ignoring the economic participation of women distorts the picture of household or family economic status in important ways. * * * Indeed, there is ample evidence that the interactions among economic factors differ for men and women, that women are less able than men to take personal advantage of inherited and earned economic and social capital, and that occupational schemes developed for men are less accurate for women.

Theorizing and measuring the economic status of members of racial and ethnic minority groups pose problems of equal magnitude. I will limit myself to only a few illustrations of the many ways in which strategies for the transmission of economic advantage from parents to children have historically been less successful for blacks than for whites.

Part of the problem is that black upward mobility is so recent a phenomenon for many black families. In a study of intergenerational elements of educational attainment in the black middle class, Zena Smith Blau found that when black and white families of seemingly similar socioeconomic status (measured by the occupational status of the higher ranking parent and both parents' educational attainment) were compared, black families "in fact, possess fewer resources than those white families." The key difference was that white parents' own socioeconomic status translated into a more privileged social milieu. This means, Blau concluded, that parental occupational and educational gains in white families "are more readily translated into access to middle-class influences and role models than is usually the case for black families." There is also evidence, from Coleman, that although "black parents . . . show a greater interest in their child's education and greater aspirations for his success in education than do white parents of the same economic level," the interests of black, Hispanic, and Native American parents do not translate as well into improved academic performance for the child.

More generally, the past and present effects of discrimination mean that blacks and whites who appear to have the same occupation, education, or residential situation when a simple metric is used may well not occupy the same status in reality. When black families live in the suburbs, they tend to live in predominantly black suburbs that lie closer to the inner city and that are less advantaged in their public and private services. Blacks are more likely to be employed in the public sector, where civil-service employment rules diminish the ability of parents to use their influence to provide jobs for children in their community. Although patterns of segregation are breaking down, black professionals are historically more likely to serve within the black community, which means that having professionals in the family opens up a less advantaged social network for blacks than for whites. Blacks in the professions remain more likely than whites to be employed in occupations at the lower end of the category in credentials, prestige, and income. Blacks have less wealth than whites of the same income level. And skin color remains a powerful obstacle to the translation of wealth, occupation, income, education, and cultural capital into even the most basic dignity in public life. As one Jewish carpenter explained to an ethnographer in Brooklyn, New York, my hometown: "The problem is that we see blacks as a mass. It is unfortunate. We can't tell the difference between a black pimp and a black mailman. When I look at a white man, I can tell what social class he is, but if he is colored, I can't tell." There is little gain to be had from class mobility if its public indicia are overwhelmed by the more socially salient reality of race.

These examples demonstrate that if an overly simplistic measurement of class is used, systematic differences in the present and historical economic condition of blacks will be ignored, and the socioeconomic privilege of middle class blacks will be overstated. It is highly likely, given the complexity of the phenomenon, that even the most earnest efforts at designing an adequate metric will fail. And the result of failure will likely be that the law's official discourse will falsely proclaim that in the contest for economic equality, class has been "held constant"—and that if blacks still lose, their loss must be because of some postulated lack of individual or collective merit. That is a significant danger for anyone concerned with racial justice in this country.

———

NOTES AND QUESTIONS

1. Class position. How would you describe your class position? What was your parents' class position when you were growing up? Has it changed over time? Of the factors Malamud lists as relevant to the determination of a person's "class," which do you think are the most determinative? Is class a relevant category in American life?

2. The American Dream. A central ideology of American democracy and markets is that economic mobility is fully open to all citizens with talent and a strong work ethic. The asserted classlessness of American society remains a cherished characterization of the opportunity structure here. Americans venerate our tradition of individual achievement. Opposition to the accumulation of great wealth and the hereditary privileges associated with such concentrations of political, social and economic power have been a feature of American political rhetoric since the founding of the nation.

Political scientist Jennifer Hochschild uses a quote from former President Bill Clinton to encapsulate the "American Dream":

> The American Dream that we were all raised on is a simple but powerful one—if you work hard and play by the rules you should be given a chance to go as far as your God-given ability will take you.

President Bill Clinton, Speech to Democratic Leadership Council, 1993.

> In one sentence, President Clinton has captured the bundle of shared, even unconsciously presumed, tenets about achieving success that make up the ideology of the American Dream. Those tenets answer the questions: *Who* may pursue the American Dream? In *what* does the pursuit consist? *How* does one successfully pursue the dream? *Why* is the pursuit worthy of our deepest commitment?

> The answer to "who" in the standard ideology is "everyone, regardless of ascriptive traits, family background, or personal history." The answer to "what" is "the reasonable anticipation, though not the promise, of success, however it is defined." The answer to "how" is "through actions and traits under one's control." The answer to "why" is "true success is associated with virtue."

JENNIFER L. HOCHSCHILD, FACING UP TO THE AMERICAN DREAM: RACE, CLASS, AND THE SOUL OF THE NATION 18 (1995). How does belief in the American Dream shape attitudes toward class?

3. The immigrant story. Related to the American Dream is another central ideology in American life, one that relates to the possibility of group rather than individual class mobility. The United States is a nation of immigrants, and many Americans can tell stories of a great-grandfather or grandfather who came to this country with "nothing" and was able to "work his way up," eventually passing wealth along to his children. Nathan Glazer puts this kind of story into a larger framework:

> [T]he American polity has * * * been defined by a steady expansion of the definition of those who may be included in it to the point where it now includes all humanity; * * * the United States has become the first great nation that defines itself not in terms of ethnic origin but in terms of adherence to common rules of citizenship; * * * no one is now excluded from the broadest access to what the society makes possible; and * * * this access is combined with a considerable concern for whatever is necessary to maintain group identity and loyalty.

Nathan Glazer, *The Emergence of an American Ethnic Pattern, in* FROM DIFFERENT SHORES: PERSPECTIVES ON RACE AND ETHNICITY IN AMERICA 13, 14 (Ronald Tataki ed., 1987).

Is the immigrant story of individual and group social and economic mobility despite ethnic difference a story that can be told about all groups? Robert Blauner argues that there is a key historical difference between "colonized" and "immigrant" minorities. As he sets forth his argument, he identifies three assumptions on which it rests:

The first assumption is that racial groups in America are, and have been, colonized peoples; therefore their social realities cannot be understood in the framework of immigration and assimilation that is applied to European ethnic groups. The second assumption is that the racial minorities share a common situation of oppression, from which a potential political unity is inferred. The final assumption is that there is a historical connection between the third world abroad and the third world within.

Robert Blauner, *Colonized and Immigrant Minorities, in* From Different Shores: Perspectives on Race and Ethnicity in America 149, 149 (Ronald Takaki ed., 1987).

4.   *San Antonio Independent School District v. Rodriguez.* Malamud is pessimistic about American law's ability to adequately deal with issues of class. As you read *San Antonio Independent School District v. Rodriguez,* think about how Justice Powell is trying to conceptualize wealth discrimination. Does he adequately distinguish this case from the precedents he discusses? Does "class" fit into the ways lawyers think about "discrimination"? How might Malamud conceptualize the issues faced by the litigants in the case?

B.   The Constitution: Wealth and Class

San Antonio Independent School District v. Rodriguez

411 U.S. 1 (1973).

■ Mr. Justice Powell delivered the opinion of the Court.

This suit attacking the Texas system of financing public education was initiated by Mexican–American parents whose children attend the elementary and secondary schools in the Edgewood Independent School District, an urban school district in San Antonio, Texas. They brought a class action on behalf of schoolchildren throughout the State who are members of minority groups or who are poor and reside in school districts having a low property tax base. * * *

I

The first Texas State Constitution, promulgated upon Texas' entry into the Union in 1845, provided for the establishment of a system of free schools. Early in its history, Texas adopted a dual approach to the financing of its schools, relying on mutual participation by the local school districts and the State. As early as 1883, the state constitution was amended to provide for the creation of local school districts empowered to levy ad valorem taxes with the consent of local taxpayers for the "erection . . . of school buildings" and for the "further maintenance of public free schools." Such local funds as were raised were supplemented by funds distributed to each district from the State's Permanent and Available School Funds. * * *

Until recent times, Texas was a predominantly rural State and its population and property wealth were spread relatively evenly across the State. Sizable differences in the value of assessable property between local school districts became increasingly evident as the State became more industrialized and as rural-to-urban population shifts became more pronounced. The location of commercial and industrial property began to play a significant role in determining the amount of tax resources available to each school district. These growing disparities in population and taxable property between districts were responsible in part for increasingly notable differences in levels of local expenditure for education.

In due time it became apparent to those concerned with financing public education that contributions from the Available School Fund were not sufficient to ameliorate these disparities. * * *

Recognizing the need for increased state funding to help offset disparities in local spending and to meet Texas' changing educational requirements, the state legislature in the late 1940's undertook a thorough evaluation of public education with an eye toward major reform. In 1947, an 18-member committee, composed of educators and legislators, was appointed to explore alternative systems in other States and to propose a funding scheme that would guarantee a minimum or basic educational offering to each child and that would help overcome interdistrict disparities in taxable resources. The Committee's efforts led to the passage of the Gilmer–Aikin bills, named for the Committee's co-chairmen, establishing the Texas Minimum Foundation School Program. Today, this Program accounts for approximately half of the total educational expenditures in Texas.

The Program calls for state and local contributions to a fund earmarked specifically for teacher salaries, operating expenses, and transportation costs. The State, supplying funds from its general revenues, finances approximately 80% of the Program, and the school districts are responsible—as a unit—for providing the remaining 20%. The districts' share, known as the Local Fund Assignment, is apportioned among the school districts under a formula designed to reflect each district's relative taxpaying ability. * * *

In the years since this program went into operation in 1949, expenditures for education—from state as well as local sources—have increased steadily.

* * *

The school district in which appellees reside, the Edgewood Independent School District, has been compared throughout this litigation with the Alamo Heights Independent School District. This comparison between the least and most affluent districts in the San Antonio area serves to illustrate the manner in which the dual system of finance operates and to indicate the extent to which substantial disparities exist despite the State's impressive progress in recent years. Edgewood is one of seven public school districts in the metropolitan area. Approximately 22,000 students are enrolled in its 25 elementary and secondary schools. The district is situated in the core-city sector of San Antonio in a residential neighborhood that has little commercial or industrial property. The residents are predominantly of Mexican–American descent: approximately 90% of the student population is Mexican–American and over 6% is Negro. The average assessed property value per pupil is $5,960—the lowest in the metropolitan area—and the median family income ($4,686) is also the lowest. At an equalized tax rate of $1.05 per $100 of assessed property—the highest in the metropolitan area—the district contributed $26 to the education of each child for the 1967–1968 school year above its Local Fund Assignment for the Minimum Foundation Program. The Foundation Program contributed $222 per pupil for a state-local total of $248. Federal funds added another $108 for a total of $356 per pupil.

Alamo Heights is the most affluent school district in San Antonio. Its six schools, housing approximately 5,000 students, are situated in a residential community quite unlike the Edgewood District. The school population is predominantly "Anglo," having only 18% Mexican–Americans and less than 1% Negroes. The assessed property value per pupil exceeds $49,000, and the median family income is $8,001. In 1967–1968 the local tax rate of $.85 per $100 of valuation yielded $333 per pupil over and above its contribution to the Foundation Program. Coupled with the $225 provided from that Program, the district was able to supply $558 per student. Supplemented by a $36 per-pupil grant from federal sources, Alamo Heights spent $594 per pupil.

* * *

The District Court held that the Texas system discriminates on the basis of wealth in the manner in which education is provided for its people.[1] Finding that wealth is a "suspect" classification and that education is a "fundamental" interest, the District Court held that the Texas system could be sustained only if the State could show that it was premised upon some compelling state interest.[2] On this issue the court concluded that "[n]ot only are defendants unable to demonstrate compelling state interests . . . they fail even to establish a reasonable basis for these classifications."[3]

Texas virtually concedes that its historically rooted dual system of financing education could not withstand the strict judicial scrutiny that this Court has found appropriate in reviewing legislative judgments that interfere with fundamental constitutional rights or that involve suspect classifications. If, as previous decisions have indicated, strict scrutiny means that the State's system is not entitled to the usual presumption of validity, that the State rather than the complainants must carry a "heavy burden of justification," that the State must demonstrate that its educational system has been structured with "precision," and is "tailored" narrowly to serve legitimate objectives and that it has selected the "less drastic means" for effectuating its objectives, the Texas financing system

1. 337 F. Supp., at 282.   **3.** *Id.*, at 284.
2. *Id.*, at 282–284.

and its counterpart in virtually every other State will not pass muster. The State candidly admits that "[n]o one familiar with the Texas system would contend that it has yet achieved perfection." Apart from its concession that educational financing in Texas has "defects" and "imperfections," the State defends the system's rationality with vigor and disputes the District Court's finding that it lacks a "reasonable basis."

This, then, establishes the framework for our analysis. We must decide, first, whether the Texas system of financing public education operates to the disadvantage of some suspect class or impinges upon a fundamental right explicitly or implicitly protected by the Constitution, thereby requiring strict judicial scrutiny. If so, the judgment of the District Court should be affirmed. If not, the Texas scheme must still be examined to determine whether it rationally furthers some legitimate, articulated state purpose and therefore does not constitute an invidious discrimination in violation of the Equal Protection Clause of the Fourteenth Amendment.

II

The District Court's opinion does not reflect the novelty and complexity of the constitutional questions posed by appellees' challenge to Texas' system of school financing. In concluding that strict judicial scrutiny was required, that court relied on decisions dealing with the rights of indigents to equal treatment in the criminal trial and appellate processes, and on cases disapproving wealth restrictions on the right to vote. Those cases, the District Court concluded, established wealth as a suspect classification. Finding that the local property tax system discriminated on the basis of wealth, it regarded those precedents as controlling. It then reasoned, based on decisions of this Court affirming the undeniable importance of education, that there is a fundamental right to education and that, absent some compelling state justification, the Texas system could not stand.

We are unable to agree that this case, which in significant aspects is *sui generis*, may be so neatly fitted into the conventional mosaic of constitutional analysis under the Equal Protection Clause. Indeed, for the several reasons that follow, we find neither the suspect-classification nor the fundamental-interest analysis persuasive.

A

The wealth discrimination discovered by the District Court in this case, and by several other courts that have recently struck down school-financing laws in other States, is quite unlike any of the forms of wealth discrimination heretofore reviewed by this Court. Rather than focusing on the unique features of the alleged discrimination, the courts in these cases have virtually assumed their findings of a suspect classification through a simplistic process of analysis: since, under the traditional systems of financing public schools, some poorer people receive less expensive educations than other more affluent people, these systems discriminate on the basis of wealth. This approach largely ignores the hard threshold questions, including whether it makes a difference for purposes of consideration under the Constitution that the class of disadvantaged "poor" cannot be identified or defined in customary equal protection terms, and whether the relative—rather than absolute—nature of the asserted deprivation is of significant consequence.

* * *

The case comes to us with no definitive description of the classifying facts or delineation of the disfavored class. Examination of the District Court's opinion and of appellees' complaint, briefs, and contentions at oral argument suggests, however, at least three ways in which the discrimination claimed here might be described. The Texas system of school financing might be regarded as discriminating (1) against "poor" persons whose incomes fall below some identifiable level of poverty or who might be characterized as functionally "indigent," or (2) against those who are relatively poorer than others, or (3) against all those who, irrespective of their personal incomes, happen to reside in relatively poorer school districts. Our task must be to ascertain whether, in fact, the Texas system has been shown to discriminate on any of these possible bases and, if so, whether the resulting classification may be regarded as suspect.

The precedents of this Court provide the proper starting point. The individuals, or groups of individuals, who constituted the class discriminated against in our prior cases shared two distinguishing characteristics: because of their impecunity they were completely unable to pay for some desired benefit, and as a consequence, they sustained an absolute deprivation of a meaningful opportunity to enjoy that benefit. In *Griffin v. Illinois*[4] and its progeny, the Court invalidated state laws that prevented an indigent criminal defendant from acquiring a transcript, or an adequate substitute for a transcript, for use at several stages of the trial and appeal process. The payment requirements in each case were found to occasion *de facto* discrimination against those who, because of their indigency, were totally unable to pay for transcripts. And the Court in each case emphasized that no constitutional violation would have been shown if the State had provided some "adequate substitute" for a full stenographic transcript. * * *

Likewise, in *Douglas v. California*,[5] a decision establishing an indigent defendant's right to court-appointed counsel on direct appeal, the Court dealt only with defendants who could not pay for counsel from their own resources and who had no other way of gaining representation. *Douglas* provides no relief for those on whom the burdens of paying for a criminal defense are relatively speaking, great but not insurmountable. Nor does it deal with relative differences in the quality of counsel acquired by the less wealthy.

Williams v. Illinois[6] and *Tate v. Short*[7] struck down criminal penalties that subjected indigents to incarceration simply because of their inability to

4. 351 U.S. 12 (1956).   **6.** 399 U.S. 235 (1970).

5. 372 U.S. 353 (1963).   **7.** 401 U.S. 395 (1971).

pay a fine. Again, the disadvantaged class was composed only of persons who were totally unable to pay the demanded sum. Those cases do not touch on the question whether equal protection is denied to persons with relatively less money on whom designated fines impose heavier burdens. The Court has not held that fines must be structured to reflect each person's ability to pay in order to avoid disproportionate burdens. Sentencing judges may, and often do, consider the defendant's ability to pay, but in such circumstances they are guided by sound judicial discretion rather than by constitutional mandate.

Finally, in *Bullock v. Carter*[8] the Court invalidated the Texas filing-fee requirement for primary elections. Both of the relevant classifying facts found in the previous cases were present there. The size of the fee, often running into the thousands of dollars and, in at least one case, as high as $8,900, effectively barred all potential candidates who were unable to pay the required fee. As the system provided "no reasonable alternative means of access to the ballot",[9] inability to pay occasioned an absolute denial of a position on the primary ballot.

Only appellees' first possible basis for describing the class disadvantaged by the Texas school-financing system—discrimination against a class of defineably "poor" persons—might arguably meet the criteria established in these prior cases. Even a cursory examination, however, demonstrates that neither of the two distinguishing characteristics of wealth classifications can be found here. First, in support of their charge that the system discriminates against the "poor," appellees have made no effort to demonstrate that it operates to the peculiar disadvantage of any class fairly definable as indigent, or as composed of persons whose incomes are beneath any designated poverty level. Indeed, there is reason to believe that the poorest families are not necessarily clustered in the poorest property districts. A recent and exhaustive study of school districts in Connecticut concluded that "[i]t is clearly incorrect . . . to contend that the 'poor' live in 'poor' districts. . . . Thus, the major factual assumption of *Serrano*—that the educational financing system discriminates against the 'poor'—is simply false in Connecticut." Defining "poor" families as those below the Bureau of the Census "poverty level," the Connecticut study found, not surprisingly, that the poor were clustered around commercial and industrial areas—those same areas that provide the most attractive sources of property tax income for school districts. Whether a similar pattern would be discovered in Texas is not known, but there is no basis on the record in this case for assuming that the poorest people—defined by reference to any level of absolute impecunity—are concentrated in the poorest districts.

Second, neither appellees nor the District Court addressed the fact that, unlike each of the foregoing cases, lack of personal resources has not occasioned an absolute deprivation of the desired benefit. The argument here is not that the children in districts having relatively low assessable property values are receiving no public education; rather, it is that they are

---

8.   405 U.S. 134 (1972).   **9.**   *Id.*, at 149.

receiving a poorer quality education than that available to children in districts having more assessable wealth. Apart from the unsettled and disputed question whether the quality of education may be determined by the amount of money expended for it, a sufficient answer to appellees' argument is that, at least where wealth is involved, the Equal Protection Clause does not require absolute equality or precisely equal advantages. Nor indeed, in view of the infinite variables affecting the educational process, can any system assure equal quality of education except in the most relative sense. Texas asserts that the Minimum Foundation Program provides an "adequate" education for all children in the State. * * *

For these two reasons—the absence of any evidence that the financing system discriminates against any definable category of "poor" people or that it results in the absolute deprivation of education—the disadvantaged class is not susceptible of identification in traditional terms.

As suggested above, appellees and the District Court may have embraced a second or third approach, the second of which might be characterized as a theory of relative or comparative discrimination based on family income. Appellees sought to prove that a direct correlation exists between the wealth of families within each district and the expenditures therein for education. That is, along a continuum, the poorer the family the lower the dollar amount of education received by the family's children. * * *

If, in fact, these correlations could be sustained, then it might be argued that expenditures on education—equated by appellees to the quality of education—are dependent on personal wealth. Appellees' comparative-discrimination theory would still face serious unanswered questions, including whether a bare positive correlation or some higher degree of correlation is necessary to provide a basis for concluding that the financing system is designed to operate to the peculiar disadvantage of the comparatively poor, and whether a class of this size and diversity could ever claim the special protection accorded "suspect" classes. These questions need not be addressed in this case, however, since appellees' proof fails to support their allegations or the District Court's conclusions. * * *

This brings us, then, to the third way in which the classification scheme might be defined—*district* wealth discrimination. Since the only correlation indicated by the evidence is between district property wealth and expenditures, it may be argued that discrimination might be found without regard to the individual income characteristics of district residents. Assuming a perfect correlation between district property wealth and expenditures from top to bottom, the disadvantaged class might be viewed as encompassing every child in every district except the district that has the most assessable wealth and spends the most on education. Alternatively, as suggested in Mr. Justice Marshall's dissenting opinion, * * * the class might be defined more restrictively to include children in districts with assessable property which falls below the statewide average, or median, or below some other artificially defined level.

However described, it is clear that appellees' suit asks this Court to extend its most exacting scrutiny to review a system that allegedly discriminates against a large, diverse, and amorphous class, unified only by the common factor of residence in districts that happen to have less taxable wealth than other districts. The system of alleged discrimination and the class it defines have none of the traditional indicia of suspectness: the class is not saddled with such disabilities, or subjected to such a history of purposeful unequal treatment, or relegated to such a position of political powerlessness as to command extraordinary protection from the majoritarian political process. * * *

[The Court turns to the question of whether education is a fundamental right protected by the Constitution.]

Lindsey v. Normet,[10] decided only last Term, firmly reiterates that social importance is not the critical determinant for subjecting state legislation to strict scrutiny. The complainants in that case, involving a challenge to the procedural limitations imposed on tenants in suits brought by landlords under Oregon's Forcible Entry and Wrongful Detainer Law, urged the Court to examine the operation of the statute under "a more stringent standard than mere rationality."[11] The tenants argued that the statutory limitations implicated "fundamental interests which are particularly important to the poor," such as the "need for decent shelter" and the "right to retain peaceful possession of one's home."[12] MR. JUSTICE WHITE'S analysis, in his opinion for the Court is instructive:

> "We do not denigrate the importance of decent, safe and sanitary housing. But the Constitution does not provide judicial remedies for every social and economic ill. We are unable to perceive in that document any constitutional guarantee of access to dwellings of a particular quality or any recognition of the right of a tenant to occupy the real property of his landlord beyond the term of his lease, without the payment of rent.... *Absent constitutional mandate*, the assurance of adequate housing and the definition of landlord-tenant relationships are legislative, not judicial, functions."[13]

Similarly, in *Dandridge v. Williams*,[14] the Court's explicit recognition of the fact that the "administration of public welfare assistance ... involves the most basic economic needs of impoverished human beings,"[15] provided no basis for departing from the settled mode of constitutional analysis of legislative classifications involving questions of economic and social policy. * * *

[The Court concludes that education is not a fundamental right and that the Texas system survives the rational basis test.]

■ MR. JUSTICE MARSHALL, with whom MR. JUSTICE DOUGLAS concurs, dissenting.

* * * In my view, * * * it is inequality—not some notion of gross inadequacy—of educational opportunity that raises a question of denial of

---

10. 405 U.S. 56 (1972).

11. *Id.*, at 73.

12. *Ibid.*

13. *Id.*, at 74 (emphasis supplied).

14. 397 U.S. 471 (1970).

15. *Id.*, at 485.

equal protection of the laws. I find any other approach to the issue unintelligible and without directing principle. Here, appellees have made a substantial showing of wide variations in educational funding and the resulting educational opportunity afforded to the schoolchildren of Texas. This discrimination is, in large measure, attributable to significant disparities in the taxable wealth of local Texas school districts. This is a sufficient showing to raise a substantial question of discriminatory state action in violation of the Equal Protection Clause.

———

NOTES AND QUESTIONS

1. **Economic inequality.** One issue that bears both on how we measure class and on our understanding of the American Dream is the issue of economic inequality. In this section, we look at readings that investigate economic inequality along two of the dimensions of class described by Malamud—income and wealth.

2. **The right to education under state constitutions.** Forty-eight out of fifty states have education clauses in their state constitutions. *See* Michael Heise, *State Constitutions, School Finance Litigation, and the "Third Wave": From Equity to Adequacy*, 68 Temple L. Rev. 1151, 1163 (1995). See Paul L. Tractenberg, *Using the Law to Advance the Public Interest: Rutgers Law School and Me*, 51 Rutgers L. Rev. 1001, 1011–12 (Rutgers Law Review Symposium 1999); Susan H. Bitensky, *Theoretical Foundations for a Constitutional Right to Education Under the U.S. Constitution: A Beginning to the End of a National Education Crisis*, 86 Nw. U. L. Rev. 550 (1992); Molly McUsic, *The Use of Education Clauses in School Finance Reform Litigation*, 28 Harv. J. on Legis. 307 (1991); James S. Liebman, *Three Strategies for Implementing Brown Anew, in* Race in America: The Struggle for Equality 112, 120–21 (Herbert Hill & James E. Jones, Jr. eds., 1993).

C. Class and Inequality—Historical Perspectives

● Income Inequality

Economic Development in Indian Country: Will Capitalism or Socialism Succeed?

80 Oreg. L. Rev. 757 (2001).

■ Robert J. Miller

* * * European settlers and early Americans misunderstood tribal economies and property rights. Even today, there seems to be an almost universal misunderstanding that American Indian cultures had and still

have little or no appreciation or understanding of private property owner-ship and private, free market, capitalist economic activities. This mistaken idea could not be further from the truth. It appears to be based almost exclusively on the idea that most American Indian tribes did not consider that land could be privately owned but instead thought that tribal lands were communally owned. Thus, the European and American colonists came to believe that Indians did not believe in or understand private property and capitalist principles.

In contrast, as in all societies, Indians and their governing bodies had to provide for the daily needs of their families and their tribes. Hence, Indians were continuously involved in the production of food, tools, cloth-ing, shelter and all sorts of objects for personal use. Indians also regularly traded goods with other peoples from near and far both for survival and to make life as comfortable as possible. The majority, if not all, of this trade was conducted in free market situations where private individuals volun-tarily came together to buy and sell items they had manufactured for sale and which they exchanged by barter and sometimes even sold for money. Startlingly, perhaps, it appears that the only way in which Indian princi-ples of economics and private property differed from the European/Ameri-can concepts was in the conflicting views these societies had on the private ownership of land. The actual purpose for the European and American settlers to discount or intentionally to ignore how Indians viewed and used private property may have been to provide justification for stealing Indian property rights with a clear conscience. * * *

From its inception, the United States copied the long-standing English political and economic policies towards tribes. The economic goal of the English government had been to make Indians dependent on English goods by integrating them into the colonial marketplace. Politically, England wanted to keep the peace with tribes by preventing the colonists and traders from provoking the tribes to warfare through the colonists' uncon-trolled trade and land grabs. Thus, England and the American colonial governments established regulations and bonding and licensing schemes to control who traded with Indians and how the trade was conducted. * * *

* * * Government trading houses were operated at twenty-eight loca-tions all across the frontier from 1795–1822. This process assisted in making Indians dependent on the federal government as they bought their supplies at the federal stores, and it also contributed to shutting the door to free trade and free markets in Indian country.

The federal control of free trade and economic activities in Indian country inhibited the operation of a free capitalist market and most economic development in Indian country. In essence, Congress preempted the American free market and became "a surrogate for Indian decision making in . . . economic relations with the settlers." The federal executive branch also participated in this isolation of Indian country from the American capitalist economy. Most treaties with tribes required that the tribe limit their previous trading habits or only trade with the United States government. Many tribes later realized that they were suffering from an absence of access to trade and they negotiated in subsequent treaties to take steps to increase trade and to gain better access to goods.

One result of the Trade and Intercourse Era policy, intentional or not, was to start the process of shutting Indians, tribes, and their lands and resources out of the American capitalist economy and free trade market. Congress caused this result by refusing to allow any use of tribal assets, such as for leasing land for grazing or farming, or for mineral or timber development, by imposing strict limits on traders interacting with Indians, and by creating the federal trading houses which dominated the early American trade with Indians. The policy had the concrete impact of cutting Indian and tribal assets out of the American economy. Indians were thus severely limited if not totally prevented from participating in the American capitalist economy to whatever extent they might have wished to participate. Consequently, Indians have lived in governmentally controlled, quasi-socialist economies since 1790.

* * *

For decades preceding the 1880s, liberal thinkers, politicians, "Friends of the Indians," and Christian reformers had been closely examining federal Indian policy. The predominant idea on how to deal with tribes was to civilize and christianize individual Indians and liberate them from the control and communal living of tribal life. This policy was designed to bring Indians into the American "melting pot" by assimilating them into mainstream society. This era in federal Indian policy also had the explicit goals of breaking up tribal ownership of land, ending tribal existence, and, most importantly, opening reservation lands to non-Indian settlement. In fact, the desire of non-Indians to own reservation lands and to open tribal lands and assets to the American economy may have been the prime motivation behind the allotment policy.

The allotment aspect of the policy was designed to break up the communally owned tribal lands into individual plots, or allotments, to be owned by individual Indians and operated as farms. The General Allotment Act and the tribal-specific allotment acts that followed during 1890–1910, generally provided for the division or allotment of reservations into 160 or 80 acre plots to be given to individual tribal members who could later become U.S. citizens. To protect economically unsophisticated Indians, the United States retained legal ownership of these allotments by holding the land in trust for twenty-five year periods during which the land was inalienable and not taxable by the states. The idea was that Indians over time would become astute in business affairs and farming and could eventually handle their own business matters. Significantly, reservation land not allotted to Indians was considered "surplus" and was sold for non-Indian settlement. Most tribes did not have sufficient populations to allot their entire reservation to just tribal members. Hence, the United States sold the surplus lands to non-Indians and today many reservations have much higher non-Indian than Indian populations.

In the 1890s, Congress also began opening reservation assets to the American economy, which had been closed by the Trade and Intercourse policy, by allowing the development of minerals and timber in Indian country and the leasing of reservation land to non-Indians for grazing and farming. Congress also utilized Indian lands for other purposes for the U.S. economy, such as for telephone, telegraph, and railroad rights of ways. Indian lands have also often been used for dams and reclamation and irrigation projects that benefitted non-Indians.

An important aspect of the Allotment Era policy did provide for individual Indians to gain private ownership of land free from tribal and federal governmental restraints. It appears, however, to be an exaggeration to state that the policy had the economic goal to make Indians and tribal economies capitalist in nature. Rather than having economic goals, the purpose of allotment was to turn Indians into "civilized" and "christian-ized" American citizens and small scale farmers based on the model of white Americans. In regard to its effect on the economy in Indian country, the Allotment policy ultimately created long-term problems that have stifled individual Indian and tribal economic activity to this very day.

Subsequent events severely limited any private benefits accruing to Indians from the allotment and ownership of ex-tribal lands. Many Indians quickly sold or lost their allotments to tax foreclosures once they received alienable patents or deeds to their land. Thus, the lands are no longer in Indian ownership to help Indians or tribal governments with economic development. Another problem, which was not foreseen, is the "fractionali-zation" of ownership of the individual allotments that remain in Indian ownership, which occurred because the original allottees died and their property passed intestate to ever larger numbers of heirs. Many individual allotments on reservations today have hundreds of Indian owners. This has led to a serious lack of coordinated ownership and decision making over allotments and a nightmare of record keeping and legal work to manage and utilize these lands for tribal and federal governments. In this situation, many Indians today have severe problems putting together and operating viably sized pieces of real property to make economic endeavors feasible. It is often easier for Indians passively to lease these properties than to gain consensus on projects or to consolidate enough land to develop a business or project involving allotments on reservation. * * *

The Indian Reorganization Era of Federal Indian policy ran from the early 1930s to about 1945 and was marked by passage of the Indian Reorganization Act (IRA) in 1934. Under the IRA, the United States completely reversed its allotment policy of breaking up reservations and attempting to destroy tribal governments and instead decided to support tribal governments. By the 1930s, it had become obvious that allotment of tribal lands and the attempt to assimilate Indians had led to disaster. A two-year study of Indian country showed that reservation Indians were living in far worse economic and social conditions after four decades of allotment and assimilation than they had been in 1887. Consequently, among many other goals, the IRA ended the federal policy of allotting tribal lands to individuals and placed a freeze on the sale or loss of any remaining trust allotments still held by individual Indians.

The federal government now actively encouraged and assisted tribes to organize governments and adopt constitutions and bylaws. The IRA also had a very explicit goal to increase economic activity and development in Indian country. The IRA attempted to accomplish this goal by providing for the formation of federally chartered tribal corporations to engage in economic development and business. This provision is very significant to the modern day predominant role of tribal governments in reservation economies.

The IRA allowed tribes to apply to the Secretary of the Interior for federal charters to create tribal corporations through which they could operate businesses, hire attorneys, enter contracts, and engage in litigation. The official policy of the IRA was to encourage tribal business and economic development to be undertaken by tribal governments and tribal institutions even if it worked to exclude individual Indians from the economic activity. The tribal corporations formed under section 17 of the IRA were granted the power to manage their own property, to buy and sell and manage any property, and "such further powers as may be incidental to the conduct of corporate business. . . ." Tribal corporations could also borrow money from a ten million dollar revolving loan fund authorized by Congress for tribal economic development purposes. The loan fund was created primarily to serve tribal economic enterprises although tribes could transfer loans to tribal members. The IRA arguably had a significant socialistic impact on the economic life on reservations because the federal and tribal efforts and concentration on economic development became focused on the tribal government as the entity to start and operate reservation businesses, even to the exclusion of individuals.

For this very reason, when the IRA was proposed it encountered virulent opposition by groups claiming that it promoted socialism and communism. The various opponents of the IRA thought, among other things, that assimilation of Indians should continue, that Indians were inhibited in their liberty and citizenship rights by being subject to tribal governmental control, and that reservation lands and assets should continue to be available to the American market. The charges of communism and socialism that were used to fight and later to reverse the IRA might have only been a form of "red-scare" politics in the 1930s. However, many different groups and persons described the IRA and the alleged intention to keep Indian people segregated from white society and living in a communal, tribal society as being the start of communism and socialism in America. Even Congresspersons opposed the Act and worked to amend and repeal it because of concerns about socialism.

Notwithstanding any "red scare" claims of socialism, and the serious doubts about the IRA in the 1930s, it is certain that the IRA established strong tribal governments in Indian country that today have pervasive control over the economic life and economies of reservations. Modern day observers contend that the IRA imposed tribal governments, tribally controlled economies, and artificial economies on Indian country. In fact, the IRA had such an all encompassing tribal business orientation that many of the tribal governmental entities that were formed under the IRA are today officially called the tribal business committee or tribal business council. This is no surprise since the IRA encouraged tribes "to organize along the lines of modern business corporations" and demanded that economic development proceed with a "tribal approach." Tribal governments and their role in operating tribal businesses have become so intertwined that even the federal government and others have often confused and failed to distinguish between the activities and identity of the tribal governments formed under IRA section 16 and the tribal corporations formed under IRA section 17. Commentators agree that the IRA has led to tribal governments starting and operating businesses, something they are ill-equipped to do.

The economic aspects of the IRA have led to problems for tribes and individual Indians with regard to economic development in Indian country. The primary problem beyond leading tribal governments to becoming the main economic force on reservations is that the IRA also helped create pervasive federal bureaucratic control over Indian economic activity. For example, while tribes could now hire their own attorneys, the "choice of counsel and fixing of fees [was] subject to the approval of the Secretary of the Interior." Furthermore, federal control of tribal economic activity had already been greatly increased in 1871 when Congress enacted a statute that required the Secretary of the Interior to approve all contracts tribes might sign "relative to their lands." The 1871 act and the IRA's creation of new tribal governments and businesses led to extensive federal agency oversight and direction of tribal governments in their political and business decisions. The federal control and direction of tribes became overwhelming in the IRA Era and for decades afterwards. It is universally accepted, however, that federal bureaucratic review and approval authority over tribal economic activities is a death knell to effective and efficient business decision making, yet this is the situation tribal economic development found itself in during the IRA Era and thereafter. It is no surprise, then, that tribal economies did not develop well under the IRA and the subsequent federal control over tribal decisions, assets and resources. Tribal and federal management of reservation economies and direct control over most of the reservation jobs and economic activity since the IRA Era has not created economic success. Indeed, the IRA has almost prevented the success on reservations of individual entrepreneurship and free market capitalism and instead has created governmentally controlled economies that do not function very well.

Black Wealth/White Wealth: New Perspectives on Racial Inequality

■ MELVIN L. OLIVER & THOMAS M. SHAPIRO 12–13, 13–16, 16–18 (1995).

Disparities in wealth between blacks and whites are not the product of haphazard events, inborn traits, isolated incidents or solely contemporary individual accomplishments. Rather, wealth inequality has been structured over many generations through the same systemic barriers that have hampered blacks throughout their history in American society: slavery, Jim Crow, so-called de jure discrimination, and institutionalized racism. How these factors have affected the ability of blacks to accumulate wealth, however, has often been ignored or incompletely sketched. * * *

The close of the Civil War transformed four million former slaves from chattel to freedmen. Emerging from a legacy of two and a half centuries of legalized oppression, the new freedmen entered Southern society with little or no material assets. With the north's military victory over the South freshly on the minds of Republican legislators and white abolitionists, there were rumblings in the air of how the former plantations and the property of Confederate soldiers and sympathizers would be confiscated and divided among the new freedmen to form the basis of their new status in society. The slave's often-cited demand of "forty acres and a mule" fueled great anticipation of a new beginning based on land ownership and a transfer of skills developed under slavery into the new economy of the South. Whereas slave muscle and skills had cleared the wilderness and made the land productive and profitable for plantation owners, the new vision saw the freedmen's hard work and skill generating income and resources for the former slaves themselves. W.E.B. DuBois, in his *Black Reconstruction in America*, called this prospect America's chance to be a modern democracy.

Initially it appeared that massive land redistribution from the Confederates to the freedmen would indeed become a reality. Optimism greeted Sherman's March through the South, and especially his Order 15, which confiscated plantations and redistributed them to black soldiers. Such wartime actions were eventually rescinded and some soldiers who had already started to cultivate the land and build new lives were forced to give up their claims. Real access to land for the freedman had to await the passage of the Southern Homestead Act in 1866, which provided a legal basis and mechanism to promote black landownership. In this legislation public land already designated in the 1862 Homestead Act, which applied only to non-Confederate whites but not blacks, was now opened up to settlement by former slaves in the tradition of homesteading that had helped settle the West. The amount of land involved was substantial, a total of forty-six million acres. Applicants in the first two years of the Homestead Act were limited to only eighty acres, but subsequently this amount increased to 160 acres. The Freedmen's Bureau administered the program, and there was every reason to believe that in reasonable time slaves would be transformed from farm laborers to yeomanry farmers.

This social and economic transformation never occurred. The Southern Homestead Act failed to make newly freed blacks into a landowning class or to provide what Gunnar Myrdal in *An American Dilemma* called "a basis of real democracy in the United States." Indeed, features of the legislation worked against its use as a tool to empower blacks in their quest for land. First, instead of disqualifying former Confederate supporters as the previous act had done, the 1866 legislation allowed all persons who applied for land to swear that they had not taken up arms against the Union or given aid and comfort to the enemies. This opened the door to massive white applications for land. One estimate suggests that over three-quarters (77.1 percent) of the land applicants under the act were white. In addition, much of the land was poor swampland and it was difficult for black or white applicants to meet the necessary homesteading requirements because they could not make a decent living off the land. What is more important, blacks had to face the extra burden of racial prejudice and discrimination along with the charging of illegal fees, expressly discriminatory court challenges and court decisions, and land speculators. While these barriers faced all poor and illiterate applicants, Michael Lanza has stated in his *Agrarianism and Reconstruction Politics* that "The freedmen's badge of color and previous servitude complicated matters to almost incomprehensible proportions."

Gunnar Myrdal's *An American Dilemma* provides the most cogent explanation of the unfulfilled promise of land to the freeman in an anecdotal passage from a white Southerner. Asked, "Wouldn't it have been better for the white man and the Negro" if the land had been provided?

The old man remarked emphatically:

> "No, for it would have made the Negro 'uppity.'" ... and "the real reason ... why it wouldn't do, is that we are having a hard time now keeping the nigger in his place, and if he were a landowner, he'd think he was a bigger man than old Grant, and there would be no living with him in the Black District.... Who'd work the land if the niggers had farms of their own?"

Nevertheless, the extent of black landowning was remarkable given the economically deprived backgrounds from which the slaves emerged. * * *

The suburbanization of America was principally financed and encouraged by actions of the federal government, which supported suburban growth from the 1930s through the 1960s by way of taxation, transportation, and housing policy. Taxation policy, for example, provided greater tax savings for businesses relocating to the suburbs than to those who stayed and made capital improvements to plants in central city locations. As a consequence, employment opportunities steadily rose in the suburban rings of the nation's major metropolitan areas. In addition, transportation policy encouraged freeway construction and subsidized cheap fuel and mass-produced automobiles. These factors made living on the outer edges of cities both affordable and relatively convenient. However, the most important government policies encouraging and subsidizing suburbanization focused on housing. In particular, the incentives that government programs gave for the acquisition of single-family detached housing spurred both the development and financing of the tract home, which became the hallmark of suburban living. While these governmental policies collectively enabled over thirty-five million families between 1933 and 1978 to participate in homeowner equity accumulation, they also had the adverse effect of constraining black Americans' residential opportunities to central-city ghettos of major U.S. metropolitan communities and denying them access to one of the most successful generators of wealth in American history—the suburban tract home.

This story begins with the government's initial entry into home financing. Faced with mounting foreclosures, President Roosevelt urged passage of a bill that authorized the Home Owners Loan Corporation (HOLC). According to Kenneth Jackson's *Crabgrass Frontier*, the HOLC "refinanced tens of thousands of mortgages in danger of default or foreclosure." Of more importance to this story, however, it also introduced standardized appraisals of the fitness of particular properties and communities for both individual and group loans. In creating "a formal and uniform system of appraisal, reduced to writing, structured in defined procedures, and implemented by individuals only after intensive training, government appraisals institutionalized in a rational and bureaucratic framework a racially discriminatory practice that all but eliminated black access to the suburbs and to government mortgage money." Charged with the task of determining the "useful or productive life of housing" they considered to finance, government agents methodically included in their procedures the evaluation of the racial composition or potential racial composition of the community. Communities that were changing racially or were already black were deemed undesirable and placed in the lowest category. The categories, assigned various colors on a map ranging from green for the most desirable, which included new, all-white housing that was always in demand, to red, which included already racially mixed or all-black, old, and undesirable areas, subsequently were used by Federal Housing Authority (FHA) loan officers who made loans on the basis of these designations.

Established in 1934, the FHA aimed to bolster the economy and increase employment by aiding the ailing construction industry. The FHA ushered in the modern mortgage system that enabled people to buy homes on small down payments and at reasonable interest rates, with lengthy repayment periods and full loan amortization. The FHA's success was remarkable: housing starts jumped from 332,000 in 1936 to 619,000 in 1941. The incentive for home ownership increased to the point where it became, in some cases, cheaper to buy a home than to rent one. As one former resident of New York City who moved to suburban New Jersey pointed out, "We had been paying $50 per month rent, and here we come up and live for $29.00 a month." This included taxes, principal, insurance, and interest.

This growth in access to housing was confined, however, for the most part to suburban areas. The administrative dictates outlined in the original act, while containing no antiurban bias, functioned in practice to the neglect of central cities. Three reasons can be cited: first, a bias toward the financing of single-family detached homes over multifamily projects favored open areas outside of the central city that had yet to be developed over congested central-city areas; second, a bias toward new purchases over repair of existing homes prompted people to move out of the city rather than upgrade or improve their existing residences; and third, the continued use of the "unbiased professional estimate" that made older homes and communities in which blacks or undesirables were located less likely to receive approval for loans encouraged purchases in communities where race was not an issue.

While the FHA used as its model the HOLC's appraisal system, it provided more precise guidance to its appraisers in its *Underwriting Manual*. The most basic sentiment underlying the FHA's concern was its fear that property values would decline if a rigid black and white segregation was not maintained. The *Underwriting Manual* openly stated that "if a neighborhood is to retain stability, it is necessary that properties shall continue to be occupied by the same social and racial classes" and further recommended that "subdivision regulations and suitable restrictive covenants are the best way to ensure such neighborhood stability. The FHA's recommended use of restrictive covenants continued until 1949, when, responding to the Supreme Court's outlawing of such covenants in 1948 (*Shelley v. Kraemer*), it announced that 'as of February 15, 1950, it would not insure mortgages on real estate subject to covenants.'"

Even after this date, however, the FHA's discriminatory practices continued to have an impact on the continuing suburbanization of the white population and the deepening ghettoization of the black population. While exact figures regarding the FHA's discrimination against blacks are not available, data by county show a clear pattern of "redlining" in central-city counties and abundant loan activity in suburban counties.

The FHA's actions have had a lasting impact on the wealth portfolios of black Americans. Locked out of the greatest mass-based opportunity for wealth accumulation in American history, African Americans who desired and were able to afford home ownership found themselves consigned to central-city communities where their investments were affected by the "self-fulfilling prophecies" of the FHA appraisers: cut off from sources of new investment their homes and communities deteriorated and lost value in comparison to those homes and communities that FHA appraisers deemed desirable. One infamous housing development of the period—Levittown—provides a classic illustration of the way blacks missed out on this asset-accumulating opportunity. Levittown was built on a mass scale, and housing there was eminently affordable, thanks to the FHA's and VHA's accessible financing, yet as late as 1960 "not a single one of the Long Island Levittown's 82,000 residents was black."

Race, Gender & Work: A Multicultural Economic History of Women in the United States

(1991)

■ TERESA AMOTT & JULIE MATTHEI

Chapter 4—The Soul of the *Tierra Madre*: Chicano Women

Much of the complex economic history of the Chicana/o people centers on struggles over land and national boundaries. The earliest ancestors of today's Chicanas were members of many different Indian nations who inhabited the lands now known as Mexico and the U.S. Southwest, including the Aztec, Pueblo, and Tlaxcalán. Beginning in the sixteenth century, these indigenous peoples were conquered by Spanish invaders. Sexual relations, many of them forced, between Spanish men and indigenous (and African slave) women soon produced a *mestiza/o* population. Through colonization and settlement, the Spanish extended their territories north. The vast country of Mexico was formed after independence from Spain in 1821, stretching from what we know today as Guatemala up through Texas, California, Arizona, Colorado, New Mexico, and Nevada, and even into parts of Oregon, Utah, and Idaho.

In the early nineteenth century, Anglo settlers from the deep South migrated to Texas, sowing the seeds for a war between Mexico and the United States that eventually led to the annexation of almost half of Mexico's territories in 1848. From then up until the present, Mexican citizens have migrated to the United States in search of work, and many have become U.S. citizens. * * *

As a result of this history, the economics and politics of the U.S. Chicana population are inextricably linked to those of Mexico. * * *

* * * [In Mexico, t]he period between 1834 and 1846 has been called the "Golden Age of the ranchos" because land became increasingly concentrated in the hands of a few wealthy ranchers, all of them of Spanish ancestry (or claiming to be). Next in the class hierarchy were *mestiza/o* small ranchers and farmers. Following them were *mestiza/o* artisans, skilled workers, laborers, and seasonal workers in the cattle industry. Lowest of all were the Indians, the chief source of manual labor.

The new country quickly became engaged in a bitter struggle with Anglo settlers in what we know now as Texas, culminating in the Mexican–American War of 1846. Anglo settlers began arriving in Mexico's northern territories in the early 1800s, granted land first by the Spanish government and later by Mexico, which encouraged migration to the sparsely settled area. Most anglo settlers came to farm or raise cattle, but starting in 1829, an increasing number brought slaves from the deep South to work cotton plantations. Although there were some landed Mexicans in Texas, by the 1830s, Anglo Texans outnumbered Mexicans by five to one. To discourage slavery and stem further Anglo immigration, Mexico prohibited importation of slaves in 1830. In 1835, Anglo Texans, chafing under these restrictions, began the Texas Revolt to free themselves from Mexican rule. After losses at the Alamo and Goliad, they defeated Mexican forces in 1837 and set up the Lone Star Republic. In 1845, Texas became part of the United States. One researcher documented the transfer of land ownership from Mexicans to Anglos in Nueces County, Texas in the 1800s: "at the beginning of the Texas Revolt in 1835 every foot of land in Nueces County was held under

Mexican land grants, two years prior to the Civil War all but one had passed out of Mexican hands, and by 1883 none was held by Mexicans.''

* * * The [Mexican–American] war ended with the Treaty of Guadalupe Hidalgo in 1848, in which Mexico was forced to give up more than half her territory—including California, New Mexico, Utah, Nevada, Colorado, and Arizona—in exchange for $15 million. In the annexation, the United States acquired lands populated by over 80,000 Spanish-speaking people, most of them *mestiza/o* and *criolla/o*. The quarter of a million Indian peoples in these lands now faced U.S. rather than Mexican efforts to subordinate or exterminate them.

While the language of the Treaty contained protections for Mexican land titles and water rights, the United States government made no attempt to safeguard these rights. Thus the annexation of Mexican territories placed annexed Mexicans in a vulnerable position. As Anglo settlers flooded into the Southwest, they took over the lands and wealth of the Mexican inhabitants, reducing most of the Mexican population in the Southwest to a landless, politically disempowered group.

Some of the *ricos* were able to protect their landholdings by intermarrying with Anglo newcomers. In San Antonio, for instance, marriage records between 1837 and 1860 show that one daughter from almost every *rico* family had married an Anglo. Such marriages were attractive to Anglo men since daughters as well as sons inherited property in Mexican families.

But many other Mexicans, particularly those with smaller landholdings or subsistence plots, lost their lands through a variety of devices familiar to us from the history of American Indians. Anglo domination of the political and judicial systems, along with the use of force and violence, ensured Anglo economic domination. For instance, when floods, drought, or economic downturns made it difficult for Mexican ranchers to pay taxes imposed by the Anglo-controlled government, their lands were quickly sold to Anglos. California passed a law in 1851 that encouraged squatters to take over Mexican lands. Lynching was also a common tool employed by Anglos to terrorize Mexicans into leaving their lands. Some estimate that more Mexicans were lynched between 1850 and 1930 than African Americans during the same period.

　　　　* * *

During the second half of the nineteenth century, the southwestern economy expanded rapidly. Subsistence farming began to give way to huge ranches and cash crops as railroads made it possible for southwestern products to reach eastern markets. Displaced Mexicans found jobs as seasonal agricultural workers, domestic workers, or miners in isolated, company-controlled towns.

　　　　* * *

Chapter 7—Climbing Gold Mountain: Asian American Women

From 1840 through World War II, Asian immigrants—first Chinese, then Japanese, and finally Filipinas/os—were recruited as a low-wage second-class labor force by employers in the western United States and Hawaii. The U.S. legal system denied Asian immigrants the legal rights which had been accorded their European counterparts, relying on the 1790 naturalization law that restricted the privilege of citizenship to "free white persons." When the law was revised after the Civil War to make African Americans eligible for citizenship, the phrase "persons of African descent" was added, and the law continued to bar Asian immigrants from naturalizing. Unable to become citizens, Asian immigrants remained permanent "aliens" (non-citizens), and whites were able to pass numerous laws which restricted their rights simply by referring to their alien status. For example, in the early twentieth century California passed laws which prevented Asian immigrants from purchasing land. However, children of immigrant Asians were allowed to become citizens and escape these restrictions if they were born in the United States.

On the West Coast, where the vast majority of Asians lived, whites bolstered their own relative economic status at the expense of Asian immigrants. White employers achieved higher profits by using Asians as low-wage replacements for white workers and as strikebreakers. White workers resented the threat Asians appeared to pose to wages and unionizing efforts. Self-employed whites felt threatened by Asian successes in small business.

To defend their economic positions, whites formed broad-based movements to restrict Asian immigration and even to send migrants back to Asia. Filipino historian Paul Valdez wrote of the anti-"Oriental" movement of the 1920s, "They used to pass out leaflets saying that the Japanese were taking the lands from the Americans, the Chinese were taking the businesses, and the Filipinos were taking the women." Under these pressures, white-controlled federal and state governments passed close to 50 laws specifically aimed at restricting and subordinating Asian immigrants between 1850 and 1950. These sentiments culminated in laws excluding further immigration. Chinese immigration was cut off in 1882 and 1892; Japanese in 1907–08 and 1924; Indian in 1917; and Filipina/o in 1934.

Whites also discriminated against second-generation Asians who, unlike white ethnics, could not disguise their ethnicity by speaking English and adopting European American ways. These barriers to upward mobility in the labor market compelled many Asian Americans to seek advancement through self-employment in family-based businesses—for the Chinese, laundries and restaurants; for the Japanese, truck farming; and for the Koreans, grocery stores.

D. Wealth, Class and Economic Mobility—The Intergenerational Effects

In what follows, three writers: two influential Princeton economists, Alan B. Krueger and Paul Krugman, as well as conservative *New York Times* columnist, David Brooks, explore the emerging problem of decreasing economic mobility and pinched opportunity structures arising from inherited economic status across all socio-economic groups. This research and argument poses a direct challenge to that part of our national story that depends on belief in the power of individual effort, merit, and achievement. If parent-child wealth correlations are as strong as these economists argue, it reveals a largely hidden force that will preserve economic inequality for a long time. This force could be described as the new "invisible hand," shaping markets and posing a threat to the democratic distribution of political power.

The Sticky Ladder

N.Y. TIMES, Jan. 25, 2005, at A19.

■ DAVID BROOKS

In his Inaugural Address President Bush embraced the grandest theme of American foreign policy—the advance of freedom around the world. Now that attention is turning to the State of the Union address, it would be nice if he would devote himself as passionately to the grandest theme of domestic policy—social mobility.

The United States is a country based on the idea that a person's birth does not determine his or her destiny. Our favorite stories involve immigrants climbing from obscurity to success. Our amazing work ethic is predicated on the assumption that enterprise and effort lead to ascent. "I hold the value of life is to improve one's condition," Lincoln declared.

The problem is that in every generation conditions emerge that threaten to close down opportunity and retard social mobility. Each generation has to reopen the pathways to success.

Today, for example, we may still believe American society is uniquely dynamic, but we're deceiving ourselves. European societies, which seem more class driven and less open, have just as much social mobility as the United States does.

And there are some indications that it is becoming harder and harder for people to climb the ladder of success. *The Economist* magazine gathered much of the recent research on social mobility in America. The magazine concluded that the meritocracy is faltering: "Would-be Horatio Algers are finding it no easier to climb from rags to riches, while the children of the privileged have a greater chance of staying at the top of the social heap."

Economists and sociologists do not all agree, but it does seem there is at least slightly less movement across income quintiles than there was a few decades ago. Sons' income levels correlate more closely to those of their fathers. The income levels of brothers also correlate more closely. That suggests that the family you were born into matters more and more to how you will fare in life. That's a problem because we are not supposed to have a hereditary class structure in this country.

But we're developing one. In the information age, education matters more. In an age in which education matters more, family matters more, because as James Coleman established decades ago, family status shapes educational achievement.

At the top end of society we have a mass upper-middle class. This is made up of highly educated people who move into highly educated neighborhoods and raise their kids in good schools with the children of other highly educated parents. These kids develop wonderful skills, get into good colleges (the median family income of a Harvard student is now $150,000), then go out and have their own children, who develop the same sorts of wonderful skills and who repeat the cycle all over again.

In this way these highly educated elites produce a paradox—a hereditary meritocratic class.

It becomes harder for middle-class kids to compete against members of the hypercharged educated class. Indeed, the middle-class areas become more socially isolated from the highly educated areas.

And this is not even to speak of the children who grow up in neighborhoods in which more boys go to jail than college, in which marriage is not the norm before child-rearing, in which homes are often unstable, in which long-range planning is absurd, in which the social skills you need to achieve are not even passed down.

In his State of the Union address, President Bush is no doubt going to talk about his vision of an ownership society. But homeownership or pension ownership is only part of a larger story. The larger story is the one Lincoln defined over a century ago, the idea that this nation should provide an open field and a fair chance so that all can compete in the race of life.

Today that's again under threat, but this time from barriers that are different than the ones defined by socialists in the industrial age. Now, the upper class doesn't so much oppress the lower class. It just outperforms it generation after generation. Now the crucial inequality is not only finance capital, it's social capital. Now it is silly to make a distinction between economic policy and social policy.

We can spend all we want on schools. But if families are disrupted, if the social environment is dysfunctional, bigger budgets won't help.

President Bush spoke grandly and about foreign policy last Thursday, borrowing from Lincoln. Lincoln's other great cause was social mobility. That's worth embracing too.

Economic Scene; The Apple Falls Close to the Tree, Even in the Land of Opportunity

N.Y. TIMES, Nov. 14, 2002, at C1.

■ ALAN B. KRUEGER

It seems increasingly apparent that the secret to success is to have a successful parent. Consider some prominent examples: George H. W. Bush and George W. Bush; Bobby Bonds and Barry Bonds; Henry Fonda and Jane Fonda; Estee Lauder and Ronald Lauder; Julio Iglesias and Enrique Iglesias; Sam Walton and Jim, John, S. Robson and Alice Walton.

As more recent and better data have become available, economists have marked up their estimate of the impact of parents' socioeconomic status on their children's likelihood of economic success.

It turns out that the famous line attributed to Andrew Carnegie—"from shirt-sleeves to shirt-sleeves in three generations"—is an understatement. Five or six generations are probably required, on average, to erase the advantages or disadvantages of one's economic origins.

This represents a marked departure from past thinking. In the 1980s, when Gary S. Becker of the University of Chicago pioneered the economic theory of intergenerational transmission of economic status, it was believed that the correlation between a father's and son's income was only around 0.15—less than half the correlation between fathers' and sons' heights.

The early studies suggested that if a father's income was twice the average, his son's expected income would be 15 percent above average, and his grandson's just 2 percent above average. This is fast "regression to the mean," a concept Sir Francis Galton used to describe the progression of offspring toward the average height.

Landmark studies published by Gary Solon of the University of Michigan and David J. Zimmerman of Williams College in The American Economic Review a decade ago, however, led economists to revise substantially upward the estimate of the similarity of fathers' and sons' incomes. They noted that income fluctuated for idiosyncratic reasons from year to year—an employee could lose a job, for example—so estimates that depended on a single year were based on "noisy" data. Also, the samples previously analyzed represented only a narrow slice of the population at different points in individual careers. These factors caused the correlation in annual incomes to understate the correlation in "lifetime" incomes.

Averaging earnings over five years produced a correlation of around 0.40 for fathers' and sons' earnings—the same as the correlation between their heights. If people's incomes were represented by their heights, the similarity in income between generations would resemble the similarity observed in the heights of fathers and sons.

New studies by Bhashkar Mazumder of the Federal Reserve Bank of Chicago suggest that the similarity in income is even greater. Using Social Security records, he averaged fathers' earnings over 16 years (1970 through 1985) and sons' earnings over four years (1995 through 1998), and found that around 65 percent of the earnings advantage of fathers was transmitted to sons. The wider window provides a better reflection of lifetime earnings.

Also, the samples previously analyzed represented only a narrow slice of the population at different points in individual careers. These factors caused the correlation in annual incomes to understate the correlation in "lifetime" incomes.

The relationship between fathers' and daughters' earnings was just as strong.

So that grandson (or granddaughter) mentioned previously could expect to earn 42 percent more than average. After five generations, the earnings advantage would still be 12 percent.

Furthermore, the degree of persistence across generations is strong for both rich and poor. Thomas Hertz of American University finds that a child born in the bottom 10 percent of families ranked by income has a 31 percent chance of ending up there as an adult and a 51 percent chance of ending up in the bottom 20 percent, while one born in the top 10 percent has a 30 percent chance of staying there and a 43 percent chance of being in the top 20 percent.

In another study, David I. Levine of Berkeley and Dr. Mazumder found that the impact of parental income on adult sons' income increased from 1980 to the early 1990s.

Why is there such a strong connection between parents' socioeconomic status and their children's? A large part of the answer involves intergenerational transmission of cognitive ability and educational level.

But these factors can "explain at most three-fifths of the intergenerational transmission of economic status," Samuel Bowles and Herbert Gintis of the University of Massachusetts wrote in the latest issue of The Journal of Economic Perspectives. They suggest that the intergenerational transmission of race, geographical location, height, beauty, health status and personality also plays a significant role.

Arthur S. Goldberger of the University of Wisconsin has long questioned whether knowledge of the "heritability" of income is of much use. Even if the father-son correlation is high because traits that affect earning power are inherited, well-designed interventions could still be cost effective and improve the lot of the disadvantaged.

To take an extreme example, the correlation in incomes between fathers and sons was high in South Africa under apartheid because race is an inherited trait. The abolition of apartheid reduced the correlation. The organization of society matters.

Perhaps the only legitimate use of the intergenerational correlation in income is to characterize economic mobility. The data challenge the notion that the United States is an exceptionally mobile society. If the United States stands out in comparison with other countries, it is in having a more static distribution of income across generations with fewer opportunities for advancement.

Anders Bjorklund of Stockholm University and Markus Jantti of the University of Tampere in Finland, for example, find more economic mobility in Sweden than in the United States. Only South Africa and Britain have as little mobility across generations as the United States.

Luke Skywalker and Darth Vader are an unusual father-son pair; in most families, the apple does not fall so far from the tree.

————

The Sons Also Rise

N.Y. TIMES, Nov. 22, 2002, at A27.

■ PAUL KRUGMAN

America, we all know, is the land of opportunity. Your success in life depends on your ability and drive, not on who your father was.

Just ask the Bush brothers. Talk to Elizabeth Cheney, who holds a specially created State Department job, or her husband, chief counsel of the Office of Management and Budget. Interview Eugene Scalia, the top lawyer at the Labor Department, and Janet Rehnquist, inspector general at the Department of Health and Human Services. And don't forget to check in with William Kristol, editor of The Weekly Standard, and the conservative commentator John Podhoretz.

What's interesting is how little comment, let alone criticism, this roll call has occasioned. It might be just another case of kid-gloves treatment by the media, but I think it's a symptom of a broader phenomenon: inherited status is making a comeback.

It has always been good to have a rich or powerful father. Last week my Princeton colleague Alan Krueger wrote a column for The Times surveying statistical studies that debunk the mythology of American social mobility. "If the United States stands out in comparison with other countries, he wrote, 'it is in having a more static distribution of income across generations with fewer opportunities for advancement.' " And Kevin Phillips, in his book "Wealth and Democracy," shows that robber-baron fortunes have been far more persistent than legend would have it.

But the past is only prologue. According to one study cited by Mr. Krueger, the heritability of status has been increasing in recent decades. And that's just the beginning. Underlying economic, social and political trends will give the children of today's wealthy a huge advantage over those who chose the wrong parents.

For one thing, there's more privilege to pass on. Thirty years ago the C.E.O. of a major company was a bureaucrat—well paid, but not truly wealthy. He couldn't give either his position or a large fortune to his heirs. Today's imperial C.E.O.'s, by contrast, will leave vast estates behind—and they are often able to give their children lucrative jobs, too. More broadly, the spectacular increase in American inequality has made the gap between the rich and the middle class wider, and hence more difficult to cross, than it was in the past.

Meanwhile, one key doorway to upward mobility—a good education system, available to all—has been closing. More and more, ambitious parents feel that a public school education is a dead end. It's telling that Jack Grubman, the former Salomon Smith Barney analyst, apparently sold his soul not for personal wealth but for two places in the right nursery school. Alas, most American souls aren't worth enough to get the kids into the 92nd Street Y.

Also, the heritability of status will be mightily reinforced by the repeal of the estate tax—a prime example of the odd way in which public policy and public opinion have shifted in favor of measures that benefit the wealthy, even as our society becomes increasingly class-ridden.

It wasn't always thus. The influential dynasties of the 20th century, like the Kennedys, the Rockefellers and, yes, the Sulzbergers, faced a public suspicious of inherited position; they overcame that suspicion by demonstrating a strong sense of noblesse oblige, justifying their existence by standing for high principles. Indeed, the Kennedy legend has a whiff of Bonnie Prince Charlie about it; the rightful heirs were also perceived as defenders of the downtrodden against the powerful.

But today's heirs feel no need to demonstrate concern for those less fortunate. On the contrary, they are often avid defenders of the powerful against the downtrodden. Mr. Scalia's principal personal claim to fame is his crusade against regulations that protect workers from ergonomic hazards, while Ms. Rehnquist has attracted controversy because of her efforts to weaken the punishment of health-care companies found to have committed fraud.

The official ideology of America's elite remains one of meritocracy, just as our political leadership pretends to be populist. But that won't last. Soon enough, our society will rediscover the importance of good breeding, and the vulgarity of talented upstarts.

For years, opinion leaders have told us that it's all about family values. And it is—but it will take a while before most people realize that they meant the value of coming from the right family.

TABLE 2.1. "Like Parent, Like Child—Recent Studies Find That There Is Less Income Mobility from One Generation to Another than Previously Believed."

	Chance of Children Attaining Each Income Level		
Parent's Income	Top Quintile	Middle Quintile	Bottom Quintile
Top 20%	42.3%	16.5%	6.3%
Middle 20%	15.3%	25.0%	17.3%
Bottom 20%	7.3%	18.4%	37.3%

SOURCE: *Thomas Hertz, American University.*

For Richer

N.Y. TIMES, Oct. 20, 2002, § 6 (magazine), at 62.

■ PAUL KRUGMAN

I.   THE DISAPPEARING MIDDLE

When I was a teenager growing up on Long Island, one of my favorite excursions was a trip to see the great Gilded Age mansions of the North

Shore. Those mansions weren't just pieces of architectural history. They were monuments to a bygone social era, one in which the rich could afford the armies of servants needed to maintain a house the size of a European palace. By the time I saw them, of course, that era was long past. Almost none of the Long Island mansions were still private residences. Those that hadn't been turned into museums were occupied by nursing homes or private schools.

For the America I grew up in—the America of the 1950's and 1960's—was a middle-class society, both in reality and in feel. The vast income and wealth inequalities of the Gilded Age had disappeared. Yes, of course, there was the poverty of the underclass—but the conventional wisdom of the time viewed that as a social rather than an economic problem. Yes, of course, some wealthy businessmen and heirs to large fortunes lived far better than the average American. But they weren't rich the way the robber barons who built the mansions had been rich, and there weren't that many of them. The days when plutocrats were a force to be reckoned with in American society, economically or politically, seemed long past.

Daily experience confirmed the sense of a fairly equal society. The economic disparities you were conscious of were quite muted. Highly educated professionals—middle managers, college teachers, even lawyers—often claimed that they earned less than unionized blue-collar workers. Those considered very well off lived in split-levels, had a housecleaner come in once a week and took summer vacations in Europe. But they sent their kids to public schools and drove themselves to work, just like everyone else.

But that was long ago. The middle-class America of my youth was another country.

We are now living in a new Gilded Age, as extravagant as the original. Mansions have made a comeback. Back in 1999 this magazine profiled Thierry Despont, the "eminence of excess," an architect who specializes in designing houses for the superrich. His creations typically range from 20,000 to 60,000 square feet; houses at the upper end of his range are not much smaller than the White House. Needless to say, the armies of servants are back, too. So are the yachts. Still, even J.P. Morgan didn't have a Gulfstream.

As the story about Despont suggests, it's not fair to say that the fact of widening inequality in America has gone unreported. Yet glimpses of the lifestyles of the rich and tasteless don't necessarily add up in people's minds to a clear picture of the tectonic shifts that have taken place in the distribution of income and wealth in this country. My sense is that few people are aware of just how much the gap between the very rich and the rest has widened over a relatively short period of time. In fact, even bringing up the subject exposes you to charges of "class warfare," the "politics of envy" and so on. And very few people indeed are willing to talk about the profound effects—economic, social and political—of that widening gap.

Yet you can't understand what's happening in America today without understanding the extent, causes and consequences of the vast increase in inequality that has taken place over the last three decades, and in particular the astonishing concentration of income and wealth in just a few hands. To make sense of the current wave of corporate scandal, you need to understand how the man in the gray flannel suit has been replaced by the imperial C.E.O. The concentration of income at the top is a key reason that the United States, for all its economic achievements, has more poverty and lower life expectancy than any other major advanced nation. Above all, the growing concentration of wealth has reshaped our political system: it is at the root both of a general shift to the right and of an extreme polarization of our politics.

But before we get to all that, let's take a look at who gets what.

II. THE NEW GILDED AGE

The Securities and Exchange Commission hath no fury like a woman scorned. The messy divorce proceedings of Jack Welch, the legendary former C.E.O. of General Electric, have had one unintended benefit: they have given us a peek at the perks of the corporate elite, which are normally hidden from public view. For it turns out that when Welch retired, he was granted for life the use of a Manhattan apartment (including food, wine and laundry), access to corporate jets and a variety of other in-kind benefits, worth at least $2 million a year. The perks were revealing: they illustrated the extent to which corporate leaders now expect to be treated like *ancien régime* royalty. In monetary terms, however, the perks must have meant little to Welch. In 2000, his last full year running G.E., Welch was paid $123 million, mainly in stock and stock options.

Is it news that C.E.O.'s of large American corporations make a lot of money? Actually, it is. They were always well paid compared with the average worker, but there is simply no comparison between what executives got a generation ago and what they are paid today.

Over the past 30 years most people have seen only modest salary increases: the average annual salary in America, expressed in 1998 dollars (that is, adjusted for inflation), rose from $32,522 in 1970 to $35,864 in 1999. That's about a 10 percent increase over 29 years—progress, but not much. Over the same period, however, according to Fortune magazine, the average real annual compensation of the top 100 C.E.O.'s went from $1.3 million—39 times the pay of an average worker—to $37.5 million, more than 1,000 times the pay of ordinary workers.

The explosion in C.E.O. pay over the past 30 years is an amazing story in its own right, and an important one. But it is only the most spectacular indicator of a broader story, the reconcentration of income and wealth in the U.S. The rich have always been different from you and me, but they are far more different now than they were not long ago—indeed, they are as different now as they were when F. Scott Fitzgerald made his famous remark.

That's a controversial statement, though it shouldn't be. For at least the past 15 years it has been hard to deny the evidence for growing inequality in the United States. Census data clearly show a rising share of income going to the top 20 percent of families, and within that top 20 percent to the top 5 percent, with a declining share going to families in the middle. Nonetheless, denial of that evidence is a sizable, well-financed industry. Conservative think tanks have produced scores of studies that try to discredit the data, the methodology and, not least, the motives of those who report the obvious. Studies that appear to refute claims of increasing inequality receive prominent endorsements on editorial pages and are eagerly cited by right-leaning government officials. Four years ago Alan Greenspan (why did anyone ever think that he was nonpartisan?) gave a keynote speech at the Federal Reserve's annual Jackson Hole conference that amounted to an attempt to deny that there has been any real increase in inequality in America.

* * * Meanwhile, politically motivated smoke screens aside, the reality of increasing inequality is not in doubt. In fact, the census data understate the case, because for technical reasons those data tend to undercount very high incomes—for example, it's unlikely that they reflect the explosion in C.E.O. compensation. And other evidence makes it clear not only that inequality is increasing but that the action gets bigger the closer you get to the top. That is, it's not simply that the top 20 percent of families have had bigger percentage gains than families near the middle: the top 5 percent have done better than the next 15, the top 1 percent better than the next 4, and so on up to Bill Gates.

Studies that try to do a better job of tracking high incomes have found startling results. For example, a recent study by the nonpartisan Congressional Budget Office used income tax data and other sources to improve on the census estimates. The C.B.O. study found that between 1979 and 1997, the after-tax incomes of the top 1 percent of families rose 157 percent, compared with only a 10 percent gain for families near the middle of the income distribution. Even more startling results come from a new study by Thomas Piketty, at the French research institute Cepremap, and Emmanuel Saez, who is now at the University of California at Berkeley. Using income tax data, Piketty and Saez have produced estimates of the incomes of the well-to-do, the rich and the very rich back to 1913.

The first point you learn from these new estimates is that the middle-class America of my youth is best thought of not as the normal state of our society, but as an interregnum between Gilded Ages. America before 1930 was a society in which a small number of very rich people controlled a large share of the nation's wealth. We became a middle-class society only after the concentration of income at the top dropped sharply during the New Deal, and especially during World War II. The economic historians Claudia Goldin and Robert Margo have dubbed the narrowing of income gaps during those years the Great Compression. Incomes then stayed fairly equally distributed until the 1970's: the rapid rise in incomes during the first postwar generation was very evenly spread across the population.

Since the 1970's, however, income gaps have been rapidly widening. Piketty and Saez confirm what I suspected: by most measures we are, in fact, back to the days of "The Great Gatsby." After 30 years in which the income shares of the top 10 percent of taxpayers, the top 1 percent and so on were far below their levels in the 1920's, all are very nearly back where they were.

And the big winners are the very, very rich. One ploy often used to play down growing inequality is to rely on rather coarse statistical breakdowns—dividing the population into five "quintiles," each containing 20 percent of families, or at most 10 "deciles." * * * For example, a conservative commentator might concede, grudgingly, that there has been some increase in the share of national income going to the top 10 percent of taxpayers, but then point out that anyone with an income over $81,000 is in that top 10 percent. So we're just talking about shifts within the middle class, right?

Wrong: the top 10 percent contains a lot of people whom we would still consider middle class, but they weren't the big winners. Most of the gains in the share of the top 10 percent of taxpayers over the past 30 years were actually gains to the top 1 percent, rather than the next 9 percent. In 1998 the top 1 percent started at $230,000. In turn, 60 percent of the gains of that top 1 percent went to the top 0.1 percent, those with incomes of more than $790,000. And almost half of those gains went to a mere 13,000 taxpayers, the top 0.01 percent, who had an income of at least $3.6 million and an average income of $17 million.

A stickler for detail might point out that the Piketty–Saez estimates end in 1998 and that the C.B.O. numbers end a year earlier. Have the trends shown in the data reversed? Almost surely not. In fact, all indications are that the explosion of incomes at the top continued through 2000. Since then the plunge in stock prices must have put some crimp in high incomes—but census data show inequality continuing to increase in 2001, mainly because of the severe effects of the recession on the working poor and near poor. When the recession ends, we can be sure that we will find ourselves a society in which income inequality is even higher than it was in the late 90's.

So claims that we've entered a second Gilded Age aren't exaggerated. In America's middle-class era, the mansion-building, yacht-owning classes had pretty much disappeared. According to Piketty and Saez, in 1970 the top 0.01 percent of taxpayers had 0.7 percent of total income—that is, they earned "only" 70 times as much as the average, not enough to buy or maintain a mega-residence. But in 1998 the top 0.01 percent received more than 3 percent of all income. That meant that the 13,000 richest families in America had almost as much income as the 20 million poorest households; those 13,000 families had incomes 300 times that of average families.

And let me repeat: this transformation has happened very quickly, and it is still going on. * * *

III.   UNDOING THE NEW DEAL

In the middle of the 1980's, as economists became aware that something important was happening to the distribution of income in America, they formulated three main hypotheses about its causes.

The "globalization" hypothesis tied America's changing income distribution to the growth of world trade, and especially the growing imports of manufactured goods from the third world. Its basic message was that blue-collar workers—the sort of people who in my youth often made as much money as college-educated middle managers—were losing ground in the face of competition from low-wage workers in Asia. A result was stagnation or decline in the wages of ordinary people, with a growing share of national income going to the highly educated.

A second hypothesis, "skill-biased technological change," situated the cause of growing inequality not in foreign trade but in domestic innovation. The torrid pace of progress in information technology, so the story went, had increased the demand for the highly skilled and educated. And so the income distribution increasingly favored brains rather than brawn.

Finally, the "superstar" hypothesis—named by the Chicago economist Sherwin Rosen—offered a variant on the technological story. It argued that modern technologies of communication often turn competition into a tournament in which the winner is richly rewarded, while the runners-up get far less. The classic example—which gives the theory its name—is the entertainment business. As Rosen pointed out, in bygone days there were hundreds of comedians making a modest living at live shows in the borscht belt and other places. Now they are mostly gone; what is left is a handful of superstar TV comedians.

The debates among these hypotheses—particularly the debate between those who attributed growing inequality to globalization and those who attributed it to technology—were many and bitter. I was a participant in those debates myself. But I won't dwell on them, because in the last few years there has been a growing sense among economists that none of these hypotheses work.

　　　* * *

The Great Compression—the substantial reduction in inequality during the New Deal and the Second World War—also seems hard to understand in terms of the usual theories. During World War II Franklin Roosevelt used government control over wages to compress wage gaps. But if the middle-class society that emerged from the war was an artificial creation, why did it persist for another 30 years?

Some—by no means all—economists trying to understand growing inequality have begun to take seriously a hypothesis that would have been considered irredeemably fuzzy-minded not long ago. This view stresses the role of social norms in setting limits to inequality. According to this view, the New Deal had a more profound impact on American society than even its most ardent admirers have suggested: it imposed norms of relative equality in pay that persisted for more than 30 years, creating the broadly middle-class society we came to take for granted. But those norms began to unravel in the 1970's and have done so at an accelerating pace.

Exhibit A for this view is the story of executive compensation. In the 1960's, America's great corporations behaved more like socialist republics than like cutthroat capitalist enterprises, and top executives behaved more like public-spirited bureaucrats than like captains of industry. I'm not exaggerating. Consider the description of executive behavior offered by John Kenneth Galbraith in his 1967 book, "The New Industrial State": "Management does not go out ruthlessly to reward itself—a sound management is expected to exercise restraint." Managerial self-dealing was a thing of the past: "With the power of decision goes opportunity for making money. . . . Were everyone to seek to do so . . . the corporation would be a chaos of competitive avarice. But these are not the sort of thing that a good company man does; a remarkably effective code bans such behavior. Group decision-making insures, moreover, that almost everyone's actions and even thoughts are known to others. This acts to enforce the code and, more than incidentally, a high standard of personal honesty as well."

Thirty-five years on, a cover article in Fortune is titled "You Bought. They Sold." "All over corporate America," reads the blurb, "top execs were cashing in stocks even as their companies were tanking. Who was left holding the bag? You." As I said, we've become a different country.

Let's leave actual malfeasance on one side for a moment, and ask how the relatively modest salaries of top executives 30 years ago became the gigantic pay packages of today. * * * The key reason executives are paid so much now is that they appoint the members of the corporate board that determines their compensation and control many of the perks that board members count on. So it's not the invisible hand of the market that leads to those monumental executive incomes; it's the invisible handshake in the boardroom.

* * * That is, the explosion of executive pay represents a social change rather than the purely economic forces of supply and demand. We should think of it not as a market trend like the rising value of waterfront property, but as something more like the sexual revolution of the 1960's—a relaxation of old strictures, a new permissiveness, but in this case the permissiveness is financial rather than sexual. * * *

How did this change in corporate culture happen? Economists and management theorists are only beginning to explore that question, but it's easy to suggest a few factors. One was the changing structure of financial markets. In his new book, "Searching for a Corporate Savior," Rakesh Khurana of Harvard Business School suggests that during the 1980's and 1990's, "managerial capitalism"—the world of the man in the gray flannel suit—was replaced by "investor capitalism." Institutional investors weren't willing to let a C.E.O. choose his own successor from inside the corporation; they wanted heroic leaders, often outsiders, and were willing to pay immense sums to get them. The subtitle of Khurana's book, by the way, is "The Irrational Quest for Charismatic C.E.O.'s"

* * *

Economists also did their bit to legitimize previously unthinkable levels of executive pay. During the 1980's and 1990's a torrent of academic papers—popularized in business magazines and incorporated into consultants' recommendations—argued that Gordon Gekko was right: greed is good; greed works. In order to get the best performance out of executives, these papers argued, it was necessary to align their interests with those of stockholders. And the way to do that was with large grants of stock or stock options.

* * *

What economists like Piketty and Saez are now suggesting is that the story of executive compensation is representative of a broader story. Much more than economists and free-market advocates like to imagine, wages—particularly at the top—are determined by social norms. What happened during the 1930's and 1940's was that new norms of equality were established, largely through the political process. What happened in the 1980's and 1990's was that those norms unraveled, replaced by an ethos of "anything goes." And a result was an explosion of income at the top of the scale.

IV.   THE PRICE OF INEQUALITY

It was one of those revealing moments. Responding to an e-mail message from a Canadian viewer, Robert Novak of "Crossfire" delivered a little speech: "Marg, like most Canadians, you're ill informed and wrong. The U.S. has the longest standard of living—longest life expectancy of any country in the world, including Canada. That's the truth."

But it was Novak who had his facts wrong. Canadians can expect to live about two years longer than Americans. In fact, life expectancy in the U.S. is well below that in Canada, Japan and every major nation in Western Europe. On average, we can expect lives a bit shorter than those of Greeks, a bit longer than those of Portuguese. Male life expectancy is lower in the U.S. than it is in Costa Rica.

Still, you can understand why Novak assumed that we were No. 1. After all, we really are the richest major nation, with real G.D.P. per capita about 20 percent higher than Canada's. And it has been an article of faith in this country that a rising tide lifts all boats. Doesn't our high and rising national wealth translate into a high standard of living—including good medical care for all Americans?

Well, no. Although America has higher per capita income than other advanced countries, it turns out that that's mainly because our rich are much richer. And here's a radical thought: if the rich get more, that leaves less for everyone else.

That statement—which is simply a matter of arithmetic—is guaranteed to bring accusations of "class warfare." If the accuser gets more specific, he'll probably offer two reasons that it's foolish to make a fuss over the high incomes of a few people at the top of the income distribution. First, he'll tell you that what the elite get may look like a lot of money, but it's still a small share of the total—that is, when all is said and done the rich aren't getting that big a piece of the pie. Second, he'll tell you that trying to do anything to reduce incomes at the top will hurt, not help, people further down the distribution, because attempts to redistribute income damage incentives.

These arguments for lack of concern are plausible. And they were entirely correct, once upon a time—namely, back when we had a middle-class society. But there's a lot less truth to them now.

First, the share of the rich in total income is no longer trivial. These days 1 percent of families receive about 16 percent of total pretax income, and have about 14 percent of after-tax income. That share has roughly doubled over the past 30 years, and is now about as large as the share of the bottom 40 percent of the population. That's a big shift of income to the top; as a matter of pure arithmetic, it must mean that the incomes of less well off families grew considerably more slowly than average income. And they did. Adjusting for inflation, average family income—total income divided by the number of families—grew 28 percent from 1979 to 1997. But median family income—the income of a family in the middle of the distribution, a better indicator of how typical American families are doing—grew only 10 percent. And the incomes of the bottom fifth of families actually fell slightly.

Let me belabor this point for a bit. We pride ourselves, with considerable justification, on our record of economic growth. But over the last few decades it's remarkable how little of that growth has trickled down to ordinary families. Median family income has risen only about 0.5 percent per year—and as far as we can tell from somewhat unreliable data, just about all of that increase was due to wives working longer hours, with little or no gain in real wages. * * *

Still, many people will say that while the U.S. economic system may generate a lot of inequality, it also generates much higher incomes than any alternative, so that everyone is better off. That was the moral Business Week tried to convey in its recent special issue with "25 Ideas for a Changing World." One of those ideas was "the rich get richer, and that's O.K." High incomes at the top, the conventional wisdom declares, are the result of a free-market system that provides huge incentives for performance. And the system delivers that performance, which means that wealth at the top doesn't come at the expense of the rest of us.

A skeptic might point out that the explosion in executive compensation seems at best loosely related to actual performance. Jack Welch was one of the 10 highest-paid executives in the United States in 2000, and you could argue that he earned it. But did Dennis Kozlowski of Tyco, or Gerald Levin of Time Warner, who were also in the top 10? A skeptic might also point out that even during the economic boom of the late 1990's, U.S. productivity growth was no better than it was during the great postwar expansion, which corresponds to the era when America was truly middle class and C.E.O.'s were modestly paid technocrats.

* * *

Many Americans assume that because we are the richest country in the world, with real G.D.P. per capita higher than that of other major advanced countries, Americans must be better off across the board—that it's not just our rich who are richer than their counterparts abroad, but that the typical American family is much better off than the typical family elsewhere, and that even our poor are well off by foreign standards.

But it's not true. Let me use the example of Sweden, that great conservative bete noire.

A few months ago the conservative cyberpundit Glenn Reynolds made a splash when he pointed out that Sweden's G.D.P. per capita is roughly comparable with that of Mississippi—see, those foolish believers in the welfare state have impoverished themselves! Presumably he assumed that this means that the typical Swede is as poor as the typical resident of Mississippi, and therefore much worse off than the typical American.

But life expectancy in Sweden is about three years higher than that of the U.S. Infant mortality is half the U.S. level, and less than a third the rate in Mississippi. Functional illiteracy is much less common than in the U.S.

How is this possible? One answer is that G.D.P. per capita is in some ways a misleading measure. Swedes take longer vacations than Americans, so they work fewer hours per year. That's a choice, not a failure of economic performance. Real G.D.P. per hour worked is 16 percent lower than in the United States, which makes Swedish productivity about the same as Canada's.

But the main point is that though Sweden may have lower average income than the United States, that's mainly because our rich are so much richer. The median Swedish family has a standard of living roughly comparable with that of the median U.S. family: wages are if anything higher in Sweden, and a higher tax burden is offset by public provision of health care and generally better public services. And as you move further down the income distribution, Swedish living standards are way ahead of those in the U.S. Swedish families with children that are at the 10th percentile—poorer than 90 percent of the population—have incomes 60 percent higher than their U.S. counterparts. And very few people in Sweden experience the deep poverty that is all too common in the United States. One measure: in 1994 only 6 percent of Swedes lived on less than $11 per day, compared with 14 percent in the U.S.

The moral of this comparison is that even if you think that America's high levels of inequality are the price of our high level of national income, it's not at all clear that this price is worth paying. The reason conservatives engage in bouts of Sweden-bashing is that they want to convince us that there is no tradeoff between economic efficiency and equity—that if you try to take from the rich and give to the poor, you actually make everyone worse off. But the comparison between the U.S. and other advanced countries doesn't support this conclusion at all. * * *

And we might even offer a challenge from the other side: inequality in the United States has arguably reached levels where it is counterproductive. That is, you can make a case that our society would be richer if its richest members didn't get quite so much.

I could make this argument on historical grounds. The most impressive economic growth in U.S. history coincided with the middle-class interregnum, the post-World War II generation, when incomes were most evenly distributed. But let's focus on a specific case, the extraordinary pay packages of today's top executives. Are these good for the economy?

* * *

It's easy to get boggled by the details of corporate scandal—insider loans, stock options, special-purpose entities, mark-to-market, round-tripping. But there's a simple reason that the details are so complicated. All of these schemes were designed to benefit corporate insiders—to inflate the pay of the C.E.O. and his inner circle. That is, they were all about the "chaos of competitive avarice" that, according to John Kenneth Galbraith, had been ruled out in the corporation of the 1960's. But while all restraint has vanished within the American corporation, the outside world—including stockholders—is still prudish, and open looting by executives is still not acceptable. So the looting has to be camouflaged, taking place through complicated schemes that can be rationalized to outsiders as clever corporate strategies.

Economists who study crime tell us that crime is inefficient—that is, the costs of crime to the economy are much larger than the amount stolen. Crime, and the fear of crime, divert resources away from productive uses: criminals spend their time stealing rather than producing, and potential victims spend time and money trying to protect their property. Also, the things people do to avoid becoming victims—like avoiding dangerous districts—have a cost even if they succeed in averting an actual crime.

The same holds true of corporate malfeasance, whether or not it actually involves breaking the law. Executives who devote their time to creating innovative ways to divert shareholder money into their own pockets probably aren't running the real business very well (think Enron, WorldCom, Tyco, Global Crossing, Adelphia . . .). Investments chosen because they create the illusion of profitability while insiders cash in their stock options are a waste of scarce resources. And if the supply of funds from lenders and shareholders dries up because of a lack of trust, the economy as a whole suffers. Just ask Indonesia.

* * *

VI.   PLUTOCRACY?

* * *

America in the 1920's wasn't a feudal society. But it was a nation in which vast privilege—often inherited privilege—stood in contrast to vast misery. It was also a nation in which the government, more often than not, served the interests of the privileged and ignored the aspirations of ordinary people.

Those days are past—or are they? Income inequality in America has now returned to the levels of the 1920's. Inherited wealth doesn't yet play a big part in our society, but given time—and the repeal of the estate tax—we will grow ourselves a hereditary elite just as set apart from the concerns of ordinary Americans as old Horace Havemeyer. And the new elite, like the old, will have enormous political power.

Kevin Phillips concludes his book *Wealth and Democracy* with a grim warning: "Either democracy must be renewed, with politics brought back to life, or wealth is likely to cement a new and less democratic regime—plutocracy by some other name." It's a pretty extreme line, but we live in extreme times. Even if the forms of democracy remain, they may become meaningless. It's all too easy to see how we may become a country in which the big rewards are reserved for people with the right connections; in which ordinary people see little hope of advancement; in which political involvement seems pointless, because in the end the interests of the elite always get served.

Am I being too pessimistic? Even my liberal friends tell me not to worry, that our system has great resilience, that the center will hold. I hope they're right, but they may be looking in the rearview mirror. Our optimism about America, our belief that in the end our nation always finds its way, comes from the past—a past in which we were a middle-class society. But that was another country.

NOTES AND QUESTIONS

1.   Other factors influencing income inequality. Besides intergenerational economic position, what are other factors that could explain income inequality in America?

2.   Intergenerational economic mobility: racial implications. The above-cited study by Charles and Hurst portrays the strong correlation between individuals' parents' incomes and their own economic futures. Are such findings consistent for all demographic groups? In other words, are members of one ethnic or racial group more likely to break free of their parents' economic status than members of another demographic group?

American University professor of economics Tom Hertz encountered this question in a study of economic mobility. Using data compiled from the Panel Study of Income Dynamics, consisting of a sample of 6,723 black and white families observed over thirty two years and in two generations, Hertz found that African Americans are more likely to remain in lower income brackets than their white counterparts. The study revealed that blacks' rate of persistence at low-income levels was 42 percent, while their rate of persistence at high income levels was only 4 percent. On the other hand, for whites, the rate of persistence at the bottom was approximately half that at the top (17 percent versus 30 percent). Adjusted for age, the study revealed blacks' persistence to remain in a lower income bracket was 41 percent, while whites' persistence to remain at the bottom was 25 percent. Also, for white families, extreme upward mobility is more likely than downward mobility (14 percent versus 9 percent), but the reverse is true for blacks—blacks have a 35 percent chance of substantially sliding down the income scale, and only have a 4 percent chance of substantially moving up the scale. These findings all point to the conclusion that black families have a significantly lower rate of upward mobility from the bottom income bracket than do whites. Tom Hertz, *Rags, Riches and Race: The Intergenerational Mobility of Black and White Families in the United States*, under review for inclusion in: UNEQUAL CHANCES: FAMILY BACKGROUND AND ECONOMIC SUCCESS (Samuel Bowles, et al. eds., forthcoming).

What are the reasons for income differences among demographic groups?

———

● WEALTH INEQUALITY

Wealth and Inequality in America

BLACK WEALTH/WHITE WEALTH: A NEW PERSPECTIVE ON RACIAL INEQUALITY 53–90 (1997).

■ MELVIN L. OLIVER & THOMAS M. SHAPIRO

[A] thorough analysis of economic well-being and social and racial equality must include a wealth dimension. A lack of systematic, reliable data on wealth accumulation, however, partly explains the general absence of such an analysis until now. * * *

The bulk of our analysis and discussion of wealth is drawn from the Survey of Income and Program Participation. SIPP is a sample of the U.S. population that interviews adults in households periodically over a two-and-a-half-year period. A new panel is introduced every year. Data for this study came from the 1987 Panel. Household interviews began in June 1987, and the same households were reinterviewed every four months through 1989. The full data set of eight interviews was available for 11,257 households. * * *

What is wealth? How does one define it? What indicators of wealth are the best ones to use? Definitional and conceptual questions about wealth have produced a diverse and sometimes confusing set of approaches to the topic. Indeed, a major difficulty in analyzing wealth is that people define it in different ways with the result that wealth measures lack comparability. After working with the literature for several years, we decided to measure wealth by way of two concepts. The first, *net worth* (NW) conveys the straightforward value of all assets less any debts. The second, *net financial assets* (NFA), excludes equity accrued in a home or vehicle from the calculation of a household's available resources.

Net worth gives a comprehensive picture of all assets and debts; yet it may not be a reliable measure of *command over future resources* for one's self and family. Net worth includes equity in vehicles, for instance, and it is not likely that this equity will be converted into other resources, such as prep school for a family's children. Thus one's car is not a likely repository in which to store resources for future use. Likewise, viewing home equity as a reasonable and unambiguous source of future resources for the current generation raises many vexing problems. Most people do not sell their homes to finance a college education for their children, start a business, make other investments, buy medical care, support political candidates, or pay lobbyists to protect their special interests. Even if a family sells a home, the proceeds are typically used to lease or buy replacement housing. An exception to the general rule may involve the elderly. Mortgage payments, especially in times of high housing inflation, may be seen as a kind of "forced savings" to be cashed in at retirement or to pass along to one's children.

* * * The specific differences between net worth and net financial assets is that equity in vehicles and homes is excluded from the latter, although debts are subtracted from NFA. In contrast to net worth, net financial assets consists of more readily liquid sources of income and wealth that can be used for a family's immediate well-being. Because the distinction between net worth and net financial assets is somewhat controversial and still open to debate, we usually present both measures. Generally, in our view, however, net financial assets seem to be the best indicator of the current generation's command over future resources, while net worth provides a more accurate estimate of the wealth likely to be inherited by the next generation.

Let us now turn to the substantive questions at the heart of our study. How has wealth been distributed in American society over the twentieth century? What about the redistribution of wealth that took place in the decade of the eighties? And finally, what do the answers to these questions imply for black-white inequality?

The 1980s and Beyond Bigger Shares for the Wealthy

Available information concerning wealth in the twentieth century, until very recently, comes mainly from national estate-tax records for the very wealthy collected between 1922 and 1981, and from sporadic cross-sectional household surveys starting in 1953. Drawing from these data bases, we track trends in the distribution of wealth, paying particular attention to whether inequality is falling, remaining stable, or rising, into the late 1980s and early 1990s.

Estate-tax data show consistently high wealth concentrations throughout the early part of the twentieth century. According to Edward Wolff's

"The Rich Get Increasingly Richer," the top 1 percent of American house-holds possessed over 25 percent of total wealth between 1922 and 1972. Beginning in 1972, however, the data indicate a significant decline in wealth inequality. The share of the top percentile declined from 29 percent to 19 percent between 1972 and 1976. While this decline was unexpected, it was not permanent. In fact in the next five-year period, from 1976 to 1981, a sharp renewal of wealth inequality occurred. Between 1976 and 1981 the share of the richest 1 percent expanded from 19 to 24 percent.

The standard theory explaining wealth inequality associates the phenomenon with the process of industrialization. Stable, low levels of inequality characterize preindustrial times; the onset of modern economic growth is characterized by rapid industrialization, which ushers in a sharp increase in inequality; and then advanced, mature industrial societies experience a gradual leveling of inequality and finally long-term stability. This explanation highlights industrialization as a universal, master trend in the evolution of market economies. The twentieth century in particular is said to represent a clear pattern, specifically from 1929 on, when, according to Jeffrey Williamson's and Peter Lindert's *American Inequality*, wealth imbalance "seems to have undergone a permanent reduction." One must question the persistence of this reduced inequality into the 1990s, especially in light of growing income inequalities.

Estimates of household wealth inequality from two relatively consistent sources of household survey data, the 1962 Survey of Financial Characteristics of Consumers and the Surveys of Consumer Finances conducted in the 1980s, furnish more recent information. Responses to these surveys indicate that wealth inequality remained relatively fixed between 1962 and 1983. The top 3 percent of wealth holders held 32 percent of the wealth in 1962 and 34 percent in 1983. The Gini coefficient, which measures equality over an entire distribution rather than as shares of the top percentile, rose slightly, from 0.73 in 1962 to 0.74 in 1983. The Gini ratio is a statistic that converts levels of inequality into a single number and allows easy comparisons of populations. Gini figures range from 0 to 1. A low ratio indicates low levels of inequality; a high ratio indicates high levels of inequality. Thus Ginis closer to 0 illustrate more distributional equality, while figures closer to 1 indicate more inequality. While the Gini coefficient is a very useful summary measure of inequality, it is probably most helpful and meaningful as a way of comparing distributions of wealth between time periods, given its sensitivity to small changes and its clear indication of the direction of change.

What happened during the 1980s? Quite simply, the very rich increased their share of the nation's wealth. One leading economist dubbed the resulting wealth imbalance an "unprecedented jump in inequality to Great Gatsby levels." Notably, inequality had risen very sharply by 1989, with the wealthiest 1 percent of households owning 37.7 percent of net worth. An examination of net financial assets suggests even greater levels of inequality. In 1983 the top 1 percent held 42.8 percent of all financial assets, a figure that increased to 48.2 percent in 1989. The Gini coefficient reflects this increase in inequality, rising 0.04 during the period. Wealth inequality by the end of the 1980s closely approximated historically high levels not seen since 1922.

Our review of other wealth indicators and studies corroborates the finding that wealth is reconcentrating. It also goes a way toward revealing the relationship between trends toward wealth concentration and growing inequality and [a] lower standard of living * * *. The evidence presented by Edward Wolff in "The Rich Get Increasingly Richer" and by others using [Survey of Consumer Finances] data suggests that while the concentration of wealth decreased substantially during the mid–1970s, it increased sharply during the 1980s. In particular the *mean* net worth of families grew by over 7 percent from 1983 to 1989. However, *median* net worth grew much more slowly than mean wealth, at a rate of 0.8 percent. According to Wolff, this discrepancy "implies that the upper-wealth classes enjoyed a disproportionate share [of wealth]" between 1983 and 1989. Wolff's median net financial assets declined 3.7 percent during this period. Thus the typical family disposed of fewer liquid resources in 1989 than in 1983. In stark contrast, the wealth of the "superrich," defined as the top one-half of 1 percent of wealth-holders, increased 26 percent from 1983 to 1989. Over one-half (55 percent) of the wealth created between 1983 and 1989 accrued to the richest one-half of one percent of families, a fact that vividly illustrates the magnitude of the 1980s increase in their share of the country's wealth. Not surprisingly, the Gini coefficient increased sizably during this period, from 0.80 to 0.84. Indeed, U.S. wealth concentration in 1989 was more extreme than at any time since 1929.

SIPP as well as SCF data confirm that the wealth pie is being resliced, and that the wealthy are getting larger pieces of it. In a 1994 update on its ongoing SIPP study, the Census Bureau reports that the median net worth of the nation's households dropped 12 percent between 1988 and 1991. The drop in median wealth is associated with a sharp decline in the middle classes' largest share of net worth: home equity. The median home equity declined by 14 percent between 1988 and 1991 as real estate values fell.

The trends of increasing income and wealth inequality have disrupted long-standing post-World War II patterns. The movement toward income equality and stability expired by the mid–1970s, while the trend toward wealth equality extended into the early 1980s. By 1983 wealth inequality began to rise. The time lag in these reversals is important. Along with declining incomes, a growth in debt burden, and fluctuations in housing values and stock prices, the actions of government—and the Reagan tax cuts of the early 1980s—can only be viewed as prime causes of the increase in wealth inequality.

How has this redistribution of wealth in favor of the rich affected the middle class? Examining wealth groups by ranking all families into wealth fifths provides one way to get at this question. The average holdings of the lower-middle and bottom wealth groups (fifths) declined in real terms by 30 percent. The wealth of the middle group remained unchanged, while that of the upper-middle group increased by slightly less than 1 percent a year.

The average wealth of the top group increased by over 10 percent. Combining this with previous information showing a decline in median net financial assets strengthens the argument that the economic base of middle-class life is becoming increasingly fragile and tenuous.

During the 1980s the rich got much richer, and the poor and middle classes fell further behind. One obvious culprit was the Reagan tax cuts. These cuts provided greater discretionary income for middle-and upper-class taxpayers. However, most middle-class taxpayers used this discretionary income to bolster their declining standards of living or decrease their debt burden instead of saving or investing it. Although Reagan strategists had intended to stimulate investment, the upper classes embarked on a frenzy of consumer spending on luxury items. Wolff's "The Rich Get Increasingly Richer" explains the redistribution of wealth in favor of the rich during the 1980s as resulting more from capital gains reaped on existing wealth than from increased savings and investment. He attributes 70 percent of the growth in wealth over the 1983–1989 period to the appreciation of existing financial assets and the remaining 30 percent to the creation of wealth from personal savings. Led by rapid gains in stocks, financial securities, and liquid assets, existing investments grew at an impressive rate at a time when it was difficult to convert earnings into personal savings.

One asset whose value grew dramatically during the eighties was real estate. Home ownership is central to the average American's wealth portfolio. Housing equity makes up the largest part of wealth held by the middle class, whereas the upper class and wealthy more commonly own a greater degree of their wealth in financial assets. The percentage of families owning homes peaked in the mid–1970s at 65 percent and has subsequently declined by a point or two. Forty-three percent of blacks own homes, a rate 65 percent lower than that of whites. Housing equity constitutes the most substantial portion of all wealth assets by far. SIPP results clearly demonstrate this assertion: housing equity represented 43 percent of median household assets in 1988. It is even more significant, however, in the wealth portfolios of blacks than of whites, accounting for 43.3 percent of white wealth and 62.5 percent of black assets. This initial glance at the role of housing in overall wealth carries ramifications for subsequent in-depth analysis. Thus, owning a house—a hallmark of the American Dream—is becoming harder and harder for average Americans to afford, and fewer are able to do so. The ensuing analysis of racial differences in wealth requires a thorough investigation of racial dynamics in access to housing, mortgage and housing markets, and housing values.

The eighties ushered in a new era of wealth inequality in which strong gains were made by those who already had substantial financial assets. Those who had a piece of the rock, especially those with financial assets, but also those with real estate, increased their wealth holdings and consolidated a sense of economic security for themselves and their families. Others, a disproportionate share of them black, saw their financial status improve only slightly or decline.

In *Warm Hearts and Cold Cash* Marcia Millman notes that for most of this century, the primary legacy of middle-class parents to children has been "cultural" capital, that is, the upbringing, education, and contacts that allowed children to get a good start in life and to become financially successful and independent. Now some parents have more to bestow than cultural capital. In particular, middle-class Americans who started rearing families after World War II have amassed a huge amount of money in the value of their homes and stocks that they are now in the process of dispatching to the baby boom generation through inheritances, loans, and gifts. Millman says this money is "enormously consequential in shaping the lives of their adult children."

Much of this wealth was built by their parents between the late 1940s and the late 1960s when real wages and saving rates were higher and housing costs were considerably lower. For the elderly middle class, the escalation of real estate prices over the last twenty years has been a significant boon. * * *

Access to Assets

The potential for assets to expand or inhibit choices, horizons, and opportunities for children emerged as the most consistent and strongest common theme in our interviews. Since parents want to invest in their children, to give them whatever advantages they can, we wondered about the ability of the average American household to expend assets on their children. This section thus delves deeper into the assets households command by (1) considering the importance of home and vehicle equity in relation to other kinds of assets; (2) inspecting available financial assets for various groups of the population; and (3) looking at children growing up in resource-deficient households. We found a strong relationship between the amount of wealth and the composition of assets. Households with large amounts of total net worth control wealth portfolios composed mostly of financial assets. Financial investments make up about four-fifths of the assets of the richest households. Conversely, home and vehicle equity represents over 70 percent of the asset portfolio among the poorest one-fifth of American households, one in three of which possesses zero or negative financial assets.

Table 4.5 reports households with zero or negative net financial assets for various racial, age, education, and family groups. It shows that one-quarter of white households, 61 percent of black households, and 54 percent of Hispanic households are without financial resources. A similar absence of financial assets affects nearly one-half of young households; circumstances steadily improve with age, however, leaving only 15 percent of those households headed by seniors in a state of resource deficiency. The educational achievement of householders also connects directly with access to resources, as 40 percent of poorly educated household heads control no financial assets while over 80 percent of households headed by a college graduate control some NFA. Findings reported in this table also demonstrate deeply embedded disparities in resource command between single and married-couple parents. Resource deprivation characterizes 62 percent of single-parent households in comparison to 37 percent of married couples raising children.

TABLE 4.5 Who is on the Edge?

	Households with 0 or Negative NFA*	Households without NFA* for 3 months**	Households without NFA* for 6 months**
Sample	31.0%	44.9%	49.9%
Race			
White	25.3	38.1	43.2
Black	60.9	78.9	83.1
Hispanic	54.0	72.5	77.2
Age of Householder			
15–35	48.0	67.0	72.8
36–49	31.7	45.0	50.7
50–64	22.1	32.0	36.2
65 or older	15.1	26.4	30.6
Education			
Less than high school	40.3	55.5	60.0
High school degree	32.2	48.0	63.2
Some college	29.9	45.3	61.4
College degree	18.9	26.8	31.2
Family Type* * *			
Single parent	61.9	79.2	83.2
Married Couple	36.9	53.8	59.9

* Net financial worth
** NFA reserves to survive at the poverty line of $968 per month
*** Includes only households with children

Besides looking at resource deprivation, table 4.5 also sets criteria for "precarious-resource" circumstances. Households without enough NFA reserves to survive three months at the poverty line ($2,904) meet these criteria. Nearly 80 percent of single-parent households fit this description. Likewise 38 percent of white households and 79 percent of black households live in precarious-resource circumstances.

Among our interviewees, parents with ample assets planned to use them to create a better world for their children. Those without them strategized about acquiring some and talked about their "wish list." Parents talked about ballet lessons, camp, trips for cultural enrichment or even to Disney World, staying home more often with the children, affording full-time day care, allowing a parent to be home after day care. The parents discussed using assets to provide better educational opportunities for their children. Kevin takes great pride in paying for his son's college and being able to offer him advanced training. Stacie wants to be able to afford private school for Carrie. Ed and Alicia told us about the private school choices and dilemmas facing their children.

FIGURE 4.2 Percent of Children in Resource–Deficient Households, by Race

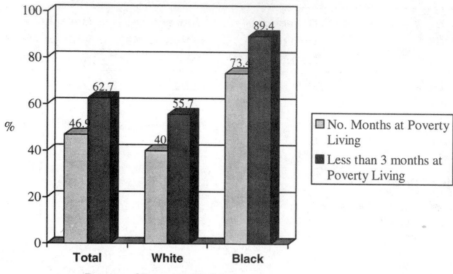

Degree of Resource Deficiency

Figure 4.2 looks at the percentage of children in resource-poor households by race. It provides information both on households with no net financial assets and on those with just enough assets to survive above the poverty line for at least three months. Close to one-half of all children live in households with no financial assets and 63 percent live in households with precarious resources, scarcely enough NFA to cushion three months of interrupted income.

A further analysis of this already disturbing data discloses imposing and powerful racial and ethnic cleavages. For example, 40 percent of all white children grow up in households without financial resources in comparison to 73 percent of all black children. Most telling of all perhaps, only 11 percent of black children grow up in households with enough net financial assets to weather three months of no income at the poverty level. Three times as many white kids live in such households.

According to Richard Steckel and Jayanthi Krishnan, cross-sectional measures of wealth acquisition and inequality may disguise underlying changes in wealth status. Analyzing surveys from 1966 and 1976, Steckel and Krishnan found that changes in marital status were associated with changes in wealth. The largest increase in wealth occurred for single women who later married. Other groups who experienced increases in wealth included households headed by the young, those with at least twelve years of schooling, and individuals who married. The greatest loss in wealth occurred among households headed by older individuals, single men, and those experiencing marital disruption.

SUMMARY

Financial wealth is the buried fault line of the American social system. The wealth distribution portrait drawn in this chapter has disclosed the existence of highly concentrated wealth at the top; a pattern of steep resource inequality; the disproportionate asset reserves held by various demographic groups; the precarious economic foundation of middle-class life; and how few financial assets most American households can call upon. This chapter has also provided documentation concerning the relationship between income inequality and wealth inequality. At one level, income makes up the largest component of potential wealth. At the same time, however, distinctive patterns of income and wealth inequality exist. Put another way, substituting what is known about income inequality for what is not known about wealth inequality limits, and even biases, our understanding of inequality. A thorough understanding of inequality must therefore pay more attention to resources than has been paid in the past.

Perhaps no single piece of information conveys the sense of fragility common to those on the lowest rungs of the economic ladder as the proportion of children who grow up in households without assets. Reducing all life's chances for success to economic circumstances no doubt overlooks much, but resources nonetheless provide an accurate measure of differential access to educational, career, health, cultural, and social opportunities. In poignantly reciting the hopes they have for their children, parents recognize the importance of resources. Our interviews show how parents use assets to bring these hopes to life, or wish they had ample assets so they could bring them to life. Nearly three-quarters of all black children, 1.8 times the rate for whites, grow up in households possessing no financial assets. Nine in ten black children come of age in households that lack sufficient financial reserves to endure three months of no income at the poverty line, about four times the rate for whites.

————

NOTES AND QUESTIONS

1. Some data on poverty rates. During the era of Gunnar Myrdal's classic study of American society, *An American Dilemma*, the majority of African Americans in the United States lived in the South; white supremacy relegated blacks to an inferior socioeconomic status; and social, political, and economic opportunity for African Americans was virtually non-existent. Ronald F. Ferguson, *Shifting Challenges: Fifty Years of Economic Change Toward Black-White Earnings Equality*, in AN AMERICAN DILEMMA REVISITED: RACE RELATIONS IN A CHANGING WORLD 76 (Obie Clayton, Jr. ed., 1996). Though almost sixty years have passed since Myrdal's commentary on the socioeconomic status of African Americans during the period between the Great Depression and World War II, grave economic inequalities continue to plague minorities, maintaining a systematic socioeconomic hierarchy in society. *Id.*, at xxiii.

Sociologists Melvin L. Oliver and Thomas M. Shapiro conclude that several variables account for wealth differences among racial and ethnic communities, including geographic region, educational attainment, the number of workers in the household, marital status, gender, and age.[16] As we have just discussed, intergenerational wealth effects are stronger than was once thought to be the case. For the poor this economic and social immobility creates brutal traps in a world of disadvantage. A study by Thomas Hertz of American University found that a child born to a family in the bottom 10 percent income bracket has a 31 percent chance of remaining in that same caste as an adult and a 51 percent chance of moving into the bottom 20 percent. However, a child born in the top 10 percent has a 30 percent chance of remaining in that income bracket and a 43 percent chance of moving into the top 20 percent.[17]

Hidden Cost of Being African American

HIDDEN COST OF BEING AFRICAN AMERICAN 141 (2004).

■ THOMAS M. SHAPIRO

In the 20 largest metropolitan areas, where 36 percent of all African Americans live, segregation pervades basic dimensions of community life. The residential color line means that blacks have greater difficulty overcoming problems associated with poor communities, especially crime, violence, housing abandonment, unstable families, poorer health and higher mortality, environmental degradation, and failing schools. No other group experiences segregation to the extent that blacks do. In many geographical areas, two decades of rising income inequality and budget cuts have produced a concentration of poverty that further compounds problems of segregation. Poor black neighborhoods are crowded, highly concentrated, and isolated far more severely than neighborhoods where poor whites, Latinos, or Asians live.

---

16. MELVIN L. OLIVER & THOMAS M. SHAPIRO, *Wealth and Inequality, in* BLACK WEALTH/ WHITE WEALTH: A NEW PERSPECTIVE ON RACIAL INEQUALITY 67–90 (1997).

17. Alan B. Krueger, *Economic Scene; The Apple Falls Close to the Tree, Even in the Land of Opportunity*, N.Y. TIMES, Nov. 14, 2002, at C1.

TABLE 2.2.

1984 Residence	1994 Residence			
	Predominately White Area	Racially Mixed Area	Predominately Black Area	Total
WHITE FAMILIES				
Predominately White Area	95.6%	4.4%	-	100.0% (456)
Racially Mixed Area	40.2%	58.8%	1.0%	100.0% (97)
Predominately Black Area	-	-	-	100.0%
TOTAL	85.9% (475)	13.9% (77)	0.2% (1)	100.0% (553)
BLACK FAMILIES				
Predominately White Area	66.7%	33.3%	-	100.0% (21)
Racially Mixed Area	6.5%	79.0%	14.5%	100.0% (214)
Predominately Black Area	8.5%	56.4%	66.3%	100.0% (166)
TOTAL	8.5% (34)	56.4% (226)	35.2% (141)	100% (401)

Source: *Id.* at 138.

Sheryll Cashin argues that "housing [is] the last plank in the civil rights revolution ... [s]egregated residential housing contributes to pervasive inequality in this country."[18]

The Price of Segregation—Unconventional Wisdom: New Facts From the Social Sciences

Wash. Post, Dec. 28, 1997, at C5.

■ Richard Morin

THE PRICE OF SEGREGATION

FOR SALE: Three-bedroom, two-bath ranch-style house. Near good schools and good neighbors. Low taxes, low crime. Located in a white neighborhood.

How much would you pay for this house? If you're white, a new study of housing prices suggests that you'll pay, on average, about 13 percent more than if the same house were located in a racially integrated part of town.

That's the premium that whites appear to be willing to pay to live in the typical segregated white neighborhood, say Harvard economists David Cutler, Edward Glaeser and Jacob Vigdor.

And it's this extra cost that's now primarily either responsible for keeping America's neighborhoods predominantly black or white decades after legal segregation officially ended, Cutler argues.

---

18. Sheryll Cashin, The Failures of Integration: How Race and Class are Undermining The American Dream 3 (2004) infra at 484.

To measure just how much whites will pay to live in white neighbor-hoods, Cutler and his colleagues collected a mountain of data on every neighborhood in three American cities: Cleveland, Atlanta and Sacramento. They selected these cities because they were "representative of the urban experience of the past century." The information they gathered included Census data, neighborhood characteristics and federal reports on housing prices back to 1940, the first year such information was collected.

They found that the whiter the neighborhood, the higher the housing prices. "We can say that the premium that a white pays in a segregated city (such as Cleveland) in 1990 is 18 percent, while the premium that a white pays in a relatively integrated city (such as Sacramento) in 1990 is 12 percent," Glaeser said.

These researchers also said [they] were able to track the shifting patterns of residential segregation, from a system enforced by laws to one sustained by market forces.

Through the 1950s, segregation was enforced by law and the "collective actions taken by whites to exclude blacks from their neighborhoods."

Real estate covenants written into deeds in some neighborhoods barred homeowners from selling or renting to blacks (or Jews or sometimes even unmarried people). When laws and covenants didn't work, Cutler said "whites took bats, broke some windows and threw things at the house to run off black families who dared to move into white neighborhoods, as well as to warn other African–Americans to stay out. You can't do that any more."

Now, Cutler said it's sticker shock that is keeping many African-Americans out.

———

The Failures of Integration, How Race and Class are Undermining the American Dream

Public Affairs, New York, at 4 (2004).

■ SHERYLL CASHIN

"Housing—where we live—is fundamental in explaining American separatism. Housing was the last plank in the civil rights revolution, it is the realm in which we have experienced the fewest integration gains. When it comes to integration, housing is also the realm in which Americans most seem to agree that separation is acceptable. We may accept, even desire, integrated workplaces and integrated public spheres. But when it come to our private life space, more visceral personal needs of comfort and security take precedence-especially for families with children. In this context, for many, integration is simply irrelevant or perceived as a threat to more fundamental concerns...."

"How do you decide where to live? Eleven years ago, I bought a lovely bungalow in Shepherd Park, in integrated, albeit a majority-black, upper-middle-class neighborhood in the northwest quadrant of Washington, D.C. My goal at the time was to acquire a house in the best and safest neighborhood I could afford. The race or class of my would-be neighbors was not at the forefront of my thinking. But many communities were beyond consideration. As a committed urbanite and a hater of traffic living outside the Beltway was out of the question. As a black woman with a strong racial identity, I found the overwhelmingly white neighborhoods west of Rock Creek Park, such as Georgetown, American University Park, and Bethesda, inherently unattractive. I was not prepared, even if investment wisdom counseled otherwise, to make the profound personal sacrifice of living totally among 'others' with who I could not identify and who likely could not identify with me. Implicit in my choice about where to live was the understanding that I wanted to be among more than just a smattering of black people. If I had been forced to describe my ideal neighborhood, I suppose I would have said it was an integrated one."

NOTES AND QUESTIONS

1.   Note on wealth and income inequalities. Why do parents and children have similar wealth? Availability of economic resources accounts for some of the correlation, but Charles and Hurst conclude spending patterns and comparable portfolio investment decisions between parents and their children have a considerable impact on the relationship between parents' wealth and their offspring's. They argue that when parents make investment choices, they set an example for their children to follow. For example, a mother who owns a company can advise her children on the tools necessary to succeed in running an enterprise and may pass on the company to her children. In addition, a wealthy parent may allow his children to take on investment decisions, such as stock ownership early in life. Kerwin Kofi Charles & Erik Hurst, *The Correlation of Wealth Across Generations* (National Bureau of Economic Research (NBER), Working Paper 9314, Oct. 2002), *at* http://www.nber.org/papers/w9314. *See also* Dalton Conley, The Pecking Order: Which Siblings Succeed and Why (2004).

Can Charles and Hurst's conclusion be extended to a large demographic group? For example, is it possible for children to learn about and mimic spending patterns and investment decisions, from not only their parents, but also from members of their own ethnic community? The Federal Reserve Board issued a Survey of Consumer Finances in 1998, reporting that the net wealth of the typical African American household was $15,500 that year; this figure is less than one-quarter that of the net wealth of the typical American household (including blacks)—$71,000. The study also revealed considerable differences in self-reported financial behavior between African American families and all families about investments, spending and income, savings tendencies, and risk aversion. Black households are much more likely than all households to have a shorter fiscal planning perspective, spend more rather than less of their earnings, not save and not save consistently, and be less willing to take monetary risks when saving or investing.

Is it possible for African Americans to persistently remain in the lower wealth brackets because members of the black community share similar ill-advised spending behaviors? Other factors influence the difference in wealth between black families and other families; for example, fewer African American households reported having received an inheritance, and black inheritors reported receiving lower bequests. Stephen Brobeck, Executive Director of the Consumer Federation of America, believes financial education is needed to aid the black community in revamping their financial behavior in order to increase wealth. However, he maintains that financial education should be shaped to meet the cultural needs of the African–American community:

> [F]inancial education needs to recognize important ethnic and cultural differences. Obviously, this education can be most effective if it uses language with which targeted populations are comfortable. But it also may be more effective if the education appeals to unique ethnic identities. For example, a Black American Saves initiative may well have more appeal to African Americans than does a more generalized America Saves initiative. Stephen Brobeck, *Black American Personal Wealth: Current Status* (Consumer Federation of America, Aug. 2002), *at* http://www.americasaves.org/back_page/BlackWealthReport082902.doc.

A recent study, "The Lives and Times of the Baby Boomers" by Duke sociology professors Angela M. O'Rand and Mary Elizabeth Hughes, suggests that the children of African American "baby boomers" are not doing as well as their parents. *See* Darryl Fears, *Black Baby Boomers' Income Gap Cited; Study Says That, Economically, Generation Has Not Improved Over Its Parents'*, WASH. POST, Dec. 17, 2004, at A02.

2.   Wealth distribution and residential segregation. Though segregation is no longer enforced by explicitly racist laws, residential segregation is still prevalent. Due to the stark differences in wealth among racial groups, richer white families live in more affluent areas, while poorer minorities often live in meager surroundings. Though this proposition logically makes sense, it fails to consider other implications, like the dependency of housing prices on the racial makeup of the neighborhood. Harvard economists David Cutlen, Edward Glaeser, and Jacob Vigdor performed a study in 1997 and found that on average a white individual is willing to pay thirteen percent more for a house not located in a racially integrated part of town. The study intimated that because whites are willing to pay a premium to live in the typical segregated white neighborhood, housing prices are higher in white areas. In turn, residential segregation continues to prevail, standing as a clear reminder that socioeconomic inequalities based on background still exist.

3.   College admissions. Educational attainment is one variable that aids in determining an individual's socioeconomic position in American society. For this reason, the prominence of one's college background plays an influential role in developing cultural capital. Parents invest tremendous amounts of time and resources in preparing their children for college by sending them to prestigious secondary schools, hoping their children's academic excellence will ensure them a prosperous lifestyle in the future.

One impressive institution, the Groton School in Massachusetts, sends countless students to prestigious colleges and universities each year. One would assume that remarkable achievement at such a school would ensure successful results in the college admissions process. However, in a society where familial status and networking are significant factors in attaining success, scholastic honors do not always guarantee a ticket to a top university. Several affluent children of universities' alumni and celebrities often have lower academic scores and still have the opportunity to study at the nation's top colleges. These students have what college admissions officers call a "hook"—criteria for preferential treatment. Henry Park, a 1998 graduate of Groton, had no "hook" to get accepted to several leading institutions. Park's parents, middleclass Korean immigrants from New Jersey, went to college in Korea and sacrificed their finances to pay Groton's $33,000 per year tuition and room and board. However, Mr. Park was ranked fourteenth in his class, earned a 1560 on his SAT, and demonstrated mathematical prowess. How do schools like those that rejected Mr. Park—Harvard, Yale, Brown, and Columbia—justify their choices in admitting less qualified students? Some assert that favoring children of alumni and prospective donors helps to ensure the growth of their institutions through the funding of scholarships, faculty salaries, and other projects by alumni parents. They further contend that children of celebrities "enhance an institution's visibility." Daniel Golden, *For Groton Grads, Academics Aren't Only Keys to Ivy Schools*, WALL ST. J., Apr. 25, 2003, at A1.

The college admissions process has serious implications for low-income and minority students. Considering most prestigious universities have relatively few minority alumni and low-income families do not have the means to contribute to colleges, many promising students are excluded from the elite academic realm. Consequently, they will attend less prestigious schools and have trouble attaining prominent occupations in the job market. In turn, these students will fail to pass to their children the capital necessary to succeed and the socioeconomic caste in society will endure through time. Economic distribution will continue to dwindle and wealth inequalities will consistently prevail.

Is it unjust for colleges to use legacy or donation criteria in deciding to offer a student admission? Some deem that the legacy preference unfairly favors wealthy applicants:

> The reason for the legacy preference appears to be primarily economic. Harvard and Yale, along with many other academic institutions, argue that the financial support provided by alumni is critical to their fiscal health. The assumption is that alumni will stop donating to fundraising campaigns if colleges reject their children. If economics were the primary basis for admission, however, why should the wealthiest applicants always not be accepted over all others? The very purpose of a need-blind admissions policy as expounded by both Harvard and Yale is to admit students regardless of their ability to pay or their financial background. Yet by preferring legacies over other applicants based

upon economic reasons, both schools are admitting that the financial resources of an applicant's family do matter. Thus, need-blind admissions are a misnomer, for economic considerations apparently are of great importance in the admissions process. John D. Lamb, *The Real Affirmative Action Babies: Legacy Preferences at Harvard and Yale*, 26 Colum. J.L. & Soc. Probs. 491, 517–18 (1993).

Do you agree with Lamb that admissions are not truly need-blind because admissions officers take financial issues into account when evaluating applications?

Are the legacy preferences unconstitutional? Can students like Mr. Park bring an equal protection claim against schools like Harvard and Yale for denying them admission and admitting lesser qualified students whose parents donated a gymnasium to the institution? Though no cases address the legitimacy of a private institution's admissions preference for children of alumni, a North Carolina court upheld a preference for out-of-state legacies at the University of North Carolina at Chapel Hill. There, the plaintiff asserted that she was denied equal protection when the school rejected her while accepting legacies and in-state applicants. Because the plaintiff was not part of a suspect class and no fundamental criteria were involved, the state was only required to show a rational basis for its preferential treatment. The court held that because out-of-state alumni offer considerable financial support for the school, the university's preferential treatment was a rational basis and not unconstitutional. *Rosenstock v. Governors of Univ. of N.C.*, 423 F. Supp. 1321, 1322–27 (M.D.N.C. 1976). For more on affirmative action, see chapter 13.

4. Estate tax. The estate tax, also referred to by opponents as the death tax, is a means of limiting the impact of intergenerational transmission of wealth and redistributing wealth through government spending. Only about 2 percent of deaths result in estate tax liability due to exemptions and other provisions, and the average estate paid taxes of 17 percent. Iris J. Lay & Joel Friedman, *Estate Tax Repeal: A Costly Windfall for the Wealthiest Americans* (Center on Budget and Policy Priorities, rev. Feb. 6, 2001), *available at* http://www.cbpp.org/5-25-00tax.htm.

People in the highest 20 percent of the income distribution at the time of their death pay 99 percent of estate taxes. And 91 percent of decedents had annual incomes over $190,000. *Id.* Opponents to the estate tax claim that farms and small businesses bear the weight of the tax, but these estates in fact make up a small proportion of taxable estates and could be given additional relief without repealing the entire estate tax. *Id.* The complete repeal of the estate tax will cost the government about $60 billion annually; the wealthiest people in the country would receive windfalls, often in the millions of dollars; and income such as unrealized capital gains would never be taxed. *Id.*

Despite the potentially devastating effects, there is bipartisan political support for repealing the estate tax. The Economic Growth and Tax Relief Reconciliation Act of 2001 phases out the estate tax between 2002 and 2009, but it includes a sunset provision that would reinstate the estate tax in 2011 unless further legislation extends the repeal. Agnes C. Powell, *Hocus-Pocus: The Federal Estate Tax—Now You See It, Now You Don't*, Nat'l Bus. Ass'n Mag. 21 (Oct. 2001).

The repeal of the estate tax would greatly increase the intergenerational transmission of wealth, further restraining economic mobility, and leading to cutbacks of government funded programs. What could prevent further legislation limiting redistribution of wealth? What alternative means of wealth redistribution could close the economic gap between rich and poor, and between black and white?

5.   Race and taxes. Thomas and Mary Edsall argue in *Chain Reaction: The Impact of Race, Rights and Taxes on American Politics* that political party voting alignment with regards to tax policy is linked to issues of race. Specifically, they contend that "race has become a powerful wedge, breaking up what had been the majoritarian economic interests of the poor, working, and lower-middle classes in the traditional liberal coalition." Thomas Byrne Edsall & Mary D. Edsall, Chain Reaction: The Impact of Race, Rights and Taxes on American Politics 4 (1991). The general polarization between the two parties that has taken place on issues of race has been reflected in the fashioning of a "Republican populism" in which conservative politicians have devised a strategy "to persuade working and lower-middle class voters to join an alliance with business interests and the affluent." *Id.* at 13. Central to this strategy has been opposition to programs designed to benefit racial minorities, such as busing and affirmative action, along with a commitment to reduced spending and curtailed government programs, and rejection of welfare and social programs which have been portrayed as benefiting minorities to the detriment of working-class whites. *Id.* at 13–19. The Edsalls detect a new definition of taxes, in which they are not understood as resources for the funding of government, but rather as a hand-out from those who work to those who do not, the latter group implicitly being racial minorities. *Id.* at 214. *See also*, Woojin Lee & John Roemer, *Racism and Redistribution in the United States: A Solution to the Problem of American Exceptionalism*, Cowles Foundation for Research in Economics, Discussion Paper No. 1462 (2004).

In a progressive tax system, tax burdens rise with incomes. Dana Milbank & Jonathan Weisman, *Middle Class Tax Shares Set to Rise: Studies Say Burden of Rich to Decline*, Wash. Post, Jun. 4, 2003, at A1. Although progressivity is evident in much of the tax system, cuts on dividends, capital gains, and estate taxes lower the burden on the wealthiest Americans, actually increasing the burden on the middle class. *Id.* How will the tax cuts affect economic equality? Will those households identified by Oliver and Shapiro as "on the edge," and therefore least equipped to handle the economic downturn, benefit from the tax cuts? Is a progressive tax system fair, or should the poor and wealthy contribute comparable portions of their income?

6.   Financial behavior. A thriving couple in *Wealth and Inequality in America* credited their financial success to the values instilled in them by their families. Could differences in financial behaviors (such as financial planning horizons, spending compared to income, saving habits, and financial risk taking in investments) explain the wealth disparities between African Americans and other Americans? Stephen Brobeck, *Black American Personal Wealth: Current Status* (Consumer Federation of America, Aug. 2002), *available at* http://www.americasaves.org/back_page/Black-WealthReport082902.doc. According to the Consumer Federation of America, differences in financial behaviors between black Americans and all other Americans "virtually disappear" when comparing similar wealth levels. *Id.* Discrepancies in financial behavior between African Americans and the nation as a whole can be attributed to the concentration of wealth-poor people—45 percent of black Americans compared with 25 percent of all Americans. While education efforts should continue to recognize ethnic and cultural differences, effective financial education should focus on the behavior of the wealth-poor. *Id.*

———

Your Stake in America

41 ARIZ. L. REV. 249 (1999).

■ BRUCE ACKERMAN & ANNE ALSTOTT

America has become a three-class society. More than twenty-five percent of its children now graduate from a four-year college and move into the ranks of the symbol-using class. Their increasing prosperity stands in sharp contrast to the grim picture of life at the bottom. The lowest twenty percent inhabit a world of low wages, dead-end jobs, and high unemployment despite the economic boom.

Then there is the vast majority. Over the past quarter century, they have endured a long period of economic stagnation. Despite optimistic rhetoric from the right, economic growth has bypassed these forgotten Americans. The richest twenty percent has captured virtually all of the growth in the nation's wealth since the early 1980s. While income trends have been somewhat less extreme, family income for the vast middle is only modestly higher than in 1973. Even treading water has been tough. Real wages for men have declined by nearly fifteen percent, and it is only the massive entry by women into the workplace that has taken up the slack.

Trickle-down economics has utterly failed and will continue to fail in the globalizing economy of the future. The past is prologue: By 1995, the top one percent owned 38.5% of the nation's disposable wealth, up from 33.8% in 1983. During the 1990s, the share of total income earned by the top twenty percent has risen to its highest point since 1947.

Our politics has not caught up with this three-class reality. On the one hand, we heap large subsidies on the college-bound. On the other, we target the underclass with diminishing amounts of assistance. However, we have done little to aid the vast middle. While the rich have been showered with tax breaks, the middle has been treated to a series of symbolic gestures signifying nothing. The 1997 "middle-class tax cut" hid a darker agenda.

The average family took home a few hundred dollars in new tax credits for children and education, but the rich gained thousands of dollars from the capital gains tax cut and other goodies.

The result is simmering resentment and a ready reception of the protectionist nostrums of Ross Perot and Pat Buchanan. The current boom will hold these economic nationalists in check for a while, but it is past time to search for a more constructive response to economic inequality. How can we use the benefits of globalization to ensure that every American gets a fair start in life?

This is the question we set for ourselves in our new book The Stakeholder Society. Stakeholding seeks justice by rooting it in capitalism's preeminent value: the importance of private property. It points the way to a society that is more democratic, more productive, and more free. Bear with us, and you will see how a single innovation once proposed by Tom Paine can achieve what a thousand lesser policies have failed to accomplish.

The basic proposal is straightforward. As young Americans rise to maturity, they should claim a stake of $80,000 as part of their birthright as citizens. This stake should be financed by an annual wealth tax, equal to two percent of every individual's wealth in excess of $80,000. The tie between wealth-holding and stake-holding expresses a fundamental social responsibility. Every American has an obligation to contribute to a fair starting point for all.

Stakeholders are free. They may use their money for any purpose they see fit: to start a business or pay for higher education, to buy a house or raise a family or save for the future. But they must take responsibility for their choices. Their triumphs and blunders are their own.

At the end of their lives, stakeholders have a special responsibility. Since the $80,000 was central in starting them off in life, it is only fair for them to repay it at death if this is financially possible. The stakeholding fund, in short, will be enriched each year by the ongoing contributions of property-owners, and by a final payback at death.

There are many possible variations on the stakeholding theme, but we have said enough to suggest its broad political appeal. How many young adults start off life with $80,000? How many parents can afford to give their children the head-start that this implies?

Stakeholding liberates college graduates from the burdens of debt, often with something to spare. It offers unprecedented opportunities for the tens of millions who do not go to college and have often been short-changed by their high school educations. For the first time, they will confront the labor market with a certain sense of security. The stake will give them the independence to choose where to live, whether to marry, and how to train for economic opportunity. Some will fail, but fewer than today.

We should, of course, structure the program to maximize the successes. For starters, no stakeholder should be allowed free use of his $80,000 without completing high school and passing a state or national qualifying examination. High-school dropouts would have their stakes held in trust, and would have access only to the annually accruing interest. Since only three-quarters of American teenagers have high school degrees, this single requirement will prevent massive "stakeblowing" by those least capable of handling adult responsibilities. It will also provide a beacon of hope to kids locked in rural poverty or urban ghettos. Stay in school and graduate, and you will not be forgotten. You will get a solid chance to live out the American dream of economic independence.

Timing is also crucial. High school graduates should get immediate access to their money if they want to spend their $80,000 on college. Those choosing other paths should be obliged to learn a few lessons in the school of hard knocks before they can get their stakes—in $20,000 annual payments between the ages of twenty-one and twenty-four. The result will change the way young people think about themselves, their options, and their obligations to society.

Begin with the college-bound. Poor kids confront hardships unknown to their better-off peers—juggling schoolwork and jobs in ways that easily overwhelm self-confidence. The endless rounds of scholarship applications, and intermittent failures to pay tuition, take a toll by themselves. Statistics confirm that students in two-year colleges are even harder-pressed: a much higher percentage live at home, hold a job, and work more hours. It should be no surprise, then, that lower-class kids are much more likely to delay enrollment, and less likely to earn a degree, than their richer peers. At the end of the day, fifty-one percent of students from the top quarter earn bachelor's degrees, compared to twenty-two percent of middle-status students, and only 7.2% in the lowest socioeconomic quartile. For this large group of college-bound students, stakeholding will work a genuine revolution. It would allow all young men and women to focus their energies on academic work and compete with their peers on relatively equal terms.

Stakeholding would also inaugurate a new era of healthy competition in higher education. While colleges might try to raise tuition, they would face countervailing market pressures to keep costs low. Every student would enter the market with significant resources and an incentive to shop carefully. No longer would state universities or community colleges have a captive pool of in-state or low-income students without other options. These people could now choose a school in another community, or across the country, or even overseas.

This option will be especially valuable to people interested in a two-year college degree. At present, these colleges provide much smaller subsidies to their students than do more traditional universities. However, under the new system, students at two-year colleges will have the same buying power as their more academically inclined age-mates. To be sure, they will be utterly unwilling to spend their entire $80,000 on a couple of years of post-high school education. However, their stakes will create new incentives for serious programs directed at their distinctive concerns. Over time, two-year colleges will emerge from the shadow of their bigger brothers, and build their students' skills and self-confidence with increasing imagination and vigor.

We have left the best for last. Consider the millions of Americans who decide that college—even a two-year college—is not for them. These are today's forgotten Americans. Many of them have already been denied the decent high school education that should be every citizen's birthright. Now they are tossed unaided into the marketplace, while their upwardly mobile peers are given federal scholarships and state-subsidized tuitions.

This is just plain wrong. Joe Sixpack is every bit as much of an American as Joe College. And for the first time, his claim to equal citizenship will be treated with genuine respect. Since these high-school graduates are not going to college, they will have to wait until their early twenties to gain access to their stakes. Indeed, some may want to require young adults to wait until twenty-five or so before they get any of their money. We would be happy to compromise so long as the basic principle of universal stakeholding remains intact. The decision to go to college should not be required for an American to gain his country's support for the pursuit of happiness. All Americans have a fundamental right to start off as adults with a fair chance at making a decent life for themselves.

For all our precautions, some will fail to make good use of their stakes, and in ways they will bitterly regret. But the predictable failures of some should not deprive millions of others of *their* fair chance to pursue happiness. Each individual citizen has a right to a fair share of the patrimony left by preceding generations. This right should not be contingent on how others use or misuse their stakes.

Some poor Americans do face multiple social problems—inadequate education, drug or alcohol abuse, a propensity to violence—that leave them ill-equipped to handle financial responsibility for their stake. Despite pervasive media images, the size of the so-called "underclass" is quite tiny—less than four percent of the population. Most of these people would be excluded from full control of their stake by the requirement of high-school graduation.

In addition, we propose a cautious use of stakeholding as a sanction in the criminal law justice system. At the present time, the only way we have to punish young adults is to deprive them of their personal liberty. Stakeholding will, however, for the first time, also allow us to use financial sanctions against youth crime. For example, we would put nineteen year olds on notice that participation in the drug-trade would mean the loss of all or part of their stakes. For many people of eighteen or nineteen, such a threat might have more deterrence value than a prison term.

In any event, the important point is this: We should not allow trendy talk of "underclass" pathologies to divert our attention from the central problem posed by our emerging three-class society. Quite simply, there are tens of millions of ordinary Americans who are perfectly capable of responsible decision making in a stakeholding society, but are now becoming the forgotten citizens of our globalizing economy. We should confront this problem now before the wealth gap widens to Latin American proportions.

In our many conversations on the subject, somebody invariably suggests the wisdom of restricting the stake to a limited set of praiseworthy purposes—requiring each citizen to gain bureaucratic approval before spending down his $80,000. Would not this allow us to redistribute wealth and make sure the money is well spent?

This question bears the mark of the bureaucratic mindset that has haunted so much policymaking in the twentieth century. Our goal is to transcend the welfare state mentality, not transform stakeholding into another exercise in paternalistic social engineering. The point of stakeholding is to liberate each citizen from government, not to create an excuse for a vast new bureaucracy intervening in our lives. To be sure, the construction industry, the university sector, and the brokerage houses would prefer a plan that limited stakeholders' choices to home-buying, education, or investment. But if stakeholders want advice, they can buy it on the market. If people in their twenties can not be treated as adults, when will they be old enough?

We do not deny the need for a "social safety net" for Americans who make particularly bad choices, but this is not our primary focus. We are concerned with providing a fair opportunity for success for all Americans, and not only those lucky enough to be born to parents of the symbol-using classes. It is one thing to make a mess out of your life; quite another, never to have had a fair chance.

Indeed, the real problem with stakeholding is that it does not go far enough to redeem America's promise of an equal opportunity society. Does not the $80,000 come too late for all those who have been shortchanged as children?

Our short answer is yes. As a consequence, we certainly favor more spending on better versions of Head Start and the like. Nonetheless, we are skeptical of the egalitarian potential of enormous new investments in primary and secondary education. So long as suburbs can insulate themselves from central cities, there is only so much that money alone can accomplish. And, the upper classes have proven themselves adept in channeling federal aid for the disadvantaged into their own local school systems. Worse yet, school decentralization and privatization seem to be the order of the day—rather than a movement toward metropolitan-wide school systems and greater national efforts to provide poorer regions of the country with greater educational resources.

By contrast, it would be relatively easy to realize the goals of a stakeholder society. To a very large degree, the institutional infrastructure is already in place. We already have an Internal Revenue Service and a Social Security Administration. Although it is fashionable to denigrate these "bureaucracies," both agencies are full of competent people whose tasks might easily be broadened to encompass the jobs of identifying eligible stakeholders and paying out benefits. Unlike a comparable educational reform, stakeholding will not require a massive reorganization of the existing institutional framework. It builds on what we already have.

Americans could, in relatively short order, actually achieve the massive step toward equality of opportunity that stakeholding makes possible. This breakthrough, in turn, would give the lie to neo-conservative banalities about the inevitability of government failure. Having established that Americans *can* succeed in redeeming their fundamental ideals by inaugurating stakeholding, many other seemingly impossible initiatives may seem within our grasp.

Of course, real freedom and equal opportunity do not come cheap. Using conservative assumptions, the annual cost of stakeholding today would be about $255 billion—a little less than we spend on national defense. This is a big number, but we have made comparable commitments in the past: Would America have been a better place after the Second World War without the GI Bill of Rights? At that time, wealthy taxpayers were a lot poorer than they are today. They were paying far heavier taxes, and yet they did not seek to evade their obligation to give the rising generation a fair start in adult life.

The GI Bill represented the payment of a debt for the sacrifices that our soldiers made during the war. Today the ties that bind older to younger are less obvious—but no less important. Day after day, our society demands countless small acts of voluntary cooperation, as well as many larger personal sacrifices. If the younger generation is denied a fair start, how can the rest of us expect them to reciprocate as the need requires?

For the rest of their lives, stakeholders will endlessly consider how their $80,000 contributed to their individual pursuits of happiness—and at the same time reflect on their good fortune in enjoying this precious right of economic citizenship. Except for the most hardened cynics, this will lead to a deep and sustaining loyalty to the country that made stakeholding a concrete reality. Rather than dismissing the Declaration of Independence as boastful words on paper, stakeholders will hear in Jefferson's proud phrases a description of their own lives, and seek, as best they can, to repay their own debt by passing on their great American heritage on to the future.

We have talked enough about the potential benefits of stakeholding. Let us move to the revenue-raising side of the equation: How are we going to come up with the necessary quarter of a trillion dollars a year?

Well, there is never a good time for a tax hike, but now is the best time we will have for a long time. To be sure, we would not bet the ranch on the optimistic budgetary projections coming out of Washington right now. Since both Bill Clinton and Congressional Republicans are happy to take credit for restoring the nation to fiscal health, neither side emphasizes how much a sharp recession or two might dent their happy predictions of multi-trillion dollar surpluses over the next decade or so. More importantly, short-term surpluses will be swamped in the longer run. Depending on what we do with Medicare, the deficits looming by mid-century may well be horrific. Nevertheless, the happy numbers of the next decade should provide us a much-needed pause for reflection on our long-run fiscal responsibilities.

Stakeholding makes an initial intellectual contribution by exposing a question-begging assumption behind the emerging debate surrounding the budget surplus. Too often, the talk proceeds as if the only serious question is how much of the surplus should be used to save Social Security and Medicare. This begs the question whether our only exigent fiscal priority is aid to the elderly or whether the time has not come to emphasize the competing claim of the generation only now rising to maturity.

In raising stakeholding as a serious alternative, we do not suggest that it should automatically trump the claims of the older generation to a decent level of income and medical care. But we do believe that both social justice and social peace require America to redeem its promise of equal opportunity to the young no less than its promise of decency to the old. If we can not afford to do both, it is not obvious that we should entirely ignore stakeholding and lavish the lion's share of the surplus on the old.

America *is* rich enough to do both. Despite the fog of anti-tax rhetoric, our taxes remain far lower than those imposed by other rich Western nations, and they would remain so after we have paid the quarter-of-a-trillion-dollar annual bill for stakeholding. Obviously, there are lots of different ways of raising the money. For example, we would favor a hike in the income tax or a new national consumption tax whose revenues were dedicated to the stakeholding fund. But, so far as we are concerned, the best way to proceed is through a new comprehensive tax on wealth similar to the ones currently imposed by twelve other countries in the elite club of first-world nations called the Organization for Economic Cooperation and Development.

We have built many conservative assumptions into our economic analysis of the revenue-raising potential of such a tax. We have also allowed every American an $80,000 personal exemption, thereby eliminating the bottom sixty percent of the population from all liability. Nevertheless, our analysis reveals that an annual tax of two percent would be enough to fund the entire program.

Even when we focus on the top forty percent, this tax would have a vastly different impact on different groups. So far as the households falling between the sixtieth and eightieth percentile, the average tax would be $1100 a year, and the entire group would contribute only seven percent of the total fund. The big tax burden would be borne at the top, with thirty-nine percent of the total tax contributed by the top one percent of American households, whose median wealth in 1995 was $4.6 million.

The disproportionate impact of the tax on the rich strikes us as entirely fair. Since wealth is correlated with age, Americans over the age of fifty or sixty will bear the brunt of the burden. But it is precisely these people who have participated fully in the great post-war economic boom. The wealthy man or woman who is sixty in the year 2000 was born in 1940—just in time to avoid the agonies of the Great Depression and the Second World War, but just in time to reap the harvest. Graduating from college about 1960, the typical up-and-comer was in a perfect position to take advantage of the rich array of opportunities made possible by Amer-

ica's rise to world power. The best universities, the most advanced companies, the biggest pool of capital—all of these were available for Americans who seized the moment. To be sure, nobody could become wealthy without some combination of effort, insight, and luck. It would be blind for any sixty-year-old to ignore the role played by the simple fact that he was an American in an American age—and thereby gained the enormous advantages created at great sacrifice by his parents' generation. Given their existing balance of generational advantage, it is especially appropriate to ask this group of elder Americans to make a sacrifice to sustain the Republic's political and economic equilibrium.

We are calling upon older Americans to remember that they themselves were the beneficiaries of similar acts of statesmanship by earlier generations. During the New Deal and Great Society, Americans recognized the elderly as a group that was particularly threatened by the inegalitarian operation of market forces. By responding with Social Security and Medicare, our predecessors ensured a decent life for millions of elderly Americans today. Without these programs, the distribution of wealth would be even more unequal than it already is. Is it not time, then, for the elder generation to reciprocate when the market threatens to undermine the promise of economic opportunity for millions of younger Americans?

This commitment should not come at the cost of retirees who depend on their monthly Social Security checks. Rather than leading a raid on Social Security revenues, we simply urge prosperous older Americans to recognize the moral claim of younger Americans who will otherwise live out lives of quiet despair.

Or not so quiet despair. After all, the prison population has soared over the last quarter century. About 100 Americans in every 100,000 were in the nation's prisons in 1975; that number is now over 400. Young males, and increasingly females, are the prime targets for prison—men and women who might find it within themselves to take a different path in a stakeholding society. If inequality increases over the next century, are we really prepared to lock up more and more young Americans who react with rage at a system that has never delivered on its promises? If those with the greatest stake in the system do not take heed, who is supposed to?

It is time for the wealthy to accept stakeholding as part of the social compact. While wealth taxes are unfamiliar in America, they are a fixture of public finance in most other industrialized nations. Of course, every new tax generates the same old cry that it will kill the economy. Rich people are always happy to tell you the story of the goose that lays the golden eggs, but is it just a fairy tale?

Not only has our economy boomed, and busted, under very different levels of taxation, recent empirical research suggests that the link between tax rates and growth is far weaker than implied by the prevailing political rhetoric. Moreover, stakeholding will itself unleash the energies of millions of youthful entrepreneurs—while many will fail, many others will succeed ways that will enrich the lives of us all.

Two hundred years ago, Tom Paine surveyed the revolutionary world he helped create, and sensed something missing: "A revolution in the state of civilization is the necessary companion of revolutions in the system of government." This could be accomplished, he was convinced, only through stakeholding. Every citizen, Paine insisted, had a right to a stake of fifteen pounds Sterling "when arrived at the age of twenty-one years." In a remarkable gesture for the eighteenth century, Paine argued that this expanded stake should go to every man *and* woman. Regardless of his or her claims on private wealth, each should be accorded an economic stake in the commonwealth.

Tom Paine was not alone. Our leading Founders acknowledged a deep relationship between property and citizenship. When Madison viewed "the merits alone," it was clear to him that "the freeholders of the Country would be the safest depositories of Republican liberty," and that the propertyless should be excluded from the suffrage. Standing before the Constitutional Convention, he did not conceal his anxiety as he glimpsed the dread day when the "great majority of the people will not only be without landed, but any other sort of, property."

But in 1787, this grim prospect could be deferred to the remote future. The Founders treated the problem of propertylessness in the way they dealt with the curse of slavery. They did not seek a definitive solution, leaving it to some later generation to confront the crisis when it became acute.

This seemed sensible enough. A vast frontier beckoned to generations of yeomen farmers. So long as the government sold virgin land at low prices, the link between property and citizenship could be more or less preserved. But as the nineteenth century moved on, this Jeffersonian vision of a farmer-republic became increasingly obsolete. By the time of the great Homestead Act of 1863, the statute's provision of free land on the frontier was already out of sync with the needs of the rising urban masses of the East. If the link between property and citizenship were to be sustained, provision of free land would no longer suffice. With the closing of the frontier, something like Tom Paine's vision of stakeholding was required to guarantee each citizen a property interest in America.

By then Paine's voice had become a muffled memory. The mainstream of reform was flowing in other directions: Populists, Progressives, New Dealers, and the partisans of the Great Society sought to regain control over the market economy, but none moved in the direction of citizen stakeholding. Rather than broadening the property-owning base, the overriding aim was to regulate property more intensely in the public interest.

We think that the intellectual climate really is changing today. Nationalization of industry is on nobody's agenda anymore. People are recognizing that "capitalism" is a Marxist label concealing the differences between economic systems built on private property and markets—some bitterly unjust, and others striving for a world of free and equal citizenry. It is time to stop dreaming about

private property and get to work creating a commonwealth in which all citizens are property owners.

This intuition has been behind some major initiatives attempted by leading politicians of our age. They have gained great followings through initiatives that bear a family resemblance to our proposal. When Margaret Thatcher became Prime Minister, thirty-two percent of all housing in England was publicly owned. Though bent on sweeping privatization, Thatcher refused to sell off these vast properties to big companies. She invited residents to buy their own homes at bargain rates. With a single stroke, she created a new class of property-owning citizens, and won vast popularity in the process.

A more sweeping initiative took place in the Czech Republic in the aftermath of 1989. The Prime Minister, Vaclav Klaus, was confronting a much larger task than Thatcher's: the state sector contained 7000 medium and large-scale enterprises, 25,000 to 35,000 smaller ones. How to distribute this legacy of Communism? Klaus saw his problem as an opportunity to create a vast new property-owning class.

The mechanism was the ingenious technique of "voucher privatization." Each Czech citizen was encouraged to subscribe to a book of vouchers that he could use to bid for shares in state companies as they were put on the auction block. An overwhelming majority—8.5 out of 10.5 million—took up Klaus' offer, and claimed their fair share of the nation's wealth as they moved into the free-market system. Klaus' creative program helped cement his position as the leading politician of the Republic. More importantly, the broad involvement of citizen-stakeholders played a central role in legitimating the country's transition to liberal democracy.

Thatcher and Klaus conceived their initiatives as one-shot affairs. However, the citizens of Alaska have made stakeholding a regular part of their political economy. Once again, the occasion was the distribution of a major public asset, in this case the revenues from North Slope oil. Rather than using it all for public expenditures, the Republican leadership designed a stakeholding scheme that is now distributing about a $1000 a year to every Alaskan citizen. Once again, the system has become broadly popular, with politicians of both parties regularly pledging that they will not raid the symbolically-named Permanent Fund.

There is no good reason to limit stakeholding to physical assets like housing or factories or oil. Americans have created other assets that are less material, but have even greater value. Most notably, the free enterprise system did not drop from thin air. It has emerged only as the result of a complex and on-going scheme of social cooperation. The "free market" requires heavy public expenditures on police, courts, and much else besides. But without billions of voluntary decisions by Americans to respect the rights of property in their daily lives, the system would collapse overnight. All Americans benefit from this cooperative activity—some much more than others. Those who benefit the most have a duty to share some of their wealth with fellow citizens whose cooperation they require to sustain the market system. This obligation is all the more exigent when the operation of the global market threatens to split the country more sharply into haves and have-nots.

This view gives our proposal a different ideological spin from those pioneered by Margaret Thatcher and Vaclav Klaus. Surely there will be some on the Right who will blanch at the implications of our proposal. But we hope that many others will come to see its justice. We expect a similar split on the Left. Some will be deeply suspicious of liberating stakeholding assets from the grip of the regulatory state, leaving each citizen free to make their own decisions. Others will be more impressed by the justice of empowering all Americans to share in the pursuit of happiness.

Stakeholding also holds out the promise of political renewal. Nobody we have met has the slightest problem grasping the idea of $80,000—or the possibility of funding the program by taxing wealth. Lots of people do not like the initiative, but at least they know what they are disagreeing with—and this is absolutely essential for a rebirth of democratic politics in this country. Unless progressives come up with projects that are transparent to the common understanding, the politics of scandal will have no real competitor. The general public has no patience for a policy debate that speaks a technocratic language accessible only to people with advanced degrees.

If Beltway babble is the alternative, ordinary Americans will turn with relief to news of the latest personal indiscretion by leading politicos. Only a program like stakeholding can focus the public mind on the prospects for real change. It raises—in a straightforward and concrete way—the leading questions of our age: Is America more than a libertarian marketplace? Can we preserve a sense of ourselves as a nation of free and equal citizens?

Stakeholding really does bring power back to the people. It marks a radical break with the elitist tradition of social engineering. We do not need a host of experts to minister to ordinary Americans. Give citizens their stakes and let them inaugurate a new age of freedom.

This call can unify a badly fractured nation. Even many Americans in the top twenty percent may recognize its power. Do they really want their own children to live in gated communities locked away from the rest of American life?

The stakeholder society is no utopia, but it does provide an alternative to our current moral drift. Perhaps we will never fully realize the American Dream of equal opportunity. But without that dream, this country will become a very ugly place.

NOTES AND QUESTIONS

1. Ackerman & Alstott's proposal. Do you think the stakeholder idea effectively addresses the problems of inequality outlined in this section? Will it do what the authors think it will? Is it politically feasible?

2. The stakeholder society and African American reparations. Does Ackerman & Alstott's proposal address racialized disparities in wealth? What can minority groups do to overcome obstacles to economic opportunity? Claud Anderson of The Harvest Institute (a think tank whose goal is to reform the social and economic aspects of African American life) offers several suggestions to African Americans to escape financial inequality, including mastering the principles of capitalism and group economics, vertically integrating industries and businesses, expanding business in minority communities, and increasing black leadership. CLAUD ANDERSON, BLACK LABOR WHITE WEALTH: THE SEARCH FOR POWER AND ECONOMIC JUSTICE 188 (1994). Another notable recommendation by Anderson is for African Americans to ask the government for reparations: "Reparation payments should be directed into black communities . . . to repair the socioeconomic damages that the dominant society and government have inflicted in 16 generations of black Americans." *Id.* at 182. Is Anderson's request too radical? If only five or six generations are needed to eradicate the indicia of slavery, why is Anderson asking for *sixteen* generations to be compensated? *See* Emma Coleman Jordan, *A History Lesson: Reparations for What?*, 58 N.Y.U. ANN. SURV. AM. L. 1,557 (2003). *See also*, ROY L. BROOKS, ATONEMENT AND FORGIVENESS: A NEW MODEL FOR BLACK REPARATIONS (2004).

3. Stakeholding and inequality. Why do income and wealth inequality matter? After all, capitalism is premised on the notion of competition, and not everyone can be a winner. Do Ackerman and Alstott explain why we should care about rising inequality?

CHAPTER 7

LIFE IN A CLASS SOCIETY

A. DOWN AND OUT

Number of People Living in Poverty Increases in U.S.

N.Y. TIMES, Sept. 25, 2002, at A1.

■ ROBERT PEAR

The proportion of Americans living in poverty rose significantly last year, increasing for the first time in eight years, the Census Bureau reported today. At the same time, the bureau said that the income of middle-class households fell for the first time since the last recession ended, in 1991.

The Census Bureau's annual report on income and poverty provided stark evidence that the weakening economy had begun to affect large segments of the population, regardless of race, region or class. Daniel H. Weinberg, chief of income and poverty statistics at the Census Bureau, said the recession that began in March 2001 had reduced the earnings of millions of Americans.

The report also suggested that the gap between rich and poor continued to grow.

All regions except the Northeast experienced a decline in household income, the bureau reported. For blacks, it was the first significant decline in two decades; non-Hispanic whites saw a slight decline. Even the incomes of Asians and Pacific Islanders, a group that achieved high levels of prosperity in the 1990's, went down significantly last year.

"The decline was widespread," Mr. Weinberg said.

The Census Bureau said the number of poor Americans rose last year to 32.9 million, an increase of 1.3 million, while the proportion living in poverty rose to 11.7 percent, from 11.3 percent in 2000.

Median household income fell to $42,228 in 2001, a decline of $934 or 2.2 percent from the prior year. The number of households with income above the median is the same as the number below it.

A family of four was classified as poor if it had cash income less than $18,104 last year. The official poverty levels, updated each year to reflect changes in the Consumer Price Index, were $14,128 for a family of three, $11,569 for a married couple and $9,039 for an individual.

The bureau's report is likely to provide fodder for the Congressional campaigns. The White House said the increase in poverty resulted, in part, from an economic slowdown that began under President Bill Clinton. But Democrats said the data showed the failure of President Bush's economic policies and his tendency to neglect the economy.

Mr. Bush said today that he remained optimistic. "When you combine the productivity of the American people with low interest rates and low inflation, those are the ingredients for growth," Mr. Bush said.

But Senator Paul S. Sarbanes, Democrat of Maryland, said the administration should "start paying attention to the economic situation." Richard A. Gephardt of Missouri, the House Democratic leader, expressed amazement that Mr. Bush, after being in office for 20 months, was still blaming his predecessor.

Rudolph G. Penner, a former director of the Congressional Budget Office, said: "The increase in poverty is most certainly a result of the recession. The slow recovery, the slow rate of growth, has been very disappointing. Whether that has a political impact this fall depends on whether the election hinges on national conditions or focuses on local issues."

Although the poverty rate, the proportion of the population living in poverty, rose four-tenths of a percentage point last year, it was still lower than in most of the last two decades. The poverty rate exceeded 12 percent every year from 1980 to 1998. As the economy grew from 1993 to 2000, the rate plunged, to 11.3 percent from 15.1 percent, and the poverty rolls were reduced by 7.7 million people, to 31.6 million.

The latest recession showed an unusual pattern, seeming to raise poverty rates among whites more than among minority groups, Mr. Weinberg said.

Increases in poverty last year were concentrated in the suburbs, in the South and among non-Hispanic whites, the Census Bureau said. Indeed, non-Hispanic whites were the only racial group for whom the poverty rate showed a significant increase, to 7.8 percent in 2001, from 7.4 percent in 2000.

Poverty rates for minority groups were once much higher. But last year, the bureau said, they remained "at historic lows" for blacks (22.7 percent), Hispanics (21.4 percent) and Asian Americans (10.2 percent).

With its usual caution, the Census Bureau said the data did not conclusively show a year-to-year increase in income inequality. But the numbers showed a clear trend in that direction over the last 15 years.

The most affluent fifth of the population received half of all household income last year, up from 45 percent in 1985. The poorest fifth received 3.5 percent of total household income, down from 4 percent in 1985. Average income for the top 5 percent of households rose by $1,000 last year, to $260,464, but the average declined or stayed about the same for most other income brackets.

Robert Greenstein, executive director of the Center on Budget and Policy Priorities, a liberal research institute, said, "The census data show that income inequality either set a record in 2001 or tied for the highest level on record."

Median earnings increased 3.5 percent for women last year, but did not change for men, so women gained relative to men.

"The real median earnings of women age 15 and older who worked full time year-round increased for the fifth consecutive year, rising to $29,215— a 3.5 percent increase between 2000 and 2001," Mr. Weinberg said. The comparable figure for men was unchanged at $38,275. So the female-to-male earnings ratio reached a high of 0.76. The previous high was 0.74, first recorded in 1996.

Democrats said the data supported their contention that Congress should increase spending on social welfare programs, resisted by many Republicans. But Wade F. Horn, the administration's welfare director, said the number of poor children was much lower than in 1996, when Congress overhauled the welfare law to impose strict work requirements.

Of the 32.9 million poor people in the United States last year, 11.7 million were under 18, and 3.4 million were 65 or older. Poverty rates for children, 16.3 percent, and the elderly, 10.1 percent, were virtually unchanged from 2000. But the poverty rate for people 18 to 64 rose a half percentage point, to 10.1 percent.

Median household income for blacks fell last year by $1,025, or 3.4 percent, to $29,470. Median income of Hispanics, at $33,565, was virtually unchanged. But household income fell by 1.3 percent for non-Hispanic whites, to $46,305, and by 6.4 percent for Asian Americans, to $53,635.

The Census Bureau report also included these findings:

There were 6.8 million poor families last year, up from 6.4 million in 2000. The poverty rate for families rose to 9.2 percent, from a 26-year low of 8.7 percent in 2000.

The rate in the South rose to 13.5 percent, from 12.8 percent in 2000. The South is home to more than 40 percent of all the nation's poor, and it accounted for more than half of the national increase in the number of poor last year.

The poverty rate for the suburbs rose to 8.2 percent last year, from 7.8 percent in 2000. The number of poor people in suburban areas rose by 700,000, to 12 million. There was virtually no change in the rates in central cities (16.5 percent) and outside metropolitan areas (14.2 percent).

The bureau said the number of "severely poor" rose to 13.4 million last year, from 12.6 million in 2000. People are considered to be severely poor if their family incomes are less than half of the official poverty level.

Just Trying to Survive

Rosa Lee: A Mother and Her Family In Urban America 39–47 (1996).

■ Leon Dash

Rosa Lee guided her eleven-year-old grandson through the narrow aisles of a thrift shop in suburban Oxon Hill, Maryland, past the crowded racks of secondhand pants and shirts, stopping finally at the row of children's jackets and winter coats. Quickly, the boy selected a mock-leather flight jacket with a big number on the back and a price tag stapled to the collar.

"If you want it," Ross Lee said, "then you're going to have to help me get it."

"Okay, Grandmama," he said nervously. "But do it in a way that I won't get caught."

Like a skilled teacher instructing a new student, Rosa Lee told her grandson what to do. "Pretend you're trying it on. Don't look up! Don't look around! Don't laugh like it's some kind of joke! Just put it on. Let Grandma see how you look."

The boy slipped off his old, coat and put on the new one. Rosa Lee whispered, "Now put the other one back on, over it." She pushed down the new jacket's collar so that it was hidden.

"What do I do now?" he asked.

"Just walk on out the door," Rosa Lee said. "It's your coat."

Four days later, Rosa Lee is recounting this episode for me, recreating the dialogue by changing her voice to distinguish between herself and her grandson. It is January 1991. By now, I have spent enough time with Rosa Lee that her shoplifting exploits no longer surprise me.

The previous November, Rosa Lee took her eight-year-old granddaughter into the same thrift shop on a Sunday morning to steal a new winter coat for the girl one week after they were both baptized in a Pentecostal church. On the Sunday of the shoplifting lesson, Rosa Lee had decided she did not want to take her granddaughter back to the church because her winter coat was "tacky and dirty."

In the thrift shop, Rosa Lee told her granddaughter to take off her coat and hang it on the coatrack. Next, she told the grinning child to put on the attractive pink winter coat hanging on the rack.

"Are we going to take this coat, Grandma?" asked the skinny little girl.

"Yes," Rosa Lee told her. "We are exchanging coats. Now walk out the door."

A month later, a week before Christmas, Rosa Lee was searching for something in a large shopping bag in her bedroom and dumped the contents onto the bed. Out spilled dozens of bottles of expensive men's cologne and women's perfume, as well as leather gloves with their sixty-dollar price tags still attached. She leaves the tags on when she sells the goods as proof of the merchandise's newness and quality.

"Did you get all this in one trip?" I ask.

"Oh, no," she says. "This is a couple of weeks' worth."

In Rosa Lee's younger years especially, shoplifting was a major source of income, supplementing her welfare payments and the money she made during fifteen years of waitressing at various nightclubs. With eight children to feed and clothe, stealing, she says, helped her survive. Later on, when she began using heroin in the mid-1970s, her shoplifting paid for drugs.

She stole from clothing stores, drugstores, and grocery stores, stuffing items inside the torn liner of her winter coat or slipping them into one of the oversized black purses that she carries wherever she goes. When her children were young—the ages of the grandson and granddaughter—she taught them how to shoplift as well.

"Every time I went somewhere to make some money, I would take my children," she said. "I would teach them or they would watch me. 'Just watch what Mama does. I'm getting food for y'all to eat.' "

In supermarkets, she could count on her children "to distract the security guard while I hit the meat freezer. The guards would always watch groups of children before they'd watch an adult."

Her favorite targets were the department stores. One of her two older brothers, Joe Louis Wright, joked with me one day that Rosa Lee "owned a piece" of Hecht's and had put Lansburgh's out of business. "Man, she would get coats, silk dresses," he recalled. "A cloth coat with a mink collar. She got me a mohair suit. Black. Three-piece. I don't know how the hell she'd get them out of there."

Her stealing has caused divisions and hard feelings in her family, and is one reason why Rosa Lee's relationships with several of her brothers and sisters are strained. They see Rosa Lee's stealing as an extreme and unjustified reaction to their impoverished upbringing. And her sons Alvin and Eric have always refused to participate in any of their mother's illegal activities.

Rosa Lee has served eight short prison terms for various kinds of stealing during the past forty years, dating back to the early 1950s. Her longest stay was eight months for trying to steal a fur coat from a Maryland department store in 1965. She says that she went to prison rehabilitation programs each time but that none had much of an effect on her. "I attended those programs so it would look good on my record when I went before the parole board," she says. "What they were talking about didn't mean anything to me. I didn't have the education they said would get me a job. I couldn't read no matter how many programs I went to."

Nothing seems to deter her from shoplifting, not even the specter of another jail term. On the day she directed her grandson in stealing the flight jacket, she was four days away from sentencing at the city's Superior Court for stealing the bedsheets from Hecht's the previous summer.

"I'm just trying to survive," she says.

Rosa Lee had chosen her clothes carefully for her appearance before Commissioner John Treanor in November. She wanted to look as poor as possible to draw his sympathy.

She wore an ill-fitting winter coat, gray wool overalls and a white wool hat pulled back to show her graying hair. She had removed her upper dental plate to give herself a toothless look when she smiled. "My homey look," she calls it. "No lipstick. No earrings. No nothing!"

Rosa Lee did not expect to go home that day. She saw a heavyset female deputy U.S. marshal move into place behind the defense table when the courtroom clerk called her name. It was a certain sign that Treanor had already decided to "step her back" and send her to jail. She hastily handed me her purse with all her documents.

"Hold on to these papers for me, Mr. Dash," she whispered. "Looks like I'm going to get some jail time. Tell my children where I'm at. You better come see me!"

Her lawyer's statements matched her downtrodden look. Rosa Lee's life was a mess, Elmer D. Ellis told Treanor. She was addicted to heroin, a habit she had developed in 1975. She was HIV positive. She was caring for three grandchildren because their mother was in jail.

Rosa Lee told Treanor that she was trying hard to turn herself around. She was taking methadone every day to control her heroin addition and had turned again to the church. "I got baptized Sunday, me and my three grandchildren," she said, her voice breaking. "And I'm asking you from the bottom of my heart, give me a chance to prove that I'm taking my baptize seriously, 'cause I know I might not have much longer."

Tears ran down her cheeks. "I'm asking you for a chance, please," she begged Treanor. "I know I have a long record."

Rosa Lee was stretching the truth. Yes, she had been baptized, and yes, she was taking methadone. But no, she wasn't caring for her grandchildren alone. Their mother's jail term had ended in July, and she had returned to Rosa Lee's two-bedroom apartment to take care of the children, with help from Rosa Lee.

Treanor looked unimpressed with Rosa Lee's performance. He glowered at her, and Rosa Lee braced for the lecture she knew was coming. Both had played these roles before.

"Every time you pump yourself full of drugs and spend money to do it," he said, "you're stealing from your grandchildren. You're stealing food from their plates, clothes from their backs, and you're certainly jeopardizing their future. You're going to be the youngest dead grandmother in town. And you're going to have three children that will be put up for adoption or going out to some home or some junior village or someplace."

That had been Rosa Lee's opening. "Can I prove to you that my life has changed?"

"Yeah, you can prove it to me, very simply," Treanor answered. "You can stay away from dope. Now I'll make a bargain with you. . . . You come back here the end of January and tell me what you've been doing, and then we'll think about it. But you're looking at jail time. You're looking at the cemetery."

Rosa Lee had won. Treanor postponed the sentencing. The marshal, who had moved in closer behind Rosa Lee at the start of Treanor's lecture, moved back. Treanor, red-faced with anger, called a ten-minute recess and hurriedly left the bench. Ellis shook Rosa Lee's hand.

Rosa Lee came over to me, her cheeks still tearstained but her face aglow. "Was I good?" she asked.

"Yeah," I said, startled at her boldness.

"Thank you," she said, smiling.

The marshal walked up to Rosa Lee. She too was smiling. She had escorted Rosa Lee and her daughters to the jail several times in the not-so-distant past. "You were going to jail, honey," she said to Rosa Lee. "You stopped him with those three grandchildren. He didn't want to have to deal with making arrangements for those children if he had sent you to jail. Is their mama still over the jail?"

"Yes, she is," Rosa Lee lied, putting on a sad face.

Five days before the hearing Rosa Lee was teaching her grandchild how to shoplift. Through most of November and December, Rosa Lee stole cologne, perfume, gloves, and brightly colored silk scarves to sell to people who used them as Christmas presents. The day before her court appearance, she and a fellow drug-clinic patient, Jackie, were shoplifting in a drugstore one block from the Superior Court building shortly after they had drunk their morning meth.

When she returns for sentencing on January 22, a transformed Rosa Lee enters the courthouse. She looks good. She has a clean report from the methadone clinic. She stopped injecting heroin and cocaine in November, after her last seizure. She seems to have done everything Commissioner Treanor asked.

She always dresses well, but she has outdone herself today: she's wearing a two-piece, white-and-gray cotton knit suit with tan leather boots and a tan pocketbook. A gold-colored watch on a gold-colored chain hangs around her neck, both items she stole from the drugstore.

Before they enter Treanor's courtroom, Elmer Ellis has a word with Rosa Lee. "Please don't cry, Mrs. Cunningham," her lawyer says gently. "If you start crying again, you're only going to make Treanor angry." Rosa Lee laughs and agrees not to cry.

"What would you like to say, Mrs. Cunningham?" Treanor asks Rosa Lee when she stands in front of him.

"Well, Your Honor, I know I haven't been a good person. I know it," she begins.

Treanor cuts her off. His demeanor is softer, his words more sympathetic than in November. "Wait a minute, now. Why do you say that? . . . You're taking care of those three grandchildren, isn't that right?"

"Yes, Sir," Rosa Lee says, keeping up the pretense.

"All right," he says. "Now you've raised one family, and now you have another one."

"Yes, Sir," she says.

"Which is really too much to ask of anybody, so I don't think you should sell yourself short. You're doing the Lord's work. Your daughter's in jail for drugs, right?"

"Yes, sir," Rosa Lee says.

"And you have or have had a bad drug problem yourself."

"Yes, Sir."

Then Treanor launches into another lecture about drugs. He doesn't ask Rosa Lee why she steals. "You steal to support your habit," he says. "It's as plain as the nose on your face."

But it isn't that plain. Rosa Lee began stealing long before she became a drug addict.

Finally, Treanor announces his decision: no jail. Instead, he gives her a suspended sentence and one year of probation with drug counseling. "Now, don't come back here," he says.

Rosa Lee sometimes puts on a public mask, the way she wants the world to see her. She fudges a little here, omits a little there, even when she is trying to be candid about her behavior. By her account, her stealing started when she was a teenager. It was her eldest brother, Ben Wright, who told me that Rosa Lee's stealing started when she was nine years old. Her target: the lunch money that her fourth-grade classmates at Giddings Elementary School kept in their desks.

"JESUS, BEN!" Rosa Lee shouts when I ask her about it.

"What's the matter?" I laugh. "You said I could interview Ben."

It is a late afternoon in January, not long after her court appearance. We are talking in my car, which is parked outside Rosa Lee's apartment. We watch the teenage crack dealers come and go, making the rounds of the low-rent housing complex. Two of Rosa Lee's grandchildren are playing nearby on a patch of dirt where the grass has been worn away. The sun is beginning to sink behind the buildings as she tells me about her first theft.

The year was 1946, and Giddings's imposing red-brick building at Third and G streets, S.E., was a bustling part of the District's then-segregated education system. The school served black children living in Capitol Hill neighborhoods; some, like Rosa Lee, came from poor sharecropping families who had moved to Washington during the Depression, and

they did not have the new clothes and spending money that their better-off classmates did.

Rosa Lee's father, Earl Wright, never made much money. He worked for a paving contractor as a cement finisher but he was never given that title; instead, he was always classified as a "helper" and paid a lower wage. Eventually, drinking became the primary activity of his life. Rosa Lee's mother, Rosetta Lawrence Wright, brought in most of the family's money, working as a domestic on Capitol Hill during the day.

"She used to call it 'day work,'" remembers Rosa Lee. "That's what she used to do down in the country" in North Carolina. "Clean white people's houses."

Rosetta also sold dinners from the family's kitchen in the evening and on weekends, always for cash. "She wanted cash because she was getting a welfare check for us," says Rosa Lee. The welfare payments began several years before her father's death because he spent all his time drinking and did not work. After he died, Rosetta had four additional children by another man. "Back in those days, they gave you a check for each child. Seventeen dollars a check. You never want the welfare to know how much money you got. They'll cut the check."

Ben contends that his sister's memory is faulty, that the family did receive monthly deliveries of surplus government food in this period, as did all of the poorest families in Washington, but his mother did not receive a monthly welfare stipend.

Whatever the truth, Rosa Lee and Ben agree that their family—there were eleven children in all—was poor. For much of her childhood, they lived in a ramshackle wooden row house within a mile of the Capitol, since replaced with a public housing project. None of the houses they rented over the years had electricity. The toilet for each dwelling was an outhouse along the edge of the property in the back yard. Water came from a standpipe spigot in the center of the yard.

"I hated them!" says Rosa Lee of the houses, her mouth turning down in a grimace. "No privacy. People knew what you were doing when you went into" the outhouse. "No bathtub. I was always afraid of the kerosene lamps. I was scared they'd turn over and we'd all burn up in those houses."

Other girls came to school with change to buy "brownie-thins"—penny-a-piece cookies that the teachers sold to go with free milk at lunch. Rosa Lee's family was too poor to spare even a few pennies. Rosa Lee was determined to steal her classmates' money so she too could buy cookies. And she did. She knew it was wrong to steal from her classmates' desks, she says. But she couldn't stand being poor, either.

Rosa Lee soon found that she had plenty of opportunities to steal, if she were daring enough. During the summer of 1948, a sinewy Rosa Lee was the only girl among the many "roughneck" boys selling the *Baltimore-Washington Afro–American* newspaper door-to-door on Tuesday and Thursday evenings. She was eleven. The newspaper sales were timed to catch

middle-class black people—low-level federal and city civil servants—when they had just come from work.

Rosa Lee was not concerned about tough neighborhood bullies taking her money or trying to force her off the blocks where an *Afro* seller was sure to be successful. "Rosa Lee would fight quick," remembers Ben. "Fight anybody! Beat up most girls and a good many boys. I don't remember ever having to stick up for her."

Selling the *Afro* also gave Rosa Lee a chance to slip into neighborhood row houses and rifle through the pocketbooks that women often left on the dining room table or the living room couch. Washington was a safer place in those days, and Rosa Lee discovered that many families would leave their front screen doors unlatched while they chatted in their back yards, trying to cool off on hot summer evenings after returning home from work.

"I would walk down Fourth Street," says Rosa Lee, in front of the row houses across from Mount Joy Baptist Church, where her family worshipped. "I would go and knock on their screen door. *'Afro!* Anybody want an *Afro?'* I would open the screen door and if no one answered, I'd go in. I could look through the house and see them out back," she remembers. "Some people would leave their pocketbooks on the chair in the front room or on their table. I would go into so many peoples' houses." * * *

———

Mathematics

BLACK ON BOTH SIDES (Priority Records 1999).

■ MOS DEF

* * *

Yo, it's one universal law but two sides to every story

Three strikes and you be in for life, mandatory

* * *

Young soldiers tryin' to earn they next stripe

When the average minimum wage is $5.15

You best believe you gotta find a new ground to get cream

The white unemployment rate, is nearly more than triple for black

so frontliners got they gun in your back

Bubblin' crack, jewel theft and robbery to combat poverty

and end up in the global jail economy

Stiffer stipulations attached to each sentence

Budget cutbacks but increased police presence

And even if you get out of prison still livin'

join the other five million under state supervision

This is business, no faces just lines and statistics

from your phone, your zip code, to S-S-I digits

The system break man child and women into figures

Two columns for who is, and who ain't niggaz

Numbers is hardly real and they never have feelings

but you push too hard, even numbers got limits

Why did one straw break the camel's back? Here's the secret:

the million other straws underneath it—it's all mathematics.

* * *

Homelessness and the Issue of Freedom

39 UCLA L. Rev. 295, 299–302 (1991).

■ Jeremy Waldron

Estimates of the number of homeless people in the United States range from 250,000 to three million. A person who is homeless is, obviously enough, a person who has no home. One way of describing the plight of a homeless individual might be to say that there is no place governed by a private property rule where he is allowed to be.

In fact, that is not quite correct. Any private proprietor may invite a homeless person into his house or onto his land, and if he does there *will* be some private place where the homeless person is allowed to be. A technically more accurate description of his plight is that there is no place governed by a private property rule where he is allowed to be whenever *he* chooses, no place governed by a private property rule from which he may not at any time be excluded as a result of someone else's say-so. As far as being on private property is concerned—in people's houses or gardens, on farms or in hotels, in offices or restaurants—the homeless person is utterly and at all times at the mercy of others. And we know enough about how this mercy is generally exercised to figure that the description in the previous paragraph is more or less accurate as a matter of fact, even if it is not strictly accurate as a matter of law.

For the most part the homeless are excluded from *all* of the places governed by private property rules, whereas the rest of us are, in the same sense, excluded from *all but one* (or maybe all but a few) of those places. That is another way of saying that each of us has at least one place to be in a country composed of private places, whereas the homeless person has none.

Some libertarians fantasize about the possibility that *all* the land in a society might be held as private property ("Sell the streets!") This would be catastrophic for the homeless. Since most private proprietors are already disposed to exclude him from their property, the homeless person might discover in such a libertarian paradise that there was literally *nowhere* he was allowed to be. Wherever he went he would be liable to penalties for trespass and he would be liable to eviction, to being thrown out by an owner or dragged away by the police. Moving from one place to another would involve nothing more liberating than moving from one trespass liability to another. Since land is finite in any society, there is only a limited number of places where a person can (physically) be, and such a person would find that he was legally excluded from all of them. (It would not be entirely mischievous to add that since, in order to exist, a person has to be *somewhere*, such a person would not be permitted to exist.)

Our society saves the homeless from this catastrophe only by virtue of the fact that some of its territory is held as collective property and made available for common use. The homeless are allowed to *be*—provided they are on the streets, in the parks, or under the bridges. Some of them are allowed to crowd together into publicly provided "shelters" after dark (though these are dangerous places and there are not nearly enough shelters for all of them). But in the daytime and, for many of them, all through the night, wandering in public places is their only option. When all else is privately owned, the sidewalks are their salvation. They are allowed to *be* in our society only to the extent that our society is communist.

This is one of the reasons why most defenders of private property are uncomfortable with the libertarian proposal, and why that proposal remains sheer fantasy. But there is a modified form of the libertarian catastrophe in prospect with which moderate and even liberal defenders of ownership seem much more comfortable. This is the increasing regulation of the streets, subways, parks, and other public places to restrict the activities that can be performed there. What is emerging—and it is not just a matter of fantasy—is a state of affairs in which a million or more citizens have no place to perform elementary human activities like urinating, washing, sleeping, cooking, eating, and standing around. Legislators voted for by people who own private places in which they can do all these things are increasingly deciding to make public places available only for activities other than these primal human tasks. The streets and subways, they say, are for commuting from home to office. They are not for sleeping; sleeping is something one does at home. The parks are for recreations like walking and informal ball-games, things for which one's own yard is a little too confined. Parks are not for cooking or urinating; again, these are things one does at home. Since the public and the private are complementary, the activities performed in public are to be the complement of those appropriately performed in private. This complementarity works fine for those who have the benefit of both sorts of places. However, it is disastrous for those who must live their whole lives on common land. If I am right about this, it is one of the most callous and tyrannical exercises of power in modern times by a (comparatively) rich and complacent majority against a minority of their less fortunate fellow human beings.

NOTES AND QUESTIONS

1. **Illicit activity as means for survival.** Traditionally, the majority of African American women have been obliged, by necessity, to work outside the home to support their families. LEITH MULLINGS, ON OUR OWN TERMS: RACE, CLASS, AND GENDER IN THE LIVES OF AFRICAN AMERICAN WOMEN 90 (1997). Due to severe levels of unemployment of black men, the labor force participation rate of black females has become approximately equal to that of black males. *Id.* Though black women comprise a considerable proportion of the labor force, women like Rosa Lee still face several obstacles to achieve economic stability and must therefore resort to either government assistance and/or illicit activity to support their families. In a study performed in Central Harlem in 1990, for example, 54.7 percent of women eligible to work were not in the labor force, with 28.9 percent of individuals residing in Harlem receiving Aid to Families with Dependent Children. *Id.* at 91 (citing *Persons 16 Years and Over by Labor Force Status and Sex, New York City, Boroughs and Community Districts.* (New York: Department of City Planning, no. 317, 1990)). Furthermore, that study found that more than half of all households in Harlem headed by females that include children under age eighteen have incomes below the poverty line. *Id.* (citing *Socioeconomic profiles: A Portrait of New York City's Community Districts from the 1980 and 1990 Census of Population and Housing* (New York: Department of City Planning)). Faced with poor odds of achieving economic stability, and in "just trying to survive," what can women like Rosa Lee do but break the law to support their families?

University of Pennsylvania Professor of Law Regina Austin explains that though illegal activity may be disparaged, it may be the only means for underprivileged African Americans to survive in America:

> [F]or some poor blacks, breaking the law is not only a way of life: it is the only way to survive. Thus, what is characterized as economic deviance in the eyes of a majority of people may be viewed as economic resistance by a significant number of blacks. Regina Austin, *"An Honest Living": Street Vendors, Municipal Regulation, and The Black Public Sphere*, 103 YALE L.J. 2119, 2119 (1994).

Austin reaches this conclusion based on her study of black street vendors in major cities like New York, Washington, D.C., and Philadelphia. These vendors are part of an informal economy where merchants work without a license and in violation of applicable regulations and sales tax laws. Though illegal, street vending by black workers gives people jobs, supplies African Americans with their preferred products, contributes to the maintenance of African American culture, and assists individuals in gaining the necessary capital and knowledge to operate a business in the formal sector. Because of street vending's benefits for afflicted black communities, Austin stresses that such activity should not immediately be written off, and should instead be respected:

> As blacks in America, we must not fall into the trap of automatically equating legitimacy with legality. Just because an enterprise is small,

informal, and illegal does not mean that it is not valuable or that it should be disparaged. *Id.* at 2130.

Based on her comments, how do you think Austin would react to Rosa Lee's illegal behavior? Would she disagree with Rosa Lee's actions because stealing, like street vending, does not achieve legitimate objectives such as promoting African American black entrepreneurial activity?

2. Sociology of deviance. Are lawbreakers innately inclined to transgress social norms, or are they simply reacting to society's imposed institutions? In other words, are individuals like Rosa Lee instinctively prone to deviate from societal standards, or are they simply products of their insolvent, unstable environments? Howard S. Becker addressed these questions in *Outsiders: Studies in the Sociology of Deviance*, and proposed the premise that deviant peoples violate rules because social groups establish laws whose breach constitutes deviance, and by applying those laws and penalties to an "offender." Becker defines an outsider as an individual who others deem deviant and therefore unworthy of inclusion in society's "normal" social functions.

Would Howard Becker maintain that Rosa Lee is an outsider—one who is judged by law-abiders and stands outside of conventional social groups? Is she more likely to be labeled as an outsider because she is an African American? Becker elaborates on the implications of being an outsider:

> The degree to which an act will be treated as deviant depends also on who commits the act and who feels he has been harmed by it. Rules tend to be applied more to some persons than others. Studies of juvenile delinquency make the point clearly. Boys from middleclass areas do not get as far in the legal process when they are apprehended as do boys from slum areas. The middle-class boy is less likely, when picked up by the police, to be taken to the station; less likely when taken to the station to be booked; and it is extremely unlikely that he will be convicted and sentenced. This variation occurs even though the original infraction of the rule is the same in the two cases. Similarly, the law is differentially applied to Negroes and whites. It is well known that a Negro believed to have attacked a white woman is much more likely to be punished than a white man who commits the same offense; it is only slightly less well known that a Negro who murders another Negro is much less likely to be punished than a white man who commits murder.

HOWARD S. BECKER, OUTSIDERS: STUDIES IN THE SOCIOLOGY OF DEVIANCE 12–13 (1973).

Consider Becker's proposition and Rosa Lee's case. Recall that Rosa Lee was acquitted when she returned to court for a shoplifting charge. Though she is African American and a "deviant outsider," she was able to receive approval from the judge and continue to maintain her freedom. However, was Rosa Lee not trying to portray herself as an "insider" by wearing more respectable attire and emotionally appealing to the judge?

3. "Underclass" and "culture of poverty." Since the 1970s, conservative scholars and critics have attempted to highlight the role of "culture" in maintaining poverty, arguing that poverty becomes intergenerational when poor people lack self-discipline, initiative, and "soft skills" required for success in the working world. These arguments played a large part in welfare reform from the 1970s through the turn of the twenty-first century. A similar debate has gone on about the so-called "underclass," identified as a group of people (Marx would have called them an "industrial reserve army") so chronically lacking regular employment that they can be seen as having effectively been marginalized from the economy altogether. In the late 1980s, the media spent a lot of time worrying about the "underclass," which was said to epitomize all the cultural deviance (lack of initiative, dependency, and so on) exhibited by the poor more generally, and which was thought to be a breeding ground for street crime. For scholarly discussions of the "underclass," *see, e.g.*, WILLIAM JULIUS WILSON, THE TRULY DISADVANTAGED: THE INNER CITY, THE UNDERCLASS, AND PUBLIC POLICY (1987); CHRISTOPHER JENCKS, RETHINKING SOCIAL POLICY: RACE, POVERTY, AND THE UNDERCLASS (1992).

Is it "culture" or material conditions that account for the large gaps that remain in family income, wages, and employment between African Americans and whites? For a "cultural" explanation, *see, e.g.*, STEPHEN THERNSTROM & ABIGAIL THERNSTROM, *America in Black and White* (1997); for a "material" explanation, *see, e.g.*, MICHAEL K. BROWN, ET AL., WHITEWASHING RACE: THE MYTH OF A COLOR-BLIND SOCIETY 66–103 (2003). Does a material explanation account for the behavior of people like Rosa Lee?

4. *"Underclass"* and prison industrial complex. Some might argue that to the extent that an underclass exists, it is, ironically, the effect as much as the cause of state policy. The "war on drugs" and the "war on crime" more generally have created an incarceration crisis for many poor communities. African American and Latino men are incarcerated for long periods at dramatic rates, which creates a social ripple effect of poverty: ex-felons find it difficult to get jobs when they get out of prison; the removal of these men from families and neighborhoods places extra economic and social stress on the people left behind. This social disorganization, in turn, leads to more crime in the increasingly impoverished and dangerous neighborhoods of inner cities. *See* Tracey Meares, *Social Organization and Drug Law Enforcement,* 35 AM. CRIM. L. REV. 191 (1998); Dorothy Roberts, *The Social and Moral Cost of Mass Incarceration in African American Communities,* 56 STAN. L. REV. 1271 (2004).

Some scholars argue that this vicious circle is coupled with another vicious circle: the increasing dependency of strapped towns and counties on prisons as economic engines, which leads to the increased political power of prison guards and prison officials unions, which leads in turn to a continuation of punitive criminal justice policies. *See* Stephen C. Thaman, *Is America a Systematic Violator of Human Rights in the Administration of Criminal Justice?* 44 ST. LOUIS L.J. 999 (2000). Another element in the continuing appeal of punitive policies, some scholars argue, is the declining influence of criminal justice experts: criminal justice policy today tends to be seen as a populist issue and not an issue about which experts should have any particular say. In this environment, politicians promising to be "tough on crime" and prosecutors dominate the legislative process. *See* Franklin Zimring, *Populism, Democratic Government, and the Decline of Expert Authority: Some Reflections on "Three Strikes" in California,* 28 PAC. L.J. 243 (1996); William Stuntz, *The Pathological Politics of Criminal Law,* 100 MICH. L. REV. 505 (2001).

5. Crime, class, and race. The United States mass incarceration policy does not seem to have been either effective at stopping crime nor economically efficient. Why, then, has it persisted? Some scholars argue that punitive criminal justice policy serves ideological functions that are more powerful than their economic or social functions. *See, e.g.,* JEFFREY REIMAN, THE RICH GET RICHER AND THE POOR GET PRISON: IDEOLOGY, CLASS, AND CRIMINAL JUSTICE (7TH ED. 2003); MICHAEL TONRY, MALIGN NEGLECT: RACE, CRIME, AND PUNISHMENT IN AMERICA (1996); DAVID COLE, NO EQUAL JUSTICE: RACE AND CLASS IN THE AMERICAN CRIMINAL JUSTICE SYSTEM (2000).

6. Homelessness and criminal justice policy. Like "the underclass," "the homeless" are frequently a target of fear and loathing in American culture; like the poor generally, some make an effort to distinguish the innocent or involuntary homeless from those who have "chosen" their situation; and like poverty generally, homelessness and crime are closely connected in the public mind, resulting in, ironically, more criminalization. *See* CHRISTOPHER JENCKS, THE HOMELESS (1995); PETER H. ROSSI, DOWN AND OUT IN AMERICA: THE ORIGINS OF HOMELESSNESS (1991). For a lively discussion of how not only law but architecture and urban planning are affected by the desire to make homeless people invisible in city spaces, see MIKE DAVIS, CITY OF QUARTZ: EXCAVATING THE FUTURE IN LOS ANGELES (1992).

B. RELATIONS OF (RE)PRODUCTION

The Working Poor: Invisible in America

39–44 50, 64–67 (2004).

■ DAVID K. SHIPLER

Christie did a job that this labor-hungry economy could not do without. Every morning she drove her battered '86 Volkswagen from her apartment in public housing to the YWCA's child-care center in Akron, Ohio, where she spent the day watching over little children so their parents could go to work. Without her and thousands like her across the country, there would have been fewer people able to fill the jobs that fueled America's prosperity. Without her patience and warmth, children could have been harmed as well, for she was more than a baby-sitter. She gave the youngsters an emotionally safe place, taught and mothered them, and sometimes even rescued them from abuse at home.

For those valuable services, she received a check for about $330 every two weeks. She could not afford to put her own two children in the day-care center where she worked.

Christie was a hefty woman who laughed more readily than her predicament should have allowed. She suffered from stress and high blood pressure. She had no bank account because she could not keep enough money long enough. Try as she might to shop carefully, she always fell behind on her bills and was peppered with late fees. Her low income entitled her to food stamps and a rental subsidy, but whenever she got a little pay raise, government agencies reduced the benefits, and she felt punished for working. She was trapped on the treadmill of welfare reform, running her life according to the rules of the Personal Responsibility and Work Opportunity Reconciliation Act of 1996. The title left no doubt about what Congress and the White House saw as poverty's cause and solution.

Initially the new law combined with the good economy to send welfare caseloads plummeting. As states were granted flexibility in administering time limits and work requirements, some created innovative consortiums of government, industry, and charity to guide people into effective job training and employment. But most available jobs had three unhappy traits: They paid low wages, offered no benefits, and led nowhere. "Many who do find jobs," the Urban Institute concluded in a 2002 report, "lose other supports designed to help them, such as food stamps and health insurance, leaving them no better off—and sometimes worse off—than when they were not working."

Christie considered herself such a case. The only thing in her wallet resembling a credit card was a blue-green piece of plastic labeled "Ohio" and decorated with a drawing of a lighthouse projecting a beam into the night. Inside the "O" was a gold square—a computer chip. On the second working day of every month, she slipped the card into a special machine at Walgreen's, Save-A-Lot, or Apple's, and punched in her identification number. A credit of $136 was loaded into her chip. This was the form in which her "food stamps" were now issued—less easy to steal or to sell, and less obvious and degrading in the checkout line.

The card contained her first bit of income in every month and permitted her first expenditure. It could be used for food only, and not for cooked food or pet food. It occupied the top line in the balance sheet she kept for me during a typical October.

"2nd Spent 136.00 food stamps," she wrote. So the benefit was all gone the day she got it. Three days later she had to come up with an additional $25 in cash for groceries, another $54 on October 10, and $15 more on the twelfth. Poor families typically find that food stamps cover only one-half to three-quarters of their grocery costs.

Even the opening balance on the card was chipped away as Christie inched up in salary. It makes sense that the benefit is based on income: the less you need, the less you get. That's the economic side. On the psychological side, however, it produces hellish experiences for the beneficiaries. Every three months Christie had to take half a day off from work (losing half a day's wages) and carry an envelope full of pay stubs, utility bills, and rent receipts to be pawed over by her ill-tempered caseworker, who applied a state-mandated formula to figure her food stamp allotment and her children's eligibility for health insurance. When Christie completed a training course and earned a raise of 10 cents an hour, her food stamps dropped by $10 a month.

That left her $6 a month ahead, which was not nothing but felt like it. Many former welfare recipients who go to work just say good riddance to the bureaucracies that would provide food stamps, medical coverage, and housing. Some think wrongly that they're no longer eligible once they're off welfare; others would rather forfeit their rights than contend with the hassle and humiliation. Quiet surrender ran against Christie's grain, however. She was smart and insistent, as anyone must be to negotiate her way through the system. She never flinched from appealing to higher authority. When she once forgot to put a utilities bill in her sheaf of papers, her caseworker withheld her food stamps. "I mailed it to her the next day," Christie said. Two weeks passed, and the card remained empty. Christie called the caseworker. "She got really snotty," Christie remembered. " 'Well, didn't I tell you you were supposed to send some documentation?' "

"I was like, 'Have you checked your mail?' " No, as it turned out, the caseworker's mail had piled up unread. "She was like, 'Well, I got people waiting up to two, three months on food stamps.' And she didn't get back with me. I had to go to her supervisor." The benefits were then restored.

It is easy to lose your balance having one foot planted tentatively in the working world and the other still entwined in this thicket of red tape. Managing relations with a boss, finding reliable child care, and coping with a tangle of unpaid bills can be daunting enough for a single mother with little such experience; add surveillance by a bureaucracy that seems more prosecutor than provider, and you have Christie's high blood pressure.

While she invoked the system's rules to get her due, she also cheated—or thought she did. Living with her surreptitiously was her boyfriend, Kevin, the father of her son. She was certain that if the Housing Authority knew, she would be evicted, either because he was a convicted felon (two years for assault) or because his earning power, meager though it was, would have lifted her beyond eligibility. So slight are the margins between government assistance and outright destitution that small lies take on large significance in the search for survival.

Kevin looked like a friendly giant—a solid 280 pounds, a shaved head, and a small earring in his right ear. His income was erratic. In decent weather he made $7.40 an hour working for a landscaper, who rewarded him with a free turkey to end the season at Thanksgiving—and then dumped him onto unemployment for the winter. He wanted to drive a truck or cut meat. He had received a butcher's certificate in a training course during imprisonment, but when he showed the document from the penitentiary, employers didn't rush to put a knife in his hand.

The arithmetic of Christie's life added up to tension, and you had to look hard through her list of expenditures to find fun or luxury. On the fifth she received her weekly child support check of $37.66 from Kevin (she got nothing from her daughter's father, who was serving a long prison sentence for assault). The same day, she put $5 worth of gas in her car, and the next day spent $6 of her own money to take the day-care kids to the zoo. The eighth was payday, and her entire $330 check disappeared in a flash. First, there was what she called a $3 "tax" to cash her check, just one of several such fees for money orders and the like—a penalty for having no checking account. Immediately, $172 went for rent, including a $10 late fee, which she was always charged because she never had enough to pay by the first of the month. Then, because it was October and she had started to plan for Christmas, she paid $31.47 at a store for presents she had put on layaway, another $10 for gasoline, $40 to buy shoes for her two kids, $5 for a pair of corduroy pants at a secondhand shop, another $5 for a shirt, $10 for bell-bottom pants, and $47 biweekly car insurance. The $330 was gone. She had no insurance on her TVs, clothes, furniture, or other household goods.

Utilities and other bills got paid out of her second check toward the end of the month. Her phone usually cost about $43 a month, gas for the apartment $34, electricity $46, and prescriptions between $8 and $15. Her monthly car payment ran $150, medical insurance $72, and cable TV $43. Cable is no longer considered a luxury by low-income families that pinch and sacrifice to have it. So much of modern American culture now comes through television that the poor would be further marginalized without the broad access that cable provides. Besides, it's relatively cheap entertainment. "I just have basic," Christie explained. "I have an antenna, but you can't see anything, you get no reception." And she needed good reception because she and Kevin loved to watch wrestling.

One reason for Christie's tight budget was the abundance of high-priced, well-advertised snacks, junk food, and prepared meals that provide an easy fallback diet for a busy working mother—or for anyone who has never learned to cook from scratch. Besides the staples of hamburgers, and chicken, "I buy sausages," Christie said, "I buy the TV dinners 'cause I might be tired some days and throw it in the oven—like Salisbury steaks and turkey and stuff like that. My kids love pizza. I get the frozen pizzas.... I buy my kids a lot of breakfast things 'cause we're up early and we're out the door. You know, those cereal bars and stuff like that, they're expensive! You know? Pop Tarts, cereal bars, Granola." The cheaper breakfasts, like hot cereal, came only on weekends, when she had time. "They eat the hot cereal, but during the week we're on the go. So I give them cereal in the bag. My son likes to eat dry cereal, so I put him some cereal in the lunch bag. Cocoa Puffs. They got Cocoa Dots." She laughed. "Lucky Charms. He's not picky. My daughter's picky." Those candylike cereals soak up dollars. At my local supermarket, Lucky Charms cost dearly: $4.39 for a box of just 14 ounces, while three times as much oatmeal goes for nearly the same price, $4.29. * * *

Her mother, "Gladys," had dropped out of high school, spent years on welfare, and nurtured the fervent dream of seeing her three children in college. The ambition propelled two of them. Christie's brother became an accountant, and her sister, a loan officer. But Christie never took to higher education. She began reluctantly at the University of Akron, lived at home, and finally got fed up with having no money. The second semester of her sophomore year, she went to work instead of to school, a choice that struck her then as less momentous than it turned out to be.

"She didn't take things as serious as they really were," Gladys complained. "Now she sees for herself how serious this is." Just how serious depended on what she wanted to do. She loved working with children but now discovered that without a college degree she would have trouble getting hired at a responsible level in the Head Start preschool program, much less as a teacher in a regular school; she was limited to a YWCA day-care center whose finances were precarious. Since 95 percent of the Y's children came from low-income families, the fees were essentially set by the center's main source of income, Ohio's Department of Human Services, which paid $99 to $114 a week for full-time care. Given the center's heavy expenses, the rates were not enough to pay teachers more than $5.30 to $5.90 an hour.

Christie's previous jobs had also imprisoned her close to the minimum wage as a hostess-cashier at a Holiday Inn, a cashier at Kmart, a waitress in a bar, a cook and waitress and cashier in various restaurants. She had become a veteran of inadequate training programs designed to turn her into a retail salesperson, a bus driver, and a correctional officer, but the courses never enabled her and her classmates to pass the tests and get hired. She had two words to explain why she had never returned to college. "Lazy. Lazy."

It was strange that she thought of herself as lazy, because her work was exhausting, and her low wage required enormous effort to stay afloat. * * *

The new millennium arrived in a crescendo of American riches. The nation wallowed in luxury, burst with microchips, consumed with abandon, swaggered globally. Everything grew larger: homes, vehicles, stock portfolios, life expectancy. Never before in the sweep of human history had so many people been so utterly comfortable.

Caroline Payne was not one of them. A few weeks after New Year's Day, she sat at her kitchen table and reflected on her own history. Two of her three goals had been achieved: She had earned a college diploma, albeit just a two-year associate's degree. And she had gone from a homeless shelter into her own house, although it was mostly owned by a bank. The third objective, "a good-paying job," as she put it, still eluded her. Back in the mid–1970s, she earned $6 an hour in a Vermont factory that made plastic cigarette lighters and cases for Gillette razors. In 2000, she earned

$6.80 an hour stocking shelves and working cash registers at a vast Wal-Mart superstore in New Hampshire. * * *

Anyone who walked all the way around the outside of the Wal-Mart superstore on Route 103 would walk a mile, Caroline said. The place was immense. It sold everything from lawn mowers to ground beef, underpricing smaller stores that were struggling to survive in the center of town. Its 300 to 330 employees, who came and went seasonally, wore Wal-Mart's uniform of blue smocks and friendly smiles, trained as they were to be surprisingly helpful to customers.

Mark Brown, the manager, could pay his people more without raising prices, he conceded. He sat at a table in the store's snack bar, watching the part of the grocery section he could see, listening to the public address system's call for help at the registers, his eyes darting around this corner of his fiefdom like a school principal waiting for the next catastrophe. He was thirty-one, but he looked as young as a college kid and spoke with the twang of his native southeast Missouri. He had come from another store in Georgia and was learning to ski here in New Hampshire.

His employees started at $6.25 an hour, earned an extra dollar at night and another 25 cents "for going to the front end," which meant working one of the twenty-four cash registers. And if he started them at $8 an hour, say, instead of $6.25, how would that change the economics of the store? "Hmmmm. I don't think it would change at all." He wouldn't have to raise prices? "No. We've got a corporate pricing structure. And the way we do things, we go out and we check our competition every single week. Every department manager in this store goes out once a week and checks competition, and that's what determines our prices. We have a core price structure that we set regionally, by areas. Definitely the base price here would be probably higher than what it is in Arkansas, where there's a cheap cost of living. So it would be higher here, but it would still be standard to this area. And then after they give us that base, then we go out and check our competition, and if we're gettin' beat, we lower our prices."

So there's enough profit to absorb an increase from $6.25 to $8? "There would be, because if we were having to raise our wages, then evidently everybody else would be too, and if we make sure we're low enough, our competitors' customers are gonna shop with us." Would wage increases have any effect at all? "We'd have to cut corners on other things like, you know, we may not be able to put all the pretty balloons up all over the store. The non-necessities we'd have to cut back on."

Three days later Wal-Mart Stores, Inc., announced a net income of $5.58 billion for 1999, up 26 percent from the previous year.

Caroline was bouncing from one department to another, from one shift to another, but her pay stayed within a narrow range, beginning at $6.25, going to $6.80, sometimes up to $7.50 if she worked at night. So unpredictable were her hours that she couldn't work a second job, which would have helped her cash flow. She kept applying to higher positions and kept hearing that she needed a bit more experience. * * *

In more depressed parts of the country and during recessions,* * * some Wal-Mart managers were accused of forcing employees to work before punching in or after punching out to avoid paying overtime as required by law. "Wal-Mart management doesn't hold itself to the same standard of rectitude it expects from its low-paid employees," wrote Barbara Ehrenreich, who worked at a Wal-Mart in Minnesota while researching her book *Nickel and Dimed*. "When I applied for a job at Wal-Mart in the spring of 2000, I was reprimanded for getting something 'wrong' on this test: I had agreed only 'strongly' to the proposition, 'All rules have to be followed to the letter at all times.' The correct answer was 'totally agree.' Apparently the one rule that need not be slavishly adhered to at Wal-Mart is the federal Fair Labor Standards Act, which requires that employees be paid time and a half if they work more than forty hours in a week." Workers were warned against "time theft," which meant "doing anything other than working during company time, anything at all," she reported. "Theft of *our* time is not, however, an issue."

Caroline never had the overtime problem in her New Hampshire store, but in six Southern states employees filed a class-action suit against the company for ordering them off the clock as their weekly time approached forty hours. Their attorney calculated the benefits to the firm: If each of 250 hourly wage "associates" in a single store worked just one hour of unpaid overtime a week, that would total 250 unpaid hours a week, 1,000 a month, 12,000 a year—and there were over 300 Wal-Mart stores in Texas, producing savings in that state alone of more than $30 million that should have been paid to employees.

Caroline did not suffer from any violations of law, as far as she could tell, but her career went nowhere. Mark Brown, the manager who liked her, got transferred to Pennsylvania, dimming her prospects for advancement. So after a year and a half at Wal-Mart, she signed up with a temp agency, which found her a $7.50–an-hour daytime job Monday through Friday assembling wallpaper sample books. And she had the pleasure of telling Wal-Mart's assistant manager that she was leaving for higher pay.

Down and Out in Discount America

The Nation, Dec. 16 2004, http://www.thenation.com/doc.mhtml?i=20050103&s= featherstone).

■ Liza Featherstone

On the day after Thanksgiving, the biggest shopping day of the year, Wal-Mart's many progressive critics—not to mention its business competitors—finally enjoyed a bit of schadenfreude when the retailer had to admit to "disappointing" sales. The problem was quickly revealed: Wal-Mart hadn't been discounting aggressively enough. Without low prices, Wal-Mart just isn't Wal-Mart.

That's not a mistake the big-box behemoth is likely to make again. Wal-Mart knows its customers, and it knows how badly they need the discounts. Like Wal-Mart's workers, its customers are overwhelmingly female, and struggling to make ends meet. Betty Dukes, the lead plaintiff in *Dukes v. Wal-Mart*, the landmark sex-discrimination case against the company, points out that Wal-Mart takes out ads in her local paper the same day the community's poorest citizens collect their welfare checks. "They are promoting themselves to low-income people," she says. "That's who they lure. They don't lure the rich. . . . They understand the economy of America. They know the haves and have-nots. They don't put Wal-Mart in Piedmonts. They don't put Wal-Mart in those high-end parts of the community. They plant themselves right in the middle of Poorville."

Betty Dukes is right. A 2000 study by Andrew Franklin, then an economist at the University of Connecticut, showed that Wal-Mart operated primarily in poor and working-class communities, finding, in the bone-dry language of his discipline, "a significant negative relationship between median household income and Wal-Mart's presence in the market." Although fancy retailers noted with chagrin during the 2001 recession that absolutely everybody shops at Wal-Mart—"Even people with $100,000 incomes now shop at Wal-Mart," a PR flack for one upscale mall fumed— the Bloomingdale's set is not the discounter's primary market, and probably never will be. Only 6 percent of Wal-Mart shoppers have annual family incomes of more than $100,000. A 2003 study found that 23 percent of Wal-Mart Supercenter customers live on incomes of less than $25,000 a year. More than 20 percent of Wal-Mart shoppers have no bank account, long considered a sign of dire poverty. And while almost half of Wal-Mart Supercenter customers are blue-collar workers and their families, 20 percent are unemployed or elderly.

Al Zack, who until his retirement in 2004 was the United Food and Commercial Workers' vice president for strategic programs, observes that appealing to the poor was "Sam Walton's real genius. He figured out how to make money off of poverty. He located his first stores in poor rural areas and discovered a real market. The only problem with the business model is that it really needs to create more poverty to grow." That problem is cleverly solved by creating more bad jobs worldwide. In a chilling reversal of Henry Ford's strategy, which was to pay his workers amply so they could buy Ford cars, Wal-Mart's stingy compensation policies—workers make, on average, just over $8 an hour, and if they want health insurance, they must pay more than a third of the premium—contribute to an economy in which, increasingly, workers can only afford to shop at Wal-Mart.

To make this model work, Wal-Mart must keep labor costs down. It does this by making corporate crime an integral part of its business strategy. Wal-Mart routinely violates laws protecting workers' organizing rights (workers have even been fired for union activity). It is a repeat offender on overtime laws; in more than thirty states, workers have brought wage-and-hour class-action suits against the retailer. In some cases, workers say, managers encouraged them to clock out and keep working; in others, managers locked the doors and would not let employees go home at the end of their shifts. And it's often women who suffer most from Wal-Mart's labor practices. *Dukes v. Wal-Mart*, which is the largest civil rights class-action suit in history, charges the company with systematically discriminating against women in pay and promotions. * * *

Solidarity Across the Checkout Counter

Given the poverty they have in common, it makes sense that Wal-Mart's workers often express a strong feeling of solidarity with the shoppers. Wal-Mart workers tend to be aware that the customers' circumstances are similar to their own, and to identify with them. Some complain about rude customers, but most seem to genuinely enjoy the shoppers.

One longtime department manager in Ohio cheerfully recalls her successful job interview at Wal-Mart. Because of her weight, she told her interviewers, she'd be better able to help the customer. "I told them I wanted to work in the ladies department because I'm a heavy girl." She understands the frustrations of the large shopper, she told them: " 'You know, you go into Lane Bryant and some skinny girl is trying to sell you clothes.' They laughed at that and said, 'You get a second interview!' "

One plaintiff in the *Dukes* lawsuit, Cleo Page, who no longer works at Wal-Mart, says she was a great customer service manager because "I knew how people feel when they shop, so I was really empathetic."

Many Wal-Mart workers say they began working at their local Wal-Mart because they shopped there. "I was practically born in Wal-Mart," says Alyssa Warrick, a former employee now attending Truman State University in Missouri. "My mom is obsessed with shopping. . . . I thought it would be pretty easy since I knew where most of the stuff was." Most assumed they would love working at Wal-Mart. "I always loved shopping there," enthuses *Dukes* plaintiff Dee Gunter. "That's why I wanted to work for 'em."

Shopping is traditionally a world of intense female communication and bonding, and women have long excelled in retail sales in part because of the identification between clerk and shopper. Page, who still shops at Wal-Mart, is now a lingerie saleswoman at Mervyn's (owned by Target). "I do enjoy retail," she says. "I like feeling needed and I like helping people, especially women."

Betty Dukes says, "I strive to give Wal-Mart customers one hundred percent of my abilities." This sentiment was repeated by numerous other Wal-Mart workers, always with heartfelt sincerity. Betty Hamilton, a 61-year-old clerk in a Las Vegas Sam's Club, won her store's customer service award last year. She is very knowledgeable about jewelry, her favorite department, and proud of it. Hamilton resents her employer—she complains about sexual harassment and discrimination, and feels she has been penalized on the job for her union sympathies—but remains deeply devoted to her customers. She enjoys imparting her knowledge to shoppers so "they can walk out of there and feel like they know something." Like Page,

Hamilton feels she is helping people. "It makes me so happy when I sell something that I know is an extraordinarily good buy," she says. "I feel like I've done somebody a really good favor."

The enthusiasm of these women for their jobs, despite the workplace indignities many of them have faced, should not assure anybody that the company's abuses don't matter. In fact, it should underscore the tremendous debt Wal-Mart owes women: This company has built its vast profits not only on women's drudgery but also on their joy, creativity and genuine care for the customer.

Why Boycotts Don't Always Work

Will consumers return that solidarity and punish Wal-Mart for discriminating against women? Do customers care about workers as much as workers care about them? Some women's groups, like the National Organization for Women and Code Pink, have been hoping that they do, and have encouraged the public not to shop at Wal-Mart. While this tactic could be fruitful in some community battles, it's unlikely to catch on nationwide. A customer saves 20–25 percent by buying groceries at Wal-Mart rather than from a competitor, according to retail analysts, and poor women need those savings more than anyone.

That's why many women welcome the new Wal-Marts in their communities. *The Winona* (Minnesota) *Post* extensively covered a controversy over whether to allow a Wal-Mart Supercenter into the small town; the letters to the editor in response offer a window into the female customer's loyalty to Wal-Mart. Though the paper devoted substantial space to the sex discrimination case, the readers who most vehemently defended the retailer were female. From the nearby town of Rollingstone, Cindy Kay wrote that she needed the new Wal-Mart because the local stores didn't carry large-enough sizes. She denounced the local anti-Wal-Mart campaign as a plot by rich and thin elites: "I'm glad those people can fit into and afford such clothes. I can barely afford Shopko and Target!"

A week later, Carolyn Goree, a preschool teacher also hoping for a Winona Wal-Mart, wrote in a letter to the *Post* editor that when she shops at most stores, $200 fills only a bag or two, but at Wal-Mart, "I come out with a cart full top and bottom. How great that feels." Lacking a local Wal-Mart, Goree drives over the Wisconsin border to get her fix. She was incensed by an earlier article's lament that some workers make only $15,000 yearly. "Come on!" Goree objected. "Is $15,000 really that bad of a yearly income? I'm a single mom and when working out of my home, I made $12,000 tops and that was with child support. I too work, pay for a mortgage, lights, food, everything to live. Everything in life is a choice. . . . I am for the little man/woman—I'm one of them. So I say stand up and get a Wal-Mart."

Sara Jennings, a disabled Winona reader living on a total of $8,000, heartily concurred. After paying her rent, phone, electric and cable bills, Jennings can barely afford to treat herself to McDonald's. Of a recent trip to the LaCrosse, Wisconsin, Wal-Mart, she raved, "Oh boy, what a great treat. Lower prices and a good quality of clothes to choose from. It was like heaven for me." She, too, strongly defended the workers' $15,000 yearly income: "Boy, now that is a lot of money. I could live with that." She closed with a plea to the readers: "I'm sure you all make a lot more than I. And I'm sure I speak for a lot of seniors and very-low-income people. We *need* this Wal-Mart. There's nothing downtown."

FROM CONSUMERS TO WORKERS AND CITIZENS

It is crucial that Wal-Mart's liberal and progressive critics make use of the growing public indignation at the company over sex discrimination, low pay and other workers' rights issues, but it is equally crucial to do this in ways that remind people that their power does not stop at their shopping dollars. It's admirable to drive across town and pay more for toilet paper to avoid shopping at Wal-Mart, but such a gesture is, unfortunately, not enough. As long as people identify themselves as consumers and nothing more, Wal-Mart wins.

The invention of the "consumer" identity has been an important part of a long process of eroding workers' power, and it's one reason working people now have so little power against business. According to the social historian Stuart Ewen, in the early years of mass production, the late nineteenth and early twentieth centuries, modernizing capitalism sought to turn people who thought of themselves primarily as "workers" into "consumers." Business elites wanted people to dream not of satisfying work and egalitarian societies—as many did at that time—but of the beautiful things they could buy with their paychecks.

Business was quite successful in this project, which influenced much early advertising and continued throughout the twentieth century. In addition to replacing the "worker," the "consumer" has also effectively displaced the citizen. That's why, when most Americans hear about the Wal-Mart's worker-rights abuses, their first reaction is to feel guilty about shopping at the store. A tiny minority will respond by shopping elsewhere—and only a handful will take any further action. A worker might call her union and organize a picket. A citizen might write to her congressman or local newspaper, or galvanize her church and knitting circle to visit local management. A consumer makes an isolated, politically slight decision: to shop or not to shop. Most of the time, Wal-Mart has her exactly where it wants her, because the intelligent choice for anyone thinking as a consumer is not to make a political statement but to seek the best bargain and the greatest convenience.

To effectively battle corporate criminals like Wal-Mart, the public must be engaged as citizens, not merely as shoppers. What kind of politics could encourage that? It's not clear that our present political parties are up to the job. Unlike so many horrible things, Wal-Mart cannot be blamed on George W. Bush. The Arkansas-based company prospered under the state's native son Bill Clinton when he was governor and President. Sam Walton and his wife, Helen, were close to the Clintons, and for several years Hillary Clinton, whose law firm represented Wal-Mart, served on the company's board of directors. Bill Clinton's "welfare reform" has provided Wal-Mart with a ready workforce of women who have no choice but to accept its poverty wages and discriminatory policies.

Still, a handful of Democratic politicians stood up to the retailer. California Assemblywoman Sally Lieber, who represents the 22nd Assembly District and is a former mayor of Mountain View, was outraged when she learned about the sex discrimination charges in *Dukes v. Wal-Mart*, and she smelled blood when, tipped off by dissatisfied workers, her office discovered that Wal-Mart was encouraging its workers to apply for public assistance, "in the middle of the worst state budget crisis in history!" California had a $38 billion deficit at the time, and Lieber was enraged that taxpayers would be subsidizing Wal-Mart's low wages, bringing new meaning to the term "corporate welfare."

Lieber was angry, too, that Wal-Mart's welfare dependence made it nearly impossible for responsible employers to compete with the retail giant. It was as if taxpayers were unknowingly funding a massive plunge to the bottom in wages and benefits—quite possibly their own. She held a press conference in July 2003, to expose Wal-Mart's welfare scam. The Wal-Mart documents—instructions explaining how to apply for food stamps, Medi-Cal (the state's healthcare assistance program) and other forms of welfare—were blown up on posterboard and displayed. The morning of the press conference, a Wal-Mart worker who wouldn't give her name for fear of being fired snuck into Lieber's office. "I just wanted to say, right on!" she told the assemblywoman.

Wal-Mart spokespeople have denied that the company encourages employees to collect public assistance, but the documents speak for themselves. They bear the Wal-Mart logo, and one is labeled "Wal-Mart: Instructions for Associates." Both documents instruct employees in procedures for applying to "Social Service Agencies." Most Wal-Mart workers I've interviewed had co-workers who worked full time for the company and received public assistance, and some had been in that situation themselves. Public assistance is very clearly part of the retailer's cost-cutting strategy. (It's ironic that a company so dependent on the public dole supports so many right-wing politicians who'd like to dismantle the welfare state.)

Lieber, a strong supporter of the social safety net who is now assistant speaker pro tempore of the California Assembly, last year passed a bill that would require large and mid-sized corporations that fail to provide decent, affordable health insurance to reimburse local governments for the cost of providing public assistance for those workers. When the bill passed, its opponents decided to kill it by bringing it to a statewide referendum. Wal-Mart, which just began opening Supercenters in California this year, mobilized its resources to revoke the law on election day this November, even while executives denied that any of their employees depended on public assistance.

Citizens should pressure other politicians to speak out against Wal-Mart's abuses and craft policy solutions. But the complicity of both parties in Wal-Mart's power over workers points to the need for a politics that squarely challenges corporate greed and takes the side of ordinary people. That kind of politics seems, at present, strongest at the local level.

Earlier this year, labor and community groups in Chicago prevented Wal-Mart from opening a store on the city's South Side, in part by pushing through an ordinance that would have forced the retailer to pay Chicago workers a living wage. In Hartford, Connecticut, labor and community advocates just won passage of an ordinance protecting their free speech rights on the grounds of the new Wal-Mart Supercenter, which is being built on city property. Similar battles are raging nationwide, but Wal-Mart's opponents don't usually act with as much coordination as Wal-Mart does, and they lack the retail behemoth's deep pockets.

With this in mind, SEIU president Andy Stern has recently been calling attention to the need for better coordination—and funding—of labor and community anti-Wal-Mart efforts. Stern has proposed that the AFL-CIO allocate $25 million of its royalties from purchases on its Union Plus credit card toward fighting Wal-Mart and the "Wal-Martization" of American jobs. * * *

Such efforts are essential not just because Wal-Mart is a grave threat to unionized workers' jobs (which it is) but because it threatens all American ideals that are at odds with profit—ideals such as justice, equality and fairness. Wal-Mart would not have so much power if we had stronger labor laws, and if we required employers to pay a living wage. The company knows that, and it hires lobbyists in Washington to vigorously fight any effort at such reforms—indeed, Wal-Mart has recently beefed up this political infrastructure substantially, and it's likely that its presence in Washington will only grow more conspicuous.

The situation won't change until a movement comes together and builds the kind of social and political power for workers and citizens that can balance that of Wal-Mart. This is not impossible: In Germany, unions are powerful enough to force Wal-Mart to play by their rules. American citizens will have to ask themselves what kind of world they want to live in. That's what prompted Gretchen Adams, a former Wal-Mart manager, to join the effort to unionize Wal-Mart. She's deeply troubled by the company's effect on the economy as a whole and the example it sets for other employers. "What about our working-class people?" she asks. "I don't want to live in a Third World country." Working people, she says, should be able to afford "a new car, a house. You shouldn't have to leave the car on the lawn because you can't afford that $45 part."

NOTES AND QUESTIONS

1. Wal-Mart as avatar of new economy. Simon Head notes the phenomenal success of Wal-Mart:

Within the corporate world Wal-Mart's preeminence is not simply a matter of size. In its analysis of the growth of U.S. productivity, or output per worker, between 1995 and 2000—the years of the "new economy" and the high-tech bubble on Wall Street—the McKinsey Global Institute has found that just over half that growth took place in two sectors, retail and wholesale, where, directly or indirectly, Wal-Mart "caused the bulk of the productivity acceleration through ongoing managerial innovation that increased competition intensity and drove the diffusion of best practice." This is management-speak for Wal-Mart's aggressive use of information technology and its skill in meeting the needs of its customers.

In its own category of "general merchandise," Wal-Mart has taken a huge lead in productivity over its competitors, a lead of 44 percent in 1987, 48 percent in 1995, and still 41 percent in 1999, even as competitors began to copy Wal-Mart's strategy. Thanks to the company's superior productivity, Wal-Mart's share of total sales among all the sellers of "general merchandise" rose from 9 percent in 1987 to 27 percent in 1995, and 30 percent in 1999, an astonishing rate of growth which recalls the rise of the Ford Motor Company nearly a century ago. McKinsey lists some of the leading causes of Wal-Mart's success. For example, its huge, ugly box-shaped buildings enable Wal-Mart "to carry a wider range of goods than competitors" and to "enjoy labor economies of scale."

McKinsey mentions Wal-Mart's "efficiency in logistics," which makes it possible for the company to buy in bulk directly from producers of everything from toilet paper to refrigerators, allowing it to dispense with wholesalers. McKinsey also makes much of the company's innovative use of information technology, for example its early use of computers and scanners to track inventory, and its use of satellite communications to link corporate headquarters in Arkansas with the nationwide network of Wal-Mart stores. Setting up and fine-tuning these tracking and distribution systems has been the special achievement of founder Sam Walton's (the "Wal" of Wal-Mart) two successors as CEOs, David Glass and the incumbent Lee Scott.

Simon Head, *Inside the Leviathan*, 51 N.Y. REV. BOOKS 80 (2004), *available at* http://www.nybooks.com/archives. Wal-Mart's success has also, however, crucially relied on its ability to keep wages and benefits low. Like Featherstone, Head argues for stronger and better enforced labor laws, asserting that "Wal-Mart has reached back beyond the New Deal to the harsh, abrasive capitalism of the 1920s." *Id*.

2. Wal-Mart and gender discrimination. In the summer of 2004, a federal district court certified a sex discrimination class action against Wal-Mart on behalf of 1.6 million women who had worked at Wal-Mart since December 26, 1998. The plaintiffs in *Dukes v. Wal-Mart*, 222 F.R.D. 137 (N.D. Cal. 2004), the largest private civil rights case in United States history, alleged that Wal-Mart discriminated against its female employees in making promotions, job assignments, pay decisions and training, and retaliated against women who complained about such practices. *See* http://www.walmartclass.com.

3. Markets in poverty. Many services as well as goods are targeted to the poverty market. As David Shipler describes in his book, *The Working Poor: Invisible in America* (2004), tax preparers, check-cashing outlets, credit card companies, and mortgage and other loan providers often market their services to poor people. Services to the poor, however, tend to cost more money than the same services to the middle-class or the wealthy. The "subprime" market is a lucrative one because the customers have few options, urgent need, and often little information about their rights. Shipler offers an example of how poverty costs money:

> Say you're short of cash, and the bills are piling up, along with some disconnection notices. Payday is two weeks away, and your phone and electricity will be shut off before then. The guy at the local convenience store, who has a booth for cashing checks, throws you a lifeline. If you need $100 now, you write him a check for $120, postdated by two weeks. He'll give you the $100 in cash today, hold your check until your wages are in your bank account, and then put the check through. Or you can give him the $120 in cash when you get it, and he'll return your check. Either way, 20 percent interest for two weeks equals 1.438 percent a day, or 521 percent annually. * * *

> Furthermore, the loans are not technically loans in some states, because there's a check. And if a check bounces, more severe penalties apply than those for unrepaid loans. Borrowing $300, for instance, an Indiana woman paid a $30 fee and wrote a check for $330. When the check bounced, her bank and the payday loan establishment charged $80 in fees. Then the lender took her to court, won triple damages of $990, lawyer's fees of $150, and $60 in court costs. The total charge on the $300 loan: $1,310.

Shipler, The Working Poor, *supra* at 18–19.

4. Health care and bankruptcy. A recent study found that about half of personal bankruptcy filers interviewed cited "medical causes" as the reason for their filing bankruptcy. Among those whose illnesses led to bankruptcy, out-of-pocket costs averaged $11,854 since the start of illness; 75.7 percent had insurance at the onset of illness. David U. Himmelstein et al., *Market Watch: Illness and Injury as Contributors to Bankruptcy*, Health Affairs, Feb. 2, 2005, http://content.healthaffairs.org/cgi/content/full/hlthaff.w5.63/DC1. The authors of the study concluded that "Even middle-class insured families often fall prey to financial catastrophe when sick." *Id.*

Nanny Diaries and Other Stories: Imagining Immigrant Women's Labor in the Social Reproduction of American Families[a]

52, 809, 813, 814–22, 832–47 (2003).

■ MARY ROMERO

Wanted: One young woman to take care of four-year-old boy. Must be cheerful, enthusiastic, and selfless—bordering on masochistic. Must relish sixteen-hour shifts with a deliberately nap-deprived preschooler. Must love getting thrown up on, literally and figuratively, by everyone in his family. Must enjoy the delicious anticipation of ridiculously erratic pay. Mostly, must love being treated like fungus found growing out of employer's Hermes bag. Those who take it personally need not apply.

INTRODUCTION

Two former nannies employed on the Upper East Side of Manhattan offer this want advertisement as an illustration of employers' expectations and working conditions awaiting potential employees. Although it is a fictionalized account of their total six-year experience as nannies while attending college, Emma McLaughlin and Nicola Kraus's *The Nanny Diaries: A Novel* has spurred significant attention from the media. * * * * * *

II. *THE NANNY DIARIES*: REALITY OR FANTASY?

Given the media attention and public discourse generated by the novel, it is worth asking the question: How representative is *The Nanny Diaries?* * * *

Given the large number of undocumented immigrants and United States workers employed "off the books," workers with temporary or permanent visas, and the broad category that the Department of Labor and the Census classify as domestic service, precise numbers of domestics and nannies are difficult to obtain. Assessing the United States Bureau of Labor Statistics, Human Rights Watch estimates that 800,000 private household workers were officially recorded in 1998, of which 30% were immigrant women. Regions exporting the largest number of women to labor as domestic servants are Asia, Africa, Latin America, and Eastern Europe. Research conducted on domestics in the United States include immigrants from Latin America, the Caribbean, and the Philippines.

A distinctive characteristic of domestic service in the United States is the race and ethnic differences between employer and employee. The intersection of class, race, and ethnicity has been a prominent component to the study of African-American, Chicana and Japanese-American domes-

---

a. For further discussion of the racial, national and class dimensions of the U.S. domestic labor market, see chapter 11 at 919.

tics. Racial distinctions remain a striking feature identifying caregivers from their charges and employers. Reflecting on the playground scene in Central Park depicted in *The Nanny Diaries*, one onlooker contrasted the faces of children and caretakers:

> There are also adults there, but curiously, the faces of the two groups (adults and children) don't match. For every white child in a stroller, there is a black woman leaning down, to guide a juice box into their mouth. If she isn't black, she is Hispanic or Asian. The women are the children's nannies. In many cases, they are stepping in for white parents, who are working full-time.

Apparent differences between native-born and immigrant women of color employed as maids and nannies are education and previous work experience. African-American, Chicana and Japanese-American women rarely have more than a high school education. A growing number of Latina and Caribbean immigrants are high school and college graduates, and some have held white-collar positions in their homeland. Helma Lutz noted the international trend toward older and better educated third-world immigrant women in her survey of research on the globalization of domestic service. Unlike younger and single European immigrant women at the turn of the twentieth century, these women work to cope with financial crisis, to support families, and to educate their children. Thus, Nan's race, marital status, and citizenship are not characteristic of many women employed as nannies in the United States. With the exception of European women immigrating to the United States with J-1 visas to work as *au pairs* while pursuing their education, most immigrant women are not part-time college students. Nan's career trajectory is obviously destined for a professional or managerial position; whereas, older immigrant working mothers find little if any social mobility. For these women, domestic service is best described as a ghetto occupation rather than a bridging occupation.

Nan informs the reader of the existing continuum of childcare arrangements which she designates as three types of nanny gigs: (1) "a few nights a week for people who work all day and parent most nights;" (2) " 'sanity time' a few afternoons a week to a woman who mothers most days and nights;" and (3) "provide twenty-four/seven 'me time' to a woman who neither works nor mothers." Embedded in this classification are live-in positions (twenty-four hours a day, seven days a week) and day workers that might work solely for one employer full-time or for a number of employers. Employers make arrangements with agencies, franchises, collectives, or directly with the employee. Employees working on their own include some that are bonded and considered self-employed, and others working in the underground economy. However, the actual distinctions are reflected in the working conditions: hours of employment, wages, lack of benefits, and the inclusion of all household work alongside childcare.

Researchers and labor advocates reporting wages for immigrant women over the last decade point to the variability in the market. Grace A. Rosales found wages ranging from $100 to $400 a week in Los Angeles. In her study of immigrant women employed as domestics and nannies in Los

Angeles, Pierrette Hondagneu-Sotelo states that many Latina live-in workers do not receive minimum wage, whereas day workers averaged a higher wage of $5.90 an hour. Doreen Mattingly interviewed current and former Latina domestics in San Diego during the same period and found the average hourly rate for day workers was $8.02 and for live-ins was $2.72. Rhacel Salazar Parreñas reports that Filipina women migrating to Los Angeles earned an average of $425 a week for providing elderly care and $350 a week for live-in housekeeping and childcare. In a survey conducted in 2000, the Center for the Childcare Workforce in Washington, D.C., found that half of childcare providers earned less than $4.82 an hour and worked 55 hours a week. Human Rights Watch reviewed 43 egregious cases among domestic workers with special visas in the United States, and found a median hourly rate of $2.14.

Variation in wages and working conditions among employees points to the hierarchical structure in domestic service reinforced by employers' preferences. Obviously the hierarchy was not completely lost by McLaughlin and Kraus. In a reading at a Barnes & Noble bookshop, Kraus acknowledged the privileged subject position she and her colleague experienced: "We were the Hermès bags of nannies. . . . [A]s white, middle-class and university-educated nannies they [she and McLaughlin] were able to avoid the seamier elements of the industry." Latina and Caribbean immigrants are more vulnerable in the labor market than European immigrants. Skills do appear to be taken into consideration under certain circumstances. For instance, in her study of language between nannies and children in Los Angeles, Patricia Baquedano–López concluded that speaking English and a high school education were assets that domestics used in their negotiations with employers.

McLaughlin and Kraus portray a typical day of nanny tasks as "spent schlepping Grayer to French class, music lessons, karate, swimming, school and play dates." Although consistent with the image of Maria Rainer, the governess that Captain Von Trapp hired to care for his children in the film *The Sound of Music*, most employers with a live-in nanny assign employees a wide range of household tasks. While the distinction between housekeepers and nannies is frequently used to distinguish workers employed primarily to care for children, housekeepers may occasionally be asked to assist in childcare and nannies may be expected to cook, wash dishes, "pick-up," and do other household work directly related to the care of children. A consistent complaint among nannies is the expectation that they do housework and cook, alongside caring for children. Distinctions between domestic workers or private household workers and nannies are blurred in the everyday reality of employees as they engage in a broad range of household and caregiving activities, including cleaning, cooking, laundry, nursing the sick, supervising, playing with children, and grocery shopping.

Obviously, the most lucrative and sought after positions are the ones that make a clear distinction between tasks and recognize employees' skills, expertise, and experience. Immigrant women, particularly those who are undocumented, are more likely to be hired for live-in, as well as day work, positions that do not have clearly defined job descriptions. These nannies are unlikely to have much authority over the children or in planning activities. Instead, they find themselves at the beck and call of children as they serve and wait on them. Given the number of immigrant women nannies that McLaughlin and Kraus saw in the park, it is not surprising that they wrote, "[E]very playground has at least one nanny getting the shit kicked out of her by an angry child." *San Francisco Chronicle* reporter Adair Lara differentiated job descriptions offered to non-immigrant women: "At the other end of the spectrum, a professional nanny often works weekends, engages the child in imaginative play, knows CPR. . . . She will want her hours guaranteed, will expect a bonus, and might be persnickety about doing more than the dishes and the baby's laundry."

Nan's life implies that work as a nanny is filled with new learning opportunities and adventures, from learning to cook exotic foods for Grayer to vacationing among the rich and famous. This depiction does not capture the overwhelming sense of isolation reported by immigrant women, particularly among live-in workers. Since Lucy Salmon's sociological study at the turn of the century, extreme isolation continues to be cited among live-in workers as one of the worst aspects of the job. Isolation from relatives, friends, and other domestic workers removes them from gaining resources to find employment elsewhere. Separation from their own children is frequently identified as a major force in developing strong emotional attachment to their charges. Domestics' loneliness is not countered by stimulating tasks. In the transformation of domestic labor from the unpaid work of mothers to low-wage work, physical demands are increased and more creative aspects are eliminated. The transformation from unpaid to paid childcare results in assigning immigrant nannies to the least pleasant tasks. Childcare advocates Suzanne W. Helburn and Barbara R. Bergmann describe the division as follows: "The parents try to reserve the more interesting child-rearing tasks for themselves. They do the storytelling and reading, supervise homework, and organize outings and parties in order to spend 'quality time' with their children."

Like the public discourse generated by the Nannygate scandals over the last decade, *The Nanny Diaries* examined the impact on employers and their children rather than on the employees and their children. Editorials and book reviews focus on employer rights to privacy, poor parenting, and the suffering and deprivation of "the poor little rich boy, Grayer." Since the novel's fictionalized couple who hired the nanny was portrayed as a cheating husband and an unemployed trophy wife, the stage is set against a public debate over the needs of working parents. Labor issues are contexualized as interpersonal gender relationships between women (and their competing expectations and emotions in doing "women's work") and the difficulty of employees identifying as a servant. Reference to immigrant nannies are curtailed to discussions concerning the impact that their limited English skills and cultural differences have on children under their care.

However, when immigrant women speak for themselves, the following list of labor issues are similar to the concerns expressed by workers in the United States: low wages, unpaid hours, lack of decent standards, absence of health insurance and other employee benefits, and constant supervision. In the case of live-in domestics, employer abuses include violations of their human rights. Grievances reported in Bridget Anderson and Philzacklea's international study that are also found in the United States include:

> denial of wages in cases of dismissal following trial or probation periods, refusal by employers to arrange legal resident status (for tax reasons, etc.); control and sexual harassment; pressure to do additional work (for friends and colleagues); excessive workloads, especially where in addition to caring for children and elderly people they are responsible for all other household chores; and finally the very intimate relationship between the domestic helpers and their employers.

Human Rights Watch cites the following additional employer abuses in the United States: "basic telephone privileges, prohibiting them from leaving employers' homes unaccompanied, and forbidding them to associate or communicate with friends and neighbors." "To prevent domestic workers from leaving exploitative employment situations, employers confiscate the workers' passports and threaten them with deportation if they flee. In the most severe cases of abuse, migrant domestic workers—both live-in and day workers—have reported instances of sexual assault, physical abuse, and rape." Health hazards posed by cleaning chemicals "causing everything from skin irritation and rashes to serious respiratory problems from inhaling toxic fumes" is another grievance reported by human rights and labor advocates.

* * *

IV. IMMIGRANT NANNY CARE AND THE REPRODUCTION OF PRIVILEGE

Globalization of childcare is based on income inequality between women from poor countries providing low-wage care work for families in wealthier nations. Even with the low wages and variability in the market cited above, hiring a nanny is recognized as the most expensive childcare option. Researchers recognize this reality: "The grim truth is that some women's access to the high-paying, high-status professions is being facilitated through the revival of semi-indentured servitude. Put another way, one woman is exercising class and citizenship privilege to buy her easy way out of sex oppression." The largest number of domestic workers are located in areas of the country with the highest income inequality among women. In regions with minimal income inequality, the occupation is insignificant. Particular forms of domestic labor that affirm and enhance employers' status, shift the burden of sexism to low-wage women workers, and relegate the most physically difficult and dirty aspects of domestic labor. However, little attention has been given to the ways that privilege is reproduced through childcare arrangements and the significance that third-world immigrant women's labor plays in the reproduction of privilege.

Intensive and competitive mothering revolves around individuality, competition, and the future success of their children. Competition and individualism are values embedded in children's activities. Annette Lareau refers to this version of child rearing as "concerted cultivation" geared toward "deliberate and sustained effort to stimulate children's development and to cultivate . . . cognitive and social skills." Concerted cultivation aims to develop children's ability to reason by negotiating with parents and placing value on children's opinions, judgments, and observations. Family leisure time is dominated by organized children activities, such as sports, clubs, and paid lessons (e.g., dance, music, tennis). Most children's time is adult-structured rather than child-initiated play. "Play is not just play anymore. It involves the honing of 'large motor skills,' 'communication skills,' 'hand-eye coordination,' and the establishment of 'developmentally appropriate behavior.' "

Qualities of intensive and competitive mothering are at odds with demanding careers. Everyday practices of intensive mothering [require] immense emotional involvement, constant self-sacrificing, exclusivity, and a completely child-centered environment. These mothering activities are financially draining and time-consuming. Mothers with disposable income use commodities to fulfill areas of intensive and competitive mothering that they find themselves falling short of. In *The Mother Puzzle*, Judith D. Schwartz argues that advertising companies use guilt as significant child leverage:

> Companies who are marketing to our guilt inevitably start marketing the guilt itself in order to keep us shopping. This toy will help your child develop motor skills (implicit message: his motor skills will suffer without it). This line of clothing is made of the softest cotton (implicit message: other, less expensive fabrics may be abrasive).

By the 1990s, "babies and children were firmly entrenched as possessions that necessitated the acquisition of other commodities (and that became more valuable with further investment in goods and services)." Advertisers targeted the new "Skippies" market (*s*chool *k*ids with *i*ncome and *p*urchasing *p*ower). Quoting *People* magazine, Schwartz characterizes parents of these "gourmet children" as "rapaciously grabbing kudos for their kids with the same enterprise applied to creating fortunes on Wall Street." She suggests that, "Teaching values to our children has been replaced by building value into them . . . by preparing them to compete and giving them what we think they need to do so."

Hiring a live-in immigrant worker is the most convenient childcare option for juggling the demands of intensive mothering and a career. Purchasing the caretaking and domestic labor of an immigrant [woman] commodificates reproductive labor and reflects, reinforces, and intensifies social inequalities. The most burdensome mothering activities (such as cleaning, laundry, feeding babies and children, and chauffeuring children to their various scheduled activities) are shifted to the worker. Qualities of intensive mothering, such a sentimental value, nurturing, and intense emotional involvement, are not lost when caretaking work is shifted to an employee. Employers select immigrant caretakers on the basis of perceived "warmth," "love for children," and "naturalness in mothering." Different racial and ethnic groups are stereotyped by employers as ideal employees for housework, childcare, or for live-in positions. Stereotyping is based on a number of individual characteristics—race, ethnicity, class, caste, education, religion, and linguistic ability—and results in a degree of "otherness" for all domestic servants. However, such a formalization of difference does not always put workers in the subordinate position, and employers' preferences can vary from place to place. Janet Henshall Momsen notes that, "Professionally-trained British nannies occupy an élite niche in Britain and North America." Interviewing employers in Los Angeles and New York City, Julia Wrigley observed Spanish-speaking nannies were identified by employers for their ability to broaden the cultural experience of their children, particularly in exposing them to a second language in the home. Employers referenced the growing Latino population in their community and the long-term benefits of their children learning Spanish. However, the socialization to race and culture politics may be the most significant consequence of the current commodification of reproductive labor.

The primary mission of reproductive labor in contemporary mothering is to assure their children's place in society. This is partially accomplished through socialization into class, gender, sexual, ethnic and race hierarchies. Employment of immigrant women as caregivers contributes to this socialization. Reinforced by their parents' conceptualization of caretaking as a "labor of love," children learn a sense of entitlement to receiving affection from people of color that is detached from their own actions. Children learn to be "consumers of care" rather than providers of caregiving. Caretaking without parental authority does not teach children reciprocal respect but rather teaches that the treatment of women of color as "merely means, and not as ends in themselves." The division of labor between mother and live-in caretaker domestic stratifies components of reproductive labor and equates burdensome, manual and basic maintenance labor with immigrant women of color. This gendered division of labor serves to teach traditional patriarchal privilege. Privilege is learned as they acquire a sense of entitlement to having a domestic worker always on call to meet their needs.

Stratified reproductive labor of a live-in immigrant domestic assures "learned helplessness and class prejudice in the child," and teaches "[dependence], aggressiveness, and selfishness." Systems of class, racial, ethnic, gender and citizenship domination are taught to children by witnessing "the arbitrary and capricious interaction of parents and servants or if they are permitted to treat domestic servants in a similar manner." As children move from their homes located in class (and frequently racially) segregated neighborhoods to schools (also likely to be segregated), power relationships and the larger community's class and racial etiquette are further reinforced. "As care is made into a commodity, women with greater resources in the global economy can afford the best-quality care for their family." If mothering is directed toward assuring their child's social and economic status in society—a society that is racist, capitalist, and patriarchal—then her goals are strengthened by employing a low wage, full-time or live-in immigrant woman. Conditions under which immigrant women of color are employed in private homes is structured by systems of privilege and, consequently, employers' children are socialized into these norms and values.

V. Prolongation of Immigrant Women Subordination

Paid reproductive labor in the United States is structured along local, national and international inequalities, positioning third-world immigrant women as the most vulnerable workers. Careworkers are sorted by the degree of vulnerability and privilege. Consequently, paid domestic labor is not only structured around gender but is stratified by race and citizenship status, relegating the most vulnerable worker to the least favorable working conditions and placing the most privileged in the best positions. A major initiative in the American childcare movement is addressing low wages in the childcare industry. However, the plight of live-in caregivers and immigrant women as a specific group is rarely addressed. The solution of hiring a live-in domestic, used by a relatively privileged group, is a component of reproductive labor in the United States, and serves to intensify inequalities between women: first, by reinforcing childcare as a private rather than public responsibility; and second, by reaping the benefits gained by the impact of globalization and restructuring on third-world women. The globalization of domestic service contributes to the reproduction of inequality between nations in transnational capitalism and cases reported of domestic servitude is increasingly characterized as global gender apartheid.

Devaluation of immigrant women in the international division of labor begins in the home as unpaid labor; then is further devalued in the segregated labor forces within third-world countries used by wealthier nations for cheap labor. Women are relegated to low-wage factory work in textiles and electronics industries with no opportunities available for better-paid positions. Migrating and working as domestics becomes the primary strategy for sustaining households for both poor and middle-class women. The demand for low-wage migrant workers expands the pool of cheap labor that unemployment and welfare regulations are unable to maintain. Theorists have traditionally argued that women's unpaid domestic labor in the home served as a reserve labor force. Applying this qualification to immigrant domestic workers, the employment of third-world women becomes a significant source for reproducing a labor reserve, similar to the function of the unemployed and underemployed. Saskia Sassen states this proposition in the following question: "Does domestic service—at least in certain locations—become one of the few alternatives and does it, then, function, as a privatized mechanism for social reproduction and maintenance of a labor reserve?" The transnational export of women from global south to the rich industrialized countries of the north has resulted in promoting domestics as a major "export product." Transnational division of labor is determined "simultaneously by global capitalism and systems of gender inequality in both sending and receiving countries of migration."

A prominent feature of globalized reproductive labor is commodification. Parreñas argues that, "Commodified reproductive labor is not only low-paid work but declines in market value as it gets passed down the international transfer of caretaking." However, Anderson argues that the commodification process in globalization is not limited to the labor but is extended to the worker. In her work on the global politics of domestic labor, she points out that employers "openly stipulate that they want a particular type *person* justifying this demand on the grounds that they will be working in the home." Having hired the preferred racialized domestic caretaker on the basis of personal characteristics rather than former experience or skills, the emotional labor required is not recognized by the employer but the worker's caring "brings with it no mutual obligations, no entry into a community, no 'real' human relations, only money."

Employers' hiring preferences for employees who are a particular race, ethnicity, and nationality contributes to the hierarchical chain of domestic caretakers. Hondagneu-Sotelo notes that African Americans are no longer the preferred employee in Los Angeles homes because [they] are portrayed as "bossy" and with "terrifying images associated with young black men." Similar images are applied to Caribbean women in New York and are cautioned against coming "across in interviews as being in any way aggressive." Latina immigrants in Los Angeles are perceived as "responsible, trustworthy, and reliable" workers as well as "exceptionally warm, patient, and loving mothers." In the case of Filipina women, Dan Gatmaytan argues that their labor is distinctively featured in international division of labor as "docile and submissive," and thus, ideally packaged to be imported "by other countries for jobs their own citizens will not perform and for wages domestic citizens would not accept." Parreñas's findings suggest that employers view Filipinas as providing a "higher-quality" service because they speak English and generally have a higher education than Latina immigrants.

However, without state regulations of labor and immigration policies, employers' preferences are irrelevant in the racialization of reproductive labor in the United States. Joy Mutanu Zarembka, director of the Campaign for Migrant Domestic Workers' Rights, argues that the estimated four thousand special visas issued annually for third-world immigrant women contributes to commodification of these workers into a "maid to order" in the United States. Three visas perpetuating the subordination of immigrant women of color as live-in domestic workers are:

> A-3 visas to work for ambassadors, diplomats, consular officers, public ministers, and their families; G-5 visas to work for officers and employees of international organizations or of foreign missions to international organizations and their families; and B-1 visas to accompany U.S. citizens who reside abroad but are visiting the United States or assigned to the United States temporarily for no more than four years, or foreign nations with nonimmigrant status in the United States.

In contrast to special visas given primarily to third-world immigrant women, the J-1 visa is increasingly used to bring young and middle-class

European immigrant women as nannies or *au pairs* with "educational and cultural exchange" their primary purpose. Under this visa, each nanny receives an orientation session and is placed in geographical locations near other nannies. After her placement, she attends an orientation session and "receives information on community resources, educational opportunities and contacts for a local support network." Counselors have monthly sessions with each employer and nanny to "report any problems and resolve disputes." "In contrast, with the G-5, A-1 and B-1 domestic worker programs, there are no official orientations, no information, no contact numbers, no counselors, and no educational programs. In practice, as well, there is often no freedom—many are systematically (though illegally) forbidden from contacting the outside world."

Human Rights Watch further asserts that special visas intensify workers' vulnerability to abuse and facilitate the violation of other human rights. Procedures, guidelines, laws, and regulations governing special domestic worker visas construct circumstances that tolerate and conceal employer abuses, and restrict workers' rights. Among the problems cited by Human Rights Watch are the lack of INS follow-up monitoring or investigations to verify employer compliance with employment contracts, and the Department of Labor's lack of involvement with administrating these visas. Consequently, no governmental agency is responsible for enforcing contracts. Zarembka asserts that the secrecy of the whereabouts of G-5, A-3 and B-1 workers makes "them some of the most vulnerable and easily exploited sectors of the American workforce" and violation of human rights is silenced by their invisibility. In addition to low wages, long hours, and the lack of both privacy and benefits that are common among live-in conditions, immigrant women experience other abuses. They include passport confiscation, limited freedom of movement and ability to communicate with others, employer threats of deportation, assault and battery, rape, servitude, torture, and trafficking. Changing employers under live-in conditions has always been difficult for workers, and for women with employment-based visas, they are faced with weighing "respect for their own human rights and maintaining their legal immigration status." For similar reasons, women are reluctant to report abuse because they fear losing their jobs, deportation, unfamiliarity with the American legal system, social and cultural isolation, and fear that "their retaliation powerful employers will retaliate against their families in their countries of origin."

Exclusion from a number of labor policies contribute to the hardships immigrant women experience as live-in domestics. They are excluded from overtime provisions provided in the Fair Labor Standard Act, from the right to organize, strike, and bargain collectively in the National Labor Relations Act, and from regulations in the Occupational Safety and Health Act. "In practice, too, live-in domestic workers are rarely covered by Title VII protections against sexual harassment in the workplace, as Title VII only applies to employers with fifteen or more workers."

Third-world immigrant domestics experience first hand the inequalities of caregiving as they provide labor for parents in rich industrialized countries while leaving their own children. Sarah Blaffer Hrdy equates mothers leaving their children with relatives in their homelands to European infants left in foundling homes or sent to wet nurses during the eighteenth century: "Solutions differ, but the tradeoffs mothers make, and the underlying emotions and mental calculations, remain the same." Anderson notes that immigrant women's care for their children is limited "in the fruits of hard labour, in remittances, rather than in the cuddles and 'quality time' that provide so much of the satisfaction of care." Transnational mothering cannot provide the "physical closeness, seen as healthy and 'normal' in the Western upbringing of a child, are not given, because most of the women are not allowed to take their children with them." These conditions reduce mothering to the basic function of economic support. In her research on Filipina women in Rome and Los Angeles, Parrenas observed the impact of economic ties rather than affective ties between mother and child departed from each over a long period of time. The use of material good, financial assistance, and school tuition result in commodifying family relationships and motherhood. Inequalities in the distribution and quality of domestic labor and caregiving is a cost borne by the children of live-in workers. The absence of retirement benefits pension assures that workers will not be able to contribute financially to their children's future, but rather will need their assistance.

VI. CONCLUSION

Before the September 11 attacks, the Federation for American Immigration Reform (FAIR), Patrick Buchanan, Pete Wilson and others vilified immigrants as the cause of all problems in the United States. Homeland security has further fanned the flames of xenophobia and support for vilifying immigrants. Yet, within the intimacy of many American homes, immigrant women (primarily Latina and Caribbean immigrants) continue to provide assisted reproductive labor that fulfills the basic tasks of maintaining families of dual career couples and contribute to middle-upper- and upper-class lifestyles. Popular culture functions to normalize the hiring of immigrant women by depicting domestic service as a bridging occupation that offers social mobility, opportunities to learn English, and other cultural skills that assist in the assimilation process. The characterization of nannies and private household workers in *The Nanny Diaries*, as well as in films and sitcoms, serves to reduce the significance of immigrant women in fulfilling childcare needs in the United States and to erase issues of employee rights from the American imagination. Instead, employers are classified as good or bad: good employers who are benevolent and provide immigrant women with a modernizing experience, or bad employers who are rich couples ignoring their children. Popular culture does not contextualize paid reproductive labor. Economic, political and legal structures surrounding the migration of Latina, Caribbean and Filipina women are ignored along with the circumstances that relegate their labor to low-wage dead-end jobs. Consequently, we can maintain our illusions of Latina domestics as sexually out of control and utterly colorful spitfire, the self-deprecating accented smart-mouthed, or the rosary-praying maid. We can continue to see these images and sing out, "Yes, that's what maids are like."

* * *

Centering immigration on questions of "belonging" (and related concepts, e.g., assimilation, ethnic differences, and ethnic loyalty) blinds us to inquiries into the role of immigration in sustaining systems of privilege and perpetuating myths and ideologies central to national identity. Immigration and labor regulations reproduce race, class, gender and citizenship inequalities and privileges. In the case of immigrant women employed as private household workers or caregivers, the social reproduction of inequalities begins in the employer's home. Managing the contradictions of intimacy and vilification of immigrants through cultural images that falsify employee-employer relationships, allows Americans to reap the benefits of retaining a vulnerable labor force unprotected from exploitation while arguing humanitarian positions. The popular version of nannies depicted in *The Nanny Diaries* assists in normalizing privilege and erases issues of economic injustice. Our complacency in the subordination of immigrant women is once again obtained by our fascination with chatty gossip on sex, drugs, money, and family values of the wealthy on Park Avenue. Moreover, our illusion that there is no greater state of being than Americans is further enhanced by denying the privileges gained by third-world assisted social reproduction.

The Hidden Injuries of Class

79–87 (1972).

■ Richard Sennett & Jonathan Cobb

Josiah Watson Grammar School is an old red-brick building with a simple but well-kept playground. It is a large school, in the midst of an urban neighborhood of mostly three-decker houses. In the community surrounding the school live groups of Irish, Italian, and old-stock New Englanders, but almost all are manual laborers. The median family income in the neighborhood is about $8000—neither poor nor affluent.

The rooms at the Watson School evoke the interiors of the children's homes: old, rather run down, and yet clean, almost austere. In each schoolroom the only decorations consist of an American flag, a bound set of maps, and a plaque with the Pledge of Allegiance. The school desks are new—tubular steel legs holding up flat wooden boxes. In them, children's supplies are neatly arranged, even for the littlest children. The teachers take a certain pride in this, but they apologize to the visitor for the tops scratched with the obscene words, drawings, and initials that children always seem to inflict on such objects.

The classes in Watson School, even as low as the second grade, jolt the outsider who has lost touch with the institutional life of children. Everything that goes on in the second-grade class, from reading preparedness to play with toys, is directed by the teacher. She takes great pains to see that the children act "good and proper." The visitor who is aware of his own presence in these classrooms at first thinks this show of discipline, this constant commanding and watching, is the teacher's response to that presence. After the teacher relaxes and forgets he is there, however, the discipline continues. It varies among the teachers from harsh to loving; but all those in charge of classrooms at the Watson School act like conductors who must bring potentially unruly mobs of musicians under their direction. As the principal remarks, "It is by establishing authority that we make this school work."

In Watson School, teachers restrict the freedom of the children because these figures of authority have a peculiar fear of the children. It is the mass who seem to the teachers to threaten classroom order, by naughty or unruly behavior; only a few are seen as having "good habits" or the right attitude. As one teacher explained, "These children come from simple laborers' homes where the parents don't understand the value of education." Yet in the early grades the observer noticed few examples of disruptive behavior. He sensed among the six-and seven-year olds a real desire to please, to accept the teacher's control and be accepted by her. One pathetic incident, although extreme, stands out. In the middle of a reading-preparedness class, a child wet his pants because he was absorbed in his lesson. "What can you do with children like that?" the teacher later remarked in a tone of disgust.

What happens is that the teachers act on their expectations of the children in such a way as to *make* the expectations become reality. Here is how the process worked in one second-grade class at Watson School—unusual in that it was taught by a young man. In this class there were two children, Fred and Vincent, whose appearance was somewhat different from that of the others: their clothes were no fancier than the other children's, but they were pressed and seemed better kept; in a class of mostly dark Italian children, these were the fairest-skinned. From the outset the teacher singled out these two children, implying that they most closely approached his own standards for classroom performance. He never praised them openly by comparison to the other children, but a message that they were different, were better, was spontaneously conveyed. As the observer watched the children play and work over the course of the school year, he noticed these two boys becoming more serious, more solemn, as the months passed. Obedient and never unruly from the first, by the end of the year they were left alone by the other children.

By then they were also doing the best work in the class. The other children had picked up the teacher's hidden cues that their performance would not be greeted with as much enthusiasm as the work of these two little boys. "It's not true of the other children that they generally have less potential," the teacher remarked. "It's a question of not developing their ability like Fred and Vincent. I know you're right, I tend to encourage them more despite myself, but I—it's obvious to me these little boys are going to make something of themselves."

In the Watson School, by the time the children are ten or eleven the split between the many and the few who are expected to "make something of themselves" is out in the open; the aloofness developing in the second grade has become open hostility by the sixth. Among the boys, this hostility is expressed by images which fuse sex and status. Boys like Fred and Vincent are described by the "ordinary" students as effeminate and weak, as "suck-ups." The kids mean by this both that the Freds and Vincents are getting somewhere in school because they are so docile, and that only a homosexual would be so weak; the image of a "suck-up" crystallizes this self-demeaning, effeminate behavior that to them marks off a student whom the institution can respect.

What has happened, then, is that these children have directed their anger at their schoolmates who are rewarded as individuals rather than at the institution which is withholding recognition of them. Indeed, the majority of boys in the fifth and sixth grades are often not consciously in conflict with the school at all. Something more complex is happening to them.

These "ordinary" boys in class act as though they were serving time, as though schoolwork and classes had become something to wait out, a blank space in their lives they hope to survive and then leave. Their feeling, apparently, is that when they get out, get a job and some money, *then* they will be able to begin living. It is not so much that they are bored in school— many in Watson School like their classes. It is rather that they have lost any expectation that school will help them, that this experience will change them or help them grow as human beings.

One teacher in this school, an enthusiastic young woman who liked to work with "ordinary" students, said her greatest problem was convincing the students that they could trust her. The other teachers and the principal disapprove of her because she runs her class in an informal manner. They feel she lets the students "get away with anything," "that she can't keep discipline." Permissiveness is a vice, order a necessity, in the minds of the other teachers; they believe that most of their charges, due to family class background and past school performances, will resist following the rules which to an educated adult seem so logical and beneficial. It is not that these teachers are intentionally mean, but that they unwittingly set in motion in the classroom a vicious circle that produces exactly the kind of behavior they expect.

There is a counterculture of dignity that springs up among these ordinary working-class boys, a culture that seeks in male solidarity what cannot be found in the suspended time that comprises classroom experience. This solidarity also sets them off from the "suck-ups." Hanging around together, the boys share their incipient sexual exploits, real and imagined; sex becomes a way to compete within the group. What most cements them as a group, however, is the breaking of rules—smoking, drinking, or taking drugs together, cutting classes. Breaking the rules is an act "nobodies" can share with each other. This counterculture does not come to grips with the labels their teachers have imposed on these kids; it

is rather an attempt to create among themselves badges of dignity that those in authority can't destroy.

A full circle: outsider observers—parents, teachers, and others—who see only the external aspects of this counterculture, are confirmed in their view that "hanging around" is destructive to a child's self-development. Dignity in these terms exacts a toll by the standards of the outer world.

The division of children, in schools like Watson, into groups with a shared sense of loyalty and individuals alone but "getting somewhere," characterizes many levels of education; it is not something unique to, say, college-bound youth as opposed to vocational school boys. Studies of trade schools show the same phenomenon occurring: boys who are good at car mechanics in school start to feel cut off from others, even though the possession of those skills might make them admired by their less-skilled peers outside of school. It is an institutional process that makes the difference, a question of mere toleration versus active approval from those in power.

The drama played out in the Watson School has as its script the assigning and the wearing of badges of ability like those described earlier, worn by adults. The teachers cast the Freds and Vincents into the role of Andrew Carnegie's virtuous man. Ability will make these children into individuals, and as individuals they will rise in social class. The mass find themselves in a role similar to that which Lipset assigns to adult workers: their class background allegedly limits their self-development, and the counterculture of compensatory respect they create reinforces, in a vicious circle, the judgments of the teachers.

The teacher has the *power* to limit the freedom of development of his or her students through this drama. But why is he or she moved to act in this repressive way? This question is really two questions: it is first a matter of a teacher legitimizing in his own mind the power he holds, and second, a matter of the students taking that power as legitimate.

The teachers are in a terrible existential dilemma. It is true that they are "prejudiced" against most of their students; it is also true that they, like all human beings, want to believe in the dignity of their own work, no matter how difficult the circumstances in which they have to work seem to them. If a teacher believed that every single student would perpetually resist him, he would have no reason to go on teaching—his power in the classroom would be empty. A teacher needs at least a responsive few in order to feel he has a *reason* to possess power. The few will confirm to him that his power to affect other people is real, that he can truly do good. To sort out two classes of ability, then, in fear of the "lower" class of students, is to create a meaningful image of himself as an authority rather than simply a boss.

It is true that an analysis at this level of teachers, or other power figures dealing with working-class people, is by itself inadequate. A teacher may be having an existential crisis, but that doesn't explain why images of social class and classes of ability have come to fuse in his mind, nor does it

explain how useful, how convenient, this crisis of self-legitimacy is in keeping the present class structure going. Still, it is important to keep before ourselves the experiential reality facing a person who has power over others. The teachers at Watson did not think of themselves as tools of capitalism, or even as repressive. They felt they had to legitimize their own work's dignity in the face of working-class students; and making a moral hierarchy on the basis of ability—however artificially and unjustifiably— was the natural means they used.

The perceptions the children had of the teachers similarly concerned not their power, but their legitimacy.

The observer is playing marbles with Vinny, a third-grader, described by his teacher as an "unexceptional average student who tolerates school," and Vinny begins absentmindedly to arrange the marbles in sets by color. The observer points out to him that he is doing something like what the teacher had asked him to do in arithmetic hour and he hadn't then been able to do. Vinny replies, "I didn't want to give her no trouble"—an answer the observer notes without, at the time, understanding what Vinny meant. In a class on grammar, Stephanie gives a past participle incorrectly; the teacher asks her to try again, but while she is thinking, one of the bright children interrupts with the right answer. The teacher—the experimental and "permissive" woman already described—tells the bright child to shut up and gives Stephanie another answer to work out. Stephanie looks at her in total surprise, wondering why the teacher should still care about whether *she* can learn to do it, if the right answer has already been provided. Max, an obnoxious fifth-grade bully, has somehow formed an interest in writing doggerel rhymes. During a composition hour he reads one, but when he finishes, the teacher makes no reply, merely smiles and calls on the next pupil. Asked later how he felt, Max looks a little crestfallen and says with characteristic grace, "Lookit, shithead, she ain't got time to waste on me."

––––––––

NOTES AND QUESTIONS

1. "Globalization" at top and bottom of economy. Saskia Sassen argues that "globalization" has produced both transnational marginalized labor classes and transnational privileged classes: while the elite of "global cities" such as New York, Hong Kong, and Paris are increasingly intertwined through networks of education and training, the "underclass" in such cities are also intertwined, through networks of migration and the demand for low-end service work. Saskia Sassen, *Toward a Feminist Analytics of the Global Economy*, 4 IND. J. GLOBAL LEGAL STUD. 7 (1996). Sassen argues that migration (legal and illegal), which is often treated as only a problem for the government sector to be solved through immigration law, should be seen as intimately connected to trade policy and economic policy more generally.

How might the increasing income and wealth inequality brought about by globalization affect women as a group? Sassen is hopeful that the globalizing economy, as it pulls more women into wage work, will empower them within their families and in the public sector. *Id.*, at 27. At the same time, she acknowledges that women are "constituted as an invisible and disempowered class of workers in the service of the strategic sectors constituting the global economy." *Id.*, at 26.

2. Modern-day slavery. The very lowest caste of contemporary workers is made up of those whose labor power is forcibly expropriated by others. Kevin Bales argues that slavery is alive and well today, although it takes different legal and social forms than the "old" slavery:

> *My best estimate of the number of slaves in the world today is 27 million.*
>
> This number is much smaller than the estimates put forward by some activists, who give a range as high as 200 million, but it is the number I feel I can trust * * *. The biggest part of that 27 million, perhaps 15 to 20 million, is represented by *bonded labor* in India, Pakistan, Bangladesh, and Nepal. Bonded labor or debt bondage happens when people give themselves into slavery as security against a loan or when they inherit a debt from a relative * * *. Otherwise slavery tends to be concentrated in Southeast Asia, northern and western Africa, and parts of South America (but there are some slaves in almost every country in the world, including the United States, Japan, and many European countries). There are more slaves alive today than all the people stolen from Africa in the time of the transatlantic slave trade. Put another way, today's slave population is greater than the population of Canada, and six times greater than the population of Israel.
>
> These slaves tend to be used in simple, nontechnological, and traditional work. The largest group work in agriculture. But slaves are used in many other kinds of labor: brickmaking, mining or quarrying, prostitution, gem working and jewelry making, cloth and carpet making, and domestic service; they clear forests, make charcoal, and work in shops. Much of this work is aimed at local sale and consumption, but slave-made goods reach into homes around the world. Carpets, fireworks, jewelry, and metal goods made by slave labor, as well as grains, sugar, and other foods harvested by slaves, are imported directly to North America and Europe. In addition, large international corporations, acting through subsidiaries in the developing world, take advantage of slave labor to improve their bottom line and increase the dividends to their shareholders.

KEVIN BALES, DISPOSABLE PEOPLE: NEW SLAVERY IN THE GLOBAL ECONOMY 8–9 (1999).

Bales argues that the new slavery differs from the old slavery in several ways. Among these differences are the following: slaveholders no longer assert legal ownership over their slaves; slaveholders do not contribute to the maintenance costs of their slaves; ethnic differences between slaveholding and slave classes are less important than they were in, for example, American slavery; slaves produce very high profits; the relationship between slaveholder and slave tends to be short-term rather than long-term; and there is a surplus rather than a shortage of potential slaves. *Id.*, at 15.

The International Labor Organization defines "forced labor" as "all work or service which is exacted from any person under the menace of any penalty and for which the said person has not offered himself voluntarily." International Labor Organization, Convention Concerning Forced Labor (No. 29). Using this definition, a team of researchers at the University of California at Berkeley, working with a nonprofit antislavery organization, examined the nature and scope of forced labor in the United States from January 1998 to December 2003. According to their report:

> Over the past five years, forced labor operations have been reported in at least ninety U.S. cities. These operations tend to thrive in states with large populations and sizable immigrant communities, such as California, Florida, New York, and Texas—all of which are transit routes for international travelers.

> Forced labor is prevalent in five sectors of the U.S. economy: prostitution and sex services (46%), domestic service (27%), agriculture (10%), sweatshop/factory (5%), and restaurant and hotel work (4%) * * *. Forced labor persists in these sectors because of low wages, lack of regulation and monitoring of working conditions, and a high demand for cheap labor. These conditions enable unscrupulous employers and criminal networks to gain virtually complete control over workers' lives.

Human Rights Center & Free the Slaves: Forced Labor in the United States 1 (2004), *available at* http://www.hrcberkeley.org/download/hiddenslaves_report.pdf. (posted September 2004) (last visited, Mar. 6, 2005). The researchers estimated that approximately 10,000 people are working as forced laborers in the United States at any given time. *Id.*, at 10.

In the United States, slavery and human trafficking are subject to the federal Victims of Trafficking and Violence Protection Act of 2000, § 107, 22 U.S.C. §7105 (2004). The act, among other things, establishes mandatory restitution from convicted traffickers, and an amendment allows survivors to sue their captors for civil damages for violations of the statute. *See* Trafficking Victims Protection Reauthorization Act of 2003, 18 U.S.C. §1595 (2004) (civil damages provision). The act also provides social services and immigration status to victims of a "severe form of trafficking" who cooperate with law enforcement to prosecute the traffickers.

3. Women, prostitution and sex work: abolitionists versus labor activists. Feminists have long argued over whether prostitution and other forms of sex work should be abolished as forms of violence against women, or legalized and regulated as just another kind of labor. Jane Larson argues that the dichotomy is unhelpful and that prostitution, like sweatshop labor, child labor, and various forms of bonded and indentured labor, should be examined more closely to help us think more generally about what kinds of labor are acceptable and why:

> Instead of fruitless debates about the "essential nature" of the commodity relation of prostitution, I urge instead a common project aimed at defining the material, moral, and legal differences between free and unfree labor, describing with empirical depth and range what conditions of work characterize commercial sex in its various forms and locales, and measuring the sex industry against the free labor standard. What is force and compulsion in the sex labor setting? Is the definition of force such that the exchange of money refutes the claim of compulsion, or can the liberal concern for substantive freedom in labor relations translate into international standards? What working conditions render prostitution a per se unacceptably exploitative practice for children? Is it different for adults? Why or why not? What kinds of discrimination on the basis of sex or race are unacceptable? Does the demographic constitution of the market for sexual labor demonstrate such discrimination? If prostitution is one of women's best economic options, how does this shape other economic opportunities for women? Does female prostitution violate the equality ideal?

Jane E. Larson, *Prostitution, Labor, and Human Rights,* 37 U.C. DAVIS L. REV. 673, 698–99 (2004).

4. Public education and construction of failure. Cobb and Sennett were concerned primarily with the education and socialization of the sons of white working class "ethnic" immigrants. Other scholars have found that public education similarly sets up African American and Latino/a working class children, especially boys, to fail. For example, Theresa Glennon observes:

> First, African American boys are much more likely to be identified as disabled or delinquent than other children, including African American girls. Second, they are more likely than other children to be placed in educational, mental health, and juvenile justice programs that exert greater external control and deliver fewer services despite identified needs. Third, these negative experiences lead African American boys to stay away from or exit these institutional settings.

Theresa Glennon, *Knocking Against the Rocks: Evaluating Institutional Practices and the African American Boy*, 5 J. HEALTH CARE L. & POL'Y 10, 11 (2002). Glennon argues that these disparities are a result of racism.

Sociologist John Ogbu found another dynamic among African American children similar to that identified by Sennett and Cobb: black students both underperform and pressure one another to underperform by associating school success with "acting white." Signithia Fordham & John U. Ogbu, *Black Students' School Success: Coping with the "Burden of Acting White,"* 18 URB. REV. 176 (1986). Ogbu and Fordham's findings have been controversial in African American communities.

———

The Overworked American: The Unexpected Decline of Leisure

17–24 (1991).

■ JULIET B. SCHOR

Time squeeze has become big news. In summer 1990, the premiere episode of Jane Pauley's television show, "Real Life," highlighted a single father whose computer job was so demanding that he found himself at 2:00 A.M. dragging his child into the office. A Boston-area documentary featured the fourteen-to sixteen-hour workdays of a growing army of moonlighters. CBS's "Forty–Eight Hours" warned of the accelerating pace of life for everyone from high-tech business executives (for whom there are only two types of people—"the quick and the dead") to assembly workers at Japanese-owned automobile factories (where a car comes by every sixty seconds). Employees at fast-food restaurants, who serve in twelve seconds, report that the horns start honking if the food hasn't arrived in fifteen. Nineteen-year-olds work seventy-hour weeks, children are "penciled" into their parents' schedules, and second-graders are given "half an hour a day to unwind" from the pressure to get good grades so they can get into a good college. By the beginning of the 1990s, the time squeeze had become a national focus of attention, appearing in almost all the nation's major media outlets. * * *

The time squeeze surfaced with the young urban professional. These high achievers had jobs that required sixty, eighty, even a hundred hours a week. On Wall Street, they would regularly stay at the office until midnight or go months without a single day off. Work consumed their lives. And if they weren't working, they were networking. They power-lunched, power-exercised, and power-married. As the pace of life accelerated, time became an ever-scarcer commodity, so they used their money to buy more of it. Cooking was replaced by gourmet frozen foods from upscale delis. Eventually the "meal" started disappearing, in favor of "grazing." Those who could afford it bought other people's time, hiring surrogates to shop, write their checks, or even just change a light bulb. They cut back on sleep and postponed having children. ("Can you carry a baby in a briefcase?" queried one Wall Street executive when she was asked about having kids.)

High-powered people who spend long hours at their jobs are nothing new. Medical residents, top corporate management, and the self-employed have always had grueling schedules. But financiers used to keep bankers' hours, and lawyers had a leisured life. Now bankers work like doctors, and lawyers do the same. A former Bankers Trust executive remembers that "somebody would call an occasional meeting at 8 A.M. Then it became the regular 8 o'clock meeting. So there was the occasional 7 A.M. meeting.... It just kept spreading." On Wall Street, economic warfare replaced the clubhouse atmosphere—and the pressure forced the hours up. As women and new ethnic groups were admitted into the industry, competition for the plum positions heightened—and the hours went along. Twenty-two-year-olds wear beepers as they squeeze in an hour for lunch or jogging at the health club.

What happened on Wall Street was replicated throughout the country in one high-income occupation after another. Associates in law firms competed over who could log more billable hours. Workaholics set new standards of survival. Even America's sleepiest corporations started waking up; and when they did, the corporate hierarchies found themselves coming in to work a little earlier and leaving for home a little later. As many companies laid off white-collar people during the 1980s, those who remained did more for their monthly paycheck. A study of "downsizings" in auto-related companies in the Midwest found that nearly half of the two thousand managers polled said they were working harder than two years earlier.

At cutting-edge corporations, which emphasize commitment, initiative, and flexibility, the time demands are often the greatest. "People who work for me should have phones in their bathrooms," says the CEO from one aggressive American company. Recent research on managerial habits reveals that work has become positively absorbing. When a deadline approached in one corporation, "people who had been working twelve-hour days and Saturdays started to come in on Sunday, and instead of leaving at midnight, they would stay a few more hours. Some did not go home at all, and others had to look at their watches to remember what day it was." The recent growth in small businesses has also contributed to overwork. When Dolores Kordek started a dental insurance company, her strategy for survival was to work harder than the competition. So the office was open from 7 A.M. to 10 P.M. three hundred and sixty-five days a year. And she was virtually always in it.

This combination of retrenchment, economic competition, and innovative business management has raised hours substantially. One poll of senior executives found that weekly hours rose during the 1980s, and vacation time fell. Other surveys have yielded similar results. By the end of the decade, overwork at the upper echelons of the labor market had become endemic—and its scale was virtually unprecedented in living memory.

If the shortage of time had been confined to Wall Street or America's corporate boardrooms, it might have remained just a media curiosity. The number of people who work eighty hours a week and bring home—if they ever get there—a six-figure income is very small. But while the incomes of these rarefied individuals were out of reach, their schedules turned out to be downright common. As Wall Street waxed industrious, the longer schedules penetrated far down the corporate ladder, through middle management, into the secretarial pool, and even onto the factory floor itself. Millions of ordinary Americans fell victim to the shortage of time.

The most visible group has been women, who are coping with a double load—the traditional duties associated with home and children and their growing responsibility for earning a paycheck. With nearly two-thirds of adult women now employed, and a comparable fraction of mothers on the job, it's no surprise that many American women find themselves operating in overdrive. Many working mothers live a life of perpetual motion, effectively holding down two full-time jobs. They rise in the wee hours of the morning to begin the day with a few hours of laundry, cleaning, and other housework. Then they dress and feed the children and send them off to school. They themselves then travel to their jobs. The three-quarters of employed women with full-time positions then spend the next eight and a half hours in the workplace.

At the end of the official workday, it's back to the "second shift"—the duties of housewife and mother. Grocery shopping, picking up the children, and cooking dinner take up the next few hours. After dinner there's clean-up, possibly some additional housework, and, of course, more child care. Women describe themselves as "ragged," "bone-weary," "sinking in quick-sand," and "busy every waking hour." For many, the workday rivals those for which the "satanic mills" of the Industrial Revolution grew justly infamous: twelve-or fourteen-hour stretches of labor. By the end of the decade, Ann Landers pronounced herself "awestruck at the number of women who work at their jobs and go home to another full-time job . . . How do you do it?" she asked. Thousands of readers responded, with tales ranging from abandoned careers to near collapse. According to sociologist Arlie Hochschild of the University of California, working mothers are exhausted, even fixated on the topic of sleep. "They talked about how much they could 'get by on': . . . six and a half, seven, seven and a half, less, more . . . These women talked about sleep the way a hungry person talks about food."

By my calculations, the total working time of employed mothers now averages about 65 hours a week. Of course, many do far more than the average—such as mothers with young children, women in professional positions, or those whose wages are so low that they must hold down two jobs just to scrape by. These women will be working 70 to 80 hours a week. And my figures are extremely conservative: they are the lowest among existing studies. A Boston study found that employed mothers *average* over 80 hours of housework, child care, and employment. Two nationwide studies of white, married couples are comparable: in the first, the average week was 87 hours; in the second, it ranged from 76 to 89, depending on the age of the oldest child.

One might think that as women's working hours rose, husbands would compensate by spending less time on the job. But just the opposite has occurred. Men who work are also putting in longer hours. The 5:00 Dads of the 1950s and 1960s (those who were home for dinner and an evening with the family) are becoming an "endangered species." Thirty percent of men with children under fourteen report working fifty or more hours a week. And many of these 8:00 or 9:00 Dads aren't around on the weekends either. Thirty percent of them work Saturdays and/or Sundays at their regular employment. And many others use the weekends for taking on a second job.

A twenty-eight-year-old Massachusetts factory worker explains the bind many fathers are in: "Either I can spend time with my family or support them—not both." Overtime or a second job is financially compelling: "I can work 8–12 hours overtime a week at time and a half, and that's when the real money just starts to kick in.... If I don't work the OT my wife would have to work much longer hours to make up the differences, and our day care bill would double.... The trouble is, the little time I'm home I'm too tired to have any fun with them or be any real help around the house." Among white-collar employees the problem isn't paid overtime, but the regular hours. To get ahead, or even just to hold on to a position, long days may be virtually mandatory.

Overwork is also rampant among the nation's poorly paid workers. At $5, $6, or even $7 an hour, annual earnings before taxes and deductions range from $10,000 to $14,000. Soaring rents alone have been enough to put many of these low earners in financial jeopardy. For the more than one-third of all workers now earning hourly wages of $7 and below, the pressure to lengthen hours has been inexorable. Valerie Connor, a nursing-home worker in Hartford, explains that "you just can't make it on one job." She and many of her co-workers have been led to work two eight-hour shifts a day. According to an official of the Service Employees International Union in New England, nearly one-third of their nursing-home employees now hold two full-time jobs. Changes in the low end of the labor market have also played a role. Here is less full-time, stable employment. "Twenty hours here, thirty hours there, and twenty hours here. That's what it takes to get a real paycheck," says Domenic Bozzotto, president of Boston's hotel and restaurant workers union, whose members are drowning in a sea of work. Two-job families? Those were the good old days, he says. "We've got four-job families." The recent influx of immigrants has also raised hours. I.N. Yazbeck, an arrival from Lebanon, works ninety hours a week at three jobs. It's necessary, he says, for economic success.

This decline of leisure has been reported by the Harris Poll, which has received widespread attention. Harris finds that since 1973 free time has fallen nearly 40 percent—from a median figure of 26 hours a week to slightly under 17. Other surveys, such as the 1989 Decision Research Corporation Poll, also reveal a loss of leisure. Although these polls have serious methodological drawbacks, their findings are not far off the mark. A majority of working Americans—professionals, corporate management, "working" mothers, fathers, and lower-paid workers—*are* finding themselves with less and less leisure time.

Life.com

THE BERKELEY MONTHLY, October 1999.

■ CLIVE THOMPSON

The elevator door slides open and Jess slides in, looking slightly rumpled. Tara sizes her up.

"Didn't get much sleep last night?"

"You can tell?"

"Well, you're wearing the same clothes as yesterday."

Jess laughs. Her music show, Freq, broadcast live over the internet here at the new-media house Pseudo, went late last night and the staff wound up hanging around till dawn. Now it's 10:30 a.m. and she's back from breakfast to make some calls and set up meetings.

"At some point I'm gonna have to shower," she mutters as she wanders off to her desk.

Tara and I tour the studios, strolling through Pseudo's odd mix of high camp and high tech. The office is a study in chaos and energy, each room reflecting the peculiar pop-cultural animus of the twenty-somethings who work here. There's the room for the women's net shows, done up in late-'70s drag with a rainbow-colored bead-curtain entrance. There's a group of goateed musicians hanging out in one room, holding keyboards and a computer monitor. Who are they? "I have no idea," Tara says.

"Sorry," she apologizes at one point, yawning. "I'm a bit burnt out today."

I'm not surprised. In new media it's difficult to find anyone who can boast a full night's rest. Later in the day I visit a 23-year-old acquaintance at a website design firm across town and find him collapsed on a sofa in the staff room.

Late night? "Yeah." He's been setting up a database for a website that's set to go live in two days. The deadline looms and the client—a major corporation—is getting twitchy. Some deeply caffeinated all-nighters will be called for.

"It's intense but it's going pretty well," he says, his hair out of whack with a minor case of bed-head. "I figure I have another two days like this. But it's cool. It's a really cool project."

He pours himself a thick coffee in the well-stocked kitchen and heads back to his workstation, plopping down beside some two dozen other coders and designers clacking away at their keyboards as a stereo pumps out ambient techno in an endless loop. Most of them figure they'll be here until 4 in the morning.

Working till sunup, destroying your eyesight, playing Quake on the company lan, hanging out in a funky office with your dog: in the modern digital workplace this sort of stuff is de rigueur. Indeed, for young Turks in new media—software, website development or the amorphous zone of "content"—aggressively casual and freewheeling is the signature office style.

On the surface it has to do with making work seem a lot more fun and thus a lot less like work. It is, as it were, the master narrative of the New Work, which we could sketch out like this: young digital employees have thrown off the 9-to-5 straitjacket in which their parents so miserably toiled. No more suits, no more rigid corporate hierarchies, no more dull, repetitive tasks. Today work means getting to wear your Star Wars T-shirt, sport multiple piercings and hang out in an office with homey perks: massagetherapist visits, pets, wacky furniture, toys and lots of beer. The staff dines together and parties together. It works hard, sure, but it plays hard too, and usually at the same time. And the workers aren't chained to one job. Instead they hop at will from company to company, forcing hapless employers to scramble after them, offering ever more perks and stock options to lure their portable, highly paid talents. These kids hold all the cards.

It's a story that has fascinated the media. Reporters covering the industry regularly marvel at the scenes of controlled chaos and pop-cultural riot. In Mountain View [California], Netscape staff members are willing to quit if they can't bring their dogs to work. *USA Today* once breathlessly noted that the office at Organic Online "has been the scene of a dance party, complete with disc jockeys, for 400 people."

Which is precisely the problem.

The studied hipness of new media is a rather devious cultural illusion. Those ultracool offices cover up a seldom-discussed truth: that the jobs themselves often demand intense work and devotion for relatively low pay and zero security. By making work more like play, employers neatly erase the division between the two, which ensures that their young employees will almost never leave the office.

High-tech employees hang out at work long after the city has gone to bed. They'll kill themselves over deadlines, putting in up to 80 hours a week. Then they'll smile and thank their lucky stars that they're part of the digital revolution, the cultural flashpoint of the '90s. For employers, of course, it's a sweet deal—you can't buy flexibility like that. As more than one worker has told me, a website design company can almost always hold a meeting at 2 o'clock on a Saturday afternoon because, well, everyone's there. Where else would they be?

New-media companies are notorious for employee burnout and nanosecond turnover. It's not surprising: given the insane hours, the payoffs are rather slim. We're hit relentlessly with media hype about digital workers' high pay, desirability and stock options. But none of these myths holds up under statistical scrutiny. The vast majority of new-media workers in New York, for example, make less than junior accountants, enjoy the job security of fast-food workers and have a laughably small chance of getting offered any stock anytime anywhere. As for programmers, most are paid surprisingly little and hurled overboard as soon as they hit their mid-30s.

Enamored of its distorted image, the digital workforce is reluctant to accept the facts. "People do not want to face reality," says Bill Lessard, a veteran of the industry who runs NetSlaves, a website that compiles true tales of new-media burnout. "Someone will tell you, 'Oh, I'm a producer.' But they're just a schmuck who's working 90 hours a week. You give these companies body and soul and you really get nothing back."

These workers are touted as the most renegade, the most entrepreneurial generation in years. Yet they are, in traditional labor terms, amazingly compliant. Chained to their keyboards, working far longer hours than they're paid for and blurring the boundaries between their jobs and their lives, digital employees paradoxically present the kind of servile workforce that would have pleased Henry Ford, Nelson Rockefeller and probably Chairman Mao.

When I visit Fred Kahl he's busy designing a computer game based on the TV cartoon "Space Ghost." I peer over his shoulder at the screen, where Fred is fiddling with a sequence: Space Ghost chasing the arch-villain Lokar, who is impersonating Santa Claus. In a few days this will air on the website of the Cartoon Network, one of the major clients of Funny Garbage, the new-media design firm that Kahl works for.

It's hard to deny that new-media workplaces are, aesthetically anyway, extremely pleasant places to be. Kahl shows me around Funny Garbage—a firm respected for its right-brained, creative web animations—and it's not unlike wandering through a gallery of '70s kitsch. Workstations are cluttered with retro-pop toys and icons. One of the company's founders, 33-year-old Peter Girardi, has three different video-game systems in his office.

This is not to suggest that everyone is horsing around. Over by the animation computers, three designers are hunkering down for a long haul, even though it's already past 5 o'clock on a Friday night. By 9, staff members will likely launch into a Quake tournament on the company lan. ("I had to stop," Kahl says. "I almost destroyed my wrists.") In this context, it's easy to see how work and life inexorably bleed into each other. It's also easy to see how new-media employers can capitalize on the confusion. For people involved in digital culture, a highly wired office—replete with digital toys and fueled by a T1 connection—can be a more inviting place to hang out than a cramped apartment or a bar or club.

In fact, sometimes work offers even better partying than a club.

One of Psuedo's longest-serving staff members, a 29-year-old programmer named Joey Fortuna, remembers arriving on his first day four years ago to find the office in a fantastic mess from a party held the night before. Pseudo CEO Josh Harris staggered in from his on-site apartment wearing nothing but boxer shorts and instantly set Fortuna to work, even though Fortuna had never written a line of code in his life.

To get up to speed on HTML, Fortuna—like most of the staff—put in months of 12-hour days. In 1996 he spent Christmas Day writing code for a video-publishing database. "It was just insane!" he says. "I was working all the time. I lived here. But I didn't mind. It was like a clubhouse."

He gestures around the loft, pointing to its kooky mix of high-and low-tech. "You know, it's ironic," he grins, "but in the last century this used to be a sweatshop."

If there's an archetypal success story in new media it's probably that of Jeff Dachis and Razorfish. In spring 1995, Dachis and his friend Craig Kanarick, both in their late 20s, founded the website design company in their living rooms. Last year they had 350 employees in eight offices and did $30 million in business.

Companies like Razorfish have built the mythos of gold-rush success in new media: start a firm in your garage, wow senior executives at Fortune 500 companies, then take occasional breaks from your PlayStation to watch the dough roll in. "The trappings of power have changed," wrote *Time* magazine in an October 1997 survey of the "cyber-elite."

But here too the hype outstrips the reality. True, there are dozens of fantastic entrepreneurial successes. But when you look at the statistics the New Work starts to look like an old story: low pay, no security and those who no longer suit the company profile pitched instantly overboard.

In 1997 the New York New Media Association did a study of the local scene. It discovered that high-tech jobs paid an average of $37,212. That's middling at best for a city as expensive as New York. It's also far outpaced by the average salaries in other media: advertising, $71,637; periodicals, $69,849; TV broadcasting, $85,938.

The churn rate in new-media jobs is amazingly high. The New York study found that almost half the work in new media is freelance or part time. More than two-thirds of all freelance contracts last fewer than six months, most are three-month stints. Part-time jobs are growing four-times faster than full-time positions.

In place of decent pay and regular work, new media offers the lure of instant wealth—the fabled stock options that turned the creators of Amazon.com or TheGlobe.com into overnight multimillionaires. It's a seductive tale, and those who have won the game have won huge. Berkeley's Adam Sah, who was in on the ground floor at Inktomi, cashed in some stocks when the company went public. The years of 400-hour months paid off. "It wasn't fun," he says, "but it did turn out all right for me."

Sah previously worked at Microsoft, which pretty much invented the stock-options trick, knowing that the lure of the market is one of the few things that will motivate coders to impale themselves upon unshippable products with unmeetable deadlines. "It's amazing what people will do for money," Sah laughs wryly.

The stock payoff, though, is about as chimerical as you can get. There are no stats on new-media stock cash-ins but high-tech hunters counsel their clients that the chance of getting lucrative options are slim.

"To cash in on stock you have to stick around for several years at a company," says Alex Santic, head of Silicon Valley Connections, one of the first headhunting firms to specialize in new media. "But few people really want to. They want to move on after a year. They get lured in by the promise of stock but rarely see it through." Indeed, as the New York new-media study found, the only folks who own substantial equity are management and founders—worker bees have a statistically insignificant slice of the pie.

Perhaps the most persistent myth of recent years, though, is that of the "programmer shortage." According to this tale, the geeks now run the show. There isn't enough programming talent to go around, so companies are fighting tooth and nail over warm bodies. Mainstream media have taken up the story like a mantra. "Business leaders say the shortage has reached near-crisis proportions," wrote the *Washington Post* in an article detailing—with a sort of horrified fascination—the incredible perks offered to lure programmers, from "signing bonuses like professional athletes" to $70-an-hour rates for temp work.

Again, the facts contradict the hype. Last year Norman Matloff, a professor of computer science at UC Davis, released one of the few studies ever done on the programmer job market. He surveyed the hiring practices of software and new-media firms and concluded that there was, in fact, no shortage of programmers. Companies were hiring only two to four percent of the people they interviewed, a rate far below that for other types of engineers.

Older programmers, meanwhile, are ruthlessly squeezed out. Age discrimination, Matloff says, is "amazingly rampant." He found that after age 35 and increasingly as they get older, programmers are ditched in favor of the fresh-scrubbed kids released each year from technical colleges. By their early 40s fewer than one-fifth of all trained programmers are still working in the field. One 47-year-old programmer Matloff talked to was fluent in C++, Perl, Unix and a host of other languages, but when he went looking for a new job he landed only two interviews in 15 months of searching. Another man had been programming since 1976. "I can't get so much as an interview," he told Matloff. "I now earn about $24,000 a year in retail sales and management."

When you look at the facts you begin to realize the incredible power of new-media workplace culture. It sells a lifestyle of liberation and autonomy that is wildly out of sync with reality. Then you begin to realize why those Quake marathons, those cappuccino machines in the staff kitchen and all those dogs at work are important. Absent decent pay and a commitment from your boss, maybe a game of Quake is the best you can get.

————

The Law and Economics of Critical Race Theory

112 Yale L.J. 1757, 1789–93, 1795–96, 1797–99, 1801–14 (2003) (reviewing Crossroads, Directions, and a New Critical Race Theory (Francisco Valdes et al. eds., 2002)).

■ Devon W. Carbado & Mitu Gulati

A starting point for thinking about workplace discrimination is to raise the question of whether today's workplace is buttressed by institutionalized racial norms. With respect to explicit racial norms, the answer is no: That would violate antidiscrimination law. But do implicit racial norms structure today's workplace culture? [Critical race theory, or CRT] answers this question affirmatively, pointing to workplace practices like English-only rules and grooming regulations (e.g., rules prohibiting employees from braiding their hair) that restrict the expression of particular identities and, in so doing, marginalize them.

There is, however, a subtle form of institutional discrimination to which CRT scholars have not paid attention. This discrimination derives from a commitment on the part of many employers, particularly employers who use teams to manage their workplace culture to achieve trust, fairness, and loyalty (TFL). Why? TFL reduces transaction costs. Empirical evidence suggests that the effectiveness of teams is enhanced when employers engender TFL among their employees. Employees who perceive that they are a part of a "TFL community" work hard, cooperate, police each other, and share valuable information. Based on this evidence, scholars have argued that law should be structured to facilitate the creation of TFL workplaces. In addition to its efficiency gains, TFL values seem normatively appealing.

TFL's normative surface appeal helps to explain why the institutional discrimination story we articulate below has not yet been told. Central to our story is not the fact that employers are invested in TFL but rather how they go about realizing that investment—by aggressively promoting homogeneity. Evidence suggests that, at least in the short term, a manager with a demographically homogeneous work team has a better chance of producing TFL than one with a diverse team. If, as is often suggested, managers focus primarily on short-term results, there is an incentive for managers to seek demographically homogeneous teams.

The relationship between the pursuit of demographic homogeneity and racial discrimination is direct. In short, workplaces organized to achieve homogeneity are likely to discriminate because homogeneity norms, by their very nature, reflect a commitment to sameness (favoring people perceived to be members of the in-group ("insiders")) and a rejection of difference (disfavoring people perceived to be members of the out-group ("outsiders")). Coupled with the fact that, within most professional settings, whites are insiders and nonwhites are outsiders, the relationship between discrimination and homogeneity becomes clear.

The foregoing suggests that race-neutral workplace norms institutionalize insider racial preference. Is this a reason for concern? The answer is not obviously yes. One might argue that, even to the extent that there are incentives for employers to create and maintain homogeneous workplaces, the threat of antidiscrimination sanctions undermines that incentive. Richard Epstein famously worried about exactly this effect of antidiscrimination law. According to Epstein, part of the problem with antidiscrimination law is that it compromises workplace efficiency by preventing employers from establishing homogeneous workplace cultures. One might conclude, then, that given the threat of legal sanctions, the institutionalized racism problem we have identified is theoretical—not real.

Moreover, there are institutional legitimacy concerns that militate against the establishment of homogenous workplaces. White-only work forces can create public relations problems. Perhaps not surprisingly, there is no employer-driven movement afoot to have antidiscrimination laws repealed because they prohibit employers from establishing demographically homogenous workplaces. To the contrary, even a cursory examination of the management and organizational behavior literature reveals (at least rhetorically) an institutional commitment to manage, and not to eliminate, heterogeneity. Thus, all seems well: Law prevents institutions from privileging homogeneity, and institutions perceive the pursuit of homogeneity to be problematic.

Our claim, however, is that all is not well. Neither antidiscrimination law nor the affirmative pursuit of diversity operates as a meaningful barrier to, or substantially undermines the incentives for employers to achieve, workplace homogeneity. Epstein need not worry. To be sure, the law prohibits blatant racial animus in hiring and promotion. But that is a minimal barrier to the managerial pursuit of racial homogeneity. To move from a phenotypic conception of race to a performative conception is to find that, to a significant extent, judges can (and, we surmise, do) apply antidiscrimination law to actually *protect* the pursuit of racial homogeneity. They do so by failing to capture employment discrimination based on *intraracial* distinctions—distinctions employers make among people within a particular racial group.

Driving these distinctions is a question about racial stereotypes and racial salience. Other things being equal, employers prefer nonwhites whose racial identity is not salient and whose identity performance is inconsistent with stereotypes about their racial group. In other words, employers screen for racial palatability. With respect to Asian Americans, for example, employers determine whether, notwithstanding phenotypic difference, a particular Asian American is (based on how she performs her identity) sufficiently like insiders to be successfully assimilated into a homogenized workplace.

To date, there are no Title VII cases that render a racial palatability discrimination claim cognizable. Thus, employers can make these kinds of intraracial distinctions with legal impunity. And to the extent employers engage in this practice, their associated institutional legitimacy remains intact because the practice anticipates and produces at least some workplace racial integration. Finally, because the racial diversity employers achieve by making intraracial distinctions is literally skin deep, it comfortably coexists with their commitment to homogeneity.

The foregoing sets forth a theory of institutional racism—that it is a function of an investment on the part of employers to realize the efficiency gains of homogeneity. Because many institutions operate under what we call a *diversity constraint*—a constraint that requires the firm to hire at least some nonwhites—employers will determine which nonwhites to hire on evidence of racial palatability. The more racially palatable employers perceive a potential employee to be, the less concerned they will be over the possibility that that potential employee will (racially) disrupt workplace homogeneity. * * *

B. *The Incentive for Employers To Pursue Homogeneity*

   * * *

1. *Theories*

There are at least three theories suggesting that employers are motivated to pursue homogeneity: social identity theory, similarity-attraction theory, and statistical judgments theory.

Social identity theory suggests that people have an affinity for those they perceive to be part of their in-group. In concrete terms, people are more likely to demonstrate TFL (which, again, is shorthand for trust, fairness, and loyalty) to those they perceive to be members of their in-group. Conversely, they are more likely to discriminate against those they perceive to be members of an out-group. Race, being both socially salient and facially visible, is one of the primary categories along which people make initial in-group and out-group categorizations. One explanation is that people assume that those of a similar race are likely to share similar values and to have had similar experiences. As a result, racial outsiders are vulnerable to discrimination from their racial insider colleagues. To avoid this distrust and dislike (which will likely undermine workplace efficiency by increasing transaction costs), employers will want to hire people who are similar to insiders.

The similarity-attraction theory is largely analogous. It posits that people are attracted to those who are similar. The theory is that race is one of the primary categories used to determine similarity and that this similarity, in turn, translates into attraction. * * *

The final theory suggesting that employers are motivated to pursue homogeneity is statistical judgments theory. Most often attributed to economics (though also central to psychology), this theory claims that racial differences often activate *statistical judgments* about likely behavioral tendencies. These statistical judgments are a type of mental shortcut, a resource-saving device. For example, white workers may see a new black colleague as likely to be lazy, untrustworthy, disloyal (especially to her white colleagues), frequently angry (perhaps as a result of oversensitivity about race), and difficult to communicate with (due to her likely having different values, different interests, and different cultural and experiential points of reference). Under this theory, whether an insider-employer will hire a black person turns on the currency of the foregoing statistical judgments. The stronger the statistical judgment, the stronger the employer's perception that a prospective black employee will not fit into the institution.

These theories suggest that there is a disincentive for employers to hire outsiders and a corresponding incentive for employers to hire insiders. Difference engenders distrust, dislike, disconnection, disidentification, and disassociation. Each of these characteristics (and certainly all of them together) undermines a necessary condition for the effective operation of teams—cooperative behavior—and therefore increases the transaction costs of managing the workplace.

2. *Empirical Evidence*

   a. *The Basic Story*

In addition to the theoretical literature, there is empirical evidence predicting that racially heterogeneous teams are likely to be less effective than homogenous ones. Studies consistently show what the above theories suggest: Racial heterogeneity undermines trust and cooperation. Team members in heterogeneous teams tend not to communicate as well as team members in homogeneous teams. Turnover rates in heterogeneous teams are higher. And managerial attempts to spur innovation by diversifying their teams have "met with mixed success."

b. *The More Complicated Account*

Recent scholarship on diversity management suggests that the empirical story about workplace homogeneity may be more complicated than we have thus far described. The complication is that heterogeneity can operate as a double-edged sword. To appreciate how this is so, it is helpful to conceptualize heterogeneity/diversity as operating in a two-stage process. At stage one, superficial differences in terms of variables like race cause distrust, difficulties in communication, and a reluctance to cooperate. However, under the right conditions of intergroup contact—equal status, opportunities for self-revelation, egalitarian norms, and tasks that require cooperative interdependence—diverse team members can, at stage two, gain each other's trust, begin to see commonalities, work cooperatively, and realize the benefits of working as a diverse team. Central to this theory is the notion that there are meaningful things an employer can do at stage one—the initial contact stage—to facilitate cooperative behavior at stage two. * * *

C. *Summary*

There is theoretical and empirical evidence suggesting that employers are motivated to pursue homogeneity: Put simply, homogeneous workplaces facilitate trust, loyalty, and cooperative behavior. The story with respect to heterogeneous work teams is different. First, at an institutional level, heterogeneity is difficult and costly to manage. Second, the most cost-effective way for individual supervisors to manage heterogeneity is to "socialize away" outsider difference. Thus, it is more accurate to characterize this strategy as eliminating, rather than managing, heterogeneity. Third, even assuming that heterogeneity can be effectively managed, the benefits of a heterogeneous workplace are speculative, and they are realized primarily over the long term.

Acknowledging the homogeneity incentive is helpful to CRT in at least two ways. First, it provides critical race theorists with a different perspective on colorblindness. The homogeneity incentive exists because of the transaction costs of heterogeneity. Like colorblindness, then, the homogeneity incentive requires the submersion of racial difference. Second, the existence of the homogeneity incentive supports CRT's claim that an employer's preference for racial sameness won't always be motivated by racial animus. One of the most important ideas in CRT is that racism is not just a function of individual bad actors. From here, CRT advances one of two arguments: (1) that discrimination is unconscious and (2) that discrimination is institutional. The homogeneity incentive provides an additional base from which to theorize about the latter. It demonstrates that institutional discrimination can exist in the absence of racial animosity. * * *

IV.   HOW EMPLOYERS RESPOND TO THE HOMOGENEITY INCENTIVE

Given antidiscrimination laws and social norms disfavoring racial exclusivity, institutions are unlikely to respond to the homogeneity incentive by hiring only insiders. They will hire outsiders as well. The claim we advance is that employers will use specific mechanisms to screen outsiders for evidence of racial palatability. These mechanisms select "but for outsiders"—outsiders who, but for their racial phenotype, are very similar to the insiders—and they select against "essential outsiders"—outsiders whose personal characteristics are consistent with the image of the prototypical outsider. * * *

A.   *The "Race–Neutral" Response to the Homogeneity Incentive*

1.   *The Basic Idea: Selection and Socialization*

Broadly speaking, there are two mechanisms employers can use to respond to the homogeneity incentive: "selection" and "socializing" mechanisms. Selection mechanisms operate at the hiring and the promotion stages. Here, an employer screens individuals for particular characteristics that function as proxies for determining whether a given individual (1) is willing to be homogenized into the workplace culture *and* (2) has the capacity to do so. Socializing mechanisms, in turn, are used to initiate and integrate the individual into the workplace. In other words, socializing mechanisms are the rites of passage that structure a new employee's experiential travels through the workplace after selection mechanisms are used to bring her into the firm. Constituting this passage are numerous rituals through which the individual is expected to demonstrate her commitment to homogeneity. More particularly, she must effectively prove that the employer made the right selection decision. Due to space constraints, we do not elaborate further on socialization mechanisms. We focus on selection, identifying four selection mechanisms employers can use to screen potential employees for evidence of performative (and not simply phenotypic) homogeneity.

2.   *The Selection Mechanisms*

Four interrelated selection mechanisms that we draw out of the theory and evidence on homogeneity are: similarity, comfort, differentiation, and respectable exoticism.

a.   *Similarity*

This mechanism is intuitive. The question is whether the individual exhibits personal characteristics suggesting she is similar to employees already at the firm. The more an individual appears to be similar to existing employees, the more likely an employer is to conclude that the individual has the potential to be assimilated. The potential employee's response to standard interview questions can signal her potential for assimilation to employers. Consider, for example, Johnny, who is being considered for a mid-level associate position at an elite corporate law firm. A senior partner has asked Johnny to "tell us a little bit about yourself." Johnny's response includes the following:

> *I enjoy tennis and golf, though I confess that both need improvement. I like a good Gore Vidal novel; in fact, I'm in the process of rereading* Julian, *which, by the way, I highly recommend. I'm not a huge sports fan, but I try to make time to watch a good basketball game—usually with colleagues and friends. I wasn't always fond of theater, but two years ago my wife took me to see* The Tin Man, *and I've been sold on theater—both high and low—ever since. I enjoy Italian cinema, the old Fellini stuff as well as some of the more contemporary productions. And every so often, I truly enjoy a good B movie—not a B movie masquerading as an A movie, but a B movie that knows it's a B movie. I love going to the museum with my kids. We try to go twice a month. You'd be surprised at the interpretational skills of a six-year old.*

This response provides the employer with signals about Johnny's socialized identity, information that the employer can use to make a determination as to whether Johnny is sufficiently like the firm's existing employees. Johnny plays tennis and golf, the preferred sports of corporate America. The fact that both need improvement suggests that he is available to play both sports with his colleagues and not likely to be unduly competitive when he does so. In this way, both games can function as sites for socialization. Johnny's response also indicates that he is not an avid sports fan, but that he enjoys a good basketball game. Here, Johnny signals respectable (but not hyper-) masculinity and a willingness to participate in group-based spectator sport rituals. Johnny is married with kids, which reveals his heterosexuality and possibly a certain traditionalism. He appears to be cultured (he reads Gore Vidal, watches Italian cinema, attends the theater, and visits museums), but he is not overly elitist or pompous (he enjoys the occasional B movie and attends low-brow (and just barely high-brow) theater). Finally, the fact that Johnny's wife successfully socialized him into the theater, an experience that he was not predisposed to enjoy, suggests that he will likely not resist the firm's socialization efforts.

Not every institution will select for the foregoing qualities: Similarity selection mechanisms will vary from institution to institution. The point here is twofold: (1) Most employers will have a set of characteristics that they perceive to define their workplace, and (2) without much difficulty, employers can screen for these qualities in interviews.

b.   *Comfort*

Related to similarity is comfort. Here, employers want to know whether incumbent employees will be comfortable working with the prospective hire. Again, they can select for comfort (or at least select against discomfort) by considering a prospective employee's response to standard interview questions. Stipulate once more that Johnny is interviewing for a job with an elite corporate law firm. The partner asks Johnny: "Tell us what kind of firm you're looking for." Johnny responds:

I am looking for a firm doing high-level, sophisticated corporate work. Quite frankly, most of the firms I am interviewing with seem to fall in that category—certainly your firm does. What becomes important for me, then, is firm culture. I am looking for a firm that values and respects difference. I guess I believe that people shouldn't have to lose themselves at work. They should be permitted to be who they are. I was happy to learn that your firm recently adopted a casual Friday policy.

I am also looking for a firm within which junior associates have a voice—that is, an opportunity to comment on the institutional governance of the firm, for example, the firm's billing, hiring, and pro bono policies. That sort of participation helps to make junior associates invested in the firm.

Employers could interpret Johnny's response in a number of ways. But if they are screening for comfort, a given employer may have concerns about whether Johnny "fits." Johnny's view is that individuals should be permitted to be themselves and that a firm should value difference. However, difference can be uncomfortable or discomforting. To employ what many would consider an extreme example, the firm would likely be uncomfortable with Johnny coming to work as a cross-dresser. If Johnny does cross dress, the firm would expect him to do so (if at all) outside of the workplace.

Recall that Johnny wants a voice in institutional governance and provides an indication of the kinds of issues he hopes to engage. Johnny's representations here might send a positive signal—specifically, that he wants to become a part of the firm. To the extent the employer is selecting for comfort, however, the employer could interpret Johnny's comments to suggest that he will likely make the firm uncomfortable about its hiring, pro bono, and billing practices, among other institutional governance matters.

c. *Differentiation*

Employers are most likely to utilize the differentiation mechanism when they perceive themselves to be making a "risky hire." Here, prospective employees are in a *category* that is presumed to be incapable of homogenization (or that is disinterested in socialization). Imagine that Johnny is seeking an entry-level job with a law firm. He is a third-year law student at State Law School, which is a third-tier law school. He is on law review and has an A-grade point average. His letters of recommendation are effusive; his writing sample is strong.

The firm has never hired a law student from State Law School, in part because the school is insufficiently elite and because most of the students at State Law School are from working-class backgrounds. The firm therefore assumes that these students are likely to have difficulty fitting into an elite corporate law firm. The firm might not be right for them (read: they might not be right for the firm). Given this concern, whether the employer hires Johnny will be a function of whether Johnny can differentiate himself from the category within which he is situated—that is, State law students. Consider the following exchange between Johnny and a senior partner.

Partner: Good of you to stop by. Come in and have a seat. It seems that I've left your resume elsewhere in the office. You wouldn't happen to have an extra copy, would you?

Johnny: Yes, in fact I do.

Partner: Oh yes ... I am beginning to remember this resume. I see that you went to Harvard undergrad and that you rowed crew. How did we do this year? I graduated Harvard in '75.

Johnny: We lost to Yale, second year in a row, no pun intended. I suppose if we're going to lose to any school, it ought to be Yale. Their heavyweight eight was selected to represent the country at the World Championships in London.

Partner: So you did really well at Harvard—Magna in history, 3.7 GPA, member of the debating team. I suspect that you had a lot of options when you applied to law school.

Johnny: I was fortunate to have a few. In addition to State, NYU, Columbia, and Michigan said yes. Harvard and Stanford placed me on a waiting list. Yale said no.

Partner: I didn't get into Yale, either. What's more, I've lived to tell the tale. You will, too. But, seriously, you had all these options. I'm curious as to how you made your decision.

Johnny: Well, to a considerable extent my decision was a financial one. I couldn't afford to attend any of the other schools. And I didn't want to burden my parents anymore than I had to. Besides, I hoped that if I distinguished myself at State, I would have many of the same opportunities as if I had attended, say, Michigan.

Partner: So, Johnny, tell me about how you're thinking about law firms. Big law firms are not for everyone, and as you know, we're a pretty big law firm.

Johnny: I had the good fortune of clerking for two summers at Bronton, Stevely & Kellog in Chicago.

Partner: Yes, yes, an excellent firm.

Johnny: I had a good time there. People got along well. They had interests similar to mine. I got the sense that the attorneys there felt that they were part of a larger community. Your firm describes itself in precisely that way. Most of my classmates run away from big firms. Why go through that haze, some ask?

Partner: They consider big firms a haze?

Johnny: Some do. Most simply believe that big firms treat individuals as fungible commodities. That's not my assumption but it is the predominant assumption on campus.

Partner: What's your view, then? Let me guess: You love big firms?

Johnny: Of course. Kidding aside, I'd say that, whether it's a big firm or a small firm, the question is really twofold: whether the individual is committed to becoming a part of a team and whether the firm provides him with the opportunity to play ball.

The foregoing reflects enough differentiation on Johnny's part to effectively remove him from, or at least situate him on the periphery of, the outsider group (again, students at State Law School). Presumably, few law students at State attended Harvard. Johnny's Harvard education is significant in at least three respects. First, it signifies Johnny's intellectual capacity. Second, the fact that Johnny graduated from Harvard (and rowed crew) suggests that he has the potential for socialization. Finally, Johnny's Harvard education places Johnny and the partner in a community that has significant cultural capital—the community of Harvard alumni. That the partner recognizes this shared community is evident in his question: "How did we do this year?"

Nor would many students at State have had the opportunity to attend NYU, Michigan, and Columbia or to clerk at an elite corporate law firm. Here, too, Johnny is different. Finally, Johnny is also different in terms of his strong academic performance and the fact that he does not have a bias against big-firm practice. In short, after completing the interview with Johnny, the partner could tell himself that, although, as a formal matter, Johnny belongs to the group of State Law students, in a substantive sense, he is different. It is this kind of information that the differentiation selection mechanism is designed to ascertain.

d.   *Respectable Exoticism*

Certain differences do not threaten firm homogeneity. To the extent that a given difference is both exotic (not an awful lot of people are likely to have it) and respectable (the difference is not overdetermined by a negative social meaning), firms can commodify this difference to their advantage. Thus, while hiring too many immigrants might compromise a firm's commitment to homogeneity, hiring an immigrant of royal lineage might not produce that effect. Immigrant difference that is located in the context of royal identity can be marketed—for example, to employees who might feel special because they have a royal coworker.

Another example of respectable exoticism might be an ex-NBA player in a corporate context. Note, however, that while a firm's homogeneity might tolerate one such individual, it may not be able to tolerate several. The incentive for the employer to utilize the exotic difference selection perhaps is not as strong as the employer's incentive to utilize similarity, comfort, or differentiation. In this respect, it might be more accurate to say that a firm will not select against respectable exoticism than it would be to say that the firm will actively select for that characteristic.

B.   *Explicitly Racializing the Discussion: Combining CRT Insights*

The preceding discussion does not identify the racial effects of selection mechanisms. These effects can be demonstrated by adopting CRT's meth-

odology of racializing the analysis. To borrow from Jerome Culp, we "raise
... the race question" and, in the process, make a number of empirical
assumptions about race. While we think the assumptions are plausible, the
analysis is necessarily tentative and meant only to be illustrative of the
type of analysis that might be performed.

1. *How Likely Is It That Johnny Will Be a Racial Minority?*

How likely is it that "Johnny" will be a racial minority? Consider, for
example, the Johnny who is a student at State Law School. Recall that this
Johnny attended Harvard College and rowed crew. Rowing crew often
means that one attended an elite East Coast prep school, and the number
of minorities who fit in this category will be small. Further, although
Johnny is at State Law School, he had the option of attending first-tier law
schools. Not many students of color at a third-tier law school will have had
that opportunity. In short, few minorities will have the kind of cultural
capital reflected in Johnny's background.

2. *Assuming That the Johnny at State Law School Is Black, Will He
Be "Selected"?*

Our hypothetical assumes that an elite corporate firm would select a
person like Johnny, notwithstanding the fact that Johnny does not fit the
standard profile (that is, a person who has attended a first-tier law school).
But if Johnny is black, this issue is far from clear. Few elite corporate firms
hire blacks from schools other than those in the first-tier—more specifically, in the top ten. This may be (at least in part) due to two assumptions.
The first is an assumption about affirmative action and intellectual competence—namely, that given race-based admission preferences, "smart
blacks" should end up at first-tier schools. The second is an assumption
about race and class—namely, that a black person at State Law School is
likely to be working class and thus may have difficulty fitting into the law
firm. While both assumptions can be rebutted, doing so would require an
employer to engage in more intensive (read: more costly) screening of
Johnny.

3. *As a General Matter, What Kind of Person of Color Is Johnny
Likely to Be?*

Except for respectable exoticism, each of the selection mechanisms
described above is designed to ascertain the extent to which a prospective
employee is different from firm insiders. The outsiders likely to be the least
different from the firm's insiders are those on (or who perform their
identity as if they are on) the periphery of their outsider group identity.
These "most peripheral outsiders" are likely to have grown up in predominantly white neighborhoods and to have attended elite (and predominantly
white) high schools, colleges, and law schools. Employers can use these
background characteristics as proxies for whether, and to what extent,
outsider candidates will fit comfortably into a predominantly white workplace.

But there is a more direct method the employer can use to determine
whether an outsider has the capacity to work within a homogenized

workplace. There is evidence suggesting that particular types of outsiders are, from an employer's perspective, likely to cause fewer problems in the operation of a team dominated by insiders than are other types of outsiders. Racial outsiders who are "extroverted" and effective at "self-monitoring" are more likely to succeed than those who are not. Good self-monitors assess how others perceive them and adjust their behavior accordingly; extroverts project a strong and identifiable self-identity. Presumably, the reason these types of outsiders cause minimal disruption is that they actively engage in "impression management." That is, they are constantly interacting with others, sending signals about themselves, and reacting to the impressions that others have of them. An employer's selection decision likely will take account of how well outsiders manage impressions about their racial identity (that is, at least in part, how well they disprove racial stereotypes).

4.   *How Do People of Color Signal Racial Differentiation?*

The point of differentiation strategies is to convey one of three ideas—that one does not identify as an outsider, that one is a different kind of outsider, or that what others think of outsiders is wrong. To convey the first idea, that one does not identify as an outsider, an employee would engage in disidentification or disassociation strategies—strategies that signal that the employee does not really identify with his outsider group. Imagine that, in the context of an interview with an elite firm, a partner says this to Johnny: "I have to tell you, Johnny, racial diversity at our firm is not good. We do our best. But the numbers are what they are—not pretty." That statement offers Johnny an "opportunity" to articulate his relationship to his outsider identity. To disidentify and disassociate, Johnny can say: "I appreciate your telling me this, but I am more interested in learning about how your firm cultivates and trains junior associates." Johnny's response could also reflect even stronger evidence of outsider disidentification and disassociation. He might have said: "I appreciate your telling me this, but I just don't believe in identity politics. Diversity is fine and good, but people are people." The point is that the earlier response is enough differentiation to suggest to the employer that Johnny is not a "race man."

To convey the second idea of differentiation, that one is a different kind of outsider, the outsider could adopt an individualized stereotype negation strategy. Here, the outsider would attempt to convey to the employer that stereotypes about his outsider identity do not apply to him. Imagine that the employer asks Johnny what he does with his spare time and Johnny responds: "Fishing, golfing, and catching up on foreign cinema." The employer could interpret this response to suggest that Johnny is not an ordinary black man (who, based on stereotypes, would have responded: "Watching basketball, playing basketball, and listening to hip-hop."). To the extent the employer does not perceive Johnny to be a black male prototype, the employer is less likely to attribute negative stereotypes of black men to Johnny.

Johnny can convey the final idea of differentiation—that others' assumptions about outsiders are wrong—through generalized stereotype negation. Under this strategy, Johnny attempts to persuade the employer that stereotypes about the employee's outsider group are inaccurate. This strategy is difficult and risky to perform when one is interviewing for a job. For instance, after articulating what he likes to do in his spare time (fishing, golfing, and catching up on foreign cinema), Johnny could add something like: "Not all black men like basketball. Moreover, most of the stereotypes about blacks are simply inaccurate. Consider, for example, crime...." It is unlikely that, in the context of an interview, Johnny would engage the employer in this way: The statement presupposes that the employer harbors stereotypes about blacks, a presupposition that could engender racial discomfort on the part of the employer ("This black guy thinks I am a racist."). Further, even if Johnny did make such a statement to the employer, it is unlikely that the employer would be persuaded by it. For generalized stereotype negation to work, there needs to be a level of trust, and sustained interaction, between the outsider and the employer.

Performing each of the foregoing differentiation strategies constitutes a form of work—identity work. Among other problems with this work, it can compromise one's sense of identity.

5.   *What Are the Racial Community Costs of Differentiation Strategies?*

One of the problems with the first two differentiation strategies (disidentification/disassociation and individual stereotype negation) is that they are individually oriented. To the extent that an employee feels pressured to perform these strategies, he privileges his individual advancement over that of his group. Differentiation strategies are a response to an institutionalized problem—the employer's investment in homogeneity. So long as the homogeneity incentive drives employment decisions, there is little room for racial diversification. Society ends up with minimal (or token) outsider economic advancement into the workplace. The incentives for the outsider group, therefore, should be to engage in a collective struggle to change the system to tolerate (if not welcome) greater expression and representation of outsider identities. The first two differentiation strategies undermine that goal. They encourage outsiders to disidentify with, and disassociate from, the collective interests of the outsider group. In this sense, the problem with homogeneity is not simply that it drives employers to hire only certain kinds of outsiders, but also that the outsiders whom the employer hires are not likely to lift as they climb.

To summarize, the employer's pursuit of a homogenous workforce is likely to produce the following effects (subject to the assumptions made):

- Given the negative presumption that applies to the ability and willingness of outsiders to satisfy the homogeneity requirement (and the positive presumptions that apply to whites), the quantum of cultural capital (or the price of entry) that employers require of outsiders is likely to be higher than that for their white counterparts.

• Within the outsider community, only the elite are likely to possess the quantum of cultural capital necessary to gain entry. Employers seeking to satisfy the diversity constraint will affirmatively pursue this small subset of minorities.

• The strategies that an individual outsider employee is likely to pursue, such as differentiation, may hurt the collective cause of her minority group and compromise her sense of self. The collective cause may be better served by a struggle to reduce and remove barriers, as opposed to a competition among outsiders for a few slots (and which requires outsider homogenization).

* * *

NOTES AND QUESTIONS

1. **"Lean" production and new, ruthless economy.** Changes in technology have permitted a steady rise in economic productivity for the United States in recent years. These changes, however, collectively have made labor much more insecure. William Greider discusses the case of labor unions and the manufacturing sector:

> Starting in the 1970s, U.S. companies gravitated toward a different strategy in which global price pressures were offset by extracting more from labor. Corporations discarded their long postwar truce with unions and began moving jobs, first to the low-wage South and then offshore. They closed factories and demanded wage contracts that depressed wages. They mobilized both political and economic power to weaken labor's bargaining position.

> American corporate managers might point out that they themselves were driven to these defensive actions by the global economic forces. The "virtuous circle" of the 1950s and 1960s had also been sustained by the existence of industrial oligopolies—a few big companies that dominated major sectors like autos, steel and aircraft and were powerful enough to set prices and wages in a clubby, arbitrary fashion. The rise of foreign producers, especially from Japan, broke up that comfortable arrangement forever.

> As firms shifted production to lower-wage workers, organized labor lost members and became steadily less able to discipline managements. The decline in wages was not confined to union members, however, but was more general. Retail sales workers, for instance, experienced a much sharper fall than manufacturing. In 1970, wages constituted 67 percent of all personal income in the United States, a ratio that had held constant for decades. By 1994, wages were less than 58 percent of total incomes. In 1960, wages were about 26 percent of total sales. By 1994, they were about 20 percent.

WILLIAM GREIDER, ONE WORLD, READY OR NOT: THE MANIC LOGIC OF GLOBAL CAPITALISM 77 (1997). Greider argues that these trends are symptomatic of a larger phenomenon: "wage arbitrage." Wage arbitrage "moves the production and jobs from a high-wage labor market to another where the labor is much cheaper. The producers thus reduce their costs and enhance profits by arbitraging these wage differences, usually selling their finished products back into the high-wage markets." *Id.* at 57. Since labor is much less mobile than capital, wage arbitrage means the upper hand in bargaining power for capital in particular disputes. Unions, which are usually organized within national boundaries, become vulnerable to the threat of moving jobs to lower-wage countries.

2. Law firms as internal labor markets. For an extended application of economic theory to explain the hiring and promotion practices of large law firms, see David B. Wilkins & G. Mitu Gulati, *Reconceiving the Tournament of Lawyers: Tracking, Seeding, and Information Control in the Internal Labor Markets of Elite Law Firms*, 84 Va. L. Rev. 1581 (1998).

3. Winner-take-all markets. Some economists argue that a new feature of contemporary labor markets is the existence of the "winner take all" market. In such markets there are many competitors for a very few extremely lucrative slots. The entertainment industry provides many examples: as reality shows like *American Idol* dramatically illustrate, the possibility of fame and fortune in the entertainment world draws many more people than could possibly succeed. As the economists argue, and as *American Idol* also illustrates, winner-take-all markets are socially wasteful because the possibility of extremely high rewards (coupled with the cognitive quirks identified by bounded rationality theory) draws people who would do better for themselves and the rest of society if they put their time and energy elsewhere. Winner-take-all markets also contribute to income inequality, since a very small number of players make a huge amount of money and the rest make very little. Robert Frank and Philip Cook argue that changes in tax policy, tort reform, health care finance, educational finance, and antitrust policy, among other reforms, could promote both efficiency and equity by reducing the spread and impact of winner-take-all markets. *See* Robert H. Frank & Philip J. Cook, The Winner-Take-All Society 211–31 (1995).

4. Women and emotional labor. Arlie Russell Hochschild, in *The Managed Heart: Commercialization of Human Feeling* (20th anniversary edition 2003), argues that women in the workplace often face demands not placed on men, that they display certain kinds of emotions, usually cheeriness and nurturance. Arlie Russell Hochschild, The Managed Heart: Commercialization of Human Feeling (20th anniv. ed. 2003). Thus, women may be asked to smile, will be expected to be peacemakers in workplace disputes, and are expected to defer to the emotional needs and desires of men. Hochschild argues that the requirement of emotional labor also tends to fall upon occupations that have been heavily feminized, such as secretaries and nurses, without regard to the sex of the people in those occupations. *See also* Arlie Russell Hochschild, Commercialization of Intimate Life: Notes From Home and Work (2003). Does Carbado and Gulati's analysis suggest a similar burden of emotional labor on racial minorities in the workplace?

5. Impression management. Carbado and Gulati's analysis is indebted to the work of sociologist Erving Goffman, who coined the phrase "impression management" to describe how individuals attempt to control how they are seen by others, while those others in turn attempt to discern the "real" self behind the front. *See, e.g.,* Erving Goffman, *The Arts of Impression Management, in* THE PRESENTATION OF SELF IN EVERYDAY LIFE 208–37 (1959). Goffman emphasizes that everyone in social life is constantly engaged in impression management, both in private and in public settings, and uses the metaphor of the dramatic performance throughout his analysis:

> In this report, the individual was divided by implication into two basic parts: he was viewed as a *performer*, a harried fabricator of impressions involved in the all-too-human task of staging a performance; he was viewed as a *character*, a figure, typically a fine one, whose spirit, strength, and other sterling qualities the performance was designed to evoke. The attributes of a performer and the attributes of a character are of a different order, quite basically so, yet both sets have their meaning in terms of the show that must go on. * * *

> A correctly staged and performed scene leads the audience to impute a self to a performed character, but this imputation—this self—is a *product* of a scene that comes off, and is not a *cause* of it. The self, then, as a performed character, is not an organic thing that has a specific location, whose fundamental fate is to be born, to mature, and to die; it is a dramatic effect arising diffusely from a scene that is presented, and the characteristic issue, the crucial concern, is whether it will be credited or discredited.

Id., at 252–53.

C. CLASS AND CONSUMPTION

The Overspent American: Why We Want What We Don't Need

80–91 (1998).

■ JULIET B. SCHOR

While television has long been suspected as a promoter of consumer desire, there has been little hard evidence to support that view, at least for adult spending. After all, there's not an obvious connection. Many of the products advertised on television are everyday low-cost items such as aspirin, laundry detergent, and deodorant. Those TV ads are hardly a spur to excessive consumerism. Leaving aside other kinds of ads for the moment (for cars, diamonds, perfumes), there's another counter to the argument that television causes consumerism: TV is a *substitute* for spending. One of the few remaining free activities, TV is a popular alternative to costly recreational spending such as movies, concerts, and restaurants. If it causes us to spend, that effect must be powerful enough to overcome its propensity to save us money.

Apparently it is. My research shows that the more TV a person watches, the more he or she spends. The likely explanation for the link between television and spending is that what we see on TV inflates our sense of what's normal. The lifestyles depicted on television are far different from the average American's: with a few exceptions, TV characters are upper-middle-class, or even rich.

Studies by the consumer researchers Thomas O'Guinn and L.J. Schrum confirm this upward distortion. The more people watch television, the more they think American households have tennis courts, private planes, convertibles, car telephones, maids, and swimming pools. Heavy watchers also overestimate the portion of the population who are millionaires, have had cosmetic surgery, and belong to a private gym, as well as those suffering from dandruff, bladder control problems, gingivitis, athlete's foot, and hemorrhoids (the effect of all those ads for everyday products). What one watches also matters. Dramatic shows—both daytime soap operas and prime-time drama series—have a stronger impact on viewer perceptions than other kinds of programs (say news, sports, or weather).

Heavy watchers are not the only ones, however, who tend to overestimate standards of living. Almost everyone does. (And almost everyone watches TV.) In one study, ownership rates for twenty-two of twenty-seven consumer products were generally overstated. Your own financial position also matters. Television inflates standards for lower-, average-, and above-average-income students, but it does the reverse for really wealthy ones. (Among those raised in a financially rarefied atmosphere, TV is almost a reality check.) Social theories of consumption hold that the inflated sense of consumer norms promulgated by the media raises people's aspirations and leads them to buy more. In the words of one Los Angeles resident, commenting on this media tendency, "They try to portray that an upper-class lifestyle is normal and typical and that we should all have it."

Television also affects norms by giving us real information about how other people live and what they have. It allows us to be voyeurs, opening the door to the "private world" inside the homes and lives of others. * * *

Another piece of evidence for the TV-spending link is the apparent correlation between debt and excessive TV viewing. In the Merck Family Fund poll, the fraction responding that they "watch too much TV" rose steadily with indebtedness. More than half (56 percent) of all those who reported themselves "heavily" in debt also said they watched too much TV.

It is partly because of television that the top 20 percent of the income distribution, and even the top 5 percent within it, has become so important in setting and escalating consumption standards for more than just the people immediately below them. Television lets *everyone* see what these folks have and allows viewers to want it in concrete, product-specific ways. Let's not forget that television programming and movies are increasingly filled with product placements—the use of identifiable brands by characters. TV shows and movies are more and more like long-running ads. * * *

Part of what keeps the see-want-borrow-and-buy sequence going is lack of attention. Americans live with high levels of denial about their spending patterns. We spend more than we realize, hold more debt than we admit to, and ignore many of the moral conflicts surrounding our acquisitions. The importance of denial for dysfunctional consumers has been well documented. We've all heard the stories about people who drive around in cars full of unpaid credit card bills, who sneak into the guest room at 2:00 A.M. to make a QVC purchase, or who quietly slip off at lunchtime for a quick trip to the mall. What is not well understood is that the spending of many normal consumers is also predicated on denial. (How many times have you heard someone say, "Oh, I'm not materialistic, I'm just into books and CDs—and travel"?) * * *

Nowhere is denial so evident as with credit cards. Contrary to economists' usual portrayal of credit card debtors as fully rational consumers who use the cards to smooth out temporary shortfalls in income, the finding of the University of Maryland economist Larry Ausubel was that people greatly underestimate the amount of debt they hold on their cards— 1992's actual $182 billion in debt was thought to be a mere $70 billion. Furthermore, most people do not expect to use their cards to borrow, but, of course, they do. Eighty percent end up paying finance charges within any given year, with just under half (47 percent) always holding unpaid balances.

Not paying attention to what we spend is also very common. How many of us really keep track of where the cash from the ATM goes? Most Americans don't budget. And they don't watch. Many "fritter," as this downshifter recalled: "All I know is at the end of the month I never had anything left. And so I have to say I spent it all. I don't know what I frittered away. I really don't know what I spent the money on." * * *

Finally, denial also helps us navigate the moral conflicts associated with consumption. Most of our cherished religious and ethical teachings condemn excessive spending, but we don't really know what that means. We have a sense that money is dirty and a nagging feeling that there must be something better to do with our hard-earned dollars than give them to Bloomingdale's. As our salaries and creature comforts expand, many of us keep alive our youthful fantasies of doing humanitarian work, continuing the inner dialogue between God and Mammon. Not looking *too* hard helps keep that inner conflict tolerable. Squarely facing the fact that you spent $6,000 on your wardrobe last year and gave less than one-third of that sum to charity is a lot harder than living with a vague sense that you need to start spending less on clothes and giving away more money. * * *

In many places, private school is becoming a part of the upper-middle- (and even middle-) class standard of living—a requisite element in the basic package. Parents worry that without it their children will fall behind. Fears about education become magnified because they tap into larger, more deep-seated anxieties. Class position seems to be at stake. And, of course, as the middle and upper-middle classes abandon the public schools, the class divisions widen. Public school becomes tainted with a lower-class image. As another mother in the Los Angeles study explained, the public schools work well for her "housekeeper's child," who will have language problems, but not for her children. "Our concern with the public schools is really the safety issue. I have blond-haired, blue-eyed children who are not very physical and not very aggressive, and I worry about interactions on playgrounds."

At the same time, these parents have to deal with the complications of schooling alongside the super-wealthy. The same woman who is afraid of the public school playgrounds also worries about her children being at the bottom of the economic ladder in their private school. "The wealth of these kids is just mind-boggling. You put them in an environment in which we cannot compete, nor do we *want* them to compete and have those kinds of values. I don't want them to come home and say, 'Why don't we live in a ten-bedroom house?' " * * *

We have no problem acknowledging the "conspicuous consumption" of the early twentieth century that [Thorstein] Veblen wrote about. Middle class Americans shake their heads at what inner-city youths do to obtain expensive sneakers or gold chains. We can even get passionate about the dangers of status symbols in the Third World. Many Americans boycotted Nestle for promoting infant formula, the often deadly status alternative to breast milk. (Nestle and other companies had women in "modern" white uniforms doling out free supplies of formula in hospitals, leading to sickness, malnutrition, and even death among "bottle babies.") Many Americans deplore the entry of soft drinks and fast-food outlets into poor countries because they contribute to comerciogenic malnutrition: the poor spend their few pesos on soft drinks or French fries, forgoing nutritious food and becoming sick in the process. On the lighter side, we can chuckle at Peruvian Indians carrying rocks painted like transistor radios, Chinese who keep the brand tags on their designer sunglasses, Brazilian shanty-town dwellers with television antennae but no TV's, or the Papua New Guineans who substitute Pentel pens for boars' nose pieces. Third World status consumption seems straightforward, unambiguous in motive.

We have more trouble seeing the counterparts of these behaviors in the American middle class, and in ourselves.

No Scrubs

TLC, *on* Fanmail, La Face (1999).

■ Kevin Briggs, Kandi Burruss, Tameka Cottle

A scrub is a guy that thinks he's fly
And is also known as a buster

Always talkin' about what he wants
And just sits on his broke ass
So (no)

I don't want your number (no)
I don't want to give you mine and (no)
I don't want to meet you nowhere (no)
I don't want none of your time and (no)

Chorus:
I don't want no scrub
A scrub is a guy that can't get no love from me
Hanging out the passenger side
Of his best friend's ride
Trying to holler at me
I don't want no scrub
A scrub is a guy that can't get no love from me
Hanging out the passenger side
Of his best friend's ride
Trying to holler at me

But a scrub is checkin' me
But his game is kinda weak
And I know that he cannot approach me
Cuz I'm lookin' like class and he's lookin' like trash
Can't get wit' no deadbeat ass
So (no)

I don't want your number (no)
I don't want to give you mine and (no)
I don't want to meet you nowhere (no)
I don't want none of your time (no)

Chorus
If you don't have a car and you're walking
Oh yes son I'm talking to you
If you live at home wit' your momma
Oh yes son I'm talking to you (baby)
If you have a shorty but you don't show love
Oh yes son I'm talking to you
Wanna get with me with no money
Oh no I don't want no (oh)

No scrub
No scrub (no no)
No scrub (no no no no no)
No scrub (no no)
No

* * *

Dress As Success

BEAUTY SECRETS: WOMEN AND THE POLITICS OF APPEARANCE 79–80, 83–85, 88–93 (1986).

■ WENDY CHAPKIS

Appearance talks, making statements about gender, sexuality, ethnicity and class. In a sexually, racially and economically divided society all those visual statements add up to an evaluation of power. Economic power, or class position, is easily suggested by a man's use of the standard business suit. An expensive tailored three-piece suit says authority and privilege quietly but unmistakeably. For a woman to get that kind of attention, she must speak up more loudly. Even dressed in designer everything and costly jewelry her appearance makes a less unambiguous statement than a man's $1,000 suit.

Traditionally, a woman dressed in money has been assumed to be making a statement not about herself, but about a man. Her expensive clothing was thought to signal to the world that her husband or other male provider was so wealthy he could afford a clearly useless luxury in the form of this female. In this Veblenesque* interpretation, the woman herself is relegated to the position of a passive object much like a clothes hanger in someone else's closet. While this may well explain a husband's rationale for paying the bills, conspicuous consumption has a special purpose in a wealthy woman's life, too. * * *

Not only has consuming been one of the few pursuits open to women of a certain class, but being dressed in money demonstrates to the viewing public that the woman's one all important investment—marriage—has paid off nicely. Woman to woman we know that the marriage contract is far from an agreement between peers. At least being well-dressed serves as the visual equivalent of a large pay check.

Women in the role of wife establish social position second hand. A wealthy husband provides access to power for the woman married to him. But this ascribed power has to be made visible. If he has it, you flaunt it—not merely to reflect well on him, but to protect yourself. Dressed in money, a woman looks like someone not to be trifled with despite her sex. She is clearly protected by someone with the ability to do the job.

Increasingly, though, women are finding a need to indicate *personal* financial authority through their dress. Many more women now are breadwinners than in the past. This change is due in part to the women's movement. However, perhaps even more important than feminism is rising male unemployment and inflation making a woman's paycheck indispensable. Higher divorce rates, too, have helped make female financial independence a necessity.

How a woman should indicate professional power through her appearance is still a subject of debate. But all those voices presuming to advise women on how to put together such an image seem to agree on two fundamental things. First, *looking* "successful" is more than half the battle

---

* Thorstein Veblen, author of *The Theory of the Leisure Class,* published in 1899.

in actually achieving professional success. And second, success is a formula not to be tinkered with—that is, women may now aspire to professional success but should not attempt to redefine it.

Both these precepts have a particular resonance for women. Haven't we always known that how we look is far more important than what we do or how we do it? And as interlopers in the man-made world of business, we tend toward gratitude if someone even takes the time to explain the rules of the game—we may feel in no position to try to change them. Success in these terms is intensely individual and conformity a useful strategy.

* * *

The carefully composed look of success is not without its fashion competition. New Wave culture and punk style are among the most radical forms of visual dissent. At a very minimum, punk is a statement about consumerism. At least initially, the fashion was put together from hand-made or second hand clothing. Jewelry was to be found or created from inexpensive materials like rubber, plastic and cheap metals.

Punk has also been an explicit message on the state of the economy. If there is a possibility of a job interview in the near future, one probably won't choose a fluorescent green hair dye or a Mohawk haircut. But when unemployment becomes a predictable long-term condition, little is put at risk by looking outrageous. Radically transforming one's personal appearance can be an exercise of personal power in a life that feels out of control. While it may not be possible for an individual to change the reality of high unemployment, housing shortages and poverty, it is possible to transform one's body into a visual shout: "No, I do not accept the goodness of your goals and expectations. No, I will not help you feel secure in your choices. Do I look frightening? Do I look angry? Do I look dangerous? Do you still feel safe in thinking that the system works just fine? Think again."

Not surprisingly, it is not the Punk but the young urban profession-als—the so-called Yuppies—who have become the darlings of contemporary media. Their aerobic bodies and expensive dress speak confidently of physical and economic health. The image is above all reassuring. The system works just fine if you play by the rules. We accept the goals and the methods and we will be among the winners.

Success as it is known in the contemporary corporate world is depen-dent on a division between winners and losers, with a built-in guarantee that more will fail than will be rewarded. Women have always been the structural losers in the system. To be a woman was to be slotted for the position of support staff, both professionally and personally. The reality remains that even today most women will not become senior executives. In fact, most women will not even marry senior executives. The majority of working women will remain on a parallel job ladder which ends in the position of executive secretary or senior administrative assistant.

As anyone with experience in the business world knows, these are the women who run the show, without whom many organizations would come to a standstill. Yet they will never have the money or the authority to accompany the responsibility.

As long as success remains an individual characteristic, only one name will go on the by-line, while research assistants will have to be satisfied with a thank you in the acknowledgements. Secretaries will continue to receive lunch invitations or roses once a year instead of colleague-to-colleague respect and recognition of their partnership in the business endeavor. And women who do make it to a position of recognized power will have to quickly switch class and gender allegiance. Too close an identification with the secretarial crowd, too much empathy with those who come up on the short end of the unequal division of rewards will only be detrimental to one's own climb toward success.

It is arguably an improvement if women as a group are no longer automatically relegated to subordinate positions. But only those who find Jeane Kirkpatrick and Margaret Thatcher shining examples of feminism will believe that this sort of individual success is the same thing as women's liberation.

* * *

In the early days of the contemporary women's movement, women created strategies of empowerment that focused on shared experience and collective labor. However, we also longed for the individual perques of authority and prestige. But we were operating in an economic structure that insured that while our efforts might allow some of us to "make it," all of us would not. Western industrial society is based on competition and scarcity; equality not of condition but of opportunity. Taking on male bastions of power like the corporate world and opening them up to women meant collectively breaking down the barriers to women's participation. We worked for and achieved legislation that guaranteed us access. But once we succeeded in opening the door, we stepped through and realized that the stairway to the top was narrow and already crowded.

Still, now that the opportunity was there, failure became evidence of personal inadequacy not a political problem. Nor was class (known in America as one's "background") a political concern—provided one knew how to hide it. An entire literature developed teaching the common woman how to reach uncommon heights by "applying" herself and dressing for the part. * * *

Once inside and part way up the corporate ladder, the need to disguise your origins becomes imperative. In order to become executive materials, you must look as if you come from executive stock—the upper middle class. Enter John T. Molloy and *Dress for Success*:

> We can increase [a woman's] chances of success in the business world; we can increase her chances of being a top executive; we can make her more attractive to various types of men.

Molloy believes at least as firmly as [Helen Gurley Brown, founder of *Cosmopolitan* magazine] that a woman's business success lies in her own hands. Failure, too, is a personal not a structural problem: "If you have to tell your boss not to send you for coffee, you must have already told him non-verbally that you were ready to go." He quotes "Two extremely successful women" to back him up on this; these women expressed the belief that "The reason most young women wouldn't succeed was because they didn't look like they wanted to succeed."

Dressed in the proper outfit and sporting the proper attitude, the political problem of sexism can be sidestepped. The trick is learning to *accept* reality, not trying to change it. "It is a stark reality that men dominate the power structure. . . . I am not suggesting that women dress to impress men simply because they are men [but rather because men have power] . . . It is not sexism; it is realism."

In the chapter entitled "Does Your Background Hurt You," Molloy dismisses class as a political problem as neatly as he does sex. Women who intend to move into "The power ranks of American society" first must "learn the manners and mores of the inner circle. And the inner circle is most emphatically upper middle class." Not to worry; his advice is exceedingly specific:

> My research showed that a woman wearing a black raincoat is definitely not automatically categorized as lower middle class. Raincoats are important for women, but not as important as they are for men. . . . The country-tweed look is very upper middle class and highly recommended. . . . The blazer, by its very nature, is upper middle class; every woman should have at least one. . . . Office sweaters . . . say lower middle class and loser. Don't wear lower middle class colors such as purple and gold.

Predictably, the colors that test best are "gray, medium range blue, beige, deep maroon, deep rust." And the colors to avoid are "most pastels, particularly pink and pale yellow, most shades of green, mustard, bright anything, any shade that would be considered exotic." What we end up with as acceptable colors in the business world are those commonly associated with men and with the white upper class. This look is then defined as "serious." Serious becomes a question of conformity not creative difference, of masculinity not femininity and of the bland over the exotic, i.e. the foreign or racially "deviant."

Racial difference is indeed problematic to success and must be minimized. The process begins with learning to lose any ethnic accent and avoiding exotic fashions. But people of color serious about success are also advised to do whatever possible to transform even their bodies. In African women's magazines, advertisements promote the skin lightner Clere:

> Clere for your own special beauty. We are a successful people and have to look successful. We use Clere for a lighter, smoother skin. Now, Clere will work its magic for you, and make you more beautiful and successful.

Of course, it is not only among dress for success advisors that one finds these prejudices. They just help make them respectable. Even among articulate critics of sexism and racism in contemporary society there is evidence that these standards have been internalized. * * *

The shift from full-time homemaking to double duty (working both for wages and in the home) has helped create a need for new symbols of identity. Women are discovering that they are expected to have not one, but several conflicting images: the wholesome mother, the coolly professional businesswoman and the sexy mistress. No wonder women turn to the magic of wardrobe and makeup to provide inspiration for their multiple selves: "Springfever by Elizabeth Arden ... New make-up. New inspiration." "I can bring home the bacon, fry it up in a pan and never let you forget you're a man ... En Jolie" "Colors that inspire ... Let L'erin do the talking." You almost can hear the poor woman sigh "gladly."

The cosmetics industry has been carefully studying how best to make use of this bewildering set of demands made upon working women. Women's wages have been a mixed blessing for the beauty trade. In 1983, *Advertising Age*, an industry trade journal, noted with some alarm an increase in the number of women working outside the home:

> Today, 49% of America's mothers with children under six years old are employed as opposed to only 18% in 1960 ... Where women in this group once spent middays at the department store, they are now in the office.... Women who formerly had the time to sample and listen and spend money are no longer shoppers. Even when they do visit the store, they do so as buyers.

The subtle distinction between "shopping" and "buying," *Advertising Age* points out, is that the former implies leisure. This distinction seems to be borne out by figures on grocery store cosmetic sales (cheap and fast). In the U.S., they increased by 35 percent from 1980 to 1982.

Without the leisure to linger and shop, a woman may buy what is handy and in the process discover that what she is buying for convenience is not substantially different than the more expensive brand she used to carefully seek out. *Advertising Age* warns: "This is a dangerous conclusion for the industry."

And indeed after decades of constant growth, the beauty trade is now faced with a leveling off of sales and, in some cases, even a slight decline. Not all product lines have felt the squeeze, though. "Customers seem to be turning away from medium price products," the vice-president for marketing of one of America's largest cosmetic companies notes. "They are buying better goods or switching to generic, low-price products." * * *

Often the expensive and cheap products are not only produced by different divisions of the same conglomerate, but they are made of nearly identical ingredients. Even when we know this to be true, we often will buy the more expensive item because the fantasy it offers is more attractive. Psychologist Erika Freeman explains,

> An item that promises a fantasy by definition must be priced fantastically.... If a cream begins to sell at 50 cents it will not sell as well nor will it be considered as miraculous as a cream that sells for $30.
> * * *

Why do women buy costly beauty products that demonstrably have little purpose other than participation in a fantasy? The purchase of a new cosmetic, the decision to change the color or style of one's hair, the start of a new diet are the female equivalent of buying a lottery ticket. Maybe *you* will be the one whose life is transformed. Despite daily experience to the contrary, we continue to hope that maybe this time, maybe this product, will make a difference in our lives. And if it doesn't, it is still a relatively inexpensive way to visit the mysterious orient of Shiseido, the elite circle of Chanel, the smouldering, sensuous world of Dior. Everything that is so difficult to attain in real life is promised for the price of a new perfume or eye shadow.

NOTES AND QUESTIONS

1. **Thorstein Veblen and social meaning of consumption.** Thorstein Veblen [1857–1929] was an American economist whose work focused on the embeddedness of economic activity in a larger social world in which the desire for prestige in the eyes of others is as central as the desire for purely material gain. Two of the concepts he elaborated—"conspicuous consumption" and "pecuniary emulation"—illustrate this focus. Veblen argued that wealthy people desire to signal to others that they are wealthy, and that buying and displaying luxury goods is an important means by which this is done. Thus, "Conspicuous consumption is how the wealthy demonstrate their wealth, and thus their success in war or in business. By purchasing the finest houses, autos, suits, and shoes—all visible and public signs of financial success—they gain the respect and admiration of their peers and subordinates." Janet Knoedler, *Thorstein Veblen and the Predatory Nature of Contemporary Capitalism, in* INTRODUCTION TO POLITICAL ECONOMY 66 (Charles Sackrey & Geoffrey Schneider eds., 3d ed. 2002).

Veblen also argued that people in all economic classes make consumption decisions based not only on their rational desire for goods and services to make their life better, but out of envy of those who are more successful. This desire to be like and to be seen as like those with more money and social success he named "pecuniary emulation":

> [T]he standard of expenditure which commonly guides our efforts is not the average, ordinary expenditure already achieved; it is an ideal of consumption that lies just beyond our reach ... The motive is emulation—the stimulus of an invidious comparison which prompts us to outdo those with whom we are in the habit of classing ourselves ... [e]ach class envies and emulates the class next above it in the social scale, while it rarely compares itself with those below or with those who are considerably in advance.

THORSTEIN VEBLEN, THE THEORY OF THE LEISURE CLASS 81 (HOUGHTON MIFFLIN Co. 1973) (1899).

2. Crisis of over-production and creation of desire. Economic historians argue that after 1890, as modern forms of industrial production began to take shape and more and more mass-produced goods began to flood American markets, American business interests began a campaign to change consumption patterns away from patterns of thrift, self-denial, and self-reliance. As William Leach argues:

> From the 1890s on, American corporate business, in league with key institutions, began the transformation of American society into a society preoccupied with consumption, with comfort and bodily well-being, with luxury, spending, and acquisition, with more goods this year than last, more next year than this. American consumer capitalism produced a culture almost violently hostile to the past and to tradition, a future-oriented culture of desire that confused the good life with goods. It was a culture that first appeared as an alternative culture—or as one moving largely against the grain of earlier traditions of republicanism and Christian virtue—and then unfolded to become the reigning culture of the United States. It was the culture that many people the world over soon came to see as *the* heart of American life.

William Leach, Land of Desire: Merchants, Power, and the Rise of a New American Culture, xiii (1993); *see also* Stuart Ewen, Captains of Consciousness: Advertising and the Social Roots of the Consumer Culture (2001).

Consumer culture is partly a response to what Veblen identified as an incipient crisis within capitalist societies: the threat of overproduction, too many goods chasing too few buyers. As William Greider puts it:

> As economist Thorstein Veblen taught several generations ago, the problem of capitalist enterprise is always the problem of supply: managing the production of goods in order to maximize profit and the return on invested capital. * * *

> The great virtue of capitalism—the quality that always confounded socialist critics and defeated rival economic systems—is its ability to yield more from less. Its efficient organization of production strives to produce more goods from less input, whether the input is capital, labor or raw resources. Assuming markets are stable, the rising productivity increases the profit per unit, the yields that get distributed as returns to invested capital or as rising wages for labor or in lower product prices for consumers and, in the happiest circumstances, all three.

> But this expanding potential to produce more goods also poses the enduring contradiction for capitalist enterprise: how to dispose of the surplus production. You can make more things, but can you sell them? An undisciplined expansion of productive capacity will be self-defeating, even dangerous for a firm, if all it accomplishes are continuing supply surpluses that degrade prices and undermine the rate of return. The problem of surplus capacity drives not only the competition among firms for market shares but also the imperative to discover new markets.

WILLIAM GREIDER, ONE WORLD, READY OR NOT: THE MANIC LOGIC OF GLOBAL CAPITALISM 44–45 (1997).

2.   Branding and consumption. As the culture of consumption has matured, advertising strategies have changed as well. In the early 1990s, American corporations began to shift even more profoundly away from advertising what Karl Marx would have called the use-value of their products, to focus instead on using advertising to create an affective link between their products and the consumer's dreams and fantasies. This new technique relied on "branding," and the advertising of the brand rather than the product. As Naomi Klein observes:

> Overnight, "Brands, not products!" became the rallying cry for a marketing renaissance led by a new breed of companies that saw themselves as "meaning brokers" instead of product producers. What was changing was the idea of what—in both advertising and branding—was being sold. The old paradigm had it that all marketing was selling a product. In the new model, however, the product always takes a back seat to the real product, the brand, and the selling of the brand acquired an extra component that can only be described as spiritual.
> * * *
>
> On Marlboro Friday [a day in 1993 when Marlboro announced plans to dramatically reduce its prices in an attempt to compete with bargain cigarette brands], a line was drawn in the sand between the lowly price slashers and the high-concept brand builders. The brand builders conquered and a new consensus was born: the products that will flourish in the future will be the ones presented not as "commodities" but as concepts: the brand as experience, as lifestyle.

NAOMI KLEIN, NO LOGO: TAKING AIM AT THE BRAND BULLIES 21 (1999).

Does the ever-more-ephemeral link between products and the consumer's actual need for them threaten the pursuit of happiness?

Advertising At the Edge of the Apocalypse

Available at http://www.sutjhally.com/onlinepubs/onlinepubs_frame.html (n.d.)

■ SUT JHALLY

In this article I wish to make a simple claim: 20th century advertising is the most powerful and sustained system of propaganda in human history and its cumulative cultural effects, unless quickly checked, will be responsible for destroying the world as we know it. As it achieves this it will be responsible for the deaths of hundreds of thousands of non-western peoples and will prevent the peoples of the world from achieving true happiness. Simply stated, our survival as a species is dependent upon minimizing the threat from advertising and the commercial culture that has spawned it. I am stating my claims boldly at the outset so there can be no doubt as to what is at stake in our debates about the media and culture as we enter the new millennium.

Colonizing Culture

Karl Marx, the pre-eminent analyst of 19th century industrial capitalism, wrote in 1867, in the very opening lines of *Capital* that: "The wealth of societies in which the capitalist mode of production prevails appears as an 'immense collection of commodities'". * * * In seeking to initially distinguish his object of analysis from preceding societies, Marx referred to the way the society showed itself on a surface level and highlighted a *quantitative* dimension—the number of objects that humans interacted with in everyday life.

Indeed, no other society in history has been able to match the immense productive output of industrial capitalism. This feature colors the way in which the society presents itself—the way it *appears*. Objects are everywhere in capitalism. In this sense, capitalism is truly a revolutionary society, dramatically altering the very landscape of social life, in a way no other form of social organization had been able to achieve in such a short period of time. (In *The Communist Manifesto* Marx and Engels would coin the famous phrase "all that is solid melts into air" to highlight capitalism's unique dynamism.) It is this that strikes Marx as distinctive as he observes 19th century London. The starting point of his own critique therefore is not what he believes is the dominating agent of the society, *capital*, nor is it what he believes creates the value and wealth, *labor*—instead it is the *commodity*. From this surface appearance Marx then proceeds to peel away the outer skin of the society and to penetrate to the underlying essential structure that lies in the "hidden abode" of production.

It is not enough of course to only produce the "immense collection of commodities"—they must also be sold, so that further investment in production is feasible. Once produced commodities must go through the circuit of distribution, exchange and consumption, so that profit can be returned to the owners of capital and value can be "realized" again in a money form. If the circuit is not completed the system would collapse into stagnation and depression. Capitalism therefore has to ensure the sale of commodities on *pain of death*. In that sense the problem of capitalism is not mass production (which has been solved) but is instead the *problem of consumption*. That is why from the early years of this century it is more accurate to use the label "the consumer culture" to describe the western industrial market societies.

So central is consumption to its survival and growth that at the end of the 19th century industrial capitalism invented a unique new institution—the advertising industry—to ensure that the "immense accumulation of commodities" are converted back into a money form. The function of this new industry would be to recruit the best creative talent of the society and to create a culture in which desire and identity would be fused with commodities—to make the dead world of things come alive with human and social possibilities (what Marx would prophetically call the "fetishism of commodities"). And indeed there has never been a propaganda effort to match the effort of advertising in the 20th century. More thought, effort, creativity, time, and attention to detail has gone into the selling of the immense collection of commodities that any other campaign in human history to change public consciousness. One indication of this is [simple] the amount of money that has been exponentially expended on this effort. Today, in the United States alone, over $175 billion a year is spent to sell us things. This concentration of effort is unprecedented.

It should not be surprising that something this central and with so much being expended on it should become an important presence in social life. Indeed, commercial interests intent on maximizing the consumption of the immense collection of commodities have colonized more and more of the spaces of our culture. For instance, almost the entire media system (television and print) has been developed as a delivery system for marketers—its prime function is to produce audiences for sale to advertisers. Both the advertisements it carries, as well as the editorial matter that acts as a support for it, celebrate the consumer society. The movie system, at one time outside the direct influence of the broader marketing system, is now fully integrated into it through the strategies of licensing, tie-ins and product placements. The prime function of many Hollywood films today is to aid in the selling of the immense collection of commodities. As public funds are drained from the non-commercial cultural sector, art galleries, museums and symphonies bid for corporate sponsorship. Even those institutions thought to be outside of the market are being sucked in. High schools now sell the sides of their buses, the spaces of their hallways and the classroom time of their students to hawkers of candy bars, soft drinks and jeans. In New York City, sponsors are being sought for public playgrounds. In the contemporary world everything is sponsored by someone. The latest plans of Space Marketing Inc. call for rockets to deliver mile-wide Mylar billboards to compete with the sun and the moon for the attention of the earth's population.

With advertising messages on everything from fruit on supermarket shelves, to urinals, and to literally the space beneath our feet (Bamboo lingerie conducted a spray-paint pavement campaign in Manhattan telling consumers that "from here it looks likes you could use some new underwear"), it should not be surprising that many commentators now identify the realm of culture as simply an *adjunct* to the system of production and consumption.

Indeed so overwhelming has the commercial colonization of our culture become that it has created its own problems for marketers who now worry about how to ensure that their *individual* message stands out from the "clutter" and the "noise" of this busy environment. In that sense the main competition for marketers is not simply other brands in their product type, but all the other advertisers who are competing for the attention of an increasingly cynical audience which is doing all it can to avoid ads. In a strange paradox, as advertising takes over more and more space in the culture the job of the individual advertisers becomes much more difficult.

Therefore even greater care and resources are poured into the creation of commercial messages—much greater care than the surrounding editorial matter designed to capture the attention of the audience. Indeed if we wanted to compare national television commercials to something equivalent, it [would be] the biggest budget movie blockbusters. Second by second, it costs more to produce the average network ad than a movie like *Jurassic Park*.

The twin results of these developments are that advertising is everywhere and huge amounts of money and creativity are expended upon them.

If Marx were writing today I believe that not only would he be struck by the presence of even more objects, but also by the ever-present "discourse through and about objects" that permeates the spaces of our public and private domains. * * * This commercial discourse is the *ground* on which we live, the space in which we learn to think, the *lens* through which we come to understand the world that surrounds us. In seeking to understand where we are headed as a society, an adequate analysis of this commercial environment is essential.

Seeking this understanding will involve clarifying what we mean by the power and effectiveness of ads, and of being able to pose the right question. For too long debate has been concentrated around the issue of whether ad campaigns create demand for a particular product. If you are Pepsi Cola, or Ford, or Anheuser Busch, then it may be the right question for your interests. But, if you are interested in the social power of advertising—the impact of advertising on society—then that is the wrong question.

The right question would ask about the *cultural* role of advertising, not its marketing role. Culture is the place and space where a society tells stories about itself, where values are articulated and expressed, where notions of good and evil, of morality and immorality, are defined. In our culture it is the stories of advertising that dominate the spaces that mediate this function. If human beings are essentially a storytelling species, then to study advertising is to examine the central storytelling mechanism of our society. The correct question to ask from this perspective, is not whether particular ads sell the products they are hawking, but what are the consistent stories that advertising spins as a whole about what is important in the world, about how to behave, about what is good and bad. Indeed, it is to ask what values does advertising consistently push.

Happiness

Every society has to tell a story about happiness, about how individuals can satisfy themselves and feel both subjectively and objectively good. The cultural system of advertising gives a very specific answer to that question for our society. *The way to happiness and satisfaction is through the consumption of objects through the marketplace.* Commodities will make us happy. * * * In one very [important sense] that is the consistent and explicit message of every single message within the system of market communication.

Neither the fact of advertising's colonization of the horizons of imagination or the pushing of a story about the centrality of goods to human satisfaction should surprise us. The immense collection of goods have to be consumed (and even more goods produced) and the story that is used to ensure this function is to equate goods with happiness. Insiders to the system have recognized this obvious fact for many years. Retail analyst Victor Liebow said, just after the second world war:

> Our enormously productive economy ... demands that we make consumption our way of life, that we convert the buying and the selling of goods into rituals, that we seek our spiritual satisfaction, our ego satisfaction in commodities ... We need things consumed, burned up, worn out, replaced, and discarded at an ever increasing rate. * * *

So economic growth is justified not simply on the basis that it will provide employment (after all a host of alternative non-productive activities could also provide that) but because it will give us access to more things that will make us happy. This rationale for the existing system of ever-increasing production is told by advertising in the most compelling form possible. In fact it is this story, that human satisfaction is intimately connected to the provisions of the market, to economic growth, that is the major motivating force for social change as we start the 21st century.

The social upheavals of eastern Europe were pushed by this vision. As Gloria Steinhem described the East German transformation: "First we have a revolution then we go shopping." * * * The attractions of this vision in the Third World are not difficult to discern. When your reality is empty stomachs and empty shelves, no wonder the marketplace appears as the panacea for your problems. When your reality is hunger and despair it should not be surprising that the seductive images of desire and abundance emanating from the advertising system should be so influential in thinking about social and economic policy. Indeed not only happiness but political freedom itself is made possible by access to the immense collection of commodities. These are very powerful stories that equate happiness and freedom with consumption—and advertising is the main propaganda arm of this view.

The question that we need to pose at this stage (that is almost never asked) is, "Is it true?" Does happiness come from material things? Do we get happier as a society as we get richer, as our standard of living increases, as we have more access to the immense collection of objects? Obviously these are complex issues, but the general answer to these questions is "no."

* * *

In a series of surveys conducted in the United States starting in 1945 (labeled "the happiness surveys") researchers sought to examine the link between material wealth and subjective happiness, and concluded that, when examined both cross-culturally as well as historically in one society, there is a very *weak* correlation. Why should this be so?

former so called "socialist" societies of eastern Europe. These repressive societies never found a way to connect to people in any kind of pleasurable way, relegating issues of pleasure and individual expression to the non-essential and distracting aspects of social life. This indeed was the core of the failure of Communism in Eastern Europe. As Ehrenreich reminds us, not only was it unable to deliver the material goods, but it was unable to create a fully human "ideological retort to the powerful seductive messages of the capitalist consumer culture." * * * The problems are no less severe domestically:

> Everything enticing and appealing is located in the (thoroughly private) consumer spectacle. In contrast, the public sector looms as a realm devoid of erotic promise—the home of the IRS, the DMV, and other irritating, intrusive bureaucracies. Thus, though everyone wants national health insurance, and parental leave, few are moved to wage political struggles for them. 'Necessity' is not enough; we may have to find a way to glamorize the possibility of an activist public sector, and to glamorize the possibility of public activism. * * *

The imperative task for those who want to stress a different set of values is to make the struggle for social change fun and sexy. By that I do not mean that we have to use images of sexuality, but that we have to find a way of thinking about the struggle against poverty, against homelessness, for healthcare and child-care, to protect the environment, in terms of *pleasure and fun and happiness.*

To make this glamorization of collective issues possible will require that the present commercial monopoly of the channels of communication be broken in favor of a more democratic access where difficult discussion of important and relevant issues may be possible. While the situation may appear hopeless we should remind ourselves of how important capitalism deems its monopoly of the imagination to be. The campaigns of successive United States government against the Cuban revolution, and the obsession of our national security state with the Sandinista revolution in Nicaragua in the 1980s, demonstrates the importance that capitalism places on smashing the alternative model. Even as the United States government continues to support the most vicious, barbarous, brutal and murderous regimes around the world, it takes explicit aim at those governments that have tried to redistribute wealth to the most needy—who have been prioritized collective values over the values of selfishness and greed. The monopoly of the vision is vital and capitalism knows it.

The End of the World as We Know It

The consumer vision that is pushed by advertising and which is conquering the world is based fundamentally, as I argued before, on a notion of *economic growth*. Growth requires resources (both raw materials and energy) and there is a broad consensus among environmental scholars that the earth cannot sustain past levels of expansion based upon resource-intensive modes of economic activity, especially as more and more nations struggle to join the feeding trough.

When we examine this process more closely the conclusions appear to be less surprising than our intuitive perspective might suggest. In another series of surveys (the "quality of life surveys") people were asked about the kinds of things that are important to them—about what would constitute a good quality of life. The findings of this line of research indicate that if the elements of satisfaction were [divided up] into social values (love, family, friends) and material values (economic security and success) the former outranks the latter in terms of importance. What people say they really want out of life is: autonomy and control of life; good self-esteem; warm family relationships; tension-free leisure time; close and intimate friends; as well as romance and love. This is not to say that material values are not important. They form a necessary component of a good quality of life. But above a certain level of poverty and comfort, material things stop giving us the kind of satisfaction that the magical world of advertising insists they can deliver.

These conclusion[s] point to one of the great ironies of the market system. The market is good at providing those things that can be bought and sold and it pushed us—via advertising—in that direction. But the real sources of happiness—social relationships—are outside the capability of the marketplace to provide. The marketplace cannot provide love, it cannot provide real friendships, it cannot provide sociability. It can provide other material things and services—but they are not what makes us happy.

The advertising industry has known this since at least the 1920s and in fact have stopped trying to sell us things based on their material qualities alone. If we examine the advertising of the end of the 19th and first years of the 20th century, we would see that advertising talked a lot about the properties of commodities—what they did, how well they did it, etc. But starting in the 1920s advertising shifts to talking about the relationship of objects to the social life of people. It starts to connect commodities (the things they have to sell) with the powerful images of a deeply desired social life that people say they want.

No wonder then that advertising is so attractive to us, so powerful, so seductive. What it offers us are images of the real sources of human happiness—family life, romance and love, sexuality and pleasure, friendship and sociability, leisure and relaxation, independence and control of life. That is why advertising is so powerful, that is what is real about it. The cruel illusion of advertising however is in the way that it links those qualities to a place that by definition cannot provide it—the market and the immense collection of commodities. The falsity of advertising is not in the appeals it makes (which are very real) but in the answers it provides. We want love and friendship and sexuality—and advertising points the way to it through objects.

To reject or criticize advertising as false and manipulative misses the point. Ad executive Jerry Goodis puts it this way: "Advertising doesn't mirror how people are acting but how they are dreaming." * * * It taps into our real emotions and repackages them back to us connected to the world of things. What advertising really reflects in that sense is the nonexistent role in conventional microeconomic markets shaped by strangers. Needless to say, feminist economists have criticized both Becker's assumptions and conclusions.

In the cases that follow, we take up questions often put on the back burner of analysis in both family law and constitutional doctrine: What are the economic imperatives within living units that foster social cohesion for both individuals and society? Do legal rules incorporate social constructs about the "natural," pre-political norms of how a family should be configured? Does state intervention or refusal to intervene create economic incentives or disincentives for caring bonds that flow outside of conventional arrangements? Do legal rules privilege some family cultural practices over others, thus placing an economic burden on already disfavored groups? How are the tensions we referred to earlier between community, equality and individual rights resolved in these cases? Can Mrs. Moore's decision to provide housing for her grandchild be explained by Becker's rational choice theory?

A. NUCLEAR FAMILY VS. EXTENDED FAMILY

Moore v. City of East Cleveland, Ohio

Supreme Court of the United States, 431 U.S. 494 (1977).

■ MR. JUSTICE POWELL announced the judgment of the Court, and delivered an opinion in which MR. JUSTICE BRENNAN, MR. JUSTICE MARSHALL, and MR. JUSTICE BLACKMUN joined.

[In an earlier, related case, *Village of Belle Terre v. Boraas*, 416 U.S. 1 (1974), the Supreme Court rejected a challenge to the constitutionality of a zoning ordinance of the Village of Belle Terre, New York, restricting land use to one-family dwellings, and prohibiting occupancy of a dwelling by more than two unrelated persons as a "family," while permitting occupancy by any number of persons related by blood, adoption, or marriage. Justice Douglas, expressing the view of seven members of the court, held that the zoning ordinance (a) was not unconstitutional since it did not violate any right of interstate travel; (b) involved no procedural disparity inflicted on some but not on others; (c) involved no fundamental constitutional right, such as the rights of association or privacy; and (d) was reasonable and bore a rational relationship to a permissible state objective, thus not violating equal protection.

Justice Marshall's dissent argued that the challenged ordinance was unconstitutional. Marshall would have found that it unnecessarily burdened tenants' fundamental rights of association and privacy guaranteed by the First and Fourteenth Amendments. Marshall argued that since the village's legitimate interests in controlling land use and population density could be protected by limiting the number of occupants without discriminating on the basis of such occupants' constitutionally protected choices of life style.]

East Cleveland's housing ordinance, like many throughout the country, limits occupancy of a dwelling unit to members of a single family. § 1351.02.[1] But the ordinance contains an unusual and complicated definitional section that recognizes as a "family" only a few categories of related individuals. § 1341.08.[2] Because her family, living together in her home, fits none of those categories, appellant stands convicted of a criminal offense. The question in this case is whether the ordinance violates the Due Process Clause of the Fourteenth Amendment.

I

Appellant, Mrs. Inez Moore, lives in her East Cleveland home together with her son, Dale Moore, Sr., and her two grandsons, Dale, Jr., and John Moore, Jr. The two boys are first cousins rather than brothers; we are told that John came to live with his grandmother and with the elder and younger Dale Moore after his mother's death.

In early 1973, Mrs. Moore received a notice of violation from the city, stating that John was an "illegal occupant" and directing her to comply with the ordinance. When she failed to remove him from her home, the city filed a criminal charge. Mrs. Moore moved to dismiss, claiming that the ordinance was constitutionally invalid on its face. Her motion was overruled, and upon conviction she was sentenced to five days in jail and a $25 fine. The Ohio Court of Appeals affirmed after giving full consideration to her constitutional claims and the Ohio Supreme Court denied review. We noted probable jurisdiction of her appeal, 425 U.S. 949 (1976).

II

The city argues that our decision in *Village of Belle Terre v. Boraas, 416 U.S. 1 (1974),* requires us to sustain the ordinance attacked here. Belle

---

1. All citations by section number refer to the Housing Code of the city of East Cleveland, Ohio.

2. Section 1341.08 (1966) provides:

" 'Family' means a number of individuals related to the nominal head of the household or to the spouse of the nominal head of the household living as a single housekeeping unit in a single dwelling unit, but limited to the following:

"(a) Husband or wife of the nominal head of the household.

"(b) Unmarried children of the nominal head of the household or of the spouse of the nominal head of the household, provided, however, that such unmarried children have no children residing with them.

"(c) Father or mother of the nominal head of the household or of the spouse of the nominal head of the household.

"(d) Notwithstanding the provisions of subsection (b) hereof, a family may include not more than one dependent married or unmarried child of the nominal head of the household or of the spouse of the nominal head of the household and the spouse and dependent children of such dependent child. For the purpose of this subsection, a dependent person is one who has more than fifty percent of his total support furnished for him by the nominal head of the household and the spouse of the nominal head of the household.

"(e) A family may consist of one individual."

Terre, like East Cleveland, imposed limits on the types of groups that could occupy a single dwelling unit. Applying the constitutional standard announced in this Court's leading land-use case, *Euclid v. Ambler Realty Co.*, 272 U.S. 365 (1926),[6] we sustained the Belle Terre ordinance on the ground that it bore a rational relationship to permissible state objectives.

But one overriding factor sets this case apart from *Belle Terre*. The ordinance there affected only *unrelated* individuals. It expressly allowed all who were related by "blood, adoption, or marriage" to live together, and in sustaining the ordinance we were careful to note that it promoted "family needs" and "family values." 416 U.S., at 9. East Cleveland, in contrast, has chosen to regulate the occupancy of its housing by slicing deeply into the family itself. This is no mere incidental result of the ordinance. On its face it selects certain categories of relatives who may live together and declares that others may not. In particular, it makes a crime of a grandmother's choice to live with her grandson in circumstances like those presented here.

When a city undertakes such intrusive regulation of the family, neither *Belle Terre* nor *Euclid* governs; the usual judicial deference to the legislature is inappropriate. "This Court has long recognized that freedom of personal choice in matters of marriage and family life is one of the liberties protected by the Due Process Clause of the Fourteenth Amendment." * * * A host of cases * * * have consistently acknowledged a "private realm of family life which the state cannot enter." * * * Of course, the family is not beyond regulation. * * * But when the government intrudes on choices concerning family living arrangements, this Court must examine carefully the importance of the governmental interests advanced and the extent to which they are served by the challenged regulation. * * *

When thus examined, this ordinance cannot survive. The city seeks to justify it as a means of preventing overcrowding, minimizing traffic and parking congestion, and avoiding an undue financial burden on East Cleveland's school system. Although these are legitimate goals, the ordinance before us serves them marginally, at best.[7] For example, the ordinance permits any family consisting only of husband, wife, and unmarried children to live together, even if the family contains a half dozen licensed drivers, each with his or her own car. At the same time it forbids an adult brother and sister to share a household, even if both faithfully use public

---

6. *Euclid* held that land-use regulations violate the Due Process Clause if they are "clearly arbitrary and unreasonable, having no substantial relation to the public health, safety, morals, or general welfare." 272 U.S., at 395. See *Nectow v. Cambridge*, 277 U.S. 183, 188 (1928). Later cases have emphasized that the general welfare is not to be narrowly understood; it embraces a broad range of governmental purposes. See *Berman v. Parker*, 348 U.S. 26 (1954). But our cases have not departed from the requirement that the government's chosen means must rationally further some legitimate state purpose.

7. It is significant that East Cleveland has another ordinance specifically addressed to the problem of overcrowding. See *United States Dept. of Agriculture v. Moreno*, 413 U.S. 528, 536–537 (1973). Section 1351.03 limits population density directly, tying the maximum permissible occupancy of a dwelling to the habitable floor area. Even if John, Jr., and his father both remain in Mrs. Moore's household, the family stays well within these limits.

transportation. The ordinance would permit a grandmother to live with a single dependent son and children, even if his school-age children number a dozen, yet it forces Mrs. Moore to find another dwelling for her grandson John, simply because of the presence of his uncle and cousin in the same household. We need not labor the point. Section 1341.08 has but a tenuous relation to alleviation of the conditions mentioned by the city.

III

The city would distinguish the cases based on *Meyer* and *Pierce*. It points out that none of them "gives grandmothers any fundamental rights with respect to grandsons," * * * and suggests that any constitutional right to live together as a family extends only to the nuclear family— essentially a couple and their dependent children.

To be sure, these cases did not expressly consider the family relationship presented here. They were immediately concerned with freedom of choice with respect to childbearing, * * * or with the rights of parents to the custody and companionship of their own children, *Stanley v. Illinois, supra,* or with traditional parental authority in matters of child rearing and education. *Yoder, Ginsberg, Pierce, Meyer, supra.* But unless we close our eyes to the basic reasons why certain rights associated with the family have been accorded shelter under the Fourteenth Amendment's Due Process Clause, we cannot avoid applying the force and rationale of these precedents to the family choice involved in this case.

Understanding those reasons requires careful attention to this Court's function under the Due Process Clause. Mr. Justice Harlan described it eloquently:

"Due process has not been reduced to any formula; its content cannot be determined by reference to any code. The best that can be said is that through the course of this Court's decisions it has represented the balance which our Nation, built upon postulates of respect for the liberty of the individual, has struck between that liberty and the demands of organized society. If the supplying of content to this Constitutional concept has of necessity been a rational process, it certainly has not been one where judges have felt free to roam where unguided speculation might take them. The balance of which I speak is the balance struck by this country, having regard to what history teaches are the traditions from which it developed as well as the traditions from which it broke. That tradition is a living thing. A decision of this Court which radically departs from it could not long survive, while a decision which builds on what has survived is likely to be sound. No formula could serve as a substitute, in this area, for judgment and restraint."

". . . [T]he full scope of the liberty guaranteed by the Due Process Clause cannot be found in or limited by the precise terms of the specific guarantees elsewhere provided in the Constitution. This 'liberty' is not a series of isolated points pricked out in terms of the taking of property; the freedom of speech, press, and religion; the right to keep and bear arms; the freedom from unreasonable searches and seizures; and so on. It is a rational continuum which, broadly speaking, includes a freedom from all substantial arbitrary impositions and purposeless restraints, . . . and which also recognizes, what a reasonable and sensitive judgment must, that certain interests require particularly careful scrutiny of the state needs asserted to justify their abridgment." *Poe v. Ullman,* supra, at 542–543 (dissenting opinion).

Substantive due process has at times been a treacherous field for this Court. There *are* risks when the judicial branch gives enhanced protection to certain substantive liberties without the guidance of the more specific provisions of the Bill of Rights. As the history of the *Lochner* era demonstrates, there is reason for concern lest the only limits to such judicial intervention become the predilections of those who happen at the time to be Members of this Court. That history counsels caution and restraint. But it does not counsel abandonment, nor does it require what the city urges here: cutting off any protection of family rights at the first convenient, if arbitrary boundary—the boundary of the nuclear family.

Appropriate limits on substantive due process come not from drawing arbitrary lines but rather from careful "respect for the teachings of history [and] solid recognition of the basic values that underlie our society." * * * Our decisions establish that the Constitution protects the sanctity of the family precisely because the institution of the family is deeply rooted in this Nation's history and tradition.[12] It is through the family that we inculcate and pass down many of our most cherished values, moral and cultural.

---

12. In *Wisconsin v. Yoder,* 406 U.S. 205 (1972), the Court rested its holding in part on the constitutional right of parents to assume the primary role in decisions concerning the rearing of their children. That right is recognized because it reflects a "strong tradition" founded on "the history and culture of Western civilization," and because the parental role "is now established beyond debate as an enduring American tradition." *Id.,* at 232. In *Ginsberg v. New York,* 390 U.S. 629 (1968), the Court spoke of the same right as "basic in the structure of our society." *Id.,* at 639. *Griswold v. Connecticut, supra,* struck down Connecticut's anticontraception statute. Three concurring Justices, relying on both the Ninth and Fourteenth Amendments, emphasized that "the traditional relation of the family" is "a relation as old and as fundamental as our entire civilization." 381 U.S., at 496 (Goldberg, J., joined by Warren, C.J., and Brennan, J., concurring). Speaking of the same statute as that involved in *Griswold,* Mr. Justice Harlan wrote, dissenting in *Poe v. Ullman,* 367 U.S. 497, 551–552 (1961):

"[H]ere we have not an intrusion into the home so much as on the life which characteristically has its place in the home. . . . The home derives its pre-eminence as the seat of family life. And the integrity of that life is something so fundamental that it has been found to draw to its protection the principles of more than one explicitly granted Constitutional right."

Although he agrees that the Due Process Clause has substantive content, Mr. Justice White in dissent expresses the fear that our recourse to history and tradition will "broaden enormously the horizons of the Clause." *Post,* at 549–550. To the contrary, an approach grounded in history imposes limits on the judiciary that are more meaningful than any based on the abstract formula taken from *Palko v. Connecticut,* 302 U.S. 319 (1937), and apparently suggested as an alternative. Cf. *Duncan v. Louisiana, supra,* at 149–150, n.14 (rejecting the *Palko* formula as the basis for deciding what procedural protections are required of a State, in favor of a

Ours is by no means a tradition limited to respect for the bonds uniting the members of the nuclear family. The tradition of uncles, aunts, cousins, and especially grandparents sharing a household along with parents and children has roots equally venerable and equally deserving of constitutional recognition.[14] Over the years millions of our citizens have grown up in just such an environment, and most, surely, have profited from it. Even if conditions of modern society have brought about a decline in extended family households, they have not erased the accumulated wisdom of civilization, gained over the centuries and honored throughout our history, that supports a larger conception of the family. Out of choice, necessity, or a sense of family responsibility, it has been common for close relatives to draw together and participate in the duties and the satisfactions of a common home. Decisions concerning child rearing, which *Yoder, Meyer, Pierce* and other cases have recognized as entitled to constitutional protection, long have been shared with grandparents or other relatives who occupy the same household—indeed who may take on major responsibility for the rearing of the children.[15] Especially in times of adversity, such as the death of a spouse or economic need, the broader family has tended to come together for mutual sustenance and to maintain or rebuild a secure home life. This is apparently what happened here.[16]

Whether or not such a household is established because of personal tragedy, the choice of relatives in this degree of kinship to live together may not lightly be denied by the State. *Pierce* struck down an Oregon law requiring all children to attend the State's public schools, holding that the Constitution "excludes any general power of the State to standardize its children by forcing them to accept instruction from public teachers only." 268 U.S., at 535. By the same token the Constitution prevents East Cleveland from standardizing its children—and its adults—by forcing all to live in certain narrowly defined family patterns.

Reversed.

historical approach based on the Anglo–American legal tradition). Indeed, the passage cited in MR. JUSTICE WHITE's dissent as "most accurately reflect[ing] the thrust of prior decisions" on substantive due process, *post*, at 545, expressly points to history and tradition as the source for "supplying . . . content to this Constitutional concept." *Poe* v. *Ullman, supra*, at 542 (Harlan, J., dissenting).

14. See generally B. Yorburg, The Changing Family (1973); Bronfenbrenner, The Calamitous Decline of the American Family, Washington Post, Jan. 2, 1977, p. C1. Recent census reports bear out the importance of family patterns other than the prototypical nuclear family. In 1970, 26.5% of all families contained one or more members over 18 years of age, other than the head of household and spouse. U.S. Department of Commerce, 1970 Census of Population, vol. 1, pt. 1, Table 208. In 1960 the comparable figure was 26.1%. U.S. Department of Commerce, 1960 Census of Population, vol. 1, pt. 1, Table 187. Earlier data are not available.

15. Cf. *Prince v. Massachusetts*, 321 U.S. 158 (1944), which spoke broadly of family authority as against the State, in a case where the child was being reared by her aunt, not her natural parents.

16. We are told that the mother of John Moore, Jr., died when he was less than one year old. He, like uncounted others who have suffered a similar tragedy, then came to live with the grandmother to provide the infant with a substitute for his mother's care and to establish a more normal home environment. Brief for Appellant 25.

■ Mr. Justice Brennan, with whom Mr. Justice Marshall joins, concurring.

I join the plurality's opinion. I agree that the Constitution is not powerless to prevent East Cleveland from prosecuting as a criminal and jailing[1] a 63-year-old grandmother for refusing to expel from her home her now 10-year-old grandson who has lived with her and been brought up by her since his mother's death when he was less than a year old. I do not question that a municipality may constitutionally zone to alleviate noise and traffic congestion and to prevent overcrowded and unsafe living conditions, in short to enact reasonable land-use restrictions in furtherance of the legitimate objectives East Cleveland claims for its ordinance. But the zoning power is not a license for local communities to enact senseless and arbitrary restrictions which cut deeply into private areas of protected family life. East Cleveland may not constitutionally define ''family'' as essentially confined to parents and the parents' own children.[3] The plurality's opinion conclusively demonstrates that classifying family patterns in this eccentric way is not a rational means of achieving the ends East Cleveland claims for its ordinance, and further that the ordinance unconstitutionally abridges the ''freedom of personal choice in matters of . . . family life [that] is one of the liberties protected by the Due Process Clause of the Fourteenth Amendment.'' *Cleveland Board of Education v. LaFleur*, 414 U.S. 632, 639–640 (1974). I write only to underscore the cultural myopia of the arbitrary boundary drawn by the East Cleveland ordinance in the light of the tradition of the American home that has been a feature of our society since our beginning as a Nation—the ''tradition'' in the plurality's words, ''of uncles, aunts, cousins, and especially grandparents sharing a household along with parents and children. . . .'' *Ante,* at 504. The line drawn by this ordinance displays a depressing insensitivity toward the economic and emotional needs of a very large part of our society.

In today's America, the ''nuclear family'' is the pattern so often found in much of white suburbia. J. Vander Zanden, Sociology: A Systematic Approach 322 (3d ed. 1975). The Constitution cannot be interpreted, however, to tolerate the imposition by government upon the rest of us of white suburbia's preference in patterns of family living. The ''extended family'' that provided generations of early Americans with social services and economic and emotional support in times of hardship, and was the

---

1. This is a criminal prosecution which resulted in the grandmother's conviction and sentence to prison and a fine. Section 1345.99 permits imprisonment of up to six months, and a fine of up to $1,000, for violation of any provision of the Housing Code. Each day such violation continues may, by the terms of this section, constitute a separate offense.

3. The East Cleveland ordinance defines ''family'' to include, in addition to the spouse of the ''nominal head of the household,'' the couple's childless unmarried children, but only one dependent child (married or unmarried) having dependent children, and one parent of the nominal head of the household or of his or her spouse. Thus an ''extended family'' is authorized in only the most limited sense, and ''family'' is essentially confined to parents and their own children. Appellant grandmother was charged with violating the ordinance because John, Jr., lived with her at the same time her other grandson, Dale, Jr., was also living in the home; the latter is classified as an ''unlicensed roomer'' authorized by the ordinance to live in the house.

beachhead for successive waves of immigrants who populated our cities, remains not merely still a pervasive living pattern, but under the goad of brutal economic necessity, a prominent pattern—virtually a means of survival—for large numbers of the poor and deprived minorities of our society. For them compelled pooling of scant resources requires compelled sharing of a household.[5]

The "extended" form is especially familiar among black families.[6] We may suppose that this reflects the truism that black citizens, like generations of white immigrants before them, have been victims of economic and other disadvantages that would worsen if they were compelled to abandon extended, for nuclear, living patterns.[7] Even in husband and wife house-

5. See, *e.g.,* H. Gans, The Urban Villagers 45–73, 245–249 (1962).

"Perhaps the most important—or at least the most visible—difference between the classes is one of family structure. *The working class subculture* is distinguished by the dominant role of the family circle. . . .

"The specific characteristics of the family circle may differ widely—from the collateral peer group form of the West Enders, to the hierarchical type of the Irish, or to the classical three-generation extended family. . . . What matters most—and distinguishes this subculture from others—is that there be a family circle which is wider than the nuclear family, and that all of the opportunities, temptations, and pressures of the larger society be evaluated in terms of how they affect the ongoing way of life that has been built around this circle." *Id.,* at 244–245 (emphasis in original).

6. Yorburg, *supra,* n. 4, at 108. "Within the black lower-class it has been quite common for several generations, or parts of the kin, to live together under one roof. Often a maternal grandmother is the acknowledged head of this type of household which has given rise to the term 'matrifocal' to describe lower-class black family patterns." See J. Scanzoni, The Black Family in Modern Society 134 (1971); see also Anderson, The Pains and Pleasures of Old Black Folks, Ebony 123, 128–130 (Mar. 1973). See generally E. Frazier, The Negro Family in the United States (1939); Lewis, The Changing Negro Family, in E. Ginzberg, ed., The Nation's Children 108 (1960).

The extended family often plays an important role in the rearing of young black children whose parents must work. Many such children frequently "spend all of their growing-up years in the care of extended kin. . . . Often children are 'given' to their grandparents, who rear them to adulthood. . . . Many children normally grow up in a three-generation household and they absorb the influences of grandmother and grandfather as well as mother and father." J. Ladner, Tomorrow's Tomorrow: The Black Woman 60 (1972).

7. The extended family has many strengths not shared by the nuclear family.

"The case histories behind mounting rates of delinquency, addiction, crime, neurotic disabilities, mental illness, and senility in societies in which autonomous nuclear families prevail suggest that frequent failure to develop enduring family ties is a serious inadequacy for both individuals and societies." D. Blitsten, The World of the Family 256 (1963).

Extended families provide services and emotional support not always found in the nuclear family:

"The troubles of the nuclear family in industrial societies, generally, and in American society, particularly, stem largely from the inability of this type of family structure to provide certain of the services performed in the past by the extended family. Adequate health, education, and welfare provision, particularly for the two nonproductive generations in modern societies, the young and the old, is increasingly an insurmountable problem for the nuclear family. The unrelieved and sometimes unbearably intense parent-child relationship, where childrearing is not shared at least in part by others, and the loneliness of nuclear family units, increasingly turned in on themselves in contracted and relatively isolated settings, is another major problem." Yorburg, *supra,* n. 4, at 194.

holds, 13% of black families compared with 3% of white families include relatives under 18 years old, in addition to the couple's own children.[8] In black households whose head is an elderly woman, as in this case, the contrast is even more striking: 48% of such black households, compared with 10% of counterpart white households, include related minor children not offspring of the head of the household.[9]

I do not wish to be understood as implying that East Cleveland's enforcement of its ordinance is motivated by a racially discriminatory purpose: The record of this case would not support that implication. But the prominence of other than nuclear families among ethnic and racial minority groups, including our black citizens, surely demonstrates that the "extended family" pattern remains a vital tenet of our society. It suffices that in prohibiting this pattern of family living as a means of achieving its objectives, appellee city has chosen a device that deeply intrudes into family associational rights that historically have been central, and today remain central, to a large proportion of our population.

Moreover, to sanction the drawing of the family line at the arbitrary boundary chosen by East Cleveland would surely conflict with prior decisions that protected "extended" family relationships. For the "private realm of family life which the state cannot enter," recognized as protected in *Prince v. Massachusetts*, 321 U.S. 158, 166 (1944), was the relationship of aunt and niece. And in *Pierce v. Society of Sisters*, 268 U.S. 510, 534–535 (1925), the protection held to have been unconstitutionally abridged was "the liberty of parents and *guardians* to direct the upbringing and education of children under their control" (emphasis added). See also *Wisconsin v. Yoder*, 406 U.S. 205, 232–233 (1972). Indeed, *Village of Belle Terre v. Boraas*, 416 U.S. 1 (1974), the case primarily relied upon by the appellee, actually supports the Court's decision. The Belle Terre ordinance barred only unrelated individuals from constituting a family in a single-family zone. The village took special care in its brief to emphasize that its ordinance did not in any manner inhibit the choice of *related* individuals to constitute a family, whether in the "nuclear" or "extended" form. This was because the village perceived that choice as one it was constitutionally powerless to inhibit. Its brief stated: "Whether it be the extended family of a more leisurely age or the nuclear family of today the role of the family in raising and training successive generations of the species makes it more important, we dare say, than any other social or legal institution.... *If any freedom not specifically mentioned in the Bill of Rights enjoys a 'preferred position' in the law it is most certainly the family.*" (Emphasis supplied.) * * * The cited decisions recognized, as the plurality recognizes today, that the choice of the "extended family" pattern is within the "freedom of

---

8. R. Hill, The Strengths of Black Families 5 (1972).

9. *Id.*, at 5–6. It is estimated that at least 26% of black children live in other than husband-wife families, "including foster parents, the presence of other male or female relatives (grandfather or grandmother, older brother or sister, uncle or aunt), male or female nonrelatives, [or with] only *one* adult (usually mother) present...." Scanzoni, *supra*, n. 6, at 44.

personal choice in matters of . . . family life [that] is one of the liberties protected by the Due Process Clause of the Fourteenth Amendment." 414 U.S., at 639–640.

* * *

■ MR. JUSTICE STEVENS, concurring in the judgment.

In my judgment the critical question presented by this case is whether East Cleveland's housing ordinance is a permissible restriction on appellant's right to use her own property as she sees fit.

Long before the original States adopted the Constitution, the common law protected an owner's right to decide how best to use his own property. This basic right has always been limited by the law of nuisance which proscribes uses that impair the enjoyment of other property in the vicinity. But the question whether an individual owner's use could be further limited by a municipality's comprehensive zoning plan was not finally decided until this century.

The holding in *Euclid v. Ambler Realty Co.*, 272 U.S. 365, that a city could use its police power, not just to abate a specific use of property which proved offensive, but also to create and implement a comprehensive plan for the use of land in the community, vastly diminished the rights of individual property owners. It did not, however, totally extinguish those rights. On the contrary, that case expressly recognized that the broad zoning power must be exercised within constitutional limits.

In his opinion for the Court, Mr. Justice Sutherland fused the two express constitutional restrictions on any state interference with private property—that property shall not be taken without due process nor for a public purpose without just compensation—into a single standard: "[B]efore [a zoning] ordinance can be declared unconstitutional, [it must be shown to be] clearly arbitrary and unreasonable, *having no substantial relation to the public health, safety, morals, or general welfare.*" *Id.*, at 395 (emphasis added). This principle was applied in *Nectow v. Cambridge*, 277 U.S. 183; on the basis of a specific finding made by the state trial court that "the health, safety, convenience and general welfare of the inhabitants of the part of the city affected" would not be promoted by prohibiting the landowner's contemplated use, this Court held that the zoning ordinance as applied was unconstitutional. * * *

Litigation involving single-family zoning ordinances is common. Although there appear to be almost endless differences in the language used in these ordinances, they contain three principal types of restrictions. First, they define the kind of structure that may be erected on vacant land.[4]

---

4. As this Court recognized in *Euclid,* even residential apartments can have a negative impact on an area of single-family homes.

"[O]ften the apartment house is a mere parasite, constructed in order to take advantage of the open spaces and attractive surroundings created by [a single-family dwelling area]. . . . [T]he coming of one apartment house is followed by others, interfering by their height and bulk with the free circulation of air and monopolizing the rays of the

Second, they require that a single-family home be occupied only by a "single housekeeping unit." Third, they often require that the housekeeping unit be made up of persons related by blood, adoption, or marriage, with certain limited exceptions.

Although the legitimacy of the first two types of restrictions is well settled, attempts to limit occupancy to related persons have not been successful. The state courts have recognized a valid community interest in preserving the stable character of residential neighborhoods which justifies a prohibition against transient occupancy. Nevertheless, in well-reasoned opinions, the courts of [several states] have permitted unrelated persons to occupy single-family residences notwithstanding an ordinance prohibiting, either expressly or implicitly, such occupancy.

These cases delineate the extent to which the state courts have allowed zoning ordinances to interfere with the right of a property owner to determine the internal composition of his household. The intrusion on that basic property right has not previously gone beyond the point where the ordinance defines a family to include only persons related by blood, marriage, or adoption. Indeed, as the cases in the margin demonstrate, state courts have not always allowed the intrusion to penetrate that far. The state decisions have upheld zoning ordinances which regulated the identity, as opposed to the number, of persons who may compose a household only to the extent that the ordinances require such households to remain nontransient, single-housekeeping units.

There appears to be no precedent for an ordinance which excludes any of an owner's relatives from the group of persons who may occupy his residence on a permanent basis. Nor does there appear to be any justification for such a restriction on an owner's use of his property. The city has failed totally to explain the need for a rule which would allow a homeowner to have two grandchildren live with her if they are brothers, but not if they are cousins. Since this ordinance has not been shown to have any "substantial relation to the public health, safety, morals, or general welfare" of the city of East Cleveland, and since it cuts so deeply into a fundamental right normally associated with the ownership of residential property—that of an owner to decide who may reside on his or her property—it must fall under the limited standard of review of zoning decisions which this Court preserved in *Euclid* and *Nectow*. Under that standard, East Cleveland's unprecedented ordinance constitutes a taking of property without due process and without just compensation.

sun which otherwise would fall upon the smaller homes, and bringing, as their necessary accompaniments, the distributing noises incident to increased traffic and business, and the occupation, by means of moving and parked automobiles, of larger portions of the streets, thus detracting from their safety and depriving children of the privilege of quiet and open spaces for play, enjoyed by those in more favored localities,—until, finally, the residential character of the neighborhood and its desirability as a place of detached residences are utterly destroyed. Under these circumstances, apartment houses, which in a different environment would be not only entirely unobjectionable but highly desirable, come very near to being nuisances." 272 U.S., at 394–395.

For these reasons, I concur in the Court's judgment.

■ MR. CHIEF JUSTICE BURGER, with whom MR. JUSTICE STEWART and MR. JUSTICE WHITE join, dissenting.

* * *

". . . Courts are forced to add more clerks, more administrative personnel, to move cases faster and faster. They are losing . . . time for reflection, time for the deliberate maturation of principles." [Department of Justice Committee on Revision of The Federal Judicial System, Report on the Needs of the Federal Courts 3–4 (1977).]

■ MR. JUSTICE STEWART, with whom MR. JUSTICE REHNQUIST joins, dissenting.

* * *

The *Belle Terre* decision * * * disposes of the appellant's contentions to the extent they focus not on her blood relationships with her sons and grandsons but on more general notions about the "privacy of the home." Her suggestion that every person has a constitutional right permanently to share his residence with whomever he pleases, and that such choices are "beyond the province of legitimate governmental intrusion," amounts to the same argument that was made and found unpersuasive in *Belle Terre*.

To be sure, the ordinance involved in *Belle Terre* did not prevent blood relatives from occupying the same dwelling, and the Court's decision in that case does not, therefore, foreclose the appellant's arguments based specifically on the ties of kinship present in this case. Nonetheless, I would hold, for the reasons that follow, that the existence of those ties does not elevate either the appellant's claim of associational freedom or her claim of privacy to a level invoking constitutional protection.

* * *

The "association" in this case is not for any purpose relating to the promotion of speech, assembly, the press, or religion. And wherever the outer boundaries of constitutional protection of freedom of association may eventually turn out to be, they surely do not extend to those who assert no interest other than the gratification, convenience, and *economy* [emphasis added] of sharing the same residence.

* * *

The appellant also challenges the single-family occupancy ordinance on equal protection grounds. Her claim is that the city has drawn an arbitrary and irrational distinction between groups of people who may live together as a "family" and those who may not. While acknowledging the city's right to preclude more than one family from occupying a single-dwelling unit, the appellant argues that the purposes of the single-family occupancy law would be equally served by an ordinance that did not prevent her from sharing her residence with her two sons and their sons.

This argument misconceives the nature of the constitutional inquiry. In a case such as this one, where the challenged ordinance intrudes upon no substantively protected constitutional right, it is not the Court's business to decide whether its application in a particular case seems inequitable, or even absurd. The question is not whether some other ordinance, drafted more broadly, might have served the city's ends as well or almost as well. The task, rather, is to determine if East Cleveland's ordinance violates the Equal Protection Clause of the United States Constitution. And in performing that task, it must be borne in mind that "[w]e deal with economic and social legislation where legislatures have historically drawn lines which we respect against the charge of violation of the Equal Protection Clause if the law be ' "reasonable, not arbitrary" ' (quoting *Royster Guano Co. v. Virginia*, 253 U.S. 412, 415) and bears 'a rational relationship to a [permissible] state objective.' *Reed v. Reed, 404 U.S. 71, 76.*" *Village of Belle Terre v. Boraas*, 416 U.S., at 8. "[E]very line drawn by a legislature leaves some out that might well have been included. That exercise of discretion, however, is a legislative, not a judicial, function." *Ibid.* (footnote omitted).[8]

Viewed in the light of these principles, I do not think East Cleveland's definition of "family" offends the Constitution. The city has undisputed power to ordain single-family residential occupancy. *Village of Belle Terre v. Boraas, supra; Euclid v. Ambler Realty Co.*, 272 U.S. 365. And that power plainly carries with it the power to say what a "family" is. * * *

     * * *

For these reasons, I think the Ohio courts did not err in rejecting the appellant's constitutional claims. Accordingly, I respectfully dissent.

■ Mr. Justice White, dissenting.

The Fourteenth Amendment forbids any State to "deprive any person of life, liberty, or property, without due process of law," or to "deny to any person within its jurisdiction the equal protection of the laws." Both provisions are invoked in this case in an attempt to invalidate a city zoning ordinance.

I

The emphasis of the Due Process Clause is on "process." * * * As Mr. Justice Harlan once observed, it has been "ably and insistently argued in response to what were felt to be abuses by this Court of its reviewing power," that the Due Process Clause should be limited "to a guarantee of procedural fairness." *Poe v. Ullman*, 367 U.S. 497, 540 (1961) (dissenting

---

8. The observation of Mr. Justice Holmes quoted in the *Belle Terre* opinion, 416 U.S., at 8 n. 5, bears repeating here.

"When a legal distinction is determined, as no one doubts that it may be, between night and day, childhood and maturity, or any other extremes, a point has to be fixed or a line has to be drawn, or gradually picked out by successive decisions, to mark where the change takes place. Looked at by itself without regard to the necessity behind it the line or point seems arbitrary. It might as well or nearly as well be a little more to one side or the other. But when it is seen that a line or point there must be, and that there is no mathematical or logical way of fixing it precisely, the decision of the legislature must be accepted unless we can say that it is very wide of any reasonable mark." *Louisville Gas Co. v. Coleman*, 277 U.S. 32, 41 (dissenting opinion).

opinion). These arguments had seemed "persuasive" to Justices Brandeis and Holmes, *Whitney v. California*, 274 U.S. 357, 373 (1927), but they recognized that the Due Process Clause, by virtue of case-to-case "judicial inclusion and exclusion," *Davidson v. New Orleans*, 96 U.S. 97, 104 (1878), had been construed to proscribe matters of substance, as well as inadequate procedures, and to protect from invasion by the States "all fundamental rights comprised within the term liberty." *Whitney v. California*, supra, at 373.

* * *

Although the Court regularly proceeds on the assumption that the Due Process Clause has more than a procedural dimension, we must always bear in mind that the substantive content of the Clause is suggested neither by its language nor by preconstitutional history; that content is nothing more than the accumulated product of judicial interpretation of the Fifth and Fourteenth Amendments. This is not to suggest, at this point, that any of these cases should be overruled, or that the process by which they were decided was illegitimate or even unacceptable, but only to underline Mr. Justice Black's constant reminder to his colleagues that the Court has no license to invalidate legislation which it thinks merely arbitrary or unreasonable. And no one was more sensitive than Mr. Justice Harlan to any suggestion that his approach to the Due Process Clause would lead to judges "roaming at large in the constitutional field." *Griswold v. Connecticut, supra*, at 502. No one proceeded with more caution than he did when the validity of state or federal legislation was challenged in the name of the Due Process Clause.

* * *

* * * Here the head of the household may house himself or herself and spouse, their parents, and any number of their unmarried children. A fourth generation may be represented by only one set of grandchildren and then only if born to a dependent child. The ordinance challenged by appellant prevents her from living with both sets of grandchildren only in East Cleveland, an area with a radius of three miles and a population of 40,000. Brief for Appellee 16 n. 1. The ordinance thus denies appellant the opportunity to live with all her grandchildren in this particular suburb; she is free to do so in other parts of the Cleveland metropolitan area. If there is power to maintain the character of a single-family neighborhood, as there surely is, some limit must be placed on the reach of the "family." Had it been our task to legislate, we might have approached the problem in a different manner than did the drafters of this ordinance; but I have no trouble in concluding that the normal goals of zoning regulation are present here and that the ordinance serves these goals by limiting, in identifiable circumstances, the number of people who can occupy a single household. The ordinance does not violate the Due Process Clause.

IV

For very similar reasons, the equal protection claim must fail, since it is not to be judged by the strict scrutiny standard employed when a fundamental interest or suspect classification is involved[.] * * * Rather, it is the generally applicable standard of *McGowan v. Maryland*, 366 U.S. 420, 425 (1961):

> "The constitutional safeguard [of the Equal Protection Clause] is offended only if the classification rests on grounds wholly irrelevant to the achievement of the State's objective. State legislatures are presumed to have acted within their constitutional power despite the fact that, in practice, their laws result in some inequality. A statutory discrimination will not be set aside if any state of facts reasonably may be conceived to justify it."

* * * Under this standard, it is not fatal if the purpose of the law is not articulated on its face, and there need be only a rational relation to the ascertained purpose.

On this basis, as already indicated, I have no trouble in discerning a rational justification for an ordinance that permits the head of a household to house one, but not two, dependent sons and their children.

Respectfully, therefore, I dissent and would affirm the judgment.

NOTES AND QUESTIONS

1. Teachings of history and sanctity of family. What limits can one expect to impose on the murky concepts of substantive due process as applied to government regulation of family life? Justice Powell, writing for the Court, thought that the "appropriate limits on due process come not from drawing arbitrary lines but rather from careful respect for the 'teachings of history [and] solid recognition of the basic values that underlie our society.'" *Moore*, supra at ___. *See also* Snyder v. Massachusetts, 291 U.S. 97, 105 (1934); Griswold v. Connecticut, 381 U.S. 479, 501 (1965) (Harlan, J., concurring). Powell goes on to say that the Court's "decisions establish that the Constitution protects the sanctity of the family precisely because the institution of the family is deeply rooted in this Nation's history and tradition." *Moore, supra*, at 503.

Is there a cultural consensus about what the "teachings of history" are? Even if we could agree on the definition of the composition of the family, there remain important differences about the norms that should apply within the family system. Disputes about "family values" are a staple of divisive political campaigns today. Families certainly make intensely different decisions as to methods of discipline, breast feeding, intra-family privacy, individual space expectations, the sharing of bathrooms, young children's nakedness in the home, the appropriate age to begin dating, and the willingness of family to discuss biology and emotional components of human sexuality, just to name a few. *See* Gill Jagger & Caroline Wright, CHANGING FAMILY VALUES (eds., 1999).

Has Justice Powell assumed the existence of a stable, widely shared set of values about family in our very diverse society?

Is the model of deference to history likely to produce stagnant or dynamic approaches to constitutional interpretation of state restrictions on family preferences? What should be the role of the legal system in these intra-family debates? What is the role of economic analysis in Justice Powell's approach? What would Fran Olson's arguments about how the law should view the concepts of non-intervention, privacy, and the private/public distinction suggest about Powell's basis of reasoning (see chapter 6)?

2. **Extended family vs. nuclear family.** Justices Brennan and Marshall's concurrence focuses on the central role that the extended family has played for immigrant groups throughout American history, as well as African Americans today. The predominance of non-nuclear family structures in America, especially among ethnic and racial minority groups, suggests that the "extended family" pattern remains a vital tenet of our society. *See* ANDREW BILLINGSLEY, CLIMBING JACOB'S LADDER: THE ENDURING LEGACY OF AFRICAN-AMERICAN FAMILIES (1992); Ronald Angel & Marta Tienda, *Determinants of Extended Household Structure: Cultural Pattern or Economic Need?*, 87 AM. J. SOC. 1360 (1982). Under the reasoning in Brennan's concurrence, should associational forms which have been historically utilized by such populations in this country receive special protection?

If a minority group traditionally practiced polygamy in order to aid in pooling resources and to avoid the social problems associated with destitute widows and single motherhood, would Brennan's reasoning protect that group's definition of family? What about in the opposite case of polyandry? What about membership in a potentially criminal organization? *See* Linda Kelly, *Family Planning, American Style*, 52 ALA. L. REV. 943 (2001); Alison Harvison Young, *Reconceiving the Family: Challenging the Paradigm of the Exclusive Family*, 6 AM. U. J. GENDER & L. 505 (1998).

3. **Drawing the line.** What sociological theories are and could be employed by the Court to decide where to draw the line defining what is and is not a family? Are courts competent to make use of the often conflicting theories of social science research? Should people not related by blood have similar associational rights as the traditional family? *See* Smith v. Organization of Foster Families, 431 U.S. 816 (1977). What about unmarried parents? *See* Stanley v. Illinois, 405 U.S. 645 (1972). What about people engaging in casual sex? *See* FW/PBS, Inc. v. City of Dallas, 493 U.S. 215 (1990). How would economic theory shape this debate?

4. **Strict scrutiny, rational basis, and *Moore v. East Cleveland*.** At the time of *Moore v. East Cleveland*, Fourteenth Amendment Due Process analysis required that if a regulation excluded a suspect class of people, then that regulation must satisfy a "strict scrutiny" test. If the regulation did not discriminate against a suspect class, however, it needed only to pass a much more forgiving "rational basis" standard of review. Though the plurality opinion in *Moore* did not state that the ordinance in question should be subjected to strict scrutiny review, it does seem to be advocating more than a rational basis standard. Does *Moore* create another standard of review between strict scrutiny and rational relationship? If so, does the standard extend past the regulation of families? *See* Robert J. Hopperton,

The Presumption of Validity in American Land-Use Law: A Substitute for Analysis, A Source of Significant Confusion, 23 B.C. ENVTL. AFF. L. REV. 301 (1996).

5. Race, economics, and family definitions. Brennan and Marshall decry the "cultural myopia" of the plurality. In today's America, the "nuclear family" is the pattern so often found in much of white suburbia. The Constitution cannot be interpreted, however, to tolerate the imposition by government of white suburbia's preference in patterns of living. *See also* PEGGY COOPER DAVIS, NEGLECTED STORIES: THE CONSTITUTION AND FAMILY VALUES (1997); DOROTHY ROBERTS, KILLING THE BLACK BODIES (1998).

On the relevance of racial variation in patterns of family formation, the dissent of Justices Stewart and Rehnquist takes the opposite position than the plurality and concurring opinions:

> The opinion of MR. JUSTICE POWELL and MR. JUSTICE BRENNAN'S concurring opinion both emphasize the traditional importance of the extended family in American life. But I fail to understand why it follows that the residents of East Cleveland are constitutionally prevented from following what MR. JUSTICE BRENNAN calls the "pattern" of "white suburbia," even though that choice may reflect "cultural myopia." In point of fact, East Cleveland is a predominantly Negro community, with a Negro City Manager and City Commission.

Moore, supra at 537, n.7.

6. Additional reading. For an annotated catalog of cases and articles relating to the definition of "family" in zoning regulations and restrictive covenants, see James L. Rigelhaupt, Jr., *Annotation What Constitutes a "Family" Within Meaning of Zoning Regulation or Restrictive Covenant*, 71 A.L.R.3D 693 (2004). For a description of how housing codes can be used as tools for discrimination, see Ellen J. Pader, *CLUSTER VI: Class, Economics, and Social Rights: Space of Hate: Ethnicity, Architecture and Housing Discrimination*, 54 RUTGERS L. REV. 881 (2002). For an interesting proposal for defining family, see Angie Smolka, Note, *That's the Ticket: A New Way of Defining Family*, 10 CORNELL J. L. & PUB. POL'Y 629 (2001).

B. UNMARRIED HETEROSEXUAL COUPLES

Marvin v. Marvin

557 P.2d 106 (Cal. 1976).

◼ JUSTICE TOBRINER delivered the opinion of the court.

During the past 15 years, there has been a substantial increase in the number of couples living together without marrying. Such nonmarital relationships lead to legal controversy when one partner dies or the couple separates. Courts of Appeal, faced with the task of determining property rights in such cases, have arrived at conflicting positions: two cases * * * have held that the Family Law Act (Civ. Code, § 4000 et seq.) requires division of the property according to community property principles, and one decision * * * has rejected that holding. We take this opportunity to resolve that controversy and to declare the principles which should govern distribution of property acquired in a nonmarital relationship.

We conclude: (1) The provisions of the Family Law Act do not govern the distribution of property acquired during a nonmarital relationship; such a relationship remains subject solely to judicial decision. (2) The courts should enforce express contracts between nonmarital partners except to the extent that the contract is explicitly founded on the consideration of meretricious sexual services. (3) In the absence of an express contract, the courts should inquire into the conduct of the parties to determine whether that conduct demonstrates an implied contract, agreement of partnership or joint venture, or some other tacit understanding between the parties. The courts may also employ the doctrine of quantum meruit, or equitable remedies such as constructive or resulting trusts, when warranted by the facts of the case.

In the instant case plaintiff and defendant lived together for seven years without marrying; all property acquired during this period was taken in defendant's name. When plaintiff sued to enforce a contract under which she was entitled to half the property and to support payments, the trial court granted judgment on the pleadings for defendant, thus leaving him with all property accumulated by the couple during their relationship. Since the trial court denied plaintiff a trial on the merits of her claim, its decision conflicts with the principles stated above, and must be reversed.

1.   THE FACTUAL SETTING OF THIS APPEAL.

Since the trial court rendered judgment for defendant on the pleadings, we must accept the allegations of plaintiff's complaint as true, determining whether such allegations state, or can be amended to state, a cause of action. * * *

Plaintiff avers that in October of 1964 she and defendant "entered into an oral agreement" that while "the parties lived together they would combine their efforts and earnings and would share equally any and all property accumulated as a result of their efforts whether individual or combined." Furthermore, they agreed to "hold themselves out to the general public as husband and wife" and that "plaintiff would further render her services as a companion, homemaker, housekeeper and cook to ... defendant."

Shortly thereafter plaintiff agreed to "give up her lucrative career as an entertainer [and] singer" in order to "devote her full time to defendant ... as a companion, homemaker, housekeeper and cook;" in return defendant agreed to "provide for all of plaintiff's financial support and needs for the rest of her life."

Plaintiff alleges that she lived with defendant from October of 1964 through May of 1970 and fulfilled her obligations under the agreement.

During this period the parties as a result of their efforts and earnings acquired in defendant's name substantial real and personal property, including motion picture rights worth over $1 million. In May of 1970, however, defendant compelled plaintiff to leave his household. He continued to support plaintiff until November of 1971, but thereafter refused to provide further support.

On the basis of these allegations plaintiff asserts two causes of action. The first, for declaratory relief, asks the court to determine her contract and property rights; the second seeks to impose a constructive trust upon one half of the property acquired during the course of the relationship.

* * *

2. *PLAINTIFF'S COMPLAINT STATES A CAUSE OF ACTION FOR BREACH OF AN EXPRESS CONTRACT.*

* * * [W]e established the principle that nonmarital partners may lawfully contract concerning the ownership of property acquired during the relationship. * * * "If a man and woman [who are not married] live together as husband and wife under an agreement to pool their earnings and share equally in their joint accumulations, equity will protect the interests of each in such property."

In the case before us plaintiff, basing her cause of action in contract upon these precedents, maintains that the trial court erred in denying her a trial on the merits of her contention. Although that court did not specify the ground for its conclusion that plaintiff's contractual allegations stated no cause of action, defendant offers some four theories to sustain the ruling; we proceed to examine them.

Defendant first and principally relies on the contention that the alleged contract is so closely related to the supposed "immoral" character of the relationship between plaintiff and himself that the enforcement of the contract would violate public policy. He points to cases asserting that a contract between nonmarital partners is unenforceable if it is "involved in" an illicit relationship. * * * A review of the numerous California decisions concerning contracts between nonmarital partners, however, reveals that the courts have not employed such broad and uncertain standards to strike down contracts. The decisions instead disclose a narrower and more precise standard: a contract between nonmarital partners is unenforceable only *to the extent* that it *explicitly* rests upon the immoral and illicit consideration of meretricious sexual services.

In the first case to address this issue, *Trutalli v. Meraviglia* * * * the parties had lived together without marriage for 11 years and had raised two children. The man sued to quiet title to land he had purchased in his own name during this relationship; the woman defended by asserting an agreement to pool earnings and hold all property jointly. Rejecting the assertion of the illegality of the agreement, the court stated that "The fact that the parties to this action at the time they agreed to invest their earnings in property to be held jointly between them were living together in an unlawful relation, did not disqualify them from entering into a lawful agreement with each other, so long as such immoral relation was not made *a consideration* of their agreement." (Emphasis added.) * * *

In *Bridges v. Bridges, supra,* * * * both parties were in the process of obtaining divorces from their erstwhile respective spouses. The two parties agreed to live together, to share equally in property acquired, and to marry when their divorces became final. The man worked as a salesman and used his savings to purchase properties. The woman kept house, cared for seven children, three from each former marriage and one from the nonmarital relationship, and helped construct improvements on the properties. When they separated, without marrying, the court awarded the woman one-half the value of the property. Rejecting the man's contention that the contract was illegal, the court stated that: "Nowhere is it expressly testified to by anyone that there was anything in the agreement for the pooling of assets and the sharing of accumulations that contemplated meretricious relations as any part of the consideration or as any object of the agreement." * * *

* * * Numerous other cases have upheld enforcement of agreements between nonmarital partners in factual settings essentially indistinguishable from the present case.

* * * Although the past decisions hover over the issue in the somewhat wispy form of the figures of a Chagall painting, we can abstract from those decisions a clear and simple rule. The fact that a man and woman live together without marriage, and engage in a sexual relationship, does not in itself invalidate agreements between them relating to their earnings, property, or expenses. Neither is such an agreement invalid merely because the parties may have contemplated the creation or continuation of a nonmarital relationship when they entered into it. Agreements between nonmarital partners fail only to the extent that they rest upon a consideration of meretricious sexual services. Thus the rule asserted by defendant, that a contract fails if it is "involved in" or made "in contemplation" of a nonmarital relationship, cannot be reconciled with the decisions.

The three cases cited by defendant which have *declined* to enforce contracts between nonmarital partners involved consideration that *was* expressly founded upon an illicit sexual services. In *Hill v. Estate of Westbrook,* * * * the woman promised to keep house for the man, to live with him as man and wife, and to bear his children; the man promised to provide for her in his will, but died without doing so. Reversing a judgment for the woman based on the reasonable value of her services, the Court of Appeal stated that "the action is predicated upon a claim which seeks, among other things, the reasonable value of living with decedent in meretricious relationship and bearing him two children.... The law does not award compensation for living with a man as a concubine and bearing him children.... As the judgment is at least in part, for the value of the claimed services for which recovery cannot be had, it must be reversed." * * * Upon retrial, the trial court found that it could not sever the contract and place an independent value upon the legitimate services performed by claimant. We therefore affirmed a judgment for the estate. * * *

In the only other cited decision refusing to enforce a contract, * * * the contract "was based on the consideration that the parties live together as husband and wife." * * * Viewing the contract as calling for adultery, the court held it illegal.[6]

The decisions in the *Hill* and *Updeck* cases thus demonstrate that a contract between nonmarital partners, even if expressly made in contemplation of a common living arrangement, is invalid only if sexual acts form an inseparable part of the consideration for the agreement. In sum, a court will not enforce a contract for the pooling of property and earnings if it is explicitly and inseparably based upon services as a paramour. The Court of Appeal opinion in *Hill*, however, indicates that even if sexual services are part of the contractual consideration, any *severable* portion of the contract supported by independent consideration will still be enforced.

The principle that a contract between nonmarital partners will be enforced unless expressly and inseparably based upon an illicit consideration of sexual services not only represents the distillation of the decisional law, but also offers a far more precise and workable standard than that advocated by defendant.

* * * Similarly, in the present case a standard which inquires whether an agreement is "involved" in or "contemplates" a nonmarital relationship is vague and unworkable. Virtually all agreements between nonmarital partners can be said to be "involved" in some sense in the fact of their mutual sexual relationship, or to "contemplate" the existence of that relationship. Thus defendant's proposed standards, if taken literally, might invalidate all agreements between nonmarital partners, a result no one favors. Moreover, those standards offer no basis to distinguish between valid and invalid agreements. By looking not to such uncertain tests, but only to the consideration underlying the agreement, we provide the parties and the courts with a practical guide to determine when an agreement between nonmarital partners should be enforced.

* * * In summary, we base our opinion on the principle that adults who voluntarily live together and engage in sexual relations are nonetheless as competent as any other persons to contract respecting their earnings and property rights. Of course, they cannot lawfully contract to pay for the performance of sexual services, for such a contract is, in essence, an

---

6. Although not cited by defendant, the only California precedent which supports his position is *Heaps v. Toy* * * * In that case the woman promised to leave her job, to refrain from marriage, to be a companion to the man, and to make a permanent home for him; he agreed to support the woman and her child for life. The Court of Appeal held the agreement invalid as a contract in restraint of marriage (Civ. Code, § 1676) and, alternatively, as "contrary to good morals" (Civ. Code, § 1607). The opinion does not state that sexual relations formed any part of the consideration for the contract, nor explain how—unless the contract called for sexual relations—the woman's employment as a companion and housekeeper could be contrary to good morals.

The alternative holding in *Heaps v. Toy, supra,* finding the contract in that case contrary to good morals, is inconsistent with the numerous California decisions upholding contracts between nonmarital partners when such contracts are not founded upon an illicit consideration, and is therefore disapproved.

agreement for prostitution and unlawful for that reason. But they may agree to pool their earnings and to hold all property acquired during the relationship in accord with the law governing community property; conversely they may agree that each partner's earnings and the property acquired from those earnings remains the separate property of the earning partner.[10] So long as the agreement does not rest upon illicit meretricious consideration, the parties may order their economic affairs as they choose, and no policy precludes the courts from enforcing such agreements.

In the present instance, plaintiff alleges that the parties agreed to pool their earnings, that they contracted to share equally in all property acquired, and that defendant agreed to support plaintiff. The terms of the contract as alleged do not rest upon any unlawful consideration. We therefore conclude that the complaint furnishes a suitable basis upon which the trial court can render declaratory relief. * * * The trial court consequently erred in granting defendant's motion for judgment on the pleadings.

3.   * * *

As we have noted, both causes of action in plaintiff's complaint allege an express contract; neither assert any basis for relief independent from the contract. In *In re Marriage of Cary,* * * * however, the Court of Appeal held that, in view of the policy of the Family Law Act, property accumulated by nonmarital partners in an actual family relationship should be divided equally. Upon examining the *Cary* opinion, the parties to the present case realized that plaintiff's alleged relationship with defendant might arguably support a cause of action independent of any express contract between the parties. The parties have therefore briefed and discussed the issue of the property rights of a nonmarital partner in the absence of an express contract. Although our conclusion that plaintiff's complaint states a cause of action based on an express contract alone compels us to reverse the judgment for defendant, resolution of the *Cary* issue will serve both to guide the parties upon retrial and to resolve a conflict presently manifest in published Court of Appeal decisions.

Both plaintiff and defendant stand in broad agreement that the law should be fashioned to carry out the reasonable expectations of the parties. Plaintiff, however, presents the following contentions: that the decisions prior to *Cary* rest upon implicit and erroneous notions of punishing a party for his or her guilt in entering into a nonmarital relationship, that such decisions result in an inequitable distribution of property accumulated during the relationship, and that *Cary* correctly held that the enactment of the Family Law Act in 1970 overturned those prior decisions. Defendant in response maintains that the prior decisions merely applied common law principles of contract and property to persons who have deliberately elected

---

10. A great variety of other arrangements are possible. The parties might keep their earnings and property separate, but agree to compensate one party for services which benefit the other. They may choose to pool only part of their earnings and property, to form a partnership or joint venture, or to hold property acquired as joint tenants or tenants in common, or agree to any other such arrangement. * * *

to remain outside the bounds of the community property system.[11] *Cary*, defendant contends, erred in holding that the Family Law Act vitiated the force of the prior precedents.

* * * This failure of the courts to recognize an action by a nonmarital partner based upon implied contract, or to grant an equitable remedy, contrasts with the judicial treatment of the putative spouse. Prior to the enactment of the Family Law Act, no statute granted rights to a putative spouse.[13] The courts accordingly fashioned a variety of remedies by judicial decision. Some cases permitted the putative spouse to recover half the property on a theory that the conduct of the parties implied an agreement of partnership or joint venture. * * * Others permitted the spouse to recover the reasonable value of rendered services, less the value of support received. * * * Finally, decisions affirmed the power of a court to employ equitable principles to achieve a fair division of property acquired during putative marriage. * * *

Thus in summary, the cases prior to *Cary* exhibited a schizophrenic inconsistency. By enforcing an express contract between nonmarital partners unless it rested upon an unlawful consideration, the courts applied a common law principle as to contracts. Yet the courts disregarded the common law principle that holds that implied contracts can arise from the conduct of the parties.[16] Refusing to enforce such contracts, the courts spoke of leaving the parties "in the position in which they had placed themselves" * * * just as if they were guilty parties *in pari delicto*.

11. We note that a deliberate decision to avoid the strictures of the community property system is not the only reason that couples live together without marriage. Some couples may wish to avoid the permanent commitment that marriage implies, yet be willing to share equally any property acquired during the relationship; others may fear the loss of pension, welfare, or tax benefits resulting from marriage * * * Others may engage in the relationship as a possible prelude to marriage. In lower socio-economic groups the difficulty and expense of dissolving a former marriage often leads couples to choose a nonmarital relationship; many unmarried couples may also incorrectly believe that the doctrine of common law marriage prevails in California, and thus that they are in fact married. Consequently we conclude that the mere fact that a couple have not participated in a valid marriage ceremony cannot serve as a basis for a court's inference that the couple intend to keep their earnings and property separate and independent; the parties' intention can only be ascertained by a more searching inquiry into the nature of their relationship.

13. The Family Law Act, in Civil Code section 4452, classifies property acquired during a putative marriage as " 'quasi-marital property,' " and requires that such property be divided upon dissolution of the marriage in accord with Civil Code section 4800.

16. "Contracts may be express or implied. These terms however do not denote different kinds of contracts, but have reference to the evidence by which the agreement between the parties is shown. If the agreement is shown by the direct words of the parties, spoken or written, the contract is said to be an express one. But if such agreement can only be shown by the acts and conduct of the parties, interpreted in the light of the subject matter and of the surrounding circumstances, then the contract is an implied one." * * * Thus, as Justice Schauer observed in *Desny v. Wilder* * * * in a sense all contracts made in fact, as distinguished from quasi-contractual obligations, are express contracts, differing only in the manner in which the assent of the parties is expressed and proved. * * *

Justice Curtis noted this inconsistency in his dissenting opinion in *Vallera*, pointing out that "if an express agreement will be enforced, there is no legal or just reason why an implied agreement to share the property cannot be enforced." * * * And in *Keene v. Keene* * * * Justice Peters observed that if the man and woman "were not illegally living together . . . it would be a plain business relationship and a contract would be implied."

* * *

Still another inconsistency in the prior cases arises from their treatment of property accumulated through joint effort. To the extent that a partner had contributed *funds* or *property*, the cases held that the partner obtains a proportionate share in the acquisition, despite the lack of legal standing of the relationship. * * * Yet courts have refused to recognize just such an interest based upon the contribution of *services*. As Justice Curtis points out "Unless it can be argued that a woman's services as cook, housekeeper, and homemaker are valueless, it would seem logical that if, when she contributes money to the purchase of property, her interest will be protected, then when she contributes her services in the home, her interest in property accumulated should be protected." * * *

Thus as of 1973, the time of the filing of *In re Marriage of Cary* * * * the cases apparently held that a nonmarital partner who rendered services in the absence of express contract could assert no right to property acquired during the relationship. The facts of *Cary* demonstrated the unfairness of that rule.

Janet and Paul Cary had lived together, unmarried, for more than eight years. They held themselves out to friends and family as husband and wife, reared four children, purchased a home and other property, obtained credit, filed joint income tax returns, and otherwise conducted themselves as though they were married. Paul worked outside the home, and Janet generally cared for the house and children.

In 1971 Paul petitioned for "nullity of the marriage." Following a hearing on that petition, the trial court awarded Janet half the property acquired during the relationship, although all such property was traceable to Paul's earnings. The Court of Appeal affirmed the award.

Reviewing the prior decisions which had denied relief to the homemaking partner, the Court of Appeal reasoned that those decisions rested upon a policy of punishing persons guilty of cohabitation without marriage. The Family Law Act, the court observed, aimed to eliminate fault or guilt as a basis for dividing marital property. But once fault or guilt is excluded, the court reasoned, nothing distinguishes the property rights of a nonmarital "spouse" from those of a putative spouse. Since the latter is entitled to half the " 'quasi marital property' " (Civ. Code, § 4452), the Court of Appeal concluded that, giving effect to the policy of the Family Law Act, a nonmarital cohabitator should also be entitled to half the property accumulated during an "actual family relationship." * * *

* * *

* * * The argument that granting remedies to the nonmarital partners would discourage marriage must fail; as *Cary* pointed out, "with equal or greater force the point might be made that the pre–1970 rule was calculated to cause the income-producing partner to avoid marriage and thus retain the benefit of all of his or her accumulated earnings." * * * Although we recognize the well-established public policy to foster and promote the institution of marriage * * * perpetuation of judicial rules which result in an inequitable distribution of property accumulated during a nonmarital relationship is neither a just nor an effective way of carrying out that policy.

In summary, we believe that the prevalence of nonmarital relationships in modern society and the social acceptance of them, marks this as a time when our courts should by no means apply the doctrine of the unlawfulness of the so-called meretricious relationship to the instant case. As we have explained, the nonenforceability of agreements expressly providing for meretricious conduct rested upon the fact that such conduct, as the word suggests, pertained to and encompassed prostitution. To equate the nonmarital relationship of today to such a subject matter is to do violence to an accepted and wholly different practice.

We are aware that many young couples live together without the solemnization of marriage, in order to make sure that they can successfully later undertake marriage. This trial period, preliminary to marriage, serves as some assurance that the marriage will not subsequently end in dissolution to the harm of both parties. We are aware, as we have stated, of the pervasiveness of nonmarital relationships in other situations.

The mores of the society have indeed changed so radically in regard to cohabitation that we cannot impose a standard based on alleged moral considerations that have apparently been so widely abandoned by so many. Lest we be misunderstood, however, we take this occasion to point out that the structure of society itself largely depends upon the institution of marriage, and nothing we have said in this opinion should be taken to derogate from that institution. The joining of the man and woman in marriage is at once the most socially productive and individually fulfilling relationship that one can enjoy in the course of a lifetime.

We conclude that the judicial barriers that may stand in the way of a policy based upon the fulfillment of the reasonable expectations of the parties to a nonmarital relationship should be removed. As we have explained, the courts now hold that express agreements will be enforced unless they rest on an unlawful meretricious consideration. We add that in the absence of an express agreement, the courts may look to a variety of other remedies in order to protect the parties' lawful expectations.[24]

---

24. We do not seek to resurrect the doctrine of common law marriage, which was abolished in California by statute in 1895. * * * Thus we do not hold that plaintiff and defendant were "married," nor do we extend to plaintiff the rights which the Family Law Act grants valid or putative spouses; we hold only that she has the same rights to enforce contracts and to assert her equitable interest

The courts may inquire into the conduct of the parties to determine whether that conduct demonstrates an implied contract or implied agreement of partnership or joint venture * * * or some other tacit understanding between the parties. The courts may, when appropriate, employ principles of constructive trust * * * or resulting trust * * *. Finally, a nonmarital partner may recover in quantum meruit for the reasonable value of household services rendered less the reasonable value of support received if he can show that he rendered services with the expectation of monetary reward. * * *[25]

Since we have determined that plaintiff's complaint states a cause of action for breach of an express contract, and, as we have explained, can be amended to state a cause of action independent of allegations of express contract,[26] we must conclude that the trial court erred in granting defendant a judgment on the pleadings.

The judgment is reversed and the cause remanded for further proceedings consistent with the views expressed herein.[27]

■ Mr. Justice Clark, concurring in part and dissenting in part.

The majority opinion properly permit recovery on the basis of either express or implied in fact agreement between the parties. These being the issues presented, their resolution requires reversal of the judgment. Here, the opinion should stop.

This court should not attempt to determine all anticipated rights, duties and remedies within every meretricious relationship—particularly in vague terms. Rather, these complex issues should be determined as each arises in a concrete case.

* * *

The general sweep of the majority opinion raises but fails to answer several questions. First, because the Legislature specifically excluded some parties to a meretricious relationship from the equal division rule of Civil Code section 4452, is this court now free to create an equal division rule? Second, upon termination of the relationship, is it equitable to impose the economic obligations of lawful spouses on meretricious parties when the latter may have rejected matrimony to avoid such obligations? Third, does not application of equitable principles—necessitating examination of the conduct of the parties—violate the spirit of the Family Law Act of 1969, designed to eliminate the bitterness and acrimony resulting from the

in property acquired through her effort as does any other unmarried person.

25. Our opinion does not preclude the evolution of additional equitable remedies to protect the expectations of the parties to a nonmarital relationship in cases in which existing remedies prove inadequate; the suitability of such remedies may be determined in later cases in light of the factual setting in which they arise.

26. We do not pass upon the question whether, in the absence of an express or implied contractual obligation, a party to a nonmarital relationship is entitled to support payments from the other party after the relationship terminates.

27. We wish to commend the parties and amici for the exceptional quality of the briefs and argument in this case.

former fault system in divorce? Fourth, will not application of equitable principles reimpose upon trial courts the unmanageable burden of arbitrating domestic disputes? Fifth, will not a quantum meruit system of compensation for services—discounted by benefits received—place meretricious spouses in a better position than lawful spouses? Sixth, if a quantum meruit system is to be allowed, does fairness not require inclusion of all services and all benefits regardless of how difficult the evaluation?

When the parties to a meretricious relationship show by express or implied in fact agreement they intend to create mutual obligations, the courts should enforce the agreement. However, in the absence of agreement, we should stop and consider the ramifications before creating economic obligations which may violate legislative intent, contravene the intention of the parties, and surely generate undue burdens on our trial courts.

By judicial overreach, the majority perform a nunc pro tunc marriage, dissolve it, and distribute its property on terms never contemplated by the parties, case law or the Legislature.

NOTES AND QUESTIONS

1.   The choice to marry. Rational Choice Theory relies on the assumption that humans have goals and sets of hierarchically ordered preferences or "utilities." In making a choice between one behavior and another, humans will weigh the utility of the behavior against its costs, including the utility of alternate behaviors and the cost of selecting this behavior over another in terms of utility foregone. In an efficient transaction between two parties, the goal is presumably to increase utility for at least one party without sacrificing utility for either party. *See* Michael Allingham, Rational Choice (1999). How do the arguments of Rational Choice Theory apply to *Marvin v. Marvin*? What are the utilities and costs of opting not to marry and instead choosing to contract as the plaintiff in *Marvin* claims? Has utility been maximized in this transaction, given the foregone utility of the alternate behavior of marriage? *See* Margaret F. Brinig, *Unmarried Partners and the Legacy of* Marvin v. Marvin: *The Influence of* Marvin v. Marvin *on Housework during Marriage*, 76 Notre Dame L. Rev. 1311 (2001). Which sex is most likely to receive the primary benefit of the express and implied contract rules? *See* Debra S. Betteridge, Note, *Inequality in Marital Liabilities: The Need for Equal Protection When Modifying the Necessaries Doctrine*, 17 U. Mich. J.L. Reform 43 (1983). Are important differences in the transaction costs likely to arise from the enforcement of the express and implied contract theories?

2.   History and tradition? Is the court ignoring legal, cultural, and religious arguments in deciding that parties who are eligible to marry but who choose not to should not be given the economic benefits of marriage? Does the court disregard the "history and tradition" of rewarding compliance with the social and legal norms of marriage? *See* Carol Weisbrod,

Gender-Based Analyses of World Religions and the Law: Universals and Particulars: A Comment on Women's Human Rights and Religious Marriage Contracts, 9 S. CAL. REV. L. & WOMEN'S STUD. 77 (1999). What is the role of cultural change and what framework of analysis did this court rely upon to assess the relevance of these changes to its decision in this case? How do the rationales employed by the court in *Marvin* relate to those employed in *Moore v. East Cleveland*?

3. Bargaining. How would you expect the pre-cohabitation bargaining dynamic to be affected by this decision? How do differences in gender correspond to differences in bargaining power? *See* Elizabeth G. Anderson, *Women and Contracts: No New Deal*, 88 MICH L. REV. 1792 (1990). Is there any way for a couple to cohabit without automatically pooling their assets, short of writing an extremely unromantic contract explicitly separating their assets? *See* Jennifer K. Robbennolt & Monica Kirkpatrick Johnson, *Therapeutic Jurisprudence: Legal Planning for Unmarried Committed Partners: Empirical Lessons for a Preventive and Therapeutic Approach*, 41 ARIZ. L. REV. 417 (1999). How does the rule announced in *Marvin* affect the cultural and economic status of the parties? Furthermore, does this rule provide disincentives for parties who have a strong competitive position in the marriage market because of beauty, wealth, or social status to ever marry? *See* Amy L. Wax, *Bargaining in the Shadow of the Market: Is There a Future for Egalitarian Marriage?*, 84 VA. L. REV. 509 (1998).

4. Meretricious consideration and prostitution. The holding of *Marvin* is limited to the extent that it does not mandate the enforcement of contracts which are made expressly in consideration of sexual services. Given that the courts, as a rule, do not examine the adequacy of consideration, does the court's decision in *Marvin* open the door to legalized prostitution? If a prostitute were to say to a client, "Those pants don't look good on you, let's get them off," would that "fashion advice" qualify as separate consideration and thus render a contract between prostitute and client enforceable under *Marvin*? What is the implication of the court referring to the relationship of two unwed cohabitants as "meretricious," defined as "of, relating to, or befitting a prostitute; having the character of a prostitute" or "showily or superficially attractive but having in reality no value or integrity." OXFORD ENGLISH DICTIONARY (drafted. 2001), *available at* www.oed.com.

5. Common law marriage. From 1920 to 1930, Charlotte Fixel-Erlanger and Abraham Lincoln Erlanger lived together. Charlotte abandoned her career as an actress to support Abraham and take care of his house. Charlotte and Abraham never married and, when Abraham died in 1930, Charlotte was left out of his will. However, in 1932, after a three-month trial, Charlotte was given rights in Abraham's estate as his common-law wife. *In re Estate of Erlanger*, 145 Misc. 1, 259 N.Y.S. 610 (N.Y. Surr. Ct. 1932). Does *Marvin* do anything more than sanction adultery? Is *Marvin* the beginning of common-law polygamy?

6. Additional reading. For more information on the law of cohabitation, see generally Ariela R. Dubler, *Wifely Behavior: A Legal History of Acting*

Married, 100 COLUM. L. REV. 957 (2000); Katherine C. Gordon, Note, *The Necessity and Enforcement of Cohabitation Agreements: When Strings Will Attach and How to Prevent Them a State Survey*, 37 BRANDEIS L.J. 245 (1998/1999). For more information on associational rights and marriage, see generally Symposium, *Liberty and Marriage-Baehr and Beyond: Due Process in 1998*, 12 BYU J. PUB. L. 253 (1998); David A. Anderson, Note, *Jail, Jail, The Gang's All Here: Senate Crime Bill Section 521, The Criminal Street Gang Provision*, 36 B.C. L. REV. 527 (1995). For information on how *Marvin* extends to same sex couples, see Sharmila Roy Grossman, Comment, *The Illusory Rights of* Marvin v. Marvin *for the Same-Sex Couple versus the Preferable Canadian Alternative—M. v. H.*, 38 CAL. W. L. REV. 547 (2002).

C. SAME-SEX COUPLES

Whorton v. Dillingham

248 Cal. Rptr. 405 (Cal. Ct. App. 1988).

■ JUDGE WORK delivered the opinion of the court.

Donnis G. Whorton appeals a judgment dismissing his action against Benjamin F. Dillingham III after the court sustained a demurrer without leave to amend. Whorton claims property rights based on an oral cohabiters' agreement with which he fully complied but which Dillingham breached after approximately seven years. The trial court found the pleadings showed the contract was unenforceable as expressly and inseparably based on sexual services. We conclude Whorton has alleged consideration for the purported contract substantially independent of sexual services, and reverse the judgment.

I

On appeal from a judgment of dismissal arising from the sustaining of a demurrer, we accept the facts pleaded in the complaint as true. *(Noguera v. N. Monterey County Unified Sch. Dist.* (1980) 106 Cal. App. 3d 64, 66, 164 Cal. Rptr. 808.)

The alleged facts include the following. At the time the parties began dating and entered into a homosexual relationship, Whorton was studying to obtain his Associate in Arts degree, intending to enroll in a four-year college and obtain a Bachelor of Arts degree. When the parties began living together in 1977, they orally agreed that Whorton's exclusive, full-time occupation was to be Dillingham's chauffeur, bodyguard, social and business secretary, partner and counselor in real estate investments, and to appear on his behalf when requested. Whorton was to render labor, skills, and personal services for the benefit of Dillingham's business and investment endeavors. Additionally, Whorton was to be Dillingham's constant companion, confidant, traveling and social companion, and lover, to terminate his schooling upon obtaining his Associate in Arts degree, and to make no investment without first consulting Dillingham.

In consideration of Whorton's promises, Dillingham was to give him a one-half equity interest in all real estate acquired in their joint names, and in all property thereafter acquired by Dillingham. Dillingham agreed to financially support Whorton for life, and to open bank accounts, maintain a positive balance in those accounts, grant Whorton invasionary powers to savings accounts held in Dillingham's name, and permit Whorton to charge on Dillingham's personal accounts. Dillingham was also to engage in a homosexual relationship with Whorton. Importantly, for the purpose of our analysis, the parties specifically agreed that any portion of the agreement found to be legally unenforceable was severable and the balance of the provisions would remain in full force and effect.

Whorton allegedly complied with all terms of the oral agreement until 1984 when Dillingham barred him from his premises. Dillingham now refuses to perform his part of the contract by giving Whorton the promised consideration for the business services rendered.

II

Adults who voluntarily live together and engage in sexual relations are competent to contract respecting their earnings and property rights. Such contracts will be enforced "unless expressly and inseparably based upon an illicit consideration of sexual services...." *(Marvin v. Marvin* (1976) 18 Cal. 3d 660, 672 [134 Cal. Rptr. 815, 557 P.2d 106].) One cannot lawfully contract to pay for the performance of sexual services since such an agreement is in essence a bargain for prostitution. *(Id.* at p. 674, 134 Cal. Rptr. 815, 557 P.2d 106.)

A standard which inquires whether an agreement involves or contemplates a sexual relationship is vague and unworkable because virtually all agreements between nonmarital (and certainly, marital) cohabiters involve or contemplate a mutual sexual relationship. Further, a compact is not totally invalid merely because the parties may have contemplated creating or continuing a sexual relationship, but is invalid only to the extent it rests upon a consideration of sexual services. *(Id.* at pp. 670–671, 134 Cal. Rptr. 815, 557 P.2d 106.) Thus, "even if sexual services are part of the contractual consideration, any *severable* portion of the contract supported by independent consideration will still be enforced." *(Id.* at p. 672, 134 Cal. Rptr. 815, 557 P.2d 106.) For instance, contracting parties may make a variety of arrangements regarding their property rights—i.e., agree to pool their earnings and to hold all property in accord with the law governing community property, or to treat monetary earnings and property as separate property of the earning partner, or to keep property separate but compensate one party for services which benefit the other, or to pool only a part of their earnings and property, etc. *(Id.* at p. 674, fn. 10, 134 Cal. Rptr. 815, 557 P.2d 106.) "So long as the agreement does not rest upon illicit meretricious consideration, the parties may order their economic affairs as they choose, and no policy precludes the courts from enforcing such agreements." (*Id.* at p. 674, 134 Cal. Rptr. 815, 557 P.2d 106.)

Regarding the issue of what constitutes adequate consideration, *Marvin* notes "[a] promise to perform homemaking services is, of course, a lawful and adequate consideration for a contract...." (*Id.* at p. 670, fn. 5, 134 Cal. Rptr. 815, 557 P.2d 106.) *Marvin* expressly rejects the argument that the partner seeking to enforce the contract must have contributed either property or services additional to ordinary homemaking services. (*Ibid.*)

In *Marvin*, the plaintiff alleged the parties orally agreed that while they lived together they would combine their efforts and earnings and would share equally all property accumulated as a result of their efforts, that they would hold themselves out to the general public as husband and wife, that plaintiff would render services as companion, homemaker, housekeeper and cook, that plaintiff would give up her career in order to provide these services full-time, and that in return defendant would provide for all of plaintiff's financial support for the rest of her life. (*Id.* at p. 666.) The court stated:

> "... plaintiff alleges that the parties agreed to pool their earnings, that they contracted to share equally in all property acquired, and that defendant agreed to support plaintiff. The terms of the contract as alleged do not rest upon any unlawful consideration." (*Id.* at pp. 674–675, 134 Cal. Rptr. 815, 557 P.2d 106.)

The holding in *Marvin* suggests the court determined that the contract before it did not *expressly* include sexual services as part of the consideration, and thus, it did not need to reach the issue of whether there were severable portions of the contract supported by independent consideration. The only reference to sexual services in *Marvin's* alleged facts was that the parties agreed to hold themselves out to the public as husband and wife, which apparently the court did not interpret as expressly indicating sexual services were part of the consideration. (See *Alderson v. Alderson* (1986) 180 Cal. App. 3d 450, 462–464, 225 Cal. Rptr. 610 [even though couple engaged in sexual relations and plaintiff perceived this as part of her "role," no evidence that implied agreement between the parties explicitly rested upon a consideration of meretricious sexual services].)

III

Unlike the facts of *Marvin*, here the parties' sexual relationship was an express, rather than implied, part of the consideration for their contract. The contract cannot be enforced to the extent it is dependent on sexual services for consideration, and the complaint does not state a cause of action to the extent it asks for damages from the termination of the sexual relationship.

The issue here is whether the sexual component of the consideration is severable from the remaining portions of the contract.[1] We reiterate the

---

1. Dillingham does not assert *Marvin* is inapplicable to same-sex partners, and we see no legal basis to make a distinction.

guiding language of *Marvin v. Marvin, supra,* 18 Cal. 3d at page 672, 134 Cal. Rptr. 815, 557 P.2d 106 "[E]ven if sexual services are part of the contractual consideration, any *severable* portion of the contract supported by independent consideration will still be enforced." One test for determining the enforceability of a contract having both lawful and unlawful factors for consideration is stated in the Restatement Second of Contracts, section 183, "If the parties' performances can be apportioned into corresponding pairs of part performances so that the parts of each pair are properly regarded as agreed equivalents and one pair is not offensive to public policy, that portion of the agreement is enforceable by a party who did not engage in serious misconduct." (See also Civ. Code, § 1599: "Where a contract has several distinct objects, of which one at least is lawful, and one at least is unlawful, in whole or in part, the contract is void as to the latter and valid as to the rest.")

Tyranski v. Piggins (1973) 44 Mich. App. 570, 205 N.W.2d 595, 596–597, evaluates the issue of severability as follows:

"Professor Corbin and the drafters of the Restatement of Contracts both write that while bargains in whole or in part in consideration of an illicit relationship are unenforceable, agreements between parties to such a relationship with respect to money or property will be enforced if the agreement is independent of the illicit relationship.

"Neither these authorities nor the large body of case law in other jurisdictions ... articulate a guideline for determining when the consideration will be regarded as 'independent' and when it is so coupled with the meretricious acts that the agreement will not be enforced. A pattern does, however, emerge upon reading the cases.

"Neither party to a meretricious relationship acquires, by reason of cohabitation alone, rights in the property accumulations of the other during the period of the relationship. But where there is an express agreement to accumulate or transfer property following a relationship of some permanence and *an additional consideration in the form of either money or of services, the courts tend to find an independent consideration.*

"Thus, a plaintiff who can show an actual contribution of money, pursuant to an agreement to pool assets and share accumulations, will usually prevail. Services, such as cooking meals, laundering clothes, 'caring' for the decedent through sickness, have been found to be adequate and independent considerations in cases where there was an express agreement." (Fns. omitted; italics added.)[2]

---

2. In *Tyranski v. Piggins, supra,* 205 N.W.2d at pages 596–597, the plaintiff cleaned the house, did the marketing, cooked the food, did the decedent's personal laundry, acted as his hostess, cared for him when he was sick, and contributed money towards the purchase of a house in which the unmarried plaintiff and the decedent resided. The court held it was proper to enforce the parties' express agreement to convey the house, which was held in the name of the decedent, to the plaintiff.

Of particular significance is the decision in *Latham v. Latham* (1976) 274 Ore. 421, 547 P.2d 144. In *Latham*, the court overruled a demurrer where complainant pleaded an agreement to live with defendant, to care for, and to furnish him with all the amenities of married life. The court recognized the alleged agreement specifically included the sexual services implicit in cohabitation. (*Id*. 547 P.2d at p. 145.) Thus, as here, the sexual aspect of the agreement appeared on the face of the complaint. In overruling a demurrer based on public policy, the court stated it was not validating an agreement in which sexual intercourse was the only or primary consideration, but only one of the factors incident to the burdens and amenities of married life. (*Id*. 547 P.2d at p. 147.)

Thus, the crux of our analysis is whether Whorton's complaint negates as a matter of law, a trier of fact finding he made contributions, apart from sexual services, which provided independent consideration for Dillingham's alleged promises pertaining to financial support and property rights. The services which plaintiff alleges he agreed to and did provide included being a chauffeur, bodyguard, secretary, and partner and counselor in real estate investments. If provided, these services are of monetary value, and the type for which one would expect to be compensated unless there is evidence of a contrary intent. Thus, they are properly characterized as consideration independent of the sexual aspect of the relationship. By way of comparison, such services as being a constant companion and confidant are not the type which are usually monetarily compensated nor considered to have a "value" for purposes of contract consideration, and, absent peculiar circumstances, would likely be considered so intertwined with the sexual relationship as to be inseparable. (Cf. *Walters v. Calderon* (1972) 25 Cal. App. 3d 863, 873, 102 Cal. Rptr. 89 [love and affection do not constitute valuable consideration necessary to support validity of contractual promise].)

We hold that Whorton—based on allegations he provided Dillingham with services of a chauffeur, bodyguard, secretary, and business partner—has stated a cause of action arising from a contract supported by consideration independent of sexual services. Further, by itemizing the mutual promises to engage in sexual activity, Whorton has not precluded the trier of fact from finding those promises are the consideration for each other and independent of the bargained for consideration for Whorton's employment.

We believe our holding does not conflict with that in *Jones v. Daly* (1981) 122 Cal. App. 3d 500, 508, 176 Cal. Rptr. 130, where services provided by the complaining homosexual partner were limited to "lover, companion, homemaker, traveling companion, housekeeper and cook...." The court there found the pleadings unequivocally established that plaintiff's rendition of sex and other services naturally flowing from sexual cohabitation was an inseparable part of the consideration for the so-called cohabitor's agreement. The court stated:

"According to the allegations of the complaint, the agreement provided that the parties would share equally the earnings and property accumulated as a result of their efforts while they lived together and that Daly would support plaintiff for the rest of his life. *Neither the property sharing nor the support provision of the agreement rests upon plaintiff's acting as Daly's traveling companion, housekeeper or cook as distinguished from acting as his lover. The latter service forms an inseparable part of the consideration for the agreement and renders it unenforceable in its entirety.*" (*Jones v. Daly, supra,* 122 Cal. App. 3d at p. 509, 176 Cal. Rptr. 130 italics added.)

Jones is factually different in that the complaining party did not allege contracting to provide services apart from those normally incident to the state of cohabitation itself. Further, Jones's complaint stated the agreement was premised on that they "would hold themselves out to the public at large as cohabiting mates...." (*Id.* at p. 505, 176 Cal. Rptr. 130.) In contrast, Whorton's complaint separately itemizes services contracted for as companion, chauffeur, bodyguard, secretary, partner and business counselor. These, except for companion, are significantly different than those household duties normally attendant to nonbusiness cohabitation and are those for which monetary compensation ordinarily would be anticipated.[5] Accepting Whorton's allegations as true, we cannot say as a matter of law any illegal portion of the contract is not severable so as to leave the balance valid and enforceable, especially where it is alleged the parties contemplated such a result when entering into their agreement.

IV

Statute of frauds

Dillingham asserts the oral agreement is invalid under the statute of frauds, requiring agreements not to be performed within one year or for the sale of an interest in real property to be written. (Civ. Code, § 1624, subds. (a) and (c).) In *Marvin v. Marvin, supra,* 18 Cal. 3d at page 674, footnote 10, 134 Cal. Rptr. 815, 557 P.2d 106, the court noted in cases involving agreements between nonmarital partners, the majority of the agreements were oral and the courts have expressly rejected defenses grounded upon the statute of frauds.

Marvin cites *Cline v. Festersen* (1954) 128 Cal. App. 2d 380, 386, 275 P.2d 149. In *Cline,* the court rejected a statute of frauds argument on the basis of estoppel, reasoning that the nonmarital partner seeking to obtain her promised share of the property had trusted and worked for many years in reliance on the promise, and her partner had never repudiated the agreement. *Cline* relies on the principle that the doctrine of estoppel to assert the statute of frauds should be applied to prevent fraud and unconscionable injury that would result from refusal to enforce oral contracts in certain circumstances—i.e., after one party has been induced by the other seriously to change position in reliance on the contract, or when

---

5. Most of the numerous cases cited in *Marvin* where nonmarital cohabiters' oral agreements to pool earnings were upheld involved contributions other than normal homemaking services. However, *Marvin* states homemaking services alone are lawful consideration. (*Marvin v. Marvin,* supra, 18 Cal. 3d, p. 670, fn. 5; see also *Watkins v. Watkins* (1983) 143 Cal. App. 3d 651, 655, 192 Cal. Rptr. 54.)

unjust enrichment would result if a party who has received the benefits of the other's performance were allowed to rely upon the statute. (*Id.* at p. 387, 275 P.2d 149.)

Whorton alleges he stopped his education earlier than planned to assist Dillingham in his business ventures in exchange for promises of support and sharing of accumulated property. These facts are sufficient to estop Dillingham from raising the statute of frauds by way of demurrer to bar enforcement of the contract.

Statute of limitations

Dillingham meritlessly asserts the action is barred by the statute of limitations.

The general rule is that a cause of action for breach of contract accrues at the time of breach. (See 3 Witkin, Cal. Procedure (3d ed. 1985) Actions, § 375, p. 402.) A *Marvin*-type contract is breached when one partner terminates the relationship. (*Estate of Fincher* (1981) 119 Cal. App. 3d 343, 352, 174 Cal. Rptr. 18.) The statute of limitations for an action upon a contract not founded on a writing is two years. (Code Civ. Proc., § 339, subd. 1.) The complaint states the breach occurred "on or about the latter part of 1984." The complaint was filed in June 1986. The complaint on its face does not show the contract cause of action is barred by the statute of limitations.

For the same reasons, the complaint on its face does not show the three-year fraud limitation has expired.[6]

Additionally, a cause of action based on equitable grounds is not barred, for which the statute of limitations is four years. (*Nelson v. Nevel* (1984) 154 Cal. App. 3d 132, 140–141, 201 Cal. Rptr. 93; Code Civ. Proc., § 343; see generally *Marvin v. Marvin*, supra, 18 Cal. 3d at p. 684, fn. 25, 134 Cal. Rptr. 815, 557 P. 2d 106.)

Terminable at will

Finally, Dillingham contends that under *Labor Code section 2922*, the contract was terminable at will.[7] That section has no applicability to the issues here. This case does not involve an employment contract within the purview of the Labor Code, but rather a cohabiters' agreement regarding how two nonmarital partners have agreed to regulate their economic affairs. Of course, one partner has a right to end the relationship, and the only issue is whether the facts support a monetary and/or property award to one of the partners.

* * *

6. The caption of the complaint does not refer to fraud, stating: "Complaint for damages for breach of express oral contract; breach of implied in fact contract; to impress a constructive trust; for declaratory relief; and for injunctive relief." However, the body of the complaint states facts in support of, and refers to, a fraud cause of action.

7. Labor Code section 2922 states: "An employment, having no specified term, may be terminated at the will of either party on notice to the other. Employment for a specified term means an employment for a period greater than one month."

Domestic Partner Ordinance Quashed: Atlanta to Appeal in Second Defeat

ATLANTA J. & CONST., Jan. 1, 1997 at D2.

■ BILL RANKIN

A Fulton County judge Tuesday struck down Atlanta's domestic partnership ordinance, the second try by the city to extend insurance benefits to live-in partners of city employees.

The city is attempting "to incorporate a 'family relationship' it has created, domestic partners, into the definition of a dependent," Superior Court Judge Isaac Jenrette said. This "is now inconsistent with state law."

The city will appeal the ruling, said Nick Gold, spokesman for Mayor Bill Campbell. Six city employees have signed up for the domestic partnership benefits, he said.

"Georgia law is clear—no matter how the city manipulates the language of its ordinance, domestic partners are neither 'family' nor 'dependents,'" said Atlanta lawyer David Reed, who argued the case for the conservative Southeastern Legal Foundation. "The taxpayers and families of Georgia have had enough of this nonsense."

Foundation lawyers have said the ordinance was an unconstitutional attempt by the city to encourage homosexuality and was a waste of taxpayers' money.

The foundation filed the lawsuit Sept. 10, the same day the U.S. Senate approved a bill denying recognition of same-sex marriages. The lawsuit challenged an ordinance passed by the City Council to authorize insurance benefits to the unmarried, live-in partners of city employees.

The new provision is a revised version of a 1993 city ordinance granting benefits for domestic partners. The Georgia Supreme Court struck down that ordinance in 1995, saying the city "exceeded its power ... by recognizing domestic partners as 'a family relationship.'" The court noted that the state uses several definitions for "dependents" when allowing insurance benefits and "domestic partners do not meet any of these statutory definitions."

On Tuesday, Jenrette said the city's new ordinance is fatally flawed for the same reasons.

Teresa Nelson, executive director of the Georgia chapter of the American Civil Liberties Union, expressed disappointment at the ruling.

"There are a number of individuals who have no dependents who are city employees, and they have shared the burden for the coverage of those employees who have dependents," Nelson said. "For those who are in partnership relationships, whether they are heterosexual or homosexual, their dependents have been denied that coverage. The city's ordinance is not a statement of morality. It is a statement of equality."

But Matthew Glavin, president of the Southeast Legal Foundation, said the City Council should realize this is not something it has the authority to do.

"If the City Council or the mayor want this kind of ordinance, they should march up the street to the state Legislature and convince it to change the law to include domestic partners," he said. "Unless they do that, anything they do will be unconstitutional, and we will stop them at every attempt."

———

NOTES AND QUESTIONS

1. Limits of consideration for homosexual couples. The Court in this case held that "Whorton—based on allegations he provided Dillingham with services of a chauffeur, bodyguard, secretary, and business partner— has stated a cause of action arising from a contract supported by consideration independent of sexual services." Of course, none of those services were provided in *Marvin*, though the services that were provided in *Marvin*—keeping house, functioning as a companion, etc. were also present in *Whorton*. Why, then, would the court choose to focus on these tasks to find consideration, and what are the implications of that decision? *See, e.g.*, Jones v. Daly, 176 Cal. Rptr. 130 (Cal. App. 1981).

2. Impact of *Whorton v. Dillingham*. Is *Whorton* a victory for homosexual rights? After all, the case is specifically premised on the idea of an express contract being enforced even though it was partially based on sexual consideration. Since this holding is completely orientation-neutral, why should *Whorton v. Dillingham* be considered significant? If it is a victory, how far does it extend? *See* Sharmila Roy Grossman, Comment, *The Illusory Rights of* Marvin v. Marvin *for the Same-Sex Couple Versus the Preferable Canadian Alternative*—M. v. H., 38 Cal. W. L. Rev. 547, 557 (2002). If homosexual couples are allowed to enter valid marriages in the state in which they reside, does the *Marvin v. Marvin* rationale apply?

3. Additional reading. For additional information on domestic partner ordinances, see generally, Jonathan Andrew Hein, *Caring for the Evolving American Family: Cohabiting Partners and Employer Sponsored Health Care*, 30 N.M. L. Rev. 19 (2000); Debbie Zielinski, Note, *Domestic Partnership Benefits: Why not Offer Them to Same-Sex Partners and Unmarried Opposite Sex Partners*, 13 J.L. & Health 281 (1998–99); William V. Vetter, *Restrictions on Equal Treatment of Unmarried Domestic Partners*, 5 B.U. Pub. Int. L.J. 1 (1995).

D. Sex Between Consenting Adults

Lawrence v. Texas

Supreme Court of the United States, 539 U.S. 558 (2003).

■ Justice Kennedy delivered the opinion of the Court.

Liberty protects the person from unwarranted government intrusions into a dwelling or other private places. In our tradition the State is not omnipresent in the home. And there are other spheres of our lives and existence, outside the home, where the State should not be a dominant presence. Freedom extends beyond spatial bounds. Liberty presumes an autonomy of self that includes freedom of thought, belief, expression, and certain intimate conduct. The instant case involves liberty of the person both in its spatial and more transcendent dimensions.

I

The question before the Court is the validity of a Texas statute making it a crime for two persons of the same sex to engage in certain intimate sexual conduct.

In Houston, Texas, officers of the Harris County Police Department were dispatched to a private residence in response to a reported weapons disturbance. They entered an apartment where one of the petitioners, John Geddes Lawrence, resided. The right of the police to enter does not seem to have been questioned. The officers observed Lawrence and another man, Tyron Garner, engaging in a sexual act. The two petitioners were arrested, held in custody over night, and charged and convicted before a Justice of the Peace * * * [of] "deviate sexual intercourse, namely anal sex, with a member of the same sex (man)." App. to Pet. for Cert. 127a, 139a. The applicable state law is Tex. Penal Code Ann. § 21.06(a) (2003). It provides: "A person commits an offense if he engages in deviate sexual intercourse with another individual of the same sex." * * *

* * *

We granted certiorari, 537 U.S. 1044 (2002), to consider three questions:

"1. Whether Petitioners' criminal convictions under the Texas 'Homosexual Conduct' law—which criminalizes sexual intimacy by same-sex couples, but not identical behavior by different-sex couples—violate the Fourteenth Amendment guarantee of equal protection of laws?

"2. Whether Petitioners' criminal convictions for adult consensual sexual intimacy in the home violate their vital interests in liberty and privacy protected by the Due Process Clause of the Fourteenth Amendment?

"3. Whether Bowers v. Hardwick, 478 U.S. 186 (1986), should be overruled?" Pet. for Cert. i.

* * *

II

We conclude the case should be resolved by determining whether the petitioners were free as adults to engage in the private conduct in the exercise of their liberty under the Due Process Clause of the Fourteenth Amendment to the Constitution. For this inquiry we deem it necessary to reconsider the Court's holding in *Bowers*.

There are broad statements of the substantive reach of liberty under the Due Process Clause in earlier cases, * * * but the most pertinent beginning point is our decision in *Griswold v. Connecticut*, 381 U.S. 479 (1965).

In *Griswold* the Court invalidated a state law prohibiting the use of drugs or devices of contraception and counseling or aiding and abetting the use of contraceptives. The Court described the protected interest as a right to privacy and placed emphasis on the marriage relation and the protected space of the marital bedroom. *Id.*, at 485.

After *Griswold* it was established that the right to make certain decisions regarding sexual conduct extends beyond the marital relationship. In *Eisenstadt v. Baird*, 405 U.S. 438 (1972), the Court invalidated a law prohibiting the distribution of contraceptives to unmarried persons. The case was decided under the Equal Protection Clause, *id.*, at 454; but with respect to unmarried persons, the Court went on to state the fundamental proposition that the law impaired the exercise of their personal rights, *ibid.* It quoted from the statement of the Court of Appeals finding the law to be in conflict with fundamental human rights, and it followed with this statement of its own:

> "It is true that in *Griswold* the right of privacy in question inhered in the marital relationship. . . . If the right of privacy means anything, it is the right of the *individual*, married or single, to be free from unwarranted governmental intrusion into matters so fundamentally affecting a person as the decision whether to bear or beget a child." *Id.*, at 453.

The opinions in *Griswold* and *Eisenstadt* were part of the background for the decision in *Roe v. Wade*, 410 U.S. 113 (1973). As is well known, the case involved a challenge to the Texas law prohibiting abortions, but the laws of other States were affected as well. Although the Court held the woman's rights were not absolute, her right to elect an abortion did have real and substantial protection as an exercise of her liberty under the Due Process Clause. The Court cited cases that protect spatial freedom and cases that go well beyond it. *Roe* recognized the right of a woman to make certain fundamental decisions affecting her destiny and confirmed once more that the protection of liberty under the Due Process Clause has a substantive dimension of fundamental significance in defining the rights of the person.

In *Carey v. Population Services Int'l*, 431 U.S. 678 (1977), the Court confronted a New York law forbidding sale or distribution of contraceptive devices to persons under 16 years of age. Although there was no single opinion for the Court, the law was invalidated. Both *Eisenstadt* and *Carey*, as well as the holding and rationale in *Roe*, confirmed that the reasoning of *Griswold* could not be confined to the protection of rights of married adults. This was the state of the law with respect to some of the most relevant cases when the Court considered *Bowers* v. *Hardwick*.

The facts in *Bowers* had some similarities to the instant case. A police officer, whose right to enter seems not to have been in question, observed Hardwick, in his own bedroom, engaging in intimate sexual conduct with another adult male. The conduct was in violation of a Georgia statute making it a criminal offense to engage in sodomy. One difference between the two cases is that the Georgia statute prohibited the conduct whether or not the participants were of the same sex, while the Texas statute, as we have seen, applies only to participants of the same sex. Hardwick was not prosecuted, but he brought an action in federal court to declare the state statute invalid. He alleged he was a practicing homosexual and that the criminal prohibition violated rights guaranteed to him by the Constitution. The Court, in an opinion by Justice White, sustained the Georgia law. * * *

The Court began its substantive discussion in *Bowers* as follows: "The issue presented is whether the Federal Constitution confers a fundamental right upon homosexuals to engage in sodomy and hence invalidates the laws of the many States that still make such conduct illegal and have done so for a very long time." *Id.*, at 190. That statement, we now conclude, discloses the Court's own failure to appreciate the extent of the liberty at stake. To say that the issue in *Bowers* was simply the right to engage in certain sexual conduct demeans the claim the individual put forward, just as it would demean a married couple were it to be said marriage is simply about the right to have sexual intercourse. The laws involved in *Bowers* and here are, to be sure, statutes that purport to do no more than prohibit a particular sexual act. Their penalties and purposes, though, have more far-reaching consequences, touching upon the most private human conduct, sexual behavior, and in the most private of places, the home. The statutes do seek to control a personal relationship that, whether or not entitled to formal recognition in the law, is within the liberty of persons to choose without being punished as criminals.

This, as a general rule, should counsel against attempts by the State, or a court, to define the meaning of the relationship or to set its boundaries absent injury to a person or abuse of an institution the law protects. It suffices for us to acknowledge that adults may choose to enter upon this relationship in the confines of their homes and their own private lives and still retain their dignity as free persons. When sexuality finds overt expression in intimate conduct with another person, the conduct can be but one element in a personal bond that is more enduring. The liberty protected by the Constitution allows homosexual persons the right to make this choice.

Having misapprehended the claim of liberty there presented to it, and thus stating the claim to be whether there is a fundamental right to engage in consensual sodomy, the *Bowers* Court said: "Proscriptions against that conduct have ancient roots." *Id.*, at 192. In academic writings, and in many of the scholarly *amicus* briefs filed to assist the Court in this case, there are fundamental criticisms of the historical premises relied upon by the majority and concurring opinions in *Bowers*. * * * We need not enter this debate in the attempt to reach a definitive historical judgment, but the following

considerations counsel against adopting the definitive conclusions upon which *Bowers* placed such reliance.

At the outset it should be noted that there is no longstanding history in this country of laws directed at homosexual conduct as a distinct matter. Beginning in colonial times there were prohibitions of sodomy derived from the English criminal laws passed in the first instance by the Reformation Parliament of 1533. The English prohibition was understood to include relations between men and women as well as relations between men and men. See, *e.g., King v. Wiseman*, 92 Eng. Rep. 774, 775 (K. B. 1718) (interpreting "mankind" in Act of 1533 as including women and girls). Nineteenth-century commentators similarly read American sodomy, buggery, and crime-against-nature statutes as criminalizing certain relations between men and women and between men and men. See, *e.g.*, 2 J. Bishop, Criminal Law § 1028 (1858); 2 J. Chitty, Criminal Law 47–50 (5th Am. ed. 1847); R. Desty, A Compendium of American Criminal Law 143 (1882); J. May, The Law of Crimes § 203 (2d ed. 1893). The absence of legal prohibitions focusing on homosexual conduct may be explained in part by noting that according to some scholars the concept of the homosexual as a distinct category of person did not emerge until the late 19th century. See, *e.g.*, J. Katz, The Invention of Heterosexuality 10 (1995); J. D'Emilio & E. Freedman, Intimate Matters: A History of Sexuality in America 121 (2d ed. 1997) ("The modern terms *homosexuality* and *heterosexuality* do not apply to an era that had not yet articulated these distinctions"). Thus early American sodomy laws were not directed at homosexuals as such but instead sought to prohibit nonprocreative sexual activity more generally. This does not suggest approval of homosexual conduct. It does tend to show that this particular form of conduct was not thought of as a separate category from like conduct between heterosexual persons.

Laws prohibiting sodomy do not seem to have been enforced against consenting adults acting in private. A substantial number of sodomy prosecutions and convictions for which there are surviving records were for predatory acts against those who could not or did not consent, as in the case of a minor or the victim of an assault. As to these, one purpose for the prohibitions was to ensure there would be no lack of coverage if a predator committed a sexual assault that did not constitute rape as defined by the criminal law. Thus the model sodomy indictments presented in a 19th-century treatise, see 2 Chitty, *supra,* at 49, addressed the predatory acts of an adult man against a minor girl or minor boy. Instead of targeting relations between consenting adults in private, 19th-century sodomy prosecutions typically involved relations between men and minor girls or minor boys, relations between adults involving force, relations between adults implicating disparity in status, or relations between men and animals.

* * * The longstanding criminal prohibition of homosexual sodomy upon which the *Bowers* decision placed such reliance is as consistent with a general condemnation of nonprocreative sex as it is with an established tradition of prosecuting acts because of their homosexual character.

The policy of punishing consenting adults for private acts was not much discussed in the early legal literature. We can infer that one reason for this was the very private nature of the conduct. Despite the absence of prosecutions, there may have been periods in which there was public criticism of homosexuals as such and an insistence that the criminal laws be enforced to discourage their practices. But far from possessing "ancient roots," *Bowers*, 478 U.S., at 192, American laws targeting same-sex couples did not develop until the last third of the 20th century. * * *

It was not until the 1970's that any State singled out same-sex relations for criminal prosecution, and only nine States have done so. * * * Post-*Bowers* even some of these States did not adhere to the policy of suppressing homosexual conduct. Over the course of the last decades, States with same-sex prohibitions have moved toward abolishing them. * * *

In summary, the historical grounds relied upon in *Bowers* are more complex than the majority opinion and the concurring opinion by Chief Justice Burger indicate. Their historical premises are not without doubt and, at the very least, are overstated.

It must be acknowledged, of course, that the Court in *Bowers* was making the broader point that for centuries there have been powerful voices to condemn homosexual conduct as immoral. The condemnation has been shaped by religious beliefs, conceptions of right and acceptable behavior, and respect for the traditional family. For many persons these are not trivial concerns but profound and deep convictions accepted as ethical and moral principles to which they aspire and which thus determine the course of their lives. These considerations do not answer the question before us, however. The issue is whether the majority may use the power of the State to enforce these views on the whole society through operation of the criminal law. "Our obligation is to define the liberty of all, not to mandate our own moral code." *Planned Parenthood of Southeastern Pa. v. Casey*, 505 U.S. 833, 850 (1992).

Chief Justice Burger joined the opinion for the Court in *Bowers* and further explained his views as follows: "Decisions of individuals relating to homosexual conduct have been subject to state intervention throughout the history of Western civilization. Condemnation of those practices is firmly rooted in Judeao–Christian moral and ethical standards." 478 U.S., at 196. As with Justice White's assumptions about history, scholarship casts some doubt on the sweeping nature of the statement by Chief Justice Burger as it pertains to private homosexual conduct between consenting adults. See, *e.g.*, Eskridge, Hardwick and Historiography, 1999 U. Ill. L. Rev. 631, 656. In all events we think that our laws and traditions in the past half century are of most relevance here. These references show an emerging awareness that liberty gives substantial protection to adult persons in deciding how to conduct their private lives in matters pertaining to sex. "History and tradition are the starting point but not in all cases the ending point of the substantive due process inquiry." *County of Sacramento v. Lewis*, 523 U.S. 833, 857 (1998) (Kennedy, J., concurring).

* * *

In *Bowers* the Court referred to the fact that before 1961 all 50 States had outlawed sodomy, and that at the time of the Court's decision 24 States and the District of Columbia had sodomy laws. 478 U.S., at 192–193. Justice Powell pointed out that these prohibitions often were being ignored, however. Georgia, for instance, had not sought to enforce its law for decades. Id., at 197–198, n. 2 ("The history of nonenforcement suggests the moribund character today of laws criminalizing this type of private, consensual conduct").

The sweeping references by Chief Justice Burger to the history of Western civilization and to Judeo–Christian moral and ethical standards did not take account of other authorities pointing in an opposite direction. A committee advising the British Parliament recommended in 1957 repeal of laws punishing homosexual conduct. The Wolfenden Report: Report of the Committee on Homosexual Offenses and Prostitution (1963). Parliament enacted the substance of those recommendations 10 years later. Sexual Offences Act 1967, § 1.

Of even more importance, almost five years before *Bowers* was decided the European Court of Human Rights considered a case with parallels to *Bowers* and to today's case. * * * The court held that the laws proscribing [consenting homosexual] conduct were invalid under the European Convention on Human Rights. *Dudgeon* v. *United Kingdom*, 45 Eur. Ct. H. R. (1981) P52. Authoritative in all countries that are members of the Council of Europe (21 nations then, 45 nations now), the decision is at odds with the premise in *Bowers* that the claim put forward was insubstantial in our Western civilization.

In our own constitutional system the deficiencies in *Bowers* became even more apparent in the years following its announcement. The 25 States with laws prohibiting the relevant conduct referenced in the *Bowers* decision are reduced now to 13, of which 4 enforce their laws only against homosexual conduct. In those States where sodomy is still proscribed, whether for same-sex or heterosexual conduct, there is a pattern of nonenforcement with respect to consenting adults acting in private. The State of Texas admitted in 1994 that as of that date it had not prosecuted anyone under those circumstances. *State v. Morales*, 869 S.W.2d 941, 943 .

Two principal cases decided after *Bowers* cast its holding into even more doubt. In *Planned Parenthood of Southeastern Pa. v. Casey*, 505 U.S. 833 (1992), the Court reaffirmed the substantive force of the liberty protected by the Due Process Clause. The *Casey* decision again confirmed that our laws and tradition afford constitutional protection to personal decisions relating to marriage, procreation, contraception, family relationships, child rearing, and education. *Id.*, at 851. In explaining the respect the Constitution demands for the autonomy of the person in making these choices, we stated as follows:

"These matters, involving the most intimate and personal choices a person may make in a lifetime, choices central to personal dignity and autonomy, are central to the liberty protected by the *Fourteenth Amendment*. At the heart of liberty is the right to define one's own concept of existence, of meaning, of the universe, and of the mystery of human life. Beliefs about these matters could not define the attributes of personhood were they formed under compulsion of the State." *Ibid.*

Persons in a homosexual relationship may seek autonomy for these purposes, just as heterosexual persons do. The decision in *Bowers* would deny them this right.

The second post-*Bowers* case of principal relevance is *Romer v. Evans*, 517 U.S. 620, (1996). There the Court struck down class-based legislation directed at homosexuals as a violation of the Equal Protection Clause. *Romer* invalidated an amendment to Colorado's constitution which named as a solitary class persons who were homosexuals, lesbians, or bisexual either by "orientation, conduct, practices or relationships," *id.*, at 624 (internal quotation marks omitted), and deprived them of protection under state antidiscrimination laws. We concluded that the provision was "born of animosity toward the class of persons affected" and further that it had no rational relation to a legitimate governmental purpose. *Id.*, at 634.

* * *

Equality of treatment and the due process right to demand respect for conduct protected by the substantive guarantee of liberty are linked in important respects, and a decision on the latter point advances both interests. If protected conduct is made criminal and the law which does so remains unexamined for its substantive validity, its stigma might remain even if it were not enforceable as drawn for equal protection reasons. When homosexual conduct is made criminal by the law of the State, that declaration in and of itself is an invitation to subject homosexual persons to discrimination both in the public and in the private spheres. The central holding of *Bowers* has been brought in question by this case, and it should be addressed. Its continuance as precedent demeans the lives of homosexual persons.

The stigma this criminal statute imposes, moreover, is not trivial. The offense, to be sure, is but a class C misdemeanor, a minor offense in the Texas legal system. Still, it remains a criminal offense with all that imports for the dignity of the persons charged. The petitioners will bear on their record the history of their criminal convictions. * * * We are advised that if Texas convicted an adult for private, consensual homosexual conduct under the statute here in question the convicted person would come within the [sexual-offender] registration laws of a least four States were he or she to be subject to their jurisdiction. * * * This underscores the consequential nature of the punishment and the state-sponsored condemnation attendant to the criminal prohibition. Furthermore, the Texas criminal conviction carries with it the other collateral consequences always following a conviction, such as notations on job application forms, to mention but one example.

* * *

* * * The right the petitioners seek in this case has been accepted as an integral part of human freedom in many other countries. There has been no showing that in this country the governmental interest in circumscribing personal choice is somehow more legitimate or urgent.

The doctrine of *stare decisis* is essential to the respect accorded to the judgments of the Court and to the stability of the law. It is not, however, an inexorable command. *Payne v. Tennessee*, 501 U.S. 808, 828 (1991) ("*Stare decisis* is not an inexorable command; rather, it 'is a principle of policy and not a mechanical formula of adherence to the latest decision' ") (quoting *Helvering v. Hallock*, 309 U.S. 106, 119 (1940))). In *Casey* we noted that when a Court is asked to overrule a precedent recognizing a constitutional liberty interest, individual or societal reliance on the existence of that liberty cautions with particular strength against reversing course. 505 U.S., at 855–856; see also *id.*, at 844 ("Liberty finds no refuge in a jurisprudence of doubt"). The holding in *Bowers*, however, has not induced detrimental reliance comparable to some instances where recognized individual rights are involved. Indeed, there has been no individual or societal reliance on *Bowers* of the sort that could counsel against overturning its holding once there are compelling reasons to do so. *Bowers* itself causes uncertainty, for the precedents before and after its issuance contradict its central holding.

The rationale of *Bowers* does not withstand careful analysis. In his dissenting opinion in *Bowers* JUSTICE STEVENS came to these conclusions:

> "Our prior cases make two propositions abundantly clear. First, the fact that the governing majority in a State has traditionally viewed a particular practice as immoral is not a sufficient reason for upholding a law prohibiting the practice; neither history nor tradition could save a law prohibiting miscegenation from constitutional attack. Second, individual decisions by married persons, concerning the intimacies of their physical relationship, even when not intended to produce offspring, are a form of "liberty" protected by the Due Process Clause of the Fourteenth Amendment. Moreover, this protection extends to intimate choices by unmarried as well as married persons." 478 U.S., at 216 (footnotes and citations omitted).

JUSTICE STEVENS' analysis, in our view, should have been controlling in *Bowers* and should control here.

* * *

The present case does not involve minors. It does not involve persons who might be injured or coerced or who are situated in relationships where consent might not easily be refused. It does not involve public conduct or prostitution. It does not involve whether the government must give formal recognition to any relationship that homosexual persons seek to enter. The case does involve two adults who, with full and mutual consent from each other, engaged in sexual practices common to a homosexual lifestyle. The petitioners are entitled to respect for their private lives. The State cannot demean their existence or control their destiny by making their private sexual conduct a crime. Their right to liberty under the Due Process Clause gives them the full right to engage in their conduct without intervention of the government. "It is a promise of the Constitution that there is a realm of personal liberty which the government may not enter." *Casey, supra,* at 847. The Texas statute furthers no legitimate state interest which can justify its intrusion into the personal and private life of the individual.

Had those who drew and ratified the Due Process Clauses of the Fifth Amendment or the Fourteenth Amendment known the components of liberty in its manifold possibilities, they might have been more specific. They did not presume to have this insight. They knew times can blind us to certain truths and later generations can see that laws once thought necessary and proper in fact serve only to oppress. As the Constitution endures, persons in every generation can invoke its principles in their own search for greater freedom.

[Reversed.]

It is so ordered.

■ JUSTICE O'CONNOR, concurring in the judgment.

The Court today overrules *Bowers v. Hardwick*, 478 U.S. 186 (1986). I joined *Bowers*, and do not join the Court in overruling it. Nevertheless, I agree with the Court that Texas' statute banning same-sex sodomy is unconstitutional. See Tex. Penal Code Ann. § 21.06 (2003). Rather than relying on the substantive component of the Fourteenth Amendment's Due Process Clause, as the Court does, I base my conclusion on the Fourteenth Amendment's Equal Protection Clause.

The Equal Protection Clause of the Fourteenth Amendment "is essentially a direction that all persons similarly situated should be treated alike." *Cleburne v. Cleburne Living Center, Inc.*, 473 U.S. 432, 439 (1985); see also *Plyler v. Doe*, 457 U.S. 202 (1982). Under our rational basis standard of review, "legislation is presumed to be valid and will be sustained if the classification drawn by the statute is rationally related to a legitimate state interest." *Cleburne v. Cleburne Living Center, supra,* at 440; see also *Department of Agriculture v. Moreno*, 413 U.S. 528, 534 (1973); *Romer v. Evans*, 517 U.S. 620, 632–633 (1996); *Nordlinger v. Hahn*, 505 U.S. 1, 11–12 (1992).

* * * We have consistently held * * * that some objectives, such as "a bare ... desire to harm a politically unpopular group," are not legitimate state interests. *Department of Agriculture v. Moreno, supra,* at 534. See also *Cleburne v. Cleburne Living Center, supra,* at 446–447; *Romer v. Evans, supra,* at 632. When a law exhibits such a desire to harm a politically unpopular group, we have applied a more searching form of rational basis review to strike down such laws under the Equal Protection Clause.

* * *

The statute at issue here makes sodomy a crime only if a person "engages in deviate sexual intercourse with another individual of the same sex." Tex. Penal Code Ann. § 21.06(a) (2003). Sodomy between opposite-sex partners, however, is not a crime in Texas. That is, Texas treats the same conduct differently based solely on the participants. Those harmed by this law are people who have a same-sex sexual orientation and thus are more likely to engage in behavior prohibited by § 21.06.

The Texas statute makes homosexuals unequal in the eyes of the law by making particular conduct—and only that conduct—subject to criminal sanction. * * * [W]hile the penalty imposed on petitioners in this case was relatively minor, the consequences of conviction are not. As the Court notes, see *ante*, at 15, petitioners' convictions, if upheld, would disqualify them from or restrict their ability to engage in a variety of professions, including medicine, athletic training, and interior design. * * * Indeed, were petitioners to move to one of four States, their convictions would require them to register as sex offenders to local law enforcement. * * *

And the effect of Texas' sodomy law is not just limited to the threat of prosecution or consequence of conviction. Texas' sodomy law brands all homosexuals as criminals, thereby making it more difficult for homosexuals to be treated in the same manner as everyone else. Indeed, Texas itself has previously acknowledged the collateral effects of the law, stipulating in a prior challenge to this action that the law "legally sanctions discrimination against [homosexuals] in a variety of ways unrelated to the criminal law," including in the areas of "employment, family issues, and housing." *State v. Morales*, 826 S.W.2d 201, 203 (Tex. App. 1992).

Texas attempts to justify its law, and the effects of the law, by arguing that the statute satisfies rational basis review because it furthers the legitimate governmental interest of the promotion of morality. * * *

This case raises a different issue than *Bowers:* whether, under the *Equal Protection Clause*, moral disapproval is a legitimate state interest to justify by itself a statute that bans homosexual sodomy, but not heterosexual sodomy. It is not. Moral disapproval of this group, like a bare desire to harm the group, is an interest that is insufficient to satisfy rational basis review under the Equal Protection Clause. See, *e.g., Department of Agriculture v. Moreno, supra*, at 534; *Romer v. Evans*, 517 U.S., at 634–635. Indeed, we have never held that moral disapproval, without any other asserted state interest, is a sufficient rationale under the Equal Protection Clause to justify a law that discriminates among groups of persons.

* * *

Whether a sodomy law that is neutral both in effect and application, see *Yick Wo v. Hopkins*, 118 U.S. 356, 30 L. Ed. 220, 6 S. Ct. 1064 (1886), would violate the substantive component of the Due Process Clause is an issue that need not be decided today. I am confident, however, that so long as the Equal Protection Clause requires a sodomy law to apply equally to the private consensual conduct of homosexuals and heterosexuals alike, such a law would not long stand in our democratic society. * * *

A law branding one class of persons as criminal solely based on the State's moral disapproval of that class and the conduct associated with that class runs contrary to the values of the Constitution and the Equal Protection Clause, under any standard of review. I therefore concur in the Court's judgment that Texas' sodomy law banning "deviate sexual intercourse" between consenting adults of the same sex, but not between consenting adults of different sexes, is unconstitutional.

■ Justice Scalia, with whom the Chief Justice and Justice Thomas join, dissenting.

"Liberty finds no refuge in a jurisprudence of doubt." *Planned Parenthood of Southeastern Pa. v. Casey*, 505 U.S. 833, 844, 120 L. Ed. 2d 674, 112 S. Ct. 2791 (1992). That was the Court's sententious response, barely more than a decade ago, to those seeking to overrule *Roe v. Wade*, 410 U.S. 113, 35 L. Ed. 2d 147, 93 S. Ct. 705 (1973). The Court's response today, to those who have engaged in a 17-year crusade to overrule *Bowers v. Hardwick*, 478 U.S. 186, 92 L. Ed. 2d 140, 106 S. Ct. 2841 (1986), is very different. The need for stability and certainty presents no barrier.

Most of the rest of today's opinion has no relevance to its actual holding—that the Texas statute "furthers no legitimate state interest which can justify" its application to petitioners under rational-basis review. *Ante*, at 18 (overruling *Bowers* to the extent it sustained Georgia's anti-sodomy statute under the rational-basis test). Though there is discussion of "fundamental propositions," *ante*, at 4, and "fundamental decisions," *ibid.* nowhere does the Court's opinion declare that homosexual sodomy is a "fundamental right" under the Due Process Clause; nor does it subject the Texas law to the standard of review that would be appropriate (strict scrutiny) if homosexual sodomy *were* a "fundamental right." Thus, while overruling the *outcome* of *Bowers*, the Court leaves strangely untouched its central legal conclusion: "Respondent would have us announce ... a fundamental right to engage in homosexual sodomy. This we are quite unwilling to do." 478 U.S., at 191. Instead the Court simply describes petitioners' conduct as "an exercise of their liberty"—which it undoubtedly is—and proceeds to apply an unheard-of form of rational-basis review that will have far-reaching implications beyond this case. *Ante*, at 3.

* * *

Today's approach to *stare decisis* invites us to overrule an erroneously decided precedent (including an "intensely divisive" decision) *if*: (1) its foundations have been "eroded" by subsequent decisions, *ante*, at 15; (2) it has been subject to "substantial and continuing" criticism, *ibid.*; and (3) it has not induced "individual or societal reliance" that counsels against overturning, *ante*, at 16. The problem is that *Roe* itself—which today's majority surely has no disposition to overrule—satisfies these conditions to at least the same degree as *Bowers*.

* * *

I do not quarrel with the Court's claim that *Romer v. Evans*, 517 U.S. 620, 134 L. Ed. 2d 855, 116 S. Ct. 1620 (1996), "eroded" the "foundations" of *Bowers'* rational-basis holding. See *Romer, supra, at 640–643* (Scalia, J., dissenting).) But *Roe* and *Casey* have been equally "eroded" by *Washington v. Glucksberg*, 521 U.S. 702, 721, 138 L. Ed. 2d 772, 117 S. Ct. 2258, 117 S. Ct. 2302 (1997), which held that *only* fundamental rights which are " 'deeply rooted in this Nation's history and tradition' " qualify for anything other than rational basis scrutiny under the doctrine of "substantive due process." *Roe* and *Casey*, of course, subjected the restriction of abortion to heightened scrutiny without even attempting to establish that the freedom to abort *was* rooted in this Nation's tradition.

* * * *Bowers*, the Court says, has been subject to "substantial and continuing [criticism], disapproving of its reasoning in all respects, not just as to its historical assumptions." *Ante*, at 15. * * * Of course, *Roe* too (and by extension *Casey*) had been (and still is) subject to unrelenting criticism, including criticism from the two commentators cited by the Court today. See Fried, *supra*, at 75 ("Roe was a prime example of twisted judging"); Posner, *supra*, at 337 ("[The Court's] opinion in *Roe* ... fails to measure up to professional expectations regarding judicial opinions"); Posner, Judicial Opinion Writing, 62 U. Chi. L. Rev. 1421, 1434 (1995) (describing the opinion in *Roe* as an "embarrassing performanc[e]").

* * * It seems to me that the "societal reliance" on the principles confirmed in *Bowers* and discarded today has been overwhelming. Countless judicial decisions and legislative enactments have relied on the ancient proposition that a governing majority's belief that certain sexual behavior is "immoral and unacceptable" constitutes a rational basis for regulation. * * * State laws against bigamy, same-sex marriage, adult incest, prostitution, masturbation, adultery, fornication, bestiality, and obscenity are likewise sustainable only in light of *Bowers'* validation of laws based on moral choices. Every single one of these laws is called into question by today's decision; the Court makes no effort to cabin the scope of its decision to exclude them from its holding. * * * The impossibility of distinguishing homosexuality from other traditional "morals" offenses is precisely why *Bowers* rejected the rational-basis challenge. "The law," it said, "is constantly based on notions of morality, and if all laws representing essentially moral choices are to be invalidated under the Due Process Clause, the courts will be very busy indeed." 478 U.S., at 196.

What a massive disruption of the current social order, therefore, the overruling of *Bowers* entails. * * *

Texas Penal Code Ann. § 21.06(a) (2003) undoubtedly imposes constraints on liberty. So do laws prohibiting prostitution, recreational use of heroin, and, for that matter, working more than 60 hours per week in a bakery. But there is no right to "liberty" under the Due Process Clause, though today's opinion repeatedly makes that claim. * * * The Fourteenth Amendment *expressly allows* States to deprive their citizens of "liberty," *so long as "due process of law" is provided[.]*

Our opinions applying the doctrine known as "substantive due process" hold that the Due Process Clause prohibits States from infringing *fundamental* liberty interests, unless the infringement is narrowly tailored to serve a compelling state interest. *Washington v. Glucksberg*, 521 U.S., at 721. We have held repeatedly, in cases the Court today does not overrule, that *only* fundamental rights qualify for this so-called "heightened scrutiny" protection—that is, rights which are " 'deeply rooted in this Nation's history and tradition,' " *ibid*. See *Reno v. Flores*, 507 U.S. 292, 303 (1993) * * * *United States v. Salerno*, 481 U.S. 739, 751 (1987) * * * See also *Michael H. v. Gerald D.*, 491 U.S. 110, 122 (1989) * * * *Moore v. East Cleveland*, 431 U.S. 494, 503 (1977) (plurality opinion); *Meyer v. Nebraska*, 262 U.S. 390, 399 (1923) * * * All other liberty interests may be abridged or abrogated pursuant to a validly enacted state law if that law is rationally related to a legitimate state interest.

Bowers held * * * that criminal prohibitions of homosexual sodomy are not subject to heightened scrutiny because they do not implicate a "fundamental right" under the Due Process Clause, 478 U.S., at 191–194. * * *

The Court today does not overrule this holding. Not once does it describe homosexual sodomy as a "fundamental right" or a "fundamental liberty interest," nor does it subject the Texas statute to strict scrutiny. Instead, having failed to establish that the right to homosexual sodomy is " 'deeply rooted in this Nation's history and tradition,' " the Court concludes that the application of Texas's statute to petitioners' conduct fails the rational-basis test, and overrules *Bowers'* holding to the contrary, see *id.*, at 196. * * *

* * *

It is (as *Bowers* recognized) entirely irrelevant whether the laws in our long national tradition criminalizing homosexual sodomy were "directed at homosexual conduct as a distinct matter." *Ante*, at 7. Whether homosexual sodomy was prohibited by a law targeted at same-sex sexual relations or by a more general law prohibiting both homosexual and heterosexual sodomy, the only relevant point is that it *was* criminalized—which suffices to establish that homosexual sodomy is not a right "deeply rooted in our Nation's history and tradition." The Court today agrees that homosexual sodomy was criminalized and thus does not dispute the facts on which *Bowers actually* relied.

* * * [T]he Court makes the claim, again unsupported by any citations, that "[l]aws prohibiting sodomy do not seem to have been enforced against consenting adults acting in private." *Ante*, at 8. The key qualifier here is "acting in private"—since the Court admits that sodomy laws *were* enforced against consenting adults (although the Court contends that prosecutions were "infrequent," *ante*, at 9). I do not know what "acting in private" means; surely consensual sodomy, like heterosexual intercourse, is rarely performed on stage. If all the Court means by "acting in private" is "on private premises, with the doors closed and windows covered," it is entirely unsurprising that evidence of enforcement would be hard to come by. (Imagine the circumstances that would enable a search warrant to be obtained for a residence on the ground that there was probable cause to believe that consensual sodomy was then and there occurring.) Surely that

lack of evidence would not sustain the proposition that consensual sodomy on private premises with the doors closed and windows covered was regarded as a "fundamental right," even though all other consensual sodomy was criminalized. * * *

* * *

[A]n "emerging awareness" is by definition not "deeply rooted in this Nation's history and traditions," as we have said "fundamental right" status requires. Constitutional entitlements do not spring into existence because some States choose to lessen or eliminate criminal sanctions on certain behavior. Much less do they spring into existence, as the Court seems to believe, because *foreign nations* decriminalize conduct. The *Bowers* majority opinion *never* relied on "values we share with a wider civilization," *ante*, at 16, but rather rejected the claimed right to sodomy on the ground that such a right was not " 'deeply rooted in *this Nation's* history and tradition,' " 478 U.S., at 193–194 (emphasis added). * * *

* * *

The Texas statute undeniably seeks to further the belief of its citizens that certain forms of sexual behavior are "immoral and unacceptable," *Bowers, supra*, at 196—the same interest furthered by criminal laws against fornication, bigamy, adultery, adult incest, bestiality, and obscenity. *Bowers* held that this *was* a legitimate state interest. The Court today reaches the opposite conclusion. The Texas statute, it says, "furthers *no legitimate state interest* which can justify its intrusion into the personal and private life of the individual," *ante*, at 18 (emphasis added). * * * This effectively decrees the end of all morals legislation. If, as the Court asserts, the promotion of majoritarian sexual morality is not even a *legitimate* state interest, none of the above-mentioned laws can survive rational-basis review.

* * *

[As for JUSTICE O'Connor's Equal Protection Clause analysis, m]en and women, heterosexuals and homosexuals, are all subject to [the statute's] prohibition of deviate sexual intercourse with someone of the same sex. To be sure, § 21.06 does distinguish between the sexes insofar as concerns the partner with whom the sexual acts are performed: men can violate the law only with other men, and women only with other women. But this cannot itself be a denial of equal protection, since it is precisely the same distinction regarding partner that is drawn in state laws prohibiting marriage with someone of the same sex while permitting marriage with someone of the opposite sex.

* * * A racially discriminatory purpose is always sufficient to subject a law to strict scrutiny, even a facially neutral law that makes no mention of race. See *Washington v. Davis*, 426 U.S. 229, 241–242 (1976). No purpose to discriminate against men or women as a class can be gleaned from the Texas law, so rational-basis review applies. That review is readily satisfied here by the same rational basis that satisfied it in *Bowers*—society's belief that certain forms of sexual behavior are "immoral and unacceptable," 478

U.S., at 196. This is the same justification that supports many other laws regulating sexual behavior that make a distinction based upon the identity of the partner—for example, laws against adultery, fornication, and adult incest, and laws refusing to recognize homosexual marriage.

JUSTICE O'CONNOR argues that the discrimination in this law which must be justified is not its discrimination with regard to the sex of the partner but its discrimination with regard to the sexual proclivity of the principal actor.

"While it is true that the law applies only to conduct, the conduct targeted by this law is conduct that is closely correlated with being homosexual. Under such circumstances, Texas' sodomy law is targeted at more than conduct. It is instead directed toward gay persons as a class." *Ante*, at 5.

Of course the same could be said of any law. A law against public nudity targets "the conduct that is closely correlated with being a nudist," and hence "is targeted at more than conduct"; it is "directed toward nudists as a class." But be that as it may. Even if the Texas law *does* deny equal protection to "homosexuals as a class," that denial *still* does not need to be justified by anything more than a rational basis, which our cases show is satisfied by the enforcement of traditional notions of sexual morality.

* * *

Today's opinion is the product of a Court, which is the product of a law-profession culture, that has largely signed on to the so-called homosexual agenda, by which I mean the agenda promoted by some homosexual activists directed at eliminating the moral opprobrium that has traditionally attached to homosexual conduct. * * *

One of the most revealing statements in today's opinion is the Court's grim warning that the criminalization of homosexual conduct is "an invitation to subject homosexual persons to discrimination both in the public and in the private spheres." *Ante*, at 14. It is clear from this that the Court has taken sides in the culture war, departing from its role of assuring, as neutral observer, that the democratic rules of engagement are observed. Many Americans do not want persons who openly engage in homosexual conduct as partners in their business, as scoutmasters for their children, as teachers in their children's schools, or as boarders in their home. They view this as protecting themselves and their families from a lifestyle that they believe to be immoral and destructive. The Court views it as "discrimination" which it is the function of our judgments to deter. So imbued is the Court with the law profession's anti-anti-homosexual culture, that it is seemingly unaware that the attitudes of that culture are not obviously "mainstream[.]" * * *

* * * [P]ersuading one's fellow citizens is one thing, and imposing one's views in absence of democratic majority will is something else. I would no more *require* a State to criminalize homosexual acts—or, for that matter, display *any* moral disapprobation of them—than I would *forbid* it to do so. What Texas has chosen to do is well within the range of traditional democratic action, and its hand should not be stayed through the invention of a brand-new "constitutional right" by a Court that is impatient of democratic change. It is indeed true that "later generations can see that laws once thought necessary and proper in fact serve only to oppress," *ante*, at 18; and when that happens, later generations can repeal those laws. But it is the premise of our system that those judgments are to be made by the people, and not imposed by a governing caste that knows best.

* * *

■ JUSTICE THOMAS, dissenting.

I join JUSTICE SCALIA'S dissenting opinion. I write separately to note that the law before the Court today "is ... uncommonly silly." *Griswold v. Connecticut*, 381 U.S. 479, 527 (1965) (Stewart, J., dissenting). If I were a member of the Texas Legislature, I would vote to repeal it. Punishing someone for expressing his sexual preference through noncommercial consensual conduct with another adult does not appear to be a worthy way to expend valuable law enforcement resources.

Notwithstanding this, I recognize that as a member of this Court I am not empowered to help petitioners and others similarly situated. My duty, rather, is to "decide cases 'agreeably to the Constitution and laws of the United States.'" *Id.*, at 530. And, just like Justice Stewart, I "can find [neither in the Bill of Rights nor any other part of the Constitution a] general right of privacy," *ibid.*, or as the Court terms it today, the "liberty of the person both in its spatial and more transcendent dimensions," *ante*, at 1.

———

NOTES AND QUESTIONS

1. *Moore* **in context of** *Lawrence*. The plurality opinion in *Moore* relied on the primary place that the extended family has traditionally occupied in United States history. This reasoning is similar to that used in *Bowers v. Hardwick*, 478 U.S. 186 (1986), where a history and tradition of intolerance for homosexual conduct was used to support an anti-sodomy law. However, now that *Lawrence v. Texas*, 539 U.S. 558 (2003) has overruled *Bowers*, is the history and tradition argument which was invoked by the plurality in *Moore* on shaky ground? *See* David M. Wagner, *Hints, Not Holdings: Use of Precedent in* Lawrence v. Texas, 18 BYU J. PUB. L. 681 (2004); Susan Austin Blazier, Note, *The Irrational Use of Rational Basis Review in* Lawrence v. Texas, 26 CAMPBELL L. REV. 21 (2004).

2. **Justice O'Connor's concurrence.**

a. **Domestic partners and O'Connor's concurrence in** *Lawrence*. In her concurring opinion in *Lawrence v. Texas*, 539 U.S. 558 (2003) (O'Connor, J., concurring), Justice O'Connor notes that the conduct targeted by the Texas sodomy law was "closely correlated with being homosexual," and that this contributed to her decision that that law violated the equal protection clause. Under that rationale, it would seem that the state law that forbids recognition of domestic partners as dependants would also violate the equal protection clause, given that, as long as homosexuals are not allowed to marry, they will be forced into domestic partnership arrangements. Does this mean, under O'Connor's equal protection argument, that the state would be required to extend positive benefits (like domestic partner benefits) to homosexuals if those benefits are extended to heterosexuals?

In May 1992, MCA Corporation announced that it would provide health benefits to employees' same-sex partners, but not heterosexual domestic partners. William V. Vetter, *Restrictions on Equal Treatment of Unmarried Domestic Partners*, 5 B.U. Pub. Int. L.J. 1, 3 (1995). Is this asymmetric treatment of same-sex and opposite domestic partnerships discriminatory, or is some level of asymmetry necessary in order to compensate for the asymmetry in marriage laws between same-sex and opposite-sex couples?

     b. **Heterosexual domestic partnership.** Domestic partnership arrangements are certainly not limited to same-sex couples. Would the "correlated with" approach O'Conner uses to equal protection sweep too broadly and end up refuting legislative intent by requiring domestic partner benefits for all cohabiting couples? However, if you reject a "correlated with" approach to equal protection, what would prevent a legislature from enacting a law which fell much more heavily on some disfavored group but had an ostensibly neutral purpose, like promoting marriage?

3. **Morality as a state interest.** Justice Scalia's dissent is longer than the opinion of the court itself, yet in eleven pages of dissent, he devotes only two paragraphs to the majority opinion, and those two paragraphs merely observe that no other society has decreed that morality is a sufficient basis for the enactment of a law. Does this mean that Scalia believes that enforcing public morality should be considered a legitimate state interest? *See* TracyLee Schimelfenig, Note, *Recognition of the Rights of Homosexuals: Implications of* Lawrence v. Texas, 40 Cal. W. L. Rev. 149, 158–59 (2003). If that is the case, under Scalia's philosophy, can any law *ever* fail a rational basis review, since, presumably, the public elected the legislature and the legislature writes laws that are consistent with the social norms of the society that elected them? In other words, if morality alone is a legitimate state interest, is there anything left of due process?

4. **Silly laws and legitimate state interests.** Justice Thomas' dissent begins by stating that the Texas anti-sodomy law is "uncommonly silly." Given that Justice Thomas does not believe that enforcing this law is a "worthy" use of government resources, how can he support the idea that it survives a due process attack for lacking a rational relation to a legitimate state interest? Is Thomas' version of due process something closer to "a silly relation to an unworthy government interest?" *See* Kris Franklin, *Homophobia and the "Matthew Shepard Effect": In* Lawrence v. Texas, 48 N.Y.L. Sch. L. Rev. 657, 667 at n.51 (2004).

5.   The limits of *Lawrence*. The holding of the court in this case is that "[t]he Texas statute furthers no legitimate state interest which can justify its intrusion into the personal and private life of the individual." However, this holding raises an interesting question: is the Texas statute unconstitutional because it furthers no legitimate state interest, or because it intrudes into the private life of the individual? If the former is true, then it would seem that all morals-based legislation is illegitimate and, unless it has some ancillary benefits, will most likely be struck down. If the latter is the case, *Lawrence* is a much more limited victory for gay rights, essentially stating that individuals have the right to be homosexual in their bedrooms, but nowhere else. *See* Wagner, *supra* at 655, n.1.

6.   Response of the church to changing social norms. In response to the decision in *Lawrence v. Texas*, televangelist Pat Robertson issued a national call for Christians to pray for the retirement of Justices O'Connor, Stevens, and Ginsburg. Interview by Paula Zahn with Pat Robertson, *Pat Robertson: Pray For Justices to Retire*, July 17, 2003, *available at* http://www.cnn.com/2003/LAW/07/17/cnna.robertson/.   Additionally,   the Catholic Church has issued a statement condemning homosexual marriage. Victor L. Simpson, *Vatican Issues Offensive on Gay Marriages*, ASSOCIATED PRESS, July 28, 2003.

7.   Additional reading. For additional information on morality laws, see generally Peter M. Cicchino, *Reason and the Rule of Law: Should Bare Assertions of "Public Morality" Qualify as Legitimate Government Interests for the Purposes of Equal Protection Review?*, 87 GEO. L.J. 139 (1998); Steve Sheppard, *The State Interest in the Good Citizen: Constitutional Balance Between the Citizen and the Perfectionist State*, 45 HASTINGS L.J. 969 (1994). For a look at existing methods of gaining state recognition of same-sex marriages, see Phyllis Randolph Frye & Alyson Dodi Meiselman, *Same–Sex Marriages Have Existed Legally in the United States for a Long Time Now*, 64 ALB. L. REV. 1031 (2001). For an overview of the evolving definition of family with respect to same-sex unions, see Paula Ettelbrick, *Domestic Partnership, Civil Unions, or Marriage: One Size Does Not Fit All*, 64 ALB. L. REV. 905 (2001).

E.   A FAMILY BASED ON SAME SEX MARRIAGE

Goodridge v. Department of Public Health

798 N.E.2d 941 (Mass. 2003).

■ MARSHALL, C.J.

Marriage is a vital social institution. The exclusive commitment of two individuals to each other nurtures love and mutual support; it brings stability to our society. For those who choose to marry, and for their children, marriage provides an abundance of legal, financial, and social benefits. In return it imposes weighty legal, financial, and social obligations. The question before us is whether, consistent with the Massachusetts Constitution, the Commonwealth may deny the protections, benefits, and obligations conferred by civil marriage to two individuals of the same sex who wish to marry. We conclude that it may not. The Massachusetts Constitution affirms the dignity and equality of all individuals. It forbids the creation of second-class citizens. In reaching our conclusion we have given full deference to the arguments made by the Commonwealth. But it has failed to identify any constitutionally adequate reason for denying civil marriage to same-sex couples.

We are mindful that our decision marks a change in the history of our marriage law. Many people hold deep-seated religious, moral, and ethical convictions that marriage should be limited to the union of one man and one woman, and that homosexual conduct is immoral. Many hold equally strong religious, moral, and ethical convictions that same-sex couples are entitled to be married, and that homosexual persons should be treated no differently than their heterosexual neighbors. Neither view answers the question before us. * * *

[In *Lawrence*,] the Court affirmed that the core concept of common human dignity protected by the Fourteenth Amendment to the United States Constitution precludes government intrusion into the deeply personal realms of consensual adult expressions of intimacy and one's choice of an intimate partner. The Court also reaffirmed the central role that decisions whether to marry or have children bear in shaping one's identity. * * *

Barred access to the protections, benefits, and obligations of civil marriage, a person who enters into an intimate, exclusive union with another of the same sex is arbitrarily deprived of membership in one of our community's most rewarding and cherished institutions. That exclusion is incompatible with the constitutional principles of respect for individual autonomy and equality under law.

I

The plaintiffs are fourteen individuals from five Massachusetts counties. * * *

In March and April, 2001, each of the plaintiff couples attempted to obtain a marriage license from a city or town clerk's office. * * * In each case, the clerk either refused to accept the notice of intention to marry or denied a marriage license to the couple on the ground that Massachusetts does not recognize same-sex marriage. Because obtaining a marriage license is a necessary prerequisite to civil marriage in Massachusetts, denying marriage licenses to the plaintiffs was tantamount to denying them access to civil marriage itself, with its appurtenant social and legal protections, benefits, and obligations.

[The District Court ruled in favor of the defendants, concluding "prohibiting same-sex marriage rationally furthers the Legislature's legitimate interest in safeguarding the 'primary purpose' of marriage, 'procreation.' "]

* * *

e of the statutory
nto civil marriage
ncome tax filing,
use who does not
eased employee].

re also directly or
special legal and
standing the Com-
tinctions between
pport and care of
eap a measure of
r parents' legally
adily accessible, to
, such as the en-
g a marital child.
ss to family-based
of one's parentage.

as for its intimate-
en termed a "civil

right to choose to
an experience and
commitment to an
se civil marriage is
he community, our
rry against undue
y and substantially

y (including Massa-
e and black Ameri-
Court of California
nterracial marriage
Fourteenth Amend-
s later, the United
interracial marriage
inia, * * * As both
s little if it does not
bject to appropriate
health, safety, and
ust yield to a more
y of the discrimina-

artment claims, government
arriage constitutes a legiti-
ate conduct, or whether, as
xclusion violates the Massa-
he long-standing statutory
that "marriage" means the
history cannot and does not

triction violates the Massa-
ways. Does it offend the
law? Or do the liberty and
nstitution secure the plain-
tters implicating marriage,
two constitutional concepts

marriage itself. Simply put,
chusetts, civil marriage is,
what its name implies: a

ough exercise of the police
e's power to enact rules to
e "necessary to secure the
elfare of the community."

he "welfare of the commu-
importance." * * * Civil
aging stable relationships
Commonwealth identifies
of property, ensures that
l whenever possible from
rtant epidemiological and

nd social advantages on
t once a deeply personal
y public celebration of the
delity, and family. * * *

from marriage. The mar-
hose who meet the entry
erwise be a burdensome
* * *

age license are enormous,
e department states that
and to marital benefits.

With no attempt to be comprehensive, we note that som
benefits conferred by the Legislature on those who enter
include, as to property [including: joint Massachusetts
automatic rights to inherit the property of a deceased sp
leave a will, and entitlement to wages owed to a de

* * *

Where a married couple has children, their children
indirectly, but no less auspiciously, the recipients of the
economic protections obtained by civil marriage. Notwith
monwealth's strong public policy to abolish legal dis
marital and nonmarital children in providing for the su
minors, * * * the fact remains that marital children
family stability and economic security based on thei
privileged status that is largely inaccessible, or not as re
nonmarital children. Some of these benefits are socia
hanced approval that still attends the status of bein
Others are material, such as the greater ease of acce
State and Federal benefits that attend the presumptions

It is undoubtedly for these concrete reasons, as well
ly personal significance, that civil marriage has long be
right." * * *

Without the right to marry—or more properly, the
marry—one is excluded from the full range of hum
denied full protection of the laws for one's "avowed
intimate and lasting human relationship." * * * Becau
central to the lives of individuals and the welfare of t
laws assiduously protect the individual's right to ma
government incursion. Laws may not "interfere directl
with the right to marry." * * *

B

For decades, indeed centuries, in much of this countr
chusetts) no lawful marriage was possible between whi
cans. That long history availed not when the Supreme
held in 1948 that a legislative prohibition against i
violated the due process and equality guarantees of the
ment, *Perez v. Sharp,* * * * or when, nineteen year
States Supreme Court also held that a statutory bar to
violated the Fourteenth Amendment, *Loving v. Virg*
Perez and *Loving* make clear, the right to marry mean
include the right to marry the person of one's choice, s
government restrictions in the interests of public
welfare. * * * As it did in *Perez* and *Loving,* history
fully developed understanding of the invidious qualit
tion. * * *

The individual liberty and equality safeguards of the Massachusetts Constitution protect both "freedom from" unwarranted government intrusion into protected spheres of life and "freedom to" partake in benefits created by the State for the common good. * * * Both freedoms are involved here. Whether and whom to marry, how to express sexual intimacy, and whether and how to establish a family—these are among the most basic of every individual's liberty and due process rights. * * * And central to personal freedom and security is the assurance that the laws will apply equally to persons in similar situations. "Absolute equality before the law is a fundamental principle of our own Constitution." * * * The liberty interest in choosing whether and whom to marry would be hollow if the Commonwealth could, without sufficient justification, foreclose an individual from freely choosing the person with whom to share an exclusive commitment in the unique institution of civil marriage.

* * *

The department posits three legislative rationales for prohibiting same-sex couples from marrying: (1) providing a "favorable setting for procreation"; (2) ensuring the optimal setting for child rearing, which the department defines as "a two-parent family with one parent of each sex"; and (3) preserving scarce State and private financial resources. We consider each in turn.

The judge in the Superior Court endorsed the first rationale, holding that "the state's interest in regulating marriage is based on the traditional concept that marriage's primary purpose is procreation." This is incorrect. Our laws of civil marriage do not privilege procreative heterosexual intercourse between married people above every other form of adult intimacy and every other means of creating a family. * * * People who have never consummated their marriage, and never plan to, may be and stay married. * * * While it is certainly true that many, perhaps most, married couples have children together (assisted or unassisted), it is the exclusive and permanent commitment of the marriage partners to one another, not the begetting of children, that is the sine qua non of civil marriage.

Moreover, the Commonwealth affirmatively facilitates bringing children into a family regardless of whether the intended parent is married or unmarried, whether the child is adopted or born into a family, whether assistive technology was used to conceive the child, and whether the parent or her partner is heterosexual, homosexual, or bisexual. If procreation were a necessary component of civil marriage, our statutes would draw a tighter circle around the permissible bounds of nonmarital child bearing and the creation of families by noncoital means. The attempt to isolate procreation as "the source of a fundamental right to marry," * * * overlooks the integrated way in which courts have examined the complex and overlapping realms of personal autonomy, marriage, family life, and child rearing. Our jurisprudence recognizes that, in these nuanced and fundamentally private areas of life, such a narrow focus is inappropriate.

* * *

The department's first stated rationale, equating marriage with unassisted heterosexual procreation, shades imperceptibly into its second: that confining marriage to opposite-sex couples ensures that children are raised in the "optimal" setting. Protecting the welfare of children is a paramount State policy. Restricting marriage to opposite-sex couples, however, cannot plausibly further this policy. * * * The "best interests of the child" standard does not turn on a parent's sexual orientation or marital status. * * *

The department has offered no evidence that forbidding marriage to people of the same sex will increase the number of couples choosing to enter into opposite-sex marriages in order to have and raise children. There is thus no rational relationship between the marriage statute and the Commonwealth's proffered goal of protecting the "optimal" child rearing unit. Moreover, the department readily concedes that people in same-sex couples may be "excellent" parents. These couples (including four of the plaintiff couples) have children for the reasons others do—to love them, to care for them, to nurture them. But the task of child rearing for same-sex couples is made infinitely harder by their status as outliers to the marriage laws. * * * Given the wide range of public benefits reserved only for married couples, we do not credit the department's contention that the absence of access to civil marriage amounts to little more than an inconvenience to same-sex couples and their children. Excluding same-sex couples from civil marriage will not make children of opposite-sex marriages more secure, but it does prevent children of same-sex couples from enjoying the immeasurable advantages that flow from the assurance of "a stable family structure in which children will be reared, educated, and socialized." * * *

The third rationale advanced by the department is that limiting marriage to opposite-sex couples furthers the Legislature's interest in conserving scarce State and private financial resources. The marriage restriction is rational, it argues, because the General Court logically could assume that same-sex couples are more financially independent than married couples and thus less needy of public marital benefits, such as tax advantages, or private marital benefits, such as employer-financed health plans that include spouses in their coverage.

An absolute statutory ban on same-sex marriage bears no rational relationship to the goal of economy. First, the department's conclusory generalization—that same-sex couples are less financially dependent on each other than opposite-sex couples—ignores that many same-sex couples, such as many of the plaintiffs in this case, have children and other dependents (here, aged parents) in their care. The department does not contend, nor could it, that these dependents are less needy or deserving than the dependents of married couples. Second, Massachusetts marriage laws do not condition receipt of public and private financial benefits to married individuals on a demonstration of financial dependence on each other; the benefits are available to married couples regardless of whether they mingle their finances or actually depend on each other for support. * * *

It has been argued that, due to the State's strong interest in the institution of marriage as a stabilizing social structure, only the Legislature can control and define its boundaries. * * * The Massachusetts Constitution requires that legislation meet certain criteria and not extend beyond certain limits. It is the function of courts to determine whether these criteria are met and whether these limits are exceeded. In most instances, these limits are defined by whether a rational basis exists to conclude that legislation will bring about a rational result. The Legislature in the first instance, and the courts in the last instance, must ascertain whether such a rational basis exists. To label the court's role as usurping that of the Legislature, * * * is to misunderstand the nature and purpose of judicial review. We owe great deference to the Legislature to decide social and policy issues, but it is the traditional and settled role of courts to decide constitutional issues.

* * *

The history of constitutional law "is the story of the extension of constitutional rights and protections to people once ignored or excluded." * * * As a public institution and a right of fundamental importance, civil marriage is an evolving paradigm. * * * Marriage has survived [many] transformations, and we have no doubt that marriage will continue to be a vibrant and revered institution.

* * *

■ [Greaney, J. concurred in the opinion]

■ [Spina, J. and Sosman, J. dissented, with Cordy, JJ. joining both opinions].

■ Cordy, J. (dissenting, with whom Spina and Sosman, JJ., join).

* * *

Civil marriage is the institutional mechanism by which societies have sanctioned and recognized particular family structures, and the institution of marriage has existed as one of the fundamental organizing principles of human society. * * * Marriage has not been merely a contractual arrangement for legally defining the private relationship between two individuals (although that is certainly part of any marriage). Rather, on an institutional level, marriage is the "very basis of the whole fabric of civilized society," * * * and it serves many important political, economic, social, educational, procreational, and personal functions.

Paramount among its many important functions, the institution of marriage has systematically provided for the regulation of heterosexual behavior, brought order to the resulting procreation, and ensured a stable family structure in which children will be reared, educated, and socialized. * * * Admittedly, heterosexual intercourse, procreation, and child care are not necessarily conjoined (particularly in the modern age of widespread effective contraception and supportive social welfare programs), but an orderly society requires some mechanism for coping with the fact that sexual intercourse commonly results in pregnancy and childbirth. The institution of marriage is that mechanism.

The institution of marriage provides the important legal and normative link between heterosexual intercourse and procreation on the one hand and family responsibilities on the other. * * * The alternative, a society without the institution of marriage, in which heterosexual intercourse, procreation, and child care are largely disconnected processes, would be chaotic.

The marital family is also the foremost setting for the education and socialization of children. Children learn about the world and their place in it primarily from those who raise them, and those children eventually grow up to exert some influence, great or small, positive or negative, on society. The institution of marriage encourages parents to remain committed to each other and to their children as they grow, thereby encouraging a stable venue for the education and socialization of children. * * *

It is difficult to imagine a State purpose more important and legitimate than ensuring, promoting, and supporting an optimal social structure within which to bear and raise children. At the very least, the marriage statute continues to serve this important State purpose. * * *

Taking all of this available information into account, the Legislature could rationally conclude that a family environment with married opposite-sex parents remains the optimal social structure in which to bear children, and that the raising of children by same-sex couples, who by definition cannot be the two sole biological parents of a child and cannot provide children with a parental authority figure of each gender, presents an alternative structure for child rearing that has not yet proved itself beyond reasonable scientific dispute to be as optimal as the biologically based marriage norm. * * *

NOTES AND QUESTIONS

1. **Economic framework for same sex marriage.**

    a. **Orderly distribution of property, private support for children's care.**

    "It is central to the way the Commonwealth identifies individuals, provides for the orderly distribution of property, ensures that children and adults are cared for and supported whenever possible from private rather than public funds...."

    b. **Property rights to those who choose to marry.**

    "The marriage license grants valuable property rights to those who meet the entry requirements, and who agree to what might otherwise be a burdensome degree of government regulation of their activities."

2. **Justifications for ban on same sex marriage.**

    a. Providing a "favorable setting for procreation"

    b. Ensuring the optimal setting for child rearing, which the department defines as "a two-parent family with one parent of each sex"

    c. Preserving scarce state and private financial resources

Which of the above listed rationales for banning same-sex marriage are based upon libertarian arguments for limited government and maximum personal autonomy?

3.   Neo-classical economics and same sex marriage.

Libertarian economist Milton Friedman has argued that there were four duties of government: (1) to protect citizens from military invasion, (2) to protect citizens from violence by fellow citizens, (3) to create and maintain the public works infrastructure and (4) to provide for "irresponsibles." Does a state or federal ban on same-sex marriage fit into any of these categories?

What position would you guess Milton and Rose Friedman take in the same-sex marriage debates? Would their position be consistent with economic libertarianism? If not, what rationale would they give for any inconsistency?

4.   Queer theory arguments against same sex marriage?

Can you imagine what the arguments of gay advocates might be against same sex marriage? For a representative selection of such arguments, see WILLIAM H. ESKRIDGE & NAN D. HUNTER, *Families We Choose, in* SEXUALITY, GENDER AND THE LAW 1008–99 (2d ed. 2004), (featuring gay argument and counter arguments for same sex marriage).

Paula Ettelbrick argues that:

"Marriage runs contrary to two of the primary goals of the lesbian and gay movement: the affirmation of gay identity and culture and the validation of many forms of relationships.... At this point in time, making legal marriage for lesbian and gay couples a priority would set an agenda of gaining rights for a few, but would do nothing to correct power imbalances between those who are married (whether gay or straight) and those who are not. Thus justice would not be gained.... Being queer means pushing the parameters of sex, sexuality, and family, and in the process transforming the very fabric of society.... The thought of emphasizing our sameness to married heterosexuals in order to obtain this 'right' terrifies me. It rips away the very heart and soul of what I believe it is to be a lesbian in this world. It robs me of the opportunity to make a difference. We end up mimicking all that is bad about the institution of marriage in our effort to appear to be the same as straight couples."

Id. at 1098 (excerpted from Paula Ettelbrick, *Since When is Marriage a Path to Liberation*, OUTLOOK, Autumn 1989, at 8–12).

CHAPTER 9

CULTURE AND IDENTITY

Introduction

The assumptions of conventional economic theory largely ignore questions of race, class, or other variables that affect individual identity. The rational actor of economics is assumed to be, like the reasonable person of law, a male member of the dominant culture. This assumption allows the values and perspectives of the dominant groups to serve as a crude surrogate for a more refined understanding of other perspectives.

The major consequence of omitting identity from economic reasoning is that economic theory has been unable to provide effective tools for diagnosing some of the most critical issues of economic inequality. This omission is present in both theoretical models and empirical research assumptions. The "thin" accounts of how race, gender, and other identity variables play a role in creating economic distribution are now being vigorously challenged by more robust models that for the first time are explicitly concerned with the economic impact of identity.

In 2003, George Akerlof, a Nobel laureate in economics, and Rachel Kranton, a professor of economics, introduced an important model of economic behavior that explicitly addresses critical questions of race, class and other identity factors and their relationship to the distribution of economic resources.

In this chapter, we begin with Akerlof and Kranton's model that offers a persuasive account of identity and culture in the sphere of economic activity. Next, we take up the insights of social norm theory, which draws upon modern sociological theory and turns attention to the dynamics of social group interaction. Finally, we look at race itself, a major identity variable. In this section, we explore the two competing theories about race and economics, and we look at law professor Ian Ayres' pathbreaking empirical study of evidence of pervasive racial discrimination in the market for the second-largest consumer retail purchase: new cars. Ayres has extended his empirical studies of racial discrimination to include transactions as varied as kidney transplants, taxi tipping practices, and bail setting. From these investigations he has argued, with some success in actual litigation, for a more sensitive test of the disparate impact theory of racial discrimination. Ayres' view does not require proof of discriminatory intent, and relies instead upon statistical disparities that show discriminatory impact upon subordinated groups.

A. CULTURE AND IDENTITY

Economics and Identity

115 Q. J. ECON. 715 (2000).

GEORGE A. AKERLOF AND RACHEL E. KRANTON

This paper considers how identity, a person's sense of self, affects economic outcomes. We incorporate the psychology and sociology of identity into an economic model of behavior. In the utility function we propose, identity is associated with different social categories and how people in these categories should behave. We then construct a simple game-theoretic model showing how identity can affect individual interactions. The paper adapts these models to gender discrimination in the workplace, the economics of poverty and social exclusion, and the household division of labor. In each case, the inclusion of identity substantively changes conclusions of previous economic analysis.

I. INTRODUCTION

This paper introduces identity—a person's sense of self—into economic analysis. Identity can account for many phenomena that current economics cannot well explain. It can comfortably resolve, for example, why some women oppose "women's rights," as seen in microcosm when Betty Friedan was ostracized by fellow suburban housewives for writing *The Feminine Mystique*. Other problems such as ethnic and racial conflict, discrimination, intractable labor disputes, and separatist politics all invite an identity-based analysis. Because of its explanatory power, numerous scholars in psychology, sociology, political science, anthropology, and history have adopted identity as a central concept. This paper shows how identity can be brought into economic analysis, allowing a new view of many economic problems.

We incorporate identity into a general model of behavior and then demonstrate how identity influences economic outcomes. Specifically, we consider gender discrimination in the labor market, the household division of labor, and the economics of social exclusion and poverty. In each case, our analysis yields predictions, supported by existing evidence, that are different from those of existing economic models. The Conclusion indicates many other realms where identity almost surely matters.

Our identity model of behavior begins with social difference. Gender, a universally familiar aspect of identity, illustrates. There are two abstract social categories, "man" and "woman." These categories are associated with different ideal physical attributes and prescribed behaviors. Everyone in the population is assigned a gender category, as either a "man" or a "woman." Following the behavioral prescriptions for one's gender affirms one's self-image, or identity, as a "man" or as a "woman." Violating the prescriptions evokes anxiety and discomfort in oneself and in others. Gender identity, then, changes the "payoffs" from different actions.

This modeling of identity is informed by a vast body of research on the salience of social categories for human behavior and interaction. We present in the next section a series of examples of identity-related behavior. These examples, and other evidence, indicate that (1) people have identity-based payoffs derived from their own actions; (2) people have identity-based payoffs derived from others' actions; (3) third parties can generate persistent changes in these payoffs; and (4) some people may choose their identity, but choice may be proscribed for others.

The concept of identity expands economic analysis for at least four corresponding reasons.

First, identity can explain behavior that appears detrimental. People behave in ways that would be considered maladaptive or even self-destructive by those with other identities. The reason for this behavior may be to bolster a sense of self or to salve a diminished self-image.

Second, identity underlies a new type of externality. One person's actions can have meaning for and evoke responses in others. Gender again affords an example. A dress is a symbol of femininity. If a man wears a dress, this may threaten the identity of other men. There is an externality, and further externalities result if these men make some response.

Third, identity reveals a new way that preferences can be changed. Notions of identity evolve within a society and some in the society have incentives to manipulate them. Obvious examples occur in advertising (e.g., Marlboro ads). As we shall explore, there are many other cases, including public policies, where changing social categories and associated prescriptions affects economic outcomes.

Fourth, because identity is fundamental to behavior, choice of identity may be the most important "economic" decision people make. Individuals may—more or less consciously—choose who they want to be. Limits on this choice may also be the most important determinant of an individual's economic well-being. Previous economic analyses of, for example, poverty, labor supply, and schooling have not considered these possibilities. * * *

B. *Psychology and Experiments on Group Identification*

The prominence of identity in psychology suggests that economists should consider identity as an argument in utility functions. Psychologists have long posited a self or "ego" as a primary force of individual behavior. They have further associated an individual's sense of self to the social setting; identity is bound to social categories; and individuals identify with people in some categories and differentiate themselves from those in others.

While experiments in social psychology do not show the existence of a "self" or this identification per se, they do demonstrate that even arbitrary social categorizations affect behavior. Consider the Robbers Cave experiment. In its initial week, two groups of boys at a summer camp in Oklahoma were kept apart. During this period, the boys developed norms of behavior and identities as belonging to *their* group. When they met for a tournament in the second week, the eleven-year-old equivalent of war broke out, with name-calling, stereotyping, and fighting. Later experiments show that competition is not necessary for group identification and even the most minimal group assignment can affect behavior. "Groups" form by nothing more than random assignment of subjects to labels, such as even or odd. Subjects are more likely to give rewards to those with the same label than to those with other labels, even when choices are anonymous and have no impact on own payoffs. Subjects also have higher opinions of members of their own group.

Our modeling of identity exactly parallels these experiments. In the experiments ... there are social categories; there is an assignment of subjects to those social categories; finally, subjects have in mind some form of assignment-related prescriptions, else rewards would not depend on group assignment.

C. *Examples of Identity–Related Behavior*

We next present a set of "real-world" examples of four different ways, outlined in the introduction and formalized in our utility function, that identity may influence behavior.

Our *first* set demonstrates that people have identity-related payoffs from their own actions. The impact of an action a_j *on utility* U_j depends in part on its effect on identity I_j.

Self-Mutilation. The first of these examples is perhaps the most dramatic: people mutilate their own or their children's bodies as an expression of identity. Tattooing, body-piercing (ear, nose, navel, etc.), hair conking, self-starvation, steroid abuse, plastic surgery, and male and female circumcision all yield physical markers of belonging to more or less explicit social categories and groups. In terms of our utility function, these practices transform an individual's physical characteristics to match an ideal. The mutilation may occur because people believe it leads to pecuniary rewards and interactions such as marriage. But the tenacity and defense of these practices indicate the extent to which belonging relies on ritual, and people have internalized measures of beauty and virtue.

Gender and Occupations. Female trial lawyer, male nurse, woman Marine—all conjure contradictions. Why? Because trial lawyers are viewed as masculine, nurses as feminine, and a Marine as the ultimate man. People in these occupations but of the opposite sex often have ambiguous feelings about their work. In terms of our utility function, an individual's actions do not correspond to gender prescriptions of behavior. A revealing study in this regard is Pierce's [1995] participant-observer research on the legal profession. Female lawyers thought of themselves as women, yet being a good lawyer meant acting like a man. Lawyers were told in training sessions to act like "Rambo" and to "take no prisoners." In the office, trial attorneys who did not "win big" were described as "having no balls." Intimidation of witnesses was "macho blasts against the other side." A Christmas skit about two partners dramatized the gender conflict:

[O]ne secretary dressed up as Rachel and another dressed up as Michael. The secretary portraying Michael ... ran around the stage barking orders and singing, "I'm Michael Bond, I'm such a busy man. I'm such a busy man." The other secretary followed suit by barking orders and singing. "I'm Rachel Rosen, I'm such a busy man, I mean woman. I'm such a busy man, I mean woman...." Michael responded to the spoof in stride.... Rachel, on the other hand, was very upset [Pierce, 1995, p. 130].

Female lawyers expressed their ambivalence in many discussions. "Candace," another partner, told Pierce: "I had forgotten how much anger I've buried over the years about what happened to the woman who became a lawyer ... To be a lawyer, somewhere along the way, I made a decision that it meant acting like a man. To do that I squeezed the female part of me into a box, put on the lid, and tucked it away" [Pierce 1995, p. 134].

Alumni Giving. Charitable contributions may yield a "warm glow" [Andreoni 1989], but how do people choose one organization over another? Charity to the organization with the highest marginal return would maximize its economic impact. Yet, at least for higher education, contributions may well reflect identity. Graduates give to *their own* alma mater. Alumni giving could enhance the value of a degree by maintaining an institution's reputation. But this explanation suffers from the collective action problem. And it does not account for student loyalty and identification with an institution, as expressed in such lyrics as "For God, for country, and for Yale."

Mountaineering. Why do people climb mountains? Loewenstein [1998] argues that facing the extreme discomfort and danger of mountaineering enhances an individual's sense of self.

Our *second* set of examples demonstrates that people have identity-related payoffs from others' actions. The effect of an action a_j on utility includes an impact on I_j.

Gender and Occupations. A woman working in a "man's" job may make male colleagues feel less like "men." To allay these feelings, they may act to affirm their masculinity and act against female coworkers. In her study of coal handlers in a power plant, Padavic [1991] interpreted the behavior of her male coworkers in this way. On one occasion, they picked her up, tossed her back and forth, and attempted to push her onto the coal conveyer belt (jokingly, of course). In the case of another worker, no one trained her, no one helped her, and when she asked for help, she was refused assistance that would have been routine for male coworkers.

To further assay the reasons for such behavior, we took a random-sample telephone survey relating a vignette about a female carpenter at a construction company who was "baited and teased" by a male coworker. We see in Table I that among the six possible explanations, 84 percent of the respondents said it was "somewhat likely," "likely," or "very likely" that the male worker behaved in this way because he felt less masculine. This explanation was one of the most popular, and more than three-quarters of the respondents thought that a woman in a man's job "frequently" or "almost always" faces such treatment.

Manhood and Insult. For a man, an action may be viewed as an insult which, if left unanswered, impugns his masculinity. As in the example above, an action a_{-j} impacts I_j, which may be countered by an action a_j. Psychologists Nisbett and Cohn [1996] have detected such identity concerns in experiments at the University of Michigan. These experiments, they argue, reveal remnants of the white antebellum Southern "culture of honor" in disparate reactions to insult of males from the U. S. South and North. Their experiments involved variations of the following scenario: an associate of the experimenters bumped subjects in the hallway as they made their way to the experiment. Rather than apologizing, the associate called the subject "asshole." Insulted Southerners were more likely than insulted Northerners and control Southerners to fill in subsequent word-completion tests with aggressive words (for example, g-un rather than f-un), and had raised cortisol levels.

TABLE I

VIGNETTE CONCERNING HARASSMENT AND EVALUATION OF POSSIBLE EXPLANATIONS

Vignette: Paul is a carpenter for a construction company. The company has just hired Christine, its first female carpenter, for 3 dollars *less* per hour than it pays Paul and the other carpenters. On Christine's first day of work, Paul and two of his coworkers bait and tease Christine, making it difficult for her to do her job.

Try to imagine why Paul behaved as he did. Rate each of the following explanations for Paul's behavior as not-at-all likely, not likely, somewhat likely, likely, or very likely.

Explanation	Fraction somewhat likely, likely, or very likely[a,b]	Average Score[c]
Paul put Christine down because he is afraid that by hiring a woman the company can lower his wage.	.36 (.06)	2.5 (.12)
Paul put Christine down because he does not feel that it is fair that Christine is getting a lower wage.	.13 (.04)	1.7 (.12)
Paul put Christine down because he feels less masculine when a woman is doing the same job.	.84 (.04)	3.4 (.12)
Paul put Christine down because he feels he and his friends will not be able to joke around if a woman is present.	.84 (.04)	3.6 (.12)

Explanation	Fraction likely, likely, or very likely[a,b]	Average Score[c]
Paul put Christine down because he is afraid that other men will tease him if a woman is doing the same job.	.76 (.05)	3.3 (.13)
Paul put Christine down because he is afraid that people will think that his requires less skill if a woman is doing the same job.	.64 (.06)	2.9 (.12)
Paul put Christine down because he is afraid that if he does not, then his male coworkers will start to tease him.	.80 (.05)	3.4 (.13)
Paul put Christine down because he feels that it is wrong for women to work in a man's job.	.77 (.05)	3.2 (.14)

a. Sample size is 70 households. Households were selected randomly from the Fremont, CA phonebook.

b. Standard errors are in parentheses.

c. Average with not-at-all likely = 1, not likely = 2, somewhat likely = 3, likely = 4, very likely = 5.

Most revealing that the insult affected identity, insulted Southerners were also more likely to fear that the experimenter had a low opinion of their masculinity. They will probably never meet the experimenter or the hallway accomplice again; their encounter in the experiment is otherwise anonymous. Their concern about the experimenter then can only be a concern about how they feel about themselves, about their own sense of identity, as perceived through the "mirror of the opinions and expectations of others" [Gleitman 1996, p. 343]. We see the same psychology in other examples.

Changing Groups or Violating Prescriptions. Because of j's *identification* with others, it may affect j's identity when another person in j's social category violates prescriptions or becomes a different person. A common response is scorn and ostracism, which distances oneself from the maverick and affirms one's own self-image. Such behavior occurs daily in school playgrounds, where children who behave differently are mocked and taunted. Those who seek upward mobility are often teased by their peers, as in *A Hope in the Unseen* [Suskind 1998], which describes Cedric Jennings' progress from one of Washington's most blighted high schools to Brown University. The book opens with Cedric in the high-school chemistry lab, escaping the catcalls of the crowd at an awards assembly. Those who try to change social categories and prescriptions may face similar derision because the change may devalue others' identity, as for the housewives in Betty Friedan's suburb.

Our *third* set of examples demonstrates that to some extent people choose their identity; that is, c_j may be partially a choice. Many women in the United States can choose either to be a career woman or a housewife (see Gerson [1986]). Parents often choose a school—public versus private, secular versus parochial—to influence a child's self-image, identification with others, and behavior. The choice of where to live at college can both reflect and change how students think of themselves. Fraternities, sororities, African–American, or other "theme"-oriented dorms are all associated with social groups, self-images, and prescribed behavior. The list can continue. The choice for an immigrant to become a citizen is not only a change in legal status but a change in identity. The decision is thus often fraught with ambivalence, anxiety, and even guilt.

Identity "choice," however, is very often limited. In a society with racial and ethnic categories, for example, those with nondistinguishing physical features may be able to "pass" as a member of another group. But others will be constrained by their appearance, voice, or accent.

Our *fourth* set of examples demonstrates the creation and manipulation of social categories **C** and prescriptions **P**.

Advertising. Advertising is an obvious attempt to manipulate prescriptions. Marlboro and Virginia Slims advertisements, for example, promote an image of the ideal man or woman complete with the right cigarette.

Professional and Graduate Schools. Graduate and professional programs try to mold students' behavior through a change in identity. As a "one-L" Harvard Law School student said: " 'They are turning me into someone else. They're making me different' " [Turow 1977, p. 73]. In medicine, theology, the military, and the doctorate, a title is added to a graduate's name, suggesting the change in person.

Political Identity. Politics is often a battle over identity. Rather than take preferences as given, political leaders and activists often strive to change a population's preferences through a change in identity or prescriptions. Again, examples abound. Fascist and populist leaders are infamous for their rhetoric fostering racial and ethnic divisions, with tragic consequences. Symbolic acts and transformed identities spur revolutions. The ringing of the Liberty Bell called on the colonists' identities as Americans. Gandhi's Salt March sparked an Indian national identity. The French Revolution changed subjects into *citizens*, and the Russian Revolution turned them into *comrades*.

III. ECONOMICS AND IDENTITY: A PROTOTYPE MODEL

In this section we construct a prototype model of economic interaction in a world where identity is based on social difference. In addition to the usual tastes, utility from actions will also depend on identity. Identity will depend on two social categories—Green and Red—and the correspondence of own and others' actions to behavioral prescriptions for their category.

A. A Prototype Model

We begin with standard economic motivations for behavior. There are two possible activities, Activity One and Activity Two. There is a population of individuals each of whom has a taste for either Activity One or Two. If a person with a taste for Activity One (Two) undertakes Activity One (Two), she earns utility V. An individual who chooses the activity that does not match her taste earns zero utility. In a standard model of utility maximization, each person would engage in the activity corresponding to her taste.

We next construct identity-based preferences. We suppose that there are two social categories, Green and Red. We assume the simplest division of the population into categories; all persons think of themselves and others as Green. We add simple behavioral prescriptions: a Green should engage in Activity One (in contrast to Reds who engage in Activity Two). Anyone who chooses Activity Two is not a "true" Green—she would lose her Green identity. This loss in identity entails a reduction in utility of I_s, where the subscript s stands for "self." In addition, there are identity externalities. If an i and j are paired, Activity Two on the part of i diminishes j's Green identity. j has a loss in utility I_o, where the subscript o denotes "other." After i has committed Activity Two, j may "respond." The response restores j's identity at a cost c, while entailing a loss to i in amount L.

Figure I represents an interaction between an individual with a taste for Activity One ("Person One") and an individual with a taste for Activity Two ("Person Two"). Person One chooses an activity first.

This model can be expressed by ideas central to the psychodynamic theory of personality, found in almost any psychology text. In personality development, psychologists agree on the importance of *internalization* of rules for behavior. Freud called this process the development of the *superego*. Modern scholars disagree with Freud on the importance of psychosexual factors in an individual's development, but they agree on the importance of *anxiety* that a person experiences when she violates her internalized rules. One's *identity*, or *ego*, or *self*, must be constantly "defended against anxiety in order to limit disruption and maintain a sense of unity" [Thomas 1996, p. 284]. In terms of our model, Person Two's internalization of prescriptions causes her to suffer a loss in utility of I_s if she chooses Activity Two. To avoid this anxiety, she may refrain from that activity.

Identification is a critical part of this internalization process: a person learns a set of values (prescriptions) such that her actions should conform with the behavior of some people and contrast with that of others. If Person One has internalized prescriptions via such identifications, another person's violation of the prescriptions will cause anxiety for Person One. In our model, this anxiety is modeled as a loss in utility of I_o. Person One's response, in our language, restores her identity, and in terms of the psychology textbook relieves her anxiety and maintains her sense of unity. Person One no longer loses I_o, although she does incur c.

* * *

IV.   IDENTITY, GENDER AND ECONOMICS IN THE WORKPLACE

An identity theory of gender in the workplace expands the economic analysis of occupational segregation. As recently as 1970, two-thirds of the

United States' female or male labor force would have had to switch jobs to achieve occupational parity. This measure of occupational segregation remained virtually unchanged since the beginning of the century. Yet, in twenty years, from 1970 to 1990, this figure declined to 53 percent. An identity model points to changes in societal notions of male and female as a major cause.

The model we propose captures the "auras of gender" [Goldin 1990a] that have pervaded the labor market. Occupations are associated with the social categories "man" and "woman," and individual payoffs from different types of work reflect these gender associations. This model can explain patterns of occupational segregation that have eluded previous models. It also directly captures the consequences of the women's movement and affords a new economic interpretation of sex discrimination law.

Identity also provides a microfoundation for earlier models. The "distaste" of men for working with women, as in the crudest adaptations of racial discrimination models [Becker 1971; Arrow 1972], can be understood as due to loss in male identity when women work in a man's job. Similarly women's assumed lower desire for labor force participation (as in Mincer and Polachek [1974], Bulow and Summers [1986], and Lazear and Rosen [1990]) can be understood as the result of their identity as homemakers.

A. *The Model*

There are two social categories, "men" and "women," with prescriptions of appropriate activities for each. A firm wishes to hire labor to perform a task. By the initial prescriptions, this task is appropriate only for men; it is a "man's job." Relative to a "woman's job," women lose identity in amount I_s by performing such work. In this situation, male coworkers suffer a loss I_o. They may relieve their anxiety by taking action against women coworkers, reducing everyone's productivity.

To avoid these productivity losses, the firm may change gender-job associations at a cost. The firm is likely to create a "woman's job" alongside the "man's job," rather than render the whole task gender neutral, when a new job description can piggyback on existing notions of male and female. A well-known historical example illustrates. In the nineteenth century, Horace Mann (as Secretary of Education for Massachusetts) transformed elementary school teaching into a woman's job, arguing that women were "more mild and gentle," "of purer morals," with "stronger parental impulses." Secondary school teaching and school administration remained jobs for men.

The model also indicates why gender-job associations may persist. If associations are sector-wide or economy-wide, and not firm-specific, perfectly competitive firms will underinvest in new job categories. Benefits would accrue to other firms. In the absence of market power or technological change, a shift in social attitudes and legal intervention would be necessary for changes in employment patterns.

The model easily extends to the decision to participate in the labor force. If women's identity is enhanced by work inside the home, they will have lower labor force attachment than men. Historically, female labor force participation rates, relative to male rates, have been both lower and more cyclically variable.

B. Implications for Labor Market Outcomes

This identity model explains employment patterns arising from associations between gender and type of work. These patterns go beyond what can be explained by women's assumed lower labor force attachment as in Mincer and Polachek [1974], where women work in occupations that require little investment in firm-specific human capital.

In our model, women will dominate jobs whose requirements match construed female attributes and inferior social status; men eschew them. Historically, three occupations illustrate: secretaries (97.8 percent female in 1970) have often been called "office wives," and elements of sexuality are inscribed in the working relationship (boss = male, secretary = female) [MacKinnon 1979; Pringle 1988]. Secretaries are expected to serve their bosses, with deference, and to be attentive to their personal needs [Davies 1982; Kanter 1977; Pierce 1996]. Elementary school teachers (83.9 percent female), in contrast to secondary school teachers (49.6 percent female), are supposed to care for young children. Nurses (97.3 percent female) are supposed to be tender and care for patients, as well as be deferential to doctors [Fisher 1995; Williams 1989].

In our model, women do not enter male professions because of gender associations. Historically, many male professions have required similar levels of education and training to female professions and could have been amenable to part-time and intermittent work. Contrast nursing and teaching with accounting and law. All require college degrees and certification, and sometimes have tenure and experience-based pay. Only the very top of these professions have required continuity in employment and full-time work.

Rhetoric surrounding job shifts from male to female further demonstrates the salience of gender-job associations. The recruitment of women into "men's jobs" during World War II, for example, was accompanied by official propaganda and popular literature picturing women taking on factory work without loss of femininity [Milkman 1987; Honey 1984; Pierson 1986]. In addition, the jobs were portrayed as temporary; only the wartime emergency excused the violation of the usual gender prescriptions.

C. Effects of the Women's Movement

The model gives a theoretical structure for how the women's movement may have impacted the labor market. The movement's goals included reshaping societal notions of femininity (and masculinity) and removing gender associations from tasks, both in the home and in the workplace. In the model, such changes would decrease women's gains (men's losses) in identity from homemaking, and decrease the identity loss I_s of women

(men) working in traditionally men's (women's) jobs, as well as the accompanying externalities I_o. These shifts would increase women's labor force participation and lead to a convergence of male and female job tenure rates. More women (men) would work in previously male (female) jobs.

All these outcomes are observed coincidental with and following the women's movement. Gender-job associations diminished, reflected in changes in language (e.g., firemen became firefighters). In 1998 the median job tenure of employed women over 25 was 0.4 years lower than that of men; in 1968 that gap had been 3.3 years. Changes in sex composition within occupations accounted for the major share of decline in occupational segregation from 1970–1990 [Blau, Simpson, and Anderson, 1998]. Of the 45 three-digit Census occupations that were 0.0 percent female in 1970, only one (supervisors: brickmasons, stonemasons, and tile setters), was less than 1 percent female twenty years later. Many incursions of females into male-dominated professions were very large. Consider again accounting and law. In 1970 (1990) females were 24.6 (52.7) percent of auditors and accountants, and 4.5 (24.5) percent of lawyers. Not only did the proportion of women in men's jobs increase, but so did the proportion of men in women's jobs (albeit much less dramatically). Of the triumvirate of explanations for such increases—technology, endowments, and tastes—elimination makes tastes the leading suspect, since there was no dramatic change in technology or endowments that would have caused such increased mixing on the job. Legal initiatives discussed next reflect such changes in tastes.

D.   Gender–Job Associations and Sex Discrimination Law

Legal interpretations of sex discrimination correspond to earlier economic models as well as our own. Title VII of the Civil Rights Act of 1964 makes it unlawful for an employer to discriminate "against any individual . . . with respect to . . . compensation, terms, conditions of employment" or "to [adversely] limit, segregate, or classify his employees . . . because of . . . sex." At its most basic, this law prohibits a discriminatory exercise of "tastes" against women (analogous to Becker [1971] and Arrow [1972]). Courts also interpret Title VII as outlawing statistical discrimination by sex or criteria correlated with, even when women on average lack a desirable job qualification. Discriminatory hiring because of women's presumed lower workplace attachment, as in Lazear and Rosen [1990], was precisely the issue addressed in *Phillips v. Martin-Marietta*.

Our model, where sex discrimination occurs because jobs have gender associations, corresponds to a wider interpretation of Title VII. This interpretation is at the forefront of current legal debate and is supported by a number of precedents. In *Diaz v. Pan American World Airways*, the Court outlawed sex bans in hiring. The airline originally pleaded for their prohibition of male flight attendants because women were better at "the nonmechanical aspects of the job." But this association of gender with the job was disallowed on appeal since feminine traits were deemed irrelevant to the "primary function or services offered" (cited in MacKinnon [1979, p.

180]). *Price Waterhouse v. Hopkins* set a precedent for workers already hired. The plaintiff had been denied a partnership after negative evaluations for her masculine deportment. The Supreme Court ruled that "an employer who objects to aggressiveness in women but whose positions require this trait places women in an intolerable and impermissible Catch 22" (cited in Wurzburg and Klonoff [1997, p. 182]). Cases have also involved harassment of women working in men's jobs as, in the terminology of our model, male coworkers protect themselves from loss of identity I_o. *Berkman v. City of New York* reinstated a firefighter who had been dismissed because of substandard work performance. The Court ruled that the interference and harassment by her male coworkers made it impossible for her to perform her job adequately [Schultz 1998, p. 1770]. This expansive interpretation of a "hostile work environment," a category of sexual harassment which is in turn a category of sex discrimination, has been exceptional. Judges have viewed sexual desire as an essential element of sexual harassment. However, Schultz [1998] and Franke [1995] argue that any harassment derived from gender prescriptions has discriminatory implications (as depicted in our model) and are thus violations of Title VII.

V. IDENTITY AND THE ECONOMICS OF EXCLUSION AND POVERTY

This section will consider identity and behavior in poor and socially excluded communities. In an adaptation of the previous model of Greens and Reds, people belonging to poor, socially excluded groups will choose their identity. Greens identify with the dominant culture, while those with Red identity reject it and the subordinate position assigned to those of their "race," class, or ethnicity. From the point of view of those with Green identities, Reds are often making bad economic decisions; they might even be described as engaging in self-destructive behavior. Taking drugs, joining a gang, and becoming pregnant at a young age are possible signs of a Red identity. This aspect of behavior has not been explored in previous models, but it is implicit in Wilson's account of black ghetto poverty [1987, 1996]. It also is implicit in every study that finds significant dummy variables for "race," after adjustment for other measures of socioeconomic status. The Green/Red model of this section offers an explanation for the significance of such dummy variables. Furthermore, it yields a less monolithic view of poverty than current economic theories that emphasize conformity (e.g., Akerlof [1997] and Brock and Durlauf [1995]).

A. *Motivation for Model*

Our model reflects the many ethnographic accounts of "oppositional" identities in poor neighborhoods. MacLeod's [1987] study of teenagers in a Boston area housing project, for example, contrasts the murderous and alcoholic Hallway Hangers to their obedient and athletic peers, the Brothers. In *Learning to Labour* Willis [1977] describes the antagonism between the unruly "lads" and the dutiful "earholes" in a working-class English secondary school. Similarly, Whyte's [1943] description of Boston's Italian North End circa 1940 contrasts the Corner Boys to the College Boys. Yet earlier, turn-of-the century accounts of the Irish in the United States contrast the "lace curtain" Irish of poor districts to their neighbors (see, e.g., Miller [1985]).

Our model further evokes the psychological effects of social exclusion in the colonial experience analyzed by Bhabha [1983] and Fanon [1967], and in the context of African–Americans in the United States by Anderson [1990], Baldwin [1962], Clark [1965], DuBois [1965], Frazier [1957], Hannerz [1969], Rainwater [1970], Wilson [1987, 1996], and others. In these settings, individuals from particular groups can never fully fit the ideal type, the ideal "Green," of the dominant culture. Some in excluded groups may try to "pass" or integrate with the dominant group, but they do so with ambivalence and limited success. A series of autobiographies tells of the pain and anger of discovering that one is not really "Green." Former *New York Times* editor Mel Watkins [1998] titles the chapter on his freshman year at Colgate as "stranger in a strange land." Gandhi [1966], Fanon [1967], Fulwood [1996], Staples [1994], and Rodriguez [1982] all relate strikingly similar experiences of perceived or real rejection and alienation. This social exclusion may create a conflict: how to work within the dominant culture without betraying oneself. As Jill Nelson [1993, p. 10] explains her exhaustion after a long day of interviewing for a job at *The Washington Post*:

> I've also been doing the standard Negro balancing act when it comes to dealing with white folks, which involves sufficiently blurring the edges of my being so that they don't feel intimidated, while simultaneously holding on to my integrity. There is a thin line between Uncle-Tomming and Mau-Mauing. To fall off that line can mean disaster. On one side lies employment and self-hatred; on the other, the equally dubious honor of unemployment with integrity.

These reactions, it must be emphasized, reflect how dominant groups define themselves by the exclusion of others. The creation and evolution of such social differences are the subject of much historical research. Said [1978] documents the emergence of the Western idea of the "Oriental," a concept that had significant implications for colonialism. In the United States Roediger [1991] and other historians show how workers of European descent in the nineteenth century increasingly were defined as "white." Prior to Emancipation, this identity evoked the contrast between white freedom and African-American enslavement. In the model we construct, the key interaction is between such social differences and the adoption of oppositional identities by those in excluded groups.

Lack of economic opportunity may also contribute to the choice of an oppositional identity. Wilson [1987, 1996] underscores the relation between the decline in remunerative unskilled jobs, the loss of self-respect by men who cannot support their families, and the rise in inner city crime and drug abuse. This process is illustrated in microcosm by "Richard" in *Tally's Corner* [Liebow 1967]. Unable to find decent-paying work, he abandoned his family and joined Tally's group of idlers on the street corner. By adopting a different identity, Richard no longer suffered the guilt of a failed provider.

Red activities have negative pecuniary externalities. Richard's wife and children had to find alternative means of support. The prime goal of the "lads" in Willis' secondary school was to get a "laff," through vandalism, picking fights, and returning drunk to school from the local pub. Running a school with lads is difficult. The situation corresponds to the externalities in Benabou's [1993, 1996] models of high schooling costs in poor neighborhoods. Further externalities accrue from drug dealing, crime, and other "pathological" behavior. In our model, there are also identity-based externalities. A Red is angered by a Green's complicity with the dominant culture, while a Green is angered by a Red's "breaking the rules." Again consider Willis' lads and earholes. As the lads define themselves in contrast to the earholes, the earholes define themselves in contrast to the lads. The earholes are even more proestablishment than the teachers—feeling that the teachers should be stricter. The lads, in turn, bait the earholes. This situation is just one (relatively tame) example of how interaction between the two groups generates antagonism on both sides.

B. Identity Model of Poverty and Social Exclusion

As in the prototype model, there are two activities, One and Two. Activity One can be thought of as "working" and Activity Two as "not working." There is a large community, normalized to size one, of individuals. The economic return to Activity One for individual i is v_i which we assume is uniformly distributed between zero and one, to reflect heterogeneity in the population and to ensure interior solutions. The economic return to Activity Two is normalized to zero.

As for identity, there are two social categories, Green and Red. A Green suffers a loss in identity r, representing the extent to which someone from this community is not accepted by the dominant group in society. Those with the less adaptive Red identity do not suffer this loss. Behavioral prescriptions say that Greens (Reds) should engage in Activity One (Two). Thus, a Green (Red) loses identity from Activity Two (One) in amount I^G_s ($I^R_s il$). Because Reds reject the dominant Green culture, they are also likely to have lower economic returns to Activity One than Greens. A Red individual i will only earn v_i—a from Activity One, as well as suffer the loss I^R_s. There are also identity externalities when Greens and Reds meet. A Green (Red) suffers a loss I^G_o (I^R_o). In addition, Reds who have chosen Activity Two impose a pecuniary externality k on those who have chosen Activity One.

Each person i chooses an identity and activity, given the choices of everyone else in the community. We assume that people cannot modify their identity or activity for each individual encounter. Rather, individuals choose an identity and activity to maximize expected payoffs, given the probabilities of encounters with Greens who choose Activity One, Greens who choose Two, Reds who choose One, and Reds who choose Two.

* * *

D.   Further Lessons from the Model

The model and its solution also afford interpretations of policies designed to reduce poverty and the effects of social exclusion.

First, the model indicates why residential Job Corps programs may succeed while other training programs fail [Stanley, Katz, and Krueger 1998]. According to the model, taking trainees out of their neighborhoods would eliminate, at least for a time, the negative effects of interaction with those with Red identities. Moreover, being in a different location may reduce a trainee's direct loss r from being Green and pursuing Activity One. That is, this loss may be both individual-specific and situational, and leaving a poor neighborhood is likely to generate a lower r than otherwise. In a somewhat controlled experiment, the U.S. government tried to save money with JOBSTART, which preserved many of the features of Job Corps except the expensive housing of trainees. Follow-up studies of JOBSTART show little or no improvement in employment or earnings.

Second, the model affords an interpretation of different education initiatives for minority students. Like Job Corps, the Central Park East Secondary School (CPESS) in East Harlem may succeed because it separates Green students from Red students. Students, for example, must apply to the school, indicating their and their parents' willingness to adopt its rules (see Fliegel [1993] and Meier [1995] for this and other details). Another interpretation of CPESS and other successes (e.g., Comer [1980] in New Haven) parallels the logic of the all-Red equilibrium where some people nonetheless pursue Activity One. The schools take measures to reduce the loss in identity of Red students, I^R_s, in activities such as learning Standard English. Delpit's [1995] award-winning book *Other People's Children* proposes numerous ways to reduce the alienation that minority students may experience in school.

Finally, the model illuminates a set of issues in the affirmative action debate. Much of this debate concerns the success or failure of specific programs (see, e.g., Dickens and Kane [1996]). Yet, more is at stake. The rhetoric and symbolism of affirmative action may affect the level of social exclusion r. On the one hand, Loury [1995] argues that portraying African-Americans as victims, a portrayal necessary to retain affirmative action programs, is costly to blacks. In terms of the model, such rhetoric will increase r and the adoption of Red identities. On the other hand, affirmative action will decrease r, to the extent it is seen as an apology for previous discrimination and an invitation for black admission to the dominant culture. Reversal of affirmative action would negate this effect. To cite a recent example, our analysis suggests that removing affirmative action admissions criteria at the University of California and University of Texas Law Schools could have behavioral implications that far exceed the impact on applicants.

The identity model of exclusion, then, explains why legal equality may not be enough to eliminate racial disparities. If African-Americans choose to be Red because of exclusion and if whites perpetuate such exclusions, even in legal ways, there can be a permanent equilibrium of racial inequality. The negative externalities and their consequences, however, would disappear when the community is fully integrated into the dominant culture, so that $r = \mathbf{a} = 0$, and everyone in the community adopts a Green identity. This, of course, is the American ideal of the melting pot, or the new ideal of a mosaic where difference can be maintained within the dominant culture.

VI.   IDENTITY AND THE ECONOMICS OF THE HOUSEHOLD

An identity model of the household, unlike previous models, predicts an asymmetric division of labor between husbands and wives. Theories based on comparative advantage (e.g., Becker [1965] and Mincer [1962]) predict that whoever works more outside the home will work less inside the home, whether it be the husband or the wife. Yet, the data we present below indicate a gender asymmetry. When a wife works more hours outside the home, she still undertakes a larger share of the housework.

Hochschild's [1990] study *The Second Shift* reveals the details of such asymmetries. One of the couples in her study found an ingenious way to share the housework. "Evan Holt," a furniture salesman, took care of the lower half of the house (i.e., the basement and his tools). His wife "Nancy," a full-time licensed social worker, took care of the upper half. She took care of the child. He took care of the dog.

Quantitative evidence from Hochschild's sample and our data analysis suggest that the Holts conform to a national pattern. Figure III shows the low average of husbands' share of housework and its low elasticity with respect to their share of outside work hours. The figure plots shares of housework reported by married men in the Panel Study of Income Dynamics, as computed from answers to the question(s): "About how much time do you (your wife) spend on housework in an average week? I mean time spent cooking, cleaning, and doing other work around the house?" The intent of the question was to exclude child care. The figure plots men's share of housework as a fourth-order polynomial of their share of outside hours, for households by age of youngest child. When men do all the outside work, they contribute on average about 10 percent of housework. But as their share of outside work falls, their share of housework rises to no more than 37 percent. As shown in the figure the presence of children of different ages makes a small difference to the function. Similar results obtain when the independent variable is shares of income rather than shares of outside work hours.

Predicted values from tobit estimation

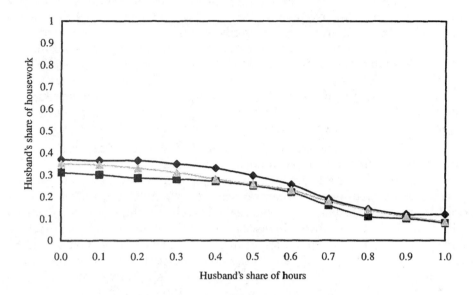

FIGURE III

Husband's Share of Housework versus Their Share of Outside Work Hours

Existing theories do not predict this asymmetry. Consider the following variant based on comparative advantage. Husband and wife both have the same utility function, which is increasing in quantity of a household public good that derives from their joint labor. Utility is decreasing in own labor inputs in outside and home production. We assume equal bargaining power, so that each marriage partner enjoys the same level of utility. With this framework, returns to specialization explain the observed division of labor when a wife has a comparative advantage in home production. Women who put in less than half of the outside work hours put in more than half the housework, as seen in the right-hand side of the graph of Figure III. But this model is inconsistent with the left-hand side of the graph.

Identity considerations can explain the high shares of housework of wives who undertake a large share of outside work hours. Add to the above model two social categories, "men" and "women." Prescriptions dictate that "men" should not do "women's work" in the home and "men" should earn more than their wives. Hochschild's interviews suggest that many men, and some women, hold these prescriptions. In the amended model, the husband loses identity when he does housework and when his wife earns more than half the household income. Equality of utility is restored when the wife undertakes more housework than her husband. Hochschild reports that in the "Tanagawa" household, for example, "Nina" earned more than half the family income, but she worked more than "Peter" at home to assuage his unease with the situation. Eventually, she quit her job.

VII. CONCLUSION

This paper considers how identity affects economic outcomes. Following major themes in psychology and sociology, identity in our models is based on social difference. A person's sense of self is associated with different social categories and how people in these categories should behave. This simple extension of the utility function could greatly expand our understanding of economic outcomes. In a world of social difference, one of the most important economic decisions that an individual makes may be the type of person to be. Limits on this choice would also be critical determinants of economic behavior, opportunity, and well-being.

Identity affects economic behavior in our models through four avenues. First, identity changes the payoffs from one's own actions. We capture this possibility by a value I_s in our models. In our study of gender in the workplace, for example, a woman working in a "man's" job suffers a loss in utility, affecting the labor supply. Second, identity changes the payoffs of others' actions. We capture this externality by a value I_o in our models. A "Red" in our poverty model, for example, is harmed by a member of his own community who complies with the dominant culture. Third, the choice, or lack thereof, of different identities affects an individual's economic behavior. In our poverty model, while individuals could choose between Green or Red, they could never be a "true" Green. The greater the extent of this social exclusion, the greater the possibility of equilibria in which individuals eschew remunerative activities. Finally, the social categories and behavioral prescriptions can be changed, affecting identity-based preferences. This possibility expanded the scope of employment policy in our model of gender in the workplace and of education policy in our study of social exclusion.

This paper has only scratched the surface of the economic implications of identity. A first tack in future research would be continued analysis of particular settings. Identity is likely to affect economic outcomes, for example, in areas of political economy, organizational behavior, demography, the economics of language, violence, education, consumption and savings behavior, retirement decisions, and labor relations. As in this paper, models that incorporate well-documented existing social categories and prescriptions could yield new results. A second tack in this agenda is comparative, examining identity across space and time. Researchers, for example, could consider why notions of "class" or "race" vary across countries; why might gender and racial integration vary across industries; what might explain the rise and fall of ethnic tensions. Such comparative studies would be a fruitful way to explore the formation of identity-based preferences.

In peroration, this paper explores how to incorporate identity into economic models of behavior. Many standard psychological and sociological concepts—*self-image, ideal type, in-group and out-group, social category, identification, anxiety, self-destruction, self-realization, situation*—fit naturally in our framework, allowing an expanded analysis of economic outcomes. This framework is then perhaps one way to incorporate many different nonpecuniary motivations for behavior into economic reasoning, with considerable generality and a common theme.

———

Identity in Mashpee

THE PREDICAMENT of Culture: TWENTIETH-CENTURY ETHNOGRAPHY, LITERATURE, AND ART 277–346 (1988).

JAMES CLIFFORD

In August 1976 the Mashpee Wampanoag Tribal Council, Inc., sued in federal court for possession of about 16,000 acres of land constituting three-quarters of Mashpee, "Cape Cod's Indian Town." (The township of Mashpee extends inland from the Cape's southern shore, facing Martha's Vineyard, between Falmouth and Barnstable.) An unprecedented trial ensued whose purpose was not to settle the question of land ownership but rather to determine whether the group calling itself the Mashpee Tribe was in fact an Indian tribe, and the same tribe that in the mid-nineteenth century had lost its lands through a series of contested legislative acts.

The Mashpee suit was one of a group of land-claim actions filed in the late 1960s and 1970s, a relatively favorable period for redress of Native American grievances in the courts. Other claims were being initiated by the Gay Head Wampanoag Tribe on Martha's Vineyard; the Narragansets of Charlestown, Rhode Island; Western Pequots, Schaghticokes, and Mohegans in Connecticut; and Oneidas, St. Regis Mohawks, and Cayugas in New York. The Mashpee action was similar in conception to a much-publicized suit by the Passamaquoddy and Penobscot tribes laying claim to a large portion of the state of Maine. Their suit, after initial successes in Federal District Court, direct intervention from President Jimmy Carter, and five years of hard negotiation, resulted in a favorable out-of-court settlement. The tribes received $81.5 million and the authority to acquire 300,000 acres with Indian Country status.

The legal basis of the Penobscot-Passamaquoddy suit, as conceived by their attorney, Thomas Tureen, was the Non-Intercourse Act of 1790. This paternalist legislation, designed to protect tribal groups from spoliation by unscrupulous whites, declared that alienation of Indian lands could be legally accomplished only with permission of Congress. The act had never been rescinded, although throughout the nineteenth century it was often honored in the breach. When in the 1970s Indian groups appealed to the Non-Intercourse Act, they were attempting, in effect, to reverse more than a century of attacks on Indian lands. The alienations had been particularly severe for eastern groups, whose claim to collective land was often unclear. When court decisions confirmed that the Non–Intercourse Act applied to non-reservation Indians, the way was opened for suits, like those of the Maine tribes, claiming that nearly two centuries of Indian land transfers, even ordinary purchases, were invalid since they had been made without permission of Congress.

Although the Mashpee claim was similar to the Maine Indians', there were crucial differences. The Passamaquoddy and Penobscot were generally recognized Indian tribes with distinct communities and clear aboriginal roots in the area. The Mashpee plaintiffs represented most of the nonwhite inhabitants of what, for over three centuries, had been known as an "Indian town" on Cape Cod; but their institutions of tribal government had long been elusive, especially during the century and a half preceding the suit. Moreover, since about 1800 the Massachusett language had ceased to be commonly spoken in Mashpee. The town was at first largely Presbyterian then Baptist in its public religion. Over the centuries inhabitants had intermarried with other Indian groups, whites, blacks, Hessian deserters from the British Army during the Revolutionary War, Cape Verde islanders. The inhabitants of Mashpee were active in the economy and society of modern Massachusetts. They were businessmen, schoolteachers, fishermen, domestic workers, small contractors. Could these people of Indian ancestry file suit as the Mashpee Tribe that had, they claimed, been despoiled of collectively held lands during the mid-nineteenth century? This was the question a federal judge posed to a Boston jury. Only if they answered yes could the matter proceed to a land-claim trial.

The forty-one days of testimony that unfolded in Federal District Court during the late fall of 1977 bore the name *Mashpee Tribe v. New Seabury et al.*, shorthand for a complex, multipartied dispute. Mashpee Tribe referred to the plaintiffs, the Mashpee Wampanoag Tribal Council, Inc., described by its members as an arm of the Mashpee Tribe. A team of lawyers from the Native American Rights Fund, a nonprofit advocacy group, prepared their suit. Its chief architects were Thomas Tureen and Barry Margolin. In court the plaintiffs' case was argued by the trial lawyer Lawrence Shubow, with assistance from Tureen, Margolin, Ann Gilmore, and Moshe Genauer. New Seabury et al. referred to the New Seabury Corporation (a large development company), the Town of Mashpee (representing over a hundred individual landowners), and various other classes of defendant (insurance companies, businesses, property owners). The case for the defense was argued by James St. Clair (Richard Nixon's Watergate attorney) of the large Boston firm Hale and Dorr, and Allan Van Gestel of Goodwin, Proctor, and Hoar. They were assisted by a team of eight other lawyers.

The presence of the Town of Mashpee among the defendants requires explanation. It was not until 1869 that the community living in Mashpee was accorded formal township status. From 1869 until 1964 the town government was overwhelmingly in the hands of Indians. During this period every selectman but one was an Indian or married to an Indian. Genealogical evidence presented at the trial showed that the families of town officers were closely interrelated. No one contested the fact that before the 1960s Mashpee was governed by Indians. The disagreement was over whether they governed as an "Indian tribe."

This basic demographic and political situation, which had not altered drastically for over three centuries, was revolutionized during the early 1960s. Before then census figures showed a population in Mashpee fluctuating in the neighborhood of 350 Indians and "negroes," "coloreds," or "mulattoes" (the official categories shifted), and 100 or fewer whites. A reliable count of 1859, which served as a benchmark in the trial, listed only one white resident. After 1960 for the first time white were recorded in the majority and by 1970 whites outnumbered Indians and other people of color by 982 to 306. By 1968 two of the town's selectmen were whites, the third Indian. This proportion was in effect at the time of the lawsuit. Mashpee's white selectmen voted that the town should legally represent the non-Indian majority of property holders who were threatened by the land claim.

"Cape Cod's Indian Town" had finally been discovered. For centuries a backwater and a curiosity, in the 1950s and 1960s Mashpee became desirable as a site for retirement, vacation homes, condominiums, and luxury developments. Fast roads now made it accessible as a bedroom and weekend suburb of Boston. The new influx of money and jobs was first welcomed by many of Mashpee's Indian residents, including some of the leaders of the land-claim suit. They took advantage of the new situation. The town government, still run by Indians, enjoyed a surge in tax revenues. But when local government passed out of Indian control, perhaps for good, and as the scale of development increased, many Indians began to feel qualms. What they had taken for granted—that this was their town—no longer held true. Large tracts of undeveloped land formerly open for hunting and fishing were suddenly ringed with "No Trespassing" signs. The New Seabury development, on a choice stretch of coastline, with its two golf courses and expansionist plans, seemed particularly egregious. Tensions between traditional residents and newcomers increased, finally leading to the suit, filed with the support of most, but not all, of the Indians in Mashpee. The land claim, while focusing on a loss of property in the nineteenth century, was actually an attempt to regain control of a town that had slipped from Indian hands very recently.

Earl Mills

Earl Mills has taught high school in the Falmouth Public School system for over twenty-five years. Between 1952 and 1967 he lived in Falmouth, ten miles from Mashpee. Mills has taught physical education, health, and social studies. He advises the student council and directs various other extracurricular activities.

In Mashpee he shares ownership of the town's best restaurant with his ex-wife, Shirley. He is its principal cook.

Since the mid-fifties Mills has held the title of Chief Flying Eagle of the Mashpee Wampanoag Tribe.

On the witness stand he is earnest, engaging, very much the coach or Boy Scout leader. Forty-eight years old, trim, athletic-looking, he wears a striped necktie, blue blazer, loafers.

Mills recalls his youth in Mashpee during the thirties and forties. He was never as good a hunter as his brother, Elwood, so he often skipped the frequent hunting trips. Early on he asked questions and read books. He questioned his grandmother, "the strong arm" behind his uncle (who had held the formal title of chief and was "a drifter"), and also his mother, the treasurer and tax collector of the town, "the strong arm behind me."

In the thirties, Mills recalls, some townspeople wore regalia occasionally, and a few spoke a little Indian dialect. He remembers the festive atmosphere of a close community—selling corn at town meetings, the yearly beach outings, the annual herring run.

As a child he was shown the location of "Indian taverns." These were not drinking places, according to Mills, but just places where paths crossed. You would pick up a stick, spit on it, and throw it on a heap to appease spirits in the area.

Mills says he can still identify two "Indian taverns," but most have long since been cleared away because the sticks, piled high, were a fire hazard.

This is the extent of the Indian rituals Mills reports. Raised a Baptist, he does not now consider himself a Christian; but he believes in a creator, "something greater than me."

Mills says that when he inquired after Indian artifacts, especially the traditional Mashpee plaited baskets, he was told by his father that "those fellows up around Cambridge must've taken them" (a reference probably to the Harvard Anthropology Department). His father showed him how to plait bark baskets, a skill he had acquired as a young man from Eben Queppish, a master basket maker in Mashpee.

Mills recalls that as a boy he made fun of the old-timers, including the medicine man of the period, William James.

In Falmouth High School Mills excelled in athletics. ("You had to be a scrapper to make it.") Sports were a road to confidence in a threatening environment. Outside of school, like his father and other Mashpee Indians, he served as a guide for hunting and fishing parties in the region.

Q.: "How was your youth different from that of any small-town youth?"

A.: "We were different. We knew we were different. We were told we were different."

Only in the late forties did Mills learn Indian dancing—in the army. On a lonely evening during basic training at Fort Dix two comrades, a Montana Chippewa and a New York Iroquois, performed their dances. Mills was chagrined to admit that he knew none himself.

Earl Mills tells about his five children-four by his first wife, who is part Navajo, and one by his second wife, who is Caucasian. The eldest, Roxanne, is married to a Choctaw. Earl Jr. (called "Chiefy") lives in Falmouth and in recent years has become a champion drummer at various Indian gatherings and powwows. Shelly, also a fine drummer, attends Native American festivals all over the Northeast. Robert lives on Commonwealth Avenue in Boston. "He's into quill work, leather work, skins." Nancy, the child of Mills's second marriage, is now six years old. She does Indian dances. Her parents agree that she is a Wampanoag.

Mills explains his duties as tribal chief. He teaches beadwork, leather-work, and basketry in Mashpee. Overall his job is to be a mediator, to keep his people "on balance."

Under questioning he cannot or will not give any specific examples of his mediations. Mills tells how in the late fifties and early sixties he and three whites formed a committee to restore the Old Indian Meeting House in Mashpee. The meeting house, which had fallen into disrepair, had for many years been the most visible symbol of Indian life in the town.

During the fifties there had been a tribal constitution of some sort (the document is introduced into evidence), but Mills testifies that the tribe did not follow the constitution as written. Tribal meetings were held irregularly, with notice passed by word of mouth. (Where, St. Clair asks on cross-examination, are the minutes for these purported tribal meetings?)

In the early seventies, Mills says, he attended a grant-writing seminar at Dartmouth College, along with Amelia Bingham, a state employee (sister of John Peters, the tribal medicine man, and Russell Peters, chairman of the Tribal Council, Inc.). Mills says he had little originally to do with the land suit. As chief he simply approved the action of the incorporated body on behalf of the tribe. It was discussed in his restaurant kitchen.

Earl Mills testifies that he respects John Peters. The two of them represent the Mashpee traditionalist wing. The modernists, he says, people like Russell Peters, are the legal arm of the tribe and represent its interests in dealings with the government, the courts, and foundations.

St. Clair's questions portray Chief Flying Eagle as an opportunist following rather than leading his people. They reveal that Mills's traditional authority was recently challenged by Russell Peters and others who wanted to sell beer at the annual Mashpee powwow, a festival attended by a considerable number of tourists and other outsiders. Over the chief's objections beer was sold. St. Clair harps on this evidence of lack of leadership. Rebuttals follow, concerning different tribal responsibilities and roles. There are references to President Carter's inability to control the (beer-related) behavior of his brother, Billy.

On the stand Chief Flying Eagle often sounds like a social studies teacher; his speech is larded with pat anecdotes and homilies.

Only once, toward the end of his testimony, does he do something unexpected. Asked whether he often wears Indian regalia, Mills answers no, only at powwows. Then he suddenly lugs at his necktie, pulling two thin strings of beads from under his shirt. One, he says, is turquoise, from the Southwest. The other small strand was a gift from his father.

Many people in the courtroom are surprised by this apparently sponta-neous revelation—surprised and, as Mills stuffs the beads back into his shirt and fumbles to readjust his tie, a little embarrassed.

Images

At the end of the trial Federal Judge Walter J. Skinner posed a number of specific questions to the jurors concerning tribal status at

certain dates in Mashpee history; but throughout the proceedings broader questions of Indian identity and power permeated the courtroom. Although the land claim was formally not at issue, the lawyers for New Seabury et al. sometimes seemed to be playing on a new nightmare. At the door of your suburban house a stranger in a business suit appears. He says he is a Native American. Your land has been illegally acquired generations ago, and you must relinquish your home. The stranger refers you to his lawyer.

Such fears, the threat of a "giveaway" of private lands, were much exploited by politicians and the press in the Penobscot-Passamaquoddy negotiations. Actually small holdings by private citizens were never in danger; only large tracts of undeveloped land held by timber companies and the state were in question. In Mashpee the plaintiffs reduced their claim to eleven thousand acres, formally excluding all private homes and lots up to an acre in size. Large-scale development, not small ownership, was manifestly the target; but their opponents refused pretrial compromises and the kinds of negotiation that had led to settlement of the Maine dispute.

According to Thomas Tureen the sorts of land claims pursued in Maine, Mashpee, Gay Head, and Charlestown were always drastically circumscribed. At that historical moment the courts were relatively open to Native American claims, a situation unlikely to last. In a decision of 1985 permitting Oneida, Mohawk, and Cayuga Non-Intercourse Act suits the Supreme Court made it abundantly clear, in Tureen's words, "that Indians are dealing with the magnanimity of a rich and powerful nation, one that is not about to divest itself or its non-Indian citizens of large acreage in the name of its own laws." In short, the United States will permit Indians a measure of recompense through the law—indeed, it has done so to an extent far greater than any other nation in a comparable situation—but it ultimately makes the rules and arbitrates the game. (Tureen 1985:147; also Barsh and Henderson 1980:289–293).

Seen in this light, the Mashpee trial was simply a clarification of the rules in an ongoing struggle between parties of greatly unequal power. But beneath the explicit fear of white citizens losing their homes because of an obscure past injustice, a troubling uncertainty was finding its way into the dominant image of Indians in America. The plaintiffs in the Non-Intercourse Act suits had power. In Maine politicians lost office over the issue, and the Mashpee case made national headlines for several months. Scandalously, it now paid to be Indian. Acting aggressively, tribal groups were doing sophisticated, "nontraditional" things. All over the country they were becoming involved in a variety of businesses, some claiming exemption from state regulation. To many whites it was comprehensible for Northwest Coast tribes to demand traditional salmon-fishing privileges; but for tribes to run high-stakes bingo games in violation of state laws was not.

Indians had long filled a pathetic imaginative space for the dominant culture; they were always survivors, noble or wretched. Their cultures had been steadily eroding, at best hanging on in museumlike reservations. Native American societies could not by definition be dynamic, inventive, or expansive. Indians were lovingly remembered in Edward Curtis' sepia

photographs as proud, beautiful, and "vanishing." But Curtis, we now know, carried props, costumes, and wigs, frequently dressing up his models. The image he recorded was carefully staged (Lyman 1982). In Boston Federal Court a jury of white citizens would be confronted by a collection of highly ambiguous images. Could a group of four women and eight men (no minorities) be made to believe in the persistent "Indian" existence of the Mashpee plaintiffs without costumes and props? This question surrounded and infused the trial's technical focus on whether a particular form of political-cultural organization called a tribe had existed continuously in Mashpee since the sixteenth century.

The image of Mashpee Indians, like that of several other eastern groups such as the Lumbee and the Ramapough, was complicated **by** issues of race (Blu 1980; Cohen 1974). Significant intermarriage **with** blacks had occurred since the mid-eighteenth century, and the Mashpee were, at times, widely identified as "colored." In court the defense occasionally suggested that they were really blacks rather than Native Americans. Like the Lumbee (and, less successfully, the Ramapough) the Mashpee plaintiffs had struggled to distinguish themselves from other minorities and ethnic groups, asserting tribal status based on a distinctive political-cultural history. In court they were not helped by the fact that few of them looked strongly "Indian." Some could pass for black, others for white.

* * *

Borderlines

Mashpee Indians suffered the fate of many small Native American groups who remained in the original thirteen states. They were not accorded the reservations and sovereign status (steadily eroded) of tribes west of the Mississippi. Certain of the eastern communities, such as the Seneca and the Seminoles, occupied generally recognized tribal lands. Others—the Lumbee, for example—possessed no collective lands but clustered in discrete regions, maintaining kinship ties, traditions, and sporadic tribal institutions. In all cases the boundaries of the community were permeable. There was intermarriage and routine migration in and out of the tribal center—sometimes seasonal, sometimes longer term. Aboriginal languages were much diminished, often entirely lost. Religious life was diverse—sometimes Christian (with a distinctive twist), sometimes a transformed tradition such as the Iroquois Longhouse Religion. Moral and spiritual values were often Native American amalgams compounded from both local traditions and pan-Indian sources. For example the ritual and regalia at New England powwows now reflect Sioux and other western tribal influences; in the 1920s the feathered "war bonnet" made its appearance among Wampanoag leaders. Eastern Indians generally lived in closer proximity to white (or black) society and in smaller groups than their western reservation counterparts. In the face of intense pressure some eastern communities have managed to acquire official federal recognition as tribes, others not. During the past two decades the rate of applications has risen dramatically.

Within this diversity of local histories and institutional arrangements the long-term residents of Mashpee occupied a gray area, at least in the eyes of the surrounding society and the law. The Indian identity of the Penobscot and Passamaquoddy was never seriously challenged, even though they had not been federally recognized and had lost or adapted many of their traditions. The Mashpee were more problematic. Partisans of their land claim, such as Paul Brodeur (1985), tend to accept without question the right of the tribal council, incorporated in 1974, to sue on behalf of a group that had lost its lands in the mid-nineteenth century. They see the question of tribal status as a legal red herring, or worse, a calculated ploy to deny the tribe its birthright. However procrustean and colonial in origin the legal definition of tribe, there was nonetheless a real issue at stake in the trial. Although tribal status and Indian identity have long been vague and politically constituted, not just anyone with some native blood or claim to adoption or shared tradition can be an Indian; and not just any Native American group can decide to be a tribe and sue for lost collective lands.

Indians in Mashpee owned no tribal lands (other than fifty-five acres acquired just before the trial). They had no surviving language, no clearly distinct religion, no blatant political structure. Their kinship was much diluted. Yet they did have a place and a reputation. For centuries Mashpee had been recognized as an Indian town. Its boundaries had not changed since 1665, when the land was formally deeded to a group called the South Sea Indians by the neighboring leaders Tookonchasun and Weepquish. The Mashpee plaintiffs of 1977 could offer as evidence surviving pieces of Native American tradition and political structures that seemed to have come and gone. They could also point to a sporadic history of Indian revivals continuing into the present.

The Mashpee were a borderline case. In the course of their peculiar litigation certain underlying structures governing the recognition of identity and difference became visible. Looked at one way, they were Indian, seen another way, they were not. Powerful ways of *looking* thus became inescapably problematic. The trial was less a search for the facts of Mashpee Indian culture and history than it was an experiment in translation—part of a long historical conflict and negotiation of "Indian" and "American" identities.

◆

I offer vignettes of persons and events in the courtroom that are obviously composed and condensed. Testimony evoked in a page or two may run to hundreds of pages in the transcript. Some witnesses were on the stand for several days. Moreover, real testimony almost never ends the way my vignettes do; it trails off in the quibbles and corrections of redirect and recross-examination. While I have included for comparison a verbatim excerpt from the transcript, I have generally followed my courtroom notes, checked against the record, and have not hesitated to rearrange, select, and highlight. Where quotation marks appear, the statement is a fairly exact quotation; the rest is paraphrase.

Overall, if the witnesses seem flat and somewhat elusive, the effect is intentional. Using the usual rhetorical techniques, I could have given a more intimate sense of peoples' personalities or of what they were really trying to express; but I have preferred to keep my distance. A courtroom is more like a theater than a confessional.

Mistrustful of transparent accounts, I want mine to manifest some of its frames and angles, its wavelengths.

* * *

History I

The case against the plaintiffs was straightforward: there never had been an Indian tribe in Mashpee. The community was a creation of the colonial encounter, a collection of disparate Indians and other minorities who sought over the years to become full citizens of the Commonwealth of Massachusetts and of the Republic. Decimated by disease, converted to Christianity, desirous of freedom from paternalistic state tutelage, the people of mixed Indian descent in Mashpee were progressively assimilated into American society. Their Indian identity had been lost, over and over, since the mid-seventeenth century.[2]

The plague. When the English Pilgrims arrived at Plymouth in 1620, they found a region devastated by a disease brought by white seamen. The settlers walked into empty Indian villages and planted in already cleared fields. The region was seriously underpopulated. In the years that followed Puritan leaders like Myles Standish pressed steadily to limit Indian territories and to establish clear "properties" for the growing number of newcomers. Misunderstandings inevitably ensued: for example whites claimed to own unoccupied land that had been ceded to them for temporary use.

Richard Bourne of Sandwich, a farmer near what is now Mashpee Pond and a tenant on Indian lands, studied the language of his landlords and soon became an effective mediator between the societies. He was friendly to the area's inhabitants, remnants of earlier groups, who came to be called South Sea Indians by the settlers to the north. He believed that they needed protection; becoming their advocate, he negotiated formal title to a large tract adjoining his farm (which in the meantime he had managed to purchase). His ally in these transactions was Paupmunnuck, a leader of the nearby Cotachesset.

---

2. The two "histories" that follow represent the best brief interpretive accounts I could construct of the contending versions of Mashpee's past. They draw selectively on the expert testimony presented at the trial—testimony much too long, complex, and contested to summarize adequately. The overall shape of the two accounts reflects the summation provided at the end of the testimony by each side's principle attorney. "History I" owes a good deal to Francis Hutchins' book *Mashpee: The Story of Cape Cod's Indian Town* (1979). This book takes a somewhat more moderate position than the courtroom testimony on which it is based. "History II" owes something to the general approach of James Axtell's book *The European and the Indian* (1981). Axtell was a witness for the plaintiffs.

Bourne's "South Sea Indian Plantation" was to become a refuge for Christian converts, for as white power increased, it became increasingly dangerous for Indians to live around Cape Cod unless they came together as a community of "praying Indians." Under Bourne's tutelage the Mashpee plantation was a center for the first Indian church on the Cape, organized in 1666.

Thus Mashpee was originally an artificial community, never a tribe. It was created from Indian survivors in an area between the traditional sachemdoms of Manomet and Nauset—the former centered on the present town of Bourne at the Cape's western edge, the latter near its tip.

Conversion to Christianity. Badly disorganized after the plague and confronted by a growing number of determined settlers, the Cape Cod Indians made accommodations. Live and let live was not the Puritan way, especially once their power had been consolidated. Tensions and conflicts grew, leading to war in 1675 with the forces of the Wampanoag Supreme Sachem Metacomet ("King Philip"). After Metacomet's defeat Indians who sympathized with him were expelled from their lands. Many, including some who had remained neutral, were sold into slavery.

The price for living on ancestral lands in eastern New England was cooperation with white society. The Mashpee, under Bourne's tutelage became model Christians. By 1674 ninety Mashpee inhabitants were counted as baptized, and twenty-seven were admitted to full communion. The "praying Indians" were entering a new life. They stopped consulting "powwows" (medicine men, in seventeenth-century usage); they respected the Sabbath and other holy days, severed ties with "pagans," altered child-rearing practices, dressed in new ways, washed differently. The changes were gradual but telling. They reflected not only a tactical accommodation but also a new belief, born of defeat, that the powerful white ways must be superior. When Bourne died in 1682, his successor as protestant minister was an Indian, Simon Popmonet, son of Bourne's old ally Paupmunnuck. This was a further sign that the Indians were willingly giving up their old ways for the new faith.

"Plantation" status. Once the South Sea Indian Plantation had been established, its inhabitants' claim to their land rested on a written deed and on English law rather than on any aboriginal sovereignty. Like other "plantations" in New England, the community at Mashpee was a joint-ownership arrangement by a group of "proprietors." Under English law proprietors were licensed to develop a vacant portion of land, reserving part for commons, part for the church, and part for individual holdings. All transfers of land were to be approved collectively. This plantation-proprietory form, as applied to early Cape Cod settlements such as Sandwich and Barnstable, was intended to evolve quickly into a township where freemen held individual private property and were represented in the General Court of the colony. The white plantations around Mashpee did evolve directly into towns. From the late seventeenth century on their common lands were converted into private individual holdings in fee simple. Mashpee followed the same course, but more slowly. As late as 1830 its lands were the joint property of proprietors.

For complex historical reasons Mashpee's progress toward full citizenship lagged almost two centuries behind that of its neighbors. An enduring prejudice against Indians, and their supposed lack of "civility" certainly played a part, for during the early and mid-eighteenth century the Indian plantation was governed in humiliating ways by white "guardians." Nonetheless, development toward autonomy, while delayed, did occur. In 1763, after a direct appeal to King George III, Mashpee won the right to incorporation as a district, a step on the road to township status and a liberation from oppressive meddling by white outsiders. Then, beginning in 1834 and culminating in 1870, a series of acts of the Massachusetts legislature changed the Mashpee plantation into an incorporated town. Its inhabitants had overcome the prejudice and paternalism that had so long hemmed them in. They were now full-fledged citizens of Massachusetts.

Taking the colonists' side. From early on the Indian inhabitants of Mashpee gave signs of active identification with the new white society. During King Philip's War a certain Captain Amos, probably a Nauset from near Sandwich, led a group of Indians against Metacomet. Amos became a prominent inhabitant of Mashpee after the conflict ended. A century later the district of Mashpee sent a contingent to fight in the Revolutionary War against the British, a commitment of troops even greater than that of the surrounding white towns. Reliable accounts estimate that about half the adult male population died in the war. A Mashpee Indian, Joshua Pocknet, served at Valley Forge with George Washington. At these critical moments, therefore, the descendants of the South Sea Indians showed something more than simple acquiescence under colonial rule. Their enthusiastic patriotism strongly suggests that they had identified with white society, relinquishing any sense of a separate tribal political identity.

Intermarriage. Mashpee's population showed two significant periods of expansion. During the 1660s and 1670s there had been an influx of Indians from elsewhere on the Cape. Then after a century of relative equilibrium the population rose again in the 1760s and 1770s. Census figures are inexact and subject to interpretation, but it seems clear that before 1760 the principal newcomers were a steady trickle of New England Indians: Wampanoags from Gay Head and Herring Pond, Narragansets and Mohicans from Connecticut, Long Island Montauks. Immigration was restrained by the tutelage of outside "guardians," some of whom had an interest in keeping Mashpee small so that "unused" Indian lands could be made available for whites. After 1763, however, the newly incorporated district opened its borders to a variety of new settlers. A few whites entered by marriage but maintained a separate legal status. Their progeny, if one parent was Indian, could become proprietors. A least one white man "went native," living in a wigwam—just as the Indian residents of Mashpee were abandoning the last of theirs. Four Hessian mercenaries stayed on after the Revolutionary War and married Mashpee women. It is recorded that they accepted Indian manners.

The 1776 census counted fourteen "negroes" in a total population of 341. Significant intermarriage with freed black slaves occurred in this period, but it is difficult to say how much since common parlance, reflected in the census, sometimes mixed diverse peoples of brownish skin color in categories such as "Indian," "mulatto," or "negro." Intermarriage between blacks and Indians was encouraged by a common social marginality and by a relative shortage of men among the Indians and of women among the blacks. The local racial mix also included Cape Verde islanders and exotic imports resulting from the employment of Mashpee men in the far-flung sailing trades and women in domestic service: a Mexican and an Indian from Bombay are mentioned in the written sources.

By 1789 Mashpee's white minister, the Reverend Gideon Hawley, had become so concerned about Mashpee being overrun by blacks and foreigners that he engineered a return to plantation status, with himself as guardian of the town's threatened authenticity. This return to a restrictive paternalism was a setback for Mashpee's ability to grow and develop into a distinctive, independent nonwhite community. It was not until the 1840s, after a long conflict with Hawley's successor, the Reverend Phineas Fish, that local leaders finally rid themselves of outside tutelage. The struggle for citizenship had been slowed but not stopped. By the time of the final transition from plantation to township status in the four decades after 1830 the American citizens of Mashpee had become a complex mix—"colored" in contemporary parlance—that included several American Indian, black, and foreign ingredients.

Mashpee becomes a town. In 1834, following a popular rebellion against the outside authority of the Presbyterian minister Fish, district status was again accorded by the Massachusetts General Court. The Mashpee were no longer wards of the state and, like other towns, were governed by three elected selectmen. But full citizenship did not follow, largely because the proprietors of Mashpee wished to preserve traditional restraints on the sale of lands to outsiders. Leaders such as Daniel Amos argued that many inhabitants of Mashpee were not yet ready for the responsibilities of citizenship and unrestricted property rights. They might sell their lands irresponsibly or be maneuvered into debt; the community would be invaded and broken up. In practice the entailment on property did not seal off Mashpee from growth. To qualify as a landowner one had to trace ancestry to at least one Indian proprietor; and by the mid-nineteenth century quite a few individuals around the Cape could make this claim. In 1841–42, at the urging of Indian entrepreneurs such as Solomon Attaquin, who had returned to Mashpee with the end of state tutelage, most of the district's common lands were divided among its individual proprietors—men, women, and children. Lands could now be freely bought and sold, but still only among proprietors.

This progress did not go uncontested. Mashpee was divided among those who, like Attaquin—self-made men reflecting the era's dominant laissez-faire capitalist ethos—wanted to move quickly to remove all barriers to individual initiative and others who wanted to move more slowly or who saw in the old plantation entailments a guarantee of community integrity. In 1868 matters finally came to a head. A petition to the General Court from two of Mashpee's three selectmen and twenty-nine residents requested an end to all land-sale restrictions and the granting of full state and federal voting rights. This petition was promptly countered by a "remonstrance" signed by the third selectman and fifty-seven Mashpee residents urging that the district's status not be altered. A public hearing was called to air the differing views.

The hearing, which took place in early 1869, marks a crucial turning point in Mashpee history. Records of its disagreements offer a rare access to a diversity of local voices and opinions. Those who spoke in favor of the proposed changes evoked centuries of degrading state tutelage and second-class status. It was time, they said, for Mashpee inhabitants to be full citizens, to stand on their own. If this meant that some would fail or be displaced from their lands, so be it. They spoke also of the commercial advantages to the region of making portions of its land available for outside capital investment. Representatives of Mashpee's "colored non-proprietors" (a status that gave certain mulattoes and blacks all rights of proprietorship except title to land) also favored the changes in legal status. As valued members of the community they felt the restriction on landholding to be an insult and a reminder of an inferior condition they had in every other respect left behind.

Others opposed the changes. They argued that the influx of outside capital would be a very mixed blessing, and without the present protections many who were not wealthy and wise to the ways of business would soon be displaced. They would find themselves, in the words of one speaker, "ducking and dodging from one city to another, and gain no residence." Some proprietors did not think the right to vote in state and federal elections worth the risk; the present system, providing real control over Mashpee's government, seemed sufficient to local needs. The Reverend Joseph Amos ("Blind Joe" Amos), the community's most influential spiritual voice and leader of a successful Indian Baptist movement three decades earlier, opposed the changes. He said that another generation of preparation was needed before the proposed step could safely be taken. Solomon Attaquin, who owned the Hotel Attaquin, a renowned hunting lodge in Mashpee, spoke for abandoning the district's special status. He evoked a lifelong dream of full citizenship and equality, a dream shared with others in the community. Those who had worked long and hard for this day should not have to die without gaining the status of free men in the commonwealth and the nation.

A vote was taken. Eighteen favored participation in federal and state elections, eighteen were opposed. The removal of land restrictions was sharply rejected, twenty-six to fourteen. Despite this vote by a minority of the total population the recorded discussions clearly showed a consensus in favor of ultimately ending Mashpee's special status, with disagreements only on the timing. The Massachusetts General Court, recognizing this fact and more impressed by Mashpee's "progressive" voices, in 1870 formally abolished the status of "Mashpee proprietor." All lands were henceforth held in fee simple with no restrictions on alienation. All residents, whatever their ancestry, now enjoyed equal status before the law. The transfer of town lands to outsiders began immediately.

This turning point marked the end of Mashpee's distinctive institutional status stemming from its Indian past. Though the community was divided on the change, the most dynamic, forward-looking leaders favored it; whatever their hesitations on timing, community members willingly embraced their future as Massachusetts and United States citizens.

Assimilation. During the years between 1670 and the 1920s Indians throughout the nation were forced to abandon tribal organizations and to become individual citizen-farmers, workers, and businessmen. This was the period of the Dawes Act with its extensive land-allotment projects west of the Mississippi. Not until the twenties was there much evidence anywhere of tribal dynamism. Mashpee residents continued to live as before, working as hunting and fishing guides, servants, and laborers in various trades. The town remained a backwater. To find steady work people often had to move to nearby towns or even farther afield. The historical record contains little evidence of any distinctly Indian life in Mashpee before the Wampanoag revival movements of the twenties. The town apparently did not undergo any major demographic or social changes and remained a rather cohesive community of long-term residents, most of whom were of varying degrees of Indian descent. Significantly, between 1905 and 1960 the category "Indian" disappeared from Mashpee's federal census records. The more than two hundred individuals who had previously been so classified were now listed as either "colored" (distinct from "negro") or "other." Only in 1970 would they again be called Indian. In the eyes of the state the majority of Mashpee's inhabitants were simply Americans of color.

Some of these Americans participated in the founding of the Wampanoag Nation in the late twenties. At that time various more-or-less theatrical revivals of Indian institutions were under way. People in Mashpee showed interest, but the daily life and government of the town were not materially affected. The Wampanoags did not, like many other Indian groups in the thirties, take advantage of the turnaround in policy at John Collier's Bureau of Indian Affairs (BIA) to reorganize themselves as a federally recognized "tribal" unit. The new sense of Indianness around Mashpee was a matter of county fairlike powwows, costumes, and folkloric dances.

The individuals of Indian ancestry from Mashpee who filed suit in 1976 were American citizens similar to Irish-or Italian–Americans with strong ethnic attachments. Individuals such as Earl Mills and John and Russell Peters had simply taken advantage of the latest wave of pan-Indian revivalism and the prospect of financial gain to constitute themselves as a Mashpee Tribe. Mashpee's distinctive history was in fact a story of Indian–Christian remnants who over the centuries had repeatedly given up their customs and sovereignty. Theirs had been a long, hard struggle for equality and respect in a multiethnic America.

Vicky M. Costa

Vicky Costa is seventeen years old; her father is Portuguese, her mother Indian. She considers herself an Indian. She looks like any American teenager.

Q.: How do you know you're an Indian? A.: My mother told me.

She speaks softly. Judge Skinner asks her to speak up so the court can hear. "Think of yourself shouting across a field to those people," indicating the jury, "over there." (The "field" is a courtroom cluttered with lawyers tables, papers, documents, items of evidence.)

Vicky Costa does not shout, and everyone listens closely. She tells about the values she is currently learning in Mashpee: "To walk on Mother Earth in balance, and to respect every living thing."

Q.: How often do you dance? A.: All the time. Q.: When did you dance most recently? A.: Last night.

She describes her Indian dancing. She says she first learned at a powwow "a long time ago." Now she attends powwows regularly.

She names the dances: animal names, "blanket dance," "fancy dance." In the "round dance" they turn and dance to the good and bad spirit, moving in both directions so neither of the spirits will be offended. Is there music? Singing? Just the round-dance song. The purpose of the animal dances? To imitate the animals, mocking them. To thank the Creator for that animal.

(The mood in these questions and answers is conversational, quiet. Is it partly because this time Ann Gilmore of the plaintiffs' trial team is conducting the examination? It is one of the rare moments in the trial when a woman speaks directly with another woman. For whatever reasons the prevailing sense of contest and performance is gone.)

Costa testifies that she has been studying what she calls the "Wampanoag language" for one-and-a-half years. She says that as a girl she had to go to the Baptist church but now believes in Indian values.

On cross-examination she assents to hostile questions with the devastating American teenage shrug: "Yeah . . . yeah . . . yeah . . ."

History II

The case against the Mashpee plaintiffs was based on a reading of Cape Cod history. Documents were gathered, interpreted, and arranged in a coherent sequence. The story emerged of a small mixed community fighting for equality and citizenship while abandoning, by choice or coercion, most of its aboriginal heritage. But a different, also coherent, story was constructed by the plaintiffs, drawing on the same documentary record. In this account the residents of Mashpee had managed to keep alive a core of Indian identity over three centuries against enormous odds. They had done so in supple, sometimes surreptitious ways, always attempting to control, not reject, outside influences.

The plague. Aboriginally the concept of tribe has little meaning. The "political" institutions of Native American groups before contact with Europeans varied widely. Cape Cod Indian groupings seem to have been flexible, with significant movement across territories. Communities formed and reformed. In this context it is unclear whether the elders of local villages or sachems or supreme sachems should be identified as "tribal" leaders. These individuals had supreme power in some situations, limited authority in others. The plague was a disaster, but it did not decimate the Cape to the extent that it did the Plymouth area. In any event the response of the survivors at Mashpee, regrouping to form a cohesive unit, was a traditional political response, albeit to an unusual emergency. Written sources reflect only the views of whites, such as the evangelist Bourne, who saw his "praying Indians" paternalistically as passive remnants. The intentions of leaders such as Paupmunnuck and his kin are not recorded.

Thus it is anachronistic to say that the community gathered at what would later be called Mashpee was not a tribe. It is well known that the political institutions of many bona fide American Indian "tribes" actually emerged during the nineteenth and twentieth centuries in response to white expectations and power. Neat analytic categories such as "political organization," "kinship," "religion," and "economy" do not reflect Indian ways of seeing things. The simple fact remains that Bourne's South Sea Indian Plantation was a discrete community of Cape Cod Indians living on traditional Indian land—an arrangement that, through many modifications, survived until the mid-twentieth century.

Conversion to Christianity. Accounts of conversion as a process of "giving up old ways" or "choosing a new path" usually reflect a wishful evangelism rather than the more complex realities of cultural change, resistance, and translation. Recent ethnohistorical scholarship has tended to show that Native Americans' response to Christianity was syncretic over the long run, almost never a radical either-or choice. Moreover, in situations of drastically unequal power, as on Puritan Cape Cod, one should expect the familiar response of colonized persons: outward agreement and inner resistance.

The disruptions caused by disease, trade, and military conquest were extreme. All Indian societies had to adjust, and they developed varying strategies for doing so. Some passed through revitalization movements in the late eighteenth and early nineteenth centuries, led by messianic figures: the Delaware Prophet or Handsome Lake. These movements incorporated Christian features in a new "traditional" religion. Other groups renewed native culture by using Christianity for their own purposes. The white man's religion could be added on to traditional deities and rites. Beliefs that appeared contradictory to Puritan evangelists coexisted in daily life. Native American religions are generally more tolerant, pragmatic, and inclusive than Christianity, a strongly evangelical, exclusive faith.

This is not to say that groups such as the South Sea Indians did not embrace Christianity in good faith or find there a source of spiritual strength. It is only to caution against the either-or logic of conversion as seen by the outsiders whose accounts dominate the written record. The gain of Christian beliefs did not necessarily mean the loss of Indian spirituality. It is easy to be impressed by surface transformations of clothing and public behavior and to forget that continuous kin ties and life on a familiar piece of land also carry potent "religious" values.

Adopting Christianity in Mashpee was not merely a survival strategy in an intolerant, hostile environment. The faith of the "praying Indians" kept a distinctly indigenous cast. Beginning with Richard Bourne's successor, Simon Popmonet, Indian ministers in Mashpee preached in Massachusett, a practice that continued throughout the eighteenth century. When white missionaries were imposed from outside, they were forced to use some Massachusett or to compromise, like Gideon Hawley, who conducted bilingual services in tandem with a respected Indian pastor, Solomon Briant. Moreover, the historical record before 1850 is filled with conflict between authoritarian missionaries and Indian church members. Hawley, who served from 1757 to 1807, progressively alienated his parishioners, especially after Solomon Briant's death in 1775. His successor, Phineas Fish, lost virtually all local support and in 1840, after a protracted struggle, was physically ejected from the Old Indian Meeting House by irate Indian Christians.

Baptist revivalism had already won over most of the congregation, a change tied to a political assertion of Indian power. As in many nativist revitalization movements, an Indian outsider took a leading role—in this case William Apes, a young Pequot Baptist preacher. Blind Joe Amos had already acquired a larger following for his all-Indian Baptist meetings than the Congregationalist minister, Fish.

The situation was volatile. Apes, a firebrand with a vision of united action by "colored" peoples against white oppressors, stimulated a Masphee "Declaration of Independence" in 1833 on behalf of a sovereign Mashpee Tribe. (This was one of the few times before the twentieth century that the word tribe appears in the historical record.) The effect of the declaration and of the political maneuvers that ensued was to wrest control of the town's religion from the outsider Fish, reclaiming the Meeting House and funds from Harvard University supporting Indian Christianity for the majority faith, which was now Baptist. Mashpee returned to district status, free of outside governors.

Over the centuries Indians in Mashpee fought to keep control first of their Presbyterian and then their Baptist institutions. Religion was a political as well as a spiritual issue. Well into the 1950s the New England Baptist Convention habitually referred to Mashpee as "our Indian church." The exact nature of Mashpee Christian belief and practice over the centuries is obscure. The historical record does not inform us, for example, of exactly what took place in Blind Joe Amos' insurgent Baptist services during the 1830s; but even the partial written record makes it clear that Christianity in Mashpee, symbolized by the Old Indian Meeting House, was a site of local power and of resistance to outsiders. At recurring intervals it was a focus of openly Indian, or "tribal," power.

"Plantation" Status. Leaders of the South Sea Indians probably recognized, with Bourne, that title to land under white law was needed if it was not to be despoiled by an aggressive colonization; but seventeenth-century English proprietory forms did not unduly restrict their ability to function as an Indian community. Collective ownership of land, with individual use rights, could be maintained. The legal status that to some appeared an impediment to progress in fact protected the traditional life ways of Indian proprietors.

Although eastern Indians were not accorded reservation lands, Mashpee's plantation status created a de facto reservation. Unlike all its neighbors Mashpee did not quickly become a town but had the status forced on it in 1869. The plantation was widely considered to be Indian land held collectively in a distinctive manner. The reasons for keeping Mashpee "backward," a pupil of the state, were often racist and paternalist; but from the viewpoint of a small group struggling to maintain its collective identify, the proprietorship arrangement was an effective way of having legal status while also maintaining a difference. While there was internal disagreement at times, the majority of Mashpee proprietors consistently favored keeping the plantation land system. This was changed only by legislative fiat in 1969, against their expressed wishes. Until then an "archaic" status had been effectively used to preserve Indian lands in a collective form through rapidly changing times. The land claim suit aimed to restore a situation illegally altered by the Massachusetts legislature.

Taking the colonists' side. The fact that some South Sea Indians fought against Metacomet in King Philip's War does not prove that they were abandoning their Indian sovereignty or independence. More did not fight, and the motivations of those who did are a matter of speculation. There was nothing new about Indians making war on other Indians. Moreover they may have had little choice. Puritan authorities were on the warpath, and even "loyal" Indians were punished during and after the war by loss of lands and slavery.

As for the war against England, again we should be wary of imputing motives. The Mashpee Indians who served in the Revolutionary Army may not have done so primarily as "American" patriots. They were, among other things, rebelling against the authority of their missionary Hawley, an ardent Tory. Moreover, as Indian status has evolved in the United States, it has been legally recognized that the privileges of citizenship (including the decision to unite in war against a common enemy) do not contradict other arrangements establishing special group identity and status. One can be fully a citizen and fully an Indian.

To expect Cape Cod Indians to hold themselves apart from the historical currents and conflicts of the dominant society would be to ask them to commit suicide. Survival in changing circumstances meant participation, wherever possible on their own terms. Staying separate or uninvolved would be to yield to the dangerous fantasies of protectors, like Hawley, who worked to keep the Mashpee pure—and under his tutelage. The inhabitants of Mashpee again and again resisted this restrictive "authenticity." The record confirms that they wanted integrity but never isolation.

Intermarriage. There was a good deal of racial mixing In Mashpee, but the exact extent is hard to determine, given the shifting categories of different censuses and doubts about how race was actually measured. Mashpee was a refuge for misfits, refugees, and marginal groups. At certain times a natural alliance against dominant white society formed between the town's Indian "survivors" and newly freed blacks. The crucial issue is whether the core Indian community absorbed the outsiders or were themselves absorbed in the American melting pot.

Historical evidence supports the former conclusion. Since whites and people of color who settled in Mashpee during the eighteenth and most of the nineteenth centuries could not become proprietors, this limited the influx; non-Indians remained a significant but small minority. Children with one Indian parent could become full community members. Intermarriage frequently occurred, and thus the purity of Indian blood was much diluted; but the legal and social structure consistently favored Indian identification. With land entailment and the maintenance of close kin ties among property holders a core was maintained. In any event blood is a debatable measure of identity, and to arrive at quotas for determining "tribal" status is always a problematic exercise. There are federally recognized tribes as mixed as the Mashpee, and organized Indian groups vary widely in the amount of traceable ancestry they actually require for membership.

Ethnohistorical studies show that in New England mixing of different communities was common well before the Pilgrims' arrival. Adoption was frequent, and it was customary to capture and incorporate opponents in war. Indians were in this respect color blind. In colonial times a large number of white captives stayed with their captors, adopting Indian ways, some even becoming chiefs. Mashpee's later openness to outsiders—as long as the newcomers intermarried and conformed to Indian ways—was a continuation of an aboriginal tradition, not a loss of distinct identity.

In 1859, after more than a century of intermarriage and sporadic population growth (the dilution of Indian stock lamented by the missionary Hawley), a detailed report by the commissioner for Indian affairs, John Earle, offered a census of the "Mashpee Tribe" that included 371 "natives" and 32 "foreigners." The latter were people living on the land without proprietary rights and not lineal descendants of Indians. They were described as "Africans" and "colored." Only one "white" was listed. The names of "natives" listed on the 1859 census served in the trial as a benchmark of continuous "tribal" kinship ties.

Mashpee becomes a town. There is strong documentary evidence that most of the proprietors between 1834 and 1869 wanted to hold on to Mashpee's special land restrictions. Commissioner Earle asserts this in his report. "Progressives" such as Attaquin were more vocal, and their testimony thus receives more weight in the record than the less articulate majority who in 1869 voted decisively against township status. Spokesmen (note how few female voices are "heard" by history, although the role of women at the center of community life was undoubtedly crucial) such as Blind Joe Amos and his brother Daniel urged postponing the transition. They argued that most people in Mashpee were too "immature," not "ready" to dispose of their land individually. Give us just one more generation, Daniel Amos asked in the 1830s. His brother asked the same thing in the late 1860s. What do these arguments signify?

For those who see Mashpee's "development" and assimilation as inevitable, such statements require no interpretation: they simply show that even the traditionalists in Mashpee were ready eventually to give up their special status. But this is to assume the historical outcome. The Indian proprietors of Mashpee valued community integrity and possessed effective public and informal leadership. They had shown much strength and initiative in dealing with their various "protectors." The early historical record reveals a steady stream of petitions—1748, 1753, 1760—on behalf of the "poor Indians of Mashpee called the South Sea Indians" protesting abuses by the agents appointed to watch over them. More recently they had successfully asserted their autonomy against the missionaries Hawley and Fish. They were hardly "immature." Yet throughout the mid-nineteenth century Mashpee proprietors temporized, hesitated in the face of an "inevitable" progress. Their ability to protect their community from the coercions and enticements of white society was evidently precious to them.

The modified plantation status they had secured in 1834 gave them a way of keeping collective control over land and immigration while not isolating the community from interaction with the surrounding society. Even the "allotment" of lands sanctioned at that time reproduced an aboriginal land arrangement. Parcels were traditionally given to families for exclusive use while ultimate collective ownership was maintained. (In 1834, moreover, three thousand acres were formally kept as common land.) Continuing entailments on land sales outside the community guaranteed a flexible nineteenth-century tribalism. In this context public arguments about Mashpee's "immaturity" should be seen as ways of addressing an outside audience, the Massachusetts General Court, which still thought of the plantation as a ward of the state and which had already decided and again would arbitrarily decide its fate. It would be impolitic in addressing this body to say that Mashpee rejected full township status in the name of a distinctive vision of Indian community and citizenship. An argument for delay couched in paternalist rhetoric was more likely to succeed.

This interpretation of the debates in 1869 is at least as plausible as a literal reading of the recorded public utterances. Mashpee, like Indian communities throughout their recent history, was split between modernists and traditionalists. The traditionalists prevailed in the vote, but the modernists swayed the authorities. In changing Mashpee's land entailment the legislature violated both simple democracy and, the Federal Non–Intercourse Act of 1790. But even the forced change—although it ultimately brought much land into non-Indian hands—was not fatal. The Mashpee

Indians used their new imposed status as they had their former one. For almost a century local government was kept firmly in the hands of a closely interrelated group of town officers. Mashpee remained "Cape Cod's Indian Town."

Assimilation. The Mashpee Indians did not "assimilate." The term's linear, either-or connotations cannot account for revivalism and for changes in the cultural and political climate between 1869 and 1960. There have been better and worse times in the United States to be publicly Indian. The late nineteenth and early twentieth centuries were among the worst. Government policy strongly favored tribal termination and the dispersal of collective lands. It was not until the late 1920s that the failure of allotment schemes was recognized and a "New Indian Policy" instituted at the BIA that favored tribal reorganization. If there is little evidence in the historical record of "tribal" life in Mashpee between 1869 and 1920, it is no surprise. Many groups all over the nation that would emerge later as tribes kept a low profile during these years. Mashpee seemed to be simply a sleepy town run by Indians, known for its good hunting and fishing. There was no political need or any wider context for them to display their Indianness in spectacular ways. Everyone knew who they were. A few attended the Carlisle Indian School in Pennsylvania during this period. Traditional myths and stories were told around kitchen tables; the piles of sticks at Mashpee's "Indian taverns" or "sacrifice heaps" grew into enormous mounds; life close to the land went on.

The history of Indian tribes in the United States has been punctuated by revival movements. The 1920s saw the organization of the Wampanoag Nation, with various explicit tribal institutions including a supreme sachem and a renewed interest in more public Indian displays: dances, regalia, powwows, and the like. As in all revitalization movements "outside" influences from other Indian groups played a major role. Eben Queppish, who had once ridden with Buffalo Bill's Wild West Show, taught traditional basket making and on demand donned his Sioux war bonnet. Individuals from Mashpee participated in nationally known groups such as the Thunderbird Indian Dancers. The effects of these revivals were largely cultural. There was little need for political reorganization in Mashpee, for the town was still governed by an unchallenged Indian majority. Political reorganization of a more explicit "tribal" structure would occur during a later revivalist period, the ferment spurred by the loss of town control after 1968.

Like other tribal groups the Mashpee have been opportunists, taking advantage of propitious historical contexts and undergoing external influences. They have survived as Indians because they have *not* conformed to white stereotypes. They have lived since aboriginal times in a traditional locale. They have maintained their own hybrid faith. Over the centuries they have controlled the rate of intermarriage and have fought for the political autonomy of their community. Explicitly tribal political structures have sometimes been visible to the outside world, as in 1833, the 1920s, and the 1970s, but for the most part these structures have been informal.

Often the "tribe" in Mashpee was simply people deciding things by consensus in kitchens or at larger ad hoc gatherings where no records were kept. The chief in Mashpee, when there was one, shared authority with a variety of respected leaders, women and men. Politics was not hierarchical and did not need much in the way of institutional forms. The "tribe" in Mashpee was simply shared Indian kinship, place, history and a long struggle for integrity without isolation. Sometimes the Baptist parish served as an arm of the tribe; so did the town government. When the Mashpee Wampanoag Tribal Council, Inc. filed suit in 1976, it did so as a new legal arm of the tribe.

* * *

◆

The jurors were sequestered, accompanied by a large pile of documents. After twenty-one hours of deliberation they emerged with a verdict:

Did the proprietors of Mashpee, together with their spouses and children, constitute an Indian tribe on any of the following dates:

July 22, 1790? No.	June 23, 1869? No.
March 31, 1834? Yes.	May 28, 1870? No.
March 3, 1842? Yes.	

Did the plaintiff groups, as identified by the plaintiff's witnesses, constitute an Indian tribe as of August 26, 1976? No.

If the people living in Mashpee constituted an Indian tribe or nation on any of the dates prior to August 26, 1976, did they continuously exist as a tribe or nation from such date or dates up to and including August 26, 1976? No.

◆

The verdict was a clear setback for the Indians' suit. But as a statement about their tribal history it was far from clear. Judge Skinner, after hearing arguments, finally decided that despite its ambiguity—the apparent emergence of a tribe in 1834—the jury's reply was a denial of the required tribal continuity. His dismissal of the suit has since been upheld on appeal.

The verdict remains, however, a curious and problematic outcome. We can only speculate on what happened in the jury room—the obscure chemistry of unanimity. What was done with the pile of historical documents during the twenty-one hours of discussion? Did the jurors search for a false precision? Asked to consider specific dates, did they conscientiously search the record for evidence of tribal institutions, for mention of the word *tribe*? If so, their literalism was nonetheless different from that encouraged by the particularist history of the defense, for the jury found that Mashpee Indians were inconsistently a tribe. Violating the judge's instructions, they found that a tribe first did not, then did, then did not again exist in Mashpee. Historical particularism does not by itself yield coherent developments or stories. Entities appear and disappear in the record.

The jurors' response contained an element of subversion. In effect it suggested that the trial's questions had been wrongly posed. Asked to apply consistent criteria of tribal existence over three centuries of intense change and disruption, the jury did so and came up with an inconsistent verdict.

Afterthoughts

The court behaved like a philosopher who wanted to know positively whether a cat was on the mat in Mashpee. I found myself seeing a Cheshire cat now a head, now a tail, eyes, ears, nothing at all, in various combinations. The Mashpee "tribe" had a way of going and coming; but something was persistently, if not continuously, there.

The testimony I heard convinced me that organized Indian life had been going on in Mashpee for the past 350 years. Moreover a significant revival and reinvention of tribal identity was clearly in process. I concluded that since the ability to act collectively as Indians is currently bound up with tribal status, the Indians living in Mashpee and those who return regularly should be recognized as a "tribe."

Whether land improperly alienated after 1869 should be transferred to them, how much, and by what means was a separate issue. I was, and am, less clear on this matter. A wholesale transfer of property would in any case be politically unthinkable. Some negotiation and repurchase arrangement—such as that in Maine involving local, state, and federal governments—could eventually establish a tribal land base in some portion of Mashpee. But that, for the moment, is speculation. In the short run the outcome of the trial was a setback for Wampanoag tribal dynamism.

In Boston Federal Court, Cape Cod Indians could not be seen for what they were and are. Modern Indian lives—lived within and against the dominant culture and state—are not captured by categories like tribe or identity. The plaintiffs could not prevail in court because their discourse and that of their attorneys and experts was inevitably compromised. It was constrained not simply by the law, with its peculiar rules, but by powerful assumptions and categories underlying the common sense that supported the law.

Among the underlying assumptions and categories compromising the Indians' case three stand out: (1) the idea of cultural wholeness and structure, (2) the hierarchical distinction between oral and literate forms of knowledge, and (3) the narrative continuity of history and identity.

The idea of cultural wholeness and structure. Although the trial was formally about "tribal" status, its scope was significantly wider. The *Montoya* definition of tribe, featuring race, territory, community and government, did not specifically mention "cultural" identity. The culture concept in its broad anthropological definition was still new in 1901; but the relatively loose *Montoya* definition reflected this emerging notion of a multifaceted, whole way of life, determined neither by biology nor politics. By 1978 the modern notion of culture was part of the trial's common sense.

In the courtroom an enormous amount of testimony from both sides debated the authenticity of Indian culture in Mashpee. Often this seemed to have become the crucial point of contention. Had the Mashpee lost their distinct way of life? Had they assimilated? In his summation for the plaintiffs Lawrence Shubow took time to define the term culture anthropologically, distinguishing it from the "ballet and top hat" conception. Closely paraphrasing E. B. Tylor's classic formula of 1871, he presented culture as a group's total body of behavior. He said that it included how people eat as well as how they think. Using the anthropological definition, he argued that ecology, the special feeling for hunting and fishing in Mashpee, the herring eaten every year, spitting on a stick at an "Indian tavern," these and many other unremarkable daily elements were integral parts of a whole, ongoing way of life.

It is easy to see why the plaintiffs focused on Indian culture in Mashpee. Culture, since it includes so much, was less easily disproven than tribal status. But even so broadly defined, the culture concept posed problems for the plaintiffs. It was too closely tied to assumptions of organic form and development. In the eighteenth century culture meant simply "a tending to natural growth." By the end of the nineteenth century the word could be applied not only to gardens and well-developed individuals but to whole societies. Whether it was the elitist singular version of a Matthew Arnold or the plural, lower-case concept of an emerging ethnography, the term retained its bias toward wholeness, continuity, and growth. Indian culture in Mashpee might be made up of unexpected everyday elements, but it had in the last analysis to cohere, its elements fitting together like the parts of a body. The culture concept accommodates internal diversity and an "organic" division of roles but not sharp contradictions, mutations, or emergences. It has difficulty with a medicine man who at one time feels a deep respect for Mother Earth and at another plans a radical real estate subdivision. It sees tribal "traditionalists" and "moderns" as representing aspects of a linear development, one looking back, the other forward. It cannot see them as, contending or alternating futures.

Groups negotiating their identity in contexts of domination and exchange persist, patch themselves together in ways different from a living organism. A community, unlike a body, can lose a central "organ" and not die. All the critical elements of identity are in specific conditions replaceable: language, land, blood, leadership, religion. Recognized, viable tribes exist in which any one or even most of these elements are missing, replaced, or largely transformed.

The idea of culture carries with it an expectation of roots, of a stable, territorialized existence. Weatherhead (1980:10–11) shows how the *Montoya* definition of tribe was designed to distinguish settled, peaceful Indian groups from mobile, marauding "bands." This political and military distinction of 1901 between tribe and band was debated again, in technical, anthropological terms, during the Mashpee trial. How rooted or settled should one expect "tribal" Native Americans to be—aboriginally, in specific contact periods, and now in highly mobile twentieth century America?

Common notions of culture persistently bias the answer toward rooting rather than travel.

Moreover the culture idea, tied as it is to assumptions about natural growth and life, does not tolerate radical breaks in historical continuity. Cultures, we often hear, "die." But how many cultures pronounced dead or dying by anthropologists and other authorities have, like Curtis' "vanishing race" or Africa's diverse Christians, found new ways to be different? Metaphors of continuity and "survival" do not account for complex historical processes of appropriation, compromise, subversion, masking, invention, and revival. These processes inform the activity of a people not living alone but "reckoning itself among the nations." The Indians at Mashpee made and remade themselves through specific alliances, negotiations, and struggles. It is just as problematic to say that their way of life "survived" as to say that it "died" and was "reborn."

The related institutions of culture and tribe are historical inventions, tendentious and changing. They do not designate stable realities that exist aboriginally "prior to" the colonial clash of societies and powerful representations. The history of Mashpee is not one of unbroken tribal institutions or cultural traditions. It is a long, relational struggle to maintain and recreate identities that began when an English-speaking Indian traveler, Squanto, greeted the Pilgrims at Plymouth. The struggle was still going on three-and-a-half centuries later in Boston Federal Court, and it continues as the "Mashpee Tribe" prepares a new petition, this time for recognition from the Department of the Interior.

The hierarchical distinction between oral and literate. The Mashpee trial was a contest between oral and literate forms of knowledge. In the end the written archive had more value than the evidence of oral tradition, the memories of witnesses, and the intersubjective practice of fieldwork. In the courtroom how could one give value to an undocumented "tribal" life largely invisible (or unheard) in the surviving record?

As the trial progressed the disjuncture of oral and literate modes sharpened. The proceedings had been theatrical, full of contending voices and personalities, but they ended with a historian's methodical recitation of particulars. In the early portions of the trial the jurors had been asked to piece together and imagine a tribal life that showed recurring vitality but no unimpeachable essence or institutional core. Indianness in Mashpee often seemed improvised, ad hoc. The jury heard many wishful, incomplete memories of childhood events and debatable versions of recent happenings. In what may be called the "oral-ethnographic" parts of the trial many—too many—voices contended, in its "documentary" ending too few. A historian's seamless monologue was followed by attorneys' highly composed summations, two fully documented stories. There was no way to give voice to the silences in these histories, to choose the unrecorded.

The court imposed a literalist epistemology. Both sides searched the historical records for the presence or absence of the word and institution *tribe*. In this epistemology Indian identity could not be a real yet essentially contested phenomenon. It had to exist or not exist as an objective documentary fact persisting through time. Yet oral societies—or more accurately oral domains within a dominant literacy—leave only sporadic and misleading traces. Most of what is central to their existence is never written. Thus until recently nearly everything most characteristically Indian in Mashpee would have gone unrecorded. The surviving facts are largely the records of missionaries, government agents, outsiders. In the rare instances when Indians wrote—petitions, deeds, letters of complaint—it was to address white authorities and legal structures. Their voices were adapted to an imposed context. The same is true even in the rare cases in which a range of local *voices* was recorded, for example the public debates of 1869 on township status.

History feeds on what finds its way into a limited textual record. A historian needs constant skepticism and a willingness to read imaginatively, "against" the sources, to divine what is not represented in the accumulated selection of the archive. Ultimately, however, even the most imaginative history is tied to standards of textual proof. Anthropology, although it is also deeply formed and empowered by writing, remains closer to orality. Fieldwork—interested people talking with and being interpreted by an interested observer—cannot claim to be "documentary" in the way history can. For even though the origin of evidence in an archive may be just as circumstantial and subjective as that in a field journal, it enjoys a different value: archival data has been found, not produced, by a scholar using it "after the fact."

The distinction between historical and ethnographic practices depends on that between literate and oral modes of knowledge. History is thought to rest on past—documentary, archival—selections of texts. Ethnography is based on present—oral, experiential, observational—evidence. Although many historians and ethnographers are currently working to attenuate, even erase this opposition, it runs deeper than a mere disciplinary division of labor, for it resonates with the established (some would say metaphysical) dichotomy of oral and literate worlds as well as with the pervasive habit in the West of sharply distinguishing synchronic from diachronic, structure from change. As Marshall Sahlins (1985) has argued, these assumptions keep us from seeing how collective structures, tribal or cultural, reproduce themselves historically by risking themselves in novel conditions. Their wholeness is as much a matter of reinvention and encounter as it is of continuity and survival.

The narrative continuity of history and identity. Judge Skinner instructed the jury to decide whether the Indians of Mashpee had continuously constituted a tribe prior to filing suit in 1976. For the land claim to go forward the same tribal group had to have existed, without radical interruption, from at least the eighteenth century. The court's common sense was that the plaintiffs' identity must be demonstrated as an unbroken narrative, whether of survival or change. Both attorneys in their summations duly complied.

St. Clair's story of a long struggle for participation in plural American society and Shubow's "epic of survival and continuity" had in common a linear teleology. Both ruled out the possibility of a group existing disconti-nuously, keeping open multiple paths, being both Indian and American.

An either-or logic applied. St. Clair argued that there had never been a tribe in Mashpee, only individual Indian Americans who had repeatedly opted for white society. His story of progress toward citizenship assumed a steady movement away from native tradition. Identity as an American meant giving up a strong claim to tribal political integrity in favor of ethnic status within a national whole. Life as an American meant death as an Indian. Conversely Shubow's Mashpee had "survived" as a living tribe and culture from aboriginal times; but the historical record often contradicted his claim, and he sometimes strained to assert continuity. The plaintiffs could not admit that Indians in Mashpee had lost, even voluntarily aban-doned, crucial aspects of their tradition while at the same time pointing to evidence over the centuries of reinvented "Indianness." They could not show tribal institutions as relational and political, coming and going in response to changing federal and state policies and the surrounding ideo-logical climate. An identity could not die and come back to life. To recreate a culture that had been lost was, by definition of the court, inauthentic.

But is any part of a tradition lost if it can be remembered, even generations later, caught up in a present dynamism and made to symbolize a possible future?

The Mashpee were trapped by the stories that could be told about them. In this trial "the facts" did not speak for themselves. Tribal life had to be emplotted, told as a coherent narrative. In fact only a few basic stories are told, over and over, about Native Americans and other "tribal" peoples. These societies are always either dying or surviving, assimilating or resisting. Caught between a local past and a global future, they either hold on to their separateness or "enter the modern world." The latter entry—tragic or triumphant—is always a step toward a global future defined by technological progress, national and international cultural rela-tions. Are there other possible stories?

Until recently the "history" accorded to tribal peoples has always been a Western history. They may refuse it, embrace it, be devastated by it, changed by it. But the familiar paths of tribal death, survival, assimilation, or resistance do not catch the specific ambivalences of life in places like Mashpee over four centuries of defeat, renewal, political negotiation, and cultural innovation. Moreover most societies that suddenly "enter the modern world" have already been in touch with it for centuries.

The Mashpee trial seemed to reveal people who were sometimes separate and "Indian," sometimes assimilated and "American." Their history was a series of cultural and political transactions, not all-or-nothing conversions or resistances. Indians in Mashpee lived and acted between cultures in a series of ad hoc engagements. No one in Boston Federal Court, expert or layperson, stood at the end point of this historical series, even though the stories of continuity and change they told implied that they did. These stories and the trial itself were episodes, turns in the ongoing engagement. Seen from a standpoint not of finality (survival or assimilation) but of emergence, Indian life in Mashpee would not flow in a single current.

Interpreting the direction or meaning of the historical "record" always depends on present possibilities. When the future is open, so is the meaning of the past. Did Indian religion or tribal institutions disappear in the late nineteenth century? Or did they go underground? In a present context of serious revival they went underground; otherwise they disappeared. No continuous narrative or clear outcome accounts for Mashpee's deeply contested identity and direction. Nor can a single development weave together the branching paths of its past, the dead ends and hesitations that, with a newly conceived future, suddenly become prefigurations.

◆

(Hesitations. In 1869 Blind Joe Amos and the majority of Mashpee proprietors agreed that they were not yet ready to become citizens of Massachusetts, separate entrepreneurs with individual control over their lands. They held back, declining a "progressive" step imposed by the legislature. Was it from backwardness? Confusion? Fear? Or something else: an alternate vision? A different voice?

What Susan Howe (1985) has written about a woman—Emily Dickinson, working during the same decade from another place of New England "isolation"—echoes strangely the Indian predicament: the problem of finding a different way through capitalist America.

HESITATE from the Latin, meaning to stick. Stammer. To hold back in doubt, have difficulty speaking. "*He* may pause but *he* must not hesitate"—Ruskin. Hesitation circled back and surrounded everyone in that confident age of aggressive industrial expansion and brutal Empire building. Hesitation and Separation. The Civil War had split America in two. *He* might pause, *She* hesitated. Sexual, racial, and geographical separation are at the heart of Definition. Tragic and eternal dichotomy—if we concern ourselves with the deepest Reality, is this world of the imagination the same for men and women? What voice when we hesitate and are silent is moving to meet us? (p. 22)

In 1869 Joe Amos and the others did not go on record as resisting full citizenship. Separation and dichotomy were not their agenda: they were already more than half-caught up in a new America. It is important to distinguish hesitation from resistance, for hesitation need not oppose or acquiesce in the dominant course. It can be an alert waiting, thinking, anticipating of historical possibilities. Along with the history of resistances we need a history of hesitations.)

Stories of cultural contact and change have been structured by a pervasive dichotomy: absorption by the other *or* resistance to the other. A fear of lost identity, a Puritan taboo on mixing beliefs and bodies, hangs over the process. Yet what if identity is conceived not as a boundary to be maintained but as a nexus of relations and transactions actively engaging a subject? The story or stories of interaction must then be more complex, less linear and teleological. What changes when the subject of "history" is no longer Western? How do stories of contact, resistance, and assimilation appear from the standpoint of groups in which exchange rather than identity is the fundamental value to be sustained? Events are always mediated by local cultural structures. By focusing on the peripheral places, the neglected "islands of history" In Sahlins' words, "we ... multiply our conceptions of history by the diversity of structures. Suddenly there are all kinds of new things to consider" (1985:72).

In the diversity of local histories—like that of Mashpee—we find distinctive processes and directions. The channeled, inevitable flow of events begins to loop, waver, and fork. In 1830, for example, was the proprietary status of the Mashpee Indians an eroded "survival" from archaic English law, a social form destined to disappear? Or by the nineteenth century had it become a specific invention, a novel way to live on Indian land in modern America, a possible future? Neither story is false; both can be amply documented from the historical record. To say that the strange "tribal" integrity of the Mashpee Plantation was destined to disappear is to accept the history of the victors. But the suit filed a century later was an attempt to reopen this foregone conclusion. Mashpee's semiautonomous plantation, a specific mix of individual citizenship and collective entailment, now appeared not as a historical dead end but as a precursor of reinvented tribalism. No return to a pure Wampanoag tradition was at issue, but rather a reinterpretation of Mashpee's contested history in order to act—with other Indian groups—powerfully, in an impure present-becoming-future.

Whatever the trial's outcome "tribal" life had once again become powerful in Mashpee. Only a literal, backward-looking sense of authenticity (one no group would willingly apply to itself, only to others) could deny this emergent reality. The Wampanoag Supreme Sachem, Elsworth Oakley, commented after the verdict: "How can a white majority decide on whether we are a tribe? We know who we are."

The future of Native American life on Cape Cod after the setback in court is uncertain.

◆

The years immediately following the verdict were marked by disarray in Mashpee. An anticipated petition to the Department of the Interior for tribal status was slow to emerge. During this period the Bureau of Indian Affairs standardized its procedure for recognition claims, following criteria similar to those required by the court in *Mashpee v. New Seabury et al.* (Weatherhead 1980:17). The Indians in Mashpee watched with misgivings the progress of a petition by their fellow Wampanoags at Gay Head. In 1986 the petition was turned down in a preliminary finding. Government experts cited an insufficient degree of community specificity over the years and a loss of tribal political authority after Gay Head became a township in 1870. Gay Head's history was similar to Mashpee's.

Appealing the preliminary finding, the Native American Rights Fund presented additional evidence, compiled by Jack Campisi, of continuing social networks among Gay Head Indians and of a line of tribal authority after 1870. On February 8, 1987, for the first time ever the Bureau of Indian Affairs reversed a negative preliminary finding. The Gay Head Wampanoags were given full tribal recognition.

Quotations from a Native American Rights Fund press release:

Henry Sockbeson, the Penobscot attorney representing the tribe: "This decision means that the Gay Head will be able to settle their land claim within a few months. Under the terms of the settlement the Tribe will receive approximately 250 acres of land that can be developed. We anticipate that they will use it for housing and economic development."

Gladys Widdiss, chairperson of the Wampanoag Tribal Council of Gay Head, Inc.: "I am delighted. This now means that the Tribe can function in a formally recognized manner. Our status as a tribe can no longer be in doubt. Recognition means that our survival as a tribe for generations to come is assured."

Jack Campisi and Native American Rights Fund attorneys are working on Mashpee's petition.

TWO SNAPSHOTS

Mrs. Pells is an Indian born in Mashpee. She is seventy-one years old, now living eighteen miles away near the Bourne Bridge, and is an active member of the Tribal Council, Inc. She is dignified, slow-speaking.

She shows an enlarged photograph of her grandmother, Rebecca Hammond, Blind Joe Amos' daughter.

She has been a member of the Mashpee Wampanoag tribe "since birth."

She testifies that she lived in New York between 1928 and 1972 where she was active in a number of Native American organizations. During the 1940s she was secretary of the "American Indian Thunderbird Dancers." Most of the dancers did not originate in Massachusetts, and only one of the dancers was from Cape Cod.

◆

"Chiefy" Mills is Earl Mills's teenage son. He says he knows he is an Indian because his father told him. He likes to hunt and hang around with his cousins in Mashpee. A champion drummer, he participates often in Native American gatherings around New England. Recently he was among the young people arrested at a camping retreat held to promote Indian consciousness on the fifty-five acres of tribal land in Mashpee.

* * *

Whiteness as Property

106 HARV. L. REV. 1707 (June 1993).

CHERYL I. HARRIS

Issues regarding race and racial identity as well as questions pertaining to property rights and ownership have been prominent in much public discourse in the United States. In this article, Professor Harris contributes to this discussion by positing that racial identity and property are deeply interrelated concepts. Professor Harris examines how whiteness, initially constructed as a form of racial identity, evolved into a form of property, historically and presently acknowledged and protected in American law. Professor Harris traces the origins of whiteness as property in the parallel systems of domination of Black and Native American peoples out of which were created racially contingent forms of property and property rights. Following the period of slavery and conquest, whiteness became the basis of racialized privilege—a type of status in which white racial identity provided the basis for allocating societal benefits both private and public in character. These arrangements were ratified and legitimated in law as a type of status property. Even as legal segregation was overturned, whiteness as property continued to serve as a barrier to effective change as the system of racial classification operated to protect entrenched power.

Next, Professor Harris examines how the concept of whiteness as property persists in current perceptions of racial identity, in the law's misperception of group identity and in the Court's reasoning and decisions in the arena of affirmative action. Professor Harris concludes by arguing that distortions in affirmative action doctrine can only be addressed by confronting and exposing the property interest in whiteness and by acknowledging the distributive justification and function of affirmative action as central to that task.

> she walked into forbidden worlds
>
> impaled on the weapon of her own pale skin
>
> she was a sentinel
>
> at impromptu planning sessions
>
> of her own destruction . . .

Cheryl I. Harris, *poem for alma*[1]

[P]etitioner was a citizen of the United States and a resident of the state of Louisiana of mixed descent, in the proportion of seven eighths Caucasian and one eighth African blood; that the mixture of colored blood was not discernible in him, and that he was entitled to every recognition, right, privilege and immunity secured to the citizens of the United States of the white race by its Constitution and laws . . . and thereupon entered a

---

1. Cheryl I. Harris, *poem for alma* (1990) (unpublished poem, on file at the Harvard Law School Library).

passenger train and took possession of a vacant seat in a coach where passengers of the white race were accommodated.

Plessy v. Ferguson[2]

I.   INTRODUCTION

In the 1930s, some years after my mother's family became part of the great river of Black migration that flowed north, my Mississippi-born grandmother was confronted with the harsh matter of economic survival for herself and her two daughters. Having separated from my grandfather, who himself was trapped on the fringes of economic marginality, she took one long hard look at her choices and presented herself for employment at a major retail store in Chicago's central business district. This decision would have been unremarkable for a white woman in similar circumstances, but for my grandmother, it was an act of both great daring and self-denial, for in so doing she was presenting herself as a white woman. In the parlance of racist America, she was "passing."

Her fair skin, straight hair, and aquiline features had not spared her from the life of sharecropping into which she had been born in anywhere/nowhere, Mississippi—the outskirts of Yazoo City. But in the burgeoning landscape of urban America, anonymity was possible for a Black person with "white" features. She was transgressing boundaries, crossing borders, spinning on margins, traveling between dualities of Manichean space, rigidly bifurcated into light/dark, good/bad, white/Black. No longer immediately identifiable as "Lula's daughter," she could thus enter the white world, albeit on a false passport, not merely passing, but *tres*passing.

Every day my grandmother rose from her bed in her house in a Black enclave on the south side of Chicago, sent her children off to a Black school, boarded a bus full of Black passengers, and rode to work. No one at her job ever asked if she was Black; the question was unthinkable. By virtue of the employment practices of the "fine establishment" in which she worked, she could not have been. Catering to the upper-middle class, understated tastes required that Blacks not be allowed.

She quietly went about her clerical tasks, not once revealing her true identity. She listened to the women with whom she worked discuss their worries—their children's illnesses, their husbands' disappointments, their boyfriends' infidelities—all of the mundane yet critical things that made up their lives. She came to know them but they did not know her, for my grandmother occupied a completely different place. That place—where white supremacy and economic domination meet—was unknown turf to her white co-workers. They remained oblivious to the worlds within worlds that existed just beyond the edge of their awareness and yet were present in their very midst.

Each evening, my grandmother, tired and worn, retraced her steps home, laid aside her mask, and reentered herself. Day in and day out, she made herself invisible, then visible again, for a price too inconsequential to

---

2.   163 U.S. 537, 538 (1896).

do more than barely sustain her family and at a cost too precious to conceive. She left the job some years later, finding the strain too much to bear.

From time to time, as I later sat with her, she would recollect that period, and the cloud of some painful memory would pass across her face. Her voice would remain subdued, as if to contain the still remembered tension. On rare occasions she would wince, recalling some particularly racist comment made in her presence because of her presumed, shared group affiliation. Whatever retort might have been called for had been suppressed long before it reached her lips, for the price of her family's well-being was her silence. Accepting the risk of self-annihilation was the only way to survive.

Although she never would have stated it this way, the clear and ringing denunciations of racism she delivered from her chair when advanced arthritis had rendered her unable to work were informed by those experiences. The fact that self-denial had been a logical choice and had made her complicit in her own oppression at times fed the fire in her eyes when she confronted some daily outrage inflicted on Black people. Later, these painful memories forged her total identification with the civil rights movement. Learning about the world at her knee as I did, these experiences also came to inform my outlook and my understanding of the world.

My grandmother's story is far from unique. Indeed, there are many who crossed the color line never to return. Passing is well-known among Black people in the United States and is a feature of race subordination in all societies structured on white supremacy. Notwithstanding the purported benefits of Black heritage in an era of affirmative action, passing is not an obsolete phenomenon that has slipped into history.

The persistence of passing is related to the historical and continuing pattern of white racial domination and economic exploitation that has given passing a certain economic logic. It was a given to my grandmother that being white automatically ensured higher economic returns in the short term, as well as greater economic, political, and social security in the long run. Becoming white meant gaining access to a whole set of public and private privileges that materially and permanently guaranteed basic subsistence needs and, therefore, survival. Becoming white increased the possibility of controlling critical aspects of one's life rather than being the object of others' domination.

My grandmother's story illustrates the valorization of whiteness as treasured property in a society structured on racial caste. In ways so embedded that it is rarely apparent, the set of assumptions, privileges, and benefits that accompany the status of being white have become a valuable asset that whites sought to protect and that those who passed sought to attain—by fraud if necessary. Whites have come to expect and rely on these benefits, and over time these expectations have been affirmed, legitimated, and protected by the law. Even though the law is neither uniform nor explicit in all instances, in protecting settled expectations based on white privilege, American law has recognized a property interest in whiteness that, although unacknowledged, now forms the background against which legal disputes are framed, argued, and adjudicated.

My Article investigates the relationships between concepts of race and property and reflects on how rights in property are contingent on, intertwined with, and conflated with race. Through this entangled relationship between race and property, historical forms of domination have evolved to reproduce subordination in the present. * * * I examine the emergence of whiteness as property and trace the evolution of whiteness from color to race to status to property as a progression historically rooted in white supremacy and economic hegemony over Black and Native American peoples. The origins of whiteness as property lie in the parallel systems of domination of Black and Native American peoples out of which were created racially contingent forms of property and property rights. I further argue that whiteness shares the critical characteristics of property even as the meaning of property has changed over time. In particular, whiteness and property share a common premise—a conceptual nucleus—of a right to exclude. This conceptual nucleus has proven to be a powerful center around which whiteness as property has taken shape. Following the period of slavery and conquest, white identity became the basis of racialized privilege that was ratified and legitimated in law as a type of status property. After legalized segregation was overturned, whiteness as property evolved into a more modern form through the law's ratification of the settled expectations of relative white privilege as a legitimate and natural baseline.

[I examine] the two forms of whiteness as property—status property and modern property—that are the submerged text of two paradigmatic cases on the race question in American law, *Plessy v. Ferguson* and *Brown v. Board of Education.* As legal history, they illustrate an important transition from old to new forms of whiteness as property. Although these cases take opposite interpretive stances regarding the constitutional legitimacy of legalized racial segregation, the property interest in whiteness was transformed, but not discarded, in the Court's new equal protection jurisprudence.

[I then consider] the persistence of whiteness as property. I first examine how subordination is reinstituted through modern conceptions of race and identity embraced in law. Whiteness as property has taken on more subtle forms, but retains its core characteristic—the legal legitimation of expectations of power and control that enshrine the status quo as a neutral baseline, while masking the maintenance of white privilege and domination. I further identify the property interest in whiteness as the unspoken center of current polarities around the issue of affirmative action. As a legacy of slavery and de jure and de facto race segregation, the concept of a protectable property interest in whiteness permeates affirmative action doctrine in a manner illustrated by the reasoning of three important affirmative action cases—*Regents of the University of California v. Bakke, City of Richmond v. J. A. Croson & Co.,* and *Wygant v. Jackson Board of Education.*

* * *, I offer preliminary thoughts on a way out of the conundrum created by protecting whiteness as a property interest. I suggest that affirmative action, properly conceived and reconstructed, would de-legitimate the property interest in whiteness. I do not offer here a complete reformulation of affirmative action, but suggest that focusing on the distortions created by the property interest in whiteness would provoke different questions and open alternative perspectives on the affirmative action debate. The inability to see affirmative action as more than a search for the "blameworthy" among "innocent" individuals is tied to the inability to see the property interest in whiteness. Thus reconstructed, affirmative action would challenge the characterization of the unfettered right to exclude as a legitimate aspect of identity and property.

II. THE CONSTRUCTION OF RACE AND THE EMERGENCE OF WHITENESS AS PROPERTY

The racialization of identity and the racial subordination of Blacks and Native Americans provided the ideological basis for slavery and conquest. Although the systems of oppression of Blacks and Native Americans differed in form—the former involving the seizure and appropriation of labor, the latter entailing the seizure and appropriation of land—undergirding both was a racialized conception of property implemented by force and ratified by law.

The origins of property rights in the United States are rooted in racial domination. Even in the early years of the country, it was not the concept of race alone that operated to oppress Blacks and Indians; rather, it was the *interaction* between conceptions of race and property that played a critical role in establishing and maintaining racial and economic subordination.

The hyper-exploitation of Black labor was accomplished by treating Black people themselves as objects of property. Race and property were thus conflated by establishing a form of property contingent on race—only Blacks were subjugated as slaves and treated as property. Similarly, the conquest, removal, and extermination of Native American life and culture were ratified by conferring and acknowledging the property rights of whites in Native American land. Only white possession and occupation of land was validated and therefore privileged as a basis for property rights. These distinct forms of exploitation each contributed in varying ways to the construction of whiteness as property.

A. Forms of Racialized Property: Relationships Between Slavery, Race, and Property

1. The Convergence of Racial and Legal Status.—Although the early colonists were cognizant of race, racial lines were neither consistently nor sharply delineated among or within all social groups. Captured Africans sold in the Americas were distinguished from the population of indentured or bond servants—"unfree" white labor—but it was not an irrebuttable presumption that all Africans were "slaves" or that slavery was the only appropriate status for them. The distinction between African and white indentured labor grew, however, as decreasing terms of service were introduced for white bond servants. Simultaneously, the demand for labor intensified, resulting in a greater reliance on African labor and a rapid increase in the number of Africans imported into the colonies.

The construction of white identity and the ideology of racial hierarchy also were intimately tied to the evolution and expansion of the system of chattel slavery. The further entrenchment of plantation slavery was in part an answer to a social crisis produced by the eroding capacity of the landed class to control the white labor population. The dominant paradigm of social relations, however, was that, although not all Africans were slaves, virtually all slaves were not white. It was their racial otherness that came to justify the subordinated status of Blacks. The result was a classification system that "key[ed] official rules of descent to national origin" so that "[m]embership in the new social category of 'Negro' became itself sufficient justification for enslaveability." Although the cause of the increasing gap between the status of African and white labor is contested by historians, it is clear that "[t]he economic and political interests defending Black slavery were far more powerful than those defending indentured servitude."

By the 1660s, the especially degraded status of Blacks as chattel slaves was recognized by law. Between 1680 and 1682, the first slave codes appeared, codifying the extreme deprivations of liberty already existing in social practice. Many laws parceled out differential treatment based on racial categories: Blacks were not permitted to travel without permits, to own property, to assemble publicly, or to own weapons; nor were they to be educated. Racial identity was further merged with stratified social and legal status: "Black" racial identity marked who was subject to enslavement; "white" racial identity marked who was "free" or, at minimum, not a slave. The ideological and rhetorical move from "slave" and "free" to "Black" and "white" as polar constructs marked an important step in the social construction of race.

2. Implications for Property.—The social relations that produced racial identity as a justification for slavery also had implications for the conceptualization of property. This result was predictable, as the institution of slavery, lying at the very core of economic relations, was bound up with the idea of property. Through slavery, race and economic domination were fused.

Slavery produced a peculiar, mixed category of property and humanity—a hybrid possessing inherent instabilities that were reflected in its treatment and ratification by the law. The dual and contradictory character of slaves as property and persons was exemplified in the Representation Clause of the Constitution. Representation in the House of Representatives was apportioned on the basis of population computed by counting all persons and "three-fifths of all other persons"—slaves. Gouveneur Morris's remarks before the Constitutional Convention posed the essential question: "Upon what principle is it that slaves shall be computed in the representation? Are they men? Then make them Citizens & let them vote? Are they property? Why then is no other property included?"

The cruel tension between property and humanity was also reflected in the law's legitimation of the use of Blackwomen's bodies as a means of increasing property. In 1662, the Virginia colonial assembly provided that "[c]hildren got by an Englishman upon a Negro woman shall be bond or free according to the condition of the mother...." In reversing the usual common law presumption that the status of the child was determined by the father, the rule facilitated the reproduction of one's own labor force. Because the children of Blackwomen assumed the status of their mother, slaves were bred through Blackwomen's bodies. The economic significance of this form of exploitation of female slaves should not be underestimated. Despite Thomas Jefferson's belief that slavery should be abolished, like other slaveholders, he viewed slaves as economic assets, noting that their value could be realized more efficiently from breeding than from labor. A letter he wrote in 1805 stated: "I consider the labor of a breeding woman as no object, and that a child raised every 2 years is of more profit than the crop of the best laboring man."

Even though there was some unease in slave law, reflective of the mixed status of slaves as humans and property, the critical nature of social relations under slavery was the commodification of human beings. Productive relations in early American society included varying forms of sale of labor capacity, many of which were highly oppressive; but slavery was distinguished from other forms of labor servitude by its permanency and the total commodification attendant to the status of the slave. Slavery as a legal institution treated slaves as property that could be transferred, assigned, inherited, or posted as collateral. For example, in *Johnson v. Butler,* the plaintiff sued the defendant for failing to pay a debt of $496 on a specified date. Because the covenant had called for payment of the debt in "money or negroes," the plaintiff contended that the defendant's tender of one negro only, although valued by the parties at an amount equivalent to the debt, could not discharge the debt. The court agreed with the plaintiff. This use of Africans as a stand-in for actual currency highlights the degree to which slavery "propertized" human life.

Because the "presumption of freedom [arose] from color [white]" and the "black color of the race [raised] the presumption of slavery," whiteness became a shield from slavery, a highly volatile and unstable form of property. In the form adopted in the United States, slavery made human beings market-alienable and in so doing, subjected human life and personhood—that which is most valuable—to the ultimate devaluation. Because whites could not be enslaved or held as slaves, the racial line between white and Black was extremely critical; it became a line of protection and demarcation from the potential threat of commodification, and it determined the allocation of the benefits and burdens of this form of property. White identity and whiteness were sources of privilege and protection; their absence meant being the object of property.

Slavery as a system of property facilitated the merger of white identity and property. Because the system of slavery was contingent on and conflated with racial identity, it became crucial to be "white," to be identified as white, to have the property of being white. Whiteness was the characteristic, the attribute, the property of free human beings.

B.   Forms of Racialized Property: Relationships Between Native American Land Seizure, Race, and Property

Slavery linked the privilege of whites to the subordination of Blacks through a legal regime that attempted the conversion of Blacks into objects of property. Similarly, the settlement and seizure of Native American land supported white privilege through a system of property rights in land in which the "race" of the Native Americans rendered their first possession rights invisible and justified conquest. This racist formulation embedded the fact of white privilege into the very definition of property, marking another stage in the evolution of the property interest in whiteness. Possession—the act necessary to lay the basis for rights in property—was defined to include only the cultural practices of whites. This definition laid the foundation for the idea that whiteness—that which whites alone possess—is valuable and is property.

Although the Indians were the first occupants and possessors of the land of the New World, their racial and cultural otherness allowed this fact to be reinterpreted and ultimately erased as a basis for asserting rights in land. Because the land had been left in its natural state, untilled and unmarked by human hands, it was "waste" and, therefore, the appropriate object of settlement and appropriation. Thus, the possession maintained by the Indians was not "true" possession and could safely be ignored. This interpretation of the rule of first possession effectively rendered the rights of first possessors contingent on the race of the possessor. Only particular forms of possession—those that were characteristic of white settlement—would be recognized and legitimated. Indian forms of possession were perceived to be too ambiguous and unclear.

The conquest and occupation of Indian land was wrapped in the rule of law. The law provided not only a defense of conquest and colonization, but also a naturalized regime of rights and disabilities, power and disadvantage that flowed from it, so that no further justifications or rationalizations were required. A key decision defending the right of conquest was *Johnson and Graham's Lessee v. M'Intosh,* in which both parties to the action claimed the same land through title descendant from different Indian tribes. The issue specifically presented was not merely whether Indians had the power to convey title, but to whom the conveyance could be made—to individuals or to the government that "discovered" land. In holding that Indians could only convey to the latter, the Court reasoned that Indian title was subordinate to the absolute title of the sovereign that was achieved by conquest because "[c]onquest gives a title which the Courts of the conqueror cannot deny...." If property is understood as a delegation of sovereign power—the product of the power of the state—then a fair reading of history reveals the racial oppression of Indians inherent in the American regime of property.

In *Johnson* and similar cases, courts established whiteness as a prerequisite to the exercise of enforceable property rights. Not all first possession or labor gave rise to property rights; rather, the rules of first possession and labor as a basis for property rights were qualified by race. This fact infused whiteness with significance and value because it was solely through being white that property could be acquired and secured under law. Only whites possessed whiteness, a highly valued and exclusive form of property.

C. Critical Characteristics of Property and Whiteness

The legal legacy of slavery and of the seizure of land from Native American peoples is not merely a regime of property law that is (mis)informed by racist and ethnocentric themes. Rather, the law has established and protected an actual property interest in whiteness itself, which shares the critical characteristics of property and accords with the many and varied theoretical descriptions of property.

Although by popular usage property describes "things" owned by persons, or the rights of persons with respect to a thing, the concept of property prevalent among most theorists, even prior to the twentieth century, is that property may "consist[] of rights in 'things' that are intangible, or whose existence is a matter of legal definition." Property is thus said to be a right, not a thing, characterized as metaphysical, not physical. The theoretical bases and conceptual descriptions of property rights are varied, ranging from first possessor rules, to creation of value, to Lockean labor theory, to personality theory, to utilitarian theory. However disparate, these formulations of property clearly illustrate the extent to which property rights and interests embrace much more than land and personality. Thus, the fact that whiteness is not a "physical" entity does not remove it from the realm of property.

Whiteness is not simply and solely a legally recognized property interest. It is simultaneously an aspect of self-identity and of personhood, and its relation to the law of property is complex. Whiteness has functioned as self-identity in the domain of the intrinsic, personal, and psychological; as reputation in the interstices between internal and external identity; and, as property in the extrinsic, public, and legal realms. According whiteness actual legal status converted an aspect of identity into an external object of property, moving whiteness from privileged identity to a vested interest. The law's construction of whiteness defined and affirmed critical aspects of identity (who is white); of privilege (what benefits accrue to that status); and, of property (what *legal* entitlements arise from that status). Whiteness at various times signifies and is deployed as identity, status, and property, sometimes singularly, sometimes in tandem.

1. Whiteness as a Traditional Form of Property.—Whiteness fits the broad historical concept of property described by classical theorists. In James Madison's view, for example, property "embraces every thing to which a man may attach a value and have a right," referring to all of a person's legal rights. Property as conceived in the founding era

> included not only external objects and people's relationships to them, but also all of those human rights, liberties, powers, and immunities that are important for human well-being, including: freedom of expression, freedom of conscience, freedom from bodily harm, and free and equal opportunities to use personal faculties.

Whiteness defined the legal status of a person as slave or free. White identity conferred tangible and economically valuable benefits and was jealously guarded as a valued possession, allowed only to those who met a strict standard of proof. Whiteness—the right to white identity as embraced by the law—is property if by property one means all of a person's legal rights.

Other traditional theories of property emphasize that the "natural" character of property is derivative of custom, contrary to the notion that property is the product of a delegation of sovereign power. This "bottom up" theory holds that the law of property merely codifies existing customs and social relations. Under that view, government-created rights such as social welfare payments cannot constitute legitimate property interests because they are positivistic in nature. Other theorists have challenged this conception, and argued that even the most basic of "customary" property rights—the rule of first possession, for example—is dependent on its acceptance or rejection in particular instances by the government. Citing custom as a source of property law begs the central question: whose custom?

Rather than remaining within the bipolar confines of custom or command, it is crucial to recognize the dynamic and multifaceted relationship among custom, command, and law, as well as the extent to which positionality determines how each may be experienced and understood. Indian custom was obliterated by force and replaced with the regimes of common law that embodied the customs of the conquerors. The assumption of American law as it related to Native Americans was that conquest *did* give rise to sovereignty. Indians experienced the property laws of the colonizers and the emergent American nation as acts of violence perpetuated by the exercise of power and ratified through the rule of law. At the same time, these laws were perceived as custom and "common sense" by the colonizers. The Founders, for instance, so thoroughly embraced Lockean labor theory as the basis for a right of acquisition because it affirmed the right of the New World settlers to settle on and acquire the frontier. It confirmed and ratified their experience.

The law's interpretation of those encounters between whites and Native Americans not only inflicted vastly different results on them, but also established a pattern—a *custom*—of valorizing whiteness. As the forms of racialized property were perfected, the value and protection extended to whiteness increased. Regardless of which theory of property one adopts, the concept of whiteness—established by centuries of custom (illegitimate custom, but custom nonetheless) and codified by law—may be understood as a property interest.

2. *Modern Views of Property as Defining Social Relations.*—Although property in the classical sense refers to everything that is valued and to which a person has a right, the modern concept of property focuses on its function and the social relations reflected therein. In this sense, modern property doctrine emphasizes the more contingent nature of property and has been the basis for the argument that property rights should be expanded.

Modern theories of property reject the assumption that property is "objectively definable or identifiable, apart from social context." Charles Reich's ground-breaking work, *The New Property,* was an early effort to focus on the function of property and note the changing social relations reflected and constructed by new forms of property derived from the government. Property in this broader sense encompassed jobs, entitlements, occupational licenses, contracts, subsidies, and indeed a whole host of intangibles that are the product of labor, time, and creativity, such as intellectual property, business goodwill, and enhanced earning potential from graduate degrees. Notwithstanding the dilution of new property since *Goldberg v. Kelly* and its progeny as well as continued attacks on the concept, the legacy of new property infuses the concept of property with questions of power, selection, and allocation. Reich's argument that property is not a natural right but a construction by society resonates in current theories of property that describe the allocation of property rights as a series of choices. This construction directs attention toward issues of relative power and social relations inherent in any definition of property.

3. *Property and Expectations.*—"Property is nothing but the basis of expectation," according to Bentham, "consist[ing] in an established expectation, in the persuasion of being able to draw such and such advantage from the thing possessed." The relationship between expectations and property remains highly significant, as the law "has recognized and protected even the expectation of rights as actual legal property." This theory does not suggest that all value or all expectations give rise to property, but those expectations in tangible or intangible things that are valued and protected by the law are property.

In fact, the difficulty lies not in identifying expectations as a part of property, but in distinguishing which expectations are reasonable and therefore merit the protection of the law as property. Although the existence of certain property rights may seem self-evident and the protection of certain expectations may seem essential for social stability, property is a legal construct by which selected private interests are protected and upheld. In creating property "rights," the law draws boundaries and enforces or reorders existing regimes of power. The inequalities that are produced and reproduced are not givens or inevitabilities, but rather are conscious selections regarding the structuring of social relations. In this sense, it is contended that property rights and interests are not "natural," but are "creation[s] of law."

In a society structured on racial subordination, white privilege became an expectation and, to apply Margaret Radin's concept, whiteness became the quintessential property for personhood. The law constructed "whiteness" as an objective fact, although in reality it is an ideological proposition imposed through subordination. This move is the central feature of "reification": "Its basis is that a relation between people takes on the character of a thing and thus acquires a 'phantom objectivity,' an autonomy that seems so strictly rational and all-embracing as to conceal every trace of its fundamental nature: the relation between people." Whiteness was an "object" over which continued control was—and is—expected. The protection of these expectations is central because, as Radin notes: "If an object you now control is bound up in your future plans or in your anticipation of your future self, and it is partly these plans for your own continuity that make you a person, then your personhood depends on the realization of these expectations."

Because the law recognized and protected expectations grounded in white privilege (albeit not explicitly in all instances), these expectations became tantamount to property that could not permissibly be intruded upon without consent. As the law explicitly ratified those expectations in continued privilege or extended ongoing protection to those illegitimate expectations by failing to expose or to radically disturb them, the dominant and subordinate positions within the racial hierarchy were reified in law. When the law recognizes, either implicitly or explicitly, the settled expectations of whites built on the privileges and benefits produced by white supremacy, it acknowledges and reinforces a property interest in whiteness that reproduces Black subordination.

4. The Property Functions of Whiteness.—In addition to the theoretical descriptions of property, whiteness also meets the functional criteria of property. Specifically, the law has accorded "holders" of whiteness the same privileges and benefits accorded holders of other types of property. The liberal view of property is that it includes the exclusive rights of possession, use, and disposition. Its attributes are the right to transfer or alienability, the right to use and enjoyment, and the right to exclude others. Even when examined against this limited view, whiteness conforms to the general contours of property. It may be a "bad" form of property, but it is property nonetheless.

(a) Rights of Disposition.—Property rights are traditionally described as fully alienable. Because fundamental personal rights are commonly understood to be inalienable, it is problematic to view them as property interests. However, as Margaret Radin notes, "inalienability" is not a transparent term; it has multiple meanings that refer to interests that are non-salable, non-transferable, or non-market-alienable. The common core of inalienability is the negation of the possibility of separation of an entitlement, right, or attribute from its holder.

Classical theories of property identified alienability as a requisite aspect of property; thus, that which is inalienable cannot be property. As the major exponent of this view, Mill argued that public offices, monopoly privileges, and human beings—all of which were or should have been inalienable—should not be considered property at all. Under this account, if inalienability inheres in the concept of property, then whiteness, incapable of being transferred or alienated either inside or outside the market, would fail to meet a criterion of property.

As Radin notes, however, even under the classical view, alienability of certain property was limited. Mill also advocated certain restraints on alienation in connection with property rights in land and probably other natural resources. In fact, the law has recognized various kinds of inalienable property. For example, entitlements of the regulatory and welfare states, such as transfer payments and government licenses, are inalienable; yet they have been conceptualized and treated as property by law. Although this "new property" has been criticized as being improper—that is, not appropriately cast as property—the principal objection has been based on its alleged lack of productive capacity, not its inalienability.

The law has also acknowledged forms of inalienable property derived from nongovernmental sources. In the context of divorce, courts have held that professional degrees or licenses held by one party and financed by the labor of the other is marital property whose value is subject to allocation by the court. A medical or law degree is not alienable either in the market or by voluntary transfer. Nevertheless, it is included as property when dissolving a legal relationship.

Indeed, Radin argues that, as a deterrent to the dehumanization of universal commodification, market-inalienability may be justified to protect property important to the person and to safeguard human flourishing. She suggests that non-commodification or market-inalienability of personal property or those things essential to human flourishing is necessary to guard against the objectification of human beings. To avoid that danger, "we must cease thinking that market alienability is inherent in the concept of property." Following this logic, then, the inalienability of whiteness should not preclude the consideration of whiteness as property. Paradoxically, its inalienability may be more indicative of its perceived enhanced value, rather than its disqualification as property.

(b) Right to Use and Enjoyment.—Possession of property includes the rights of use and enjoyment. If these rights are essential aspects of property, it is because "the problem of property in political philosophy dissolves into . . . questions of the will and the way in which we use the things of this world." As whiteness is simultaneously an aspect of identity and a property interest, it is something that can both be experienced and deployed as a resource. Whiteness can move from being a passive characteristic as an aspect of identity to an active entity that—like other types of property—is used to fulfill the will and to exercise power. The state's official recognition of a racial identity that subordinated Blacks and of privileged rights in property based on race elevated whiteness from a passive attribute to an object of law and a resource deployable at the social, political, and institutional level to maintain control. Thus, a white person "used and enjoyed" whiteness whenever she took advantage of the privi-

leges accorded white people simply by virtue of their whiteness—when she exercised any number of rights reserved for the holders of whiteness. Whiteness as the embodiment of white privilege transcended mere belief or preference; it became usable property, the subject of the law's regard and protection. In this respect whiteness, as an active property, has been used and enjoyed.

(c) Reputation and Status Property.—In constructing whiteness as property, the ideological move was to conceptualize white racial identity as an external thing in a constitutive sense—an "object [] or resource [] necessary to be a person." This move was accomplished in large measure by recognizing the reputational interest in being regarded as white as a thing of significant value, which like other reputational interests, was intrinsically bound up with identity and personhood. The reputation of being white was treated as a species of property, or something in which a property interest could be asserted. In this context, whiteness was a form of status property.

The conception of reputation as property found its origins in early concepts of property that encompassed things (such as land and personalty), income (such as revenues from leases, mortgages, and patent monopolies), and one's life, liberty, and labor. Thus, Locke's famous pronouncement, "every man has a 'property' in his own 'person,'"undergirded the assertion that one's physical self was one's property. From this premise, one's labor, "the work of his hands," combined with those things found in the common to form property over which one could exercise ownership, control, and dominion. The idea of self-ownership, then, was particularly fertile ground for the idea that reputation, as an aspect of identity earned through effort, was similarly property. Moreover, the loss of reputation was capable of being valued in the market.

The direct manifestation of the law's legitimation of whiteness as reputation is revealed in the well-established doctrine that to call a white person "Black" is to defame her. Although many of the cases were decided in an era when the social and legal stratification of whites and Blacks was more absolute, as late as 1957 the principle was reaffirmed, notwithstanding significant changes in the legal and political status of Blacks. As one court noted, "there is still to be considered the social distinction existing between the races," and the allegation was likely to cause injury. A Black person, however, could not sue for defamation if she was called "white." Because the law expressed and reinforced the social hierarchy as it existed, it was presumed that no harm could flow from such a reversal.

Private identity based on racial hierarchy was legitimated as public identity in law, even after the end of slavery and the formal end of legal race segregation. Whiteness as interpersonal hierarchy was recognized externally as race reputation. Thus, whiteness as public reputation and personal property was affirmed.

(d) The Absolute Right to Exclude.—Many theorists have traditionally conceptualized property to include the exclusive rights of use, disposition, and possession, with possession embracing the absolute right to exclude.

The right to exclude was the central principle, too, of whiteness as identity, for mainly whiteness has been characterized, not by an inherent unifying characteristic, but by the exclusion of others deemed to be "not white." The possessors of whiteness were granted the legal right to exclude others from the privileges inhering in whiteness; whiteness became an exclusive club whose membership was closely and grudgingly guarded. The courts played an active role in enforcing this right to exclude—determining who was or was not white enough to enjoy the privileges accompanying whiteness. In that sense, the courts protected whiteness as any other form of property.

Moreover, as it emerged, the concept of whiteness was premised on white supremacy rather than mere difference. "White" was defined and constructed in ways that increased its value by reinforcing its exclusivity. Indeed, just as whiteness as property embraced the right to exclude, whiteness as a theoretical construct evolved for the very purpose of racial exclusion. Thus, the concept of whiteness is built on both exclusion and racial subjugation. This fact was particularly evident during the period of the most rigid racial exclusion, as whiteness signified racial privilege and took the form of status property.

At the individual level, recognizing oneself as "white" necessarily assumes premises based on white supremacy: It assumes that Black ancestry in any degree, extending to generations far removed, automatically disqualifies claims to white identity, thereby privileging "white" as unadulterated, exclusive, and rare. Inherent in the concept of "being white" was the right to own or hold whiteness to the exclusion and subordination of Blacks. Because "[i]dentity is ... continuously being constituted through social interactions," the assigned political, economic, and social inferiority of Blacks necessarily shaped white identity. In the commonly held popular view, the presence of Black "blood"—including the infamous "one-drop" consigned a person to being "Black" and evoked the "metaphor ... of purity and contamination" in which Black blood is a contaminant and white racial identity is pure. Recognizing or identifying oneself as white is thus a claim of racial purity, an assertion that one is free of any taint of Black blood. The law has played a critical role in legitimating this claim.

D. White Legal Identity: The Law's Acceptance and Legitimation of Whiteness as Property

The law assumed the crucial task of racial classification, and accepted and embraced the then-current theories of race as biological fact. This core precept of race as a physically defined reality allowed the law to fulfill an essential function—to "parcel out social standing according to race" and to facilitate systematic discrimination by articulating "seemingly precise definitions of racial group membership." This allocation of race and rights continued a century after the abolition of slavery.

The law relied on bounded, objective, and scientific definitions of race—what Neil Gotanda has called "historical race"—to construct whiteness as not merely race, but race plus privilege. By making race determinant and the product of rationality and science, dominant and subordinate positions within the racial hierarchy were disguised as the product of natural law and biology rather than as naked preferences. Whiteness as racialized privilege was then legitimated by science and was embraced in legal doctrine as "objective fact."

Case law that attempted to define race frequently struggled over the precise fractional amount of Black "blood"—traceable Black ancestry—that would defeat a claim to whiteness. Although the courts applied varying fractional formulas in different jurisdictions to define "Black" or, in the terms of the day, "Negro" or "colored," the law uniformly accepted the rule of hypodescent—racial identity was governed by blood, and white was preferred.

This legal assumption of race as blood-borne was predicated on the pseudo-sciences of eugenics and craniology that saw their major development during the eighteenth and nineteenth centuries. The legal definition of race was the "objective" test propounded by racist theorists of the day who described race to be immutable, scientific, biologically determined—an unsullied fact of the blood rather than a volatile and violently imposed regime of racial hierarchy.

In adjudicating who was "white," courts sometimes noted that, by physical characteristics, the individual whose racial identity was at issue appeared to be white and, in fact, had been regarded as white in the community. Yet if an individual's blood was tainted, she could not claim to be "white" as the law understood, regardless of the fact that phenotypically she may have been completely indistinguishable from a white person, may have lived as a white person, and have descended from a family that lived as whites. Although socially accepted as white, she could not *legally* be white. Blood as "objective fact" dominated over appearance and social acceptance, which were socially fluid and subjective measures.

But, in fact, "blood" was no more objective than that which the law dismissed as subjective and unreliable. The acceptance of the fiction that the racial ancestry could be determined with the degree of precision called for by the relevant standards or definitions rested on false assumptions that racial categories of prior ancestors had been accurately reported, that those reporting in the past shared the definitions currently in use, and that racial purity actually existed in the United States. Ignoring these considerations, the law established rules that extended equal treatment to those of the "same blood," albeit of different complexions, because it was acknowledged that, "[t]here are white men as dark as mulattoes, and there are pure-blooded albino Africans as white as the whitest Saxons."

The standards were designed to accomplish what mere observation could not: "That even Blacks who did not look Black were kept in their place." Although the line of demarcation between Black and white varied from rules that classified as Black a person containing "any drop of Black blood," to more liberal rules that defined persons with a preponderance of white blood to be white, the courts universally accepted the notion that white status was something of value that could be accorded only to those persons whose proofs established their whiteness as defined by the law. Because legal recognition of a person as white carried material benefits, "false" or inadequately supported claims were denied like any other unsubstantiated claim to a property interest. Only those who could lay "legitimate" claims to whiteness could be legally recognized as "white," because allowing physical attributes, social acceptance, or self-identification to determine whiteness would diminish its value and destroy the underlying presumption of exclusivity. In effect, the courts erected legal "No Trespassing" signs.

In the realm of *social* relations, racial recognition in the United States is thus an act of race subordination. In the realm of *legal* relations, judicial definition of racial identity based on white supremacy reproduced that race subordination at the institutional level. In transforming white to whiteness, the law masked the ideological content of racial definition and the exercise of power required to maintain it: "It convert[ed] [an] abstract concept into [an] entity."

1. Whiteness as Racialized Privilege.—The material benefits of racial exclusion and subjugation functioned, in the labor context, to stifle class tensions among whites. White workers perceived that they had more in common with the bourgeoisie than with fellow workers who were Black. Thus, W. E. B. Du Bois's classic historical study of race and class, *Black Reconstruction,* noted that, for the evolving white working class, race identification became crucial to the ways that it thought of itself and conceived its interests. There were, he suggested, obvious material benefits, at least in the short term, to the decision of white workers to define themselves by their whiteness: their wages far exceeded those of Blacks and were high even in comparison with world standards. Moreover, even when the white working class did not collect increased pay as part of white privilege, there were real advantages not paid in direct income: whiteness still yielded what Du Bois termed a "public and psychological wage" vital to white workers. Thus, Du Bois noted:

> They [whites] were given public deference ... because they were white. They were admitted freely with all classes of white people, to public functions, to public parks.... The police were drawn from their ranks, and the courts, dependent on their votes, treated them with ... leniency.... Their vote selected public officials, and while this had small effect upon the economic situation, it had great effect on their personal treatment.... White schoolhouses were the best in the community, and conspicuously placed, and they cost anywhere from twice to ten times as much per capita as the colored schools.

The central feature of the convergence of "white" and "worker" lay in the fact that racial status and privilege could ameliorate and assist in "evad[ing] rather than confront[ing] [class] exploitation." Although not accorded the privileges of the ruling class, in both the North and South, white workers could accept their lower class position in the hierarchy "by fashioning identities as 'not slaves' and as 'not Blacks.'" Whiteness produced—and was reproduced by—the social advantage that accompanied it.

Whiteness was also central to national identity and to the republican project. The amalgamation of various European strains into an American identity was facilitated by an oppositional definition of Black as "other." As Hacker suggests, fundamentally, the question was not so much "who is white," *but* "who may be considered white," as the historical pattern was that various immigrant groups of different ethnic origins were accepted into a white identity shaped around Anglo–American norms. Current members then "ponder[ed] whether they want[ed] or need[ed] new members as well as the proper pace of new admissions into this exclusive club." Through minstrel shows in which white actors masquerading in blackface played out racist stereotypes, the popular culture put the Black at " 'solo spot centerstage, providing a relational model in contrast to which masses of Americans could establish a positive and superior sense of identity[,]' . . . [an identity] . . . established by an infinitely manipulable negation comparing whites with a construct of a socially defenseless group."

It is important to note the effect of this hypervaluation of whiteness. Owning white identity as property affirmed the self-identity and liberty of whites and, conversely, denied the self-identity and liberty of Blacks. The attempts to lay claim to whiteness through "passing" painfully illustrate the effects of the law's recognition of whiteness. The embrace of a lie, undertaken by my grandmother and the thousands like her, could occur only when oppression makes self-denial and the obliteration of identity rational and, in significant measure, beneficial. The economic coercion of white supremacy on self-definition nullifies any suggestion that passing is a logical exercise of liberty or self-identity. The decision to pass as white was not a choice, if by that word one means voluntariness or lack of compulsion. The fact of race subordination was coercive and circumscribed the liberty to self-define. Self-determination of identity was not a right for all people, but a privilege accorded on the basis of race. The effect of protecting whiteness at law was to devalue those who were not white by coercing them to deny their identity in order to survive.

2.   Whiteness, Rights, and National Identity.—The concept of whiteness was carefully protected because so much was contingent upon it. Whiteness conferred on its owners aspects of citizenship that were all the more valued because they were denied to others. Indeed, the very fact of citizenship itself was linked to white racial identity. The Naturalization Act of 1790 restricted citizenship to persons who resided in the United States for two years, who could establish their good character in court, and who were "white." Moreover, the trajectory of expanding democratic rights for whites was accompanied by the contraction of the rights of Blacks in an ever deepening cycle of oppression. The franchise, for example, was broadened to extend voting rights to unpropertied white men at the same time that Black voters were specifically disenfranchised, arguably shifting the property required for voting from land to whiteness. This racialized version of republicanism—this Herrenvolk republicanism—constrained any vision of democracy from addressing the class hierarchies adverse to many who considered themselves white.

The inherent contradiction between the bondage of Blacks and republican rhetoric that championed the freedom of all men was resolved by positing that Blacks were different. The laws did not mandate that Blacks be accorded equality under the law because nature—not man, not power, not violence—had determined their degraded status. Rights were for those who had the capacity to exercise them, a capacity denoted by racial identity. This conception of rights was contingent on race—on whether one could claim whiteness—a form of property. This articulation of rights that were contingent on property ownership was a familiar paradigm, as similar requirements had been imposed on the franchise in the early part of the republic.

For the first two hundred years of the country's existence, the system of racialized privilege in both the public and private spheres carried through this linkage of rights and inequality, and rights and property. Whiteness as property was the critical core of a system that affirmed the hierarchical relations between white and Black.

* * *

IV. THE PERSISTENCE OF WHITENESS AS PROPERTY

In the modern period, neither the problems attendant to assigning racial identities nor those accompanying the recognition of whiteness have disappeared. Nor has whiteness as property. Whiteness as property continues to perpetuate racial subordination through the courts' definitions of group identity and through the courts' discourse and doctrine on affirmative action. The exclusion of subordinated "others" was and remains a central part of the property interest in whiteness and, indeed, is part of the protection that the court extends to whites' settled expectations of continued privilege.

The essential character of whiteness as property remains manifest in two critical areas of the law and, as in the past, operates to oppress Native Americans and Blacks in similar ways, although in different arenas. This Part first examines the persistence of whiteness as valued social identity; then exposes whiteness as property in the law's treatment of the question of group identity, as the case of the Mashpee Indians illustrates; and finally, exposes the presence of whiteness as property in affirmative action doctrine.

A. *The Persistence of Whiteness as Valued Social Identity*

Even as the capacity of whiteness to deliver is arguably diminished by the elimination of rigid racial stratifications, whiteness continues to be perceived as materially significant. Because real power and wealth never have been accessible to more than a narrowly defined ruling elite, for many whites the benefits of whiteness as property, in the absence of legislated privilege, may have been reduced to a claim of relative privilege only in comparison to people of color. Nevertheless, whiteness retains its value as a "consolation prize": it does not mean that all whites will win, but simply that they will not lose, if losing is defined as being on the bottom of the social and economic hierarchy—the position to which Blacks have been consigned.

Andrew Hacker, in his 1992 book *Two Nations,* recounts the results of a recent exercise that probed the value of whiteness according to the perceptions of whites. The study asked a group of white students how much money they would seek if they were changed from white to Black. "Most seemed to feel that it would not be out of place to ask for $50 million, or $1 million for each coming black year." Whether this figure represents an accurate amortization of the societal cost of being Black in the United States, it is clear that whiteness is still perceived to be valuable. The wages of whiteness are available to all whites regardless of class position, even to those whites who are without power, money, or influence. Whiteness, the characteristic that distinguishes them from Blacks, serves as compensation even to those who lack material wealth. It is the relative political advantages extended to whites, rather than actual economic gains, that are crucial to white workers. Thus, as Kimberlé Crenshaw points out, whites have an actual stake in racism. Because Blacks are held to be inferior, although no longer on the basis of science as antecedent determinant, but by virtue of their position at the bottom, it allows whites—all whites—to "include themselves in the dominant circle. [Although most whites] hold no real power, [all can claim] their privileged racial identity."

White workers often identify primarily as white rather than as workers because it is through their whiteness that they are afforded access to a host of public, private, and psychological benefits. It is through the concept of whiteness that class consciousness among white workers is subordinated and attention is diverted from class oppression.

Although dominant societal norms have embraced the idea of fairness and nondiscrimination, removal of privilege and antisubordination principles are actively rejected or at best ambiguously received because expectations of white privilege are bound up with what is considered essential for self-realization. Among whites, the idea persists that their whiteness is meaningful. Whiteness is an aspect of racial identity surely, but it is much more; it remains a concept based on relations of power, a social construct predicated on white dominance and Black subordination.

B. *Subordination Through Denial of Group Identity*

Whiteness as property is also constituted through the reification of expectations in the continued right of white-dominated institutions to control the legal meaning of group identity. This reification manifests itself in the law's dialectical misuse of the concept of group identity as it pertains to racially subordinated peoples. The law has recognized and codified racial group identity as an instrumentality of exclusion and exploitation; however, it has refused to recognize group identity when asserted by racially oppressed groups as a basis for affirming or claiming rights. The law's approach to group identity reproduces subordination, in the past through "race-ing" a group—that is, by assigning a racial identity that equated with inferior status, and in the present by erasing racial group identity.

In part, the law's denial of the existence of racial groups is predicated not only on the rejection of the ongoing presence of the past, but is also grounded on a basic tenet of liberalism—that constitutional protections inhere in individuals, not groups. As informed by the Lockean notion of the social contract, the autonomous, free-will of the individual is central. Indeed, it is the individual who, in concert with other individuals, elects to enter into political society and to form a state of limited powers. This philosophical view of society is closely aligned with the antidiscrimination principle—the idea being that equality mandates only the equal treatment of individuals under the law. Within this framework, the idea of the social group has no place.

Although the law's determination of any "fact," including that of group identity, is not infinitely flexible, its studied ignorance of the issue of racial group identity insures wrong results by assuming a pseudo-objective posture that does not permit it to hear the complex dialogue concerning the identity question, particularly as it pertains to historically dominated groups.

Instead, the law holds to the basic premise that definition from above can be fair to those below, that beneficiaries of racially conferred privilege have the right to establish norms for those who have historically been oppressed pursuant to those norms, and that race is not historically contingent. Although the substance of race definitions has changed, what persists is the expectation of white-controlled institutions in the continued right to determine meaning—the reified privilege of power—that reconstitutes the property interest in whiteness in contemporary form.

In undertaking any definition of race as group identity, there are implicit and explicit normative underpinnings that must be taken into account. The "riddle of identity" is not answered by a "search for essences" or essential discoverable truth, nor by a search for mere "descriptions and re-descriptions." Instead, when handling the complex issue of group identity, we should look to "purposes and effects, consequences and functions." The questions pertaining to definitions of race then are not principally biological or genetic, but social and political: what must be addressed is who is defining, how is the definition constructed, and why is the definition being propounded. Because definition is so often a central part of domination, critical thinking about these issues must precede and adjoin any definition. The law has not attended to these questions. Instead, identity of "the other" is still objectified, the complex, negotiated quality of identity is ignored, and the impact of inequitable power on identity is masked. These problems are illustrated in the land claim suit brought by the Mashpee, a Massachusetts Indian tribe.

In *Mashpee Tribe v. Town of Mashpee,* the Mashpee sued to recover land that several Indians had conveyed to non-Indians in violation of a statute that barred alienation of tribal land to non-Indians without the approval of the federal government. In order to recover possession of the land, the Mashpee were required to prove that they were a tribe at the time of the conveyance. Although the trial judge admitted to some preliminary

confusion about the appropriate definition of "tribe," he ultimately accepted the standard articulated in prior case law that defined tribe as "a body
of Indians of the same or similar race, united in a community under one
leadership or government, and inhabiting a particular though sometimes
ill-defined territory." The Mashpee were held not to be a tribe at the time
the suit was filed, so that their claim to land rights based on group identity
were rejected.

The Mashpee's experience was filtered, sifted, and ultimately rendered
incoherent through this externally constituted definition of tribe that
incorporated outside criteria regarding race, leadership, territory, and
community. The fact that the Mashpee had intermingled with Europeans,
runaway slaves, and other Indian tribes signified to the jury and to the
court that they had lost their tribal identity.

But for the Mashpee, blood was not the measure of identity: their
identity as a group was manifested for centuries by their continued relationship to the land of the Mashpee; their consciousness and embrace of
difference, even when it was against their interest; and, their awareness
and preservation of cultural traditions. Nevertheless, under the court's
standard, the tribe was "incapable of *legal* self-definition." Fundamentally,
then, the external imposition of definition maintained the social equilibrium that was severely challenged by the Mashpee land claims.

The Mashpee case presents new variations on old themes of race and
property. Previous reified definitions of race compelled abandonment of
racial identity in exchange for economic and social privilege. Under the
operative racial hierarchy, passing is the ultimate assimilationist move—
the submergence of a subordinate cultural identity in favor of dominant
identity, assumed to achieve better societal fit within prevailing norms. The
modern definition of "tribe" achieved similar results by misinterpreting
the Mashpee's adaptation to be assimilation. The Mashpee absorbed and
managed, rather than rejected and suppressed, outsiders; yet the court
erased their identity, assuming that, by virtue of intermingling with other
races, the Mashpee's identity as a people had been subsumed. The Mashpee
were not "passing," but were legally determined to have "passed"—no
longer to have distinct identity. This erasure was predicated on the assumption that what is done from necessity under conditions of established
hierarchies of domination and subordination is a voluntary surrender for
gain.

Beyond the immediate outcome of the case lies the deeper problem
posed by the hierarchy of the rules themselves and the continued retention
by white-controlled institutions of exclusive control over definitions as they
pertain to the identity and history of dominated peoples. Although the law
will always represent the exercise of state power in enforcing its choices,
the violence done to the Mashpee and other oppressed groups results from
the law's refusal to acknowledge the negotiated quality of identity. Whiteness as property assumes the form of the exclusive right to determine rules;
it asserts that, against a framework of racial dominance and unequal
power, fairness can result from a property rule, or indeed any other rule,

economic discrimination, does that mean that economic developments that tend to reduce the incidence of such non-market identities are desirable as a means of reducing discrimination? Would the aggressively paternalistic practices that led to the partial assimilation of the Mashpee tribe discussed on pages 695–96 be viewed as desirable practices because they reduce the incidence of the "Red" identity? What about even more intrusive measures such as taking children away from "Red" parents so that they can be raised in a "Green" environment?

2.   Akerlof, Kranton and McAdams. The identity payoff model presented in this paper, and the group-status production model presented by McAdams, *infra* at 744, both attempt to explain the persistence of economic inequality when classical economic theory states that the free market should eliminate discrimination. However, while the goals of the two papers might be similar, their approaches are quite different. First, McAdams' approach is group based; all individuals are looked upon as basically the same, with differences created by quasi-market forces. By contrast, the model presented by Akerlof and Kranton focuses on individuals and assumes that, even in the absence of markets, some individuals would have a predisposition to be "Red" while others would be "Green." Additionally, McAdams sees discrimination as the result of self-interested behavior on the part of the majority, while Akerlof and Kranton see identity differentiation as arising partially as a survival strategy by the minority. Given these differences between the two explanations for discrimination, is there any way that the Akerlof–Kranton and McAdams positions can be reconciled?

3.   Different identities or different settings? Are the "Red" and "Green" cultures of the Akerlof-Kranton model necessarily representative of different identities, or could they be thought of more accurately as different manifestations of the same identity when faced with different circumstances? When Malcolm X began hustling, his mentor gave him the following advice: "[g]et here early ... everything in place ... you never need to waste motion." ALEX HALEY & MALCOLM X, THE AUTOBIOGRAPHY OF MALCOLM X 46 (1965). When Malcolm X became a more successful drug dealer he demonstrated considerable capitalist acumen. He reinvested his profits into his business, developed rational strategies for dealing with law enforcement and entered new markets when government regulation became too tight. *Id.* at 99–102. Given the effort and business skills required to succeed as a hustler, as well as Malcolm X's success when he was able to find non-criminal employment with the Nation of Islam, does it seem more likely that Malcolm's "Red" identity was different from a mainstream "Green" identity, or that it was simply a "Green" identity expressing itself in "Red" surroundings?

4.   Definition of tribe. This case was presented as a contest between history and anthropology, with history winning in the end. However, aren't broad historical and anthropological definitions of the word tribe ultimately beside the point? Shouldn't the definition of tribe be that used by the drafters of the Non-Intercourse Act?

that imposes an entirely externally constituted definition of gro...
Reality belies this presumption. In *Plessy,* the Court affirmed th...
the state to define who was white, obliterating aspects of social ac...
and self-identification as sources of validation and identity. The M...
were similarly divested of their identity through the state's excl...
retention of control over meaning in ways that reinforced group oppress...
When group identity is a predicate for exclusion or disadvantage, the la...
has acknowledged it; when it is a predicate for resistance or a claim of righ...
to be free from subordination, the law determines it to be illusory. This
determinist approach to group identity reproduces racial subordination and
reaffirms whiteness as property.

C. *Subjugation Through Affirmative Action Doctrine*

The assumption that whiteness is a property interest entitled to
protection is an idea born of systematic white supremacy and nurtured over
the years, not only by the law of slavery and "Jim Crow," but also by the
more recent decisions and rationales of the Supreme Court concerning
affirmative action. In examining both the nature of the affirmative action
debate and the legal analysis applied in three Supreme Court cases involving affirmative action—*Regents of University of California v. Bakke, City of
Richmond v. J. A. Croson Co.,* and *Wygant v. Jackson Board of Education,*
it is evident that the protection of the property interest in whiteness still
lies at the core of judicial and popular reasoning.

* * *

VI. CONCLUSION

Whiteness as property has carried and produced a heavy legacy. It is a
ghost that has haunted the political and legal domains in which claims for
justice have been inadequately addressed for far too long. Only rarely
declaring its presence, it has warped efforts to remediate racial exploitation. It has blinded society to the systems of domination that work against
so many by retaining an unvarying focus on vestiges of systemic racialized
privilege that subordinates those perceived as a particularized few—the
"others." It has thwarted not only conceptions of racial justice but also
conceptions of property that embrace more equitable possibilities. In protecting the property interest in whiteness, property is assumed to be no
more than the right to prohibit infringement on settled expectations,
ignoring countervailing equitable claims that are predicated on a right to
inclusion. It is long past time to put the property interest in whiteness to
rest. Affirmative action can assist in that task. Affirmative action, if
properly conceived and implemented, is not only consistent with norms of
equality, but is essential to shedding the legacy of oppression.

NOTES AND QUESTIONS

1. Identity, economics, and multiculturalism. If, as this article seems
to imply, non-market-oriented identities will invariably arise in response to

5. Performative identity. The Indians of Mashpee lost their case because they didn't behave in a way that comported with the jury's view of how an Indian tribe should act, thus their performative identity was not that of a tribe. Isn't this a rather odd way to structure a lawsuit? Modern anti-discrimination laws generally take the opposite approach: the more a minority has assimilated into mainstream culture, the greater chance that minority has of winning an anti-discrimination claim. Devon W. Carbado & Mitu Gulati, *The Law and Economics of Critical Race Theory: Crossroads, Directions, and a New Critical Race Theory*, 112 Yale L.J. 1757, 1822 (2003) (book review). Why is it that in this case, assimilation was (from the standpoint of the outcome of the suit) a bad thing? Does a legal regime which encourages rejection of mainstream culture provide perverse incentives from an anti-discrimination viewpoint?

6. The point of all this. How did the disposition of this case effect the "tribe?" According to the plaintiffs, the tribe was based on culture, shared traditions, kinship, and other intangible bonds. Would those bonds have been strengthened if the "tribe" had won its suit? Would they have been diluted by the effects of a large settlement? Since the "tribe" was not simply an amalgam of individuals, could it possibly have been aided in any way by a positive verdict? Is it more likely that the "tribe" would have been destroyed by the ascendancy of Tribal Council, Inc., which was organized specifically to provide a structure for interaction with the non-tribal world? Would victory for the corporation have helped the "tribe" of Mashpee?

7. Taint of whiteness. According to Professor Harris, "[a]t the individual level, recognizing oneself as 'white' necessarily assumes premises based on white supremacy ... privileging 'white' as unadulterated, exclusive, and rare." *Supra* p. 729. Is it constructive to tar all people who recognize themselves as white with the implication of white supremacy? It would seem likely that recognition of the social power of whiteness is necessary in order to try to eliminate discrimination against blacks. How, under Professor Harris' conception of whiteness as property, is it possible for a white person to work against racism, when by acknowledging the social privileges accorded to whiteness, white people assume the premises of white supremacy?

8. Neutrality of affirmative action. Professor Harris asserts that, "[b]ecause affirmative action can only be implemented through conscious intervention and requires constant monitoring and reevaluation, it does not function behind a mask of neutrality in the realm beyond scrutiny." Of course, chattel slavery was also implemented through conscious intervention and required constant monitoring and reevaluation (not to mention terroristic violence). The same is true of Jim Crow segregation. Does this mean that segregation and slavery did not function to distort white expectations because they did not "function behind a mask of neutrality?" Further, how could any meaningful affirmative action program not change black expectations? Will expectations not change if affirmative action is effective and reliable? Is Professor Harris arguing that blacks can never be beneficiaries of racism in the future because they have been its victims in the past?

9. Additional reading. For a non-technical perspective on economics and identity, see Gerald D. Jaynes, *Identity and Economic Performance*, 568 ANNALS AM. ACAD. POL. & SOC. SCI. 128 (2000). For an interesting description of an interaction between cultures, see *Ann Southerland, Complexities of U.S. Law and Gypsy Identity*, 45 AM. J. COMP. L. 393 (1997). For additional information on anthropological issues in the courts, see generally Larry Cata Backer, *Chroniclers in the Field of Cultural Production: Courts, Law and the Interpretive Process*, 20 B.C. THIRD WORLD L.J. 291 (2000); Glen Stohr, Comment, *The Repercussions of Orality in Federal Indian Law*, 31 ARIZ. ST. L.J. 679 (1999). For additional information on Indian tribes in the courts, see generally Jennifer L. Tomsen, Note, *"Traditional" Resource Uses and Activities: Articulating Values and Examining Conflicts in Alaska*, 19 ALASKA L. REV. 167 (2002); Neu Jessup Newton, *Sovereignty and the Native American Nation: Memory and Misrepresentation: Representing Crazy Horse*, 27 CONN. L. REV. 1003 (1995). For additional information on the Mashpee case, see Gerald Torres & Kathryn Milun, *Frontier of Legal Thought III: Translating Yonnondio by Precedent and Evidence: The Mashpee Indian Case*, 1990 DUKE L.J. 625 (1990). For an approach to white privilege outside of the property framework, see Sylvia A. Law, *White Privilege and Affirmative Action*, 32 AKRON L. REV. 603 (1999). For an article that, notwithstanding Harris, espouses the idea of Blackness as property, see Jim Chen, *Affirmative Action: Diversity of Opinions: Embryonic Thoughts on Racial Identity as New Property*, 68 U. COLO. L. REV. 1123 (1997). For a Marxist approach to identity as property, see e. christi cunningham, *Identity Markets*, 45 HOW. L.J. 491 (2002). For an analysis of whiteness as property explored through a fictionalized dialogue with a space alien, see Derrick Bell, *Xerces and the Affirmative Action Mystique*, 57 GEO. WASH. L. REV. 1595 (1989).

B.   RACIAL DISCRIMINATION: TWO COMPETING THEORIES AND EMPIRICAL EVIDENCE OF DISPARATE RACIAL IMPACT

A major dispute between scholars who are interested in the problem of persistent racial discrimination is whether the market can be expected to provide a self-correction for racial discrimination that locks members of racial minorities out of participation in basic transactions and therefore wealth accumulation. We return to economics Nobel laureate, Gary Becker for his economic model which treats racial discrimination like any other private preference that can be expressed as a "taste" with monetary value in the marketplace. Legal scholar Richard McAdams draws on sociological theories of group status production to offer an alternative view of the mechanisms fueling persistent racial discrimination. Legal scholar and economist Ian Ayres enters this debate with a powerful new tool: empirical studies of actual marketplace racial dynamics in important transactions.

1.   A RATIONAL CHOICE THEORY OF RACIAL DISCRIMINATION IN THE MARKETPLACE

The Forces Determining Discrimination in the Market Place

THE ECONOMICS OF DISCRIMINATION 13–18 (2d ed. 1971).

GARY BECKER

In the socio-psychological literature on this subject one individual is said to discriminate against (or in favor of) another if his behavior toward the latter is not motivated by an "objective" consideration of fact. It is difficult to use this definition in distinguishing a violation of objective facts from an expression of tastes or values. For example, discrimination and prejudice are not usually said to occur when someone prefers looking at a glamorous Hollywood actress rather than at some other woman; yet they are said to occur when he prefers living next to whites rather than Negroes. At best calling just one of these actions "discrimination" requires making subtle and rather secondary distinctions. Fortunately, it is not necessary to get involved in these more philosophical issues. It is possible to give an unambiguous definition of discrimination in the market place and yet get at the essence of what is usually called discrimination.

1.   THE ANALYTICAL FRAMEWORK

Money, commonly used as a measuring rod, will also serve as a measure of discrimination. If an individual has a "taste for discrimination," he must act *as if* he were willing to pay something either directly or in the form of a reduced income, to be associated with some persons instead of others. When actual discrimination occurs, he must, in fact, either pay or forfeit income for this privilege. This simple way of looking at the matter gets at the essence of prejudice and discrimination.

Social scientists tend to organize their discussion of discrimination in the market place according to their disciplines. To the sociologist, different levels of discrimination against a particular group are associated with different levels of social and physical "distance" from that group or with different levels of socioeconomic status; the psychologist classifies individuals by their personality types, believing that this is the most useful organizational principle. The breakdown used here is most familiar to the economist and differs from both of these: all persons who contribute to production in the same way, e.g., by the rent of capital or the sale of labor services, are put into one group, with each group forming a separate "factor of production." The breakdown by economic productivity turns out to be a particularly fruitful one, since it emphasizes phenomena that have long been neglected in literature on discrimination.

By using the concept of a *discrimination coefficient* (this will be abbreviated to "DC"), it is possible to give a definition of a "taste for discrimination" that is parallel for different factors of production, employers, and consumers. The *money* costs of a transaction do not always completely measure *net* costs, and a DC acts as a bridge between money and net costs. Suppose an *employer* were faced with the money wage rate π of a particular factor; he is assumed to act as $\pi(1 + d_i)$ were the net wage rate, with di as his DC against this factor. An *employee*, offered the money wage rate π_i for working with this factor, acts as if $\pi(1-d_j)$ were the *net* wage rate, with dj as his DC against this factor. A *consumer*, faced with a unit money of p for the commodity "produced" by this factor, acts as if the net price were $p(1 + d_k)$ with dk as his DC against this factor. In all three instances a DC gives the percentage by which either money costs or money returns are changed in going from money to net magnitudes: the employer uses it to estimate his net wage costs, the employee his net wage rate, and the consumer the net price of a commodity.

A DC represents a non-pecuniary element in certain kinds of transactions, and it is positive or negative, depending upon whether the non-pecuniary element is considered "good" or "bad." Discrimination is commonly associated with *dis*utility caused by contact with some individuals and this interpretation is followed here. Since this implies that d_i, d_j, and d_k are all greater than zero, to the employer this coefficient represents a non-monetary cost of production, to the employer a non-monetary cost of employment, and to the consumer a non-monetary cost of consumption. "Nepotism" rather than "discrimination" would occur if they were less than zero, and they would then represent non-monetary returns of production, employment, and consumption to the employer, employee, and consumer, respectively.

The quantities πd_i, $\pi j d_j$, and $p d_k$ are the exact money equivalents of these non-monetary costs; for given wage rates and prices, these money equivalents are larger, the larger di, dj, and dk are. Since a DC can take on any value between zero and plus infinity, tastes for discrimination can also vary continuously within this range. This quantitative representation of a taste for discrimination provides the means for empirically estimating the quantitative importance of discrimination.

2.   TASTES FOR DISCRIMINATION

The magnitude of a taste for discrimination differs from person to person, and many investigators have directed their energies toward discovering the variables that are most responsible for these differences. I also attempt to isolate and estimate the quantitative importance of some of these variables; the following discussion briefly describes several variables that receive attention in subsequent chapters.

The discrimination by an individual against a particular group (to be called N) depends on the social and physical distance between them and on their relative socioeconomic status. If he works with N in production, it may also depend on their substitutability in production. The relative number of N in the society at large also may be very important: it has been argued that an increase in the numerical importance of a minority group increases the prejudice against them, since the majority begins to fear their growing power; on the other hand, some argue that greater numbers bring greater knowledge and that leads to a decline in prejudice. Closely related to this variable are the frequency and regularity of "contact" with N in different establishments and firms.

According to our earlier definition, if someone has a "taste for discrimination," he must act *as if* he were willing to forfeit income in order to avoid certain transactions; it is necessary to be aware of the emphasis on the words "as if." An employer may refuse to hire Negroes solely because he erroneously underestimates their economic efficiency. His behavior is discriminatory not because he is prejudiced against them but because his is ignorant of their true efficiency. Ignorance may be quickly eliminated by the spread of knowledge, while a prejudice (i.e. preference) is relatively independent of knowledge. This distinction is essential for understanding the motivation of many organizations, since they either explicitly or implicitly assume that discrimination can be eliminated by a wholesale spread of knowledge.

Since a taste for discrimination incorporates both prejudice and ignorance, the amount of knowledge available must be included as a determinant of tastes. Another proximate determinant is geographical and chronological location: discrimination may vary from country to country, from region to region within a country, from rural to urban areas within a region, and from one time period to another. Finally, tastes may differ simply because of differences in personality.

3. MARKET DISCRIMINATION

Suppose there are two groups, designated by W and N, with members of W being perfect substitutes in production for members of N. In the absence of discrimination and nepotism and if the labor market were perfectly competitive, the equilibrium wage rate of W would equal that of N. Discrimination could cause these wage rates to differ; the market discrimination coefficient between W and N (this will be abbreviated "MDC") is defined as the proportional difference between these wage rates. If π_w and π_n represent the equilibrium wage rates of W and N, respectively, then

$$\text{MDC} = \frac{\pi_w - \pi_n}{\pi_n}$$

If W and N are imperfect substitutes, they may receive different wage rates even in the absence of discrimination. A more general definition of the MDC sets it equal to the difference between the ratio of W's and N's wage rate with and without discrimination. In the special case of perfect substitutes, this reduces to the simpler definition given previously, because $\pi_{\overset{\circ}{w}}$ would equal $\pi_{\overset{\circ}{n}}$.

It should be obvious that the magnitude of the MDC depends on the magnitude of individual DC's. Unfortunately, it is often implicitly assumed that it depends only on them; the arguments proceed as if a knowledge of the determinants of tastes was sufficient for a complete understanding of market discrimination. This procedure is erroneous; many variables in addition to tastes take prominent roles in determining market discrimination, and, indeed, tastes sometimes play a minor part. The abundant light thrown on the other variables by the tools of economic analysis has probably been the major insight gained from using them.

The MDC does depend in an important way on each individual's DC; however, merely to use some measure of the average DC does not suffice. The complete distribution of DC's among individuals must be made explicit because the size of the MDC is partly related to individual *differences* in tastes. It also depends on the relative importance of competition and monopoly in the labor and product markets, since this partly determines the weight assigned by the market to different DC's. The economic and quantitative importance of N was mentioned as one determinant of tastes for discrimination; this variable is also an independent determinant of market discrimination. This independent effect operates through the number of N relative to W and the cost of N per unit of output relative to the total cost per unit of output. Both may be important, although for somewhat different reasons, in determining the weight assigned by the market to different DC's. Reorganizing production through the substitution of one factor for another is a means of avoiding discrimination; the amount of substitution available is determined by the production function.

The MDC is a direct function of these variables and an indirect function of other variables through their effect on tastes. Our knowledge of the economic aspects of discrimination will be considered satisfactory only when these relationships are known exactly. In subsequent chapters I present the results of my own attempts to close some gaps in this knowledge. * * *

2.   A SOCIOLOGICAL THEORY OF RACIAL DISCRIMINATION IN THE MARKETPLACE

Cooperation and Conflict: The Economics of Group Status Production and Race Discrimination

108 HARV. L. REV. 1003 (1995).

RICHARD H. MCADAMS

In Shakespeare's history of King Henry V, when the time comes for the young King to ready his troops to battle a much larger French force at Agincourt, he delivers a stirring speech that many regard as a masterpiece of inspirational rhetoric. Rejecting his advisor's lament for more men, he responds: "No, my fair cousin:/ If we are marked to die, we are enow/ To do our country loss: and if to live,/ The fewer men, the greater share of honour." The King proclaims his personal desire for honor, offers safe passage back to England for those who do not wish to fight, and then describes how those who stay will be celebrated on future anniversaries of this day of battle, known as the Feast of St. Crispian:

And Crispin Crispian shall ne'er go by,

From this day to the ending of the world,

But we in it shall be remembered;

We few, we happy few, we band of brothers:

For he to-day that sheds his blood with me

Shall be my brother....

And gentlemen in England, now a-bed,

Shall think themselves accursed they were not here;

And hold their manhoods cheap, whiles any speaks

That fought with us upon Saint Crispin's day.

For those of us who strive to be hard-headed theorists of human behavior, and who use economics and game theory to reveal the consequences of legal rules, our initial response to this speech is likely to be: "What a disaster." The King and his soldiers are about to risk their lives. Yet he denies wanting more men though additional troops would obviously better their odds of surviving and winning. Such a non sequitur can only raise doubts about the clarity of Henry's thinking, which in turn can only increase the chances that his officers will question his commands. And, one might ask, what are the meaning and value of "honor" and "brotherhood"? If Henry wishes to motivate his men, a better strategy would be to spell out the potential material benefits (perhaps promising them more pay) or to remind them of the serious penalties for breaking their promise to fight. Offering to pay their way home, after the enhanced risk of loss has caused Henry's troops to regret their decision to join him in France, is sheer insanity. Finally, those "gentlemen in England now a-bed" will likely count themselves lucky for the opportunity to free-ride on a victory. After all, most of the benefits of victory—the general peace and prosperity of England—cannot be withheld from those who do not fight.

Economics, especially "law and economics," prides itself on the universal application of its method. Yet a theory of human motivation that did not grasp the meaning and power of this speech would be seriously flawed. Military leaders are among the more pragmatic and hard-headed people around and would likely scoff at this economic analysis of Henry's speech. Military rhetoric frequently appeals to honor and brotherhood. If such words prod men and women to risk their lives, one can only imagine how much greater is the power of such words relative to smaller material sacrifices. Consider, for example, the possible economic consequences of the following words:

> Standing in the presence of this multitude, sobered with the responsibility of the message I deliver to the young men of the South, I declare that the truth above all others to be worn unsullied and sacred in your hearts, to be surrendered to no force, sold for no price, compromised in no necessity, but cherished and defended as the covenant of your prosperity, and the pledge of peace to your children, is that the white race must dominate forever in the South, because it is

the white race, and superior to that race by which its supremacy is threatened.

A principal purpose of this Article is to illuminate the economic power of this white supremacist oration by Henry Grady and of Henry V's justly celebrated speech, as well as to examine the precise parallel between the two.

Each speech appeals to *group* interests, *group* loyalty, and *group* identity. The ubiquity of social groups says something of their importance: groups include not just firms, trade associations, and families, but groups based on demographic traits such as race, gender, or age, and those based on membership, such as fraternities or sororities, amateur sports teams, gangs, the Rotary or Elks Clubs, or private lunch clubs. Undoubtedly, some or all of these groups, like the firm, serve the individual's interest by minimizing the transaction costs she incurs while acting to satisfy her preference for whatever interest or function the group facilitates. But that explanation offers no insight into the meaning or power of the speeches of Henry V and Henry Grady.

This Article offers an economic theory to explain why individuals make material sacrifices for group welfare. My thesis is that a material view of human motivation underestimates both the level of cooperation that groups elicit from their members and the level of conflict that groups elicit from each other. A single group dynamic connects these added increments of cooperation and conflict: groups achieve solidarity and elicit loyalty beyond what economic analysis conventionally predicts, but solidarity and loyalty within groups lead predictably, if not inevitably, to competition and conflict between groups. The connection is the desire for esteem or status. Groups use intra-group status rewards as a non-material means of gaining material sacrifice from members, but the attendant desire for inter-group status causes inter-group conflict. This theory explains the power of King Henry's speech, which appeals to the individual's identification with the group ("we band of brothers") and effectively describes the status reward by contrasting other members of the group (those gentlemen left in England) who will not share in it. At the same time, the war itself was the product of England's desire for esteem and status—more specifically, Henry's desire for honor—which can only be achieved by conquering France.

This two-fold importance of status is essential to a genuine understanding of race discrimination, which has eluded economics. Discrimination is a means by which social groups produce status for their members, but pivotal to understanding this form of inter-group *conflict* is the role that status plays in generating the intra-group *cooperation* necessary to make discrimination effective. Absent the desire for intra-group status, selfish individuals would not make the material sacrifices that discrimination requires. In this context, Henry Grady's racist speech is an economically explicable (if unusually candid) means of enlisting white troops in the ongoing status warfare, urging them to "compromise[ ] in no [material] necessity" the process of discriminating against, and thereby subordinating, the blacks whose inferior position produces a status gain for whites.

The rhetoric helps establish a norm of white behavior, the abrogation of which will lower the in-group status of non-conforming whites.

Race discrimination is the best and most important illustration of what I view as a more general phenomenon of intra-group cooperation and inter-group conflict. Before discussing race, however, I must articulate the general theory—to establish empirically that, because of concern for status, cooperation arises within groups and conflict occurs between groups. Part I sets forth puzzling instances of intra-group cooperation in experimental "dilemma" situations and elsewhere, which are not explained by existing economic theory but are well explained by concern for the esteem of other group members. Part I then proposes a model that describes how 'esteem payments' afford groups a novel means of solving their collective action problems and, finally, how this same mechanism leads inevitably to inter-group status conflict. Part II considers the particular problem of race discrimination—the deficiencies in existing economic theory, the superior ability of a status-production model to explain many race-related phenomena, and the implications of such a model. In particular, if race discrimination is a means of producing group status—if groups are engaged in a form of status "warfare"—then discrimination presents the same case for government prohibition that exists for more traditional government restraints on force and fraud.

I. EXPLAINING "EXCESS" COOPERATION AND CONFLICT: AN ECONOMIC THEORY OF SOCIAL GROUPS

Current economic theory fails to predict the prevalence of cooperation and conflict in human affairs. Considerable evidence supports David Hume's observation that "[w]hen men are once inlisted on opposite sides, they contract an affection to the persons with whom they are united, and an animosity against their antagonists: And these passions they often transmit to their posterity." Economics has been slow to address the function of social groups and the means by which they engender levels of loyalty and hostility in apparent defiance of conventional notions of material selfishness. But the psychic motivations that explain these "passions"— and the resulting intra-group cooperation and inter-group conflict—are reconcilable with rational self-interest.

This Part presents the modern evidence that supports Hume's claim. Initially, section A examines the empirical evidence that people cooperate beyond conventionally predicted levels. This "excess" cooperation is explained neither by sophisticated rational choice mechanisms such as reciprocity, nor by unselfish motives such as altruism. Instead, the experimental data indicate that cooperation is related to group membership. Section B advances a theory to account for this data: individuals who seek to maximize the esteem they receive from others have selfish reasons to contribute to group status. Two concepts of "group" are advanced: one defined externally by common characteristics observable by third-parties, and one defined internally by relationships among the members. In each case, there are selfish but non-pecuniary reasons for cooperating with one's group members. Finally, section C suggests reasons that the very mechanisms that increase cooperation within groups also increase conflict between groups, and considers evidence that such status-based "excess" conflict exists.

A.   The Empirical Evidence of "Excess" Cooperation

To understand conflict among social groups, we must first understand how groups elicit cooperation from their members. Game theorists study the strategic interactions of individuals, and their most compelling contribution is their description of the difficulties groups face in procuring the cooperation of members. In contrast to Adam Smith's "invisible hand," which guides society to desirable outcomes though individuals are selfishly motivated, game theory describes "collective action problems"—situations in which individually rational decisions lead to sub-optimal collective outcomes. The classic example is the prisoner's dilemma, but the basic problem exists in more complex situations with more than two parties: each individual faces a choice essentially between cooperation and defection, where the dominant strategy for each individual is defection, but where mutual defection is worse for everyone than mutual cooperation. The interest in studying such "games" is generated by the belief that they represent a fundamental feature of social life. Whether it is the undersupply of "public goods," the overconsumption of common resources, or related difficulties, the problem of collective action is commonly offered as a rationale for government regulation. Conversely, many private economic practices can best be understood as mechanisms for solving collective action problems.

The focus of this section and the next is a particular mechanism for solving collective action problems commonly ignored by legal economists: groups achieve cooperation by allocating intra-group status. To persuade the skeptical that the desire for esteem exists and is necessary to explain important examples of cooperation, I could begin with a number of real-world examples of group cooperation. It is difficult, however, to distinguish subtle motivations in complex, uncontrolled events. Some might plausibly assert that, for any number of reasons, the individual's pecuniary self-interest in such examples happens to conform to the group interest. Others, including some critics of economic analysis, would argue that cooperation indicates the existence, not of a selfish interest in status, but of genuine altruism. Given these difficulties, I turn first to laboratory experiments, which can control for alternative motivations for cooperation.

1.   Dilemma Experiments: Evidence of Non–Material Motivations for Cooperation.—Since the 1950s, social scientists have conducted experiments with the prisoner's dilemma game, its multi-party variants, public goods problems, and common resource problems. In each test, experimenters structure monetary payoffs to make defection or free-riding the dominant strategy. Despite the logical force of the monetarily dominant strategy, researchers have not found uniform defection. Many individuals defect, but a significant proportion—one-quarter to two-thirds—chooses to cooperate.

After more than two thousand social dilemma experiments, one of the "generally accepted" conclusions is that, when pecuniary incentives appear to compel defection, "many subjects do *not* defect." For those who employ game theory to predict the consequences of legal rules, this residuum of cooperation demands explanation.

One immediate and material explanation is *reciprocity*. When future interactions are likely, reciprocity is possible, and defection may no longer be the dominant strategy. One reciprocal strategy is "tit-for-tat," in which one begins by cooperating and then responds in future rounds by doing whatever the other player did in the previous round. Considerable evidence demonstrates the success of tit-for-tat in preventing mutual defection in iterated prisoner's dilemmas.

Reciprocity does not, however, explain the cooperation observed in the dilemma experiments discussed above. Reciprocity requires future interaction in which players can reciprocate past decisions. Theorists still predict mutual defection for "one-shot" prisoner's dilemmas. Yet a large number of the empirical tests of collective action problems were intentionally designed as "one-shot" games to exclude the opportunity for reciprocity, and these tests have repeatedly found significant amounts of cooperation. In the very circumstance in which there is no material reason to cooperate, there is the undeniable fact of cooperation. Thus, however powerful reciprocity may be in some contexts, a significant residual level of cooperation remains unexplained.

One might note, finally, that the material stakes in these experiments typically involve only a few dollars or less. Though higher stakes might cause people to free-ride, the question is what explains subjects' consistent failure to free-ride when low material stakes suggest they should. After all, entire industries arise to capture stakes of a similar size; what seems low in isolation is vast when aggregated over a large population. Whether we can say the same of the motivations causing this residual cooperation requires us first to discover what those motivations are.

2.   Dilemma Experiments: Evidence of Non–Altruistic Motivations for Cooperation.—Critics and reformers of economic modeling have pointed to the dilemma experiments described above as proof of altruism or a commitment to principles of fairness. Yet a full review of the psychological research on collective dilemmas refutes this thesis. Some sense of "group identity," rather than altruism or fairness, explains the variations in cooperation researchers have observed. Of particular note are studies revealing that individuals cooperate more frequently in dilemma games than do groups of individuals and studies revealing that discussion increases the level of cooperation in dilemma games.

First, many prisoner's dilemma studies have contrasted games between individual subjects with games between groups of subjects. Holding the payoffs constant, these studies consistently find significantly more cooperation when individuals play individuals than when teams play teams. One study, for example, found that three-person groups defected an average of 8.73 times in twenty rounds, compared to an average of 1.8 defections out of twenty when individuals played each other. This individual-group "discontinuity" is consistent with research finding that the formation of a purely experimental "group" can elicit a bias in favor of in-group members, against out-group members, or both. Psychologists discovered this when they set out to create a base line in which individuals would have no reason to favor their own group. To their surprise, whenever subjects were divided into groups, people consistently evaluated members of their own group more favorably than members of other groups. Summarizing this effect, one pair of researchers stated that "more awareness of the presence of an out-group is sufficient to provoke intergroup competitive or discriminatory responses on the part of the in-group."

Additional confirmation of the importance of groups is provided by dilemma experiments in which researchers elicited differences in cooperation by symbolically invoking 'real-world' group memberships. In one study, psychologists observed significantly more cooperation from subjects sharing a common resource when they told the subjects that they were being evaluated as a single group against groups not then a part of the experiment (for example, college students versus non-students) than when they told the subjects that they were being evaluated as members of one of two subgroups in the experiment (for example, psychology majors versus economics majors).

These studies appear to confirm David Hume's insight that individuals "have such a propensity to divide into personal factions, that the smallest appearance of real difference will produce them." The experimenter's arbitrary division of subjects into groups is sufficient to "factionalize" them, causing more competitive behavior between groups than between individuals and favoritism for members of one's own 'group.' Neither a general concern for the welfare of others nor a concern for fairness explains why subjects were so much less cooperative with other subjects whom the experimenter placed in a different group.

The second body of studies that challenge the altruism-fairness explanation are those involving discussion. Repeated study shows that permitting communication between the subjects in a prisoner's dilemma situation dramatically increases the level of cooperation; indeed, discussion as much as doubles cooperation rates. Yet "in none of these experiments does group discussion change the fact of defection's dominance"; given the structure of the experiments, there is no reason for any threat or promise to be credible.

To explain this puzzle, researchers varied the conditions of discussion in multi-party prisoner's dilemmas. In one study, the experimenters randomly divided subjects into two groups and placed each group in a separate room. The experimenters permitted ten minutes of discussion in half the groups and no discussion in the others. In addition, half the groups were told that their decisions would affect the payoff for their own group, while the other half were told that their decisions would determine the payoff for the other group and, conversely, that the decisions of the other group would determine the payoff for their group. The results were striking. When subjects believed their decisions would affect the payoffs of members of their own group, discussion increased cooperation from thirty-four percent to sixty-nine percent. But when subjects believed that their decisions affected payoffs for the *other* group, discussion slightly reduced cooperation. The researchers concluded that "discussion does *not* enhance contribution when beneficiaries are strangers." Of course, *all* of these subjects were "strangers" to each other in the sense that they had never met before the experiment and were randomly assigned to the different groups. Yet with ten minutes of discussion about their upcoming decisions, they were, in an important economic sense, no longer strangers. Limited discussion was sufficient to dramatically increase cooperation if and only if the discussants were the beneficiaries of the cooperation.

These findings further demonstrate that altruism and fairness do not fully explain excess cooperation in the prisoner's dilemma. If discussion invoked a general concern for others or for fairness, it should not matter that the beneficiaries are arbitrarily placed in another room. Instead, discussion seems to permit formation of a group identity that creates a special reason for discussants to cooperate. In the transcripts of the subjects' pre-decision discussion, people frequently referred to what "we"— the members of the group—should do. Moreover, where one group knew that its decisions would affect only the other group, there were "frequent statements that the best results would occur if we all keep and they all give to us." The motive seems to fall far short of altruism or fairness. The kind of speech that so effectively increases cooperation tends to be an appeal not to principle, but to solidarity. Thus, successful inspirational rhetoric—like Henry Grady's racist speech—is often centered around repeated invocations of an "us against them" image.

3. Cooperation Outside the Laboratory: Further Evidence That Groups Matter.—Although laboratory experiments more easily control for alternative explanations, it is also appropriate to consider two real-world collective action problems: social protest and war. Although law and economics scholars have criticized Title VII, none has attempted to explain why individual blacks participated in the civil rights protests that led to its enactment. Social protests—such as marches, boycotts, and "sit-ins"—are costly to the individual. Although a group may benefit from collective protest, the gains will likely be enjoyed by all members of the group, regardless of whether they participated in the protest. Thus, social movements are rife with collective action problems, which usually prevents such movements from forming or succeeding. Posing this problem, Dennis Chong inquires how the civil rights movement of the 1950s and 1960s succeeded in mobilizing considerable collective action. Given the violence of white resisters, Chong rejects the possibility that material rewards explain the participation, recounting instead the importance of social incentives within small, pre-existing groups such as black churches.

Consider also the high-stakes collective action problems in war. If all soldiers attempt to free-ride on the combat efforts of others, the result is a rout. S.L.A. Marshall argues forcefully that, for the bulk of soldiers, the only thing that stops them from fleeing in the face of fire is the *opinion* of those with whom the soldiers have formed social ties. Marshall's evaluation is based on the fighting effectiveness of "battle stragglers," soldiers separated from their fighting unit who temporarily join an unfamiliar company. He found that individual stragglers had almost no "combat value" in a new unit, while small squads of stragglers "tended to fight as vigorously as any element:"

> Within the group increments the men were still fighting alongside old friends, and though they were now joined to a new parent body, they were under the same compulsion to keep face and share in the common defense. The individual stragglers were simply responding to the first law of nature which began to apply irresistibly the moment they were separated from the company of men whom they knew and who knew them.

Even in the face of death—high stakes indeed—individuals cooperate not merely to secure material rewards, but also to preserve the opinion that group members hold of them. This, of course, is the very dynamic King Henry manipulates in his St. Crispian speech.

B.   Economic Explanations of "Excess" Cooperation: The Production of Inter-Group and Intra-Group Status

If neither material self-interest nor altruism explains the residuum of cooperation, what can? And why does the level of cooperation vary so significantly with the manner in which individuals are categorized by group? This section proposes an answer: group-based status production. In the experiments discussed above, individuals behave selfishly, not altruistically, but their selfish end is the production of the non-material good of esteem. If individuals seek such non-material ends, members of social groups have another means of solving collective action problems—by allocating esteem to induce members to make contributions to group welfare. Once we add esteem consequences to the material payoffs of individual decisions in such settings, we can explain both the fact and the nature of residual cooperation.

This section argues that human beings seek esteem from others; in aggregate terms, they seek social status. Individuals derive status from groups in two ways: first, individuals gain esteem from strangers based on visible group memberships; and second, within a socially connected group, individuals are especially concerned with the esteem of fellow members. In each case, though for different reasons, status production creates a non-material incentive for group cooperation.

1.   The Individual Preference for Esteem and Status.—If one assumes that individuals behave rationally, the only explanation for the subjects' behavior in the experiments discussed in Part I.A is that the subjects receive benefits from cooperation, or avoid costs from defection, that are not part of the formal, pecuniary payoff structure of the game. One simple way of explaining the cooperation is that the benefit they receive is the esteem of their fellow game-players.

In an earlier article, I described the pervasiveness and power of what I called "negative relative preferences—preferences for approaching or surpassing the consumption level of others." In particular, I offered evidence that people care greatly about achieving a relative social rank or social status. What one gains by attaining 'status,' however, is merely a state of mind—the opinion of others in society—that one is particularly worthy in some way. To understand "excess" cooperation, we should start with precisely this point: that one of the "basic pleasures" people seek in life is the esteem of others.

That people care what others think of them is a parsimonious explanation of many phenomena. The desire for esteem explains, for example, why people are obsessed with the impression their goods make on others. The desire for esteem also underlies the common emotion of embarrassment: individuals feel a momentary but acute pain from loss of esteem at having others observe their missteps or indiscretions. And this desire for esteem helps explain the well-established finding that individuals conform dramatically in the face of a group judgment. Even when there is no material cost to disagreement, individuals appear to fear that dissent will adversely affect how others view them.

Given this behavior, it is not implausible to say that some individuals would cooperate in what is nominally a prisoner's dilemma solely to preserve the minimal esteem strangers (in that community) normally feel for one another. Individuals add the "esteem rewards" and "esteem penalties" to the material payoffs and choose accordingly. Esteem concerns may change the total payoffs enough to make cooperation rational.

2. Members of "Shared-Trait" Groups Cooperate to Produce Inter-Group Status.—To explain the dilemma experiments adequately, an esteem theory must also explain why the level of cooperation varies with "group identity" measures. The concept of "shared-trait groups" explains the existence and variation in the level of cooperation observed in the experiments. By "shared-trait" group, I mean a collection of individuals who have in common some readily observable feature. In American society, people can roughly agree on how to group individuals—for example, by age, by language, or by physical characteristics we refer to as "race." In each case, on the basis of casual observation, one can determine reasonably well whether individuals fall within the category.

Observable traits are important because, when individuals encounter a stranger, they have no other basis for making an esteem judgment. If individuals feel particularly high or low esteem for others with the same trait, they tend to extend that judgment to the stranger. I am not describing irrational prejudice, but a simple application of the economics of information. Given the scarcity of information, it is rational to use cheaper information—proxies—to infer the existence of more expensive, individualized information. The economics literature describes the use of proxies for making decisions of material consequence (such as employment), but proxies can also be used for the allocation of status. Shared-trait group membership is a proxy people use for granting or withholding esteem to individuals they do not know personally.

The use of observable traits as proxies gives individuals a reason to care about the esteem-generating behavior of those with whom they share an observable trait. If an individual shares a trait with others, she expects strangers to extend her the esteem they have for the group that shares the trait. If these third-party observers know only an individual's putative group membership, the individual expects them to judge her entirely on the basis of that membership. She therefore has a selfish concern that the group be highly esteemed in comparison to other groups. Even though the "members" of a group may not know or feel any affinity for each other, third-party categorization gives these members a reason to care about the group's status.

This proxy effect provides a parsimonious explanation of the variation in cooperation observed in the experiments reviewed above: in the laboratory, the experimenter is the third party who categorizes individuals. Any set of subjects the experimenter designates as constituting a group has a "shared trait" for purposes of the experiment. The subjects know that the researcher is observing and evaluating them as members of the group she created. In collective action experiments, the only means of distinguishing successful from unsuccessful groups is the extent to which the group cooperates and achieves the best collective result. Subjects in such experiments may earn additional benefits for cooperating or face additional costs for defecting—thus, esteem consequences may make cooperation a rational strategy.

Further, in the prisoner's dilemma studies, individuals playing the game against individuals cooperated at higher levels than teams playing the same game against teams. With team-play, individuals expect that the esteem they receive depends on the success of the arbitrarily created groups to which they belong. The proxy effect works to raise the payoff of defecting when the other team cooperates (the one way of "beating" the other team) and to lower the payoff of cooperating when the other team defects (thereby "losing"). With individual play, however, either there is no cognizable "group," or the group contains both of the subjects in the game. Thus any proxy effect works toward cooperation. If subjects understand that the experimenter will have other pairs play the game, they may imagine themselves being evaluated as a pair against other pairs, which raises the payoff of mutual cooperation (the best "pair" outcome) and lowers the payoff of mutual defection (the worst "pair" outcome).

To the experiments previously reviewed, we may now add studies on relative deprivation as a cause of social protest. Relative deprivation refers to the fact that individuals react strongly to deprivation when others have what they lack. "Psychologists hypothesize that a central component of people's angry feelings over deprivation is a comparison between themselves and others who have the desired thing." Numerous studies have demonstrated the importance of comparison with others to feelings of relative deprivation and to behavior motivated by such feelings. Most important, many of these studies find that attitudes about inter-group comparisons predict participation in social protest, whereas attitudes about interpersonal comparisons do not. People are more likely to protest when they feel that the group to which they belong is relatively deprived than when they simply feel that they as individuals are relatively deprived.

In sum, laboratory experiments show that, even when the group is an entirely arbitrary construct, individuals seek to acquire esteem from "non-group" members by raising the status of what, in the eyes of those non-group members, is the individuals' group. Outside the laboratory, concern with how one's shared-trait group is regarded also motivates significant action.

3. *Members of "Socially Connected" Groups Cooperate to Produce Intra–Group Status.*—A second, more conventional understanding of the group posits that the members are, in some manner, socially connected. These socially connected groups are comprised of people who know each other, the paradigm cases being families, networks of friends, or social clubs. Such groups have two noteworthy features, each of which contributes to the group's ability to overcome collective action problems: individuals tend to care especially about the esteem of their fellow group members, and individuals tend to grant esteem to members who contribute to group welfare.

The first feature of socially connected groups is that individuals tend to value the esteem of fellow group members more than they value the esteem of non-members. If we care what others think of us, we care more intensely the more well-informed an opinion is; those with whom we have frequent interaction—group members—know us best. Moreover, the dilemma experiments in which the simple act of discussion generated greater cooperation among discussants indicate that even minimal social connection can significantly increase the concern for the esteem of another. In addition, the very reason many social groups exist is that the members share some skill, trait, or interest; members tend to value the esteem of in-group members more than outsiders because members share a sense of what skills or traits are worth possessing. Finally, there is a self-reinforcing aspect to the concern for intra-group status: we tend to value most the opinion of those we esteem highly, and we prefer to belong to social groups including such people.

Given the especially high concern for esteem from socially connected group members, we can better understand high-stakes cooperation in the collective action problems presented by social protest and war. Military and social protest groups elicit cooperation by rewarding members with esteem or prestige based on how much they contribute to the group's welfare. Yet even if people *seek* intra-group esteem, the question remains why individual group members *provide* intra-group esteem to those who contribute to group welfare. The second noteworthy feature of socially connected groups is that members readily provide esteem to those who benefit the group; even without a central authority, members tend not to free-ride completely on the "esteem payments" of other members.

People provide esteem to members who benefit the group because, up to a point, thinking well of others is not a cost. To the contrary, esteeming others is a valuable "consumption good." A person deprived of this good—who finds no one in the world worth esteeming—is far less happy than one who has located a small collection of worthy souls. Nor is an individual who esteems twenty others necessarily poorer than someone who esteems only ten others to the same degree. To the extent that esteem is not costly, there is no reason to free-ride by withholding esteem from others. Instead, group members tend to allocate esteem in a way that brings them some return by rewarding those who contribute materially to group welfare and, at a secondary level, by rewarding those who allocate esteem in a manner that benefits the group. Imagine, as an analogy, that people have a kind of currency that is useless except for making group members feel better. It would be irrational to keep the currency or to distribute it randomly; one might as well provide it as a reward for those who contribute to group welfare and withhold it to punish those who do not.

Departing briefly from an economic description of human behavior, I can state the point in more realistic psychological terms. "Thinking well of others" is often reflexive rather than deliberate. People who might free-ride on material payments tend not to free-ride on esteem "payments" because they reflexively admire and respect those who benefit the group. Imagine, for example, a chessmaster, a person who not only intensely studies the game, but also socializes predominantly with others who do the same. Taking egoism seriously means that this person will consider chess-playing ability to be an important measure by which others can be judged. Individuals elevate the importance of those traits or skills that they possess. This process helps the individual secure self-esteem. But a consequence of thinking that a particular trait is desirable is to esteem *others* who possess the trait and to esteem them in relation to how much of the trait they possess. It is neither plausible nor coherent for the chessmaster to withhold esteem from other people who excel in chess. Barring an overshadowing negative trait, an individual will more or less *automatically* esteem others who have the traits the individual most values in herself, or the traits the individual would most like to acquire for herself.

Frequently, people reflexively esteem traits or behaviors that increase the welfare of the group. A player's success at chess tournaments raises the prestige of the chess club to which she belongs and earns her esteem within the club. A soldier whose skill or effort saves the lives of his fellow squad members earns their esteem. Moreover, if one who is known to value a particular trait withholds esteem from those who possess it, she risks appearing envious and losing the esteem of others. Especially within a group of people who desire a particular trait, refusing to esteem the trait (or at least to appear to esteem it) calls into question the dissenter's commitment to or understanding of shared values. Of course, some members may nonetheless be envious and refuse to provide esteem. But since esteem is at least partially reflexive, there is less than complete free-riding in allocating esteem, and the group can achieve a significant level of coordination.

Sociological evidence supports the theory that socially connected groups allocate esteem to overcome collective action problems. Socially connected groups, as I have defined them, consist of relatively small numbers of people who know each other. Sociologists have long been interested in how, within larger groups in society, "norms" arise as an important decentralized mechanism of social control. Esteem allocation, it turns out, provides the necessary micro-level explanation for social norms; the functioning of social norms, in turn, demonstrates the full power of intra-group cooperation.

Although economically inclined theorists have mostly ignored norms, one important exception is Robert Ellickson. *In Order Without Law*, Ellickson summarizes and supplements the empirical literature on the success of norms in regulating individual behavior. Ellickson's empirical contribution is his study of norms that govern the resolution of various disputes over livestock between neighbors in Shasta County, California. Like other social norms that arise within "close-knit groups," the Shasta County norms are a means of enhancing group welfare. The norms are a non-legal means by which the group facilitates desirable collective action. To some degree, what Ellickson and others identify as efficient norms are enforced by reciprocity between neighbors who expect to interact indefinitely, and the norms are therefore explicable in material terms. But the unique contribution norms make to cooperation—the additional power of norms beyond reciprocity—is third-party enforcement. What Ellickson has in mind are sanctions administered not by the immediate "victim" of a norm violation, but by "friends, relatives, gossips, vigilantes, and other nonhierarchical third-party enforcers." Third parties sanction—by gossip, scorn, ostracism, or physical retaliation—those who violate the norms or informal rules of the group.

My point, however, is that this informal third-party enforcement cannot exist without the desire for esteem. There is no material incentive to obey norms unless there is a material cost attached to violating them. There is no material cost associated with violation unless someone imposes a material penalty. And there is no material incentive for others to bear the cost of inflicting such a penalty; after all, norm-enforcement is, for the group, a public good, and like all public goods, faces the problem of free-riding. Ellickson says that there is a secondary enforcement norm that compels people to punish those who violate norms and that those who fail to do so will also be sanctioned. But then the question arises why anyone would bear the cost of sanctioning those who failed to sanction a substantive norm violator. As Jon Elster argues, "People do not frown upon others when they fail to sanction people who fail to sanction people who fail to sanction people who fail to sanction a norm violation." As one moves away from the original norm violation, "the cost of receiving disapproval falls rapidly to zero." Yet if the cost of refusing to enforce a norm at any level falls to zero, there is no reason for anyone to enforce the norm, and hence no reason for anyone to follow the norm.

A concern for esteem as an end in itself, however, is sufficient to defend norm enforcement against the infinite regress Elster describes.

Elster's argument assumes that mechanisms like gossip, scorn, and ostracism work only to signal who is to be subject to material sanctions and are only as effective as those material sanctions. But if disapproval *itself* exerts a real force, then the gossip, scorn, and ostracism are themselves sufficient to enforce norms; they punish the violator by lowering the esteem she receives from the community. In addition to this direct support, the desire for esteem may produce a secondary enforcement norm that requires material sanctions for violators of the primary norm. To avoid esteem punishment, individuals may have to bear some cost incurred by imposing material sanctions on norm violators. Thus, the considerable body of evidence that shows that social norms govern behavior further supports the significance of esteem motives, especially within socially connected groups.

In sum, individuals care particularly for esteem within socially connected groups. Even without a central authority, individuals tend to provide esteem to those who contribute to the welfare of such groups, and this process of esteem allocation facilitates wider social norms that bring about further cooperation. Of course, group members will still free-ride when their desire for material well-being outweighs their desire for intra-group status, but esteem allocation will ameliorate, if not eliminate, collective action problems.

C.   The Consequences of Intra–Group Cooperation: Inter–Group Conflict

Intra-group cooperation increases inter-group conflict. Status is both an additional *means* of ensuring intra-group cooperation and a new *end* of intra-group cooperation, and it contributes in both ways to conflict between groups. Given that social groups often conflict over material resources, the desire for intra-group status means that group members will cooperate more effectively in such disputes, which ensures that groups will be more effective 'combatants' whenever material conflict arises. More important, the very mechanism that facilitates greater intra-group cooperation will ensure a new form of conflict: competition for *inter-group* status. This latter result is the unfortunate and inevitable connection between cooperation and conflict.

Groups sometimes engage in zero-sum competition with other groups. A classic example is lobbying. When interest groups pursue what economists call "rent-seeking" legislation, such as farm subsidies and tax "loopholes," they seek merely to transfer resources from one group to another. Cartels similarly seek to extract the profits of non-competitive pricing from consumers. For lobbying groups and cartels, individual contributions to the group's rent-seeking endeavor tend to be undersupplied; selfish members free-ride on the efforts of other members. But the cooperation secured by intra-group status production means that individuals contribute more heavily than they otherwise would toward their group's effort to win a conflict.

Indeed, intra-group esteem production, and social norms based on such esteem, may provide the only explanations for the success of very large groups in lobbying despite powerful incentives for individuals to free-ride.

Judge Richard Posner has conceded some uncertainty, for example, in explaining how farmers cooperate in legislative activities. I propose that the answer is the same for farmers as it is for the ranchers Ellickson studied in Shasta County. Although the occupational status of farmers or ranchers is not as observable as, for example, their race, it is one of the first things strangers detect about them. And within a geographic area, farmers and ranchers tend to be socially connected. Thus, farmers and ranchers have an interest in the status generally accorded their occupation and a means of inducing contributions to that status. Intra-group esteem allocation elicits material contributions to group material welfare, such as monetary contributions to lobbying efforts. For individual farmers and ranchers, the amount contributed may be small, but multiplication by a large number produces considerable political clout.

There is a second reason intra-group esteem allocation increases group conflict. Individuals compete for esteem. One arena of competition is *group status competition*, in which individuals seek to produce status for themselves by raising the status of their groups. Under certain conditions, status is zero-sum, so that satisfaction of the status preferences of one group's members necessarily means non-satisfaction of the status preferences of another group's members.

In another article, I detailed the conditions under which relative preferences "inherently" conflict—that is, the circumstances under which the relative position is genuinely zero-sum. Although I focused there primarily on individual status-seeking, those conditions exist for social groups when members of different groups seek incompatible positions for their groups along some common, observable, and reasonably objective dimension. When these conditions do not hold, group status production is socially benign. But the conditions do hold, for example, when groups compare themselves along the "common dimension" of generalized social status and seek a position of superiority on that scale. Under such circumstances, social status is entirely relative. Investment in such zero-sum competition is therefore socially wasteful; the extent of the investment measures the size of the inefficiency. In particular, note the social waste of an obvious group optimizing strategy: *one way to raise the status of one's group is to invest in lowering the status of other groups.* Thus, the desire for esteem may lead to "subordination" as groups attempt to sabotage each other's general social position.

The status theory of cooperation and conflict may now be summarized. First, individuals seek, as an end, the esteem of others; in aggregate terms, they seek social status. Second, because socially connected group members are a key source of esteem, individuals will make material sacrifices on behalf of the group to gain intra-group status. Conversely, the group will reward such status to those who contribute to its welfare. Third, because another source of status is the larger society beyond one's social groups, one measure of group welfare is its status within society. Consequently, groups will use intra-group status "payments" to encourage members to contribute materially to inter-group status. Finally, because general social status is relative, one group can raise its inter-group status by lowering the status of other groups.

> * * *

The novelty of these otherwise non-instrumental beliefs is that the normal economic correctives to false belief formation do not apply. For expressive purposes, a "good" belief is not necessarily an accurate belief, but rather one that is pleasurable to express. Of course, even if a category of beliefs serves only expressive ends, there are some constraints on belief formation. Our cognitive mechanisms may make it difficult for us to believe certain things that are manifestly contradicted by experience. Moreover, we may not experience the full pleasure of expressing our beliefs if others find them palpably false in an uninteresting way.

Most important for our purposes, however, is the constraint of self-esteem. Some beliefs are more pleasant than others. For expressive purposes, people are more likely to adopt beliefs that enhance, rather than degrade, their self-esteem. If the issue is the talent of a celebrity, for example, a person is more likely to think highly of the celebrity if, through some connection—having attended the same school, for example—the celebrity's talent will enhance the individual's self-esteem. If esteem can influence expressive belief formation in this manner, esteem can also affect conventionally instrumental beliefs—beliefs concerning how best to satisfy one's preferences. As long as the gain in esteem from the bias toward esteem-producing beliefs is larger than any instrumental loss from the bias, then such a bias serves the individual's overall interests. There is considerable evidence to support this claim: research shows, for example, that people tend systematically to overevaluate their own performance and characteristics. Such a bias may even be essential to mental well-being. Self-evaluation is clearly an instrumental belief—one needs to know what one's talents and abilities are—yet the need for self-esteem is sufficient to create some deviation from strictly impartial beliefs about oneself.

If esteem production favorably biases one's self-evaluations, esteem production may also cause a positive bias toward the social groups to which one belongs. One may gain pleasure from believing positive things about one's groups. Moreover, groups will reward status to those who hold beliefs that are conducive to group welfare. A favorable bias regarding group members may strengthen intra-group cooperation by increasing the apparent material advantage available from transacting with members rather than non-members.

But groups may encourage and reward beliefs more complex than simple bias. For example, although he does not explain how belief distortion occurs, Richard Posner has invoked such distortion to explain how certain cartels solve collective action problems. According to Posner, the distinguishing feature of certain successful cartels—which he terms "guilds"—is their having an "ideology." A guild is a social as well as an economic institution in which members have adopted a common "personal morality" of loyalty, conformity, and craftsmanship, and which has achieved a certain "mystique" involving the idealization of quality over quantity. The "mutually reinforcing combination" of this morality and mystique comprises "the *ideology* of guild production," which serves the "the self-interest of producers in the cartelization of production."

Posner appears to mean that guild members convince themselves that the public interest is served by the restrictions on market entry and production necessary to cartelize an industry. This analysis implies that a principled concern for the public good has some force in motivating behavior, so that cartel members would be even more likely to free-ride if they realized that cartel pricing is contrary to the public interest. Ideology, however, turns the moral force against free-riding. An ideological commitment to quality allows the guild member to believe that conduct that would undermine the cartel—lowering quality and expanding output—would harm the public. Self-interested self-deception thus serves the cartel's long run interests by curbing the individual's impulse to free-ride on the restraint of others.

Return now to racial beliefs. In Posner's terms, negative stereotypes are part of a racial "guild's" efforts to monopolize production of esteem. Even for beliefs that serve an instrumental purpose (such as evaluating potential employees), the desire for esteem will cause an individual to adopt distorted beliefs about racial groups as long as the esteem benefit exceeds the instrumental cost. Consequently, the status-production model can explain differences in voting behavior between blacks and whites. A person may gain esteem by believing positive things about political candidates from her own group and, at least in a relative sense, negative things about politicians of other races. If people do not vote for instrumental reasons, there is no instrumental check on the accuracy of these beliefs. A small bias may suffice to explain a significant difference in voting behavior because, for different racial groups, the bias works in opposite directions.

If one assumes that this analysis correctly explains the existence and direction of racial bias, the question remains how to explain the *evolution* of white attitudes regarding race. Recall that status production commonly involves the denial that one's motive is status production. When one seeks to gain status by lowering the status of others, it is all the more important to deny that one is degrading others in order to look better by comparison. Consequently, "guild ideology" never acknowledges its self-serving nature. Members of Posner's representative guild do not openly declare, even among themselves, that they desire to restrain competition in order to charge higher prices and earn monopoly profits. Similarly, whites never explain their discriminatory behavior as serving the function of status production. Even in the Jim Crow South, whites attempted to justify segregation not by reference to naked self-interest but by claims that blacks were inherently inferior, that blacks preferred segregation, or that segregation somehow reflected the natural order of things. Toward this end, the Jim Crow doctrine of "separate but equal" was ideal. Separation was a means of expressing contempt; the pretense of equality served to deny the status motivation.

When proponents of a status-driven ideology can no longer confidently deny the status motivation of their beliefs, the ideology fails and proponents must search for another ideology. This insight may explain the evolution of white attitudes toward segregation. Although the exact causal strands are difficult to disentangle, events leading up to and including the modern civil rights movement undermined the ability of whites to believe that their existing racial beliefs were anything other than a self-serving ideology. World War II provided one ideological shock, as revulsion to Nazi claims of racial superiority was difficult to square with rationalization of southern racial practices. Rising levels of black education and job skills put a material strain on racial ideology by raising the attractiveness of black labor and thus the cost of absolute racial exclusion. I suspect the most immediate cause of ideological breakdown occurred during the civil rights movement, when photographs captured segregation extremists using violent means, often against women and children, to suppress peaceful protests. Violence against peaceful demonstrators was, even for some southern supporters of Jim Crow, irrefutable evidence that whites were not (at least morally) superior, that blacks were indisputably unhappy with segregation, and that segregation was not a naturally ordained moral order. One of the constraints I have suggested for non-instrumental beliefs is "palpable falsity"; the events of the 1950s and 1960s made salient to whites the falsity of the belief that intentional racial segregation is something other than selfishly hurtful.

Whatever the causal mechanism, many whites have come genuinely to believe that segregation is wrong. This shift does not mean, however, that a psychological veil of prejudice has simply been lifted from their eyes. The expressive beliefs whites adopt about race can no longer be of the crude form needed to justify segregation, but the quest for the production of status continues. Having abandoned the older ideology, whites still tend to oppose policies and candidates that would increase the social status of blacks. Whites can give up old, extreme stereotypes and still embrace negative views of blacks. Unless one consciously scrutinizes the statistical validity of one's generalizations about other groups—an unlikely scenario—even false stereotypes will rarely be *palpably* false. Thus, one may acknowledge the good faith and intellectual integrity of conservative arguments on political issues concerning race—like busing, affirmative action, and welfare—and still worry that the same status-maximizing bias that first rationalized slavery and then segregation infects much of the public thinking on these matters. It is more pleasant to believe that one lives in a society in which everyone (or at least everyone else) is being treated as well as she deserves, that past transgressions have been righted, and that fairness and justice require no further sacrifice. The evolution of white attitudes, therefore, reflects an ideological adjustment to status production under changed circumstances. The final descriptive virtue of the status-production theory is that it offers some insight into this otherwise puzzling evolution of white attitudes.

C. Implications of the Status Production Model of Discrimination

The associational model of discrimination has two key implications: market competition will erode discrimination and, partly for that reason, prohibiting race discrimination is inefficient. The status-production model leads to different conclusions on both points.

1. The Persistence of Race Discrimination.—Becker drew an analogy between race discrimination and transportation costs, both of which increase the cost of certain trades. It is uncontroversial that, other things being equal, those who can minimize transportation costs achieve a competitive advantage over those who cannot. If the analogy with discrimination is sound, we should also expect that whites with less intense tastes for discrimination will enjoy a competitive advantage over those with more intense tastes and will tend to dominate a competitive market.

Under the status-production model, discrimination is not the result of costs that discriminators incur from contact with members of other groups, but is a means of producing status. The discriminator does bear a cost in discriminating—forgoing otherwise beneficial trade with the objects of the discrimination—but that cost is an *investment* in the production of status. As long as such investments are cost-effective for the discriminator, the status-production model predicts that race discrimination will persist in the face of market competition. Consequently, the transportation analogy is inapt. Discrimination may exist in a competitive equilibrium for at least three reasons: the power of discriminatory social norms; the existence of reciprocity between whites; and, under certain circumstances, the effect of esteem-producing racial biases. I will examine each of these in turn.

(a) The Stability of Discriminatory Norms.—This section presents a theory of discriminatory social norms. I begin with George Akerlof's economic theory of a racial caste system. I then raise and respond to two key objections to Akerlof's theory—that it does not explain why anyone enforces the caste-based norms, and that it does not capture the complexities of modern American society. I conclude that, despite market competition, status production can support a stable system of discriminatory norms.

Akerlof has provided an explanation for the resiliency of the discriminatory customs of a caste society. It is the essence of a caste-system, Akerlof says, that "any transaction that breaks the caste taboos changes the subsequent behavior of uninvolved parties" who may act to punish the caste-breaker. Third party reactions change the calculus for those who have not internalized the norm:

> Those who fail to follow, or even to enforce the caste customs do not gain the profits of the successful arbitrageur but instead suffer the stigma of the outcaste. If the punishment of becoming an outcaste is predicted to be sufficiently severe, the system of caste is held in equilibrium irrespective of individual tastes, by economic incentives; the predictions of the caste system become a self-fulfilling prophecy.

Thus, Akerlof applies to race discrimination the same view of social norm enforcement that Ellickson has applied to property law—because people boycott norm breakers, it often pays to follow norms.

This insight would be trivial, however, if it only applied when *everyone* in society was willing to boycott those who break the caste rules. Surely a few individuals will always be willing to deal with social outcasts (such as other social outcasts or near outcasts). One could argue that, as long as the number of people willing to violate the discriminatory norms exceeds the number of people targeted by the norm, violators need suffer no harm. Further, one might predict that if a few people violate the norm intially, their violation will weaken the norm and induce other violations to follow, eventually leading to the norm's complete unraveling.

Akerlof responds to these arguments with a simple point that depends merely on the existence of transaction costs. Suppose there are search costs for firms seeking buyers or sellers; because of imperfect information about the existence and reputation of buyers and sellers, firms cannot instantly replace existing trading partners but must incur costs inversely proportional to the number of potential trading partners in the relevant geographic market. Under these circumstances, assuming that there are any parties who will boycott "innovators" (those who violate discriminatory norms), the innovators necessarily incur higher search costs in finding trading partners. Thus, each boycotter raises the likely search costs the innovator will incur before locating a trading partner. Further, when the innovator locates a non-boycotter, its higher search costs will place it "in a weaker bargaining position, since the cost of failing to make a trade is greater to [it] than to noninnovators." If the costs of innovation are higher than the benefits, the discriminatory norm will be stable in a competitive market.

There are, however, weaknesses in Akerlof's explanation. First, Akerlof simply posits that some discriminators will boycott those who fail to follow the discriminatory norm. He offers no explanation of why these boycotters are willing to bear such costs. The status-production model does offer such an explanation. The model shows how individuals gain from adhering to and enforcing certain norms, why the kind of norms individuals benefit from enforcing include norms of discrimination, and why the groups for which this process is frequently employed are racial groups. As I argued above, individuals within racial groups benefit from raising the status of their shared traits. One means of contributing to one's racial status is by subordinating members of other races. With sufficient overlap between racial and socially connected groups, whites have a status benefit to exploit and the cooperative means to exploit it.

Consider, however, a second possible weakness in Akerlof's model. A simple caste society is an appropriate starting point, but American society is more complex. Unquestionably, a norm exists against racial discrimination (or at least against certain forms of racial discrimination), and some whites, as well as blacks, boycott those who overtly discriminate. Given this reality, one might reject the Akerlof caste model.

Yet, even with blacks and some whites "counter-boycotting" discriminators, the equilibrium may entail significant discrimination. Discriminators will bear a cost when targeted for a counter-boycott (or other sanction), but unless that cost exceeds the cost that discriminators create for non-discriminators, it will pay to continue discriminating. The relative costs depend largely on the relative size and economic power of the two groups. Because whites constitute a large majority and possess disproportionate wealth, the costs from white boycotts is likely to exceed the costs from black counter-boycotts. At some point, the participation by a sufficient number of whites in the counter-boycott would tip the balance the other way, but this outcome seems unlikely. First, one cannot infer from the fact that opponents of discrimination are more vocal today—when discrimination in various forms is illegal—that white opponents of discrimination exceed supporters. Second, those who rely on the power of white counter-boycotts rely on the force of moral principle (or altruism) to overcome the selfish force of status production. Under existing theory, selfishness is thought to undermine discrimination. But given the status productivity of discrimination, the power of selfishness suggests the more pessimistic outcome.

One might object that discriminatory norms do not exist if any whites are willing to act against them. That some whites will boycott discriminators merely reflects, however, the fact that American whites do not constitute a single group. "Whites" include various ethnic, religious, political, regional, and class subgroups. How much a particular subgroup invests in subordination as a means of producing status will depend on what its various status options are. Low-status whites have fewer options and tend to discriminate more than high-status whites. Further, white condemnation of the blatant racial discrimination common in an earlier era is consistent with a more subtle discriminatory norm. Subordination works only as long as one can deny that one is acting for the purpose of producing status. Whites are less able to deny this function of racial derogation now than in the past; consequently, overt discrimination is no longer as productive of status as it once was. Just as a "nouveau riche" may undermine her own status by engaging in ostentatious and wasteful consumption, a "redneck" or bigot undermines her own status by expressing contempt solely on the basis of race. But, there is still status in wealth if one displays it more deftly, with the appearance of not calculating to make a display. Likewise, there is status to be gained from race discrimination of a more subtle form, especially when one can plausibly deplore its more flagrant manifestations.

One might nevertheless assert that there are significant numbers of whites who oppose even subtle forms of discrimination. One interpretation of this behavior is that high-status whites who condemn low-status whites for their discrimination may gain more by distinguishing themselves from other whites than by investing in the subordination of blacks or other minorities. In fact, certain classes of whites may enjoy free-riding on the status that other whites secure and then further increase their status by subordinating those whites for being discriminatory. A second, more sanguine interpretation begins with Ellickson's claim that norms tend to be efficient, at least from the perspective of the group in which they arise. Ellickson does not discuss norms that span a group as large as an entire society, but a weaker concern for the esteem of strangers might give rise to norms between strangers. If a weak counter-norm arises against discrimination, perhaps it is because discrimination is inefficient from the perspective of the entire society. But because the norm arises at a different and more diffuse level, it can exist alongside more powerful discriminatory norms that arise within or between socially connected groups.

Becker's model does not contemplate the existence of discriminatory social norms. Thus, I cannot be certain how he would respond to the claim I make here. But Robert Cooter, who embraces Becker's prediction that competition will drive out discrimination, does consider social norms. Cooter argues that the proper economic model for discrimination is that of a cartel and that during the Jim Crow era, southern whites advanced their material ends by using law to gain monopoly power in various markets. Like all cartels, whites faced the inherent problem of instability—that is, the incentive for each member to cheat. Cooter agrees that discriminatory social norms countered the incentives to free-ride, but asserts that the effectiveness of the norms probably depended on their being supported by Jim Crow legislation. Thus, Cooter expresses the conventional economic skepticism that the norms that supported the white "cartel" could survive absent such legal restrictions. The material incentives in an unfettered market, in his view, provide a strong lure for individuals to defect from the group enterprise.

The theory of intra-group cooperation and inter-group conflict offers a reason for thinking otherwise. Cooter's skepticism about the independent strength of social norms would be well-founded if the only ends that individuals seek are material. Indeed, I argued previously that social norms add nothing to our understanding of cooperation beyond what can be explained by reciprocity unless people value the esteem of others as an end in itself. Therefore Cooter's argument might be right if the only purpose of the white cartel were to advance the material ends of whites and the only means of inducing cooperation were material rewards. The whole thrust of the status-production model, however, is that the cartel-like behavior of whites serves to maximize the non-material end of status production (the cartel seeks to monopolize social status) and that the cartel employs the non-material means of intra-group status rewards and punishments. If this fundamental point is right, then social norms can support discrimination notwithstanding market competition.

Nevertheless, Cooter's basic insight is quite helpful. Whites do act like a cartel. But whites are more accurately described as the subset of cartels that Posner calls "guilds," that is, cartels with "social cohesiveness." Based on a morality emphasizing loyalty and conformity, these guilds have an "ideology"—a set of beliefs that serves to inhibit free-riding—specifically that blacks tend to be inferior, that whites should not interact with blacks in certain ways, and that whites must "stick together." Posner contends that farmers and lawyers—very large industrial groups—manage to cooperate in legislative lobbying efforts despite incentives to free-ride. Racial groups may similarly succeed. For reasons explained above, the more observable the trait that links a group of people, the more status members have to gain by cooperating and the greater the reason to expect such groups to become socially connected as a means of achieving cooperation. Given that race is more observable than these industrial affinities, there is reason to believe racial groups can better succeed in overcoming their collective action problems despite their large size.

Consider, then, a new economic analogy for race discrimination: not transportation costs, but an analogy to the acquisition of a public reputation. An entrepreneur donates a large sum of money to a local museum, or a corporate president agrees to sponsor a marathon. No doubt, the economically inclined theorist would assert that such behavior occurs not because it serves an individual's "taste" for fame, but because it produces greater profits for entrepreneurs and firms by bolstering their reputation or name recognition. I suspect the main force behind this view, however, is nothing as contingent as empirical data on the profitability of such donations, but an inference that economic actors would not give money away unless it was productive to do so. I merely argue for a similar inference with respect to race discrimination. Discrimination exists because it is productive for its practitioners.

(b) Reciprocity as a Basis for Market Discrimination.—There is a second reason to believe that race discrimination will persist in the face of market competition. Becker's theory does not argue that market competition erodes social discrimination. Yet because social interaction facilitates more commercial reciprocity, social discrimination may cause persistent "market" discrimination.

According to Axelrod's analysis of iterated prisoner's dilemmas, it often pays to seek cooperation through a reciprocal strategy such as tit-for-tat when there is sufficient likelihood of future interaction with another. Axelrod emphasizes that the more likely future interactions are, the more likely it is that those who employ reciprocal strategies will prosper. Thus, to increase the prospects of cooperation with a particular individual, Axelrod advises (consciously) increasing the durability and frequency of interactions with that individual. One time-honored means of implementing Axelrod's strategy is to pursue social interaction with the group of individuals with whom one wishes to cooperate. When prospective business partners eat, talk, or play together, they are not merely acquiring information about each other. Social interaction also supports reciprocity; by joining a social group, one increases the likelihood of future interaction with members of the group. Most important, social interactions may themselves be relatively inexpensive but might increase the chance of cooperation's emerging in a business or market setting, where the benefits of cooperation are greater. Joining a country club, a "businessman's"club, or a particular neighborhood may "lock" one into a particular social group, raising one's ability to cooperate with members in non-social settings.

We can now understand more fully the power of discriminatory norms. Even in the absence of a social norm that restrains market trading with other racial groups, social norms could significantly impede such trades. A norm limited to preventing social contacts with members of another race is sufficient to harm such members economically. Since social contacts affect the probability of reciprocity, the absence of such contacts places the isolated individual or the disfavored group at a comparative disadvantage in economic trades. Consequently, norm-based discrimination in one setting, such as social clubs or housing, may cause discrimination in other settings, such as business or employment. Social clubs that exclude women and minorities thus cause them more harm than simply denying them information about, and the chance to become known to, market players. They deny them the opportunity to make reciprocity work.

(c) The Power of Esteem-Producing Racial Biases.—A final factor that contributes to the persistence of discrimination is racially biased beliefs or stereotypes. As noted above, discriminatory norms invoke rationalization mechanisms; discriminators prefer to have reasons for discriminating other than a bare interest in status production. Indeed, because status production is inconsistent with an overt strategy of subordination, it is important that discriminators have an explanation—an "ideology"—apart from status production. Such an explanation can most easily take the form of negative stereotypes—that the failure of blacks to succeed is their own fault, due to their own shortcomings in ability, integrity, or dependability. This ideology buttresses discriminatory norms. Whatever the social cost of violating the norm, biased evaluations of blacks make it appear that the material benefits of norm violation are less than they are. Self-deception prevents cheating that would undermine the cartel.

Indeed, even if there were no discriminatory social norms, ideologically based racial stereotypes might sustain a stable level of discrimination. One might argue, to the contrary, that absent norms, market competition would discipline whites whose evaluations of blacks were biased. If some white employers fail to perceive black workers accurately, for example, they will lose a competitive advantage to more discerning whites. Yet there is one condition under which stereotypes alone will sustain discrimination—when the material costs of one's miscalculation is zero. In the employment setting, for example, the employer may believe in some cases that the applicants are essentially "tied," that is, they appear to have equal marginal productivities. A white employer would suffer no harm from the decision to hire a white applicant who was tied with a black applicant. Of course, given the white employer's ideology, the employer may not actually perceive the two candidates as being equal, but rather will think that the white candidate is better. The point, however, is that there will be no market correction for such a perception; having white job applicants win all "ties" is a market equilibrium. The question remains how frequently such ties occur in the real world—an interesting empirical question that I, like opponents of Title VII, leave to be answered by others. I simply note that, if such ties were frequent, stereotyping could itself add to the persistence of race discrimination.

In sum, the status-production model provides three reasons to suppose that race discrimination will survive market competition: the power of discriminatory social norms; the existence of reciprocity between whites; and, under certain circumstances, the effect of esteem-producing racial biases.

2. *The Efficiency of Anti-Discrimination Laws.*—Many legal economists have contended that federal anti-discrimination laws are efficient only to the extent that they nullify state laws mandating discrimination. These theorists view such laws as inefficient when they prohibit private discrimination because their only function is to frustrate discriminatory preferences. But the new descriptive theory I propose requires a rethinking of this normative claim. The status-production model views anti-discrimination laws as potentially correcting a market failure in which individuals invest in essentially confiscatory behavior. That discrimination is a market failure would not itself prove that government action is desirable. We must consider whether the regulation can correct the failure and whether the benefits of such intervention exceed the costs.

(a) *Discrimination as Market Failure: The Theft Analogy.*—Welfare economics provides a justification for laws that prohibit theft (and other forms of force and fraud) that is not dependent on discounting the gains to the thief (or other criminals). Even assuming that the transfer accomplished by theft itself causes no wealth loss, because the thief gains what the owner loses, a system that permits theft "results in a very substantial diversion of resources to fields where they essentially offset each other, and produce no positive product." In other words, absent laws against theft, individuals must expend resources merely to protect their property from seizure. They will also forgo certain wealth-creating activities to protect what they already have and because it may be too costly to protect some forms of wealth from theft. In response, the thief invests in gaining tools and knowledge to circumvent anti-theft practices and technology. These dynamic reactions to the risk of theft result in deadweight losses to society. Less is produced, and part of what is produced (burglar alarms and burglars' tools) provides no greater satisfaction of an individual's preferences, but merely helps the individual to retain or confiscate goods that will satisfy preferences. The net effect is to decrease wealth. The same argument applies for laws against violence. It is, of course, Thomas Hobbes's justification for the state: that the only alternative, the "warre ... of every man, against every man," is worse.

It follows from the status-production model that a society without discrimination laws permits an unfettered status war of "every group against every group." What is striking about Richard Epstein's *Forbidden Grounds*, which argues for the repeal of laws that prohibit employment discrimination, is not so much his controversial claim that the only role of government is to prevent force or fraud, but that he never considers how laws against race discrimination may fall precisely within this libertarian principle. Status "warfare" may not be as violent as literal combat, but the term is more than just a metaphor. Hobbes identifies competition for honor as one of the three causes of war; he warns that violent conflict results from attempted subordination. Similarly, Hume warned of the tendency of factions to produce "the fiercest animosities." Competition for group status has generated much of America's history of interracial violence, as when whites lynched blacks to preserve their social position or when blacks retaliated against repeated acts of derogation and dishonor.

Of course, laws prohibit such violence. But even with such laws, unregulated status competition mirrors the inefficiency of a regime without laws prohibiting theft. First, racial status preferences inherently conflict. Race discrimination exists because members of (at least) one race seek for their group a status position that is incompatible with the position sought by members of one or more other groups. Even when only one group seeks superiority, if the other group seeks equality, the struggle for social status is zero sum. Consequently, the appropriation of status by subordinating behavior is, like theft, a mere wealth transfer; the gain to the discriminator is at least matched by the loss to the victim. Second, this form of transfer—using discrimination as a mechanism of subordination—generates extremely high costs. By definition, the discriminator makes a material sacrifice (giving up an otherwise favorable trade or engaging in costly behavior) as a means of lowering the status of the victim. The size of the material sacrifice measures the investment that the discriminator makes in status appropriation. This investment determines the initial cost of the process of racial group status production.

But that is not the whole story. As I noted at the outset of this Part, economic analysis of discrimination strikes many non-economists as barren because it fails to acknowledge the full benefit to its practitioners or the full harm to its victims. The status-production model takes as its central premise that whites gain status by discriminating against blacks. To determine the full extent of the investment in, and therefore the costs of, status competition, we must consider the full range of status defense mechanisms employed by victims of discrimination. Such defense mechanisms include the sometimes desperate reactions of those who live as targets of discrimination. These reactions represent further investment in status production and increase the wastefulness of the unregulated process, much like added investment in theft-protection devices constitute waste in a society without theft laws. Of course, the psychological mechanisms at work are vastly more complex. I will attempt merely a brief summary of the reactions within the framework of the status-production model.

First, enraged victims may respond in kind by attempting to disparage and subordinate the original discriminator. Such behavior may take the form of discrimination, which means the victim also makes a wasteful material sacrifice for the sake of status. The victim may, however, lack the opportunity or wealth to respond in kind and may seek a cheaper means of disparagement such as an insult. Violence is the extreme form of such an insult; it inflicts the loss of dignity inherent in an intentional deprivation of bodily integrity. Even if an African American counters with some means other than violence, the original subordinator may resort to violence to ensure the effectiveness of the original insult and to counter any responsive insult. Hobbes identified this escalation over dishonor as a primary source of war.

A second response is to seek to regain status by subordinating someone *other* than the original discriminator. If whites present too difficult a target, other minority groups may be within reach. Thus, the long and unpleasant history of status competition between minority groups exemplifies a predictable response to subordination. The original victim may also focus on vulnerable members of her own group, such as women or those of a different economic class. Evidence suggests, for example, that African Americans discriminate against one another on the basis of the relative lightness or darkness of their skin. Finally, because the original victim may lack any non-violent means of responding to discrimination, some of what appears to be "senseless violence" among discrimination victims may actually be a rational attempt to produce status by subordinating others.

The victim's responses are not limited to subordinating others. The victim may also withdraw from competition—by which status is generally determined—by adopting beliefs that such competitions are without merit. When a subordinated subgroup fails according to the prevailing cultural values, its members may decide to reject those values completely. For example, minorities facing discrimination may decide, rather than be judged by standards of academic or economic success, that education or employment is an overrated "white" value. Like the processes of rationalization, the belief that academics is unimportant may preserve self-esteem; however, such a belief may prove destructive in the long run because it depresses efficient investment in human capital.

Finally, a victim of subordination may wholeheartedly adopt the beliefs of the subordinators, including those that members of her group are deserving of their low status. Such a response might seem unlikely; however, for some it may be easier to accept a lower status with the belief that such a role is natural and proper than to live out such a role every day believing it is arbitrarily imposed. The result, however, is a form of self-loathing.

In sum, many of the effects of discrimination, well-explored in other disciplines, should be of central concern to an economic assessment of the system of race discrimination. In many cases, these effects represent investments that the victims make in defending their status. Combined with the investments made by the original discriminators, these resources represent the deadweight loss of race discrimination. Consequently, considerable evidence demonstrates that race discrimination is a grossly inefficient market failure.

(b) An Efficiency Argument for Anti-Discrimination Laws.—As with laws against theft, the benefit of prohibiting a form of discrimination is to prevent the wasteful investment of resources in such discrimination. When laws prohibit theft, the primary alternative by which the former thief can make material gains is to engage in lawful, productive activity. The argument for laws that prohibit subordination as a means of acquiring

status is exactly parallel: by raising the costs of subordination, such laws induce people to switch to socially productive, or at least socially benign, means of acquiring status (either at an individual or a group level). Subordination is not the only means of group status production, and inter-group status production is not the only means of gaining esteem.

A possible distinction from theft, however, is the availability of equally wasteful substitutes to blatant discrimination. A group with a dispropor-tionately large share of political power, economic wealth, and symbols of status will have at its disposal a number of alternative means of subordi-nating a minority group. Prohibiting one form of subordinating behavior may simply cause a shift to an equally wasteful form of acquiring status. Such a concern, however, may be overstated. After all, common law larceny initially required a trespass in the taking and thus exempted what we now think of as embezzlement and fraud. Even though thieves were free to switch to non-trespassory means of confiscation, the initial prohibition was nonetheless efficient. The opportunities remaining were more limited and costly; a complete substitution would not occur. The same argument can be made for prohibiting private discrimination in certain key areas, such as employment and housing. These forms of discrimination probably represent the most productive means of subordination and therefore induce the greatest 'investment' by whites. As I previously pointed out, employment discrimination offers for whites a double insult to blacks: not only the insult inherent in shunning someone, but also the consequence of lowering black income in a society that accords status to wealth. Similarly, excluding blacks from neighborhoods is not only a very public symbol of subordina-tion, but also denies them the material benefits of reciprocity that may arise among neighbors. Effectively prohibiting employment and housing discrimination would deprive whites of their most productive private means of subordination and would thereby lower the resources invested in this wasteful confiscatory activity.

Second, anti-discrimination laws may lower the investment in status confiscation by increasing the incidence of "cross-membership." *Ceteris paribus*, an individual prefers subordinating a group to which she does not belong to subordinating a group to which she does belong. An individual always bears a cost from subordination of her own group and that cost gives her an incentive to avoid such behavior. In fact, an individual who is a member of group *A* and group *B* might find it in her interest to invest in efforts to prevent members of group *A* from seeking to subordinate group *B*. Therefore, the more "cross-membership" between two groups, the fewer the resources that will be invested by the two groups in subordinating each other.

Laws forbidding race discrimination may increase the occurrence of cross-membership and thereby undermine the effectiveness of racial subor-dination as a status strategy. Race has been and remains highly correlated with other demographic factors. If a white individual lives in an all-white neighborhood, attends an all-white school, works in an all-white firm, worships at an all-white church, belongs to an all-white amateur sports league, and patronizes all-white hobby clubs, she will never face the problem of cross-membership. If, however, anti-discrimination laws were to integrate neighborhoods, schools, firms, and private clubs, more whites would find themselves in a position in which racial minorities belong to some of *their* groups. Consequently, racial subordination would lower the status of these integrated groups. One response will be for whites to flee the groups that become integrated, but if the costs are too high, as when the law integrates a number of social groups at the same time, the effect might be to lower the effectiveness of racial subordination as a status strategy for many whites.

Finally, anti-discrimination laws may serve to correct the market failure of discrimination by undermining the credibility of rationalizations for discrimination. Several commentators have noted that the law shapes preferences, and that Title VII and other civil rights laws may have reduced the preference for discrimination. The status-production model explains this evolution not as a change in the taste for discrimination, but as a change in the productive capacity of certain forms of subordination. Individuals who seek status require some rationalization for their behavior. Admitting that one seeks to subordinate others for the sake of status conflicts with obtaining such status. Law affects the credibility of any alternative explanation. Take Posner's example of a guild that survives on an ideology of quality to justify restrictions on competition. Consider the long-term effect Posner's critique might have on such ideology were it sufficiently publicized. Exposing the naked self-interest behind platitudes of public concern erodes their effectiveness.

Law is more crude than an intellectual critique, yet it is inherently more public, and can carry more weight. When Jim Crow laws mandated certain forms of segregation, whites confidently spoke of segregation as the natural order of things; when the laws forbade segregation, discriminatory whites had a greater difficulty believing their own ideology. Rationalizations can be fragile things; sometimes they require that dissent be held to a minimum. In the South and elsewhere, Title VII constituted a very powerful 'dissent,' an indication that a large number, perhaps a majority, of Americans no longer believed the explanations of discrimination. If people care about esteem, the law can change behavior merely by signaling on what grounds the majority will henceforth give and withhold esteem.

In sum, law may correct the market failure of discrimination in three ways: by raising the costs and lowering the productive returns of certain forms of subordination; by increasing the racial diversity of socially connected groups, which raises selfish resistance to the subordination strategy; and by symbolizing a consensus that the rationalizations for the subordination strategy are, in fact, mere rationalizations. Whether such laws are efficient depends on the magnitude of these benefits relative to the administrative and opportunity costs of the system that adjudicates discrimination claims. But under the status-production model, the efficiency question is, like it is for the prohibition of theft, an empirical one; one can no longer simply assert that laws prohibiting satisfaction of discriminatory preferences are presumptively inefficient.

One might inquire about the implications of the status-production model of discrimination for affirmative action. In what may seem like an evasion, I believe the model provides no clear answer for affirmative action, but does reveal the consequential tensions the policy represents. The "cross-membership" effect of anti-discrimination laws provides a theoretical foundation for the claim that affirmative action serves to combat discrimination more effectively than a mere non-discrimination policy. Indeed, the benefit of cross-membership might justify a very aggressive affirmative action program. The utility of integrating social groups by race is not limited by any principle of past wrongful discrimination. The status-production model indicates that we can reduce investment in future status subordination by decreasing racial stratification in society.

Conversely, affirmative action creates a "common fate" for those of the same race and thus raises the salience of race. As critics of affirmative action have claimed, this fact may cause whites to identify themselves more fully with their race. The status-production model adds this insight: raising the salience of race may increase the return from racial subordination and enhance the power of whites to elicit intra-group cooperation for the remaining avenues of racial subordination. Affirmative action likely has already had this effect, which offsets the positive effects of cross-membership. However difficult it is to ascertain the present net effect, the more important and difficult question is what the future effects will be. Affirmative action has, so far, done little to integrate effectively American society. Therefore, we have no reason to expect the positive consequences of that policy to have emerged. In the end, the status-production model reveals what I think we knew already: affirmative action is an investment in which we bear certain costs today for the hope of a greater return tomorrow. The model illuminates, but does not resolve, the empirical question of whether the future benefits will outweigh the present costs.

III.   CONCLUSION

Groups inherently tend to elicit a level of cooperation from their members and to incur a level of conflict with other groups. The cooperation, in fact, facilitates the conflict. Intra-group esteem allocation permits groups to overcome certain collective action problems that would otherwise make conflict impossible. At the same time, the desire for esteem provides a new objective of group conflict—competition over social status.

What I have termed the theory of intra-group cooperation and inter-group conflict is merely the logical extension of three other steps in political and economic theory. First, Hobbes, among others, justified the state as necessary to avoid perpetual conflict in the state of nature; thus the state's role is to facilitate peaceful cooperation. Second, economists have persuasively contended that certain forms of peaceful cooperation, such as price-fixing, are detrimental to society. Consequently, the government should act in such cases to prevent cooperation. Third, Ellickson, among others, has written that groups use social norms to solve collective action problems without the centralized coercive power of the state, namely to bring about a cooperative "order without law." The next step, I propose, is to recognize that significant instances of this decentralized cooperation will inevitably be socially destructive and, therefore, that government should obstruct these forms of cooperation. Groups inherently tend to use their powers of decentralized cooperation to produce status through the socially wasteful process of subordination. As with cartels, cooperation in such cases is a social threat that justifies state action.

Aside from these general political implications, the theory of intra-group cooperation and inter-group conflict illuminates the complex problem of race discrimination. Status production explains both the historic and contemporary contours of race discrimination far better than the prevailing associational model of discrimination. Understanding race discrimination as a means of producing status helps us explain its tenacity in the face of market competition and reveals, within an economic model, the full costs of the practice of discrimination. The effort to gain status by taking status away from others, and the responsive measures this effort elicits, are socially wasteful in the same way that confiscation of material property is wasteful. The inefficiency in the system of status competition is measured by the investments each group makes in gaining or protecting its status. Prohibiting the more productive forms of investments can reduce the wastefulness of such actions even if it does not eliminate it.

In criticizing the associational preference model of discrimination, I focused intensively on a single form of discrimination—racial discrimination—and within that category, exclusively on discrimination against African Americans. The points I made in this context, however, apply to other forms of racial and ethnic discrimination. When substantial overlap exists between groups that share publicly observable traits and groups that are socially connected, the theory predicts substantial investment in status production, including the subordination of other groups. With more than two racial and ethnic groups, greater opportunity exists for movement in social position, and there is, therefore, reason to expect greater investment in maintaining or improving status.

* * * * *

Groups matter. Groups form for simple informational reasons, as economics describes in considerable detail: to minimize the transaction costs people incur in the course of satisfying their preferences. Yet the formation of groups has another consequence. People have a loyalty to groups that goes beyond what serves their narrow pecuniary self-interest. I have sought to explain that solidarity in self-interested terms; doing so requires an expanded understanding of self-interest that includes a powerful desire for esteem and status. Given the ubiquity of groups, this broader social science perspective on their function should prove useful in understanding legal issues beyond racial discrimination. For now, I have argued for a sober appreciation that solidarity for some often means enmity for others.

NOTES AND QUESTIONS

1.   Comparing Rational Choice Theory with Group Status Production Theory.

Is it possible to compare the Becker and McAdams Models? What are the starting assumptions of each piece? Does McAdams accept any part of the rational choice heuristic?

2.   Groups vs. individuals.

One possible difference between the Becker and McAdams models is how they treat groups. McAdams is primarily concerned with the operation of intergroup processes for enforcing subordination. In contrast, Becker treats the individual as the central unit of measuring preferences for discrimination. Becker does, however, note that "it has been argued that an increase in the numerical importance of a minority group increases the prejudice against them, since the majority begins to fear their growing power; on the other hand, some argue that greater numbers bring greater knowledge and that leads to a decline in prejudice." To what use does Becker's theory of discrimination put this observation about group size?

3.   Racial discrimination, the moral argument.

If racial discrimination is simply a preference with exactly the same entitlement to expression in the marketplace as a taste for strawberry ice cream, how does rational choice distinguish between morally repugnant choices (child pornography) and morally neutral choices? Does rational choice theory require a normative view of racial discrimination to work?

Becker observes that : "[f]or example, discrimination and prejudice are not usually said to occur when someone prefers looking at a glamorous Hollywood actress rather than at some other woman; yet they are said to occur when he prefers living next to whites rather than Negroes. At best, calling just one of these actions "discrimination" requires making subtle and rather secondary distinctions. Fortunately, it is not necessary to get involved in these more philosophical issues."

4.   Adam Smith and Group Status Production Theory.

Recall that Adam Smith argued, p. 144, self interest, modified by benevolence born of conscience, or the influence of the moral spectator are the primary motivations for human economic behavior. Now, compare Smith to McAdams' thesis "that a material view of human motivation underestimates both the level of cooperation that groups elicit from their members and the level of conflict that groups elicit from each other. A single group dynamic connects these added increments of cooperation and conflict: groups achieve solidarity and elicit loyalty beyond what economic analysis conventionally predicts, but solidarity and loyalty within groups lead predictably, if not inevitably, to competition and conflict between groups. The connection is the desire for esteem or status. Groups use intra-group status rewards as a non-material means of gaining material sacrifice from members, but the attendant desire for inter-group status causes inter-group conflict.''

―――――

3.   AN EMPIRICAL STUDY OF RACIAL DISCRIMINATION

Fair Driving: Gender and Race Discrimination in Retail Car Negotiations

104 HARV. L. REV. 817 (1991).

IAN AYRES

The struggle to eradicate discrimination on the basis of race and gender has a long history in American law. Based on the widely held belief that such discrimination will occur only in markets in which racial or gender animus distorts competition, regulatory efforts have been limited to areas in which interpersonal relations are significant and ongoing, such as housing and employment. In this Article, Professor Ayres offers empirical evidence that seriously challenges faith in the ability of competitive market forces to eliminate racial and gender discrimination in other markets. His Chicago based research demonstrates that retail car dealerships systematically offered substantially better prices on identical cars to white men than they did to blacks and women. Professor Ayres details the nature and startling degree of the discrimination his testers encountered and evaluates various theoretical explanations for their disparate treatment. Based on his conclusions, Professor Ayres explores routes by which "fair driving" plaintiffs might bring suits against dealerships and mechanisms through which regulators might effectively rid the retail car market of such discrimination.

[The] civil rights laws of the 1960s prohibit race and gender discrimination in the handful of markets—employment, housing, and public accommodations—in which discrimination was perceived to be particularly acute. In recent years, lawsuits have increasingly presented claims of more subtle and subjective forms of discrimination within these protected markets. Both legislators and commentators, however, have largely ignored the possibility of discrimination in the much broader range of markets left uncovered by civil rights laws. Housing and employment may be the two most important markets in which people participate, but women and racial minorities may also be susceptible to discrimination when spending billions of dollars on other goods and services. Of these unprotected markets, the market for new cars is particularly ripe for scrutiny because, for most Americans, new car purchases represent their largest consumer investment after buying a home. In 1986, for example, more than $100 billion was spent on new cars in the United States.

This Article examines whether the process of negotiating for a new car disadvantages women and minorities. More than 180 independent negotiations at ninety dealerships were conducted in the Chicago area to examine how dealerships bargain. Testers of different races and genders entered new car dealerships separately and bargained to buy a new car, using a uniform negotiation strategy. The study tests whether automobile retailers react differently to this uniform strategy when potential buyers differ only by gender or race.

The tests reveal that white males receive significantly better prices than blacks and women. As detailed below, white women had to pay forty percent higher markups than white men; black men had to pay more than twice the markup, and black women had to pay more than three times the markup of white male testers. Moreover, the study reveals that testers of different race and gender are subjected to several forms of nonprice discrimination. Specifically, testers were systematically steered to salespeople of their own race and gender (who then gave them worse deals) and were asked different questions and told about different qualities of the car.

At the outset it is difficult to choose how, linguistically, to characterize the results that black and female testers were treated differently from white male testers using the same bargaining strategy. The term "discrimination," although surely a literal characterization, unfortunately connotes to many the notion of animus (even though in antitrust, for example, "price discrimination" is not taken to imply any hatred by sellers). "Disparate treatment," in contrast, connotes to others a strictly technical legal meaning developed in civil rights case law. For the moment, the terms "discrimination" and "disparate treatment" are both used to refer to the result that sellers' conduct was race-and gender-dependent; sellers took race and gender into account and treated differently testers who were otherwise similarly situated. These terms are not meant to imply that salespeople harbored any animus based on race or gender.

In recent years, the Supreme Court has struggled in the employment context to enunciate workable evidentiary standards to govern claims of subtle and possibly unconscious forms of discrimination. Although the 1960s civil rights laws do not reach retail car sales, the finding that car retailers bargain differently with different races might give rise to disparate treatment suits under 42 U.S.C. §§ 1981 and 1982, which originated in the 1866 Civil Rights Act. The test results, by focusing on an unexplored manifestation of disparate treatment, push us to define more clearly what constitutes discrimination generally.

Furthermore, the results highlight a gaping hole in our civil rights laws regarding gender discrimination. Although sections 1981 and 1982 prohibit racial discrimination in contracting and the sale of real and personal property, no federal laws bar intentional discrimination on the basis of gender in the sale of most goods or services. The civil rights laws of the 1960s fail to fill this gap, leaving unregulated a legion of markets in which women contract. Put simply, car dealers can legally charge more or refuse to sell to someone *because* she is a woman. Intentional gender (or race) discrimination of this kind might alternatively be attacked as an "unfair or deceptive" trade practice under state and federal consumer protection laws. In the end, however, courts might perceive that the quintessentially individualized and idiosyncratic nature of negotiation places such disparate treatment entirely outside the purview of either the civil rights or consumer protection laws.

The goal of Congress in passing the Civil Rights Act of 1866 was to guarantee that "a dollar in the hands of a Negro will purchase the same thing as a dollar in the hands of a white man." The standard argument against enacting civil rights laws has been grounded in the conviction that the impersonal forces of market competition will limit race and gender discrimination to the traditionally protected markets, in which there is significant interpersonal contact. Yet the results of this study give lie to such an unquestioning faith in competition: in stark contrast to congressional objectives, this Article indicates that blacks and women simply cannot buy the same car for the same price as can white men using identical bargaining strategies. The price dispersion engendered by the bargaining process implicates basic notions of equity and indicates that the scope of the civil rights laws has been underinclusive. The process of bargaining, already inefficient in many ways, becomes all the more problematic when it works to the detriment of traditionally disadvantaged members of our society.

Part I of this Article describes how the tests of race and gender discrimination were conducted. Part II reports the results of the tests. An analysis of disparate treatment in price, sales tactics, and steering is combined with a regression analysis focusing on the determinants of final offers. Part III explores theoretical explanations of the results. Animus-based theories of disparate treatment are compared with theories of statistical discrimination and tested against the results of the study. Particular attention is paid to the role of competition at both the wholesale and retail level in limiting and channeling the form of race and gender discrimination. Finally, Part IV explores the legal implications of the study. This Part considers whether and how "fair driving" plaintiffs could legally challenge this disparate treatment under consumer protection laws and sections 1981 and 1982. The Article concludes by considering the need for legal reform.

I. Methodology of the Test

To test whether there is disparate treatment by car retailers on the basis of race or gender, pairs of consumers/testers (for example, a white male and a black female) used the same bargaining strategy in negotiating at new car dealerships. A white male tester was included in each pair of testers. The white male results provide a bench-mark against which to measure the disparate treatment of the non-"whitemale" tester. Three consumer pairs (black female and white male, black male and white male, and white female and white male) conducted approximately 180 tests at ninety Chicago dealerships.

Each tester followed a bargaining script designed to frame the bargaining in purely distributional terms: the only issue to be negotiated was the price. The script instructed the testers to focus quickly on buying a particular car, and testers offered to provide their own financing. The testers elicited an initial price from the dealers and then, after waiting five minutes, the testers responded with an initial counteroffer that equalled an estimate of the dealer's marginal cost. After the tester's initial counteroffer, the salesperson could do one of three things: (1) attempt to accept the tester's offer, (2) refuse to bargain further, or (3) make a lower offer. If the salesperson attempted to accept the tester's offer or refused to bargain further, the test was over (and the tester left the dealership). If the salesperson responded by making a lower offer, the script instructed the tester to wait five minutes and to split the difference. After the tester split the difference, the salesperson again had the same three choices, and the rounds of bargaining continued until the salesperson accepted a tester offer or refused to bargain further. Testers jotted down each offer and counteroffer, as well as options on the car and the sticker price. Upon leaving the dealership, the testers completed a survey recording information about the test.

This design produced results that permit two tests for discrimination. The first, "short test" of discrimination simply compares the dealer's response to the testers' initial question, "How much would I have to pay to buy this car?" The "long test" of discrimination, on the other hand, compares instead the final offers given to testers after the multiple rounds of concessionary bargaining. By focusing on the initial offer, the short test is well controlled because salespeople had little information from which to draw inferences. By focusing on the final offer, the long test isolates more closely the price a real consumer would pay, but it increases the risk that individual differences among the testers influenced the results.

In order to minimize the possibility of non-uniform bargaining, particular attention was paid to issues of experimental control. A major goal of the study was to choose uniform testers and to train them to behave in a standardized manner. Testers were chosen to satisfy the following criteria for uniformity:

1. *Age*: All testers were twenty-four to twenty-eight years old.

2. *Education*: All testers had three or four years of college education.

3. *Dress*: All testers were dressed similarly during the negotiations. Testers wore casual "yuppie" sportswear: the men wore polo or buttondown shirts, slacks, and loafers; the women wore straight skirts, blouses, minimal make-up, and flats.

4. *Economic Class*: Testers volunteered that they could finance the car themselves.

5. *Occupation*: If asked by a salesperson, each tester said that he or she was a young urban professional (for example, a systems analyst for First Chicago Bank).

6. *Address*: If asked by the salesperson, each tester gave a fake name and an address for an upper-class, Chicago neighborhood (Streeterville).

7. *Attractiveness*: Applicants were subjectively ranked for average attractiveness.

The testers were trained for two days before visiting the dealerships. The training included not only memorizing the tester script, but also participating in mock negotiations designed to help testers gain confidence and learn how to negotiate and answer questions uniformly. The training emphasized uniformity in cadence and inflection of tester response. In addition to spoken uniformity, the study sought to achieve tester uniformity in non-verbal behavior.

* * *

Readers should focus, therefore, not merely on statistical significance but also on the *amount* of the reported discrimination. Although perfect control of such complex bargaining is impossible, the amounts of discrimination reported in the next Part cannot be plausibly explained by idiosyncratic divergence from uniform bargaining.

II. RESULTS OF THE TEST

The results from the tester surveys provide a rich database for investigating how salespeople bargain and whether they treat testers of a different race or gender differently. This Part presents the results of these tests in three sections. The first section reports disparate treatment regarding the prices that dealerships were willing to offer the testers. This section includes an analysis of both initial and final offers as well as refusals to bargain and differences in the bargaining paths (the sequence of offers made in succeeding rounds). In the second section, nonprice dimensions of the bargaining process are analyzed. The tests reveal that salespeople asked testers different types of questions and used different tactics in attempting to sell the cars. Finally, the third section uses multivariate regression analysis to analyze the determinants of the final offers. The regressions reveal a fairly sophisticated seller strategy. In particular, the size of final offers is sensitive not only to the race and gender of both the tester and the salesperson, but also to the information revealed by the tester in the course of bargaining.

A. Price Discrimination

1. *Final Offers.*—The final offer of each test was the lowest price offered by a dealer after the multiple rounds of bargaining. By comparing these final offers with independent estimates of dealer cost, it was possible to calculate the dealer profit associated with each final offer (final offer minus dealer cost). For a sample of 165 tester visits, the average dealer profits for the different classes of tester are presented in Table 1.

TABLE 1: AVERAGE DEALER PROFIT FOR FINAL OFFERS	
White Male	$ 362
White Female	504
Black Male	783
Black Female	1237

Black female testers were asked to pay over three times the markup of white male testers, and black male testers were asked to pay over twice the white male markup. Moreover, race and gender discrimination were synergistic or "superadditive": the discrimination against the black female tester was greater than the combined discrimination against both the white female and the black male tester.

The reliability of these results is buttressed by an analysis of the relative unimportance of individual effects. The average dealer profits on the non-"white male" testers were statistically different from the average profits on the white males at a five percent significance level. The average profits for the three individual white males were, however, not significantly different from each other. This last result lends support to the proposition that the idiosyncratic characteristics of at least the white male testers did not affect the results.

* * *

Dealer discrimination in early rounds will cause disparate concessions by testers that may preclude equal treatment in final rounds. The possibility that early offers matter, however, is not an embarrassment of design. Bargainers engage in time consuming initial rounds of bargaining because they individually believe that these rounds will affect the final price. The tests provide strong evidence that if consumers use the same "split the difference" strategy, they will receive different final offers that are determined by their race and gender. * * *

2. *Initial Offers.*—This study also constructed a test of disparate treatment on the basis of the initial offers sellers made to the testers. * * *

The average dealer profit on offers made to white female testers was not significantly different from the average profit on offers made to white male testers. Sellers, however, offered both black males and black females significantly higher prices: sellers asked black males to pay almost twice the markups they charged white males, and they asked black females to pay two and one-half times that markup.

TABLE 2: AVERAGE DEALER PROFIT FOR FINAL OFFERS	
White Male	$ 818
White Female	829
Black Male	1534
Black Female	2169

3. *Willingness to Bargain.*—Another potentially important form of disparate treatment concerns the sellers' willingness to bargain. Consumers are hurt if the sellers either refuse to bargain or force the consumers to spend more time bargaining to achieve the same price. An analysis of the number of bargaining rounds reveals that the average number of rounds for different types of testers did not differ significantly, as shown in Table 3. The amount of time black male and white female testers spent bargaining (both total and per round) was not statistically longer than the amount spent by white male testers. Although black female testers clearly had to pay the most for cars, it was not because dealers refused to spend time bargaining with them. * * *

TABLE 3:
DIFFERENCES IN ROUNDS

	Average Number of Rounds	Average Length of Test (Minutes)	Average Length per Round (Minutes)
White Male	2.43	35.8	14.8
White Female	2.21	32.9	14.9
Black Male	2.32	49.1	21.2
Black Female	3.08	34.6	11.2

* * *

B. Nonprice Discrimination

The study also examined other ways in which sellers may have treated the testers differently. Although these other types of disparate treatment do not directly concern the sales price, they could facilitate price discrimination. Moreover, these comparisons suggest something about the racial and sexual perceptions that determine the behavior of salespeople.

1. *Customer Steering.*—As designed, the script allowed dealerships to steer testers to different types of salespeople or different types of cars. The script instructed testers to go to the center of the showroom and wait for a salesperson to approach them. The salespeople chose the tester, so that the testers could be steered to salespeople of a particular race or gender. In the sample of 119 encounters, sellers paired with testers as reported in Table 4.

The salesperson's race and gender was not randomly distributed across testers. Instead, sellers steered testers to persons of their own race and gender: white male sellers were more likely to serve white male testers; white female sellers were more likely to serve white female testers; and black male sellers were more likely to serve black testers.

TABLE 4:
STEERING TO PARTICULAR TYPES OF SALESPEOPLE

	Seller Type Percentages		
	White Male	White Female	Black Male
All testers	83.2%	7.5%	9.3%
White Male	89.5	3.5	7.0
White Female	71.4	19.1	9.5
Black Male	83.4	5.5	11.1
Black Female	82.6	4.3	13.1

In addition, the study was designed to uncover a second type of dealer steering. Upon entering the dealership, the testers told the salesperson that they were interested in buying a certain car model with certain options and then allowed the salesperson to show them specific cars. However, no statistically significant disparate treatment was found. The test results reveal that dealers did not systematically steer different types of testers to cars of different cost.

2. Disparate Questioning.—The testers recorded how often they were asked specific types of questions. Statistical tests were then conducted to evaluate whether sellers asked non-"white male" testers particular questions significantly more or less often than white male testers. These tests indicate the following:

> Sellers asked black female testers *more* often about their occupation, about financing, and whether they were married. Sellers asked black female testers *less* often whether they had been to other dealerships and whether they had offers from other dealers.

> Sellers asked black male testers *less* often if they would like to test drive the car, whether they had been to other dealerships, and whether they had offers from other dealers.

> Sellers asked white female testers *more* often whether they had been to other dealerships. Sellers asked white female testers *less* often what price they would be willing to pay.

These differences may indicate ways that dealers try to sort consumers in order to price discriminate effectively. For example, the fact that salespeople asked black testers less often about whether they had been to other dealerships (or had other offers) may indicate that salespeople do not think that interdealer competition is as much of a threat with black customers as with white customers. Because the price that sellers are willing to offer any customer may be sensitive to that customer's responses, the disparity among who is questioned may facilitate a seller's attempt to price discriminate.

3. Disparate Sales Tactics.—The testers also recorded the different tactics that the salespeople used in trying to sell the car. Test statistics were calculated to evaluate whether particular sales tactics were used significantly more or less often with white male testers than with non-"white male" testers. These tests indicate the following:

> Salespeople tried to sell black female testers *more* often on gas mileage, the color of the car, dependability, and comfort, and asked them more often to sign purchase orders.

> Salespeople tried to sell white female testers more often on gas mileage, the color of the car, and dependability.

> With black male testers, salespeople *more* often offered the sticker price as the initial offer and forced the tester to elicit an initial offer

from the seller. Salespeople asked black male testers to sign a purchase order less often.

These tests suggest that salespeople believe women are more concerned with gas mileage, color, and dependability than are men. The tests also indicate that salespeople try to "sucker" black males into buying at the sticker price by offering the sticker price or refusing to make an initial offer until asked.

4. Cost Revelation.—The script also elicited information about the dealers' willingness to reveal their marginal cost to consumers. In half of the bargaining sessions, the testers were told to ask the seller (at the end of the test) what the dealer had paid the car manufacturer. Thirty-five per cent of the sellers represented a specific dollar cost in response to the testers' inquiries. These disclosures, however, were not evenly distributed across the tester groups. Disaggregated by tester type, the disclosure rates indicate that salespeople were less willing to disclose cost data to black testers, especially black female testers, as presented in Table 5.

TABLE 5:
DISCLOSURE OF COST DATA

Tester Type	Percentage of Salespeople Disclosing Cost Figure
All Testers	35%
White Male	47
White Female	42
Black Male	25
Black Female	0

Instead of disclosing their cost information to black testers, the salespeople were more likely to dissemble and claim that they did not know the car's cost. To the extent that such cost disclosure is valuable, the failure to disclose costs to black testers undermines their ability to bargain as effectively as white testers and thus facilitates price discrimination based on race.

Based on this sample, however, it is unclear whether such disclosure would actually put white testers at a competitive advantage. When the seller did reveal his cost, the represented cost was substantially higher than independent estimates of seller cost for the same models, as seen in Table 6. Thus, although salespeople are more likely to disclose cost figures to white testers, they systematically overstate their costs. The greatest mis-representations were made to white female testers.

* * *

Although the individual interaction variables are not statistically significant, the regressions indicate that the linear constraints in Model Two are binding. * * *

TABLE 6:
SELLER MISREPRESENTATION OF COST DATA

	Average Misrepresentation
White Male Tester	$ 849
White Female Tester	1046
Black Male Tester	752
Black Female Tester	—

White male testers received best deals from white female sellers.

White female testers received best deals from black male sellers.

Black male testers received best deals from white female sellers.

Black female testers received best deals from white male sellers.

The social psychology literature would not suggest this result to be expected. Several studies, for example, have shown that parties tend to bargain more cooperatively with an opponent of their own race and gender than with a person of a different race or gender. The interaction effects revealed in Model Three (although not statistically significant) suggest, however, that salespeople may try to take strategic advantage of consumers' perceptions. This result is especially plausible when combined with the earlier finding that testers were systematically steered to salespeople of the same race and gender. The data thus paints a clear picture: sellers steered testers to salespeople of their own race and gender, who then proceeded to give them the worst deals.

III.   TOWARD A THEORETICAL EXPLANATION

The preceding Part detailed race and gender discrimination that was not only statistically significant but also surprisingly pronounced. This Part explores possible explanations for why dealers would discriminate in this manner. Only with an accurate understanding of the reasons for dealer behavior can regulators hope to determine what, if any, governmental intervention can effectively protect black and female customers. With this goal in mind, this Part examines two broad theories of discrimination: animus-based theories and theories of statistical discrimination.

A.   *Animus–Based Theories of Discrimination*

Animus theories of discrimination posit that a certain group is treated differently because that group is disliked or hated. A variety of market participants can interject animus into a market. A dealership, for example, might charge blacks more because the dealership dislikes blacks, because the dealership's employees dislike blacks, or because the dealership's other customers dislike blacks. As originally formulated by Gary Becker, these sources of bigotry could force sellers to charge blacks higher prices as an animus-compensating tax.

The source of bigotry might partially determine the specific form that animus-based discrimination takes. For example, in the fair housing context, consumer animus has led to steering and refusals to bargain. In the "fair driving" context, employee animus against blacks or women might cause salespeople to bargain frivolously. Because testers visited the dealerships during the least busy times of the day, bigoted dealers—with nothing better to do with their time—might have gained satisfaction in frustrating or wasting the time of women or blacks. Finally, the testers also might have experienced "role-based" bigotry: dealers might have discriminated against buyers who acted in ways that diverged from the dealer's expectation. Female testers could have faced prejudice for speaking with "a male voice"; black testers could have faced prejudice for not "staying in their place." In sum, the animus of various market participants can manifest itself as disparate treatment not only in the prices offered but also in other aspects of seller behavior.

                    * * *

C.   A Tentative Explanation

1.   Statistical Discrimination as an Explanation for Dealer Behavior.—The preceding discussion presented three broad theories of discrimination: animus-based, cost-based, and revenue-based. The fair driving tests, like their fair housing analogues, were designed primarily to identify the existence of disparate treatment—not to determine its cause. As a result, ancillary evidence must be used to determine which of the three competing theories best explains seller behavior. Although more study is warranted, it appears that the revenue-based theory best explains the discrimination that the testers encountered.

The cost-based theories of statistical discrimination are perhaps the weakest. The testers' script was explicitly structured to eliminate cost-based differences among the testers. The testers volunteered that they did not need financing—a potentially major source of disparate dealer cost. Notwithstanding these uniform representations, it is possible that the dealers inferred residual differences among the tester types. As an empirical matter, however, differences in net dealership cost simply do not explain why black female testers paid over three times the markup of white male testers. Moreover, on a cost-based theory, the observed seller inferences about profits from ancillary sales might predict a different pattern of disparate treatment.

Animus theories find more support in the data. The testers, for example, recorded several instances of overtly sexist and racist language by sellers. Nonetheless, animus theories do not appear to explain the magnitude of the discrimination. For example, under a theory of salesperson animus, the seller required a higher price from black females as compensation for having to deal with a black customer whom the seller disliked. The data would then imply that the dealer-required compensation must have been an implausible $900 per hour.

Consumer-based animus also fails to explain adequately disparate treatment by sellers. First, each class of testers received its best treatment from salespeople of a different race and gender and, in many cases, the worst treatment from salespeople of the same race and gender. For example, although all salespeople discriminated against black male testers, black salesmen gave them their worst deals. This result runs counter to the standard notion that a person's bigotry is usually directed at another race. Second, the amount of price discrimination black testers encountered at all dealerships did not vary with the racial makeup of the dealership's customer base. One-third of Chicago dealerships are located in neighborhoods with a greater than ninety percent black population, yet the offers these dealerships made to black testers did not differ from offers black testers received elsewhere. If disparate treatment were caused by white consumers' dislike of blacks, there should be less discrimination by sellers in neighborhoods where most consumers are black. Because the data do not confirm this prediction, the animus theory seems an unlikely explanation for the disparate treatment. Finally, consumer animus is inconsistent with observed salesperson behavior: salespeople did not attempt to reduce the length of bargaining sessions with the non-"white male" testers. If disparate treatment of black consumers were caused by sellers' concern for white consumers' desire not to associate with blacks, dealerships should have discouraged black consumers from bargaining for lengthy periods.

Although any conclusions based on this evidence must remain tentative, the case for revenue-based statistical discrimination is strongest. Despite the large amount of randomness (or unexplained variance) in bargaining outcomes, the dealerships seem to display a great deal of sophistication in bargaining. The systematic steering of customers to salespeople who charge them higher markups may be evidence of revenue-based statistical discrimination. Salespeople of the consumer's race and gender may, for example, be better able to infer that consumer's willingness to pay—and thus more finely tune the price discrimination.

* * *

Yet the conundrum persists as to why race and gender would be proxies for consumers' firm-specific reservation price that disfavor women and blacks. Even accepting that firm-specific willingness to pay is more a function of search costs than of ability to pay, why would blacks and women be disfavored? George Stigler has predicted that consumers with high opportunity costs will search less for a particular good than those consumers with lower opportunity costs. Because white males earn more on average than other tester types, under Stigler's theory a dealer should rationally infer that white males search less than members of other race and gender classes. If race and gender serve as proxies for dealer-specific willingness to pay, these proxies would seem to lead sellers to charge higher prices to white males, and not the lower prices revealed by this study.

Nevertheless, group differences in search costs, information, and aversion to bargaining may explain why profit-maximizing dealers charge white males less. The caricatured assertion that white males have higher opportunity costs (because they forgo higher wages when searching) ignores other effects that on balance may make it more difficult for blacks and women to search for a car. For example, white males may have a greater ability to take time off from work or family responsibilities to search for a car.

Moreover, blacks are less likely to have a trade-in car with which to search when purchasing a new car. If, on net, blacks and women experience higher search costs than do white males, revenue-based statistical discrimination might lead dealers to make lower offers to white males. Knowing that blacks and women tend to incur higher search costs, a dealer could "safely" charge members of those groups higher prices, because the dealer would effectively have less competition for members of those groups from other dealers. White men may also have superior access to information about the car market. A large proportion of white men know that automobiles can be purchased for less than the sticker price, and white men may more easily be able to discover the customary size of negotiated discounts from the sticker price.

* * *

2. The Reinforcing Role of Dealer Competition.—Many commentators have argued that competition among sellers will tend to eliminate certain forms of race and gender discrimination against buyers. The following discussion examines how market competition among dealerships may in fact reinforce the opportunities for statistical discrimination.

As a first intuition, competition should quickly eliminate revenue-based statistical discrimination, slowly eliminate animus-based discrimination, and never eliminate cost-based statistical discrimination. Competition should quickly eliminate revenue-based discrimination because rival dealers would immediately move to undercut any supra-competitive prices offered to high-valuing car buyers. Competition should slowly eliminate animus discrimination because bigoted sellers would be at a competitive disadvantage and so would eventually be driven out of the market. By contrast, competition should not eliminate cost-based statistical discrimination because no dealer would have a market-based incentive to offer prices that fall below the best estimates of that dealer's actual costs.

The preceding analysis, however, tentatively suggested just the opposite causal ordering. Cost-based statistical discrimination is the least plausible explanation, and revenue-based statistical discrimination is the most plausible. The simple competitive story thus poses a major challenge to the assertion that revenue-based statistical discrimination caused the disparate treatment. In a large city such as Chicago, with hundreds of car dealerships, how could rival dealerships successfully charge individual consumers significantly more than dealership marginal costs?

* * *

The dealers' reliance on high-markup buyers lends additional credibility to the notion that dealership disparate treatment of consumers might be a form of revenue-based statistical discrimination. The dealers' search for high-markup buyers may be tailored to focus on specific racial or gender groups. In their quest to locate high-markup buyers, dealers are not guided by the amount that the *average* black woman is willing to pay. Rather, they focus on the proportion of black women who are willing to pay close to the sticker price. Even a small difference in the percentage of high-markup buyers represented by consumers of any one race or gender class may lead to large differences in the way dealers treat that entire class. Thus, the previous explanations of racial- or gender-based differences in search costs, information, or aversion to bargaining need not be true for the average members of a consumer group in order for those differences to generate significant amounts of revenue-based disparate treatment. The Consumer Federation of America recently completed a survey which revealed that thirty-seven percent of consumers do not understand that the sticker price is negotiable. These responses varied greatly across both race and gender. Sixty-one percent of black consumers surveyed did not realize that the sticker price is negotiable, whereas only thirty-one percent of white consumers made this error. This fact by itself could easily explain dramatic disparate treatment by sellers. Profit maximizing dealers may rationally quote higher prices to blacks even if the average black consumer in fact has a lower willingness to pay.

In sum, although simple economic theory suggests that dealer competition should quickly eliminate price dispersion, dealers in the market for new cars nevertheless sell the same car for different prices. Highly concentrated profits give dealers incentives to search for high-markup buyers through the process of bargaining. In particular, the dealers' search for high-markup buyers may reinforce incentives to discriminate on the basis of race or gender. The concentration of profits is a central pathology of retail car sales and one to which we will return below.

IV.   LEGAL IMPLICATIONS

The results of the bargaining tests show that car dealerships treat black and female testers differently than they do white men who use the same bargaining strategy. Whether these findings constitute actionable racial or gender discrimination in a traditional legal sense, however, is a separate matter. The differential treatment of consumers might be seen as a natural consequence of any bargaining process. Market economies sanction such treatment by allowing sellers to pursue high-markup sales through a variety of bargaining methods. The pre-contractual interplay between a potential buyer and seller may seem, in some sense, outside the purview of the law.

This Part argues, however, that the findings presented in this Article constitute compelling evidence of unlawful racial and gender discrimination under both the civil rights and consumer protection laws. In particular, the following section explores whether the car sellers' dealings with black testers constitute unlawful disparate treatment violative of sections 1981 and 1982. Such a claim does not necessarily imply that sellers dislike black or female customers—only that sellers take their customers' race and gender into account when deciding how to bargain. Section B then proposes legal reforms to strengthen sections 1981 and 1982 and to extend their coverage to currently unprotected groups.

A.   Liability Under Sections 1981 and 1982

Sections 1981 and 1982 mandate that all people shall have the same rights "to make and enforce contracts" and to "purchase ... personal property," respectively, "as is enjoyed by white citizens." Although a racial discrimination suit has never been brought against a retail car dealership under section 1981 or section 1982, there seems little doubt that one or both these laws covers discrimination relating to retail car price bargaining between private parties. In *Jones v. Alfred H. Mayer Co.*, the Supreme Court emphatically stated that section 1982 (and by implication section 1981) applies to acts of private discrimination. Since *Jones*, courts have applied these sections' prohibitions of private discrimination to contexts similar to retail car price bargaining.

Even if car dealership bargaining falls within the scope of sections 1981 and 1982, a fair driving plaintiff would have a number of hurdles to overcome in winning a claim under these statutes. The substantive legal standard under sections 1981 and 1982 is straightforward: plaintiffs claiming disparate treatment must prove that the defendant intentionally discriminated against them and caused them an identifiable injury. Although the Supreme Court has stated that intentional discrimination "can *in some situations* be inferred from the mere fact of differences in treatment," no civil rights case has ever concluded that a showing of disparate treatment was insufficient to establish intentional discrimination. Thus, it appears that courts will find intentional discrimination whenever the defendant's conduct was conditioned on the plaintiff's race. To establish liability in this context, the typical fair driving plaintiff would need to show that the specific car dealer with whom he or she had bargained considered the plaintiff's race in deciding how to bargain.

On the other hand, because of the difficulties in obtaining direct proof that a defendant's conduct was race-dependent, the law has developed a method for allocating the burdens of proof under sections 1981 and 1982 that in effect allows intent to be inferred from indirect evidence. In particular, courts hearing section 1981 or 1982 claims have imported from the title VII context the shifting burdens of proof scheme articulated in *McDonnell Douglas v. Green*.

Applying the *McDonnell Douglas* reasoning to fair driving suits, the plaintiff bears the initial burden of establishing disparate treatment: that sellers took race into account when deciding how to bargain. If the plaintiff can establish a prima facie violation of section 1981 or section 1982, a burden of production shifts to the defendant "to articulate some legitimate, nondiscriminatory reason" for its differential behavior. Finally, if the defendant can offer such a reason, the burden shifts back to the plaintiff to show that the defendant's response is a mere "pretext."

A black tester from the present study who wanted to make out a successful prima facie case against a particular dealership would have to persuade the court of two things. First, she would have to persuade the court that the study was sufficiently controlled—that is, that she and the white tester visiting the defendant's car dealership appeared similar in every objective respect except for the color of their skin. If courts' attitudes in housing cases under sections 1981 and 1982 are any indication, the fair driving tests conducted in this study were more than sufficiently controlled. Although the typical fair housing test is similarly controlled with respect to timing of the tests, it is less controlled with respect to verbal and nonverbal conduct than was the testing in this study.

Second, fair driving plaintiffs would have to persuade the court that the instances of differential treatment are sufficiently numerous so that the results can not be explained by chance. Again, analogy to the fair housing context suggests that the results of one pair of well controlled testers should suffice. Under this standard, the present study could theoretically give rise to dozens of actionable instances of discrimination against individual dealers.

Although comparisons with the fair housing context are generally apposite, courts may be much more reluctant to find the existence of prima facie cases in the fair driving context because society has differing presumptions about the pervasiveness of the two kinds of discrimination. The long and ongoing history of housing discrimination in the United States is so well known and well documented that courts may require relatively less proof. Discrimination in car negotiations may have a similarly long and deep-seated history, but the size and nature of such discrimination may be masked by the processes of bargaining. As a result, a court hearing a fair driving claim may require that the tests be that much more controlled, that the disparity of treatment be that much greater, or that there be that many more instances of disparate treatment by the same dealer.

Once a court finds that a fair driving plaintiff has made out a prima facie case of disparate treatment, the burden shifts to the defendant-dealer to articulate a legitimate, nondiscriminatory explanation for why it treated white buyers and black buyers differently. If the defendant does not directly rebut the plaintiff's evidence of disparate treatment, it might put forward two distinct arguments that the disparate treatment was not "intentional" discrimination. First, the dealer may argue that the disparate treatment was unintentional because the dealer's motive was to make money, not to harm black people. Under this theory, the dealer might openly admit that its behavior flowed from consciously drawn, economically rational inferences based on the race of prospective buyers—revenue-based inferences, for example, about the proportion of blacks willing to pay a higher markup. It is, however, precisely these sorts of inferences—inferences based on the color of a person's skin—that sections 1981 and 1982 do not countenance. As Judge Posner recently held, "[d]iscrimination may be instrumental to a goal not itself discriminatory, just as murder may be instrumental to a goal not itself murderous (such as money); it is not any less—it is, indeed, more clearly—discriminatory on that account."

Alternatively, defendants might claim that their disparate treatment was unintentional in the sense that they were not conscious of it. The D.C. Circuit rejected this argument in *Hopkins v. Price Waterhouse*:

[Plaintiff demonstrated] that she was treated less favorably than male candidates because of her sex. This is sufficient to establish discriminatory motive; the fact that some or all of the partners at Price Waterhouse may have been unaware of that motivation, even within themselves, neither alters the fact of its existence nor excuses it.

Once a plaintiff has proven that a defendant has treated blacks differently from identically situated whites, it is fair and reasonable to conclude as a matter of law that the dealer at some level of consciousness must have been aware of the testers' race. Such a legal inference conforms with our common moral intuition that a dealer who must consciously decide what initial price to offer every customer who walks through the door must be aware of the skin color of those to whom it consistently offers a higher initial price. Thus, so long as the fair driving plaintiff can persuade the factfinder that sellers treated similarly situated blacks differently from whites, the disparate treatment discussed in this Article violates sections 1981 and 1982.

B. Legal Reform

1. Modernizing Civil Rights Laws.—Lawmakers could respond to bargaining discrimination by expanding the current coverage of the civil rights and consumer protection laws. Most important, Congress could amend sections 1981 and 1982 to extend to women (and other protected classes) the right to be free from discrimination in contracting to buy and sell services as well as goods. Modernized versions of sections 1981 and 1982 could also allow plaintiffs to bring disparate impact suits, currently actionable under title VII, which require no showing of intent. Disparate impact litigation would allow suits to challenge the bargaining practices of sellers that are facially neutral (in the sense that they do not consciously take a buyer's race or gender into account) but have significant discriminatory effects. In sum, creating an additional roman numeraled civil rights "title" to cover the sale of goods and services would provide a remedy for the kinds of discrimination examined in this Article.

Although this Article has argued that the sellers' search for high-markup consumers causes sellers to discriminate against blacks and women, the proposal to extend civil rights protection to the sale of all goods and services is based on the notion that racial and gender-based disparate treatment may well exist in a broader variety of markets. The problem of disparate treatment in new car sales has been perpetuated by the fact that the bargaining process conceals from black and female consumers the prices received by their white male counterparts. Without such information, blacks and women cannot directly learn of disparate treatment. Black and female consumers may also be deprived of this crucial bench-mark in retail markets in which bargaining does not occur. Although uniform stated-pricing eliminates the potential for gender or race discrimination in pricing for most goods, such discrimination may still exist along such different dimensions as product or service quality. Again, although blacks and women can gather information about how other retailers treat them, they face difficulty in learning how retailers treat white men.

The 1960s civil rights laws outlawed discrimination in those markets—most notably housing and employment—in which conspicuous accessible bench-marks disclosed disparate treatment. But the absence of a manifest bench-mark does not imply the absence of discrimination; there is no reason to think that animus or statistical causes of discrimination manifest themselves only in markets in which interracial comparisons of treatment can be readily made. Indeed, as various overt forms of discrimination have become illegal, more subtle and covert manifestations have often replaced them. This Article seeks fundamentally to expand the domain of the civil rights inquiry.

2. *Reinvigorating Consumer Protection Laws.*—State and federal governments might also attempt to enforce more rigorously consumer protection laws to reduce the type of discrimination revealed in this Article. Indeed, recent Supreme Court decisions hostile to civil rights suits suggest the wisdom of pursuing a remedy under consumer protection laws. In *Patterson v. McLean Credit Union*, for example, the Court, although refusing to apply section 1981 to what it considered "postformation conduct," suggested instead that the victims of discrimination turn to traditional contractual remedies. To the extent that consumer protection laws codify common law remedies such as fraud and duress, they may provide a viable alternative to civil rights remedies. Thus, although consumer protection laws have not yet been used to attack racial disparate treatment as a "deceptive" misrepresentation, this history does not preclude more extensive governmental intervention in the future.

The Federal Trade Commission (FTC) Act and the numerous baby FTC acts passed by the individual states outlaw the use of "unfair or deceptive" trading practices. Utilizing such acts to reach discrimination in bargaining for a new car purchase will require a reconceptualization of what we consider unfair or deceptive. Attacking sellers' disparate treatment in bargaining as being "deceptive" strikes at closely held beliefs about what is appropriate in the normal course of negotiations. The complexity of these beliefs is demonstrated by contrasting the effect of seller misrepresentation in the context of car sales with seller misrepresentation in housing sales. Fair housing cases often gain their moral authority from the egregious nature of seller misrepresentations such as "the apartment is no longer available." In the retail car bargaining context, however, some forms of misrepresentation are broadly accepted. Few would believe, for example, that a seller would be held liable for misrepresenting "I can't reduce the price any further"—even if the seller did reduce the price for another consumer. Seller misrepresentation is present in both the housing market and in the new car market. The distinction in our response turns, if at all, on which types of misrepresentation we deem acceptable.

Nevertheless, consumer protection laws do provide a framework for attacking disparate treatment in bargaining. Courts have construed consumer protection statutes to prohibit implied as well as express misrepresentation. Courts could attack disparate treatment in negotiations for new cars by finding an implied representation that the dealer would not treat black consumers differently from white consumers. In other words, courts may preserve the "essence" of bargaining—by conceding that all consumers should expect inconsistent and unpredictable treatment at the hands of car dealers—but refuse to sanction "discrimination" by rejecting regimes in which the unpredictable behavior is in fact predicated on race or gender.

Such a finding would be completely consistent with freedom of contract. Sellers could avoid making this implicit representation by expressly reserving the right to bargain differently with customers of different races. A judicial or legislative finding of an implicit representation of no racial disparate treatment would simply be "filling a gap" in the parties' contract. Finding an implied representation of no racial disparate treatment is at least as reasonable as finding an implied representation that sellers reserve the right to treat different races differently: few explicit contracts would ever opt for the latter provision. Once lawmakers established a default rule of no disparate treatment, plaintiffs bringing implied misrepresentation cases would then face the same burden as traditional section 1981 plaintiffs: the burden of demonstrating disparate treatment.

The Supreme Court's decision in *Patterson v. McLean Credit Union* strongly supports this analysis. In restricting civil rights protection under section 1981 to discrimination in the formation of a contract, the *Patterson* Court suggested that victims of discrimination should turn to traditional contractual remedies: racial harassment "amounting to a breach of contract under state law is precisely what the language of § 1981 does not cover. That is because, in such a case . . . the plaintiff is free to enforce the terms of the contract in state court." Although the contract at issue was silent as to whether post-formation discrimination was permissible, the court implied that nondiscrimination provisions could be read into state contract remedies. Following the *Patterson* rationale, finding an implicit representation not to treat consumers differently in bargaining because of their race or gender would offer a free market alternative to civil rights interventionism.

3. Structural Reforms.—The expansion of traditional civil rights and consumer protection laws is unlikely to completely eliminate disparate treatment in bargaining based on race or gender. Victims of disparate bargaining treatment will most likely be restricted to suing individual dealerships—instead of manufacturers or groups of dealerships. Even if plaintiffs bring class actions and courts consistently grant testers standing to sue, the piecemeal approach of such suits, combined with the protracted nature of litigation, is unlikely to be sufficient to deter race- and gender-dependent behavior.

In light of these conditions, policymakers might consider structural reforms to improve the workings of the market. Structural changes should grow out of specific causal theories of disparate treatment in order quickly and effectively to erase such treatment. For example, if animus is inducing price discrimination, a law that outlawed price discrimination might induce some sellers to refuse to bargain. However, if the disparate treatment is caused by inferences about different consumer demand, then outlawing price discrimination should not generate such refusals. Simply put, to formulate effective intervention, policymakers must understand why sellers discriminate.

The earlier analysis of competition suggested that high-markup customers (and the ensuing concentration of profits) are a central cause of dealer price discrimination. As a result, if policymakers can find a way to reduce significantly the profits on these sucker sales, the manner in which dealerships conduct the retail sale of *all* cars would become dramatically more competitive. Without the pathological effects of highly concentrated profits, dealers would no longer have an incentive to force consumers to expend real and psychic resources in bargaining.

Policymakers could use three different strategies to eliminate high-markup sales. Most directly, courts could strengthen current notions of substantive unconscionability to prohibit high-markup sales. This strategy, however, is unlikely to occur: courts in the past have shown extreme reluctance to distinguish conscionable from unconscionable markups. Although courts voided contracts for unconscionable markups in two well-known cases, *Frostifresh Corp. v. Reynoso* and *American Home Improvement v. MacIver*, few courts since the early 1960s have reached similar holdings. The likelihood of courts taking the dramatic step of expanding this rarely used doctrine becomes even smaller in light of the special nature of bargaining for retail cars and society's solicitude toward such bargaining.

As a second regulatory strategy, policymakers might restrict the amount of price dispersion permissible in the car market. Regulators might, for example, allow dealerships to engage in bargaining, but void sales with markups that are more than twenty percent above the average markup. Unlike direct unconscionability regulation, firms would retain the freedom to set the average markup for any one model as high as the market would bear but would be prohibited from selling similar cars at significantly different prices. At its most extreme, this form of regulation would prohibit bargaining and mandate that dealerships sell at advertised prices. Restraining price dispersion is an attractive form of regulation because it might benefit all would-be car buyers. If the number of high-markup sales is reduced, sellers may find that bargaining (and the transaction costs that it imposes on all consumers) is no longer profitable. Once high-markup consumers are protected, sellers may no longer subject their low-markup consumers to costly and unpleasant bargaining.

Finally and least intrusively, regulators might reduce the number of sales with disparately high markups by mandating various types of disclosure from dealerships to consumers. Dealerships, for example, might be required to reveal the average price for which each make of car is sold. Knowing that the dealership is attempting to charge $3000 more than the average price would allow high-markup consumers to protect themselves. Alternatively, regulation might force dealerships to reveal the size of the markup on each individual transaction. Clay Miller and I have argued elsewhere that markup disclosure could improve both the equity and efficiency of retail car sales: "markup revelation would truncate the bargaining process at each dealership. The possibility of hoodwinking uninformed buyers into purchasing at a high markup would diminish as the excessive profits would be directly revealed."

In sum, mandating disclosure and restraining price dispersion are plausible strategies to reduce the importance that dealerships place on high-markup sales. A central prediction of this Article is that at some point reducing the concentration of dealership profits would rationalize dealership competition by giving individual dealerships an incentive to opt for high-volume, stated-price selling strategies. The relatively unintrusive nature of disclosure and price-dispersion regulation makes them politically and administratively more viable.

Before choosing a strategy to eliminate price dispersion, policy-makers should determine whether a single price equilibrium is "sustainable": that is, whether competitive dealerships that charge a single price could break even and thus survive price dispersion. In markets with high fixed costs, if sellers were required (directly or indirectly through disclosure) to charge a single price, competition might drive that price to a level below sellers' average cost. Such markets have "hollow cores" (because the "core" set of viable single-price equilibriums is empty or "hollow").

If the retail car market has a hollow core, government intervention to eliminate price dispersion would tend to drive dealerships from the market. In such markets, high-markup sales help dealers cover their fixed costs. In the airline industry, for example, the high-markup sales to business travelers may be necessary to meet industry fixed costs. Indeed, business travelers may benefit from the presence of lower-price tourist fares because "cheap" seats defray part of these fixed costs. If regulation eliminated price dispersion and mandated a single fare per route, business travelers might have to pay higher prices than under the current regime. Tourist travelers would stop buying, and the airline would then pass its fixed costs along to the smaller group of business travelers.

Regulator concerns should be allayed, however, because the retail car market does not resemble hollow core markets. Retail car dealerships do not experience significant high fixed costs (especially when compared to many other single price markets such as the market for electronic appliances and stereo equipment). Moreover, it is implausible that white males would (like tourist travelers) stop purchasing in a single price equilibrium. Mandating a single fare for airlines might lead to an inflated price that only businesspeople could afford, but mandating a single price for automobiles would not leave blacks and females alone to shoulder even higher proportions of the retailers' fixed costs.

Although this discussion of potential regulatory strategies is impressionistic, at the very least it suggests that regulators have a variety of choices beyond traditional civil rights and consumer protection remedies to attack the inequalities uncovered in this Article. Naturally, implementing one of these structural interventions would impose enforcement costs that must be weighed against the benefits of regulation. Dealers may attempt to circumvent such regulations in several ways. Nevertheless, in evaluating the efficacy of structural changes, policymakers should pay particular attention to the concentration of profits and the prevalence of high-markup sales.

V. CONCLUSION

The negotiation of contracts occupies a mysterious and somewhat mythical position in the law and in our society. In *The Wealth of Nations*, Adam Smith opined that people have a natural propensity to "truck and barter" over the sale of goods. Law-and-economic scholars at times extend this insight, suggesting that people will tend to negotiate whenever resources are misallocated: if I want to sit on a crowded subway, I will negotiate with the other passengers for a seat.

Common experience indicates, however, that many people in the United States are averse to bargaining. The frustration that many consumers experience in bargaining for a car is largely attributable to the ludicrously inefficient manner in which cars are marketed. Although Smith and others attach almost mythic qualities to the process of bargaining, this Article has thrown the equity and efficiency of car negotiations into question. The process of retail car negotiations becomes even more problematic when traditionally disadvantaged members of our society effectively pay a bargaining tax whenever they purchase a new car.

Earlier this year, I asked a car dealer during an interview whether the bulk of his profits were concentrated in a few sales. He told me that his dealership made a substantial number of both "sucker" and "non-sucker" sales. He added: "My cousin, however, owns a dealer-ship in a black neighborhood. He doesn't sell nearly as many [cars], but he hits an awful lot of home runs. You know, sometimes it seems like the people that can least afford it have to pay the most." Although it is dangerous to extrapolate from the results of a single study, the amounts of discrimination uncovered, if representative of a larger phenomenon, are truly astounding. A $500 overcharge per car means that blacks annually pay $150 million more for new cars than they would if they were white males. There are substantial reasons to uncover *and eliminate* such discrimination.

———

For further reading, *see also* Peter Siegelman, *Gender and Race Discrimination in Retail Car Negotiations, in* PERVASIVE PREJUDICE?: UNCONVENTIONAL EVIDENCE OF RACE AND GENDER DISCRIMINATION 19 (Ian Ayres ed., 2001).

CHAPTER 10

THE MARKET VALUE OF CULTURE

Introduction

Between culture and commerce lies an ocean of mostly unexplored misunderstandings. In a thousand ways, the captains of commerce and the giants of creative invention live in the perpetual paradox of mutual hostility and mutual dependence. When race and ethnic pluralism are tossed into this already volatile mix, the questions multiply even as the answers diminish in inverse proportion.

This chapter takes up some of the most troublesome issues at the intersection of culture, race, gender and identity in the marketplace. In what follows we consider four central queries: *First*, can economic behavior be fully understood, without an attentive account of the cultural context in which economic transactions occur? The paucity of attention of neoclassical strands of economic analysis to the cultural variables that we discuss in what follows has produced a largely impotent set of models for predicting many crucial items of economic behavior. These thin models, devoid of cultural context, have dominated the legal discourse about economics. We identify a more complex set of ideas that incorporates culture and its tension with commerce. *Second*, what is the impact of racial dominance on the ownership and control of cultural property? We ask whether the rules of intellectual property support or undermine the growth of economic autonomy for members of culturally subordinated groups. Is the economic structure that frames the labor of musicians, artists, singers, songwriters, actors, and other creators just? *Third*, how does subordination express its effect in the valuation of the human capital components of language, hairstyle, sexual difference, and modes of expressive autonomy in the workplace? *Fourth,* if we reconceptualize the relationship of culture and markets, can we elevate the level of human flourishing for a broader group of citizens?

A. ACCENTS

In this passage, novelist Amy Tan vividly captures the problem of an immigrant mother's effort to communicate her hope for cultural transformation, even while clinging to the project of symbolic and creative preservation of cultural memory. The mother dreams of speaking without an accent.

The old woman remembered a swan she had bought many years ago in Shanghai for a foolish sum. This bird, boasted the market vendor, was once a duck that stretched its neck in hopes of becoming a goose, and now look! It is too beautiful to eat.

Then the woman and the swan sailed across an ocean many thousands of *li* wide, stretching their necks toward America. On her journey she cooed to the swan: 'In America, I will have a daughter just like me. But over there nobody will say her worth is measured by the loudness of her husband's belch. Over there nobody will look down on her, because I will make her speak perfect American English. And over there she will always be too full to swallow any sorrow! She will know my meaning, because I will give her this swan—a creature that became more than what was hoped for.'

But when she arrived in the new country the immigration officials pulled her swan away from her, leaving the woman fluttering her arms and with only one swan feather for a memory. And then she had to fill out so many forms she forgot why she had come and what she had left behind.

Now the woman was old. And she had a daughter who grew up speaking only English and swallowing more Coca–Cola than sorrow. For a long time now the woman had wanted to give her daughter the single swan feather and tell her, "This feather may look worthless, but it comes from afar and carries with it all my good intentions." And she waited, year after year, for the day she could tell her daughter this in perfect American English.

AMY TAN, *Feathers From a Thousand* Li *Away, in* THE JOY LUCK CLUB (1989).

Voices of America: Accent, Antidiscrimination Law, and a Jurisprudence for the Last Reconstruction

100 YALE L.J. 1329 (1991).

■ MARI J. MATSUDA

I.   INTRODUCTION

* * * This Article opens with stories of some of the accents that gave rise to the existing judicial decisions. The influence of the "turn to narrative"—the suggestion that human beings understand and form their worlds through stories—is evident here. These narratives create a doctrinal puzzle. * * * The puzzle is this: Courts recognize that discrimination against accent can function as the equivalent of prohibited national origin discrimination. The fact that communication is an important element of job performance, however, tends to trump this prohibition against discrimination, such that it is impossible to explain when or why plaintiffs will ever win in accent cases. In fact, they almost never do. Much of this section will sound like a positivist's plea for logic.

[This article] attempts to understand the cultural context of accent discrimination by considering the role of speech in society, and the ways in which prejudice and status assumptions are tied inextricably to speech evaluation. Given this sociolinguistic reality, I argue * * * for a doctrinal reconstruction that will apply Title VII to accent cases in a rational way. I criticize the current, conclusory reasoning of most accent decisions, while acknowledging the difficulties courts face. This is positivism plus sociology of law—a kind of thinking I associate with the Yale Law School. It demands that we apply our faculties of reason to the social reality of lived experience.

Having set forth what I believe is a rational and just application of Title VII principles to accent cases, [I will then] consider the ethical implications of accepting or rejecting a doctrinal scheme intended to promote linguistic pluralism. [This article] explores liberal justifications for linguistic tolerance, and * * * considers accent from within the perspective of emerging progressive theories of law, including Critical Legal Studies, Critical Race Theory, and feminist jurisprudence. Utilizing these critical theories, I inquire into the deeper meaning of accent discrimination as situated in structures of subordination. This part is influenced by the critical theorists who have confronted the issue of audience: for whom do we write, and why? I attempt to make explicit my intended and multiple audiences, and my political goals.

> * * *

II. THE STORIES

I come from a place that is farther away from any place than any place. The islands of Hawaii, geographically isolated and peopled from all corners of the world, are a linguist's dream. The linguistic and ethnic heritage of the islands is more diverse than that of any other state in the United States. In the voices of the islands one hears traces of Hawaiian, Portuguese, New England English, Japanese, Chinese, Filipino, and Spanish. It is thus no accident that two significant Title VII cases falling in the middle of the doctrinal puzzle of accent discrimination come from Hawaii.

Perhaps in explaining the puzzle, it is best to begin where all cases begin, with a person and the story they bring to court.

A. *Manuel Fragante's Story*

> * * *

In 1981 Manuel Fragante took a civil service examination along with over 700 other applicants. He is an intelligent and educated man, and he was not surprised when he received the highest score of all applicants who took the test. Fragante was ranked first on the list of eligibles, but, after a brief interview, he was turned down for the job of clerk in the Division of Motor Vehicles. When he asked why, he learned that he was rejected because of his Filipino accent. Manuel Fragante, combat veteran of two wars and true believer in the rhetoric of equality, promptly contacted a

Filipino American state legislator, who in turn recommended that Fragante visit the run-down office of a neighborhood public interest law firm.

* * *

Because the DMV creates constant demand for new employees, the personnel department sent a specialist to study the job and devise a screening test to help identify a large pool of prospective clerks. This is a well-established procedure used by large employers. The specialist observed clerks on the job. The key skills she identified included alphabetizing, reproducing numbers and letters with accuracy, making change, exhibiting courtesy, and other routine clerical skills. A test was devised to measure these skills.

* * *

This was the premise Manuel Fragante relied on when he took the civil service examination and out-tested his 700 competitors. He was proud of his score and felt assured of the job. While others thought the job was beneath him given his age and experience, he was looking forward to the simplicity of its tasks, to the official feel of working for the government in an air-conditioned building, and to the chance to earn some spending money instead of wasting his time in boring idleness. He found warnings that the job was stressful mildly amusing. Having lived through invasion, war, and economic uncertainty, Manuel Fragante figured he could handle an irate taxpayer complaining about a long wait in line. He thus walked in for his interview with a calm and assured dignity. He knew the job was his.

* * *

Manuel Fragante was passed over for the job. The administrator in charge of hiring recommendations stated, "because of his accent, I would not recommend him for this position." The interviewers heard what any listener would hear in a brief conversation with Mr. Fragante: he speaks with a heavy Filipino accent, one that he is unlikely to lose at his age.

* * *

The linguist sat through the trial and noted the proceedings with interest. Attorneys for both sides suffered lapses in grammar and sentence structure, as did the judge. Mr. Fragante's English, a review of the transcript confirmed, was more nearly perfect in standard grammar and syntax than any other speaker in the courtroom. Mr. Fragante testified for two days, under the stress of both direct and cross-examination. The judge and the examiners spoke to Fragante in English and understood his answers. A court reporter understood and took down his words verbatim. In the functional context of the trial, everyone understood Manuel Fragante's speech. Yet the defendant's interviewers continued to claim Fragante could not be understood well enough to serve as a DMV clerk.

In an irony particularly noticeable to the linguist, lawyers for both sides, as well as the defendant's witnesses, spoke with the accent characteristic of non-whites raised in Hawaii—the Hawaiian Creole accent that would become the subject of another significant Title VII accent case discussed below. * * * The linguist, trained as he was to recognize accents as intriguing differences rather than handicaps, was troubled by the legal result in the *Fragante* case.

* * * The judge was on assignment from Arizona. He listened to four days of testimony and concluded that Manuel Fragante was denied the job *not* because of national origin, but because of legitimate difficulties with his accent. The opinion was somewhat of a puzzle. The judge found, as fact, that Manuel Fragante "has extensive verbal communication skill in English" but paradoxically that he has a "difficult manner of pronunciation" and a "military bearing," and that some listeners would "stop listening" when they hear a Filipino accent. The court made much of the high-stress communication required for the job, and found that speech was a bona fide occupational qualification. Finally, the court applied the *McDonnell Douglas* test, and found no proof of discriminatory intent or subterfuge.

Manuel Fragante was upset by the opinion. Soon after losing out on the DMV job, he was hired by the State of Hawaii as a statistician. Much of his work involved telephone interviews. Fragante felt his employment with the State proved his claim that the city misjudged his accent. He told his attorneys he wanted to press forward with his case.

Fragante lost on appeal before the Ninth Circuit although he did gain the symbolic victory of the court's sympathetic recognition that accent discrimination could violate Title VII. The U.S. Supreme Court denied certiorari.

* * *

B. *The Weather Forecasters*

* * *

In 1985, the National Weather Service advertised for a vacancy in the Honolulu forecast office. Coursework in meteorology, climatology, physics, and mathematics was identified in the vacancy announcement as relevant to the position, as was meteorology experience. James Kahakua, a native Hawaiian, proudly possessed years of experience in meteorology, and a Bachelor of Science degree with coursework in all of the areas identified in the announcement. He applied for a promotion to the open position, but was turned down in favor of a "haole"—or white—newcomer to Hawaii. A speech consultant had rated Kahakua's Creole-tinged speech unacceptable for weather broadcasts. The white applicant had no college degree, and minimal experience in meteorology. He was selected because of his "excellent" broadcasting voice. Kahakua, along with other applicants who felt that the promotion of a neophyte constituted discrimination, sued the Weather Service and lost.

* * *

The district judge, a visitor from Fresno, found that race was not a factor in the promotion. The white candidate was selected because he had "better diction, better enunciation, better pronunciation, better cadence, better intonation, better voice clarity, and better understandability." The judge credited the testimony of speech experts that "standard English is that used by radio and TV announcers" and that "standard English pronunciation should be used by radio broadcasters." The court added, "there is no race or physiological reason why Kahakua could not have used standard English pronunciations." The judge discounted the testimony of the linguist who stated that Hawaiian Creole pronunciation is not incorrect, rather it is one of the many varieties of pronunciation of standard English. The linguist, the judge stated, was not an expert in speech.

C.   *More Stories, More Voices*

In 1988, A. L. Hahn, a young Korean American, ran for city council in Santa Clara, California. The editorial page of the San Jose Mercury News, an award-winning California newspaper, recommended against voting for Hahn, in spite of the paper's general agreement with Hahn on the issues. This seemed odd in an editorial that welcomed change and opened with criticism of the "old guard" of "powerful insiders," arguing against candidates with established real estate and institutional ties. Why would a pro-change editor reject a bright newcomer? The editorial stated:

> *We like Hahn, 34, who was born in South Korea and whose positions on controlling growth are much like our own. Unfortunately, we think his heavy accent and somewhat limited contacts would make it difficult for him to be a councilman.*

* * *

III.   THE DOCTRINAL PUZZLE OF ACCENT AND ANTIDISCRIMINATION LAW

This is the doctrinal puzzle presented by these stories:

1. Title VII absolutely disallows discrimination on the basis of race and national origin.

2. A fortiori, Title VII absolutely disallows discrimination on the basis of traits, like accent, when they are stand-ins for race and national origin.

3. Title VII absolutely allows employers to discriminate on the basis of job ability.

4. Communication, and therefore accent, employers will insist, are elements of job ability.

The puzzle in accent cases is that accent is often derivative of race and national origin. Only Filipino people speak with Filipino accents. Yet, within the range of employer prerogatives, it is reasonable to require communication skills of employees. The claim that accent impedes job ability is often made with both sincerity and economic rationality. How, then, should Title VII squeeze between the walls of accent as protected trait and speech as job requirement?

This puzzle is evident in every reported case considering accent and Title VII. The courts recognize that discrimination against a trait that is a stand-in for a protected category is prohibited. An employer who says, "I'm not discriminating against people of color, I just don't want to hire people with dark skin," is in violation of Title VII. The EEOC has found that discrimination against an accent associated with foreign birth is the equivalent of discrimination against foreign birth, relying in part on evidence that it is nearly impossible for an adult to eliminate their natural accent. Even the skilled mimics of new accents frequently overcorrect. That is, they blankelty apply stereotypical traits of the acquired accent, even in circumstances in which native speakers would drop the trait. To acquire natural, unself-conscious, and native-sounding speech with a new accent is a feat accomplished easily only by young children, who are still in the process of language acquisition. Given this near-immutability, discrimination against accent is the functional equivalent of discrimination against foreign origin.

* * *

A second complicating factor is the role of speech in the job. In some jobs—say a 911 operator—speech is a critical and central job function. In other jobs, such as a bricklayer or a graphic artist, speech is helpful but not central to the work. In some cases the employer may want a certain accent because of its prestige value—say a French accent in a French restaurant. The range of reasons for wanting speech clarity will vary with the range of jobs.

* * *

Given the pervasive, unconscious bias against low-status accents, it is reasonable to inquire of employers exactly what they mean when they declare an accent nonfunctional for the job. If they mean consciously or unconsciously "I don't like foreign sounds and neither will my customers," they are arguing that discrimination is a justification for discrimination. This kind of tautology is obviously insufficient to surmount Title VII's prohibition against discrimination.

* * *

IV. WHAT IS SPEECH?

* * *

B. *What is Accent?*

Accent, as used in this Article, refers to pronunciation rather than choice of words. A linguist might break down the lay concept of accent into smaller components of phonology, including intonation, stress, and rhythm. While this Article focuses on accent, much of the analysis is also relevant to dialect, or word choice. There are many dialects of English, some more prestigious than others, providing many opportunities for discrimination.

As feminist theorists have pointed out, everyone has a gender, but the hidden norm in law is male. As critical race theorists have pointed out, everyone has a race, but the hidden norm in law is white. In any dyadic relationship, the two ends are equidistant from each other. If the parties are equal in power, we see them as equally different from each other. When the parties are in a relationship of domination and subordination we tend to say that the dominant is normal, and the subordinate is different from normal.

And so it is with accent. Everyone has an accent, but when an employer refuses to hire a person "with an accent," they are referring to a hidden norm of non-accent—a linguistic impossibility, but a socially constructed reality. People in power are perceived as speaking normal, unaccented English. Any speech that is different from that constructed norm is called an accent.

The unstated norm—the so-called standard American accent—is an odd choice for a norm, because only a minority of citizens speak it. Most speakers of North American English have an accent that reflects their regional affiliations, their ethnicity, or their age. An odd recent phenomenon, the geographically dispersed, upper-middle-class, youth-based accent known as "valley" or "sunbelt-speak" is heard increasingly among law students across the country. Because I grew up in a world in which accents tended to attach to races, it seems odd to me as a teacher to hear my students of different races speaking in this new, youth-based accent. (They might characterize a racist decision, for example, as "ruhley" unfair or "see-oh" ridiculous.)

If almost no one speaks with standard pronunciation—or, as they call it in Great Britain, "received pronunciation"—the claim that standardization is important for comprehension loses some force. Variability is the master rule of spoken North American English, and if variability impedes comprehension, then we are already living in the tower of Babel.

We are not. We understand each other, particularly when we are motivated to do so. One of the interesting lessons of sociolinguistics is that comprehension is as much a function of attitude as it is of variability. Human beings can and do adjust to marked variation in pitch, intonation, and pronunciation in ways that scores of computer engineers working in the fields of fuzzy logic and artificial intelligence have been unable to duplicate. The seemingly simple ability of a tiny child to recognize its own name whether spoken at Mom's pitch or at Dad's, is in actuality a complex feat of comprehension. The magnificent switchboard that converts sound to understanding in the human mind can account for gaps, pauses, variations, and distortions of many kinds.

Thus a twentieth-century North American can listen to the long-dead accents in a Shakespeare play and—after perhaps a moment of disorientation—soon follow the dialogue with ease. A traveler to a new region of English-speakers, after a sometimes hilarious miscue, will understand more and more of the local speech, especially if motivated by the need to get a bite to eat or a moment of human company. We have all, at various times, performed the miracle of comprehension across a vast sea of phonological difference.

The ability to comprehend across variations is accompanied by a clumsy inability to alter speech across variations. Most of us feel noticeably uncomfortable and phony when we try to imitate other accents, and few succeed at the task of acquiring a permanent, unself-conscious, new accent.

When the Beatles were an unknown Liverpool band trying to make it in the new world of rock and roll, they inserted "R's" in their pronunciation in order to sound more American. As the British invasion captured the fancy of young whites in America, it became more acceptable to sound British. By the time the Beatles hit superstar status, they had reverted to the "R" dropping that characterized their working class, British backgrounds. The Sergeant Pepper album—which established the Beatles as musicians destined to go down in popular history as more than just another pretty band—is notably authentic in its "R"-lessness.

Meanwhile, back in the midwest, U.S.A.—land of "R" pronunciation so abundant it appears even in words like "wash"—a young white musician named Bob Dylan regularly dropped "R's" in his singing. He did this not because he wanted to sound British, but because he wanted to sound like his idols—the African Americans who regularly dropped "R's" in their creation of the indigenous American art form known as the blues. The boys from Liverpool had made a characteristic imitator's error of overcorrection. In adding R's prodigiously to their early recordings they ended up sounding more like Pat Boone than like their African American inspiration, Little Richard. Bob Dylan, more sophisticated in his understanding of "R" usage in the United States, knew that in the world of contemporary American music, status moved south in more ways than one. Sounding Black, sounding down in the power hierarchy, sounding blue, was the definition of cool among the truly down, downtown, non-"R" pronouncers.

The view of most sociolinguists, grounded as they are in the field of anthropology, is that accent is a societal and cultural creation. It situates people socially and helps them sort through social contexts. Most of us do this unconsciously—we speak differently at work, at play, to children, to authority figures.

Sitting on my porch in Honolulu one day, I was talking long distance to my friend Barb in California. Because I lived in L.A. as a child, it's easy for me to shift into a voice that matches hers when we talk. Shifting closer in accent to someone we like is a common signal of intimacy. As we spoke, the newspaper girl, a thirteen-year-old Tongan-Samoan immigrant, walked by and I called out a friendly greeting and asked her a question.

"Oh, how cute, you're talking local," Barb said over the phone. I laughed, because I hadn't realized I had made a shift, but Barb recognized the melodic, inquiring intonation of "local" Hawaii talk that was so absent when I was speaking to an L.A. friend. Because she has lived in Hawaii and liked it, the accent had a good connotation for her.

Accents sometimes charm us with difference. Barb and I both laugh over the accent of the man who cuts our hair. His is a marked Italian accent, sometimes incomprehensible to both of us. In the West L.A. shop where he works, his accent adds the cachet of difference that recalls an old

Beverly Hills joke about the patient who refused a local anesthetic, insisting instead on the imported.

At other times accents can repel us. In that same West L.A. salon, I overheard a beautiful stylist complaining to a client in Brooklynese, "I can't stand the way I talk, it sounds so low class." Media stereotyping can make some accents sound ignorant or threatening. These evaluations are imposed, not natural. As much as we may believe that certain accents "just sound better" or "sound so harsh," our judgments are mediated judgments. The evidence suggests there is no such thing as an inherently pleasant accent. What sounds "low-class, vulgar, rough" in one culture can sound "interesting, pretty" to someone from another culture unfamiliar with the status position of the accent.

I cling to certain notions of accent attitudes as pure and not culturally generated. I am fond of saying that the Hawaiian language sounds beautiful, as though this were absolutely true rather than true to my ears, in relation to the English I am used to, and in connection with my knowledge of the generous, loving aspects of Hawaiian culture that infuse the language. Similarly, I am fond of saying that a particular person has a beautiful voice or a sexy voice as though that were absolutely true, rather than true as a convocation of Hollywood, Madison Avenue, Motown, and my own desires.

We want to believe, when we say of an accent that it is good, or bad, or easy, or difficult, that we are speaking of facts rather than social constructions. Facts, especially when the alternative conclusion is that our evaluations are produced by bigotry or our own feelings of fear and inadequacy.

While the sociolinguists tell us that accent is a social phenomenon, some experts in the field called "speech" or "communications" hold quite a different view. Books on accents are typically found in two separate places in the libraries: under Sociolinguistics and under Speech Pathology. In the Speech Pathology section, accent is considered a disease in need of a cure. There, chapters on accent are side-by-side with chapters on stuttering and aphasia. Rather than seeing accent as a social phenomenon marking speakers as equidistant from each other, the speech pathology view sees an "accent" as an unfortunate deviation from a standard. This deviation is at once labeled disease and declared curable with a series of exercises and manipulations. This view persists in spite of the evidence that eliminating one's native accent is nearly impossible for most adults.

The presumption behind the speech pathology view is that variability is harmful, both for the speaker and the community. Private accent-elimination classes now exist in some cities to help immigrants sound "less foreign." Speech consultants help employers pick "good" voices. In the *Kahakua* case, the employer's speech consultant discussed the joys of eradicating an ethnic accent in almost sexual tones. Writing of one Japanese American candidate, she stated:

> [H]e needs specific help in the area of developing good speech habits through deleting "pidgin" from his daily vocabulary in order to

insure that Standard English can become his automatic model. This will take disciplined work by means of professional help, but he should make every effort to receive such help. It is my belief that he would experience a most gratifying surge of renewed self-confidence and pride in his accomplishment.

* * *

The language of "control" and "handicap" is typical of the speech pathology view. In referring to the accent as "pidgin" the speech consultant shows unfamiliarity with linguistic terminology. Pidgin is a broken English that is spoken by non-native speakers. Neither speaker evaluated in the passages above was speaking pidgin when evaluated. Both were lifelong, native speakers of English. They were reading a weather report written in standard English. The horrible handicap, subject to control through disciplined study, was simply the local accent native to most non-whites who grow up in Hawaii.

The linguist's evaluation of speakers in the *Kahakua* case differed notably from the speech consultant's. The linguist found that both speakers used an acrolectal variety of Hawaiian Standard English. That is, their speech was quite close to standard mainland pronunciation with certain phonological features characteristic of Hawaiian Creole speakers, such as occasional substitution of the "d" sound for the "th" sound.

The linguist concluded that both speakers

> speak what a large portion of Hawaiian-born, educated, professional people (e.g. the governor and most state legislators) speak: Hawaii Standard English ... both use an acrolectal and highly intelligible English. The HCE [Hawaiian Creole English] features that are observable are phonetic ones that do mark their identity as non-Caucasians, however, they are not accurately viewed as linguistic deficiencies of any kind. Just as one would not fault the southern accent of former President Jimmy Carter or Jim Lehrer (of the McNeil/Lehrer News Hour). . . .

The linguist thus viewed the accents as acceptable and intelligible, while the speech consultant viewed them as handicaps in need of correction. The linguist's view is supported by research that shows that language variability is inevitable and that moderate accent differences rarely impede communication when listeners are motivated and nonprejudiced. The speech consultant's view is supported by a widely held belief that speech standardization is necessary, good, and attainable, and that accent interferes with intelligibility.

* * *

V.   TOWARD A DOCTRINAL RECONSTRUCTION

* * *

This doctrinal framework is not intended as a complete guide to the intricacies of Title VII as applied to accent cases. Title VII is one of the most litigated of all federal statutes, and the many significant nuances of Title VII litigation are beyond the scope of this piece. Rather, the intent here is to suggest the critical areas of inquiry that must be part of the analysis of any Title VII accent case, and to suggest why and how a conscientious court would conduct such inquiry.

I suggest that courts should consider four separate questions in accent cases:

1. What level of communication is required for the job?

2. Was the candidate's speech fairly evaluated?

3. Is the candidate intelligible to the pool of relevant, nonprejudiced listeners, such that job performance is not unreasonably impeded?

4. What accommodations are reasonable given the job and any limitations in intelligibility?

* * *

A.   *Step One: The Level of Communication Required for the Job*

There are many jobs that people do in silence. In some work places, the level of industrial noise is so high that conversation is impossible. Jobs that rely on visual, manual, and intellectual skills have traditionally comprised the employment of the deaf. The deaf, however, are proving that even jobs that require regular communication can be done by individuals with little or no speech. Our assumption that speech is integral to a job may reflect "hearie" bias.

There are some jobs, however, in which speech is central. Broadcasters and telephone operators, for example, regularly use speech in their jobs.

* * *

The paradigmatic job requiring maximum oral clarity is the 911 operator. Several elements mark the importance of speech in that position:

1. The consequences of miscommunication are grave.

2. Giving and receiving oral communication are a substantial part of the job.

3. The speech interactions are under high stress, where time is of the essence, increasing probability of miscommunication.

4. The interactions are typically one-time calls, such that the caller has little time to adjust in listening and comprehension patterns.

If one or more of these elements is absent, the degree of importance of speech decreases. For example, if time is not of the essence, but clarity of communication is important to avoid grave consequences, forms of communication other than speech—such as writing—may be more appropriate. If interactions are repeated, such that listeners can adjust, again a difference in speech style becomes less of a barrier. Consider, for example, the way in which the regulars at a pier-side fish auction can understand an auctioneer's rapid-fire babble, while newcomers find it incomprehensible.

As one moves farther away from the 911 paradigm, there are a range of jobs in which facility in oral communication is useful but not critical if other job skills are present. Computer programmers, word processors, janitors, dancers, assembly line workers, parking lot attendants, architects, and laboratory technicians, for example, all fall somewhere between the polar opposites of "speech is critical" and "speech is inconsequential."

* * *

In a range of jobs in which speech seems critical—doctor, bank teller, police officer, teacher, lawyer—consideration of the actual job tasks and needs of patients/customers/clients is useful. Is "bedside manner" the equivalent of oral facility? Not necessarily. Some very articulate doctors have weak skills in empathy. Care, concern, and understanding are communicated by nonspeech—posture, eye contact, touch, and taking the time to listen—as well as speech.

* * *

The principle that there are gradations of communication skills required in different jobs was recognized by the Ninth Circuit Court of Appeals in *Nanty v. Barrows*. In that case, the employer refused to hire Mr. Nanty, a Native American, for a job as a furniture mover, claiming, among other things, that Nanty was "inarticulate." That claim alone, without any evidence of why articulate speech was essential for the job, was unpersuasive to the court. The applicant was an experienced furniture mover. The court was suspicious of the claim that Mr. Nanty was inarticulate, especially given the fact that the employer had not even conducted an interview. An employer who is serious about the necessity for oral communication will have some job screening mechanism that rationally measures oral skills. The next section discusses applicant screening and fair evaluation.

B. *Step Two: Fair Evaluation*

An employer who claims speech is a critical job function, but who does not fairly evaluate speech of candidates, is behaving irrationally, or discriminatorily, or both. As Justice Rehnquist suggested in the *Furnco* case, we reasonably presume that economic entities act rationally. When they do not—when they prefer less-qualified applicants, for example—it is probable that prejudice is entering into the process. Evaluation of accent is particularly susceptible to bias and distortion, and thus it is appropriate for courts to examine the evaluation process.

* * *

When we hear a different voice we are likely to devalue it, particularly when it triggers the collective xenophobic unconscious that is the ironic legacy of a nation populated largely by people from other continents. Because misevaluation of speech, and particularly of speech associated with historical targets of discrimination, is common, claims that accent impedes job performance are not credible unless they stem from fair evaluation. An informal answer-a-few-questions interview is less reliable than an evaluation of on-the-job performance, whether simulated or actual. Rather than assuming an accent would be unintelligible over the phone, for example, a candidate might be asked to complete an actual or simulated phone call to see whether breakdowns in communication occur.

Similarly, evaluations that rely on subjective impressions of untrained interviewers are less credible. Interviewers and others making employment decisions can be trained to avoid accent bias. The State of California, for example, has produced a training manual that explains in simple language the danger of bias and prejudice in evaluation of accents.

* * *

C. *Step Three: Comprehension by the Relevant, Nonprejudiced Listener at the Level Required for the Job*

If the employer fairly evaluates the speaker, and if speech is an important job function, then it is reasonable to reject a speaker whose accent impedes intelligibility by the relevant, nonprejudiced listener.

* * *

In public contact jobs, the listener pool is identifiable by region and demography. A bank teller, for example, generally serves clientele from within one city. Having a regional accent, when most of one's clients are from the same region, can enhance rather than impede communication. The point here is that intelligibility is not absolute. It is relational. To whom we speak determines whether our accent helps or hurts communication.

* * *

The testimony of experts familiar with speech interactions in the relevant listener pool is thus entitled to considerable weight in meeting the plaintiff's burden of persuasion. In the *Kahakua* case, the speech pathologist who declared the Creole-accented speech substandard was not from Hawaii, nor did she purport to speak from knowledge of the relevant listener pool. Instead, she used a generic "broadcasting" standard to conclude that a white candidate's accent was superior.

The plaintiff's expert was a linguist whose field of expertise was speech interactions within the relevant listener pool. She testified that the local-accented speech of the plaintiffs was easily intelligible to *all* residents of Hawaii, including white newcomers, and that for the majority of residents who themselves have some level of a local accent, communication was enhanced by speech in that accent.

The court in *Kahakua* apparently applied the speech pathologist's generic standard, rather than the linguist's contextualized standard. The problem with the court's approach is that it imposes a standard on the community without any rationale for choosing the standard. It is not a majoritarian standard, since most Americans speak with an ethnic or regional accent. It is not an intelligibility standard, because there is no evidence that there is a generic accent that is always more intelligible than any other accent in a given listener pool.

The hidden rationale thus becomes a nationalist/monocultural one. That is, holding people in a nation as radically diverse in accents as ours to one standard of pronunciation is a declaration that this is a nation of one voice. In the same way that some insist ours is a Christian nation with Christianity the norm against which all other religions are seen as different, the fiction of a generic American accent implies that this is a white, upper-class nation, and all non-white, ethnic, regional, and lower-class accents are subnormal. Rather than imagining a fictional generic listener, the unbiased court would look to the actual listeners.

* * *

D. *Rejecting the Gift: The Problem of the Prejudiced Listener*

What should we do when members of the relevant listener pool are prejudiced and can't or won't tolerate an accent? In applying Step 3 above, the principles of Title VII require removing prejudiced listeners from analysis of the relevant listener pool.

It is well established under Title VII that bigoted preferences of customers, however real and economically effective, may not govern employment decisions. Even when employers can prove that they will lose customers who prefer not to do business with women, for example, Title VII requires employers to hire qualified women. By holding all employers to this nondiscriminatory standard, Title VII intervenes in the market and disallows an economic advantage to those employers who are otherwise eager to accede to the racist or sexist demands of customers. Title VII was designed to alter business practices in order to eliminate racism and sexism as a factor in hiring, promotion, and setting conditions of work.

* * *

The claim that customers will refuse to do business with employees with ethnic accents raises two problems. First is the problem that customer preference claims are often made without empirical foundation, reflecting false assumptions about the inability of customers to comprehend certain accents. Given the linguistic evidence that comprehension adjustments are relatively easy for motivated listeners, claims of customer preference, at a minimum, should be supported by some evidence of actual refusal to deal.

At the second level is the problem of actual prejudice. Certain accents, to certain listeners, sound "untrustworthy," for example, regardless of the sincerity of the speaker. An employer concerned with establishing customer confidence might be tempted to exclude from the workplace ethnic accents that key customers find untrustworthy. This is not allowed under Title VII. A particular accent sounds untrustworthy, or lazy, or ignorant to a listener when the listener has attached a cultural meaning, typically a racist cultural meaning, to the accent. In matched guise tests, linguists have shown that these cultural meanings rather than any combination of pronunciation or inflection, create the negative impression. Under the matched guise method, listeners hear tapes of the same words spoken by an actor using different accents. The listeners are not told that one person is acting out the different accents. They are then asked to evaluate what they assume are different speakers for qualities such as intelligence, confidence, trustworthiness, and warmth. The use of the same text and same speaker eliminates the role of personality traits or voice quality of the speaker in evaluation. The subjects are also tested separately to determine what racial stereotypes and prejudices they harbor. In repeated studies of this type, there is a high correlation between negative stereotyping of certain races and negative evaluation of accents associated with those races. The listener who thinks X people are lazy will evaluate a speaker with an X accent as lazy. Listeners can even internalize stereotypes about themselves. Members of subordinated groups in one study evaluated speakers of their own accent as "less intelligent" and "more warm" indicating in-group loyalties, as well as internalization of dominant group stereotypes about intellect.

* * *

E. *Step Four: Can the Employee Be Understood with Reasonable Accommodation of Linguistic Difference?*

To determine whether prejudice rather than unintelligibility motivates linguistic discrimination, it is useful to ask whether the employer can make reasonable changes in the workplace that would increase communication within the relevant listener pool. The concept of reasonable accommodation is well developed in the law governing employment of the differently-abled. It asks not that employers go broke in order to accommodate physical differences. Rather, it asks that employers make those alterations which are either costless or impose costs that, while they may cut into short-term returns, will have the long-term benefit of bringing qualified handicapped individuals into the labor force. Wheelchair ramps, braille in elevators, and grab-bars in restroom stalls are all accommodations we have grown accustomed to in recent years. We have made a collective decision that the costs, while not inconsequential, are reasonable in light of the benefits gained.

* * *

There are several specific inquiries that help separate legitimate communication difficulty from biased evaluation. First, as discussed above, expert witnesses can help in identifying the relevant, nonprejudiced listeners, and in determining whether the accent discrepancies are so divergent as to impede communication. Second, accommodations, including assistance to both speakers and listeners in bridging communication gaps, help show that any residual non-understanding reflects a genuine, irremediable intelligibility problem. Finally, the court can inquire into the level of prejudice against the accent. If the accent is one historically subjected to discrimination, for example, this cautions particular scrutiny and special efforts at accommodation in order to avoid the probability of biased evaluations. Again, experts are useful in determining whether there is a demonstrable history of prejudice against a particular accent, and in identifying kinds of phonological differences that actually do impede comprehension.

* * *

G. *Application*

How would the doctrinal reconstruction suggested above apply to the facts of the existing cases? This section will suggest briefly the ways in which the framework of inquiry presented in this Article would have altered the outcome in cases like *Fragante* and *Kahakua*.

1.   Fragante *Reconsidered*

* * * The evaluation of *Fragante* was shoddy. Given the care and effort put into the civil service examination process, the cursory interview by untrained office workers seems an irrational allocation of resources. The interviewers who found Fragante's accent "difficult" did not identify any incidences of misunderstanding during the interview. The lack of standard interview questions, the irrationality of the rating sheet, and the absence in the interview process of training or instruction in either speech assessment or the obligation of nondiscrimination, reveal a weak system of evaluation. This weakness is unjustified given the size and the resources of the employer, and the regular turnover in the job. Significantly, the evaluation process did not include a functional component. That is, Fragante's speech was never tested in a real or simulated job setting. There was no evidence other than presumption that Fragante could not communicate with customers at the DMV.

* * *

The trial judge, as well as the employer's interviewers, found Fragante's accent "difficult." There is no distinction in the trial court opinion between "difficult" meaning "foreign, unusual, a strain on my ears because it is not how most people I know talk," and intelligibility at the level necessary to perform job tasks. The failure to make this critical distinction would, at a minimum, require a remand for clarification. The only legitimate inquiry, given the Title VII rule of nondiscrimination, is whether the speaker can communicate at the level required for the job.

The Ninth Circuit opinion in *Fragante* fails to make this distinction. The court found that there was no proof of discriminatory pretext and that the individuals selected in lieu of Fragante "had superior qualifications." The only "superior qualification" on record is speaking without a Filipino accent. The opinion seems to allow the employer to select a favored accent in lieu of a "foreign" accent. If the intent of the court is to prohibit accent discrimination, clarification is required on this point. The court should state unequivocally that once a person's speech is found functional, the employer may not reject it because a competitor's speech is "less foreign."

* * *

Finally, if the courts had considered the possibility of reasonable accommodation, they might well have altered their ultimate conclusions in *Fragante*. If, as the employer claims, customers are frequently frustrated and confused when they visit the DMV, perhaps there are other alterations to procedures, written information, and staffing, that could ease this burden. If a Filipino accent will "turn off" some listeners, those listeners could, perhaps, be directed to another line, or they could ask for a slower repetition of instructions.

* * *

VII.   Accent and Antisubordination: A Radical Critique

This Article is written out of contradiction, and this part enters the theoretical world that sees contradiction at the core of meaning in life and law. The contradiction in this Article, the irony of it, is that a self-conscious radical, schooled in the postmodern world, argues from cases, rules, and principles for a result that she sees as liberating. That same system of cases, rules, and principles has enslaved and excluded, taken lives and stilled dissent. That same system of cases, rules, and principles has entrenched ideas of objectivity, neutrality, necessity, and right that have made enslavement, exclusion, murder, and oligarchy seem natural and inevitable. These are the teachings of the feminists, critical legal scholars, and critical race scholars who are the voices of dissent in the world of legal theory. These critical voices constitute the community of scholar-activists whom I consider my colleagues in a most-serious quest for a just world. This part is my tribute to them.

It looks at accent discrimination from within that critical world, to try to understand what is really going on in accent cases, and to suggest an explicitly political justification for the doctrinal position set forth above. If the doctrinal section was "do the logical thing," and the preceding section was "do the liberal thing," I add now, not in jest and not because I reject either logic or liberalism, a section to plead, "do the right thing." This Article is an attempt to do legal scholarship using the tools of critical legal analysis. The method of the following sections follows a pattern emerging within such scholarship:

— First, it attempts to unmask false claims of objectivity, merit, neutrality, and necessity in the rhetoric of accent cases;

— Second, it examines the context of power in which accent cases arise, and draws from an emerging phenomenonology of subordination to understand how accent discrimination fits into broader social, historical, and psychological structures of subordination;

— Third, it is explicit, partisan, and non-neutral in its commitment to the ends of dismantling structures of subordination and promoting radical pluralism;

— Fourth, it understands doctrinal puzzles concerning accent and Title VII as cites of contestation with both ideological and material consequences; and

— Finally, it employs a strategy of legal analysis designed to promote both reformist and radical agendas by exploiting existing tensions in civil rights law. More specifically, by delineating a fair and logical application of Title VII doctrine to accent cases, I hope to affect three constituencies:

a. Readers—including judges, lawyers, possible litigants, and legal theorists of goodwill—who are committed to the values I draw upon in this Article but who are unclear about how or whether those values should apply in accent cases;

b. Activists and theorists seeking to form and critique strategies for radical social change; and

c. Gatekeepers of the established order, whom I hope to reveal as self-interested and politically motivated should they choose to reject a logical argument for accent egalitarianism.

A. *Accent and the Critique of Objectivity*

Which accent is seen as normal, intelligent, most-likely-to-succeed, is a function of power distribution. Thus the key inquiry in understanding accent cases is "what are the power distributions." Attempting to apply Title VII without asking that question is what allows courts to suggest that employers can pick the best accent out of many, without seeing that "best" points up the racial hierarchy. Unmasking the hidden center reveals accent evaluation for what it is: an exercise in power.

Seeing accent evaluation as an exercise of power helps refute the typical justifications for excluding or repressing certain accents, which include:

1. *The inherent superiority of the standard accent.* The claim here is that the standard accent is more pure, more eloquent, more expressive, more valuable.

2. *The universality of the standard accent.* Most people speak it and everyone understands it, therefore it is reasonably designated the national standard.

3. *Standardization is efficient.* Even if the standard is somewhat arbitrary, having a standard increases communication among diverse speakers. It reduces misunderstanding and saves time.

4. *The standard is unifying.* Having a standard helps forge a national identity and avoids the balkanizing disarray that comes with language variation.

The concept of positioned perspective, developed by feminists and critical race theorists, and the critique of neutrality associated with Foucault and the critical legal theorists, rejects the idea of a universal measure of accent quality. Add to this critique the empirical work of sociolinguists, and the argument that standard pronunciation is inherently superior and universal disappears. While most people in power speak the standard, the critical technique of challenging false norms as creations of power helps show how the seemingly absolute universality of standard pronunciation is actually an imposed universality.

This leaves the final two arguments of efficiency and unity. The argument that uniformity is efficient presumes that uniformity is attainable and that variability impedes communication. Both claims are historically and empirically false. Uniformity never has been and by all indications never will be the reality of spoken English. Language is a living, moving thing. Linguistic geographers show this graphically in an obscure but fascinating form of cartography that charts the journeys of words and pronunciation over space and time. The names we call things by are born, expand outward gathering more speakers of those names, and die, as other names take over. The word "orts" for scraps of garbage traveled from England to Massachusetts in the time of the colonies, where it thrived and then faded until only one informant in Bar Harbor and one in New Bedford could tell field researchers what it meant. Similarly, "standard pronunciation" varies both regionally in our time and historically over time. The teachers of "correct enunciation" of fifty years ago would hang their heads in sorrow over what passes for correct on Cable News Network today.

   * * *

B.   *What Fear Is This? Accent and the Culture of Domination*

   * * *

When certain accents are deemed inappropriate for the workplace, for political life, for use in schools and boardrooms, a policing of public and private boundaries occurs. Who may speak, when, and where, is a typical mechanism for distributing power. Who is competent to testify in court, who may speak at political meetings, who is an expert authority—answers to these questions stand at the border between the public realm of power and the private realm of the personal.

As it has become increasingly unacceptable to deny public speech on the basis of race or gender, accent becomes a significant means of maintaining boundaries. The recent push for English-only laws, and the attack on bilingual education, may represent new outlets for racial anxiety now that many traditional outlets are denied. The angry insistence that "they" should speak English serves as a proxy for a whole range of fears displaced by the social opprobrium directed at explicit racism.

   * * *

Accents thus construct social boundaries, and social boundaries reinforce accents. The circumstances that perpetuate accents—including residential segregation, tracking systems in schools, and social distancing—are socially created. In distributing social standing according to accent, we distribute according to accents we have, in part, created.

   * * *

C.   *Producing Counter-Ideology: Antisubordination Strategies in Law*

   * * *

Progressive legal theorists seek to include antisubordination ideology in the law through such strategies as affirmative action, reparations, and restriction of hate speech. All of these legal positions recognize that ours is a non-neutral world in which legal attention to past and present injustice requires rules that work against the flood of structural subordination. Anyone who has swum against the tide knows that it requires effort. Staying still means moving backward.

The accent cases illustrate some of what we know about subordination. We know that subordination has material and ideological dimensions. In the case of accent, the material dimensions include the real denial of life chances: jobs, housing, and educational opportunity may depend on talking the right way. Whether one can speak persuasively before the law—before a police officer or a judge or a legislature or a jury—may determine life or death, freedom or jail, protection or neglect. The ideological dimension of accent discrimination is the creation and maintenance of a belief system that sees some as worthy and others as unworthy based on accent, such that disparities in wealth and power are naturalized.

* * *

Immutability arguments feed into this hierarchical ideology. In arguing for accent tolerance, the rationale of accent as immutable is thus a dangerous one. A more progressive argument is that even if accent is changeable, no citizen should have to alter core parts of identity in order to participate in society. A true antisubordination agenda would apply reasonable accommodation to all differences, whether chosen or immutable, that are historically subject to exploitation or oppression by dominant groups.

In arguing that Title VII should prohibit accent discrimination, the more powerful justification is a notion of radical pluralism, not a notion of charitable concern for the immutably afflicted. Indeed, I am coming to see the antisubordination principle and the radical pluralism principle as necessarily linked.

D. *Accent and Radical Pluralism*

* * *

If language is the nest of culture, and cultural diversity is an absolute good, than linguistic tolerance is a legitimate end of the law. Saying this raises questions of how radical pluralism will work in practice as our imaginations call up much that is ugly when we speak of pluralism, including bitter cultural clashes and domination disguised as cultural expression, to name two.

* * *

In summary, the antisubordination rationale for accent tolerance suggests a radically pluralistic re-visioning of national identity. The only center, the only glue, that makes us a nation is our many-centered cultural heritage. Just as our use of language is rich, varied, interactive, and changeable, so is our national culture. We are the only country in which an Okinawan vendor serves Kosher pastrami and stir-fried vegetables wrapped in a tortilla to young white punk rockers at 3:00 a.m. in the morning. We are the only country in which a white child sleeps blissfully under a quilt lovingly stitched by his aunt, emblazoned with a life-sized portrait of an

African American basketball star. We are the only country in which a group of parents planning a little league fundraiser around a transvestite beauty contest would call the ACLU to defend their right to use a public park for the event, and convince a mayor named Hannibal Tavares to change his mind about a permit. From the oversized plaster chickens and donuts that mark our highways to the exquisite wisps of nouvelle Franco-Latin-Japanese cuisine set before our expense-account diners, we are a nation fantastic and wide-ranging in our vernacular and our juxtapositions. From the Grand Ole Opry to neo-metal, from zydeco to the Met, we are a range of tastes and sounds wider than ever before known to the nations of this planet. That is the defining centrality of the American culture I grew up in and love: a broad and delightfully incongruous coming together of difference. In acknowledging plural culture as a strength, and in recognizing and dismantling the false hierarchies that place one culture over another, it may come to pass that we live together in celebration and peace.

E. *To Save Our Own Souls: Law for the Last Reconstruction*

Throughout this Article, I have written to persuade readers of good will to adopt legal rules and ethical positions that promote linguistic pluralism. I have used existing legal doctrine, traditional liberal theory, and new critical theories in this effort. This eclecticism might seem as odd as the kosher burrito and as dangerous as the Ku Klux Klan to those who see impassioned pleas for favored constituencies and eclectic borrowing from many traditions as unprincipled and undisciplined. I believe the antisubordination principle is a principle, and that it can inform our law in a way that is as principled and as disciplined as the ideas of property, equality, and due process that are our constitutional legacy. I have tried to show that accent discrimination is rooted in a culture of dominance fundamentally at odds with the creed of this nation—at odds both with the Enlightenment ideals of liberalism that attended our national birth and the ideal of antisubordination that has constituted the core of our defining struggles against slavery, against fascism, against Jim Crow.

* * *

In suggesting a reconstructed interpretation of Title VII that responds to both liberal and radical critiques, I intended to suggest a model of what law can be and what lawyers can do to work toward justice. The great legal historians of our time have said of Americans that they are users of law. They use it, they believe in it, they constructed a nation around it. Law is part of our culture and it is, therefore, a place to begin in making the changes we need to make.

* * *

VIII. EPILOGUE: VOICES OF AMERICA

* * *

In recounting the tale of the world's many languages coming to America, I have not forgotten that the journey was often hard. We lost most of our native American languages, as we lost their speakers, in a dark part of our history. Also in darkness, the round sounds of West African languages came to America in the bellies of slave ships. Out of pain and poverty, waves of immigrants came from all corners of the earth. Refugees from war came, survivors of persecution came, all came with their tongues and palates shaping newly-learned English words in ways that echoed their years in other places. That is the American accent, the multiplicity of sound bearing the history of our nation, bearing the struggle of its many-voiced people.

————

NOTES AND QUESTIONS

1.   Differences in accents. In her discussion of the accent and the anti-subordination principle, Matsuda argues that the unequal evaluation of differences in accents is directly linked to the frame work of racism and ethnic power relationships. Do you have an accent? What is your accent? Is your accent associated with power and authority in our settings? Consider the complaint of a mafia member's child who was in the witness protection program from New Jersey, to Salt Lake City, then Seattle, and asked to "blend in."

2.   Preference of some accents to others. Matsuda discusses minorities who were discriminated against for having accents. But she also distinguishes between minority accents and those associated with Europeans. She writes that a plaintiff is most likely to be successful with:

> a slight trace of a European accent, but for the most part ... has adopted the speech patterns associated vaguely with North American television newscasters. She is qualified in every other respect for a job that requires some basic communication ability. Speech, is not however, a major job function.

Matsuda, supra at 1351. This suggests that not all accents are created equal. As the case law demonstrates, a large number of the plaintiffs are members of minority groups. Is it safe to say that a Norwegian or Swedish person would be treated differently upon applying for a communication position than a Hispanic or Filipino? According to Sandra Del Valle, language and accent are not separate from national origin. Because of this, an accent easily marks minorities as the "other." *See* SANDRA DEL VALLE, LANGUAGE RIGHTS AND THE LAW IN THE UNITED STATES: FINDING OUR VOICES 144 (2003).

3.   Immutability of accents. Del Valle argues that accents are immutable traits. Foreigners, whether they are Hispanic, European, or Asian, will retain traces of their native origins and language. The immutable nature of accents suggests that it is not a choice when people speak with accents. So, why do courts regard accents differently than they do an Afro? In particular, courts have ruled that employees cannot prohibit Afros because they are an immutable trait of blacks. However, numerous courts have ruled that accents can validly eliminate job applicants from consideration. What concept lies within in the court's distinction? Del Valle asserts that regardless of how vital public speaking is to the position, whenever it is just a small component of the job, courts have allowed employers to eliminate candidates with accents without much debate or question.

4. Can Title VII and the Equal Employment Opportunity Commission interpretation be read as contradictory? As Del Valle argues, Title VII does not ban accent discrimination, but the EEOC bans discrimination based on "cultural or linguistic characteristics." Does that not ban accent discrimination? After all, accents stem from one's cultural background and constitute a linguistic characteristic.

5. The four-pronged test articulated by the Supreme Court in *McDonnell Douglas Corp. v. Green* is not always a clear cut indicator that discrimination can be successfully proven. The Court laid out these requirements to have a *prima facie* case of discrimination:

1. That the plaintiff belongs to a protected class;
2. That he or she applied and was qualified for the position sought or held;
3. That despite such qualifications, he or she was rejected or fired; and
4. that after his or her rejection, the position sought or terminated from either remained open and the employer continued to seek similarly qualified applicants or was filled by equally or less qualified individuals not of the protected group.

See 411 U.S. 792, 802 (1973). The fact that fulfilling the four-pronged test can be insufficient is exemplified by *Fragante*. The employer felt he spoke with a heavy, difficult to comprehend Filipino accent that would be difficult to understand. However, it was noted in court that the plaintiff was only asked to repeat his answer on two occasions. Matsuda, *supra* at 1338, n.28.

B.   ENGLISH-ONLY RULES

Garcia v. Spun Steak Co.
998 F.2d 1480 (9th Cir. 1993).

■ O'SCANNLAIN, CIRCUIT JUDGE, delivered the opinion of the court.

* * *

I

Spun Steak Company ("Spun Steak") is a California corporation that produces poultry and meat products in South San Francisco for wholesale distribution. Spun Steak employs thirty-three workers, twenty-four of whom are Spanish-speaking. Virtually all of the Spanish-speaking employees are Hispanic. While two employees speak no English, the others have varying degrees of proficiency in English. Spun Steak has never required job applicants to speak or to understand English as a condition of employment.

Approximately two-thirds of Spun Steak's employees are production line workers or otherwise involved in the production process. Appellees Garcia and Buitrago are production line workers; they stand before a conveyor belt, remove poultry or other meat products from the belt and place the product into cases or trays for resale. Their work is done individually. Both Garcia and Buitrago are fully bilingual, speaking both English and Spanish.

Appellee Local 115, United Food and Commercial Workers International Union, AFL–CIO ("Local 115"), is the collective bargaining agent representing the employees at Spun Steak.

Prior to September 1990, these Spun Steak employees spoke Spanish freely to their co-workers during work hours. After receiving complaints that some workers were using their bilingual capabilities to harass and to insult other workers in a language they could not understand, Spun Steak began to investigate the possibility of requiring its employees to speak only English in the workplace. Specifically, Spun Steak received complaints that Garcia and Buitrago made derogatory, racist comments in Spanish about two co-workers, one of whom is African–American and the other Chinese-American.

The company's president, Kenneth Bertelson, concluded that an English-only rule would promote racial harmony in the workplace. In addition, he concluded that the English-only rule would enhance worker safety because some employees who did not understand Spanish claimed that the use of Spanish distracted them while they were operating machinery, and would enhance product quality because the U.S.D.A. inspector in the plant spoke only English and thus could not understand if a product-related concern was raised in Spanish. Accordingly, the following rule was adopted:

> [I]t is hereafter the policy of this Company that only English will be spoken in connection with work. During lunch, breaks, and employees' own time, they are obviously free to speak Spanish if they wish. However, we urge all of you not to use your fluency in Spanish in a fashion which may lead other employees to suffer humiliation.

> * * *

In November 1990, Garcia and Buitrago received warning letters for speaking Spanish during working hours. For approximately two months thereafter, they were not permitted to work next to each other. Local 115 protested the English-only policy and requested that it be rescinded but to no avail.

> * * *

Garcia, Buitrago, and Local 115, on behalf of all Spanish-speaking employees of Spun Steak, (collectively, "the Spanish-speaking employees") filed suit, alleging that the English-only policy violated Title VII. On September 6, 1991, the parties filed cross-motions for summary judgment.

The district court denied Spun Steak's motion and granted the Spanish-speaking employees' motion for summary judgment, concluding that the English-only policy disparately impacted Hispanic workers without sufficient business justification, and thus violated Title VII. Spun Steak filed this timely appeal and the EEOC filed a brief amicus curiae and participated in oral argument.

II

As a preliminary matter, we must consider whether Local 115 has standing to sue on behalf of the Spanish-speaking employees at Spun Steak. If Local 115 does not have standing, we will consider the application of the policy only to Garcia and Buitrago, both of whom speak English fluently.

* * * [T]he claim asserted and the relief requested do not require the participation of individual members. Local 115 claims that the policy has a per se discriminatory impact on all Spanish-speaking employees. Further, the union is seeking only injunctive relief on behalf of its members, not damages.

In short, Local 115 has standing.

III

Sections 703(a)(1) and (2) of Title VII provide:

(a) It shall be an unlawful employment practice for an employer—

(1) to fail or refuse to hire or to discharge any individual, or otherwise to discriminate against any individual with respect to his compensation, terms, conditions, or privileges of employment, because of such individual's race, color, religion, sex or national origin; or

(2) to limit, segregate, or classify his employees or applicants for employment in any way which would deprive or tend to deprive any individual of employment opportunities or otherwise adversely affect his status as an employee, because of such individual's race, color, religion, sex, or national origin.

42 U.S.C. § 2000e–2(a). It is well-settled that Title VII is concerned not only with intentional discrimination, but also with employment practices and policies that lead to disparities in the treatment of classes of workers. *See, e.g., Griggs v. Duke Power Co.,* 401 U.S. 424, 430–31, (1970). Thus, a plaintiff alleging discrimination under Title VII may proceed under two theories of liability: disparate treatment or disparate impact. *Watson v. Fort Worth Bank & Trust,* 487 U.S. 977, 986–87 (1987). While the disparate treatment theory requires proof of discriminatory intent, intent is irrelevant to a disparate impact theory. *Id. at 988.* "[I]mpact analysis is designed to implement Congressional concern with 'the consequences of employment practices, not simply the motivation.'" *Rose v. Wells Fargo & Co.,* 902 F.2d 1417, 1424 (9th Cir. 1990) (citations omitted).

A

The Spanish-speaking employees do not contend that Spun Steak intentionally discriminated against them in enacting the English-only policy. Rather, they contend that the policy had a discriminatory impact on them because it imposes a burdensome term or condition of employment exclusively upon Hispanic workers and denies them a privilege of employment that non-Spanish-speaking workers enjoy.

* * *

This case, by contrast, does not fall within the language of section 703(a)(2). While policies that serve as barriers to hiring or promotion clearly deprive applicants of employment opportunities, we cannot conclude that a burdensome term or condition of employment or the denial of a privilege would "limit, segregate, or classify" employees in a way that would "deprive any individual of employment opportunities" or "otherwise adversely affect his status as an employee" in violation of section 703(a)(2). *See Nashville Gas Co. v. Satty*, 434 U.S. 136, 144 (1977) (deprivation of benefits does not fall under § 703(a)(2)). Such claims, therefore, must be brought directly under section 703(a)(1). We have never expressly considered, however, whether disparate impact theory applies to claims under section 703(a)(1), and the Supreme Court has explicitly reserved the issue. *Id.*

* * *

B

To make out a prima facie case of discriminatory impact, a plaintiff must identify a specific, seemingly neutral practice or policy that has a significantly adverse impact on persons of a protected class. *Teal*, 457 U.S. at 446. If the prima facie case is established, the burden shifts to the employer to "demonstrate that the challenged practice is job related for the position in question and consistent with business necessity." 42 U.S.C.A. § 2000e–2(k)(1)(A) (Supp. 1992). In this case, the district court granted summary judgment in favor of the Spanish-speaking employees, concluding that, as a matter of law, the employees had made out the prima facie case and the justifications offered by the employer were inadequate.

1

We first consider whether the Spanish-speaking employees have made out the prima facie case. "[T]he requirements of a prima facie disparate impact case ... are in some respects more exacting than those of a disparate treatment case." *Spaulding v. University of Washington*, 740 F.2d 686, 705 (9th Cir. 1984) (citation omitted). In the disparate treatment context, a plaintiff can make out a prima facie case merely by presenting evidence sufficient to give rise to an inference of discrimination. *McDonnell Douglas Corp. v. Green*, 411 U.S. 792, 802–06 (1973). In a disparate impact case, by contrast, plaintiffs must do more than merely raise an inference of discrimination before the burden shifts; they "must actually prove the discriminatory impact at issue." *Rose*, 902 F.2d at 1421. In the typical disparate impact case, in which the plaintiff argues that a selection criterion excludes protected applicants from jobs or promotions, the plaintiff proves discriminatory impact by showing statistical disparities between the number of protected class members in the qualified applicant group and those in the relevant segment of the workforce. *Wards Cove Packing Co. v. Atonio*, 490 U.S. 642, 650 (1988). While such statistics are often difficult to compile, whether the protected group has been disadvantaged turns on quantifiable data. When the alleged disparate impact is on the conditions, terms, or privileges of employment, however, determining whether the protected group has been adversely affected may depend on subjective factors not easily quantified. The fact that the alleged effects are subjective, however, does not relieve the plaintiff of the burden of proving disparate impact. The plaintiff may not merely assert that the policy has harmed members of the group to which he or she belongs. Instead, the plaintiff must prove the existence of adverse effects of the policy, must prove that the impact of the policy is on terms, conditions, or privileges of employment of the protected class, must prove that the adverse effects are significant, and must prove that the employee population in general is not affected by the policy to the same degree.

* * *

The crux of the dispute between Spun Steak and the Spanish-speaking employees, however, is not over whether Hispanic workers will disproportionately bear any adverse effects of the policy; rather, the dispute centers on whether the policy causes any adverse effects at all, and if it does, whether the effects are significant. The Spanish-speaking employees argue that the policy adversely affects them in the following ways: (1) it denies them the ability to express their cultural heritage on the job; (2) it denies them a privilege of employment that is enjoyed by monolingual speakers of English; and (3) it creates an atmosphere of inferiority, isolation, and intimidation. We discuss each of these contentions in turn.

* * *

a

The employees argue that denying them the ability to speak Spanish on the job denies them the right to cultural expression. It cannot be gainsaid that an individual's primary language can be an important link to his ethnic culture and identity. Title VII, however, does not protect the ability of workers to express their cultural heritage at the workplace. Title VII is concerned only with disparities in the treatment of workers; it does not confer substantive privileges. *See, e.g., Garcia v. Gloor*, 618 F.2d 264, 269 (5th Cir. 1980), cert. denied, 449 U.S. 1113 (1981). It is axiomatic that an employee must often sacrifice individual self-expression during working hours. Just as a private employer is not required to allow other types of self-expression, there is nothing in Title VII which requires an employer to allow employees to express their cultural identity.

b

Next, the Spanish-speaking employees argue that the English-only policy has a disparate impact on them because it deprives them of a privilege given by the employer to native-English speakers: the ability to converse on the job in the language with which they feel most comfortable. It is undisputed that Spun Steak allows its employees to converse on the job. The ability to converse—especially to make small talk—is a privilege of employment, and may in fact be a significant privilege of employment in an assembly-line job. It is inaccurate, however, to describe the privilege as broadly as the Spanish-speaking employees urge us to do.

* * *

c

Finally, the Spanish-speaking employees argue that the policy creates an atmosphere of inferiority, isolation, and intimidation. Under this theory, the employees do not assert that the policy directly affects a term, condition, or privilege of employment. Instead, the argument must be that the policy causes the work environment to become infused with ethnic tensions. The tense environment, the argument goes, itself amounts to a condition of employment.

i

The Supreme Court in *Meritor Savings Bank v. Vinson*, 477 U.S. at 66, held that an abusive work environment may, in some circumstances, amount to a condition of employment giving rise to a violation of Title VII. The Court quoted with approval the decision in *Rogers v. EEOC*, 454 F.2d 234, 238 (5th Cir. 1971), cert. denied, 406 U.S. 957 (1972):

> [T]he phrase 'terms, conditions or privileges of employment' in [Title VII] is an expansive concept which sweeps within its protective ambit the practice of creating a working environment heavily charged with ethnic or racial discrimination. . . . One can readily envision working environments so heavily polluted with discrimination as to destroy completely the emotional and psychological stability of minority group workers.

Although *Vinson* is a sexual harassment case in which the individual incidents involved behavior that was arguably intentionally discriminatory, its rationale applies equally to cases in which seemingly neutral policies of a company infuse the atmosphere of the workplace with discrimination. The *Vinson* Court emphasized, however, that discriminatory practices must be pervasive before an employee has a Title VII claim under a hostile environment theory.

* * *

The Spanish-speaking employees in this case have presented no evidence other than conclusory statements that the policy has contributed to an atmosphere of "isolation, inferiority or intimidation." The bilingual employees are able to comply with the rule, and there is no evidence to show that the atmosphere at Spun Steak in general is infused with hostility toward Hispanic workers. Indeed, there is substantial evidence in the record demonstrating that the policy was enacted to prevent the employees from intentionally using their fluency in Spanish to isolate and to intimidate members of other ethnic groups. In light of the specific factual context of this case, we conclude that the bilingual employees have not raised a genuine issue of material fact that the effect is so pronounced as to amount to a hostile environment. * * *

ii

* * *

We do not reject the English-only rule Guideline lightly. We recognize that "as an administrative interpretation of the Act by the enforcing agency, these Guidelines . . . constitute a body of experience and informed judgment to which courts and litigants may properly resort for guidance." *Meritor Sav. Bank*, 477 U.S. 57 at 65 (internal quotations and citations omitted). But we are not bound by the Guidelines. *See Espinoza v. Farah Mfg. Co., Inc.*, 414 U.S. 86, 94 (1973). We will not defer to "an administrative construction of a statute where there are 'compelling indications that it is wrong.'" *Id.*

* * *

2

Because the bilingual employees have failed to make out a prima facie case, we need not consider the business justifications offered for the policy as applied to them. On remand, if Local 115 is able to make out a prima facie case with regard to employees with limited proficiency in English, the district court could then consider any business justification offered by Spun Steak.

IV

In sum, we conclude that the bilingual employees have not made out a prima facie case and that Spun Steak has not violated Title VII in adopting an English-only rule as to them. Thus, we reverse the grant of summary judgment in favor of Garcia, Buitrago, and Local 115 to the extent it represents the bilingual employees, and remand with instructions to grant summary judgment in favor of Spun Steak on their claims. * * *

REVERSED and REMANDED.

■ BOOCHEVER, CIRCUIT JUDGE, dissenting in part:

I agree with most of the majority's carefully crafted opinion. I dissent, however, from the majority's rejection of the EEOC guidelines. The guidelines provide that an employee establishes a prima facie case in a disparate impact claim by proving the existence of an English-only policy, thereby shifting the burden to the employer to show a business necessity for the rule. *See* 29 C.F.R. § 1606.7(b) (1991) ("An employer may have a rule requiring that employees speak only in English at certain times where the employer can show that the rule is justified by business necessity.''). I would defer to the Commission's expertise in construing the Act, by virtue of which it concluded that English-only rules may "create an atmosphere of inferiority, isolation and intimidation based on national origin which could result in a discriminatory working environment." *Id.* § 1606.7(a).

* * *

It is true that EEOC regulations are entitled to somewhat less weight than those promulgated by an agency with Congressionally delegated rulemaking authority. *General Elec. Co. v. Gilbert*, 429 U.S. 125, 141 (1976). Nevertheless, the EEOC guideline is entitled to "great deference" in the absence of "compelling indications that it is wrong." *Espinoza v. Farah Mfg. Co.*, 414 U.S. 86, 94–95 (1973). While one may reasonably differ with the EEOC's position as a matter of policy, I can find no such "compelling indications" in this case. The lack of directly supporting language in § 703(a)(1) or the legislative history of Title VII, relied on by the majority, does not in my opinion make the guideline "inconsistent with an obvious congressional intent not to reach the employment practice in question." *Id.* at 94.

I conclude that if appropriate deference is given to the administrative interpretation of the Act, we should follow the guideline and uphold the district court's decision that a prima facie case was established. I believe, however, that triable issues were presented whether *Spun Steak* established a business justification for the rule, and I would remand for trial of that issue.

———

Yniguez v. Arizonans For Official English

69 F.3d 920 (9th Cir. 1995), *vacated by* 520 U.S. 43 (1997).

■ REINHARDT, Circuit Judge:

I.

* * *

State employees who fail to obey the Arizona Constitution are subject to employment sanctions. For this reason, immediately upon passage of Article XXVIII, Yniguez ceased speaking Spanish on the job. She feared that because of Article XXVIII her use of Spanish made her vulnerable to discipline.

In November 1988, Yniguez filed an action against the State of Arizona, Governor Rose Mofford, Arizona Attorney General Robert Corbin, and Director of the Arizona Department of Administration Catherine Eden, in federal district court. She sought an injunction against state enforcement of Article XXVIII and a declaration that the provision violated the

First and Fourteenth Amendments of the Constitution, as well as federal civil rights laws.

* * *

II.

* * *

We agree with the district court's construction of Article XXVIII. The article's plain language broadly prohibits all government officials and employees from speaking languages other than English in performing their official duties, save to the extent that the use of non-English languages is permitted pursuant to the provision's narrow exceptions section. * * *

III.

* * *

Arizonans for Official English argues vehemently that First Amendment scrutiny should be relaxed in this case because the decision to speak a non-English language does not implicate pure speech rights. Rather, the group suggests, "choice of language . . . is a mode of conduct"—a *"nonverbal* expressive activity." * * * Accordingly, it compares this case to those involving only "expressive conduct" or "symbolic speech." E.g., *Texas v. Johnson*, 491 U.S. 397 (1989) (burning American flag for expressive reasons); *Tinker v. Des Moines Independent Community School Dist.*, 393 U.S. 503 (1969) (wearing arm band for expressive reasons); *United States v. O'Brien*, 391 U.S. 367 (1968) (burning draft card for expressive reasons). In such cases, the government generally has a wider latitude in regulating the conduct involved, but only when the regulation is not directed at the communicative nature of that conduct. *Johnson*, 491 U.S. at 406.

We find the analysis employed in the above cases to be inapplicable here, as we are entirely unpersuaded by the comparison between speaking languages other than English and burning flags. Of course, speech in any language consists of the "expressive conduct" of vibrating one's vocal chords, moving one's mouth and thereby making sounds, or of putting pen to paper, or hand to keyboard. Yet the fact that such "conduct" is shaped by a language—that is, a sophisticated and complex system of understood meanings—is what makes it speech. Language is by definition speech, and the regulation of any language is the regulation of speech.

* * *

In sum, we most emphatically reject the suggestion that the decision to speak in a language other than English does not implicate pure speech concerns, but is instead akin to expressive conduct. Speech in any language is still speech, and the decision to speak in another language is a decision involving speech alone.

* * *

Arizonans for Official English next contends, incorrectly, that Yniguez seeks an affirmative right to have government operations conducted in foreign tongues. Because the organization misconceives Yniguez's argument, it relies on a series of cases in which non-English-speaking plaintiffs have unsuccessfully tried to require the government to provide them with services in their own language. *See Guadalupe Org. Inc.*, 587 F.2d at 1024 (no right to bilingual education); *Carmona v. Sheffield*, 475 F.2d 738 (9th Cir. 1973) (no right to unemployment notices in Spanish); *Toure v. United States*, 24 F.3d 444 (2d Cir. 1994) (no right to notice of administrative seizure in French); *Soberal-Perez v. Heckler*, 717 F.2d 36 (2d Cir. 1983) (no right to Social Security notices and services in Spanish), *cert. denied*, 466 U.S. 929 (1984); *Frontera v. Sindell*, 522 F.2d 1215 (6th Cir. 1975) (no right to civil service exam in Spanish). These cases, however, hold only that (at least under the circumstances there involved) non-English speakers have no affirmative right to compel state government to provide information in a language that they can comprehend. The cases are inapplicable here.

In the case before us, there is no claim of an affirmative right to compel the state to provide multilingual information, but instead only a claim of a negative right: that the state cannot, consistent with the First Amendment, gag the employees currently providing members of the public with information and thereby effectively preclude large numbers of persons from receiving information that they have previously received. *Cf. Board of Educ. Island Trees Union Free School Dist. No. 26 v. Pico*, 457 U.S. 853, 866–67 (1982). Such a claim falls squarely within the confines of traditional free speech doctrine, and is in no way dependent on a finding of an affirmative duty on the part of the state.

> * * *

If this case involved a statewide ban on all uses of languages other than English within the geographical jurisdiction of the state of Arizona, the constitutional outcome would be clear. A state cannot simply prohibit all persons within its borders from speaking in the tongue of their choice. Such a restriction on private speech obviously could not stand. *Meyer v. Nebraska*, 262 U.S. 390, 401 (1923). However, Article XXVIII's restraint on speech is of more limited scope. Its ban is restricted to speech by persons performing services for the government. Thus, we must look beyond first principles of First Amendment doctrine and consider the question of what limitations may constitutionally be placed on the speech of government servants.

> * * *

Thus, the Court has made it clear that it is the government's interest in performing its functions efficiently and effectively that underlies its right to exercise greater control over the speech of public employees. * * *

In deciding whether to afford constitutional protection to prohibited employee speech, we must consider both the general interest of the public servant in speaking freely, as described in *Perry* and *Rutan,* and the importance to the public of the speech involved. *See Connick*, 461 U.S. at 149 (considering the public's interest in the speech in determining whether to protect it); *Pickering*, 391 U.S. at 571–72 (same). The employee speech banned by Article XXVIII is unquestionably of public import. It pertains to the provision of governmental services and information. Unless that speech is delivered in a form that the intended recipients can comprehend, they are likely to be deprived of much needed data as well as of substantial public and private benefits. The speech at issue is speech that members of the public desire to hear. Indeed, it is most often the recipient, rather than the public employee, who initiates the dialogue in a language other than English. * * *

For example, monolingual Spanish-speaking residents of Arizona cannot, consistent with the article, communicate effectively with employees of a state or local housing office about a landlord's wrongful retention of a rental deposit, nor can they learn from clerks of the state court about how and where to file small claims court complaints. They cannot obtain information regarding a variety of state and local social services, or adequately inform the service-givers that the governmental employees involved are not performing their duties properly or that the government itself is not operating effectively or honestly. Those with a limited command of English will face commensurate difficulties in obtaining or providing such information. * * * Moreover, as we suggested earlier, the restrictions that Article XXVIII imposes severely limit the ability of state legislators to communicate with their constituents concerning official matters. For example, the provision would preclude a legislative committee from convening on a reservation and questioning a tribal leader in his native language concerning the problems of his community. A state senator of Navajo extraction would be precluded from inquiring directly of his Navajo-speaking constituents regarding problems they sought to bring to his attention. So would his staff. The legislative fact-finding function would, in short, be directly affected.

Arizonans for Official English claims, as it and others did when the initiative was on the ballot, that Article XXVIII promotes significant state interests. The organization enumerates these interests as; protecting democracy by encouraging "unity and political stability"; encouraging a common language; and protecting public confidence. We note at the outset that the sweeping nature of Article XXVIII's restriction on public employee speech weighs significantly in our evaluation of the state's alleged interests. In *National Treasury Employees Union,* the Court explained that when the government seeks to defend a "wholesale deterrent to a broad category of expression by a massive number of potential speakers," 513 U.S. at ___, 115 S.Ct. at 1013, its burden is heavier than when it attempts to defend an isolated disciplinary action. *Id.* Thus, we must examine the state's asserted justifications with particular care.

There is no basis in the record to support the proponents' assertion that any of the broad societal interests on which they rely are served by the provisions of Article XXVIII. * * *

Accordingly, the appellants have not demonstrated that the benefits to be obtained outweigh the burdens imposed on First Amendment rights, particularly given the all-encompassing scope of the restriction they seek to defend. *See National Treasury Employees Union,* 513 U.S. at ___, 115 S.Ct. at 1014 (explaining that the government's "burden is greater" in such cases).

We also reject the justifications for even more basic reasons. Our conclusions are influenced primarily by two Supreme Court cases from the 1920s in which nearly identical justifications were asserted in support of laws restricting language rights. *See Meyer v. Nebraska,* 362 U.S. 390 (1923); *Farrington v. Tokushige,* 273 U.S. 284 (1927). *Meyer* involved a Nebraska statute that prohibited the teaching of non-English languages to children under the eighth grade level; *Tokushige,* similarly, involved a Hawaii statute that singled out "foreign language schools," such as those in which Japanese was taught, for stringent government control.

Like the Court in *Meyer* and *Tokushige, we* recognize the importance of (1) promoting democracy and national unity and (2) encouraging a common language as a means of encouraging such unity. *See Guadalupe Organization, Inc., supra.* The two primary justifications relied on by the article's proponents are indeed closely linked. We cannot agree, however, that Article XXVIII is in any way a fair, effective, or appropriate means of promoting those interests, or that even under a more deferential analysis its severely flawed effort to advance those goals outweighs its substantial adverse effect on first amendment rights. As we have learned time and again in our history, the state cannot achieve unity by prescribing orthodoxy. * * * (forced "Americanization" violates American tradition of liberty and toleration). Notwithstanding this lesson, the provision at issue here "promotes" English only by means of proscribing other languages and is, thus, wholly coercive. Moreover, the goals of protecting democracy and encouraging unity and stability are at most indirectly related to the repressive means selected to achieve them. Next, the measure inhibits rather than advances the state's interest in the efficient and effective performance of its duties. Finally, the direct effect of the provision is not only to restrict the rights of all state and local government servants in Arizona, but also to severely impair the free speech interests of a portion of the populace they serve.

    * * *

V.

    * * *

We affirm the district court's judgment that Article XXVIII of the Arizona Constitution is facially overbroad and violates the First Amendment, and that the article is unconstitutional in its entirety. We reverse and remand the district court judgment insofar as it denies Yniguez an award of nominal damages.

Affirmed in Part, Reversed in Part and Remanded.

    * * *

■ Fernandez, Circuit Judge, with whom Chief Judge Wallace and Judges Hall and Kleinfeld join, dissenting:

    * * * Maria–Kelley F. Yniguez does not like Article XXVIII as a matter of policy. I can understand and sympathize with that. It is when she goes

beyond the realm of policy and seeks to show that the Article violates the First Amendment to the United States Constitution that she goes astray. It is there that we part company.

She, in effect, proceeds from the fundamentally flawed assumption that while performing government business an official or employee has much the same freedom as a private citizen. That leads her into a thicket of incorrect assumptions and assertions about the nature of her speech rights, the nature of language, and the rights and duties of the State when it chooses to speak for itself. As a result, she has left the proper analytical pathway and become hopelessly lost in a forest of her own hopes.

* * * Certainly, if the State can require teaching in a particular language, it can itself choose to use a particular language to express the content of what it has to say.

In fine, the people of the State of Arizona did not violate the First Amendment when they adopted Article XXVIII. For good or ill, it was a question "for the people to decide." *Id*.

Therefore, I respectfully dissent.

NOTES AND QUESTIONS

1.   English-only rules as route to socioeconomic mobility? Arizona Representative Dave Carson (R–Prescott) was the key supporter of the bill in 1987. *See* RAYMOND TATALOVICH, NATIVISM REBORN: THE OFFICIAL ENGLISH LANGUAGE MOVEMENT AND THE AMERICAN STATES 131 (1995). Tatalovich, Carson and his supporters argued English-only rules would serve as a positive impetus to draw Hispanics out of the "language and economic ghettoes" of Arizona. *Id*. at 132. The bill's supporters regarded English-only rules as a barrier against social and economic segregation in the state. But, it did not seem to take into account the tools needed when immigrants did not understand English. The notion that English is needed to combat segregation and marginalization is reasonable but it ignores the fact that people need the tools, i.e., English fluency, to participate in the marketplace.

2.   Bilingual education initiatives and counterinitiatives—the first rung on the ladder. In the primary and secondary public school arena, advocates of bilingual education have made the argument that children from homes in which English is a second language will secure the full benefit of educational opportunity only if they are given a graduated educational experience, in which they are taught in both their primary language and English in the same curriculum. The opponents of bilingual education, like the English-only advocates for government communication, insist that English is the official language, and that other languages should be banished to the margins of authoritative discourse.

For an explanation of the dynamics of these two political positions, see Charu A. Chandrasekhar, Comment, *The Bay State Buries Bilingualism: Advocacy Lessons from Bilingual Education's Recent Defeat in Massachusetts*, 24 CHICANO-LATINO L. REV. 4 (2003). Chandrasekhar argues that:

> by a vote of 68 to 32 percent, Massachusetts voters endorsed Question 2, a ballot initiative sponsored by anti-bilingual education activist Ron Unz that eviscerates bilingual education and erodes parents' and teachers' rights. . . . The successful passage in Massachusetts of Question 2 marked another legislative triumph for Unz, who previously crafted Propositions 227 and 203 (successful bills similar to Question 2 banning bilingual education as an instructional method in California and Arizona, respectively).

2. Effectiveness of the EEOC when English-only rules are applied in the workplace. *Garcia* illustrates the success employers can have by enforcing English-only rules. This was especially the case in *Garcia* because the court placed emphasis on the fact that bilingual employees would not be negatively impacted by an English-only rule. In particular, the court argued bilingual employees have the freedom and choice to switch to English while in the workplace. It was noted that only one of Spun Steak's employees did not speak English. The *Garcia* ruling suggests that the EEOC's guidelines cannot be assumed to be automatically applied in English-only environments.

3. Additional reading. *See* Drucilla Cornell & William W. Bratton, *Deadweight Costs & Intrinsic Wrongs of Nativism: Economics, Freedom and Legal Suppression of Spanish*, 84 CORNELL L. REV. 595, 629–34 (1999).

C. CULTURAL PROPERTY

Protecting Folklore of Indigenous Peoples: Is Intellectual Property the Answer?

30 CONN. L. REV. 1 (1997).

■ CHRISTINE HAIGHT FARLEY

INTRODUCTION

What can the Navajos do to prevent non-Navajos from using Navajo rug patterns to produce rugs overseas using cheap materials and labor, thereby undercutting the Navajos themselves in a market for their famous rugs? What can the Australian Aboriginal peoples do when their sacred and secret imagery is reproduced on carpets they did not make, and sold to non-Aboriginals, who will inevitably walk on them? Do these communities have any legal rights to these pieces of their culture? Does the law provide any means for them to take back their culture or to prevent further poaching?

Due to the increasingly widespread commercial appropriation of indigenous images, patterns, designs, and symbols, indigenous rights groups have turned to intellectual property schemes for protection. But indigenous art and folklore present many problems for intellectual property protection, and existing western legal mechanisms may be illsuited to protect certain types of indigenous art.

* * *

[T]he Article begins by recounting a recent incident of commercial use of indigenous art in order to both illustrate the harm caused by this phenomenon and to suggest the challenges in achieving meaningful protection. Part II of this Article describes the particular situation of the indigenous populations and the growing trend toward commercialization and commodification of their art forms. It also explains the particular nature of indigenous art and why this use is so troubling to them. Part III provides an in-depth analysis of the obstacles to copyright protection of folklore, including the duration of the rights, the originality requirement, the fixation requirement, the individual nature of the rights, the fair use exception, the economic focus of the remedies, and considers possible ways of overcoming these obstacles. Part IV evaluates international proposals to develop *sui generis* rights to protect folklore. Part V appraises the possibility of coupling copyright with other laws to achieve protection of folklore. It analyzes moral rights, public domain statutes, and unfair competition laws. Finally, Part VI assesses these strategies with regard to the particular motivations of the indigenous peoples and concludes that the existing intellectual property regime is well-suited to protect those groups who want to participate in and control the marketing of their arts and crafts. But for those who want to preclude any use of their imagery, the existing intellectual property regime is deficient. Application of intellectual property laws, whose underlying logic is to facilitate dissemination, is fundamentally inappropriate to prevent sacred indigenous images from circulation and re-use.

I.   A CASE OF PIRATING CULTURAL HERITAGE

The Australian carpet incident alluded to earlier presents an excellent illustration of the harm caused by the commercial poaching of indigenous art. In 1991, Mr. Bethune, an Australian entrepreneur, went into the business of importing hand-knotted, wool carpets into Australia. After a failed attempt to sell carpets with traditional Oriental designs, he decided to have Australian Aboriginal designs reproduced on the carpets, which he thought would generate more interest. After selecting ten designs from reproductions of Aboriginal artists' paintings, Bethune instructed a factory in Vietnam to produce carpets copying these designs, only making them "less busy." In all, he had 266 carpets manufactured. These carpets were sold for up to $4,252 each. Each carpet was affixed with a swing tag that read:

> These unique wall hangings and rugs have been designed by Aboriginal artists from areas throughout Australia. These artists are

paid royalties on every carpet sold.... As carpet weaving is not a tradition of the Aboriginal people, the rugs are produced in Vietnam where we can combine the artistic skills of the Aboriginal people with the weaving traditions of the Vietnamese.... [W]e have achieved a blending of the talents of these peoples to produce original artistic creations. Each carpet is a unique piece of art.

But Bethune had no agreement with the Aboriginal artists whose paintings he copied. He neither had their authorization to reproduce the designs, nor did he pay them any royalties.

* * *

The artists whose paintings were copied sued Bethune, his company, and its two directors in federal court for copyright infringement. They claimed they had a valid copyright in the paintings and that Bethune had violated their exclusive rights under the Australian Copyright Act. The court agreed, and *Milpurrurru v. Indofurn Pty. Ltd.* became the first case in which a court declared that Aboriginal artists must be compensated for the unauthorized use of their art. This case was seen as a big victory for Aboriginal peoples and as marking the end to the continued pilfering of their heritage. But has it solved the problem? Although the indigenous artists were able to assert copyright successfully, its requirements may still pose problems for other indigenous works. In addition, other copyright problems that are not present in this case have yet to be overcome.

II. The Uses and Abuses of Indigenous Art

The *Milpurrurru* case is not an isolated example. Instead, it is indicative of a trend. Over the last decade there has been a proliferation of reproductions of indigenous peoples' artworks. Increasingly, indigenous designs are being appropriated and used commercially throughout the world. Technological advances have only fanned this fire. Indigenous motifs are used to sell everything from Japanese automobiles like the Mazda Navajo to Barbie dolls to back-to-school clothes. Indigenous art has been reproduced and sold as art reproductions and as craft items, but more commonly it has been reproduced and sold as cheaper commodities, such as T-shirts, tea towels, and other souvenirs. Indigenous art has also been reproduced and used in advertising and marketing. Thus we are seeing indigenous designs more often and in new contexts.

* * *

Significantly, nearly all of these reproductions are unauthorized. Most are reproduced without so much as a request for permission. The consequence is that the indigenous peoples who created the art are not being compensated for its use. Another consequence is that indigenous communities are not exercising control over how their art is being used. This lack of control means that they cannot refuse to have their work put to particular uses and that they cannot ensure that their work is reproduced in a way that maintains its integrity or the reputation of the creator. To better understand the consequences of this unauthorized use, we need to better understand the traditional place of art in indigenous communities.

A. *The Nature of Indigenous Art*

Art is central to the practice of religion in most indigenous communities. Most spiritual rituals involve visual displays, dance, and/or music and song. In the words of one well-known Aboriginal artist, "In song and dance, in rock engraving and bark painting we re-enact the stories of the Dreamtime, and myth and symbol come together to bind us inseparably from our past, and to reinforce the internal structures of our society."

* * *

Often, due to the spiritual connections to art, a song, dance, or image may be reserved for special ceremonies. Often "certain works of folklore ... cannot be shown, nor can the themes in them be disclosed, except to those few who have been admitted to knowledge of ritual secrets and mysteries by undergoing initiation or other special ceremonies" due to the sacred nature of the work. Only members of the community who have achieved a certain level of initiation may be permitted to observe these rituals. Thus, the "law of art" will also dictate who may see these images and dances and who may hear these songs.

* * *

B. *The Poaching of Indigenous Culture*

The theft of cultural symbols and art must be placed in historical perspective to grasp its implications fully. Many would agree that the survival of indigenous folklore is threatened. For the indigenous communities, the theft of their folklore represents the final blow to their civilization from "invaders." It is simply an extension of the plunder mentality. It signifies "that culture is open to pillage in the same way that Aboriginal lands and resources have been for over 200 years. Survival for indigenous peoples the world over is not merely a question of physical existence, but depends upon maintaining spiritual links with the land and their communities." Protection of their culture has become recognized as a fundamental human right.

* * *

III.   COPYRIGHT PROTECTION FOR FOLKLORE

Over the last few decades there has been an outcry in the United States, Canada, and Australia for governments to do something to protect indigenous communities from the poaching of their artworks. Naturally, indigenous peoples and advocacy groups are concerned about this problem and have sought legal avenues of redress. In an effort to prevent the appropriation and manipulation of their cultural images and texts, indigenous peoples, fighting for their cultural survival, are increasingly turning to intellectual property laws to protect their cultural heritage from external poaching. Significantly, indigenous groups are willing to participate in the western intellectual property rights scheme from which they feel they have been excluded and therefore disadvantaged. They have invoked intellectual property laws to use as a shield to prevent further intrusions into their already pillaged culture.

* * *

What to the consumer market may look like the same problem actually involves two different sets of concerns. First, some indigenous peoples want to be able to benefit from the economic rights provided by intellectual property laws. They want to be compensated for their contribution to the artwork through licensing, and they want to exclude non-indigenous competitors from the market by preventing unauthentic products from being marketed as made by indigenous people. Assuming that the circulation of indigenous art is inevitable, some indigenous artists want to be sure to participate in this celebration of indigenous culture. By gaining control over the circulation of their imagery, they want to ensure that the public gets an accurate account of indigenous culture and that the investment in that culture goes back to their communities. These concerns are illustrated in the first example described at the beginning of this Article involving the use of the Navajo rug patterns. Perhaps a subset of this group is the individual artists who want to be able to draw on and develop the imagery of their ancestors in a way that may lead to commercial success. Throughout this Article, I will refer to this first group as the "realist group."

But the second set of concerns is more profound. Some indigenous peoples also want to use intellectual property laws to prevent what may be characterized as a cultural or psychological harm caused by the unauthorized use of their art. They see intellectual property laws as offering a means to control the circulation of their art. * * *

It is said that indigenous communities are vulnerable to this kind of theft because their artworks do not enjoy comprehensive protection under existing intellectual property regimes. Unfortunately, this claim has been made without supporting analysis. Most commentators begin with the normative question of whether indigenous art should be protected with intellectual property laws. Few even get to the descriptive question of whether or not indigenous art is protected by simply assuming that it is not. By beginning from the standpoint that indigenous art should be protected by intellectual property laws, and by accepting that it is not currently protected based on generalized notions of the originality of indigenous works as a unified group, commentators have failed to understand how indigenous peoples will best be able to meet their needs. Thus this Article will now proceed to that descriptive level and analyze whether some indigenous art is excluded from protection under existing intellectual property laws, whether the protection intellectual property laws offer is adequate and appropriate, or whether intellectual property laws must be reformulated to accommodate the unique challenges that folklore poses.

Of all the existing legal mechanisms, copyright law initially appears to be the best suited to protect indigenous folklore. Copyright law is a logical choice because copyright law is designed to protect artistic works from unauthorized reproduction. Likewise, indigenous groups are seeking to control the reproduction of their paintings, songs, and dances. Why shouldn't copyright law protect indigenous art? Indigenous artists feel that they should be protected to the same extent as non-indigenous artists. In one article, a well-known Aboriginal artist argued that Aboriginal artists should be accorded "the same recognition [as non-Aboriginal artists], that our works be respected and that we be acknowledged as the rightful owners of our own works of art." Thus the question arises as to whether copyright law is capable of accommodating this art form and satisfactorily meeting the needs of the community.

The copyright doctrine, however, presents a myriad of barriers to the full protection of indigenous art and folklore. These barriers include the duration of the protection, the originality requirement, the fixation requirement, the individual nature of the rights, the fair use exception, and the economic focus of the remedies. Each of these barriers will be analyzed in turn to understand whether they are preclusive or whether they can be overcome.

A. *The Duration of the Rights*

The first problem of affording copyright protection to folklore is the term of protection. In all Berne Convention member states, the term of the protection is the life of the author plus fifty years. In addition to the problem of identifying a particular author by whose life the term may be measured, the more significant problem is that the term is insufficient. Many indigenous rights advocates argue that perpetual protection should be granted to folklore because "the protection of the expression of folklore is not for the benefit of individual creators but a community whose existence is not limited in time." Even assuming that works would be protected, say, for one hundred years as an unpublished anonymous work, that period is still insignificant in the life of artistic traditions that date back thousands of years. One hundred years from now, indigenous peoples will not want to release their sacred texts to the outside to be exploited. Thus, this term of protection is insufficient for the "traditional group." It is also inadequate for the "realist group." This limited term of protection means that most folkloric works may already be in the public domain and may therefore be used without authorization. Therefore, the "realist group" will not be able to prevent outsiders from copying their works or their basic underlying symbols.

* * *

B. *The Originality Requirement*

The second barrier to the protection of folklore is that copyright law requires that a work be original to be eligible for protection. As the U.S. Supreme Court pronounced in its most recent decision concerning the subject matter of copyright: "The sine qua non of copyright is originality." And, indeed, American (and Continental) copyright law is premised on the concept of authorship and the concomitant notion of originality. The Copyright Act provides protection only to "original works of authorship."

* * *

Still, this requirement may present problems for folklore. Folkloric work is most often ancient, many of the art forms having been developed generations ago. Australian Aboriginal art, for instance, "draw[s] upon custom and tradition" and "represent[s] a ... continuation of ... time-honoured myths and legends." Although folklore can be entirely new, it is most often directly derived from preexisting works. Folklore is the product of a slow process of creative development. It is not stagnant, but evolves slowly.

* * *

Therefore, to protect folklore adequately, copyright would need to be extended "beyond the borders of originality." Furthermore, because the underlying work is unprotected, an outsider could adapt a public domain work and copyright her new translation, thereby obtaining a monopoly over the use of those designs. This would obviously be very problematic for indigenous groups.

* * *

C. *The Fixation Requirement*

Often it may be an outsider who first fixes an indigenous work in a tangible medium—a documentary film maker who videotapes a ritual, or a researcher who notes the steps of a dance, or a musician who writes down the words or notes of a song for the first time. These persons, however, are not the authors, and therefore not the initial copyright owners just as a stenographer is not the "author" for copyright purposes of what he or she transcribes. Under the copyright doctrine, the author is the party who actually "creates" the work. The "fixer" is the author in only the original expression that originates with her. That is, the film-maker is the author of the film, not of the underlying dances or music that she captures on film. Furthermore, the U.S. Copyright Act, for example, requires that the work be fixed "by or under the authority of the author." So, unauthorized fixation will not result in copyright, nor will it preclude indigenous artists from thereafter fixing and copyrighting the work.

* * *

D. *Group Rights*

The fourth problem for the application of copyright to folklore is more fundamental. Copyright law is premised on individual rights, and recognizes group rights only in limited situations. At its core, copyright is intended to reward individual authors for their creation of intellectual property. Indigenous art, in contrast, is not thought to be owned by the particular artist who created it. Instead, it is seen as the property of the group or clan. That is, it is something passed down through the generations for the enrichment of all.

* * *

This custom poses a problem for copyright law since copyright law vests the rights in the one who executes the work. It is this owner alone who has the exclusive right to reproduce the work. But this formulation is contrary to indigenous custom where the art is seen as something owned by the community.

* * *

Three mechanisms in copyright law could be utilized to attempt to overcome this problem: (1) joint authorship; (2) the transfer of rights; and (3) the work made-for-hire provision. These mechanisms may, however, in the end, be unsatisfactory. The most logical possibility is the provision for joint authorship. This provision is the only nod to collective ownership in the acts. It allows the multiple authors of a work to be co-owners of the copyright in the work. Unfortunately, this provision is very narrow. In order to be deemed a joint author, two requirements must be satisfied. First, the joint authors must in fact collaborate in the work's preparation, and second, they must intend, at the time the work is prepared, that their contributions be merged into "inseparable or interdependent parts of a unitary whole." Thus, under the first requirement, joint authorship vests the rights only in the persons who actually make the work (or their designees). That is, only those clan members who are involved in the creation of the work can be joint authors. The rest of the clan or community could not be considered co-owners unless they actually contributed to the creation of the work. Furthermore, to be a joint author each person's contribution must be copyrightable. Thus, a clan elder who dictates the composition to an artist who executes it will not be a joint author with the artist.

* * *

E.   *Fair Use*

Under most copyright regimes, the monopoly on speech that the law permits is balanced by a provision that allows the unauthorized use of a copyrighted work where that use is fair—the so-called "fair use" exception. Whether or not an unauthorized use is deemed fair is determined on a case-by-case basis by considering various factors such as the purpose of the use, the nature of the copyrighted work, the amount of the copyrighted work used, and the effect of the use on the value of the copyrighted work. Thus, where a copyrighted work is used for comment or criticism or for an educational purpose, the author of the work may not be able to preclude its use.

* * *

In all instances, the nature of the copyrighted work also makes a harder case for fair use because creative works are thought to deserve more protection than informational works. Even though most indigenous art is used to communicate information to the community, as in the case of art that depicts creation stories, the work itself will still be judged to be creative. Original songs, dances, and paintings, unlike most databases, have a creative element that is impossible to separate from their underlying facts. That is, it is impossible to take only the information about the creation without also taking the design or expression. Moreover, courts are more prone to protect works that are not yet published. Thus, where unpublished sacred texts are used, it will mitigate against a finding of fair use.

* * *

F. *Damages*

Lastly, some copyright laws may not provide adequate remedies for the unauthorized use of indigenous art. Surely, injunctive relief and the impounding and destruction of infringing works would be helpful. However, the threat of injunctions and destruction of infringing goods may not be enough to deter individuals and companies from using indigenous art without authorization. Damages may be the only way to ensure that outsiders will respect the copyright in indigenous art. For instance, a small company that manufactures infringing T-shirts at a profit may deliberately do so, knowing that the worst that can happen is that it may be ordered to cease at some point. If it were threatened with surrendering its profits, it might not embark on that plan.

Recovering significant damages, however, may not be possible for infringement of indigenous art. Under some copyright laws, only actual damages are awarded for economic harm caused by infringement. The "realist group" will not be negatively affected by this regime since it will be able to show economic harm. But the "traditional group" will fare worse. Where indigenous art would never be put to a economical use by the copyright owners, it may not be possible to prove that the infringement caused any economic loss. That is, where a work is a sacred text, reproduction of which would never be allowed for commercial gain, an infringing use of their work would not deprive the copyright owners of any financial gain. Thus, the true harm done to the copyright owners—the denigration and release of sacred texts—would go unpunished, although it would be halted. This lack of punishment may not adequately deter future infringements.

* * *

IV. International Proposals

* * *

B. *Model Law on Copyright*

The Tunis Model Law on Copyright (1976) was written to provide a model for developing countries to enact comprehensive copyright legislation. This model act explicitly refers to folklore at several places "because in developing countries national folklore constitutes an appreciable part of the cultural heritage and is susceptible of economic exploitation, the fruits of which should not be denied to those countries." In Section 6(2) the act provides that "[w]orks of national folklore are protected by all means in accordance with subsection (1), without limitation in time." Thus it seems that the protection of folklore is perpetual under this act. There is, however, no mention of retroactivity of protection. Therefore, although newer works will be protected forever, much folklore will already be in the public domain.

* * *

C. *Model Provisions*

* * *

The Model Provisions enable the collective ownership and control of folklore, grant perpetual protection, and do not require fixation. The major tenet of the Model Provisions is that utilizations of folklore are subject to authorization by the competent authority "when they are made ... with gainful intent and outside their traditional or customary context." According to the Working Group on the Intellectual Property Aspects of Folklore Protection, three criteria should be used to determine whether a use is unauthorized: (1) whether the intent is gainful; (2) whether the use was made by members or non-members of the community where the expression is derived from; and (3) whether the use is outside of the traditional context of the usual use.

* * *

D. *The Mataatua Declaration*

In June 1993, over 150 representatives from indigenous populations of fifteen countries convened in New Zealand for the first International Conference on Cultural and Intellectual Property Rights of Indigenous Peoples. There they passed The Mataatua Declaration on Cultural and Intellectual Property Rights of Indigenous Peoples. The Declaration states that existing intellectual property regimes are inadequate to the needs of indigenous peoples and calls for, among other things, new intellectual property mechanisms that provide for collective ownership, retroactive coverage of historical works, protection against debasement of culturally significant items, and multigenerational coverage span. Moreover, the Declaration urges indigenous peoples to define for themselves their own intellectual property and develop a code of ethics that outsiders must observe when interacting with that property. This document thus identifies the key challenges in reconciling the copyright regime with the needs of the indigenous community. However, because it is more a call to action than a proposal, it offers little guidance as to how to achieve a reconciliation. Unfortunately, no action has been taken in response to this declaration thus far.

V. Stretching the Boundaries of Copyright Law

Another possibility in the protection of folklore may be to look beyond copyright law. Without reformulating the copyright law, it may be that the law, when coupled with other rights, provides sufficient protection to folklore. The following mechanisms may provide a means to stretch and strengthen copyright law's protection of folklore.

A. *Moral Rights*

Moral Rights, although distinct from economic rights, are usually grouped in with copyright. Moral Rights basically consist of the rights of divulgation, paternity, and integrity. These rights, which are usually inalienable, allow artists to protect their artwork from being denigrated. Indigenous artists may be protected under this doctrine from having their work first published without their authorization, published without attribution, reproduced in poor quality, reproduced only partially causing the message to be distorted, or put to a use which would be inappropriate to the nature of the original work.

* * * The term of protection may also be a problem for folklore, as protection may be extinguished upon the death of the author, or after a set time. The indigenous community, however, would want to ensure the integrity of the work beyond this limited time since it is the community's interest in the work and not the reputation of the artist with which they are concerned. The community's interest in the work is perpetual. On the other hand, moral rights, if applied too zealously, may frustrate the interests of the "realist group" by protecting sacred imagery from any commercial exploitation.

B. *Public Domain Statutes and Domaine Public Payant*

Public Domain statutes basically provide moral rights in perpetuity. Public Domain legislation is intended to "prevent or sanction use of public domain works in such a way as to prejudice their authenticity or identity." Public domain works can be used as the basis of derivative works so long as the use does not violate the work's essence, cultural value, or reputation. Thus, this scheme appears to provide the appropriate safeguard to the indigenous community's cultural interests, especially those who want to protect sacred imagery. Protection is extended, however, only to works whose copyright protection has expired and to works that would have qualified for copyright protection had the legislation existed at the time they were created. For these reasons, folklore will have the same difficulties that it does with copyright law. Namely, the originality and fixation requirements may prevent it from enjoying protection. Furthermore, authority to control public domain works rests with a designated state agency. Public Domain legislation therefore does not present the problem of individual ownership for indigenous peoples, but it may be problematic to have the state exercise this degree of control over indigenous folklore, especially where the state is not representative of the indigenous community.

* * *

C. *The Law of Unfair Competition*

Combining copyright protection with an additional source of intellectual property protection may be a means of providing adequate protection to folklore. Trademark law may provide additional protection against some kinds of unauthorized copying.

In the United States, Canada, and Australia, indigenous arts and crafts have faced competition in their market from cheaper imitations made by non-indigenous persons, often from overseas. The problem is that as soon as any of their art forms gains popularity with the general public, the market is flooded with imitations. Each of these governments has taken special measures to ensure the authenticity of indigenous products.

In the United States, for example, the Indian Arts and Crafts Act of 1935 was enacted to protect Native American Arts and Crafts. The Act attempts to assure authenticity of Native American works by issuing certification marks * * *. The Act provides civil and criminal penalties for counterfeiting the Board's marks and for misrepresenting the works as "Indian made." The Act, however, appears to be "only a paper tiger" since there has never been a single prosecution in the history of the Act. In fact, after more than sixty years on the books, the Interior Department has not even promulgated any regulations for its enforcement.

* * *

Another possible means of supplementing copyright law's protection is through general unfair competition laws. Unfair competition laws are designed to protect consumers and competitors from the misrepresentation of products on the market. Indigenous groups may use these laws to prevent outsiders from marketing goods as "Indian made" or as being produced on indigenous lands. Trademark law has the advantage of granting rights collectively and of providing perpetual protection. To gain protection under these laws, however, folklore must qualify as a commercial good or service. Some aspects of folklore, however, such as rituals or dance, may not generally qualify as commercial activities. Thus this law would benefit the first group of concerns more than it would the second.

* * *

VI.   Arriving at the Normative Question

Finally, with the benefit of an analysis of the extent to which indigenous art and folklore are currently protected by intellectual property regimes, we can now ask the normative question: Should indigenous art and folklore be protected by intellectual property regimes? The answer to this question should not be assumed. Along with it one might ask: What are the implications of the application of existing intellectual property laws to folklore? Stated otherwise, what are the consequences of fitting folklore into the existing scheme?

One consequence is that these artistic traditions will be forced to conform to a set of assumptions that are at odds with their traditions. The underlying rationale of intellectual property law privileges individual ownership, economic exploitation, and the dissemination of new expressions of ideas. Intellectual property rights are driven by the economics of free enterprise and profit. The objective is the creation of a limited monopoly right as an incentive for individuals to disseminate their original expressions. However, indigenous art, especially in its sacred forms, is not something that can be owned by any individual, is not something that should be commercially exploited, is not something that can be freely disseminated, and is not something that can be reinterpreted or adapted. These works, which are often sacred in nature, are unlike the types of works anticipated by the copyright law and may require different types of protections. Thus, in some cases, indigenous groups may seek to use intellectual property laws, which imply dissemination, to withhold the circulation of their art. Although they may use the intellectual property regime to get partial protection, they are using it for a purpose that is alien to it.

* * *

CONCLUSION

* * *

The first revelation that the analysis unveils is that those indigenous peoples who want to gain control of their imagery in order to participate in its circulation are, in fact, adequately protected by the existing legal regime. Certainly their protection could be strengthened, but anything more may inhibit free expression and upset the delicate balance that the copyright law has achieved. To the extent we want to grant special protection to these works, this goal may be better achieved through unfair competition law.

———

NOTES AND QUESTIONS

1. Copyright law as a Western concept. Copyrights are widely used in Western countries to protect artists' creations and works but this does not easily translate to indigenous cultures. *See* Dieter Dambiec, *Protecting indigenous peoples' folklore through copyright law, available at* http://www.proutworld.org/features/copyrightindigen.itra (1999). According to Dambiec, copyright law does not easily apply in indigenous cultures because of the differences in the concept of ownership. Western cultures tend to think of ownership in individual terms while many indigenous cultures think in terms of community ownership. An intriguing argument on this point can be found in MICHAEL I. BROWN, WHO OWNS NATIVE CULTURE, Harvard University Press (2003).

2. Questions of identity and ownership. Another important issue in indigenous folklore is identification of the artists and ownership. Unlike Western cultures, it is not as easy to identify work that may have been created hundreds of years ago in indigenous communities. Some works contain the contribution of a successive groups of artists, whose work accumulates overtime in a serial dynamic process of revision and change. Dambiec says that New Zealand's Maori society has assumed ownership of tribal creations through various levels, meaning different people in the tribe control specific aspects of the creations. This is a possible avenue in giving ownership to indigenous tribes in a manner that allows community ownership and participation.

3. **Moral rights or copyrights?** As Dambiec argues, copyrights are often insufficient when dealing with indigenous culture and folklore. Because of this, a viable solution could be to merge the moral and legal to best meet the needs of indigenous cultures. According to Dambiec, moral rights comprise three types of rights: the power to control the publication or dissemination of a work; the right to have the artist's or tribe's name associated with the work; and the right to prevent misuse, mutilation or distortion of a work. *See* Dambiec, *supra* at 847, n.1. Because of the various issues involved in ownership and folklore culture, the most viable means of compensating indigenous peoples is to merge Western and indigenous concepts to best protect their interests. Obviously, the Western concept of ownership and copyright is often insufficient to address indigenous people's concerns, just as their ideas of ownership and identity are often dismissed in the Western legal system.

D.　BUSINESS–LIKE IMAGE

Rogers v. American Airlines, Inc.

Southern District of New York, 527 F.Supp. 229 (S.D.N.Y. 1981).

■ JUDGE SOFAER delivered the opinion of the court:

Plaintiff is a black woman who seeks $10,000 damages, injunctive, and declaratory relief against enforcement of a grooming policy of the defendant American Airlines that prohibits employees in certain employment categories from wearing an all-braided hairstyle. Plaintiff has been an American Airlines employee for approximately eleven years, and has been an airport operations agent for over one year. Her duties involve extensive passenger contact, including greeting passengers, issuing boarding passes, and checking luggage. She alleges that the policy violates her rights under the Thirteenth Amendment of the United States Constitution, under Title VII of the Civil Rights Act, 42 U.S.C. § 2000e et seq. (1976), and under 42 U.S.C. § 1981 (1976), in that it discriminates against her as a woman, and more specifically as a black woman. She claims that denial of the right to wear her hair in the "corn row" style intrudes upon her rights and discriminates against her.* * *

[The court dismissed the plaintiff's Thirteenth Amendment claim]. The [motion to dismiss] is also meritorious with respect to the statutory claims insofar as they challenge the policy on its face. * * * The policy is addressed to both men and women, black and white. Plaintiff's assertion that the policy has practical effect only with respect to women is not supported by any factual allegations. Many men have hair longer than many women. Some men have hair long enough to wear in braids if they choose to do so. Even if the grooming policy imposed different standards for men and women, however, it would not violate Title VII. * * * The complaint does not state a claim for sex discrimination.

The considerations with respect to plaintiff's race discrimination claim would clearly be the same, see *Smith v. Delta Air Lines*, 486 F.2d 512 (5th Cir. 1973), except for plaintiff's assertion that the "corn row" style has a special significance for black women. She contends that it "has been, historically, a fashion and style adopted by Black American women, reflective of cultural, historical essence of the Black women in American society." * * * "The style was 'popularized' so to speak, within the larger society, when Cicely Tyson adopted the same for an appearance on nationally viewed Academy Awards presentation several years ago. * * * It was and is analogous to the public statement by the late Malcolm X regarding the Afro hair style. * * * At the bottom line, the completely braided hair style, sometimes referred to as corn rows, has been and continues to be part of the cultural and historical essence of Black American women." * * * "There can be little doubt that, if American adopted a policy which foreclosed Black women/all women from wearing hair styled as an 'Afro/bush,' that policy would have very pointedly racial dynamics and consequences reflecting a vestige of slavery unwilling to die (that is, a master mandate that one wear hair divorced from ones historical and cultural perspective and otherwise consistent with the 'white master' dominated society and preference thereof)." * * *

Plaintiff is entitled to a presumption that her arguments, largely repeated in her affidavit, are true. But the grooming policy applies equally to members of all races, and plaintiff does not allege that an all-braided hair style is worn exclusively or even predominantly by black people. Moreover, it is proper to note that defendants have alleged without contravention that plaintiff first appeared at work in the all-braided hairstyle on or about September 25, 1980, soon after the style had been popularized by a white actress in the film "10." Plaintiff may be correct that an employer's policy prohibiting the "Afro/bush" style might offend Title VII and section 1981. But if so, this chiefly would be because banning a natural hairstyle would implicate the policies underlying the prohibition of discrimination on the basis of immutable characteristics. * * * An all-braided hair style is an "easily changed characteristic," and, even if socioculturally associated with a particular race or nationality, is not an impermissible basis for distinctions in the application of employment practices by an employer. * * * The Fifth Circuit recently upheld, without requiring any showing of business purpose, an employer's policy prohibiting the speaking of any language but English in the workplace, despite the importance of Spanish to the ethnic identity of Mexican–Americans. * * *

Although the Act may shield "employees' psychological as well as economic fringes" from employer abuse * * * plaintiff's allegations do not amount to charging American with "a practice of creating a working environment heavily charged with ethnic or racial discrimination," or one "so heavily polluted with discrimination as to destroy completely the emotional and psychological stability of minority group workers." * * * If an even-handed English-only policy that has the effect of prohibiting a Mexican–American from speaking Spanish during working hours is valid without a showing of business purpose, the policy at issue here, even if ill-advised, does not offend the law.

Moreover, the airline did not require plaintiff to restyle her hair. It suggested that she could wear her hair as she liked while off duty, and permitted her to pull her hair into a bun and wrap a hairpiece around the bun during working hours. * * *

Plaintiff has failed to allege sufficient facts to require defendants to demonstrate that the policy has a bona fide business purpose. * * * In this regard, however, plaintiff does not dispute defendant's assertion that the policy was adopted in order to help American project a conservative and business-like image, a consideration recognized as a bona fide business purpose. E.g., *Fagan v. National Cash Register Co.*, 481 F.2d 1115, 1124–25 (D.C. Cir. 1973). * * *

Plaintiff also asserts in her complaint that the regulation has been applied in an uneven and discriminatory manner. She claims that white women in particular have been permitted to wear pony tails and shag cuts. She goes on to claim, in fact, that some black women are permitted to wear the same hairstyle that she has been prohibited from wearing. These claims seriously undercut her assertion that the policy discriminates against women, and her claim that it discriminates against black women in particular. Conceivably, however, the complaint could be construed as alleging that the policy has been applied in a discriminatory manner against plaintiff because she is black by some representative of the defendant. On its face, this allegation is sufficient, although it might be subject to dismissal on a summary judgment motion if it is not supplemented with some factual claims.

This remaining claim-of racially discriminatory application-by its nature is not appropriate for class action treatment. In light of plaintiff's assertions that both white and black women in the purported class have been permitted to wear the all-braided style, she seems to be saying, ultimately, that there are no similarly situated people, and she does not identify any. Therefore, the motion for class certification is denied. * * * Indeed, even as broadly alleged, plaintiff's claims would not warrant certification of a class. Plaintiff seeks specific retroactive monetary relief only for herself and not for any class members. With respect to the class, plaintiff seeks a change in company policy, and a victory in plaintiff's case, with an injunctive and declaratory order, would afford relief to all similarly situated people. * * *

A Hair Piece: Perspective on the Intersection of Race and Gender

1991 DUKE L.J. 365.

Paulette M. Caldwell

I.   OF SMALL BEGINNINGS

A.   *Rediscovering My Hair*

When will I cherish my hair again, the way my grandmother cherished it, when fascinated by its beauty, with hands carrying centuries-old secrets of adornment and craftswomanship, she plaited it, twisted it, cornrowed it, finger-curled it, olive-oiled it, on the growing moon cut and shaped it, and wove it like fine strands of gold inlaid with semiprecious stones, coral and ivory, telling with my hair a lost-found story of the people she carried inside her?

* * *

B.   *On Being the Subject of a Law School Hypothetical*

The case of *Rogers v. American Airlines* upheld the right of employers to prohibit categorically the wearing of braided hairstyles in the workplace. The plaintiff, a black woman, argued that American Airline's policy discriminated against her specifically as a black woman. In effect, she based her claim on the interactive effects of racial and gender discrimination. The court chose, however, to base its decision principally on distinctions between biological and cultural conceptions of race. More importantly, it treated the plaintiff's claims of race and gender discrimination in the alternative and independent of each other, thus denying any interactive relationship between the two.

* * *

I discovered *Rogers* while reading a newspaper article describing the actual or threatened firing of several black women in metropolitan Washington, D.C. solely for wearing braided hairstyles. The article referred to *Rogers* but actually focused on the case of Cheryl Tatum, who was fired from her job as a restaurant cashier in a Hyatt Hotel under a company policy that prohibited "extreme and unusual hairstyles."

The newspaper description of the Hyatt's grooming policy conjured up an image of a ludicrous and outlandishly-coiffed Cheryl Tatum, one clearly bent on exceeding the bounds of workplace taste and discipline. But the picture that accompanied the article revealed a young, attractive black woman whose hair fell neatly to her shoulders in an all-American, common, everyday pageboy style, distinguished only by the presence of tiny braids in lieu of single strands of hair.

* * *

C.   *Why Would Anyone Want to Wear Their Hair That Way?*

* * *

Hair seems to be such a little thing. Yet it is the little things, the small everyday realities of life, that reveal the deepest meanings and values of a culture, give legal theory its grounding, and test its legitimacy.

II.   TO CHOOSE MYSELF: INTERLOCKING FIGURATIONS
IN THE CONSTRUCTION OF RACE AND GENDER

A.   *A Black Woman's Hair, A Black Woman's Place*

SUNDAY. School is out, my exams are graded, and I have un-braided my hair a few days before my appointment at the beauty parlor to have it braided again. After a year in braids, my hair is healthy again: long and thick and cottony soft. I decide not to french roll it or twist it or pull it into a ponytail or bun or cover it with a scarf. Instead, I comb it out and leave it natural, in a full and big "Angela Davis" afro style. I feel full and big and regal. I walk the three blocks from my apartment to the subway. I see a white male colleague walking in the opposite direction and I wave to him from across the street. He stops, squints his eyes against the glare of the sun and stares, trying to figure out who has greeted him. He recognizes me and starts to cross over to my side of the street. I keep walking, fearing the possibility of his curiosity and needing to be relieved of the strain of explanation.

MONDAY. My hair is still unbraided, but I blow it out with a hair dryer and pull it back into a ponytail tied at the nape of my neck before I go to the law school. I enter the building and run into four white female colleagues on their way out to a white female lunch. Before I can say hello, one of them blurts out, "It IS weird!" Another drowns out the first: "You look so young, like a teenager!" The third invites me to join them for lunch while the fourth stands silently, observing my hair. I mumble some excuse about lunch and, interject, almost apologetically, that I plan to get my hair braided again the next day. When I arrive at my office suite and run into the white male I had greeted on Sunday, I realize immediately that he has told the bunch on the way to lunch about our encounter the day before. He mutters something about how different I look today, then asks me whether the day before I had been on my way to a ceremony. He and the others are generally nice colleagues, so I half-smile, but say nothing in response. I feel a lot less full and big and regal.

TUESDAY. I walk to the garage under my apartment building, again wearing a big, full "Angela Davis" afro. Another white male colleague passes me by, not recognizing me. I greet him and he smiles broadly saying that he has never seen me look more beautiful. I smile back, continue the chit chat for a moment more and try not to think about whether he is being disingenuous. I slowly get into my car, buckle up, relax, and turn on the radio. It will take me about forty-five minutes to drive uptown to the beauty parlor, park my car, and get something to eat before beginning the long hours of sitting and braiding. I feel good, knowing that the braider will be ecstatic when she sees the results of her healing handiwork. I keep my movements small, easy, and slow, relish-ing in a rare, short morning of being free.

B. *When Race and Gender Intersect*

My initial outrage notwithstanding, *Rogers* is an unremarkable decision. Courts generally protect employer-mandated hair and dress codes, and they often accord the greatest deference to codes that classify individuals on the basis of socially-conditioned rather than biological differences. And although *Rogers* rests on one line of authority without acknowledging the existence of another, grooming codes are governed by decisional law that clearly lacks conceptual coherence. All in all, such cases are generally considered only marginally significant in the battle to secure equal employment rights.

But *Rogers* is regrettably unremarkable in an important respect. It rests on suppositions that are deeply imbedded in American culture—assumptions so entrenched and so necessary to the maintenance of interlocking, interdependent structures of domination that their mythological bases and political functions have become invisible, especially to those to whom their existence is most detrimental. *Rogers* proceeds from the premise that, although racism and sexism share much in common, they are nonetheless fundamentally unrelated phenomena—a proposition proved false by history and contemporary reality. Racism and sexism are interlocking, mutually-reinforcing components of a system of dominance rooted in patriarchy. No significant and lasting progress in combating either can be made until this interdependent aspect of their relation is acknowledged, and until the perspectives gained from considering their interaction are reflected in legal theory and public policy.

* * *

C. *The Limitations of the Assumptions of Race–Sex Correspondence and Independence*

* * *

Correlative to the assumption of race-sex correspondence, there exists an equally powerful assumption of race-sex independence or distinctiveness. Also rooted in American history, particularly in the politics of emancipation and suffrage, this assumption has contemporary manifestations in the existence of distinct political movements against racism and sexism, the development of social policy along exclusively gender or race lines, and the legal conceptualization of distinct approaches to issues of race and gender.

* * *

Problems arise in the development of legal theory and social policy when the possibility of other relationships between race and gender, such as intersection, are not considered. Black women's issues "slip through the cracks" of legal protection, and the gender components of racism and the race components of sexism remain hidden.

* * *

In one category, courts have considered whether black women may represent themselves or other race or gender discriminatees. Some cases deny black women the right to claim discrimination as a subgroup distinct from black men and white women. Others deny black women the right to represent a class that includes white women in a suit based on sex discrimination, on the ground that race distinguishes them. Still other cases prohibit black women from representing a class in a race discrimination suit that includes black men, on the ground of gender differences. These cases demonstrate the failure of courts to account for race-sex intersection, and are premised on the assumption that discrimination is based on either race or gender, but never both.

A second category of cases concerns the interaction of race and gender in determining the limits of an employer's ability to condition work on reproductive and marital choices associated with black women. Several courts have upheld the firing of black women for becoming pregnant while unmarried if their work involves association with children—especially black teenage girls. These decisions rest on entrenched fears of and distorted images about black female sexuality, stigmatize single black mothers (and by extension their children) and reinforce "culture of poverty" notions that blame poverty on poor people themselves. They also reinforce the notion that the problems of black families are attributable to the deviant and dominant roles of black women and the idea that racial progress depends on black female subordination.

A third category concerns black women's physical images. These cases involve a variety of mechanisms to exclude black women from jobs that involve contact with the public—a tendency particularly evident in traditionally female jobs in which employers place a premium on female attractiveness—including a subtle, and often not so subtle, emphasis on female sexuality. The latter two categories sometimes involve, in addition to the intersection of race and gender, questions that concern the interaction of race, gender, and culture.

* * *

D.   *The Rogers Opinion*

The *Rogers* decision is a classic example of a case concerning the physical image of black women. Renee Rogers, whose work for American Airlines involved extensive passenger contact, claimed that American's prohibition of braided hairstyles in certain job classifications discriminated against her as a woman in general, and as a black woman in particular. The court did not attempt to limit the plaintiff's case by forcing her to proceed on either race or gender grounds, nor did it create a false hierarchy between the two bases by treating one as grounded in statutory law and the other as a "plus" factor that would explain the application of law to a subgroup not technically recognized as a protected group by law. The court also appeared to recognize that the plaintiff's claim was not based on the cumulative effects of race and gender.

* * *

The court gave three principal reasons for dismissing the plaintiff's claim. First, in considering the sex discrimination aspects of the claim, the court disagreed with the plaintiff's argument that, in effect, the application of the company's grooming policy to exclude the category of braided hairstyles from the workplace reached only women. Rather, the court stressed that American's policy was even-handed and applied to men and women alike. Second, the court emphasized that American's grooming policy did not regulate or classify employees on the basis of an immutable gender characteristic. Finally, American's policy did not bear on the exercise of a fundamental right. The plaintiff's racial discrimination claim was analyzed separately but dismissed on the same grounds: neutral application of American's anti-braid policy to all races and absence of any impact of the policy on an immutable racial characteristic or of any effect on the exercise of a fundamental right.

* * *

In support of its view that the plaintiff had failed to establish a factual basis for her claim that American's policy had a disparate impact on black women, thus destroying any basis for the purported neutral application of the policy, the court pointed to American's assertion that the plaintiff had adopted the prohibited hairstyle only shortly after it had been "popularized" by Bo Derek, a white actress, in the film "10." Notwithstanding the factual inaccuracy of American's claim, and notwithstanding the implication that there is no relationship between braided hair and the culture of black women, the court assumed that black and white women are equally motivated (i.e., by the movies) to adopt braided hairstyles.

* * *

The court's reference to Bo Derek presents us with two conflicting images, both of which subordinate black women and black culture. On the one hand, braids are separated from black culture, and, by implication are said to arise from whites. Not only do blacks contribute nothing to the nation's or the world's culture, they copy the fads of whites. On the other hand, whites make fads of black culture, which, by virtue of their popularization, become—like all "pop"—disposable, vulgar, and without lasting value. Braided hairstyles are thus trivialized and protests over them made ludicrous.

* * *

III.   Truths and Sojourns: Stereotyping at the Intersection of Race and Gender

A.   *Of Changes and More*

1985. In a few days I will teach in a four-day workshop for fifty black women. The participants have been chosen primarily because of their status in the corporate world of business and finance. My feelings of performance anxiety seem greatly overshadowed by feelings of happy excitement and expectancy at the prospect of navigating my peers through the murky waters of possibilities and pitfalls for black women in leadership positions. I arrive at the beauty parlor for the grooming of my hair, which, after a year in braids, has grown to my shoulders. Time is short and the hairdresser is late. When she arrives, on impulse,

I decide to forgo braids and ask her to apply a chemical straightener to my virgin hair. I return to work a day later and the "significant other" of a male colleague addresses me in that chastising, condescending tone of voice reserved for slaves and women in domestic service: "Every time I see you, you've done something else to your hair!"

Days later I arrive at the workshop site and greet the participants, my hair arranged in a style reminiscent of my former for-profit corporate self. Over the next four days, I am frequently complimented for my competence, unusual insights, and mastery of subject matter, but mostly—especially from those who over the years have watched me alternate between closely-cropped Afros and short, straight bobs—for the beauty of my long, straight hair.

B.   *Hair and the Timeless Search for Legitimacy*

* * *

Unlike skin color and other physical manifestations of race, hair has both mutable and immutable characteristics. Change in the mutable and in the appearance of the immutable characteristics of hair can be accomplished with relative ease, albeit, for many blacks, not without long-term consequences. Hair can be cut off, straightened out, curled up, or covered over either in the exercise of individual preference or to comply with the tastes or preferences of others. The uniqueness of hair among physical characteristics correlating with race lies not only in the ability of its true nature to be disguised, but also in its susceptibility to external control.

* * *

Today, Afro hairstyles—or at least some of them—are widely accepted in all forms of employment, although the extent of their legal protection is far from certain. They are considered by many to reflect personal style—aesthetic choice—and are not generally associated with the politics of the period of their origin. However, the rationalizations that accompanied opposition to Afro hairstyles in the 1960s—extreme, too unusual, not businesslike, inconsistent with a conservative image, unprofessional, inappropriate with business attire, too "black" (i.e., too militant), unclean—are used today to justify the categorical exclusion of braided hairstyles in many parts of the workforce, particularly in jobs that are either traditionally conservative or highly structured, involve close immediate supervision, or require significant contact with the public.

C.   *In Whose Image? The Application of Antidiscrimination Principles to Employer Grooming and Image Preferences*

By focusing on neutrality, immutability, and the exercise of fundamental rights, the *Rogers* court obscured an underlying principle in the application of antidiscrimination law to a variety of employer image preferences, including—but not limited to—those expressed through grooming codes. A careful analysis of cases in this area reveals that courts pay close attention to the eradication of stereotypes, attention in no way evidenced in *Rogers*.

These cases also make clear that stereotyping is impermissible whether or not the standards set forth in *Rogers* are satisfied.

* * *

* * * *Image Discrimination in the Airline Industry*. The fact that the *Rogers* case was brought against a major airline is itself of considerable significance. The airline industry's history of discrimination against women is nothing short of malevolent. Perhaps no industry has fought as hard to control its image and to seek competitive advantage by exploiting stereotypical cultural attitudes concerning the physical appearance, proper place in society, and supposed personal characteristics of blacks and women.

* * *

D. *Public Degradation of Black Women*

Many employers express shock that black women who refuse to unbraid their hair take such a strong stance, one that could cost them their jobs, in defense of a hairstyle. More shocking is the recurrence among unrelated employers of virtually identical solutions to the issue of braids, solutions that embody overt racist caricatures of the past expressed in the subtle, symbolic code of contemporary racism. Invariably, black women are told either to unbraid their hair or to disguise their braids by pulling them into a bun or cover them up with a wig or hairpiece. This latter solution—the forcible covering up of a black woman's hair—connotes a demeaning servitude that persists even in the face of changes in one of America's most cherished and enduring symbols. For the first time in the more than one hundred years of the Aunt Jemima trademark's existence, its current owner has deemed it profitable to reveal Aunt Jemima's hair. But for the color of her skin, the new Aunt Jemima could pass for Betty Crocker. There is nothing wrong or offensive about the similarity of these trademarks, but the marketing judgment of Aunt Jemina's owner does reflect the assumption that the public equates progress for black women with the imitation of white women. Because being black is an occasion for oppression, avoiding blackness and its attached cultural associations becomes the essential mechanism of liberation.

* * *

Judgments about aesthetics do not exist apart from judgments about the social, political, and economic order of a society. They are an essential part of that order. Aesthetic values determine who and what is valued, beautiful, and entitled to control. Thus established, the structure of society at other levels also is justified. What appears to be merely an aesthetic judgment in *Rogers* is part of the subordination of black women and is inextricably connected to the more obvious economic judgments reflected in other cases that affect black women.

IV. The Nature of Kinship

The issues in *Rogers* defy resolution by resort to arguments about mere aesthetic judgments, doctrinal confusion, or minimal effect on employment rights. The application of *Willingham* in *Rogers* reflects patriarchal assumptions about women generally and competing stereotypical images about womanhood determined by race. These competing images limit black women's choices in ways far more fundamental than is readily apparent in controversies about hair. And although *Willingham* and *Rogers* appear to reserve to white women the privilege of their personal and cultural choices, these cases are based on stereotypes that constitute a ready mechanism for denying employment opportunity to white women who refuse to express themselves in ways that satisfy their employers' notions of "white femaleness." These decisions effectively lock men—black and white—and black women out of choices associated with "true" womanhood; read in reverse, they lock white women into such choices.

* * *

V.   HEALING THE SHAME

Eliminating the behavioral consequences of certain stereotypes is a core function of antidiscrimination law. This function can never be adequately performed as long as courts and legal theorists create narrow, inflexible definitions of harm and categories of protection that fail to reflect the actual experience of discrimination. Considering the interactive relationship between racism and sexism from the experiential standpoint and knowledge base of black women can lead to the development of legal theories grounded in reality, and to the consideration by all women of the extent to which racism limits their choices *as women* and by black and other men of color of the extent to which sexism defines their experiences as men of subordinated races.

* * *

NOTES AND QUESTIONS

1. **Impact of *Rogers*.** The ruling in the case upheld employers' right to prohibit their employees from wearing braided hairstyles. The case relied on *Carswell v. Peachford Hospital*, which upheld the right of a psychiatric hospital to dismiss an employee for wearing beads in their braided hairstyle. The court held that the decision was based on a rule that banned the wearing of jewelry by employees. According to the hospital, the rule was mandated for the patients' safety rather than as a form of racial discrimination. Both cases rely on the premise that braided hairstyles are not the exclusive province of black women. For example, American Airlines claimed the plaintiff only began wearing the braided hairstyle after it was "popularized" by Bo Derek in the movie *10*. This argument succeeded because it operated on the premise that braided hairstyles are not immutable physical traits such as an Afro. *See* Caldwell, *supra*.

2. **Employee discrimination or customer preference?** Caldwell learned of the *Rogers* decision while reading an article concerning Cheryl Tatum, a black woman dismissed from Hyatt Hotel in Washington, D.C. for wearing an inappropriate hairstyle. According to Caldwell, the accompany-

ing picture showed a black woman with a pageboy hairstyle that had small braids also. Tatum claims a Hyatt manager said, "I can't understand why you would want to wear your hair like that anyway. What would our guests think if we allowed you all to wear your hair like that?" *See* Caldwell, *supra* at 850, n.7. The managers' statements exhibit the frequency in which employers invoke customer preference as the reason for banning certain hairstyles. But as Caldwell states, customer preference is usually nothing more than the employer stating its appearance preferences.

3. Black women's place in appearance-focused industries. In the article, Caldwell argues that black women often experience a precarious position in appearance-focused, feminine industries such as airline stewardesses. For example, do the appearance regulations speak to gender or race? Caldwell's article seems to suggest that gender and race are significant factors in the regulations and that black women particularly face both issues. As mentioned in the article, scores of black women have been dismissed from jobs for having inappropriate hairstyles such as braids. In addition, these appearance rules are seen as particularly restricting upon women and decided by men. In this sense black women's appearance has to be pleasing to the white and male eye.

4. Distinction between immutable and mutable traits. American Airlines and the court felt the plaintiff's hairstyle was a voluntary choice. It was not like an Afro which is an immutable biological trait of blacks. In this sense, the court distinguished between physical and cultural traits and choices. Furthermore, the argument concerning Bo Derek was used by the court and American Airlines to suggest that the prohibition against braided hairstyles was not racial in nature because it was also a style popular with white women. Because of this, it was difficult for the plaintiff to successfully argue that black women were exclusively targeted by the prohibition.

5. Narrow definition of discrimination. Caldwell's article suggests that Rogers was unsuccessful because the court used such a narrow scope of the harm caused by discrimination. She suggests that a more flexible interpretation would take into account the reality of racism and the manner in which it constricts the choices and options of black women and other minorities. Upon suing under the Thirteenth Amendment prohibition on slavery, Rogers' arguments were not supported because the court ruled she was not forced to stay on the job.

E. THE MARKET VALUE OF POPULAR IMAGES

Madonna: Plantation Mistress or Soul Sister?

BLACK LOOKS: RACE AND REPRESENTATION 157–64 (1992).

BELL HOOKS

White women "stars" like Madonna, Sandra Bernhard, and many others publicly name their interest in, and appropriation of, black culture as yet another sign of their radical chic. Intimacy with that "nasty" blackness good white girls stay away from is what they seek. To white and other non-black consumers, this gives them a special flavor, an added spice. After all it is a very recent historical phenomenon for any white girl to be able to get some mileage out of flaunting her fascination and envy of blackness. The thing about envy is that it is always ready to destroy, erase, take-over, and consume the desired object. That's exactly what Madonna attempts to do when she appropriates and commodifies aspects of black culture. Needless to say this kind of fascination is a threat. It endangers. Perhaps that is why so many of the grown black women I spoke with about Madonna had no interest in her as a cultural icon and said things like, "The bitch can't even sing." It was only among young black females that I could find die-hard Madonna fans. Though I often admire and, yes at times, even envy Madonna because she has created a cultural space where she can invent and reinvent herself and receive public affirmation and material reward, I do not consider myself a Madonna fan.

    * * *

Fascinated yet envious of black style, Madonna appropriates black culture in ways that mock and undermine, making her presentation one that upstages. This is most evident in the video "Like a Prayer." Though I read numerous articles that discussed public outrage at this video, none focused on the issue of race. No article called attention to the fact that Madonna flaunts her sexual agency by suggesting that she is breaking the ties that bind her as a white girl to white patriarchy, and establishing ties with black men. She, however, and not black men, does the choosing. The message is directed at white men. It suggests that they only labeled black men rapists for fear that white girls would choose black partners over them. Cultural critics commenting on the video did not seem at all interested in exploring the reasons Madonna chooses a black cultural backdrop for this video, i.e., black church and religious experience. Clearly, it was this backdrop that added to the video's controversy.

    * * *

Eager to see the documentary *Truth or Dare* because it promised to focus on Madonna's transgressive sexual persona, which I find interesting, I was angered by her visual representation of her domination over not white men (certainly not over Warren Beatty or Alek Keshishian), but people of color and white working-class women. I was too angered by this to appreciate other aspects of the film I might have enjoyed. In *Truth or Dare* Madonna clearly revealed that she can only think of exerting power along very traditional, white supremacist, capitalistic, patriarchal lines. That she made people who were dependent on her for their immediate livelihood submit to her will was neither charming nor seductive to me or the other black folks that I spoke with who saw the film. We thought it tragically ironic that Madonna would choose as her dance partner a black male with dyed blonde hair. Perhaps had he appeared less like a white-identified black male consumed by "blonde ambition" he might have upstaged her. Instead he was positioned as a mirror, into which Madonna and her audience could look and see only a reflection of herself and the worship of "whiteness" she embodies-that white supremacist culture wants everyone to embody. Madonna used her power to ensure that he and the other non-white women and men who worked for her, as well as some of the white subordinates would all serve as the backdrop to her white-girl-makes-good drama. Joking about the film with other black folks, we commented that Madonna must have searched long and hard to find a black female that was not a good dancer, one who would not deflect attention away from her. And it is telling that when the film directly reflects something other than a positive image of Madonna, the camera highlights the rage this black female dancer was suppressing. It surfaces when the "subordinates" have time off and are "relaxing".

* * *

I can only say this doesn't sound like liberation to me. Perhaps when Madonna explores those memories of her white working-class childhood in a troubled family in a way that enables her to understand intimately the politics of exploitation, domination, and submission, she will have a deeper connection with oppositional black culture. If and when this radical critical self-interrogation takes place, she will have the power to create new and different cultural productions, work that will be truly transgressive—acts of resistance that transform rather than simply seduce.

NOTES AND QUESTIONS

1.   Minority gay males in the image of white women. The hooks essay suggests that minority gay males often impersonate and aspire to white womanhood. She also suggests that Madonna capitalizes on this by using a black male dancer who sports blond hair. According to hooks, Madonna is able to look into a mirror and see a similar reflection staring back. *See* bell hooks *Madonna: Plantation Mistress or Soul Sister?, in* BLACK LOOKS: RACE AND REPRESENTATION, 157–64 (1992). As a doubly oppressed minority, many impoverished minority gay males impersonate famous white women including Madonna. In particular, if one looks at the "drag ball" phenomenon depicted in *Paris Is Burning*, it seems that many poor minority gay males aspire to the "power that is clustered around whiteness, wealth and heterosexuality." *See* Darren Lenard Hutchinson, *Out Yet Unseen: A Racial Critique of Gay and Lesbian Legal Theory and Political Discourse*, CONN. L. REV. 561 (1997). Similarly, hooks contends that Madonna uses her whiteness as power and property that enable her dominance over her minority subordinates. In particular, hooks criticizes the manner in which Madonna often humiliates and condescends to her minority dancers and backup singer. It somewhat echoes Hutchinson's argument that subjugated minorities will often suffer various harms to gain entry into the white world. *See* hooks, *supra*.

2.   Class as a division between women. In *Feminist Theory: From Margin to Center*, hooks suggests that class is a divider in addition to race between white and black women. BELL HOOKS, FEMINIST THEORY FROM MARGIN TO CENTER (1984). According to hooks, to deny that there is a class division is equivalent to denial of a class struggle in the United States. To hooks, it is insufficient for an affluent woman to take a poor woman to lunch and cite this as an example of female unity. In the same sense, it is insufficient for Madonna to hire the services of minorities and still subjugate them to abuse. In hooks' opinion, the documentary film *Truth or Dare: In Bed with Madonna* only reinforces the notion of white dominance over minorities. In particular, she argues that the movie and its images connote white patriarchal power. HOOKS, *supra* at 159.

3.   The different perceptions of black and white female sexuality. Perhaps an excellent example of this is the recent Super Bowl controversy over Janet Jackson and Justin Timberlake's performance. Here is a sample of some of the headlines in leading national and international newspapers: *FCC is Investigating Super Bowl Show*, THE WASH. POST, Feb. 3, 2004, at A1; *Singer's Boob Sparks Outrage in US*, THE GUARDIAN, Feb. 3, 2004; *Halftime incident sparks FCC inquiry*, ATLANTA J–CONST., Feb. 3, 2004; *Janet's Sorry for Super strip*, N.Y. DAILY NEWS, Feb. 3, 2004. Interestingly enough, Timberlake's participation was notably absent in much of the outrage and debate. A majority of media outlets treated Jackson as if she were the lone participant in the performance. A number of reasons could explain this. Some view her as solely responsible for the planning of the performance and him as an unknowing accomplice. On the other hand, some argue that Jackson has been severely criticized due to her race. In particular, some have wondered if this would have happened if she were white or Timberlake black. Another issue has been whether Timberlake would have been criticized if he were a black man ripping the bodice of a white female performer.

4.   Race, sex and advertising hyperbole: crossing the line.

Although hooks's essay was written in 1992, sexuality, race, and power continue to be very controversial topics. The Super Bowl controversy illustrates the notion that the public still rejects certain presentations of female sexuality. In the essay, hooks asserts that Madonna has built a career on bold sexuality while still being able to retreat to her whiteness. For hooks, this means Madonna has been able to project sexuality without having the same derogatory labels and exploitation affixed to her suffered by generations of black women.

What accounts for the different reactions to black and white sexuality? The reactions to Madonna and Janet Jackson were disparate. The latter was pilloried and drew major criticism in terms of her morals and values. Of course, there are several possible reasons for this. First, it occurred during the "family hour" of the Super Bowl. Many adults contend that the half-time show was inappropriate for children. Second, it occurred during one of the biggest events of the year. It is the highest rated show and that could account for the large outpouring of reaction and opinion. Third, she is a black woman who was exposed on national television. The last possibility is one that has been mainly voiced by minority groups. The majority of the mainstream press has not discussed the event as a racial issue. Regardless, the aftermath of the Super Bowl suggests that the public has different standards and notions regarding black and white sexuality.

By contrast to the nearly uniform negative outcry over the Janet Jackson nipple baring "wardrobe malfunction," public reaction was mixed in response to an ad that aired during ABC's Monday Night Football. The ad featured white actress Nicollette Sheridan dropping her towel to flash her naked body to black Philadelphia Eagles receiver Terrell Owens. One columnist thought that the initial public criticism was an "overaction." *Moral Standards; Under Assault, But Holding Their Own*, Orlando Senti-nel, Dec. 7, 2004, at A15. Other critics called the "towel-dropping teaser everything from racist to pornographic."

F.   Market Value of Sexual Differences

The Sexual Continuum: Transsexual Prisoners

Note, 24 New Eng. J. on Crim. & Civ. Confinement 599 (1998).

■ Anita C. Barnes

I.   Introduction

In a society so bent on the absolute, within a legal system so dependent on identifiable categories, the transsexual prisoner presents a serious problem. Transsexualism protests the confines of gender and sex, questioning the very essence of what is man and what is woman, what is masculine and what is feminine. Transgendered individuals challenge the relationship of sex to gender, specifically, sex does not control gender.

The transsexual inmate faces an even greater struggle due to the narrow definition of sex employed by prison authorities. Courts and prisons strain to place pre-and postoperative transsexuals into recognizable categories and fail to appreciate the uniqueness that transsexualism creates. In effect, transgendered prisoners encounter two forms of imprisonment: (1) they are trapped in a body not their own, and (2) they are oppressed within a legal system just beginning to understand their plight.

* * *

II.   Legal Recognition of Gender and Sex

A.   *The Definition of Sex and Gender*

Sex refers to one's anatomy, biology, and physiology. This includes one's genitalia, chromosomal structure, and internal sexual organs. Gender refers to an individual's self-image, how others perceive the individual, and the underlying stereotypes surrounding sex. Gender represents the social construction of sex, "gender is to sex as feminine is to female and masculine is to male." Sex defines the system, and gender the function: "sex is the act and gender is the classification."

* * *

Yet gender is largely more determinative of a person's sex than anatomy or biology. In underestimating the importance of gender in defining sex, "the legal community refuses to accept ... that one's gender is as much an indication of sex as is biology." Gender encompasses one's private experience of sexual roles and his or her public expression of them. Gender influences how sex is perceived, and, ultimately, how society determines identity. Gender identity—the sense of maleness or femaleness—" 'pervades one's entire concept of one's place in life, of one's place in society.' " This pervasiveness culminates in actual facts of biology becoming secondary. As Dr. Richard Green, Director of the Gender Identity Research and Treatment Clinic at the University of California School of Medicine in Los Angeles noted, "[g]ender is the usually unshakable conviction of being male or female." The social construction of gender challenges the notion that sex is somehow irrevocably assigned at birth, and that sex in its biological sense exclusively dictates the formation of gender. The medical profession acknowledges that gender identity is generally established early in life. Medical practitioners also recognize that genetic make-up does not wholly determine gender or sexual identity; rather, socialization plays a crucial role as well. In order to better understand the dilemma of the transsexual prisoner, the legal community must embrace the notion that anatomy does not conclusively define gender, and gender identity does not necessarily stem from biological sex. As Leslie Pearlman concluded:

> It is the semantic distinction between sex and gender and the subsequent jurisprudential construction of gender which the legal community has failed to understand, but that cannot be ignored. The separate concepts of gender and sex must be respected and accorded their true, individual meanings. If they are not, the uniqueness of the transsexual situation cannot be understood.

B. *Legal Recognition of Gender: Gender Discrimination*

Though the United States Supreme Court hesitates to differentiate gender from sex or to acknowledge gender as separate from sex, Supreme Court cases implicitly focus on gender stereotyping as grounds for sex discrimination. In *Orr v. Orr*, for example, the Court struck down an Alabama statute that required husbands, but not wives, to pay alimony. Recognizing traditional gender roles of men as breadwinners, and women as homemakers as the impetus behind the statute, the Court reasoned that, in order to survive constitutional scrutiny, the statute must rest on some basis other than antiquated gender stereotypes. The Court in *Orr* concentrated on whether sex is a viable criteria for judging financial need. In analyzing this viability, the Court focused on sex not in terms of biology, but rather in terms, of how society dictates gender *on the basis of sex*.

III. LEGAL DYNAMICS OF TRANSSEXUALISM

A. *The Definition of Transsexualism*

* * *

Much of the debate surrounding how the law should recognize transsexuality revolves around the search for the root causes of transsexualism, particularly, whether the origin is psychological or physical. Regardless, transsexualism occurs early in life. Though transsexualism is traditionally viewed as a mental disorder, the medical profession recognizes neurological causes for transsexualism. Studies point to brain size and the role of sexual differentiation during fetal development as the sources of transsexuality. Specifically, research concludes that gender identity is the result of "an interaction between the developing brain and sex hormones." Studies suggest that " 'transsexuals are right. Their sex was judged in the wrong way at the moment of birth because people look only to the sex organs and not to the brain' " to determine sex. Given the medical research regarding brain structure and the sexual differentiation of the brain which occurs after birth, assigning a child's sex on the basis of external genitalia amounts to "an act of faith."

* * *

In *Pinneke v. Preisser*, the United States Court of Appeals for the Eighth Circuit concluded that sex reassignment surgery is medically necessary, therefore, Medicaid cannot deny coverage. Likewise, in *G.B. v. Lackner*, the California Court of Appeals rejected the California Department of Health's argument that sex reassignment amounted to cosmetic surgery, which is excluded from Medi–Cal coverage. Instead, the court concluded that transsexual surgery constitutes a reasonable and medically necessary approach to treating transsexuality.

B. *Transsexualism and Sex Discrimination*

* * *

In analyzing sex discrimination claims brought by transgendered individuals, courts employ circular reasoning. Courts disallow claims of discrimination on the basis of transsexuality, yet would recognize similar actions if based on a transsexual's anatomic or perceived sex. To succeed, transgendered individuals must prove discrimination due to their sex, whether male or female, not their transsexuality. *Dobre* attests to how difficult a burden this places on transsexuals. In *Dobre* the court went so far as to assume that the plaintiff was female and still found that Dobre failed to state an adequate claim that she was discriminated against as a female. The court concluded, "[if] the plaintiff was discriminated against at all, it was because she was perceived as a male who wanted to become a female."

* * *

By clinging to narrow definitions of sex and gender, courts fail to understand the continuum of sexual identity that transgendered individuals create. Instead, courts continue to struggle to assign pre-and postoperative transsexuals an identifiable "sex" according to the traditional definitions of gender and sex. Some courts adopt the rule that completion of surgery determines sex, recognizing postoperative transsexuals with their new sex while classifying preoperative transsexuals according to their anatomy. For the transitioning transsexual, however, this assignment of gender based on biology and genitalia is essentially a form of "institutionalized oppression."

* * *

C.   *Transsexualism and Disability Discrimination*

Title VII of the Americans with Disabilities Act (ADA), which bars discrimination against people with disabilities, expressly excludes transsexuals from such protection. Meanwhile, state and federal courts have struggled to define transsexualism and determine whether it is a handicap. In *Leyland v. Orr*, the Ninth Circuit recognized transsexuality as a disability when it upheld the honorable discharge of a postoperative transsexual from the Air Force Reserves. The Air Force concluded that undergoing transsexual surgery significantly impairs an individual's ability to perform his or her duties, and that such surgery rendered Leyland "psychologically unsuitable and physically unfit" for military service.

* * *

In *Doe v. Blue Cross & Blue Shield of Rhode Island*, a Rhode Island district court recognized the "highly sensitive" nature of transsexuality and the stigma associated with the condition when it allowed a transsexual litigant to pursue his claim under a fictitious name. The judge noted the need for anonymity "[p]articularly in this era of seemingly increased societal intolerance toward 'unconventional' sexual behavior." The judge concluded, "I will not strip [the] plaintiff of the cloak of privacy, which shields him from the stigmatization he. might otherwise endure."

* * *

Transsexuality should fall within this protection. Transsexual individuals are socially marginalized due to intolerance, prejudice, and stereotypes surrounding gender and sexual identity. Transgendered individuals are likely to face any or all of the following pervasive social problems: dismissal from employment upon discovery of their transsexuality, termination of parental rights, being labeled as handicapped by the military due to sex reassignment, and being discriminated against by school boards which perpetuate intolerance. Unfortunately, these consequences all occur with the approval of the legal system. This tolerated marginalization challenges Title VII's exclusion of transsexuality as a disability. Transsexualism, therefore, should fall within the definition of a perceived disability.

IV.   THE TRANSSEXUAL PRISONER

* * *

The Eighth Amendment directly addresses the treatment of prisoners and the conditions surrounding incarceration. Specifically, it prohibits the infliction of cruel and unusual punishment, thereby imposing on prison authorities a duty to provide humane conditions of confinement and to ensure that inmates receive adequate food, clothing, shelter, and medical care. The Eighth Amendment also requires that prison officials "'take reasonable measures to guarantee the safety of the inmates.'" As noted:

> "[W]hen the State by the affirmative exercise of its power [through incarceration] so restrains an individual's liberty that it renders him unable to care for himself, and at the same time fails to provide for his basic human needs ... it transgresses the substantive limits on state action set by the Eighth Amendment."

The Supreme Court defines cruel and unusual punishment as the wanton and unnecessary infliction of pain, which includes harm that serves no legitimate penological interest and treatment that is grossly disproportionate to the sentence imposed. The standard underlying the Eighth Amendment is not static; rather, its meaning derives from the evolving principles of dignity, decency, and humanity.

* * *

A. *Placement of Transsexual Prisoners*

In *Farmer v. Brennan*, the Court articulated the standard for use with the Eighth Amendment as one of "deliberate indifference." Under this standard, the petitioner must prove that the deprivation was serious and also show that prison officials acted with a culpable state of mind. In defining culpability, the Court rejected an objective test-that prison officials knew or should have known of the risk—and instead set out that to be culpable, an official must be aware of, yet disregard, an excessive risk to a prisoner's health or safety. This subjective standard requires that an officer "be aware of facts from which the inference could be drawn that a substantial risk of serious harm exists, and he [or she] must also draw the inference." A showing of reckless disregard of a substantial risk satisfies this "culpable state of mind" requirement.

* * *

The Court further stated that an official would not escape liability by refusing to verify, or failing to confirm, a strong suspicion that a substantial risk existed. Likewise, the Court recognized that membership within an identifiable group from which members are frequently singled out for attack, establishes a sufficiently serious risk that warrants Eighth Amendment protection.

* * *

Placing preoperative transsexuals with prisoners of the same anatomical sex exacerbates the risk of harm to transsexual prisoners and challenges the constitutionality of this practice. Adherence to the strict construction that genitalia determines sex places transitioning transsexuals in a "Catch–22." The inevitable dangers of being placed in the general population forces prison officials to segregate transsexual prisoners into protective custody. As the court in Crosby concluded, due to the inherent risk involved in placing preoperative transsexuals according to their biological sex and the limitations associated with segregation, the best solution is to house transsexual prisoners according to their gender identity.

B. *Medical Care of Transsexual Prisoners*

In *Phillips v. Michigan Department of Corrections*, a district court in Michigan granted a transsexual's preliminary injunction for the continued use of female hormones. In so doing, the court recognized that transsexualism represents a serious medical disorder and that failure to provide treatment constitutes cruel and unusual punishment. The court specifically ordered prison officials to continue estrogen therapy and to afford the plaintiff with "the same standard of care she was receiving prior to incarceration." The *Phillips* court further observed that the failure to provide female hormones to the plaintiff reversed the transitional process, thus adversely affecting the plaintiff by worsening her physical and emotional state. As the court noted,

> [i]t is one thing to fail to provide an inmate with care that would improve his or her medical state, such as refusing to provide sex reassignment surgery or to operate on a long-endured cyst. Taking measures which actually reverse the effects of years of healing medical treatment ... is measurably worse, making the cruel and unusual determination much easier.

Ironically, prisons continue to support treatment approaches that the medical profession and most courts recognize as futile. Outside the prison walls, courts denounce policies that summarily dismiss hormone treatment and sex reassignment as unnecessary and inappropriate treatment for transsexualism. Instead, courts conclude that such treatment is medically necessary and required to "cure" transsexualism. Prison officials' insistence on providing counseling alone, a treatment recognized as unsuccessful, constitutes the unnecessary and wanton infliction of pain, in violation of the Eighth Amendment.

* * *

C. *Use of Protective Custody*

Administrative segregation, also known as protective custody or administrative detention, is a form of confinement utilized to separate an inmate from the general population. It is designed to segregate inmates for short periods of time. Where protective custody is not voluntary, heightened standards will attach. Prison officials may place an inmate in administrative detention when that inmate poses a serious threat to the security of the institution, the lives of staff, other inmates, or to him or herself. In addition, prisoners may voluntarily choose segregation for their own protection. Wherever possible, the conditions of administrative detention should mirror those of the general population. Administrative segregation, for nonpunitive reasons, "is the sort of confinement that inmates should reasonably anticipate receiving at some point in their incarceration." Accordingly, the Fourteenth Amendment does not independently protect inmates from such segregation. Conditions of confinement, however, fall under the scrutiny of the Eighth Amendment. The " 'evolving standards of decency' " and human dignity govern such protective custody.

* * *

States may create liberty interests governing the use of protective custody. In *Hewitt v. Helms*, for example, the United States Supreme Court held that a Pennsylvania statute created a liberty interest for a prisoner to remain in the general prison population. Focusing on the mandatory language contained in the statute, the Court recognized that the Pennsylvania legislature went "beyond simple procedural guidelines" toward creating a liberty interest in not being held in administrative segregation without first complying with due process requirements. The Court also, recognized how administrative detention puts restraints on an inmate's freedom. As dictated by the statute, the Court emphasized that "administrative segregation may not be used as a pretext for indefinite confinement of an inmate." Prison officials, however, must conduct periodic reviews to prevent such abuse. The lower court in *Hewitt* analogized protective custody with solitary confinement absent a showing of misconduct, and concluded that "inmates' interests in avoiding confinement in Administrative Custody are no less real" than those of the prisoner seeking to avoid solitary confinement.

* * *

The United States Supreme Court has recognized that conditions beyond one's control are not punishable. For example, punishing someone for uncontrollable conduct resulting from a disease or illness violates the Eighth Amendment. In *Robinson v. California*, the Court struck down a California statute making drug addiction a criminal offense. The Court determined that addiction represents a status or condition and not a punishable offense. As such, to punish addiction imposes " 'a continuing offense ... [that] is chronic rather than acute; that it continues after it is complete and subjects the offender to arrest at any time.' " Addiction may also occur innocently or involuntarily, further implicating the Eighth Amendment. In concluding that the punishment of addiction violated the Eighth Amendment, the Court analogized that a statute criminalizing mental illness would undoubtedly entail cruel and unusual punishment as well. As the Court explained:

> A state law which imprisons a person thus afflicted [with addiction] as a criminal, inflicts a cruel and unusual punishment in violation of the Fourteenth Amendment. To be sure, imprisonment for ninety days is not, in the abstract, a punishment which is either cruel or unusual. But the question cannot be considered in the abstract. Even one day in prison would be a cruel and unusual punishment for the "crime" of having a common cold.

* * *

Transsexualism falls within the definition of a status. Specifically, it is beyond the person's control, it is acquired innocently and involuntarily, possibly at birth, and those afflicted are powerless to overcome the condition. Transsexualism is the constant, inflexible, and immutable conviction of imprisonment in the wrong body. Placing transsexual prisoners in protective custody, given their status, compounds the unconstitutionality of such a practice.

* * *

V. CONCLUSION

Present policies regarding the placement, treatment, and conditions of confinement of transsexual prisoners raise serious constitutional issues. Prisons house transsexual prisoners according to their sex as assigned at birth without recognizing the significance of gender in determining identity. This practice ignores the fact that gender plays a far more crucial role than sex in an individual's self-definition, and in how others perceive that individual. Transsexual prisoners constitute an identifiable group due to their gender identity. Intolerance by other inmates sets transsexual inmates apart and encourages attacks' upon them. Prison authorities' insistence on placing preoperative transsexuals according to their biology represents a conscious disregard, or deliberate indifference, toward the obvious risks inherent in such a policy.

Refusal to Hire, or Dismissal From Employment, on Account of Plaintiff's Sexual Lifestyle or Sexual Preference As Violation of Federal Constitution or Federal Civil Rights Statutes

Annotation, 42 A.L.R. FED. 189, 191, 204–05 (1979 & Supp. 2004).

■ RUSSELL J. DAVIS

[a] Scope

This annotation collects and analyzes the federal and state cases, and relevant decisions of the Equal Employment Opportunity Commission which decide whether it is a violation of the United States Constitution or of any federal civil rights statute to dismiss an employee or to refuse to hire an applicant for employment because of his "sexual lifestyle" or "sexual preference." The latter terms are given a rather broad definition for purposes of this annotation and include such matters as homosexuality, transsexuality, "adulterous" relationships, and cohabitation without benefit of marriage; however, the annotation does not include decisions involving isolated instances of unorthodox or disapproved sexual behavior.

* * *

5. Transsexuality

* * *

In *Grossman v. Bernards Township Board of Education*, [538 F.2d 319 (D.C.N.J. 1975)], the court dismissed the civil rights action of an elementary school music teacher who was dismissed from the school system after undergoing a "sex reassignment operation," holding that jurisdiction over the action could not be based on 42 U.S.C.A. § 1981. The court pointed out that the purpose of § 1981 was clearly to afford protection from discrimination based on race, and that no allegation of racial discrimination appeared anywhere in the plaintiff teacher's pleading.

Plaintiff, who was prospective transsexual and employee in beauty salon operated on premises of department store and who was terminated from employment for not dressing and acting as man while at work, failed to state cause of action under 42 U.S.C.A. § 1985(3), where, under statute, plaintiff must allege that defendants' refusal to allow her to continue work while dressing and acting as woman denied her equal protection, or equal privileges and equal immunities, and where there was no allegation that any other employees who were biologically men, were protected, privileged, or immune so as to have right to work while dressed and acting as women (or vice versa); therefore, plaintiff had failed to allege any manner in which she was treated other than as all other (biological) men were. Further, transsexuals are not suspect class for purposes of equal protection analysis and clearly there was rational basis for employer's requiring its employees who dealt with public to dress and act as persons of their biological sex since allowing employees to do otherwise would disturb customers and cause them to take their business elsewhere. *Kirkpatrick v. Seligman & Latz, Inc.*, [475 F.Supp. 145 (M.D. Fla. 1979)].

[b] Title VII of Civil Rights Act of 1964

Finding a failure to state a cause of action under Title VII of the Civil Rights Act of 1964, 42 U.S.C.A. § 2000e–2(a)(1), the court in *Grossman v. Bernards Township Board of Education*, [538 F.2d 319 (D.C.N.J. 1975)], dismissed an action brought by a transsexual who had been discharged from her position as a music teacher for elementary schools after undergoing a "sex reassignment operation." As affirmed by the state's commissioner of education, the dismissal resulted from school officials' conclusion that the plaintiff teacher was incapable of teaching children because of the potential that her presence in the classroom would cause them psychological harm. Assuming for the purpose of the instant case that the plaintiff teacher was "a member of the female gender," the court found it apparent that she was discharged by the school board not because of her status as a female, but rather because of her change in sex. Noting the scarcity of legislative history relating to the inclusion of sex as a prohibited source of employment discrimination in Title VII, the court expressed its reluctance to ascribe import to this term other than its plain meaning.

Defendant former employer was entitled to dismissal of sex-discrimination complaint by transsexual, since discrimination against sex-change process is not discrimination based on stereotypic notions of males and females and not within congressional intent in prohibiting "sex" discrimination under Title VII. *Dobre v. National R.R. Passenger Corp.*, [850 F.Supp. 284 (E.D. Pa. 1993)].

NOTES AND QUESTIONS

1. **Transsexual prisoners' rights and housing.** One of the most divisive and controversial issues concerning imprisoned transsexuals is their housing. It is a highly delicate issue in terms of the prisoners' concerns for safety and other inmates' concern for privacy. A determinate of where to place the prisoners is whether the prisoner has had genital replacement surgery. Under *Farmer v. Brennan,* 511 U.S. 825, 829 (1994), prisoners who have not had the surgery will be placed according to their birth sex while those who have will be placed in the reassigned gender space. However positive that sounds, there are also negative aspects. In particular, those reassigned are often excluded from educational and occupational opportunities and associational rights. *See* Darren Rosenblum, *"Trapped" in Sing Sing: Transgendered Prisoners Caught in the Gender Binarism,* 6 MICH. J. GENDER & L. 499, 530 (2000).

2. **Hormone therapy use in prison.** Like housing, the issue of hormone use for transsexual prisoners has not been clear-cut. While courts have ruled that transsexual prisoners have a right to continue hormone therapy, prison officials have not been strictly required to provide the treatments. Because of this, scores of prisoners have not received hormone therapy while imprisoned. *See* Rosenblum, *supra* at 545, note 62.

3. **Placement rights over privacy issues.** Whose rights should receive priority in housing situations? Many female prisoners have felt threatened by male to female prisoners sharing the same quarters with them. On the other hand male to female prisoners are threatened in male quarters. For many, the issue of providing separate quarters for transsexuals rings of special treatment that is unfair. None of these issues are simplified by the overcrowding and violence that are prevalent in the United States prison system. If transsexual prisoners are placed in separate facilities, does that mean people should be segregated by race, handicaps, and sexual orientation also?

4. **Impact of unconscious attitudes on sexual orientation discrimination.** Some argue that it has been difficult to prove sexual orientation discrimination because courts take a narrow view that overlook the impact of unconscious attitudes toward gays. *See* Elvia R. Arriola, *Gendered Inequality Lesbians, Gays, and Feminist Legal Theory*, 9 BERKELEY WOMEN'S L.J. 103 (1994). Arriola contends that courts should examine how attitudes toward sexual identity and stereotypes lead to discrimination.

G.   THE MARKET FOR COUNTERCULTURE

"The price we pay when pursuing any art or calling, is an intimate knowledge of its ugly side"
—James Baldwin

Black But Not Beautiful: Negative Black Stereotypes Abound in Rap Lyrics, on Music Videos, in Movies and on Cable—and Blacks Are Among Those Doing the Stereotyping

NEWSDAY, Oct. 24, 1993, at 6.

■ ESTHER IVEREM

Spike Lee Tells a college audience that Hollywood only wants to make black films about urban violence and drugs.

Bill Cosby calls "Russell Simmons' Def Comedy Jam" a "minstrel show."

The Rev. Calvin Butts thunders from his Harlem pulpit about black musical artists who refer to all women as "bitches" and "whores."

Is this Blaxploitation II?

* * *

"What's happening now I call the black-on-black film crime, the black-on-black television crime, because a lot of people creating this stuff happen to be African–American," Townsend says. "Nobody wants to blow the whistle because they say, 'Hey, that's a brother trying to make some money. He's getting paid.' "

Women in the entertainment industry are concerned about how young female fans will build self-esteem and self confidence in the face of misogynist lyrics characterizing women as sex-for-sale gold diggers—lyrics embraced by many young male artists who find that their newfound money and fame attract groupies who would otherwise shun them. In a recent interview, rapper Dr. Dre described his Los Angeles-area home as a place where he hangs out with friends "and about twenty to thirty women."

Another element that distinguishes the new blaxploitation from that of 20 years ago is the degree to which much of the art by blacks is also consumed by whites. Artists such as Ice-T, Ice Cube and L.L. Cool J. generate more sales in America's suburban malls than in city shopping districts. "Def Comedy Jam" has an audience that is 60 percent white.

* * *

MUSIC

* * *

To pinpoint the beginning of the current cultural wave is difficult, but by 1989, there was already criticism of artists in the male-dominated world of rap such as Slick Rick, Too Short, and the group N.W.A. for their sexist lyrics.

Slick Rick, for example, included on his 1989 album, "The Great Adventures of Slick Rick," the cut, "Treat Her Like a Prostitute." The group N.W.A. was one of the first groups to refer to all women as "bitches" and "hos" in its seminal "Straight Outta Compton." Even after N.W.A. disbanded, solo acts spawned by the group, including Dr. Dre, continued the tradition. And as the first popular gangster rappers, N.W.A. also launched a barrage of violent images across the country: "When I'm called off / I gotta sawed off / Squeeze the trigger / And bodies are hauled off," the group also rapped in "Straight Outta Compton."

* * *

But most of the violence in black video (and film) depicts black-on-black crime. And rather than being afraid, young white America embraced gangster rap. During the late '80s, as hip-hop's popularity grew, many white pop and dance-music stations played controversial rap groups banned on black radio stations—and lured young black listeners. Though white pop stations traditionally target youth, black radio stations such as New York's WBLS have historically served a wide variety of musical tastes. Even as some black stations have loosened their restrictions to woo back listeners, it's not uncommon for Onyx, Ice-T and 2Pac to receive their first airplay on white pop stations.

* * *

VIDEO AND PERFORMANCE

Nothing has had a greater impact on the overall music industry in the past decade than music videos. Though record companies were slower to provide video budgets for black artists and MTV was slow to give videos by blacks airplay, videos are now an integral part of the marketing strategy for most artists. Today "MTV Jams," which highlights black music, is one of the most popular programs on the cable channel. Like radio, MTV competes successfully against black-owned BET for young black listeners, even though BET plays a wider variety of black artists.

* * *

Butts, pastor of Harlem's Abyssinian Baptist Church, a leader in the black community's response to offensive messages, says that coming across three videos—one by Luther Campbell, Apache's "Gangsta Bitch" and "Ain't Too Proud to Beg" by TLC—in part spurred him to get involved.

"I was appalled at what I saw and heard," says Butts, sitting at his desk at the church's office. "It was so vulgar. I had seen some things in music before that didn't quite jibe with my sensibilities, but I knew that these things were doing important commentary. However, what I saw that particular night had no socially redemptive value at all."

* * *

FILM

Taken as a whole, the new wave of black filmmakers is producing diverse films such as Mario Van Peebles' "Posse," Spike Lee's "Malcolm X" and Charles Lane's "Sidewalk Stories." But there is no doubt that Hollywood sees green in what some directors call "hood" films, centering on criminal elements of the black community—starting with "New Jack City," and "Boyz in the Hood" in 1991 and followed by films such as "Juice," "South-Central," "Trespass," "A Rage in Harlem" and, this year, "Menace II Society." Some have starred rap artists.

"It becomes a self-fulfilling prophecy," says Helena Echegoyen, director of development for New Line Cinema, which released "Menace II Society." "We have to look at the movies being made, at what is making money, and you make movies like those."

* * *

And once their films are in the market, black filmmakers contend with a virtually all-white corps of arts writers and critics, many of whom, directors say, feel more comfortable with ghetto stereotypes and violence than with other depictions of black life.

For example, when Kenneth Turan panned "Boomerang" last year in the Los Angeles Times, he cited his feeling that the movie's star, Eddie Murphy, had been better in his previous hustler roles, and his sense that an all-black cast playing successful professionals was "silly and arbitrary." The review provoked a rare written outcry from Murphy, Hudlin and members of the public.

"If this were a movie about gun-totin' drug dealers, it would be praised for its gritty authenticity while the complaints would be about encouraging violent behavior in the wake of national riots," Hudlin wrote in a letter to the Times.

* * *

COMEDY

At 36 years of age, Russell Simmons is certainly old enough to have been shaped by the race debates of the 1960s and 1970s. But, in his role as head of Rush Communications, which includes the record label and "Def Comedy Jam," he finds himself championing artists and trends of what writer Nelson George calls the post-soul culture of black America. And Simmons is not concerned that many of his artists as well as "Def Comedy Jam" serve a largely white audience. Reflecting a general comedy explosion in this country, several black comedy shows have cropped up in the past two years, including The Uptown Comedy Club, The Apollo Comedy Hour and Comic View. But none of these draws the audience or controversy of HBO's "Def Comedy Jam." A recent show, for example, peppered with what is the standard profanity, included several comedians graphically illustrating oral sex.

Responding to criticism leveled by Bill Cosby, Simmons says of his program, "I don't feel it's a minstrel show. If he's offended by their language or whatever they do, hey, those are real people. And they are mostly moral and very straightforward people."

Stan Lathan, director and executive producer of "Comedy Jam," says the show fairly represents the kinds of material being presented in black comedy clubs across the country. "The problem is that people zero in on the raunchy material," Lathan says.

* * *

Sandy Wernick, another executive producer of the show and president of Brillstein–Grey Entertainment, which manages several "Saturday Night Live" artists, including Dana Carvey and Adam Sandler, says the show appeals to whites in part because blacks have become secure enough to laugh at themselves.

Wernick, who is white, says he was intrigued by Simmons' idea because of its crossover appeal, and thought Simmons, who sold rap music to white America, was the right man to make the concept successful.

* * *

WHAT'S NEXT

If those concerned about black messages and images in pop culture are searching for relief, they might find it in the fact that the entertainment machine has to get new parts when the current ones wear down. What is coming could be a backlash against current artists who have reduced the panorama of black life to a single grim snapshot.

Artists who followed Public Enemy in the last wave of "conscious rap," such as X–Clan, A Tribe Called Qwest, Chubb Rock, Heavy D, Queen Latifah, De La Soul, and Poor Righteous Teachers, are being joined by newer artists rejecting images of death and nihilism, such as Arrested Development, Nefertitti, Das EFX and Get Set V.O.P.

"People are tired of hearing about people shooting somebody with their nine," said the rapper Heavy D. "Now it's getting monotonous. In the beginning, it was creative because it was somebody telling the rest of the world about a certain place they are from. Now you have a million and one people making those records who aren't even from the ghettos."

* * *

Status Censorship Report

Entertainment Weekly, June 29, 1990.

In an unprecedented legal decision, a federal judge in Florida ruled on June 6 that As Nasty as They Wanna Be, the controversial, sexually explicit rap album by the Miami-based 2 Live Crew, violated community obscenity laws. Within days, three members of the band and a local record-store owner had been arrested for their involvement in the performance and sale of the record, which has been bought by nearly 2 million people nation-wide—and has jumped 29 places on the Billboard chart since the ruling.

With that announcement, the music censorship movement appeared to lose steam-everywhere but in Florida. There, the 2 Live Crew has been at the center of an antiporn campaign by Gov. Bob Martinez (who called Nasty "audio pornography") and Miami attorney Jack Thompson since the release of the album last year. In March, a record-store clerk in Sarasota, Fla., was arrested for selling Nasty to an 11–year-old girl; charges were dropped, but the message to the record business was clear. In response to that incident and other attempts by local police to quell album sales, Luther Campbell (leader of the 2 Live Crew and owner of Luke's Records, which released Nasty) brought a civil suit against Broward County Sheriff Nick Navarro for prohibiting sales of the album by threatening arrest. But on June 6, in a 62–page decision (which began "This is a case between two ancient enemies: Anything Goes and Enough Already"), U.S. District Court Judge Jose Gonzalez ruled that the album's lyrics were legally obscene under the 1973 Miller v. California Supreme Court decision.

In a related development, police attended a Madonna concert in Toron-to on May 29 after complaints of "lewdness" during her Blond Ambition tour, including simulations of masturbation and other sexual acts. No legal action followed. For the moment Madonna is safe, as are most rap albums in local record stores. But developments in the censorship battle have proven that the law can be as nasty as it wants to be, too.

––––––

A NOTE ON CONFLICTING VALUES WITHIN AFRICAN AMERICAN COMMUNITIES

A discernable tension has developed between some traditional civil rights leaders and the performers in the Gangsta Rap genre of hip-hop. The conflict of values is in part generational. Older civil rights leaders see the sex and violence-laden lyrics of rappers as an affront to more conservative, traditional values of many church-based civil rights activists.

The conflicts between these opposing views within the black communi-ty have often included intellectual property litigation and tort claims for interference with contract, trademark infringement, violation of rights of publicity, defamation, with countercharges of conspiracy, extortion, and fraud.

How would critical race theorists analyze the Rosa Parks and C. Delores Tucker's legal disputes described below? How would law and economics scholars analyze these disputes? Are these primarily economic disputes with political implications, or primarily political disputes with economic implications?

Parks v. LaFace Records

329 F.3d 437 (6th Cir. 2003).

■ JUDGE HOLSCHUH delivered the opinion of the court:

This is a dispute over the name of a song. Rosa Parks is a civil rights icon who first gained prominence during the Montgomery, Alabama bus boycott in 1955. She brings suit against LaFace Records, a record producer, and OutKast, a "rap" (or "hip-hop") music duo, as well as several other named affiliates, for using her name as the title of their song, *Rosa Parks*. Parks contends that Defendants' use of her name constitutes false advertising under § 43(a) of the Lanham Act, 15 U.S.C. § 1125(a), and intrudes on her common law right of publicity under Michigan state law. Defendants argue that they are entitled to summary judgment because Parks has failed to show any violation of the Lanham Act or her right of publicity. Defendants further argue that, even if she has shown such a violation, their First Amendment freedom of artistic expression should be a defense as a matter of law to each of these claims. Parks also contends that Defendants' conduct renders them liable under Michigan law for defamation and tortious interference with a business relationship; Defendants have also denied liability with respect to these claims.

* * *

For the reasons hereafter set forth, [the court concludes that the district court erred in granting Defendants' motion for summary judgment on the Lanham Act and right of publicity claim, but that that the district court properly granted summary judgment in favor of Defendants on Rosa Parks' state law claims of defamation and tortious interference with a business relationship].

I.   BACKGROUND

A.   Facts

Rosa Parks is an historical figure who first gained prominence as a symbol of the civil rights movement in the United States during the 1950's and 1960's. In 1955, while riding in the front of a segregated bus in Montgomery, Alabama, she refused to yield her seat to a white passenger and move to the back of the bus as blacks were required to do by the then-existing laws requiring segregation of the races. A 381-day bus boycott in Montgomery flowed from that one event, which eventually became a catalyst for organized boycotts, sit-ins, and demonstrations all across the South. Her single act of defiance has garnered her numerous public accolades and awards, and she has used that celebrity status to promote various civil and human rights causes as well as television programs and books inspired by her life story. She has also approved a collection of gospel recordings by various artists entitled *Verity Records Presents: A Tribute to Mrs. Rosa Parks* (the *"Tribute"* album), released in 1995.

Defendants are OutKast, comprised of recording artists André "Dré" Benjamin and Antwan "Big Boi" Patton; their record producers, LaFace— * * * and LaFace's record distributors, Arista Records and BMG Entertainment—* * *. In September 1998, Defendants released the album *Aquemini.* The album's first single release was a song titled *Rosa Parks,* described as a "hit single" by a sticker on the album. The same sticker that contained the name *Rosa Parks* also contained a Parental Advisory warning of "explicit content." Because, as later discussed, the critical issue in this case is a determination of the artistic relevance of the title, *Rosa Parks,* to the content of the song, the lyrics obviously must be considered in their entirety. They are as follows:

(Hook)

Ah ha, hush that fuss
Everybody move to the back of the bus
Do you wanna bump and slump with us
We the type of people make the club get crunk

Verse 1: (Big Boi)

Many a day has passed, the night has gone by
But still I find the time to put that bump off in your eye
Total chaos, for these playas, thought we was absent
We takin another route to represent the Dungeon Family
Like Great Day, me and my nigga decide to take the back way
We stabbing every city then we headed to that bat cave
A–T–L, Georgia, what we do for ya
Bull doggin hoes like them Georgetown Hoyas
Boy you sounding silly, thank my Brougham aint sittin pretty
Doing doughnuts round you suckas like then circles around titties
Damn we the committee gone burn it down
But us gone bust you in the mouth with the chorus now

(Hook)

Verse 2: (André)

I met a gypsy and she hipped me to some life game
To stimulate then activate the left and right brain
Said baby boy you only funky as your last cut
You focus on the past your ass'll be a has what
Thats one to live by or either that one to die to
I try to just throw it at you determine your own adventure
Andre, got to her station here's my destination
She got off the bus, the conversation lingered in my head for hours
Took a shower kinda sour cause my favorite group ain't comin with it
But I'm witcha you cause you probably goin through it anyway
But anyhow when in doubt went on out and bought it
Cause I thought it would be jammin but examine all the flawsky-wawsky

Awfully, it's sad and it's costly, but that's all she wrote
And I hope I never have to float in that boat Up shit creek it's weak is the last quote
That I want to hear when I'm goin down when all's said and done
And we got a new joe in town
When the record player get to skippin and slowin down
All yawl can say is them niggas earned that crown but until then ...
* * *

II. DISCUSSION

* * *

B. The Lanham Act

Section 43(a) of the Lanham Act creates a civil cause of action against any person who identifies his or her product in such a way as to likely cause confusion among consumers or to cause consumers to make a mistake or to deceive consumers as to association of the producer of the product with another person or regarding the origin of the product or the sponsorship or approval of the product by another person. * * *

[The court discusses the Lanham Act's primary application to "disputes between producers of commercial products and their competitors," but states that it] also permits celebrities to vindicate property rights in their identities against allegedly misleading commercial use by others. * * *

In order to prevail on a false advertising claim under § 43(a), a celebrity must show that use of his or her name is likely to cause confusion among consumers as to the "affiliation, connection, or association" between the celebrity and the defendant's goods or services or as to the celebrity's participation in the "origin, sponsorship, or approval" of the defendant's goods or services. * * *

Parks contends that Defendants have violated the Lanham Act because the *Rosa Parks* title misleads consumers into believing that the song is about her or that she is affiliated with the Defendants, or has sponsored or approved the *Rosa Parks* song and the *Aquemini* album. * * *

Defendants respond that Parks' Lanham Act claim must fail for two reasons. First, they claim that Parks does not possess a trademark right in her name and Defendants have not made a trademark use of her name, as allegedly required for a cause of action under the Lanham Act. Second, they contend that even if use of the title posed some risk of consumer confusion, the risk is outweighed by Defendants' First Amendment right to free expression.

1. *Trademark Right In and Trademark Use of Parks' Name*
* * *

We find Parks' prior commercial activities and international recognition as a symbol of the civil rights movement endow her with a trademark interest in her name the same as if she were a famous actor or musician.

* * * We turn then to Defendants' second argument, that even if Parks could establish some likelihood of confusion, the First Amendment protects Defendants' choice of title.

2. *The First Amendment Defense—Three Approaches*

* * *

[The court discusses the defendants' First Amendment defenses at length, and determines that the *Rogers v. Grimaldi*, 875 F.2d 994 (1989) test should apply.]

* * * The *Rogers* court, finding that overextension of Lanham Act restrictions in the area of titles might intrude on First Amendment values * * * adopted a two-pronged test:

> In the context of allegedly misleading titles using a celebrity's name, that balance [between avoiding consumer confusion and protecting free expression] will normally not support application of the Act unless [1] the title has no artistic relevance to the underlying work whatsoever, or, if it has some artistic relevance, unless [2] the title explicitly misleads as to the source or the content of the work.

* * *

3. **Application of the Rogers Test**

a. *Artistic Relevance Prong*

The first prong of Rogers requires a determination of whether there is any artistic relationship between the title and the underlying work. Parks contends that a cursory review of the *Rosa Parks* title and the lyrics demonstrates that there is no artistic connection between them. Parks also submits two articles in which members of OutKast are purported to have admitted that the song was not about her. As further evidence, she offers a "translation" of the lyrics of the song *Rosa Parks,* derived from various electronic "dictionaries" of the "rap" vernacular to demonstrate that the song truly has nothing to do with Parks herself. * * *

Defendants respond that their use of Parks' name is "metaphorical" or "symbolic." They argue that the historical association between Rosa Parks and the phrase "move to the back of the bus" is beyond dispute and that Parks' argument that the song is not "about" her in a biographical sense is simply irrelevant.

* * *

Contrary to the opinion of the district court, we believe that the artistic relationship between the title and the content of the song is certainly not obvious and, indeed, is "open to reasonable debate" for the following reasons.

It is true that the phrase "move to the back of the bus" is repeatedly used in the "hook" or chorus of the song. When the phrase is considered *in the context of the lyrics,* however, the phrase has absolutely nothing to do with Rosa Parks. * * * The composers did *not* intend it to be about Rosa

Parks, and the lyrics are *not* about Rosa Parks. The lyrics' sole message is that OutKast's competitors are of lesser quality and, therefore, must "move to the back of the bus," or in other words, "take a back seat." We believe that reasonable persons could conclude that there is no relationship of any kind between Rosa Parks' name and the content of the song—a song that is nothing more and nothing less than a paean announcing the triumph of superior people in the entertainment business over inferior people in that business. . . . Choosing Rosa Parks' name as the title to the song unquestionably enhanced the song's potential sale to the consuming public.

* * *

While Defendants' lyrics contain profanity and a great deal of "explicit" language (together with a parental warning), they contain absolutely nothing that could conceivably, by any stretch of the imagination, be considered, explicitly or implicitly, a reference to courage, to sacrifice, to the civil rights movement or to any other quality with which Rosa Parks is identified. If the requirement of "relevance" is to have any meaning at all, it would not be unreasonable to conclude that the title *Rosa Parks* is *not* relevant to the content of the song in question. The use of this woman's name unquestionably was a good marketing tool—*Rosa Parks* was likely to sell far more recordings than *Back of the Bus*—but its use could be found by a reasonable finder of fact to be a flagrant deception on the public regarding the actual content of this song and the creation of an impression that Rosa Parks, who had approved the use of her name in connection with the *Tribute* album, had also approved or sponsored the use of her name on Defendants' composition.

It is certainly not dispositive that, in response to an interview following the filing of this lawsuit, one of the OutKast members said that using Rosa Parks' name was "symbolic." Where an artist proclaims that a celebrity's name is used merely as a "symbol" for the lyrics of a song, and such use is highly questionable when the lyrics are examined, a legitimate question is presented as to whether the artist's claim is sincere or merely a guise to escape liability. Our task, it seems to us, is not to accept without question whatever purpose Defendants may now claim they had in using Rosa Parks' name. It is, instead, to make a determination as to whether, applying the law of *Rogers,* there is a genuine issue of material fact regarding the question of whether the title is artistically relevant to the content of the song. * * *

There is a genuine issue of material fact whether the use of Rosa Parks' name as a title to the song and on the cover of the album is artistically related to the content of the song or whether the use of the name Rosa Parks is nothing more than a misleading advertisement for the sale of the song.

b. Misleading Prong

In *Rogers,* the court held that if the title of the work is artistically relevant to its content, there is no violation of the Lanham Act *unless* the "title explicitly misleads as to the source or the content of the work." * * *

We considered all the facts presented to us and concluded that, with reference to the first prong of the *Rogers* analysis, the issue of artistic relevance of the title *Rosa Parks* to the lyrics of the song is highly questionable and cannot be resolved as a matter of law. However, if, on remand, a trier of fact, after a full evidentiary hearing, concludes that the title *is* used in some symbolic or metaphorical sense, application of the *Rogers* analysis, under the particular facts of this case, would appear to be complete. In the present case, the title *Rosa Parks* "make[s] no explicit statement that the work is about that person in any direct sense." In other words, Defendants did not name the song, for example, *The True Life Story of Rosa Parks* or *Rosa Parks' Favorite Rap*.

 * * *

C. Right of Publicity

1. *Applicable Law*

The right of publicity protects the identity of a celebrity from exploitive commercial use. *See Carson v. Here's Johnny Portable Toilets, Inc.,* 698 F.2d 831, 835 (6th Cir.1983). "The theory of the right is that a celebrity's identity can be valuable in the promotion of products, and the celebrity has an interest that may be protected from the unauthorized commercial exploitation of that identity." *Id.* As such, the common law right of publicity forms a species of property right. * * *

Parks' right of publicity argument tracks that of her Lanham Act claim. She alleges that Defendants have profited from her fame by using her name solely for a commercial purpose. * * *

2. *Analysis*

A right of publicity claim is similar to a false advertising claim in that it grants a celebrity the right to protect an economic interest in his or her name. However, a right of publicity claim does differ from a false advertising claim in one crucial respect; a right of publicity claim does not require any evidence that a consumer is likely to be confused. All that a plaintiff must prove in a right of publicity action is that she has a pecuniary interest in her identity, and that her identity has been commercially exploited by a defendant.

The parties have stipulated that Parks is famous and that she has used her name to promote other goods and services. She has therefore established an economic interest in her name. Furthermore, Defendants admit that they have used Parks' name as the name of their song, and have used that name to sell the song and their album. * * *

For the same reasons we have stated earlier and need not repeat, we believe that Parks' right of publicity claim presents a genuine issue of material fact regarding the question of whether the title to the song is or is not "wholly unrelated" to the content of the song. A reasonable finder of fact, in our opinion, upon consideration of all the evidence, could find the title to be a "disguised commercial advertisement" or adopted "solely to attract attention" to the work.

D. Other Michigan State Law Claims

* * *

1. Defamation

Parks argues that the song defames her character or places her in a false light. To succeed on a defamation claim, a public figure must prove actual malice. *See New York Times Co. v. Sullivan*, 376 U.S. 254, 279–80 (1964). In turn, actual malice requires a showing, by clear and convincing evidence, that a defendant made a false statement with knowledge of the falsity or with reckless disregard for the truth. * * * The song is plainly not about Parks in any biographical sense of the term, and certainly does not make any factual statements about her. As there is no factual statement about her, Parks cannot show even the first element of a defamation claim. Therefore, we find this argument meritless.

Parks' defamation-by-implication argument is likewise meritless. As with a traditional defamation claim, a plaintiff in a defamation-by-implication claim must establish a material falsity. Parks has not done so.* * *

[The court found the plaintiff's claim of intentional interference with a business relationship meritless because there was no "wrongful act" must have hastened a contract breach or another breakdown of a business relationship].

For the reasons stated, as to Rosa Parks' Lanham Act claim and her common law right of publicity claim, the judgment of the District Court is REVERSED and this case is REMANDED for future proceedings not inconsistent with this Opinion. With respect to Rosa Parks' claims of defamation and tortious interference with a business relationship, the judgment of the District Court is AFFIRMED.

———

Delores Tucker, Gangsta Busta: She's Playing Defense in Her Offensive Against Rap

WASH. POST, Nov. 29, 1995, at C1.

■ JUDITH WEINRAUB

* * *

C. Delores Tucker, 68, entered the fight for civil rights more than 50 years ago and never left. She is a glamorous, well-to-do master of fund-raising—for black causes, black mayors, Democrats, anyone whose needs matched her own need to make a difference. She says she's motivated by "a passionate love affair for God and my people," but she's ready to give it up. "I wish other people could do what I'm doing so I could step back and retire," she says.

Instead she finds herself in deeper than ever. Through the National Political Congress of Black Women, an organization she co-founded more than a decade ago, Tucker has waged her latest and perhaps loudest battle—the one against gangsta rap, the one that has made her the target of two lawsuits.

The plaintiffs are Interscope Records and Death Row Records, music companies whose controversial artists she has campaigned against. They charge Tucker with conspiracy and extortion. Though she has high-profile allies in her campaign—notably former secretary of education William Bennett and Connecticut Sen. Joseph Lieberman—only Tucker is being sued.

The suits contend that last summer Tucker tried to persuade rap impresario Suge Knight, head of Death Row Records, to take his business away from Interscope, a distributor. They charge that Tucker offered to distribute Knight's records through a new company that Tucker would control and from which she would profit. They also allege conspiracy, threats, extortion and bribery.

"The allegations are fictional," says Tucker. "The whole charge was simply to restrain me. They were afraid I was going to damage their business."

* * *

She's been crusading for more than two years, picketing stores that sell the music, blocking their entrances and risking arrest. Distributing anti-gangsta-rap petitions and getting statements of support from dozens of African American organizations. Demanding congressional hearings. Buying stock in Nobody Beats the Wiz, Musicland, Sony and Time Warner in order to protest at shareholder meetings.

* * *

Each side in the legal battle, of course, presents a different version. David Kenner, an attorney for Knight and Death Row Records, says he heard Tucker offer $80 million to Knight to leave Interscope and join her in a black-owned distribution company that Time Warner would back.

But Tucker describes a more benign version: She agreed to a meeting with Knight, along with Warwick and Moore. She encouraged Knight to get his gangsta rap clients to use their talents to deliver positive messages. When she asked him what it would take to produce such music, he said he needed distribution. So Tucker asked Warwick and Moore to identify women in the business who might be interested.

"I was trying to assist [the record industry women] in getting what they came to me to get in the first place," she says.

* * *

The Making of a Leader

* * *

Her husband of 44 years calls her "one of the most fearless individuals I have ever known. She will take on anyone, anything, if that is what she thinks is right. . . . I tell her there are times you have to compromise, but she is not one who will readily entertain the idea of compromise about anything.''

* * *

Tucker herself has run for office three times—unsuccessfully—most recently for Congress in Philadelphia three years ago. She says she was urged to run by African American women who wanted representation, and she's not interested in doing it again. "Everything that's happened in my life," she says, "I never planned it. I never sought it."

Now she is focused on causes, like the Bethune–DuBois Fund, an organization she founded to provide educational and training programs for black youth, and a newly formed coalition of African American women intent on voter registration.

* * *

CLOUDY DAYS

The rap lawsuits are not the first time Tucker's activities have been questioned. She was fired as secretary of state of Pennsylvania in 1977 by Gov. Milton Shapp, who had hired her. She had been reprimanded two years earlier, after charges that she used state workers and resources to produce speeches for which she received $65,000 in 28 months.

She brushes aside questions about those problems, maintaining that they started when she refused to support Shapp's designated successor as governor. "That's when the henchmen moved in," she says.

In the battle over gangsta rap, opponents describe her as "robotic . . . unable to discuss complicated issues." Industry executives say she has been promoting her own interests by singling out Time Warner for attention over other major rap distributors: Polygram, Sony and BMG. "She wasn't interested in a serious conversation about a complex issue," says one. "She was interested in going on 'Nightline.' "

* * *

"WE . . . HAVE POWER"

Despite the lawsuits, Tucker claims victory in her gangsta rap campaign.

* * *

Tucker's masterstroke was to stand up at the Time Warner stockholder meeting in May and read Tupac Shakur and Snoop Doggy Dogg lyrics aloud. Through the summer and fall, she and Bennett—joined by Lieberman in the Senate—kept up a steady beat of news conferences, television appearances and radio ads. By September, the Warner Music Group had sold its $115 million interest in Interscope.

* * *

Nevertheless, the day after the Interscope sale, Tucker clenched her fist in triumph. "They said it couldn't be done," she crowed. "It shows that we the people have power."

————

Does a Song By Any Other Name Still Sound as Sweet? Digital Sampling and Its Copyright Implications

Comment, 43 AM. U. L.R. 231 (1993).

■ RANDY S. KRAVIS

INTRODUCTION

Much controversy has emerged over the new technology of digital sampling. Simply put, sampling is the process that recording artists use to include previously recorded portions of another artist's work in a new recording. While some people in the music industry believe that sampling without permission is tantamount to stealing, others view sampling as an art form no more plagiaristic than any other. The popularity of "rap" music, which relies heavily on the use of sampling, has pushed the technique into the spotlight of the music industry. As a result, a debate has arisen over the practice of sampling and its legal implications.

The primary area of debate focuses on the Copyright Act of 1976. The Act governs the making and the use of artistic creations such as books, works of art, and musical compositions. Although it requires artists to obtain permission before using another's sound recordings in certain instances, for the most part, the Act is ill equipped to deal effectively with digital sampling. Congress simply could not have foreseen the myriad of issues that the advanced technology of sampling would present.

* * *

Another test that the Copyright Act uses to determine whether a use is a fair use is the "effect on the market" test, which asks whether the imitation or re-creation of a copyrighted song adversely affects the market for the copyrighted song. Again, when it formulated the effect on the market test, Congress did not and could not have taken into account sampling, where actual sounds of a song are used. Some commentators have questioned whether Congress would have outlawed digital sampling under the Act if it could have foreseen the advent of such technologies. Nevertheless, because Congress could not have considered the unique nature of sampling when it created and last amended the Act, legal scholars must analyze digital sampling without direct congressional guidance.

Surprisingly, despite the confusion, debate, and controversy surrounding sampling and its widespread use, it was not until December 1991 in *Grand Upright Music Ltd. v. Warner Bros. Records, Inc.* that a court handed down the first decision regarding the use of sampling. In that case, Judge Kevin Duffy for the U.S. District Court for the Southern District of New York enjoined the production and sale of rap artist Biz Markie's album "I Need a Haircut" because it contained sampled portions of Gilbert O'Sullivan's 1972 hit "Alone Again (Naturally)." In addition to issuing the injunction, Judge Duffy referred the case to the U.S. Attorney for consideration of possible criminal penalties.

The *Grand Upright Music* decision is significant for two reasons. First, the Southern District of New York, which issued the opinion, handles a large percentage of this country's copyright cases; thus the court has a substantial impact on copyright law. Second, the decision is the first and, so far, the only judicial attempt to provide guidance on applying current copyright law to digital sampling.

* * *

I. DIGITAL SAMPLING

* * *

While the use of the sampling process is a fairly recent phenomenon, digital sampling actually traces its roots back to the 1960s when disc jockeys (DJs) began experimenting with "dub," a form of art created when DJs mix different sounds together into a single musical work. Dub originated in Jamaica, where DJs mixed Jamaican and non-Jamaican records together. It continued to be solely a Jamaican practice until a Jamaican-born DJ named Kool DJ Herc, along with other early DJs, introduced dub in the United States by experimenting with early sound techniques that would become precursors to modern-day sampling.

II. COPYRIGHT LAW

The Copyright Act of 1976, which is the statutory body of law governing digital sampling, addresses four main issues: (1) What qualifies for copyright protection?; (2) If a work qualifies for protection, what rights does the owner of the copyright have with respect to the work?; (3) What constitutes infringement of that copyright?; and (4) If infringement is found, what remedies are available to the copyright owner? This Part addresses each question separately.

A. *What Qualifies for Copyright Protection?*

The 1976 Copyright Act protects only "original works of authorship fixed in any tangible medium of expression." Thus, for a work to qualify for copyright protection, it must satisfy certain criteria. First, a "work of authorship" must be at issue. The Act specifically lists seven categories that constitute works of authorship: literary works; dramatic works; pantomimes and choreographic works; pictorial, graphic, and sculptural works; motion pictures and audiovisual works; and sound recordings. Sampled songs are works of authorship because, as "musical ... works," they fall under the category of "sound recordings."

Second, only "original" works of authorship receive copyright protection under the Act. The Act itself does not define "original"; the courts, however, are in general agreement that the originality threshold is a very low one. In *L. Batlin & Son, Inc. v. Snyder*, for example, the U.S. Court of Appeals for the Second Circuit held that an author need only contribute something more than a "merely trivial" variation for the court to consider the work at issue to be original. The author's work simply has to be "recognizably his own." An original work must also possess "independent creation," but it need not be invention in the sense of striking uniqueness, ingeniousness, or novelty. Rather, an original work simply must be a distinguishable creation of the author.

Third, copyright law does not protect ideas, but expressions of those ideas in fixed forms. Thus, only ideas reduced to concrete form are copyrightable. For example, a copyright extends to the arrangement of words in a book, but not to the idea conveyed by the words. Similarly, a tune or melody that an individual hums is not protected. To gain protection, the melody must be recorded.

B. Rights of the Copyright Owner

Once an author has met the criteria for establishing a valid copyright and has completed the proper copyright registration procedure, the author then has certain exclusive rights under § 106 of the Act with respect to the copyrighted work. These exclusive rights include the rights to reproduce the work, to prepare derivative works, and to sell copies of the work to the public. A copyright's term lasts for fifty years after the death of the sound recording artist.

C. Infringement

Section 501(a) of the Copyright Act provides that "anyone who violates any of the exclusive rights of the copyright owner . . . is an infringer of the copyright." To show infringement of the copyright, a plaintiff must show proof of ownership of a valid copyright and demonstrate that the defendants copied the work. To prove actual copying, which is difficult to do, a plaintiff must establish the following two elements: "(1) defendant's access to the copyrighted work prior to creation of defendant's work, and (2) substantial similarity of both general ideas and expression between the copyrighted work and the defendant's work."

1. Ownership

To prove copyright infringement, the owner of a sound recording must prove ownership. Under § 201 of the Act, the author of a particular work initially receives ownership of the copyright. In most cases, then, a copyright owner may prove ownership simply by showing authorship. Under certain exceptional circumstances, however, the author of a work is not the owner of the copyright. For example, if the author were hired to create the work, then the copyright would rest not in the author, but in the employer for whom the work was made. In this instance, the employer must demonstrate that the work was created for hire to establish rightful ownership. Similarly, if the author previously conveyed all or part of the copyright to someone else, then the new owner has the burden of proving proper receipt of copyright ownership.

2. Copying

To prove infringement, the plaintiff in a copyright suit must prove that the defendant copied the sound recording by demonstrating that the defendant had "access" to the recording and that the two works are substantially similar.

a. Access

Without proof of access, the similarity between two works may be purely coincidental. Courts generally agree that the test for access is whether the defendant had a reasonable opportunity to view the copyrighted work. In sampling cases, access is rarely an issue because, by definition, sampling involves the purposeful usurpation of, and thus access to, another's work.

b. Substantial similarity

Unlike the access determination, the question of substantial similarity is an important issue in most sampling cases. The test for substantial similarity is whether a reasonable person would recognize that the defendant took the copyrighted work and incorporated it into a new work. A general impression of similarity is not sufficient to constitute "substantial" similarity. Rather, the "total concept" and "feel" of the two works must be similar. At the same time, however, a copyright owner does not have to show that every small detail of the protected work was duplicated. In fact, the duplication of only a small part of the work may be considered substantial if the part taken was an important and material part of the work.

3. The defense of fair use

In determining whether an act constitutes infringement, courts recognize that certain acts, such as fair use, are defensible. Specifically, § 107 provides an affirmative defense to potential infringers of the fair use doctrine. Section 107 does not define "fair use," but merely lists four factors for courts to weigh in determining whether the use of a copyrighted work is fair. The Act is silent, however, as to how much weight courts should allocate to each factor. The Supreme Court has also provided little guidance, explaining only that "[s]ection 107 requires a case-by-case determination whether a particular use is fair."

The first factor listed in § 107 is the purpose and character of the use. If the work is used for nonprofit educational purposes, for example, fair use may be presumed. A work used for commercial purposes, however, would not constitute a fair use. The second consideration is the nature of the copyrighted work. Courts generally permit the use of a longer portion of a protected work if the work is an informational collection of facts as opposed to a creative piece. The third factor is the amount and substantiality of the portion used. When determining whether this element has been met, courts look to the same considerations set forth in the substantial similarity element of infringement; specifically, courts consider both quantitative and qualitative similarity. If a court finds substantial similarity, it generally will find that the use was not fair. The fourth and final factor is the effect of the use on the potential market for the copyrighted work. A use that produces a negative effect on the sales market for the original work will tend to deny a finding of fair use.

D.   Remedies

Section 504 of the Copyright Act provides damage awards for the copyright owner once infringement has been proven. The Act states that the infringer is liable for either actual damages and profits or statutory damages. Actual damages generally are measured by the market value of profits lost by the copyright owner. Infringer's profits, which the owner is entitled to, are determined by deducting certain costs from the infringer's gross revenue. Statutory damages are available even without evidence that the plaintiff has suffered actual damages. The court has wide discretion in determining the amount of damages as long as it remains within the statutory limits.

* * *

Finally, if the court finds that the infringement is willful, the court can impose criminal sanctions. Courts are split, however, on the question of what level of intent constitutes willfulness. Some courts hold that only a general intent to act constitutes willfulness, even if the defendant did not realize that he or she was acting in an illegal manner; other courts require a specific intent to break the law.

III.   The Controversy Surrounding Digital Sampling

A.   The Debate Over Substantial Similarity

The legality of unauthorized digital sampling has divided the music industry. One issue that has caused much debate is the role of "substantial similarity" in a digital sampling suit. The controversy arises over the use of the word "actual" in § 114(b) of the Copyright Act. On one hand, this term can be viewed as prohibiting the usurpation of any exact sound from a song. But on the other hand, a plaintiff in a copyright suit must demonstrate substantial similarity between the two works in order to prove infringement. This substantial similarity requirement thus suggests that the Copyright Act might allow some actual use of a copyrighted song without that use rising to the level of infringement.

* * *

B.   The Debate Over Originality

Proponents of sampling often argue that sampling is no different from other art forms that rely on older works, and should thus be accorded the favorable legal treatment that these other art forms presently receive. They do not understand why samplers are penalized when other artists also borrow from earlier works of art without criticism. They maintain that all artists borrow from past works and assert that even great composers such as Bach, Handel, and Vivaldi borrowed from preexisting works.

* * *

On the other hand, this argument based on artistic originality might be out of place in a legal context because it has been held that "artistic originality is not the same thing as the legal concept of originality in the Copyright Act." In *Gracen v. Bradford Exchange*, the Seventh Circuit held that although a slight change or diversion from the original work might constitute artistic originality, it does not necessarily constitute legal originality. Consequently, samplers' claims that their works are original and independent creations might be misplaced because they focus on artistic originality, not legal originality.

* * *

C.   The Debate Over the Effect of Sampling on a Song's Market

The effect that sampling has on a song's potential market is one element courts use to decide whether the use of the song is a fair one. It is an affirmative defense for one accused of copyright infringement to argue that the infringement did not adversely affect the market for the copyrighted song. Given that digital samplers often borrow from older songs, samplers argue that use of these songs does not adversely affect their potential market because the people who would buy these older songs will not buy rap albums in their place. Therefore, even if it is conceded that sampling is a copyright infringement, it is still a fair use because it does not harm the market for the original song. In fact, some argue that sampling actually helps the potential market for older songs by reviving interest in relatively forgotten music.

Critics of sampling could suggest, however, that a market analysis that only examines the effect on the original song is incomplete because it fails to account for the effect on other potential or derivative uses of the song. For example, if the owner of an older song re-released the song as a rap version, any prior sampling would affect the market for that derivative work by potentially interfering with sales of the owner's new version. In this way, sampling may hurt the market for protected songs, thus proving to be an unfair use of the original songs.

* * *

Advocates of sampling could respond by asserting that § 107 does not mention the effect on the potential market for the musician. Rather, the Act only mentions the effect on the market for the actual work. Under this approach, while the effect on the common studio musician is unfortunate, it has no bearing on the question of fair use.

D.   The Copyright Act's Ambiguous Legislative History

Both sides of the digital sampling debate have interpreted the language of the Copyright Act differently when arguing whether digital sampling constitutes copyright infringement. Attempting to find answers in the Act's legislative history, however, is difficult. When Congress last made major changes to the Act in 1976, digital sampling did not exist. Any analysis of legislative history thus can only speculate on what Congress would have done had it considered digital sampling. As a result, the Act's legislative history has spawned further debate over how Congress would have responded to digital sampling.

* * *

IV. THE CASE: *GRAND UPRIGHT MUSIC LTD. v. WARNER BROS. RECORDS, INC.*

Before December 1991, the controversy surrounding the copyright implications of digital sampling could only take the form of a debate as to what the law should be with regards to sampling. With no judicial decisions addressing the issue and with a controlling statute that predated the development of sampling technology, the debate was necessarily and uncomfortably theoretical. On December 16, 1991, however, the Southern District of New York, "[a]fter many years of anticipation and speculation," announced the first judicial opinion to address the issues presented by digital sampling, *Grand Upright Music Ltd. v. Warner Bros. Records, Inc.*

A. *The Factual Background*

Grand Upright Music Ltd., the alleged copyright owner of pop artist Gilbert O'Sullivan's 1972 hit "Alone Again (Naturally)," brought a copyright infringement action to enjoin all production and sales of rap artist Biz Markie's album "I Need a Haircut." Grand Upright Music based its claim on the fact that Biz Markie's album contained a song entitled "Alone Again" that used three words and a portion of the music from the master recording of the Gilbert O'Sullivan song. Before the infringement action arose, Biz Markie's attorney had tried to get permission to use the 1972 song from Terry O'Sullivan, the artist's brother and agent, by sending a letter requesting use of the song along with a cassette copy of Biz Markie's recording. Before the two reached an agreement, however, Biz Markie released the "I Need a Haircut" album. Mr. O'Sullivan subsequently refused to grant permission to use the song and, after repeated demands to remove the album from the market, he filed suit.

B. *The Opinion*

The defendants in this case, Biz Markie and the record companies that produced "I Need a Haircut," conceded that the Biz Markie song used words and music from the Gilbert O'Sullivan song. On the basis of this admission, the district court concluded that Biz Markie's use constituted infringement of the original song's copyright and that the only remaining issue was whether Grand Upright Music was the true owner of the "Alone Again (Naturally)" copyright. The court ruled that Grand Upright Music was the owner of the copyright based on three categories of proof: (1) copies of the copyrights and deeds vesting title to the copyrights in Gilbert O'Sullivan and then from O'Sullivan to Grand Upright Music; (2) testimony of Gilbert O'Sullivan acknowledging Grand Upright Music as the copyright owner; and (3) the defendants' attempt to contact Gilbert and Terry O'Sullivan. With regard to the third element of proof of ownership, the court held that the defendants' attempt to discuss terms for use of the song with Terry and Gilbert O'Sullivan was evidence that the plaintiff owned a valid copyright. The court reasoned that the defendants would not have attempted to discuss terms with O'Sullivan if the latter were not the copyright owner.

The court further concluded that Biz Markie's use of the song violated Grand Upright Music's valid copyright to the song. As a result, the court enjoined the sale of Biz Markie's album. The court also found that the defendants intended "to sell thousands upon thousands of records" by knowingly violating the copyright. Consequently, the court referred the case to the U.S. Attorney for the Southern District of New York for possible criminal prosecution of the defendants for willful copyright infringement.

V. THE EFFECT OF *GRAND UPRIGHT MUSIC* ON THE LAW REGARDING DIGITAL SAMPLING

A. *The Decision's Effect on the Law Regarding Digital Sampling*

There are two reasons to believe that *Grand Upright Music* will have a strong impact on digital sampling law. First, the Southern District of New York, which decided *Grand Upright Music*, handles a substantial percentage of all the copyright and entertainment law cases in this country. The *Grand Upright Music* decision, which is binding authority on all cases that come out of the Southern District of New York, will thus serve as controlling authority on a large percentage of future digital sampling cases.

Second, because *Grand Upright Music* is the only judicial pronouncement on the issue of digital sampling, it is likely to be persuasive authority in other jurisdictions. Considering the vagueness of the outdated body of statutory law, and the lack of judicial assistance in applying the statutory law to digital sampling, future digital sampling cases from other jurisdictions will at least address the *Grand Upright Music* decision. Other jurisdictions, therefore, may use this case as a starting point from which to rule on digital sampling simply because it is the first and only court ruling on digital sampling. For purposes of a detailed legal review of this decision, then, this Note assumes that the *Grand Upright Music* decision will influence the law.

B. *How the Decision Will Influence the Law Regarding Digital Sampling*

Although long awaited as the first digital sampling decision, *Grand Upright Music* left many questions unanswered. One prominent entertainment lawyer said, " '[T]his isn't the seminal case everyone wanted.' " While the court ruled that Biz Markie's sampling violated the copyright law, the court failed to mention the elements necessary to prove copyright infringement, with the exception of the copyright ownership element. Although the decision failed to clear up many of the theoretical legal questions regarding digital sampling, it still will have a significant impact on the music and entertainment industry.

1. The impact on the questions of law presented by digital sampling

The *Grand Upright Music* decision explicitly focuses on ownership, one of the elements a plaintiff must demonstrate to prove infringement. This issue, however, is not the real problem that digital sampling brings to copyright law. Observers had hoped that this case would address some of the questions that the issue of fair use presents to digital sampling, such as sampling's effect on the market and the role of substantial similarity in a digital sampling suit. Yet, without addressing any defense of fair use issues, the court ruled that, once the plaintiff proved ownership, infringement had occurred by the simple fact that Biz Markie had sampled Gilbert O'Sullivan's song.

* * *

Grand Upright Music also fails to clarify the issue of willful infringement. In *Grand Upright Music*, the district court referred the case to the U.S. Attorney for possible criminal sanctions because it had found willful infringement. In particular, the defendants' actions and testimony indicated that they knew Mr. O'Sullivan owned a valid copyright. The court, however, omitted any discussion of whether willfulness requires a specific intent to break the law or only a broader intent to commit an act that is an infringement of a copyright. The fact that the defendants knew that they were sampling a copyrighted song without authorization was sufficient for the court to find the defendants guilty of copyright infringement. Nevertheless, the court's utter failure to explain what level of intent is needed for sampling to constitute infringement perpetuates the confusion surrounding willful infringement.

* * *

2. The impact on the music industry

Even though the court in *Grand Upright Music* did not expressly rule out the possibility that the limited use of a song may be legal, the court's strong condemnation of unauthorized sampling could be construed as a declaration that sampling constitutes infringement per se. Thus, while *Grand Upright Music* provides little guidance on the legal questions of digital sampling, it will still have a major impact on the music industry because it is a strong judicial denunciation of the practice of unauthorized sampling. For this reason, samplers will have to alter their behavior.

* * *

VI. Solutions

A. Congress Should Amend the Copyright Act

Grand Upright Music's shortcomings suggest that the Copyright Act is so outdated that it simply cannot provide answers to the digital sampling problem. A revision of the Act may thus be the only solution to the sampling dilemma.

* * *

A revision of the current copyright law to accommodate sampling would be consistent with both the Copyright Act's history of periodic adjustment due to technological advancements and the purposes of copyright law. The Copyright Act has two major objectives: securing an adequate return for the artist, and securing public access to artistic works through the prevention of monopolies. When copyright laws become outdated, new technologies escape regulation and the Act's policy goals are thwarted. * * *

B. Congress Should Institute a Compulsory Licensing Provision for Digital Sampling

Copyright law's two competing policy goals, public access to works of art and protection of copyright owners' rights to profit, are diametrically opposed objectives. For example, a prohibition on sampling would disregard the policy of access to others' works. At the same time, allowing unrestricted unauthorized sampling would compromise the copyright owners' interests in seeking an adequate return on their works. To achieve the optimal balance between these two goals, the law should take the middle ground.

* * *

CONCLUSION

In modern musical culture, digital sampling has emerged as a popular technique for exploring and reexamining older music. Because the sampling phenomenon is more far-reaching in its technological capabilities than any previous musical technology, sampling has transcended the scope of the existing law, forcing lawyers, musicians, and others in the music entertainment business to analyze this new musical technique in a legal vacuum, and leaving them only to speculate as to how the old law applies to sampling. As a result, much debate and controversy among those interested in the entertainment law field have produced a whole spectrum of opinions on digital sampling's place in the law. In fact, even the judiciary appears confused and undecided on how the law should treat sampling, as evidenced by the *Grand Upright Music* decision.

* * *

_____

A NOTE ON ARTISTIC REPARATIONS

In the following excerpt, we catch a glimpse of black rock 'n' roll icon Little Richard's bitterness about the economic impact of racism that many black artists endured in the 1930s through 1970s. After he suffered bankruptcy, Little Richard describes his economic subordination in the industry as follows: "I was taken for everything except my toenails—and they would've got them as well, but they were too short to cut."

The exploitation of African American talent during this period is a double tragedy because many of the individual artists who are still alive today do not have a secure retirement, or the financial security of many of their less talented white contemporaries. The second misfortune is that the black music of this period is generally agreed around the world to be the most uniquely American contribution to music. It is a paradox that the cultural contributions of African American artists serve as the foundation of American cultural identity worldwide, while these contributions have not provided a foundation of stable wealth for the communities from which they emerged.

The difficulty in law is fashioning a legal theory that will permit the wealth of the music industry to be redirected to rectify past economic injustice. As we see in *Merchant v. Levy*, below, formal legal rules such as laches (delay in pursuing the claim), estoppel (preclusion to pursue the claim because of some earlier action by the claimant), or statutes of limitation (statutory time limitations imposed on the injured party's right to sue for redress) present formidable barriers to redress.

Can you think of other theories of compensation? What about reparations theory? Equitable restitution and constructive trusts? For a careful exploration of the moral and ethical premises of restitution, see Hanoch Dagan, *The Distributive Foundation of Corrective Justice*, 98 Mich. L. Rev. 138, (1999) (exploring the corrective justice approach to the doctrine of restitution for wrongs and especially for appropriations); Hanoch Dagan, The Fourth Pillar: The Law and Ethics of Restitution (2004).

————

A Session With Little Richard

Jim Jerome, Life Mag., Dec. 1992, at p. 48.

With a crash of piano keys, a flash of mascaraed eyelashes and a dash of awop-bop-aloo-bop-awop-bam-boom, Little Richard baptized a new musical style.—born Richard Penniman in Macon, GA., and raised on gospel music, he ran away from home with Dr. Hudson's traveling medicine show.—he later toured small nightclubs in the south and cut records for RCA and the Peacock label in Houston.—commercial success eluded him—until September 14, 1955, when he entered J & M studios in New Orleans for Specialty Records. That recording session produced "Tutti Frutti," a hit in early 1956. More sessions quickly followed, and out of them came such rock standards as "Long Tall Sally," "Rip it Up," "Keep a Knockin'" and "Good Golly, Miss Molly." Then, suddenly, during a tour of Australia in late 1957, Little Richard renounced rock and roll, saying he had dreamed of his own damnation. He went on to become a minister in the Seventh–Day Adventist church, and over the years, while mounting several unsuccessful comebacks, he has preached against drugs and sex (particularly homosexuality), but it was his quavering falsetto shriek that gathered most converts. Jim Jerome talked with the 56 or 59–year–old musician (depending on whether you believe him or his mother) in a Hollywood hotel, his home away from his Riverside, Calif., home, as flamboyant and outrageous as ever. Little Richard didn't hesitate to claim his rightful place in the history of rock and roll.

"Tutti Frutti" was really an accident, wasn't it?

Yes. See, they wanted me to sing like Ray Charles and B.B. King. I did it just to record; it wasn't what I wanted. So after one session I got on the piano and did awop-bop-aloo-bop-awop-bam-boom. They said, "That's the hit. Ain't no one ever put out mess like that." I had to clean up the lyrics. I had "Tutti frutti, good booty" instead of "aw-rooty." And there was worse, believe me.

Does any one show stick in your mind?

I remember one of those early Madison Square Garden shows in New York—runnin' out there with my brothers and my entourage, the lights come up and those screams, and it just ran through my whole body like a shock. I stood there with my arms out, then I sat at the piano, screamin' to the top of my lungs and tears comin' out of my eyes. My orgasm was the stage, gettin' out there and touchin' the piano and goin' wild. You can't buy that feeling.

But money did buy you plenty.

I remember before one of his big New York shows Alan Freed walked up to me—it was my birthday or some celebration—and he handed me an envelope with $10,000 in it, all in hundred dollar bills. He kissed me on the jaw. I put it all in the trunk of my custom gold-and-white Cadillac with the leopard interior. I bought my mother a mansion in L.A., right behind Joe Louis, and my bed was packed with money. My sisters would just count it over and over.

What impact did racism have on your early career?

I was blocked from playing a lot of places. We'd have to drive all night in the car, 'cause there wasn't no blacks allowed in the hotel. If we wanted a sandwich, you had to go to the back door of a restaurant and ask the chef if he would fix you one. This is even after all of those big hits. And no hospitals for us if we got sick on the road down south.

Do you see any link between your music and rap?

Yes. When I see Hammer, I see me. Michael Jackson—I look at him, I see Little Richard. And he's the greatest entertainer ever lived. Little Richard suffered, he went through hell, he was denied, he was deprived. I helped build that bridge across despair. Now the road is paved. That's why Michael Jackson gets a billion-dollar guarantee.

So is Elvis the King of Rock and Roll?

I know they call him the King, but if he is, who crowned him? When was the ceremony—and why was I not invited? How can a white boy be King of Rock and Roll? I'm not downin' white singers. But I been imitated by more people. I, too, have been called the King of Rock and Roll. I been called the Queen. I earned the throne 'cause I am the Originator, the Architect, the Emancipator—The Founding Father of Rock and Roll.

————

The Fight Over The Golden Oldies

MACLEAN'S, March 2, 1987, at 36.

■ NICHOLAS JENNINGS

Even from an artist renowned for outrageous behavior, the action was a shocking sight. In August, 1984, Richard Penniman—better known as Little Richard, the flamboyant 1950s rocker—began picketing an office building in downtown Los Angeles. The rock star was not on strike; he was on a crusade. The offices belonged to ATV Music Corp., one of the world's largest song publishers. Little Richard's claim: that ATV, along with Specialty Records and Venice Music, owed him millions of dollars in royalties for *Tutti-Frutti, Good Golly Miss Molly* and other classic Little Richard hits. Four months later his $115–million lawsuit against those companies was thrown out of U.S. Federal Court.

Bankrupt: Now, Little Richard, 54, is pondering his next move. But in a recent *Maclean's* interview he said bitterly, "I was taken for everything except my toenails—and they would've got them as well, but they were too short to cut." Little Richard has a new recording contract with Warner Bros. and says that *Lifetime Friend,* his new album on that label, will be the first to earn him money in 30 years of recording.

* * *

Beatles: Even the biggest and presumably best-advised artists have made deals they now regret. Since 1969 Paul McCartney has tried unsuccessfully to recover ownership rights to the highly prized Beatles' songs he wrote with John Lennon, currently owned by ATV. The Beatles' songs are part of the corporation's catalogue, now valued at more than $65 million.

* * *

At last, however, artists have someone to champion their cause. He is Chuck Rubin, described by *The New York Times* as the "white knight of rock." Rubin, 48, runs the Artists Rights Enforcement Corp., a New York firm that seeks to regain royalties for performers. His list of about 200 clients reads like a *Who's Who* of early rock 'n' roll, with enough vintage pop songs to their credit to fill a rec room full of jukeboxes. Among them: The Shirelles (*I Met Him on a Sunday*); Huey (Piano) Smith (*Sea Cruise*); The Marvelettes (*Please Mr. Postman*); and the estate of Clyde McPhatter (*Money Honey*).

* * *

An even more bizarre case involves the estate of Frankie Lymon, the teenage singing sensation who died in 1968. Lymon and his group, the Teenagers, enjoyed a Top 10 hit in 1956 with *Why Do Fools Fall in Love,* which later was used on several TV shows. Rubin successfully won performance royalties for the artists, including Lymon's estate, in 1982. But it was not until a year later, while pursuing further royalties, that Rubin located Lymon's widow, Emira Lymon, a schoolteacher in Augusta, Ga. She was naturally delighted, but surprised that she was entitled to any royalties; she had been told by Lymon's attorney that she had no legal claim. When Rubin tried to help her renew the claim on her husband's composition, he discovered that Lymon's record company owner had come to court with two other women, each claiming to be the singer's widow and heir. The case is now pending in the New York courts. Rubin estimates that the royalties in question could be worth more than $1.4 million.

Payments: In some cases the loss of rights was clearly the artist's own fault. In 1957 Richard Berry sold copyrights to seven of his songs to his publisher for $750 because, he said later, he needed money to get married. One of those songs, a three-chord tune called *Louie Louie*, later became a rock classic, with more than 400 recorded versions. Had Berry retained ownership, industry experts say that he would have earned about $5 million from the song. But his story has a happy ending. Last year, after seven years of perseverance, Berry, 51, won his share of the copyright back and is now entitled to future payments.

* * *

Merchant v. Levy

92 F.3d 51 (2d Cir. 1996).

■ JON O. NEWMAN, CHIEF JUDGE.

BACKGROUND

Plaintiffs Merchant and Santiago are two of the original members of the singing group "The Teenagers," which was formed in 1955. Plaintiffs testified that in 1955 they jointly wrote the initial version of the song *Fools*. Frankie Lymon made a number of changes to the song when he subsequently joined the group, which then became known as "Frankie Lymon and The Teenagers." The jury found that Merchant, Santiago, and Lymon were co-authors of *Fools*. At the time Lymon was 12 years old and Plaintiffs were each 15.

In 1956 the Teenagers recorded *Fools* for Gee Records, then owned and operated by George Goldner, now deceased. Plaintiffs testified that they relied upon Goldner to handle the formalities of copyrighting the song, and that Goldner informed them that only two of the three authors could be listed on the copyright. Subsequently, Goldner filed the *Fools* copyright with the Copyright Office in 1956, listing himself and Lymon as sole co-authors. The Levy Defendants maintain that Goldner was properly listed as an author because he was personally involved in writing and arranging *Fools*. The Levy Defendants also contend that Goldner was a co-author of *Fools* under the "work for hire" doctrine because, during the Fools recording session, a saxophone solo composed by a studio musician was incorporated into the song. The jury, however, found that Goldner was not an author of *Fools*.

Sometime in the 1950s Lymon agreed to let Goldner exploit Lymon's interest in the song. In 1968 Lymon died, survived by his wife Emira Lymon.

In 1964, defendant Morris Levy purchased Goldner's interest in several music companies, including the music publishing company that held the copyright for *Fools*. In a letter to the Copyright Office dated June 24, 1965, Goldner stated that Levy, rather than Goldner, had co-authored *Fools* with Lymon. The copyright registration was amended to reflect this statement and, thereafter, the copyright was held by Levy's company, Big Seven Music.

Although *Fools* became a hit and continues to be popular today (Diana Ross has recorded a popular version), Plaintiffs have never received any royalties from their claimed co-authorship of *Fools*.

* * *

Beginning in the late 1970s, Plaintiffs took various steps in pursuit of their claim, including hiring an attorney and investigator to look into the status of the copyright. Plaintiffs did not take formal legal action, however, until 1987.

A. Procedural History

Plaintiffs brought the instant Complaint against the Levy Defendants and Emira Lymon on October 7, 1987. Plaintiffs asked for a declaration that they were co-owners with Lymon of the copyright to *Fools* and for an accounting of royalties. Plaintiffs also alleged copyright infringement, Sherman Act and Lanham Act violations, unfair competition, fraud and misappropriation, and negligence and breach of fiduciary duty. Before trial the District Court (Vincent L. Broderick, Judge) dismissed all claims against Emira Lymon, but allowed the action to proceed against the Levy Defendants.

* * *

The Court granted Plaintiffs' basic request for a declaration of copyright co-ownership, rejecting the three defenses advanced by the Levy Defendants, all based on the long delay in Plaintiffs' assertion of their claim.

1. *Duress and Statute of Limitations.* The Court interpreted the three-year statute of limitations, applicable to civil copyright actions, 17 U.S.C. § 507(b), as limiting Plaintiffs' recovery to damages accruing within three years of the filing of the suit, rather than as an absolute bar to Plaintiffs' cause of action. Merchant, 828 F. Supp. at 1056. The important question for the Court then became whether the statute of limitations had been tolled for any period before the filing of the suit, thereby allowing

Plaintiffs to recover damages that accrued even prior to three years before the suit. *Id.*

* * *

2. *Laches.* Responding to the Levy Defendants' laches defense, the Court, relying on equity's "clean hands" principle, refused to allow the Levy Defendants to profit from their "untoward actions" by asserting laches. *Id.* at 1064.

3. *Equitable Estoppel.* As to equitable estoppel, which requires proof that a defendant was misled into justifiably believing that a plaintiff would not pursue its claims against the defendant, the Court determined that the Levy Defendants offered no evidence that Plaintiffs acted in a manner that justified a belief on the part of the Levy Defendants that their copyright was free from challenge. *Id.*

B.   Subsequent Proceedings

* * *

In the final judgment entered on June 26, 1995, the Court awarded Plaintiffs an undivided one-half interest in the copyright to *Fools.* The Court also ordered the Levy Defendants and Windswept to pay money damages to Plaintiffs.

On this appeal Defendants challenge the District Court's subject matter jurisdiction, and also argue that the District Court erred in not dismissing the action for a declaration of copyright co-ownership as barred by the statute of limitations or laches. Defendants additionally contend that Plaintiffs failed to establish that they are joint authors of *Fools.* Plaintiffs cross-appeal, arguing that the Court should have applied the tolling doctrine of equitable estoppel to allow Plaintiffs to recover damages accruing from 1969 to 1984, the period during which the jury had found that Plaintiffs were subject to duress.

DISCUSSION

I.   Subject Matter Jurisdiction

Federal courts have exclusive original jurisdiction over actions arising under the federal copyright laws. See 28 U.S.C. § 1338(a). As Judge Friendly has explained, an action "arises under" the copyright laws "if the complaint is for a remedy expressly granted by the [Copyright] Act, ... or asserts a claim requiring construction of the Act ... or, at the very least and perhaps more doubtfully, presents a case where a distinctive policy of the Act requires that federal principles control the disposition of the claim." *T.B. Harms Co. v. Eliscu,* 339 F.2d 823, 828 (2d Cir. 1964), *cert. denied,* 381 U.S. 915 (1965). Plaintiffs' action seeking to establish their rights to copyright co-ownership because of their status as co-authors of a joint work falls well within these jurisdictional boundaries.

* * *

II.   Statute of Limitations

We come finally to the dispositive issue. Plaintiffs filed the instant suit in 1987, primarily seeking a declaration of their copyright ownership rights and an accounting of profits. Civil actions under the Copyright Act are subject to a three-year statute of limitations. 17 U.S.C. § 507(b). Defendants argue that since Plaintiffs did not institute suit for a declaration of copyright co-ownership within three years of the accrual of their claim, they are now time-barred.

* * *

The District Court nevertheless awarded Plaintiffs a declaration of co-ownership rights and damages for a time period beginning three years before the commencement of their suit. The Court relied on our decision in *Stone, supra.* That decision, however, which was based on "highly idiosyncratic facts," 3 *Nimmer, supra,* § 12.05 at 12–108 n.2.2, does not insulate all civil actions under the copyright law from the general three-year statute of limitations. Rather, *Stone* stands for the narrow proposition that, in certain situations, the statute of limitations will not be applied to defeat the copyright co-ownership claim of an author's relative accruing more than three years before the lawsuit where uncertainty surrounded the relative's status as a member of the author's family. Instead, if the relative prevails on the merits and if the equities permit, the Court will grant the relative a declaration of copyright co-ownership, but permit damages only for the period starting three years prior to the suit. See *Stone,* 970 F.2d at 1051.

Three Wives & The Legacy of "Love"; A Courtroom Clash Over Frankie Lyman's '56 Song

Wash. Post, Mar. 30, 1988, at C1.

■ Paula Span

It's been 32 years, but the song still shimmers and bops: first that calliope-like bass ("ehhh toom ah-ta toom ah-ta toom ah doe doe"), then a wash of "ooh-wahs," followed by the swooping soprano of 13–year-old Frankie Lymon, asking his immortal musical questions:

Why do birds sing so gay? Why does the rain fall from up above? And the true imponderable, "Why Do Fools Fall in Love?"

It is Frankie Lymon's only real legacy, that two minutes and 15 seconds of doo-wop. He recorded other songs, alone and with his group the Teenagers, but none has inspired the same affection. The only child he is known to have fathered died hours after her birth. He left no fortune; when he died of a heroin overdose 20 years ago, he was broke and troubled, trying again for a comeback he never achieved.

* * *

Depending on how the judge rules, the decision may reactivate a federal suit to wrest Lymon's royalties and publishing rights from the record industry executive who claims to own them. There may be further delays, though, while that executive faces federal extortion charges. Not to mention that two other members of the Teenagers have filed suit claiming they co-wrote "Why Do Fools Fall in Love."

* * *

ELIZABETH

They were there in Surrogate Court—the three would-be widows and their teams of lawyers and witnesses—for 10 days this past December and January, raking over the past.

Zola Taylor Lymon, now 50, one of the original Platters, had flown in from Los Angeles. Conscious of her stardom (Reporter: "Are you still performing in California?" Zola: "I perform all over the world"), she arrived at court daily in a limousine.

* * *

Neither Zola nor Elizabeth could quite figure Emira Eagle Lymon, the 48–year-old third wife from Augusta, Ga. Frankie marrying a schoolteacher? "She's a square," Zola decided, noticing that Emira was coming to court in sneakers. Zola and Elizabeth didn't get close to Emira; she didn't have anything much to say to them, either.

The essence of their dispute was which of the marriages was legally binding, given a certain laxity in some quarters about divorce. At the least, records and witnesses' recollections seem to indicate that Frankie Lymon did stand before a magistrate or minister on three occasions to promise himself to each of these women until death parted them, which turned out to be a fairly short time.

* * *

ZOLA

Zola Taylor had also been a teen-aged star. Her singing group, the Platters, was sometimes referred to as the Four Platters and a Dish; Zola, in her low-cut gowns, was the dish.

She and Frankie were riding a tour bus together in 1956, doing 81 one-nighters with a rock 'n' roll cavalcade that included Chuck Berry, the Coasters, the Penguins and Bo Diddley, as well as the Platters and the Teenagers. They became lovers, Zola testified, one night in Bangor, Maine, when Frankie had won $1,700 gambling with Clyde McPhatter and she had gotten "a little loaded drinking scotch and water." Zola, the older woman, was 17. Their affair continued off and on for several years.

* * *

The next month, according to Zola, she and Frankie drove to Tijuana and got married in a small chapel. The small wedding party celebrated by getting very drunk, not an uncommon state for Frankie at the time. Back in Los Angeles, the club where Zola was performing tossed a celebration, with a cake and champagne.

Zola has been unable to locate records documenting their Mexican wedding, or documenting her Mexican divorce from her previous marriage (her second). But her secretary and her booking agent both testified that they were witnesses to the wedding. Zola's attorneys argue that California law makes her a "putative spouse" entitled to share in Lymon's property.

* * *

EMIRA

By the time Pvt. Lymon was discharged a year later, he'd said "I do" once more. This time his bride was Emira Eagle, an educated, churchgoing elementary school teacher who lived with her family in nearby Augusta. Her sister's boyfriend introduced them; soon, Emira was cooking meals for Frankie and they were shopping for wedding rings. They were married in June 1967 at the Beulah Grove Baptist Church, with 50 members of Emira's family in attendance and a reception afterward at the Capri Lounge.

* * *

Key parts of this chronology are in dispute, of course. Emira's attorneys argue that Elizabeth and Frankie separated in mid–1965 and never lived together as man and wife thereafter, invalidating her claim to a common-law marriage. They point to the absence of documentation from Mexico as evidence that Zola and Frankie never married at all. Elizabeth's lawyers maintain her marriage is valid, which means that neither Zola's nor Emira's can be.

* * *

WHO WROTE THE BOOK OF "LOVE"?

* * *

Who wrote "Why Do Fools Fall in Love"? It is copyrighted in the names of Frankie Lymon and Morris Levy, head of Roulette Records, an independent label that bought out the Gee label, which originally released the record. Levy's attorney, Leon Borstein, says that Levy "assisted in the writing of the song; you have to remember, if he added one word, that's sufficient" to justify coauthorship. Borstein also says that Lymon, who was always pestering Levy for money, sold Levy the copyright to all his songs and that Levy has a signed document to that effect. "Remember, Frankie needed the money badly," Borstein says. "He had been busted in California again for drugs." The sum, he says, "might have been $1,500."

But in 1984 (as the original copyright term of the song was expiring) Emira Eagle Lymon brought suit in U.S. District Court in New York against Levy, his attorney, his record label and his publishing company. Her complaint charges fraud, misappropriation and copyright infringement, among other offenses. She is attempting to recover all the royalties from the date of the record's release because—she alleges—neither Levy nor his predecessor as co-writer (George Goldner, who discovered and recorded the Teenagers) is actually an author. Borstein, Levy's attorney, says the charges are "complete speculation; there's absolutely no proof."

* * *

Jimmy Merchant and Herman Santiago, the two surviving members of the original Teenagers (Sherman Garnes, the inventive bass, and Joe Negroni were the others), say they wrote "Why Do Fools Fall in Love?" with Frankie Lymon, and they have filed their own federal suit against Levy et al., with Emira also named as a defendant.

* * *

––––––

Lymon's "Teenagers" Are No Fools; Win Rights to '50s Hit in Long Fight

NEWSDAY, Nov. 19, 1992, at 45.

■ PAT WECHLER

It took 36 years, but a federal jury in Manhattan Tuesday awarded the copyright to the 1956 hit song "Why Do Fools Fall in Love?" to Jimmy Merchant and Herman Santiago, members of the 1950s rock and roll group Frankie Lymon and the Teenagers, which first performed it.

The award of the copyright could mean millions of dollars in past and future royalties for Merchant and Santiago, who have been fighting since the late 1960s for a share in the song's success. An attorney for the performers said that at least 3 million records with the song—now an American classic—were sold over the years, including a 1981 album by Diana Ross that used the song as its title. All records and performances of the song since 1969, the date the jury chose to base past royalties on, will bring them additional royalties.

* * *

Juries decided the composers should be allowed to right old wrongs, despite statutes of limitations, because the composers of '50s and '60s hits—often underage and from poor and minority neighborhoods—were unaware that sizable royalties were being paid and that they should have been receiving a portion.

In both cases, attorneys for the record companies, which will owe the back royalties, are seeking to overturn the verdicts.

* * *

Attorneys for Merchant and Santiago argued in the successful suit that the two had been the composers of the song, along with Lymon, but that music mogul George Goldner filed in 1956 the song's copyright in Lymon's and his own name.

In the 1964, the copyright to "Fools" was transferred to another music entrepreneur, Morris Levy, who took over Goldner's operation and has been linked to organized crime in articles and books on the music industry. Both Levy and Goldner are dead.

Santiago testified that he and Merchant were threatened by Levy in 1969 not to try to get the copyright back or a portion of the royalties.

SWEET SOUND OF ROYALTIES

Songwriters earn two types of royalties—mechanical and performing. For classics such as "Why Do Fools Fall In Love?", the combined royalties can easily reach into the millions of dollars over time.

Mechanical royalties have to do with the actual recording of songs. The government has set a rate of 6.25 cents for each time the song is recorded, multiplied by the number of records cut that contain the song. That amount is paid to the music publishing company which then pays a portion to the composer, determined by agreements between the two.

Performing royalties relate to how many times the song is played on the radio or performed on television, in movies and in nightclubs. These royalties are collected by either of the nation's two performance rights societies—the American Society for Composers, Artists and Performers (ASCAP) or Broadcast Music Inc. (BMI).

BMI or ASCAP collect a set fee for use of a song licensed to them. After subtracting a fee for the collection service, a portion of the total collection for each three-month quarter is paid to the publishing company of the song, based on how popular the song has been in that quarter as determined by BMI and ASCAP, through random samplings of radio and other outlets. These royalties split equally between the company and the actual composer.

Malcolm X and the Hip Hop Culture

RECONSTRUCTION II, 100–03 (1993).

■ MARTHA BAYLES

The looming billboards, the full-page ads, the T-shirts, the baseball caps, the potato chips, the automobile air fresheners—they all say "X." To many admirers of Malcolm X, the hype surrounding Spike Lee's latest movie is an insult. How dare Lee reduce Malcolm X's extraordinary, ultimately tragic life to a logo, a trademark with no more depth than, say, the Batman symbol. As Jonathan Yardley wrote in the *Washington Post*: "This implacably serious man has become that most American of creatures, a brand-name superstar. It is impossible to imagine that anything more demeaning could be done, to his name and his memory." Even Malcolm's widow, Betty Shabazz, expressed doubts, hiring a licensing firm to curb a marketing juggernaut that, in her view, "had gotten out of hand."

 * * *

This is not to say that there is nothing good about either hip-hop or Lee's film making. On the contrary, that ubiquitous "X" looks a whole lot better after seeing *Malcolm X*. My expectations for the film were modest, because although Lee is gifted in many areas of filmmaking (such as business, production design, hiring jazz composers and working with actors), he is deficient in the most important one, storytelling. To tell a good story, you must be able to think straight, and Lee shows minimal interest in that activity. Like so many other celebrities, black and white, who play at politics from the vantage point of entertainment, Lee seems, (especially in interviews) to have nothing invested in clarity, everything in obfuscation—or, at best, in a clownish incoherence that would be funny if the issues were not so grave.

* * *

Most people would agree that Malcolm X's legacy has something to do with truth-seeking, and with being unafraid to change one's life, along with one's mind, according to the truth one discovers. I hasten to add that by "truth-seeking" I do not mean total historical accuracy. Was Malcolm X's father a proud follower of Marcus Garvey, or did he beat his wife and children? Probably both, but I don't care. Let the historians quibble about whether Earl Little ever laid a hand on young Malcolm; God may be in the details in health-care reform, but not in legend. What matters is that Malcolm X's father was an upright, demanding, forceful man whose loss destroyed the family and left his most brilliant son alone with the painfully open question of what it means to be a black male in America. The film gets that essential starting point right.

* * *

Malcolm X *was* Detroit Red, of course, and one of the most powerful themes in his autobiography is his revulsion at the hypocrisy of whites, including his girlfriend, Sophia, who secretly pursued sexual liaisons with blacks. This theme is soft-pedaled in the film: there's a veil of contempt in Denzel Washington's eyes when (as Malcolm) he orders Sophia to kiss his foot and feed him like a baby. Later, there's more than a hint of revulsion in the image of Sophia's white husband, a lumpish fellow sunk in an armchair who doesn't even look up when she brings his TV dinner. And finally, there's the judgment rendered through Laura, the black girl who defies her strict upbringing to go with Malcolm, only to sink into drug abuse and prostitution when be drops her for Sophia. Together, these scenes evoke something of the indignation Malcolm X felt at the sick racist stereotypes that reduce black men to the status of stud animals and expose black women to every kind of exploitation.

* * *

Recall that Malcolm X, like so many of his followers, was a child of the Great Migration. In addition to being a Garveyite, his father was also an itinerant Baptist preacher, hailing from Georgia but preaching hellfire sermons among his fellow migrants in Philadelphia, Omaha, Milwaukee and East Lansing, Michigan. Malcolm's mother was a native of Grenada, also uprooted from the world of her black mother and the white man who had raped and impregnated her. Even before the Little family was torn apart, it must have experienced both the exhilaration and the terror of being set adrift in alien territory. It's no wonder that Malcolm and his siblings were drawn to the Nation of Islam; its peculiar ideology gave them, and millions like them, a way of coping with both the exhilaration and the terror.

* * *

The Nation of Islam appealed to this liberating impulse, but it was Malcolm X who expressed it most fully—because, although he was deeply serious, he was not, in Yardley's phrase, "implacably serious." The word "implacably" suggests a relentlessness, and especially a humorlessness, that were alien to the man. Hard as Washington works to imitate Malcolm X's oratorical style, his performance skimps on the quality that most intrigued listeners, both white and black. That quality, a function of Malcolm X's extraordinary courage and intelligence, was his comic sense. I don't mean this frivolously, that Malcolm X was a comedian. I mean comic in the classical sense of irony, detachment, distance on both one's circumstances and oneself. When Malcolm X laid down the rhetoric about the white man being a "pale thing" bred from dogs by the devil Yacub on the Isle of Patmos, the effect was, in the highest sense, satirical. The curl of his lip, the glint in his eye, seemed to say: "This is what you sound like, you dumb crackers. Try it on for size." More effective than the blind rage that followed his death, now sadly ritualized into the pumped-up woofing of young hip-hop poseurs, was this devastating mockery. Malcolm X didn't invent it; it has always been part of Afro–American culture. But he brought it out for the white folks to see.

Why was Malcolm X able to do this, when so many other angry people have not? Because he had also found a way to master the terror of his Great Migration upbringing—terror that came, as always, from uprootedness, from the loss of an accepted belief system by which human beings make sense of the cosmos and distinguish between right and wrong. On this level, the story of Malcolm X's youth is a descent into nihilism.

* * *

———

The Taming of Malcolm X

RECONSTRUCTION II, 93–99 (1993).

■ ALAN A. STONE

* * *

There are many conflicting opinions about Malcolm X, the man—what he came from, who he was, where he was going. But whether those opinions are derived from personal encounter, his autobiography, or other documentary sources, one thing seems clear: he was an intimidating human being—an electrifying presence, a burning firebrand, and a brilliant polemicist. Spike Lee, despite his obvious talents, seems to have been unwilling or unable to portray that intimidating presence. The movie lasts more than three hours and Denzel Washington is on the screen most of that time. But he never projects what Ossie Davis recognized as Malcolm's "style and hallmark, that shocking zing of fire and be damned to you." That real Malcolm X briefly appears at the end of the film to speak his famous phrase, "by any means necessary." You need only keep that jarring authentic moment in the center of your awareness as you reflect on the entire movie to get the measure of how much Lee fails to capture the real Malcolm.

* * *

Malcolm X has become increasingly important to African Americans since his death. Part of his importance is psychological. He is their hero, the oppressed Negro who transformed himself into a "Shining Black Prince," an archetype with whom proud young Black men and women, no matter how desperate their lives have become, can make a positive identification. Malcolm X's actual psychological identity as a young man is therefore of great importance. American history has made Washington (I can not tell a lie), Lincoln (Honest Abe who freed the slaves), J.F.K. (the president as martyred savior), into sanctified beings and by that hagiographic standard there is no basis for criticizing Lee's film. He has given African Americans their own saint. However, in the strange alchemy of history, Malcolm X is emerging as the most important African American of the twentieth century and to sanctify his memory is to mystify racism. The attempt here is therefore to analyze Lee's hagiographic version from a psychological perspective using the *Autobiography* and other sources as a standard for comparison to highlight the forces of racism in Malcolm's life which the hagiography suppresses.

* * *

Each of the big scenes during the first hour of the movie emphasize Malcolm, the child-rascal. Malcolm's first conk, sets the stage. As Shorty straightens Malcolm's hair, he quickly turns into a pain-stricken child as the lye reaches his scalp. That scene is reprised just before Malcolm goes to jail. Malcolm has to put his head in the toilet, when, at the crucial moment in his conking, he finds all the water in the apartment has been turned off. The two conk scenes are Lee's "comic" book ends for Malcolm's technicolor life of crime.

* * *

One of the reasons that *The Autobiography of Malcolm X* is a stunning book is because it is a psychologically coherent and believable indictment of life in a racist world whatever race the reader might be. Whether or not Malcolm invented many of the facts he told Haley, Malcolm was telling his version of his own life and it is authentic in that sense. The *Autobiography* also had a sophisticated psychological agenda. This is how the *Autobiogra-*

phy ends the section of Malcolm's life that Lee has made into a kind of glamorized musical comedy:

> I want to say before I go on that I have never previously told anyone my sordid past in detail. I haven't done it now to sound as though I might be proud of how bad, how evil, I was. But people are always speculating—why am I as I am? To understand that of any person, his whole life, from birth, must be reviewed. All of our experiences fuse into our personality. Everything that ever happened to us is an ingredient.

> Today, when everything that I do has an urgency, I would not spend one hour in the preparation of a book which had the ambition to perhaps titillate some readers. But I am spending many hours because the full story is the best way that I know to have it seen, and understood, that I had sunk to the very bottom of the American white man's society when—soon now, in prison—I found Allah and the religion of Islam and it completely transformed my life.

When Lee's Malcolm goes to jail he is still psychologically a child-man. Malcolm in contrast saw himself as an embittered hustler who had seen the most sordid side of life, and was appropriately nicknamed Satan by his fellow prisoners. Malcolm tells us how almost entirely by his own efforts he shaped that violent and ignorant man into something else in prison. In Lee's movie the child-man finds the good father in prison just as he found the good father in crime.

      * * *

Malcolm believed that both of his parents had been destroyed by White racism; his father murdered by bigots and his mother driven mad by grief and a harassing White social worker. His extended family was all the more important to Malcolm and he kept up his ties with his brothers and sisters. His older step-sister, Ella, by the father's first marriage was a strong woman who took him in when he first came to Boston. It is to his older brother's Black Muslim home in Detroit that he goes when he is released from prison. Malcolm's brothers and sisters, however, are entirely absent from Lee's film. Lee's child-man is a virtual orphan and from prison he goes to the invented Baines' home. We are led to believe that the Black Muslim faith has become his family and Malcolm has found in Elijah the father he had lost in childhood.

Lee's Malcolm has a series of particularly touching scenes with the messenger, Elijah Muhammad who is uncannily portrayed by the actor Al Freeman, Jr. Elijah has a gentle exotic spirituality. He is the ultimate kind and wise father and Malcolm, according to Lee's stage direction, is "completely humble in his presence accepting his authority totally and without reservation." Lee's Malcolm has found the answer to his inner longing and his mission is to be the good son.

      * * *

Malcolm made it clear in the *Autobiography* that he "adored" Elijah and Lee has found a way to make the scenes between the two men demonstrate that. Those scenes had stymied the previous screenwriters according to Lee. No doubt the earlier writers were unable to reconcile Malcolm's fiery independent personality with his subordination to Elijah. Lee's "tamed" Malcolm presents no such problem for him. He portrays a filial love affair made possible by Elijah's modesty and a Malcolm completely humble in the older man's presence. The scenes make for inspiring cinema, but as with Malcolm's relation to Baines, they also pose questions about his gullibility that are left unanswered when Malcolm leaves the Black Muslim faith. More importantly, just as Lee downplays the forces of White racism in Malcolm's early life, he downplays the Black racism that Malcolm espoused with his acceptance of Elijah Muhammad's religious beliefs.

* * *

The moments in the film which come closest to epic proportions are when Malcolm and his Black Muslim brothers confront police brutality. The mobilization of oppressed people transformed into a disciplined political force to be reckoned with by White America was Malcolm's dream and Lee captures it on film. Whatever criticism one has of the film's psychological veracity, this is surely a stirring moment of artistic and political achievement for Lee as an African American director.

* * *

Innocence and goodness are the constant elements of the Malcolm in Lee's film. That person is a denial not only of Malcolm's own righteous fury but of the contemporary Black rage that finds its sounding board in Malcolm's personality. Malcolm is the man who always knew the score. He was street-smart and self-educated. Malcolm never denied his rage, he used it. His conversion to the Black Muslim faith focused his grievances on the White man as the Blue-eyed devil. His rage was given an outlet in the focused hatred of Black racism which he embraced. His rage was turned from sordid self-destruction to constructive political and religious goals. From guns and hustling he came to polemics and sermons. He understood the traumas of his own family as part of the continuing degradation of slavery and White racism. Everything he said in his sermons and lectures had an impact because Malcolm X spoke as one who recognized the source of his pain. The people all know the awful truth when the angry prophet, the seer finally tells it. Malcolm, the angry prophet, who terrified his listeners with the truth, is what Lee has left out of his film.

* * *

Given the political pressures on Lee, the most difficult issue must have been the filmed account of the assassination. If Oliver Stone's film *J.F.K.* is the standard of comparison, then Lee deserves an Oscar for reasonableness. Some Blacks believe that a White conspiracy involving the F.B.I. or the C.I.A. killed Malcolm. Minister Farrakhan apparently would have preferred the film to have featured that version of the assassination. His idea is that the growing hostility between Malcolm and the Nation of Islam gave the White power structure cover for their own ends. Others have alleged that

Elijah Muhammad himself ordered members of "Temple no.25" in New Jersey to kill Malcolm. Of course, there are many conspiracy theories just as is the case with J.F.K., R.F.K., and Martin Luther King, Jr.

Lee's movie shows that White operatives of the F.B.I./C.I.A. had Malcolm under surveillance. But his screenplay leaves no doubt that the actual killers were Black Muslims. He writes: "Five Black men sit around a table. They do not speak. They are Thomas Haver, Ben Thomas, Lon Davis, William X and Wilbur Kinley. All are Muslims; all are the assassins."

* * *

Lee's depiction of the assassination is brilliant and conveys fanatic and desperate brutality. But then, in keeping with the tone he has established throughout his film, he takes us to South Africa where Black school children proudly announce their identification with Malcolm X who has been enshrined by Lee as the icon of Black pride and the catalyst of international Black unity. And finally there on the screen is the long suffering Nelson Mandela, who in his gentle demeanor is the antithesis of Malcolm X. In a voice, devoid of anger, he embraces Malcolm's credo. The prodigal son has found yet another godlike father.

* * *

The Marketing of Malcolm X; Is Spike Lee's Film Just Capitalizing on an Image?

WASH. POST, Nov. 4, 1996, at C1.

■ ELAINE RIVERA

Twenty-seven years after he was assassinated in an auditorium in upper Manhattan, and a few weeks before he is resurrected on the screen in Spike Lee's $34 million epic, Malcolm X is once again at the center of controversy.

* * *

The revolutionary black leader, who spent much of his life attacking white America, is suddenly big business.

* * *

Just what Malcolm's message is, and how he should be portrayed, remains a matter of some dispute. He began life in Omaha as Malcolm Little, transformed himself into a street hustler known as "Detroit Red," went to prison where he was introduced to the teachings of Elijah Muhammad, became a leader of Muhammad's Nation of Islam, which espoused a black separatist philosophy, then broke away to pursue a more international and interracial vision of human rights.

But the Nation of Islam, which Malcolm denounced in the last year of his life and which is now headed by Louis Farrakhan, is still selling Malcolm X tapes at its Harlem mosque. And some who condemned Malcolm for his militant views in the 1960s—or who have little idea of what he stood for—are now embracing him.

* * *

But Betty Shabazz, Malcolm X's widow and an administrator at Medgar Evers College in Brooklyn, says there is nothing wrong with marketing her husband's image.

"People want to be a part of Malcolm, and this is a way for them to do it," said Shabazz, who, as executor of her husband's estate, hired a management company earlier this year to license his name and likeness. "I think anyone who is wearing a hat or T-shirt has a basic understanding that Malcolm was for justice, equality and parity for all human beings."

Thulani Davis, who wrote the libretto for an opera about Malcolm's life, says it's all part of the process of transforming a man into a myth.

"Malcolm is a modern-day myth and a powerful one," said Davis, who has seen the movie and defends Lee's work. "If Spike is doing anything, he's making a movie about a hero."

* * *

The battle over Malcolm's legacy will likely heat up in coming weeks. Baraka says he plans to see the film, then make up his mind about Lee. But he says many people who rejected Malcolm when he was alive "are pimping off of him now."

* * *

———

NOTES AND QUESTIONS

1. What accounts for the alliance between black leaders and conservatives in the face of gangsta rap? Clarence Lusane argues that the alliance between C. Delores Tucker and William Bennett, a former Reagan official, against gangsta rap gives a false sense of cooperation between blacks and conservatives. *See* CLARENCE LUSANE, RACE IN THE GLOBAL ERA: AFRICAN AMERICANS AT THE MILLENNIUM 87 (1997). In particular, he argues that the seeming alliance between both groups ignores the social forces that have negatively impacted the black community.

Is this similar to the criticism that is being leveled at Bill Cosby for his harsh criticism of African Americans of "lower economic" status who have children who curse in public and commit acts of violence? Many blacks have complained that his comments only served to reinforce conservatives' negative stereotypes of blacks. Also, in what context should we assess the criticisms that Tucker and Cosby have leveled against rap music?

One writer likens the Cosby personal responsibility criticisms and counterreaction to them to the historic intellectual debates at the turn of the twentieth century between W.E.B. DuBois and Booker T. Washington. Kevin Merida, *Cos and Effect; Bill Cosby Sparked a Debate. Will His Own*

Troubles Snuff it Out? WASH. POST, Feb. 20, 2005, at D01 (arguing that Cosby's "tough-love tour that had been sweeping the country . . . was the kind of thing that used to go on with a lot greater frequency, part of an honored tradition of unflinching dialogue that African Americans have practiced for generations").

2.   Role of race in gangsta rap. It has long been noted that the majority of gangsta rap fans are white and much has been made of that fact. It has given rise to questions over whether whites are only willing to accept certain images of blacks. In fact, if one looks at MTV and BET, there is a proliferation of rap videos that depict black rappers as pimps and gangsters with numerous scantily clad black women. Is the image prevalent because it is the one whites are most comfortable with? Would blacks still be on MTV and BET if the images were the exact opposite of those presently shown?

In *Pale Imitation of Gangsta Life Gives Everyone a Bad Rap*, Richard Roeper, a *Chicago Sun-Times* columnist, argues that the prevalence of negative black stereotypes in music and movies negatively impacts all blacks. Roeper, Apr. 24, 2003, *available at* www.freerepublic.com. According to Roeper, most of the stereotypes depict blacks as chicken-eating, 40-ounce drinking, dancing people. He finds these clichés embarrassing and troubling. Most recently, the movie *Soul Plane* debuted to heavy criticism. The film purports to be a black take on *Airplane* and is rife with black stereotypes: chicken, dancing, and 40 ounce bottles of malt liquor.

The black community has been divided over its perception of *Soul Plane*. Some like Anne-Marie Johnson, an actress in *Hollywood Shuffle*, assert that Hollywood depictions of blacks have not improved since *Shuffle*. Some contend that the images have grown worse. On the other hand, some like Walter Latham, creator of the successful *Original Kings of Comedy* tours, feel that blacks take the movies far too seriously. *See* Wiley A. Hall III, *Commentary: Movie Offers Nothing More than a Soul Pain*, BLACKAMERI-CAWEB.COM NEWS, June 04, 2004, http://blackamericaweb.com/site.aspx/baw-news/soulplane63.

3.   Gangsta rap and violence. In *Black Liberation in Conservative America*, Manning Marable suggests that violence rates have increased with the increasing popularity of gangsta rap. MANNING MARABLE, BLACK LIBERATION IN CONSERVATIVE AMERICA (1997). Marable cites the violent lyrics coming from his daughter's bedroom and suggests that the music and its message are inescapable.

How much of the blame placed on rap might be misplaced? Don't inner city problems run deeper than rap lyrics? Many commentators have criticized the glamorization of gangsta life by such rappers as Tupac, Notorious B.I.G., and Snoop Dogg. These critics believe that rap lyrics are responsible for the violence and strife in urban communities.

4.   Malcolm X and black rage. Cornel West devotes much discussion to Malcolm X and the black rage he embodied. *See* CORNEL WEST, RACE MATTERS (1993). Malcolm X has long been associated with rage and fiery passion, but the articles suggest that Spike Lee drastically toned that part of his persona to make it more palatable to a mainstream audience. That argument can be made, but on the other hand, anytime a movie is made of one's life some parts are inevitably going to be left out. But, does concern over marketability or the movie's capacity account for Lee's decision to disregard some of the leader's more confrontational rhetoric?

5.   Race and royalties. Black artists and musicians have long struggled to own their songs. Because of this, many have led impoverished lives and died broke. Nor is this a past phenomenon; one only has to look at the travails of modern artists such as TLC and Toni Braxton to see that unfair recording and publishing contracts are still prevalent. Even more telling is that both TLC and Braxton were top-selling artists who still could not fend off bankruptcy.

As the aforementioned articles about Little Richard and Frankie Lymon highlight, struggles with the recording industry are not new. The articles depict both artists as victims of record companies who did not possess the necessary business knowledge for the industry. However, ignorance of the business side of the recording industry does not completely account for the uneven playing field. In *Kraski, Clint Black Launch Equity*, Clint Black, a country artist, discusses how the recording business works: "The system pays artists advances against future royalties, meaning that the revenues from their album sales first must repay numerous recoupable items, including the cost of the record production and marketing." Chris Lewis, *Kraski, Clint Black Launch Equity*, NASHVILLE CITY PAPER, August 1, 2003. As Black's statement illustrates, artists face an uphill battle in securing fair contracts.

The following excerpt provides an inside look at the way independent recording studios and record labels exploited African American artists.

CHARLIE ROSE: Much has been said before in the world, and during these four decades, that a lot of these black artists didn't get what they earned.

AHMET ERTEGUN: Oh, that's true. * * * There were a lot of independent record companies in the '40s, that—it mushroomed because there was a shortage of shellac. * * * And a lot of small companies that found a way of getting shellac, a way of pressing records, started to press anything that they could do. So there are all these independent companies. Many of them made jazz records. Many of them made rhythm and blues records. Many of them made country records. They made the music that the majors didn't make because of the shortage. * * *

And as a result, these—a lot of these independent record companies were owned and run by people who were not really that interested in the music. All they cared about was making a fast buck. And they had no intention of paying anybody royalties. So many of these companies were owned by people who were ex-jukebox operators, or nightclub owners, or whatever. They made these records, and unfortunately many of them [ ] never paid any royalties. And they only paid the big artists something to keep them from leaving the label.

At the same time, the big artists . . . all made 5 percent. Records sold for 75 cents. And they made 5 percent of 75 cents. That was top, that was the top royalty. Beginning artists, like country artists were paid 1 percent or 2 percent. Race record artists were paid either nothing or 1 or 2 percent. * * * In those days, a big hit record sold 50,000 or 100,000 copies. And you know, 100,000 times a nickel is not a lot of money. You know, it's $5,000. * * * [M]y first employee at Atlantic Records was a bookkeeper, . . . because we in our naive way thought that we had to pay everybody their royalties, so we had to know how much was owed. So we had a bookkeeper to figure that out. And we paid our royalties, but many companies did not.

And so it's generally said that nobody got paid correctly, or got paid at all. [T]he people who made big hits in those days, compared to people who make big hits today, got very little.

A Conversation With Ahmet Ertegun, Music Producer, Founder of Atlantic Records, CHARLIE ROSE TRANSCRIPTS, Feb. 21, 2005. *See also* AHMET ERTEGUN, WHAT'D I SAY: THE ATLANTIC STORY (2001).

6. The Paradox of Hip-Hop Sampling. *The Washington Post* writer, John Balz, discusses the increasing number of lawsuits between rappers over the use of hooks and beats. Since rap is built on sampling and appropriating old sounds this is new and unexpected phenomenon. In the article Balz focuses on disputes between unknown artists and established rappers such as I.O.F. (It's Only Family) and Ludacris. Most of these disputes center on unknown artists' allegations that popular rappers steal their hooks and beats and turn them into popular songs.

As more rappers encounter appropriation disputes, one has to wonder whether the increasing number of lawsuits reflects the influence of corporate business on the nature of rap. When rap first began it was mainly a way to entertain at parties or in parks. However, in the thirty years since it was introduced, it is the most popular music in the United States and often the background for advertising in print and media. The introduction of corporate values into what started as a homegrown music enterprise makes it safe to assume that the financial gain of rap has made settling musical disputes through litigation an attractive option for rappers, who until recently, were happy to avoid judicial resolution of their conflicts over creative and intellectual property issues. John Balz, "Hip-Hopping Mad Over Beats and Hooks", *Washington Post*, May 8, 2005, at B01.

CHAPTER 11

Cash and Carry

A. The Underground Economy

The "underground" or "informal" economy roughly consists of the total of all economic transactions minus those transactions that are in compliance with applicable government regulations. This economy can include both transactions where just *full* compliance with the law is avoided, such as in Martha Shirk's article in this chapter about domestic help, or transactions directly prohibited by the law, such as in the other articles in this chapter about the drug trade and prostitution.[a] The underground economy in the United States can include everything from the waiter who neglects to report all of his tip income, to the doctor who takes cash on the side for weekend visits, to the unlicensed street vendor who sells knockoff goods on the sidewalks of a major city.[b] In extreme situations, the underground economy—sometimes referred to as the "black market"—may actually satisfy more of the citizens' basic needs for housing, clothing, food, and the like than the formal economy.[c]

Defining exactly what the boundary is between the informal and formal economies, however, can have significant cultural and legal implications by distorting the data on which the government relies to control the economy.[d] The Internal Revenue Service, for instance, excludes the value of household labor, such as childcare done by family members or do-it-yourself activities around the house, from its calculations of income.[e] National economic welfare, furthermore, is measured by looking at annual reported income and its relation to the poverty line. But, because the income from underground economies is consistently not reported or underreported, using only reported income as a measure of poverty mixes the truly poor with those who have a much higher standard of living as a result of the underground economy.[f]

But what leads to the creation of underground economies in the first place? In some cases, informal economies arise to respond to a market failure created by a government prohibition on an activity seen as immoral

---

a. *See* George L. Priest, *The Ambiguous Moral Foundations of the Underground Economy*, 103 Yale L.J. 2259, 2259 (1994).

b. Richard A. Epstein, *The Moral and Practical Dilemmas of the Underground Economy*, 103 Yale L.J. 2157, 2157, 2164 (1994).

c. *See* Priest, *supra*, at 2268–70.

d. *Id.* at 2259.

e. *See* Morton Paglin, *The Underground Economy: New Estimates from Household Income and Expenditure Surveys*, 103 Yale L.J 2239, 2244–45 (1994).

f. *Id.* at 2250–51.

or undesired.[g] In other cases, they arise because of a governmental inability to provide a particular good or service in a way that is responsive to the demands of the citizenry.[h] And in still other cases, the underground economy rises up because the regulations surrounding certain economic transactions seem unjust or unfair, or their enforcement is seen as arbitrary.[i] As a result, individuals turn away from the formal economy to attempt to correct these problems.

Despite the negative implications of calling these systems "underground" economies, such structures can provide real benefits. Informal economic activity can significantly increase the standard of living for some of the poorest in a population, provide otherwise unavailable or inefficiently distributed goods and services which may be necessary for survival, and even provide work opportunities for those excluded from the formal economy by discrimination.[j] But, on the other hand, a large underground economy may undermine the stability and responsibility of the government institutions that control the economy, and such economies may also be seen as fundamentally dishonest.[k] Furthermore, unregulated underground economies also deprive the state of tax revenues that could otherwise be used for public services and can lead to sweatshop conditions and risks to the general welfare.[l] What do the following articles contribute to the underground-economy discourse?

————

Cashing in on Domestic Help[a]

St. Louis Post-Dispatch, Feb. 15, 1993, at 1C.

■ MARTHA SHIRK

To my mind, the most stunning revelation from the Zoe Baird controversy has been the apparent lack of interest of many Americans in the lives of the maids and baby sitters they employ in their homes.

The Internal Revenue Service says that only one out of four families with domestic workers contributes to the Social Security system for their employees, as required by law. Among the scofflaws, we've learned recently, are Secretary of Commerce Ron Brown, former attorney general nominee Zoe Baird and at least a half-dozen members of Congress.

Ask around, and you'll find that most of your neighbors and colleagues aren't paying into the Social Security system for their domestic help.

Chances are, you aren't either.

---

g. *See* Epstein, *supra*, at 2158–59.

h. Priest, *supra*, at 2271.

i. *See* Epstein, *supra*, at 2162–63.

j. *See* Priest, *supra*, at 2272–73.

k. *See* Priest, *supra*, at 2260.

l. *See* Lora Jo Foo, *The Vulnerable and Exploitable Workforce and the Need for Strengthening Worker Protective Legislation*, 103 YALE L.J. 2179, 2179–80 (1994).

a. For further discussion of the racial, national, and class dimensions of the U.S. domestic labor market, see chapter 7.

For the most part, employers cite one of two reasons for not complying with the law:

They don't know they're supposed to.

Their domestic workers don't want them to.

Few would admit that one of their motivations is the savings to themselves.

For instance, for my $50-a-half-day housecleaner, I pay $7.50 a week, or almost $400 a year, to make sure she's covered by Social Security. (The law requires the employer to pay only half that much, but I cover her legally required contribution, too.)

OK, you say, but it's not because of greed that you don't do it. It's because your maid, or your baby sitter, would quit if you did. She wants to be paid in cash, with no deductions.

It's true that their employees' resistance keeps a lot of employers from paying by the book. Some people do domestic work to supplement their welfare benefits, which, in Missouri anyway, provide only a third of the amount the federal government says a family needs to survive above the poverty level.

If they reported their income from domestic work, they'd lose part or all of their welfare checks, and they might lose Medicaid coverage for their children as well.

But a lot of household workers insist on cash, with no deductions, simply because they lack information about the consequences, which are considerable.

In the first place, if a worker is paid in cash, she's probably not filing a federal income tax return. That means that she can't claim the Earned Income Credit, a tax credit authorized by Congress to shore up the incomes of America's poorest families.

The IRS believes that 2 million eligible families failed to claim the Earned Income Credit last year, simply because they didn't realize they could. (Almost 14 million families did, becoming $11.3 billion richer—about $807 a family—as a result.)

The woman to whom I pay $50 a week will get an Earned Income Credit of $520 this year.

The tragedy for her is that she could be getting an earned income credit of $1,384, in one lump sum, if just two of her four other employers weren't paying her under the table. That's more money than she's managed to save in 20 years, the beginning of a nice little nest.

And what about 25 years from now, when it comes time for a household worker to retire? She's out of luck if her employers haven't contributed to the Social Security system for her. Social Security is not an entitlement. You have to pay into the system for at least 10 years—or have been married to someone who did—to draw benefits.

My housecleaner isn't going to be entitled to much of a retirement check 25 years from now if I'm the only employer who contributes to Social Security for her.

Most likely, my housecleaner, and yours, will end up among the 40 percent of elderly American women who live in or near poverty. She'll probably have to apply for SSI—Supplementary Security Income—which will put only $434 into her pocketbook each month.

I use the feminine pronoun here for a reason: Most household workers are women.

And as with many economic issues, this is one where race and gender converge. A higher proportion of black women than white women make their livings doing domestic work. By not taking care of their household employees' Social Security payments, many Americans are discriminating disproportionately against African-Americans, as well as against women.

Even at retirement, the lifelong disparities in income between men and women and whites and blacks persist. The median income in 1989 for black women over 65 was only $4,494, compared with $7,655 for over-65 white women. (Men over 65 had a median annual income of $13,107.)

It's something to think about the next time you pay your maid cash, under the table.

And if compassion doesn't make you do the right thing, maybe self-interest will.

At your employee's request, the IRS can come after you 25 years from now for back contributions—with interest and penalties.

NOTES AND QUESTIONS

1. **Nannygate and the Zoë Baird problem.** In 1993, President Clinton nominated Zoë Baird for Attorney General during the first days of his presidency. Support from the public and from the Senate for Baird's confirmation, however, quickly faded: Baird and her husband, it turned out, had hired an illegal-immigrant Peruvian couple to serve as their chauffer and children's nanny and neglected to pay Social Security taxes on the couple's wages. The public uproar surrounding what eventually became known as "Nannygate" effectively led to the withdrawal of Baird's nomination and cost her the position. The American public, it seemed, was unsympathetic to the troubles of a woman worth $2.3 million. *See* Gwen Ifill, *Settling In: Anatomy of a Doomed Nomination; The Baird Appointment: In Trouble From the Start, Then a Firestorm*, N.Y. Times, Jan. 23, 1993, at A8.

President Clinton's next nominee for Attorney General, Kimba Woods, also failed to pass inspection when she was asked if she had "a Zoë Baird problem," even though she had legally employed an alien as a babysitter and properly filed all her taxes. Following Zoë Baird, asking whether or not a particular nominee had hired immigrant nannies became standard during confirmation hearings:

> It was also the question that helped pluck the childless and unmarried Janet Reno from relative obscurity to become the President's nominee for the job. No kids, no nanny, no Zoe Baird problem. Reno, 54, who appears to be well qualified for the post, doesn't even have an immigrant gardener: she mows her own lawn.

Claudia Wallis, *The Lessons of Nannygate*, TIME MAG., Feb. 22, 1993, at 76. Clinton's top officials, including Vice President Al Gore, Labor Secretary Robert Reich, and U.S. Trade Representative Mickey Cantor were all asked if they had hired illegal aliens. J. Jennings Moss & Carleton R. Bryant, *Domestic Help a Taxing Issue*, WASH. TIMES, Feb. 8, 1993, at A1.

To be fair, Zoë Baird's acts were not criminal. Though, technically, undocumented alien workers are not allowed to start working until they receive their green cards, Baird and her husband, a professor at Yale Law School, reported the hiring to the Immigration and Naturalization Service and obtained a letter from the INS saying that it was aware of the situation and, that as long as Baird helped the couple obtain necessary documentation, there would be no problem. In addition, Baird did not pay taxes for the Peruvian couple because she was informed by a lawyer, albeit incorrectly, that the Internal Revenue Service would not accept payment until the workers were properly documented. STEPHEN L. CARTER, THE CONFIRMATION MESS 23–28 (1994). In January 1993, Baird and her husband made a lump-sum payment of the taxes due. Neither the failure to pay taxes nor the hiring of illegal immigrants is a criminal offense. Employers of illegal immigrants, though rarely prosecuted, are liable only for civil penalties, including fines of up to $3,000. David Johnston, *Clinton's Choice for Justice Dept. Hired Illegal Aliens for Household*, N.Y. TIMES, Jan. 14, 1993, at A1. And yet, support for Baird's confirmation became suddenly non-existent. Should the hiring of illegal immigrants be criminally punishable (*see* chapter 12)? Is what happened to Zoë Baird an example of the arbitrary enforcement of regulations that can lead to underground economies in the first place?

2. Nanny tax. At the time of Zoë Baird's confirmation hearings, federal statutes enacted over four decades earlier governing household employees mandated certain reporting and withholding requirements for household employers who paid their household employees more than $50 every three months. The law was sharply criticized as being outdated, however, especially since, given the right circumstances, it frequently applied to the casual, teenaged, neighborhood baby-sitter that many families of all economic backgrounds hire to occasionally watch their children. A year-and-a-half after Zoë Baird, Congress passed the Social Security Domestic Employment Reform Act of 1994, changing the threshold to $1,000 annually. Given individual state laws and the statutes enforced by the Department of Labor and the Immigration and Naturalization Service, however, this threshold increase has had little effect on reporting requirements. CHAD R. TURNER, THE NANNY TAX vii (1997).

3. Need for childcare. Zoë Baird was criticized primarily because she could afford to make other childcare arrangements without breaking the law. However, not only the very wealthy are avoiding immigration and taxation laws for the sake of childcare, though many may not be able to afford *in-home* childcare. Nearly two-thirds of American women with school-age children work and require some sort of childcare arrangement. Moreover, nearly 60 percent of married men with children in America have working wives. At the time of Nannygate, only one in four people who employed household help paid the Social Security taxes required. Wallis, *supra*. In single-parent or two-working-parent homes, how does the Nanny Tax affect the parent's quality of life and ability to work in the market-place?

4. Benefits now or later? Martha Shirk's article suggests that "[s]ome people do domestic work to supplement their welfare benefits, which, in Missouri anyway, provide only a third of the amount the federal government says a family needs to survive above the poverty level." She also suggests that reporting the domestic work income might decrease the amount of money the domestic worker was able to receive from welfare, while not reporting means that they won't receive an Earned Income Credit or Social Security Benefits in old age. For a family at or below the poverty line, which is worse? Is avoiding taxes merely short-sighted, or could it be necessary for immediate survival? Then again, Shirk makes the point that the Earned Income Credit would give her domestic "more money than she's managed to save in 20 years." Given Thomas Shapiro's research on intergenerational wealth (see chapter 13), what effect could this wealth accumulation have on the nanny's own children?

5. Outsourcing. In a two-parent home, a mother or father who stays out of the work force to raise the children is not paid for his or her labor, though that parent effectively does the same work as a nanny or house-keeper. As a result, the parent does not receive income, nor does he or she pay the Social Security taxes that ensure future benefits. Is it ultimately more efficient to hire a nanny regardless of the employer's financial status in order to allow the parent to enter the market to obtain greater retire-ment benefits?

6. Domestic workers and the public/private distinction. Because domestic work was traditionally done by housewives for no pay, it has been considered of little or no economic value. Considered part of the private sphere, domestic work is largely unregulated, while the regulations that do exist largely go unenforced. Given Critical Feminist Theory and Frances Olsen's suggestion that the public/private distinction is unsustainable, how does and how should the law regulate the hired domestic worker, who performs private, household work in the public marketplace? How does the reform of the Nanny Tax "protect[] the interests of the propertied class employers who benefit from the public-private distinction?" *See* Taunya Lovell Banks, *Toward a Global Critical Feminist Vision: Domestic Work and the Nanny Tax Debate*, 3 J. Gender Race & Just. 1, 6–9 (1999); *see also*

Peggie R. Smith, *Regulating Paid Household Work: Class, Gender, Race and Agendas of Reform*, 48 AM. U. L. REV. 851 (1999).

7. Nanny gendering. Could not Zoë Baird's husband, Yale Law Professor Paul Gewirtz, have stayed at home and raised the couple's children, given Baird's published annual salary of $507,000? How does the naturalized assumption that women are the caretakers of children interact with the increase of women in the marketplace? Are laws that make it more difficult for families to hire domestic workers discriminatory against women in those families where women want to work? Are those same laws discriminatory against the poor, female domestic worker? *See* Banks, *supra*, at 8–9.

8. Title, race, and national origin. Banks argues that "[t]he term 'domestic worker' invokes the historic image of a native-born Black women, the mammy, an 'ideological construct of the plantation's faithful household servant and the South's most perfect slave.' " She argues further that the "term 'nanny' invokes the image of a 'foreign' woman" and summons " 'vastly sentimentalized notions ... that a typical nanny came to change the diapers and stayed on for the weddings.' " *Id.* at 18–19. How do these terms, as Banks argues, "erase[] the most negative connotations of in-home childcare—low wage work often performed by non-white women in a potentially exploitative environment," and how does the use of such terms influence the debate about the Nanny Tax? *See id.* at 18–24. How do these terms simultaneously mask and highlight the class and racial differences between employer and employee? Given the Critical Legal Theorist's tenet that law and language are indeterminate, is there a better term to use, or are all the terms used for domestic work meant to gloss over the negative aspects of the job?

9. Non-neutrality of immigration law. In 1990, Congress limited the number of foreign "unskilled workers" that could receive permits to work in the United States to 10,000. Included in this category of occupations that require fewer than two years of experience was domestic help such as housekeepers and nannies. Given that most immigrants to the U.S. are women and that most domestic workers are also women, is this seemingly neutral immigration policy discriminatory against women? Furthermore, does it discriminate against the American woman in the workforce by decreasing the supply of child caretakers in the United States? *See* Joan Fitzpatrick, *The Gender Discrimination of U.S. Immigration Policy*, 9 YALE J.L. & FEMINISM 23, 23–37 (1997). For more about immigration law, see chapter 12.

The Diamonds As a Business Enterprise
THE GANG AS AN AMERICAN ENTERPRISE 91–116 (1992).

■ FELIX M. PADILLA

* * *

Several major questions will be considered in the examination. What are the reasons for the gang becoming a business organization? What does the gang look like as an entrepreneurial establishment? That is, what are its defining characteristics as a business enterprise? Which cultural elements are used by youngsters for cementing and reinforcing business relations among themselves? What is the gang's occupational structure? How does the gang generate income for maintaining itself as a business establishment?

* * *

The history of the Diamonds dates back approximately twenty years, a relatively short period compared to other Latino youth gangs in Chicago. At first the Diamonds were a musical group, playing their music on street corners in the neighborhood and in local neighborhood nightclubs. Some members believe that in about 1971 a member of the musical group was mistaken for a gang member and was killed by a gunshot fired by a youngster from an opposition gang. This incident sparked the reorganization of the group into a violent criminal youth gang. And for a period of about six years after that the Diamonds were on a course of vengeance and retaliation, provoking intergang fights with other groups.

Spike, a thirty-year member of the Diamonds, who is still very active in the gang, provides a clear description of the early days: "We were a band, and we would play to pass the time, you know, or in some gigs in the neighborhood. This was not one of your well-known professional bands, but we did OK. We were just a bunch of guys who would get together to have fun, to play music in the hood, you know—out on the streets. You know, we were doing the same thing that other people were doing at the park or in basements, except that we were in our hood. Then the band started to attract followers, people from the neighborhood that liked the music, and they would be there all the time. These people were like body guards, you know, to make sure the band was safe. So the group started growing, and then, all of a sudden, there was talk about forming the group into a gang, so some of them decided to do it. These were the followers and not the band. I don't know what was the problem with some of these guys; maybe one of them had a run-in with the opposition. But, anyway, it was about this time when one of the band players got shot. So, from here on they decided to become a gang and keep the name of the Diamonds, you know, the name of the band. And for a long time they were hard-core, you know— these guys were mean motherfuckers. You couldn't go by the neighborhood because they were shooting at everybody. It was really bad. It was worse than what these guys are doing today. There were times we would have these wars with the opposition, and we go out to the park, the two gangs, with bats, clubs, guns, and shit, and just have it out right there. It was crazy. I can tell you of about ten guys from our side who died from gang fights. Some of the fights were right here because the opposition would drive by shooting at us. Some of our guys got killed right here."

During most of this early period the membership of the Diamonds was quite small; the organization had not expanded and divided itself into sections. Gang members' involvement in drugs—in particular, marijuana—was essentially for their own recreational use. The Diamonds had yet to become a profit-making business enterprise. In some instances, a member would purchase a relatively sizable amount of marijuana and sell to others in the gang. Sometimes money was collected to purchase a quantity of marijuana, which would be equally distributed among contributing members, again, most of the drug was for personal and, at times, social use. As indicated by Spike, while describing the early days of the gang, "We would just get high a lot. It seemed that everybody was doing drugs at that time. It's not like today where people are trying to prevent drug use. No, before there used to be stories about movie stars smoking reefer and doing coke, and they were cool and bad. Doctors were doing drugs; attorneys were doing drugs. I tell you, everybody was doing it. So, we started doing it, too. There were the fights between us and some other gangs—that's another thing we used to do. But, besides that, we would be drinking beer and doing drugs. We were not selling drugs at this time. What we did was to buy the drugs and use them ourselves. We still did not know enough to go into business. We didn't know where to sell them, expect for to our friends, who were already one of us."

Then, in the late 1970s, a major change occurred in the operational structure of the Diamonds. It began to take on a businesslike character. No longer were retaliative, violent behavior against opposition gangs and reefer smoking the mainstays of the organization. Money-making through drug dealing came to represent the gang's emerging chief function. Although a great deal of gangbanging persisted as the Diamonds and enemy gangs maintained ongoing feuds, overall the gang embraced and carried out a program that was built around money-making activities.

Why did the Diamonds undergo this change during this particular period? Which factors and conditions were responsible for the transformation?

Controlled Substance Act

"I remember this older guy from the neighborhood who wanted me to sell for him. He asked several of us to be his dealers. He was offering good money, but I was afraid. I didn't know what he was about. We knew that he was doing something because all these people used to come to his house all the time. Hey, like some of us guys sometimes went to him to cop some smokes for us. He was offering us some good money. He said that we could work for him and that he was going to take care of us. He was even talking about cars; you know, if you do real good and if you're reliable, you know, all of that shit, that he would buy us a beamer [BMW]. And that we would not have to worry again about buying smokes because we would have it all the time. But since he had never dealt with us before and then all of sudden he wanted us to work for him, I was scared. I said no to the buy, I couldn't trust the cat."

What Carmelo is describing is in larger terms an event that had a major influence on the business development of the gang—namely, a piece of legislation: the Illinois Controlled Substance Act, which was passed in 1971 and carried heavy criminal penalties for adult heroin and cocaine dealers. The bill called for mandatory twenty-year prison sentences for drug peddling offenders eighteen years and older.

Well aware that juveniles could always beat the penalties of the newly instituted law, those adults who for the most part had controlled drug distribution and dealing up to this point began enlisting some of the youngsters from the Diamonds as well as from other gangs to work the street blocks and corners of particular neighborhoods. Some youngsters, like Carmelo, refused the job offers, while others agreed to them. It did not take some these youngsters or leaders of the gang very long to realize, however, that they could profit substantially by controlling neighborhood drug dealing. In other words, these young people began to ask the question "If this is our neighborhood and people are using it to make money, why can't we develop our own business?"

And indeed, they did. Gang leaders began reorganizing the structure of the Diamonds into a wholesale enterprise or investment; the organization became a business establishment. It now purchased wholesale merchandise itself and hired its own members, especially the younger ones, to retail the street level. Since the Diamonds viewed themselves as landlords of several *puntos* in the neighborhood (literally translated, the word *punto* stands for "points," but here it refers to street corners), the only missing ingredient for developing a business operation was the necessary capital with which to purchase large amounts of drugs for extracting a profit.

      * * *

Not one individual within the Diamonds organization possessed the necessary capital for purchasing large enough quantities of drugs for turning a profit. No single member had the money necessary for establishing himself as the sole owner or shareholder of the corporation. Therefore, some members began pooling their money: Sometimes two or three of the older members (usually the leaders, or chiefs) would "go into business"; at other times the group of investors was larger. On other occasions leaders would command all members to make an investment of a certain minimum amount (along with the lines of passing the hat) and would use this sum for purchasing the necessary amount of drugs with which to start the business. And in still other situations leaders of the gang would simply take and use the dues money for the purchase of large amounts of drugs.

Spike recounts this initial stage in the business development of the Diamonds: "At first it was real tough because we didn't have any cash. So, we would try different ways to raise enough to make a profit. You know, we would all chip in; you know there was no hassle about the money or stuff like that. We wanted the business to get off the ground, you know, make it work because we didn't have nothing for us. This was going to be something that was going to be ours, you know, for us. And once we got going we took control. But at first it was real difficult. And then we had to make sure that people did not spend gang money on themselves. So, it took a little while to get going. But we knew that there was a lot of money to be made in this business. This was a business made for us; it was something like it was sent by God. It was a business that we could do straight from the neighborhoods that we controlled and knew real well. How could you go wrong?"

To the question, "Who controlled the money made from dealing?" Spike answered, "It always was the chief or mainheads. They were the leaders. They had earned their position, and we respected them, and we had a lot of trust in them. So when we paid dues we knew that it was our money, but, in fact, it was the gang's money. And, since the chiefs and mainheads were the leaders, it was the same as the gang. That's how we used to see it then."

* * *

PERCEPTIONS OF CONVENTIONAL WORK

Youngsters' images of "traditional" jobs were perhaps the leading force that helped to transform the gang into a business venture. These young men began turning to the gang in search of employment opportunities, believing that available conventional work would not sufficiently provide the kinds of material goods they wished to secure. Some of the more common assessments I heard about conventional work available for Latino youth are captured in the following two expressions:

> There are some jobs that people can still find, but who wants them? They don't pay. I want a job that can support me. I want a job that I could use my talents—speaking, communicating, selling, and a definite goal that I'd be working toward as far as money is concerned.

> We were just tired of factory jobs. We were supposed to go to school and receive an education. For what? To be employed in factory jobs? We were tired of that. At the same time we were watching these other guys making a lot of money, so we said, "Hey, let's follow these guys. Let's do what they were doing."

These remarks also allow us to gain insight into the pessimistic outlook these young people have developed toward job prospects in the regular economy. Members of the Diamonds have become increasingly convinced that the jobs available to them are essentially meaningless, far from representing the vehicles necessary for overcoming societal barriers to upward mobility. Although these youngsters have been socialized with a view in the conventional cultural course to achieving material success, they refuse to buy into its official means. That is, they do not agree to accept the "American achievement ideology" representative of middle-class norms and shown by Horowitz (1983), Kornblum (1985), and others to be widely supported by ethnic and racial minority parents and teenagers. The ideology stresses that success in school leads to the attainment of managerial and professional jobs, which, in turn, pave the way for social and economic advancement. The youngsters' own school experiences and occasional contacts with the job market—as well as their observations of the frustrating and often futile efforts by some adults around them to achieve social advancement through menial, dead-end jobs—combine to serve as overwhelming evidence that the American achievement ideology does not necessarily apply to them. In brief, these young men do not believe in the power of education to be the "great equalizer," nor do they see existing "legitimate work" as capable of leading them to a successful, meaningful life.

The views of these young people point out the poignant paradox between having culturally defined goals and ineffective but socially legitimate means for achieving them, indicated by sociologist Robert Merton several decades ago and since confirmed by researchers and scholars writing on gangs, youth, and employment (Vigil 1988; Kornblum 1987; Horowitz 1983; Moore 1978; Cloward and Ohlin 1960). The contradiction lies in the absence of avenues and resources necessary for securing the rewards that society most values and which it purports to offer its members.

The decision by members of the Diamonds to accept participation in the gang is informed by their assessments of the lack of available opportunities in the regular economy but also by their high level of aspirations. Rather than arising as a deliberate violation of middle-class aspirations, the gang represents a "counter-organization," a response geared to fulfilling the standards of the larger society. The transformation of the gang into a business enterprise was sparked by the will to change, to alter those forces of domination weighing heavily upon its members' lives. In effect, what these youngsters did was reconstruct the "criminal" gang into a income-generating business operation—an alternate form of employment with which they could hope to "make it" in U.S. society. In the words of Spike, "We grew up at a time when people were making money and making it quick. You know, we saw on television people getting rich overnight. You had the professional athletes—these are the guys who are supposed to have natural talents, you know. That's a lot of bullshit. It's true these guys were taking steroids. You had all these reports about how these athletes were pumping iron and taking steroids so they could sell their bodies and so people could pay to watch them. That's one thing we saw. Then we saw, you know, you had the white-collar criminals—you know, those guys who are just like us but never get caught, except that everybody knows that they are crooks. You had all these guys becoming filthy rich. And what do you think that's going to tell us? Shit, it didn't tell me to and get a job at McDonalds and save my nickels and dimes. Who the fuck was doing it that way? Who the fuck is saving nickels and dimes today? You have kids coming up to you today and asking you for a buck, not for a nickel or a dime or a quarter. Where do they see this shit? You tell me. I wasn't going to save my nickels and dimes. That certainly wasn't going to be me because I would still be waiting, and I would be the only one waiting. Things are not done like that anymore. So, we decided to turn to what we have, and that was us."

"Some of us fucked up. We didn't make it. I'm thirty years old, and I'm still out here hustling everyday. But that's because certain things didn't work out the way that I wanted. I'm not going to make excuses for my mistakes. But you know what? I'm going to continue because there are many people like me, people who have jobs, people who are making only enough to pay the rent, and then they come out here or go into other kinds of illegal business because they know that what society says and gives them are two different things.''

Social and Cultural Components of the Ethnic Enterprise

What are the distinguishing characteristics of the gang which enable it to function as a business organization—a type of establishment necessarily built around a great deal of trust and commitment, which allow it to generate and sustain consistent and dependable social relations and monetary gains? That is, which social and cultural elements did the youngsters use for organizing the gang into a reliable money-making enterprise?

In the same way that the family unit teaches its young the norms, skills, values, beliefs, and traditions of the larger society, the gang has developed its own culture, including its own myths, norms, values and ways of communicating and reinforcing them. At the heart of the gang culture is a collective ideology that serves as the basis for realizing the overall welfare of all the members. For the gang collectivism is the major determinant of its efficient development as a business operation. The members' responses to their shared conditions and circumstances are collective in the sense that they lead to partnership, therefore uniting many individuals.

For the members of the Diamonds collectivism translates into an ideology of strength. These young men share the belief that their capacity to make a living or improve their life chances can only be realized through a "collective front." In Coco's view, "We are a group, a community, a family—we have to learn to live together. If we separate, we will never have a chance. We need each other even to make sure that we have a spot for selling our supply. You know, there is people around here, like some opposition, that want to take over your *negocio* [business]. And they think that they can do this very easy. So we stick together, and that makes other people thing twice about trying to take over what is yours. In our case, the opposition has never tried messing with our hood, and that's because they know it's protected real good by us fellas.''

Rafael echoes Coco's interpretation of collectivism: "Together we have the numbers. We have protection. My business is his business because we protect our interests together. So we talk about our thing—it's nobody's thing; rather, it's our thing. I think that one of the first things we learn when we start off is to feel like a group or a family. That means that we have to share and we have to protect each other and whatever belongs to us." In effect, though gang members can (and in some cases do) pursue individual financial gains, their business ventures are made possible because of the gang, and their individual work is geared to enhancing the common good and to pursuing collective ends.

The collectivist nature of the gang can he said to be an extension of the traditional Puerto Rican family. In Puerto Rican immigrant society, as well as in other societies from which ethnic and racial groups in the United

States originated, the family served as the cornerstone of the culture, defining and determining individual and social behavior. Ties between families were cemented by the establishment of *compadrazco* [godparent-godchild] relationships. Relatives by blood and ceremonial ties as well as friends of the family were linked together in an intricate network of reciprocal obligation. Individuals who suffered misfortunes were aided by relatives and friends, and when these individuals had reestablished themselves they shared their good fortunes with those who had helped them.

* * *

In addition to its stemming directly from Puerto Rican family tradition, ethnic solidarity served as another fundamental cultural element, used by the youngsters for cementing their business relations. As Puerto Ricans, they expressed feelings of a fundamental tie (blood, or kinship, solidarity), believed to represent a major unifying force. Of course, this organic bond, in turn, provided the basis for trust. One explanation about the correlation between ethnicity and group solidarity was offered by Rafael: "The fact that I knew that what I liked was at another person's house—they would talk to me about things like, 'We're going to listen to Salsa music, we're going to have *arroz con candules* [rice and potpies] and some other stuff—I would get more attracted to that than to other things. That brought us more together. And that's how things are with other people from other nationalities. Polish people—have you been over where they have all the stores not far from here? Well, they have their own neighborhood and groups, you know, like they do their own thing together. So, we do our thing together, too, as one people. We have our hood, our own Latin stores and the business we do in our gang works because we are the same people. We trust each other because we understand what we are all about."

* * *

It is clear that the collectivist, communitarian underpinning of the gang was also buttressed by a base of local consumers. Their willingness to become faithful customers, to continuously purchase available goods—drugs and stolen merchandise—is viewed by those in the gang as an indication of a sort of surrogate membership in the gang. Additionally, customers protect gang members working as street-level dealers by agreeing to withhold information when interrogated by police officers and other law enforcement agents. These customers become, in the opinion of one youngster, "one of us." Flaco elaborated on this point: "People from the neighborhood know that they can get smoke, caine, and other things from us. It's risky going to other places. They don't know what those other people be about. So they protect us because they feel secure with us. And we are safe with them. So, we think of them as part of the business."

These various sources of collective behavior are thought to have played a leading role in cementing the Diamond's business structure. The significance of collectivism for gang members can also be gleaned from their views about the idea of individualism. These youngsters do not agree with the view that the exercise of individual effort in pursuit of economic and social mobility applies to them. To them individualism means placing oneself in a precarious position: How can they survive without one another? They are fully aware that they do not possess the traditional resources, such as money and high levels of formal education, used by members of the middle class to negotiate and advance their individual life chances.

To them individual behavior leads to obliteration. Tony makes the claim that "by ourselves we are nobody." He says, "We can be had without no problem. I'm always with my partners because when you're by yourself you are easy prey. You are going to fall the bottom of the barrel because, well, who's going to be there for you? So, if people come to you as a bunch, then we need to create our bunch." Other of Tony's remarks are just as straightforward: "This is not a game that you can win by yourself. If you want to win, you do it as a team. We call ourselves a family, but, you know, when you really think about it we're also a team. And, if you want to lose, play alone. Most of our guys who fall, they fall because they sometimes do things without thinking. Sometimes just do stupid things. Myself, I have gotten busted by the police several times because I was alone. I couldn't see them coming. When you're with your boys you have more eyes to check out what's going on—you can see the cops; you can see the opposition. But when you are by yourself sometimes you feel scared, and you know there is so much you see and so much you can do. In the Diamonds we teach the young guys; we practice how to be together all the time. We think that that's our strength. Other people have money. We have each other."

One other major reason for rejecting the individualist stance is that these young people recognize that success in U.S. society, which is structured around the concept of individualism, has one major interpretative implication: As success honors those who have achieved it, failure (and economic failure in particular) stigmatizes those who suffer it. The system, thus, makes those who have "failed" the objects of criticism and scorn. It can also imply that one's inadequacies in the social system are based upon innate deficiency; failure thus evokes pity and concern. The emphasis on the individual in gauging success and failure in U.S. society is unacceptable as far as these young men are concerned. For this reason they see collectivism as a way of giving gang members a special sense of purpose— the driving force with which to pursue economic and social success.

* * *

NOTES AND QUESTIONS

1. Illinois Controlled Substance Act. The Illinois Controlled Substance Act, 720 ILL. COMP. STAT. 570/510 et seq. (2002 & Supp. 2003), was intended to effectively remove certain substances from the marketplace. Does this Act fall under one of Milton Freidman's four duties of government? (*See* chapter 3.) In what ways do the Diamonds's business enterprise respond to the market failure created by the act? Does criminalizing a substance or activity simply invite a market response such as the one seen here? Is this act, by strengthening the criminal penalties for its violation, attempting to restructure the market by increasing the risk premium of dealing in those goods it makes illicit? Can it effectively do so?

2. Gang as government. In what ways do the Diamonds function as a micro-level government for those in their neighborhood? Again, review Freidman's discussion on the duties of government in chapter 3. Does the system of drug trade among gang members function as a system of taxation? How does the Diamonds's business enterprise redistribute wealth? Is the micro-government a more efficient method of wealth redistribution than taxing the drug trade and redistributing wealth through the centralized governments of the United States?

3. Criminal law approach to the gang problem. Liza Vertinsky argues that, because American criminal law is essentially "transaction-based," where the wrongdoer is punished only for the harm attributable to his own, individual conduct, it is ineffective at controlling organized criminal activities. Liza Vertinsky, A Law and Economics Approach to Criminal Gangs 2 (1999). Where multiple actors are involved, proof of the act (*actus reus*) and intent (*mens rea*) are more difficult to establish for the specific individual charged. Furthermore, the organizations will likely have their own systems in place to diffuse responsibility for group activity among many, if not all, of their members, as well as incentive systems that offset the deterrent effect of governmental enforcement policies. *See id.* at 178–80. Vertinsky argues instead for a more "enterprise-based," law and economics approach, focusing on how the group as a whole functions as an economic system. *Id.* at 2–5. What might the policies following this approach look like? Does tort law provide any suggestions? *See id.* at 67–87. What are the potential problems with implementing more "enterprise-based" enforcement policies that might not be as problematic in tort law? How might Becker's rational choice paradigm (*see* chapter 4) be overly simplistic in the face of gang organization?

4. Gangs and the racism-oppression thesis. The racism-oppression thesis suggests that American race relations and ethnic conflict, as well as both majority and minority perceptions of race and oppression, leads to the formation of highly racially-homogenized gangs. *See* George W. Knox, An Introduction to Gangs 75 (1994). How does the homogenization of neighborhoods along racial lines contribute to the formation of gangs? How does the organization of gangs along racial lines lead to "bias crimes"? How does the functioning of gangs as vehicles of ethnic conflict promote racial and economic inequality? *See id.* at 74–96. Furthermore, is legislating to minimize the "patterns of ethnic conflict and competition in America, the social structure and institutionalized patterns or race relations, the accommodation of poor and minority group members to an affluent society, and the individual experiences, patterns of enduring racial conflict, and perceptions of racism and oppression" a better solution than the Illinois Controlled Substance Act? *Id.* at 75. Assuming the racism-oppression thesis is correct, how can wealth redistribution affect the formation of gangs? (*See* Thomas Shapiro's work in chapter's 6 & 13.)

5.   Cheap labor below minimum wage. A study of the monthly financial records of a drug-selling gang showed that although the average hourly wage for the gang members who were involved in the drug trade reached up to $11, the hourly wage for street-level drug dealers was less than minimum wage. Furthermore, the gang's largest non-wage expenditure was tribute to higher levels of the gang. While the gang leader made between $50,000 to $130,000 annually in income, "foot-soldiers" typically made less than $200 per year. However, the average hourly wage for the gang far exceeded the legitimate market wage available to those foot-soldiers, who could rarely expect to make more than minimum wage. For a foot-soldier, then, can participation in the gang be an economically rational decision? Stephen D. Levitt & Sudhir Alladi Venkatesh, *An Economic Analysis of a Drug–Selling Gang's Finances*, NATIONAL BUREAU OF ECONOMIC RESEARCH, WORKING PAPER 6592, 1–19 (1998), available at http://www.nber.org/papers/w6592.

"Measuring Impact of Crack Cocaine"

"There are three primary reasons why crack may have been so devastating to the Black community. First street gangs, which already controlled outdoor spaces, became the logical sellers of crack. Second, the increased returns associated with drug dealing attracted young Black males to gangs and may have reduced educational investment. Third, a large fraction of crack users were young women." STEVEN D. LEVITT & STEPHEN J. DUBNER, FREAKONOMICS: A ROGUE ECONOMIST EXPLORES THE HIDDEN SIDE OF EVERYTHING (2005) at (8–9).

Note on the Financial Pyramid of a Chicago Gang

Net monthly profit accruing to leader $8,500

Combined wages paid to three officers $2,100

Combined wages paid to foot soldiers $7,400

Total monthly gang wages (excluding leader) $9,500

The total monthly gang wages totals only $1,000 more than the net profits accrued to the leader excluding any side money the leader earns. The combination of danger and low profits suggests that low ranking gang members would reject crack dealing, but the hopes of reaching the top of the pyramid are often too high for them to resist. *Id.*

Carole, *Interview with Barbara, in* SEX WORK: WRITINGS BY WOMEN IN THE SEX INDUSTRY

166–74 (Frédérique Delacoste & Pricilla Alexander eds., 1987).

■ FRÉDÉRIQUE DELACOSTE & PRISCILLA ALEXANDER, EDS.

Barbara is a thirty-nine year old woman. She's worked with prostitutes' rights groups and lives in Richmond, California. I interviewed her in her home, which she shares with her daughter, mother and sister.

Carole: How long have you worked as a prostitute?

Barbara: I've been a prostitute for seventeen or eighteen years.

Carole: Where have you worked?

Barbara: Basically California. I've also worked in Alaska, Washington, Hawaii, and Nevada. I've worked on the streets and in the casinos in Nevada. But I don't work the streets anymore. What I do now is really not prostitution, it's domination. I still charge for it and still like doing it. If I could work on the streets I would, but the police make it too dangerous. They arrest you a lot so that you have to spend all your earnings to get out of jail. And then, they make you work in dark corners; you can't work out in the open for any amount of time. They come along and say, "Move on, move on." Basically, that's why I don't work the streets anymore. I'm older, too, but I think if the police didn't bother me and if it was legal, I'd be working the streets still. It's much easier and you don't have to play the boyfriend-girlfriend routine, you know, and it's quicker! (*She laughs.*) If you get a guy off the streets, it usually lasts about twenty minutes. The whole date, from there to the apartment and back.

Carole: What are your experiences with police arrests? Are tricks ever arrested?

Barbara: They never arrest johns. One time, I can remember in particular when they arrested me and four other women in San Francisco. There were five guys there and instead of arresting them, they made them testify in the trial against us.

Carole: Is that typical?

Barbara: That's typical, yes. If they catch you with the guy, no matter what the guy says, they won't arrest him. One time I can remember I was arrested and I was with a guy when the police pulled up behind us. I told him, "Look, don't say nothing, you know, just tell them, hey, I'm talking to you because as long as you don't say anything, I won't." Well, he freaked out and told the police, "Yeah, she solicited me for X amount of money," and they let him go. They wanted him to testify against me, but he didn't. The guy was into domination. At that time I didn't know what domination was, but he wanted me to whip him and beat him, and he wanted me to put him under a table and just do my commands, do whatever I told him to do. I thought he was crazy, but I also didn't know it was domination. (*She laughs.*) I knew he wasn't going to the court, because if he'd come to trial, I would have told everything. They finally dismissed the case, but I had to go to court at least five times.

And the case was not a case. I mean, the guy had actively solicited me. But I had to pay the cost. I had to bail out of jail and make five court appearances.

Carole: How many times have you been arrested?

Barbara: To be honest, I don't know. At least thirty, probably closer to fifty.

Carole: What kind of violent experiences have taken place in your work?

Barbara: Well, I don't know if this is violent or not. To me, it was. It was the first time I was arrested in San Francisco. I was with a girl. I didn't know her. She had two guys with her. She said they wanted to date her, so we walked around to the place that we were supposed to date at, and we find out that the guys were policemen. So the police said, "You're under arrest," and he said, "Bitch, if you make a move, I'll knock you down in the streets right now. Do you hear me?" I said, "I'm not going to do anything," and he said, "Did you hear me bitch?" You know, he screamed and hollered at me.

Carole: This was in San Francisco?

Barbara: Yes, the San Francisco police.

Carole: Have you been raped while working?

Barbara: Yes. The first year. I was working in Oakland. This guy pulled up to me. He was a young black guy, and he told me that he had a friend who had fifty dollars, but who was too ashamed to come in the area. He said he would take me to the guy. At the time, I didn't know any better and I was loaded on reds, so I went with him. He was supposed to take me to this hotel, but he pulled up in this remote area. And when he pulled off, he grabbed my purse and told me, "Bitch, give me all your money." I told him I wasn't going to give him anything. Okay, since then I've learned that you don't fight back. But I fought back that night. He wound up taking my purse and my coat. I wore wigs then, and he took my wig. He took everything. That was the only time something like that really happened ... and I don't blame the guy. I blame myself for it because I was loaded on reds, because I should have known better in the first place, and, believe me, after that I have. That's about the most violent thing that has happened to me.

Carole: So, he didn't rape you?

Barbara: Well, yes, he did. He raped me. But the rape part was nothing. I mean, the devastating part to me was him taking everything I had. He did rape me ... the rape was nothing. You know, he screwed for about twenty minutes, not even that long, maybe about fifteen. That part doesn't really stick with me because that wasn't the devastating part. Everything after that was.

Carole: When that happened, you didn't want to go to the police?

Barbara: I didn't even think about going to the police at all, you know. At that time I was so young. I was twenty-one. I had just started working. I thought because I was a prostitute, how dare I go to the police....

Carole: Was it because you didn't want them to know you were a prostitute?

Barbara: Well, yes. But at that time I didn't think I had any rights. And, I was loaded, too. I figured I'd be in just as much trouble as this guy would be.

Carole: Were you ever raped again while working?

Barbara: I've had them try. It's just that that's the only time anyone's succeeded. I had this guy one time. I was in Emeryville. He pulled up to me and told me he wanted to date me.

I got in his car and we drove like we were going to my apartment. All of a sudden, he pulled over and said, "I don't have any money and you're going to fuck me right now." I said, "In the front seat?" He had a small knife, it was real small, like a pen knife, and he said, "Get in the back seat." So I got in the back seat. And I said, "Look, whatever you want to do, just do it. I won't fight at all, there won't be any trouble." He started dating me and I kept on being so nice. I'd say, "Oh, and you have to put on a rubber." (*She laughs.*) I was just real sweet. He couldn't stand it. He started dating me, he started screwing me and he pushed me out of the car. I think he really wanted me to fight and jump with him. And I wasn't violent at all—"Okay, you want some, fine I understand, just don't mess up my dress, don't mess up my hair." (*She laughs.*) He didn't want anything to do with me because I wouldn't fight him.

One time I was in Alaska. This guy pulled up and when he pulled up I knew that it wasn't someone I should go with, but it was cold. We were in Anchorage, and in Anchorage you have to work on the streets. They won't let you work in any of the hotels or bars. They harass you some on the streets, but you can still work. It was freezing that night and this guy pulled up and he looked wrong, but I went with him anyway. So I'm on my way to the apartment and two blocks before we get there he grabs me. Well, I had some hair spray, those little aqua-net hair sprays, they make good mace. I took it and sprayed it in his face and it sort of blinded him. Then I just got out of the car.

* * *

Carole: Have police officers tried to get sexual favors from you?

Barbara: Several times. But not as bad as the other girls. Once two other girls and I were sharing an apartment and the landlord decided to call the police and tell them were working out of it. He flagged down this police. Well, I knew the guy flagged down and he was really good. One time, he'd seen me turning a car date, doing a blow job in a car, and he didn't do anything on that occasion. And there were a couple of other times, too. Then after about four times, he told me that I owed him a date. He told me if didn't want to go to jail, I should give him something. I said, "Well, I can't do that, I'm a prostitute, and if I do that you're gonna pay me." He wound up giving me a dollar and seventy cents. I didn't mind because I would much rather have dated him for a dollar and seventy cents then go to jail.

I've heard that happening many times. With vice officers, too. Most of the times I hear about it they're trying to scare the girls into something, you know. It's like, if you date me then I'll keep all the rest of the policemen away from you, or I'll tell you who all the police are.

Carole: Do you think it's better for the prostitutes not to give them anything?

Barbara: For me it was always better if I didn't date them. It's like dating a bartender. If you're in a place and he wants you then he'll keep letting you be there until he gets you. Then after he gets you, he won't want to see you anymore. And so that's what I did with the bartender and cops, too. I'd tease them and play like I was going to—"I can't do it right now, you remind me of a trick; you're too nice a guy." But I've dated a lot of police. Lots of them. I didn't know until afterwards.

Carole: It was during their off-hours?

Barbara: I don't know if it was or not. They said they weren't working, but they showed their badges and stuff afterwards. One cop said he wanted his money back. I said, "Bull." I wasn't afraid of him. I knew that if he told people he'd get in more trouble than I would.

Carole: I've also heard a lot more black prostitutes are arrested than white prostitutes, and that black prostitutes are kept in jail longer. Is that true?

Barbara: That's true. I can barely remember any white girls who were in jail with me in Oakland. The black girl has a much harder time on everything. She'll get kicked out of a hotel much faster than a white girl. A white girl, if she's got any kind of class about her, can work anywhere. Whereas if you're black, if you do anything wrong at all, like getting up to go to a guy in a bar when he calls you over instead of making him come over to you, they can kick you. If you're black, they kick you out faster. In Las Vegas, they arrested a lot of white prostitutes, but at first there *were* only white prostitutes.

Carole: A San Francisco study by Mimi Silbert, PhD, of the Delancey Street Foundation, of two hundred street prostitutes revealed that two-thirds had been raped or forced to do things they didn't want to do. What do you think of those numbers?

Barbara: It sounds too high, and I've known quite a few prostitutes. See, people want to downgrade prostitutes and they think that guys can just take advantage of them. But most of the time the prostitutes set the rules. Johns go where we want them to go. We run everything. They pay you first, they come to your place, they wash, they must use a rubber. People think that the tricks call out the rules but I don't know what girls they talked to. Now junkies work totally differently from prostitutes who are not junkies. And they get hurt more.

Carole: Barbara, why did you first get into prostitution?

Barbara: I did it for the money. That was the only reason I got into it. I couldn't find a job that paid more than minimum wage, whatever it was at the time, two dollars and thirty-five cents. I had two children. I had no way of supporting them besides being on welfare. I was always working two jobs but with the one or two jobs I could still barely pay rent.

Carole: At this point, how difficult would it be for you to leave prostitution if you want to?

Barbara: It would be hard. I'm not into prostitution right now. I'm into domination. But if I wanted to leave both of them alone it would be very difficult because my mother stays here with me, and my sister and my daughter. My sister and my daughter have jobs that don't pay much and my mother is on social security, so I'm the breadwinner, have to pay the rent, help take care of them. And I have to care of myself, too.

Carole: What kinds of things would you change about prostitution if you could?

Barbara: First, I'd make it legal. Lots of prostitutes feel they're guilty when they're arrested and that they don't have any rights. I'd like prostitutes to train prostitutes to change that so they don't think that they have to have pimps. If a woman wants a pimp, that's her business, she should be allowed one. But if she doesn't want one, I don't think that she should have one. I'd make it so that prostitutes had a place where they could work. If they wanted to work the streets I'd make it so that they could. I'd make it so the police would do other things besides bother prostitutes. So many times I was harassed by policemen and they'd say: "It's much easier coming here and talking with you because you're not going to do anything to me."

I was in Amsterdam last year. We had a Forum. A lot of the girls were telling me how bad it was even though they have places to work out of. At first, you know, I went along with them and said, "Yeah, I understand," but then I went down to the red light district, and if I had had a red light district when I was a prostitute, I would have loved it. They have little store fronts, and they sit in the window. Some girls wear hardly anything, some are dressed regular. The guy comes up and if he wants you, he knocks on the door. You've got your bodyguard in there in case anybody wants to go off or anybody's drunk or whatever. Now, I don't think we'd have to be limited that way. The women in Amsterdam complained that this was the only place they could work. I think that women should be able to work where they want to. They also complained that if they got a regular job in addition to the prostitution, they had to tell people that they were prostitutes. I think that's totally wrong. I don't think that I should be stigmatized if I want to sell my body.

Carole: So, that was their main complaint, that they had to stay in one area?

Barbara: Yeah. And that the landlords charged them an arm and a quarter. That if they wanted to get out of it, or just take a part-time job, they had to say they were prostitutes. Still, if we had that much! Some of the women who were with us said, "Yeah, but that's horrible—they're standing there like cows and they're taking them out like cattle." Well, fine, but I'd much rather have guys come to me than go to them. (*She laughs*.) And most prostitutes would.

* * *

Carole: Why do you think that prostitution is kept illegal in the United States?

Barbara: Because they're stupid and lazy. The politicians don't want to figure out a way to get the money, they're afraid that prostitutes will cheat and they won't get enough tax money. And men don't want women to have control over anything. Men want to run everything. Especially white middle class businessmen. They can get away with anything and they know they can.

Carole: What other things would you do, if prostitution was decriminalized?

Barbara: Well, a lot of violence would not happen if it wasn't a crime. Men take advantage of women, true enough, but if the girls were more organized and knew more, then they wouldn't let the guys take advantage of them. Beatings and robbings might not be if women would just stick together. There are so many things I could tell prostitutes so that they'd be protected but if I did that now, I'd be committing a felony because I'd be training a prostitute. It's also conspiracy to tell a girl that someone is a policeman. There are so many laws they can use on you. It's completely sickening to me. Just sitting on this bed could probably be illegal. (*Laughter*)

* * *

Carole: If you could have other work options that paid better than the minimum wage, might you leave prostitution?

Barbara: Prostitution is something I'd like to do on my own terms when I felt like doing it. What I mean is that I wouldn't want to do it all the time. I'd go out maybe twice a week instead of five, six times. I think I'd continue because I like the power I have with men. I like making them do whatever I want them to do. But it gets stressful too. You have to be on your toes. But there's so much money in it. And there's a power thing in making them pay for it and in deciding whether or not I'm going to date them. If I want to be nice to you, that's my choice, and if I want to be a straight up bitch, I can do that too. That's my choice.

Phyllis Luman Metal, *One for Ripley's, in* SEX WORKS: WRITINGS BY WOMEN IN THE SEX INDUSTRY

119–21 (Frédérique Delacoste & Priscilla Alexander eds., 1987).

■ PHYLLIS LUMAN METAL

Well, my dear, I must admit your story seems somewhat unusual . . . quite unusual as a matter of fact. I would never imagine a woman would begin being a prostitute at the age of fifty-five. I think that's one for Ripley's, if you don't mind me saying so. I guess I thought of prostitution as something unfortunate young girls got talked into by unscrupulous men. That was my impression. But to get into it at that age and of your own free will, although it does seem there was some financial pressure.... Still, there must have been something else you could have done. Tell me, what did you feel about it? Were you overwhelmed by guilt?

No, I was not. It was a hell of a lot better than marriage. And I tried that five times.

Well, I just don't understand. You seem quite normal. You are an attractive woman, of good family, well brought up. The men you married must have been monsters. But five of them? Something just does not fit.

Well ... I found it very liberating to be a prostitute, and the men must have found it liberating too, for they were much better lovers than my husbands. They seemed to feel free with me and I with them. Why are you so upset? You don't think sex is wrong do you?

Well, no, I don't think sex is wrong between two consenting adults.

You don't think it's wrong to earn a living, for a woman to earn a living that is?

Why no my dear, of course not. Women have jobs now, all sorts of jobs, married or unmarried.

Well then, why is it wrong to get paid for sex? You must be getting upset about putting the two together.

It would be like selling your organs. Some part of your body.

Well, what about selling blood? That doesn't seem to bother you.

Well, that is to save lives.

True, but you would be amazed at how desperate some of the men are to have sex in the way they need to have sex, and how uptight they are about telling their wives about what they need. And then there are always the guys who are between relationships, or can't seem to get anything going.

Well, my dear, the whole subject is quite confusing. Why don't we just go to a hotel and have some relaxation.

Are you willing to pay me?

Well now, we are good friends. You wouldn't charge me would you?

Do you treat your patients who are your friends for nothing? My body is my source of livelihood. I have upkeep to be available and appealing.

I just wouldn't feel right about paying you. It would spoil it for me. I think you should give it to me.

Sorry. We can be good friends, but forget the sex then. When I first charged for it, I had much more self respect and self worth than I ever had before. I felt appreciated. When I was a wife I was expected to do a lot of shit work and service my husbands and their desire, not mine. I felt used and abused. No trick ever broke my ribs like my husband did. No trick ever took all my money and left me when it was all gone—another husband did that. No trick ever urged me to neglect my children to accommodate him. No trick ever threw a bunch of in-laws who made my life miserable at me. No trick ever came home drunk every night like one of my husbands did. And I always had money, which I did not when I was married. And I never got a venereal disease. And something else. I got to know people of all nationalities in a way I never could have otherwise. My customers in Paris were from all nations. They were Swiss, British, German, Norwegian, Italian, Spanish, French, Syrian, Berber, Algerian, Senegalese, Saudi, Irani-an, Japanese. I felt like a citizen of the world. Prostitution made me feel that all of us on the planet were one family.

Well, my dear it is all very interesting. But I am sure you are an anomaly. I can't believe this is how it usually goes. There is something wrong about it. What would happen to the family if it were legal?

I think it is much more prevalent and accepted in Catholic countries where the family is much stronger than here.

Well, my dear, let's have a drink and talk about something else. There are so many aspects to you. You have such a varied life. This surely isn't that important to you. Why don't you just forget about it? I think you just like to take up controversial issues for causes. You just like the role of being a social reformer. What in the world do you have in common with all those girls who stand on corners? They can't do anything else. Don't tell me you are a feminist.

———

NOTES AND QUESTIONS

1. **Sex work in the economically just society.** How does economic inequality contribute to prostitution? Do the overt practices of exchanging dowries and arranging marriages for economic gain in some societies, and the less overt determinations of who pays for dates, weddings, and engagement rings reinforce economic inequality and contribute to prostitution? *See* Priscilla Alexander, *Prostitution: Still a Difficult Issue for Feminists, in* SEX WORK, *supra* at 190–92. How do the dangers of prostitution, including violence and sexually transmitted diseases, reduce the economic viability of women in the workforce and perpetuate economic inequality? Is prostitution a way for those who lack the social skills, attractiveness, or life situation that might prohibit them from competing in the non-monetized sex market of dating, marriage, and one-night stands to gain access to the type of sexual interaction they desire? *See* HELEN REYNOLDS, THE ECONOMICS OF PROSTITUTION 189–90 (1986).

Liz Highleyman, also known as Mistress Veronika Frost, suggests that "[f]rom and anticapitalist perspective, sex work is perhaps the ultimate expression of worker ownership of the means of production, as expressed in the slogan 'my body is my business,' as a person's body is the one asset that cannot be taken away from them." Liz Highleyman, *Professional Dominance: Power, Money, and Identity, in* Whores and Other Feminists 148 (Jill Nagle ed., 1997). She further suggests that, although it is true that some sex workers are badly exploited and hate their work, "body labor" in the form of sex work should not be taken away from those that lack the educational and infrastructural resources necessary for "mind labor" until alternatives are available. *Id.* at 149. If alternative job choices pay less, is paying a prostitute for sex not the most efficient use of her human resources? *See* Reynolds, *supra* at 190. Are prohibitions on the sex industry an exercise in capitalistic dominance? In an economically just society, would the sex industry still exist? *See* Highleyman, *supra* at 148–49.

2. Gender and "exploitation." Female prostitutes are traditionally regarded as victimized, degrading to all women, and in need of rescue from their circumstances. Is there anything *inherently* exploitative about adults engaging in consensual sex for money, or is it only after the actors in a sex-for-money exchange are gendered as female and male that the practice becomes seemingly exploitative? In a gay sex-for-money exchange, "[w]hose erect penis represents the 'weaker sex'?" *See* Julian Marlowe, *It's Different for Boys, in* Whores and Other Feminists, *supra* at 141–44.

3. Prostitution and civil rights. Are prostitutes being systematically deprived of their civil rights? Does prostitution violate the Thirteenth Amendment's prohibition on slavery? *See* Catherine A. Mackinnon, *Prostitution and Civil Rights, in* Applications of Feminist Legal Theory to Women's Lives 226–227 (D. Kelley Weisberg ed., 1996). Frequently, female prostitutes are arrested while the soliciting customers, usually men, are let go with a citation or a warning. *Id.* at 224. Does this violate the Equal Protection Clause of the Fourteenth Amendment? *See* People v. Superior Court of Alameda County, 562 P.2d 1315 (Cal. 1977). What about the fact that police usually send men out to solicit prostitutes, resulting in a higher percentage of women arrested than men? Mackinnon, *supra* at 224.

4. Sex work and stigma. How does the fear of being stigmatized as a "whore" interact with the economics of sex work? Does it discourage participation in the sex trade, or merely "provoke and permit violence against prostitute, and ensure poor working conditions and the inability of many sex workers to move on to other kinds of work without lying about their experience?" Alexander, *supra* at 185.

CHAPTER 12

ECONOMIC BORDERS TO COMMUNITY

Introduction

> *Beyond the calling of race or nation or creed is this vocation of sonship and brotherhood. Because I believe that the Father is deeply concerned, especially for His suffering and helpless and outcast children, I come tonight to speak for them. This I believe to be the privilege and the burden of all of us who deem ourselves bound by allegiances and loyalties which are broader and deeper than nationalism and which go beyond our nation's self-defined goals and positions. We are called to speak for the weak, for the voiceless, for the victims of our nation, for those it calls "enemy," for no document from human hands can make these humans any less our brothers.*
>
> **Dr. Martin Luther King, Jr., Beyond Vietnam: A Time to Break Silence, Address delivered to the Clergy and Laymen Concerned about Vietnam, at Riverside Church, 4 April 1967, New York City**

At the height of the Vietnam War, Dr. Martin Luther King, Jr. declared his vision of moral citizenship beyond the borders of the nation state. For Dr. King, the defined targets of national hatred became the objects of his compassion and religious commitment. In the years since this stirring oration was delivered into the conflicting passions of the Vietnam era, Dr. King's words have come to stand for something more that compassion toward enemies during wartime. His vision of shared humanity beyond citizenship, like his vision of economic distribution beyond markets, has served as a reminder, even in the academy, of the larger verities at stake in defining who may share in the bounty of this prosperous nation.

In this chapter, we look at several views of the meaning and function of national borders. The Supreme Court defines the constitutional framework for exercising the powers of excluding non citizens. The Plenary Powers doctrine which grants Congress virtually unlimited power, not explicitly enumerated in the Constitution, is a centerpiece of our legal rules and procedures for deciding who may enter, and once inside the nation, who may stay. This chapter is not designed to teach the law of immigration, a fascinating subject itself. Our purpose in what follows is to identify some of the cultural and identity related variables at work in our national definition of ourselves as citizens, and the sentiments that shape our shifting attitudes toward aliens. This chapter is intended to suggest the economic dimensions of immigration control of non citizens and the class-based exclusions that obtain in erecting borders that separate citizens from each other within the nation.

In a much debated essay, University of Chicago philosopher Martha Nussbaum joins the tradition of Dr. King's Vietnam speech by calling for an ideal of "allegiance to the worldwide community of human beings." Drawing on her work in international development ethics, she argues that even in the aftermath of the tragedy of the September 11 World Trade Center attack:

> We find ourselves feeling sympathy for many people who did not even cross our minds before, New York firefighters, that gay rugby player who helped bring down the fourth plane, ... [w]e even sometimes notice with a new attention the lives of Arab–Americans among us.... Sometimes our compassion even crosses that biggest line of all, the national boundary.... The world has come to a stop—in a way that it never has for Americans, when disaster befalls human beings in other places.

Martha Nussbaum, *Introduction: Cosmopolitan Emotions?*, *in* FOR LOVE OF COUNTRY? ix–x (Joshua Cohen ed., Beacon Press 2002) (1996).

In America, the most politically sensitive immigration issue concerns the conflicting policies and attitudes towards Mexican immigration over the southern border. This decades-long snarl of economic and human rights policy invites our attention to questions of the American role in stimulating immigration, the role that culture and household decision making in Mexico plays in sending male heads of household to work temporarily in America to support families back home in Mexico.

Finally, in keeping with our project of close examination of hidden cultural arrangements that increase economic inequality we look inward to see the way in which two facts of contemporary life create invisible domestic borders to economic inequality. First, we ask whether residential segregation sets up domestic economic borders to communities that are just as vigorously enforced as the national border is enforced against non citizens. Second, we take a look at the escalating use of prisons to fence out a burgeoning population of men and women of color who experience the civil death of felony convictions.

A.   THE BASICS: CITIZENSHIP

Patriotism and Cosmopolitanism

FOR LOVE OF COUNTRY? 3–17 (Joshua Cohen ed., Beacon Press 2002) (1996).

■ MARTHA NUSSBAUM

> When anyone asked him where he came from, he said, "I am a citizen of the world."

Diogenes Laertius, Life of Diogenes the Cynic

In Rabindranath Tagore's novel, *The Home and the World*, the young wife Bimala, entranced by the patriotic rhetoric of her husband's friend Sandip, becomes an eager devotee of the *Swadeshi* movement, which has organized a boycott of foreign goods. The slogan of the movement is *Bande Mataram*, "Hail Motherland." Bimala complains that her husband, the cosmopolitan Hindu landlord Nikhil, is cool in his devotion to the cause:

> And yet it was not that my husband refused to support *Swadeshi*, or was in any way against the Cause. Only he had not been able whole-heartedly to accept the spirit of *Bande Mataram*.

> "I am willing," he said, to serve my country; but my worship I reserve for Right which is far greater than my country. To worship my country as a god is to bring a curse upon it.'

Americans have frequently supported the principle of *Bande Mataram*, giving the fact of being American a special salience in moral and political deliberation, and pride in a specifically American identity and a specifically American citizenship a special power among the motivations to political action. I believe, with Tagore and his character Nikhil, that this emphasis on patriotic pride is both morally dangerous and, ultimately, subversive of some of the worthy goals patriotism sets out to serve—for example, the goal of national unity in devotion to worthy moral ideals of justice and equality. These goals, I shall argue, would be better served by an ideal that is in any case more adequate to our situation in the contemporary world, namely the very old ideal of the cosmopolitan, the person whose primary allegiance is to the community of human beings in the entire world.

My articulation of these issues is motivated, in part, by my experience working on international quality-of-life issues in an institute for development economics connected with the United Nations. It is motivated, as well, by the renewal of appeals to the nation, and national pride, in some recent discussions of American character and American education. In a by now well-known op-ed piece in *The New York Times* (13 February 1994), philosopher Richard Rorty urges Americans, especially the American left, not to disdain patriotism as a value, and indeed to give central importance to "the emotion of national pride" and "a sense of shared national identity." Rorty argues that we cannot even criticize ourselves well unless we also "rejoice" in our American identity and define ourselves fundamentally in terms of that identity. Rorty seems to hold that the primary alternative to a politics based on patriotism and national identity is what he calls a "politics of difference," one based on internal divisions among America's ethnic, racial, religious, and other sub-groups. He nowhere considers the possibility of a more international basis for political emotion and concern.

This is no isolated case. Rorty's piece responds to and defends Sheldon Hackney's recent call for a "national conversation" to discuss American identity. As a participant in an early phase of that project, I was made vividly aware that the project, as initially conceived, proposed an inward-looking task, bounded by the borders of the nation, rather than considering ties of obligation and commitment that join America to the rest of the world. As with Rorty's piece, the primary contrast drawn in the project was between a politics based on ethnic and racial and religious difference and a politics based on a shared national identity. What we share as both rational and mutually dependent human beings was simply not on the agenda.

One might wonder, however, how far the politics of nationalism really is from the "politics of difference." *The Home and the World* (better known, perhaps, in Satyajit Ray's haunting film of the same title) is a tragic story of the defeat of a reasonable and principled cosmopolitanism by the forces of nationalism and ethnocentrism. I believe that Tagore sees deeply when he sees that at bottom nationalism and ethnocentric particularism are not alien to one another, but akin—that to give support to nationalist sentiments subverts, ultimately, even the values that hold a nation together, because it substitutes a colorful idol for the substantive universal values of justice and right. Once one has said, "I am an Indian first, a citizen of the world second," once one has made that morally questionable move of self-definition by a morally irrelevant characteristic, then what, indeed, will stop one from saying, as Tagore's characters so quickly learn to say, "I am a Hindu first, and an Indian second," "I am an upper-caste landlord first, and a Hindu second." Only the cosmopolitan stance of the landlord Nikhil—so boringly flat in the eyes of his young wife Bimala and his passionate nationalist friend Sandip—has the promise of transcending these divisions, because only this stance asks us to give our first allegiance to what is morally good—and that which, being good, I can commend as such to all human beings. Or so I shall argue.

Proponents of nationalism in politics and in education frequently make a thin concession to cosmopolitanism. They may argue, for example, that although nations should in general base education and political deliberation on shared national values, a commitment to basic human rights should be part of any national educational system, and that this commitment will in a sense serve to hold many nations together. This seems to be a fair comment on practical reality; and the emphasis on human rights is certainly necessary for a world in which nations interact all the time on terms, let us hope, of justice and mutual respect.

But is it sufficient? As students here grow up, is it sufficient for them to learn that they are above all citizens of the United States, but that they ought to respect the basic human rights of citizens of India, Bolivia, Nigeria, and Norway? Or should they, as I think—in addition to giving special attention to the history and current situation of their own nation—learn a good deal more than is frequently the case about the rest of the world in which they live, about India and Bolivia and Nigeria and Norway and their histories, problems, and comparative successes? Should they learn only that citizens of India have equal basic human rights, or should they also learn about the problems of hunger and pollution in India, and the implications of these problems for larger problems of global hunger and global ecology? Most important, should they be taught that they are above all citizens of the United States, or should they instead be taught that they are above all citizens of a world of human beings, and that, while they themselves happen to be situated in the United States, they have to share this world of human beings with the citizens of other countries? I shall shortly suggest four arguments for the second conception of education, which I shall call *cosmopolitan education*. But first I introduce a historical digression, which will trace cosmopolitanism to its origins, in the process recovering some excellent arguments that originally motivated it as an educational project.

II

When Diogenes the Cynic replied, "I am a citizen of the world," he meant apparently that he refused to be defined by his local origins and local group memberships, so central to the self-image of a conventional Greek male; instead, he defined himself in terms of more universal aspirations and concerns. The Stoics who followed his lead developed his image of the *kosmou politês* or world citizen more fully, arguing that each of us dwells, in effect, in two communities—the local community of our birth, and the community of human argument and aspiration that "is truly great and truly common, in which we look neither to this corner nor to that, but measure the boundaries of our nation by the sun" (Seneca, *De Otio*). It is this community that is, most fundamentally, the source of our moral obligations. With respect to the most basic moral values such as justice, "we should regard all human beings as our fellow citizens and neighbors" (Plutarch, *On the Fortunes of Alexander*). We should regard our deliberations as, first and foremost, deliberations about human problems of people in particular concrete situations, not problems growing out of a national identity that is altogether unlike that of others. Diogenes knew that the invitation to think as a world citizen was, in a sense, an invitation to be an exile from the comfort of patriotism and its easy sentiments, to see our own ways of life from the point of view of justice and the good. The accident of where one is born is just that, an accident; any human being might have been born in any nation. Recognizing this, his Stoic successors held, we should not allow differences of nationality or class or ethnic membership or even gender to erect barriers between us and our fellow human beings. We should recognize humanity wherever it occurs, and give its fundamental ingredients, reason and moral capacity, our first allegiance and respect.

This clearly did not mean that the Stoics were proposing the abolition of local and national forms of political organization and the creation of a world state. The point was more radical still: that we should give our first allegiance to no mere form of government, no temporal power, but to the moral community made up by the humanity of all human beings. The idea of the world citizen is in this way the ancestor and source of Kant's idea of the "kingdom of ends," and has a similar function in inspiring and regulating moral and political conduct. One should always behave so as to treat with equal respect the dignity of reason and moral choice in every human being. It is this conception, as well, that inspires Tagore's novel, as the cosmopolitan landlord struggles to stem the tide of nationalism and factionalism by appeals to universal moral norms. Many of the speeches of the character Nikhil were drawn from Tagore's own cosmopolitan political writings.

Stoics who hold that good civic education is education for world citizenship recommend this attitude on three grounds. First, they hold that the study of humanity as it is realized in the whole world is valuable for self-knowledge: we see ourselves more clearly when we see our ways in relation to those of other reasonable people.

Second, they argue, as does Tagore, that we will be better able to solve our problems if we face them in this way. No theme is deeper in Stoicism than the damage done by faction and local allegiances to the political life of a group. Political deliberation, they argue, is sabotaged again and again by partisan loyalties, whether to one's team at the Circus or to one's nation. Only by making our fundamental allegiance that to the world community of justice and reason do we avoid these dangers.

Finally, they insist that the stance of the *kosmou politès* is intrinsically valuable. For it recognizes in persons what is especially fundamental about them, most worthy of respect and acknowledgment: their aspirations to justice and goodness and their capacities for reasoning in this connection. This aspect may be less colorful than local or national traditions and identities—and it is on this basis that the young wife in Tagore's novel spurns it in favor of qualities in the nationalist orator Sandip that she later comes to see as superficial; it is, the Stoics argue, both lasting and deep.

The Stoics stress that to be a citizen of the world one does not need to give up local identifications, which can frequently be a source of great richness in life. They suggest that we think of ourselves not as devoid of local affiliations, but as surrounded by a series of concentric circles. The first one is drawn around the self; the next takes in one's immediate family; then follows the extended family; then, in order, one's neighbors or local group, one's fellow city-dwellers, one's fellow countrymen—and we can easily add to this list groupings based on ethnic, linguistic, historical, professional, gender and sexual identities. Outside all these circles is the largest one, that of humanity as a whole. Our task as citizens of the world will be to "draw the circles somehow toward the center" (Stoic philosopher Hierocles, 1st-2nd CE), making all human beings more like our fellow city dwellers, and so on. In other words, we need not give up our special affections and identifications, whether ethnic or gender-based or religious. We need not think of them as superficial, and we may think of our identity as in part constituted by them. We may and should devote special attention to them in education. But we should work to make all human beings part of our community of dialogue and concern, base our political deliberations on that interlocking commonality, and give the circle that defines our humanity a special attention and respect.

This means, in educational terms, that the student in the United States, for example, may continue to regard herself as in part defined by her particular loves—for her family, her religious and/or ethnic and/or racial community or communities, even for her country. But she must also, and centrally, learn to recognize humanity wherever she encounters it, undeterred by traits that are strange to her, and be eager to understand humanity in its "strange" guises. She must learn enough about the different to recognize common aims, aspirations, and values, and enough about these common ends to see how variously they are instantiated in the many cultures and many histories. Stoic writers insist that the vivid imagining of the different is an essential task of education; and that requires in turn, of course, a mastery of many facts about the different. Marcus Aurelius gives himself the following advice, which might be called the basis for cosmopolitan education: "Accustom yourself not to be inattentive to what another person says, and as far as possible enter into that person's mind" (VI. 53). "Generally," he concludes, "one must first learn many things before one can judge another's action with understanding."

A favored exercise, in this process of world thinking, is to conceive of the entire world of human beings as a single body, its many people as so many limbs. Referring to the fact that it takes only the change of a single letter in Greek to convert the word "limb" (*melos*) into the word "[detached] part" (*meros*), Marcus concludes: "If, changing the word, you call yourself merely a [detached] part rather than a limb, you do not yet love your fellow men from the heart, nor derive complete joy from doing good; you will do it merely as a duty, not as doing good to yourself" (VII. 13). It is important to recall that, as Emperor, he gives himself this advice in connection with daily duties that require coming to grips with the cultures of remote and initially strange civilizations such as those of Parthia and Sarmatia.

I would like to see education adopt this cosmopolitan Stoic stance. The organic model could of course be abused—if, for example, it were to be taken to deny the fundamental importance of the separateness of persons and of fundamental personal liberties. Stoics were not always sufficiently attentive to these values and to their political salience; in that sense their thought is not always a good basis for a scheme of democratic deliberation and education. But as the image is primarily intended—as a reminder of the interdependence of all human beings and communities—it has fundamental significance. There is clearly a huge amount to be said about how such ideas might be realized in curricula at many levels. Instead of beginning that more concrete task, however, I shall now return to the present day and offer four arguments for making world citizenship, rather than democratic/national citizenship, education's central focus. (The first two are modern versions of my first two Stoic arguments; the third develops one part of my Stoic argument about intrinsic moral value; the fourth is more local, directed at the pro-patriotism arguments I am criticizing.)

III

1. *Through cosmopolitan education, we learn more about ourselves.*

One of the greatest barriers to rational deliberation in politics is the unexamined feeling that one's own current preferences and ways are neutral and natural. An education that takes national boundaries as morally salient too often reinforces this kind of irrationality, by lending to what is an accident of history a false air of moral weight and glory. By looking at ourselves in the lens of the other, we come to see what in our practices is local and non-necessary, what more broadly or deeply shared. Our nation is appallingly ignorant of most of the rest of the world. I think that this means that it is also, in many crucial ways, ignorant of itself.

To give just one example of this—since 1994 is the United Nations' International Year of the Family—if we want to understand our own history and our choices where the structure of the family and of child-rearing are involved, we are immeasurably assisted by looking around the world to see in what configurations families exist, and through what strategies children are in fact being cared for. (This would include a study of the history of the family, both in our own and in other traditions.) Such a study can show us, for example, that the two-parent nuclear family, in which the mother is the primary homemaker and the father the primary breadwinner is by no means a pervasive style of child-rearing in today's world. The extended family, clusters of families, the village, women's associations—all these groups and still others are in various places regarded as having major child-rearing responsibilities. Seeing this, we can begin to ask questions—for example, how much child abuse there is in a family that involves grandparents and other relatives in child-rearing, as compared with the relatively isolated Western-style nuclear family; how many different structures of child care have been found to support women's work, and how well each of these is functioning. If we do not undertake this kind of educational project, we risk assuming that the options familiar to us are the only ones there are, and that they are somehow "normal" and "natural" for the human species as such. Much the same can be said about conceptions of gender and sexuality, about conceptions of work and its division, about schemes of property holding, about the treatment of childhood and old age.

2. *We make headway solving problems that require international cooperation.* The air does not obey national boundaries. This simple fact can be, for children, the beginning of the recognition that, like it or not, we live in a world in which the destinies of nations are closely intertwined with respect to basic goods and survival itself. The pollution of third-world nations who are attempting to attain our high standard of living will, in some cases, end up in our air. No matter what account of these matters we will finally adopt, any intelligent deliberation about ecology—as, also, about the food supply and population—requires global planning, global knowledge, and the recognition of a shared future.

To conduct this sort of global dialogue, we need not only knowledge of the geography and ecology of other nations—something that would already entail much revision in our curricula—but also a great deal about the people with whom we shall be talking, so that in talking with them we may be capable of respecting their traditions and commitments. Cosmopolitan education would supply the background necessary for this type of deliberation.

3. *We recognize moral obligations to the rest of the world that are real, and that otherwise would go unrecognized.* What are Americans to make of the fact that the high living standard we enjoy is one that very likely cannot be universalized, at least given the present costs of pollution controls and the present economic situation of developing nations, without ecological disaster? If we take Kantian morality at all seriously, as we should, we need to educate our children to be troubled by this fact. Otherwise we are educating a nation of moral hypocrites, who talk the language of universalizability but whose universe has a self-serving, narrow scope.

This point may appear to presuppose universalism, rather than being an argument in its favor. But here one may note that the values on which Americans may most justly pride themselves are, in a deep sense, Stoic values: respect for human dignity and the opportunity for each person to pursue happiness. If we really do believe that all human beings are created equal and endowed with certain inalienable rights, we are morally required to think about what that conception requires us to do with and for the rest of the world.

Once again, that does not mean that one may not permissibly give one's own sphere a special degree of concern. Politics, like child care, will be poorly done if each thinks herself equally responsible for all, rather than giving the immediate surroundings special attention and care. To give one's own sphere special care is justifiable in universalist terms, and I think that this is its most compelling justification. To take one example, we do not really think that our own children are morally more important than other people's children, even though almost all of us who have children would give our own children far more love and care than we give other people's children. It is good for children, on the whole, that things should work out this way, and that is why our special care is good rather than selfish. Education may and should reflect those special concerns—spending more time, for example, within a given nation, on that nation's history and politics. But my argument does entail that we should not confine our thinking to our own sphere—that in making choices in both political and economic matters we should most seriously consider the right of other human beings to life, liberty, and the pursuit of happiness, and work to acquire the knowledge that will enable us to deliberate well about those rights. I believe that this sort of thinking will have large-scale economic and political consequences.

4. *We make a consistent and coherent argument based on distinctions we are really prepared to defend.* Let me now return to the defense of shared values in Richard Rorty's article and Sheldon Hackney's project. In these eloquent appeals to the common there is something that makes me very uneasy. On the one hand Rorty and Hackney seem to argue well when they insist on the centrality to democratic deliberation of certain values

that bind all citizens together. But why should these values, which instruct us to join hands across boundaries of ethnicity and class and gender and race, lose steam when they get to the borders of the nation? By conceding that a morally arbitrary boundary such as the boundary of the nation has a deep and formative role in our deliberations, we seem to be depriving ourselves of any principled way of arguing to citizens that they should in fact join hands across these other barriers.

For one thing, the very same groups exist both outside and inside. Why should we think of people from China as our fellows the minute they dwell in a certain place, namely the United States, but not when they dwell in a certain other place, namely China? What is it about the national boundary that magically converts people toward whom our education is both incurious and indifferent into people to whom we have duties of mutual respect? I think, in short, that we undercut the very case for multicultural respect within a nation by failing to make a broader world respect central to education. Richard Rorty's patriotism may be a way of bringing all Americans together; but patriotism is very close to jingoism, and I'm afraid I don't see in Rorty's argument any proposal for coping with this very obvious danger.

Furthermore, the defense of shared national values in both Rorty and Hackney, as I understand it, requires appealing to certain basic features of human personhood that obviously also transcend national boundaries. So if we fail to educate children to cross those boundaries in their minds and imaginations, we are tacitly giving them the message that we don't really mean what we say. We say that respect should be accorded to humanity as such, but we really mean that Americans as such are worthy of special respect. And that, I think, is a story that Americans have told for far too long.

IV

Becoming a citizen of the world is often a lonely business. It is, in effect, as Diogenes said, a kind of exile—from the comfort of local truths, from the warm nestling feeling of patriotism, from the absorbing drama of pride in oneself and one's own. In the writings of Marcus Aurelius (as in those of his American followers Emerson and Thoreau), one sometimes feels a boundless loneliness, as if the removal of the props of habit and local boundaries had left life bereft of a certain sort of warmth and security. If one begins life as a child who loves and trusts its parents, it is tempting to want to reconstruct citizenship along the same lines, finding in an idealized image of a nation a surrogate parent who will do one's thinking for one. Cosmopolitanism offers no such refuge; it offers only reason and the love of humanity, which may seem at times less colorful than other sources of belonging.

In Tagore's novel, the appeal to world citizenship fails—fails because patriotism is full of color and intensity and passion, whereas cosmopolitanism seems to have a hard time gripping the imagination. And yet in its very failure, Tagore shows, it succeeds. For the novel is a story of education for world citizenship, since the entire tragic story is told by the widowed Bimala, who understands, if too late, that Nikhil's morality was vastly superior to Sandip's empty symbol-mongering, that what looked like passion in Sandip was egocentric self-exaltation, and that what looked like lack of passion in Nikhil contained a truly loving perception of her as a person. If one goes today to Santiniketan, a town several hours by train from Calcutta, the town where Tagore founded his cosmopolitan university Vishvabharati—whose name means "all the world"—one feels the tragedy once more. For all-the-world university has not achieved the anticipated influence or distinction within India, and the ideals of the cosmopolitan community of Santiniketan are increasingly under siege from militant forces of ethnocentric particularism and Hindu-fundamentalist nationalism. And yet, in the very decline of Tagore's ideal—which now threatens the very existence of the secular and tolerant Indian state—the observer sees its worth. To worship one's country as a god is indeed to bring a curse upon it. Recent electoral reactions against Hindu nationalism give some grounds for optimism that this recognition of worth is widespread and may prove efficacious, averting a tragic ending of the sort that Tagore describes.

And since I am in fact optimistic that Tagore's ideal can be successfully realized in schools and universities in democracies around the world, and in the formation of public policy, let me conclude with a story of cosmopolitanism that has a happy ending. It is told by Diogenes Laertius about the courtship and marriage of the Cynic cosmopolitan philosophers Crates and Hipparchia (one of the most eminent female philosophers of antiquity), in order, presumably, to show that casting off the symbols of status and nation can sometimes be a way to succeed in love. The background is that Hipparchia is from a good family, attached, as most Greek families were, to social status and pedigree. They resent the cosmopolitan philosopher Crates, with his strange ideas of world citizenship and his strange disdain for rank and boundaries.

> [Hipparchia] fell in love with Crates' arguments and his way of life and paid no attention to any of her suitors nor to wealth or high birth or good looks. Crates, though, was everything to her. Moreover, she told her parents that she would kill herself if she were not married off to him. So Crates was called on by her parents to talk their daughter out of it; he did all he could, but in the end he didn't persuade her. So he stood up and threw off his clothes in front of her and said, "Here is your bridegroom; these are his possessions; make your decision accordingly—for you cannot be my companion unless you undertake the same way of life." The girl chose him. Adopting the same clothing and style of life she went around with her husband and they copulated in public and they went off together to dinner parties. And once she went to a dinner party at the house of Lysimachus and there refuted Theodorus the Atheist, with a sophism like this: "If it wouldn't be judged wrong for Theodorus to do something, then it wouldn't be judged wrong for Hipparchia to do it either; but Theodorus does no wrong if he beats himself; so Hipparchia too does no wrong if she beats Theodorus." And when Theodorus could not reply to her argument, he ripped off her cloak. But Hipparchia was not upset or distraught as a woman would normally be. (DL 6.96–8)

I am not exactly recommending Crates and Hipparchia as the marital ideal for students in my hypothetical cosmopolitan schools (or Theodorus the Atheist as their logic teacher). But the story does reveal this: that the life of the cosmopolitan, who puts right before country, and universal reason before the symbols of national belonging, need not be boring, flat, or lacking in love.

NOTES AND QUESTIONS

1.   Unrealistic idealism? — Consider this opposing view to Nussbaum's argument for humanitarianism:

> Many people oppose immigration reform and argue against controlling immigration because they believe in a new world order, in the rise of internationalism, and in the demise of nation-states. While their vision may be commendable and their ideals unquestionable, their sense of reality is limited. The world is divided into nations. It will be divided into nations for as long as we can see into the future. And the United States, one of the last few nations to accept any appreciable number of migrants, is one of the most desirable nations in the world in which to live. It will continue to attract as many legal immigrants as we allow to come here, and as many illegal immigrants as we refuse to deter.
>
> Another group, the humanitarian idealists, argues that the United States can help deal with world poverty through high levels of immigration. They, too, are probably sincere but unrealistic. The United States is a small part of the world—only 5 percent of the population of the earth. We can voluntarily share the world's poverty; we cannot make the world rich by sharing our wealth.

RICHARD D. LAMM & GARY IMHOFF, THE IMMIGRATION TIME BOMB: THE FRAGMENTING OF AMERICA 1–26 (1986).

2.   Beyond the nation state? Can we ever expect that national boundaries will become meaningless? Or is Nussbaum's rumination a call to philosophical ideals, not implementation in the world of practical politics and geopolitical interests?

Lamm and Imhoff object to this perspective:

> The immigration laws of the United States should be written and enforced in order to protect and preserve the interests of Americans and of this country. The test of immigration policy must be the interests of Americans. It cannot be whether it hastens the demise of nations, or whether it makes the worldwide distribution of wealth more equitable by lowering the wealth of Americans while imperceptibly raising the wealth of a small proportion of others.
>
> The first priority of any country, the first test for a nation, is to have defined, agreed-upon borders over which the movements of

citizens and noncitizens alike are controlled. By that test, the United States today would hardly qualify as a nation. We have not clearly and distinctly set and enforced the conditions under which individuals are entitled to enter this country and become participants in our polity. By failing to do so, we have failed to pay attention to the needs, the desires, and the interests of our own citizens.

Lamm & Imhoff, *supra.*

3.   The moral vision of a preacher and a philosopher. Can we afford to ignore the moral compass of our visionaries like Dr. Martin Luther King, and Martha Nussbaum? On the other hand, can we afford to apply their vision? What role does moral authority play in the process of shaping national immigration policy? What role should it play?

One commentator offers this perspective on the question:

This brings us to the role philosophers can play in resolving these issues. It is often thought that the philosopher aims to be the conscience of policymakers, advising what they ought, morally speaking, to do, and perhaps explaining how this might figure in the tough, pragmatic world of politics. * * * [This] portrays the philosopher as one with some special moral gift to impart to those who lack it.

But the moral is not an aspect separable in the way this view suggests from the world's practical or other aspects. Ethics is not a species unto itself—the department of altruistic affairs; it is practical reasoning. * * *

Of course, the philosopher is not an expert on all or even most of the issues relevant to enlightened decision-making. But then who is? ... Values cannot be wholly eliminated, but they should be revealed. They need not be arbitrary. Again philosophers can contribute their expertise, which consists not in a unique moral vision but rather in knowing how and to what extent value judgments can be supported.

Judith Litchenberg, *Mexican Migration and U.S. Policy: A Guide for the Perplexed, in* THE BORDER THAT JOINS 14 (Peter G. Brown & Henry Shue eds., 1983.)

B.   THE BASICS: CONGRESSIONAL POWER TO EXCLUDE, DETAIN, OR DEPORT, PLENARY POWER?

Fiallo v. Bell

Supreme Court of the United States, 430 U.S. 787 (1977).

[Three sets of unwed natural fathers and their illegitimate offspring brought action to permanently enjoin enforcement of those sections of the

Immigration and Nationality Act which have the effect of excluding the relationship between an illegitimate child and his natural father, as opposed to his natural mother, from the special preference immigration status accorded a "child" or "parent" of a United States citizen or lawful permanent resident. The three-judge District Court for the Eastern District of New York, Moore, Circuit Judge, rendered judgment for the Government, and plaintiffs appealed.]

■ MR. JUSTICE POWELL delivered the opinion of the Court.

This case brings before us a constitutional challenge to §§ 101(b)(1)(D) and 101(b)(2) of the Immigration and Nationality Act of 1952 [(The Act)].

I

The Act grants special preference immigration status to aliens who qualify as the "children" or "parents" of United States citizens or lawful permanent residents. Under § 101(b)(1), a "child" is defined as an unmarried person under 21 years of age who is a legitimate or legitimated child, a stepchild, an adopted child, or an illegitimate child seeking preference by virtue of his relationship with his natural mother. The definition does not extend to an illegitimate child seeking preference by virtue of his relationship with his natural father. Moreover, under § 101(b)(2), a person qualifies as a "parent" for purposes of the Act solely on the basis of the person's relationship with a "child." As a result, the natural father of an illegitimate child who is either a United States citizen or permanent resident alien is not entitled to preferential treatment as a "parent."

The special preference immigration status provided for those who satisfy the statutory "parent-child" relationship depends on whether the immigrant's relative is a United States citizen or permanent resident alien. A United States citizen is allowed the entry of his "parent" or "child" without regard to *either* an applicable numerical quota *or* the labor certification requirement.* * * On the other hand, a United States permanent resident alien is allowed the entry of the "parent" or "child" subject to numerical limitations but without regard to the labor certification requirement. * * *

Appellants are three sets of unwed natural fathers and their illegitimate offspring who sought, either as an alien father or an alien child, a special immigration preference by virtue of a relationship to a citizen or resident alien child or parent. In each instance the applicant was informed that he was ineligible for an immigrant visa unless he qualified for admission under the general numerical limitations and, in the case of the alien parents, received the requisite labor certification.

* * *

II

At the outset, it is important to underscore the limited scope of judicial inquiry into immigration legislation. This Court has repeatedly emphasized that "over no conceivable subject is the legislative power of Congress more complete than it is over" the admission of aliens. * * * Our cases "have long recognized the power to expel or exclude aliens as a fundamental sovereign attribute exercised by the Government's political departments largely immune from judicial control." * * * Our recent decisions have not departed from this long-established rule. Just last Term, for example, the Court had occasion to note that "the power over aliens is of a political character and therefore subject only to narrow judicial review." *Hampton v. Mow Sun Wong*, 426 U.S. 88, 101 n.21 (1976), citing *Fong Yue Ting v. United States*, 149 U.S. 698, 713 (1893). And we observed recently that in the exercise of its broad power over immigration and naturalization, "Congress regularly makes rules that would be unacceptable if applied to citizens." * * *

Appellants apparently do not challenge the need for special judicial deference to congressional policy choices in the immigration context, but instead suggest that a "unique coalescing of factors" makes the instant case sufficiently unlike prior immigration cases to warrant more searching judicial scrutiny. * * * Appellants first observe that since the statutory provisions were designed to reunite families wherever possible, the purpose of the statute was to afford rights not to aliens but to United States citizens and legal permanent residents. Appellants then rely on our border-search decisions in *Almeida–Sanchez v. United States*, 413 U.S. 266 (1973), and *United States v. Brignoni–Ponce*, 422 U.S. 873 (1975), for the proposition that the courts must scrutinize congressional legislation in the immigration area to protect against violations of the rights of citizens. At issue in the border-search cases, however, was the nature of the protections mandated by the Fourth Amendment with respect to Government procedures designed to stem the illegal entry of aliens. Nothing in the opinions in those cases suggests that Congress has anything but exceptionally broad power to determine which classes of aliens may lawfully enter the country. * * *

Appellants suggest a second distinguishing factor. They argue that none of the prior immigration cases of this Court involved "double-barreled" discrimination based on sex and illegitimacy, infringed upon the due process rights of citizens and legal permanent residents, or implicated "the fundamental constitutional interests of United States citizens and permanent residents in a familial relationship." * * * But this Court has resolved similar challenges to immigration legislation based on other constitutional rights of citizens, and has rejected the suggestion that more searching judicial scrutiny is required. In *Kleindienst v. Mandel*, * * *, for example, United States citizens challenged the power of the Attorney General to deny a visa to an alien who, as a proponent of "the economic, international, and governmental doctrines of World communism", was ineligible to receive a visa * * * absent a waiver by the Attorney General. The citizen-appellees in that case conceded that Congress could prohibit entry of all aliens falling into the class defined by § 1182(a)(28)(D). They contended, however, that the Attorney General's statutory discretion to approve a waiver was limited by the Constitution and that their First Amendment rights were abridged by the denial of Mandel's request for a visa. The Court held that "when the Executive exercises this [delegated] power negatively on the basis of a facially legitimate and bona fide reason, the courts will neither look behind the exercise of that discretion, nor test it by balancing its justification against the First Amendment interests of those who seek personal communication with the applicant." * * * We can see no reason to review the broad congressional policy choice at issue here under a more exacting standard than was applied in *Kleindienst v. Mandel*, a First Amendment case.

Finally, appellants characterize our prior immigration cases as involving foreign policy matters and congressional choices to exclude or expel groups of aliens that were "specifically and clearly perceived to pose a grave threat to the national security," citing *Harisiades v. Shaughnessy*, 342 U.S. 580 (1952), "or to the general welfare of this country," citing *Boutilier v. INS*, 387 U.S. 118 (1967). * * * We find no indication in our prior cases that the scope of judicial review is a function of the nature of the policy choice at issue. To the contrary, "[s]ince decisions in these matters may implicate our relations with foreign powers, and since a wide variety of classifications must be defined in the light of changing political and economic circumstances, such decisions are frequently of a character more appropriate to either the Legislature or the Executive than to the Judiciary," and "[t]he reasons that preclude judicial review of political questions also dictate a narrow standard of review of decisions made by the Congress or the President in the area of immigration and naturalization." * * * As Mr. Justice Frankfurter observed in his concurrence in *Harisiades v. Shaughnessy*:

> "The conditions of entry for every alien, the particular classes of aliens that shall be denied entry altogether, the basis for determining such classification, the right to terminate hospitality to aliens, the grounds on which such determination shall be based, have been recognized as matters solely for the responsibility of the Congress and wholly outside the power of this Court to control." 342 U.S., at 596–597.

* * *

IV

We hold that §§ 101(b)(1)(D) and 101(b)(2) of the Immigration and Nationality Act of 1952 are not unconstitutional by virtue of the exclusion of the relationship between an illegitimate child and his natural father from the preferences accorded by the Act to the "child" or "parent" of a United States citizen or lawful permanent resident.

Affirmed.

■ MR. JUSTICE MARSHALL, with whom MR. JUSTICE BRENNAN joins, dissenting.

Until today I thought it clear that when Congress grants benefits to some citizens, but not to others, it is our duty to insure that the decision comports with Fifth Amendment principles of due process and equal protection. Today, however, the Court appears to hold that discrimination among citizens, however invidious and irrational, must be tolerated if it occurs in the context of the immigration laws. Since I cannot agree that Congress has license to deny fundamental rights to citizens according to the most disfavored criteria simply because the Immigration and Nationality Act is involved, I dissent.

* * *

This case, unlike most immigration cases that come before the Court, directly involves the rights of citizens, not aliens. "[C]oncerned with the problem of keeping families of United States citizens and immigrants united," Congress extended to American citizens the right to choose to be reunited in the United States with their immediate families. The focus was on citizens and their need for relief from the hardships occasioned by the immigration laws. The right to seek such relief was given only to the citizen, not the alien. * * * If the citizen does not petition the Attorney General for the special "immediate relative" status for his parent or child, the alien, despite his relationship, can receive no preference. * * * It is irrelevant that aliens have no constitutional right to immigrate and that Americans have no constitutional right to compel the admission of their families. The essential fact here is that Congress did choose to extend such privileges to American citizens but then denied them to a small class of citizens. When Congress draws such lines among citizens, the Constitution requires that the decision comport with Fifth Amendment principles of equal protection and due process. The simple fact that the discrimination is set in immigration legislation cannot insulate from scrutiny the invidious abridgment of citizens' fundamental interests.

* * *

————

Zadvydas v. Davis

Supreme Court of the United States, 533 U.S. 678 (2001).

■ JUSTICE BREYER, delivered the opinion of the Court.

* * *

We note at the outset that the primary federal habeas corpus statute, * * * confers jurisdiction upon the federal courts to hear these cases. * * * Before 1952, the federal courts considered challenges to the lawfulness of immigration-related detention, including challenges to the validity of a deportation order, in habeas proceedings. * * * Beginning in 1952, an alternative method for review of *deportation orders,* namely, actions brought in federal district court under the Administrative Procedure Act (APA), became available. * * * And in 1961 Congress replaced district court APA review with initial *deportation order* review in courts of appeals. * * * The 1961 Act specified that federal habeas courts were also available to hear statutory and constitutional challenges to *deportation* (and exclusion) *orders.* * * * These statutory changes left habeas untouched as the basic method for obtaining review of continued *custody after* a deportation order had become final. * * *

More recently, Congress has enacted several statutory provisions that limit the circumstances in which judicial review of deportation decisions is available. But none applies here. One provision * * * simply forbids courts to construe *that section* "to create any . . . procedural right or benefit that is legally enforceable"; it does not deprive an alien of the right to rely on [the provision] to challenge detention that is without statutory authority.

Another provision * * * says that "no court shall have jurisdiction to review" decisions "specified . . . to be in the discretion of the Attorney General." The aliens here, however, do not seek review of the Attorney General's exercise of discretion; rather, they challenge the extent of the Attorney General's authority under the post-removal-period detention statute. And the extent of that authority is not a matter of discretion * * *.

We conclude that * * * habeas corpus proceedings remain available as a forum for statutory and constitutional challenges to post-removal-period detention statute.* * *

* * *

A statute permitting indefinite detention of an alien would raise a serious constitutional problem. The Fifth Amendment's Due Process Clause forbids the Government to "depriv[e]" any "person . . . of . . . liberty . . . without due process of law." Freedom from imprisonment—from government custody, detention, or other forms of physical restraint—lies at the heart of the liberty that Clause protects. * * * And this Court has said that government detention violates that Clause unless the detention is ordered in a *criminal* proceeding with adequate procedural protections * * * or, in certain special and "narrow" nonpunitive "circumstances," * * * where a special justification, such as harm-threatening mental illness, outweighs the "individual's constitutionally protected interest in avoiding physical restraint." * * *

The proceedings at issue here are civil, not criminal, and we assume that they are nonpunitive in purpose and effect. There is no sufficiently strong special justification here for indefinite civil detention—at least as administered under this statute. The statute, says the Government, has two regulatory goals: "ensuring the appearance of aliens at future immigration proceedings" and "[p]reventing danger to the community." * * * But by definition the first justification—preventing flight—is weak or nonexistent where removal seems a remote possibility at best. As this Court said in *Jackson v. Indiana,* 406 U.S. 715 (1972), where detention's goal is no longer practically attainable, detention no longer "bear[s][a] reasonable relation to the purpose for which the individual [was] committed." *Id.,* at 738.

The second justification—protecting the community—does not necessarily diminish in force over time. But we have upheld preventive detention based on dangerousness only when limited to specially dangerous individuals and subject to strong procedural protections. * * * In cases in which preventive detention is of potentially *indefinite* duration, we have also demanded that the dangerousness rationale be accompanied by some other special circumstance, such as mental illness, that helps to create the danger. * * * The civil confinement here at issue is not limited, but potentially permanent. * * * The provision authorizing detention does not apply narrowly to "a small segment of particularly dangerous individuals," * * * say, suspected terrorists, but broadly to aliens ordered removed for many and various reasons, including tourist visa violations. And, once the flight risk justification evaporates, the only special circumstance present is the alien's removable status itself, which bears no relation to a detainee's dangerousness. * * *

* * *

The Government also looks for support to cases holding that Congress has "plenary power" to create immigration law, and that the Judicial Branch must defer to Executive and Legislative Branch decisionmaking in that area. * * * But that power is subject to important constitutional limitations. See *INS v. Chadha,* 462 U.S. 919, 941–942 (1983) (Congress must choose "a constitutionally permissible means of implementing" that power); *The Chinese Exclusion Case,* 130 U.S. 581, 604 (1889) (congressional authority limited "by the Constitution itself and considerations of public policy and justice which control, more or less, the conduct of all civilized nations"). In these cases, we focus upon those limitations. In doing so, we nowhere deny the right of Congress to remove aliens, to subject them to supervision with conditions when released from detention, or to incarcerate them where appropriate for violations of those conditions. * * * The question before us is not one of " 'confer[ring] on those admitted the right to remain against the national will' " or " 'sufferance of aliens' " who should be removed. [*Post* (SCALIA, J., dissenting) (emphasis deleted).] Rather, the issue we address is whether aliens that the Government finds itself unable to remove are to be condemned to an indefinite term of imprisonment within the United States.

* * *

B

Despite this constitutional problem, if "Congress has made its intent" in the statute "clear, 'we must give effect to that intent.' " * * * We cannot find here, however, any clear indication of congressional intent to grant the Attorney General the power to hold indefinitely in confinement an alien ordered removed. And that is so whether protecting the community from dangerous aliens is a primary or (as we believe) secondary statutory purpose. [Cf. *post* (KENNEDY, J., dissenting).] After all, the provision is part of a statute that has as its basic purpose effectuating an alien's removal. Why should we assume that Congress saw the alien's dangerousness as unrelated to this purpose?

The Government points to the statute's word "may." But while "may" suggests discretion, it does not necessarily suggest unlimited discretion. In that respect the word "may" is ambiguous. Indeed, if Congress had meant to authorize long-term detention of unremovable aliens, it certainly could have spoken in clearer terms. * * *

* * *

The Fifth Circuit held Zadvydas' continued detention lawful as long as "good faith efforts to effectuate . . . deportation continue" and Zadvydas failed to show that deportation will prove "impossible." * * * But this standard would seem to require an alien seeking release to show the absence of *any* prospect of removal—no matter how unlikely or unforeseeable—which demands more than our reading of the statute can bear. The Ninth Circuit held that the Government was required to release Ma from detention because there was no reasonable likelihood of his removal in the foreseeable future. * * * But its conclusion may have rested solely upon the "absence" of an "extant or pending" repatriation agreement without giving due weight to the likelihood of successful future negotiations. * * * Consequently, we vacate the judgments below and remand both cases for further proceedings consistent with this opinion.

It is so ordered.

■ JUSTICE SCALIA, with whom JUSTICE THOMAS joins, dissenting.

I join Part I of JUSTICE KENNEDY's dissent, which establishes the Attorney General's clear statutory authority to detain criminal aliens with no specified time limit. I write separately because I do not believe that, as JUSTICE KENNEDY suggests in Part II of his opinion, there may be some situations in which the courts can order release. I believe that in both *Zadvydas v. Davis,* No. 99–7791, and *Ashcroft v. Ma,* No. 00–38, a "careful description" of the substantive right claimed, *Reno v. Flores,* 507 U.S. 292, 302 (1993), suffices categorically to refute its existence. A criminal alien under final order of removal who allegedly will not be accepted by any other country in the reasonably foreseeable future claims a constitutional right of supervised release into the United States. This claim can be repackaged as freedom from "physical restraint" or freedom from "indefinite detention," [*ante*] but it is at bottom a claimed right of release into this country by an individual who *concededly* has no legal right to be here. There is no such constitutional right.

Like a criminal alien under final order of removal, an inadmissible alien at the border has no right to be in the United States. *The Chinese Exclusion Case,* 130 U.S. 581, 603 (1889). In *Shaughnessy v. United States ex rel. Mezei,* 345 U.S. 206 (1953), we upheld potentially indefinite detention of such an inadmissible alien whom the Government was unable to return anywhere else. We said that "we [did] not think that respondent's continued exclusion deprives him of any statutory or constitutional right." * * * While four Members of the Court thought that Mezei deserved greater procedural protections the Attorney General had refused to divulge any information as to why Mezei was being detained * * * no Justice asserted that Mezei had a substantive constitutional right to release into this country. And Justice Jackson's dissent, joined by Justice Frankfurter, affirmatively asserted the opposite, with no contradiction from the Court: "Due process does not invest any alien with a right to enter the United States, *nor confer on those admitted the right to remain against the national will.* Nothing in the Constitution requires admission *or sufferance* of aliens hostile to our scheme of government." * * * Insofar as a claimed legal right to release into this country is concerned, an alien under final order of removal stands on an equal footing with an inadmissible alien at the threshold of entry: He has no such right.

* * *

■ JUSTICE KENNEDY, with whom THE CHIEF JUSTICE joins, and with whom JUSTICE SCALIA and JUSTICE THOMAS join as to Part I, dissenting.

The Court says its duty is to avoid a constitutional question. It deems the duty performed by interpreting a statute in obvious disregard of congressional intent; curing the resulting gap by writing a statutory amendment of its own; committing its own grave constitutional error by arrogating to the Judicial Branch the power to summon high officers of the Executive to assess their progress in conducting some of the Nation's most sensitive negotiations with foreign powers; and then likely releasing into our general population at least hundreds of removable or inadmissible aliens who have been found by fair procedures to be flight risks, dangers to the community, or both. Far from avoiding a constitutional question, the Court's ruling causes systemic dislocation in the balance of powers, thus raising serious constitutional concerns not just for the cases at hand but for the Court's own view of its proper authority. Any supposed respect the Court seeks in not reaching the constitutional question is outweighed by the intrusive and erroneous exercise of its own powers. In the guise of judicial restraint the Court ought not to intrude upon the other branches. The constitutional question the statute presents, it must be acknowledged, may be a significant one in some later case; but it ought not to drive us to an incorrect interpretation of the statute. The Court having reached the wrong result for the wrong reason, this respectful dissent is required.

* * *

The majority's unanchored interpretation ignores another indication that the Attorney General's detention discretion was not limited to this truncated period. Section 1231(a)(6) permits continued detention not only of removable aliens but also of inadmissible aliens, for instance those stopped at the border before entry. Congress provides for detention of both categories within the same statutory grant of authority. Accepting the majority's interpretation, then, there are two possibilities, neither of which is sustainable. On the one hand, it may be that the majority's rule applies to both categories of aliens, in which case we are asked to assume that Congress intended to restrict the discretion it could confer upon the Attorney General so that all inadmissible aliens must be allowed into our community within six months. On the other hand, the majority's logic might be that inadmissible and removable aliens can be treated differently. Yet it is not a plausible construction of § 1231(a)(6) to imply a time limit as to one class but not to another. The text does not admit of this possibility. As a result, it is difficult to see why "[a]liens who have not yet gained initial admission to this country would present a very different question."

* * *

The risk to the community posed by the mandatory release of aliens who are dangerous or a flight risk is far from insubstantial; the motivation to protect the citizenry from aliens determined to be dangerous is central to the immigration power itself. The Government cites statistical studies showing high recidivism rates for released aliens. One Government Accounting Office study cited by Congress in floor debates on the Antiterrorism and Effective Death Penalty Act of 1996, 110 Stat. 1214, put the figure as high as 77 percent. * * * It seems evident a criminal record accumulated by an admitted alien during his or her time in the United States is likely to be a better indicator of risk than factors relied upon during the INS's initial decision to admit or exclude. Aliens ordered deported as the result of having committed a felony have proved to be dangerous.

    * * *

II

The aliens' claims are substantial; their plight is real. They face continued detention, perhaps for life, unless it is shown they no longer present a flight risk or a danger to the community. In a later case the specific circumstances of a detention may present a substantial constitutional question. That is not a reason, however, for framing a rule which ignores the law governing alien status.

As persons within our jurisdiction, the aliens are entitled to the protection of the Due Process Clause. Liberty under the Due Process Clause includes protection against unlawful or arbitrary personal restraint or detention. The liberty rights of the aliens before us here are subject to limitations and conditions not applicable to citizens, however. * * * No party to this proceeding contests the initial premise that the aliens have been determined to be removable after a fair hearing under lawful and proper procedures. Section 1229a sets forth the proceedings required for deciding the inadmissibility or removability of an alien, including a hearing before an immigration judge, at which the INS carries "the burden of establishing by clear and convincing evidence that ... the alien is deportable." * * * Aliens ordered removed pursuant to these procedures are given notice of their right to appeal the decision, * * * may move the immigration judge to reconsider, * * * can seek discretionary cancellation of removal, and can obtain habeas review of the Attorney General's decision not to consider waiver of deportation. * * * As a result, aliens like Zadvydas and Ma do not arrive at their removable status without thorough, substantial procedural safeguards.

    * * *

C. NATIONAL BORDERS: ECONOMICS AND IMMIGRATION POLICY DEBATES

Border Crossings in An Age of Border Patrols: *Cruzando Fronteras Metaforicas*

26 N.M. L. REV. (1996).

■ MARGARET E. MONTOYA

    * * * Issues involving immigration, free trade, illicit drugs, affirmative action for Latinos and the English-only movement have pushed relations

with Mexico, Mexicanos, and Chicanos into a prominence in the political discourse that is unusual for recent national elections. No issue is more prominent and more hotly debated by both the Democrats and the Republicans than the legal and illegal migration of low-skilled persons from Mexico into the Southwestern portions of the United States.

Concerns about transborder movement of people, goods, capital, languages, and accompanying legal claims have become global. People throughout the globe are moving from the southern regions with their relative poverty into the northern countries in search of employment and political stability. Within this current political environment borders are embedded with symbolic meaning about national sovereignty, a desired clarity about who "belongs" and who does not, and employment security. Border crossers become media symbols and political scapegoats.

* * *

THE BORDER

The U.S./Mexico border was defined, as many international borders have been, by war, political intrigue, and river morphology. The 1848 Treaty of Guadalupe Hidalgo ended the United States' war with Mexico and established the Rio Grande as the border from the Gulf of Mexico to El Paso. Moving west, the Gila River that runs from New Mexico through Arizona at a point above Tucson and into the Colorado River was the negotiated boundary. From the Colorado River, a straight line was drawn to the Pacific Ocean at a point just below San Diego.

By 1853, Mexico, and its President Santa Anna, had land and needed money; the United States had money and wanted land for a transcontinental railroad system. So James Gadsden, the minister to Mexico, bargained to have the United States buy large portions of northern Mexico. Originally hoping for Baja California and parts of Sonora and Chihuahua, he eventually settled for a smaller section of land, approximately 30,000 acres for which the United States paid $10 million. With the so-called Gadsden Purchase, the border was now drawn below Nogales and Douglas, Arizona.

The border measures 1,951.36 miles from the Gulf of Mexico to the Pacific, with the Rio Grande accounting for 1,253.69 miles, the Colorado for 23.72 miles, and the land border for 697.67 miles. Even after the border had been officially defined, both the meandering of the alluvial channels of the Rio Grande and the cartographic mistakes in the maps which formed the basis for the Treaty of Guadalupe Hidalgo created ongoing disputes between the two governments.

Nonetheless, what has characterized the border for most of its one hundred and fifty year history has been the lack of open hostility among the people who inhabit the territory along the border. According to historians, the process of cultural lending and borrowing began almost immediately with the flows of people, capital, and ideas largely disregarding the political boundary.

During most of the past century, the United States actively encouraged the movement of workers from Mexico. In the late 1800s, miners were recruited from Sonora and Jalisco, and those immigrant laborers were responsible for the feasibility and profitability of open pit copper mines in Arizona and New Mexico. Later as the Imperial and Mesilla Valleys were irrigated, farm labor from Mexico became critical for the planting, weeding and harvesting of crops. Immigration laws were specifically drafted to protect the Mexican labor supply for agribusiness in California and elsewhere.

Much of the current political debate centers on the "violations" and "transgressions" of the border by undocumented workers who cross to work in the United States or who overstay their visas. This debate is in sharp contrast to the original desire of the two countries to facilitate transborder interactions. A series of "sister-cities" were established along the border—Mexicali and Calexico; Nogales, Arizona and Nogales, Sonora; El Paso, Texas and El Paso del Norte (now called Cuidad Juarez); Laredo, Texas, and Nuevo Laredo, Tumaulipas—with the explicit intent, at the time, to create a population along the border with facility in both cultures, a borderlands in which both languages would be spoken and goods, labor, and capital would move fairly freely. These hopes have largely been realized. Current proposals to fortify the border by building impenetrable concrete walls, electrified fences, or a human fence of border guards fail to take into account the considerable advantages of these historic connections, especially those advantages offered by a hybrid population that navigates easily through both societies.

Rep. Duncan Hunter (R–El Cajon, Ca.) has proposed the building of a triple fence along the 14–mile stretch of border from the Pacific Ocean to Otay Mesa, known colloquially as "Smugglers Alley." According to the Los Angeles Times, the idea for the fence is based on a study prepared by the Sandia National Laboratory in New Mexico, which "concluded that if one fence was good, three fences were better." * * * Nevertheless, the border continues to serve the political fortunes of jingoistic politicians.

BORDER AS METAPHOR

More recently, the border has been imbedded with metaphoric and tropic meanings. Applicable to disciplinary, cultural, and epistemological spaces, the border is seen as site, intersection, bridge, and membrane. Borders have been transformed from bilateral national boundaries to borders representing cultural and epistemic sites of contestation.

In her classic book, *Borderlands, La Frontera: The New Mestiza*, Gloria Anzaldúa transformed the concept of the "border" from geographic and physical spaces to one applicable to psychological, sexual, and spiritual sites, "present wherever two or more cultures edge each other, where people of different races occupy the same territory, where under, lower, middle and upper classes touch, where the space between two individuals shrinks with intimacy." * * * The border as an epistemic space for the exploration of cultural production has proven particularly salient to ethnographers. In 1989, the anthropologist Renato Rosaldo observed:

> [O]ur everyday lives are crisscrossed by border zones, pockets and eruptions of all kinds. Social borders frequently become salient around such lines as sexual orientation, gender, class, race, ethnicity, nationality, age, politics, dress, food or taste. Along with "our" supposedly transparent cultural selves, such borderlands should be regarded not as analytically empty transitional zones but as sites of creative cultural production that require investigation.

Dwight Conquergood extended the notion of contested sites to the self, exploring the reframing of borders for purposes of epistemology and identity formation:

> "borders bleed, as much as they contain. Instead of dividing lines to be patrolled or transgressed, boundaries are now understood as crisscrossing sites inside the post-modern subject. Difference is resituated within, instead of beyond, the self. Inside and outside distinctions, like genres, blur and wobble. . . .
>
> ". . . The major epistemological consequence of displacing the idea of solid centers and unified wholes with borderlands and zones of contest is a rethinking of identity and culture as constructed and relational, instead of ontologically given and essential. This rethinking privileges metonym, 'reasoning part-to-part' over . . . synecdoche, 'reasoning part-to-whole'; it features syntax over semantics. Meaning is contested and struggled for in the interstices, *in between* structures. Identity is invented and contingent, not autonomous: 'I' is, therefore, not a unified subject, a fixed identity, or that solid mass covered with layers of superficialities one has gradually to peel off before one can see its true face. "I' is, itself, infinite layers."

My personal favorite is Ruth Behar's *Translated Woman: Crossing the Border with Esperanza's Story.* The centerpiece story about an indigenous Mexican woman is told by Behar in her ethnographic voice, but the multilayered translation of Esperanza's story requires Behar to tell her own story. Here the border is integral to the identities of both the Cuban ethnographer and her Indian informant, but, more importantly, both Behar and Esperanza use their relation to the border to create their identity, to name themselves as illegal, as "literary wetbacks," thereby robbing the popular discourse of its power to define epithets, to construct identities, and to stigmatize experience:

> Esperanza has given me her story to smuggle across the border. Just as Mexican laborers export their bodies for labor on American soil, Esperanza has given me her story for export only. Her story, she realizes, is a kind of commodity that will have a value on the other side that it doesn't have at home-why else would I be "using up" my life to write about her life? She has chosen to be a literary wetback, and I am to act as her literary broker, the border crosser who will take her story

to the other side and make it be heard in translation. The question will be whether I can act as literary broker without becoming the worst kind of coyote, getting her across, but only by exploiting her lack of power to make it to *el otro lado* any other way.

[T]here is a special burden that authorship carries if you have ever occupied a borderland place in the dominant culture, especially if you were told at some point in your life that you didn't have what it takes to be an authority on, an author of, anything. It means writing as a "literary wetback," as the Chicana poet Alicia Gaspar de Alba puts it, without "the 'right' credentials . . . to get across."

It is not just Esperanza, then who is a literary wetback. Even though I have borne her story across to this side of the border, I recognize that I, too, in a quite different way, am a literary wetback in the world of academic letters, a wetback despite the papers that tell me I'm okay, I'm in, I'm a legal alien.

* * *

A CAVEAT

Policing the southern border of the United States has become a central issue in the political agenda of both the Democratic and Republican parties in the presidential campaigns of 1996. As this introduction is being written, the House has considered and passed sweeping new immigration legislation, further restricting legal immigration and adding 5000 new border patrol agents. In California, the Riverside police were recently videotaped in a high-speed chase that ended with them viciously billy-clubbing Enrique Funes Flores and Alicia Sotero, two Mexican nationals who put up no resistance when caught. The Mexican male driver had been transporting some twenty Mexican undocumented workers in the bed of a dilapidated truck.

And while the Mexicans were stereotyped as lazy, shiftless, passive siesta seekers, people who patronized *manhexana*, those who knew them realized that just the opposite was true. The Mexican was one of the hardest working individuals on earth, and [s]he proved it just to get into the United States. [S]he walked for weary weeks, forded muddy and violent rivers, clung to the tenuous underside of trucks and trains, stuffed him[/her]self into the sizzling engine compartment of automobiles, slipped through and over jagged fences, risked being murdered by his own people, flattened by traffic as [s]he darted across the freeway, suffocated in tightly enclosed vans and railroad cars, arrested by the Border Patrol, all so [s]he could earn minimum wages toiling with a short hoe from dawn to dusk. If [s]he wasn't an illegal, [s]he would surely have deserved commendation for bravery, perseverance, and endurance. Such are the people whom we expel from our borders.

As Peter McLaren reminds us, "Some people cross borders willingly, some people are forced to cross them, and others are shot in their attempts at crossing." So as we deploy the border as a metaphor, we need to remember that for many people throughout the world crossing borders is not cognitive or rhetorical; border crossings can be life-risking and life-losing endeavors.

We engage in disciplinary and discursive border crossings to ally ourselves with the millions in their diasporic searches for new homelands with their unfulfilled promise of work, food, security, and opportunity. We engage in disciplinary and discursive border crossings to construct new, more fluid, more complex identities, and in doing so we turn our gaze southward towards our ancestral homes. We engage in disciplinary and discursive border crossings to destabilize the meanings and inscriptions that the superordinate cultures, the Euro/Anglo/North American cultures with their Border Patrols, place on borders.

Undocumented Mexican Migration: In Search of a Just Immigration Law and Policy

28 UCLA L. Rev. 615 (1981).

■ GERALD P. LÓPEZ

    * * *

The informed consensus applies classical push-pull theory to undocumented Mexican migration. The theory's success has been well-earned in view of its broad utility in explaining world mass migration over the past century. Moreover, data taken in by the informed consensus are mostly accurate. The components seem believable, particularly because their descriptive interaction brings order to what can otherwise appear to be an incomprehensible geo-political jumble. At the same time that the theory seems to provide an objective explanation for mass migration, it implies that the destination country has a quite limited moral responsibility for the problem.

Narrow descriptive accuracy is not, for the most part, what distinguishes the informed consensus from the following alternative explanation that sees as critical certain information the informed consensus has overlooked, disregarded or negligibly weighted. The chief distinctions are ones of interpretation.

* * * The great weakness of the informed consensus lies in its central hypothesis that economic disparity is at the source of mass Mexican migration. This position could be translated into a causal relationship: "but for" economic disparity mass undocumented Mexican migration would not occur. This view derives from the obvious observation that economic disparity between the United States and Mexico has always played an important role in contributing to mass migration. Indeed, mass migration in modern times has rarely occurred except where economic disparity has been present.

There have been numerous instances, however, where economic disparity between nations—even adjoining nations—exists but mass migration is absent. In other words, economic disparity is necessary but not sufficient for migration. Certainly this is true of migration from Mexico to the United States. More than one expert has underscored that the same wage differential (13:1) between migrant earning in the United States and average agricultural wage rates in primary Mexican source regions has prevailed since the first decade of this century. In fact, the disparity was probably greater in earlier years. Nevertheless, mass migration from these regions was unknown until later years. Nor does economic disparity account for the pattern of Mexican migration. Primary Mexican source regions for today's undocumented migration are areas that provided labor earlier in this century. Yet the economic disparity between these source regions and the United States is no greater than that existing between numerous other regions in Mexico and this country. Economic disparity hardly accounts for the fact that the great majority of undocumented Mexicans are the strongest, most able-bodied workers who presumably could compete well in the Mexican labor market.

In contrast to conventional push-pull theory, the following hypothesis offers a more complete explanation for migration: Where there is substantial economic disparity between two adjoining countries and the potential destination country promotes, *de jure* or *de facto*, access to its substantially superior minimal wage, that promotion encourages migrants reasonably to rely on the continuing possibility of migration, employment, and residence, until a competitive economic alternative is made available in the source country. Substantial migration from Mexico did not begin until the United States urged and encouraged Mexican workers to fill lower echelon jobs in this country. The now discernible pattern of emigration from certain source regions coincides almost perfectly with active American promotion in those regions. The curious near-exclusivity of young males among all migrant groups is understandable when one fixes on the fact that promotional effort, particularly until recent years, sought only their services.

* * * [The author reviews over one hundred years of U.S. recruitment and solicitation of Mexican workers to show how the U.S. has induced Mexican villages to send young workers to the United States for temporary employment. After documenting how we have created this reliance by formal and informal means, he turns to the other side of the equation— Eds.]

The Decision–Making Calculus

It is necessary to examine whether the decision to migrate is, as much thinking about undocumented Mexican migration assumes, an individual economic calculation. Identifying the actual decision-making unit as the household rather than the individual allows examination of the effect of migration on the household unit and the influence that unit extends on the migrant's aspirations in the United States.

Even so perceptive a commentator as Professor [Wayne] Cornelius has written that the migratory phenomenon can be understood by taking the rational decision making of the individual as the point of departure: "For most [Mexican migrants] the decision to go to the U.S. is an eminently rational one, in terms of differential economic returns to one's labor, as well as the high probability of finding a job in the U.S." Although most evidence supports Cornelius's assertion that the decision, at least in part, is rational, it disputes his contention that the decision is an individual one. Dedicated field researchers such as Raymond Wiest and Richard Mines argue that the relevant decision-making unit is the household, not the individual. Their conclusion is modern confirmation of the findings of earlier anthropological studies: the household is the appropriate unit for analysis of decisions concerning economic cooperation and production. Despite this early consensus, few studies have subsequently examined the interaction between "wage-labor migration" and the operation of the household unit. Nonetheless, the evidence accumulated by Wiest, Mines, and even Cornelius strongly supports the conclusion that the "rational individual" is not a self-contained decision-making unit, but is part of a household that makes decisions according to the demands of its living situation.

Special reasons argue for focusing on the household unit. First, the household decision-making process may differ markedly from an individual one; the difference bears heavily on the issues of aspirational evolution. For instance, it is far more persuasive to hypothesize that values undergo inevitable change sufficient to predict permanent undocumented relocation if the migrant worker is responsible for his own needs and not those of an economic unit beyond himself than if he is a member of a household unit and responsible to it. To emphasize the importance of the household unit is not to deny that some unmarried young men, and even some married men, migrate for primarily individual reasons. It is also not to deny that some migrant workers begin to operate, after awhile, according to individual needs rather than the needs of the household unit that may have initially dictated their temporary migration. These, however, are not the "normal" cases; even the evidence gathered by Cornelius confirms this fact.

Care in identifying the proper unit of economic decision making is also important if we are to determine, in Mines's terminology, the "retentive capability" of the source village. That is, to understand the possibilities for dissuading undocumented migrant workers from leaving their source villages or, from another angle, to determine what must be done to encourage their remaining at home, we must understand the true decision-making process.

Finally, any culturally sensitive theory must select the appropriate decision-making unit. The simple fact is that Mexico's agricultural society, which still provides the bulk of undocumented workers, has long been characterized by close family ties and a communal struggle to survive. The typical household is perennially in danger of being unable to subsist and of disintegration. All working members of the family cooperate to insure the two essential conditions of household survival: adequate income and adequate composition to permit fulfillment of domestic functions (including child care). All members become committed to the notion of shared obligation within the household unit and to the overriding importance of subordinating individual desires to the extent necessary to perpetuate the household. Initially the older generation provides for the younger; in short time the obligation is shared. Finally, the generations' roles are reversed and with the arrival of the next generation the cycle repeats itself. Centuries of economic loyalty to one's household have transformed what was once essentially an economic decision into an entrenched cultural principle.

Adequate income has always been the most difficult of the two conditions of survival to insure. Households in agricultural Mexico traditionally pursued a variety of income-producing activities; dangerous as generalizations are, it is probably accurate to conclude that a household's most dependable means of producing more income to restore equilibrium was stepped-up agricultural production. Other means of intensifying the household effort were explored but inevitably proved unreliable.

Although intensification of agricultural production was the best means of augmenting income, it was at the same time a dangerous and limited solution because of short-term catastrophes, crude productive techniques, and shortages of cultivable land. These combined obstacles to income production often threatened to disintegrate agricultural household the "normal" cases; even the evidence gathered by Cornelius confirms this fact.

Access to a relatively superior wage structure in the United States created an opportunity to avoid household disintegration by selling male labor. For some households, particularly the landless, this new alternative may have been perceived as the only possibility for survival. From the beginning, the male head was selected by the household to migrate temporarily to the United States to earn badly needed income. In part, the male was chosen because he was the object of American promotion; the household also felt it was the role of the husband-father to make the arduous sacrifice.

In his absence, the household adjusted. Domestic functions—daily logistics and socialization of young family members—became the mother's primary responsibility. The more important adjustment, in terms of cultural acceptance of wage-labor migration, was that the contributing father retained his status as the head of the household. As long as his absences were temporary and associated with remittances, the husband-father's place was secure and unthreatened. In effect, the household adjusted to endure wage-labor migration as a necessity, but insisted that it be only temporary in nature.

The recurring nature of the temporary migrations was likely unforeseeable, and certainly undesirable from the household's point of view. Struggling to maintain equilibrium, households found themselves repeatedly sending their men to the United States far more often than would have been hoped by those who left and those who remained at home. Moreover, the process began to feed on itself, becoming, almost imperceptibly, institutionalized. Not only did experienced households begin to rely regularly and predictably on temporary migration, but new and different households began to perceive temporary wage-labor migration as the dominant emerging alternative during periods of economic crisis.

Vague promotional promises were given weight by the return of "wealthy" migrants, men able to provide monetary support out of line with their previous domestic endeavors and capable of relating tales, often exaggerated by "locker room" boastfulness. Word spread that, if a household needed income, relatively superior wages were available for the price of temporary migration to the United States. From the beginning, the persistence of household disequilibrium in the agricultural areas of Mexico and heightened awareness of the continuing availability of wage-producing labor opportunities in the United States ensured a dependable and ballooning response to the wage-labor migration market.

Since 1940, survival of the household has been further endangered by Mexico's extraordinary population growth. Population growth may be able to be matched by increases in arable land, but to date these lands have gone predominantly to Mexico's large landholders who have tended toward machine-intensive and not labor-intensive development if, in fact, they develop the land at all. As a result there is an excess of population relative to cultivable land and the number of nonagricultural employment opportunities. Thus the landless rural working class and *ejidatarios* have been reduced to an almost perpetually marginal economic status and forced to turn to wage-labor migration as a means of insuring household survival.

Most researchers agree that even if the population growth were controlled, the present wage disparity between Mexico and the United States would result in mass wage-labor migration. Holding other factors constant, it appears that wage disparity determines the absolute number of undocumented migrants. The critical variable is, somewhat surprisingly, not the American but the Mexican wage. When American wages have gone up, the rate of undocumented migration remains unaffected, and when Mexican wages have decreased, migration has increased. Other studies tend to support this conclusion with data tying rates of undocumented migration to Mexican agricultural productivity, commodity prices, and farm wages.

This observation about economic conditions in Mexico, combined with the earlier description of the typical Mexican household, leads to the hypothesis that the decision to migrate for wage labor remains a function of household equilibrium. If, as a result of a decrease in Mexican wages, the household's income falls below subsistence level, the household will be sufficiently "economically motivated" to send one or more of its members to the United States to help earn income from wage labor necessary to maintain the household in Mexico.

This hypothesis is supported by the characteristics of the modern undocumented Mexican. These characteristics remain remarkably similar to those that might have been compiled in the 1880s. Although in recent years there has been an increasing number of older men, the majority of migrants are and have long been young men (between twenty-two and thirty) who are usually uneducated (less than three years). Young women seldom have migrated except with a family (an unusual occurrence) or to join a male who has already established permanent residence in the United States. A majority of undocumented migrants are married but, according to one study, fewer than one percent are ever accompanied by their wives. Most come from rural areas, though small towns and larger cities still contribute their share. Although an increasing number claim an urban residence, most are actually arriving in the United States at the end of a two-or three-leg migration from a rural area. While many have held temporary urban jobs, a majority continue to have substantial ties to households in a rural area. It appears that whenever the household is sufficiently motivated, it is still considered the duty of the man to migrate and the duty of the woman to assume a disproportionate share of the domestic obligation during periods of absence.

The evidence of recent years has made increasingly apparent both the extent and permanence of the reliance on employment in the United States. Professor Cornelius reports that forty-nine percent of those who, since 1969, migrated illegally from one long-established source village also had fathers who had previously worked in the United States, primarily in the Bracero Program. Eighty-seven percent of these same undocumented workers also had brothers or sisters who had previously migrated for wage labor. Forty-three percent of the married undocumented workers since 1969 also had one or more children who had worked in the United States. Finally, fully sixty-two percent of the families in Cornelius's study had members of at least two generations simultaneously going to the United States.

The likelihood that this near-permanent reliance will change anytime soon seems remote. Richard Mines's study of Las Animas, a long-time and prototypical source pueblo in the central plateau state of Zacatecas, is illustrative. An analysis of pueblo sources of disposable income revealed that, on the average, fully 60 percent of each household's income was annually derived from wages earned in the United States.

Even destination patterns for wage-labor migrants reflect the household's increasing reliance on the American wage. Professor Wiest's study of Mexican households indicates that husband-fathers working in the United States contribute a relatively high percentage of household income; these men return predictably to the household, continuing their traditional role in the domestic scheme despite their absences. In contrast, husband-fathers migrating within Mexico usually provide only a supplementary source of income, alone insufficient for household survival; these men tend to return much less predictably and to play a far reduced role in the household.

Economically inefficient and unreliable internal wage-labor migration constitutes a genuine threat to the husband-father's traditional status. Given this fact, growing reliance on wage-labor migration to the United States, as evidenced by recent destination patterns, may be seen as the household's judicious attachment to what it perceives as the best available alternative for its economic and cultural survival. Wage-labor migration, which began as a temporary means for restoring household equilibrium, has apparently become the primary source of income for the landless and *ejidatarios* in rural Mexico.

* * * Thus, while households now rely on wage-labor migration as an economic necessity, they nonetheless view migration as a "temporary crutch." However conscious they are of their dependence, most household members still dream that something, most often the superior American wage, will enable them to permanently terminate participation in the migration cycle. Most migrant workers intend to retire to their village in Mexico when they are done with wage labor in the United States. Interestingly, one study indicates that even if offered permanent status in the United States, most Mexicans would still rather live in Mexico and temporarily migrate for wage-labor.

The persistent cyclical and temporary character of undocumented migration is additional evidence that the more significant evolution is not "aspirational" but reliant in nature. Despite years of continual contact, most Mexican migrants remain uninterested in permanent relocation. Although migration has raised many migrants' economic expectations, most remain part of a household that wants nothing more than to remain together, to survive *in* Mexico.

* * * The present predicament tests, in many ways, our capacity and will to meet the just expectations that we have generated, to admit the truth and to accept our responsibilities. What we did in the past and even now is related to what we will decide is the decent thing to do in the future. We cannot wish away past and present hypocrisy; nor should we want to if we appreciate the very nature of a political community that is even minimally just. It may be true that national boundaries and documented status can define, and indeed may once have defined, the limits of our moral obligations. But our experience with undocumented Mexican workers is fundamentally inconsistent with that comfortable and reflex-like moral posture. If we are not accountable for the present condition of undocumented Mexican workers, we are at least responsible for the commitment implicit in our long-standing relationship. If involvement and neighborhood matter, undocumented Mexican workers are part of the living and working community. They are we.

Facts cannot be ignored even by those who reject (if in fact they even consider) fundamental moral obligations. Mexican households seem to have, and certainly perceive, no short-term means of economic survival without continued access to our labor market. If, as it appears, Mexicans cannot humanely be dissuaded from coming, some form of access must be legislatively accommodated or they will simply continue to come and to work outside the boundaries of the law. The available evidence suggests that while risks and costs to present documented residents of legalized access for undocumented Mexican workers are potentially substantial, they are dwarfed by those that accompany other responses. For those who reject any moral obligation, the most compelling reason for legalizing access may well be the predictable cost of failing to do so. Selfish pragmatists may be forced to admit that legalized access encompasses, even from their perspective, the most sober, mutually advantageous and least costly short- or middle-term response to a profoundly tense and complicated dilemma.

* * *

NOTES AND QUESTIONS

1. Is there an immigration crisis? What are the basic underlying differences between, Montoya, López, and the author of the following comments:

> The immigration crisis has grown steadily and slowly, and therefore taken us by surprise. Today, immigration to the United States is massive, and it is out of control. The United States accepts for permanent resettlement twice as many immigrants as do all the other countries of the world combined. Legal immigration is three times as high as it was in the early 1960s; there are now well over 600,000 legal immigrants in an average year. Illegal immigration is estimated to be ten times greater; there are now well over a million apprehensions a year—without any corresponding increase in enforcement activities. Illegal aliens pour into the United States through Swiss-cheese borders. Legal and illegal immigration combined contribute nearly half of the population growth of the United States. And efforts to cope with the breakdown of immigration law or to moderate the high levels of legal immigration are stymied in Congress by an unlikely coalition of the far right and the far left, fueled by a coalition of big business and Hispanic pressure groups.

Richard Lamm & Gary Imhoff, *How Many Can America Absorb?*, *in* The Immigration Time Bomb: The Fragmenting of America (1986).

2. Cosmopolitanism and Border Control. Would Martha Nussbaum, who argued for Cosmopolitanism set any limits on immigration? Lamm and Imhoff note that "Some people deny that immigration can ever be a problem. They refuse to let go of the dream. They argue that treating immigration as a problem treats people, human beings, as a problem. In that, they are right: people, large numbers of people pressing against the resources of the earth, are a problem." Lamm & Imhoff, *supra*.

3. The Economic Questions: Imhoff and Lamm argue that: "at high enough levels, immigration also creates economic problems." In many areas of the world, migrants are moving from less developed to more developed countries. They generally have fewer skills than workers in their host countries, and in those cases migrants move into unskilled jobs at the bottom of the job ladders of those countries. If their numbers are large enough, they displace native workers and when economies are not vibrant and growing at fast enough rates—they contribute to the unemployment of natives and depress the salary levels for the jobs in which they specialize. In West Germany, for example, certain jobs became stigmatized in the late

1960s and 1970s as "Turkish jobs," performed by temporary migrant guestworkers from Turkey. When certain jobs become stigmatized in such a way, a society loses some of its cohesiveness, a large part of its social mobility, and a degree of respect for manual labor. In the United States, our own garment industry has now been stigmatized as a sector in which illegal immigrants work. Wages have fallen, sweatshops have been revived, a noble union has been corrupted by accepting the existence of "shadow locals" and tolerating the exploitation of illegal workers, and—in a self-fulfilling prophecy—employers have created a class of work that "Americans won't do."

4.   The competition for status between native and immigrant workers. Again we turn to Lamm and Imhoff who argue that: "Hispanic Americans—who have been misrepresented by national groups claiming to speak for them—also show overwhelming support in polls both for increased border control against illegal immigration and for lower levels of legal immigration. This should not be surprising, though it is to many people. In many areas, Hispanic Americans are exactly those who are most hurt by massive immigration, whose neighborhoods suffer the greatest impact, and whose jobs are most affected by competition. The most comprehensive poll of Hispanic and black American opinions on immigration was conducted early in 1983 by Democratic pollster Peter D. Hart and Republican pollster V. Lance Tarrance. Hart and Tarrance found that 69 percent of black and 63 percent of Hispanic citizens wanted major increases in spending to enable the Border Patrol to stop illegal aliens from entering the United States; 66 percent of blacks and 66 percent of Hispanic citizens favored penalties and fines for employers who hired illegal aliens; and only 12 percent of Hispanic and 5 percent of black citizens felt that we should admit higher levels of legal immigrants from Mexico."

5.   The Profit Motive. Is Gerald López' argument that immigration from Mexico is fueled by the economic self-interest of employers who want cheap labor? Lamm and Imhoff note that "Certainly, in agricultural areas of Texas and California, politicians are affected by the pleas of powerful growers who employ illegal migrants at wages much lower than they could pay Americans. And restaurants, taxi fleets, and ununionized 'home improvement' firms that employ illegals in our cities certainly profit. The employers' argument is ugly and full of self-interest: they want to be able to hire illegal immigrants in preference to Americans so that they don't have to raise wages or improve working conditions. Surely the employers' argument cannot be powerful. It isn't. Its power comes from the fact that it is allied both to the immigration dream and to the politically powerful and seemingly disinterested forces of internationalism, humanitarianism, and opposition to racism." IMHOFF AND LAMM, *supra*.

6.   Racism? The most powerful argument against immigration reform is the fear of acting out of racism. Is immigration reform discriminatory? Is it racist to control illegal immigration or to set ceilings on legal immigration? One fact would tend to support the contention of racism. Twenty years ago, about 80 percent of legal immigrants came from western Europe. Today 80 percent of legal immigrants come from Asia and Latin America, and over half of all immigrants speak Spanish as a native tongue. Opponents of immigration control have contended that this shift in the composition of the immigrant stream, this difference in race, culture, language, and religion, is the real cause of concern over immigration.

Legal scholar, Kevin Johnson argues that:

"[L]ike de jure segregation of the public schools, express racial exclusions in the immigration laws, . . . is primarily a problem of the past rather than the present. The real problem of race and immigration today, . . . is that facially neutral immigration laws have unmistakable racial impacts, including some that arguably are intentional. A number of examples immediately come to mind, such as the public charge exclusion, which disparately impacts poor and working people from developing nations populated primarily by people of color. Consider that the various removal grounds are facially neutral but that over ninety-two percent of the noncitizens deported in fiscal year 1999 were from Mexico or other Latin American countries. Given such glaring disparate impacts, no wonder that Latino/a scholars have been particularly attentive to immigration and immigrant law and policy."

Kevin Johnson, *Race and Immigration Law and Enforcement: A Response to Is There A Plenary Powers Doctrine?*, 14 GEO. IMMIGR. L.J. 289, 291 (2000).

Johnson also makes the persuasive claim that:

"Many Latino/as in the United States firmly believe that race is *the* determinative factor to immigration officers investigating alleged violations of the immigration laws. This belief has basis in fact. In most cases challenging stops by the Border Patrol, one of the factors that the officers have expressly relied upon was the suspect's 'Hispanic appearance.'" The government's rationale, although infrequently stated, is simple:

the government urges the fact that the driver was Hispanic tends to give the agent reasonable suspicion that the driver was involved in illegal activity. *The government reasons that most illegal immigrants in Texas are Hispanic and jumps to the conclusion that this makes it more likely that this driver was also an illegal immigrant, or was involved in the trafficking of aliens.*

Id. at 294–95 (quoting *United States v. Rubio–Hernandez*, 39 F. Supp. 2d 808, 835 (W.D. Tex. 1999)). *See also* Kevin Johnson, *The Case Against Race Profiling in Immigration Enforcement*, 78 WASH. UNIV. L.Q. 675 (2000).

NOTES AND QUESTIONS

1. *A nation of immigrants.* Imhoff claims that the history that our country was built by immigrants "was never strictly true." As support for this statement he notes that the white population grew from over three million to almost eight million between 1790 and 1820. However, since the

entire white population of the United States is a result of immigration from Europe, does Imhoff's statement about white population growth have any real significance? Shouldn't Imhoff instead be comparing the contributions of white (and non-white) immigrants with the contributions of Native Americans?

2.   *Letting go of the dream.* One recurring argument in immigration debates is that this country needs to let go of the dream embodied in the inscription on the base of the Statue of Liberty. If this view is correct, and the dream of unlimited promise in America is dead, what are the implications of its passing? Must America now emulate the "ancient lands, with their storied pomp" that the immigrants to America fled from? If America is not doomed to become a stratified society, why is the opportunity in America only something that can be gained by people who are currently American citizens, rather than by anyone who chooses to settle here?

3.   *Extrapolating to the future.* One important question is whether flows of immigration and the politics related to immigration display any discernable patterns. If there is no continuity, then can we reliably use past data to project trends in future population growth?

4.   *Immigration and population growth.* What might be the connection between world population growth and immigration. Population growth means more people in the world. Immigration means shifting people from one part of the world into another. Indeed, if Becker's analysis of the family is correct, then immigration from poor countries like Mexico into rich countries like the United States is a good thing because it will lead to a falling birthrate. Given that it seems that immigration from poor to rich nations would lead to a net decrease in the birthrate, don't arguments about world overpopulation actually support the idea of *encouraging* unlimited immigration?

5.   *Feasibility of restricting immigration.* On May 14, 2003, a trailer was discovered containing 70 illegal immigrants who had been smuggled from Mexico. The migrants were exposed to extremes of temperature and water deprivation such that nineteen of them died. Harvey Rice, *Two Plead Not Guilty in Deaths of 19 Migrants in Truck Trailer*, Hous. Chron., July 8, 2003, at 13. This was only one among many multiple fatality incidents involving immigrants trying to cross into the United States from Mexico. In the years 2000–2001 on average more than one person died each day trying to cross into the United States. Evelyn Nieves, *Illegal Immigrant Death Rate Rises Sharply in Barren Areas*, N.Y. Times, Aug. 6, 2002, at A1. The increasing death rate is intimately connected with increased border patrol activity. "To avoid the stepped-up border patrols in populated areas, the most desperate migrants cross in the more unguarded and desolate deserts of Arizona and eastern California." *Id.* Given that immigrants have demonstrated that they are willing to risk death to enter the United States, do Imhoff's proposals to control illegal immigration make sense?

6.   *Economics of immigration restriction.* It is often claimed that immigrants contribute to the unemployment of citizens and depress the salary levels for the jobs in which they specialize. However, it is unclear that this is true. Economically, there is no difference between allowing free immigration and importing labor intensive goods from countries whose laborers would otherwise immigrate. Shubha Ghosh, *The Legal, Economic, and Policy Roles of Immigrant Entrepreneurs in the Immigration Debate*, 5 UCLA ASIAN PAC. L.J. 15, 17 (1998). Furthermore, people wishing to come to the United States could be a tremendous source of public income. The prices charged by immigrant smuggling "Coyotes" generally run from $1,000 to $4,000. Eliott C. McLaughlin, *"Coyotes" Offer Hope and Danger*, ATHENS BANNER-HERALD, July 6, 2003, *available at* http://www.onlineathens.com/stories/070703/bus_20030707013.shtml. If Imhoff's figure of one and a half million illegal immigrants per year is accurate, the government could make billions of dollars (literally) by simply selling permission to work in the United States. Additionally, once in the country, the "negative economic effects of immigration are ambiguous and unsubstantiated, but the benefits are established and substantial. ... [and] basic economics argues that our laws should allow more immigration than they currently do." Larry J. Obhof, *The Irrationality of Enforcement? An Economic Analysis of U.S. Immigration Law*, 7 KAN. J.L. & PUB. POL'Y 163, 180 (2002). Given that the economics of immigration weigh so heavily on loosening controls, why do Imhoff and others argue for spending more resources on stopping immigration?

7. *Feasibility of control of international migration.* In light of the current status of illegal immigration discussed *supra* at 980, n.5, would it make any difference if there was maximum efficiency in border control strategies, supported by well-conceived and carefully implemented organizational structures?

8. *Rationale for immigration restrictions.* Piore is in favor of immigration restrictions because "over a very long period of time immigration does have the capacity to erode the employment opportunities of national workers, and because generally, a tight labor market in which labor is in short supply is more conducive to social progress than a loose one." However, might it be that the social progress he desires is thwarted by nativist impulses which can be legitimated by restrictions on immigration? For example, during the campaign in favor and following passage of California's proposition 187, which, among other things, excluded the children of undocumented immigrants from public schools, harassment of Mexican Americans increased dramatically. Nancy Cervantes et al., *Hate Unleashed: Los Angeles in the Aftermath of Proposition 187*, 17 CHICANO-LATINO L. REV. 1 (1995). Does this correlation between nativism and immigration restriction undermine Piore's arguments?

9. Developments in Immigration Reform. The Immigration Reform and Control Act, Pub. L. No. 99–603, 100 Stat. 3359 (codified as amended in scattered sections of 8 U.S.C.), was enacted in 1986 and made it illegal to hire illegal immigrants and increased the number of authorized border patrol agents by 50%. TIMOTHY J. DUNN, THE MILITARIZATION OF THE U.S.–MEXICO BORDER, 1978–1992, at 49 (1996). Additionally, the character of the border patrol has changed substantially, as the border patrol adds drug interdiction to its objectives.

Since the attacks on September 11, 2001, government action relating to immigration control has become increasingly more vigilant. Secretive preventative detentions, mostly of those detained on immigration violations, increased rapidly after September 11, totaling over 1,000 by early November 2001. Many of those detained were held for weeks or months without charges, and all proceedings were conducted in complete secrecy. Futhermore, the U.S. Patriot Act, Pub. L. No. 107–56, 115 Stat. 272 (2001), enacted swiftly after September 11, authorizes the Attorney General to subject any alien to mandatory detention with only a reasonable belief that the alien engaged in certain vaguely specified terrorist activities. Moreover, the Act allows aliens to be deported if they provide any support that they know or reasonably should know would aid an organization in conducting terrorist activities, and allows denial of entry to aliens for ideological endorsements of terrorist activity. David Cole, *Enemy Aliens*, 54 Stan. L. Rev. 953, 959–74 (2002); David Cole, Enemy Aliens (2003).

Given this recent broadening of immigration control, are the observations and arguments made by Piore still sound?

10. *Causes of fluctuations in Mexican immigration.* Piore argues that current immigration by Mexicans can be explained by unwillingness of black youth to work low-status secondary jobs. An alternative hypothesis is that the jump in illegal immigration from Mexico was brought about by the termination of the Bracero program, a program in which the United States brought in hundreds of thousands of guest workers annually from Mexico. The Bracero program ran from the years 1942 to 1964. After the end of the Bracero program, the number of deportations skyrocketed, implying that the rise in illegal immigration is caused more by changes in government policy than by changes in employment patterns among blacks. Larry J. Obhof, *The Irrationality of Enforcement? An Economic Analysis of U.S. Immigration Law*, 7 Kan. J.L. & Pub. Pol'y 163, 178 (2002).

11. *Border control.* Lichtenberg analyzes immigration from Mexico in terms solely of U.S. and Mexican interests. However, the border between the United States and Mexico joins more than just the U.S. and Mexico, it joins the U.S. with the rest of the world. A national of a third country could easily travel to Mexico and then cross the border to the United States from Mexico. In the security conscious climate caused by the attacks of September 11, 2001, is Lichtenberg's rights-based analysis, which does not consider the threats to physical security posed by international terrorism, still applicable? For more on the security implications of international migration, see, for example, Michelle Malkin, Invasion: How America Still Welcomes Terrorists, Criminals, and Other Foreign Menaces to Our Shores (2002).

12. *Cooperation with Mexico.* Lichtenberg concludes that the governments of the United States and Mexico must work together to address the issues of legal and illegal immigration. However, given her analysis that the elite of Mexico have an interest in maintaining massive migration, which is counter to the interests of both the United States and Mexico, why should the U.S. government consult with the Mexican government? If Lichtenberg is truly able to determine the true interests of the Mexican people, as well as the motivations of the Mexican elite, shouldn't the U.S. government ignore the corrupt Mexican government and simply implement policies which advance the interests of the United States and Mexico, properly understood?

13. *Consequences of the "escape valve."* If Lichtenberg's position is correct, if Mexican migration, by alleviating unemployment and dissatisfaction in Mexico is a bad thing for Mexico, is there anything to stop that logic from being applied, by analogy, to any problem? Won't any measures taken to relieve suffering alleviate the pressure for social change caused by that suffering? Should the fact that Lichtenberg's position can be invoked to justify oppressing the downtrodden work to undermine Lichtenberg's credibility?

14. *Guilty and not guilty.* The Supreme Court held in *Plyler v. Doe*, 457 U.S. 202 (1982), that it is unlawful for local governments to deny access to public education to children of illegal immigrants. The theory behind that holding is that, while illegal immigrants themselves are guilty of breaking the law, their children are not, and should not be punished for the crimes of their parents. *Plyler* has generated a great deal of controversy, including a ballot initiative in California which, had it not been enjoined by the courts, would have invalidated *Plyler*. Phillip J. Cooper, Plyler *at the Core: Understanding the Proposition 187 Challenge*, 17 Chicano-Latino L. Rev. 64 (1995). Given the discontent with providing services for the children of illegal immigrants, should *Plyler* be reconsidered? What about if a child's parents immigrated to the United States specifically to take advantage of our social services? Would the rationale of *Plyler*, that children are essentially innocent bystanders, be valid in such a case?

15. *Additional reading.* For additional information on the *Plyler* decision, as well as the ballot initiative to invalidate it, see generally, John T. Ritondo, Jr., Comment, *California's Duty to Educate the World: Proposition 187 and Mere Rationality*, 26 Cumb. L. Rev. 1045 (1995/1996); Peter H. Schuck, *The Message of Proposition 187*, 26 Pac. L.J. 989 (1995); Nancy Cervantes et al., *Hate Unleashed: Los Angeles in the Aftermath of Proposition 187*, 17 Chicano-Latino L. Rev. 1 (1995); Phillip J. Cooper, Plyler *at the Core: Understanding the Proposition 187 Challenge*, 17 Chicano-Latino L. Rev. 64 (1995); Ruben J. Garcia, Comment, *Critical Race Theory and Proposition 187: The Racial Politics of Immigration Law*, 17 Chicano-Latino L. Rev. 118 (1995). For a religious perspective on immigration law and community, see Terry Coonan, *There Are No Strangers Among Us: Catholic Social Teachings and U.S. Immigration Law*, 40 Cath. Law. 105 (2000). For a scholarly perspective on current immigration issues, see Symposium, *Beyond Belonging: Challenging the Boundaries of Nationality: Proxies for Loyalty in Constitutional Immigration Law: Citizenship and Race After September 11*, 52 DePaul L. Rev. 871 (2003). For proposals to restrict immigration for security reasons aimed at a popular audience, see

Yeh Ling–Ling, *Stop Immigration if We Are to Fight Terrorism*, TUCSON CITIZEN, Sept. 4, 2002, *available at* http://www.diversityalliance.org/docs/article_2002sep04.html; MICHELLE MALKIN, INVASION: HOW AMERICA STILL WELCOMES TERRORISTS, CRIMINALS, AND OTHER FOREIGN MENACES TO OUR SHORES (2002). For additional information on the dangers of immigration, see generally, Eliott C. McLaughlin, *"Coyotes" Offer Hope and Danger*, ATHENS BANNER–HERALD, July 6, 2003, *available at* http://www.onlineathens.com/stories/070703/bus_20030707013.shtml; Juan A. Lozano, *Alleged Leader in Deadly Texas Immigrant–Smuggling Operation Arrested*, ASSOCIATED PRESS, June 17, 2003, *available at* http://www.islandpacket.com/24hour/nation/story/920171p–6407304c.html; *INS Announces Vast International Immigrant Smuggling Bust*, CNN, Oct. 17, 2000, *available at* http://www.cnn.com/2000/US/10/17/ins.bust/.

D.   CLASS BORDERS

Brown v. Artery Organization

654 F. Supp. 1106 (D.D.C. 1987).

■ JUDGE GREENE delivered the opinion of the court.

The Fair Housing Act (42 U.S.C. §§ 3601 *et seq.*) prohibits discrimination with respect to housing, *inter alia*, on the basis of race or national origin. The most basic substantive issue involved in this case—one of first impression in this Circuit—is whether under the Act the overwhelmingly black and Hispanic tenants of a low-rent apartment complex have the right to secure injunctive relief against the conversion of such housing to high-rent units if they are able to establish that (1) the owners are engaging in the conversion for the purpose of displacing the minority tenants or (2) the displacement of these tenants will be the conversion's predictable and inevitable effect. * * *

I

Facts

Plaintiffs, tenants in the Dominion Gardens and Bruce Street apartment complexes in Alexandria, Virginia, filed this suit challenging the renovation of those complexes and the consequent displacement of its tenants, overwhelmingly black and Hispanic, as a violation of the federal Fair Housing Act. * * * Plaintiffs seek preliminary and permanent relief, that is, injunctions to restrain the defendants from taking any action to oust tenants who have already received 120–day eviction notices and from issuing any further notices to vacate. In addition, although following the institution of this action the private defendants withdrew earlier applications for co-insurance with the United States Department of Housing and Urban Development (HUD), plaintiffs also seek injunctive relief against HUD. That relief would require the Department to delete from its governing "Handbook" a provision which delegates to banks and other lenders HUD's own statutory responsibility to minimize the involuntary displacement of tenants.

* * *

IV

Framework for Substantive Decision

Plaintiffs' motion for a preliminary injunction alleges violations of the Fair Housing Act. It requests a number of specific injunctions against defendants Dominion Gardens Arlandria Limited Partnership and Potomac Village Limited Partnership, and it further requests that all the private defendants be enjoined from taking any action which would cause or contribute to the eviction of plaintiffs. Defendants oppose plaintiffs' motion primarily on the ground that plaintiffs have not satisfied their burdens under the Fair Housing Act, in that they have not established discriminatory intent or adverse effect, and their motions to dismiss for failure to state a claim upon which relief may be granted proceed on the basis of substantially similar arguments. Since the issues raised with respect to the two principal substantive motions thus overlap to a significant degree, this part of the Opinion discusses both motions within the framework of analysis for the preliminary injunction motion.

* * * Under familiar principles, in determining whether to grant a preliminary injunction, the Court is required to consider four factors: (1) whether there is a substantial likelihood that plaintiffs will prevail on the merits; (2) whether plaintiffs will be irreparably injured if the injunction does not issue; (3) the hardship to defendants if the injunction is granted is balanced against the hardship to plaintiffs if the injunction is not granted; and (4) whether the public interest favors granting the preliminary relief requested. *Virginia Petroleum Jobbers Ass'n v. Federal Power Commission*, 259 F.2d 921, 925 (D.C.Cir. 1958). Plaintiffs are not required to prevail on each of these factors; rather the factors should be viewed as a continuum— more of one factor compensating for less of another. Preliminary injunctive relief, therefore, would not be precluded, for example, by a relatively weak showing of likelihood of success on the merits if the plaintiffs demonstrated that the other three factors weighed strongly in their favor. *Washington Metropolitan Area Transit Commission v. Holiday Tours, Inc*, 559 F.2d 841, 843–44 (D.C.Cir. 1977); *Massachusetts Law Reform Institute v. Legal Services Corp.*, 581 F.Supp. 1179, 1184 (D.D.C. 1984), *aff'd*, 737 F.2d 1206 (D.C.Cir. 1984). It is with these standards in mind that the Court examines the motions and the issues they present.

V

Precedents on Housing Discrimination

As indicated above, the Fair Housing Act prohibits public and private discrimination in housing on the basis of race or national origin. A central issue here, as in several other cases which have come before the federal courts in various parts of the country, is whether the Act requires proof of the landlord's intentional discrimination, or whether the statute is violated also where no such intention is established but where the conduct can be shown to have a discriminatory effect.

The answer to that question is unfortunately not entirely clear from a reading of the decided cases. Several of the decisions are inconsistent with each other; others are incomplete in significant respects; and still others do not distinguish between the various relevant concepts. While, to be sure, proof of discriminatory intent by the landlord seems everywhere to be regarded as establishing a violation of the statute, *see Betsey v. Turtle Creek Associates*, 736 F.2d 983, 986 (4th Cir. 1984), there is a variety of opinion, usually not reconciled in any systematic fashion, whether a violation may also be predicated solely upon proof that the landlord's actions had a discriminatory effect, that is, a disproportionate effect on minorities.

Some of the decisions hold, or at least intimate, that evidence of discriminatory effect is alone sufficient to establish a *prima facie* case under the Act. *See, e.g., Betsey*, 736 F.2d at 986; *Metropolitan Housing Corp. v. Village of Arlington Heights*, 558 F.2d 1283, 1290–91 (7th Cir. 1977) (hereinafter referred to as *Arlington II*); *Residents Advisory Board v. Rizzo*, 564 F.2d 126, 147–48 (3d Cir. 1977); *United States v. City of Black Jack, Missouri*, 508 F.2d 1179, 1184–85 (8th Cir. 1974). Other decisions— sometimes the same decisions—suggest that effect by itself is never enough; that there must also be a showing that the private landowner intended to discriminate. *See generally Betsey, supra; Arlington II, supra.*

To complicate matters further, of the cases holding that proof of discriminatory effect is alone sufficient, several distinguish between two types of effect: what has been called adverse impact discrimination and what is termed ultimate effect discrimination. *See, e.g., Arlington II*, 558 F.2d at 1290–91. Adverse impact discrimination is said to be established when the practice or policy in question has a disproportionate effect upon the minorities within the group to which the policy is applied (*e.g.*, the tenants in a particular apartment complex). *Id.; see Betsey*, 736 F.2d at 987–88. Ultimate effect discrimination, on the other hand, focuses upon a different pool: the entire population of a particular community. As the court phrased it in *Arlington II*, 558 F.2d at 1290, a violation of the Act will be found if the decision or policy in question "perpetuates segregation [in the community] and thereby prevents interracial association...."

Moreover, in some of the cases involving allegations of ultimate effect discrimination, liability under the Fair Housing Act appears to depend upon whether the defendant is a governmental body or a private entity, suggesting that proof of discriminatory effect alone (without proof of discriminatory intent) is enough only when the defendant is a governmental body. Indeed, the "ultimate effect" decisions generally involve governmental defendants, *see, e.g., Rizzo*, 564 F.2d at 149; *Black Jack*, 508 F.2d at 1184–85, and some of them explicitly hold that an action against a private landlord cannot be premised upon allegations of ultimate effect discrimination. *See, e.g., Boyd v. Lefrak Organization,* 509 F.2d 1110 (2d Cir. 1975); *Dreher v. Rana Management, Inc,* 493 F. Supp. 930 (E.D.N.Y. 1980).

VI

Rules to be Applied

The Court of Appeals for this Circuit has never had occasion to decide these issues, and this Court is thus not bound by any particular rule. After analyzing the decisions elsewhere, and after considering the theoretical underpinnings of the various holdings, this Court has decided that it will apply the following set of rules.

A.   If the defendant is a governmental body, proof of discriminatory impact of its actions on the community for which it serves suffices to establish a *prima facie* case of violation of the Fair Housing Act. It is unclear from the decided cases whether the governmental body involved can overcome that *prima facie* case by proof of a neutral or positive purpose or whether, in view of the objectives of the Fair Housing Act, the perpetuation of racial segregation or other discrimination by government must be regarded as so pernicious that evidence of a benign intent will not save the activity. Since, in the present posture at least, this case does not present that issue, its resolution may properly be left to another day or another court.

B.   If the defendant is not a governmental body, the plaintiff-tenants will be deemed not to have proved a violation of the Fair Housing Act if they demonstrate no more than that the defendant's actions have had or will have a discriminatory effect or impact: some proof of discriminatory intent (*see infra*) is necessary. The reasons for this conclusion are as simple and straightforward as they are significant.

While it makes perfect sense to charge a governmental entity with violations of the statute if its actions—by way of regulations, ordinances, zoning decisions, or the like—have the effect of fostering or perpetuating racial segregation, there is no indication that the Congress had in mind the far-reaching consequences of the application of such a rule on private landlords or developers. A rule which imposed the burden of responsibility on such individuals or entities for the racial effects of their housing conversions *irrespective of their purpose or intent* would not only render them responsible for consequences over which they have no control (*e.g.,* the racial mix in the community as a whole); but for the reasons cited below, it would also be likely to halt in their tracks most, if not all, private efforts to upgrade deteriorated housing stock in many of the large cities of this nation. The perpetuation and the spread of the resulting blight is not in the public interest, and plaintiffs have cited no evidence that it represents an objective of the Fair Housing Act.

It is an unfortunate fact, for which individual private landowners have no more responsibility than any other member of the community, that the income of a disproportionate number of blacks and members of other minority groups is such that, although they are able to afford low income housing, many cannot afford the rentals being charged for upgraded or luxury housing. As a consequence, if a disproportionate effect or impact on minorities were alone sufficient to call for injunctive relief under the statute, the inhabitants of low-rent private housing largely populated by minorities would be entitled on this basis to judicial orders halting the upgrading or conversion of such housing in all or almost all circumstances. That, as indicated, is not what Congress intended.

C.   For these reasons, it is the Court's conclusion that the Act, properly construed, also requires proof of discriminatory intent. The question is—what degree of proof? Defendants suggest that such proof must be direct and convincing, and that, absent evidence of defendant expressions of racial animus or their equivalent, the complaint must be dismissed. That position is as faulty in its way as plaintiffs' claim that intent or purpose are irrelevant.

In the view of this Court, the correct standard is that alluded to by the Seventh Circuit in *Arlington II* and by the Fourth Circuit in *Smith*—that the extent of the proof of discriminatory intent required varies with the proof of discriminatory effect adduced; the more devastating to minorities the effect or impact of the landlord's actions, the less evidence will be required of his actual intentions. That is only common sense: if the impact of particular actions falls overwhelmingly on minorities, it is not unreasonable to regard that circumstance as some evidence, at least *prima facie*, that discrimination was the intended result. To put it another way, discrete evidence of discriminatory purpose is not as critical in that situation as when the impact of a landowner's actions falls alike, or more or less alike, on both minorities and non-minorities.

To be sure, for the reasons discussed above, a plaintiff must still offer some evidence of discriminatory intent in addition to the "effects" proof, but once such evidence, direct or circumstantial, has been produced, the burden falls properly upon the defendant to demonstrate that his decision was not the product in any way of racial purpose or motive.

D.   Thus, the requirements of discriminatory effect and intent should be viewed from a single perspective: the more overwhelming the proof of discriminatory effect, the less the showing of discriminatory intent that is required to establish a violation of the Fair Housing Act, and vice versa. However, in every action brought against private parties under the Act, plaintiffs must allege and offer some proof of discriminatory intent in addition to the deduction that may be made from the effects of the defendant's actions.

VII

Application of the Principles to this Case

How do these general principles find applicability here on the basis of the present record? Plaintiffs have offered extensive proof of discriminatory effect. According to them, virtually all the tenants at the Bruce Street apartments and ninety per cent of the tenants at Dominion Gardens are members of minority groups, either black or Hispanic. As a consequence of the planned rehabilitation of the Dominion Gardens and Bruce Street apartment complexes, all of the tenants of those complexes will be evicted, and the vast majority of the 2,000 or so minority tenants will be foreclosed, according to plaintiffs' allegations, from obtaining affordable housing either in the rehabilitated complexes or elsewhere in the City of Alexandria. This will be so, say the plaintiffs, because of the combination of a low vacancy rate in Alexandria (1.7 per cent); high rents for available apartments (including those at Dominion Gardens and Bruce Street when rehabilitation is completed); and the continued existence of race discrimination in Alexandria, as evidenced by a statistical study compiled in September 1986. *See* Regional Fair Housing Consortium, *Race Discrimination in the Rental Housing Market: A Study of the Greater Washington Area* at 6 (September 29, 1986). Plaintiffs also allege, with supporting affidavits, that the displacement of these 2,000 minority tenants will significantly reduce the minority population of the City of Alexandria. In sum, according to plaintiffs, such progress as may have been made in recent times with respect to the inclusion of significant numbers of blacks and other minorities in the Alexandria population will largely be wiped out: that city will, once again, be essentially lily-white.

In contrast to plaintiffs' showing of a disproportionate effect of defendants' actions on blacks and Hispanics, their proof of discriminatory intent is not strong. They have offered no direct evidence at all of such intent. In fact, defendants vigorously assert that their objectives and interests are purely economic. However, plaintiffs have alleged, and to some degree proved, the existence of circumstances from which a trier of fact could eventually find discriminatory purpose if additional evidence of such purpose were adduced. Thus, plaintiffs allege that defendants knew, or should have known, that their actions would result overwhelmingly in the displacement of blacks and Hispanics both from the two apartment complexes directly involved and from the City of Alexandria itself. The Cafritz defendants have been intimately involved in the rehabilitation of at least one other apartment complex in Alexandria occupied primarily by minority tenants, and that rehabilitation resulted in the displacement of all or most of those minority tenants.

Moreover, from the evidence presented by both parties, it appears questionable whether the relocation program established by defendants at that apartment complex, which is comparable to the programs established at Dominion Gardens and Bruce Street, was at all effective in relocating the minority tenants in Alexandria. It is not inappropriate therefore to recall the Seventh Circuit's pronouncement that "conduct that has the necessary and foreseeable consequences of perpetuating segregation can be as deleterious as purposefully discriminatory conduct ..." *Arlington II,* 558 F.2d at 1289.

Beyond this proof, however, there is the fact that plaintiffs have flatly alleged that defendants acted with discriminatory intent. To be sure, allegation is not proof, and absent some proof, in addition to that recited above, to support their allegation, plaintiffs will not be able to prevail. However, in view of the present posture of this case, plaintiffs have had precious little opportunity to engage in discovery—discovery that is particularly critical where intent is the issue.

In short, while plaintiffs have not adduced adequate evidence of intent to meet their burden of proof at trial, they have sufficiently alleged intent and presented a sufficient indication that they may be able to prove that allegation, that the Court would not be justified in foreclosing them from going forward at this juncture. Through discovery, plaintiffs may be able to bolster their showing in this regard. All that is required of plaintiffs at this preliminary stage, is that there be a substantial likelihood that they could succeed at trial. The Court concludes that plaintiffs have carried that burden.

In addition to supporting plaintiffs' case for a preliminary injunction, the above analysis also compels the conclusion that defendants' motions to dismiss must be denied. If there is any likelihood that plaintiffs will prevail on the merits, it cannot be said that they have failed to state a claim upon which relief may be granted.

VIII

Relative Injuries

Plaintiffs have clearly established that if the injunction is not issued they will be irreparably harmed. It is axiomatic that wrongful eviction constitutes irreparable injury. *Johnson v. United States Department of Agriculture*, 734 F.2d 774, 789 (11th Cir. 1984); *Edwards v. Habib*, 366 F.2d 628 (D.C. Cir. 1965). Indeed, plaintiffs allege that, if they are evicted, they will not be able to relocate in Alexandria due to the city's high rents and extremely low vacancy rate. Consequently, according to plaintiffs, many of them will have to attempt to relocate in new areas, find new jobs, and change schools for their children in mid-year. One significant consequence may be to force these generally low-income individuals and families to spend their limited funds and to waste long periods of time every day on transportation between their out-of-Alexandria housing and their in-Alexandria jobs. Others, it is said, will be forced to move into sub-standard housing in order to avoid homelessness. And some may wind up completely homeless. In addition, the search for new housing will itself cause plaintiffs to lose income—which is low and marginal even now—as they will have to take unpaid leave from their jobs and bear increased transportation costs.

By contrast, defendants can claim only that they *may* be harmed financially if the injunction is issued. Defendants assert that they may lose necessary long-term financing upon the issuance of a court order which had the effect of delaying the conversions, but little concrete support has been offered for that intrinsically not compelling speculation. They also allege, with somewhat greater justification, that the costs of rehabilitation will increase if that rehabilitation is delayed, and that even a short delay will negatively affect income from the project. These hardships, however, are not only largely speculative but they are also reparable and clearly not of the same magnitude as the injuries suffered by plaintiffs should they be wrongfully evicted. This would be so particularly if, as seems likely, plaintiffs would be able to find alternative housing only far away from Alexandria, their employment, schools, friends, and such other ties as they may have established. In short, the balance of hardships weighs heavily in favor of granting the preliminary injunction.

Finally, defendants claim that rehabilitation of the two apartment complexes in question will serve the public interest as it preserves the existing housing and neighborhoods. Issuance of an injunction, they argue, would create a strong disincentive for maintenance and rehabilitation programs for deteriorated housing. Defendants' arguments have obvious merit, and they cannot be dismissed lightly. However, since the early 1960s, the Congress has made eradication of discrimination in all facets of public life, including housing, a priority to which many otherwise private interests must give way. Based upon that strong public policy, the Court concludes that the public interest will most readily be served if prevention of the spread of racial discrimination in housing is given priority weight. This is most appropriately accomplished if allegations of race discrimination in housing which *prima facie* have a likelihood of being meritorious, are allowed fully to be developed at trial.

IX

Conclusion

Plaintiffs have alleged that their threatened evictions from the apartment complexes in which they reside were caused by a purpose or intent to discriminate against them on account of their race or national origin. Some support for that allegation is provided by the fact that the negative impact of the actions of the developers would fall almost entirely on blacks and Hispanics, and the fact that prior renovation programs of some of these same developers had the effect of clearing, or almost clearing, members of such groups both from the apartment complexes there involved and from the City of Alexandria itself.

In view of this preliminary showing, plaintiffs are entitled to prove at trial, if they can, that the developers' actions are the products, in whole or in part, of a discriminatory intent, in which case they will have made out a case of violation of the Fair Housing Act, and they will be entitled to permanent injunctive relief. It should be clear, however, that, while the allegations and the evidence before the Court are sufficient to entitle plaintiffs to a trial and to maintenance of the status quo pending that trial, that evidence will not, without more, support an ultimate judgment in plaintiffs' favor. Under the Fair Housing Act, there will have to be some additional proof, direct or circumstantial, of discriminatory intent.

An appropriate Order consistent with this Opinion is being issued herewith.

* * *

Artery's Agreements

WASH. POST, Apr. 11, 1988, at F33.

Artery sold the northernmost section (364 units) of the 960–unit Lee Gardens complex (now renamed Sheffield Court) to the private, nonprofit Arlington Housing Corporation, which paid $50,000 per unit, or a total of $18.2 million. The complex deal included a variety of components:

The Arlington Housing Authority was given a $33 million tax-exempt loan from the Virginia Housing and Development Authority for the purchase and renovation of the units.

Artery contributed $1.076 million in cash toward the purchase.

The AHC will permanently maintain 200 of the units for lower-income tenants. Section 8 moderate rehabilitation certificates were obtained from the federal Department of Housing and Urban Development to subsidize rents in these units. The remaining 164 units will be rented at market prices.

Arlington guaranteed the VHDA loan by agreeing to a "moral," but not a legal, obligation to take over the loan payments if Arlington Housing Corporation defaults.

According to Artery, 320 households were moved from Lee Gardens. Of those, 238 remained in Arlington, 39 moved to Falls Church and rest scattered.

In addition, 23 of the 320 families decided to remain at Lee in an Artery-owned unit, taking advantage of a one-year subsidy from the company on the new, higher rent.

In the agreement involving Dominion Gardens, reached among Artery, Alexandria, the VHDA and HUD, a quarter of the total 416 units at Dominion Gardens, now named Kingsport, are set aside for lower-income tenants for five years. Forty-one of these units are reserved for an additional five years, and the parties are seeking additional financing so that all 104 units can be set aside.

Section 8 vouchers from HUD will be used to subsidize rents on the units. In order to supplement these HUD payments, which do not cover the costs of renovation, maintenance and utilities on the set-aside units, a package deal was arranged in which:

Artery agreed to forego some of its costs on these units.

Alexandria contributes $450,000.

Some lower-income tenants pay more rent than the 30 percent of their income required by Section 8 vouchers.

Alexandria applied to the VHDA for a loan of between $1.7 million to $7 million that will help subsidize set-aside units and possibly allow the city to preserve all 104 units for 10 years.

According to Artery, 270 households were moved out of Dominion Gardens. Approximately 75 percent remained in Alexandria; the rest moved elsewhere in Northern Virginia or to Maryland.

Of the 270 families, 52 bought a new home or condominium, partly with the help of the relocation money they received from Artery.

Some Tenants Left Out of Lee Gardens Victory

WASH. POST, Oct. 7, 1987, at B1.

■ EVELYN HSU

Mario Castillo is bewildered.

Castillo and other members of the Lee Gardens tenants association felt as if their efforts had paid off last week when the Artery Organization of Bethesda agreed to sell 364 units in the north section of the complex to a nonprofit Arlington housing group.

The deal would set aside 200 units for low-income tenants. The sale is not, final until Artery reaches an agreement with its lenders.

But Castillo and other tenants from the south side of the complex, who were considered the most active in championing the sale to the Arlington Housing Corp., now find they may not get the coveted subsidized units.

Because of regulations governing federal housing subsidies, tenants from the north side of the 961–unit complex will have first priority for the low-income apartments, all of which are located there.

"I'm very disappointed, disheartened." Castillo, secretary of the tenants association, said through an interpreter. "We had started this fight to get something better for all the community and for ourselves. After all this, we're the ones put aside, left out."

Federal regulations vest the tenants in the north section, which will become a separate housing project, with special rights, including first preference for subsidized units, said Arlington County Manager Anton S. Gardner.

Gardner said the county had asked the U.S. Department of Housing and Urban Development for permission to give residents in the south part of Lee Gardens second priority for the units.

HUD also has been asked to allow priority to be given to south Lee Gardens tenants for housing vouchers that will subsidize their rents at privately owned apartments elsewhere in the county, he said.

"I understand how it feels ... and how personally wrenching it is to some individuals," said Gardner.

This has not mollified tenants living in the south side of the complex, some of whom were turned down when they asked permission to move to the north side of the complex to receive priority for the subsidized units. A person familiar with the negotiations said that such a move would have unfairly favored some tenants of south Lee Gardens over others.

"Now we have to move," said Patricia Rodriguez, vice president of the tenants association and a resident of the south part of Lee Gardens. "We worked very hard to help them. We thought they would help us," she said of all the parties involved in the transaction. "I feel very bad."

The Arlington Housing Corp. has begun surveying families in north Lee Gardens to determine which are eligible for federal subsidies and the sizes of the units they will need.

It appears that 19 families are too large to be accommodated at the complex under state occupancy rules, said Wayne E. Rhodes, development coordinator for the county's housing division. Those families will have to move and will be offered relocation benefits, said Rhodes.

A similar, painful sorting out process is taking place at Alexandria's Dominion Gardens. That complex is also owned by Artery, which last week agreed to set aside for five years 104 of 416 units for low-income tenants who qualify for federal housing subsidies.

The agreement was approved by a federal judge as part of a settlement of a lawsuit alleging housing discrimination.

Some Dominion Gardens tenants complained at a court hearing last week that their settlement results in too few units being set aside for them and that occupancy restrictions will force large families from the complex. Also, some tenants complained that some small families can remain at the complex until they find suitable replacement housing, yet large families have been given a deadline to move.

"I was so disappointed in the settlement," said the Rev. Eldridge Harmon, a tenant at Dominion Gardens since 1985.

Attorneys for the tenants said the majority of residents were interested in settling the case.

U.S. District Judge Harold H. Greene, who approved the settlement, said in his ruling that state occupancy laws limiting the number of tenants in a unit would have been enforced even if the tenants had been victorious in their suit.

To qualify for a subsidized unit, a tenant must receive from the city a federal Section 8 voucher that limits a tenant's rent to 30 percent of his income, said Barry Goldstein, an attorney for the NAACP Legal Defense and Education Fund who represented the tenants in the court case.

Only families of four or fewer will be eligible for the subsidized units because of the occupancy requirements, he said. So far, 129 families have applied for the vouchers, he said. Some may not qualify financially, but if there are more applicants than units a lottery may be held.

There also may be room at the nearby Bruce Street apartments, where 68 out of 275 units are being set aside for low-income tenants as a result of a separate settlement with a different developer, said Goldstein.

"This is a very tough situation," said Goldstein.

"What we got was 104 units and a substantial increase in relocation benefits" for some Dominion Gardens families, he said. "We didn't solve all the housing problems in Northern Virginia."

NOTES AND QUESTIONS

1. *Public/private dichotomy.* The district court, in granting a preliminary injunction, stated that, because the defendant was a private organization, it was necessary to show proof of discriminatory intent. However, the plaintiffs in this case were not only seeking to enjoin private defendants. In addition to Artery Organization, the plaintiffs sought to enjoin HUD from delegating its authority with respect to minimizing displacement of tenants. Furthermore, government is undoubtedly intimately involved in the business practices of the defendants in this case. Since the end of World War II, the government has actively subsidized the market for residential housing through means such as mortgage guarantees and tax deductions. William E. Nelson & Norman R. Williams, *Suburbanization and Market Failure: An Analysis of Government Policies Promoting Suburban Growth and Ethnic Assimilation*, 27 FORDHAM URB. L.J. 197, 234 (1999). If government subsidies greatly effect (or arguably create) an industry, shouldn't the responsibility for the practices of that industry, to some extent, fall on the government? Further, if the industry in question engages in policies which have a disparate impact on minorities, wouldn't it be more appropriate to use the government specific disparate impact standard rather than the private industry specific disparate intent standard? If not, how can the government be prevented from engaging in *de facto* discrimination through proxies in the private market?

2. *Theories of responsibility.* According to the court in *Brown*, 654 F. Supp. at 1116, "it is an unfortunate fact, for which individual private landowners have no more responsibility than any other member of the community, that the income of a disproportionate number of blacks and members of other minority groups is such that, although they are able to afford low income housing, many cannot afford the rentals being charged for upgraded or luxury housing." Of course, the defendants in this case are not private individuals, they are large real estate firms and private banks. Coincidentally, until the enactment of the FHA, and, to a depressing extent afterwards, large real-estate organizations and private banks engaged in systematic and continuous discrimination against minorities, particularly African–Americans. With this discriminatory history, how is it appropriate to compare the defendants in this case to the mythical "individual private landowner?"

3. *Class and race. Brown v. Artery* was decided based on the impact that proposed renovations would have had on low income minority tenants as minorities, not on the impact that proposed renovations would have had on low income minority tenants based on their class status. Is the focus on race on *Brown v. Artery* just? If there were an affluent minority community in Alexandria such that the proposed renovations would not have effective-

ly purged the city of minorities, would the same result have been warranted? What if, instead of minority tenants, Lee Gardens had been occupied by low income Caucasians? Is it possible to distinguish between discrimination based on class and discrimination based on race? Would such a distinction be desirable? For a fascinating case study of combined race and class discrimination in the small town of Shaw, Mississippi in the late 1960s, see CHARLES HAAR & DANIEL W. FESSLER, THE WRONG SIDE OF THE TRACKS (1986).

4. *Value of property.* In American society, home ownership has come to replace the ownership of productive property (e.g., a farm) as the goal to which all citizens are assumed to aspire. Phyliss Craig–Taylor, *To be Free: Liberty, Citizenship, Property, and Race*, 14 HARV. BLACKLETTER L.J. 45 (1998). With this in mind, class discrimination can be especially damaging because it not only injures directly but also denies its victims the chance to participate in the ideal American community.

5. *Fair Housing Act of 1988.* The Fair Housing Act of 1988 makes discrimination on the basis of family status illegal, specifically prohibiting five classes of behavior, including: refusing to sell or rent, or refusing to negotiate for the sale or rental of, or otherwise making unavailable or denying a dwelling to any person based on familial status. Shelly D. Cutts, *The Fair Housing Amendments Act of 1988: An Incomplete Solution to the Problem of Housing Discrimination Against Families*, 30 ARIZ. ST. L.J. 205, 207 (1998). Would these amendments have addressed the complaints voiced by individuals in large families with regard to the Artery agreements?

6. Artery *and the Emerald City.* When dissenting from denial of certiorari in *Cleveland Board of Education v. Reed*, Justice Rehnquist wrote that "[e]ven if the Constitution required it, and it were possible for federal courts to do it, no equitable decree can fashion an 'Emerald City' where all races, ethnic groups, and persons of various income levels live side by side in a large metropolitan area." *Cleveland Bd. of Educ. v. Reed*, 445 U.S. 935, 938 (1980) (Rehnquist, J., joined by Burger, C.J. & Powell, J., dissenting from denial of cert.). It would seem then that avoiding a racially integrated city was an overriding priority for Justice Rehnquist, given that it would justify ignoring the requirements of the constitution when it was practicable to abide by them. Does the agreement above, along with all statutes that forbid housing discrimination, contravene Rehnquist's imperative to avoid the "Emerald City?"

7. *Problems with the status quo?* In the case of *Brown v. Artery Organization*, 654 F. Supp. 1106 (D.D.C. 1987), there was never any allegation that the housing in question was losing money for its owners at any time. The only question seems to be lost opportunity for additional profits. Since there was never any question that the housing in question was being run at a loss, why did there have to be any changes made at all? Prevention of housing discrimination is an overriding priority for the government, and, in this case, maintaining the status quo could have solved the possible problem of evicting minority tenants, as well as allowed Artery to continue to operate its low income housing at a profit. Since that was the case, why did these agreements have to be made at all?

8. *Additional reading.* For additional information about the develop-
ment of home ownership in America, see William E. Nelson & Norman R.
Williams, *Suburbanization and Market Failure: An Analysis of Government
Policies Promoting Suburban Growth and Ethnic Assimilation*, 27 FORDHAM
URB. L.J. 197 (1999); Phyliss Craig–Taylor, *To be Free: Liberty, Citizenship,
Property, and Race*, 14 HARV. BLACKLETTER L.J. 45 (1998); SHERYLL CASHIN,
THE FAILURES OF INTEGRATION: HOW RACE AND CLASS ARE UNDERMINING THE
AMERICAN DREAM (2004). For additional information about the intersection
of race and class, see Jennifer M. Russell, *The Race/Class Conundrum and
the Pursuit of Individualism in the Making of Social Policy*, 46 HASTINGS
L.J. 1353 (1995). For additional information on housing discrimination, see
Peter E. Mahoney, *The End(s) of Disparate Impact: Doctrinal Reconstruc-
tion, Fair Housing and Lending Law, and the Antidiscrimination Principle*,
47 EMORY L.J. 409 (1998); Shelly D. Cutts, *The Fair Housing Amendments
Act of 1988: An Incomplete Solution to the Problem of Housing Discrimina-
tion Against Families*, 30 ARIZ. ST. L.J. 205 (1998); Robert F. Drinan, S.J.,
Untying the White Noose, 94 YALE L.J. 435 (1984) (book review). For
additional information on discrimination against the poor, see generally
Gene R. Nichol, *Toward a People's Constitution*, 91 CALIF. L. REV. 621 (2003)
(book review); John Shomberg, *Equity v. Autonomy: The Problems of
Private Donations to Public Schools*, 1998 ANN. SURV. AM. L. 143 (1998);
Susan H. Bitensky, *We "Had a Dream" in* Brown v. Board of Education,
1996 DET. C.L. REV. 1 (1996); Gay Gellhorn, *Justice Thurgood Marshall's
Jurisprudence of Equal Protection of the Laws and the Poor*, 26 ARIZ. ST. L.J.
429 (1994).

From the Punitive City to the Gated Community: Security and Segregation Across the Social and Penal Landscape

56 U. MIAMI L. REV. 89 (2001).

■ MONA LYNCH

INTRODUCTION

    Just over twenty years ago, criminologist Stanley Cohen articulated his
vision of a newly evolving penal world, "The Punitive City," which was
distinguished by several elements: The dispersal and penetration of social
control beyond prison walls; the blurring of spatial boundaries which mark
the differences between inside and outside, freedom and captivity, imprisoned and released, and guilty and innocent; the emergence of a corrections
continuum where intervention and control is finely graded to fit individual
"need"; and the widening of the controllable population which resulted
from fuzzier definitions of deviancy and normalcy. Cohen conceptualized
his "punitive city" as a community built on finely graded social control
mechanisms with few clear boundaries between classes and categories of
citizens.

These representations of a new form of penal control were most apparent in the emerging revolution of what is euphemistically known as "community corrections" or community-based control. Community control ideology embraces the involvement of family, schools, peers, neighborhoods, the police, and an array of community professionals in keeping the criminal in line within the community, rather than isolated in a distinctly segregated penal institution. While Cohen doubted that these new community-based forms of intervention would replace the prison, he did indicate that prison incarceration rates would likely remain static, if not decline, as the prison became a last resort on the continuum of correction, rather than the first resort for penal intervention.

Cohen's imagined new "punitive city" was not the only expression of doubt about the role and purpose of segregated penal institutions during that period. Beginning in the 1970s, the value and necessity of the prison was being broadly and fundamentally challenged by practitioners and theorists across the U.S. and western Europe. Not only were the physical institutions and day-to-day institutional practices in the critical spotlight, but the very foundations upon which they rested, the philosophies, beliefs, and cultural tenets that told all of us why we punish and with what social aims were scrutinized and challenged. As criminologist Andrew Scull suggested at the time, the movement away from incarceration and toward "community corrections" involved a direct assault on the very intellectual foundations underlying the established systems of control. The rehabilitative mission was critiqued by those on both the left and the right of the political spectrum. It was coming to be seen as a failed experiment which denied the moral autonomy of criminal actors, allowed for oppressive institutional conditions under the guise of benevolence, and simply "didn't work".

* * *

Yet what appears to have happened in the US (in particular, although not exclusively) is that this penological crisis and movement toward alternate criminal justice responses in no way lessened the reliance on prison as a central form of social control. Indeed, the explosion in the sheer numbers of people being imprisoned in this country, and in the rate at which people are imprisoned, actually began its upswing right around the time Cohen's piece on the Punitive City was published and the prison's credibility was being overtly challenged.

In this paper, I explore a potential (if partial) explanation for this somewhat ironic prison explosion by looking beyond the machinery of criminal justice, and analytically resituating the prison as a social institution within the broader socio-cultural landscape. The article begins by describing the transformation of the American prison itself over the past several decades from what was, at least in how it was explicitly idealized, an institution that aimed to reform its charges for the betterment of the inmates themselves as well as the broader society, to the current incarnation of the post-rehabilitative, security-oriented prison. Further, this article will illustrate how the underlying logic of the contemporary prison appears to inform many aspects of contemporary community life, which is a direct contrast to the projected course in which the language and elements of "community" were going to permeate and transform the penal realm. I specifically examine the rise of the "gated community" as a fitting exemplar of the segregative, security oriented society which analysts such as Gary Marx describe. This portion of the paper seeks to illustrate the parallels between "free" gated communities and the prison as an involuntary, no-frills gated community. The article concludes by analyzing what are suspected contributing factors in these social and spatial transformations, and discussing the theoretical implications of these changes and the fundamental impact of these new forms of security zone communities on contemporary social and civic life.

A DERAILED DEMISE OF THE PRISON

As noted above, all of the deep doubts openly expressed about the penal institution's purpose and function did not add up to the "death" of the prison but instead coincided with an unprecedented expansion of its use in the United States. Specifically, between 1930 and 1975, the annual prison incarceration rate in the United States was generally fairly stable, varying between the low nineties to a high of about one-hundred-nineteen (in 1961) per one-hundred thousand population. The incarceration rate began its steady and consistent climb upwards in 1976, and by 1998 the overall national rate had more than tripled in two decades to four-hundred-sixty-one per one-hundred-thousand. At the end of the 20th century, there were in excess of 1.3 million people housed in state and federal prisons in the United States, which was about 1 million more than were incarcerated just two decades earlier. When those imprisoned at the local level, in county jails and juvenile facilities are added into the count, there were more than 2,000,000 incarcerated people in the U.S. by year-end 1999. This imprisonment explosion cannot be explained away by rising crime rates. The rate of incarceration per 1000 index crimes has also nearly quadrupled in two decades, suggesting the growth was due in large part to changing crime control policy.

Besides the growth in the rate and sheer number of people imprisoned over the past several decades, there have been several other notable transformations in the use of prisons in the United States over the same period. First, the racial and ethnic composition of the incarcerated population underwent significant change. The percentage of minorities relative to whites in prison, and relative to their percentage in the general population, especially of African–Americans, grew significantly from 1960 through the 1990s, with the sharpest increase beginning around 1980. Indeed, the incarceration rate for African–American men has increased so dramatically that it has literally reshaped the social structure of entire urban communities over the past twenty years.

Second, the kinds of offenders who occupy American prisons are increasingly non-violent offenders, despite the political rhetoric that would suggest otherwise. Drug offenders in particular have made up a disproportionate percentage of the population growth over the past 2 decades, and a disproportionate number of those who are sent to prison have been African American, not white, drug offenders.

Third, life inside institutional walls has been transformed over the same general period at facilities across the country. The emphasis on incapacitation rather than on rehabilitation in the broader criminal justice sphere has meant that prisons are becoming mere containment sites of varying security levels, with fewer resources devoted to traditional rehabilitative activities. The proliferation of "super-max" prisons in the United States, with their hallmark features of extreme isolation combined with high-tech, high-level security, are just one telling example of contemporary life behind bars. Thus, institutional life itself has undergone a dramatic qualitative shift that coincides with the changes in population demographics and numbers.

If one looks at the state of California, which lays claim to one of the most populous prison systems in the country, the incredible growth of the system is also demonstrated in numbers and rates of incarceration over the last two decades. The incarceration rate in the end of the 1978 was about 95/100,000 with an institutional population of around 21,000 inmates. Twenty years later, the rate was nearly five times higher at 481 per 100,000 and a total institutional population stood at 163,000. The growth is also evident in the physical expansion of California's system. Twenty-one of thirty-three prisons in use in the state, or two-thirds of all operating prisons, have been built since 1982, at a cost of about 5.3 billion dollars. The Department of Corrections now accounts for just over seven percent of the entire state budget, up from about two point nine percent in 1980.

A number of criminal justice scholars have begun to examine why this expansion has occurred, especially directly on the heels of the deep cynicism broadly expressed about the prison's utility and necessity. Perhaps the two most prominent categories of explanations for the huge growth can be characterized as economic/structural and political/cultural. For instance, Ted Chiricos and Miriam Delone address the seemingly Marxist paradox of prison expansion in a time of economic prosperity. The researchers have demonstrated that this contemporary period does indeed have a significant surplus labor population despite appearances to the contrary, and that this population size is positively correlated to use of imprisonment. A number of scholars have also linked the vast economic restructuring brought on by post-industrial market changes and general economic globalization over the past several decades to the growth of the prison "industrial complex" especially as directed at non-Whites.

In terms of the role of politics and issue frames, Katherine Beckett has illustrated how crime as political capital, particularly in the Reagan–Bush years, in concert with media attention to state-shaped crime issues, contributed to the expansion of imprisonment as a primary criminal justice policy, especially at the federal level. Indeed, a number of researchers have pointed to the mass media's role in at least fueling, if not creating, panic over crime which can only be remediated through harsh penal policies (e.g., Scheingold's explication of the "myth of crime and punishment, Irwin and Austin's examination of the interplay between economics, politics and media that has contributed to America's 'imprisonment binge'; Chiricos's analysis of the media-hyped cocaine panic in the 1980s which spawned harsh federal mandatory minimum statutes, and Surette's description of the media influence in California's Three Strikes 1990s lawmaking frenzy, to name a few.")

Several theorists have also grappled with the process by which this penal punitiveness has been put into popular and political language. Dario Melossi describes what he calls the "changing hegemonic vocabulary of punitive motive" which flowed from society's elites to the populace during the period of 1970–1992. During this period, the instrumental value of punishment was in essence translated into a form of moral language adopted and acted upon by politicians and the public. Jonathan Simon has suggested that what he calls, "governing through crime" in which elected officials substitute punitive crime control rhetoric and new penological policy-making in the place of substantive governance, accounts in part for the changing penal practices.

There is also, as described above, an important and growing body of work that places the incarceration boom squarely within the political realm, and illuminates the changing role of crime control/penal policy in state and federal politics and governance. Thus far, though, the prison explosion has generally been most extensively documented in terms of its extent, its practical consequences, and its policy implications. Indeed, there are some underlying social and cultural changes that seem to have contributed to this prison explosion, especially in regard to its changing qualitative features, which have been less fully explored. In particular, one of the links in the process which should be addressed is how the prison itself has transformed in meaning so that it could conceptually "fit the bill" in the new post-rehabilitative era. Given its precarious position just twenty-five years ago, one could easily have imagined a new (or retro) set of punitive penal strategies emerging from the confluence of punitive crime and punishment politics, growing concern with risk management, and skepticism about the function of penal intervention, which would have subsumed the prison's role.

PRISONS AS UNDERCLASS "LIFESTYLE COMMUNITIES"

The first aspect of the changing social meaning of the prison has to do with the understanding of its very function as a populated social space. Where the prison has traditionally been understood as an institution of transformation, in which the goals of training, fixing, and rehabilitating were primary, at least rhetorically, thus analogous in some ways to the school or the factory, it is now better understood as a place to be for those sentenced; thus a form of residence. While the prison was founded and firmly rooted in a rehabilitative tradition, its very nature, as well as its social and cultural place in the larger social sphere, has been fundamentally reconstructed in recent years. Prisons today are explicitly justified primarily (although not exclusively) as being useful for incapacitation, and perhaps a bit of retribution. As a result, the contemporary prison need only function as a holding place where the primary obligation to the residents is the famed "three hots and a cot," and the central obligation to the larger community is simply to keep convicted persons out of sight and behind bars. The label that aptly captures this shift in the role of the prison from a place that reforms to an incapacitative residence is one that is applied with more and more frequency to penal institutions—the warehouse prison.

That the prison is thought of in these terms, by the public, politicians, academics, and practitioners alike, is evident in a number of small but telling ways. First, there is the ascension of a strain of criminological theories explaining criminality as a form of lifestyle or career. As David Garland suggests, the contemporary offender is "no longer [viewed as] the poorly socialized misfit in need of assistance, but instead an implicit, opportunistic consumer." Thus, for instance, the "new criminologies of everyday life" exemplified by Felson and Cohen's routine activities theory presupposes that crime is committed by a rational actor who will only choose such behavior when the rewards are greater than the costs.

Implicit in this understanding of criminality, of course, is that a criminal "career" is a matter of individual choice and personal preference. Thus, the most appropriate intervention is mere preventive containment, since the only reform that would work to get the criminal straight is a change in lifestyle choice. Indeed, one of the few transformative programs within correctional settings that is currently popular is a series of classes offered to correctional populations about changing their lifestyle choices, along with other "cognitive" adjustment programs!

It follows, then, that those who go to prison may be seen as opting for that as their lifestyle community. One hears the assumption that convicts choose to go to prison sounded in a variety of venues. My own fieldwork on parole field supervision demonstrated that parole agents and hearing officers sometimes explicitly justified returns to prison as the choice of the wayward parolee. In the public and political realms, recent demands for tougher institutional conditions such as removing weight equipment, limiting television access, smoking bans, clothing and grooming restrictions are implicitly and explicitly justified on the need to lessen the appeal of the "country club" prison for would-be felons. Some prisons have even begun to charge rent to inmates for their stays, ranging from $10–60 a day. This language also extends to the market end of contemporary prisons, as illustrated in the ad campaigns for correctional products. For instance, DLR prison architectural firm, which frequently advertises in the correctional trade periodical, *Corrections Today*, uses the ad copy "Providing Accommodations for Selected Guests," above a photograph of a jailed man's torso with his hands extending through the bars, and a cigarette dangling between his fingers, in one of its display advertisement campaigns.

Institutions themselves appear to be increasingly operating purely as self-contained communities, with fewer connections with, and obligations to, the larger community. For example, Jonathan Simon has demonstrated how corrections in California increasingly operates in terms of internally defined efficiency and accountability goals. The internal goals are employed rather than the previously dominant externally defined goals which linked correctional success to offenders' post-sentence law abiding behavior in the community. I have found on my visits to institutions in California that prison representatives explicitly describe the prison as a "little city", offering a lengthy narrative about how the prison functions like a self-contained community. The guides on these institutional tours present the main activities that go on behind the gates as ones that simply serve to keep the place functioning smoothly. For instance, they explain where bedding and clothes are laundered, how meals are handled, how to make enough coffee for so many residents, and how to move people through the institution without threatening security. Inmate jobs are generally described in terms of their functionality within the institution, not as skill building or otherwise for the rehabilitation of the inmate, as they might be under a rehabilitative model. Even the cells are referred to as "houses" by inmates and staff alike. Those in the business of corrections products can be found to have adopted the same language in their sales pitches, as is illustrated in a long running display advertisement campaign used by KLN Steel Products Company. In it, several photographs of steel bunks, tables, stools, and lockers are featured below the ad copy: "Furniture for Every Room in the House."

If the prison is better understood as a form of residential community rather than as a reformatory, understanding its proliferation may lie in examining the qualitative shifts in residential communities during the same period. First, examining the notion of community, especially as articulated by Cohen, will illuminate where his (and his contemporaries') vision of the new correctional community failed to be realized. In Cohen's imaginary punitive city that appeared on the horizon, criminal deviants intermingled with middle-class law abiding folks, living together, working together, learning together. This kind of diversified community which could be imagined at that time no longer seems so plausible. The potential for all kinds of mixed communities after the Civil Rights revolution of the 1950s, 60s, and 70s appeared to nearly vanish by the 1980s.

A number of scholars have demonstrated the persistence and intractability of race and class segregation in communities across the nation over the last two decades, although its form has changed in shape, given the explicit prohibitions against residential and other forms of discrimination that were the product of the Civil Rights era litigation and legislation. Gregory Squires documents how policies which favor free market control of housing have contributed to the solidification of residential segregation. This segregation has occurred despite laws prohibiting outright discrimination in providing mortgages and in selling and leasing residential properties. Residential areas in many regions are becoming increasingly homogenized, rather than diversified, on a number of dimensions in the post-Civil Rights era. Generally, market forces have become the proxy by which the entrenched racial and class segregation of the pre-Civil Rights period has been allowed to persist.

Perhaps the most striking development along these lines in recent years, and the one most relevant to the subject of this paper, has been the rise of "gated communities". In many ways, these developments, which are planned residential communities of varying sizes and distinguished by their use of gates and barriers to control who may enter into their space, represent the cardinal point on a continuum of segregated residential security zones that has as its opposite end-point the new "warehouse" prison.

According to urban planning scholars Edward Blakely and Mary Snyder, gated communities began to surge in number beginning in the early 1980s. By the mid–1970s there were about two-thousand five hundred of such residential communities and by the mid–1990s, there were about twenty thousand gated communities containing more than three million housing units. Blakely and Snyder suggest that the rate of building gated communities exceeds that of non-gated planned residential developments in a number of areas. This means there will be a continuation of gated community growth for at least some time.

Gated communities have several defining features. First and foremost, as just noted, they are marked by physical boundaries—walls and gates— which define the space within as private and closed to all but residents and authorized visitors. Second, those within tend to be similar to each other. Residents are homogenized by economics—each community is generally built to aim for a particular piece of the market in terms of pricing. The executive developments do not include the modestly priced two bedroom home; the pricing of units within a development ensures that economically similar buyers will become neighbors. In fact, in some of the larger developments, there are gates within gates that protect the highest-end residents from even their more modest neighbors. Residents of gated communities also tend to be relatively racially homogeneous—generally, white, as observed by Blakely and Snyder in their visits to such communities across the country. As they point out, this is one by-product of the design. "The segregation that gated communities represent is intentionally economic, but race and class are closely correlated attributes in our society." Finally, the proliferation of gated communities is driven in significant part by residents' concern for security, anxieties about crime and other social problems, and a desire to be with similar people.

If we look at the prison as another form of gated community or residential security zone, albeit involuntary and state-run, its growth over the past couple of decades is less puzzling. First, it is within the current cultural language to understand criminals as consumers of prison as a lifestyle community. For instance, criminologist Mark Fleisher, addressing a lay audience in USA Today magazine, frames "lifestyle criminals" use of prison in just these kinds of terms. "To [these criminals], prisons are sanctuaries that deliver social, medical, and recreational services.... Prison is stable and offers plenty of food, a clean bed, recreation, and access medical and dental services. Social life in prison is good, too. Some inmates continue criminal activity, such as drug dealing, while others just 'lay up' and enjoy the safety and pleasures of not having to hustle for money and food every day."

In justifying the toughening of prison conditions in California prisons in the late 1990s, former Governor Wilson's spokesman argued, "We got into the position ... of providing a rather comfortable lifestyle in prison— We should not allow prisoners to ride roughshod over the prisons. They're not there to be entertained and catered to." Louisiana state legislator Troy Hebert justified his bills to limit television and smoking in prisons, quaintly entitled the "Party is Over" package, on similar grounds. "It should be a prison; it is not a hotel you are going to when you go to jail ... Inmates now just lie around and watch baseball games and soap operas." He added that some prisoners have it better in jail than at home "with three meals a day, clean sheets and TV". In the case of prisons, the public is also at least conceived as willing consumers of the product of prisons. As the California Department of Corrections boasts on their official website, beginning in 1981, California voters, "enthusiastically supported separate bond issues totaling more than two billion dollars" to support the "most ambitious prison constructions program in the world."

One can make the analogy between prisons and gated communities fairly easily. First, like the free gated community, the prison is also first and foremost marked by physical boundaries—walls and gates—that define the space inside as inaccessible to all but the residents, staff, and authorized visitors. Second, prisons are relatively homogeneous in population, in terms of the constellation of their demographics. A 1991 national survey of American prisoners indicated that over eighty-five percent had an annual income under $25,000 prior to imprisonment (seventy percent of total had an income below $15,000); most prisoners are men who range in age from twenty to forty, and two-thirds are racial minorities, primarily African-American, who by 1997 constituted nearly half of the state and federal prison population. And, as several researchers have illustrated, the proliferation of prison is explicitly justified by concerns for security, and is offered as a remedy to quell anxieties about crime and other social problems. Further, research on racial attitudes and opinion on punishment indicates that public support for punitive crime control policies is negatively correlated with support for integrationist policies and positively associated with negative racial stereotyping by whites.

Finally, the explosion of the post-rehabilitative "warehouse" prison, and the proliferation of gated communities follow a distinctly similar regional pattern, in addition to being contemporaneous in development. In particular, the Sunbelt and the Southwest regions—states like Florida, Texas, Arizona, Nevada, and California, particularly Southern California—have been the site of the most rapid development of both forms of the "gated community". These states have been at the forefront of prison building, including the construction of post-rehabilitative "super-max" units, and in the escalation of imprisonment rates in the past twenty or so years. They are also the same ones that have the highest concentration of gated developments.

Dana Young has even suggested that gated communities might be best viewed as nearly synonymous with prisons, in that they "represent a trend more concerned with regulating and controlling the residents within its gates and demoralizing relatively powerless groups outside its walls than with reducing the overall amount of avoidable social deprivation." She goes on to conclude, "perhaps common interest developments are ironically closer to functioning like prisons rather than like the idyllic Edens they seek to emulate. The epitome of a gated community is surely a prison." Arguably, there is a profound and fundamental difference between prisons and gated communities. Namely, with prisons, people are fenced in against their will by the state, and in the other, residents pay a premium price in private transactions to fence others out. Nonetheless, as Young might suggest, this crucial distinction depends on the target resident's viewpoint of what can be seen as a similar set of underlying logics of security and segregation.

There is a point on the "residential security zone" continuum where this difference becomes blurred and turns on the fenced in/fenced out variable. Specifically, a growing trend in public housing is "gating" for security and crime control. In these developments, while the residents are nominally living there voluntarily, two aspects suggest that this type of gating is both the mid-point and turning point on the continuum suggested.

First, the gating decision is made by a state entity and imposed upon the residents, often with little or no input by them in the decision. Second, some of those living in these public housing gated communities express a sense of real confusion about whether the gates fence outsiders out or fence residents in. Residents in a recently "gated" DC housing project compared their experiences of having their housing development gated by the government to being jailed. As one resident put it, "We aren't animals. We don't need to be caged."

Finally, in Atlanta (among other cities), which has been at the forefront of gating public housing, residents of some communities are being subject to requirements that strongly resemble a criminal justice intervention. This is the case even though their only "offense" is poverty and a reliance on subsidized housing. Residents at some of these developments are subject to criminal records checks and are required to do community service. In addition, there are nightly curfews and limits imposed upon them by the Housing Authority regarding how long extended family and friends may visit in their homes. Some residents are required to carry ID cards to prove they belong, and can be evicted after two violations of these and other rules. As one resident complained to a reporter about the litany of restrictions he lived under, "This is not a prison. People should be able to come and go as they please."

The defining features, then, of these various forms of communities are the emphasis on security technology and boundary maintenance through the use of barriers to maintain variously defined segregated populations. At the "free" end, it tends to be the wealthiest who are shutting others out to maintain an "exclusive" environment, and at the other end, it is the poor and socially defined deviants who are fenced in.

GATES AND FENCES AS MECHANISMS FOR POST-CIVIL RIGHTS SEGREGATION

The question remains, why the expansion of both of these extreme forms of gated communities at this period in time? It does not appear to be happenstance that both occurred at the end of the Civil Rights revolution. Subsequent to the 1968 enactment of the Fair Housing Act and related civil rights legislation, both the free market and the state have contributed to the maintenance of social and spatial divisions that fall on racial, ethnic, and class lines through less open and direct means than those in practice up until that time. Although neither openly targets populations based on racial categories, both work in ways that result in racialized segregation. The marketers of gated communities promote the "exclusivity" of the community and promise "like-minded neighbors" as pitches to their potential customers.

The use of race restrictive covenants by private housing developments to ensure racial segregation dates back to the early part of the twentieth century. Once these explicit covenants were definitively deemed unenforceable in 1948, however, homeowner associations began to develop and enforce "race-neutral" restrictive covenants which continued to maintain racial, ethnic, and class segregation. The homeowner association was created as a response to the loss of formal racial segregative mechanisms within private residential communities.

Under this model of privatized resident screening, association members and boards had the authority to determine and enforce "qualification" requirements designed for "preserving the character [and] . . . integrity" of the housing development, including occupancy density and other "lifestyle" restrictions. While the most blatant forms of such screening were more effectively controlled by the Fair Housing Act, the increasing level of spatial, political, and governmental distance that community developers put between their developments and urban centers continued to ensure relative homogeneity within. The subsequent fortification of such residential communities with gates and barriers simply added another layer to the privatized segregation.

* * *

The question remains as to how gates, barriers, and security hardware and software become an appropriate response to concerns about security and safety, fears of crime victimization, and anxieties about racial, cultural, and class differences. The changes described above did not just happen from a top down process, where state actors and/or private developers decided to impose a new regime to maintain race and class divisions. Rather, there has been an interactive transformative process that has occurred at multiple levels of society and culture to facilitate the acceptance and spread of this phenomenon. A major component of that transformative process (but by no means the only one), I suggest, has involved the successful mass commodification of both security and "community", in the form of products, technologies, amenities, and services. In turn, this commodification process agnosticized both state punishment and civil society.

Thus, the safe and secure lifestyle community is no longer something to be created through civic participation, but rather purchased as an amenity to one's residence. Additionally, protection against crime and other social ills is no longer a problem solved by human intervention in the form of rehabilitation or social/structural problem-solving. Rather it too can be purchased through the investment in sophisticated software and hardware that promises to incapacitate the problem population, or at least keep them out of the gated neighborhood. Consequently, these aspects of social life which have not always been thought of in terms of pure marketability have now been seized upon by myriad goods and service marketers in a manner that strips each of its underlying human values. Community responsibility is reduced to paying taxes and approving bond measures to fund the expanding prison industry, on the one hand, and paying homeowners fees and assessments to maintain gates and round-the-clock security patrols, on the other. Not surprisingly, there are hordes who are willing to pay.

The growth of security as a marketable commodity in the place of socially created forms of security has been documented in the form of private police and alarm systems. The emerging literature on gated communities and other forms of exclusive communities also suggests that security, community and lifestyle are becoming products to be purchased, rather than social states that are created. Further, the segregative goal of these social spaces is made evident in the sales pitches.

The private gated communities tend to sell both security and segregation more subtly. For example, Scottsdale, Arizona's Desert Mountain development's promotional package uses the descriptive adjectives "exclusive", "gated" and "serene" as single word selling points to describe the myriad amenities and features. The package boasts that this community that offers "members only exclusivity" and is "the envy of all, reserved for a few." DC Ranch, also in Scottsdale, Arizona, which is made up of mostly gated "neighborhoods", except for the low-end developments (in the $200,000 range) on the south side of the development, tells potential buyers in its promotional materials:

> Of course, comfort in your surroundings is dependent on more than the design of your home and neighborhood. Accordingly, DC Ranch has taken a number of steps to heighten peace of mind and provide confidence in your community and its care. Private community patrols are provided on a twenty-four hours a day, seven days a week schedule by officers who are knowledgeable of, and attentive to, each neighborhood. If you happen to live in a gated area, microchip vehicle tags offer convenient access with no need to stop at the guard station. Residents simply push a button, or insert a card into a gate control mechanism. Also available is the advantage of advanced in-home security wiring, which provides for alarm monitoring and other services.

And there is at least one gated development currently under construction that makes explicit its primary emphasis on security as the theme of the community: Front Sight Master Planned Community outside of Las Vegas, Nevada, developed around firearm training, recreation, and protection. The development is centered around a massive training facility, armory, live fire simulation training ranges, more than a dozen shooting ranges, a SWAT training tower, and an underground tunnel network. Residents can partake in Uzi sub-machine gun classes, enroll in courses in how to shoot from moving vehicles, and receive low light gun-fight training.

The surrounding two hundred home residential development, protected by armed guards, includes plans for an on-site K–12 school, a shopping center to serve all the needs of the residents (including a firearms "pro shop"), a town arsenal, and an airstrip. The developer, who calls Front Sight "a Disneyland for gun lovers" and "Uzi-land", offers free Uzi submachine guns to buyers who pay for their home sites up front. The developer also markets the place to potential buyers for its safety, "Wouldn't it be nice to live in the safest town in America? We won't have any crime at Front Sight, not with everyone trained in firearms." He has even named the residential streets in the spirit of the theme; Second Amendment Drive is one of the addresses available.

Prison products are also more explicit in selling both segregation and security in their marketing campaigns aimed at corrections' managers. In fact some of the companies that sell to correctional markets also supply security products to high-end gated community developers. A 1995 display advertisement for Robot Company's electronic security system is typical of the imagery and captioning used to sell to the prison market. The ad features a photograph of a convict climbing over low-tech institutional fencing, and the caption, "His dream is your worst nightmare."

Similar themes are used in both the Intelli–FLEX fencing and the First Defence company's ad campaigns. Intelli–FLEX features a close-up of a gruff convict behind the fencing, captioned by: "Intelli–FLEX: The really smart fence. It knows the difference between bad weather and a bad guy." First Defence features a picture of a convict helplessly dangling from the inwardly curved fence top, and the copy, "A design so effective they won't get over it."

The centrality of perimeter control to the segregative function of the warehouse prison is not limited to marketers of such products. Prisons in several jurisdictions have begun to install lethal electric fences around their facilities as the ultimate barrier to the free world. These kinds of very expensive containment products, which the warehouse prison industry invests in heavily, explicitly articulate the underlying ethos of the contemporary gated community.

Investing in prisons, like investing in gated communities, literally buys boundaries to distinguish and secure differentiated lifestyle communities, both spatially and socially. So while there is recognized cynicism about the effects of imprisonment on those incarcerated, the contemporary commitment to prison asks for nothing more than containment of its residents.

Thus the social anxieties about crime, difference, and social disorder that play a part in the desire for both can be quelled through the simple investment in walls, fences and gates.

THE MEANING OF GATES

The observations made here have been articulated by many, so I make no claim to originality in identifying the nature and shape of the racialized post-rehabilitative prison, the rise of the gated community, or the growing commodification process underlying both. The goal of this article was to simply pull these individual threads of social inquiry and analysis into a single narrative that might add to our theoretical understanding of the contemporary prison explosion.

It appears that there are multiple processes at work, including those that are political, cultural, economic, social psychological, and social structural. These processes have come together in this period in such a way that our punishment policies and practices are not only "volatile and contradictory," but also brutally punitive and deeply discriminatory. What this suggests for theoretical understanding of these phenomena, then, is that a) race and ethnicity in all their varied meanings are integral to understanding punishment in the United States; b) examinations of punishment processes like imprisonment often need to be imbedded within larger social and cultural processes; and c) the broader theoretical understandings of the "commodity culture" can also give us insights into a state process like punishment.

Finally, while these late-modern developments are theoretically informative and suggest a profound change in the social, cultural, and political landscape, they also have a real and deep impact on the contemporary state of our civic life. Gregory Alexander has commented on the withdrawal for civic responsibility borne from the proliferation of "free" gated communities and related forms of private residential developments. Alexander suggests that, "the primary functions of the modern residential association are socially insulating rather than ... connective ... It does not seem too far-fetched, then, to characterize the incredible growth of these private residential governments as the enclosure movement of the late twentieth century in the United States."

Blakely and Snyder's empirical investigation of gated communities also confirms what we might suspect about such places. The residents tend to view those outside of the walls as outside of their concern, so express apathy about issues facing the surrounding communities. Some gated communities have asked to withdraw from fiscal, political, and social involvement with the larger community, and have done so successfully in several instances.

California has at least 3 fully incorporated gated cities. Places like DC Ranch in Scottsdale plan their own "public" schools on community grounds, as well as fire and police stations so residents will have still fewer reasons to go, in their words, "beyond the fence line." Of course, one outcome of this fiscal withdrawal by predominantly mid-to high income taxpayers means that those with fewer resources who remain in the communities outside the walls end up with fewer basic services and lower levels of assistance as urban tax bases shrink.

Prisons have also had their own impact on civic life. In many urban communities, the population of young men has been decimated by the imprisonment binge, contributing to a radical reshaping of family structures, social relations, and local economics. The communities that deal directly with these criminal justice casualties are the same that have been shut out of the economic prosperity enjoyed by a segment of the nation's population. Thus, these areas in many ways have become their own security zones—whether formally, as in those gated public housing, or through the civic and economic abandonment of whole sections of cities and towns where police aggressively patrol, roust, and arrest those left behind.

This is not to romanticize a time that never really was, in which socially, economically, and racially integrated communities were successfully created as the norm. However, what seems to be gone now is even the dream or vision of such communities, which is no doubt a by-product of the same factors that have driven the growth of gates and fences. Thus, we can now read Cohen's articulation of a coming "Punitive City" not with alarm over the blurring of distinctions between corrections and community as he predicted, but with a sense of loss (or at least nostalgia) over the now absent social elements embodied in both community and "corrections" that undergirded his and others' writings of that time.

NOTES AND QUESTIONS

1. *Prison and the family.* Prison is a "lifestyle community" for more than the people who are incarcerated. When parents are locked up, their families suffer. Children from such families are more likely themselves to later enter the juvenile and criminal justice systems. This dynamic transforms the prison system into, essentially, a substitute for the family. Moreover, the family members left behind suffer the ill-effects of incarceration as well in lost emotional support, income, and family cohesion. In addition, the prisoner upon release can become a vector for spreading prison acquired diseases such as AIDS. *See* Lynette Clemetson, *Links Between Prison and AIDS Affecting Blacks Inside and Out*, N.Y. TIMES, Aug. 6, 2004, at A5. Given the importance of family, discussed in *Moore v. East Cleveland*, 431 U.S. 494 (1977), *supra* at pp. 603–617, do the effects of prisons on families cast doubt on the legitimacy of our system which is premised on prison as a lifestyle choice?

2. *Gated communities as prisons.* While there are similarities between prisons and gated communities, the most striking parallel is between the treatment of those who are in prison by those who are not, and those who are not in a gated community by those who are. In both cases, walls and gates are used to restrict the freedom of movement of those who are poor or of a different race. Additionally, the divisions between gated and non-

gated and non-imprisoned and imprisoned function to insulate the favored group from problems plaguing the disfavored group.

3. *Standard of living.* Louisiana Governor Troy Hilbert says that prisoners are often better off in prison because they have three meals a day, clean sheets to sleep between and access to a television. *Supra* at 1005. His response, of course, was to worsen conditions in prisons. However, isn't it something of an embarrassment when citizens are lacking in basic necessities such as three meals a day or a clean place to sleep? This seems to be a direct example of "governing through crime" as discussed *supra* at 1001. Instead of working to ameliorate conditions outside of prison, Governor Hilbert works directly to degrade conditions inside of prison.

4. *Additional reading.* For additional information on the effects of imprisonment on families, see Dorothy E. Roberts, *Criminal Justice and Black Families: The Collateral Damage of Over–Enforcement*, 34 U.C. Davis L. Rev. 1005 (2001). For perspectives on the intersection of race and criminal law enforcement, see generally Randolph Stone, *Mass Incarceration: Perspectives on U.S. Imprisonment: Race and Imprisonment*, 7 U. Chi. L. Sch. Roundtable 127 (2000); William Moffitt, *Race and the Criminal Justice System*, 36 Gonz. L. Rev. 305 (2000).

CHAPTER 13

CORRECTIVE STRUGGLES

"Let me give you a word of the philosophy of reform. The whole history of the progress of human liberty shows that all concessions yet made to her august claims, have been born of earnest struggle. ... If there is no struggle there is no progress. Those who profess to favor freedom and yet depreciate agitation, are men who want crops without plowing up the ground, they want rain without thunder and lightening. They want the ocean without the awful roar of its many waters.

This struggle may be a moral one, or it may be a physical one, and it may be both moral and physical, but it must be a struggle. Power concedes nothing without a demand. It never did and it never will."[1]

Frederick Douglass, Canandaigua, New York,
August 3, 1857.

Introduction

This final chapter presents, perhaps, the greatest challenge within our exploration of the meaning and dimensions of economic justice. We have framed this chapter with a set of premises that we now make explicit. First, this is not a chapter of "solutions." In order for there to be a solution, there must be a stable definition of the problem. Our experience is that race and identity subordination are dynamic, changing even as new efforts to redistribute power, realign economic resources, and eliminate inequality are proposed. In this chapter, we survey the landscape of corrective struggles in order to challenge identity-based economic inequality. We have undertaken this task, with modesty born of the recognition, that as Frederick Douglass said about the end of slavery, "power concedes nothing without a demand." We recognize that the ideas and legal remedies discussed here will be no more than hollow rhetoric without a strong connection to the lives of individual people who must resist the daily indignities of economic inequality and material deprivation. Second, as scholars, we are not committed to a fixed set of remedies. Our commitment is to the process of creative resistance to the economic inequalities that we have surveyed in elaborate detail in the preceding twelve chapters. Finally, we expect that, in keeping with our view of the dynamic nature of subordinating strategies, new theories will enter the debate about correc-

---

1. Frederick Douglass, The Significance of Emancipation in the West Indies, Address delivered in Canandaigua, New York (Aug. 3, 1857), *in* 3 THE FREDERICK DOUGLASS PAPERS 204 (John W. Blassingame ed., 1985).

tive justice, even as we go to press. We look forward to bringing the most promising ideas to future editions of this book.

We begin the chapter with two cases that represent significant milestones in the development of the Supreme Court jurisprudence on the constitutionality of minority set-asides in government contracting programs These programs represent explicit economic redistribution. *Croson*, the Richmond case, presents a fascinating opportunity to see the dynamic that ensues when a subordinated group captures a majority in a local legislature. *Metro Broadcasting* has been included, nothwithstanding the fact that it has been overruled by *Adarand Constructor v. Pena*, 515 U.S. 200 (1995). In *Metro Broadcasting*, the court adopted the distinction between benign racial classifications intended to assist members of subordinated groups and invidious discrimination that preserves age-old racial stigmas and subordination. Although this view was later repudiated, it is a valuable artifact of the evolution of Supreme Court jurisprudence addressing race-conscious remedies.

Educational opportunity, as we have seen from the beginning to the end of this book, is one of the most important access points to economic mobility. As we have discussed in earlier chapters, educational attainment is also the single biggest predictor of lifetime earnings. The Constitution, however, does not treat primary or secondary education as a fundamental interest, nor is wealth a suspect classification. These two holdings of the *Rodriguez* school financing case of the 1970s, chapter 6, at 435, have served to shatter the first rung on the ladder of equal educational access. The absence of well-financed, high quality public education at the primary and secondary level has meant that colleges and universities must select from a pool of applicants that bear all the marks of wealth- and race-based inequality. As Justices Ginsburg and Breyer observe in *Grutter v. Bollinger*, 539 U.S. 306 (2003) (Ginsberg, J. Concurring): "[a]s to public education, data for the years 2000–2001 show that 71.6% of African-American children and 76.3% of Hispanic children attended a school in which minorities made up a majority of the student body.... [I]t remains the current reality that many minority students encounter markedly inadequate and unequal educational opportunities." Grutter, 539 U.S. at 345–46. It is unsurprising, therefore, that we have the much-discussed test score and grade gap between applicants of color and poor white students on one hand, and the wealthy students who, on the other hand, are able to earn high test scores and strong grades through parental support and resources.

Decreasing economic mobility in recent years has meant that, as conservative editorial writer David Brooks notes, we have a "sticky ladder" in which parental wealth is the greatest predictor of future class status for any child born in America today. Brooks argues, with substantial research support, that we have an "inherited meritocracy." Poor whites and students from racially subordinated communities must overcome formidable financial and educational challenges to secure a college education. Thomas Shapiro documents the consequences of the wealth gap and the attitudes of meritocratic entitlement that underlie the structures of economic privilege for families at the top of the economic ladder.

The Supreme Court opinions in *Grutter* give us a fascinating view of all the major arguments that are made in the debate about race-conscious affirmative action admissions policies in higher education. Justice O'Connor's opinion in *Grutter* sets an ominous time limit of twenty-five years for constitutional approval of race-conscious admissions programs. Lani Guinier offers a deep analysis of the political dimensions of admissions policies and suggests a forward-looking alternative for making admissions decisions.

As we have seen in previous chapters, another important element of the American class system is marriage. In this country, we rely on heterosexual marriage to finance the bulk of family dependency needs, from child care to elder care to care of the sick and dying. As we have seen, the place of marriage in the economic order established in the 1950s asked wives to stay out of wage work in order to provide this dependent care, while husbands would receive a "family wage." Marriage also served as a legal access point for benefits such as private health insurance and social insurance. In recent decades, however, marriage as a system for providing dependent care has steadily broken down. As the industrial economy shifted to a service economy, the family wage disappeared, and the resulting economic pressures have forced more and more wives into wage work in order to keep families afloat. Meanwhile, social changes have led to higher divorce rates, a steadily rising age of first marriage, and increasing numbers of never-married people and single mothers. This chapter examines three groups of people caught in the crossfire of these changes: stay-at-home wives, working mothers, and same-sex couples. The human capital theory offers a useful conceptual intervention in the age-old story of individual ownership of degrees earned with spousal support during the term of a marriage. Treating discrimination against mothers as sex discrimination uses litigation as a tool for restructuring the workplace. Finally, we explore the question of same-sex marriage as an interplay of symbolic issues—religious values versus secular egalitarian values—with material issues, including the continuing viability of marriage as the major conduit for dependency care.

Finally, as we have in earlier chapters, we look at the international dimensions of economic inequality. We consider the role of cultural property, and the international development questions that arise from global poverty and economic inequality.

A.   Affirmative Action

City of Richmond v. J.A. Croson Co.
Supreme Court of the United States, 488 U.S. 469, 109 S.Ct. 706 (1989).

■ Justice O'Connor announced the judgment of the Court and delivered the opinion of the Court with respect to Parts I, III–B, and IV, and opinion with respect to Part II, in which the CHIEF JUSTICE and JUSTICE WHITE join, and an opinion with respect to Parts III–A and V, in which the CHIEF JUSTICE, JUSTICE WHITE, and JUSTICE KENNEDY join.

In this case, we confront once again the tension between the Fourteenth Amendment's guarantee of equal treatment to all citizens, and the use of race-based measures to ameliorate the effects of past discrimination on the opportunities enjoyed by members of minority groups in our society. In *Fullilove v. Klutznick, 448 U.S. 448 (1980)*, we held that a congressional program requiring that 10% of certain federal construction grants be awarded to minority contractors did not violate the equal protection principles embodied in the Due Process Clause of the Fifth Amendment. Relying largely on our decision in *Fullilove*, some lower federal courts have applied a similar standard of review in assessing the constitutionality of state and local minority set-aside provisions under the Equal Protection Clause of the Fourteenth Amendment. * * *

I

On April 11, 1983, the Richmond City Council adopted the Minority Business Utilization Plan (the Plan). The Plan required prime contractors to whom the city awarded construction contracts to subcontract at least 30% of the dollar amount of the contract to one or more Minority Business Enterprises (MBE's). Ordinance No. 83–69–59, codified in Richmond, Va., City Code, § 12–156(a) (1985). The 30% set-aside did not apply to city contracts awarded to minority-owned prime contractors. * * *

The Plan defined an MBE as "[a] business at least fifty-one (51) percent of which is owned and controlled . . . by minority group members." * * * "Minority group members" were defined as "[c]itizens of the United States who are Blacks, Spanish-speaking, Orientals, Indians, Eskimos, or Aleuts." * * * There was no geographic limit to the Plan; an otherwise qualified MBE from anywhere in the United States could avail itself of the 30% set-aside. The Plan declared that it was "remedial" in nature, and enacted "for the purpose of promoting wider participation by minority business enterprises in the construction of public projects." * * * The Plan expired on June 30, 1988, and was in effect for approximately five years.

* * *

The Plan was adopted by the Richmond City Council after a public hearing. * * * Seven members of the public spoke to the merits of the ordinance: five were in opposition, two in favor. Proponents of the set-aside provision relied on a study which indicated that, while the general population of Richmond was 50% black, only 0.67% of the city's prime construction contracts had been awarded to minority businesses in the 5–year period from 1978 to 1983. It was also established that a variety of contractors' associations, whose representatives appeared in opposition to the ordinance, had virtually no minority businesses within their membership. * * *

There was no direct evidence of race discrimination on the part of the city in letting contracts or any evidence that the city's prime contractors had discriminated against minority-owned subcontractors. [Councilperson Kent said,] "[The public witnesses] indicated that the minority contractors were just not available. There wasn't a one that gave any indication that a minority contractor would not have an opportunity, if he were available."

* * *

[The district court upheld the plan. The court of appeals affirmed, applying the *Fullilove* standard and deferring to congressional findings of past discrimination. The Supreme Court vacated the decision for further consideration in light of its *Wygant* opinion.

The court of appeals struck down the plan on remand, holding that it violated the Equal Protection clause of the Fourteenth Amendment. Applying strict scrutiny according to its reading of *Wygant*, the court of appeals held that Richmond failed to show a compelling government interest for racial preferences because there was no findings of past discrimination by the local government in awarding contracts. Further, the 30% set aside figure was not narrowly tailored as the number was arbitrary. The Supreme Court affirms.]

II

The parties and their supporting *amici* fight an initial battle over the scope of the city's power to adopt legislation designed to address the effects of past discrimination. Relying on our decision in *Wygant*, appellee argues that the city must limit any race-based remedial efforts to eradicating the effects of its own prior discrimination. This is essentially the position taken by the Court of Appeals below. Appellant argues that our decision in *Fullilove* is controlling, and that as a result the city of Richmond enjoys sweeping legislative power to define and attack the effects of prior discrimination in its local construction industry. We find that neither of these two rather stark alternatives can withstand analysis.

* * *

[In *Fullilove v. Klutznick*, 448 U.S. 448 (1980), the Court upheld the Public Works Employment Act of 1977 set aside provision, which required grants to local and state governments to use 10% of the funds on minority business enterprises. MBE's were defined as businesses effectively controlled by "citizens of the United States who are Negroes, Spanish-speaking, Orientals, Indians, Eskimos, and Aleuts."

Chief Justice Burger announced the Court's judgment, which his opinion noted was not based on an traditional standard of scrutiny for equal protection claims. The inquiry instead asked whether congressional objectives were within the scope of Congress' power and whether it was permissible to carry out these objectives with racial and ethnic criteria under the equal protection of the Due Process clause. As Congress was given special remedial powers under § 5 of the Fourteenth Amendment and the legislative history evidenced past national discrimination against minority businesses in awarding federal construction grants, the objectives were permissible. The flexibility of the 10% set aside made the use of racial criteria permissible because waivers could be granted where there were too few MBEs or where an MBE price was unreasonable, even in light of past discrimination.

Justice Powell's concurring opinion noted that requirements for findings of past discrimination might vary based on the types of remedies and the authority of the government entity.]

Appellant and its supporting *amici* rely heavily on *Fullilove* for the proposition that a city council, like Congress, need not make specific findings of discrimination to engage in race-conscious relief. Thus, appellant argues "[i]t would be a perversion of federalism to hold that the federal government has a compelling interest in remedying the effects of racial discrimination in its own public works program, but a city government does not." * * *

What appellant ignores is that Congress, unlike any State or political subdivision, has a specific constitutional mandate to enforce the dictates of the Fourteenth Amendment. The power to "enforce" may at times also include the power to define situations which *Congress* determines threaten principles of equality and to adopt prophylactic rules to deal with those situations. * * *

That Congress may identify and redress the effects of society-wide discrimination does not mean that, *a fortiori*, the States and their political subdivisions are free to decide that such remedies are appropriate. Section 1 of the Fourteenth Amendment is an explicit *constraint* on state power, and the States must undertake any remedial efforts in accordance with that provision. To hold otherwise would be to cede control over the content of the Equal Protection Clause to the 50 state legislatures and their myriad political subdivisions * * *

* * *

It would seem equally clear, however, that a state or local subdivision (if delegated the authority from the State) has the authority to eradicate the effects of private discrimination within its own legislative jurisdiction. This authority must, of course, be exercised within the constraints of § 1 of the Fourteenth Amendment. Our decision in *Wygant* is not to the contrary. *Wygant* addressed the constitutionality of the use of racial quotas by local school authorities pursuant to an agreement reached with the local teachers' union. It was in the context of addressing the school board's power to adopt a race-based layoff program affecting its own work force that the *Wygant* plurality indicated that the Equal Protection Clause required "some showing of prior discrimination by the governmental unit involved." * * *

Thus, if the city could show that it had essentially become a "passive participant" in a system of racial exclusion practiced by elements of the local construction industry, we think it clear that the city could take affirmative steps to dismantle such a system. It is beyond dispute that any public entity, state or federal, has a compelling interest in assuring that public dollars, drawn from the tax contributions of all citizens, do not serve to finance the evil of private prejudice. * * *

III

A

The Equal Protection Clause of the Fourteenth Amendment provides that "[n]o State shall ... deny to *any person* within its jurisdiction the equal protection of the laws." (Emphasis added.) As this Court has noted in the past, the "rights created by the first section of the Fourteenth Amendment are, by its terms, guaranteed to the individual. The rights established are personal rights." *Shelley v. Kraemer*, 334 U.S. 1, 22 (1948). The Richmond Plan denies certain citizens the opportunity to compete for a fixed percentage of public contracts based solely upon their race. To whatever racial group these citizens belong, their "personal rights" to be treated with equal dignity and respect are implicated by a rigid rule erecting race as the sole criterion in an aspect of public decision-making.

Absent searching judicial inquiry into the justification for such race-based measures, there is simply no way of determining what classifications are "benign" or "remedial" and what classifications are in fact motivated by illegitimate notions of racial inferiority or simple racial politics. Indeed, the purpose of strict scrutiny is to "smoke out" illegitimate uses of race by assuring that the legislative body is pursuing a goal important enough to warrant use of a highly suspect tool. The test also ensures that the means chosen "fit" this compelling goal so closely that there is little or no possibility that the motive for the classification was illegitimate racial prejudice or stereotype.

Classifications based on race carry a danger of stigmatic harm. Unless they are strictly reserved for remedial settings, they may in fact promote notions of racial inferiority and lead to a politics of racial hostility. * * * We thus reaffirm the view expressed by the plurality in *Wygant* that the standard of review under the Equal Protection Clause is not dependent on the race of those burdened or benefited by a particular classification. * * *

Our continued adherence to the standard of review employed in *Wygant* does not, as Justice Marshall's dissent suggests, * * * indicate that we view "racial discrimination as largely a phenomenon of the past" or that "government bodies need no longer preoccupy themselves with rectifying racial injustice." * * *

Under the standard proposed by Justice Marshall's dissent, "race-conscious classifications designed to further remedial goals," * * * are forthwith subject to a relaxed standard of review. * * *

Even were we to accept a reading of the guarantee of equal protection under which the level of scrutiny varies according to the ability of different groups to defend their interests in the representative process, heightened scrutiny would still be appropriate in the circumstances of this case. One of the central arguments for applying a less exacting standard to "benign" racial classifications is that such measures essentially involve a choice made by dominant racial groups to disadvantage themselves. If one aspect of the judiciary's role under the Equal Protection Clause is to protect "discrete and insular minorities" from majoritarian prejudice or indifference, * * * some maintain that these concerns are not implicated when the "white majority" places burdens upon itself. * * *

In this case, blacks constitute approximately 50% of the population of the city of Richmond. Five of the nine seats on the city council are held by blacks. The concern that a political majority will more easily act to the disadvantage of a minority based on unwarranted assumptions or incomplete facts would seem to militate for, not against, the application of heightened judicial scrutiny in this case. * * *

[In *University of California Regents v. Bakke*, 438 U.S. 265 (1978), the Court struck down a racial quotas in public university medical school admissions, which were intended to remedy past societal discrimination and minority under-representation in the medical profession. Four members of the Court found that excluding nonminority applicants from a fixed portion of seats violated Title VI of the Civil Rights Act of 1964. Justice Powell's concurrence found the quota system to be unconstitutional using heightened scrutiny under the Equal Protection clause of the Fourteenth Amendment. Under his analysis, racial preferences could only be justified based on findings of past discrimination in violation of statutes or the Constitution.]

In *Wygant*, * * * four Members of the Court applied heightened scrutiny to a race-based system of employee layoffs. Justice Powell, writing for the plurality, again drew the distinction between "societal discrimination" which is an inadequate basis for race-conscious classifications, and the type of identified discrimination that can support and define the scope of race-based relief. [A] plurality of four Justices reiterating the view expressed by Justice Powell in *Bakke* that "[s]ocietal discrimination, without more, is too amorphous a basis for imposing a racially classified remedy."

* * *

B

We think it clear that the factual predicate offered in support of the Richmond Plan suffers from the same two defects identified as fatal in *Wygant*. The District Court found the city council's "findings sufficient to ensure that, in adopting the Plan, it was remedying the present effects of past discrimination in the *construction industry*." * * * Like the "role model" theory employed in *Wygant*, a generalized assertion that there has been past discrimination in an entire industry provides no guidance for a legislative body to determine the precise scope of the injury it seeks to remedy. It "has no logical stopping point." * * * "Relief" for such an ill-defined wrong could extend until the percentage of public contracts awarded to MBE's in Richmond mirrored the percentage of minorities in the population as a whole.

* * *

While there is no doubt that the sorry history of both private and public discrimination in this country has contributed to a lack of opportunities for black entrepreneurs, this observation, standing alone, cannot justify a rigid racial quota in the awarding of public contracts in Richmond, Virginia. Like the claim that discrimination in primary and secondary schooling justifies a rigid racial preference in medical school admissions, an amorphous claim that there has been past discrimination in a particular industry cannot justify the use of an unyielding racial quota.

It is sheer speculation how many minority firms there would be in Richmond absent past societal discrimination, just as it was sheer speculation how many minority medical students would have been admitted to the medical school at Davis absent past discrimination in educational opportunities. Defining these sorts of injuries as "identified discrimination" would give local governments license to create a patchwork of racial preferences based on statistical generalizations about any particular field of endeavor.

These defects are readily apparent in this case. The 30% quota cannot in any realistic sense be tied to any injury suffered by anyone. The District Court relied upon five predicate "facts" in reaching its conclusion that there was an adequate basis for the 30% quota: (1) the ordinance declares itself to be remedial; (2) several proponents of the measure stated their views that there had been past discrimination in the construction industry; (3) minority businesses received 0.67% of prime contracts from the city while minorities constituted 50% of the city's population; (4) there were very few minority contractors in local and state contractors' associations; and (5) in 1977, Congress made a determination that the effects of past discrimination had stifled minority participation in the construction industry nationally. * * *

None of these "findings," singly or together, provide the city of Richmond with a "strong basis in evidence for its conclusion that remedial action was necessary." * * * There is nothing approaching a prima facie case of a constitutional or statutory violation by *anyone* in the Richmond construction industry. * * *

The District Court accorded great weight to the fact that the city council designated the Plan as "remedial." But the mere recitation of a "benign" or legitimate purpose for a racial classification is entitled to little or no weight. * * * Racial classifications are suspect, and that means that simple legislative assurances of good intention cannot suffice.

The District Court also relied on the highly conclusionary statement of a proponent of the Plan that there was racial discrimination in the construction industry "in this area, and the State, and around the nation." * * *

Reliance on the disparity between the number of prime contracts awarded to minority firms and the minority population of the city of Richmond is similarly misplaced. There is no doubt that "[w]here gross statistical disparities can be shown, they alone in a proper case may constitute prima facie proof of a pattern or practice of discrimination" under Title VII. *Hazelwood School Dist. v. United States*. * * * But it is equally clear that "[w]hen special qualifications are required to fill particular jobs, comparisons to the general population (rather than to the smaller group of individuals who possess the necessary qualifications) may have little probative value." * * *

In the employment context, we have recognized that for certain entry level positions or positions requiring minimal training, statistical comparisons of the racial composition of an employer's work force to the racial composition of the relevant population may be probative of a pattern of discrimination. * * * But where special qualifications are necessary, the relevant statistical pool for purposes of demonstrating discriminatory exclusion must be the number of minorities qualified to undertake the particular task. * * *

In this case, the city does not even know how many MBE's in the relevant market are qualified to undertake prime or subcontracting work in public construction projects. * * * Nor does the city know what percentage of total city construction dollars minority firms now receive as subcontractors on prime contracts let by the city.

To a large extent, the set-aside of subcontracting dollars seems to rest on the unsupported assumption that white prime contractors simply will not hire minority firms. * * * Indeed, there is evidence in this record that overall minority participation in city contracts in Richmond is 7 to 8%, and that minority contractor participation in Community Block Development Grant *construction* projects is 17 to 22%. * * * Without any information on minority participation in subcontracting, it is quite simply impossible to evaluate overall minority representation in the city's construction expenditures.

The city and the District Court also relied on evidence that MBE membership in local contractors' associations was extremely low. Again, standing alone this evidence is not probative of any discrimination in the local construction industry.

* * *

Finally, the city and the District Court relied on Congress' finding in connection with the set-aside approved in *Fullilove* that there had been nationwide discrimination in the construction industry. The probative value of these findings for demonstrating the existence of discrimination in Richmond is extremely limited. By its inclusion of a waiver procedure in the national program addressed in *Fullilove*, Congress explicitly recognized that the scope of the problem would vary from market area to market area. * * *

Moreover, as noted above, Congress was exercising its powers under § 5 of the Fourteenth Amendment in making a finding that past discrimination would cause federal funds to be distributed in a manner which reinforced prior patterns of discrimination. While the States and their subdivisions may take remedial action when they possess evidence that their own spending practices are exacerbating a pattern of prior discrimina-

tion, they must identify that discrimination, public or private, with some specificity before they may use race-conscious relief. Congress has made national findings that there has been societal discrimination in a host of fields. If all a state or local government need do is find a congressional report on the subject to enact a set-aside program, the constraints of the Equal Protection Clause will, in effect, have been rendered a nullity. * * *
        * * *

In sum, none of the evidence presented by the city points to any identified discrimination in the Richmond construction industry. We, therefore, hold that the city has failed to demonstrate a compelling interest in apportioning public contracting opportunities on the basis of race. To accept Richmond's claim that past societal discrimination alone can serve as the basis for rigid racial preferences would be to open the door to competing claims for "remedial relief" for every disadvantaged group. The dream of a Nation of equal citizens in a society where race is irrelevant to personal opportunity and achievement would be lost in a mosaic of shifting preferences based on inherently unmeasurable claims of past wrongs. "Courts would be asked to evaluate the extent of the prejudice and consequent harm suffered by various minority groups. Those whose societal injury is thought to exceed some arbitrary level of tolerability then would be entitled to preferential classifications...." [*Bakke* (Powell, J.)] We think such a result would be contrary to both the letter and spirit of a constitutional provision whose central command is equality.

The foregoing analysis applies only to the inclusion of blacks within the Richmond set-aside program. There is *absolutely no evidence* of past discrimination against Spanish-speaking, Oriental, Indian, Eskimo, or Aleut persons in any aspect of the Richmond construction industry. The District Court took judicial notice of the fact that the vast majority of "minority" persons in Richmond were black. * * * It may well be that Richmond has never had an Aleut or Eskimo citizen. The random inclusion of racial groups that, as a practical matter, may never have suffered from discrimination in the construction industry in Richmond suggests that perhaps the city's purpose was not in fact to remedy past discrimination.

If a 30% set-aside was "narrowly tailored" to compensate black contractors for past discrimination, one may legitimately ask why they are forced to share this "remedial relief" with an Aleut citizen who moves to Richmond tomorrow? The gross overinclusiveness of Richmond's racial preference strongly impugns the city's claim of remedial motivation. * * *

IV

As noted by the court below, it is almost impossible to assess whether the Richmond Plan is narrowly tailored to remedy prior discrimination since it is not linked to identified discrimination in any way. We limit ourselves to two observations in this regard.

First, there does not appear to have been any consideration of the use of race-neutral means to increase minority business participation in city contracting. * * * Many of the barriers to minority participation in the construction industry relied upon by the city to justify a racial classification appear to be race neutral. * * *

Second, the 30% quota cannot be said to be narrowly tailored to any goal, except perhaps outright racial balancing. It rests upon the "completely unrealistic" assumption that minorities will choose a particular trade in lockstep proportion to their representation in the local population. * * *

Unlike the program upheld in *Fullilove*, the Richmond Plan's waiver system focuses solely on the availability of MBE's; there is no inquiry into whether or not the particular MBE seeking a racial preference has suffered from the effects of past discrimination by the city or prime contractors.

Given the existence of an individualized procedure, the city's only interest in maintaining a quota system rather than investigating the need for remedial action in particular cases would seem to be simple administrative convenience. But the interest in avoiding the bureaucratic effort necessary to tailor remedial relief to those who truly have suffered the effects of prior discrimination cannot justify a rigid line drawn on the basis of a suspect classification. * * * Under Richmond's scheme, a successful black, Hispanic, or Oriental entrepreneur from anywhere in the country enjoys an absolute preference over other citizens based solely on their race. We think it obvious that such a program is not narrowly tailored to remedy the effects of prior discrimination.

V

Nothing we say today precludes a state or local entity from taking action to rectify the effects of identified discrimination within its jurisdiction. If the city of Richmond had evidence before it that nonminority contractors were systematically excluding minority businesses from subcontracting opportunities, it could take action to end the discriminatory exclusion. Where there is a significant statistical disparity between the number of qualified minority contractors willing and able to perform a particular service and the number of such contractors actually engaged by the locality or the locality's prime contractors, an inference of discriminatory exclusion could arise. * * * Under such circumstances, the city could act to dismantle the closed business system by taking appropriate measures against those who discriminate on the basis of race or other illegitimate criteria. * * * In the extreme case, some form of narrowly tailored racial preference might be necessary to break down patterns of deliberate exclusion.

Nor is local government powerless to deal with individual instances of racially motivated refusals to employ minority contractors. Where such discrimination occurs, a city would be justified in penalizing the discriminator and providing appropriate relief to the victim of such discrimination. * * * Moreover, evidence of a pattern of individual discriminatory acts can, if supported by appropriate statistical proof, lend support to a local government's determination that broader remedial relief is justified. * * *

Even in the absence of evidence of discrimination, the city has at its disposal a whole array of race-neutral devices to increase the accessibility of city contracting opportunities to small entrepreneurs of all races. Simplification of bidding procedures, relaxation of bonding requirements, and training and financial aid for disadvantaged entrepreneurs of all races would open the public contracting market to all those who have suffered the effects of past societal discrimination or neglect. Many of the formal barriers to new entrants may be the product of bureaucratic inertia more than actual necessity, and may have a disproportionate effect on the opportunities open to new minority firms.

* * *

Proper findings in this regard are necessary to define both the scope of the injury and the extent of the remedy necessary to cure its effects. Such findings also serve to assure all citizens that the deviation from the norm of equal treatment of all racial and ethnic groups is a temporary matter, a measure taken in the service of the goal of equality itself. Absent such findings, there is a danger that a racial classification is merely the product of unthinking stereotypes or a form of racial politics. * * * Because the city of Richmond has failed to identify the need for remedial action in the awarding of its public construction contracts, its treatment of its citizens on a racial basis violates the dictates of the Equal Protection Clause. Accordingly, the judgment of the Court of Appeals for the Fourth Circuit is

Affirmed.

■ Justice Stevens, concurring in part and concurring in the judgment.

A central purpose of the Fourteenth Amendment is to further the national goal of equal opportunity for all our citizens. In order to achieve that goal we must learn from our past mistakes, but I believe the Constitution requires us to evaluate our policy decisions—including those that govern the relationships among different racial and ethnic groups—primarily by studying their probable impact on the future. I therefore do not agree with the premise that seems to underlie today's decision, as well as the decision in *Wygant,* * * * that a governmental decision that rests on a racial classification is never permissible except as a remedy for a past wrong.[1] * * * I do, however, agree with the Court's explanation of why the

---

1. In my view the Court's approach to this case gives unwarranted deference to race-based legislative action that purports to serve a purely remedial goal, and overlooks the potential value of race-based determinations that may serve other valid purposes. With regard to the former point—as I explained at some length in *Fullilove* (dissenting opinion)—I am not prepared to assume that even a more narrowly tailored set-aside program supported by stronger findings would be constitutionally justified. Unless the legislature can identify both the particular victims and the particular perpetrators of past discrimination, which is precisely what a court does when it makes findings of fact and conclusions of law, a *remedial* justification for race-based legislation will almost certainly sweep too broadly. With regard to the latter point: I think it unfortunate that the Court in neither *Wygant* nor this case seems prepared to acknowledge that some race-based policy decisions may serve a legitimate public purpose. I agree, of course, that race is so seldom relevant to legislative decisions on how best to foster the public good that legitimate justifications for race-based legislation

Richmond ordinance cannot be justified as a remedy for past discrimination, and therefore join Parts I, III–B, and IV of its opinion. I write separately to emphasize three aspects of the case that are of special importance to me.

First, the city makes no claim that the public interest in the efficient performance of its construction contracts will be served by granting a preference to minority-business enterprises. * * *

Second, this litigation involves an attempt by a legislative body, rather than a court, to fashion a remedy for a past wrong. Legislatures are primarily policymaking bodies that promulgate rules to govern future conduct. The constitutional prohibitions against the enactment of *ex post facto* laws and bills of attainder reflect a valid concern about the use of the political process to punish or characterize past conduct of private citizens. It is the judicial system, rather than the legislative process, that is best equipped to identify past wrongdoers and to fashion remedies that will create the conditions that presumably would have existed had no wrong been committed. * * *

Third, instead of engaging in a debate over the proper standard of review to apply in affirmative-action litigation, I believe it is more constructive to try to identify the characteristics of the advantaged and disadvantaged classes that may justify their disparate treatment. * * * In this case that approach convinces me that, instead of carefully identifying the characteristics of the two classes of contractors that are respectively favored and disfavored by its ordinance, the Richmond City Council has merely engaged in the type of stereotypical analysis that is a hallmark of violations of the Equal Protection Clause. Whether we look at the class of persons benefited by the ordinance or at the disadvantaged class, the same conclusion emerges.

[Justice Kennedy's opinion concurring in part and concurring in the judgment has been omitted].

■ JUSTICE SCALIA, concurring in the judgment.

I agree with much of the Court's opinion, and, in particular, with JUSTICE O'CONNOR's conclusion that strict scrutiny must be applied to all governmental classification by race, whether or not its asserted purpose is "remedial" or "benign." * * * I do not agree, however, with JUSTICE O'CONNOR's dictum suggesting that, despite the Fourteenth Amendment, state and local governments may in some circumstances discriminate on the basis of race in order (in a broad sense) "to ameliorate the effects of past discrimination." * * * The benign purpose of compensating for social disadvantages, whether they have been acquired by reason of prior discrimination or otherwise, can no more be pursued by the illegitimate means of racial discrimination than can other assertedly benign purposes we have repeatedly rejected. * * * The difficulty of overcoming the effects of past

---

will usually not be available. But unlike the Court, I would not totally discount the legitimacy of race-based decisions that may produce tangible and fully justified future benefits.

discrimination is as nothing compared with the difficulty of eradicating from our society the source of those effects, which is the tendency—fatal to a Nation such as ours—to classify and judge men and women on the basis of their country of origin or the color of their skin. A solution to the first problem that aggravates the second is no solution at all.

       * * *

A sound distinction between federal and state (or local) action based on race rests not only upon the substance of the Civil War Amendments, but upon social reality and governmental theory. * * * The struggle for racial justice has historically been a struggle by the national society against oppression in the individual States. * * * And the struggle retains that character in modern times. * * * An acute awareness of the heightened danger of oppression from political factions in small, rather than large, political units dates to the very beginning of our national history. * * *

In my view there is only one circumstance in which the States may act *by race* to "undo the effects of past discrimination": where that is necessary to eliminate their own maintenance of a system of unlawful racial classification. If, for example, a state agency has a discriminatory pay scale compensating black employees in all positions at 20% less than their nonblack counterparts, it may assuredly promulgate an order raising the salaries of "all black employees" to eliminate the differential. * * * This distinction explains our school desegregation cases, in which we have made plain that States and localities sometimes have an obligation to adopt race-conscious remedies. * * *

I agree with the Court's dictum that a fundamental distinction must be drawn between the effects of "societal" discrimination and the effects of "identified" discrimination, and that the situation would be different if Richmond's plan were "tailored" to identify those particular bidders who "suffered from the effects of past discrimination by the city or prime contractors." * * * In my view, however, the reason that would make a difference is not, as the Court states, that it would justify race-conscious action * * * but rather that it would enable race-neutral remediation. * * *

It is plainly true that in our society blacks have suffered discrimination immeasurably greater than any directed at other racial groups. But those who believe that racial preferences can help to "even the score" display, and reinforce, a manner of thinking by race that was the source of the injustice and that will, if it endures within our society, be the source of more injustice still. The relevant proposition is not that it was blacks, or Jews, or Irish who were discriminated against, but that it was individual men and women, "created equal," who were discriminated against. And the relevant resolve is that that should never happen again. Racial preferences appear to "even the score" (in some small degree) only if one embraces the proposition that our society is appropriately viewed as divided into races, making it right that an injustice rendered in the past to a black man should be compensated for by discriminating against a white. Nothing is worth that embrace. * * *

Since I believe that the appellee here had a constitutional right to have its bid succeed or fail under a decisionmaking process uninfected with racial bias, I concur in the judgment of the Court.

■ JUSTICE MARSHALL, with whom JUSTICE BRENNAN and JUSTICE BLACKMUN join, dissenting.

It is a welcome symbol of racial progress when the former capital of the Confederacy acts forthrightly to confront the effects of racial discrimination in its midst. In my view, nothing in the Constitution can be construed to prevent Richmond, Virginia, from allocating a portion of its contracting dollars for businesses owned or controlled by members of minority groups. * * *

A majority of this Court holds today, however, that the Equal Protection Clause of the Fourteenth Amendment blocks Richmond's initiative. The essence of the majority's position is that Richmond has failed to catalog adequate findings to prove that past discrimination has impeded minorities from joining or participating fully in Richmond's construction contracting industry. I find deep irony in second-guessing Richmond's judgment on this point. As much as any municipality in the United States, Richmond knows what racial discrimination is; a century of decisions by this and other federal courts has richly documented the city's disgraceful history of public and private racial discrimination. In any event, the Richmond City Council *has* supported its determination that minorities have been wrongly excluded from local construction contracting. Its proof includes statistics showing that minority-owned businesses have received virtually no city contracting dollars and rarely if ever belonged to area trade associations; testimony by municipal officials that discrimination has been widespread in the local construction industry; and the same exhaustive and widely publicized federal studies relied on in *Fullilove*, studies which showed that pervasive discrimination in the Nation's tight-knit construction industry had operated to exclude minorities from public contracting. These are precisely the types of statistical and testimonial evidence which, until today, this Court had credited in cases approving of race-conscious measures designed to remedy past discrimination.

More fundamentally, today's decision marks a deliberate and giant step backward in this Court's affirmative-action jurisprudence. Cynical of one municipality's attempt to redress the effects of past racial discrimination in a particular industry, the majority launches a grapeshot attack on race-conscious remedies in general. The majority's unnecessary pronouncements will inevitably discourage or prevent governmental entities, particularly States and localities, from acting to rectify the scourge of past discrimination. This is the harsh reality of the majority's decision, but it is not the Constitution's command.

I

As an initial matter, the majority takes an exceedingly myopic view of the factual predicate on which the Richmond City Council relied when it passed the Minority Business Utilization Plan. * * * The majority's refusal to recognize that Richmond has proved itself no exception to the dismaying pattern of national exclusion which Congress so painstakingly identified infects its entire analysis of this case.

* * *

The congressional program upheld in *Fullilove* was based upon an array of congressional and agency studies which documented the powerful influence of racially exclusionary practices in the business world. * * *

[T]here was "abundant evidence" in the public domain "that minority businesses ha[d] been denied effective participation in public contracting opportunities by procurement practices that perpetuated the effects of prior discrimination." [*Fullilove*.] Significantly, this evidence demonstrated that discrimination had prevented existing or nascent minority-owned businesses from obtaining not only federal contracting assignments, but state and local ones as well. * * *

The members of the Richmond City Council were well aware of these exhaustive congressional findings, a point the majority, tellingly, elides. * * *

So long as one views Richmond's local evidence of discrimination against the backdrop of systematic nationwide racial discrimination which Congress had so painstakingly identified in this very industry, this case is readily resolved.

II

* * * My view has long been that race conscious classifications designed to further remedial goals "must serve important governmental objectives and must be substantially related to achievement of those objectives" in order to withstand constitutional scrutiny. * * * Analyzed in terms of this two-pronged standard, Richmond's set-aside, like the federal program on which it was modeled, is "plainly constitutional." [*Fullilove* (MARSHALL, concurring in judgment).]

* * *

A

* * *

1

Turning first to the governmental interest inquiry, Richmond has two powerful interests in setting aside a portion of public contracting funds for minority-owned enterprises. The first is the city's interest in eradicating the effects of past racial discrimination. It is far too late in the day to doubt that remedying such discrimination is a compelling, let alone an important, interest. * * *

Richmond has a second compelling interest in setting aside, where possible, a portion of its contracting dollars. That interest is the prospective one of preventing the city's own spending decisions from reinforcing and perpetuating the exclusionary effects of past discrimination. * * *

The majority pays only lipservice to this additional governmental interest. * * * But our decisions have often emphasized the danger of the government tacitly adopting, encouraging, or furthering racial discrimination even by its own routine operations. * * *

The majority is wrong to trivialize the continuing impact of government acceptance or use of private institutions or structures once wrought by discrimination. When government channels all its contracting funds to a white-dominated community of established contractors whose racial homogeneity is the product of private discrimination, it does more than place its *imprimatur* on the practices which forged and which continue to define that community. It also provides a measurable boost to those economic entities that have thrived within it, while denying important economic benefits to those entities which, but for prior discrimination, might well be better qualified to receive valuable government contracts. In my view, the interest in ensuring that the government does not reflect and reinforce prior private discrimination in dispensing public contracts is every bit as strong as the interest in eliminating private discrimination—an interest which this Court has repeatedly deemed compelling. * * *

2

The remaining question with respect to the "governmental interest" prong of equal protection analysis is whether Richmond has proffered satisfactory proof of past racial discrimination to support its twin interests in remediation and in governmental nonperpetuation. Although the Members of this Court have differed on the appropriate standard of review for race-conscious remedial measures, * * * we have always regarded this factual inquiry as a practical one. Thus, the Court has eschewed rigid tests which require the provision of particular species of evidence, statistical or otherwise. At the same time we have required that government adduce evidence that, taken as a whole, is sufficient to support its claimed interest and to dispel the natural concern that it acted out of mere "paternalistic stereotyping, not on a careful consideration of modern social conditions." [*Fullilove* (MARSHALL, concurring in judgment).]

The varied body of evidence on which Richmond relied provides a "strong," "firm," and "unquestionably legitimate" basis upon which the city council could determine that the effects of past racial discrimination warranted a remedial and prophylactic governmental response. * * *

Richmond's reliance on localized, industry-specific findings is a far cry from the reliance on generalized "societal discrimination" which the majority decries as a basis for remedial action. * * * But characterizing the plight of Richmond's minority contractors as mere "societal discrimination" is not the only respect in which the majority's critique shows an unwillingness to come to grips with why construction-contracting in Richmond is essentially a whites-only enterprise. * * *

[M]ore fundamentally, where the issue is not present discrimination but rather whether *past* discrimination has resulted in the *continuing exclusion* of minorities from a historically tight-knit industry, a contrast between population and work force is entirely appropriate to help gauge the degree of the exclusion. * * * This contrast is especially illuminating in cases like this, where a main avenue of introduction into the work force— here, membership in the trade associations whose members presumably train apprentices and help them procure subcontracting assignments—is itself grossly dominated by nonminorities.* * *

When the legislatures and leaders of cities with histories of pervasive discrimination testify that past discrimination has infected one of their industries, armchair cynicism like that exercised by the majority has no place. * * * Disbelief is particularly inappropriate here in light of the fact that appellee Croson, which had the burden of proving unconstitutionality at trial, * * * has *at no point* come forward with *any* direct evidence that the city council's motives were anything other than sincere.

Finally, I vehemently disagree with the majority's dismissal of the congressional and Executive Branch findings noted in *Fullilove* as having "extremely limited" probative value in this case. * * * The majority concedes that Congress established nothing less than a "presumption" that minority contracting firms have been disadvantaged by prior discrimination. The majority, inexplicably, would forbid Richmond to "share" in this information, and permit only Congress to take note of these ample findings. * * * In thus requiring that Richmond's local evidence be severed from the context in which it was prepared, the majority would require cities seeking to eradicate the effects of past discrimination within their borders to reinvent the evidentiary wheel and engage in unnecessarily duplicative, costly, and time-consuming factfinding.

No principle of federalism or of federal power, however, forbids a state or local government to draw upon a nationally relevant historical record prepared by the Federal Government. * * * Of course, Richmond could have built an even more compendious record of past discrimination, one including additional stark statistics and additional individual accounts of past discrimination. But nothing in the Fourteenth Amendment imposes such onerous documentary obligations upon States and localities once the reality of past discrimination is apparent. * * *

B

In my judgment, Richmond's set-aside plan also comports with the second prong of the equal protection inquiry, for it is substantially related to the interests it seeks to serve in remedying past discrimination and in ensuring that municipal contract procurement does not perpetuate that discrimination. The most striking aspect of the city's ordinance is the similarity it bears to the "appropriately limited" federal set-aside provision upheld in *Fullilove*. * * *

The majority takes issue, however, with two aspects of Richmond's tailoring: the city's refusal to explore the use of race-neutral measures to increase minority business participation in contracting, and the selection of a 30% set-aside figure. The majority's first criticism is flawed in two respects. First, the majority overlooks the fact that since 1975, Richmond has barred both discrimination by the city in awarding public contracts and discrimination by public contractors. * * * The virtual absence of minority businesses from the city's contracting rolls, indicated by the fact that such businesses have received less than 1% of public contracting dollars, strongly suggests that this ban has not succeeded in redressing the impact of past discrimination or in preventing city contract procurement from reinforcing racial homogeneity. Second, the majority's suggestion that Richmond should have first undertaken such race-neutral measures as a program of city financing for small firms, * * * ignores the fact that such measures, while theoretically appealing, have been discredited by Congress as ineffectual in eradicating the effects of past discrimination in this very industry. * * *

As for Richmond's 30% target, the majority states that this figure "cannot be said to be narrowly tailored to any goal, except perhaps outright racial balancing." * * * The majority ignores two important facts. First, the set-aside measure affects only 3% of overall city contracting; thus, any imprecision in tailoring has far less impact than the majority suggests. But more important, the majority ignores the fact that Richmond's 30% figure was patterned directly on the *Fullilove* precedent. Congress' 10% figure fell "roughly halfway between the present percentage of minority contractors and the percentage of minority group members in the Nation." [*Fullilove* (Powell, concurring).] The Richmond City Council's 30% figure similarly falls roughly halfway between the present percentage of Richmond-based minority contractors (almost zero) and the percentage of minorities in Richmond (50%). In faulting Richmond for not presenting a different explanation for its choice of a set-aside figure, the majority honors *Fullilove* only in the breach.

III

* * *

Today, for the first time, a majority of this Court has adopted strict scrutiny as its standard of Equal Protection Clause review of race-conscious remedial measures. * * * This is an unwelcome development. A profound difference separates governmental actions that themselves are racist, and governmental actions that seek to remedy the effects of prior racism or to prevent neutral governmental activity from perpetuating the effects of such racism. * * *

Racial classifications "drawn on the presumption that one race is inferior to another or because they put the weight of government behind racial hatred and separatism" warrant the strictest judicial scrutiny because of the very irrelevance of these rationales. * * * By contrast, racial classifications drawn for the purpose of remedying the effects of discrimination that itself was race based have a highly pertinent basis: the tragic and indelible fact that discrimination against blacks and other racial minorities in this Nation has pervaded our Nation's history and continues to scar our society. * * *

In concluding that remedial classifications warrant no different standard of review under the Constitution than the most brutal and repugnant forms of state-sponsored racism, a majority of this Court signals that it regards racial discrimination as largely a phenomenon of the past, and that government bodies need no longer preoccupy themselves with rectifying racial injustice. I, however, do not believe this Nation is anywhere close to eradicating racial discrimination or its vestiges. In constitutionalizing its wishful thinking, the majority today does a grave disservice not only to those victims of past and present racial discrimination in this Nation whom government has sought to assist, but also to this Court's long tradition of approaching issues of race with the utmost sensitivity.

* * *

Today's decision, finally, is particularly noteworthy for the daunting standard it imposes upon States and localities contemplating the use of race-conscious measures to eradicate the present effects of prior discrimination and prevent its perpetuation. The majority restricts the use of such measures to situations in which a State or locality can put forth "a prima facie case of a constitutional or statutory violation." * * * In so doing, the majority calls into question the validity of the business set-asides which dozens of municipalities across this Nation have adopted on the authority of *Fullilove*.

* * *

To the degree that this parsimonious standard is grounded on a view that either § 1 or § 5 of the Fourteenth Amendment substantially disempowered States and localities from remedying past racial discrimination, * * * the majority is seriously mistaken. * * *

* * *

IV

The majority today sounds a full-scale retreat from the Court's long-standing solicitude to race-conscious remedial efforts "directed toward deliverance of the century-old promise of equality of economic opportunity." [*Fullilove*.] The new and restrictive tests it applies scuttle one city's effort to surmount its discriminatory past, and imperil those of dozens more localities. I, however, profoundly disagree with the cramped vision of the Equal Protection Clause which the majority offers today and with its application of that vision to Richmond, Virginia's, laudable set-aside plan. The battle against pernicious racial discrimination or its effects is nowhere near won. I must dissent.

■ JUSTICE BLACKMUN, with whom JUSTICE BRENNAN joins, dissenting.

* * *

Richmond, to its great credit, acted. Yet this Court, the supposed bastion of equality, strikes down Richmond's efforts as though discrimination had never existed or was not demonstrated in this particular litigation. * * *

So the Court today regresses. I am confident, however, that, given time, it one day again will do its best to fulfill the great promises of the Constitution's Preamble and of the guarantees embodied in the Bill of Rights—a fulfillment that would make this Nation very special.

————

Metro Broadcasting, Inc. v. F.C.C.

Supreme Court of the United States, 497 U.S. 547, 110 S.Ct. 2997 (1990).

■ JUSTICE BRENNAN delivered the opinion of the Court.

The issue in these cases, consolidated for decision today, is whether certain minority preference policies of the Federal Communications Commission violate the equal protection component of the Fifth Amendment. The policies in question are (1) a program awarding an enhancement for minority ownership in comparative proceedings for new licenses, and (2) the minority "distress sale" program, which permits a limited category of existing radio and television broadcast stations to be transferred only to minority-controlled firms. We hold that these policies do not violate equal protection principles.

I

A

The policies before us today can best be understood by reference to the history of federal efforts to promote minority participation in the broadcasting industry.* * *

Building on the results of the conference [on minority ownership policies], the recommendations of the task force [to encourage minority participation in broadcasting], the decision [in *TV 9, Inc. v. FCC,* 161 U.S. App. D. C. 349, 938 (1973) that a reasonable expectation of superior community service was sufficient to justify a preference for African American broadcasters], and a petition proposing several minority ownership policies, the FCC adopted in May 1978 its *Statement of Policy on Minority Ownership of Broadcasting Facilities.* After recounting its past efforts to expand broadcast diversity, the FCC concluded:

> [W]e are compelled to observe that the views of racial minorities continue to be inadequately represented in the broadcast media. This situation is detrimental not only to the minority audience but to all of the viewing and listening public. Adequate representation of minority viewpoints in programming serves not only the needs and interests of the minority community but also enriches and educates the non-minority audience. It enhances the diversified programming which is a key objective not only of the Communications Act of 1934 but also of the First Amendment. * * *

Describing its actions as only "first steps," * * * the FCC outlined two elements of a minority ownership policy.

First, the Commission pledged to consider minority ownership as one factor in comparative proceedings for new licenses. * * *

Second, the FCC outlined a plan to increase minority opportunities to receive reassigned and transferred licenses through the so-called "distress sale" policy. * * * As a general rule, a licensee whose qualifications to hold a broadcast license come into question may not assign or transfer that license until the FCC has resolved its doubts in a noncomparative hearing. The distress sale policy is an exception to that practice, allowing a broadcaster whose license has been designated for a revocation hearing, or whose renewal application has been designated for hearing, to assign the license to an FCC-approved minority enterprise.* * *

II

It is of overriding significance in these cases that the FCC's minority ownership programs have been specifically approved—indeed, mandated— by Congress. In *Fullilove v. Klutznick*, 448 U.S. 448 (1980), Chief Justice Burger [gave deference to agency actions making racial preferences based on congressional instructions].

* * *

Our decision last Term in *Richmond v. J. A. Croson Co.*, 488 U.S. 469 (1989), concerning a minority set-aside program adopted by a municipality, does not prescribe the level of scrutiny to be applied to a benign racial classification employed by Congress. As Justice Kennedy noted, the question of congressional action was not before the Court, * * * and so *Croson* cannot be read to undermine our decision in *Fullilove*. In fact, much of the language and reasoning in *Croson* reaffirmed the lesson of *Fullilove* that race-conscious classifications adopted by Congress to address racial and ethnic discrimination are subject to a different standard than such classifications prescribed by state and local governments. * * *

We hold that the FCC minority ownership policies pass muster under the test we announce today. First, we find that they serve the important governmental objective of broadcast diversity. Second, we conclude that they are substantially related to the achievement of that objective.

A

Congress found that "the effects of past inequities stemming from racial and ethnic discrimination have resulted in a severe under-representation of minorities in the media of mass communications." [H. R. Conf. Rep. No. 97–765.] Congress and the Commission do not justify the minority ownership policies strictly as remedies for victims of this discrimination, however. Rather, Congress and the FCC have selected the minority ownership policies primarily to promote programming diversity, and they urge that such diversity is an important governmental objective that can serve as a constitutional basis for the preference policies. We agree.

* * *

[T]he interest in enhancing broadcast diversity is, at the very least, an important governmental objective and is therefore a sufficient basis for the Commission's minority ownership policies. Just as a "diverse student body" contributing to a "robust exchange of ideas" is a "constitutionally permissible goal" on which a race-conscious university admissions program may be predicated, [*Bakke* (opinion of Powell, J.),] the diversity of views and information on the airwaves serves important First Amendment values. * * * The benefits of such diversity are not limited to the members of minority groups who gain access to the broadcasting industry by virtue of the ownership policies; rather, the benefits redound to all members of the viewing and listening audience. As Congress found, "the American public will benefit by having access to a wider diversity of information sources." * * *

We also find that the minority ownership policies are substantially related to the achievement of the Government's interest. One component of this inquiry concerns the relationship between expanded minority ownership and greater broadcast diversity; both the FCC and Congress have determined that such a relationship exists. Although we do not " 'defer' to the judgment of the Congress and the Commission on a constitutional question," and would not "hesitate to invoke the Constitution should we determine that the Commission has not fulfilled its task with appropriate sensitivity" to equal protection principles, *Columbia Broadcasting System, Inc. v. Democratic National Committee*, [412 U.S. 94 (1973),] we must pay close attention to the expertise of the Commission and the factfinding of Congress when analyzing the nexus between minority ownership and programming diversity. With respect to this "complex" empirical question, we are required to give "great weight to the decisions of Congress and the experience of the Commission." * * *

* * *

C

The judgment that there is a link between expanded minority ownership and broadcast diversity does not rest on impermissible stereotyping. Congressional policy does not assume that in every case minority ownership and management will lead to more minority-oriented programming or to the expression of a discrete "minority viewpoint" on the airwaves. Neither does it pretend that all programming that appeals to minority audiences can be labeled "minority programming" or that programming that might be described as "minority" does not appeal to nonminorities. Rather, both Congress and the FCC maintain simply that expanded minority ownership of broadcast outlets will, in the aggregate, result in greater broadcast diversity. A broadcasting industry with representative minority participation will produce more variation and diversity than will one whose ownership is drawn from a single racially and ethnically homogeneous group. The predictive judgment about the overall result of minority entry into broadcasting is not a rigid assumption about how minority owners will behave in every case but rather is akin to Justice Powell's conclusion in *Bakke* that greater admission of minorities would contribute, on average, "to the 'robust exchange of ideas.' "

* * *

D

We find that the minority ownership policies are in other relevant respects substantially related to the goal of promoting broadcast diversity. First, the Commission adopted and Congress endorsed minority ownership preferences only after long study and painstaking consideration of all available alternatives. * * * For many years, the FCC attempted to encourage diversity of programming content without consideration of the race of station owners.

* * *

Moreover, the considered nature of the Commission's judgment in selecting the particular minority ownership policies at issue today is illustrated by the fact that the Commission has rejected other types of minority preferences. For example, the Commission has studied but refused to implement the more expansive alternative of setting aside certain frequencies for minority broadcasters. * * * In addition, in a ruling released the day after it adopted the comparative hearing credit and the distress sale preference, the FCC declined to adopt a plan to require 45–day advance public notice before a station could be sold, which had been advocated on the ground that it would ensure minorities a chance to bid on stations that might otherwise be sold to industry insiders without ever coming on the market. * * * Soon afterward, the Commission rejected other minority ownership proposals advanced by the Office of Telecommunications Policy and the Department of Commerce that sought to revise the FCC's time brokerage, multiple ownership, and other policies.

* * *

The minority ownership policies are "appropriately limited in extent and duration, and subject to reassessment and reevaluation by the Congress prior to any extension or reenactment." [*Fullilove* (opinion of Burger, C. J.).] Although it has underscored emphatically its support for the minority ownership policies, Congress has manifested that support through a series of appropriations Acts of finite duration, thereby ensuring future reevaluations of the need for the minority ownership program as the number of minority broadcasters increases. In addition, Congress has continued to hold hearings on the subject of minority ownership. * * * Furthermore, there is provision for administrative and judicial review of all Commission decisions, which guarantees both that the minority ownership policies are applied correctly in individual cases, and that there will be frequent opportunities to revisit the merits of those policies. Congress and the Commission have adopted a policy of minority ownership not as an end in itself, but rather as a means of achieving greater programming diversity.

Such a goal carries its own natural limit, for there will be no need for further minority preferences once sufficient diversity has been achieved. The FCC's plan, like the Harvard admissions program discussed in *Bakke*, contains the seed of its own termination. * * *

Finally, we do not believe that the minority ownership policies at issue impose impermissible burdens on nonminorities. * * *

In the context of broadcasting licenses, the burden on nonminorities is slight. The FCC's responsibility is to grant licenses in the "public interest, convenience, or necessity," * * * and the limited number of frequencies on the electromagnetic spectrum means that "[n]o one has a First Amendment right to a license." [*Red Lion*] Applicants have no settled expectation that their applications will be granted without consideration of public interest factors such as minority ownership. Award of a preference in a comparative hearing or transfer of a station in a distress sale thus contravenes "no legitimate firmly rooted expectation[s]" of competing applicants. [*Johnson.*]

Respondent Shurberg insists that because the minority distress sale policy operates to exclude nonminority firms completely from consideration in the transfer of certain stations, it is a greater burden than the comparative hearing preference for minorities, which is simply a "plus" factor considered together with other characteristics of the applicants. * * * The distress sale policy is not a quota or fixed quantity set-aside. Indeed, the nonminority firm exercises control over whether a distress sale will ever occur at all, because the policy operates only where the qualifications of an existing licensee to continue broadcasting have been designated for hearing and no other applications for the station in question have been filed with the Commission at the time of the designation. * * * Thus, a nonminority can prevent the distress sale procedures from ever being invoked by filing a competing application in a timely manner.

In practice, distress sales have represented a tiny fraction—less than 0.4 percent—of all broadcast sales since 1979. * * *

III

The Commission's minority ownership policies bear the *imprimatur* of longstanding congressional support and direction and are substantially related to the achievement of the important governmental objective of broadcast diversity. The judgment in No. 89–453 is affirmed, the judgment in No. 89–700 is reversed, and the cases are remanded for proceedings consistent with this opinion.

It is so ordered.

[Justice Stevens's concurring opinion has been omitted]

■ JUSTICE O'CONNOR, with whom the CHIEF JUSTICE, JUSTICE SCALIA, and JUSTICE KENNEDY join, dissenting.

At the heart of the Constitution's guarantee of equal protection lies the simple command that the Government must treat citizens "as *individuals*,

not 'as simply components of a racial, religious, sexual or national class.' "
Arizona Governing Comm. for Tax Deferred Annuity and Deferred Compensation Plans v. Norris, 463 U.S. 1073, 1083 (1983). Social scientists may debate how peoples' thoughts and behavior reflect their background, but the Constitution provides that the Government may not allocate benefits and burdens among individuals based on the assumption that race or ethnicity determines how they act or think. To uphold the challenged programs, the Court departs from these fundamental principles and from our traditional requirement that racial classifications are permissible only if necessary and narrowly tailored to achieve a compelling interest. This departure marks a renewed toleration of racial classifications and a repudiation of our recent affirmation that the Constitution's equal protection guarantees extend equally to all citizens. The Court's application of a lessened equal protection standard to congressional actions finds no support in our cases or in the Constitution. I respectfully dissent.

I

As we recognized [in *J. A. Croson*], the Constitution requires that the Court apply a strict standard of scrutiny to evaluate racial classifications such as those contained in the challenged FCC distress sale and comparative licensing policies. * * * The Court abandons this traditional safeguard against discrimination for a lower standard of review, and in practice applies a standard like that applicable to routine legislation. Yet the Government's different treatment of citizens according to race is no routine concern. This Court's precedents in no way justify the Court's marked departure from our traditional treatment of race classifications and its conclusion that different equal protection principles apply to these federal actions.

In both the challenged policies, the Federal Communications Commission (FCC) provides benefits to some members of our society and denies benefits to others based on race or ethnicity. Except in the narrowest of circumstances, the Constitution bars such racial classifications as a denial to particular individuals, of any race or ethnicity, of "the equal protection of the laws." U.S. Const., Amdt. 14, § 1. * * * The dangers of such classifications are clear. They endorse race-based reasoning and the conception of a Nation divided into racial blocs, thus contributing to an escalation of racial hostility and conflict. * * * Such policies may embody stereotypes that treat individuals as the product of their race, evaluating their thoughts and efforts—their very worth as citizens—according to a criterion barred to the Government by history and the Constitution. * * * Racial classifications, whether providing benefits to or burdening particular racial or ethnic groups, may stigmatize those groups singled out for different treatment and may create considerable tension with the Nation's widely shared commitment to evaluating individuals upon their individual merit. * * *

The Constitution's guarantee of equal protection binds the Federal Government as it does the States, and no lower level of scrutiny applies to the Federal Government's use of race classifications. * * * Consistent with this view, the Court has repeatedly indicated that "the reach of the equal protection guarantee of the Fifth Amendment is coextensive with that of the Fourteenth." [*United States v. Paradise*, 480 U.S. 149 (1987) (plurality opinion).]

Nor does the congressional role in prolonging the FCC's policies justify any lower level of scrutiny. As with all instances of judicial review of federal legislation, the Court does not lightly set aside the considered judgment of a coordinate branch. Nonetheless, the respect due a coordinate branch yields neither less vigilance in defense of equal protection principles nor any corresponding diminution of the standard of review.

* * *

The guarantee of equal protection extends to each citizen, regardless of race: The Federal Government, like the States, may not "deny to any person within its jurisdiction the equal protection of the laws." * * *

The Court's reliance on "benign racial classifications," * * * is particularly troubling. " 'Benign' racial classification" is a contradiction in terms. Governmental distinctions among citizens based on race or ethnicity, even in the rare circumstances permitted by our cases, exact costs and carry with them substantial dangers. To the person denied an opportunity or right based on race, the classification is hardly benign. * * * Untethered to narrowly confined remedial notions, "benign" carries with it no independent meaning, but reflects only acceptance of the current generation's conclusion that a politically acceptable burden, imposed on particular citizens on the basis of race, is reasonable. The Court provides no basis for determining when a racial classification fails to be "benevolent." By expressly distinguishing "benign" from remedial race-conscious measures, the Court leaves the distinct possibility that any racial measure found to be substantially related to an important governmental objective is also, by definition, "benign." * * *

This dispute regarding the appropriate standard of review may strike some as a lawyers' quibble over words, but it is not. The standard of review establishes whether and when the Court and Constitution allow the Government to employ racial classifications. A lower standard signals that the Government may resort to racial distinctions more readily. The Court's departure from our cases is disturbing enough, but more disturbing still is the renewed toleration of racial classifications that its new standard of review embodies.

II

Our history reveals that the most blatant forms of discrimination have been visited upon some members of the racial and ethnic groups identified in the challenged programs. Many have lacked the opportunity to share in the Nation's wealth and to participate in its commercial enterprises. It is undisputed that minority participation in the broadcasting industry falls markedly below the demographic representation of those groups, * * * and this shortfall may be traced in part to the discrimination and the patterns of exclusion that have widely affected our society. As a nation we aspire to create a society untouched by that history of exclusion, and to ensure that equality defines all citizens' daily experience and opportunities as well as the protection afforded to them under law.

* * *

III

Under the appropriate standard, strict scrutiny, only a compelling interest may support the Government's use of racial classifications. Modern equal protection doctrine has recognized only one such interest: remedying the effects of racial discrimination. The interest in increasing the diversity of broadcast viewpoints is clearly not a compelling interest. It is simply too amorphous, too insubstantial, and too unrelated to any legitimate basis for employing racial classifications. The Court does not claim otherwise. Rather, it employs its novel standard and claims that this asserted interest need only be, and is, "important." This conclusion twice compounds the Court's initial error of reducing its level of scrutiny of a racial classification. First, it too casually extends the justifications that might support racial classifications, beyond that of remedying past discrimination. * * * Second, it has initiated this departure by endorsing an insubstantial interest, one that is certainly insufficiently weighty to justify tolerance of the Government's distinctions among citizens based on race and ethnicity. This endorsement trivializes the constitutional command to guard against such discrimination and has loosed a potentially far-reaching principle disturbingly at odds with our traditional equal protection doctrine.

An interest capable of justifying race-conscious measures must be sufficiently specific and verifiable, such that it supports only limited and carefully defined uses of racial classifications. In *Croson*, we held that an interest in remedying societal discrimination cannot be considered compelling. * * * We determined that a "generalized assertion" of past discrimination "has no logical stopping point" and would support unconstrained uses of race classifications. * * *

The asserted interest in these cases suffers from the same defects. * * * Like the vague assertion of societal discrimination, a claim of insufficiently diverse broadcasting viewpoints might be used to justify equally unconstrained racial preferences, linked to nothing other than proportional representation of various races. And the interest would support indefinite use of racial classifications, employed first to obtain the appropriate mixture of racial views and then to ensure that the broadcasting spectrum continues to reflect that mixture. We cannot deem to be constitutionally adequate an interest that would support measures that amount to the core constitutional violation of "outright racial balancing." [*Croson*.]

* * *

IV

Our traditional equal protection doctrine requires, in addition to a compelling state interest, that the Government's chosen means be necessary to accomplish, and narrowly tailored to further, the asserted interest. * * * This element of strict scrutiny is designed to "ensur[e] that the means chosen 'fit' [the] compelling goal so closely that there is little or no possibility that the motive for the classification was illegitimate racial prejudice or stereotype." [*Croson* (opinion of O'CONNOR, J.).] The chosen means, resting as they do on stereotyping and so indirectly furthering the asserted end, could not plausibly be deemed narrowly tailored. The Court instead finds the racial classifications to be "substantially related" to achieving the Government's interest, * * * a far less rigorous fit requirement. The FCC's policies fail even this requirement.

A

The FCC claims to advance its asserted interest in diverse viewpoints by singling out race and ethnicity as peculiarly linked to distinct views that require enhancement. The FCC's choice to employ a racial criterion embodies the related notions that a particular and distinct viewpoint inheres in certain racial groups, and that a particular applicant, by virtue of race or ethnicity alone, is more valued than other applicants because he/she is "likely to provide [that] distinct perspective." [Brief for FCC.] The policies directly equate race with belief and behavior, for they establish race as a necessary and sufficient condition of securing the preference. The FCC's chosen means rest on the "premise that differences in race, or in the color of a person's skin, reflect real differences that are relevant to a person's right to share in the blessings of a free society. [T]hat premise is utterly irrational and repugnant to the principles of a free and democratic society." [*Wygant* (STEVENS, J., dissenting).] The policies impermissibly value individuals because they presume that persons think in a manner associated with their race. * * *

The majority addresses this point by arguing that the equation of race with distinct views and behavior is not "impermissible" in these particular cases. * * * Apart from placing undue faith in the Government and courts' ability to distinguish "good" from "bad" stereotypes, this reasoning repudiates essential equal protection principles that prohibit racial generalizations. * * *

B

Moreover, the FCC's selective focus on viewpoints associated with race illustrates a particular tailoring difficulty.* * *

Our equal protection doctrine governing intermediate review indicates that the Government may not use race and ethnicity as "a 'proxy for other, more germane bases of classification.'" [*Mississippi Univ. for Women v. Hogan*, 458 U.S. 718 (1982).] The FCC has used race as a proxy for whatever views it believes to be underrepresented in the broadcasting spectrum. This reflexive or unthinking use of a suspect classification is the hallmark of an unconstitutional policy. * * * The ill fit of means to ends is manifest. The policy is overinclusive: Many members of a particular racial or ethnic group will have no interest in advancing the views the FCC believes to be underrepresented, or will find them utterly foreign. The policy is underinclusive: It awards no preference to disfavored individuals who may be particularly well versed in and committed to presenting those views. The FCC has failed to implement a case-by-case determination, and that failure is particularly unjustified when individualized hearings already occur, as in the comparative licensing process. * * * Even in the remedial context, we have required that the Government adopt means to ensure that the award of a particular preference advances the asserted interest. * * *

* * *

The FCC seeks to avoid the tailoring difficulties by focusing on minority ownership rather than the asserted interest in diversity of broadcast viewpoints. The Constitution clearly prohibits allocating valuable goods such as broadcast licenses simply on the basis of race. * * * Yet the FCC refers to the lack of minority ownership of stations to support the existence of a lack of diversity of viewpoints, and has fitted its programs to increase ownership. * * * This repeated focus on ownership supports the inference that the FCC seeks to allocate licenses based on race, an impermissible end, rather than to increase diversity of viewpoints, the asserted interest. And this justification that links the use of race preferences to minority ownership rather than to diversity of viewpoints ensures that the FCC's programs, like that at issue in *Croson*, "cannot be said to be narrowly tailored to any goal, except perhaps outright racial balancing." * * *

C

Even apart from these tailoring defects in the FCC's policies, one particular flaw underscores the Government's ill fit of means to ends. The FCC's policies assume, and rely upon, the existence of a tightly bound "nexus" between the owners' race and the resulting programming.* * *

Three difficulties suggest that the nexus between owners' race and programming is considerably less than substantial. First, the market shapes programming to a tremendous extent. Members of minority groups who own licenses might be thought, like other owners, to seek to broadcast programs that will attract and retain audiences, rather than programs that reflect the owner's tastes and preferences. * * * Second, station owners have only limited control over the content of programming. The distress sale presents a particularly acute difficulty of this sort. Unlike the comparative licensing program, the distress sale policy provides preferences to minority owners who neither intend nor desire to manage the station in any respect. * * * Whatever distinct programming may attend the race of an owner actively involved in managing the station, an absentee owner would have far less effect on programming.

Third, the FCC had absolutely no factual basis for the nexus when it adopted the policies and has since established none to support its existence. * * *

Even apart from the limited nature of the Court's claims, little can be discerned from the congressional action. First, the Court's survey does not purport to establish that the FCC or Congress has identified any particular deficiency in the viewpoints contained in the broadcast spectrum. Second, no degree of congressional endorsement may transform the equation of race with behavior and thoughts into a permissible basis of governmental action. Even the most express and lavishly documented congressional declaration that members of certain races will as owners produce distinct and superior programming would not allow the Government to employ such reasoning to allocate benefits and burdens among citizens on that basis. Third, we should hesitate before accepting as definitive any declaration regarding even the existence of a nexus.* * *

D

Finally, the Government cannot employ race classifications that unduly burden individuals who are not members of the favored racial and ethnic groups. * * * The challenged policies fail this independent requirement, as well as the other constitutional requirements. The comparative licensing and distress sale programs provide the eventual licensee with an exceptionally valuable property and with a rare and unique opportunity to serve the local community. The distress sale imposes a particularly significant burden. The FCC has at base created a specialized market reserved exclusively for minority controlled applicants. There is no more rigid quota than a 100% set-aside. * * * The Court's argument that the distress sale allocates only a small percentage of all license sales, * * * also misses the mark. This argument readily supports complete preferences and avoids scrutiny of particular programs: It is no response to a person denied admission at one school, or discharged from one job, solely on the basis of race, that other schools or employers do not discriminate.

* * *

■ JUSTICE KENNEDY, with whom JUSTICE SCALIA joins, dissenting.

Almost 100 years ago in *Plessy v. Ferguson, 163 U.S. 537 (1896),* this Court upheld a government-sponsored race-conscious measure, a Louisiana law that required "equal but separate accommodations" for "white" and "colored" railroad passengers. The Court asked whether the measures were "reasonable," and it stated that "[i]n determining the question of reasonableness, [the legislature] is at liberty to act with reference to the established usages, customs and traditions of the people, and with a view to the promotion of their comfort." * * * The *Plessy* Court concluded that the "race-conscious measures" it reviewed were reasonable because they served the governmental interest of increasing the riding pleasure of railroad passengers. The fundamental errors in *Plessy*, its standard of review and its validation of rank racial insult by the State, distorted the law for six decades before the Court announced its apparent demise in *Brown v. Board of Education.* * * * *Plessy*'s standard of review and its explication have disturbing parallels to today's majority opinion that should warn us something is amiss here.

* * * The interest the Court accepts to uphold the race-conscious measures of the Federal Communications Commission (Commission or FCC) is "broadcast diversity." Furthering that interest, we are told, is worth the cost of discriminating among citizens on the basis of race because it will increase the listening pleasure of media audiences. In upholding this preference, the majority exhumes *Plessy*'s deferential approach to racial classifications. The Court abandons even the broad societal remedial justification for racial preferences once advocated by JUSTICE MARSHALL, *e.g.*, [*Bakke* (separate opinion)] and now will allow the use of racial classifications by Congress untied to any goal of addressing the effects of past race discrimination. All that need be shown under the new approach, * * * is that the future effect of discriminating among citizens on the basis of race will advance some "important" governmental interest.

Once the Government takes the step, which itself should be forbidden, of enacting into law the stereotypical assumption that the race of owners is linked to broadcast content, it follows a path that becomes ever more tortuous. It must decide which races to favor. * * * The Court's reasoning provides little justification for welcoming the return of racial classifications to our Nation's laws.

I cannot agree with the Court that the Constitution permits the Government to discriminate among its citizens on the basis of race in order to serve interests so trivial as "broadcast diversity." In abandoning strict scrutiny to endorse this interest the Court turns back the clock on the level of scrutiny applicable to federal race-conscious measures. * * * Strict scrutiny is the surest test the Court has yet devised for holding true to the constitutional command of racial equality. * * *

The Court insists that the programs under review are "benign." JUSTICE STEVENS agrees. * * * A fundamental error of the *Plessy* Court was its similar confidence in its ability to identify "benign" discrimination: "We consider the underlying fallacy of the plaintiff's argument to consist in the assumption that the enforced separation of the two races stamps the colored race with a badge of inferiority. If this be so, it is not by reason of anything found in the act, but solely because the colored race chooses to put that construction upon it." * * * Although the majority is "confident" that it can determine when racial discrimination is benign, * * * it offers no explanation as to how it will do so.

* * *

The history of governmental reliance on race demonstrates that racial policies defended as benign often are not seen that way by the individuals affected by them. * * * Although the majority disclaims it, the FCC policy seems based on the demeaning notion that members of the defined racial groups ascribe to certain "minority views" that must be different from those of other citizens. Special preferences also can foster the view that members of the favored groups are inherently less able to compete on their own. And, rightly or wrongly, special preference programs often are perceived as targets for exploitation by opportunists who seek to take advantage of monetary rewards without advancing the stated policy of minority inclusion.

* * *

Though the racial composition of this Nation is far more diverse than the first Justice Harlan foresaw, his warning in dissent is now all the more apposite: "The destinies of the two races, in this country, are indissolubly linked together, and the interests of both require that the common government of all shall not permit the seeds of race hate to be planted under the sanction of law." [*Plessy* (dissenting opinion).] Perhaps the Court can succeed in its assumed role of case-by-case arbiter of when it is desirable and benign for the Government to disfavor some citizens and favor others based on the color of their skin. Perhaps the tolerance and decency to which our people aspire will let the disfavored rise above hostility and the favored escape condescension. But history suggests much peril in this enterprise, and so the Constitution forbids us to undertake it. I regret that after a century of judicial opinions we interpret the Constitution to do no more than move us from "separate but equal" to "unequal but benign."

Note: The FCC affirmative action distress sale policy reviewed in *Metro Broadcasting* was justified, in part, based upon the agency's concern for increasing the public good of diverse viewpoints and images in the broadcast industry. In the article that follows, legal scholar Jerry Kang takes up directly the relationship of broadcast images to the reinforcement of racial bias. Kang, relying on the cognitive bias research that we considered in Chapter 1 at p. 54 above, offers a provocative "thought experiment" to redirect the broadcast media to the task of "disinfecting" racial bias from the national consciousness.

———

Trojan Horses of Race

118 HARV. L. REV. 1489 (2005).

■ JERRY KANG

* * *

Mugshot. Political scientists Frank Gilliam and Shanto Iyengar created variations of a local newscast: a control version with no crime story, a crime story with no mugshot, a crime story with a Black-suspect mugshot, and a crime story with a White-suspect mugshot. The Black and White suspects were represented by the same morphed photograph, with the only difference being skin hue—thus controlling for facial expression and features. The suspect appeared for only five seconds in a ten-minute newscast; nonetheless, the suspect's race produced statistically significant differences in a criminal law survey completed after the viewing. Having seen the Black suspect, White participants showed 6% more support for punitive remedies than did the control group, which saw no crime story. When participants were instead exposed to the White suspect, their support for punitive remedies increased by only 1%, which was not statistically significant.

* * *

Shooter Bias. Social cognitionist Joshua Correll created a video game that placed photographs of a White or Black individual holding either a gun or other object (wallet, soda can, or cell phone) into diverse photographic backgrounds. Participants were instructed to decide as quickly as possible whether to shoot the target. Severe time pressure designed into the game forced errors. Consistent with earlier findings, participants were more likely to mistake a Black target as armed when he in fact was unarmed (false alarms); conversely, they were more likely to mistake a White target as unarmed when he in fact was armed (misses). Even more striking is that Black participants showed similar amounts of "shooter bias" as Whites.

What is going on here? Quite simply, a revolution. These studies are the tip of the iceberg of recent social cognition research elaborating what I call "racial mechanics"—the ways in which race alters intrapersonal, interpersonal, and intergroup interactions. The results are stunning, reproducible, and valid by traditional scientific metrics. They seriously challenge current understandings of our "rational" selves and our interrelations.

* * *

I start by asking a fundamental question: "Where does bias come from?" One important source is vicarious experience with the racial other, transmitted through the media. If these experiences are somehow skewed, we should not be surprised by the presence of pervasive implicit bias. What, then, might we do about such media programming given the rigid constraints of the First Amendment? To be sure, private actors of good faith can voluntarily adopt best practices that decrease implicit bias and its manifestations. But can the state, through law, do anything?

If there is any room for intervention, it would be in the communications realm of broadcast, which enjoys doctrinal exceptionalism. In broadcast, notwithstanding the First Amendment, we tolerate the licensing of speakers. In broadcast, we tolerate suppression of speech we dislike, such as indecency and violence. In broadcast, we tolerate encouragement of speech we like, such as educational television and local-oriented programming. All this is in the name of the "public interest," the vague standard that Congress has charged the Federal Communications Commission with pursuing.

That "public interest" standard was recently reshaped in the controversial June 2003 Media Ownership Order. There, the FCC repeatedly justified relaxing ownership rules by explaining how such changes would increase, of all things, local news. Since local news was viewed as advancing "diversity" and "localism," two of the three core elements of the "public interest," any structural deregulation that would increase local news was lauded.

* * *

For a race paper, my using social cognition and applying it to communications law are unorthodox, but purposefully so. * * * One way to break current deadlocks is to turn to new bodies of knowledge uncovered by social science, specifically the remarkable findings of social cognition. Not only do they provide a more precise, particularized, and empirically grounded picture of how race functions in our minds, and thus in our societies, they also rattle us out of a complacency enjoyed after the demise of de jure discrimination. Further calls for equality are often derogated as whining by those who cannot compete in a modern meritocracy. Social cognition discoveries dispute that resentful characterization and make us reexamine our individual and collective responsibilities for persistent racial inequality. * * *

[I] am confident that the language, methodologies, and findings of social cognition provide trenchant additions to the philosophical, anthropological, sociological, literary, and political science modes of argument that have so far dominated critical race studies. For better and worse, law has turned sharply in favor of quantified and empirical analyses. Social cognition allows a phalanx of those who study race to take that same turn, instrumentally to fight fire with fire, and substantively to profit from a body of science that supports, particularizes, and checks what we intuit as the truth of our lived experiences. * * *

Another way to generate new insights is to view old topics through new lenses. That explains my invocation of the metaphor of "Trojan Horses," which is more familiar to cyberlaw than to critical race studies. This strategy further explains why I apply my social cognitive model of racial mechanics to FCC regulations. I start with the theory and evidence of racial mechanics.

* * *

II. TROJAN HORSES

A. *Tuning In to Broadcast*

* * *

To understand my choice of topic, we must start with a fundamental question: "Where do racial meanings come from?" Racial meanings that accrete in our schemas can, on the one hand, come from "direct experiences" with individuals mapped into those categories. On the other hand, the racial meanings can arise from what I call "vicarious experiences," which are stories of or simulated engagements with racial others provided through various forms of the media or narrated by parents and our peers. Given persistent racial segregation, we should not underestimate the significance of vicarious experiences. Even if direct experience with racial minorities more powerfully shapes our schemas, vicarious experiences may well dominate in terms of sheer quantity and frequency.

The next question becomes, "Why are racial meanings biased against racial minorities?" One hypothesis is that people encounter skewed data sets—or as the computer scientists say, "garbage in, garbage out." If these principally vicarious experiences, transmitted through electronic media, are somehow "skewed," then the racial meanings associated with certain racial categories should also be skewed. This analysis invites further study of culture and mass media policy, topics that social cognitionists have largely avoided.

Suppose that social cognitionists identify which types of vicarious experiences trigger and exacerbate bias and which ameliorate it. Private parties will obviously be free to act on the basis of such discoveries. Voluntary attempts to create a "diversity" of role models on television reflect some such impulse, in addition to financial self-interest since "diversity" is sometimes good for business. But what about collective action, mediated through the state and implemented through law?

* * *

In the 1934 Act, Congress created the FCC and charged it with managing the spectrum to further the "public convenience, interest, or necessity"—the public interest standard. In addition to regulating entry by assigning frequencies, the FCC has power to mold, at least softly, the content of broadcast. * * *

In its history, the FCC has promulgated (and the courts have enforced) regulations that restrict the broadcast of content deemed "bad," such as obscenity, indecency, and excessive commercialization. Specific to antiracism, the FCC, at the instruction of the courts, has revoked the broadcast licenses of stations that favored segregation and aired anti-Black racial epithets. Conversely, the FCC has also promulgated regulations that promote content deemed "good" through informational programming guidelines, community needs and interests ascertainment requirements, the fairness doctrine, and children's educational television guidelines. Specific to questions of race, the FCC has also tried to promote "good" and diverse content by increasing minority ownership of stations through affirmative action. Finally, the FCC has regulated market structure at each stage of production, distribution, and consumption. * * *

[G]iven constitutional law as we know it, if we are curious about what the state can do to combat implicit bias transmitted through vicarious experiences, broadcast is the prime site of inquiry.

B. *Redefining the Public Interest*

The touchstone for governmental management of broadcast is the "public interest" standard. That standard has recently been explicated in an unusual way. At least in the context of ownership policy, the public interest has been functionally equated with the local news.

In June 2003, a divided FCC lifted numerous media ownership restrictions in the name of the "public interest." Some of the changes permitted greater horizontal consolidation in local markets. Specifically, the FCC liberalized the local television multiple ownership rule and the local radio ownership rule. * * * I focus on how the FCC operationalized, and thus arguably redefined, the idea of the "public interest" by equating it with the production of local news.

* * *

Local news * * * played a starring role in one other component of the public interest: "localism." Localism has never been consistently defined in the Commission's analysis. * * * In its order, the FCC did not clarify the term, but it did establish a methodology for measuring localism. It focused again on "programming responsive to local needs and interests, and local news quantity and quality." For two out of the three fundamental components of the "public interest"—diversity and localism—the FCC highlighted the significance of local news production.

* * *

In sum, "local news" has become *the* critical component of the FCC's "public interest" analysis, at least in the media ownership context. Although local news has long played an important role in the idea of "public service," its predominance in the deregulation order is striking. The supervening norm that the FCC must pursue, the "public interest," has now become practically identical to the number of hours of local news a station broadcasts. But what in fact is on the local news?

C. *Local News*

1. Crime and Punishment.—Violent crime. Crime occupies a heavy share of broadcast news programming. This is true for national news. It is also true for local news, which is "the most widely used source of information about crime." The PEJ's annual study of local news programming consistently finds that local newscasts spend about a quarter of their time on crime stories.

* * *

Violent crime news stories frequently involve racial minorities, especially African Americans. One reason is that racial minorities are arrested for violent crimes more frequently on a per capita basis than Whites. Given our social cognition review, we can predict what watching local news might do to us. If subliminal flashes of Black male faces can raise our frustration, as shown by the Computer Crash study, would it be surprising that consciously received messages couched in violent visual context have impact, too? In fact, we have already seen in the Mugshot study, described in the Introduction, that even ephemeral exposure to race can alter our opinions about crime and punishment. That study, also conducted by Gilliam and Iyengar, is one of the more sophisticated studies in a line of newscast experiments finding similar results.

* * *

2. Trojan Horse Viruses.—I now make explicit what I have so far left implicit: local news programs, dense with images of racial minorities committing violent crimes in one's own community, can be analogized to Trojan Horse viruses. A type of computer virus, a Trojan Horse installs itself on a user's computer without her awareness. That small program then runs in the background, without the user's knowledge, and silently waits to take action—whether by corrupting files, e-mailing pornographic spam, or launching a "denial of service" attack—which the user, if conscious of it, would disavow.

Typically, a Trojan Horse comes attached secretly to a program or information we actively seek. For instance, we might download a new program for a trial run, and embedded inside may be a Trojan Horse that installs itself without our knowledge. Or, we might browse some website in search of information, and a small javascript bug may be embedded in the page we view. Here is the translation to the news context: we turn on the television in search of local news, and with that information comes a Trojan Horse that alters our racial schemas. The images we see are more powerful than mere words. As local news, they speak of threats nearby, not in some abstract, distant land. The stories are not fiction but a brutal reality. They come from the most popular and trusted source.

* * *

How do we know violent crime stories can, like Trojan Horses, exacerbate implicit bias? The Mugshot study and other work by political scientists using the newscast paradigm are suggestive. Further evidence comes from studies that demonstrate media primings of racial schemas. For example, we now know that exposure to violent rap music can increase implicit bias against African Americans and that playing the video game Doom can increase one's implicit self-concept of aggressiveness—all the while having no statistically significant impact on one's explicit, self-reported views. Still further evidence comes indirectly from research Nilanjana Dasgupta calls the "third wave" of implicit bias research, which examines the malleability of implicit bias. This research demonstrates that implicit bias can be exacerbated or mitigated by the information environments we inhabit.

* * *

[C]onsuming positive images can decrease individuals' implicit bias, although they may register no difference on measures of explicit bias. Conversely, it seems reasonable to suppose that consuming negative images can exacerbate implicit bias. Recall the group in the Blair study instructed to imagine stereotypic women. And if mental imagery can produce such effects, watching direct portrayals in electronic media may well have an even stronger impact.

* * *

To summarize: Local news provides data that we use consciously in a rational analysis to produce informed opinions on, say, criminal punishment. But these newscasts also activate and strengthen linkages among certain racial categories, violent crime, and the fear and loathing such crime invokes. In this sense, the local news functions precisely like a Trojan Horse virus. We invite it into our homes, our dens, in through the gates of our minds, and accept it at face value, as an accurate representation of newsworthy events. But something lurks within those newscasts that programs our racial schemas in ways we cannot notice but can, through scientific measurements, detect. And the viruses they harbor deliver a payload with consequences, affecting how we vote for "three strikes and you're out" laws, how awkwardly we interact with folks, and even how quickly we pull the trigger.

3. *The Accuracy Objection.*—A predictable objection is that the violent content, including crime committed by racial minorities, is a feature, not a bug. In other words, the data presented are not skewed and instead faithfully reflect a reality that the local news did not create. I have three responses to this "accuracy objection": the data are likely not fairly presented; our memories and abilities to see patterns are selective; and we interpret the data in self-serving ways.

First, the information broadcast is probably not fair and balanced. There is a prima facie case that the local media give disproportionate attention to violent crime, in which Black suspects feature prominently. Furthermore, ample evidence shows that the media treats Black-perpetrator stories differently, representing and portraying suspects in a more threatening manner than comparable White perpetrators. Specifically, Robert Entman explains that because of production biases in local newscasts, Black suspects are more likely to remain unnamed and in physical custody, and less likely to speak for themselves. As a result, while there is evidence that the statistical prominence of Blacks portrayed in crime news is "not that much out of line with the actual Black arrest rate," the emphasis on violent crime appears to skew public perceptions.

Second, even if local news accurately reflected reality, we see "illusory correlations." Whenever two salient events are noticed together, that combination leaves a deep impression in our memories and leads us to overestimate its frequency. Because racial minorities are numerical minorities (and therefore often salient) and because bad acts (for example, crimes) are also unusual and salient, when racial minorities commit bad acts, the information gets more deeply imprinted and weighted than is statistically warranted.* * *

Third, even if our recollections are accurate, our interpretations may be biased * * * even if the news conveys descriptively accurate information about the *mean* criminality of racial minority groups, the public still may seriously underestimate the *variance*. This would contribute to the fallacy of thinking that simply because 50% of crimes are committed by a group *X*, 50% of group *X* commit crimes. Consider how this tendency to view members of outgroups as monolithic could affect Arab Americans during our indefinite war on terror.

Another concern is the "fundamental attribution error" (FAE). The FAE is a general tendency to attribute the causes of behavior to dispositional, instead of situational, factors. In other words, we tend to underweight contingent, environmental factors that cause a particular action and to highlight putatively stable factors such as personality traits instead.* * *

* * *

[Kang considers the possibility of placing "caps" on local news stories concerning violent crimes.] After answering the empirical question, we must also make a final normative judgment. In other words, even if implicit bias does what I claim it does, is that important enough to count as "compelling"? First Amendment doctrine does not provide a clear test to answer such a question. So we reason through close analogy to other government interests that have been deemed "compelling." We know, for example, that "safeguarding the physical and psychological well-being" of children is a compelling interest. Drawing on equal protection case law, we know that remedying racial discrimination as well as pursuing educational diversity count as compelling interests. In the end, the government interest in decreasing implicit bias should be deemed "compelling" as well.

* * *

Grutter v. Bollinger

Supreme Court of the United States, 539 U.S. 306 (2003).

■ O'CONNOR, J., delivered the opinion of the Court, in which STEVENS, SOUTER, GINSBURG, and BREYER, JJ., joined, and in which SCALIA and THOMAS, JJ., joined in part insofar as it is consistent with the views expressed in Part VII of the opinion of THOMAS, J. GINSBURG, J., filed a concurring opinion, in which BREYER, J., joined. SCALIA, J., filed an opinion concurring in part and dissenting in part, in which THOMAS, J., joined. THOMAS, J., filed an opinion concurring in part and dissenting in part, in which SCALIA, J., joined as to Parts I–VII. REHNQUIST, C. J., filed a dissenting opinion, in which SCALIA, KENNEDY, and THOMAS, JJ., joined. KENNEDY, J., filed a dissenting opinion.

■ JUSTICE O'CONNOR delivered the opinion of the Court.

This case requires us to decide whether the use of race as a factor in student admissions by the University of Michigan Law School (Law School) is unlawful.

I

A

The Law School ranks among the Nation's top law schools. It receives more than 3,500 applications each year for a class of around 350 students. Seeking to "admit a group of students who individually and collectively are among the most capable," the Law School looks for individuals with "substantial promise for success in law school" and "a strong likelihood of succeeding in the practice of law and contributing in diverse ways to the well-being of others." * * * More broadly, the Law School seeks "a mix of students with varying backgrounds and experiences who will respect and learn from each other." * * *

The hallmark of [the law school's affirmative action] policy is its focus on academic ability coupled with a flexible assessment of applicants' talents, experiences, and potential "to contribute to the learning of those around them." * * * The policy requires admissions officials to evaluate each applicant based on all the information available in the file, including a personal statement, letters of recommendation, and an essay describing the ways in which the applicant will contribute to the life and diversity of the Law School. * * * In reviewing an applicant's file, admissions officials must consider the applicant's undergraduate grade point average (GPA) and Law School Admissions Test (LSAT) score because they are important (if imperfect) predictors of academic success in law school. * * * The policy stresses that "no applicant should be admitted unless we expect that applicant to do well enough to graduate with no serious academic problems."

* * *

The policy aspires to "achieve that diversity which has the potential to enrich everyone's education and thus make a law school class stronger than the sum of its parts." * * * The policy does not restrict the types of diversity contributions eligible for "substantial weight" in the admissions process, but instead recognizes "many possible bases for diversity admissions." * * * The policy does, however, reaffirm the Law School's long-standing commitment to "one particular type of diversity," that is, "racial and ethnic diversity with special reference to the inclusion of students from groups which have been historically discriminated against, like African–Americans, Hispanics and Native Americans, who without this commitment might not be represented in our student body in meaningful numbers." * * * By enrolling a " 'critical mass' of [underrepresented] minority students," the Law School seeks to "ensure their ability to make unique contributions to the character of the Law School." * * *

The policy does not define diversity "solely in terms of racial and ethnic status." * * * Nor is the policy "insensitive to the competition among all students for admission to the Law School." * * * Rather, the policy seeks to guide admissions officers in "producing classes both diverse and academically outstanding, classes made up of students who promise to continue the tradition of outstanding contribution by Michigan Graduates to the legal profession." * * *

B

Petitioner Barbara Grutter is a white Michigan resident who applied to the Law School in 1996 with a 3.8 grade point average and 161 LSAT score. The Law School initially placed petitioner on a waiting list, but subsequently rejected her application. In December 1997, petitioner filed suit in the United States District Court for the Eastern District of Michigan against the Law School, the Regents of the University of Michigan, Lee Bollinger (Dean of the Law School from 1987 to 1994, and President of the University of Michigan from 1996 to 2002), Jeffrey Lehman (Dean of the Law School), and Dennis Shields (Director of Admissions at the Law School from 1991 until 1998). Petitioner alleged that respondents discriminated against her on the basis of race in violation of the Fourteenth Amendment, Title VI of the Civil Rights Act of 1964, and Rev Stat § 1977.

Petitioner further alleged that her application was rejected because the Law School uses race as a "predominant" factor, giving applicants who belong to certain minority groups "a significantly greater chance of admission than students with similar credentials from disfavored racial groups." Petitioner also alleged that respondents "had no compelling interest to justify their use of race in the admissions process." * * * Petitioner requested compensatory and punitive damages, an order requiring the Law School to offer her admission, and an injunction prohibiting the Law School from continuing to discriminate on the basis of race. * * * Petitioner clearly has standing to bring this lawsuit.

* * *

We granted certiorari * * * to resolve the disagreement among the Courts of Appeals on a question of national importance: Whether diversity is a compelling interest that can justify the narrowly tailored use of race in selecting applicants for admission to public universities. Compare *Hopwood v. Texas*, 78 F.3d 932 (5th Cir. 1996) (Hopwood I) (holding that diversity is not a compelling state interest), with *Smith v. University of Washington Law School*, 233 F.3d 1188 (9th Cir. 2000) (holding that it is).

II

A

We last addressed the use of race in public higher education over 25 years ago. In the landmark *Bakke* case, we reviewed a racial set-aside program that reserved 16 out of 100 seats in a medical school class for members of certain minority groups. * * * The decision produced six separate opinions, none of which commanded a majority of the Court. Four Justices would have upheld the program against all attack on the ground that the government can use race to "remedy disadvantages cast on minorities by past racial prejudice." [*Bakke*] (joint opinion of Brennan, White, Marshall, and Blackmun, JJ., concurring in judgment in part and dissenting in part). Four other Justices avoided the constitutional question altogether and struck down the program on statutory grounds. [*Id.*] (opinion of Stevens, J., joined by Burger, C. J., and Stewart and Rehnquist, JJ., concurring in judgment in part and dissenting in part). Justice Powell provided a fifth vote not only for invalidating the set-aside program, but also for reversing the state court's injunction against any use of race whatsoever. The only holding for the Court in *Bakke* was that a "State has a substantial interest that legitimately may be served by a properly devised admissions program involving the competitive consideration of race and ethnic origin." * * * Thus, we reversed that part of the lower court's judgment that enjoined the university "from any consideration of the race of any applicant." * * *

Since this Court's splintered decision in *Bakke,* Justice Powell's opinion announcing the judgment of the Court has served as the touchstone for constitutional analysis of race-conscious admissions policies. Public and private universities across the Nation have modeled their own admissions programs on Justice Powell's views on permissible race-conscious policies. * * * We therefore discuss Justice Powell's opinion in some detail.

Justice Powell began by stating that "the guarantee of equal protection cannot mean one thing when applied to one individual and something else when applied to a person of another color. If both are not accorded the same protection, then it is not equal." * * *

First, Justice Powell rejected an interest in "reducing the historic deficit of traditionally disfavored minorities in medical schools and in the medical profession" as an unlawful interest in racial balancing. * * * Second, Justice Powell rejected an interest in remedying societal discrimination because such measures would risk placing unnecessary burdens on innocent third parties "who bear no responsibility for whatever harm the beneficiaries of the special admissions program are thought to have suffered." * * * Third, Justice Powell rejected an interest in "increasing the number of physicians who will practice in communities currently underserved," concluding that even if such an interest could be compelling in some circumstances the program under review was not "geared to promote that goal." * * *

Justice Powell approved the university's use of race to further only one interest: "the attainment of a diverse student body." * * * In seeking the "right to select those students who will contribute the most to the 'robust exchange of ideas,' a university seeks to achieve a goal that is of paramount importance in the fulfillment of its mission." * * *

B

The Equal Protection Clause provides that no State shall "deny to any person within its jurisdiction the equal protection of the laws." U.S. Const., Amdt. 14, § 2. Because the Fourteenth Amendment "protects *persons,* not *groups*," all "governmental action based on race—a *group* classification long recognized as in most circumstances irrelevant and therefore prohibited—should be subjected to detailed judicial inquiry to ensure that the *personal* right to equal protection of the laws has not been infringed." *Adarand Constructors, Inc. v. Pena,* 515 U.S. 200, 227 (1995) (emphasis in original; internal quotation marks and citation omitted). We are a "free people whose institutions are founded upon the doctrine of equality." *Loving v. Virginia,* 388 U.S. 1, 11 (1967) (internal quotation marks and citation omitted). It follows from that principle that "government may treat people differently because of their race only for the most compelling reasons." [*Adarand.*]

We have held that all racial classifications imposed by government "must be analyzed by a reviewing court under strict scrutiny." *Ibid.* This means that such classifications are constitutional only if they are narrowly tailored to further compelling governmental interests. * * *

Strict scrutiny is not "strict in theory, but fatal in fact." [*Adarand*.] Although all governmental uses of race are subject to strict scrutiny, not all are invalidated by it. * * * When race-based action is necessary to further a compelling governmental interest, such action does not violate the constitutional guarantee of equal protection so long as the narrow-tailoring requirement is also satisfied.

* * *

III

A

* * *

We first wish to dispel the notion that the Law School's argument has been foreclosed, either expressly or implicitly, by our affirmative-action cases decided since *Bakke*. It is true that some language in those opinions might be read to suggest that remedying past discrimination is the only permissible justification for race-based governmental action. See, e.g., *Richmond v. J. A. Croson Co.*, [488 U.S. 469 (1989) (plurality opinion).] But we have never held that the only governmental use of race that can survive strict scrutiny is remedying past discrimination. Nor, since *Bakke*, have we directly addressed the use of race in the context of public higher education. Today, we hold that the Law School has a compelling interest in attaining a diverse student body.

The Law School's educational judgment that such diversity is essential to its educational mission is one to which we defer. The Law School's assessment that diversity will, in fact, yield educational benefits is substantiated by respondents and their *amici*. Our scrutiny of the interest asserted by the Law School is no less strict for taking into account complex educational judgments in an area that lies primarily within the expertise of the university. Our holding today is in keeping with our tradition of giving a degree of deference to a university's academic decisions, within constitutionally prescribed limits. * * *

We have long recognized that, given the important purpose of public education and the expansive freedoms of speech and thought associated with the university environment, universities occupy a special niche in our constitutional tradition. * * * In announcing the principle of student body diversity as a compelling state interest, Justice Powell invoked our cases recognizing a constitutional dimension, grounded in the First Amendment, of educational autonomy: "The freedom of a university to make its own judgments as to education includes the selection of its student body." [*Bakke*.] From this premise, Justice Powell reasoned that by claiming "the right to select those students who will contribute the most to the 'robust exchange of ideas,'" a university "seeks to achieve a goal that is of paramount importance in the fulfillment of its mission." * * * Our conclusion that the Law School has a compelling interest in a diverse student body is informed by our view that attaining a diverse student body is at the heart of the Law School's proper institutional mission, and that "good faith" on the part of a university is "presumed" absent "a showing to the contrary." * * *

As part of its goal of "assembling a class that is both exceptionally academically qualified and broadly diverse," the Law School seeks to "enroll a 'critical mass' of minority students." * * * The Law School's interest is not simply "to assure within its student body some specified percentage of a particular group merely because of its race or ethnic origin." [*Bakke.*] That would amount to outright racial balancing, which is patently unconstitutional. * * * Rather, the Law School's concept of critical mass is defined by reference to the educational benefits that diversity is designed to produce.

These benefits are substantial. As the District Court emphasized, the Law School's admissions policy promotes "cross-racial understanding," helps to break down racial stereotypes, and "enables [students] to better understand persons of different races." * * * These benefits are "important and laudable," because "classroom discussion is livelier, more spirited, and simply more enlightening and interesting" when the students have "the greatest possible variety of backgrounds." * * *

The Law School's claim of a compelling interest is further bolstered by its *amici*, who point to the educational benefits that flow from student body diversity. In addition to the expert studies and reports entered into evidence at trial, numerous studies show that student body diversity promotes learning outcomes, and "better prepares students for an increasingly diverse workforce and society, and better prepares them as professionals." [Brief for American Educational Research Association et al.]

These benefits are not theoretical but real, as major American businesses have made clear that the skills needed in today's increasingly global marketplace can only be developed through exposure to widely diverse people, cultures, ideas, and viewpoints. [Brief for 3M et al.; Brief for General Motors Corp.] What is more, high-ranking retired officers and civilian leaders of the United States military assert that, "based on [their] decades of experience," a "highly qualified, racially diverse officer corps . . . is essential to the military's ability to fulfill its principle mission to provide national security." [Brief for Julius W. Becton, Jr. et al.] The primary sources for the Nation's officer corps are the service academies and the Reserve Officers Training Corps (ROTC), the latter comprising students already admitted to participating colleges and universities. * * * At present, "the military cannot achieve an officer corps that is *both* highly qualified *and* racially diverse unless the service academies and the ROTC used limited race-conscious recruiting and admissions policies." [*Id.* (emphasis in original).] To fulfill its mission, the military "must be selective in admissions for training and education for the officer corps, *and* it must train and educate a highly qualified, racially diverse officer corps in a racially diverse setting." [*Id.* (emphasis in original).] We agree that "it requires only a small step from this analysis to conclude that our country's

other most selective institutions must remain both diverse and selective."
* * *
     * * *

Moreover, universities, and in particular, law schools, represent the training ground for a large number of our Nation's leaders. *Sweatt v. Painter*, 339 U.S. 629, 634 (1950) (describing law school as a "proving ground for legal learning and practice"). Individuals with law degrees occupy roughly half the state governorships, more than half the seats in the United States Senate, and more than a third of the seats in the United States House of Representatives. [See Brief for Association of American Law Schools.] The pattern is even more striking when it comes to highly selective law schools. A handful of these schools accounts for 25 of the 100 United States Senators, 74 United States Courts of Appeals judges, and nearly 200 of the more than 600 United States District Court judges. * * *

In order to cultivate a set of leaders with legitimacy in the eyes of the citizenry, it is necessary that the path to leadership be visibly open to talented and qualified individuals of every race and ethnicity. All members of our heterogeneous society must have confidence in the openness and integrity of the educational institutions that provide this training. As we have recognized, law schools "cannot be effective in isolation from the individuals and institutions with which the law interacts." [*Sweatt.*] Access to legal education (and thus the legal profession) must be inclusive of talented and qualified individuals of every race and ethnicity, so that all members of our heterogeneous society may participate in the educational institutions that provide the training and education necessary to succeed in America.

The Law School does not premise its need for critical mass on "any belief that minority students always (or even consistently) express some characteristic minority viewpoint on any issue." * * * To the contrary, diminishing the force of such stereotypes is both a crucial part of the Law School's mission, and one that it cannot accomplish with only token numbers of minority students. Just as growing up in a particular region or having particular professional experiences is likely to affect an individual's views, so too is one's own, unique experience of being a racial minority in a society, like our own, in which race unfortunately still matters. The Law School has determined, based on its experience and expertise, that a "critical mass" of underrepresented minorities is necessary to further its compelling interest in securing the educational benefits of a diverse student body.

B

Even in the limited circumstance when drawing racial distinctions is permissible to further a compelling state interest, government is still "constrained in how it may pursue that end: [T]he means chosen to accomplish the [government's] asserted purpose must be specifically and narrowly framed to accomplish that purpose." *Shaw v. Hunt*, 517 U.S. 899, 908 (1996). The purpose of the narrow tailoring requirement is to ensure that "the means chosen 'fit' th[e] compelling goal so closely that there is little or no possibility that the motive for the classification was illegitimate racial prejudice or stereotype." [*Croson* (plurality opinion).]

* * *

To be narrowly tailored, a race-conscious admissions program cannot use a quota system—it cannot "insulate each category of applicants with certain desired qualifications from competition with all other applicants." [*Bakke* (opinion of Powell, J.).] Instead, a university may consider race or ethnicity only as a " 'plus' in a particular applicant's file," without "insulating the individual from comparison with all other candidates for the available seats." [*Id.*] * * *

We find that the Law School's admissions program bears the hallmarks of a narrowly tailored plan. As Justice Powell made clear in *Bakke*, truly individualized consideration demands that race be used in a flexible, nonmechanical way. * * *

We are satisfied that the Law School's admissions program, like the Harvard plan described by Justice Powell, does not operate as a quota. Properly understood, a "quota" is a program in which a certain fixed number or proportion of opportunities are "reserved exclusively for certain minority groups." [*Croson* (plurality opinion).] Quotas " 'impose a fixed number or percentage which must be attained, or which cannot be exceeded,' " *Sheet Metal Workers v. EEOC*, 478 U.S. 421, 445 (1986) (O'CONNOR, J., concurring in part and dissenting in part), and "insulate the individual from comparison with all other candidates for the available seats." [*Bakke* (opinion of Powell, J.).] In contrast, "a permissible goal . . . requires only a good-faith effort . . . to come within a range demarcated by the goal itself," [*Sheet Metal Workers*,] and permits consideration of race as a "plus" factor in any given case while still ensuring that each candidate "competes with all other qualified applicants," *Johnson v. Transportation Agency, Santa Clara Cty.*, 480 U.S. 616, 638 (1987).

* * *

The Law School's goal of attaining a critical mass of underrepresented minority students does not transform its program into a quota. As the Harvard plan described by Justice Powell recognized, there is of course "some relationship between numbers and achieving the benefits to be derived from a diverse student body, and between numbers and providing a reasonable environment for those students admitted." [*Id.*] "Some attention to numbers," without more, does not transform a flexible admissions system into a rigid quota. [*Id.*] Nor, as Justice Kennedy posits, does the Law School's consultation of the "daily reports," which keep track of the racial and ethnic composition of the class (as well as of residency and gender), "suggest[ ] there was no further attempt at individual review save for race itself" during the final stages of the admissions process. * * * To the contrary, the Law School's admissions officers testified without contradiction that they never gave race any more or less weight based on the information contained in these reports. * * * Moreover, as Justice Kennedy concedes, * * * between 1993 and 2000, the number of African–American, Latino, and Native–American students in each class at the Law School varied from 13.5 to 20.1 percent, a range inconsistent with a quota.

The Chief Justice believes that the Law School's policy conceals an attempt to achieve racial balancing, and cites admissions data to contend that the Law School discriminates among different groups within the critical mass. * * * But, as the Chief Justice concedes, the number of underrepresented minority students who ultimately enroll in the Law School differs substantially from their representation in the applicant pool and varies considerably for each group from year to year. * * *

* * *

Here, the Law School engages in a highly individualized, holistic review of each applicant's file, giving serious consideration to all the ways an applicant might contribute to a diverse educational environment. The Law School affords this individualized consideration to applicants of all races. There is no policy, either *de jure* or *de facto*, of automatic acceptance or rejection based on any single "soft" variable. Unlike the program at issue in *Gratz v. Bollinger*, [123 S.Ct. 2411 (2003),] the Law School awards no mechanical, predetermined diversity "bonuses" based on race or ethnicity. * * * Like the Harvard plan, the Law School's admissions policy "is flexible enough to consider all pertinent elements of diversity in light of the particular qualifications of each applicant, and to place them on the same footing for consideration, although not necessarily according them the same weight." [*Bakke* (opinion of Powell, J.).]

We also find that, like the Harvard plan Justice Powell referenced in *Bakke*, the Law School's race-conscious admissions program adequately ensures that all factors that may contribute to student body diversity are meaningfully considered alongside race in admissions decisions. With respect to the use of race itself, all underrepresented minority students admitted by the Law School have been deemed qualified. By virtue of our Nation's struggle with racial inequality, such students are both likely to have experiences of particular importance to the Law School's mission, and less likely to be admitted in meaningful numbers on criteria that ignore those experiences. * * *

* * *

What is more, the Law School actually gives substantial weight to diversity factors besides race. The Law School frequently accepts nonminority applicants with grades and test scores lower than underrepresented minority applicants (and other nonminority applicants) who are rejected. * * * This shows that the Law School seriously weighs many other diversity factors besides race that can make a real and dispositive difference for nonminority applicants as well. By this flexible approach, the Law School sufficiently takes into account, in practice as well as in theory, a wide variety of characteristics besides race and ethnicity that contribute to a diverse student body. Justice Kennedy speculates that "race is likely outcome determinative for many members of minority groups" who do not fall within the upper range of LSAT scores and grades. * * * But the same could be said of the Harvard plan discussed approvingly by Justice Powell in *Bakke*, and indeed of any plan that uses race as one of many factors. * * *

Petitioner and the United States argue that the Law School's plan is not narrowly tailored because race-neutral means exist to obtain the educational benefits of student body diversity that the Law School seeks. We disagree. Narrow tailoring does not require exhaustion of every conceivable race-neutral alternative. * * *

We agree with the Court of Appeals that the Law School sufficiently considered workable race-neutral alternatives. The District Court took the Law School to task for failing to consider race-neutral alternatives such as "using a lottery system" or "decreasing the emphasis for all applicants on undergraduate GPA and LSAT scores." * * * But these alternatives would require a dramatic sacrifice of diversity, the academic quality of all admitted students, or both.

* * *

We acknowledge that "there are serious problems of justice connected with the idea of preference itself." [*Bakke* (opinion of Powell, J.).] Narrow tailoring, therefore, requires that a race-conscious admissions program not unduly harm members of any racial group. Even remedial race-based governmental action generally "remains subject to continuing oversight to assure that it will work the least harm possible to other innocent persons competing for the benefit." * * * To be narrowly tailored, a race-conscious admissions program must not "unduly burden individuals who are not members of the favored racial and ethnic groups." *Metro Broadcasting, Inc. v. FCC*, 497 U.S. 547, 630 (1990) (O'CONNOR, J., dissenting).

* * * We agree that, in the context of its individualized inquiry into the possible diversity contributions of all applicants, the Law School's race-conscious admissions program does not unduly harm nonminority applicants.

We are mindful, however, that "[a] core purpose of the Fourteenth Amendment was to do away with all governmentally imposed discrimination based on race." *Palmore v. Sidoti*, 466 U.S. 429, 432 (1984). Accordingly, race-conscious admissions policies must be limited in time. This requirement reflects that racial classifications, however compelling their goals, are potentially so dangerous that they may be employed no more broadly than the interest demands. Enshrining a permanent justification for racial preferences would offend this fundamental equal protection principle. We see no reason to exempt race-conscious admissions programs from the requirement that all governmental use of race must have a logical end point. The Law School, too, concedes that all "race-conscious programs must have reasonable durational limits." * * *

In the context of higher education, the durational requirement can be met by sunset provisions in race-conscious admissions policies and periodic reviews to determine whether racial preferences are still necessary to achieve student body diversity. Universities in California, Florida, and Washington State, where racial preferences in admissions are prohibited by state law, are currently engaged in experimenting with a wide variety of alternative approaches. Universities in other States can and should draw on the most promising aspects of these race-neutral alternatives as they develop. * * *

The requirement that all race-conscious admissions programs have a termination point "assure[s] all citizens that the deviation from the norm of equal treatment of all racial and ethnic groups is a temporary matter, a measure taken in the service of the goal of equality itself." [*Croson* (plurality opinion).]

We take the Law School at its word that it would "like nothing better than to find a race-neutral admissions formula" and will terminate its race-conscious admissions program as soon as practicable. * * * It has been 25 years since Justice Powell first approved the use of race to further an interest in student body diversity in the context of public higher education. Since that time, the number of minority applicants with high grades and test scores has indeed increased. * * * We expect that 25 years from now, the use of racial preferences will no longer be necessary to further the interest approved today.

* * *

It is so ordered.

■ JUSTICE GINSBURG, with whom JUSTICE BREYER joins, concurring.

* * *

It is well documented that conscious and unconscious race bias, even rank discrimination based on race, remain alive in our land, impeding realization of our highest values and ideals. * * * As to public education, data for the years 2000–2001 show that 71.6% of African–American children and 76.3% of Hispanic children attended a school in which minorities made up a majority of the student body. * * * And schools in predominantly minority communities lag far behind others measured by the educational resources available to them. [See Brief for National Urban League et al.]

However strong the public's desire for improved education systems may be, * * * it remains the current reality that many minority students encounter markedly inadequate and unequal educational opportunities. Despite these inequalities, some minority students are able to meet the high threshold requirements set for admission to the country's finest undergraduate and graduate educational institutions. As lower school education in minority communities improves, an increase in the number of such students may be anticipated. From today's vantage point, one may hope, but not firmly forecast, that over the next generation's span, progress toward nondiscrimination and genuinely equal opportunity will make it safe to sunset affirmative action.

■ CHIEF JUSTICE REHNQUIST, with whom JUSTICE SCALIA, JUSTICE KENNEDY, and JUSTICE THOMAS join, dissenting.

I agree with the Court that, "in the limited circumstance when drawing racial distinctions is permissible," the government must ensure that its means are narrowly tailored to achieve a compelling state interest. * * * I do not believe, however, that the University of Michigan Law School's (Law School) means are narrowly tailored to the interest it asserts. The Law School claims it must take the steps it does to achieve a " 'critical mass' " of underrepresented minority students. * * * But its actual program bears no relation to this asserted goal. Stripped of its "critical mass" veil, the Law School's program is revealed as a naked effort to achieve racial balancing.

As we have explained many times, "any preference based on racial or ethnic criteria must necessarily receive a most searching examination." [*Adarand* (quoting *Wygant*).] Our cases establish that, in order to withstand this demanding inquiry, respondents must demonstrate that their methods of using race "fit" a compelling state interest "with greater precision than any alternative means." [*Id.*]

Before the Court's decision today, we consistently applied the same strict scrutiny analysis regardless of the government's purported reason for using race and regardless of the setting in which race was being used. We rejected calls to use more lenient review in the face of claims that race was being used in "good faith" because "more than good motives should be required when government seeks to allocate its resources by way of an explicit racial classification system." [*Adarand*.] We likewise rejected calls to apply more lenient review based on the particular setting in which race is being used. Indeed, even in the specific context of higher education, we emphasized that "constitutional limitations protecting individual rights may not be disregarded." [*Bakke*.]

Although the Court recites the language of our strict scrutiny analysis, its application of that review is unprecedented in its deference.

Respondents' asserted justification for the Law School's use of race in the admissions process is "obtaining 'the educational benefits that flow from a diverse student body.' " * * *

In practice, the Law School's program bears little or no relation to its asserted goal of achieving "critical mass." Respondents explain that the Law School seeks to accumulate a "critical mass" of *each* underrepresented minority group. * * * But the record demonstrates that the Law School's admissions practices with respect to these groups differ dramatically and cannot be defended under any consistent use of the term "critical mass."

From 1995 through 2000, the Law School admitted between 1,130 and 1,310 students. Of those, between 13 and 19 were Native American, between 91 and 108 were African–Americans, and between 47 and 56 were Hispanic. If the Law School is admitting between 91 and 108 African–Americans in order to achieve "critical mass," thereby preventing African–American students from feeling "isolated or like spokespersons for their race," one would think that a number of the same order of magnitude would be necessary to accomplish the same purpose for Hispanics and

Native Americans. Similarly, even if all of the Native American applicants admitted in a given year matriculate, which the record demonstrates is not at all the case,* how can this possibly constitute a "critical mass" of Native Americans in a class of over 350 students? In order for this pattern of admission to be consistent with the Law School's explanation of "critical mass," one would have to believe that the objectives of "critical mass" offered by respondents are achieved with only half the number of Hispanics and one-sixth the number of Native Americans as compared to African–Americans. But respondents offer no race-specific reasons for such disparities. Instead, they simply emphasize the importance of achieving "critical mass," without any explanation of why that concept is applied differently among the three underrepresented minority groups.

These different numbers, moreover, come only as a result of substantially different treatment among the three underrepresented minority groups, as is apparent in an example offered by the Law School and highlighted by the Court: The school asserts that it "frequently accepts nonminority applicants with grades and test scores lower than underrepresented minority applicants (and other nonminority applicants) who are rejected." * * * Specifically, the Law School states that "sixty-nine minority applicants were rejected between 1995 and 2000 with at least a 3.5 [Grade Point Average (GPA)] and a [score of] 159 or higher on the [Law School Admissions Test (LSAT)]" while a number of Caucasian and Asian–American applicants with similar or lower scores were admitted. * * *

Review of the record reveals only 67 such individuals. Of these 67 individuals, 56 were Hispanic, while only 6 were African–American, and only 5 were Native American. This discrepancy reflects a consistent practice.

These statistics have a significant bearing on petitioner's case. Respondents have *never* offered any race-specific arguments explaining why significantly more individuals from one underrepresented minority group are needed in order to achieve "critical mass" or further student body diversity. They certainly have not explained why Hispanics, who they have said are among "the groups most isolated by racial barriers in our country," should have their admission capped out in this manner. * * * True, petitioner is neither Hispanic nor Native American. But the Law School's disparate admissions practices with respect to these minority groups demonstrate that its alleged goal of "critical mass" is simply a sham. Petitioner may use these statistics to expose this sham, which is the basis for the Law School's admission of less qualified underrepresented minorities in preference to her. Surely strict scrutiny cannot permit these sort of disparities without at least some explanation.

     * * *

---

* Indeed, during this 5–year time period, enrollment of Native American students dropped to as low as *three* such students. Any assertion that such a small group constituted a "critical mass" of Native Americans is simply absurd.

The Court, in an unprecedented display of deference under our strict scrutiny analysis, upholds the Law School's program despite its obvious flaws. We have said that when it comes to the use of race, the connection between the ends and the means used to attain them must be precise. But here the flaw is deeper than that; it is not merely a question of "fit" between ends and means. Here the means actually used are forbidden by the Equal Protection Clause of the Constitution.

[Justice Kennedy's dissenting opinion has been omitted].

■ JUSTICE SCALIA, with whom JUSTICE THOMAS joins, concurring in part and dissenting in part.

    * * *

[T]he "educational benefit" that the University of Michigan seeks to achieve by racial discrimination consists, according to the Court, of " 'cross-racial understanding,' " * * * and " 'better prepar[ation of] students for an increasingly diverse workforce and society,' " * * * all of which is necessary not only for work, but also for good "citizenship." * * * This is not, of course, an "educational benefit" on which students will be graded on their Law School transcript (Works and Plays Well with Others: B+) or tested by the bar examiners (Q: Describe in 500 words or less your cross-racial understanding). For it is a lesson of life rather than law—essentially the same lesson taught to (or rather learned by, for it cannot be "taught" in the usual sense) people three feet shorter and twenty years younger than the full-grown adults at the University of Michigan Law School, in institutions ranging from Boy Scout troops to public-school kindergartens. If properly considered an "educational benefit" at all, it is surely not one that is either uniquely relevant to law school or uniquely "teachable" in a formal educational setting. *And therefore:* If it is appropriate for the University of Michigan Law School to use racial discrimination for the purpose of putting together a "critical mass" that will convey generic lessons in socialization and good citizenship, surely it is no less appropriate—indeed, *particularly* appropriate—for the civil service system of the State of Michigan to do so. There, also, those exposed to "critical masses" of certain races will presumably become better Americans, better Michiganders, better civil servants. And surely private employers cannot be criticized—indeed, should be praised—if they also "teach" good citizenship to their adult employees through a patriotic, all-American system of racial discrimination in hiring. The nonminority individuals who are deprived of a legal education, a civil service job, or any job at all by reason of their skin color will surely understand.

Unlike a clear constitutional holding that racial preferences in state educational institutions are impermissible, or even a clear anticonstitutional holding that racial preferences in state educational institutions are OK, today's *Grutter-Gratz* split double header seems perversely designed to prolong the controversy and the litigation. * * *

■ JUSTICE THOMAS, with whom JUSTICE SCALIA joins as to Parts I–VII, concurring in part and dissenting in part.

Frederick Douglass, speaking to a group of abolitionists almost 140 years ago, delivered a message lost on today's majority:

"[I]n regard to the colored people, there is always more that is benevolent, I perceive, than just, manifested towards us. What I ask for the negro is not benevolence, not pity, not sympathy, but simply *justice*. The American people have always been anxious to know what they shall do with us.... I have had but one answer from the beginning. Do nothing with us! Your doing with us has already played the mischief with us. Do nothing with us! If the apples will not remain on the tree of their own strength, if they are worm-eaten at the core, if they are early ripe and disposed to fall, let them fall! ... And if the negro cannot stand on his own legs, let him fall also. All I ask is, give him a chance to stand on his own legs! Let him alone! ... [Y]our interference is doing him positive injury." What the Black Man Wants: An Address Delivered in Boston, Massachusetts, on 26 January 1865, reprinted in 4 The Frederick Douglass Papers 59, 68 (J. Blassingame & J. McKivigan eds. 1991) (emphasis in original).

Like Douglass, I believe blacks can achieve in every avenue of American life without the meddling of university administrators. Because I wish to see all students succeed whatever their color, I share, in some respect, the sympathies of those who sponsor the type of discrimination advanced by the University of Michigan Law School (Law School). The Constitution does not, however, tolerate institutional devotion to the status quo in admissions policies when such devotion ripens into racial discrimination. Nor does the Constitution countenance the unprecedented deference the Court gives to the Law School, an approach inconsistent with the very concept of "strict scrutiny."

No one would argue that a university could set up a lower general admission standard and then impose heightened requirements only on black applicants. Similarly, a university may not maintain a high admission standard and grant exemptions to favored races. The Law School, of its own choosing, and for its own purposes, maintains an exclusionary admissions system that it knows produces racially disproportionate results. Racial discrimination is not a permissible solution to the self-inflicted wounds of this elitist admissions policy.

The majority upholds the Law School's racial discrimination not by interpreting the people's Constitution, but by responding to a faddish slogan of the cognoscenti. Nevertheless, I concur in part in the Court's opinion. First, I agree with the Court insofar as its decision, which approves of only one racial classification, confirms that further use of race in admissions remains unlawful. Second, I agree with the Court's holding that racial discrimination in higher education admissions will be illegal in 25 years. * * * I respectfully dissent from the remainder of the Court's opinion and the judgment, however, because I believe that the Law School's current use of race violates the Equal Protection Clause and that the Constitution means the same thing today as it will in 300 months.

I

* * * The Constitution abhors classifications based on race, not only because those classifications can harm favored races or are based on illegitimate motives, but also because every time the government places citizens on racial registers and makes race relevant to the provision of burdens or benefits, it demeans us all. "Purchased at the price of immeasurable human suffering, the equal protection principle reflects our Nation's understanding that such classifications ultimately have a destructive impact on the individual and our society." [*Adarand* (Thomas, J., concurring in part and concurring in judgment).]

II

Unlike the majority, I seek to define with precision the interest being asserted by the Law School before determining whether that interest is so compelling as to justify racial discrimination. The Law School maintains that it wishes to obtain "educational benefits that flow from student body diversity." * * * This statement must be evaluated carefully, because it implies that both "diversity" and "educational benefits" are components of the Law School's compelling state interest. Additionally, the Law School's refusal to entertain certain changes in its admissions process and status indicates that the compelling state interest it seeks to validate is actually broader than might appear at first glance.

* * *

A distinction between these two ideas (unique educational benefits based on racial aesthetics and race for its own sake) is purely sophistic—so much so that the majority uses them interchangeably. * * * The Law School's argument, as facile as it is, can only be understood in one way: Classroom aesthetics yields educational benefits, racially discriminatory admissions policies are required to achieve the right racial mix, and therefore the policies are required to achieve the educational benefits. It is the *educational benefits* that are the end, or allegedly compelling state interest, not "diversity." * * *

One must also consider the Law School's refusal to entertain changes to its current admissions system that might produce the same educational benefits. The Law School adamantly disclaims any race-neutral alternative that would reduce "academic selectivity," which would in turn "require the Law School to become a very different institution, and to sacrifice a core part of its educational mission." * * * In other words, the Law School seeks to improve marginally the education it offers without sacrificing too much of its exclusivity and elite status.

The proffered interest that the majority vindicates today, then, is not simply "diversity." Instead the Court upholds the use of racial discrimination as a tool to advance the Law School's interest in offering a marginally superior education while maintaining an elite institution. Unless each constituent part of this state interest is of pressing public necessity, the

Law School's use of race is unconstitutional. I find each of them to fall far short of this standard.

III

A

A close reading of the Court's opinion reveals that all of its legal work is done through one conclusory statement: The Law School has a "compelling interest in securing the educational benefits of a diverse student body." * * * No serious effort is made to explain how these benefits fit with the state interests the Court has recognized (or rejected) as compelling * * * or to place any theoretical constraints on an enterprising court's desire to discover still more justifications for racial discrimination. In the absence of any explanation, one might expect the Court to fall back on the judicial policy of *stare decisis*. But the Court eschews even this weak defense of its holding, shunning an analysis of the extent to which Justice Powell's opinion in [*Bakke*] is binding, * * * in favor of an unfounded wholesale adoption of it.

* * *

B

Under the proper standard, there is no pressing public necessity in maintaining a public law school at all and, it follows, certainly not an elite law school. Likewise, marginal improvements in legal education do not qualify as a compelling state interest.

1

While legal education at a public university may be good policy or otherwise laudable, it is obviously not a pressing public necessity when the correct legal standard is applied. * * *

2

* * * Michigan has no compelling interest in having a law school at all, much less an *elite* one. Still, even assuming that a State may, under appropriate circumstances, demonstrate a cognizable interest in having an elite law school, Michigan has failed to do so here.

* * *

[T]he Law School trains few Michigan residents and overwhelmingly serves students, who, as lawyers, leave the State of Michigan. The Law School's decision to be an elite institution does little to advance the welfare of the people of Michigan or any cognizable interest of the State of Michigan. * * *

3

Finally, even if the Law School's racial tinkering produces tangible educational benefits, a marginal improvement in legal education cannot justify racial discrimination where the Law School has no compelling interest in either its existence or in its current educational and admissions policies.

IV

The interest in remaining elite and exclusive that the majority thinks so obviously critical requires the use of admissions "standards" that, in turn, create the Law School's "need" to discriminate on the basis of race. The Court validates these admissions standards by concluding that alternatives that would require "a dramatic sacrifice of . . . the academic quality of all admitted students," * * * need not be considered before racial discrimination can be employed. In the majority's view, such methods are not required by the "narrow tailoring" prong of strict scrutiny because that inquiry demands, in this context, that any race-neutral alternative work " 'about as well.' " * * * The majority errs, however, because race-neutral alternatives must only be "workable," * * * and do "about as well" *in vindicating the compelling state interest*. The Court never explicitly holds that the Law School's desire to retain the status quo in "academic selectivity" is itself a compelling state interest, and, as I have demonstrated, it is not. * * * Therefore, the Law School should be forced to choose between its classroom aesthetic and its exclusionary admissions system—it cannot have it both ways.

With the adoption of different admissions methods, such as accepting all students who meet minimum qualifications, * * * the Law School could achieve its vision of the racially aesthetic student body without the use of racial discrimination. The Law School concedes this, but the Court holds, implicitly and under the guise of narrow tailoring, that the Law School has a compelling state interest in doing what it wants to do. I cannot agree. * * *

A

The Court bases its unprecedented deference to the Law School—a deference antithetical to strict scrutiny—on an idea of "educational autonomy" grounded in the First Amendment. * * * In my view, there is no basis for a right of public universities to do what would otherwise violate the Equal Protection Clause.

* * *

B

1

The Court's deference to the Law School's conclusion that its racial experimentation leads to educational benefits will, if adhered to, have serious collateral consequences. The Court relies heavily on social science evidence to justify its deference. * * * The Court never acknowledges, however, the growing evidence that racial (and other sorts) of heterogeneity actually impairs learning among black students. * * *

* * *

The majority grants deference to the Law School's "assessment that diversity will, in fact, yield educational benefits." * * * It follows, therefore, that an HBC's [historically black college's] assessment that racial homogeneity will yield educational benefits would similarly be given deference. An HBC's rejection of white applicants in order to maintain racial homogeneity seems permissible, therefore, under the majority's view of the Equal Protection Clause. * * * Contained within today's majority opinion is the seed of a new constitutional justification for a concept I thought long and rightly rejected—racial segregation.

2

* * *

C

* * *

The sky has not fallen at Boalt Hall at the University of California, Berkeley, for example. Proposition 209's adopt[ion] of Cal. Const., Art. 1, § 31(a) [1996], bars the State from "granting preferential treatment . . . on the basis of race . . . in the operation of . . . public education." * * * [W]ithout deploying express racial discrimination in admissions * * * total underrepresented minority student enrollment at Boalt Hall now exceeds 1996 levels. Apparently the Law School cannot be counted on to be as resourceful. The Court is willfully blind to the very real experience in California and elsewhere, which raises the inference that institutions with "reputation[s] for excellence," * * * rivaling the Law School's have satisfied their sense of mission without resorting to prohibited racial discrimination.

V

Putting aside the absence of any legal support for the majority's reflexive deference, there is much to be said for the view that the use of tests and other measures to "predict" academic performance is a poor substitute for a system that gives every applicant a chance to prove he can succeed in the study of law. The rallying cry that in the absence of racial discrimination in admissions there would be a true meritocracy ignores the fact that the entire process is poisoned by numerous exceptions to "merit." For example, in the national debate on racial discrimination in higher education admissions, much has been made of the fact that elite institutions utilize a so-called "legacy" preference to give the children of alumni an advantage in admissions. This, and other, exceptions to a "true" meritocracy give the lie to protestations that merit admissions are in fact the order of the day at the Nation's universities. The Equal Protection Clause does not, however, prohibit the use of unseemly legacy preferences or many other kinds of arbitrary admissions procedures. What the Equal Protection Clause does prohibit are classifications made on the basis of race. So while legacy preferences can stand under the Constitution, racial discrimination cannot. I will not twist the Constitution to invalidate legacy preferences or otherwise impose my vision of higher education admissions on the Nation. The majority should similarly stay its impulse to validate faddish racial discrimination the Constitution clearly forbids.

* * *

[N]o modern law school can claim ignorance of the poor performance of blacks, relatively speaking, on the Law School Admissions Test (LSAT). Nevertheless, law schools continue to use the test and then attempt to "correct" for black underperformance by using racial discrimination in admissions so as to obtain their aesthetic student body. The Law School's continued adherence to measures it knows produce racially skewed results is not entitled to deference by this Court. * * *

Having decided to use the LSAT, the Law School must accept the constitutional burdens that come with this decision. The Law School may freely continue to employ the LSAT and other allegedly merit-based standards in whatever fashion it likes. What the Equal Protection Clause forbids, but the Court today allows, is the use of these standards hand-in-hand with racial discrimination. An infinite variety of admissions methods are available to the Law School. Considering all of the radical thinking that has historically occurred at this country's universities, the Law School's intractable approach toward admissions is striking.

* * *

VI

The absence of any articulated legal principle supporting the majority's principal holding suggests another rationale. I believe what lies beneath the Court's decision today are the benighted notions that one can tell when racial discrimination benefits (rather than hurts) minority groups, * * * and that racial discrimination is necessary to remedy general societal ills. This Court's precedents supposedly settled both issues, but clearly the majority still cannot commit to the principle that racial classifications are *per se* harmful and that almost no amount of benefit in the eye of the beholder can justify such classifications.

* * *

The Law School tantalizes unprepared students with the promise of a University of Michigan degree and all of the opportunities that it offers. These overmatched students take the bait, only to find that they cannot succeed in the cauldron of competition. And this mismatch crisis is not restricted to elite institutions. * * * Indeed, to cover the tracks of the aestheticists, this cruel farce of racial discrimination must continue—in selection for the Michigan Law Review * * * and in hiring at law firms and for judicial clerkships—until the "beneficiaries" are no longer tolerated. While these students may graduate with law degrees, there is no evidence that they have received a qualitatively better legal education (or become better lawyers) than if they had gone to a less "elite" law school for which they were better prepared. And the aestheticists will never address the real problems facing "underrepresented minorities," instead continuing their social experiments on other people's children.

Beyond the harm the Law School's racial discrimination visits upon its test subjects, no social science has disproved the notion that this discrimination "engenders attitudes of superiority or, alternatively, provoke[s] resentment among those who believe that they have been wronged by the government's use of race." [*Adarand* (Thomas, J., concurring in part and concurring in judgment).] "These programs stamp minorities with a badge of inferiority and may cause them to develop dependencies or to adopt an attitude that they are 'entitled' to preferences." [*Id.*]

It is uncontested that each year, the Law School admits a handful of blacks who would be admitted in the absence of racial discrimination. * * * Who can differentiate between those who belong and those who do not? The majority of blacks are admitted to the Law School because of discrimination, and because of this policy all are tarred as undeserving. This problem of stigma does not depend on determinacy as to whether those stigmatized are actually the "beneficiaries" of racial discrimination. When blacks take positions in the highest places of government, industry, or academia, it is an open question today whether their skin color played a part in their advancement. The question itself is the stigma—because either racial discrimination did play a role, in which case the person may be deemed "otherwise unqualified," or it did not, in which case asking the question itself unfairly marks those blacks who would succeed without discrimination. Is this what the Court means by "visibly open"? * * *

    * * *

VII

As the foregoing makes clear, I believe the Court's opinion to be, in most respects, erroneous. I do, however, find two points on which I agree.
    * * *

Under today's decision, it is still the case that racial discrimination that does not help a university to enroll an unspecified number, or "critical mass," of underrepresented minority students is unconstitutional.
    * * *

I * * * understand the imposition of a 25–year time limit only as a holding that the deference the Court pays to the Law School's educational judgments and refusal to change its admissions policies will itself expire. * * * With these observations, I join the last sentence of Part III of the opinion of the Court.

              * * *

For the immediate future, however, the majority has placed its *imprimatur* on a practice that can only weaken the principle of equality embodied in the Declaration of Independence and the Equal Protection Clause. "Our Constitution is color-blind, and neither knows nor tolerates classes among citizens." *Plessy v. Ferguson*, 163 U.S. 537, 559 (1896) (Harlan, J., dissenting). It has been nearly 140 years since Frederick Douglass asked the intellectual ancestors of the Law School to "[d]o nothing with us!" and the Nation adopted the Fourteenth Amendment. Now we must wait another 25 years to see this principle of equality vindicated. I therefore respectfully dissent from the remainder of the Court's opinion and the judgment.

* * *

Admissions Rituals as Political Acts: Guardians at the Gates of Our Democratic Ideals

117 Harv. L. Rev. 113 (2003).

■ Lani Guinier

* * *

Every year, selective colleges and universities engage in admissions rituals to reconstitute themselves. Institutions presumably align these high-stakes moments of civic pedagogy with their educational agenda: to produce knowledge, to promote learning, and to help individuals realize their intellectual, athletic, or artistic potential. The moment when admissions decisions are mailed is also fraught with political consequences that reach beyond the classroom to the boardroom, the legislature, and the kitchen table. At selective institutions of higher education, admissions decisions have a special political impact: rationing access to societal influence and power, and training leaders for public office and public life. Those admitted as students then graduate to become citizens who shape business, education, the arts, and the law for the next generation. Admissions decisions affect the individuals who apply, the institutional environments that greet those who enroll, and the stability and legitimacy of our democracy. They are political as well as educational acts.

* * *

Some have construed [the *Grutter* decision's focus on the role of higher education in democracy] as a warning, as Justice O'Connor's majority opinion in *Grutter* includes a puzzling clause stating that she expects the need for considerations of race in admissions decisions to expire after twenty-five years. According to former Harvard University President Derek Bok, for example, this twenty-five-year expectation is more than simply a reminder of the need to reevaluate race-consciousness in order to satisfy the narrow tailoring element of strict scrutiny: rather, it is a "warning to do something about the underlying problem." Universities, in other words, are not living up to their educational and democratic missions: they need to do more about the achievement gap that makes affirmative action necessary; the environmental gap that socially isolates white students who, unlike students of color, spend most of their time with same-race friends in college; and the teaching and learning gaps that disable professors from reaching out to mentor students of color.

At the same time, it is important to acknowledge that the appearance of sharp boundary lines in defining race is problematic for many members of the public and the Court. There is a pervasive reluctance to view race in categorical terms. This resistance to racial categorization affects members of the public, not just the crusaders against affirmative action who, despite their defeat at the Supreme Court, seem to have lost none of their zeal.

* * *

Properly deployed, racial literacy, or the ability to read race in conjunction with institutional and democratic structures, may enable the building of a coalition that starts a larger conversation at the point where educational selection and democratic values meet. Race, in other words, reveals rather than produces the stress on institutional resources that undermines the connection between education and democracy, a connection that the Court in *Grutter* and *Gratz* recognized as essential. Because race is inextricably intertwined with every period in American history, from our founding as a constitutional democracy to current patterns of private wealth formation, it is a formidable diagnostic and sociological tool. Used as a lens to peer beyond the pretense of the debate, race helps detect the deeper issues confronting public institutions of higher education.

* * *

I. The Democratic and Educational Missions of Higher Education: Admissions Judgments as Political Acts

* * *

Although education has been linked to opportunity since the early days of the republic, higher education was originally a province reserved for wealthy white men. During the first half of the twentieth century, women, Jews, and blacks were the victims of arbitrary quotas or formal exclusionary policies sanctioned by law. During the 1950s and 1960s, however, legal challenges, social movements, and a participatory conception of individual rights helped pressure these institutions of higher education to open their doors—albeit only a crack—to those who had been shut out. Institutions that had once been bastions of elite privilege began admitting women and people of color for the first time.

At the same time, American society increasingly highlighted the importance of higher education to democratic values by extending the opportunity to attend college to more people. The GI Bill, Pell Grants, the Cold War, and the move to a global and information economy made higher education instrumental to our society's understanding of the relationship between an educated populace, a representative group of leaders, a commitment to public service, and national security. These developments also turned college education into a primary engine for economic and social upward mobility in the last part of the century.

Meanwhile, as more people saw higher education as a necessity for societal as well as individual reasons, government funding for this essential public good shrunk: states shifted resources from education to the criminal justice system, the federal government cut Pell grants, and state revenues plummeted, leading to higher tuition and reduced financial aid. This shift in funding priorities was driven in part by an ideological shift during the Reagan era. Higher education was presented as a private benefit to be financed by the individual, instead of a public good to be funded by the government. As a result, higher education became a scarce, indispensable, and competitive individual resource.

As more people wanted in, colleges and universities became more selective. * * * Many of these institutions valued their "selectivity" as an element of their identity or chose for other reasons not to add sufficient resources to keep up with increased interest. * * *

[I]nstitutions began to seek a fair and efficient set of selection criteria that would preserve their elite status, which had been derived from association with bloodlines and reinforced by the appearance of unattainability. Institutions that once used evidence of "good character"—a proxy for privilege and wealth—switched to ostensibly more democratic indicia of merit. College admissions officers began to replace the pedigreed "natural" aristocracy of Edmund Burke's world that had dominated elite higher education through the middle of the twentieth century. In the 1950s a "meritocracy" began to substitute "aptitude" for "character" (or family) as the ticket into colleges and universities. Admissions would proceed from an open calculus rather than a set of private relationships. Excellence through brains, not blood, would become the basis for awarding scarce admission slots.

Excellence did not simply cloak elitism, however. It was also associated with a fairness principle, derived from scientifically designed, and thus presumably more objective, criteria. One of the primary vehicles for apportioning access to an increasingly popular yet scarce public resource was the introduction of standardized tests and other potentially objective measures of excellence; such tests enabled university administrators to compare individuals from different demographic, geographic, and social cohorts. This ability to compare had been previously either unnecessary for the public institutions that admitted almost every (white male) applicant, or reserved to headmasters at private prep schools.

Because of the perceived ability to manufacture objective evidence of desert, excellence became measurable. Applicants who outscored or outranked their peers on standardized aptitude tests were therefore presumed to be the most qualified, regardless of social class. The premium on allocating access to higher education more democratically and meritocratically led to the development of a testing industry that now functions as one of the primary gatekeepers to upward mobility.

Deciding who "deserves" to benefit from admission to selective colleges and universities now occurs within a "testocracy" that claims to sort, evaluate, and rank measurable mental aptitude. The resulting test scores, together with high school grades, purport to tell us in both real and relative terms about each applicant's potential capacity, which is then deemed the most important evidence of his or her "visible, rankable" merit.

To maintain their elite status in terms of democratic "merit" rather than inherited privilege, these institutions had to raise the stakes. Thus, applicants who receive the thick envelopes in April have higher SAT scores than their parents did a generation ago. Unfortunately, along with democratic "merit" came a sense of entitlement without the sense of obligation. Ambition replaced pedigree, but the public spiritedness * * * failed to materialize.

During the second half of the twentieth century, the pendulum swung dramatically from subjective measures of character to objective measures of excellence; for reasons I describe in the next Part, it soon swung back to more subjective evidence of character to supplement the quantifiable standards for measuring academic merit. But now character would mean motivation, work ethic, and the ability to overcome obstacles, rather than charisma, athletic skill, and the ability to fit in. Diversity rather than homogeneity became a value.

Moving back and forth from subjective to objective to subjective measures, the admissions pendulum never settled on a single, fixed view of merit. Without a stable template for admissions choices, shifts in the values and identities of those making the choices, as well as the process of selection itself, came to define qualification. Yet the choice of who attends institutions of higher education, both public and private, has personal, institutional, and societal implications. Thus, admissions decisions are both educational questions and political acts.

The task of constituting each class is a political act because it implicates the institution's sense of itself as a community, as well as the larger society's sense of itself as a democracy. Such acts allocate resources in a way that affects those who are admitted to the institution, those who are rejected, those who fail to apply, and those who simply use the institution's selection criteria as an interpretive guide. Thus, they affect all members of society, both directly, as described above, and indirectly, by helping determine future political, economic, and social leaders. Directly or indirectly, taxpayers support these institutions, which function as gateways to upward mobility and help legitimize democratic ideals of participation, fairness, and equal opportunity. At nonselective public colleges, the opportunity to attend is less a function of admissions criteria per se, and more a question of application fees and tuition costs, as well as historical patterns of recruitment, information networks, social capital, and location that determine the demographics of the student body and faculty.

* * *

The term "political act" also describes inputs that inflect the process of decisionmaking, not just the outputs that help define it. Beyond the democratic significance, the social consequences, and the individual benefits of gaining admission to these institutions, admissions choices have an internal political dynamic. They are located in the heads of the decisionmakers as well as in the world.

II: CONTEST, SPONSORED, AND STRUCTURAL MOBILITY:
ALTERNATIVE WAYS OF CONCEPTUALIZING THE
RELATIONSHIP BETWEEN EDUCATION
AND DEMOCRACY

In this Part, I explore two related aspects of admissions rituals: the process used to make admissions decisions, and the values or goals that seem to animate different views of the selection process. Starting with the goals that inform the process, I identify four important values associated with access to higher education: individualism, merit, democracy, and upward mobility. Of these four, the value that seems to integrate the other three with higher education is upward mobility. Yet although upward mobility is the value most closely associated with higher education in our collective imagination, all four values are closely intertwined.

Upward mobility and individualism are both core values of the American Dream; they legitimate our democratic ideal of equal opportunity for all. In his history of the French Enlightenment, Marshall Berman describes individualism in perhaps its most favorable light: the right to be yourself, particularly the right not to have your role or status ascribed to you, but to find it for yourself. Individualism was forged in a revolt against feudalism, a system based entirely on ascribed roles. Thus conceived, individualism is deeply connected to democratic ideals of opportunity and upward mobility.

Likewise, mobility in America means not just moving out, but also moving up; it refers to sociological as well as geographical relocation in order to take advantage of opportunity. Upward mobility also suggests that we live in a "classless" society—or at least a society in which class is floating, not fixed. At the same time, higher education has built into it the idea of nobility as well as mobility. After all, universities predate the modern state—they were historically limited to an elite. Higher education grants upward social mobility because it is a status marker, not merely a private contract that matches one's skills with an appropriate educational setting to enhance one's learning. In our society education means opportunity, higher education offers heightened opportunity, and elite higher education confers not just heightened opportunity, but also elevated status. Admissions officers may not view themselves as the "sorting hats" of our society, but many Americans construe the fat or thin envelopes mailed in April as serving just this purpose.

Like upward mobility and individualism, meritocracy formally rejects ascribed roles, awarding opportunity based on individual merit rather than inherited status. Those who succeed are presumed to be those who do their best because of effort, not birth. Meritocracy also associates selectivity with excellence. The opportunity to choose among many qualified applicants not only confers status; it automatically connotes merit. Indeed, merit has two ideas of mobility built into it. It suggests criteria for identifying individual capacity for upward mobility. It also suggests the potential to change individual capacity through educational opportunity—the opportunity to learn in an environment that values excellence, and the opportunity to learn after graduation as the educational credential opens economic and political doors.

* * *

The different processes that educational institutions employ to navigate these goals, however, reveal that the goals are often mutually inconsistent. Individualism, for example, is in tension with a democratic commitment to equal opportunity; not all who have been disadvantaged by reason of their group status benefit equally when some group members are treated as individuals. Moreover, when taken to extremes, individualism can be a divisive force, driving people to find comfort in racial stereotyping and animosity, which becomes the only respectable reason for their own failures. If "right living and hard work do lead to success," then those who fail have no one to blame but themselves—an uncomfortable conclusion. Stuck in dead-end jobs, denied access to selective institutions, or frustrated that they cannot pass on their own privileges to their children, poor and working-class whites sometimes find it easier to blame blacks, or some other scapegoat, for "stealing" the American Dream. Blacks become personally responsible for their own, as well as everyone else's, failures. This form of one-way individualism, which accepts responsibility for success but not failure, is not only dangerously polarizing; it also ignores the experience of racial disadvantage. Many Americans have been disadvantaged precisely because of their group identity; yet this reality does not recede by simple commitments to treat everyone as an individual. Because individualism values the individual over the group, and individual mobility over community stability, it can contribute to more general feelings of dislocation and disable groups of people from participating in public life.

Moreover, systems of selection often end up perpetuating inherited privilege, even as they disavow any connection to ascribed identity or natural aristocracies. A principled commitment to merit selection can perpetuate ascribed identities in covert ways that are often aligned with the identities and experiences of those in a position to define merit. Access to higher education can become a "world in which inequalities of power are natural, and individuals compete for well-being as individuals at the same time they occupy distinct social locations replete with social roles and expectations." Nor are commitments to democratic legitimacy or upward mobility necessarily satisfied by selecting just a few group members to succeed. Indeed, in many ways, the democratic role of higher education has atrophied; without significant infusions of public funds and other potential sources of accountability, it is in danger of becoming a rhetorical but unrealized ideal.

I borrow and adopt three sociological terms—contest, sponsored, and structural mobility—to help assess the often-confusing interaction among the values that underlie admissions decisions. These three concepts describe the means through which individual upward mobility can be achieved: pure competition, discretionary choice, or structural intervention.

A. Contest Mobility

The term "contest mobility" is a very rough proxy for upward mobility achieved through competitive success on standardized tests. Elite status is the goal and is achieved by the candidate's own efforts in an open contest. Numerical valuations of students provide a scoreboard for this contest, which is either won or lost, with no middle ground. Victors assume that their success, and their resulting elite status, is a justly won prize, not an opportunity for further growth. Since aptitude or ability is presumed to be fixed before the race, the best prepared, rather than the most diligent, win. The ultimate goal of contest mobility is the distribution of opportunity based on individual competition and quantifiable measures of merit.

* * *

Contest mobility reinforces the culture of meritocratic entitlement among its primary beneficiaries, upper-middle-class whites, who feel they have played by the rules and therefore deserve to win. [C]ommitment to the narrative of contest mobility has proved resistant to data refuting its validity and continues to remain extremely persuasive, particularly among affluent whites, whose children are the primary beneficiaries of the traditional admissions regime and its overreliance on narrow, "objective" indicia of success. Survey data suggest that well-educated, well-off whites are among the most antagonistic to affirmative action in higher education, even though they are more supportive of programs designed to increase the representation of people of color in legislatures, public sector jobs, and government contracting positions.

Explicit diversity criteria for admissions are controversial. They are seen as throwbacks to an earlier, now rebuked, age that relied on social criteria rather than mathematically derived ones. Critics argue that, because explicit diversity criteria categorize people rather than their output, they leave room for the subjective exercise of racial prejudice, thus subverting the fairness principle. These critics presume that, because scores are "earned," and diversity is not, diversity criteria allow less "deserving" students of color to gain admission over more "qualified" whites, even though the number of whites adversely affected by affirmative action is miniscule. For critics of affirmative action, diversity represents a dramatic departure from the background commitment to objective measures of merit. Diversity is therefore denigrated as both a process and a substantive goal. Diversity criteria bend the rules of contest mobility.

B. Sponsored Mobility

In order to admit more individuals from underrepresented demographic categories, colleges and universities have modified contest mobility by supplementing the contest with discretion. This hybrid alternative, which I call "sponsored mobility," refers to the contemporary version of the elitist system that was in place when James Conant was President of Harvard.*

---

* Following World War II . . . James Conant, then-President of Harvard University [proposed admissions reforms]. Conant wanted to see elite institutions shift from a WASP

In a system of sponsored mobility, modern elites—including admissions officers, alumni, and others who have already enjoyed the spoils of higher education—hand-pick a few candidates to ascend the ladder of higher education. Whereas contest mobility relies solely on a fixed set of "hard" numbers, sometimes called "skinny merit," sponsored mobility relies on an expandable set of "soft" criteria, which might be called "robust merit," to supplement the hard numbers.

Sponsored mobility is an intermediate position between pure contest mobility and structural mobility. This intermediate position allows decisionmakers some room to maneuver; it also acknowledges the limitations of the contest in determining the most "qualified" candidates. The use of soft variables is defended with hard data showing that a purely test-based system suffers from the fallacy of false precision.

Like the hereditary elite system it replaced, modern sponsored mobility retains a discretionary process. * * * This discretion is informed by interviews, letters of recommendation, extracurricular activities, and personal circumstances, including the applicant's race. Sponsored mobility is managed by professional admissions officers for the most part; however, alumni representatives and the headmasters of private secondary schools still play a role in "sponsoring" candidates to elite institutions. Students from elite private schools, for example, still enjoy disproportionate access to Harvard, Yale, and Princeton.

Sponsored mobility enables status elevation at the individual level, but when it comes to issues of diversity, institutions justify it in the name of the group. This justification may take several forms. An institution may believe that diversity in higher education is important because it allows students of all races to "see that people like themselves can succeed" and to "learn the value of interacting with people who are different." Or it may believe that diversity is essential to preserve a "stable polity." Or it may conclude that interracial interaction helps destabilize stereotypes and improve race relations more generally. Whatever the motivation, decisionmakers select a few deserving group members, whose presence then legitimates the institution's educational and democratic missions. The process values associated with sponsored mobility are elite selection and good-faith discretion.

       * * *

Sponsored mobility suffers from four serious flaws: First, it enables the unconscious biases of a relatively homogeneous group to thrive by relying on the judgment of individuals who do not have to explain their choices to a third party. Admissions officers rarely enjoy longstanding relationships with the inner-city principals, high school guidance counselors, individual

---

establishment of hereditary privilege that emphasized entitlement and obligation, to a more democratic accounting that fostered an even greater sense of social responsibility and a less paternalistic view toward public service. In Conant's view, such educated talent would serve the nation in exchange for support from taxpayers. But while Conant wanted to disturb the view that college was a hereditary privilege, he also desired to maintain the elite and selective status of these institutions.

teachers, or community leaders who might know and recommend a student and who can offer information that may not be apparent from the student's file. Second, sponsored mobility does not adequately embrace the idea that individuals change in relation to their environments; thus, although it moderates notions of the intrinsic worth of individuals, sponsored mobility does not adjust sufficiently for the malleability of intelligence in response to effort or encouragement. Third, sponsored mobility perpetuates reliance on the same admissions processes that enabled the current decisionmakers to succeed. Not only do the decisionmakers sponsor students who look like or remind them of themselves, but they also sponsor students who succeeded under the same criteria they faced. This commitment to self-replication is backward-looking; it tends to encourage complacency rather than self-reflection and experimentation. Finally, because adherents of sponsored mobility do not publicly and continuously rethink the relationship between their selection criteria and their mission, their criteria tend to become ends in themselves.

* * *

In the end, sponsored mobility may be only marginally better than contest mobility at allocating access to higher education in a way that is consistent with democratic principles. Although sponsored mobility uses diversity to supplement the hard numbers, it still relies extensively on "the contest" to determine the winners; in this way, diversity becomes a stabilizing norm to legitimate the status quo. Contest mobility at least assumes that individual competition will create churn to upend a complacent view of the status quo. In addition, sponsored mobility gives power to a few decisionmakers to allocate opportunity to "deserving" individuals. Contest mobility gives that power to the institutions that manufacture or referee the rules of the contest, whether a testing bureaucracy or a news magazine; the contest then allocates opportunity to those who "earn" it on their own, with individual competition serving as a tool of accountability. Sponsored mobility, because of its tendency to operate behind closed doors and in isolation from the people who know the candidate best, often lacks such accountability. Because sponsored mobility is still beholden to the hard numbers, operates without much transparency, and tends to reward a limited range of individual attributes, it can also be perceived as a means to co-opt or pacify potential challengers to the governing regime. * * *

C.   Structural Mobility

In addition to contest mobility, which uses hard numbers to measure academic merit, and sponsored mobility, which employs expandable criteria to measure diversity, there is a third conception of the relationship between opportunity and admissions: "structural mobility." A system of structural mobility seeks to identify qualified students in relation to the greater role of higher education in the political, economic, and social structure of community. A commitment to structural mobility means that an institution's commitments to upward mobility, merit, democracy, and individualism are framed and tempered by an awareness of how structures, including the institution's own admissions criteria, tend to privilege some groups of people over others. Structural mobility would require universities to change those admissions policies to provide access to large numbers of people across class, race, and geographic lines, thereby changing the very structure of educational opportunity in this country. Advocates of structural mobility understand that opening access to higher education benefits the society as a whole, not just the individual admittees.

Structural mobility differs from both contest and sponsored mobility, which are dedicated to individual advancement through a market-oriented contest or a "vote of confidence." Structural mobility places the issue of merit firmly on the table and attempts to define it in the context of democratic values. It takes a future-oriented view of the role of higher education in a multiracial democracy by linking ideas about merit directly to ideas about public service and opportunity broadly construed.

Although structural mobility is committed to *community* advancement, it is not inconsistent with ideals of individualism. Rather, structural mobility values the individual in relation to the community. Because it privileges those who have already served, or those who want to serve, their communities, structural mobility focuses society's educational resources on those who are most likely to fulfill the aims of democracy.

For proponents of structural mobility, contest mobility's preoccupation with competitive individualism fails to fulfill Conant's dream of assembling a more publicly spirited elite; contest mobility promotes short-term winners of the wrong game. Sponsored mobility does a better job of elevating individuals who remain connected to their communities or to the taxpayers who helped subsidize their success, but only through a small segment of all admittees. Structural mobility extends the emphasis on community affiliation and linked fate to all admittees, not just those who bring racial diversity to college campuses. It links the institution and its students to their communities, thereby advancing the goals of public education at the local, state, and national levels. An institution committed to structural mobility might measure its success, for example, not only by the students it admits but also by the changes it precipitates in educational opportunity at the K–12 level. Finally, structural mobility is sustained by a broadly democratic and participatory process of self-reflective and racially literate experimentalism. In a world of structural mobility, individuals are given access to educational opportunities not because they win a "contest" or because they have been hand-picked by elites, but because the relevant stakeholders come together to make a set of public-minded choices.

* * *

All of the salient features of structural mobility—a commitment to public service, the participation of grassroots voluntary organizations or indigenous actors in the construction of the program, and the escalator effect that generates broad public support—connect to democratic values.

III: ENTER THE SUPREME COURT:
THE PROMISE AND THE CAUTION OF USING RACE
AS A LENS

Selective public institutions, such as the University of Michigan and the University of Michigan Law School, are in the position to choose among a number of qualified candidates who can do the work and be expected to graduate. Because their admissions decisions have broad social purposes and important individual consequences, these institutions must be able to articulate and defend their admissions criteria and processes to their respective constituencies. Four elements of the Supreme Court's decisions in *Grutter* and *Gratz* seem particularly relevant to the challenge facing institutions of higher education like the University of Michigan that are committed to maintaining their elite status while producing racially literate graduates who contribute to both the campus community and the larger society. These elements are: the value of race-conscious diversity as it is connected to the university's educational mission; a robust view of diversity that includes class and geography, not just race; the role of democratic values; and the relationship between data, demographics, and reflective practice to inform the way institutions operationalize the concepts of diversity and democracy.

* * *

Although *Gratz* identifies how numbers cannot capture an individual's worth (or at least are over- and underinclusive as used by the University of Michigan's undergraduate program), numbers can provide relevant information in the aggregate about relationships of groups of individuals to economic, social, and political power. And while numbers do not tell us all that we need to know about an individual (if we respect the notion that individuals are unique and cannot be compared along a single metric), numbers can provide context to help situate individuals within larger domains. Numbers are informative: they are tools for assisting in making judgments but should not be confused with proxies for those judgments. If numbers should not be outcome-determinative about race, then neither should they be outcome-determinative as proxies for individual "merit" generally.

There is a direct relationship between efforts to quantify race and efforts to quantify merit. Both are driven in part by efficiency concerns. In addition, the quantification of merit hides the discretion of those who develop the quantification tools—standardized tests—which are normed to reward upper-class and upper-middle-class whites. Thus, the decision by institutions like the University of Michigan's undergraduate program to use "hard edges" to capture race is a recognized compensatory response to the "hard edges" that define quantifiable notions of merit. Both are over- and underinclusive categories. But it is the underinclusiveness of the hard variables that contributes to the hyper-visibility of race.

To the extent "merit" is considered largely quantifiable—as opposed to a set of qualitative judgments that are essentially educated guesses about future potential made in the context of an institution's educational and

public missions—individualized assessments that include race as one variable are doomed to be somewhat mechanistic, albeit less transparently so, in
order to compensate for the preferences embedded in the hard variables.
This use of race is also vulnerable to continued attack by those who feel
excluded by the admissions choices being made (mostly working-class and
poor whites, but status-seeking upper-middle-class whites as well), unless
those choices reflect not only concerns about democratic legitimacy but also
a democratic process.

Yet the likely immediate consequence of *Grutter* is that trusted admissions officials are now freer to make their decisions without a great deal of
transparency. They need not give reasons for their choices, as long as they
avoid the mechanistic use of race. If, for example, the institution has a
backward-looking purpose, then it may rely on contest mobility and continue to use admission as a reward or prize. Many universities, however, do
not like to speak of their admissions slots as rewards; law schools in
particular have a mission to train public citizens who serve their clients
and society as a whole. Such institutions might therefore embrace sponsored mobility, since they may use subjective criteria to supplement the
hard variables in making predictions about who among their applicants are
likely to serve the public. * * *

There is a caution, in other words, voiced by the very different dissents
of Justices Ginsburg and Thomas. The caution is that elite self-replication
is the problem, not affirmative action. In this sense, sponsored mobility will
be co-opted by elites in the same way contest mobility was. Diversity will
not be an aesthetic fad; instead, it will become a fig leaf to hide a
commitment to the status quo. If admissions decisions are to be made in a
more democratic fashion—that is, with transparency and accountability to
the institution's public mission and to the taxpayers who subsidize it—then
much more than the physical aesthetics of these choices needs to be
obvious.

　　　* * *

Like Conant's version of contest mobility, which used "merit" to
replace "character" and ended up reproducing privilege, sponsored mobility
may also turn out to benefit only those who are already advantaged. It is
not the goal of diversity that is the problem. Nor does adverting to
democratic legitimacy justify that goal. The problem is the failure to adopt
safeguards that ensure that the goal remains connected to its justificatory
principle.

The *Grutter* opinion, in conjunction with Chief Justice Rehnquist's
opinion for the Court in *Gratz*, holds two other potential limitations as well
as a promise. Although the Court expects institutions to sponsor individuals of color rather than racially categorized groups, and to revisit their use
of race periodically in light of the availability of race-neutral alternatives,
the Court still, paradoxically, requires institutions to consider race differently from the way they consider merit. Simultaneously, the approval of
limited forms of race-consciousness may invite complacency rather than
vigilance. However, the Court's quixotic hope that consideration of race will

be unnecessary in twenty-five years may instead prompt universities to engage the public in a larger conversation about what type of society we want to live in and what higher education institutions must do to bring us closer to that goal. Ultimately, the promise is that the introduction of a soft deadline will trigger bold new experiments in which universities demonstrate renewed involvement in K–12 education, build relationships with local communities to garner more support, and consider multiple ways to realize their twin goals of educational excellence and democratic opportunity.

IV.   PURSUING THE PROMISE AND HEEDING THE WARNING:
RACIAL LITERACY AND THE ROLE OF HIGHER
EDUCATION IN OUR DEMOCRACY

Although the *Grutter* and *Gratz* decisions vindicate the principle of diversity, they do not explain how institutions of higher education should use that principle to help make admissions decisions. This lack of guidance appears to be intentional: as long as institutions do not weight race so heavily that it overdetermines admissions outcomes, their good faith is essentially presumed. It may be that Justice O'Connor and the *Grutter* majority presume good faith because they want the meaning of diversity to emerge from a process of experimentation, feedback, and reflection. It may be that the Court is not prepared to articulate a national definition of diversity and instead prefers for educational institutions to work out the meaning of diversity locally over time. This explanation is consistent with the way Justice O'Connor interpreted narrow tailoring in the context of sponsored mobility, as well as her preference for voluntary self-correction in other contexts.

To the extent that an institution is committed to diversifying its student body, the Court's lack of specificity gives the institution leeway to experiment with ways to link the broad concept of diversity to the specific educational mission of the institution and the public values it aims to serve. For institutions committed to racial diversity, the three forms of mobility are all presumably constitutional as long as they do not use race categorically, overtly, and decisively to fix outcomes. An institution may consider race implicitly in conjunction with class and geography, as is done in percentage plans; it may consider race explicitly as part of a holistic evaluation; and it may consider other indicia of merit that provide democratic legitimacy, such as evidence of an applicant's service commitments, pluck in the face of disadvantage, or residence in an underrepresented geographic area.

In the short term, individualized, holistic review of all candidates will bring colleges and law schools into compliance with *Grutter*. Individualized review will allow institutions to admit students of color "in meaningful numbers" to ensure that students from underrepresented communities contribute to the character of the school and, in the case of law schools, to the legal profession. But in the long run, using affirmative action simply to perpetuate the status quo will likely backfire for practical, financial, and political reasons. Universities may be dogged by complaints that they are not really following *Grutter*, that their methods are too subjective, that their procedures lack transparency, or that their policies leave the decision-making power firmly in the grasp of admissions bureaucrats. Moreover, institutions committed to affirmative action as an add-on will be hard-pressed to keep up with changing demographics: admissions practices that depend on the language of critical mass may unintentionally result in an upper-limit quota that artificially suppresses the number of black and Latino admittees, despite the burgeoning number of such students in the eighteen-to twenty-four-year-old age cohort.

* * *

To gain a deeper understanding of the problem while garnering public confidence in their admissions practices, universities need to become racially literate. A racially literate institution uses race as a diagnostic device, an analytic tool, and an instrument of process.

As a diagnostic or evidentiary device, race helps identify the underlying problems affecting higher education. Racial literacy begins by redefining racism as a structural problem rather than a purely individual one. Race reveals the ways in which demography is often destiny—not just for people of color, but for working-class and poor whites as well. Race constantly influences access to public resources, while also revealing the influence of class and geographical variables. Racial literacy, therefore, continuously links the underrepresentation of blacks and Latinos to the underrepresentation of poor people generally. At a minimum, it reminds public institutions of higher learning that the "idea of access is deeply embedded in [their] genetic code" and thus, the underrepresentation of certain demographic groups illuminates their failure to fulfill their public responsibilities.

When race is engaged directly, as it was in Texas following *Hopwood*, [78 F.3d 932 (5th Cir. 1996),] it can shed light on the confluence of forces that are truly responsible for current public dissatisfaction and that adversely affect people of all colors. At one time, for example, it was commonly accepted that each generation should publicly subsidize educational opportunity for the next generation. Yet today, higher education is no longer the engine of upward mobility and democratic opportunity that it was once imagined to be. Nor has it remained focused on its original purpose: to train leaders who then go on to serve society. Instead, it has become "a national personnel department" that sorts and ranks people and grants "the high scorers a general, long-duration ticket to high status that can be cashed in anywhere." Selective universities, in particular, use their admissions practices to generate a permanent governing elite, in ways that are inconsistent with democratic values of equal opportunity, accountability, and service. * * *

Racial literacy sees the decline in government investment in higher education, along with the accompanying justificatory rhetoric of individual responsibility and individual "desert," as deeply problematic. Racial literacy suggests that admitting a more diverse class of students not only benefits individual students, but is also necessary to realize the social function and values of higher education, including democratic access, equal opportunity, and public service. The idea that each person is alone responsible for her fate and her tuition has allowed government support for higher education to plummet while costs skyrocket. Meanwhile, the goal of training future leaders—once the noble ambition of public institutions and their signature contribution to society—continues to atrophy.

* * *

Racial literacy helps institutions as they choose between contest, sponsored, and structural mobility. Using racially literate criteria to select among the three kinds of upward mobility is permissible under *Grutter*, is not jeopardized by *Gratz*, and is not only defensible, but may be politically necessary. Racial literacy discloses how all of these admissions processes use sociological proxies for assessing "merit" and future potential. Contest mobility purports to rank individuals, yet it relies on data that is closely aligned with group, not individual, attributes and assets, such as parents' education, grandparents' socioeconomic status, and other indicators of privilege. Sponsored mobility also purports to rank individuals, yet it fails to take account of group bias, which may depress individual performance, tilt the preferences of individual sponsors, and systematically distort the opportunity structure for talented individuals. Each type of mobility puts on the table a different understanding of whether merit is fixed or contextual, stable or responsive, real or imagined, performative or service-oriented. By situating merit within structures of opportunity, racial literacy encourages consideration of qualities that current admissions policies overlook. As a result, racially literate yet selective institutions may be able to relax their efforts to predict short-term outcomes and focus more on encouraging long-term commitments to service and community leadership.

* * *

Racial literacy also has a process dimension that uses race to guide participatory problem solving and accountability. In order to change the way race is understood, race has to be directly addressed rather than ignored. Race is often the subtext of public conversations about institutional goals. In fact, informed discussion about why education is now more desirable but less affordable or accessible often gets drowned out by inflammatory and polarizing rhetoric about race or by equally divisive rhetoric about individual responsibility and merit. By contrast, discussion among a diverse group of citizens about the ways race reveals rather than produces these social costs helps institutional policies become more transparent and thus more legitimate. * * *

Institutions could also make their processes more transparent by taking the views of various constituencies into account, even as they develop in the short term their new, holistic methods of reviewing candidate files. A broadly participatory process that includes the relevant stakeholders also helps satisfy the legitimacy concerns articulated by Justice O'Connor and modified by Justice Thomas's critique of elitism. Such a process would include professional educators and administrators, and would respect their expertise and specialized knowledge. But this process would also seek opportunities to communicate openly and engage with a group that is sufficiently diverse and informed to be critical, to mitigate the tendency of socially isolated decisionmakers to select those like themselves, to pay attention to issues of race and power, and to consider the connection between admissions and pedagogy.

* * *

It is out of a deliberative and interactive process that the institution should create its mission and explore the possibilities of reconstituting itself through admissions rituals. Such a process may generate a hybrid form of contest and sponsored mobility, similar to the choices made by the University of Michigan Law School and by the college post-*Gratz*. It is just as plausible, however, that a process that includes relevant stakeholders in a larger public conversation may prefer social engineering to yield structural mobility, similar to the GI Bill and current military programs, which provide educational opportunity in exchange for national or community service. Whatever the outcome, the process of choosing among contest, sponsored, and structural mobility must be understood as a political act with important societal, not just individual, consequences.

* * *

VI. CONCLUSION

* * * The *Grutter* and *Gratz* decisions may ultimately usher in a historical moment in which institutions of higher education explore issues of access to education and the scarcity of resources—issues that make limitations on that access deeply problematic in democratic terms. Universities need to explain themselves better to the broader public through a conversation rather than a declaration. It is not simply time for a public relations battle; rather, it is an occasion to align educational opportunity with its cousin, democratic participation. The question becomes who should get opportunity given the long-term goals of the institution or the needs of the larger society, rather than who "deserves" a prize because she won a race or because her presence will improve the institution's rankings in a news magazine. To find the answer, university leaders need to consider the long-term needs of the institution, the concerns of local, regional, and national constituencies, and the stability of the larger society, in a manner that is consistent with the expectation that the university will produce a new generation of citizens capable of assuming a broad range of leadership roles. The post-*Grutter* moment is an opportunity to talk more openly about, and investigate more thoroughly and in contemporary terms, the ways in which race helps reveal the relationship between education and democracy. It is a chance to make ourselves more racially literate and to understand the ways in which the choice among contest, sponsored, and structural mobility is a fundamentally political act.

By viewing their admissions decisions as political acts, in the virtuous sense of the phrase, universities can open the door to greater public support and confidence. Ultimately, this reevaluation of admissions choices may enable universities to join with others to create institutional structures that respond to the future while holding on to the best practices of the past. At the very least, it has the potential to transform the discussion from one fixated on ersatz preferences to one that actively confronts the reality of higher education's role in a multiracial democracy with the promise that education makes to us all.

NOTES AND QUESTIONS

1. **Origins of affirmative action.** In March 1961, President John F. Kennedy issued Executive Order 10925, in an effort to end employment discrimination among government contractors. It read in part, "The Contractor will take *affirmative action*, to insure that applicants are employed, and that employees are treated during employment, without regard to their race, creed, color, or national origin." Steven M. Cahn, Introduction, *in* THE AFFIRMATIVE ACTION DEBATE, XI (Steven M. Cahn ed., 2d ed. 2002) (emphasis added). Affirmative action emerged during the civil rights movement as a strategy for helping African Americans overcome the debilitating effects of racial oppression. It has since targeted other minority groups, notably Hispanics, Native Americans, and persons of Asian descent. Affirmative action refers to an array of programs that use race as a factor in the allotment of resources with the intent of benefiting racial minorities. It may take the form of generally increasing outreach to minorities, counting race as a "plus" factor in the allocation of resources, or directing a set amount of resources to minorities in specific "percentage plans." For an overview of federal affirmative action programs, see SAMUEL LEITER & WILLIAM M. LEITER, AFFIRMATIVE ACTION IN ANTIDISCRIMINATION LAW AND POLICY 7–22 (2002).

Affirmative action is among the most controversial issues in American law and politics, evoking strong feelings in both supporters and opponents. This controversy has been accompanied by uncertainty in the Supreme Court, which in thirty years of affirmative action jurisprudence has struggled to find a consistent legal framework with which to treat the issue. Political and public support for affirmative action has also been inconsistent. Democrats and the political left have historically supported affirmative action, while Republicans and conservatives have opposed it. In polls, the public generally expresses support for the goals of racial equality and diversity, but is less supportive of specific affirmative action measures. PETER H. SCHUCK, DIVERSITY IN AMERICA 170–72 (2003).

2. **The constitutionality of affirmative action.** Challenges to the constitutionality of affirmative action rest on the Equal Protection Clause of the Fourteenth Amendment. The Fourteenth Amendment reads, in part:

> *Section 1.* . . . No State shall make or enforce any law which shall abridge the privileges or immunities of citizens of the United States; nor shall any State deprive any person of life, liberty, or

property, without due process of law; nor deny any person within its jurisdiction the equal protection of the laws.

* * *

Section 5. The Congress shall have power to enforce, by appropriate legislation, the provisions of this article.

U.S. CONST. amend. XIV, §§ 2, 5.

The Thirteenth, Fourteenth, and Fifteenth Amendments were passed in the wake of the Civil War to try and protect the rights of the South's newly-freed black population. These "Reconstruction Amendments" were deemed necessary because, after the Civil War, the Southern states quickly started passing so-called "Black Codes," which returned former slaves to a position of complete social and political subordination. GEOFFREY STONE, ET AL., CONSTITUTIONAL LAW 432–33 (4th ed. 2001). The language of the amendments appears to afford minorities strong protections against governmental discrimination. However, in the years during and after Reconstruction, the Supreme Court read the amendments narrowly, typified in the *Slaughter-House Cases*, 83 U.S. (16 Wall.) 36 (1873), and especially *Plessy v. Ferguson*, 163 U.S. 537 (1896), in which the court validated the Jim Crow system of "separate but equal." The Court interpreted the amendments as having one overriding purpose, the freeing of the slaves, and showed little inclination to interpret them more ambitiously. BRUCE ACKERMAN, WE THE PEOPLE: FOUNDATIONS 81–105 (1991). As a result, governmentally sponsored racial discrimination persisted well into the twentieth century. The civil rights movement of the 1950s and 60s was in many ways an attempt to fulfill the initial promise of Reconstruction and its three constitutional amendments, and many consider affirmative action a valuable tool for the realization of this goal. *See* Eric Schnapper, *Affirmative Action and the Legislative History of the Fourteenth Amendment*, 71 VA. L. REV. 753 (1985).

Affirmative action raises Fourteenth Amendment questions because by seeking to promote a remedy for racially subordinated groups, it does not adhere to the formalistic notions of equality. This is not to say it is unconstitutional. The term "equal protection" has bedeviled courts who have tried to elucidate its meaning and apply it to governmental classifications, but some principles have emerged. It does *not* mean that all laws must treat or effect all classes of persons identically. There are many federal, state, and local laws that single out certain groups for inclusion or exclusion in receiving a benefit or suffering a detriment. However, the guarantee of equal protection also means that there are classifications that the government *cannot* lawfully make. It has been the task of the Supreme Court to decide what these unlawful classifications are.

The modern Court's approach to this problem has been to create a system of levels of review when dealing with laws that treat a discreet group or groups differently from others. The two baseline levels of review are "rational basis" review and "strict scrutiny" review, though as *Metro Broadcasting* shows these are not exclusive. The majority of classifications made by the government are subject to low-level, "rational basis" review and are overwhelmingly, but not always, upheld. These are laws which the Court believes are a proper use of governmental power and are rationally related to a legitimate governmental interest. However, the Court has held that some classifications are, by their very nature, "suspect" and should be examined with heightened scrutiny. Race is the classic "suspect" classification, and classifications based on race are normally subject to "strict scrutiny," the most stringent form of judicial review.

Some examples may help to flesh out this discussion. In *New York City Transit Authority v. Beazer*, 440 U.S. 568 (1979), the Court asked whether it was constitutional for the Transit Authority to exclude from employment users of methadone, a drug used by heroin addicts as part of their rehabilitation treatment. The Court concluded that safety concerns provided a sufficient "rational basis" for this special classification, and that it was not constitutionally significant that some qualified potential employees would be injured by the plan. The Court said that because the law "does not circumscribe a class of persons characterized by some unpopular trait or affiliation, it does not create or reflect any likelihood of bias on the part of the ruling majority." *Id.* at 593. *Beazer* is an example of a governmental classification which does not affect people equally, but is nevertheless constitutional. Under rational basis review, the Court treats classifications with a great deal of deference, and explicitly does not examine the wisdom or effectiveness of the law.

On the other end of the spectrum are laws that explicitly disadvantage persons based on their race. In *Strauder v. West Virginia*, 100 U.S. (10 Otto) 303 (1880), a West Virginia law which said that blacks may not serve on juries was invalidated as blatant discrimination, which is constitutionally impermissible. *Strauder* is an older case, but today this kind of classification would be subjected to "strict scrutiny" and would obviously be invalidated.

Traditionally, rational basis review nearly always meant a law would be upheld, and strict scrutiny review almost guaranteed disallowance. There are, however, important exceptions. For an example of a law examined under rational basis but nevertheless invalidated, see *City of Cleburne v. Cleburne Living Center*, 473 U.S. 432 (1985) (holding unconstitutional a law which negatively affected the mentally retarded because it had no rational relation to a legitimate governmental interest, but was instead motivated by "negative attitudes, or fear"). For an example of racial classifications upheld under strict scrutiny, see *Korematsu v. United States*, 323 U.S. 214 (1944) (upholding the internment of Japanese–Americans during World War II because the action was motivated by "pressing public necessity" rather than "racial antagonism"). Note that *Korematsu* has been harshly criticized. *See, e.g.,* Eugene V. Rostow, *The Japanese–American Cases–A Disaster*, in THE MASS INTERNMENT OF JAPANESE AMERICANS AND THE QUEST FOR LEGAL REDRESS 189 (Charles McClain ed., 1994).

Between the extremes of *Beazer* and *Strauder*, there are many laws which do not clearly fit into a certain level of scrutiny. These include laws which do not explicitly make racial classifications but have disparate effects on minorities, or laws that make classifications that are less clearly "suspect," such as with women or homosexuals. See, generally, STONE ET. AL., *supra* at 514–53. Affirmative action programs fall into this problematic category because of their unique position as laws which make racial classifications in the interest of *benefiting* racial minorities. This is using racial classification in quite a different way than the law in *Strauder*, and Courts have struggled to determine what level of scrutiny should apply to affirmative action programs.

3. The Bakke case. The Supreme Court first ruled on the substance of affirmative action in *Regents of University of California v. Bakke*, 438 U.S. 265 (1978). *Bakke* established the principle that voluntary use by government employers of race-conscious goals and timetables to remedy prior discrimination is not per se unconstitutional, but that explicit "quotas" are not allowable. The case involved an admissions plan at the University of California Davis Medical School, whereby sixteen seats out of a hundred were reserved for minority applicants. Four justices voted to uphold this aggressive affirmative action plan. Four justices voted to strike it down, but not on constitutional grounds. The deciding vote came from Justice Powell, who first articulated the view that affirmative action programs should be subjected to strict scrutiny. He wrote that all racial classifications, including those that are "benign," are suspect and should be treated under the strict scrutiny test. He did not believe that a general history of prior discrimination created a compelling governmental interest because in the *Bakke* case there were no judicial, administrative, or legislative findings of prior racial discrimination, and there were no findings that discrimination was a pervasive problem at the medical school. Justice Powell's other major contribution was his treatment of diversity as a rationale for affirmative action. He wrote that the interest in a diverse student body was reason enough to allow race to be used in admission decisions, but not a rigid system that isolated sixteen spots from competition with others. Justice Powell wrote only for himself, but his opinion has proven to be very influential in affirmative action decisions. Since *Bakke*, the thorny issues associated with affirmative action have led to an often sharply divided Court and few clear guidelines.

Justice Powell retired in 1987, and Justice Kennedy's appointment was seen as creating a strong conservative voting bloc on the Court. *Croson* was the first time that the Court issued a majority opinion in an affirmative action case. Many believed the case marked a shift away from a Supreme Court that had been relatively receptive to affirmative action programs. Taking a rather literalistic view of the Fourteenth Amendment, the Court found that the fact that "the Richmond Plan denies certain citizens the opportunity to compete for a fixed percentage of public contracts based solely upon their races" meant that the plan must be subjected to strict scrutiny, which it was found not to meet. The decision in *Metro Broadcasting* was therefore something of a surprise. It marked the first time a non-remedial rationale was used to validate an affirmative action plan. The other important deviation made in *Metro Broadcasting* was its use of an intermediate level of scrutiny in assessing the FCC plan.

The regime of intermediate scrutiny in affirmative action cases was short lived. In 1995, only 5 years after *Metro Broadcasting* was decided, the Court decided *Adarand Constructors v. Pena*, 515 U.S. 200 (1995), the last major case prior to *Grutter*. A majority of the Court overruled *Metro Broadcasting*'s intermediate scrutiny standard and held that strict scrutiny applies to *all* affirmative action programs. The attitude toward affirmative action among the members of the Court had shifted once again with the addition of Justice Thomas, and the decision evidences a loss of confidence in Congress's ability to deal with race. *See* Paul J. Mishkin, *Foreword: The Making of a Turning Point—Metro and* Adarand, 84 CAL. L. REV. 875 (1996). Justice Scalia wrote in concurrence that there should be *no* group-based remedies for discrimination, only for individual cases of active discrimination, but a majority of the court has never accepted this view. For a detailed review of the Supreme Court's affirmative action jurisprudence prior to *Grutter*, see GIRARDEAU A. SPANN, THE LAW OF AFFIRMATIVE ACTION (2000).

As these cases show, the Court has struggled to find a consistent view on affirmative action, disagreeing over what legal standard should apply and more generally about the value of affirmative action. In the public arena, affirmative action is perhaps best known for its contentiousness. Depending on how the issue is framed, the arguments on both sides are appealing. What makes affirmative action problematic is that it is not intended to compensate for specific acts of overt discrimination; rather, it works more broadly to attempt to correct the general discrimination that has led to the economic and political inequality that exists for minorities. In this way, it focuses on groups rather than individuals. Supporters of affirmative action believe that given this country's history of racial prejudice, race-conscious programs are necessary to compensate for the disadvantage that has been suffered by minorities. Discrimination is still a problem that cannot be overcome through colorblind policies, and active steps must be taken to eclipse racial injustice. In addition, diversity is a valuable goal in a society where racial misunderstanding has so often led to prejudice. Opponents argue that it is wrong to use race as a basis for the allocation of resources, no matter who the intended beneficiaries are. They believe it is unfair to reserve resources for minorities at the expense of whites who have not engaged in discriminatory conduct, and unjust to have "innocent whites" today pay for the sins of past generations. Many also argue that affirmative action has a stigmatizing effect on blacks, casting doubts on the legitimacy of their accomplishments as possibly the result of special treatment.

For more on the affirmative action debate, see generally Erwin Chemerinsky, *Making Sense of the Affirmative Action Debate, in* CIVIL RIGHTS AND SOCIAL WRONGS 86 (John Higham ed., 1997); BARBARA R. BERGMANN, IN DEFENSE OF AFFIRMATIVE ACTION (1996); Ronald Dworkin, *Affirming Affirmative Action*, N.Y. REV. OF BOOKS, Oct. 28, 1998, at 91; JOHN E. ROEMER, EQUALITY OF OPPORTUNITY (1998). On the possible stigmatization of the beneficiaries of affirmative action, see Linda Hamilton Krieger, *Civil Rights*

Perestroika: *Intergroup Relations After Affirmative Action*, 86 CAL. L. REV. 1251 (1998).

4. Affirmative action and equal protection. The Fourteenth Amendment says nothing about heightened standards of scrutiny for racial classifications. What precisely is it that makes racial classifications so troubling and suited for heightened scrutiny? Are they illegitimate in themselves, or only in the context of this country's history of racism against blacks and other minorities? What is the difference between a class of short men and a class of racial minorities? In a famous footnote in *United States v. Carolene Products*, 304 U.S. 144 (1938), Justice Stone argued that "more searching judicial inquiry" for classifications involving race may be necessary because "prejudice against discrete and insular minorities may be a special condition, which tends seriously to curtail the operation of those political processes ordinarily to be relied upon to protect minorities." Consider Charles R. Lawrence, *The Id, the Ego, and Equal Protection: Reckoning with Unconscious Racism*, 39 STAN. L. REV. 317, 322 (1987):

> Traditional notions of intent do not reflect the fact that decisions about racial matters are influenced in large part by factors that can be characterized as neither intentional—in the sense that certain outcomes are self-consciously sought—nor unintentional—in the sense that the outcomes are random, fortuitous, and uninfluenced by the decisionmaker's beliefs, desires, and wishes.

> Americans share a common historical and cultural heritage in which racism has played and still plays a dominant role. Because of this shared experience, we also inevitably share many ideas, attitudes, and beliefs that attach significance to an individual's race and induce negative feelings and opinions about nonwhites. To the extent that this cultural belief system has influenced all of us, we are all racists. At the same time, most of us are unaware of our racism. We do not recognize the ways in which our cultural experience has influenced our beliefs about race or the occasions on which those beliefs affect our actions. In other words, a large part of the behavior that produces racial discrimination is influenced by unconscious racial motivation.

It is evident from this language that strict scrutiny was intended as a means of *protecting* minorities from the effects of discrimination, be it overt or unconscious. Ironically, the use of strict scrutiny in affirmative action cases has led to the defeat of laws intended to *benefit* racial minorities. Does this prove that strict scrutiny in affirmative action programs is inappropriate? What aspect of affirmative action should most inform the Court's decision about the proper level of scrutiny—its goals, its effects, or its actual operation?

In *Washington v. Davis*, 426 U.S. 229 (1976), the Court held that a law that only disproportionately impacts a minority group, but is not race-specific in its application, will be subject to rational basis review. Is there a meaningful difference between a law that explicitly disadvantages minorities and one that does so only in effect? How can the Court justify treating laws which empirically disadvantage minorities with rational basis review, while treating affirmative action laws with strict scrutiny review simply because they explicitly classify using race? For a discussion of the equal protection clause and affirmative action, see MICHEL ROSENFELD, AFFIRMATIVE ACTION AND JUSTICE (1991).

5. Can racial classifications be benign? Affirmative action programs are considered "benign" forms of discrimination because they burden the majority, and are regarded as protecting rather than harming the political interests of minorities. Many opponents of affirmative action doubt the ability of the government to make benign racial classifications. Some believe that "benign racial classification" is a contradiction in terms, and that given the troubled history of racial classifications in this country the government should *never* allocate resources or give preference on the basis of race. This position is strongly articulated in Justice Kennedy's dissent in *Metro Broadcasting*, when he writes that the Court is not able to identify readily which racial classifications are benign, and equates the logic of affirmative action with the Supreme Court's infamous decision in *Plessy*. Is it true that racial classifications are so dangerous that they should never be used? Why should it be difficult to differentiate between laws that are designed to benefit a minority population and those that are designed to oppress minorities?

6. Strict or intermediate scrutiny? Inside the courtroom, perhaps the most controversial issue regarding affirmative action has been what legal standard should apply. As Justice O'Connor wrote in *Croson*, this is not a mere quibble over lawyers' words. Strict scrutiny is a very difficult standard to meet, and prior to *Grutter* no affirmative action program had survived strict scrutiny. Many predicted that *Adarand* would mark the end of affirmative action programs, believing that strict scrutiny would be "strict in theory, fatal in fact." *Grutter* has proved these predictions wrong, at least in the context of higher education. Why was the intermediate scrutiny used in *Metro Broadcasting* abandoned so quickly?

Strict scrutiny dictates that "benign" racial classifications will only be upheld if they are narrowly tailored to achieve a compelling governmental interest. How does Justice O'Connor apply strict scrutiny in *Grutter*? Do you agree that diversity in a university is a compelling state interest? Is it likely that a set-aside program such as the one in *Croson* can meet the strict scrutiny standard? In limited circumstances, the Court has found the remedying of past discrimination to be compelling governmental interest, see *Shaw v. Hunt*, 517 U.S. 899 (1996), but has stipulated that the remedy must attack "identified discrimination" which must be identified with specificity. Why is the remedying of generalized, pervasive discrimination which certainly existed at one time in this country not a compelling interest? Note Justice Marshall's strong assertion in *Croson* that the "interest in ensuring that the government does not reflect and reinforce prior discrimination is every bit as strong as the interest in eliminating private discrimination...."

The Court in *Croson* believed that attempts to remedy generalized, societal discrimination "[have] no logical stopping point." Is the absence of a clear stopping point sufficient reason to invalidate a law? In *Croson*, why did the majority determine that strict scrutiny was necessary? What were the majority's specific objections to the affirmative action plan in question? Was it appropriate for the court to speculate that the real motivation for the law was not past discrimination but simply political favoritism among African-Americans, who held a majority of City Council seats? What is the relevancy of the dissent's mention of Richmond's history as the capital of the confederacy?

Metro Broadcasting represents a relatively brief period of time when the Supreme Court applied an intermediate level of scrutiny to affirmative action programs, holding that the governmental interest served by a given program need only be "important." How does the Court rationalize this lessened standard? How much was the Court's decision in *Metro Broadcasting* a result of deference to Congressional findings and the extensive review procedures of the FCC? Justice O'Connor contends in her *Metro Broadcasting* dissent that treating groups differently based on race "may stigmatize those groups singled out for different treatment and may create considerable tension with the Nation's widely shared commitment to evaluating individuals upon their individual merit." 497 U.S. at 604. What concern is it of the Court's if the beneficiaries of affirmative action are stigmatized in the eyes of some? Does such a commitment to individual merit exist in this country? What "merits" must one possess to secure a broadcasting license? Is it possible that some racial tension must be tolerated to correct the effects of America's history of racism?

7.   Colorblindness versus race-consciousness. Justice Blackmun wrote in *Bakke* "In order to get beyond racism, we must first take account of race. There is no other way. And in order to treat some persons equally, we must treat them differently." 438 U.S. at 407. At the core of the debate over affirmative action is disagreement over whether it is possible to overcome the inequality caused by past racial discrimination without taking race into account in the remedy. Implicit in this debate is further disagreement over whether discrimination itself continues to be a problem. Some believe that while overt racism is seldom expressed in public, unconscious discrimination continues to be a very real problem, despite the improvements in race relations that have taken place over the last fifty years. Not only are colorblind solutions ineffective, they are actually detrimental because they mask the discrimination that still occurs and disengaging whites from the unique problems facing minorities. Consider:

> I believe that [whites] today, raised white in a racist society, are often ridden with white solipsism—not the consciously held belief that one race is inherently superior to all others, but a tunnel-vision which simply does not see nonwhite experience or existence as precious or significant, unless in spasmodic, impotent guilt-reflexes, which have little or no long-term, continuing momentum or political usefulness.... A remedial regime predicated on color-

blindness will have little influence at this deep level of social and legal consciousness because it cannot adequately challenge white attitudes or recognize a role for black self-definition.

T. Alexander Aleinikoff, *A Case for Race-consciousness*, 91 COLUM. L. REV. 1060, 1060 (1991). *See also* Williams, *supra*, at 544; LANI GUINIER & GERALD TORRES, THE MINER'S CANARY: ENLISTING RACE, RESISTING POWER, TRANSFORMING DEMOCRACY 32–67 (2002).

Conservative opponents of affirmative action argue that discrimination based on race is largely a thing of the past, and that colorblind policies that simply treat everyone equally can be effective. To overcome racial prejudice and inequality we must move beyond race and treat people as individuals, because the race of a person tells us nothing about her abilities, beliefs, moral worthiness, etc. *See* STEPHAN THERNSTROM & ABIGAIL THERNSTROM, AMERICA IN BLACK AND WHITE, ONE NATION, INDIVISIBLE: RACE IN MODERN AMERICA (1997). Whether or not discrimination continues to be a problem, there is considerable evidence that whites and blacks continue to have strongly divergent opinions on issues of race. *See* DONALD R. KINDER & LYNN SANDERS, DIVIDED BY COLOR: RACIAL POLITICS AND DEMOCRATIC IDEALS (1996). For a rebuttal of the Thernstroms' position that examines a range of issues, including education, crime, poverty, and voting, see Michael K. Brown, Martin Carnoy et al., WHITEWASHING RACE: THE MYTH OF A COLOR-BLIND SOCIETY (2003).

8. Purpose of affirmative action. As *Croson*, *Metro Broadcasting*, and *Grutter* show, affirmative action programs have been employed for a variety of purposes in a variety of contexts. The original rationale for affirmative action was to remedy inequality by directing the allocation of resources to those who have been historically disadvantaged by discrimination. The "set-aside" program in *Croson* was premised on the desire to counteract past discrimination and correct the disparities in access to wealth that exists between whites and minorities. The objection opponents make to set-aside programs is that it is unfair and counterproductive to disadvantage those who have not themselves engaged in the harmful, discriminatory conduct. In *Croson*, why was the large disparity between the percentage of blacks in the general population and their share of contracting dollars not proof enough that discrimination had put black businesses at a disadvantage? Does the Court offer any other explanation for this disparity?

Who was most likely to benefit from the plan in *Metro Broadcasting*? The broadcast licenses at issue in *Metro Broadcasting* are valuable commodities, yet the court uses a diversity rationale to uphold the plan. What are the economic implications of the decision? *Metro Broadcasting* has been harshly criticized as a thinly veiled attempt to further enrich a small amount of already wealthy blacks, and characterized as doing very little to help those who have actually been disadvantaged by discrimination. SCHUCK, *supra* at 142. Others have pointed out that once the remedial rationale is removed from affirmative action cases, it become very difficult to decide what groups should be receiving benefits. Paul J. Mishkin writes, "Once remedial justification is set aside, there appears to be no explanation why the goal of greater variety in broadcast content would not be equally (or better) served by including among the preferred groups others not defined by race—e.g., older people or Polish-Americans (who may be able to claim even less presence on the airwaves)." Mishkin, *supra* at 882. Even some supporters of the decision in *Metro Broadcasting* questioned the diversity rationale as being the exclusive inspiration for the court's decision:

> [A]lthough the majority described its measures as "not 'remedial' in the sense of being designed to compensate victims of past governmental or societal discrimination," its reasoning is clearly framed as a corrective for historical conditions that are hardly long buried in the shroud of some long-forgotten past, but whose effects are specifically identifiable and endlessly enumerable.

Patricia J. Williams, Metro Broadcasting, Inc. v. FCC: *Regrouping in Singular Times*, 104 HARV. L. REV. 525, 527 (1990).

The dissent in *Metro Broadcasting* strongly questions the correlation between a person's race and a specific set of views that have been underrepresented. In one sense this must be correct; it is impossible to predict someone's views based simply on the color of their skin. Nevertheless, there is a connection between culture and race, and perhaps while minority broadcasters will not bring any particular views that can immediately be identified as "diverse," increasing the minority broadcasting ownership will better represent "a shared heritage of language patterns, habits, history, and experience" that is "black culture." *See* Williams, *supra* at 529–30.

9. Controversy about affirmative action. Affirmative action, whatever its merits, is unquestionably a hot-button issue in American politics, and the divide has only deepened in the wake of *Grutter*. This may not be surprising given the strong feelings that issues of race inject into any issue. This is accompanied by the high stakes, such as seats in highly selective colleges, and the feeling by some whites that these seats are their societal entitlement. Some opponents of affirmative action have taken to inflammatory and silly methods to try and undermine its goals. At Roger Williams University in Rhode Island, members of the College Republicans who object to the university's use of race-based affirmative action, provoked controversy by awarding a whites-only scholarship, the "Students of Non-color Scholarship." Said the president of the group, "If you're going to have race-based scholarships on campus, you just cannot have it to one group of people and not the other. We say that's unequal treatment." The Republican National Committee denounced the award and severed all ties with the college group. *All Things Considered* (NPR radio broadcast Feb. 19, 2004). In another instance, the editor of the conservative magazine National Review has encouraged white college applicants to engage in "civil disobedience" by misrepresenting their race on college admissions forms. Mark Edmundson, *Civil Disobedience Against Affirmative Action*, N.Y. TIMES, Dec. 14, 2003, (Magazine) at 60.

Supporters of affirmative action have entered this fray as well. For example, some point out that white members of the elite have enjoyed the advantages of affirmative action by being the sons and daughters of alumni of elite institutions and being enrolled in prep schools that every year send many students to the nation's best universities. Supporters note the fact that George W. Bush's sub-par academic performance in high school and subsequent acceptance at Yale. "Bush clearly got [into Yale] because of affirmative action. Affirmative action for the son and grandson of alumni. Affirmative action for a member of a politically influential family. Affirmative action for a boy from a fancy prep school. These forms of affirmative action still go on." Michael Kinsley, *How Affirmative Action Helped George W.*, TIME, Jan. 27, 2003, at 70.

Despite the controversy that surrounds affirmative action, Neal Devins points out the overwhelming support that the *Grutter* decision received from universities, the business community, the military and politicians. Not a single university filed an amicus brief opposing affirmative action, the military submitted a very influential brief in support, and even the Bush administration, though supporting the plaintiff in the case, expressed support for racial diversity and did not suggest that all race-based preferences be done away with. Devins argues that as a political matter it would have been very difficult for the Supreme Court to have disallowed all considerations of race in college admissions, and that "affirmative action has become so entrenched that the costs of taking a stand against it are greater now than ever before." Neal Devins, *Explaining* Grutter v. Bollinger, 152 U. PA. L. REV. 347, 373 (2003). Should this support affect the Supreme Court's ruling? Is it proper for the Court to recognize when it is dealing with a socially and politically controversial issue and perhaps treat it differently than others?

10. Value of diversity in higher education. There is broad disagreement as to whether diversity in the classroom is a worthwhile goal, and whether it should be achieved through affirmative action, as shown in the *Hopwood* decision. While *Grutter* has settled the legal question for now, the debate will continue. Supporters of affirmative action view diversity as promoting the inclusion of marginalized segments of the population, helping to abate the broader segregation that exists in society, breaking down stereotypes, and introducing different and previously underrepresented viewpoints into the classroom. Devon W. Carbado & Mitu Gulati, *What Exactly is Racial Diversity?*, 91 CAL. L. REV. 1149 (2003) (book review).

Conservative commentators are highly skeptical of the benefits of diversity, and agree with Justice Thomas's contention that the support for affirmative action shown by universities is merely evidence of elite institutions' desire to be "aesthetically" diverse. Who benefits from classroom diversity? Is it legitimate to expect members of a certain race to bring a set of views that will be different from the white majority? consider this attack from an opponent:

> Students of minority groups may be forceful and eloquent spokesmen for their own racial views. But so what? There are many

academic courses in which the questions of race and sex are marginal at best. In the arts and sciences, none of the math and science curriculum has a racial message; the same is true of large portions of social sciences and the humanities as well. Within the law school, tax, business, and procedural courses have little if any content related to race, and it would be odd to say that they could not be taught successfully without any reference to race, or indeed without any minority or female students. After all, many of the lawyers and professors who teach today received excellent education in these subjects before the advent of any affirmative action program.

Richard A. Epstein, *A Rational Basis for Affirmative Action: A Shaky but Classical Liberal Defense*, 100 MICH. L. REV. 2036, 2040–41 (2002).

Another critique of the diversity rationale is that it presumes that certain qualities "inhere in a racial group." SCHUCK, *supra* at 165. *See also* Charles R. Lawrence, *Two Views of the River: A Critique of the Liberal Defense of Affirmative Action*, 101 COLUM. L. REV. 928 (2001) (criticizing the diversity rationale while supporting affirmative action). Notice Justice Kennedy's claim in *Grutter* that diversity may be a convenient rationale that is not the true basis for support of affirmative action. If diversity does not benefit a university, why is affirmative action overwhelmingly supported by the country's most selective colleges and graduate schools? Admission to top universities increases one's access to elite professions and social circles. Is increasing diversity not only in the classroom but in the upper echelons of society a realistic goal for affirmative action?

Another facet of the debate over university admissions is the value of the traditional tools that universities use for admission decisions, namely grades and standardized tests. Opponents of affirmative action contend that college admission should be based solely on these and other merit-based standards. However, many believe that grades, and especially standardized tests such as the SAT and LSAT, are not predictive of success in college or law school, but do correlate quite closely to race and parental income. How would the elimination of standardized testing affect admissions to elite universities? GUINIER & TORRES, *supra* at 71. Lani Guinier proposes a "structural mobility" framework in which identification of qualified applicants would move beyond traditional indicators such as standardized tests. Take for example two applicants to an Ivy League school. One is a wealthy, white, "A" student from a top prep school who scores extremely well on standardized tests and has a full compliment of extracurricular activities. The other is a black, "B+" student, from a crumbling inner-city high school whose test scores and extracurriculars are good but less impressive. How should an admissions officer assess these two candidates? Is it possible to say who "deserves" admission? What is the goal of an admissions officer in making this decision? Is it who she thinks will better succeed in college? Succeed in life? Add more to the college's student body? Add more to society as a whole? Should the fact that the second student has very likely encountered many more obstacles in her achievements be relevant to an admissions decision?

11. ***Gratz v. Bollinger.*** *Gratz v. Bollinger*, 539 U.S. 244 (2003), decided on the same day as *Grutter*, dealt with the admissions policy at the undergraduate division of the University of Michigan. The University ranked applicants on a 150 point scale. Students were primarily awarded points for academic achievement, but up to 40 points were available based on qualifications unrelated to academics. An applicant received 20 points for membership in an underrepresented minority group, attendance at a predominately minority or disadvantaged high school, or recruitment for athletics. Other non-academic factors included 10 points for residence in Michigan, 4 points for children of alumni, and up to 3 points for an outstanding essay. This admissions policy was rejected by the Court, primarily because it did not include the individualized review present in *Grutter*, and therefore too closely resembled the kind of quota system disallowed in *Bakke*. Justice Powell wrote in *Bakke* that the fact of an applicant being a minority should be "considered without being decisive," but according to Justice Rehnquist's majority opinion, under Michigan's undergraduate plan "the factor of race [is] decisive for virtually every minimally qualified underrepresented minority applicant." Justice Souter's dissent saw a meaningful difference between the quota system in *Bakke* and the system at issue in *Gratz*, because the *Bakke* plan focused only on race, whereas this plan "lets all applicants compete for all places and values an applicant's offerings for any place not solely on the grounds of [race]." He contended that the "college simply does by a numbered scale what that law school accomplishes by 'holistic review'; the distinction does not imply that applicants to the undergraduate college are denied individualized consideration...."

12. Alternate approaches. Kevin Brown presents a bleak picture of the prospects for black enrollment in selective colleges and graduate schools if affirmative action were stopped. Kevin Brown, Hopwood: *Was This the African–American Nightmare or the African American Dream?* 2 TEX. F. ON C.L. & C.R. 97 (1996):

After the *Hopwood* decision, Texas instituted a plan in which the top 10 percent of students from every public school in the state are automatically accepted by state universities. Florida and California have adopted similar programs. The plan has been described as a compromise between race and merit-based solutions. An obvious goal of the plan is to have minority students from underperforming schools and bad neighborhoods be able to attend state universities, but by not explicitly involving race it ameliorates some of the supposed unfairness of affirmative action. The Texas plan also received support from poor, rural whites who have limited access to opportunities in higher education. Justice Souter criticized these plans in his *Gratz* dissent, writing that they suffer "the disadvantage of obfuscation ... the 'percentage plans' are just as race conscious as the point scheme (and fairly so), but they get their racially diverse results without saying directly what they are doing or why they are doing it." *Id.*

at 298. These plans may also have the effect of disadvantaging minority students who attend better schools and do well, but fall outside of the top 10 percent. Does the Texas plan strike you as an effective way to meet the goals of affirmative action without employing race-based preferences?

In California, Proposition 209 prohibited preferential treatment based on race in public education. Justice Thomas contends in *Grutter* that minority admissions at Boalt Hall, the elite law school at the University of California Berkeley, have not significantly suffered since Proposition 209's passage. For a contrary view, see ANDREA GUERRERO, SILENCE AT BOALT HALL: THE DISMANTLING OF AFFIRMATIVE ACTION (2002). One scholar at the University of California-Los Angeles has claimed, based on a statistical analysis of data collected at that university's law school, that eliminating race-conscious admissions programs in law schools would actually increase the number of minority lawyers, because African American law students who are presently unable to perform adequately at top-flight schools would go to lesser schools where they could succeed spectacularly and pass the bar in greater numbers. Richard H. Sander, *A Systematic Analysis of Affirmative Action in American Law Schools*, 57 STAN. L. REV. 367 (2004). Sander's analysis has been attacked by defenders of affirmative action. *See, e.g.,* David L. Chambers et al., *The Real Impact of Eliminating Affirmative Action in American Law Schools: An Empirical Critique of Richard Sander's Stanford Law Review Study*, 58 STAN. L. REV. (forthcoming May, 2005); Cheryl I. Harris & William C. Kidder, *The Black Student Mismatch Myth in Legal Education: The Systemic Flaws in Richard Sander's Affirmative Action Study*, J. BLACKS HIGHER EDUC. 102 (2005). How can we reconcile this controversy with Brown's article?

What kinds of measures might an elite university take to sustain minority enrollment without using explicit, race-based preferences? Is it possible that admissions officers may secretly or even subconsciously continue to give preferential treatment to minorities even after a formal affirmative action program is no longer in place? Justice Ginsburg predicts in her dissent in *Gratz* that this will take place. Is there a value to having race-based preferences out in the open?

Many have argued that affirmative action in college admissions should be based on class rather than race, pointing out that academic achievement is tied to economic status, and that the beneficiaries of race-based admissions preferences are mostly middle and upper-middle class blacks who are not as in need of assistance. *See* RICHARD D. KAHLENBERG, THE REMEDY: CLASS, RACE, AND AFFIRMATIVE ACTION (1996). Despite the victory of the University of Michigan's Law School in *Grutter*, the president of the university has expressed the desire "to create a more 'diverse diversity,' based on students from wider socioeconomic backgrounds . . . not[ing] that poor kids are nearly as scarce on campus as minorities. Just one in five of Michigan's 25,000 undergrads comes from a family making less than $50,000 a year." Keith Naughton, *A New Campus Crusader*, NEWSWEEK, Dec. 29, 2003/Jan. 5, 2004, at 78. Who has the most to lose and the most to gain when affirmative action programs are in place? What should be made of poor white students who face great challenges in achieving high levels of educations—should they be the beneficiaries of affirmative action programs? Other proposals, such as those promoted by Shapiro, promote a focus on the root causes of why affirmative action is deemed necessary, namely the poor education available to minority students that renders them unable to compete on an equal footing. Is racial inequality too widespread and deeply-rooted a problem to be solved by affirmative action?

13. Is affirmative action effective? Despite the inequality that still exists, minorities have enjoyed uneven, but noteworthy, improvement in economic and social status in the past fifty years. Some argue that affirmative action has been instrumental in this progress. William Bowen and Derek Bok contend that selective colleges have succeeded in educating "sizable numbers of minority students who have already achieved significant success and seem likely in time to occupy positions of leadership throughout society." William Bowen & Derek Bok, The Shape of the River: Long-Term Consequences of Considering Race in College and University Admissions (1998). Others attribute this progress to a variety of advances and changed circumstances for black Americans unrelated to affirmative action. Schuck, *supra* at 140. To what extent should effectiveness affect future decisions about affirmative action? Justice O'Connor's *Grutter* opinion contains the prediction that in twenty-five years affirmative action will no longer be necessary. Does this seem likely? Why would she feel compelled to include this speculation?

B. The Wealth of Communities

The financial services infrastructure available to make loans and accept deposits is a critical component for creating and sustaining wealth. Two banking statutes, the Equal Credit Opportunity Act and the Community Reinvestment Act, were designed to correct the long-established patterns of discriminatory lending to women, and to poor and minority communities. In what follows, legal scholar Anthony Taibi questions whether either of these statutes contributes significantly to the reversal of financial subordination, and economic isolation that have been sustaining features of wealth and income inequality for Blacks, and other targets of racial discrimination. Taibi proposes, instead, a "community empowerment" paradigm in which local racial cultural identities and civil institutions are accorded central importance beyond the formalistic model of markets and rational choice.

Banking, Finance, and Community Economic Empowerment: Structural Economic Theory, Procedural Civil Rights, and Substantive Racial Justice
107 Harv. L. Rev. 1463 (1994).

■ Anthony D. Taibi

> Practical men, who believe themselves to be quite exempt from any intellectual influences, are usually the slaves of some defunct economist.
>
> John Maynard Keynes

I.   INTRODUCTION: PARADIGMS OF THE RELATIONSHIP BETWEEN CIVIL RIGHTS AND BANKING REGULATION

The structure of America's financial system necessarily has a profound effect on the social and economic conditions of our neighborhoods and communities. The current small business credit crunch increasingly stifles those businesses that provide the bulk of new jobs and give regular people a chance for entrepreneurial independence. The continuing discrimination and redlining in both mortgage and consumer credit hinder the ability of Black people to buy and improve their homes and therefore block asset accumulation, stakeholding, and revitalization in Black communities. The ongoing consolidation of the banking industry has had and will continue to have a profound negative impact in low- and moderate-income communities and in non-White communities. Community investment is at the intersection of civil rights and economics, yet the prevailing civil rights paradigms fail to consider the structure of the banking system as a civil rights issue.

Two paradigms dominate civil rights discourse, neither of which aids in understanding how the structure of the financial system disempowers African–American and other non-elite communities. The equality paradigm, embodied in the Equal Credit Opportunity Act (ECOA), seeks to regulate financial institutions to ensure that banks treat like customers alike and make services available according to race neutral criteria. The affirmative action paradigm considers traditional equal treatment policy insufficient to erase the legacy of past discrimination. This latter model, embodied in the Community Reinvestment Act (CRA), seeks to ensure not only that banks apply race neutral criteria in evaluating individual loan applications, but also that banks actually lend in low- and moderate-income communities.

These two prevailing civil rights paradigms cannot address the structural nature of disinvestment, because they implicitly accept a neoclassical economic ideology that is incompatible with genuine reform. According to the neoclassical economic paradigm, every competitively profitable investment will find an investor; therefore, an unfunded investment could not possibly be competitively profitable. Although this postulate has a pleasingly simple logic, it simply is not true. All investments are made with at least some degree of uncertainty. Investment decisions are made before realization, and actual return at realization can be very different from initial assumptions: some investments do not live up to initial expectations and others outperform expectations. Neoclassical ideology refuses to acknowledge that cultural and psychological forces can be as powerful as market forces. To the extent that investors continue to undervalue community investments relative to other investments—due to racial, ethnic, or class biases, or because small investments for working people seem mundane— there is systematic market failure. Neoclassical thinkers would counter that, even if market failure does occur, in the long run, someone will discover the failure and enter the underserved market. Leaving aside for the moment the fact that disinvestment can sometimes become a self-fulfilling prophecy, that "long run" may last until long after our grandchildren are dead.

The equality paradigm implicitly embraces neoclassical assumptions in that it presupposes that the competition for funds in particular real-world marketplaces can operate as competition would in the neutral, rational, theoretically "perfect" market. Thus, the equality paradigm assumes that, to the extent that African–Americans and other people from disempowered communities have an "equal opportunity" to compete for a capital investment with other credit seekers, the outcome of that competition is fair or at least efficient.

The affirmative action paradigm reinforces neoclassical assumptions in more subtle ways. It too incorporates the neoclassical assumption that capital allocations determined in particular marketplaces are in fact "market efficient," but also posits equity as a distinct and competing value from procedural fairness and efficiency and seeks to subsidize favored groups to achieve a desired distributional outcome. It never questions the structure of marketplaces that routinely produce unacceptable results. To the extent that it accepts as given the institutional structures of American life (but for racial disparity), affirmative action reinforces the legitimacy of the very institutions that effectively disempower African–American and other non-elite communities. Thus, affirmative action turns the aspirations of disempowered groups into mere special interest pleadings, and demands for justice into supplications for charity. It divides the disempowered along the lines of who does and does not benefit from "special treatment" instead of uniting them in a common struggle.

Unwittingly accepting these neoclassical assumptions, progressive observers continue to describe community investment problems in terms of industry recalcitrance and insufficient political commitment toward reform. This is a tragic error. The disinvestment faced by lower-middle-class communities is structural—a product of the globalization of markets, capital, and production. Working-class, ethnic, and minority communities must control their own destinies by wresting control of local finance away from non-local institutions; they must not simply ask those institutions to invest a little more in local neighborhoods. The structural economic problems facing America's communities can be addressed in part by creating and reinforcing financial institutions that are community specific in their control, whether in the form of a broad-based community organization or simply a local business elite focused on profits but informed by a sense of its cultural roots.

Liberal perspectives do not treat building community institutions as an end in itself; their assumptions obscure how such institutions might be both fair and efficient given a different structural grounding. Of course, even in a reformed marketplace, not all socially desired investments will be competitive. Ensuring efficiency and structuring markets does not exhaust the role of politics. From health care to roads, from the environment to housing, American citizens must make decisions about whether and how to subsidize and to regulate. But as long as we are mired in the habits of mind engendered by liberal civil rights ideology and neoclassical economics, we will make these decisions myopically.

The creation of empowered communities requires more than new policies tied to community-based political organizations: it requires creating a new economic discourse. Although the "American Dream" of strong communities and financial independence remains an essential part of our culture and politics, the idea that the purpose of economic policy should be to promote this dream has not enjoyed intellectual respectability since the downfall of the Populist movement in the late nineteenth century. The assumptions of neoclassical economic ideology implicitly underlie and undermine the debate across the political spectrum. This Article represents merely a salvo in the battle of scholarly debates, op-ed pieces, think-tank projects, and efforts to shape our understanding of "common sense." Creating a discourse of populist community-empowerment economics and public policy is an ongoing project.

Although the racial dimension is among the most pressing and morally repugnant aspects of community disinvestment, the eroding job base, the small business credit crunch, and the globalization of capital are problems that affect all Americans. These issues are racial, but they require more than racial solutions. The small business credit crunch affects all communities, and U.S. home ownership rates have dropped precipitously in the last decade for all Americans. The "redundancy" of the American workforce to global corporations is now affecting white-collar professionals and middle managers, as well as Black and White working class people. If we are to create a new populist discourse about structural economic changes in our society, our movement must be transracial and have broad appeal across the economic spectrum. Opposing the economic and cultural colonization of our particular racial, ethnic, cultural, and religious communities requires a common struggle. Ironically, we can only promote our own group's interest if we work in concert with other groups.

The creation of a new civil rights consciousness requires that we examine the successes and the failures of existing policies that were informed by the two predominant civil rights paradigms. To that end, Part II examines the expression of the equality paradigm in the Equal Credit Opportunity Act (ECOA) and the effects and shortcomings of that Act. Part II then looks critically at liberal explanations of those shortcomings and offers an understanding of the ECOA's weaknesses from the perspective of community empowerment. Part III examines the manifestation of the affirmative action paradigm in the Community Reinvestment Act (CRA). A review and critique of the CRA's successes and failures demonstrate why a community-empowerment perspective can more effectively improve people's lives and create a multi-racial political consensus than can current paradigms. Part IV describes the emergence of the various types of institutions that comprise the community development financial institutions (CDFI) industry. A critique of the Clinton administration's proposed Community Development Banking and Financial Institutions Act of 1994, informed by a community-empowerment perspective, then reveals the failure of the bill to confront the imperatives of the already-established financial structure. The Article concludes by proposing a number of steps that the government should take if it truly wishes to embrace the community-empowerment paradigm as a model for its vision of the financial sector.

II.   THE EQUAL CREDIT OPPORTUNITY ACT

A.   Background and Aims

The Equal Credit Opportunity Act (ECOA) expresses traditional liberal civil rights policy in the credit arena. The ECOA serves two purposes. First, like other consumer credit legislation, such as the Truth in Lending Act and the Fair Credit Reporting Act, the ECOA is a consumer protection statute designed to provide accurate information to or about consumers involved in credit transactions. Second, the ECOA is an antidiscrimination statute, like the Equal Employment Opportunity Act (EEOA) and the Fair Housing Act (FHA), that seeks to promote wider credit availability by prohibiting the use of stereotypes in credit decisions. For example, the Act prohibits financial institutions from discriminating between otherwise credit-worthy customers on the basis of race, color, national origin, sex, marital status, age, receipt of public assistance income, or the exercise in good faith of the rights guaranteed under the Consumer Credit Protection Act.

ECOA compliance is enforced both by government agencies and through private litigation. The Act authorizes the Federal Reserve Board to prescribe regulations that clarify and amplify specific statutory provisions in light of the Act's legislative purpose. Overall administrative enforcement of the Act rests with the Federal Trade Commission, with limited authority delegated to several other federal agencies. The ECOA and its implementing Regulation B cover all phases of a credit transaction. Regulation B identifies and addresses in detail various phases of the credit-granting procedure, with particular focus on the application process, the evaluation process, and the reporting of reasons for adverse action.

* * *

As amended, the ECOA appeared to be an imposing piece of antidiscrimination legislation. Industry spokesmen feared a substantial increase in administrative activity and litigation, as toughened public and private enforcement mechanisms combined to promote compliance with the Act. As the next section demonstrates, however, the intervening years have produced few public enforcement actions and a only a trickle of private litigation.

B.   The ECOA's Performance: Evidence of Inadequacy

Discrimination in lending decisions remains a serious problem. Both systematic study and anecdotal evidence demonstrate that widespread credit discrimination continues to block home ownership, as well as small business creation and expansion, and thereby community economic development in non-White communities. For example, a recent Federal Reserve Bank of Boston study concluded that, all other factors being equal, Black and Latino mortgage applicants are roughly sixty percent more likely to be denied a loan than White applicants. This study may even have underestimated the extent of mortgage loan discrimination by omitting those discouraged from applying for loans by pre-application screening processes, negative institutional reputation, or loan officers' attitudes. Indeed, another recent study revealed that the lack of applications from minority neighborhoods, rather than disproportionately low approval rates, is the principal reason that lenders fail to attain similar lending rates in minority neighborhoods and White neighborhoods in the lenders' service area. Home Mortgage Disclosure Act data from 1992 further revealed that the disparity between Blacks and Whites in gross denial rates for conventional home purchase loans has widened slightly: in 1992, Blacks were 2.26 times more likely to be denied loans than were Whites, compared with 2.16 times in 1991.

Business loans to Black-owned firms present an even more distressing picture. Available data are not as complete as the data on home mortgages because business lenders need not disclose the race of their borrowers, as mortgagees must under the Home Mortgage Disclosure Act; evaluation is also more difficult because business loans are less uniform than home mortgage loans. Nevertheless, the available evidence indicates that Black and White business owners with identical predictive traits—age, educational background, a close family member who is a business owner or self-employed professional, purchase of an ongoing concern, and possession of equity capital—do not receive equal treatment. Black-owned firms are denied loans more frequently than White-owned firms, and the business financing that is approved is usually for smaller amounts and on more onerous terms. Studies indicate that lender caution derived from inaccurate perceptions that similarly situated Black-owned firms are riskier than their White-owned counterparts undermines many otherwise viable Black businesses. It is thus unsurprising that, according to one 1993 study, eighty-three percent of Black entrepreneurs believe that lending bias is a very serious problem for Black-owned businesses, with another nine percent considering the issue a moderately serious problem.

C. Standard Liberal Proposals

The evidence of ongoing and pervasive lending discrimination is extremely persuasive, prompting both explanations and proposals for possible improvement. For example, the speculative nature of actual damages in discrimination cases makes statutory damages particularly important, causing some critics to propose amending the Act to include a minimum statutory recovery. Under such a scheme, even technical violations of the Act would carry a minimum $100 award, regardless of the actual damages. Although such an Amendment might have some marginal benefit for large consumer-credit class actions, as well as for suits in which many individuals claim mortgage discrimination, statutory damages would be of little help to individual small business claims, to which the technical aspects of the Act do not apply.

Other critics attribute the paucity of litigation under the ECOA to the fact that (1) although lenders must supply written notification of adverse action to individual consumers, the lenders need only provide a written statement of reasons if the consumer makes a written request; (2) business creditors need not be notified at all; and (3) a change in credit terms to which the applicant has agreed does not constitute an adverse action. * * *

Finally, some progressive critics target the historical lack of effort on the part of public enforcement bodies. The Justice Department did not file its first "pattern or practice" lawsuit until 1992; the amount of time that went by before the first suit was filed and the paucity of suits since then have left serious doubts about the government's commitment to reform. In creating the ECOA, however, Congress clearly envisioned that private litigation that alleged substantive discrimination crimination would be the main enforcement method. The Act uses the concept of the private attorney general to provide for generous class action recoveries and attorney's fee awards. Despite Congress's expectations, most of the few suits brought under the Act have been based on minor violations of the Act's technical and notification provisions. Only a tiny amount of private litigation has been reported since the enactment of the ECOA in 1974, and most of this litigation has focused on sex rather than on race. Indeed, only a handful of substantive discrimination claims, few of which rested on racial grounds, and only three class actions have been successfully prosecuted.

* * *

D. A Community–Empowerment Critique of the ECOA

This section presents a community-empowerment critique of the ECOA that attacks both the Act's unrealistic conceptual assumptions and its defective normative vision. This critique explains more compellingly than standard liberal analyses why the ECOA has met with such limited success in extending credit to Black people and shows why the Act's vision may ultimately be undesirable.

The equality paradigm embodied by the ECOA posits an acultural, meritocratic "thing" called "creditworthiness." The paradigm assumes that banks can measure "creditworthiness" objectively and neutrally, and that, having done so, banks have an equal incentive to lend equally to all similarly creditworthy customers. The notion of "equally qualified" borrowers, however, overlooks the cultural specificity of the proxies by which creditworthiness is judged. Rather than reflecting actual ability and willingness to repay debts, particular qualifications are in fact only indicia associated with, but not determinative of, what succeeded in a creditor's past—a past that was typically "White only." The available research suggests that certain credit-scoring-model criteria have different meanings for different populations. For example, credit-scoring systems have typically deemed frequent changes in residence a significant negative, indicative of instability. It may be, however, that for Black people facing housing discrimination and concomitant schooling problems for their children, frequent family moves indicate hard work and responsibility. Such frequent movers might in fact be excellent credit risks. Similarly, frequent job changes may have different meanings for different populations. Indeed, the Federal Financial Institutions Examination Council has concluded that traditional employment stability requirements are discriminatory.

* * *

In addition to the equality paradigm's unrealistic conceptual assumptions, its normative vision is inherently limited. Relatively little non-consumer credit is granted solely on the basis of objective information. For small business loans in general and start-up loans in particular, little lending can be done by the numbers alone. The decision to lend is ultimately based on an inherently subjective determination that the credit-seeker's project has merit and that the credit-seeker is of good character and will go the extra mile to repay debts. Lenders do look to objective criteria like collateral and credit history and may consider how similar projects have fared in the past, but a decision to lend is in the end a decision to trust the judgment of the debtor. Even in mortgage lending, the decision to grant credit often hinges on the lending officer's subjective sense of the applicant's creditworthiness and the officer's extra efforts to work with the borrower to make the numbers come out right. It is at these points that racism may enter the loan-granting process.

In conventional use, "racism" means allowing race, an irrelevant characteristic, to play a part in what ought to be a purely "rational" decision. Banker discretion thus creates an opportunity for conventionally understood racism (either intentional or unconscious) to enter the loan-granting process. However, although racism is conventionally understood to mean not just hate for the other, but affinity for one's own, such subjective moments are both utterly inevitable and potentially desirable. Furthermore, fully "rationalized" settings, with no discretion and thus no conventional racism, may permit worse forms of institutional racism.

* * *

A community-empowerment critique points out that subjective moments in the lending process are not always problematic. People are more comfortable with things that are familiar to them. As a matter of common sense, loan officers feel more comfortable lending money to people with whom they share a common rapport, who belong to institutions with which they are familiar, who have backgrounds similar to their own, who seek loans for homes or business projects in familiar neighborhoods, and whose business plans are for familiar projects. At worst, we can attribute this phenomenon to culturally embedded racist stereotypes that prevent loan officers from seeing good business opportunities. At best, we can see this as good business sense: it is prudent to invest only in neighborhoods that one knows, in projects that one understands, and with people whom one trusts. It not only appears unlikely that we can eliminate subjectivity—which is necessarily culturally bound—from the credit-granting process, but it also seems that we would not want to if we could; what separates good from bad investments in lower-middle-class neighborhoods and small businesses will often be unquantifiable, intangible qualities like the passion, character, and vision of the borrower, or the aesthetic quality of the houses on a particular block. We want lenders to take a chance, based on the intuition that a project will succeed, on projects whose numbers may be less than perfect. This point of subjectivity in the lending process is paradoxically the time when both the worst and the best lending practices might transpire.

* * *

[B]lacks and Whites of the same economic status typically attend different clubs and recreational facilities, send their children to different schools, and therefore serve on different PTA boards, attend different churches, and live in different neighborhoods. Without personal knowledge of a credit seeker's character and reputation in the community, a banker has no basis for a reputational judgment. Even the most well-meaning White loan officer will be unable to make character loans with an acceptable racial balance. To the extent that, in modern America, White people do not know Black people, reputational lending by White institutions cannot help being "discriminatory."

Hiring more employees from Black communities could never be more than a partial solution. To make a large, White-owned bank in a Black neighborhood more responsive to the needs of its customers by staffing that branch with African–Americans might well harm the careers of those African–American loan officers. The management fast track at most large corporations necessitates moving around from position to position rather than remaining in a single location. The best opportunities for career advancement and bonuses are unlikely to be found in lower-middle-class neighborhoods; requiring Black professionals to work in low-income areas might ghettoize these professionals and thereby run afoul of employment discrimination laws. In addition, such a solution would do nothing for the credit problems of lower-middle-class White people.

In summary, as long as the main business of the bank is outside of a particular local community, it is difficult to imagine how members of that community could be treated "equally" by the institution. Within the context of an economy and financial structure driven by highly mobile transnational capital and large corporate interests, community-based economic development will always be a charitable afterthought, not an economic imperative.

III.   THE COMMUNITY REINVESTMENT ACT

Lending discrimination contributes to neighborhood disinvestment, but such discrimination is only a part of the story. Even if all lending discrimination were eliminated, it would have little impact on low-income neighborhoods. Many Americans cannot even conceive of having sufficient economic resources to own their own home; African–Americans are significantly overrepresented in this group. Because lending in lower-income and non-White communities cannot be improved within the framework of conventional business practices, stronger steps must be taken. Such a remedial purpose is envisioned by the Community Reinvestment Act.

The equality paradigm suggests that it is beyond the scope of public policy to remedy inequality that persists after fair and equal procedures have been established. Thus, procedural fairness has no necessary connection to fair outcomes: lending outcomes are considered beyond question as long as lending criteria are arguably rational and clearly non-racial. In contrast, the affirmative action model maintains that the lingering effects of past discrimination cannot be cured by equal treatment alone, but only by affirmative steps to make equal opportunity a reality. As President Johnson stated, "[y]ou do not take a person who, for years, has been hobbled by chains and liberate him, bring him to the starting line of a race and then say, 'you are free to compete with all the others,' and still justly believe that you have been completely fair." Under the more activist affirmative action paradigm, government policy at the intersection of civil rights and banking regulation must do more than simply demand procedural equality; regulations must ensure that an appropriate level of lending actually takes place in all communities.

In this spirit, in 1977, Congress passed the Community Reinvestment Act (CRA). The Act has recently attracted much attention. Unlike the Bush administration, whose attempts to disarm the CRA were thwarted by Congress, President Clinton made community reinvestment a centerpiece of his campaign's economic platform. Clinton promised to "[e]ase the credit crunch in our inner cities by passing a more progressive Community Reinvestment Act to prevent 'redlining'; and requiring financial institutions to invest in their communities." The battle over the CRA has been joined.

A. Background and Aims

The Community Reinvestment Act (CRA) places upon each insured depository institution a "continuing and affirmative obligation to help meet the credit needs of the local communities in which [it is] chartered" and requires that each such institution be assessed on its "record of meeting the credit needs of its entire community, including low-and moderate-income neighborhoods, consistent with the safe and sound operation of such institution." Congress determined that banks were redlining or neglecting important credit needs within their communities and that regulators' efforts to deter such behavior were inadequate.

Although redlining and discrimination are somewhat different, in the credit context, the two practices are clearly interrelated. Discrimination refers to the denial of credit to an individual applicant based on race. Redlining originally referred to the practice of literally drawing a red line around certain neighborhoods on a city map and refusing to make loans for property or businesses located within the demarcated zones. Today the term refers to any set of practices that "systematically den[ies] credit to applicants from low-and moderate-income, and minority neighborhoods." Redlining decisions are sometimes based on a perception that the housing stock in certain neighborhoods is in disrepair. The practice also derives from outright racial discrimination or from the related prejudice that property values in racially changing neighborhoods must decline. Furthermore, herd behavior may result if others follow one major lender's decision not to invest. Consequently, to the extent that Black people live in distinct communities, racially disparate rejection rates indicate that Black communities suffer from systematic under-investment—redlining.

  * * *

Despite its weaknesses, the CRA did affect bank behavior by allowing community-based organizations and residents to intervene in expansion and merger application proceedings and to challenge the approval of expansion requests on the basis of alleged inadequacies in the CRA records of the applicants or institutions to be acquired. Public responses to bank expansion requests are authorized by statute or regulation. Regulators must review evidence presented through the public comment process. Community groups have thus brought an estimated three hundred challenges against expansion requests. Although only approximately fifteen applications have been denied outright on CRA grounds since the Act's inception, and although federal regulators have granted conditional approval imposing CRA requirements in only fifty to sixty cases, community groups have successfully used the CRA process to negotiate directly with the applicant institution. A majority of CRA challenges have been withdrawn after applicant institutions and local groups negotiated settlements. Such settlements often specify what measures the applicant institution must take to improve its record in low-and moderate-income and non-White communities. Although this informal dispute resolution mechanism is neither sanctioned nor enforced by regulators, it is preferred by many community groups. These agreements have generated between $7.5 and $20 billion in targeted loan commitments to low-and moderate-income areas, which far exceeds the conditions that would have been imposed by regulators. Thus, the success of the CRA-challenge process depends on how effectively community leaders can obtain specific commitments to community reinvestment from banks in independent negotiations. Furthermore, research suggests that CRA agreements have resulted in significant changes in the institutional behavior of lenders. In addition to the imposed and negotiated commitments, lenders have made additional unilateral commitments of some $23 billion to community-development lending while their expansion requests were pending. It is doubtful that these lenders would have made these commitments without the desire to head off CRA challenges. Further, in the current climate of accelerated merger activity in the banking industry, the primary CRA enforcement mechanism of denying permission for mergers may be increasingly powerful.

In addition, in 1989 Congress greatly enhanced the CRA's impact as part of the comprehensive Financial Institutions Reform, Recovery, and Enforcement Act (FIRREA). Among other changes, the 1989 Amendments mandated public disclosure of regulators' CRA evaluation results and greatly expanded the collection of Home Mortgage Disclosure Act data.

These Amendments sent a message to the regulatory agencies to strengthen their CRA enforcement, which has been amplified by the Clinton administration's proposed overhaul of the regulations under the CRA.

B. The CRA's Performance: Evidence of Inadequacy

Although the CRA has fostered many negotiated partnerships for community lending, low- and moderate-income communities remain underserved by the banking industry. The extent to which these commitments have translated into actual changes in lending practices is unclear. Although eighty-nine percent of the nation's banks and thrifts received outstanding or satisfactory CRA grades from federal banking regulators, widespread evidence indicates that the industry continues to fall short of the law's mandates.

The inadequacy of the CRA is demonstrated both by continuing and pervasive lending discrimination and by evidence demonstrating that banks continue to neglect the credit needs of low-and moderate-income communities. Redlining of many kinds is pervasive and growing. Many of America's lower-and middle-class communities—whether White or Black, urban, rural, or small town—suffer from continuing disinvestment. Even if the CRA's goals were met, it is unclear that their fulfillment would reverse these long-term, structural declines.

C. The CRA's Inherent Contradictions

The CRA has been sharply criticized from all sides. Liberals attack the Act's enforcement provisions as ineffective and argue that much of what passes for compliance is merely charitable donation instead of serious investment. Conservatives bemoan allegedly excessive compliance costs, anti-competitive effects, and inefficient impacts on market structure. To the extent that speakers on both sides of this debate are correct, these critiques highlight the limitations of the CRA strategy that creates the illusion of a fixed choice between healthy communities and profitable industry. This false dichotomy results from our intellectual and political failure to target directly the structure of the financial industry.

1. Liberal Critiques of the CRA.—Liberal critics of the CRA see much of what passes for CRA compliance as mere public relations and charitable contribution to community-group causes. According to this view, CRA enforcement merely imposes the requirement of extensive paper trails for marginal activities that have little to do with substantive investment in low- and moderate-income communities. These critics argue that banks refuse to change the way they do business and look to please regulators rather than to comply with the spirit of the law.

Liberal critics argue persuasively that regulators must, among other things, be directed to see CRA evaluation as an integral part of a regulator's job rather than as an additional burden; that better guidelines should emphasize the CRA as an aspect of normal bank operations rather than as a charitable afterthought; that only substantive lending in low- and moderate-income communities rather than negotiated gifts to community groups or other causes should constitute compliance; and that regulators need help in forming substantive policies rather than formalistic rules and in reducing paperwork. Backed by substantial bipartisan political support, various liberal reform proposals have recently emerged on both the legislative and the new administration's regulatory agendas. * * *

The CRA Reform Act also imposes CRA-type duties on non-depository mortgage banks and mortgage insurance companies: "[e]ach mortgage bank shall have an ongoing responsibility to meet the credit needs of all the communities in which such bank makes a significant number of extensions of credit or extends a significant amount of credit, including extensions of credit in low- and moderate-income neighborhoods of such communities." This provision is significant because mortgage banks account for an large share of mortgage-origination activity. The Act would establish an Office of Mortgage Bank and Insurance Supervision within the Department of Housing and Urban Development and require mortgage banks and mortgage insurers to submit reports detailing their efforts at meeting community credit needs. If the Secretary of HUD found that a mortgage bank was maintaining an "inadequate level of community support," the Secretary could issue an order requiring the institution to file a plan within ninety days detailing "concrete goals and timetables for correcting identified deficiencies." The Secretary could further prohibit the bank from using any HUD-administered program or product until all identified deficiencies were met. Violations of such orders would be subject to administrative and judicial review, cease and desist orders, and civil monetary penalties. This portion of the Act could have a dramatic impact on the behavior of mortgage lenders.

The CRA Reform Act is a well-intentioned but inherently limited step in the right direction. Liberal critiques both accept the financial market as it is currently structured and generally fail to respond adequately to the very real difficulties that the CRA creates for financial institutions. Such difficulties are the domain of the conservative critiques to which we now turn.

2. Neoclassical and Conservative Critiques of the CRA.—Despite continuing disinvestment in lower-middle-class communities and clear lack of regulatory enforcement, industry spokespeople and conservative commentators argue that, at least in part as a consequence of the 1989 amendments:

> CRA-based challenges to bank mergers and other transactions subject to CRA scrutiny are now routine, even when the institution in question has received high marks for CRA compliance in recent examinations. Some deals are actually derailed by the statute, and the costs of consummating a transaction in the face of a CRA challenge can be substantial.

Conservative commentators and industry analysts level three main criticisms at the Act: (a) compliance costs are too high, (b) banks are put at a competitive disadvantage vis-a-vis their non-bank competitors, and (c) the Act impedes market trends toward consolidation.

(a) Compliance Costs.—There is considerable disagreement about the direct compliance costs of the CRA. The CRA has been targeted as the most costly banking regulation currently in force; more troubling still, some studies reveal that smaller banks face the highest relative compliance costs. Conservative critics also charge that CRA regulations are vague and standardless and that bankers thus have little guidance about compliance with the Act. The data are not conclusive, however. Charles A. Bowsher, the Comptroller General of the United States, argues that these industry studies of compliance costs suffer from "serious methodological problems"; the regulatory agencies concluded, based on data received from financial institutions, that the paperwork requirements of the CRA are less time-consuming than the paperwork requirements of other banking consumer regulations. Nevertheless, whatever the precise burden may be, and no matter how the proposed regulatory changes may alter that burden, the CRA does generate substantial paperwork and other bureaucratic compliance costs.

(b) Anti-competitive Effects.—It is also fairly clear that the CRA places depository institutions at a competitive disadvantage compared to their less regulated non-bank competitors. Depository institutions face competition in the lending market from a wide array of other institutions, including pension funds, life insurance companies, finance companies, mortgage banks, venture capital companies, mutual funds, and commercial paper markets. As Professors Macey and Miller argue, "[t]he CRA thus effectively imposes a special, discriminatory tax on banks and savings associations, which are thereby weakened relative to other financial institutions." Given the centrality of banks to a variety of community-development goals, banks' declining importance in the U.S. finance system is troubling. To the extent that the CRA contributes to this trend, such decline runs counter to the Act's own goals.

* * *

A second issue arises if we seek to cure the problem of differential impact by extending the CRA to cover other lenders. Although some non-bank intermediaries—mortgage banks and finance companies—often operate within a geographic community, others—mutual funds, investment banks, and pension funds—operate across extended geographic areas. To bring these lenders within the ambit of CRA regulation, the idea of meeting the credit needs of a lender's "entire community" would have to be reconsidered. Yet the inclusion of this latter group is feasible. If these institutions were given a "safe harbor" from regulatory oversight in return for investing a set percentage of their assets in certain approved investments, a highly sophisticated and liquid market for CRA-approved investments would develop rather quickly. As the last decade proved, Wall Street financiers can securitize almost any investment. In addition, there are several bills before Congress that would create secondary markets—government-sponsored enterprises (GSEs) or private market mechanisms—to facilitate the securitization of small business and community-development lending. The CRA, therefore, could conceivably be extended to more sophisticated lenders with minimal logistical barriers.

* * *

(c) Impact on Market Consolidation.—Professors Macey and Miller argue that the CRA impedes the "desirable process of bank mergers and acquisitions." They contend that the consolidation of the industry is inevitable, efficient, and by implication, socially unproblematic. Although bank merger activity continues to increase and CRA protests *can* delay, derail, or raise the costs of an attempted merger, determining the normative value of this effect is a difficult task that requires both consideration of the relevant economic evidence and sensitivity to the contested nature of the implicated political values.

* * *

However, even if we accept the deeply problematic assumption that banking industry mergers take place because they promote efficiency and economies of scale, we should not necessarily permit consolidation. Efficiency is only one of many social goals, and it is legitimate for society to consider other public policy goals and to accept some sacrifice of efficiency.

In a narrow society-as-aggregate-of-individuals welfare calculus, small businesses, community institutions, and traditional forms of authority have no independent significance. But the promotion of small businesses and community institutions may be a legitimate independent political end. Small businesses and family farmers are an important bulwark in the maintenance of community and not just another interest group. Small businesses have been the engine of economic innovation and the sector of much new job creation. Additionally, small Black-owned businesses provide the best employment opportunities for Black workers. Civil rights values will therefore be best served by a structure of finance that supports such businesses.

Greater banking consolidation is inimical to small business and community institutions. Many studies show that local independent banks give small businesses better credit terms and service than do larger, more distant lenders. Local banks can evaluate and monitor the creditworthiness of small local firms more easily than large banks, know more about their small businesses customers, provide more reliable sources of credit, keep loan personnel in place longer, provide better access to these personnel, and make lending decisions faster. Local independent banks tend, therefore, to depend more on the character of the borrower in granting credit than on requiring high collateral. Branches and subsidiaries of large banks, on the other hand, are more likely to rotate personnel and to maintain final approval authority in remote head offices. For this reason, the branches or subsidiaries of out-of-town banks tend to rely on higher collateral requirements and other standardized lending criteria and "to provide less than the amount of credit requested by small" businesses. Larger banks generally do not emphasize small business lending; they view such lending as less profitable than middle market and larger business loans. Larger banks that do compete for small business customers primarily focus on established small businesses.

* * *

   3. *Further Considerations for CRA Reformers.*—Despite the limitations of the CRA as a tool of structural reform, the CRA framework will exist for some time. It is thus useful to consider how the Act could be made more effective. This section argues that, in addition to extending the CRA's reach to all financial intermediaries, the current open-ended examination of institutions' lending policies should be replaced with a determinate requirement that institutions invest a set portion of their funds in approved investments. Such an approach would both reduce the bureaucratic role in the lending process and ensure that financial institutions actually invest in community development. Although such reform stops well short of real structural change to the economic landscape, it offers the possibility that the CRA might more systematically improve the lives of low- and moderate-income Americans.

   The simplest way to extend the CRA to all lenders would be to abandon the ideology of community reinvestment and replace it with a conventional affirmative action approach that requires lenders to meet lending volume goals for certain delineated minority groups. A reform of this type would be a terrible mistake. Although the racial dimension of community disinvestment is the most visible and morally repugnant aspect of this problem, the majority of the American people suffer from the effects of disinvestment. These issues are racial, but they are not only racial. If we are to create a new populist discourse about structural economic changes in our society, our movement must be transracial and have broad appeal across the economic spectrum. Communities can only promote their own interests if they work in concert with other communities.

   I want to underscore the argument that the CRA's reach should be extended to all financial intermediaries. First, to the extent that there are costs associated with CRA compliance, the CRA puts banks at a competitive disadvantage to non-bank competitors. Given that banks are, for a variety of reasons, already in significant decline compared to their competitors, their use as a tool of reform is of declining importance to the financial structure. The victories won in the realm of banking will be increasingly irrelevant. Moreover, the increasing complexity of America's financial marketplace requires a more comprehensive and unified regulatory structure. More generally, over the past two decades, the United States financial system has been reshaped by the spread of multifunctional financial conglomerates and the emergence of an unregulated parallel banking system. Along with other powerful trends like securitization, these events have broken down the carefully compartmentalized credit and capital marketplace that was established by New Deal legislation sixty years ago. Check-cashing and pawn shops, along with home-repair second mortgage companies, offer expensive services to low-income people bypassed by mainstream financial firms. Mortgage banks constitute a less regulated parallel housing finance system and finance companies constitute a parallel business and consumer lending regime. The commercial paper market cuts banks out of the financing of corporate businesses. Mutual funds and similar services provide the public with depository-like services that banks once provided exclusively.

* * *

In poor neighborhoods, one can find many profitable but marginal, under-regulated, and exploitative institutions that fill this niche—check-cashing outlets, pawn shops, finance companies, rent-to-own stores, and home-repair second mortgage companies—but there are few conventional banks. The data indicate that community lending is no riskier than comparable lending at similar rates of return. The lack of interest that banks show toward these markets helps create the demand for fringe banking services; conventional financial institutions then cash in on the fringe banking boom by issuing lines of credit to finance companies, providing transactional services to check-cashing outlets, purchasing high-interest notes from second mortgage companies, and pursuing other such business services. Thus, conventional financial institutions do help service these markets—but in an indirect way that permits unscrupulous operators to extract a middleman's profit while the banks keep their hands clean. To the extent that these alternative financial service businesses' high prices reflect not the actual extra risks of such lending, but rather the transaction-cost effects of cultural biases, this trend represents a cultural tax on low-and moderate-income communities.

Given current political realities, the view of most CRA supporters that the existing regulatory structure should not be abolished may well be correct. Unless the investment requirements are set high enough, a safe harbor approach will not provide sufficient incentive even to institutions that could easily extend their efforts in low- and moderate-income communities. Nevertheless, if we are to create a politics that promotes market-based community empowerment, we must move beyond marginal improvement in the opportunities for home and small business ownership and ultimately seek to alter the economic power relationships that dominate life in America.

D. A Structural Critique of the CRA

* * *

The CRA is based on a very limited vision of the nature of the credit problems facing low-and moderate-income communities. Offering no plan for the structure of the financial industry, CRA-based reinvestment strategies assume that industry and firm structure are independent of the investment decisions that firms make. By raising the cost of mergers, the Act has arbitrary and uneven effects that depend upon the zeal of local community groups and the direction of the political winds. Moreover, the incentive structure of the CRA is perverse; in recognition for having engaged in a minimally acceptable level of community investment, a firm is rewarded by being allowed to contribute to undermining the long-term basis of community investment by further concentrating the market. The

CRA assumes that, with a little push, all financial institutions, regardless of size and structure, can be made to engage in significant community investment and that structural questions are separate issues. Lacking a vision of what the structure of the industry ought to be, the CRA cannot be a coherent tool of structural change.

For example, CRA ratings for banks are inexact and subjective. The Act's requirement that each depository institution "help meet the credit needs" "of its entire community, including low-and moderate-income neighborhoods, consistent with the safe and sound operation of such institution[s]" is simple and straightforward in the abstract but, as a practical matter, difficult to assess in a uniform, principled manner. The implementing regulations that are currently in place are very vague. Even under the Clinton administration's proposed new regulations, which are somewhat more determinate and emphasize performance over procedural requirements, the CRA will remain without an overall structural image for the banking industry. In an industry of banks of many types and sizes, without credit quotas and with institutional decisionmaking left to bank managers, the best the CRA can do is to prescribe inexact guidelines and then to ask that bureaucrats apply these guidelines to various real-world situations on a case-by-case basis. Unfortunately, as the literature on bureaucratic management suggests, in this sort of environment, more attention will be paid to the imperatives of the bureaucracy than to the underlying goal.

The structural inadequacy of the CRA is symptomatic of the affirmative action paradigm's insufficiency. Although the equality paradigm and the ECOA are inadequate, because they refuse to entertain the possibility that seemingly fair procedures often yield unfair outcomes, the affirmative action paradigm is inadequate because it refuses to inspect and reform the institutional structures that determine the unfair outcomes affirmative action seeks to redress. Like most affirmative action programs, the CRA does not address the way that the structural imperatives of the institutions it seeks to reform inevitably recreate the very difficulties that the Act attempts to eradicate. Unlike most affirmative action programs, the CRA does not take an individualistic and race-specific approach to regulation. The income and neighborhood-based approach mandated by the CRA is a strength of the Act, but the lack of a vision for the structure of the financial industry undermines the Act's ability to achieve its purpose; the CRA approach does not recognize the fundamental incompatibility of the regulatory requirements it seeks to impose with the system it leaves unquestioned. To borrow President Johnson's metaphor, affirmative action does not question the type of race being run or the awards that attend differences in performance.

IV.   TOWARD A COMMUNITY-EMPOWERMENT PARADIGM

The above analysis implies that the existing paradigms of civil rights reform are deeply flawed and, in spite of some important gains won under them, hopelessly contradictory and unworkable. The equality paradigm begins with several flawed premises: that neutral standards of merit exist or could exist, that those standards can be measured objectively, and that assimilation to the culture of the standards is a positive social goal upon which we all ought to agree. The affirmative action paradigm, although more realistic than the equality paradigm, is even more problematic in its premises: it seeks to ameliorate directly inequalities produced through the usual course of business in institutional life, but never questions why such institutions continually produce unacceptable results. Racial inequality is not merely an aberration of institutions that are otherwise fair and neutral and that serve the needs of all Americans equally and unproblematically. Rather, racial inequality is simply the most visible manifestation of how institutions like banks, universities, and law firms fail to serve the lower-middle-class and non-elite cultural communities. To the extent that affirmative action accepts as a given the structure of American life (but for racial disparity), it reinforces the legitimacy of the very institutions that colonize and suppress the Black community and its culture, and other non-elite communities and their distinct cultures. The equality and affirmative action paradigms reflect the views of the big business and big government elites who promote them: that cultural identity and religious belief are pathologies that must be cured so that everyone can become national-market consumers and clients of state services.

A community-empowerment paradigm seeks to escape from our current racial impasse and to allow us both to keep our particular cultural and religious identities and to live in economically healthy communities. Traditional civil rights reformers, neoclassical conservatives, and most Marxists fail to see any positive role for racial, ethnic, and cultural identification beyond the shaping of subjective preferences for individual consumption items. Any greater cultural identification is seen as an atavistic impulse, exemplified by the Klan or the tragic situation in the former Yugoslavia, that should be replaced with universal standards that apply equally to everyone. Although few would contest that the concepts of market and jural equality have created much good for the human race, man does not live by bread and procedural rights alone. A realm of authority and meaning exists at a level between the individual and the state—a realm that cannot be comprehended by neoclassical commentators and traditional civil rights reformers. Non-rational processes and forms of authority pervade the institutions—family, church, friendship—that are most central to people's lives. The local institutions of civil society are not understandable in market or bureaucratic terms.

In advocating a move toward a community-empowerment paradigm, one need not be an extreme racial or cultural particularist. Rather, one need merely believe that there is nothing pathological or wicked about the desire most people have to bond with others with whom they feel a common link of family, language, history, religion, and tradition. The universalisms of the market and government bureaucracies weaken the bonds of community. It does not derogate the individual to realize that life is given meaning in the context of family, community, religion, and culture.

* * *

The current view—that procedural fairness and outcome fairness are necessarily in conflict—traps us between two undesirables: big business and big government. Community empowerment shows us that our real interests lie in establishing economic and political structures that strengthen community-based institutions and allow the issues that most directly touch people's lives to be decided at the local level. Community empowerment advances the interests of every non-elite American, regardless of race or ethnicity, and addresses problems of middle-class anomie as well as of lower-class hopelessness. Part of the struggle must be to create a financial structure that ensures that all Americans can buy and improve their own homes, start and maintain their own businesses, and serve their own people. A community-empowerment paradigm sees lower-and middle-class Blacks and Whites as united by their desires to resist the cultural and economic colonization of their respective communities and to engage in self-determination. Moreover, a community-empowerment approach may provide a more legitimate and enduring basis for transracial politics, because unlike existing civil rights paradigms, community empowerment is based on a genuine respect for our differences. Because the structural economic forces that are eroding our communities can only be understood in their larger context, the discussion of community-empowerment public policy begins with a sobering analysis of the local effects of globalization.

* * *

B. A Community–Empowerment Approach in Practice: Community Development Financial Institutions

Despite increasing globalization, some significant positive signs have appeared on the horizon. Quietly, over the past fifteen years, with little governmental support, a billion dollar community development financial institution (CDFI) industry has emerged. Development banks, credit unions, and loan funds have collectively extended more than $2 billion in loans and are currently capitalized with more than $700 million—much of it raised from within the communities served. Although assisted by banks receiving CRA credit for investing in CDFIs, the emergence of the CDFI industry is largely a testament to what can be achieved by committed and visionary grassroots activism coupled with the support of small business.

CDFIs exist in a variety of forms: some are bank holding companies or other insured depository institutions; others are unregulated non-profit corporations. All CDFIs are responsible financial intermediaries primarily devoted to developing the community in which they operate. They are structured so as to encourage community input in making policy. Thus, CDFIs express the community-empowerment mindset: they transcend the liberal-conservative dichotomy, they are not entirely market driven but are not charities, and they are not bureaucratic government programs. Rather, they are responsible local businesses dedicated to helping their local community, institutions, and people to help themselves.

* * *

There are a variety of traditional reasons to support the assistance of the CDFI industry. Developing credit in low-and moderate-income communities is vital to our nation's economic prospects. As corporate downsizing is expected to continue, small businesses will continue to provide the bulk of new job growth; as the conventional financial industry becomes more concentrated and increasingly neglects small business, and as the possibility of direct governmental aid becomes increasingly remote, the role of CDFIs becomes ever more crucial. In addition, CDFI lending programs encourage entrepreneurship, self-sufficiency, and creative problem solving—essential qualities for national and community economic prosperity, and for breaking the cycles of poverty and welfare dependency. Notably, CDFIs measure their success not only by institutional and client economic gains, but also by their contributions to building the civic infrastructure of businesses, professions, voluntary organizations, church groups, families, and other community institutions.

To serve our communities' growing need for locally controlled credit, a national commitment to CDFIs must be cultivated. Yet there is a notable tension between the need that community-empowerment institutions have for independence, local control, and freedom from bureaucratic red tape on the one hand, and their need for active restructuring of the financial marketplace by the federal government and more initial capital input on the other. Public policy aimed at fostering the CDFI movement must do the latter without treating CDFIs as charities. Existing public purpose lenders, particularly community-development banks, community-development credit unions, community-development loan funds, and microloan funds, constitute a solid basis for a national network of CDFIs and provide potential models for structuring new institutions. The discussion that follows offers a look at some of the major models for CDFIs and concludes with a consideration of the policies on the current legislative agenda aimed at fostering CDFIs.

1. Community–Development   Banks.—A   community-development bank—the most comprehensive of the CDFI models—provides for development credit for its community through the vehicle of a commercial bank, credit union, or savings and loan. It utilizes proactive subsidiaries or affiliates to carry out its mission to develop the community. A community-development bank incorporates a broad range of services rather than specializing in a product or credit service as do other CDFIs. The depository institution subsidiaries of community-development banks are, of course, legally identical to and bound by the same regulations as their conventional insured depository counterparts.

A community-development bank, like any financial institution, must be concerned with operating in a safe and sound manner. In addition, if the institution hopes to grow—both by building on its retained earnings and by attracting additional outside capital—then it must be reasonably profitable. Nevertheless, its primary goal is the impact that both its depository institution and other affiliates have on its community or target population. Thus, a development bank has a dual standard of performance; it must

successfully operate a financial institution and support community empowerment and development. The successes of the industry to date demonstrate that these are not necessarily incompatible goals.

　* * *

2. *Community–Development   Credit   Unions.*—Community-development credit unions (CDCUs) are regulated and federally insured depository
institutions that are cooperatively owned and operated by their members
on a one-person, one-vote system regardless of the amount on deposit. As
non-profit cooperative institutions, credit unions are tax exempt. Although
their services vary depending on the credit union's size, age, level of
organization, and the desires of its members, most CDCUs offer only a
basic set of retail banking services.

　* * *

CDCUs serve as the only bank for many poor Americans. Members are
provided with basic financial services—bank accounts; check cashing; financial planning; and personal, car, tuition, and home-repair loans. By bringing people into the financial mainstream, credit unions help members to
develop mainstream creditworthiness. Membership in the credit union
offers not only reduced costs for needed services like check cashing and bill
paying, but also encouragement to save through regular deposits and
payroll deductions. Most importantly, credit union membership encourages
better attitudes toward sound personal financial management.

Lending is, of course, central to the mission of most CDCUs. All credit
unions make loans to their members, but CDCUs strive to make loans that
will contribute to community development as well as benefit individual
members. CDCUs typically encourage loans that enable members to get
and keep jobs, start and expand businesses, and improve members' property. Many CDCUs also work with other community-development organizations to make loans for such development projects as the rehabilitation of
multi-family apartment buildings.

　* * *

3. *Community–Development Loan Funds.*—Community-development
loan funds (CDLFs) are unregulated and uninsured financial intermediaries
that aggregate capital raised from individual and institutional social investors at below market interest rates. They lend this money primarily to nonprofit and cooperative housing and business developers in low-income rural
and inner-city communities. CDLFs emphasize financing projects that
provide new economic opportunities and resources in their communities. By
providing low-income people with an economic stake, CDLFs encourage
participation in community-business, social, and political affairs. "CDLFs
have been leaders in financing community land trusts, cooperative housing
(including mobile home parks), and worker/community-owned businesses."

CDLFs provide credit that is neither affordable nor available from
mainstream lenders. Frequently, CDLFs' borrowers cannot seek financing
from mainstream institutions because they lack credit histories or require
too much technical assistance. Because most community-development pro-

jects require multiple sources of funding, the loans necessary to make the projects work most often do not comport well with mainstream financial loan packages and must be individually tailored to the project. This lack of standardization means that few projects fit secondary market criteria; these projects are thus unattractive to conventional lenders. In other instances, the loans appear too risky to mainstream lenders, and sometimes the CDLFs engage in outright interest rate subsidy.

CDLFs also operate as a bridge to conventional permanent financing by providing a reliable, low-risk source of information and funding. Conventional lenders often commit to a project once a CDLF loan provides comfort about the adequacy of the project's collateral. CDLFs can provide such assurance because, by involving community members directly in loan fund decisionmaking, CDLFs are able to base lending decisions not only on by-the-numbers financial analysis, but also on direct knowledge of their borrowers, thereby reducing risk. In addition, CDLFs' small, cooperative structure allows low-cost provision of capital because of the superior access to information and a high degree of repayment loyalty. Despite the absence of traditional risk management policies, of the more than $100 million loaned by CDLFs, loan default losses have amounted to less than one percent of all loans made.

* * *

4. Microloan Funds.—Microloan fund programs "make very small, short term loans from a revolving loan fund to people who want to start up or expand very small . . . businesses that are often part-time, home-based, and minority-owned." Microloan funds most often appear as one component among many in micro-enterprise development programs that promote and teach entrepreneurship by integrating both economic and human development among low-income people. These micro-enterprise ventures include such businesses as home day care, tailoring, catering and food service, hair and nail styling, engine repair, trucking, and retail sales. Pioneered in the developing world by Accion International and Bangladesh's Grameen Bank, microloan funds are relatively new to the United States; the first such fund was established here in 1983. Approximately 150 funds now exist in the United States, and their successes have engaged the interest of President Clinton and members of the Small Business Administration.

Many microloan programs rely on a peer-group lending model, in which a small group of would-be entrepreneurs come together for the purpose of obtaining credit; after training and analyzing each other's business plans, the group selects a plan to receive the first loan. If payments on the first loan remain current for a certain length of time, other members of the group are eligible to borrow. In most programs, if one member defaults, no one else is eligible to borrow. Members meet regularly to evaluate business plans, track repayments, exchange information, and lend mutual support. Group borrowing creates tremendous peer pressure to repay loans, and by assuming administrative tasks, participants lower operating costs.

* * *

E. Toward Community Economic Empowerment

There are moments in history in which intense shifts in what constitutes common-sense occur. The Great Depression was such a time. In the wake of the Great Depression, the American people lost their faith in the financial system and the business leadership of the society. The persistence of the Depression and the revelation of scandals involving the most prominent financiers caused a massive shift—one that transcended class—in notions about the proper role of government and the appropriate structure of the financial economy. President Roosevelt's answer was the New Deal's restructuring of financial markets, which was part of the foundation for a generation of expanding economic opportunity. That system collapsed as a result of "deregulation and destabilizing macroeconomic policies." In a similar fashion, shortly after Richard Nixon announced, "I am now a Keynesian," the neoclassical ideal of laissez faire again became the dominant economic paradigm in the United States. We are once more about to undergo such a change in world view.

I have attempted to demonstrate how a community-empowerment paradigm highlights the inadequacy of dominant civil rights paradigms that are based on neoclassical economic thinking; far from solving the problems they address, civil rights paradigms have instead obscured how the structure of the financial system harms all non-rich Americans and their communities, with particularly deleterious effects on the communities of African–Americans. This Article attempts both to disrupt the dominant paradigms and to begin to replace them. The latter ambition requires ongoing commitment, debate, and discussion. The ideas that follow are thus presented as tenuous indicators of potentially fruitful avenues of exploration, designed as much to provoke discussion and suggest areas for further research as to advocate a particular political trajectory.

Changing the nature of financial policy requires a broad-based coalition. Financial debate in Washington currently expresses little more than the scramble for advantage of different segments of the financial industry: big banks versus small banks, securities firms versus banks, and insurance companies versus securities firms. Consumer groups and community activists typically engage in the politics of finance with little more than interest-group aspirations. To achieve far-reaching reform, these groups must go beyond thinking about a hot scandal or a few bits of legislation and integrate financial reform into a larger politics. The logical source of financial reform is all nonrich Americans, whose interests are not addressed by the current financial economy. The interests of those who seek community reinvestment and those who seek decent, union-wage work are linked with those whose savings are inadequate, unguaranteed, or poorly invested, or whose pensions are jeopardized by weak regulatory and guaranty mechanisms. "These seemingly irreconcilable positions can only dovetail to drive reform if both organizing tracks explicitly promote greater financial sector stability and more dynamism in the underlying economy." Savers and borrowers must work together to effect changes in regulatory policy and in the tax code to support a more long-term perspective for investors and managers and to strengthen the foundational assets of the paper economy. "No matter where they fall on the risk-reward spectrum, most non-rich capital suppliers and capital users win when their political demands define the public obligations of financial markets in terms of strengthening domestic employment and living standards."

* * *

V. CONCLUSION

According to the influential philosopher Thomas Kuhn, when old modes of thought no longer provide a satisfactory explanation of reality or a guide to future activity, a shift in paradigms takes place so that activity and analysis can progress. This Article argues that the old liberal and conservative paradigms have exhausted their power to explain, inspire, or guide public policy. A new community-empowerment paradigm, however, is emerging. I have avoided making any highly specific claims as to the content of this emerging paradigm because, like the modes of thought I believe it will supplant, it is more a sensibility and an approach than it is a body of doctrine.

* * *

As the major parties stumble in the old grooves and grope toward a new politics, a variety of thriving grassroots organizations are meeting in living rooms and union halls across America to organize working class communities around such issues as hazardous waste dumping, community investment, and affordable housing. Unlike those who lead major activist and lobbying groups, grassroots activists come not from the professional classes, but from among the more typically alienated lower middle classes. "For them, democracy means building their own political organizations, drawing people together in a relationship that leads to real political power. In a sense, they are reinventing democracy from the ground up, starting in their own neighborhoods."

Despite the many local successes that grassroots community groups have won, the community-organizing movement has developed neither a national political presence nor a coherent body of doctrine or theory. Liberals and conservatives, bereft of any workable plans to deal with the nation's ills, look increasingly to community-based organizations for ideas. Unfortunately, mainstream politicians too often attempt to use ideas from the community-organizing movement for their own purposes and develop government programs that adopt the form but reject the substance of community empowerment. Technocratic attempts to "empower" people without challenging the entrenched power of the dominant elite are hollow. This hollowness is evident in the administration's CDFI initiative; although President Clinton genuinely seeks to give low-income communities the tools with which they can help themselves, his plan refuses to confront how the financial industry's structure undermines the economic base of our communities. Politicians now quote the old saying "give a man a fish and you feed him for a day. Teach a man to fish and you feed him for life." A community-empowerment approach argues that what really matters is who owns the fish pond, because skills and tools are not enough to ensure long-term community prosperity, and because man does not live by bread alone.

* * *

Moral values and social policies must be understood in the material economic context out of which they emerge. Moral values in the abstract have little content, and social policies meant to effectuate these values will be of no avail without concrete structural analysis of the nature of the problems being addressed. Racial justice is a moral value, and although the problems caused by the absence of racial justice are manifest everywhere, our old paradigms and attendant mindset obscure the structure within which these problems exist. Manifestations of our absence of racial justice include disinvestment in African–American communities and the difficulties that African–American people face when seeking access to capital. Continuing to understand these social problems solely in terms of the old paradigms, however, will cause us to continue to make largely ineffective public policy. The Equal Credit Opportunity Act and the Community Reinvestment Act, for all their good intentions, have failed to stem the tide of structural economic forces that are disempowering African–American and other low- and moderate-income communities.

The lack of access to capital that disempowers Black people and their communities is only the most visible and extreme manifestation of how the economic structure disempowers all non-elite people and their communities. The old formulations of anti-discrimination, equal treatment, and affirmative action policies are not up to the task of challenging the structural imperatives of the emerging global financial system; indeed, these policies tend to legitimate the very structures that are doing the damage. Within a community-empowerment paradigm, the devastation of particular communities is understood within the structural economic context, and the intellectual, rhetorical, and cultural foundation is laid for the creation of a broad-based transracial politics that can challenge the power of the emerging global business and professional elite.

The Hidden Cost of Being African American

OXFORD UNIV. PRESS (2004) at 183–200 (2004).

■ THOMAS SHAPIRO

CONCLUSION: ASSETS FOR EQUALITY

The enormous racial wealth gap perpetuates racial inequality in the United States. Racial inequality appears intransigent because the way families use wealth transmits advantages from generation to generation. Furthermore, the twenty-first century marks the beginning of a new racial dilemma for the United States: Family wealth and inheritances cancel gains in classrooms, workplaces, and paychecks, worsening racial inequality. I see no means of seriously moving toward racial equality without positive asset policies to address the racial wealth gap.

The racial wealth gap is more then obdurate historical legacy that lives in the present, because it also springs from contemporary public policy and institutional discrimination, not to mention individuals' behavior.

Children's Savings Accounts

Children growing up in families with assets go to school secure in the knowledge that their families will support their dreams and future wellbeing. However, many children in American grow up without such confidence. The majority of children come from families who cannot provide a positive asset legacy. About 4 in 10 of all children grow up in asset poor families. More distressing, over half of African American children grow up asset poor. What difference would it make if every child in America grew up knowing that (s)he had a net egg to use to go to college, buy a home, or start a business? As a result of acquiring start up money, they would be more confident and competent; they would feel more invested in themselves, their communities, and the future. They would have dreams and a way of making them come true. Benefits would accrue to individuals, families, and society as a whole.

There are many models for Children's Savings Accounts, such as initial government or private contributions at birth, matches of family contributions for low income families throughout the child's formative years, and limited use of account balances at age 18 and older. Imagine, for example, that every child born in the United States had an initial deposit of $1,000 in such an account. Additional yearly deposits would be encouraged and possibly tied to achievements such as school graduations, summer employment, and community service. Acquiring financial literacy throughout the school years would be a strong program component, providing a relevant and stimulating educational content. Government would match contributions from low income parents.

Individual Development Accounts

The vast majority of Americans have not accumulated many assets and are not about to inherit a large nest egg. This lack of assets impedes them from moving ahead, and they watch people jumping ahead who they know have not worked harder, have not tried harder, and do not deserve financial success any more than they do. Start up assets for opportunities like education, businesses and retirement could improve dramatically the lives of average Americans.

Latoya Miton, who would do anything for her daughter's education, dreams of moving to a community with better schools, even calculating sacrifices like going without telephone service and auto insurance. If Latoya's job of managing a dry-cleaning establishment paid a living wage and offered health and pension benefits, moving to Kirkwood, Missouri might not be just a dream. She is an ideal candidate for a program that motivates savings for future mobility. Smart and hardworking, she might use it for higher education or even start a dry-cleaning business of her own.

Individual Development Accounts (IDA) are the first and larges policy initiative in asset-development policy, spearheaded by Michael Sherraden's book *Assets and the Poor,* promoted by policy makers and advocacy groups, and backed by several national foundations. Individual Development Accounts reward savings by asset poor families who aim to buy their first home, acquire postsecondary education, or start a small business. For every dollar a family saves, matching funds that typically come from a variety of private and public sources provide strong incentive. The IDA Tax Credit would work by providing financial institutions with a dollar for dollar tax credit for every dollar they contribute as matching funds for IDAs, up to $500 per IDA per year.

Down Payment Accounts

Homeownership is a signature of the American Dream and, as I have emphasized throughout this book, frames class status, family identity, and schooling opportunities. We also know that homeownership provides the nexus for transformative assets of family wealth. For this reason, and others, I think a hallmark policy idea is Down Payment Accounts for first time homebuyers.

The chief purpose of Down Payment Accounts is to allow families to acquire assets for down payment and closing costs. How would these accounts work? Similar to the home mortgage interest deduction, renters could deduct a portion of their rent on their tax form and have it put aside in a dedicated account to match their own savings for homeownership on a one to one basis. This money would be used for first time homebuyers.

A revealing contrast is that in U.S. history government policies have been very effective in giving other kinds of families start ups to acquire property and assets. I am thinking specifically of the Homestead Act, begun in 1862, which provided up to 160 acres of land, self-reliance, and ultimately wealth to millions of American families. This remarkable government policy set in motion opportunities for upward mobility and a more secure future for oneself and one's children by giving nearly 1.5 million families title to 246 million acres of land, nearly the size of California and Texas combined. One study puts the number of homestead descendents living today at 46 million adults. This means that up to a quarter of the adult population potentially traces its legacy of property ownership, upward mobility, economic stability, class status, and wealth directly to one national policy—-a policy that in practice essentially excluded African Americans.

Matching Social Assistance to Asset Policy

Traditional welfare policies have failed to launch families out of poverty, just as they have failed to promote independence and self reliance. Asset policies will not work by themselves, either. In tandem, asset and income policies promise supporting pillars for mobility. To make sure that asset building policies do not become a shell game simply transferring costs from federal to state or from public to private–or creaming monies from social assistance–policy need to be crafted so that asset and traditional social assistance policies synergize one another rather than cancel each other out. For example, Children's Savings Accounts should not replace a public commitment to higher education. Tuition at public institutions of higher education should not rise just because 18 year olds have accumulated a small net egg to make college affordable. A worst case scenario involves a family raiding their fledgling IDA account, losing matching payments in the process, to buy food at the end of the month because their food stamp allocation was too small. Families should not miss medical appointments, delay renewing prescriptions, stretch out the time between dental visits, or skip meals to scrape together money for monthly IDA contributions. These sacrifices to contribute to asset accounts are damaging bargains families should not be forced to consider because of public policy failures. One lesson from the national IDA demonstration project indicates that these temptations are real and should be avoided.

The single most important housing policy is the home mortgage interest deduction. Because it lowers taxes in proportion to a family's tax rate, the majority of this $55 billion subsidy goes to the highest income families; one third of it goes to families in the top 10 percent.

The nation's housing priorities must change. First, the dynamic housing markets—that is, laws of supply and demand incentives for new housing construction, and the location of new housing—must change. I like an idea that, instead of rewarding taxpayers who pay higher marginal tax rates, converts the interest one can deduct into a flat percentage rate. All families, say, could take 25% of home mortgage interest off their taxes, regardless of earnings or whether they choose the standard deduction or the itemized tax schedule.

Given the increasing prevalence of automated underwriting systems in scoring mortgage applications, fair lending enforcement agencies should develop tools to test for discrimination so that factors weighted against minorities do not become codified into uniform industry standards. Especially as loan pricing according to risk becomes common practice, lenders should be discouraged from generating greater profits by designing systems that make minorities appear to be riskier mortgages.

Mortgage lenders and insurance redliners should be held accountable for the racially specific damages they have imposed on communities of color. Why can't we sue predatory lenders and their suppliers of capital, mortgage and insurance redliners for what they have done to cities and communities?

Without these changes, the extra capital made available to families through various asset policies and other government policies would likely fail because the two tiered housing market would still generate more wealth for the affluent.

Where a family lives largely determines school quality and family wealth largely determines where people live. Local property taxes fund the leading portion of school finances, 45–50 percent; therefore, it is easy to understand how the wealth of a community, its resource base, governs educational resources and the opportunities that go with them. (The federal share is actually only about 5–10 percent, with the state contributing the remaining 45–50 percent.) The disadvantage of low resource communities and the advantage of higher resource communities can be addressed by shifting local school financing up to state and federal levels.

Part of the big picture I have been describing is how communities, families, and individuals try to trap resources and hoard them for their own benefit. Because individuals believe they can personally benefit from it, and because they do not trust government to act in the civic interest, they attempt to buy their way out of social problems on a one at a time basis. This encourages a privatized notion of citizenship at the expense of solutions that work for all.

We can no loner ignore tremendous wealth inequities as we struggle with the thorny issue of racial inequality. Without attending to how equal results–especially concerning wealth–we will continue to repeat the deep and disturbing patterns of racial inequality and conflict that plague our republic. A just society would not wish racial legacies and inheritance to block opportunities and make a mockery of merit, and just individual will rejoice to give merit and democracy a fairer chance to triumph.

NOTE: The following case represents an innovative use of the Uniform Commercial Code and common law doctrine of unconscioniability to challenge the propensity of banks to increase fee income by introducing new fees, for automatic teller transactions for example, or by raising existing fees, such as bounced check (NSF) fees. The trend to unlimited increases in bounced check fees became a point of consumer activism in the 1990's in the immediate aftermath of Federal rules ending the interest rate ceilings on deposit account. Banks lost the government protection from having to pay market rates of interest of deposit accounts, and were forced to compete for deposits by paying higher and higher interest rates. The deposit rate wars created pressures on the profitability of the once secure bank balance sheet. This pressure was relieved in the early 1980's by introducing fees that were unrelated to cost, and that were not disclosed to depositors when the initial deposit agreement was signed.

Although, the *Perdue* case represents a victory. It did not result in a permanent reconfiguration of the fee structure for bounced checks. It did, however, introduce the use of unconscionability doctrine in class actions by plaintiffs seeking to limit the fee structure imposed on retail deposit customers in the federally regulated banking industry. The unconscionability doctrine that you encountered in your contracts course served the more limited purpose of defending a single consumer against a default enforcement action by retail sellers who sought judicial enforcement of a variety of unfair terms contained in boilerplate agreements. When you finish reading Perdue, can you think of any other retail price structures that might be suitable for unconscionability challenges?

Perdue v. Crocker National Bank

702 P.2d 503 (Cal. 1985)

■ BROUSSARD, JUSTICE

Plaintiff filed this class action to challenge the validity of charges imposed by defendant Crocker National Bank for the processing of checks drawn on accounts without sufficient funds. (The parties refer to such checks as NSF checks and to the handling charge as an NSF charge.) He appeals from a judgment of the trial court entered after that court sustained defendant's general demurrer without leave to amend.

On July 3, 1978, plaintiff filed suit on behalf of all persons with checking accounts at defendant bank and a subclass of customers who have paid NSF charges to the bank. The complaint first alleges a contract under which the bank furnishes checking service in return for a maintenance charge. It then asserts that "It is the practice of defendants to impose and collect a unilaterally set charge for processing checks presented against plaintiffs' accounts when such accounts do not contain sufficient funds to cover the amount of the check." "Defendants have at various times unilaterally increased the NSF charge to an amount the defendants deemed appropriate, without reference to any criteria, and defendants imposed and collected the said increased amount without any explanation or justification by defendants to plaintiffs." At the time of filing of the suit, the charge was $6 for each NSF check, whether the check was honored or returned unpaid, even though "the actual cost incurred by the defendants in processing an NSF check is approximately $0.30."

The bank requires each depositor to sign a signature card which it uses "to determine and verify the authenticity of endorsements on checks." In extremely small (6 point) type, the signature card states that the undersigned depositors "agree with Crocker National Bank and with each other that ... this account and all deposits therein shall be ... subject to all applicable laws, to the Bank's present and future rules, regulations, practices and charges, and to its right of setoff for the obligations of any of us." The card does not identify the amount of the charge for NSF checks, and the bank does not furnish the depositor with a copy of the applicable bank rules and regulations.

On the basis of these allegations, plaintiff asserts five causes of action: (1) for a judicial declaration that the bank's signature card is not a contract authorizing NSF charges; (2) for a judicial declaration that such charges are oppressive and unconscionable; (3) to recover damages for unjust enrichment derived from the bank's collection of illegal NSF charges; (4) to enjoin alleged unfair and deceptive practices—the bank's failure to inform customers of the contractual nature of the signature card, and its practice of waiving NSF charges as to certain preferred customers; and (5) to recover the difference between the NSF charges and defendant's actual expenses in processing NSF checks on the theory that the charges represent an unreasonable attempt to fix liquidated damages.

* * *

Plaintiff's third alleged cause of action is derivative; its charge of unjust enrichment depends upon a finding pursuant to some other cause of action that the NSF charges were invalid or excessive. This cause of action raises no issues for decision in the present appeal. The other four alleged causes of action, however, present independent and substantial issues. We review each in turn, applying the established principle that [factual allegations in the demurrer are assumed true upon review]. * * *

I.   Plaintiff's First Cause of Action: Whether the Signature Card is a Contract Authorizing NSF Charges.

The complaint alleges that "The signature card prepared by the defendants does not identify the amount of any charge to be paid by the plaintiffs for processing NSF checks and is not an agreement for such payment. The card does not constitute mutual assent to NSF charges in any particular sum or at all and accordingly is not a contract conferring authority to do the acts complained of herein." "Based upon the language of the signature card, the plaintiffs believed and expected that the signature card was intended as a handwriting example for purposes of identification and verification only." Plaintiff therefore seeks a judicial declaration "as to whether the signature card is a valid or enforceable contract and . . . a lawful basis for the imposition of the NSF charge."

The cases unanimously agree that a signature card such as the Crocker Bank card at issue here is a contract.

* * *

Plaintiff argues, however, that even if a signature card is a contract to establish a checking account, it is not a contract authorizing NSF charges. He contends that the contract is illusory because it permits the bank to set and change the NSF charges at its discretion, and without assent from the customer except such as may be inferred from the fact that the customer does not cancel his account after the bank posts notice of its rates.[6]

Plaintiff relies on the rule that "[an] agreement that provides that the price to be paid, or other performance to be rendered, shall be left to the will and discretion of one of the parties is not enforceable." [*Automatic Vending Co. v. Wisdom*, 182 Cal. App. 2d 354 (1960).] That rule, however, applies only if the total discretion granted one party renders the contract lacking in consideration. * * * If there are reciprocal promises, as in the present case, the fact that the contract permits one party to set or change the price charged for goods or services does not render the contract illusory. * * *

The recent decision in *Lazar v. Hertz Corp.*, [143 Cal. App. 3d 128 (1983)] offers an analogy to the present litigation. Hertz' car rental agreement permitted it to determine unilaterally the price charged for gas used to fill the tanks of returned rental cars. Plaintiff's suit alleged that

---

6. Financial Code section 865.4, subdivision (b)(1) requires a bank to give customers 15 days' notice of any change in charges imposed on bank accounts.

Hertz fixed unreasonably high prices, in breach of its duty of good faith and fair dealing. Discussing this cause of action, the court said that "[the] essence of the good faith covenant is objectively reasonable conduct. Under California law, an open term in a contract must be filled in by the party having discretion within the standard of good faith and fair dealing." * * *

We conclude that plaintiff here is not entitled to a judicial declaration that the bank's signature card is not a contract authorizing NSF charges. To the contrary, we hold as a matter of law that the card is a contract authorizing the bank to impose such charges, subject to the bank's duty of good faith and fair dealing in setting or varying such charges. Plaintiff may, upon remand of this case, amend his complaint to seek a judicial declaration determining whether the charges actually set by the bank are consonant with that duty.

II.   Plaintiff's Second Cause of Action: Whether the Bank's NSF Charges are Oppressive, Unreasonable, or Unconscionable.

Plaintiff's second cause of action alleges that the signature card is drafted by defendant bank which enjoys a superior bargaining position by reason of its greater economic power, knowledge, experience and resources. Depositors have no alternative but to acquiesce in the relationship as offered by defendant or to accept a similar arrangement with another bank. The complaint alleges that the card is vague and uncertain, that it is unclear whether it is intended as an identification card or a contract, that it imposes no obligation upon the bank, and permits the bank to alter or terminate the relationship at any time. It then asserts that "The disparity between the actual cost to defendants and the amount charged by defendants for processing an NSF check unreasonably and oppressively imposes excessive and unfair liability upon plaintiffs." Plaintiff seeks a declaratory judgment to determine the rights and duties of the parties.

Plaintiff's allegations point to the conclusion that the signature card, if it is a contract, is one of adhesion. The term contract of adhesion "signifies a standardized contract, which, imposed and drafted by the party of superior bargaining strength, relegates to the subscribing party only the opportunity to adhere to the contract or reject it." [*Neal v. State Farm Ins. Co.*, 188 Cal. App. 2d 690 (1961).] The signature card, drafted by the bank and offered to the customer without negotiation, is a classic example of a contract of adhesion; the bank concedes as much.

In *Graham v. Scissor–Tail, Inc.*, [28 Cal. 3d 807 (1981),] we observed that

> To describe a contract as adhesive in character is not to indicate its legal effect.... [A] contract of adhesion is fully enforceable according to its terms * * * unless certain other factors are present which, under established legal rules—legislative or judicial—operate to render it otherwise. * * * Generally speaking * * * there are two judicially imposed limitations on the enforcement of adhesion contracts or provisions thereof. The first is that

such a contract or provision which does not fall within the reasonable expectations of the weaker or "adhering" party will not be enforced against him. * * * The second—a principle of equity applicable to all contracts generally—is that a contract or provision, even if consistent with the reasonable expectations of the parties, will be denied enforcement if, considered in its context, it is unduly oppressive or 'unconscionable.' * * *

In 1979, the Legislature enacted Civil Code section 1670.5, which codified the established doctrine that a court can refuse to enforce an unconscionable provision in a contract.[10] Section 1670.5 reads as follows:

(a) If the court as a matter of law finds the contract or any clause of the contract to have been unconscionable at the time it was made the court may refuse to enforce the contract, or it may enforce the remainder of the contract without the unconscionable clause, or it may so limit the application of any unconscionable clause as to avoid any unconscionable result.

(b) When it is claimed or appears to the court that the contract or any clause thereof may be unconscionable the parties shall be afforded a reasonable opportunity to present evidence as to its commercial setting, purpose, and effect to aid the court in making the determination.

* * *

Plaintiff bases his claim of unconscionability on the alleged 2,000 percent differential between the NSF charge of $6 and the alleged cost to the bank of $0.30. * * *

To begin with, it is clear that the price term, like any other term in a contract, may be unconscionable. * * * Allegations that the price exceeds cost or fair value, standing alone, do not state a cause of action. * * * Instead, plaintiff's case will turn upon further allegations and proof setting forth the circumstances of the transaction.

The courts look to the basis and justification for the price, * * * including "the price actually being paid by ... other similarly situated consumers in a similar transaction." [*Bennett v. Behring Corp.*, 466 F.Supp. 689 (S.D. Fla. 1979).] The cases, however, do not support defendant's contention that a price equal to the market price cannot be held unconscionable. * * * Thus courts consider not only the market price, but also the cost of the goods or services to the seller, * * * the inconvenience imposed on the seller, * * * and the true value of the product or service. * * *

In addition to the price justification, decisions examine what Justice Weiner in *A & M Produce* called the "procedural aspects" of unconscionability. See *A & M Produce Co.*, [135 Cal. App. 3d 473 (1982).] Cases may

---

10. Section 1670.5 is based upon Uniform Commercial Code section 2–302, but expands coverage to include noncommercial contracts.

turn on the absence of meaningful choice, * * * the lack of sophistication of the buyer, * * * and the presence of deceptive practices by the seller. * * *

Applying this analysis to our review of the complaint at hand, we cannot endorse defendant's argument that the $6 charge is so obviously reasonable that no inquiry into its basis or justification is necessary. In 1978 $6 for processing NSF checks may not seem exorbitant, but price alone is not a reliable guide. Small charges applied to a large volume of transactions may yield a sizable sum. The complaint asserts that the cost of processing NSF checks is only $0.30 per check, which means that a $6 charge would produce a 2,000 percent profit; even at the higher cost estimate of $1 a check mentioned in plaintiff's petition for hearing, the profit is 600 percent. Such profit percentages may not be automatically unconscionable, but they indicate the need for further inquiry.[15]

* * *

In short, the bank structured a totally one-sided transaction. The absence of equality of bargaining power, open negotiation, full disclosure, and a contract which fairly sets out the rights and duties of each party demonstrates that the transaction lacks those checks and balances which would inhibit the charging of unconscionable fees. In such a setting, plaintiff's charge that the bank's NSF fee is exorbitant, yielding a profit far in excess of cost, cannot be dismissed on demurrer. Under Civil Code section 1670.5, the parties should be afforded a reasonable opportunity to present evidence as to the commercial setting, purpose, and effect of the signature card and the NSF charge in order to determine whether that charge is unconscionable.

III. *Plaintiff's Fourth Cause of Action: Whether the Bank has Performed Acts of Unfair Competition.*

Business and Professions Code section 17200 defines "unfair competition" to include any "unlawful, unfair, or fraudulent business practice." This language is intended to protect consumers as well as business competitors; its prohibitory reach is not limited to deceptive or fraudulent conduct but extends to any unlawful business conduct. * * *

The complaint charges two acts of unfair competition. First, it asserts that the "signature card is used in a manner which is unfair, deceptive and misleading, in that plaintiffs are led to believe that it is a signature card for identification purposes and the defendants treat the signature card, without disclosure of said fact, as the legal authority to impose the NSF charge on plaintiffs' checking accounts." Second, it asserts that "defendants arbitrarily and capriciously waive the NSF charge for preferred or commercial accounts," thus shifting the costs of processing NSF checks from those preferred customers to others whose accounts are charged.

---

15. We observe that the bank charges the same fee whether it honors or rejects an NSF check. The fee, consequently, cannot be intended as compensation for the credit risk arising from paying such a check, or for the interest on the amount loaned.

Neither allegation is clear and precise. [W]e are uncertain whether plaintiff contends that the signature card itself is deceptive, or whether he contends that the bank employs misrepresentations or other deceptive practices in presenting the card to the depositor. If the latter is plaintiff's contention, the complaint should set out the challenged representations or practices.

It is, of course, clear that if plaintiff can show that the card or the manner in which it is presented to the customer is deceptive and misleading, he can prove a cause of action for unfair competition. Since he seeks only injunctive relief under this cause of action, he need not show that he himself was misled; he need only prove that "members of the public are likely to be deceived." * * * Thus the defect in plaintiff's allegation is not one of substance, but only of lack of certainty. Such a defect would not justify the sustaining of a demurrer without leave to amend. * * *

Plaintiff's assertion * * * that the bank arbitrarily waives NSF charges for some customers contains a more serious defect. Although price discrimination is often unlawful, depending upon the context of the act and the intent of the perpetrator, * * * "arbitrary" price discrimination in itself is not necessarily illegal. This defect is one of substance; while plaintiff's accusation * * * of deceptive and misleading practices describes acts of unfair competition, albeit in very general terms, his accusation of arbitrary waiver of NSF charges does not.

* * *

IV.   Plaintiff's Fifth Cause of Action: Whether the Bank's Charge for NSF Checks is an Unlawful Penalty.

[T]he complaint states that "[causing] NSF checks to be presented for payment is a breach by plaintiffs of their contractual obligations to defendant. . . ." The NSF charge collected by defendants, however, "is a penalty and is not imposed to compensate defendants for damages incurred by plaintiffs' breach," and therefore violates Civil Code sections 1670 and 1671. The complaint concludes that "[plaintiffs] are entitled to recover the difference between the unlawful charges collected and defendants' actual damages. . . ."

By these allegations, plaintiff seeks to invoke the rule that a contractual provision specifying damages for breach is valid only if it "[represents] the result of a reasonable endeavor by the parties to estimate a fair average compensation for any loss that may be sustained." [*Better Food Mkts. v. Amer. Dist. Teleg. Co.*, 40 Cal.2d 179 (1953).] An amount disproportionate to the anticipated damages is termed a "penalty." A contractual provision imposing a "penalty" is ineffective, and the wronged party can collect only the actual damages sustained.

Two Court of Appeal decisions have addressed plaintiff's contention and concluded that the writing of an NSF check is not a breach of contract, and thus the fee charged for processing the check is not a penalty. [See *Hoffman v. Security Pacific Nat. Bank*, 121 Cal. App. 3d 964 (1981) ("the depositor has no statutory or contractual obligation to refrain from drawing checks for amounts in excess of the balance in his account"); accord, *Shapiro v. United California Bank*, 133 Cal. App. 3d 256 (1982).]

We agree with those decisions * * * that because the depositor has never agreed to refrain from writing NSF checks, the writing of such a check is not a breach of contract. The fee that the bank may charge for processing such a check is limited by principles of good faith, reasonableness, unconscionability, and the like, but it is not limited to the amount which a bank could recover in a suit for breach of contract. We conclude that the court correctly sustained the demurrer to plaintiff's fifth cause of action without leave to amend.

---

* * *

NOTES AND QUESTIONS

1. **Community economic development.** The intransigence of urban poverty and discrimination against African Americans and other minorities has led politicians, legal scholars, and public policy advocates to look beyond affirmative action and to seek out different legal and economic strategies with which to attack inequality. Many of these proposals have been market-based, grounded in the theory that the most effective ways to alleviate the burden of discrimination and poverty are new approaches to economic development and investment in disadvantaged communities. During the economic boom of the 1990s "community economic development...emerged as the dominant approach to poverty alleviation, touted by politicians as a market-based alternative to outdated welfare policies and championed by civil rights leaders as a critical link to economic equality." Scott L. Cummings, *Community Economic Development as Progressive Politics: Towards a Grassroots Movement for Economic Justice*, 54 STAN L. REV. 399, 400 (2001). Similarly, some argue that the primary obstacle to minority advancement is the lack of assets such as inheritance and homeownership. Asset-based policy, such as the measures Shapiro proposes in the second excerpted portion of his book, focuses on giving the poor monetary benefits they can use to lift themselves out of poverty. Financial assets are seen as providing the poor with the opportunity to attain the keys to success in American society, such homeownership, business ownership, and quality education. *See* MICHAEL SHERRADEN, ASSETS AND THE POOR: A NEW AMERICAN WELFARE POLICY (1991).

2. **Economic versus social equality.** The debate over whether blacks should focus on achieving economic or social equality goes back to the origins of the modern civil rights movement. Booker T. Washington emphasized economic self-sufficiency and downplayed the struggle for civil rights. W.E.B. DuBois rejected this "politically acquiescent strategy," and came to be identified with his concept of building a 'Talented Tenth' of college-trained black leaders to direct the fight for racial equality. Cummings,

supra at 410–11. Should the goals of economic and social equality be sought in the same manner? Does one naturally follow from the other?

3.   Community Economic empowerment. The kind of community development encouraged by Anthony Taibi is a model of economic investment wherein the betterment of the individual and community reinforce each other. Taibi expresses skepticism about the value of affirmative action, writing "the affirmative action paradigm is inadequate because it refuses to inspect and reform the institutional structures that determine the unfair outcomes affirmative action seeks to redress." How might a proponent of affirmative action respond to this critique? His proposals are very consciously economic, and this approach has been criticized as ignoring the "political dimensions of poverty." The poor are not only economically disadvantaged. Their interests are also woefully underrepresented in mainstream political discourse, and some believe that it is only through political advocacy as well as sound economic policy that the problems of inequality can truly be eradicated. The localism emphasized by Taibi has also been criticized. Scott L. Cummings argues it inhibits multiracial solutions and "works within the existing spatial distribution of poverty and does not address the nexus between poverty concentration and residential segregation–leaving unchallenged the racial cleavages that dissect urban geographies." Cummings, *supra* at 457.

What is your assessment of Taibi's proposals? Is it true that by focusing so exclusively on economics and localism his proposals will fall short of the broad-based changes many deem necessary? Why does Taibi reject the "equality paradigm" and "affirmative action paradigm" as outmoded approaches to improving the lives of minorities and the poor?

4.   Asset-based policy. Thomas Shapiro, in his book, *The Hidden Cost of Being African American: How Wealth Perpetuates Inequality* (2004), proposes several methods for providing actual monetary assets to those in need to try and foster "wealth" in disadvantaged communities. Affirmative action may also be seen as an attempt to put some minorities on the road to "wealth." What is the importance of "wealth"? Should the government take an active role in providing financial assets to those who lack them? If educational and employment opportunities are severely limited for many minorities, and the government does not take steps to improve the economic condition of minorities, what are the prospects for narrowing economic inequality?

5.   Unconscionabilty doctrine. Judicially developed legal doctrine has also been used as a method for combating the problems of racial and social inequality. The doctrine of unconscionability represents an attempt to protect the interests of those who are disadvantaged in knowledge and/or resources in contractual dealings. The doctrine was introduced in the D.C. Circuit Court case *Williams v. Walker-Thomas Furniture Co.*, 350 F.2d 445 (D.C. Cir. 1965), in response to what the court regarded as oppressive and unfair credit arrangements in low-income communities. Judge Skelly-Wright wrote that in "many cases, the meaningfulness of choice is negated by gross inequality of bargaining power." *Id.*, at 450. Unconscionability can be seen as undermining the general legal principle of freedom of contract, an extension of market-based rational choice theory, in which individuals are viewed as autonomous actors with perfect information, who may enter into any contractual arrangement they choose, as long as it is not illegal. The argument that the unconscionability doctrine does not violate freedom of contract is that the target of the doctrine, contracts of adhesion, are *not* entered into freely and therefore do not enjoy the same deference as truly bargained-for transactions. Many perceive a fundamental unfairness in form contracts between one economically sophisticated corporation, which writes a lengthy contract in dense, legalistic language, and a party who has no knowledge of contract law and limited resources for finding a different contractual partner. Despite its good intentions, the usefulness of unconscionability has been widely questioned, and there is well-developed criticism of the paternalistic nature of the doctrine. Is it the individual consumer's responsibility to understand every contract he or she enters into?

6. NSF fees and open price terms. One critic of the affirmative use of unconscionability doctrine to limit bank fees, argues that "[j]udicial attempts at limiting bank discretion in setting NSF and other fees have been wholly unsuccessful in compensating injured depositors. Rising prices and industry practices . . . are used to maximize the number of NSF checks and have created increasing consumer hostility." Stephanie J. Weber, Note, *Excessive Bank Fees: Theories of Liability and the Need for Legislative Action*, 25 U. MEM. L. REV. 1439, 1474 (1995). Is it inherently unfair for a contract to have an open price term which the seller may fill with little or no oversight, only a vague duty to engage in "good faith and fair dealing"? Are open price terms in contracts especially subject to abuse when sellers are dealing with individuals it knows have little business knowledge and will be less likely to mount a legal challenge? For an exhaustive discussion of unconscionability doctrine in California, see Harry G. Prince, *Unconscionability in California: A Need for Restraint and Consistency*, 46 HASTINGS L.J. 459 (1995).

7. Economic effects of discrimination. Shapiro contends that "studies using matching white and black couples with identical job, income, and credit information consistently reveal discrimination by real estate agents and banks." He argues that despite the reduction in overt racism, blacks and other minorities continue to be the victims of unconscious discrimination and stereotyping in employment, housing, loan application, and any number of other areas. Many contend in even stronger terms that white subordination of minorities is alive and well. Eduardo Bonilla-Silva detects a "new racism," in which racial inequality is reproduced in subtler and less facially offensive ways. In the example of housing segregation, "covert behaviors and strategies have largely replaced Jim Crow practices and have maintained the same outcome." Eduardo Bonilla-Silva, *"New Racism," Color–Blind Racism, and the Future of Whiteness in America, in* WHITE OUT: THE CONTINUING SIGNIFICANCE OF RACISM 271, 273 (Ashley "Woody" Doane & Eduardo Bonilla–Silva eds., 2003). *See also* GLENN C. LOURY, THE ANATOMY OF RACIAL INEQUALITY (2003).

The economic inequality that exists in the United States, and its relation to race, must have an explanation, and since very few people would contend that blacks are less intelligent or less naturally able to succeed, many draw the conclusion that the best possible explanation is the preservation of subtle forms of white prejudice. What is your experience with racial discrimination, either observing or experiencing it?

David Dante Troutt makes the argument that the promotion of the ideal white-American middle-class neighborhood, the "metamarket," has contributed to the development of ghettoes populated largely by minorities, the "antimarket":

> A metamarket * * * describes the dynamic interaction of wealth- and welfare-enhancing public and private forces that stabilize life in middle-income neighborhoods. Meta links not only economic and noneconomic factors, but also the cultural, political, public, and private forces. A metamarket's specific elements reflect degrees of realized psychic and cultural ideals regarding "the good life". * * *

> In contrast, the antimarket involves more than just ghetto. It is the antinorm of the metamarket, the urban place never designed to hold stability. The antimarket encompasses the economic, political, and psychic marginalization of inner-city consumers through the subversion of middle-class rules. Its elements typically include a low-credit, high-risk milieu of struggling stores, inadequate public and private services, a preponderance of undermaintained and disproportionately public rental housing, weak schools, unregulated and unlawful commerce, a lack of public safety, a dearth of political capital, and virtually no personal wealth. * * *

> African American ghetto poverty remains the quintessential form of inner-city or "underclass" poverty because exclusion of, and discrimination against, African Americans have been the most essential means to sustaining middle-class metamarkets. In many respects, such as the siting of undesirable land uses or the deprivation of basic public infrastructure and maintenance services, ghettoes have made middle-class residential markets possible.

David Dante Troutt, *Ghettoes Made Easy: The Metamarket/Antimarket Dichotomy and the Legal Challenges of Inner-City Economic Development*, 35 HARV. C.R.-C.L. L. REV. 427, 429–33 (2000); *see also* WILLIAM JULIUS WILSON, WHEN WORK DISAPPEARS: THE WORLD OF THE NEW URBAN POOR (1997).

Troutt also agues that the worst thing that can happen to a poor community is success, because of the inevitable gentrification and displacement of minorities that will follow. Troutt, *supra* at 502. Shapiro shows the importance that one's neighborhood can have for his or her economic prospects, especially with regards to property values and quality public education. There are some who argue that the increased economic viability of currently disadvantaged communities will benefit society. On the other hand, if society has limited resources, and whites are the overwhelming beneficiaries of them, is it likely they will support policies that transfer these resources to others? Is it possible for everyone to live in a good neighborhood and attend a good school? How do Shapiro's points about educational opportunity among African–Americans relate to the goals of affirmative action?

C.   RETHINKING THE FAMILY AS AN ECONOMIC INSTITUTION

In Re Marriage of Sullivan

691 P.2d 1020 (Cal. 1984).

■ BIRD, C. J.

Is a spouse, who has made economic sacrifices to enable the other spouse to obtain a professional education, entitled to any compensation for his or her contribution upon dissolution of the marriage?

I

Janet and Mark Sullivan were married in September of 1967. The following year, Mark (respondent) entered medical school at Irvine and Janet (appellant) began her final year of undergraduate college at UCLA.

Appellant gives the following abbreviated account of the ensuing years. From 1968 through 1971, respondent attended medical school. Until 1969, appellant worked part time while completing her undergraduate education. After graduation, she obtained a full-time position which she held through 1971.

In 1972, respondent began his internship at Portland, Oregon. Appellant gave up her full-time job to accompany him there. Shortly after the move, she obtained part-time employment.

The couple's daughter, Treisa, was born in May of 1974. Appellant ceased work until 1975 when she resumed part-time employment. From 1976 through 1977, she worked full-time. During this period, respondent completed his residency.

Both parties then moved back to California. Shortly afterward, they separated. In August 1978, respondent petitioned for dissolution of the marriage.

During the marriage, the couple had accumulated some used furniture and two automobiles, both with payments outstanding. This property was disposed of by agreement. Appellant received $500, some used furniture and her automobile, including the obligation to complete the payments.

At the dissolution proceeding, appellant sought to introduce evidence of the value of respondent's medical education. She argued that the education was obtained by the joint efforts and sacrifices of the couple, that it constituted the greatest asset of the marriage, and that—accordingly—both parties should share in its benefits.

The superior court rejected these arguments and granted respondent's motion *in limine* to exclude all evidence pertaining to the value of the education. At the same time, the court granted partial summary judgment to the effect that respondent's education did not constitute community property. The court indicated that it was barred from awarding appellant any compensation for her contribution to respondent's education by the rule of *In re Marriage of Aufmuth*, [89 Cal. App. 3d 446 (1979)] (professional education does not constitute community property).

In May of 1980, the court issued its interlocutory judgment of dissolution. Appellant was awarded no spousal support, but the court reserved jurisdiction for five years to modify that determination. The parties were awarded joint custody of their daughter. Respondent was ordered to pay appellant $250 per month for child support and to reimburse her for half the cost of the child's medical insurance. Finally, the court directed respondent to pay appellant $1,250 in attorney fees and $1,000 in costs.

Both parties appealed.

II

This court originally granted a hearing in this case primarily to determine whether a spouse, who has made economic sacrifices to enable the other spouse to obtain an education, is entitled to compensation upon dissolution of the marriage. While the case was pending before this court, the Legislature amended the Family Law Act to provide compensation in all cases not yet final on January 1, 1985. * * *

The Amendments provide for the community to be reimbursed, absent an express written agreement to the contrary, for "community contributions to education or training of a party that substantially enhances the earning capacity of the party." [Civ. Code, § 4800.3.] The compensable community contributions are defined as "payments made with community property for education or training or for the repayment of a loan incurred for education or training." * * * The reimbursement award may be reduced or modified where an injustice would otherwise result.[4] * * *

4. The reimbursement provision states in full: "Section 4800.3 is added to the Civil Code, to read:

4800.3. (a) As used in this section, 'community contributions to education or training' means payments made with community property for education or training or for the repayment of a loan incurred for education or training.

(b) Subject to the limitations provided in this section, upon dissolution of marriage or legal separation:

(1) The community shall be reimbursed for community contributions to education or training of a party that substantially enhances the earning capacity of the party. The amount reimbursed shall be with interest at the legal rate, accruing from the end of the calendar year in which the contributions were made.

(2) A loan incurred during marriage for the education or training of a party shall not be included among the liabilities of

In addition to providing for reimbursement, the amendments require the court to consider, in awarding spousal support, "the extent to which the supported spouse contributed to the attainment of an education, training, or a license by the other spouse." Civ. Code, § 4801.

Since the property settlement in the present proceeding will not be final on January 1, 1985, appellant is entitled to the benefit of the new amendments. * * *

III

Respondent has cross-appealed from that portion of the trial court's judgment ordering him to pay $1,250 for appellant's attorney fees and $1,000 for her costs. He contends that the decision was an abuse of the trial court's discretion.

Civil Code section 4370 provides that "[in] respect to services rendered or costs incurred after the entry of judgment, the court may award such costs and attorneys' fees as may be reasonably necessary to maintain or defend any subsequent proceeding...." The purpose of the award is to provide one of the parties, if necessary, with an amount adequate to properly litigate the controversy.

In making its determination as to whether or not attorney fees and costs should be awarded, the trial court considers the respective needs and incomes of the parties. * * * Further, the trial court is not restricted in its assessment of ability to pay to a consideration of salary alone, but may

the community for the purpose of division pursuant to Section 4800 but shall be assigned for payment by the party.

(c) The reimbursement and assignment required by this section shall be reduced or modified to the extent circumstances render such a disposition unjust, including but not limited to any of the following:

(1) The community has substantially benefited from the education, training, or loan incurred for the education or training of the party. There is a rebuttable presumption, affecting the burden of proof, that the community has not substantially benefited from community contributions to the education or training made less than 10 years before the commencement of the proceeding, and that the community has substantially benefited from community contributions to the education or training made more than 10 years before the commencement of the proceeding.

(2) The education or training received by the party is offset by the education or training received by the other party for which community contributions have been made.

(3) The education or training enables the party receiving the education or training to engage in gainful employment that substantially reduces the need of the party for support that would otherwise be required.

(d) Reimbursement for community contributions and assignment of loans pursuant to this section is the exclusive remedy of the community or a party for the education or training and any resulting enhancement of the earning capacity of a party. However, nothing in this subdivision shall limit consideration of the effect of the education, training, or enhancement, or the amount reimbursed pursuant to this section, on the circumstances of the parties for the purpose of an order for support pursuant to Section 4801."

(e) This section is subject to an express written agreement of the parties to the contrary."

consider all the evidence concerning the parties' income, assets and abilities. * * *

Finally, a motion for attorney fees and costs in a dissolution proceeding is left to the sound discretion of the trial court. * * * In the absence of a clear showing of abuse, its determination will not be disturbed on appeal. * * *

Review of the total financial situation of each of the parties reveals that there is substantial evidence to support the trial court's order. The record reflects that the trial court considered the financial statements of both the appellant and respondent before making its award. Appellant's financial statement disclosed a net monthly income that was several hundred dollars less than her monthly expenses. Further, appellant's total separate property assets amounted to even less than her net monthly income. According to her statement, then, appellant's assets would have been depleted within a matter of months and her expenses would continue to exceed her net income.

Respondent's financial statement, prepared in the spring of 1980, also reflected monthly expenses which exceeded his net monthly income by over $800. Similarly, respondent's assets, although greater than appellant's, would also have been depleted within a few months if his income and expenses remained the same.

However, the court also had before it a comparative statement of respondent's business revenue and expenditures for the years 1978 and 1979, respondent's first two years of medical practice. Significantly, this comparative statement demonstrated that the fees which respondent collected during his second year of practice were more than double the fees he collected during the first. His annual net income increased by over $40,000 in one year. On the other hand, there was no corresponding statement or testimony to indicate any likelihood of an increase in appellant's income.

Given this evidence, this court can only conclude that the trial court made the reasonable inference that respondent's burgeoning medical practice would continue to flourish and that his income would increase dramatically. The facts of this case fall woefully short of establishing any abuse of discretion by the trial court. "[The] cases have frequently and uniformly held that the court may base its decision on the [paying spouse's] ability to earn, rather than his [or her] current earnings . . ." for the simple reason that in cases such as this, current earnings give a grossly distorted view of the paying spouse's financial ability. [*Meagher v. Meagher*, 190 Cal. App. 2d 62 (1961).]

IV

That portion of the judgment ordering respondent to pay appellant's costs and attorney fees is affirmed. The judgment denying compensation for contributions to spousal education is reversed and the cause remanded for further proceedings consistent with the views expressed in this opinion. Appellant to recover costs on both appeals.

■ MOSK, J., dissenting in part.

While I agree this matter should be returned to the trial court for consideration in the light of recent legislation, I fear that inappropriate language in the majority opinion may mislead the bench and bar. Several times in the majority opinion—indeed, in framing a question at the outset—there is reference to "compensation" for contributions to education. I must assume the repetition of that term was calculated and not inadvertent.

At no place in the relevant legislation does the word "compensation" appear. With clarity and precision, the Legislature referred instead to "reimbursement." The terms are not synonymous; there is a significant distinction that extends beyond mere semantics. Reimbursement implies *re-payment* of a debt or obligation; that is what the Legislature obviously contemplated. Compensation, on the other hand, may be payment in any sum for any lawful purpose; the Legislature also obviously did not intend to give such a blank check to trial courts.

Furthermore, the majority, in their creative reference to "compensation," fail to emphasize to whom it is to be paid. It is not to an individual spouse, in response to the initial query of the majority. The Legislature was crystal clear: reimbursement is to be made to the *community*. The community consists of both the husband and the wife, not one or the other. Thus when reimbursement is made to the community, that reclaimed community asset should be divided between the husband and wife in the same manner as all other community property.

* * *

To review the legislation: Civil Code section 4800.3, subdivision (b)(1), provides "The *community* shall be *reimbursed* for community contributions to education or training of a party that substantially enhances the earning capacity of the party. The amount *reimbursed* shall be with interest...." Subdivision (c) provides "The *reimbursement* and assignment required by this section shall be reduced or modified...." Subdivision (d) is even more precise: *"Reimbursement for community contributions and assignment of loans pursuant to this section is the exclusive remedy of the community or a party for the education or training and any resulting enhancement of the earning capacity of a party."* (Italics added.)

One searches in vain in the statute for a single use of the word "compensation." Thus I find it curious that the majority choose to employ that term rather than to consistently adhere to "reimbursement," the only monetary claim authorized by the Legislature. I trust that trial courts will not be misled into making awards of any sums for any purpose other than that permitted in what the Legislature described with remarkable emphasis as "the exclusive remedy."

Beyond the Glass Ceiling: The Maternal Wall as a Barrier to Gender Equality

26 T. JEFFERSON L. REV. 1 (2003).

■ JOAN C. WILLIAMS

My subject is motherhood. More specifically, the intertwining of motherhood, economic vulnerability, and social stigma. We've all heard about the glass ceiling and I'm sad to say that the glass ceiling is alive and well in America. But most women never get near it because they are stopped long before by the maternal wall.

Over eighty percent of women become mothers. And although the wage gap between men and women is actually narrowing, the wage gap between mothers and other adults has actually risen in recent decades. Although young women now earn about ninety percent of the wages of men, mothers still earn only about sixty percent of the wages of fathers. This is what's called the family gap, as distinguished from the wage gap.

Much of this family gap stems from the ways we organize the relationship of market work to family work. We still define the ideal worker as someone who starts to work in early adulthood and works full-time, full force, for forty years straight, taking no time off for childbearing, childrearing, or really anything else. That's not an ungendered norm. Because, after all, who needs time off for childbirth? It's women. And who needs time off for childcare? American women still do seventy to eighty percent of it. In my book *Unbending Gender*, I argue that designing workplace ideals around this "ideal worker" means that they are designed around men's bodies and men's traditional life patterns in a way that discriminates against women.

For the past several years, with very generous support from the Alfred P. Sloan Foundation to the Program on Work/Life Law, I have followed up on this discrimination analysis through two interrelated efforts.

First, we did a comprehensive survey and looked at every state and federal case in the country that involved family caregivers suing when they felt that they had been unfairly treated. We looked at cases involving men as well as women; in fact, some of the most interesting cases involved men, although, of course, the overwhelming majority involved women. What we found was that family caregivers were beginning to sue, and were beginning to have some success when they sued on the basis of being unfairly disadvantaged due to caregiving responsibilities.

The second major effort, of which Professor William Bielby was a part, was to establish a Cognitive Bias Working Group, to bring together experienced litigators with law professors and social psychologists (both psychologists and sociologists). The Working Group reviewed the existing literature on stereotyping and cognitive bias and tried to shift the framework from thinking not only about *women as opposed to men*, but also about mothers—and fathers—on the front lines of family care. Today I will first discuss the case law. Then I'll discuss the patterns of stereotyping that affect family caregivers. I will end by situating my discussion within feminist theory.

First, the case law. As people know, there is no federal statute that forbids discrimination against adults with caregiving responsibilities. Some state statutes do this. The best ones that we found are in Alaska and D.C. D.C. really is the model here. It's a statute that forbids discrimination against people with family responsibilities. In the absence of that kind of statute, plaintiffs have used more than a dozen legal theories when they go into court to challenge what they see as bias, usually against mothers, sometimes against fathers.

For instance, there have been cases brought under the Equal Protection Act and the Equal Pay Act, as well as causes of action that have utilized state statutes such as D.C.'s. In addition, we found some causes of action brought under state common law theories, notably wrongful discharge. We found between twenty and thirty cases in which plaintiffs either won, settled successfully, or survived an employer's summary judgment motion—after which the parties often settle. The recoveries in some cases have been substantial. One reported tentative settlement was for $495,000; another settled for $625,000; and the settlement for another was $665,000. There have been jury verdicts in the millions. One jury verdict (later reversed) was for $3 million, and another in a Family Medical Leave Act case was for over $11 million. One company has actually now been sued three times by three different mothers.

These kinds of numbers can really make employers sit up and take notice. About three quarters of these successful cases were brought after 1990, with the majority brought in the past five years. Plaintiffs are winning in large part because of a very open pattern of stereotyping that occurs in these cases, what I call "loose lips." These are remarkably frank and open statements by employers reflecting the view that mothers don't belong in the workplace, and that fathers don't belong on the front lines of family care.

Here are some examples. In a Tenth Circuit case, *Moore v. Alabama*, a woman's supervisor looked at her walking across campus; she was eight months pregnant. He stared at her belly and said, "I was going to make you head of the office, but look at you now."

In a Virginia state wrongful discharge case, *Bailey v. Scott–Gallaher*, a mother called up her employer to find out when she was supposed to return from maternity leave. He told her that a mother's place was at home with her child, and that she was fired "because she was no longer dependable since she had delivered a child."

A third was the $3 million jury verdict, where the president of a woman's company said, "Look, you've got to decide, do you want a baby or do you want a career here?" All these cases involve what psychologists call hostile prescriptive stereotyping.

In fact, we find not only gender policing of women into caregiving roles, but also gender policing of men out of caregiving roles. Here the leading case is *Knussman v. Maryland*. In that case, Trooper Knussman wanted to take three months paid leave off under a Maryland state statute and the Family Medical Leave Act. Because his wife had been put on bed rest due to complications concerning the pregnancy, he wanted three months off after she delivered. His supervisor told him that in order for him to be eligible his wife would have to be "in a coma or dead."

These cases suggest that employers now know enough not to say, "we don't hire women here," but they don't get it when it comes to caregiving. The cases suggest that mothers encounter statements that track documented comments of gender stereotyping, which employers evidently consider no more than "hard truths" or "tough love" rather than gender bias. The result is hostile prescriptive stereotyping, in the forms of statements that prescribe traditionalist roles for both men and women. In addition to this pattern, we also see what's called benevolent stereotyping.

Here, the best story emerged from an interview on a project I co-direct with Cynthia Calvert, called the Project on Attorney Retention (PAR), which studies work/life issues in the legal profession. We heard of two lawyers, a husband and wife, who worked for the same firm. After they had a baby, the wife was sent home like clockwork at 5:30–after all, she had a baby to take care of. The husband was kept late almost every night—after all, he had a family to support. That's called benevolent stereotyping. It's stereotyping done in a very different tone of voice than hostile stereotyping, but the effect is much the same: the employer polices men and women into traditionalist bread-winner/housewife roles—clearly an inappropriate role for an employer to play.

Another example of benevolent stereotyping is in *Trezza v. The Hartford, Inc.* The Hartford is the company that's been sued three times by three different mothers. *Trezza* involved a woman who was going great guns until she had kids, and then, like many women, she began to experience problems. In one context she was not considered for a promotion; when she asked why, they told her that it was because the job required travel. That's benevolent stereotyping. The appropriate thing for the employer to do is to ask the woman what she wants to do; many mothers don't mind travel.

In the caregiver context, one key study by Susan Fiske and her colleagues, ranked stereotypes by perceived competence. Fiske and her colleagues found that businesswomen were rated as very high in competence, similar to businessmen and millionaires. Housewives, on the other hand, were rated as very low in competence—similar to—(here I quote the researchers) the elderly, blind, "retarded," and "disabled."

To see how the caregiver stereotype operates in practice, let's recall the famous story of the Boston attorney who returned from maternity leave and found she was given the work of a paralegal. She said, "I wanted to say, 'Look I had a baby, not a lobotomy.' " What happened? She was taken out of the high competence "business woman" category and put into the low competence caregiver category.

Understanding this process is very important for understanding the kinds of problems mothers often experience at one of three particular moments in time: when they get pregnant, return from maternity leave, or go on a flexible work arrangement.

In many workplaces, of course, mothers do not experience any problems. But, in some workplaces, stereotyping begins immediately when a woman gets pregnant. Thus, in one law firm case, a pregnant woman lawyer found that she was subject to rumors and isolated from participation in firm activities upon announcing her pregnancy. In other cases, as in the case of the Boston lawyer, the stereotyping occurs when a woman returns from maternity leave.

But, in many cases, women who have not had problems when they got pregnant or returned from maternity leave, find they do have problems if they go part-time or on a flexible work arrangement. For example, in work-family studies, there is a lot of talk now about the job detriments associated with the use of family friendly policies. Combining this finding with empirical social psychology suggests that the flexible work arrangements so often are viewed as career stoppers because they trigger the stereotype of the housewife or caregiver. This seems particularly true when the business-women-housewife studies are juxtaposed with another earlier study that shows that women who work part-time are viewed primarily as homemakers rather than as employees or workers and a more recent study that reports that working mothers are rated as more similar to housewives than to businesswomen.

The psychological literature that provides insights into what's going on with women also provides very important insight into what's going on with men. One significant study is by Monica Biernat and Diane Kobrynowicz. They compared the "good father" to the "good mother," and they found a lot of overlap. But they also found one key difference, in the time culture of parenthood. The "good mother" was viewed as someone who was always available to her children. Consequently, a man who rated himself as a very good father actually spent about the same amount of time away from his kids as a woman who rated herself as only an alright mother. When a woman cuts back her hours, she may trigger stigma of various sorts and cease to be considered an ideal worker, at least she'll often be considered an ideal mother. The same is not true of many fathers. Nick Townsend, in a wonderful recent book, *The Package Deal*, pointed out that our ideals of fatherhood retain a strong emphasis on fathers as the providers. And studies of masculinity by Scott Coltrane and others document how we still tie masculinity very tightly into the size of a paycheck. These studies help us understand why the chilly climate for mothers at work often becomes a frigid climate for fathers who take an active role in family care. This frigid climate can give rise to some troubling situations. For example, in another PAR interview, we heard of men who literally had been told different things about the availability of part-time work than the women in their law firms. This does not look good from a legal standpoint, for it involves disparate treatment of women and men.

The stigma that's associated with flexible work arrangements also reflects various patterns of unexamined bias. Here again, I will refer to an interview from PAR:

> Before I went part-time and people called and found that I wasn't at my desk, they assumed I was somewhere else at a business meeting. But after I went part-time, the tendency was to assume that I wasn't there because of my part-time schedule, even if I was out at a meeting. Also, before I went part-time, people sort of gave me the benefit of the doubt. They assumed that I was giving them as fast a turn-around as was humanly possible. This stopped after I went part-time. Then they assumed that I wasn't doing things fast enough because of my part-time schedule.

As a result, she said, she used to get top-of-the-scale performance reviews, but now she didn't, "even though, as far as I can tell, the quality of my work has not changed." Here we can identify three types of unexamined bias.

The first is attribution bias. When she was full-time and was not there, her co-workers attributed her absence to legitimate business reasons. But when she was part-time, and they found her not there, they attributed her absence to family reasons—even if she was at a business meeting.

The second kind of bias is called in-group favoritism. The in-group for this purpose is full-timers, and the out-group is part-timers, who are almost exclusively female. When the informant was in the in-group, she was given the benefit of the doubt. But after she went part-time, she was in the out-group and that stopped. The literature on in-group favoritism provides fascinating and important insights into objective rules, which have often been considered to be the key to eliminating bias. According to Marilyn Brewer, one of the leading scholars in this area, "Coldly objective judgment may be reserved for outsiders." Thus, when this attorney was in the in-group they gave her the benefit of the doubt, whereas when she went part-time they threw the book at her.

Finally, in this PAR interview, we recall the businesswoman housewife studies, and, in particular, the study that found that women employed part-time were viewed similar to "housewives." In other words, women who worked part-time were viewed more as housewives rather than as business-women.

The implication of all these studies is that the chilly climate for family caregivers at work, including the stigma that attaches to many part-time and other flexible work arrangements, stems in part from gender stereotyping. Gender stereotyping, in certain fact patterns, may be successfully challenged in court.

This is important for several reasons. It's important, first because this stereotyping could give rise to liability; that's an important message for employers. Yet, at this point, you need very particular sets of facts in order for liability to arise. But the case law suggests, even at this early point, that if an employer has a family-hostile workplace and an employee with "loose lips,'' family caregiving issues can take on a legal dimension. For an employer, that's a sobering message, because how many employers know what every single employee is doing? All an employer needs is a few employees with extremely traditional attitudes, and you are looking at a situation that could become very uncomfortable.

This is particularly true given that maternal wall cases can be litigated as "family values" cases. Consider the case of *Walsh v. National Computer Systems*. *Walsh* was the $625,000 case covered by CBS Nightly News when we issued our initial *New Glass Ceiling* report. The facts of this case are vivid: the plaintiff's supervisor is alleged to have thrown a phone book at her and told her to find a new pediatrician because her son got a series of ear infections. Jim Caster represented the mother. The story he told in court was that his client was being made to choose between being a good mother and being a good worker. "And you know," he said, "that made the jury really mad"—$625,000 mad.

These cases can, and should, be framed around family values. There is a very widespread and uncontroversial sense that children need and deserve time with their parents. That's one of the things that give these cases "legs."

Our case law survey not only shows that the threat of legal liability is real, it also has important implications outside the courtroom. The literature on the new institutionalism shows that once a social situation begins to be perceived through the lens of discrimination, employers often go far beyond what legal cases initially require. Take for example sexual harassment initiatives that end up with no dating policies.

Are no dating policies required by Title VII? Of course not. So why do they emerge? One reason is that, in the United States, anti-discrimination law operates as a language of social ethics. When people begin to see something as "discrimination" in the U.S., they begin to act quite differently, without tight reference to the specific contours of case law. This is a peculiarity of American legal culture.

The institutionalism reminds us that lawyers, as litigators, are not the key delivery system for law-fueled social change. What drives change on the ground is really the response of intermediaries to the threat of litigation. For example, in a recent speech to the Association of Work–Life Professionals, I said that for twenty years work/life professionals have tried to encourage employers to implement work-life policies with reference to the "business case"—the argument that family-friendly policies help employers' bottom line. Today, part of that business case is the potential for legal liability and work/life professionals stand to play a crucial role in shaping our sense of social entitlements in this arena.

At the Program on Work/Life Law, we work with employers, with employees, and with intermediaries such as work-life professionals and diversity experts. We're also working with attorneys on the management side as well as on the plaintiffs' side. Management side attorneys may ultimately play a more important role than plaintiffs' attorneys; if you're talking about fueling social change, the key role is not the lawyer as litigator, but lawyer as counselor. In response to the *New Glass Ceiling* report, one firm of management side employment lawyers advised their clients to review personnel policies to assess whether they adversely affect employees with family responsibilities; to "consider prorating at least some benefits for part-time employees"; to consider permitting flexible schedules and/or telecommuting unless this would impede productivity; to consider allowing employees to "borrow" sick leave from future years or other employees when they need it; and to avoid asking questions or making assumptions about employees' family situations, and "Instead, inquire about the ability to perform job functions and meet attendance and other job requirements."

* * *

Women don't need sameness if that means the ability to live up to the ideal worker norm without the flow of family work that supports men who are ideal workers. And they don't need difference if that means a marginalized mommy track. What they really need is simple equality. But what simple equality requires is deconstructing the ideal worker norm and replacing that with a norm of a balanced worker: a worker whose life requires him to balance work obligations and family obligations, because he is not relying on the erased labor of a stigmatized and economically vulnerable partner. We need to deconstruct gender, for men as well as for women—and to offer both men and women a re-imagined world where family work and market work mesh.

––––––

Seeking Normal? Considering Same–Sex Marriage
2 SEATTLE J. SOC. JUST. 459 (2004).

■ JODI O'BRIEN

Like many lesbians and gay men, until recently I'd given little personal thought to marriage. It was just another one of those cultural institutions that didn't apply to me. As a sociologist, I am well-versed in the discourses by which marriage is deconstructed in order to reveal its patriarchal (read inequitable and unjust) foundations. As a sexualities scholar, I am also well aware of the many economic and legal benefits that accompany state-sanctioned definitions of family. When discussions of marriage have come up in my own long-term relationships, the impetus has been consideration of these benefits. Like many same-sex couples, my partner and I have spent thousands of dollars to file legal papers that would enable us to act on one another's behalf, secure legal recognition of our joint property, and grant power of decision in matters such as a living will. Each of these considerations is focused around worst case, "what if" scenarios (what if one of us dies and the family tries to take away the house from the living partner? what if one of us is terminally ill and the other is not allowed to participate in medical decisions?).

The relevance of marriage ceremonies in my own life has involved the weddings of my six siblings. All lavish affairs, I have attended each in arm with my partner (and had her introduced as such to family friends and relatives). When I was contemplating a break-up, my Mormon mother (who opposed the break-up) reminded me sternly, "this is just like a divorce you know." My parents became much more open and accepting of my sexuality as soon as I found a nice girl with whom to take up housekeeping. Although it would never have occurred to any of my family that I should seek marriage, my partner and I at least felt some comfort in this family recognition. Although we were acknowledged, we were still separate— separate and but not equal in the eyes of the law, and separate as two lesbians in an extended family of prolific heterosexual Mormons. Separate and acknowledged is certainly not separate but equal.

The trouble with this equation, as many lesbian and gay families have discovered through difficult legal and social entanglements, is that when a situation of inequality exists, "acknowledgement" is at the whim of those who hold power. To borrow a phrase from the poet June Jordan, "there is difference and there is power; who has the power decides the meaning of difference." The current "marriage wars" can be viewed and analyzed as a battle for the power to define complete inclusion in U.S. culture. For many supporters of same-sex marriage, the battle is about the simple justice of being able to define one's own family and have this definition recognized and respected as a basic human right * * *. For others, the battle is about who holds the power to determine justice in any form—what some observers have referred to as the "just-us" justice defined by those who see themselves as the keepers of a pre-determined cultural truth.

RADICAL OR ASSIMILATIONIST?

The so-called struggle for gay marriage is additionally complicated by the fact that homosexuality is not a monolith. Lesbians and gay men represent a full spectrum of colors, creeds, political and religious affiliations and economic circumstances. There are lesbian and gay Republicans, lesbian and gay criminals, lesbian and gay ministers, lesbian and gay parents, and yes, some lesbians and gay men who would like to have their committed unions recognized by the state and possibly even blessed by their church. One of the long-standing debates in lesbian and gay studies and social movements centers on the question of "seeking the normal." There are two well-recognized discourses framing this debate. One is the argument that as marginal members of society, lesbians and gay men should push the boundaries of acceptance as far as we can by demanding recognition for even the queerest among us. The other is that assimilation is the best and most politically and socially rewarding route to general acceptance.

Both positions are strongly represented in lesbian and gay history. For instance, ACT–UP protests strove to focus public attention on the rights of HIV-positive gay men who were being discriminated against in health care on the basis of a distinctly non-normative sexuality. At the same time,

Madison Avenue was actively courting lesbian and gay dollars by featuring same-sex relationships in mainstream advertising. This marketing era, now known as the "gay media marketing moment," is credited with providing an economic basis for mainstream awareness and increasing tolerance of homosexuality. In the United States, purchasing power is one route to increased political and public acceptance. As advertisers realized that gay dollars were just as green as straight ones and just as likely to increase sales, mainstream media became more bold in the portrayal of lesbians and gay men. We moved from being background characters usually intended to draw laughs or convey moral missives to front-and-center TV-land companions. The appearance of shows such as Ellen, Will and Grace, Queer as Folk, and Queer Eye for the Straight Guy brought lesbians and gays into the living rooms of middle America and paved the way for mildly edgy straight-based identities such as the "metrosexual" and "lesbian chic." Around this time, in the early 1990s, some queer studies scholars began to note that the original ACT–UP chant, "we're here, we're queer, get used to it," was beginning to look more and more like "we're here, we're queer, let's go to IKEA."

This assimilationist trend has had many critics. Some critiques focused on the raced (white), classed (upper-middle) and gendered (predominantly male) demographics of those featured in the positive media representations of lesbian and gay characters. Others noted the increasing polarization between legions of lesbians, gay men, and transgendered persons who don't fit the assimilation mold (i.e., young runaways, poor, "too butch" or "too feminine" or "too queer") and those who were buying homes, expensive vehicles and seeking to have children. Critics of various lesbian and gay task forces and rights groups advocates observed that these groups seemed increasingly concerned with winning "mainstream" assimilation battles (e.g., same-sex adoption rights, military service, and religious participation) than in fighting the longstanding battles against forms of brutal discrimination that mark the daily lives of many queer folk. The mainstreaming of some aspects of lesbian and gay life were accompanied by an increased distancing among self-described queers who either did not relate to these representations of "normalcy" or felt obligated to actively—resist the narrow definitions of acceptability they reinforced.

Mainstream inclusion as portrayed in media [and] popular culture has also not only drawn resistance from some queers, but has resulted in a growing tide of backlash rising among heteronormative groups, most notably evangelical Christians. These anti-gay groups perceive the arrival of lesbians and gay men in the media and the winning of some basic anti-discrimination legislation as signs of the proliferation of a radical "gay agenda." This backlash has escalated into a full-blown social movement organized around attempts to legislate political and cultural exclusion. Most recently, anti-gay groups, who perceive persistent gay advancement on the cultural terrain, have drawn the line of acceptance at marriage. Amidst this climate of overt hostility and attempts to create legal discrimination, many lesbians and gay men have felt compelled to redraw the battle lines and call for a unified fight in the struggle for matrimony. The battle for legal marriage, even more than the issue of gays in the military, has forced many uneasy alliances among otherwise widely diverse individuals who claim no other commonality than shared discrimination along the dimension of (non-normative) sexuality. Ironically, to the extent that a "gay agenda" does exist, it can be defined as the collective spirit of defense that has coalesced *in response* to an anti-gay political movement. Most individuals who share a marginalized social position (race, ethnicity, gender, religion, sexuality) understand the quandary presented by the call for solidarity that such "anti-movements" provoke.

THE TYRANNY OF SOLIDARITY AND RHETORICAL AMBIVALENCE

In the case, of same-sex marriage, the quandary of solidarity is manifest among lesbians and gay men who begin conversations by claiming, "I really don't believe in marriage, *but* ..." and then attempt to justify why all lesbians and gays must fight for the *right* to marry. The most common justification is framed in economic and legal terms. To date, there are 1,138 federal benefits automatically bestowed on legally married couples. Certainly this is a compelling instance of social (in)justice that should be addressed. But my own observations indicate that the rush for marriage is about much more than the economic and legal benefits the union provides. Long before questions about legalizing same-sex marriages appeared before the courts, lesbians and gay men were seeking the blessing of religious communities for committed unions.

In recent months much talk has been spun among proponents of same-sex marriage about the legal and economic benefits that accompany state-sanctioned definitions of the family. Intriguingly, less has been said about the seemingly more obvious and long-enduring symbolic aspects of marriage. Yet, it is the symbolic, or cultural, meaning of marriage that is the central point of struggle for those opposed to same-sex unions. Lesbian and gay rights activists are correct in their focus on the discrimination that is inherent in state-sanctioned benefits that accrue through adherence to one and only one culturally accepted definition of family. We miss the mark however when we assume that U.S. legal and economic policy is grounded solely in rational arguments based on the discourse of individual "rights." The mistake often made in such debates is a conflation of "is" and "ought"—according to advocates of same-sex marriage, the U.S. government "ought" to protect individual citizens from unequal treatment. In reality, however, U.S. economic and legal policy has always reflected (and often protected) cultural hierarchies of inclusion and belonging.

Thus, the two sides currently represented in the marriage debate are not arguing about the same thing. Anthropologically, marriage is one of the only uniformly recognized rites of passage and signs of cultural achievement and social inclusion in U.S. society. In its ideal form, the union is recognized by the state and blessed by a church, symbolizing its deeply rooted cultural significance and legitimacy. Opponents of same-sex marriage are scrambling to conserve/preserve this symbolic institution of inclusion and belonging precisely because there are so few symbolic achievements that cut across the many cultural divides the define the landscape of U.S. society. Proponents of same-sex marriage are arguing for governmentally recognized access to the economic and legal benefits that accompany marriage without (appearing to be) paying genuine homage to the cultural institution itself.

The preponderance of marriage = rights/benefits rhetoric can be interpreted as an expression of the lack of consensual solidarity among lesbians and gay men regarding cultural assimilation and normalcy. Queers who have never given much thought to the cultural institution of marriage, precisely because it doesn't seem to apply to us, now feel compelled to fight for the rights of same-sex couples to marry, but are only willing to do so within a framework of "equal access to benefits" logic. At the same time, many lesbian and gay couples are seeking not only the related economic benefits of marriage, but the full cultural package. And why wouldn't they? Culturally, we are saturated with notion that marriage is truly the pinnacle of inter-relational attainment (the "happiest moment of your life"). Given similar acculturation, it stands to reason that many lesbians and gay men would grow up desiring the same cultural rites of belonging. If for the sake of argument we assume that lesbians and gays want to win the battle for same-sex marriage, then the problem, from a political/rhetorical perspective, is not whether lesbians and gays should seek this form of cultural belonging, but the failure of same-sex marriage proponents to fully acknowledge the cultural significance of marriage and the desire of some queers to participate in it.

My interpretation is that lesbian and gay activists have been slow to engage in this line of defense ("we really do want to belong as fully as we possibly can") precisely because it requires articulating a desire for normalcy that many lesbians and gay men are loathe to acknowledge. Many of the activists at the front line of this debate are ambivalent about the level of cultural normalcy they want for themselves. Many are long-time critical feminists who have been key voices in deconstructing the normative family. At the same time, as cultural acceptance and belonging has increased for these individuals, largely oriented around economic, professional, and family achievements, they find themselves enjoying more and more of the cultural benefits of inclusion and belonging. It makes sense that they would want the full recognition (legal and even religious acknowledgement) that completes this cultural package. Is this radical? Will it revolutionize, or even reform, current cultural hierarchies of belonging? That's another question entirely.

* * *

CONSIDERATIONS AND COMPLICATIONS

Legal and political recognition of same-sex unions is probably inevitable in the near future. Whether it be in the form of civil unions or the full recognition of legal marriage as currently defined, this struggle will expand the repertoire for many lesbians and gay men regarding the freedom to choose "normalcy" if they so desire. At the same time, the institution itself, which stands as a citadel of normalcy, will have its walls of inclusion stretched while simultaneously strengthening and polishing its standing as the ultimate icon of cultural belonging. In this regard, the recognition of same-sex couples will be both radical and assimilationist.

At the same time, I don't expect that this expansion will change anything at all for single parents who are poor, or for extended families with dependent relatives who do not qualify for healthcare and related benefits under current guidelines for "dependency." Same-sex unions will not alter the current political/economic arrangement whereby an average individual has access to healthcare only through corporate employment or its equivalent for one or more family members recognized as such through the legal definition of marriage/family. Most middle-class and working poor citizens will still bear a disproportionate tax burden relative to benefits received. Should so many economic and legal benefits be connected, uncritically, to the cultural institution of marriage? Certainly not. As [Zac] Kramer argues * * * and as [Nancy] Polikoff and [Martha] Fineman have argued convincingly, welfare states (of which the United States is one) should define and convey benefits and assurances based on realistic estimations of dependency. To this end, Kramer, Polikoff and Fineman call for a complete redefinition of the family as a basis for assessing economic households.

I appreciate these more complicated analyses and add that the question of the same-sex marriage, particularly as it is sometimes framed in terms of the implications of "seeking normal" needs to be problematized more complexly still on at least two dimensions: we should seek more comprehensive/comprehending analyses of the *significance* of cultural institutions in shaping lives and in reinforcing cultural hierarchies that are a basis for resource allocation; and we should interrogate the methodological and rhetorical practices by which implications regarding "radical" and "assimilationist" are falsely dichotomized. I conclude with a brief discussion of each of these points.

1) We need to pay more attention to the meaning and significance inscribed in particular cultural institutions, in this case, the institution of marriage. Whether one agrees with this meaning, it is empirically unsound and politically foolish to ignore cultural significance. Feminists scholars, myself included, have been deconstructing the institution of marriage for decades; successfully demonstrating the tremendous social and economic burden this small unit (the "couple") carries in corporate capitalist economy as well as [its] tremendous "compulsory" grip on our sense of self and accomplishment. Despite these insights, we have not done the best job at achieving an additional feminist methodological creed, comprehending the "field of relations" on its own terms. Clearly marriage stands for more than 1,138 federal benefits. We do ourselves and our work an injustice when we fail to explore the very complex, and often contradictory, reasons for the tenacity of marriage in its current cultural form.

Likewise, lesbians and gay men (and all heterosexuals for that matter) should reflect more critically on the reasons for wanting marriage. A desire for cultural acceptance and belonging is understandable, but we do ourselves an injustice when we fail to fully explore the meaning and implications of participation in any highly significant cultural institution. To the extent that marriage is seen as a pinnacle of cultural achievement and a marker of acceptance, same-sex marriages will do nothing to alter this equation except in allowing for the possibility that the two-person unit (who is now responsible for most social and economic welfare of the "family") can be a same-sex unit. Certainly, in a gender-role obsessed society such as this, same-sex marital units will be radical. But in terms of more general cultural equations connected to hierarchies of belonging and used to determine who gets what, we shouldn't fool ourselves into believing that same-sex unions will pose much of a challenge to the existing status quo.

2) We also need more complicated discourses about who seeks belonging and what that reflects and, in turn, what consequences it carries in terms of change to cultural institutions. We need classed/gendered/raced analyses of who is seeking belonging in so-called "normalizing" institutions. We need nuanced, complex studies of variations among these groups (e.g., gay Christians) before any conclusions can be drawn about what is and isn't radical. One noteworthy consequence of the debate over the *right* to marry for lesbians and gays is that it cuts across other cultural fault lines. The resulting shifts are causing some interesting shake-ups and creating some bridges across long entrenched fissures of difference. For instance, many traditionally conservative parents of lesbian and gay men find themselves speaking out in favor of same-sex marriage. They imagine the cultural acceptance it will convey on their otherwise ostracized child and end up breaking stride with long-established political, religious and cultural allies. Even the *Economist*, the top-buttoned British news weekly, covered the story complete with glossy front picture. [Its] stance? "What's all the fuss about?" From the libertarian perspective, which the magazine espouses, this position makes perfect sense. It doesn't sit so well, of course, with cultural conservatives who consider themselves economic libertarians. But is has been a reminder to many fence-sitting Republicans that it is possible for them to be more libertarian in their political views than they are conservative in their cultural commitments.

And my own stance? Some will find it contradictory, but that's often a consequence of the critical feminist inquiries I attempt to practice. Just as I understand why someone could find meaning and a sense of belonging as a queer practicing Christianity, I understand the considerable cultural draw of marriage. * * * I comprehend the significance of this cultural institution to spin a binding web of commitment to one another and to convey a deeper sense of belonging in society generally. However, this is not the form of inclusion I seek. While I understand the desire of many lesbians and gay men to have their unions recognized by state and religion, I prefer the recognition, acceptance, respect and love granted me by my (Mormon) family, my colleagues, students and friends. Personally, I have never been compelled by the marital bug. But I would be disappointed if my family did not understand the need to support same-sex marriage legislation as it has been currently framed—i.e., one is either pro or anti-gay human rights.

* * * I support the fight for everyone to make choices regarding how they wish to author their own lives and the meaning they seek for themselves and those they wish to define as "family." Simultaneously, I work to educate others about the fundamental need to forge a strong disconnect between culturally accepted definitions of "family" and political economic assessments of the distribution of benefits and assurances for U.S. citizens. In contemporary U.S. society, the power to define difference and the power to define economic well-being rest too strongly in the same "family." The dismantling of this particular union is long overdue.

NOTES AND QUESTIONS

1. Value of human capital. What is the relationship between *Sullivan* and the other materials in this chapter? States have taken different approaches to the issue of educational costs upon divorce. California stands alone as the only community property jurisdiction that permits the community estate to be reimbursed for the educational contributions of the working spouse to the degree awarded upon the dissolution of a marriage. New York courts have held that professional degrees, education leading to professional degrees, and professional licenses are marital property when earned during marriage. Raj Rajan, *Medical Degree in Divorce: New York Versus California*, 11 Contemp. Legal Issues 240 (1997). Texas courts have concluded that the costs of financial support incurred by the supporting spouse are not reimbursable even though made with community funds. Katherine M. Willis, *The True Value of an Education: The Texas Approach to Characterizing and Valuing a Professional Education Degree Upon Dissolution of Marriage*, 31 Tex. Tech L. Rev. 1117 (2000).

Recall the discussion of non-marital contractual relationships in *Marvin* and *Whorton*, *supra* chapter 8. Consensual sexual relationships are by nature intimate and in many ways opaque to those outside them. Can courts do an adequate job of deciding what is "fair" when these relationships dissolve? Does the existence of separate family-law courts in many jurisdictions prove that normal courts do not have the necessary expertise in marital and sexual relationships to adjudicate regarding them?

The court in *Marvin* wrote:

The mores of the society have indeed changed so radically in regard to cohabitation that we cannot impose a standard based on alleged moral considerations that have apparently been so widely abandoned by so many. Lest we be misunderstood, however, we take this occasion to point out that the structure of society itself largely depends upon the institution of marriage, and nothing we have said in this opinion should be taken to derogate from that institution. The joining of the man and woman in marriage is at once the most socially productive and individually fulfilling relationship that one can enjoy in the course of a lifetime.

Marvin, 557 P.2d 684.

Is this stamp of approval for marriage appropriate for a court? Have societal attitudes towards marriage changed significantly since *Marvin* was decided in 1976?

2.   Dependency, marriage, and the state. As the Williams excerpt points out, caretaking, which involves the dependency needs of both children and adults, has traditionally been considered a "private" matter and thus ceded to the heterosexual nuclear family, while at the same time supported by extensive state subsidies and extensive social privileges. This service to the larger society can be seen as a public good of economic and social value. In a time in which (1) divorce rates are very high; (2) women can no longer carry the entire burden of caretaking given the economic pressures forcing them into the workplace (not to mention many women's desire to work for wages); and (3) sexual minorities are both struggling for social recognition and denied access to marriage, what should state policy toward marriage and dependency look like? What are the "legitimate state interests" that the government should be able to directly support, or to indirectly incentivize? What should feminists and sexual minorities be fighting for?

3.   Discrimination against homosexuals? Most agree that homosexuals have historically been a marginalized population, and that a moral and religious stigma attached to same-sex relationships has existed throughout this country's history. However, some do not believe that homosexuals deserve to be treated as a "minority" in the same sense that blacks and Hispanics are. This belief may stem from the view that gays are now generally accepted in society and have every opportunity to attain material success equivalent to straight people. Indeed, gays and lesbians are sometimes painted as an economically privileged group, on the theory that they are less likely to have children. Colorado for Family Values, the group supporting Colorado's Amendment 2, made the disputed claim that "gay and lesbian Americans enjoyed substantially better salaries and higher education levels, and that they tended to be managers and professionals who travel around the world on ample supplies of disposable income . . . [thus] seeking to destroy the image of gays and lesbians as somehow disadvantaged before the law." Sharon E. Debbage Alexander, Romer v. Evans *and the Amendment 2 Controversy: The Rhetoric and Reality of Sexual Orientation Discrimination in America*, 6 TEX. F. ON C.R. & C.L. 261, 278 (2002). Others, especially those on the "Christian right" continue to believe that moral condemnation of homosexuality is acceptable.

Romer has been hailed by many as a landmark decision for the protection of the rights of homosexuals. In this view, Amendment 2 was struck down "for seeking to impose second-class status on gays and lesbians," and by striking down the law "the Supreme Court illuminated the core of equal protection: government must respect the principle that all persons have equal intrinsic worth." Supporters of the decision tend to have little doubt that Amendment 2 was inspired by hostility towards gays and lesbians, but even barring animosity they believe the law invalid because "the principle [of equal protection] bars laws that seek to entrench a social hierarchy—to keep a group 'in its place.' " Joseph S. Jackson, *Persons of Equal Worth:* Romer v. Evans *and the Politics of Equal Protection*, 45 UCLA L. REV. 453, 454 (1997). Why do you think Amendment 2 was passed? Should the legality of the Amendment be affected if it was principally inspired by hostility towards homosexuals? Scalia's dissent strongly criticizes the court's decision as having "no foundation in American constitutional law." If so, why did the court decide as it did? Was Amendment 2 the same as laws prohibiting polygamy, as Scalia suggests? Is the protection of "traditional sexual mores," endorsed by Scalia, an appropriate governmental goal?

The federal courts have not regarded homosexuals as a protected class. On the other hand, many states and municipalities have passed anti-discrimination laws that cover sexual orientation. For example, by 1999, eleven states and the District of Columbia had legislation prohibiting employment discrimination based on sexual orientation, and eighteen states and the District of Columbia prohibited discrimination based on sexual orientation in public employment specifically. By 1999, over half of the Fortune 500 companies included sexual orientation in their anti-discrimination policies, and anti-discrimination policies in universities had become commonplace. Alexander, *supra* at 271. Is the passage of anti-discrimination laws regarding homosexuals proof that they are discriminated against? If the claim made by CFV about homosexuals' material success is accurate, is that proof that they are not being discriminated against?

4. Homosexuality and the Supreme Court. The success of gays and lesbians before the Supreme Court has been mixed post-*Romer*. In *Lawrence v. Texas*, *supra* chapter 8, the court struck down laws which outlawed homosexual sex. But in *Boy Scouts of America v. Dale*, 530 U.S. 640 (2000), the Supreme Court allowed private discrimination against homosexuals by ruling that a New Jersey anti-discrimination law violated the Boy Scouts' First Amendment expressive association right to exclude homosexuals from membership.

Same-sex marriage abruptly moved to the foreground of gay and lesbian legal rights in 2003. As Phyllis Bossin recounts:

> The most dramatic legal development in the United States in 2003 was the Massachusetts Supreme Court's decision in *Goodridge v. Department of Public Health* [798 N.E.2d 941, *supra* at chapter 8.] It was without question the shot heard around the world, or at least around the United States. The decision became a call to arms for conservatives to press for a federal constitutional amendment. Although the decision was based upon the Massachusetts, not the United States, Constitution, concern about the spread of legalized same-sex marriage was profound. Numerous amicus briefs were filed by groups presenting legal, religious, and mental health perspectives. The court had amassed before it a wealth of information related to all possible aspects of this highly controversial issue. It is clear from a reading of the opinion that the court weighed all of the information before it, and also considered

much of the dicta of *Lawrence*, in rendering its opinion. The court distinguished the Massachusetts Constitution from the federal Constitution, noting that: "The Massachusetts Constitution is, if anything, more protective of individual liberty and equality than the Federal Constitution; it may demand broader protection for fundamental rights; and it is less tolerant of government intrusion into the protected sphere of private life."

The court divided the question before it—whether the marriage restriction violated the Massachusetts Constitution—into two queries: whether the restriction was a denial of equal protection and whether the restriction violated due process of law. It pointed out, however, that in matters of marriage and children, the two concepts overlap. The court recognized the substantial benefits enjoyed by those in marriages and pointed out that: "Because it fulfils yearnings for security, safe haven, and connection that express our common humanity, civil marriage is an esteemed institution, and the decision whether and whom to marry is among life's momentous acts of self-definition." The court then discussed some of the benefits attached to marriage that are not available to unmarried persons, concluding that: "It is undoubtedly for these concrete reasons, as well as for its intimately personal significance, that civil marriage has long been termed a 'civil right.'"

Significantly, the court analogized the prohibition on same-sex marriage to the earlier prohibition on interracial marriage, stating:

> As both *Perez* and *Loving* make clear, the right to marry means little if it does not include the right to marry the person of one's choice, subject to appropriate government restrictions in the interests of public health, safety and welfare. In this case, as in *Perez* and *Loving*, a statute deprives individuals of access to an institution of fundamental legal, personal, and social significance—the institution of marriage—because of a single trait: skin color in *Perez* and *Loving*, sexual orientation here. As it did in *Perez* and *Loving*, history must yield to a more fully developed understanding of the invidious quality of the discrimination.

After analyzing the safeguards of the Massachusetts Constitution to protect liberty and equality, the court found that: "The liberty interest in choosing whether and whom to marry would be hollow if the Commonwealth could, without sufficient justification, foreclose an individual from freely choosing the person with whom to share an exclusive commitment in the unique institution of civil marriage." The court went on to find that the marriage ban could not meet the rational basis test under either due process or equal protection analysis. * * *

The court stayed its order for 180 days to permit the legislature to enact legislation consistent with its decision. Subsequently, the legislature requested an advisory opinion from the court as to whether the enactment of a civil union law would comply with the court's order.

The court unequivocally found that it would not. The court found that the proposed legislation suffered from an inherent defect, specifically, that it continued to define "marriage" as between one man and one woman and attempted to create an institution that is parallel but not the same as marriage. The court stated emphatically that "the history of our nation has demonstrated that separate is seldom, if ever, equal." Therefore, the court ordered that only full marriage rights for same-sex couples would pass constitutional muster.

Although the *Goodridge* decision made abundantly clear that the Massachusetts Constitution affords greater protections than does the United States Constitution and further acknowledged that its decision can and should go no further than the state's own borders, the national reaction to the decision was nothing short of mass hysteria. Afraid that homosexual marriage would be imposed throughout the land, Congress and many states urged the passage of constitutional amendments forever banning same-sex marriage.

Phyllis G.Bossin, *Same-Sex Unions: the New Civil Rights Struggle or an Assault on Traditional Marriage?*, 40 TUL. L. REV. 381 (2005).

5. Proposal to create Private Enforcement of Anti Discrimination Employment Policies Against Gays through Intellectual Property Law. Legal scholars Ian Ayres and Jennifer Gerarda Brown have proposed an interesting new corrective opinion to expand the range of possible remedies in the struggle against employment discrimination against homosexuals. Ayres and Brown have created a certification mark, a registered trademark. The trademark is **FE** in a circle. The symbol is called the "Fair Employment" mark. Registration with the Patent Office gives the trademark holder the right to enforce the terms of the mark. The non-discrimination policy is provided by Ayres and Brown on an online licensing site that states a detailed non-discrimination policy. Any employer, who adopts this mark, becomes liable to individual lawsuits from employees who believe they have suffered discrimination because of their sexual orientation. Although the conventional method for enforcing such licenses is for the holder of the intellectual property interest to police and initiate a lawsuit, this mark was created to extend "express third party beneficiary" status to any employee of a covered employer.

Why would any employer ever adopt this mark? If you were the lawyer for an employer with a good record of non-discrimination against homosexuals what advice would you give your client about whether or not to opt into the FE. What would be the relationship of this private remedy to any future federal employment discrimination law? What might the risk calculus for an employer look like? Are employers who are now free to discriminate, including, religious institutional employers, likely to adopt this mark? Would this work for race discrimination? As a matter of legal policy is privatizing antidiscrimination law a sound idea? Ian Ayres & Jennifer Gerarda Brown, "Privatizing Gay Rights with Nondiscrimination Promises

Instead of Policies", *The Economists' Voice*: Vol. 2: No. 2, Article 11 (2002) *available at* http://www.bepress.com/ev/vol2/iss2/art11.

D.   Reparations

The idea that the federal government owed former slaves material compensation for the economic, social, and psychological injuries of the "peculiar institution of slavery," gained currency with the end of the Civil War. On January 16, 1865, General Sherman's Special Field Order No. 15 granted to former slaves, who were the heads of households, 40 acres of land formerly belonging to land-owning whites in the low lands of South Carolina, and a mule to plow the land. Eric Foner, Reconstruction: American's Unfinished Revolutions, 1863–1877 (1988). From this order, soon vetoed by President Johnson, grew the phrase, Forty Acres and a Mule, now emblematic of all forms of reparations for slavery. Through the years, virtually every black liberation movement, from Marcus Garvey to Martin Luther King, called upon the obligation of the federal government to provide redress to the descendents of former slaves.

The twenty-first century has witnessed a revival of earlier calls for reparations in the form of litigation seeking legal compensation for slavery. The defendants have ranged from insurance companies, to elite universities with proven ties to the profit from slavery. The contemporary reparations movement raises complex questions of legal standing, statutes of limitations, the problems of calculating damages, and identifying suitable plaintiffs.

Legal scholar, Roy Brooks takes up many of these questions in his book, *Atonement and Forgiveness: A New Model for Black Reparations*. In the passages that follow, Brooks advances his core conception of the atonement rationale for reparations.

―――――

Atonement and Forgiveness: A New Model for Black Reparations

University of California Press, (2004) pages 155–63.

■ Roy L. Brooks

THE ANATOMY OF REPARATIONS

Essence of Reparations

Once the perpetrator of an atrocity has apologized, it now has the burden of making its precious words believable. It must solidify its apology. In other words, the perpetrator of an atrocity cannot expiate the sin it has committed against an innocent people until it has undertaken a great and heroic task of redemption. That task of redemption is a reparation. The second element of the atonement model, a reparation can thus be defined as *the revelation and realization of apology*. It is the act that transforms the rhetoric of apology into a meaningful, material reality. Simply saying "I'm sorry" is never enough when righting an atrocity.

A reparation is by nature asymmetrical. Only victims of the atrocity are eligible to receive a reparation. A scholarship program for African Americans as a form of redress for slavery is a reparation. But a scholarship program for "minority and women students" even when presented as a form of redress for slavery is no more a reparation than are Holocaust payments to American gentiles, including blacks. It is important to understand, however, that asymmetrical civil rights policies-reparations-are not intended to displace ongoing civil rights enforcement or other social reforms. On this point, I wholeheartedly agree with Elazar Barkan. I would add that symmetrical human rights measures, such as traditional U.S. civil rights legislation, are designed to be equally accessible to all victims of discrimination. Employment discrimination laws, for example, are open to blacks, other persons of color, women, and whites. Although there may be some duplication, symmetrical and asymmetrical human rights measures are not mutually exclusive. Japanese Americans who have received reparations from the federal government were not excluded from traditional civil rights laws or even precluded from participating in social welfare programs. That is how it should be. Symmetrical and asymmetrical human rights measures serve different purposes.

Forms of Reparations

Reparations can come in many forms. They need not be directed toward the victims personally nor involve cash payments. Indeed, when one looks

> at the ways in which governments have responded to atrocities committed under their authority, a pattern begins to emerge. A basic distinction is made between what can be called *compensatory* and *rehabilitative* reparations. Compensatory reparations are directed toward the individual victim or the victim's family. They are intended to be compensatory, but only in a symbolic sense; for nothing can undo the past or truly return the victim to the status quo ante. In contrast, rehabilitative reparations are directed toward the victim's group, or community. They are designed to benefit the victim's group, to nurture the group's self-empowerment and, thus, aid in the nation's social and cultural transformation.

Whether compensatory or rehabilitative, reparations can come in monetary or nonmonetary forms. Unrestricted cash payments or restricted cash payments (such as scholarship funds) given directly to the victims or their immediate families are monetary compensatory reparations. In contrast, unrestricted cash payments or restricted cash payments to the victim's group (such as, scholarship funds or an atonement trust fund that provides an estate for educational purposes or venture capital to eligible members of the victim's group) are examples of monetary rehabilitative reparation. Although nonmonetary reparations can be compensatory, such as a statute commemorating a family member, they are more likely to be rehabilitative.

r to the United
lave narratives
ve the visitor a
umbing drudg-
o sundown and

tional Conven-
ccession can be
of slave-related
union with the
nion ultimately
y or to save the
r states' rights?
How are blacks
ll listen to the
r opinions as to
the results, the
nions may have

ld be a racially
est hour in our
e effect. Like the
ched event in TV
d nation together
ome cases, empa-
valuable lessons.

tragedy. Millions
ere broken up for
ment of our coun-
orst so that other
st. We must take
d at the hands of

ne of us was there
continue to suffer
ology and socioeco-

e who view human
pursuit of personal
all human beings.
ne to see on which

dom, tolerance, and
inion flows against

nd a museum memorializing the
ery's contribution to our nation
ive reparations.

ately has the responsibility of
of reparations. In so doing, the
ctims' needs or desires. This, of
perpetrator's atonement. What
es of reparations that may be
s to be illustrative rather than
s so that we have a pretty good
ernment ought to be moving.

row

ir government could make its
Compensatory reparations in
endants, usually broached in
d the most attention in the
reparations are inappropriate
are far more appropriate, for
esigned to reach a greater
be both more effective than
apology for slavery and Jim
nciliation. Second, rehabilita-
arms visited upon slaves and
ted at the group level-blacks
individually, but because of
rations proceed at this level
to the individual.

r most are a museum of
er would be a memorial to
tal response to some of the
d from their ancestors. As
slavery envisioned here is
the "National Museum of
it Bush signed into law in

Museum in Washington,
um of Tolerance in Los
nd every state capital to
our country and educate
ing effects slavery has on
rough high-tech, interac-
to witness the horrors of
e passage, and, finally, to
en will be able to walk
s of blacks were packed
spaces as the ship made

its way from West Africa to the American colonies (and late
States). Visitors will also be able to listen to recordings of s
spoken by the slaves themselves. This experience should gi
close-up view of life on the plantation, including the mind-n
ery of working in the fields under the hot sun from sunup t
the dehumanizing conditions of the slave quarters.

Reenactments of the debates on slavery at the Constit
tion in 1787 and in Congress on the eve of southern su
presented in a "Point of View Diner" that serves a menu
topics on video jukeboxes. Was the North's creation of a
South a necessary evil or merely a convenience? Was that
good for the slaves? Did Union soldiers fight to end slaver
Union? Did Confederate soldiers fight to keep slavery or f
What contributions have slaves made to our nation?
disadvantaged by slavery? What is racism? Visitors wi
debates on these and similar topics, and then input thei
which side of the debate won. After instant tabulation of
visitors might be surprised to learn how little our opi
changed over time.

Some might argue that a museum of slavery wou
divisive reparation, because it would dwell on the dark
nation's past. But I believe it would have just the opposit
fabulous 1970s TV series *Roots*—at the time, the most wat
history—the museum of slavery will pull a racially divide
through a mixture of awareness, understanding, and, in s
thy. The museum of slavery will, in fact, teach many
Among these are:

- Slavery was more than just another everyday
  of innocent lives were sacrificed and families w
  personal profit and the socioeconomic develop
  try. Human beings were denied liberty at its v
  human beings could enjoy liberty at its fulle
  into our hearts and minds those who perishe
  our country. They were great Americans.

- We need to learn and remember, because nor
  to see slavery, and because many Americans
  from the lingering effects of slavery-the psych
  nomics of slavery.

- There is a line drawn in time between those
  life, liberty, and well-being as expendable in
  gain, and those who believe in the dignity of
  We must always look down from time to tir
  side of the line we stand.

- We must rededicate ourselves to the cause of free
  human dignity, even when the tide of public op

us. These are the values that make our nation exceptional. These are the values worth fighting for.

- The emancipation of black slaves redefined our ideas of democracy and freedom. It made America a better nation, truer to her ideals. In this sense, emancipation and slavery transcended skin color.
- By remembering the nation's resolve to end slavery, we gain a positive racial perspective that enables us to move forward with probity and intelligence on racial matters. This racial outlook reminds us that we are on a mission of racial justice, that we must come together to complete this mission, that this is our history's call, which we must answer.

The museum of slavery, in short, will be a national symbol that gives voice to the millions of nameless slaves who made possible the aspirations of others. For the vast majority of Americans, the museum will challenge their thinking about slavery and, it may be hoped, transform them. Certainly, the construction of the museum will cost taxpayers money. But if it was worth constructing memorials to mourn the death of the some 3,000 innocent people who perished in the World Trade Center, the Pentagon, and on a field near Shanksville, Pennsylvania, at the hands of terrorists, then it is surely worth constructing a tribute to the millions of slaves who died in forced service to this country.

My second proposal is the atonement trust fund. As envisioned here, the federal government would finance, and reputable trust administrators selected by prominent black Americans would administer, a trust fund for every newborn black American child born within a certain period of time-five, ten, or more years. The Supreme Court seems to view racial progress in increments of twenty-five years, a generation, but the eligibility period can certainly be negotiated. The purpose of the trust fund is to provide a core group of blacks with one of the most important resources slavery and Jim Crow have denied them-financial capital, family resources, or an estate, handed down from generation to generation. Subject to the restrictions mentioned in a moment, each black child within this group would receive the proceeds from the trust fund annually or upon reaching a certain age. He or she would then have the financial wherewithal to take a meaningful step toward a successful future, including enrolling in and graduating from college. The atonement estate would also be ear-marked for elementary and secondary education, allowing parents to take their children out of inferior public schools.

Before sketching the contours of the atonement trust fund, I should like to take a moment to explain why this particular reparation applies only to slave descendants and not to other racial minorities, who, nonetheless, would continue to receive symmetrical social benefits. Slavery created and Jim Crow sustained a racial hierarchy based on color. Under this system of racial favoritism, presumptions of beauty and intelligence and other manifestations of group privilege are determined in large part by the group's proximity to the European (or white) phenotype. Asians, Latinos, or other racial groups whose phenotype is closer to the European model than that of blacks experience less disadvantage than blacks, although more than whites, *owing to slavery and Jim Crow*. This is true even among blacks. For example, in American society, black women who are admired for their beauty—such as Halle Berry, Tyra Banks, and Vanessa Williams—have predominantly European rather than Negroid features. One could argue, however, that because nonblack minorities experience at least some disadvantage from the lingering effects of slavery and Jim Crow-which is to say, the "black-white paradigm," or "black-white binary," which sees the color line only in black and white, is invalid-the atonement trust fund, which after all is designed to redress the lingering effects of slavery, should be made available to all racial minorities. But to do this, we would have to determine the relative degree of disadvantage each racial group actually sustains because of slavery and Jim Crow. We would have to determine, for example, what percentage of the social problems Latinos experience are fueled by the continuous flow of poor and unskilled immigrants into Latino communities, or how much harm slavery and Jim Crow visits on Asians who continue to experience housing discrimination yet have higher incomes and educational levels than even whites. This exercise would simply run the idea of reparations into the ground-it would make a mockery of an otherwise laudable principle. For that reason, a line has to be drawn somewhere.

I draw the line at blacks for several reasons. First, blacks were the *main target* of slavery and Jim Crow. No other American group inhabited the peculiar institution. No other American group sustained more casualties or lengthier suffering from slavery and Jim Crow. No other American group harbors as much ill will against the federal government for slavery and Jim Crow. Second, this gives blacks a connection to slavery and Jim Crow-both familial and psychological-that no other racial minority has. There is a collective memory here that only blacks have, and a collective emotional need that only the government can satisfy. Third, unlike Asians and Latinos, blacks did not volunteer for this tour of duty. Blacks were kidnapped from their homeland and brought to this country by brutal force, the likes of which we have not seen before or since in American history. In short, although blacks, Asians, Latinos, Native Americans, Indians, and other people of color are victims of what Joe Feagin calls "systemic racism" (or the "white-created" paradigm of racial subordination), they do not experience and hence do not react to racial subordination in exactly the same way. Each experiences a different pattern, or syndrome, of white oppression, which sometimes overlaps, and each reacts differently, from despair to disregard, from levels of resistance to total acceptance. White-on-black oppression is just different from other white-oppression syndromes, whether racial or gender. "As Patricia Rodriguez has observed, 'White means mostly privilege and black means overcoming obstacles, a history of civil rights. As a Latina, I can't try to claim one of these.' " Black Americans carry the weight of the atrocities-slavery and Jim Crow—for which atonement is being sought. But, again, all racial minorities, including blacks, should continue to receive the protection of symmetrical social measures, including the civil rights laws.

Although the atonement trust fund would apply primarily to blacks, several restrictions would be imposed on the management, transfer, and use of trust funds. Each trust fund would have a life of twenty-five years (the amount of time it would take each child to get through college or many graduate or professional schools) and be maintained by the federal government. A board of commissioners, consisting of reputable citizens selected by blacks, would oversee fund operations in their respective regions of the country. Commissioners and their staff would, for example, help fund recipients make the right choices in schools and business opportunities. All payments from the trust fund would be by electronic transfer. Recipients would never really see or handle the funds.

Money accumulated in the atonement trust fund would only be spent for education or to start or invest in a business. Good primary and secondary education, graduation from a prestigious college or university, and small businesses are important ingredients in building family resources and sustaining their accumulation from one generation to the next. The trust fund would provide resources to help black children escape poor-performing public schools, alleviate the financial burden that causes many black students to leave college before graduating, and finance business opportunities for blacks who do not go to college. Venture capital funds would not, however, be made available until the recipient's twenty-fifth birthday (or later). An eighteen-year-old simply lacks the maturity to know his or her aspirations or to make sound investment decisions. For that reason, vocational education and mandatory consultations with a managerial advisory board, consisting of retired business persons selected by the board of commissioners, would be additional requirements for the receipt of venture capital. Finally, wealthy black families would be excluded from the program. Because wealth is relative-$100,000 in Tupelo, Mississippi, is not the same as $100,000 in New York City-the income level would be set regionally by the board of commissioners.

The amount of money each black recipient should receive for education or business investment could be determined in numerous ways. One way is to base it on projected educational costs. A broader approach is offered by Boris I. Bittker, whose calculation operates upon the relevant assumption that the purpose of monetary relief is to close the considerable net family wealth gap between blacks and whites, discussed in chapter 3. Bittker takes the difference between the average earnings between whites and blacks (let us call this value EG, for earnings gap) and multiplies EG by the number of black Americans (BA) to arrive at the amount of money blacks as a group should receive. This sum (the reparations amount, or RA) is determined annually, and is the amount Congress funds each year until the net family wealth gap is closed. Bittker does not say how long it would take to close the net family wealth gap. I would suggest that the funding period be consistent with the life of the atonement trust fund-twenty-five years for each beneficiary. Bittker's formula, then, is roughly, EG x BA = RA.

Another approach, offered by a former student of mine, the attorney Darrell L. Pugh, takes the racial income gap figure (EG) and capitalizes it to determine the present value of the investment required to realize the income necessary to close the gap. "For example, assume an average income gap of $5,000 a year and an average market rate of return of zero per-cent. Under the capitalization approach, it would take $50,000 of investment capital per eligible worker to close the gap— 5,000/.10 = $50,000. This figure could then be multiplied by the number of African Americans available in the adult workforce." Pugh's approach would permit funding to be phased in over time, "not only to encourage capacity building but to make the political feasibility of funding more likely."

Bittker and Pugh demonstrate that it is quite possible to calculate a monetary amount to be paid to slave descendants either per capita or through some program of eligibility like the atonement trust fund. Indeed, calculating the value of human life is rather routine in our society. Government agencies, juries, and insurance companies do it everyday. It is also important to note, as one thinks about the reparations calculations, that these calculations are always subject to second guessing. For example, when the Environmental Protection Agency did a cost-benefit analysis of a clean-air proposal that valued the life of a person over seventy years old at $1.4 million less than the life of a younger person-the so-called "senior death discount"—it was criticized by economists on several grounds, including that the calculation was faulty.

I offer the museum of slavery and atonement trust fund as forms of redress for slavery and Jim Crow, not as substitutes for ongoing civil rights reforms. The U.S. government still has an obligation to do what governments are supposed to do-protect its citizens from invidious discrimination. The museum of slavery and atonement trust fund should be viewed as special addenda to the struggle for racial justice in the United States. When viewed in juxtaposition to the milestones of this struggle—the abolition of slavery and Jim Crow—the museum of slavery and the atonement trust fund present easy burdens for our government. The hard question is whether white self-interest or perception of the public good will, once again, impede racial justice.

E.   REDRESS IN THE GLOBAL POLITICAL ECONOMY

What Role for Humanitarian Intellectual Property? The Globalization of Intellectual Property Rights

6 MINN. J.L. SCI. & TECH. 191 (2004).

■ SUSAN K. SELL

* * *

The 1995 Agreement on Trade–Related Aspects of Intellectual Property Rights (TRIPS), administered by the World Trade Organization (WTO), is the most important international law governing intellectual property rights. TRIPS extends patent rights to a wide variety of agricultural biotechnology innovations, including pharmaceutical products, pesticides, and plant varieties. It establishes a twenty-year patent term for these innovations. TRIPS requires states to provide adequate and effective enforcement mechanisms both internally and at their borders. The price of information and technology is increased under TRIPS because monopoly privileges are extended to patent-holders and TRIPS makes WTO dispute settlement procedures available to patent holders claiming violation of intellectually property rights. If a complaining government is successful in its claim, the WTO can authorize trade sanctions against the violating state. These settlement procedures and powers to punish make TRIPS a real force in the world.

Intellectual property rights reflect an inherent tension between the strong desire to promote and reward creative energy and the desire to make the fruits of that creativity available to the public. The granting of exclusive rights must be balanced against the economic effects of higher product and transaction costs and the potential "exclusion from the market of competitors who may be able to imitate or adapt the invention in such a way that social value is increased." Thus, the question is whether intellectual property rights should be treated as "a public goods problem for which the remedy is commodification, or a monopoly of information problem for which the remedy is unfettered competition[?]"

Strong intellectual property protection is justified by a market approach, because such protection provides incentives to "increase the number of commercially available products and thereby serve the public interest." However, it is important to question which public interests these rights serve. In the context of agricultural biotechnology, stakeholders include private sector seed companies, public corporations, research institutions, and resource-poor farmers. Intellectual property rights holders benefit from exclusive control of their innovations, as do those who have the resources to gain access to these innovations via the commercial market. Yet market-based solutions have failed to serve marginalized populations, such as the millions of people afflicted with HIV/AIDS and smallholder subsistence farmers in developing countries. The fact that smallholder farmers account for seventy-five percent of the world's undernourished population is evidence of this failure. In contemporary life science industries, market mechanisms fail to deliver innovation into the public domain. Indeed, "[i]nternational markets for technologies are inherently subject to failure due to distortions attributable to concerns about appropriability, problems of valuing information by buyers and sellers, and market power, all strong justifications for public intervention at both the domestic and global levels." There is a great need to strike a balance between a patent-holder's exclusive rights and the provision of agricultural technology to marginalized populations throughout the world. Solutions that will maximize the benefit of protecting innovation and yet minimize the risk of harm created by the potential overextension of this protection must be explored. It is therefore essential that policymakers consider "humanitarian" policies that promote social goals, such as protecting public health and alleviating malnutrition.

* * *

The contemporary global intellectual property regime is embedded in a broad structural context characterized by asymmetrical power relationships. Over the past thirty years, the globalization of financial markets and the shift towards an unfettered faith in laissez faire markets ideology pursued by the Reagan and Thatcher administrations has resulted in an increase in corporate transnational power vis-à-vis the state. States, seeking to be globally competitive, have liberalized markets, engaged in deregulation and privatization, and implemented new regulatory structures designed to promote efficiency and enforce market-friendly behavior. According to Philip Cerny, "[t]he institutions and practices of the state itself are increasingly marketized or 'commodified,' and the state becomes the spearhead of structural transformation to international market norms both at home and abroad." States have increasingly privatized once-public services, such as prisons, hospitals, military support services and even "mission-critical" functions, such as providing protection for the head of the 2003 Coalition Provisional Authority in Iraq, L. Paul Bremer III. The expansion of intellectual property rights and the privatization of federally funded research under the Bayh–Dole Act must be seen as an instance of this larger trend.

These broad economic changes have profoundly affected developing countries. Earlier models of economic development such as import-substituting industrialization, popular in Latin America and India, were discredited by economic stagnation and the debt crises of the 1970s–1980s. Meanwhile, the success of the East Asian "Tigers" vindicated export-led development and integration into global markets. Many developing countries subsequently reversed decades-old policies of economic nationalism in favor of market liberalization and privatization and consequently slashed public budgets. Governments in developing countries began to compete to attract foreign investment and eased former restrictions of foreign investors' activities. The new push toward export-led growth meant that developing countries needed access to industrialized country markets. The dependence of developing nations on trade gave the United States considerable economic leverage. Those developing countries sought access to the expansive United States market. Using the U.S. Trade Act of 1974, the Office of the United States Trade Representative, at the behest of high-technology firms, threatened trade sanctions against developing countries unless they adopted and enforced highly protective intellectual property policies. Such economic coercion was an important factor behind developing countries' ultimate acceptance of TRIPS.

This liberalizing agenda favors "finance capital and other mobile factors of production." Transnational firms in knowledge-intensive sectors such as pharmaceuticals, chemicals, software, and entertainment "have the resources, motivations and capabilities to roam the world searching for the kind of opportunities that promise lucrative rewards." These privileged sectors participate in "globalized" markets insofar as "there are a small number of participants who know one another and operate across countries with a common conception of control." TRIPS reflects the wishes of these privileged sectors and globalizes their preferred conception of control by establishing a high level of protection.

Beyond extending property rights, competitiveness concerns moved the United States to relax its antitrust policies. The Reagan administration codified this approach in the Antitrust Division's Merger Control Guidelines of 1982. Reflecting the influence of the Chicago School of Economics, the new guidelines abandoned the populist focus on market structure in favor of the Chicago school's focus on price theory. "In this view, only business practices that reduce output and increase prices are anti-competitive; business practices that expand output are pro-competitive." In contrast to earlier approaches, according to the Chicago school, "[h]igh levels of market concentration and the exercise of market power may be indicative of efficiencies." The 1982 guidelines presented an expanded definition of relevant markets. The guidelines allowed the introduction of non-structural factors, such as foreign competition or the possession of new technology that was important to long-term competitiveness. The Justice Department argued that "anti-trust laws should not be applied in a way that hinders the renewed emphasis on . . . competitiveness."

This new thinking removed most intellectual property licensing from antitrust scrutiny. As Thomas Hayslett points out, under Reagan's administration, "executive agencies viewed the economic incentives provided by intellectual property rights as legitimate means of extracting the full economic benefit from innovation." In effect then, "[i]ntellectual property rights acted as a 'magic trump card' allowing many previously suspect arrangements to proceed without challenge from the [Federal Trade Commission] or [Department of Justice]." Keith Maskus and Jerome Reichman suggest that today:

> There are virtually no products sold on the general products market that do not come freighted with a bewildering and overlapping array of exclusive property rights that discourage follow-on applications of routine technical know-how. Weak enforcement of antitrust laws then further reinforces the barriers to entry erected upon this thicket of rights, while the need to stimulate and coordinate investment in complex innovation projects justifies patent pools, concentrations of research efforts, and predatory practices formerly thought to constitute misuses of the patent monopoly.

So-called patent "thickets" have proliferated, in which overlapping patent rights require those seeking to commercialize new technology to obtain licenses from multiple patent holders. "A growing thicket of rights surrounds gene fragments, research tools, and other upstream inputs of scientific research, and the resulting transaction costs impede and delay research and development undertaken in both the public and private sectors."

III. ISSUES IN AGRICULTURE

What are the implications of the foregoing for agriculture? "Increasingly ... [intellectual property] rights have invaded the research commons itself and made it both costly and difficult to obtain cutting-edge technologies needed for public health, agricultural production, environmental protection, and the provision of other public goods." Critics of the increasing commodification of what was once treated as the public domain have raised at least six issues of concern: (1) threats to traditional agriculture and food security; (2) abuses of monopoly power; (3) increased dependence on costly commercial agriculture; (4) threats to biodiversity; (5) "biopiracy;" and (6) questions of benefit sharing. The discussion in this article focuses on the first three issues of concern.

Technological, judicial, and legislative changes together have produced a radical shift from public to private provision of seeds. As Professor Keith Aoki points out, "[t]he private seed market for grains was almost nonexistent at the beginning of the twentieth century, due to free government seed distribution and the widespread practice of farmer seed saving." According to Professor Aoki, "the intersection of biotechnical knowledge and methods and expanded legal protections for plant breeders transforms seed germplasm into a paradigm commodity." Legislative changes, including the United States Plant Variety Protection Act of 1970, "increased expectations of seed industry profits and thereby helped to stimulate an upsurge in mergers and acquisitions...." Life sciences corporations "emerged out of a wave of mergers, acquisitions, joint ventures and strategic partnerships involving companies in a wide range of fields such as chemicals, seeds, processed foods, dietary supplements and pharmaceuticals." Advances in biotechnology spurred the consolidation process throughout the 1970s and particularly in the 1980s. The 1973 development of the recombinant DNA technique, "which enabled foreign genes to be inserted into microorganisms," helped launch the era of commercial biotechnology. Notably, although "the Cohen–Boyer method for combining DNA from different organisms" was patented, "the patents were licensed nonexclusively and cheaply to encourage firms to take licenses rather than to challenge the patents." This technology had been federally funded, and "[m]any observers attribute the rapid progress of the biotechnology industry to the fact that this technology was made widely available rather than licensed exclusively to a single firm." In 1980, the U.S. Supreme Court ruled in Diamond v. Chakrabarty that a man-made, oil-eating bacterium could be patented. This case led to the expansion of rights to own living organisms and injected greater certainty into the development of commercial biotechnology. The ability to acquire patents on altered life forms helped biotechnology startup companies to raise venture capital.

The combination of expanded intellectual property rights and relaxed antitrust enforcement has led to marked economic concentration in the life sciences industries. The "vertical integration" of plant breeding, agrochemical, and food processing corporations has led to a situation in which the top ten seed companies control thirty percent of the world's $23 billion commercial seed market. Corporate plant breeders are obtaining broad patents that will have "far reaching" consequences. "Breeders are patenting entire species (cotton), economic characteristics (oil quality), plant reproductive behaviour (apomixes), and basic techniques in biotechnology (gene transfer tools)." Six major industrial groups now control most of the technology " 'which gives freedom to undertake commercial research and development in the area of [genetically modified] crops.' These are (i) Agrevo and Plant Genetic Systems (PGS); (ii) Du Pont and Pioneer; (iii) ELM, DNAP, Asgrow and Seminis; (iv) Monsanto, Calgene, DeKalb, Agracetus, PBI, Hybritech and Delta and Pine Land Co.; (v) Novartis; and (vi) Zeneca, Mogen and Avanta." Furthermore, six agricultural biotechnology companies alone hold seventy-five percent of all U.S. patents granted to the top thirty patent-holding firms: Monsanto, Du Pont, Syngenta, Dow, Aventis, and Grupo Pulsar. This combination of economic concentration with extensive and broad patenting means that a handful of global corporations are making huge inroads toward control of the world's food supply and are entangling farmers and indigenous peoples in an increasingly complex web of licensing and royalty obligations. As Keith Maskus and Jerome Reichman suggest:

> [T]he natural competitive disadvantages of follower countries may become reinforced by a proliferation of legal monopolies and related entry barriers that result from global minimum [intellectual property] standards. Such external restraints on competition could consign the poorest countries to a quasi-permanent status at the bottom of the technology and growth ladder.

The current system skews research towards rich and middle-income countries' markets and sectors. Most notably, there is a tendency in the public health sector to neglect tropical diseases in favor of focusing on cancer and so-called lifestyle afflictions, requiring drugs to combat obesity, balding, and erectile dysfunction. Consequently, only thirteen of 1,233 new drugs marketed between 1975 and 1997 were approved for tropical diseases in particular. As Professor Hammer suggests, "the rhetoric of strong intellectual property rights leading to innovation that meets social needs rings particularly hollow" for poorer countries most afflicted by tropical diseases. Similarly, there is a focus on the interests of higher-income markets in the agriculture sector, resulting in the development of crops unsuitable for subsistence and smallholder farming and a dearth of research beneficial for less lucrative micro-climates. The disproportionate emphasis on wealthier countries' market needs can be corrected through changes in private-public collaboration and through the allocation of more funding towards "the goal of helping subsistence farmers." Historically, seed companies preferred to develop hybrids because farmers must purchase new hybrid seed every planting season. Since the offspring of hybrid plants do not breed true-to-type, hybrid seeds offer a "form of biological protection." However, for plant varieties that lack this built-in biological protection, plant breeders can appeal to plant breeders' rights. Plant breeders' rights "generally do not encourage breeding related to minor crops with small markets." As a result, the private sector under invests in crops and technologies suitable for smallholder farmers, and these public goods are underprovided.

With the advent of genetic engineering, plant breeders sought to safeguard their investments through strong patent protections. Depending on national law, patents may be available for "the use of the new gene to transform a plant, on the transformation process, and most significantly on the transformed plant itself." The protection of transgenic plants enables genetic engineering firms to have "more confidence in their ability to reap the fruits of their research." That is because transfer or insertion of the patented gene into other plants constitutes patent infringement. Before the adoption of the 1991 Union for the Protection of New Varieties of Plants (UPOV91), plant breeders were forced to choose to protect their plant varieties with either a plant breeders' right or a patent. However, UPOV91 "removed the 1978 [UPOV's] ban on dual protection and now permits member states to protect the same plant variety with both a breeders' right and a patent." Professor Robert Lettington argues that this expansion of intellectual property rights into the agricultural sector has threatened the public sector's traditional focus on the needs of smallholder farmers. First of all, "private sector intellectual property rights may limit public sector access to innovations and germplasm that may be adaptable to smallholder needs and conditions while also limiting public sector research options due to concerns over the unhindered distribution of the products of its research." Second, the "failure of intellectual property systems to preserve the integrity of the public domain, and the consequent development of intellectual property rights strategies in public institutions, risks distorting research priorities to the detriment of smallholder farmers."

In developing countries, a large number of farmers are smallholders who do not participate in the transgenic seed market in any substantial way. Instead, these farmers engage in seed-saving, replanting, and "across-the-fence" exchange. This is particularly the case in many African countries where the public and private sectors play a minimal role in seed production and distribution. The smallholder farming sector plays an important role in contributing to national food needs. For example, such farmers produce "fifty-one percent of Latin America's maize, seventy-seven percent of its beans and sixty-one percent of its potatoes." In Africa, smallholder farmers produce the "majority of grains and legumes and almost all root, tuber and plantain crops." Furthermore, fifty to sixty percent of Peruvians and seventy to eighty percent of Kenyans depend on smallholder agriculture for their livelihood.

According to Professor Lettington, subsistence farmers traditionally save seeds for reuse, trade, and experimentation with new hybrids. Such experimentation contributes to the planet's biodiversity, as evidenced by the farmers in Professor Lettington's study who produced "as many as [thirty or forty] distinct varieties of potato, and [five or ten varieties] of maize, on farms of little more than a hectare." In the past, American laws covering plant varieties incorporated the notion of farmers' rights in which farmers retained their freedom to engage in these important and traditional activities. However, in August 1994 the U.S. Congress amended the Plant Variety Protection Act and removed the farmer's exemption. As a result, "it is now expressly illegal for farmers to sell or save seeds from proprietary crop varieties without receiving permission from breeders and paying royalties." Ironically, according to Professor Aoki, while the U.S. Patent Office in the "early 19th century began to collect and catalogue and make" seed freely available, by the early twenty-first century, the commodification of germplasm had transformed the U.S. patent office, into a "primary means" of attacking the longstanding "practice of farmer seed-saving." Grassroots activists are convinced that American industries are seeking these same results through TRIPS by pushing a particular interpretation of sui generis protection under Article 27.3(b).

Ultimately, TRIPS restricted the patenting of life forms, but Article 27.3(b) requires that members provide intellectual property protection for plant varieties or an "effective sui generis" system. However, there really is no consensus on what a sui generis system needs to include. Additionally, the negotiations leading to the adoption of Article 27 provide little guidance because they provide no record on the meaning of sui generis. American plant breeders have been pushing the UPOV as the model sui generis system. American support of UPOV may be due in part to how generous UPOV is to the corporate plant breeder. Fifty-one countries, many of which are industrialized, have joined the UPOV, which was last amended in 1991. The 1978 version of UPOV provided two limitations on the monopoly rights of plant breeders. First, other breeders could freely use UPOV-protected varieties for research purposes. Second, farmers could reuse the seed for the following year's harvest under certain conditions. The 1991 revision narrowed down the exemption for competing breeders, deleted the so-called farmers' privilege, and extended the breeders' monopoly right to the products of the farmer's harvest. "Although the UPOV system allows on-farm replanting, its rules restrict farmers' freedom to buy seed from sources other than the original breeders." UPOV91 "does not authorize farmers to sell or exchange seeds with other farmers for propagating purposes." To join UPOV today, nations must sign the 1991 treaty. Countries eschewing the UPOV system can adopt sui generis systems of protection that allow "farmers to acquire ... protected seed from any source and/or requiring protected varieties to display qualities that are genuinely superior to existing varieties."

In a comparative study of smallholder farming in Peru and Kenya, Robert J. L. Lettington did not find evidence that plant variety protection (PVP) legislation harmed smallholder agriculture. However, he argued that "the current system of PVP [legislation] is failing to create solutions to existing problems." In particular, PVP legislation has created incentives that direct resources away from subsistence farmers' needs in favor of those of large commercial agricultural enterprises. It also promotes the use of commercial seed as opposed to landraces or "wild" cultivars. "The end result has been a hastening of the deterioration of food security in these areas...." Professor Lettington suggests that governments that seek to limit the cost of seed in economically and climatically marginal areas may "need to place limits on the nature of intellectual property rights."

IV. THE REGULATORY ENVIRONMENT

In examining the regulatory environment in this context, the central question is what degree of discretion states have in limiting intellectual property rights to support smallholder agriculture. There are at least two dimensions to the answer: one addresses the letter of the law, the other addresses the broader context of asymmetrical power. Focusing on the formal features of intellectual property law, texts, and institutions, one sees plenty of room for state discretion and flexibility in adapting the global minimum standards to local concerns. However, this formal universe is embedded in a system of asymmetrical power relationships and global capitalism that constrain weaker states' abilities to exploit the flexibilities crafted into the law.

TRIPS provides substantial flexibility for developing countries. Article 27.3(b) specifies that countries may adopt an "effective sui generis system" to protect plant varieties. Under TRIPS, countries may adopt patent protection for plant varieties, UPOV91, an alternative sui generis system, or some combination of these forms of protection. While corporate plant breeders would prefer that developing countries adopt UPOV91 as their domestic legislative standard, these countries are by no means required to do so. The UPOV treaties are one type of sui generis protection designed to serve the interests of plant breeders. In a searching and thorough analysis of developing countries' options, Professor Laurence Helfer has arrayed the options on a spectrum ranging from maximum discretion to minimal discretion for developing countries to tailor their systems to meet their particular needs. States that adopt TRIPS and ratify or accede to UPOV91 have the least discretion. According to Professor Helfer, states wishing to retain maximum flexibility and discretion to serve the needs of smallholder agriculture would be well-advised to adopt TRIPS only.

The advantages of TRIPS are that its provisions on plant varieties "do not refer to or incorporate any preexisting intellectual property agreements, including the 1978 and 1991 UPOV Acts." TRIPS members are neither required "to become members of UPOV nor to enact national laws consistent with either UPOV Act in order to comply with their obligations under TRIP[S]." Article 27.3(b) preserves "significant leeway for national governments to work out the precise manner in which they will balance protection of IPRs against other international obligations and national objectives." "The chances are, that for a poor nation, neither a UPOV nor a regular patent approach will actually encourage private-sector research. Hence, such a nation is probably best-off adopting minimum compliance with TRIPS...." TRIPS, unlike UPOV91, preserves the right of subsistence farmers to exchange seed. For a nation in which the exchange is an issue, it would be wise to incorporate both subsistence farmer exemptions resist the high-pressure tactics of the United States Trade Representative and the industries that it represents.

In these circumstances it is imperative that public institutions take the lead in assisting developing countries in the implementation of suitable legislation that conforms to their international legal obligations. Public institutions, such as land grant universities, must also continue to make the fruits of their research available to those who need it most on terms that the recipients accept. The 1980 Bayh–Dole Act allowed "grantees to seek patent rights in government-sponsored research results." The idea behind this was that many inventions with commercial potential lay fallow in university laboratories, and that patenting opportunities would give universities incentives to search research labs for significant and marketable inventions. The Bayh–Dole Act has resulted in at least a ten-fold increase of university patenting activity since 1979. This flurry of patenting activity has had the beneficial effect of generating revenue for cash-strapped public universities. For instance, the patent infringement award that the University of Minnesota won for the development of the drug Ziagen has provided much-needed funding for research and graduate student support. University patent portfolios also help to attract private sector funding, especially in biotechnology.

However, the Bayh–Dole Act also has created new divisions within universities. As Professors Arti Rai and Rebecca Eisenberg point out, the legislation makes no distinction between upstream and downstream research, and as a result, an increasing number of research tools have become patent-protected. An unintended consequence of the Bayh–Dole Act has been the dramatic reduction of open access to research tools. Technology transfer offices are charged with patenting and licensing technology to generate revenue for the institution. Research scientists are more interested in having access to "open science." The Bayh–Dole Act also has increased university collaboration with private sector biotechnology firms, raising many questions about academic freedom, research priorities, and incentives. Some critics have gone so far as to assert that universities have lost their sense of "public mission."

Yet the choices may not be so stark, and there may be ways to navigate the contours of the current system to better balance competing imperatives. For example, in the pharmaceutical sector, there could be clauses in agreements to allow a university to sublicense to generic manufacturers if its patent conflicts with efforts to distribute affordable drugs for HIV/AIDS victims in sub-Saharan Africa. Professors Rai and Eisenberg offer a similarly modest and sensible suggestion for publicly-funded research. They suggest that "decisions about the dividing line between the public domain and private property should be made by institutions that are in a position to appreciate the tensions between widespread access and preservation of commercial incentives without being unduly swayed by institutional interests that diverge from the overall public interest." In other words, they argue that public funding agencies should decide what fruits of their investments to patent. They also advocate addressing the upstream/downstream research tool issue by devising "a system that distinguishes cases in which proprietary claims make sense from cases in which they do not." Research tool exemptions would be useful to help to preserve the domain of "open science."

and research exemptions in national plant breeders' rights legislation. Countries wishing to adopt the stronger UPOV91 system should consider incorporating waivers or exemptions for subsistence and smallholder farmers. In countries lacking significant private sector competition, as is often the case in poor countries, public sector seed provision will be important to promote competition to stimulate both variety and lower prices.

Public-private partnerships in agriculture might stimulate the transfer of technology so that public sector seed providers could adapt technology to subsistence farmers' needs. In order for such arrangements to work, private firms would need to retain opportunities to capture economic benefits in the market sector, while keeping the technology affordable for the subsistence sector. This two-tiered arrangement has some parallels in the control of access to medicines and would require safeguards against diverting subsistence-priced technology into the market sector.

Focusing on TRIPS and the letter of the law, one can conclude, as does Professor Helfer, that:

> States that implement the four core TRIP[S] requirements in good faith—that is, states that grant breeders intellectual property rights and enforcement measures applicable to varieties in all species and botanical genera and that provide those same rights and measures to breeders from other TRIP[S] member states—are unlikely to have their laws challenged successfully.

However, public international law such as TRIPS is embedded in a broader context of asymmetrical power relationships between developed and developing countries, and between producers and consumers of the fruits of biotechnology. This context reduces the amount of leeway that poor states have in devising regulatory approaches most suitable for their individual needs and stages of development. In particular, developing countries increasingly have been subject to bilateral and regional pressure to surrender the flexibilities afforded by TRIPS. Bilateral investment treaties, bilateral intellectual property agreements, and regional free trade agreements concluded between the United States and developing countries and between the European Union and developing countries invariably have been considered to be "TRIPS–Plus."

For example, in the intellectual property provisions covering agriculture in the Central American Free Trade Agreement framework, developing countries are most often required to ratify or accede to UPOV91 as their sui generis system of protection and "to undertake 'all reasonable efforts' to make patent protection available for plants."

Furthermore, developing countries have failed to take full advantage of TRIPS flexibilities not only in the agricultural marketplace, but the pharmaceutical market as well. This is largely because such nations are eager to attract foreign investment and are concerned about alienating potential investors. They also are eager to have access to technologies that may aid in their development, provide reliable nutrition, and which have the potential to address a myriad of pressing social and economic problems. Most of these countries lack significant bargaining leverage and the capacity to

V. CONCLUSION

This brief overview of some major issues involved in intellectual property protection and agricultural biotechnology underscores the fact that "the institution of property is extremely complex, and more importantly, political." Yet we are no closer to resolving these controversies. "More often than not, rather than being an answer, the issue of property rights is only the beginning of a long series of vexing questions." Developing countries should do what they can to preserve their autonomy in adopting intellectual property policies that suit their levels of development. They should resist TRIPS-plus initiatives in bilateral and regional trade and investment agreements and insist upon TRIPS as their maximum standard. Developing nations should seek technical assistance that encourages them to use existing TRIPS flexibilities. They also need to participate in global standard-setting exercises concerning competition policy and address the ways in which they would prefer to regulate foreign firms' acquisition of local firms.

Promoting genuine competition is an important policy objective. "Nations in which there is limited private sector competition in the seed industry should ensure that public sector varieties are available in competition with private sector ones." Professor Lettington recommends:

> The activities of smallholder farmers, in particular the saving, use, exchange, and sale of farm-saved seed, should be explicitly stated as not subject to the rights of intellectual property rights holders. In accordance with the purposes and objectives of TRIPS, effort should be made to develop effective incentives for research targeted at smallholder farmers . . . . Limited exceptions to intellectual property rights should be permitted to promote the adaptation of protected products to the needs of smallholder farmers. These should apply to both research and development and to manufacturing and distribution.

Universities may feel caught between the conflicting imperatives of attracting private sector funding and generating revenue through patenting activity on the one hand, and promoting public goods through "humanitarian intellectual property" policies on the other. It is clear that universities have an important role to play in preserving the balance between exclusion and access as well as paving the way to more informed, effective, and socially responsible agricultural intellectual property policies.

Civil Resistance and the "Diversity of Tactics" in the Anti–Globalization Movement: Problems of Violence, Silence, and Solidarity in Activist Politics

41 Osgoode Hall L.J. 505 (2003).

■ Janet Conway

I. INTRODUCTION

With the November 1999 mobilization that shut down the World Trade Organization (WTO) meetings in Seattle, the "anti-globalization" movement erupted onto the world stage. Between the Seattle protest and the events of September 11, 2001 (9/11), massive and growing anti-globalization demonstrations confronted neo-liberal elites wherever they convened. These demonstrations, especially their North American and European variants, have been the forum for the emergence of a debate over "diversity of tactics." The debate has revolved around the acceptability of more disruptive or confrontational forms of direct action, the putative role of property damage, and the use of veiled threats of the escalation of violence in the struggle against neo-liberal globalization.

* * *

In the name of creativity, resistance, and democracy, many anti-globalization activists advocate "respect for diversity of tactics" as a non-negotiable basis of unity. Solidarity with the full range of resistance has meant that no tactics are ruled out in advance and that activists refrain from publicly criticizing tactics with which they disagree. However, embracing diversity of tactics is not without ambiguity and risk: both strategically in terms of provoking repression and losing public support, but also in terms of democratic practice and culture within the movement itself where it may damage any prospect for broad coalition politics.

* * *

II. CIVIL DISOBEDIENCE AND DIRECT ACTION

The terms "civil disobedience" and "direct action" have been used interchangeably in both activist and academic circles; their meanings are often conflated. Further, the meaning of these terms often suffers as assumptions of illegality and violence are imported into their use.

Civil disobedience is a specific form of extra-parliamentary political action involving the deliberate, principled, and public breaking of a law that is perceived to be unjust. Acts of civil disobedience are premised on the existence of liberal democratic institutions and the rule of law. The public and principled breaking of a law by otherwise law-abiding persons is meant to call attention to the unjustness of that law, both through heroic witness (being willing to risk arrest or jail), and through using or gumming-up legal channels themselves (for example, through a trial). Classic examples of the use of civil disobedience from recent movement history include the lunch counter sit-ins of the civil-rights movement, the burning of draft cards in the anti-Vietnam War movement, and the blockades and occupations of the anti-nuclear movement.

Direct action is a larger and more generic category than is civil disobedience. The term refers to forms of political action that bypass parliamentary or bureaucratic channels to directly ameliorate or eliminate an injustice, or to slow down or obstruct regular operations of an unjust system or order. Strikes, street demonstrations, and occupations are classic forms of direct action.

Virtually all contemporary forms of direct action are in some sense symbolic as the action dramatizes conflict of system-wide problems. For example, the act of squatting (moving into and living in) in a vacant building may provide housing for a dozen homeless people thus directly ameliorating their situation. However, as forms of political action, most squats point to a much larger phenomenon of homelessness and create pressure for public agencies to act against the squat or to provide affordable housing. In this sense, a single squat constitutes direct action and is symbolic at the same time.

Direct action can be legal, illegal, or extra-legal (extra-legal is used here to refer to practices that are not currently contemplated by the law). It may or may not be an occasion of police action and arrests. While all civil disobedience is a form of direct action, not all direct action involves the intentional and principled breaking of an unjust law with the purpose of calling attention to it. Direct action can be situated anywhere on what young activists call "the violence/non-violence continuum." Likewise, direct action can be situated anywhere on the illegal/extra-legal/legal continuum. There is no necessary correlation between non-violence and legality or, as activist victims of police brutality are quick to point out, between violence and illegality.

Both civil disobedience and direct action can involve property destruction and can still be considered non-violent by many activists. Here, non-violence is generally understood to mean the eschewing of the use of physical force against another human being. Generally, the mass street actions of the anti-globalization movement have been forms of direct action, some of them legal but many of them not, and have been almost completely non-violent on the part of the protesters. Within the demonstrations, there have been numerous direct actions of a great variety of types. The intensifying debate over diversity of tactics in the movement must be understood within a context of expanding commitment to, and enactment of, a wide variety of expressions of direct action.

III. DIVERSITY OF TACTICS

The debate over diversity of tactics in the anti-globalization movement initially emerged in the context of the Seattle demonstrations in November 1999. By the April 2001 anti-Free Trade Area of the Americas (FTAA) demonstrations in Quebec City, there was a full and specific articulation of the meaning of the term. Respect for diversity of tactics implies support for a bundle of organizing approaches, attitudes, and tactics. Since the Seattle demonstrations, proponents of diversity of tactics in the Canadian anti-globalization movement have argued both for an escalation and for a diversification of tactics beyond the routines of lobbying and legal, stage-managed demonstrations. They have argued for the valuing of a wider range of political activity especially in the institutionalized power centres of the movement such as labour unions and non-governmental organizations

(NGOs). Proponents of diversity of tactics have called for and have engaged in popular education, cultural work, and grassroots-community organizing. Driven by a sense of urgency resulting from mounting social and ecological crises, these activists have argued for a return to more militant and confrontational tactics, including direct action and civil disobedience. In the name of both escalation and diversity they have also called for and defended property destruction, from stickering, spray painting, and guerrilla murals, to window smashing and the defacing of signs.

Respect for diversity of tactics as an ethical framework presupposes the existence of "affinity groups" as the unit of organization and democratic decision making. Affinity group organizing has its roots in feminist, anarchist, and anti-nuclear movements in which small, autonomous groups decide on the nature of their participation in a direct action, organizing independently of any centralized movement authority. Commitment to affinity group organizing often implies a repudiation of representative forms of democracy, institutions of the liberal democratic state, as well as labour unions and more bureaucratized movement organizations. Respect for diversity of tactics is part of a commitment to and practice of direct and participatory democracy in which all practitioners participate directly in decision making about tactics within their affinity groups. Large-scale anti-globalization demonstrations have been organized in significant part by networks of affinity groups who gather in spokescouncils. Theoretically, these groups strive for consensus, but practically work towards coordination and mutual tolerance.

The decisive feature of respect for diversity of tactics is an ethic of respect for, and acceptance of, the tactical choices of other activists. This tolerance of pluralism involves an explicit agreement not to publicly denounce the tactics of other activists–most controversially, rock-throwing, window-breaking, garbage can burning, and vandalism. So respect for diversity of tactics precludes, for example, the kind of non-violence agreement proposed by the Direct Action Network (DAN) that undergirded the Seattle organizing. The debate about diversity of tactics first emerged under that name when DAN organizers and other key movement leaders condemned the people throwing rocks and breaking windows in Seattle.

By the time of the demonstrations in Quebec City, those who were advocating diversity of tactics were also repudiating the dogmatism of non-violence, which they understood to be an authoritarian move to render certain forms of political resistance illegitimate. They criticized the overly rigid violence/non-violence binary that characterizes much of the discourse around non-violence. They also critiqued the highly ritualized forms of civil disobedience that had evolved during the peace movement, where protesters passively handed themselves over to the police.

* * *

V.   PERSPECTIVES ON PROPERTY DESTRUCTION
IN THE ANTI–GLOBALIZATION MOVEMENT

The most contentious debates about violence and non-violence in the North American anti-globalization movement revolve around the nature and status of property destruction as a tactic. Proponents of diversity of tactics specify that property damage includes such political staples as stickering, billboard "corrections," or graffiti. Few activists would dispute the value and creativity of these tactics, either within the context of large demonstrations and in their own right.

They rightly argue that the label violent is used somewhat indiscriminately, both within and beyond the movement, to refer to anyone acting outside the bounds of legitimate, that is routinized, legalized, and bureaucratized, forms of dissent. Those within the movement (including those engaged in non-violent direct action) tend to single out property damage, particularly window breaking, as violent. Notably, the debate here is not about physical violence against persons, but about whether destruction of property is encompassed within the meaning of violent.

The smashing of corporate windows, police cruisers, and media vehicles remain very controversial and have occasionally given rise to fisticuffs on the spot between activists who try to prevent those who attempt to pursue these tactics. Proponents of property destruction in Seattle pointed out the irony of self-proclaimed non-violent protesters physically tackling those targeting corporate property. They reject the notion that property destruction is violent unless it involves causing pain to, or death of, people. Rather than an expression of rage or reaction, proponents claim that property damage is "strategically and specifically targeted direct action against corporate interests." Proponents distinguish between private (capitalist) property and personal (use-value) property, targeting the former. They maintain that, as a tactic, property destruction unsettles middle-class culture and the reification of private property that is so entrenched in North America. "Property destruction allows for a change in landscape, a visual punctuation."

Therefore, proponents argue both ideologically and strategically for certain *kinds* of property destruction. But within the discourse of respect for diversity of tactics there seems to be little room for discussion between affinity groups of what kinds of property can be destroyed and what kinds of damage are appropriate. Further, there is little discussion between groups about the relation of these acts to the larger political context or to any broader movement strategy.

It is a fact that both the mainstream and alternative media are captivated by property destruction and the climate of uncertainty and disorder that it fosters through its threat of escalating conflict. Some forms of property destruction—notably window breaking—have trumped all other movement tactics in terms of the mass production of images. This fact is not recognized as problematic among the proponents of property destruction, despite their rhetoric of respect for (and presumably, a valuing of) diversity of tactics.

VI. THE BLACK BLOC

Finally, while I support a clear distinction between the destruction of property and violence to people, discussions about property damage in the context of the anti-globalization movement are unavoidably haunted by the spectre of the Black Bloc and the host of political and strategic issues it raises. Because it is the most prominent apologist for, and practitioner of, property destruction, the Black Bloc's discourses and practices as a whole overdetermine the debate about property destruction in the context of the anti-globalization movement.

The Black Bloc originated in the European Autonomen movement in which masked and black-clad anarchists engaged in a range of militant and confrontational tactics and defend each other from the police. In Seattle, the Black Bloc concentrated their efforts on property damage and avoided engaging the police. In post-Seattle actions in Toronto, Ottawa, and Quebec City, the Black Bloc appeared to me to be a masked and costumed group of youths beating tattoos on poles and stop signs and marching in formation within large demonstrations. Yet in other situations, notably in Europe, all manners of mayhem have been attributed to the Black Bloc–hurling rocks, sticks, and Molotov cocktails at the police and looking for a fight. They played particularly explosive roles in Prague and Genoa.

* * *

Numerous activists do engage in various forms of property destruction without masks and without any identification with the Black Bloc. Moreover, many are explicitly non-violent in their interactions with police. There are also traditions of property destruction in the anti-nuclear movement that are part of traditions of non-violent civil disobedience. But in the current context of the anti-globalization movement, property destruction has also become a tactic favoured by the Black Bloc. And it is this relationship, created by the discourses and practices of the Black Bloc, between property destruction in the context of the large anti-globalization demonstrations and a readiness, even an eagerness, to confront the police physically, that has so problematized property destruction as an acceptable tactic in the current context. Furthermore, when property destruction is enacted by masked activists, it is also vulnerable to appropriation, manipulation, and escalation by masked others: the police or their paid agitators, fascists, or criminal elements, some of whom appear to have participated in Genoa.

According to George Lakey, at its best, non-violent protest is a form of prefiguration. Its power lies in its contrast to the violent power of the state in the theatre of protest–solidarity and pacifism in the face of naked aggression. However, these assumptions were challenged in Seattle, particularly by those who engaged in and defended property destruction, not as a form of violence, but as embodying a distinct (and more militant and therefore better) political and strategic logic. As such, property destruction continues to raise troubling and challenging questions for the movement. In the post-Seattle period, Barbara Ehrenreich states:

> Clearly the left, broadly speaking, has come to a creative impasse. We need to invent some new forms of demonstrating that minimize the danger while maximizing the possibilities for individual self-expression.... We need ways of protesting that are accessible to the uniniti-

ated, untrained, nonvegan population as well as to the seasoned veteran. We need to figure out how to capture public attention while, as often as possible, directly accomplishing some not-entirely-symbolic purpose, such as gumming up a WTO meeting or, for that matter, slowing down latte sales at a Starbucks.

Rock-throwing doesn't exactly fit these criteria, nor did the old come-as-you-are demos of the sixties. But neither do the elaborately choreographed rituals known as "nonviolent" civil disobedience.

* * *

IX. ELITE RETREAT TO KANANASKIS AND HARD LESSONS FOR THE MOVEMENT

In response to the events of Genoa, the June 2002 meeting of the G8 was set for the remote Rocky Mountain town of Kananaskis. With five thousand troops, fifteen hundred Royal Canadian Mounted Police (RCMP), and an enforced no-fly zone, it was the "largest security operation in Canadian history," with a price tag of three to 500,000,000 dollars. Activists spent months planning a week-long Solidarity Village only to be outspent and outmaneuvered by governments and security forces at every turn. Negotiations with the Stoney Point First Nation over use of land came to an abrupt halt amid accusations of federal interference. The City of Calgary refused permission to use parks. According to David Robbins, an organizer with the Council of Canadians, "there's a desire to disorganize and frustrate coherent organizing around this particular summit in order to create confrontation and discredit opposition to the G–8 and corporate globalization."

Nevertheless, several thousand people turned up to the summit, the snake march, and the picnic without a permit, to muddy corporate facades, and to demonstrate with and without their clothes on. Again, the actions were organized under the rubric of diversity of tactics. Significantly, unions, NGOs, and direct-action protesters in Canada were working together again after a post–9/11 hiatus. In Calgary, unionists were visible in all the activities, including the snake marches that disrupted traffic during Monday morning rush hour, and had participated in the convergence table leading up to and during the events. The demonstrations were completely non-violent, although not without some heated moments. Protesters actively intervened to defuse potentially explosive situations between police and the more confrontational activist factions. Police in Calgary were on bicycles and in soft hat rather than riot gear.

Several thousand people also turned up in Ottawa in response to a call to "take the capital." As in Calgary, the framework for organizing was respect for diversity of tactics. Coordinated separation of spaces allowed for different kinds of events, from an explicitly non-violent World March of Women-led "revolutionary knitting action" to a diversity of tactics, CLAC [La Convergence des Luttes Anti-Capitalistes]-led snake march. A large non-violent convergence march was organized on the second day around the theme that "no one is illegal" in response to repressive anti-terrorist laws.

In the lead-up to Calgary and Ottawa, new language had begun to appear among proponents of diversity of tactics advocating forms of resistance "that maximize respect for life." This did not mean that organizing, especially in Ottawa, was not extremely fractious. A refusal by CLAC, in the name of respect for diversity of tactics, to exclude violent tactics created a serious split in the Ottawa activist community. Most church-, labour-, and NGO-based activists (including Global Democracy Ottawa) simply stayed away from all Take the Capital activities. As a result, the CLAC-organized snake march in particular represented a much narrower cross-section of the movement; it was comprised almost exclusively of young people with a high proportion of self-identified anarchists, including a number who were masked and carrying batons. The batons were used to produce the trademark rhythmic drumming on any available metal surface—stop signs, guardrails, and street grates.

Throughout both the snake march and the "no one is illegal" march, CLAC organizer Jaggi Singh kept reiterating over the bullhorn that "anything could happen," and that people should and will directly confront actions they perceive to be unjust in ways that they deem legitimate. As a participant in both events, I experienced this rhetoric as inflammatory and manipulative. Singh was holding open the possibility of violence as an acceptable aspect of protest in general and in the context of the event in which we were participating. As someone willing to support a militant action organized under the rubric of diversity of tactics, I felt that my presence was being manipulated to support a threat of violent escalation over which I had no say.

On the other hand, the Raging Granny marching beside me had this to say: "Some of our members are uncomfortable taking part in these kinds of events because they're worried about what might happen. But, I think, when you consider the violence all around us, these (gesturing to the sea of young people) are just the lambs."

In Ottawa, there was some spray-painting and paint-bombing of banks. The windows of a police car were smashed during the snake march, but this action was immediately booed by protesters and did not escalate. Police were in regular uniform and kept their distance. Like the events in Calgary, Ottawa was acclaimed by police, press, and protesters alike as completely non-violent, despite the tensions created by those insisting on "solidarity with the full scope of resistance."

In the aftermath of these actions, Starhawk published what amounted to a thorough rethinking of diversity of tactics. Coming from an activist with demonstrated commitment to both non-violent direct action and respectful dialogue with the Black Bloc, her comments are especially persuasive. She argued that the time (post–9/11) and place (oil-rich and right-wing Calgary) demanded a powerful, militant, disruptive, and explicitly non-violent direct action. However, such action could not happen because diversity of tactics had become the movement's default mode.

Although offering a critique of the morality of much non-violence politics and the staleness of its tactics, Starhawk argues that a commitment to strategic non-violence opens up political space that diversity of tactics has, in effect, shut down:

> Strategic nonviolence lets us mobilize broadly around actions that are more than symbolic, that actually interfere with the operations of an institution of power. Unions and NGOs, and at-risk groups can support and participate in such actions, which contain many necessary roles at varied levels of risk.

> Committing to nonviolence as a strategic move for a particular action allows us to organize openly, without security culture and with broad participation in decision-making.... Transparency allows us to actually educate, mobilize, and inspire people to join us. While security culture may be necessary at times, it works against empowerment and direct democracy. People can only have a voice in the decisions that affect them if they know what is being decided....

> If we are to regain momentum in the post–9–11 climate for issues of global justice, we need actions that can mobilize large numbers of people to do more than simply march. We need to embrace discussion and debate, and trust that our movement is strong, resilient, and mature enough to tolerate our differences of opinion. We might agree that a diversity of tactics are [sic] needed in the long run to undermine global corporate capitalism, and still be willing to commit to strategic nonviolence for an action when it seems the strongest option. Otherwise, we end up without either diversity or tactics.

X. CONCLUSIONS

The first G8 summit in Europe since Genoa, 9/11, and the war in Iraq is currently taking place in Evian, France and with it has come the return of massive anti-globalization protests. Organizers claim that 120,000 people demonstrated in the mass march on Sunday, June 1, 2003. Through the winter of 2003, the anti-globalization movement was transformed by the explosion of a massive, global anti-war movement in opposition to an American-led attack on Iraq. On February 15, 2003, over four million people took to the streets in over six hundred towns and cities across the world in an extraordinary, globally-coordinated effort to prevent war. In January 2003, over 100,000 people gathered in Porto Alegre, Brazil for the third annual World Social Forum to march against the American Empire, to showcase the existence of political and economic alternatives to neoliberalism, and to assert that another world is possible. Global opposition to neo-liberalism has been fueled by the war on Iraq. United States-led military aggression is increasingly recognized as an imperial civilizational project of global proportion.

In this new climate, the debate about diversity of tactics appeared increasingly marginalized. Organizers of mass anti-war demonstrations in Canada and elsewhere negotiated routes with police and marshaled the protests. Protesters carefully avoided property destruction or confrontation with police.

Anti-globalization activists were very prominent in the organizing and protesting against the war. But the movement against the war also broadened dramatically, incorporating many more people of color, notably from Muslim and Arab communities, and people who have never before protested anything. New movement coalitions included the more traditional peace groups with their strong traditions of pacificism and non-violent civil disobedience.

There will almost certainly be renewed debates within the movement about tactics. Property destruction has re-appeared in Lausanne, Switzerland, as part of the most recent round of anti-G8 protests. So have non-violent direct actions blockading roads and bridges. But these activities are in the wake of massive anti-war coalitions and demonstrations that may change the conditions for debate within the movement. Most powerfully, in the face of such naked use of deadly force by the United States, Starhawk's argument for strategic non-violence may have greater purchase in the movement.

In Canada, from the late 1990s into the early years of this century, the notion of "respect for diversity of tactics" held great appeal, especially among young activists. Against the historical backdrop of several decades of highly institutionalized forms of movement politics, it both named and validated important new activist practices in the face of growing global crises. More than ever, the movement and the world needs the creativity and courage of this new generation of activists in advancing non-violent strategies for social transformation. But in the face of unprecedented forces of power and domination, we also need to nurture the movement as a space of freedom and democracy, genuine diversity and pluralism, respect for life, and a love of peace in prefiguring the world we want.

————

NOTES AND QUESTIONS

1. Global security and poverty: In February of 2005, UN Secretary General Kofi Annan said "We will not defeat terrorism unless we also tackle the causes of conflict and misgovernment in developing countries. And we will not defeat poverty so long as trade and investment in any major part of the world are inhibited by fear of violence or instability."

In an extended interview with *Mother Jones* magazine, Jeffrey Sachs, an international development economist, author of *The End of Poverty*, laid out his own strategies for eradicating global poverty by 2025. Sachs headed a United Nations panel of development experts that were given the task of drafting global development goals to be met by the year 2015.

Why is it that decades of development economics haven't achieved the elimination of poverty? What makes Sachs' proposals so special? Is eradicating poverty a feasible goal to achieve in our lifetime? Sachs recently discussed his views with *Mother Jones Magazine*. Onnesha Roychoudhuri, *The End of Poverty: An Interview with Jeffrey Sachs*, MOTHER JONES MAG., May 6, 2005, *available at* http://www.motherjones.com/news/qa/2005/05/jeffrey_sachs.html.

2. Practical investment strategy. Sachs proposes that the "rich countries need to help poor countries make practical investments that are often really very basic.... For instance, one issue that has been tragically neglected ... is malaria. That's a disease that kills up to 3 million people every year." Sachs decries the failure to address this practical problem "that could be controlled quite dramatically and easily". Sachs argues that development issues got sidetracked during the post-911 crisis period. However, he notes that the tsunami in the Indian Ocean in which we could all see the scope of the devastation on our television screens, shifted discussion towards the plight of the world's poor.

3. The point seven percent solution. Sachs has proposed that the rich countries, such as the United States, devote 0.7 percent of our Gross National Product to development aid. This proposal has been criticized by former World Bank economist, William Easterly. Easterly calls instead for "piecemeal reform", in which more limited projects are tried, monitored and measured to see what really works before a major commitment is given. Sachs' reply to the piecemeal approach is that "I don't think that we should be choosing between whether a young girl has immunizations or water, or between whether her mother an father are alive, because they have access of treatment for AIDS, or whether she has a meal at school, or whether her father and mother, who are farmers are able to grow enough food to feed their family.... Those strike me as quite doable and practical things that can be done at once.... I am proposing that we help people help themselves."

4. Corruption. Rich countries frequently cite the problem of corruption as a reason to withhold significant contributions of foreign aid. Sachs says, "my experience is that there's corruption everywhere: in the U.S., in Europe, in Asia, and in Africa. It's a bit like infectious disease—you can control it, but it's very hard to eradicate it ... I don't have any magic solution for those situations....Nothing is done on trust. Everything should be done on a basis of measurement and monitoring.... Don't just send money: send bed nets, send in auditors, make targets quantitative."

5. Teaching development economics in the universities. Sachs proposes a major change in the way advanced students are taught development economics. "Students in economics write dissertations about countries that they never stepped foot in because their advisor gives them a database from Nigeria or Kenya or some place else, and they do their thesis that way. That is like becoming a doctor without ever seeing a patient. We don't do case studies" Sachs proposes that development economists be trained with "clinical economics." In this mode students would meet in the field of study, then conference with professors to analyze the results of their efforts. This would approximate the hospital "rounds" for residents in training.

6.   Shocking disengagement of World Bank from the aids crisis. "I was absolutely shocked and aghast when I learned that in the late 1990s the World Bank and other donors weren't paying a penny to help treat people dying of AIDS. . . . Rarely do rich countries say, 'Look we're just not prepared to spend money to save poor people's lives'. Instead you get a lot of skepticism. 'You can't do this, this is impossible. We're doing everything we can after all. We've tried everything. Let's go slowly. Let's do one thing at a time' I don't buy those arguments."

7.   Modern direct action. Attempts to affect social change through courts or legislatures can often be a cumbersome process, characterized by delays, compromises and setbacks. Social activists have often sought more immediate strategies, such as protests and boycotts. Socially and economically disruptive activity has the advantage of gaining immediate and widespread attention from the public, and they may be more forceful both in their methods and results. These tactics include risks as well. Their failure may also be more visible, and they may engender backlash from the public.

The most famous example of a boycott from the American civil rights movement is the Montgomery Bus Boycott. In 1955, Montgomery, Alabama had a municipal law which required black citizens to ride in the back of the city's buses. On December 1, Rosa Parks sparked the boycott when she was arrested for refusing to relinquish her seat at the front of the bus to white passengers. Over the weekend of December 3 and 4, the leaders of Montgomery's black community, including Dr. Martin Luther King, planned a large scale boycott of Montgomery's bus system, in protest of the South's segregation laws. Black ministers urged their congregations to join the boycott, and pamphlets were distributed throughout the city. The boycott was remarkably successful. According to the bus company receipts, about 90 percent of blacks who usually rode the buses joined the boycott and found other means of transportation. The boycott continued into 1956, during which time the leaders and participants of the boycott were subjected to harassment and violence. Bombs were set off at the houses of both Dr. King and E. D. Nixon. In November of 1956, the Supreme Court declared that segregation on public buses was unconstitutional, and the boycott ended. *See* Thomas J. Gilliam, *The Montgomery Bus Boycott of 1955–56, in* THE WALKING CITY: THE MONTGOMERY BUS BOYCOTT (David J. Garrow ed., 1989).

The protest was an invaluable tool for the civil rights movement. Clayborne Carson describes the movement, or in his preferred term the "Black Freedom Struggle," as involving "local protest movements" engaged in by "thousands of protesters, including large numbers of working class blacks, and local organizers who were more concerned with local issues, including employment opportunities and political power, than with achieving national legislation." Clayborne Carson, *Civil Rights Reform and the Black Freedom Struggle, in* THE CIVIL RIGHTS MOVEMENT IN AMERICA 19, 23–4 (Charles W. Eagles ed., 1986). Martin Luther King highly valued the peaceful protest, and admired its participants. In his famous "Letter from a

Birmingham Jail," Dr. King responded to criticism made by eight Alabama clergymen of the demonstrations going on in Birmingham in 1963. He wrote:

> I wish you had commended the Negro sit-inners and demonstrators of Birmingham for their sublime courage, their willingness to suffer and their amazing discipline in the midst of great provocation. One day the South will recognize its real heroes. They will be the James Merediths, with the noble sense of purpose that enables them to face jeering, and hostile mobs, and with the agonizing loneliness that characterizes the life of the pioneer. They will be old, oppressed, battered Negro women, symbolized in a seventy-two-year-old woman in Montgomery, Alabama, who rose up with a sense of dignity and with her people decided not to ride segregated buses, and who responded with ungrammatical profundity to one who inquired about her weariness: "My feets is tired, but my soul is at rest." They will be the young high school and college students, the young ministers of the gospel and a host of their elders, courageously and nonviolently sitting in at lunch counters and willingly going to jail for conscience' sake. One day the South will know that when these disinherited children of God sat down at lunch counters, they were in reality standing up for what is best in the American dream and for the most sacred values in our Judeo–Christian heritage, thereby bringing our nation back to those great wells of democracy which were dug deep by the founding fathers in their formulation of the Constitution and the Declaration of Independence.

8. Protests and boycotts today. Today, protests and boycotts continue to be employed by social activists and others. The war in Iraq has led to worldwide demonstrations by those opposed to it. *See* Evelyn Nieves, *Worldwide Civil Disobedience; Protesters Speak and Act Out Against War*, WASH. POST, Mar. 21, 2003, at A28. On the other side, political pundit Bill O'Reilly has repeatedly called for a boycott of French goods for that country's refusal to support the United States' actions in Iraq. Bill O'Reilly, *No Brie for Me*, BillOReilly.com, Jul. 1, 2004, *available at* http://www.billoreilly.com/site/product?pid=18712. The goals of protesting groups are not necessarily politically progressive causes, as evidenced by Baptists' boycott of Disney for its supposed friendliness to homosexuals. The goals of the civil rights movement are now nearly universally seen as laudable and worth the civil strife they caused, though of course they were not so understood at the time by everyone. How should society react to protesters and boycotters whose goals do not seem as worthwhile or important as those engaged in during the civil rights movement? Are protests valuable if they allow insular yet tenacious minorities to sway large majorities against their interests?

Does the boycott seem like an effective strategy for achieving long-term changes, or do they seem more appropriate for combating specific incidents of perceived injustice? The rationale behind the boycott is that by economically attacking one's opponent, boycotters will hurt the target of the boycott in tangible, undeniable ways. Is it possible that boycotts will harm those who are not responsible for the offending activity?

9. **Boycotts in Colorado.** Following the passage of Amendment 2, homosexual groups and others called for a boycott of the state of Colorado. The Conference of Mayors, the National Association of Hispanic Journalists, and the American Library Association were among dozens of groups which cancelled events they had planned in the state. The mayors of New York, Chicago and Los Angeles, among others, endorsed the boycott. The boycott gained nationwide attention, prompted by support from celebrities such as Barbara Streisand. Colorado's dependence on tourism caused special concern in the state's business community. The effects of the boycott appear to have been mixed. It attained some success in financial terms, and brought the Amendment 2 issue to national prominence. However, the boycott appears to have had limited effect on public opinion in Colorado. A *Denver Post* poll taken at the time reported that 94 percent of the 606 adults interviewed in mid-December said they had not changed their minds about Amendment Two in response to the boycott. There may even have been some backlash: 43 percent said the boycott had lessened their interest in repealing Amendment 2. *Homosexuals: Fuming on the Slopes*, THE ECONOMIST, Feb. 6, 1993, at 30. A similar boycott took place in Arizona as a result of the state's refusal to declare Martin Luther King Day a holiday. It involved more than 166 meeting cancellations, costing Arizona more than $190 million. In 1992, the holiday was declared in the state, and the boycott was given much of the credit. Shari Caudron, *The Colorado Boycott: A Wake-up Call to all Businesses?*, INDUSTRY WEEK, Mar. 1, 1993, at 48.

10. **Anti-globalization struggles and guerrilla theater.** In addition to the direct action tactics of violent and non-violent mass action described by Conway, activists in the anti-globalization movement have engaged in other kinds of tactics. In *No Logo: Taking Aim at the Brand Bullies* (1999), Naomi Klein describes "culture jamming," "the practice of parodying advertisements and hijacking billboards in order to drastically alter their messages." KLEIN, *supra* at 280. Klein explains:

> [J]ammers * * * insist that they aren't inverting ad messages but are rather improving, editing, augmenting or unmasking them. * * * A good jam, in other words, is an X-ray of the subconscious of a campaign, uncovering not an opposite meaning but the deeper truth hiding beneath the layers of advertising euphemisms. So, according to these principles, with a slight turn of the imagery knob, the now-retired Joe Camel turns into Joe Chemo, hooked up to an IV machine. That's what's in his future, isn't it? * * * Apple computers' "Think Different" campaign of famous figures both living and dead has been the subject of numerous simple hacks: a photograph of Stalin appears with the altered slogan "Think Really Different"; the caption for the ad featuring the Dalai Lama is changed to "Think Disillusioned" and the rainbow Apple logo is morphed into a skull * * *. My favorite

truth-in-advertising campaign is a simple jam on Exxon that appeared just after the 1989 Valdez spill: "Shit Happens. New Exxon," two towering billboards announced to millions of San Francisco commuters.

KLEIN, *supra* at 281–82.

11.   Grassroots global anti-poverty campaigns: the Jubilee movement. "Jubilee 2000" was an international grassroots campaign that mobilized twenty four million people over a five year period, beginning in 1996, to cancel the "unpayable debts of the poorest countries by the year 2000." The term comes from the Old Testament book of Leviticus, which describes a Year of Jubilee that comes once every fifty years, during

> which slaves are freed and debt is canceled. The Jubilee 2000 campaign—which launched the slogan "Drop the Debt"–was supported by celebrities, including musicians Bono of U2, Bob Geldof, Youssou Ndour, Thom Yorke and others, as well as by mainline Protestant and evangelical church organizations. In 1999, at the Cologne G8 Summit, world leaders agreed to $34 billion in debt relief for 22 countries, 18 of them in Africa.

> *See http://www.jubilee2000uk.org/* (visited June 9, 2005); Jeff M. Sellers, *How To Spell Debt Relief*, CHRISTIANITY TODAY, May 21, 2001, *available at http://www.christianitytoday.com/ct/2001/007/6.64.html.*

Grassroots organizing under the Jubilee name continues in various countries. According to the Jubilee USA Network website, the United States network began in 1997 "when a diverse gathering of people and organizations came together in response to the international call for Jubilee debt cancellation. Now over sixty organizations including labor, churches, religious communities and institutions, AIDS activists, trade campaigners and over 9,000 individuals are active members of the Jubilee USA Network. Together we are a strong, diverse and growing network dedicated to working for a world free of debt for billions of people." Jubilee USA Network, *About the network, http://www.jubileeusa.org* (visited June 9, 2005).

12.   Porto Allegre grassroots movement. In January 2001, as a counter to the World Economic Forum—an exclusive annual gathering of economic elites in Davos, Switzerland—a committee of Brazilian non-governmental organizations hosted the first "World Social Forum" in Porto Alegre, Brazil. The World Social Forum became an annual international grassroots event. According to its Charter of Principles, the World Social Forum:

> is an open meeting place for reflective thinking, democratic debate of ideas, formulation of proposals, free exchange of experiences and interlinking for effective action, by groups and movements of civil society that are opposed to neoliberalism and to domination of the world by capital and any form of imperialism, and are committed to building a planetary society directed towards fruitful relationships among Humankind and between it and the Earth.

World Social Forum Charter of Principles, available at http://www.forumso-cialmundial.org.br/main.php?id_menu=4 & cd_language=2 (visited June 9, 2005).

Porto Alegre itself is a place open to alternatives to traditional economic practices. An article reports on "participatory budgeting" in the city:

Porto Alegre is a regional capital of 1.3 million people which since 1989 has been governed by the Partido dos Trabalhadores (PT or Workers' Party), Brazil's largest Left-wing party. Its flagship policy—the Participatory Budget—involves thousands of city residents in decisions about municipal expenditures. In a country where public funds are typically spent through a mixture of corruption, patronage and obscure technocratism, this is a revolution in political practice.

It sprang from a political party's desire to live up to its policy platform, an aim seldom achieved in the world of politics. Since it was formed in the 1980s, the Workers' Party proclaimed its commitment to both citizen participation and redirecting government priorities toward the poor. But when it was elected to municipal office in January 1989, the party found an administration deeply indebted, lacking basic supplies and with buildings and machinery in shambles. At the first neighbourhood assemblies to discuss the budget, community leaders called for hundreds of investments. Not a penny was available.

The local government spent its first year controlling costs and passing tax increases in city council but opinion polls showed high levels of dissatisfaction. So a group within the administration proposed both participatory decision-making and that priority be given to basic infrastructure in the poorest neighbourhoods. This translated as a total commitment, backed by funds, to the decisions made by the neighbourhood budget assemblies.

Since then, residents have met in their neighbourhoods annually to discuss needs for community infrastructure, electing delegates to each of 16 'district budget forums'. Through intense and often conflictual negotiations among neighbourhood representatives, these delegates list priorities for each type of capital expenditure such as basic sanitation, street paving and parks. Every year, open assemblies in each district also elect two members to a city-wide Municipal Budget Council which devises criteria for distributing funds among districts and approves an investment plan that respects the priorities of each one.

This policy gained such popularity in its first years that the administration expanded the programme beyond neighbourhood issues when it was re-elected in 1992. A year later, a series of Thematic Forums were created to discuss city-wide expenditures in areas such as urban planning, transportation and economic development. These forums also elect members to the Municipal Budget Council.

As it has grown, the Council has gained force. Not only does it now approve the entire capital budget but it also deliberates on all city expenditures. Over time a series of other participatory councils have

also been created to discuss more qualitative aspects of city programmes on issues such as housing, health, culture and the environment.

The timing was ideal for building support for the idea. The first
half of the 1990s was a period of great popular outrage in Brazil
against government corruption, leading to the impeachment of President Collor de Mello. By contrast, at a local level, the Participatory
Budget demonstrated that the administration was committed to
change by challenging 'back room decision-making', mobilizing large
numbers of people and visibly improving the quality of life in the
poorest neighbourhoods. While opposition politicians privately questioned participatory decision-making, which effectively eliminated
them as patronage brokers, they were forced to approve the investment
plans since their own supporters were increasingly participating. After
just one electoral term, all candidates promised to maintain the Participatory Budget.

As the policy began to gain international recognition, the government also gained local popularity for being innovative and responsible.
Those people participating in the Municipal Budget Council gained a
certain 'moral authority'. This helped garner the support of groups
that still questioned the policy, such as technical personnel within the
bureaucracy who doubted the ability of ordinary people to make budget
decisions. The result was a bureaucracy that worked better, responding
with agility to the demands of budget participants.

One of the outstanding achievements of the Participatory Budget
has been its effectiveness in bringing the poor into public decision-
making. The poorest neighbourhoods participate in much greater numbers than middle-class ones where streets have already been paved,
sewers built and children are sent to private schools. Surveys show
assembly participants have lower incomes and education levels than
averages for the city as a whole.

However, the most enduring value of the Participatory Budget is
that citizen participation has now become a way of life, accepted by
people as well as politicians as the modus operandi in all realms of
public decision-making. What is more, citizen groups have grown and
strengthened in response to increased opportunities for effectively
influencing government actions. Contrary to the common assumption
that civil society must strengthen before government will improve, in
Porto Alegre a state-initiated policy that has encouraged civic organizing has helped consolidate the new practices at all levels.

While promoting citizen participation may often seem politically
risky, in Porto Alegre it has helped build political success for the
Workers' Party. Since 1989 the party has been re-elected three times
and has gained a reputation for effective administration elsewhere.
Today it governs five cities of more than a million people, including
São Paulo, as well as three states. Its local successes have directly
challenged the idea that the Workers' Party—a party once identified

with radical social movements–does not know how to govern. These successes have served as credentials for the Workers' Party in this year's national election campaign, which delivered the presidency to the party's leader, 'Lula' da Silva.

By 2000, more than 100 Brazilian cities were implementing the policy (about half of which are not Workers' Party controlled). Not always have the results been so impressive as in Porto Alegre. In most cases participatory control has remained limited to a small portion of expenditures. Even so, it is clear that the policy has a tremendous potential to mobilize: in major Brazilian cities such as Belém, Brasília and Belo Horizonte, participatory budget programmes have involved hundreds of thousands of participants. In São Paulo alone, 55,000 people participated in budget forums this year.

Rebecca Abers, *Daring Democracy*, NEW INTERNATIONALIST 352 (December 2002), *available at http://www.newint.org/issue352/daring.htm*. In fall, 2004, however, the Workers' Party was voted out of office. The World Social Forum has now moved to a biannual schedule; the next meeting will be in 2007, in Africa.

COPYRIGHT PERMISSIONS

Professors Jordan and Harris, along with Foundation Press, would like to gratefully acknowledge the authors and copyright holders of the following works, who permitted their inclusion in this work:

Ackerman, Bruce & Alstott, Anne, *Your Stake in America*, 41 ARIZ. L. REV. 249, 249–261 (1999). Copyright © 1999 by Bruce Ackerman, Ann Alstott and the Arizona Law Review. Reprinted with permission of the Arizona Law Review in the format Textbook via the Copyright Clearance Center.

Ackerman, Frank & Heinzerling, Lisa, *Priceless: On Knowing the Price of Everything and the Value of Nothing* 35–40 (2004). Copyright © 2003 *Priceless: On Knowing the Price of Everything and the Value of Nothing* by Frank Ackerman and Lisa Heinzerling. Reprinted by permission of The New Press. www.thenewpress.com.

Akerlof, George A. & Kranton, Rachel E., *Economics and Identity*, 115 Q.J. OF ECON. 715 (Aug. 2000). Copyright © 2000 by the Quarterly Journal of Economics. Reprinted by permission of The MIT Press.

Amar, Akhil Reed, *Forty Acres and a Mule: A Republican Theory of Minimal Entitlements*, 13 HARV. J.L. & PUB. POL'Y 37 (1990). Copyright © 1990 by Akhil Reed Amar, the President and Fellows of Harvard College and the Harvard Journal of Law and Public Policy. Reprinted by permission.

Amott, Teresa L. & Matthei, Julie A., *Race Gender & Work: A Multicultural Economic History of Women in the United States* 63–64, 70–72, 73, 194–95 (1991) (excerpts from chapter 4 "The Soul of the *Tierra Madre*: Chicano Women" and chapter 7 "Climbing Gold Mountain: Asian American Women"). Copyright © 1991 by Teresa L. Amott, Julie A. Matthei and South End Press. Reprinted by permission of South End Press.

Associated Press, *Uneasy Rider! Jury Finds Wynona Guilty in Shoplift Case*, N.Y. DAILY NEWS, Nov. 6, 2002. Copyright © 2002 by the Associated Press. Reprinted by permission.

Averitt, Neil W. & Lande, Robert H., *Consumer Sovereignty: A Unified Theory of Antitrust and Consumer Protection Law*, 65 ANTITRUST L.J. 713 (1997). Copyright © 1997 by the Antitrust Law Journal. Reprinted by permission.

Ayres, Ian, *Pervasive Prejudice? Unconventional Evidence of Race and Gender Discrimination* 3–7 (2001). Copyright © 2001 by Ian Ayres and the University of Chicago Press. Reprinted by permission.

Ayres, Ian, *Fair Driving and Race Discrimination in Retail Car Negotiations*, 104 HARV. L. REV. 817 (1991). Copyright © 1991 by the Harvard Law Review Association. Reprinted by permission.

Barnes, Anita C., *The Sexual Continuum: Transsexual Prisoners*, 24 NEW ENG. J. ON CRIM. & CIV. CONFINEMENT 599 (1998). Copyright © 1998 by

Carole, *Interview with Barbara*, in Sex Work: Writings by Women in the Sex Industry 166–74 (Frederique Delacoste & Priscilla Alexander eds., 1987). Copyright © 1987 by the Cleis Press. Reprinted by permission.

Chapkis, Wendy, *Dress as Success*, in *Beauty Secrets: Women and the Politics of Appearance* 79–80, 83–85, 88–93 (1986). Copyright © 1986 by Wendy Chapkis and South End Press. Reprinted by permission.

Clifford, James, *Identity in Mashpee*, in The Predicament of Culture: Twentieth-Century Ethnography, Literature, and Art 277–346 (1988). "Identity in Mashpee" reprinted by permission of the publisher of THE PREDICAMENT OF CULTURE: TWENTIETH-CENTURY ETHNOGRAPHY, LITERATURE, AND ART by James Clifford, pp. 277–346, Cambridge, Mass.: Harvard University Press, Copyright © 1988 by the President and Fellows of Harvard College.

Coase, Ronald H., *Adam Smith's View of Man*, 19 J.L. & Econ. 529 (1976). Copyright © 1976 by Ronald Coase and The Journal of Law and Economics. Reprinted by permission in the format Textbook via the Copyright Clearance Center.

Cohen, Richard, *Closing the Door on Crime*, Wash. Post Mag., Sept. 7, 1986, at W13. Copyright © by Richard Cohen and the Washington Post Writers Group. Reprinted by permission in the format Textbook via the Copyright Clearance Center.

Conway, Janet, *Civil Resistance and the "Diversity of Tactics" in the Anti-Globalization Movement: Problems of Violence, Silence, and Solidarity in Activist Politics*, 41 Osgoode Hall L.J. 505 (2003). Copyright © 2003 by Janet Conway and the Osgoode Hall Law Journal. Reprinted by permission of Janet Conway.

Dash, Leon, *Just Trying to Survive*, in Rosa Lee: A Mother and Her Family in Urban America 39–47 (1996). Copyright © 1996 Leon Dash and Basic Books, a subdivision of Harper Collins Publishing. Reprinted by permission of Harper Collins Publishing.

Davis, Peggy C., *Popular Legal Culture: Law as Microaggression*, 98 Yale L.J. 1559 (1989). Reprinted by permission of The Yale Law Journal Company and William S. Hein Company from The Yale Law Journal, Vol. 98, pages 1559–1577.

Davis, Russell J., *Refusal to Hire, or Dismissal from Employment on Account of Plaintiff's Sexual Lifestyle or Sexual Preference as Violation of Federal Constitution of Federal Civil Rights Statutes*, 42 A.L.R. Fed. 189 (2002). Copyright © 2002 by Thomson West and Russell J. Davis. Reprinted by permission.

Farley, Christine Haight, *Protecting Folklore of Indigenous Peoples: Is Intellectual Property the Answer?*, 30 Conn. L. Rev. 1 (1997). Copyright © 1997 by Christine Haight Farley and the Connecticut Law Review. Reprinted by permission of Christine Haight Farley.

Featherstone, Liza, *Down and Out in Discount America*, TheNation.Com, *available at* http://thenation.com/doc.mhtml?i=20050103 &

s=featherstone (posted Dec. 16, 2004) (last visited Mar. 6, 2005). Copyright © 2004 by Liza Featherstone and TheNation.Com. Reprinted by permission from the Janury 3, 2005 issue of *The Nation*. For subscription information, call 1–800–333–8536. Portions of each week's Nation magazine can be accessed at http://www.thenation.com.

Feinman, Jay M., *Un-Making Law: The Classical Revival in the Common Law*, 28 Seattle U. L. Rev. 1 (2004). Copyright © 2004 by Jay M. Feinman and the Seattle University Law Review. Reprinted by permission.

Forbath, William E., *The New Deal Constitution in Exile*, 51 Duke L.J. 165, 176–222 (2001). Copyright © 2001 by William E. Forbath and The Duke University Law Review. Reprinted by permission in the format Textbook via the Copyright Clearance Center.

Friedman, Milton, *Take it to the Limits: Milton Friedman on Libertarianism*, broadcasted on American Public Television, February 10, 1999 *available at* http:// www-hoover.stanford.edu/main/uncom mon/99winter/324.html. Copyright © 1999 by American Public Television and the Hoover Institution. Reprinted by permission.

Friedman, Milton & Friedman, Rose D., *Created Equal*, *in* Free to Choose: A Personal Statement 128–49 (1980). Excerpts "Created Equal" from FREE TO CHOOSE: A PERSONAL STATEMENT, copyright © 1980 by Milton Friedman and Rose D. Friedman, reprinted by permission of Harcourt, Inc.

Glendon, Mary Ann, *Rights in Twentieth–Century Constitutions*, 59 U. Chi. L. Rev. 519, 523–26, 535–36 (1992). Copyright © 1992 by Mary Ann Glendon and the University of Chicago Law Review. Reprinted by permission in the format Textbook via the Copyright Clearance Center.

Greider, William, *One World, Ready or Not: The Manic Logic of Global Capitalism* 77 (1997). Copyright © 1997 by Simon & Schuster Publishing and William Grieder. Reprinted by permission.

Guinier, Lani, *Admissions Rituals as Political Acts: Guardians at the Gates of Our Democratic Ideals*, 117 Harv. L. Rev. 113 (2003). Copyright © 2003 by the Harvard Law Review Association and Lani Guinier. Reprinted by permission of the Harvard Law Review Association.

Harris, Cheryl I., *Whiteness as Property*, 106 Harv. L. Rev. 1707 (1993). Copyright © 1993 by the Harvard Law Review Association and Cheryl I. Harris. Reprinted by permission of the Harvard Law Review Association.

Harris, Ron, *The Uses of History in Law and Economics*, 4 Theoretical Inquiries in Law 659 (2003) *available at* http://www.bepress.com/til/default/vol4/iss2/art9. Copyright © 2003 by The Cegla Institute and Ron Harris. Reprinted by permission of Ron Harris.

hooks, bell, *Madonna: Plantation Mistress or Soul Sister?*, *in* Black Looks: Race and Representation 157–64 (1992). Copyright © 1992 by South End Press and bell hooks. Reprinted by permission of South End Press.

Hsu, Evelyn, *Some Tenants Left Out of Lee Gardens Victory*, Wash. Post, Oct. 7, 1987, at B01. Copyright © 1987 by the Washington Post

Publishing Company. Reprinted by permission of The New York Times Publishing Company.

Kuttner, Robert, *Everything For Sale* 16 (1996). From EVERYTHING FOR SALE by Robert Kuttner, copyright © 1996 by the Twentieth Century Fund, Inc. Used by permission of Alfred A. Knopf, a division of Random House, Inc.

Lamm, Richard D. & Imhoff, Gary, *How Many Can America Absorb?*, *in* The Immigration Time Bomb: The Fragmenting of America (1986). Copyright © 1986 by Richard D. Lamm, Gary Imhoff, and Penguin Publishing. Reprinted by permission.

Lenhardt, R.A., *Understanding the Mark: Race, Stigma, and Equality in Context*, 79 N.Y.U. L. Rev. 803 (2005). Copyright © 2005 by R.A. Lenhardt and the New York University Law Review. Reprinted by permission of the New York University Law Review in the format Textbook via the Copyright Clearance Center.

Lopez, Gerald P., *How Much Responsibility Does the U.S. Bear for Undocumented Mexican Migration?, in Undocumented Mexican Migration: In Search of a Just Immigration Law and Policy*, 28 UCLA L. Rev. 615 (1980). Copyright © 1980 by Gerald P. Lopez and the University of California at Los Angeles Law Review. Reprinted by permission of Gerald P. Lopez.

Lynch, Mona, *From Punitive City to Gated Community: Security and Segregation Across the Social and Penal Landscape, Symposium*, 56 U. Miami L. Rev. 89 (2001). Copyright © 2001 by Mona Lynch and the University of Miami Law Review.

Malamud, Deborah C., *Class Based Affirmative Action: Lessons and Caveats*, 74 Tex. L. Rev. 1847 (1996). Copyright © 1996 by Deborah C. Malamud and the University of Texas Law Review. Reprinted by permission of the University of Texas Law Review and Deborah C. Malamud.

Mathematics, Words and Music by Dante Beze and Christopher Martin © 1999 EMI BLACKWOOD MUSIC INC., EMPIRE INTERNATIONAL, MEDINA SOUND MUSIC, EMI APRIL MUSIC INC., and GIFTED PEARL MUSIC All Rights for EMPIRE INTERNATIONAL and MEDINA SOUND MUSIC Controlled and Administered by EMI BLACKWOOD MUSIC INC. All Rights for GIFTED PEARL MUSIC Controlled and Administered by EMI APRIL MUSIC INC. All Rights Reserved. International Copyright Secured. Used by Permission.

Matsuda, Mari J., *Voices of America: Accent, Antidiscrimination Law, and a Jurisprudence for the Last Reconstruction*, 100 Yale L.J. 1329 (1991). Copyright © 1991 by Mari J. Matsuda and The Yale Law Journal. Reprinted by permission of The Yale Law Journal Company and William S. Hein Company from The Yale Law Journal, Vol. 100, pages 1329–1407.

McAdams, Richard, *Cooperation and Conflict: The Economics of Group Status Production and Race Discrimination*, 108 Harv. L. Rev. 1003 (1995). Copyright © 1995 by Richard McAdams and the Harvard Law Review

Association. Reprinted by permission of the Harvard Law Review Association.

Metal, Phyllis Luman, *One for Ripley's*, in Sex Work: Writings by Women in the Sex Industry 119–21 (Frederique Delacoste & Priscilla Alexander eds., 1987). Copyright © 1987 by Phyllis Luman Metal and The Cleis Press. Reprinted by permission of The Cleis Press.

Miller, Robert J., *Economic Development in Indian Country: Will Capitalism or Socialism Succeed?*, 80 Oreg. L. Rev. 757 (2001). Copyright © 2001 by Robert J. Miller and the Oregon Law Review. Reprinted by permission in the format Textbook via the Copyright Clearance Center.

Montoya, Margaret E., *Border Crossings in an Age of Border Patrols: Cruzando Fronteras Metaforicas*, 26 N.M. L. Rev. 1 (1996). Copyright © 1996 by Margaret E. Montoya and the New Mexico Law Review. Reprinted by permission of the New Mexico Law Review in the format Textbook via the Copyright Clearance Center.

Moran, Rachel F., Symposium, *The Elusive Nature of Discrimination*, 55 Stan. L. Rev. 2365 (2003) (book review). Copyright © 2003 by Rachel F. Moran and the Stanford Law Review. Reprinted by permission in the format Textbook via the Copyright Clearance Center.

Morin, Richard, *The Price of Segregation–Unconventional Wisdom: New Facts from the Social Sciences*, Wash. Post, Dec. 28, 1997, at C05. Copyright © 1997 by Richard Morin and the Washington Post Writer's Group. Reprinted by permission in the format Textbook via the Copyright Clearance Center.

No Scrubs, Words and Music by Kandi L. Burruss, Tameka Cottle and Kevin Brigs, © 1999 EMI APRIL MUSIC INC., AIR CONTROL MUSIC, KANDACY MUSIC, TINY TAM MUSIC, SHEK'EM DOWN MUSIC, HIT-CO-MUSIC SOUTH, WARNER–TAMERLANE PUBLISHING CORP., PEPPER DRIVE MUSIC, WB MUSIC CORP. and TONY MERCEDES MUSIC. All Rights for AIR CONTROL MUSIC, KANDACY MUSIC and TINY TAM MUSIC Controlled and Administered by EMI APRIL MUSIC INC. All Rights for PEPPER DRIVE MUSIC Controlled and Administered by WARNER–TAMERLANE PUBLISHING CORP. All Rights for TONY MERCEDES MUSIC Controlled and Administered by WB MUSIC CORP. All Rights Reserved. International Copyright Secured. Used by Permission.

Nussbaum, Martha, *Introduction*, in For Love of Country? ix (2002). Copyright © 2002 by Martha Nussbaum and Beacon Press. Reprinted by permission of Beacon Press.

Nussbaum, Martha, *Patriotism and Cosmopolitanism*, in For Love of Country? 3–17 (2002). Copyright © 2002 by Martha Nussbaum and Beacon Press. Reprinted by permission of Beacon Press.

O'Brien, Jodi, *Seeking Normal? Considering Same-Sex Marriage*, 2 Seattle J. for Soc. Justice 459 (2004). Copyright © 2004 by Jodi O'Brien and the Seattle Journal for Social Justice. Reprinted by permission of Jodi O'Brien and the Seattle Journal for Social Justice.

*

INDEX

References are to pages

†